Masterplots

Fourth Edition

Masterplots

Fourth Edition

Volume 9
Poetry of Campion—Saul

Editor
Laurence W. Mazzeno
Alvernia College

12/10
SALEM PRESS
Pasadena, California   Hackensack, New Jersey

Editor in Chief: Dawn P. Dawson

Editorial Director: Christina J. Moose　　*Editorial Assistant:* Brett S. Weisberg
Development Editor: Tracy Irons-Georges　　*Research Supervisor:* Jeffry Jensen
Project Editor: Desiree Dreeuws　　*Research Assistant:* Keli Trousdale
Manuscript Editors: Constance Pollock,　　*Production Editor:* Joyce I. Buchea
Judy Selhorst, Andy Perry　　*Design and Graphics:* James Hutson
Acquisitions Editor: Mark Rehn　　*Layout:* William Zimmerman

Cover photo: V. S. Naipaul (Ulf Andersen/Getty Images)

Library of Congress Cataloging-in-Publication Data

Masterplots / editor, Laurence W. Mazzeno. — 4th ed.
　　v.　cm.
Includes bibliographical references and indexes.
ISBN 978-1-58765-568-5 (set : alk. paper) — ISBN 978-1-58765-577-7 (v. 9 : alk. paper)
1. Literature—Stories, plots, etc.　2. Literature—History and criticism.　I. Mazzeno, Laurence W.
PN44.M33 2010
809—dc22
2010033931

Fourth Edition
First Printing

Contents

Contents

Complete List of Titles

Volume 1

Volume 2

Contents lvii

Complete List of Titles. lxi

Volume 3

Volume 4

Volume 5

Volume 6

Volume 7

Contents ccxlvii
Complete List of Titles ccli

Volume 8

Volume 9

Contents cccxxiii
Complete List of Titles cccxxvii

Volume 10

Volume 11

Volume 12

Contents . . . . cdxxxvii
Complete List of Titles. . . . . cdxxxix

Indexes

Masterplots

Fourth Edition

Poetry of Campion

Author: Thomas Campion (1567-1620)
First published: 1595-1617; includes *Poemata*, 1595; *A Booke of Ayres*, 1601; *Two Bookes of Ayres*, 1613; *The Third and Fourth Booke of Ayres*, 1617
Type of work: Poetry

Of the lyric poets of the English Renaissance, Thomas Campion is for some readers one of the most difficult to appreciate and value. He is not a "difficult" poet in the way John Donne, his more famous contemporary, is difficult, for he is not a poet, as is Donne, with whom one must struggle because of the density of his language, meaning, and imagery. Campion's language is transparent, his meaning is seldom in doubt, and his imagery is both simple and conventional. Campion comes close to being a pure lyricist whose excellence is not to be described by an appeal to intellectual complexity or to originality, in the Romantic sense of the term, but by an appeal to art, artifice, technique, and the elegant handling of tradition.

Though he wrote some fine religious lyrics and an occasional moral apostrophe, Campion's true subject is love—not the immediate and frankly sexual love of Donne's early poetry, but rather the politely erotic game of literary and aristocratic love. The poetry never pretends to be anything but an elegant and highly artificial kind of play, and the poems are full of the conventions, both thematic and stylistic, of the highly formal love poetry of the Renaissance. Amarillis, Laura, shepherds and shepherdesses, rosy cheeks, tears and sighs, Cupids, nymphs, gods and goddesses, and cruel maids and faithless swains abound in Campion. The stylized voices in the poems never utter so immediate and passionate a statement as that which opens Donne's "Canonization": "For God's sake hold your tongue, and let me love." Campion's speakers utter words that evoke not an immediate situation but a set of general literary conventions: "O Love, where are thy shafts, thy quiver, and thy bow?"

One must understand the special skills and concerns of a poet such as Campion, who wrote within a set of traditional conventions (many of them unfamiliar to modern readers), before one can appreciate the excellence of his verse. Campion was a highly educated man who wrote for a highly sophisticated and educated society. He was trained in both law and medicine, and his schooling and his literary tastes, in both reading and writing, were strongly classical. His first publication was a group of greatly admired Latin poems, the

Poemata. In many of his English poems there are verbal echoes of the great Roman poets—Horace, Martial, and, particularly, Catullus, the Roman lyricist of love par excellence. In addition to specific references to the ancient poets in Campion's work, the atmosphere of many of the poems is powerfully classical, even those poems that have no definite Latin ancestors and those in which the settings are, as is most often the case, English and Renaissance modern (for example, "Jacke and Jone they thinke no ill" and "There is a Garden in her face").

The classical influence is not merely a matter of allusions to ancient poets and mythology. Such allusions are frequent enough—for example, Campion's imitation of Catullus's most famous poem in "My sweetest Lesbia let us live and love"—but not overwhelmingly present. More important is the stylistic influence. The sharply turned epigrammatic statements, the tightly controlled form and language, the avoidance of metaphor and other spectacular figures of speech, the bittersweet and ironic tone that characterizes Campion's verse—these and other such things are largely the product of the poet's imitation in English of classical Latin poetry. The significance of all this is enhanced by the fact that the people for whom Campion wrote were also widely read in or at least familiar with ancient poetry. A reference or turn of speech that might puzzle later readers would seem natural, elegant, and effective to Campion's original audience.

Related to these matters is Campion's advocacy of writing English poetry in classical meters. The poet, in a very controversial pamphlet titled *Observations in the Art of English Poesie* (1602), argued that for English poetry to achieve the highest excellence, poets should avoid rhyme, as did the ancients, and should count poetic feet in terms of the quantitative lengths of vowel sounds rather than in the more natural to English (as opposed to Latin and Greek) method of counting strong and weak accentual stresses. Campion and others who espoused this argument had little effect, and their crusade is now thought of as a literary curiosity. As a matter of fact, Campion himself managed to write only one truly successful rhymeless poem in classical meters ("Rose-cheekt

Lawra, come"); all of his most admired pieces are in standard English accentual meters and are in rhyme. It is significant, however, that Campion was involved in this controversy. It shows how important classical practice was to him, how intensely he was involved in the literary arguments of his time, and how concerned he was with the most technical aspects of his art.

As important as the classical aspect of Campion's art is, however, it must be made clear that much of the traditional material in the poems is drawn from the late medieval courtly love tradition as it was filtered into Renaissance English letters through the poetry of the Italian Petrarchan tradition and the sixteenth century French tradition (itself heavily influenced by the Italian accomplishment) exemplified in the poetry of Pierre de Ronsard and his followers. Nor should the native English tradition of amatory verse from Geoffrey Chaucer through Sir Thomas Wyatt and Edmund Spenser be minimized, although it, too, was heavily influenced by the Italian tradition at every stage. In this literary complex, readers were made familiar with the sighing lover, the abandoned maid, and many other such conventions. It is enough to recognize that Campion wrote within the multifaceted, cosmopolitan tradition of the Renaissance love lyric and that the classics, although not the whole of Campion's interest, were the most conscious non-English focus of his attention and taste.

Just as readers must be aware of the various literary factors that helped shape Campion's work, they must also be aware of the influence music had on the poetry. Campion, in addition to being a poet, was a talented composer who wrote almost all of his verse to be set to his own music. In fact, the poet did not often think of his music and his poetry separately. He composed each with an eye to the other, and his overall artistic goal, as he said, was to join his "words and notes lovingly together." In his work, song gives meaning to the poem, and poem gives meaning to the song.

Campion's success as a poet-composer had much to do with the fact that he lived in a great age of English music, the age of such composers (many of whom he knew) as William Byrd, John Wilbye, Thomas Morley, John Dowland, Thomas Weelkes, and Orlando Gibbons. The great achievements of all of these composers were in the area of vocal music, and their age thought music and poetry to be much more interdependent than did later ages. The most widely known form of English Renaissance music was the madrigal, a complex kind of song for two to seven voices (though sometimes instruments were substituted for some of the voices). Each voice sang a different melodic line, and thus the simple lyric of the madrigal tended to be dominated by the complexity of the performance. Campion did not concentrate on writing madrigals; rather, he focused on the "ayre," a relatively simple, clear melodic line composed to be sung by one or two voices to the accompaniment of the lute. As was not true in the madrigal, in the ayre the melody and the poetry were of equal value, and neither dominated the other.

Readers of Campion's poetry should always remember that the poems alone are less than half the artistic effect Campion originally created. Both the music and, crucially, the artistry of the performer are left out. The reader should also remember that any judgment of the poems separate from the available music, no matter how sensitive, is bound to be less than adequate. An analogy might be made to the twentieth century popular song: How flat would be the experience of reading an anthology of such song poems as compared to the effect of hearing the poems and the music in performance. This analogy breaks down, for those song poems seldom claimed to be distinguished poetry, whereas Campion's lyrics (and the lyrics of many of his contemporaries, including William Shakespeare) do claim to be fine poems as well as good words to accompany good music. As for Campion's idea of how music should be composed and how the nature of poetry is analogous to the nature of music, there is his statement from the preface to his first *Booke of Ayres*: "What Epigrams are in Poetrie, the same are Ayres in musicke, then in their chiefe perfection when they are short and well seasoned."

Even though his technical mastery and art seldom fail, Campion is better read in selection than in his entirety. His poetic world of love is narrow and can become monotonous. Among those poems of Campion most often admired are "When to Her lute Corinna Sings," "There is a Garden in her face," "Follow Your Saint, Follow with Accents Sweet," "I Care Not for these Ladies," "Shall I Come, sweet Love, to thee?," "Never love unless You Can Beare With All the Faults of a Man," "Rose-cheekt Lawra, come," "When Thou Must Home to Shades of Underground," and "Harke, all you ladies that do sleep." Many other poems might be named here, but these provide a fair and wide sample of the poet's excellence.

Further Reading

Coren, Pamela. "In the Person of Womankind: Female Persona Poems by Campion, Donne, Jonson." *Studies in Philology* 98, no. 2 (Spring, 2001): 225-250. Examines Campion's "A secret love or two, I must confesse" and poems by John Donne and Ben Jonson to describe the different ways in which each of these male poets creates and uses a female voice.

Davis, Walter R. *Thomas Campion*. Boston: Twayne, 1987. Provides information on Campion's life and reputation as well as discussion of his poetry, music, and masques. Thorough and accessible; an excellent resource for readers beginning the study of Campion's works.

Eldridge, Muriel T. *Thomas Campion: His Poetry and Music (1567-1620)*. New York: Vantage Press, 1971. Straightforward examination of Campion begins with a brief introduction to English poetry before 1600. Includes information on Campion's life as well as discussion of his poetry and music.

Kastendieck, Miles Merwin. *England's Musical Poet: Thomas Campion*. New York: Oxford University Press, 1938. Reprint. New York: Russell & Russell, 1963. One of the first studies of Campion's poetry to consider the importance of the influences of his music.

Lindley, David. *Thomas Campion*. New York: Brill, 1986. Comprehensive work examines Campion's poetry, music, and court masques. Pays special attention to Campion's metrical theories and the relationships between his poetry and his music.

Ryding, Erik S. *In Harmony Framed: Musical Humanism, Thomas Campion, and the Two Daniels*. Kirksville, Mo.: Sixteenth Century Journal Publishers, Northeast Missouri State University, 1993. Explores why Campion's theoretical writings favor unrhymed quantitative verse, whereas his own poetry is nearly all rhymed. Includes an interesting chapter on his lyric poetry.

Poetry of Carducci

Author: Giosuè Carducci (1835-1907)

First published: 1857-1899; includes *Rime*, 1857; *Levia gravia*, 1868; *Odi barbare*, 1877 (*Barbarian Odes*, 1939, rev. 1950); *Nuove odi barbare*, 1882 (*New Barbarian Odes*, 1939, rev. 1950); *Terze odi barbare*, 1889 (*Third Barbarian Odes*, 1939, rev. 1950); *Rime e ritmi*, 1899 (*Lyrics and Rhythms*, 1942)

Type of work: Poetry

Rarely has a poet in modern times been awarded the admiration and adulation that Italians accorded to Giosuè Carducci during his lifetime. Regarded as a national prophet as well as the unofficial poet laureate of Italy, he was something of an Italian institution. In addition to his career as poet and essayist, he was a highly successful academic. Although derided in his time by some groups, he served as a professor of literature at the University of Bologna for more than forty years. In 1906, he was awarded the Nobel Prize in Literature, one of the earliest recipients of the prize.

For most of his career, Carducci was, until converting to monarchism, a nonconformist, a republican supporter of Giuseppe Garibaldi and Giuseppe Mazzini during the unification wars. As a poet, he was an outspoken anti-Romantic and an anticleric. These stances contributed to his popularity in Italy. His importance in the history of Italian literature rests on the quantity and quality of his neoclassical poetry, which is rife with references to Roman glory, and a vocabulary to match. When he began his career in the middle of the nineteenth century, Romanticism was in full flower and entering its decadent phase. Carducci's neoclassical poems represent a different poetic, one addressing political topics and advocating political vigor for the Italians engaged in the unification movement—poetry that stressed the greatness of Rome over the theocratic Roman Catholicism of medieval Italy.

Carducci fervently believed that his, if not all, poetry should be an effective instrument in the great awakening—political, religious, and literary—that was taking place in Italy against the papacy and foreign occupiers. Carducci was dogmatically convinced that his neoclassical verses, vocabulary, and references would revitalize Italian poetry and put it back on the right and true track furnished by its Romano-classical ancestry. Literary history has proven his program misguided. His purely neoclassical poems are restrained, controlled, and intellectual. The bulk of his poetry is too often occasional, polemic, sententious, or tied to places and bygone people and events—factors that account for his poetry lacking a high readership today. Many readers dislike Carducci's grandiloquence, but his Romantic poetry is often exquisite.

Carducci continued writing in the spirit of the neoclassical movement that was initiated by J. J. Winckelmann and his groundbreaking *Gedanken über die Nachamung der griechischen Werke in der Malerei und Bildhauerkunst* (1775; *Reflections on the Imitation of Greek Works in Painting and Sculpture*, 1987). Winckelmann wrote this work after he discovered, as a librarian in Rome, what he assumed were Greek works of art. Carducci, however, chose ancient Rome, and not the Greeks, as his model. To modern readers, his neoclassical poetry rings stentorian and lacks, to compare it with another art form by neoclassical artists, the grace and charm of the neo-Greek statuary of fellow Italian Antonio Canova. Nevertheless, Carducci outshone his contemporaries and was, in the absence of other signal poets, the major Italian poet of the nineteenth century; he was a successor to the greats Ugo Foscolo and Giacomo Leopardi and a precursor to Giovanni Pascoli and Gabriele D'Annunzio.

Carducci's second published poem is the still-famous "Hymn to Satan" (1857). It shocked Italy and reaped outcries of blasphemy from his continual enemy, the Catholic Church. The poem ascribes, as Johann Wolfgang von Goethe did half a century earlier in his *Faust: Ein Fragment* (1790; *Faust: A Fragment*, 1980), creative and constructive power to the revolutionary, fallen fourth archangel and invokes Satan as other poems had invoked the Muses. In the hymn, Carducci complains that Christianity is moribund and is carrying the world to destruction. He invokes paganism as a means of freeing the human mind. Satan in the poem is presented as a spirit of paganism, the spirit that evoked the sculpture, the pictures, and the literature of classical antiquity. Thus, Satan becomes for Carducci a helper, not an adversary, of humanity and humanism, a symbol of progress, intellectuality, anticlericalism, and a positive influence on classical thought.

When not slavishly adhering to Roman locales and models, to abstruse vocabulary, or to the lambasting of other Romantic poets, Carducci wrote some first-rate poetry, ironically, mostly poems on romantic love and nature. Among these are "The Song of Love," which ends, antithetically, with heartfelt sympathy for the pontiff; "The Sonnet," an homage to the poetic form invented by a thirteenth century Italian poet; and "Crossing the Tuscan Marshland," a strong paean to the vigorous people of the region in which Carducci grew up. Others includes "Classical Spring" and "Romantic

Autumn," two poems highlighting Carducci's dialectical nature as poet; "Ancient Lament," an exquisitely elegiac nature poem bemoaning the loss of his youngest son; "St. Martin," aurally musical in its original Italian; "Classicism and Romanticism," which lauds the work that goes into a poem of neoclassical tenor and savagely disparages the poetry of the Romantics; "Congedo," a self-justifying poem, but not a cloying one; "Commemoration of the Founding of Rome," an accessible example of his Rome-inspired poetry; "Tuscan Hills," a fine example of an occasional poem, the wedding of one of Carducci's daughters; and "Alpine Noon," an exquisite nature poem, set in one of the few landscapes outside the poet's native central Italy.

Another poem, "At the Station on an Autumn Morning," is classical in strophic form and early modern in content. It is an elegy on the departure of one of Carducci's mistresses from the train station in Bologna, one of the first times a railroad train, depicted as modern monster, figures in a poem. It displays an impressive onomatopoeia of railway workers striking hotboxes, punching tickets, and shutting compartment doors.

Although a cliché, it is especially true that what gets lost when translated into English is Carducci's particular poetic voice. English tends to flatten Carducci's exalted vocabulary, his celebratory Italian. This in part explains why his work is not known by a large number of anglophone readers. The poems cited above, however, warrant reading in translation, ideally as a bridge to the reward of reading them in Italian.

Revised by Robert B. Youngblood

Further Reading

Arapaia, Paul. "Constructing a National Identity from a Created Literary Past: Giosuè Carducci and the Development of a National Literature." *Journal of Modern Italian Studies* 7, no. 2 (Summer, 2002): 192-214. Explains how Carducci created a literary history to construct a cultural identity and a sense of political mission for the emerging Italian nation.

Barricelli, Jean-Paul. "Giosuè Carducci." In *European Authors: 1000-1900: A Biographical Dictionary of European Literature*, edited by Stanley J. Kunitz and Vineta Colby. New York: H. W. Wilson, 1967. Describes Carducci's life and works. Part of a general collection of biographical essays on European writers active through the nineteenth century. Includes a bibliography.

Carducci, Giosuè. *Selected Verse.* Edited with a translation, introduction, and commentary by David H. Higgins. Warminster, England: Aris & Phillips, 1994. Collection of fifty-two poems, including "Hymn to Satan," published in Italian with English translations on the facing pages. Includes one of the best critical introductions in English to Carducci and his poetry.

Davis, J. Madison. "Giosuè Carducci." In *Critical Survey of Poetry*, edited by Rosemary M. Canfield Reisman. 4th ed. Pasadena, Calif.: Salem Press, 2011. An expansive dis-

cussion of Carducci and his work. Recommended as a good starting place for students new to his work.

Dombroski, Robert. "Carducci and Classicism." In *The Cambridge History of Italian Literature*, edited by Peter Brand and Lino Pertile. 2d ed. New York: Cambridge University Press, 1999. Though brief, this essay addresses the question of Carducci's neoclassicism versus his Romanticism.

Poetry of Carew

Author: Thomas Carew (1594-1640)
First published: Coelum Britannicum, 1634; *Poems*, 1640
Type of work: Poetry

Thomas Carew unites, with more success than any of his contemporary poets at the court of Charles I, the classical clarity of Ben Jonson with the intellectual wit of John Donne; at his best he produced work worthy of both his masters, and almost all of his poems are polished and entertaining. Like the other best-known Cavalier poets, Sir John Suckling, Richard Lovelace, Thomas Randolph, and William Davenant, he devoted much of his attention to the song and the love lyric, complimenting real or imaginary ladies. Few poems of this type are lovelier than Carew's "Ask Me No More":

> Aske me no more where Jove bestowes,
> When June is past, the fading rose:
> For in your beauties orient deepe,
> These flowers as in their causes, sleepe.
>
> Aske me no more whether doth stray,
> The golden Atomes of the day:
> For in pure love heaven did prepare
> Those powders to inrich your haire.
>
> . . . .
> Aske me no more if East or West,
> The Phenix builds her spicy nest:
> For unto you at last shee flies,
> And in your fragrant bosome dyes.

The images of the fading rose, the golden atoms, and the phoenix are the traditional ones of Renaissance love poetry, made fresh by the purity of Carew's diction, and they com-

bine to form a tribute that, in effect, transcends the compliment of a single lover to a particular lady and becomes a tribute to all beauty.

Like Ben Jonson, Carew builds much of his love poetry on the imagery and the themes of the Greek and Roman lyric poets. Classical deities, especially Cupid, find their way into many of his poems, and countless of his verses are variations on the familiar "carpe diem" theme of Horace, the notion expressed so well by Robert Herrick in his "Gather Ye Rosebuds While Ye May." Typical of Carew's treatment of the transience of beauty are these lines from one of his longer works, "To A. L., Persuasions to Love":

> For that lovely face will faile
> Beautie's sweet, but beautie's fraile
> 'Tis sooner past, 'tis sooner done
> Then Summers raine, or winters Sun:
> Most fleeting when it is most deare,
> 'Tis gone while wee but say 'tis here.

While the language and imagery of Carew's love poems, his skill at handling a variety of stanza forms, and the melodious quality of his verses, which were often sung, reveal his place as one of the "Sons of Ben," he adopts in many of his lyrics the cynical tone and, occasionally, the bizarre imagery of Donne's early works. He borrows the Metaphysical poets' practice of speaking of love in terms of religion, commerce, or geography, and he uses the device skillfully; however, his language almost always seems derivative, whereas that of

Donne impresses the reader as revelation of new and vital relationships. The song "To my inconstant Mistress" shows Carew's use of a theological vocabulary to speak of his lady:

> When thou, poore excommunicate
> From all the joyes of love, shalt see
> The full reward, and glorious fate,
>   Which my strong faith shall purchase me,
>   Then curse thine owne inconstancie.

Carew's court poetry is witty, elegant, and amusing, but it very rarely, even at its most sensual, conveys anything of the emotional or intellectual power of Donne's work. It is in this sense typical of the writing of the Caroline poets, who were, like their French contemporaries, the *precieux*, generally concerned with form rather than with the expression of either ideas or feelings. (The presence of Charles I's queen, Henrietta Maria, sister of Louis XIII, at the English court ensured some influence of contemporary French culture on English writers.) Even the highly erotic "A Rapture," a glorification of physical love, is so metaphorical in its language that it evokes little sense of real passion.

Carew was, on occasion, capable of breaking out of the conventional bonds of his generation, and he reveals an unexpected strength in his brilliant elegy on Donne, in which he follows his predecessor's techniques closely in paying tribute to him. At the very beginning of the poem, Carew imitates Donne's abrupt, terse style and his strikingly original imagery. He asks why the age has offered no epitaph for one of its great men:

> Can we not force from widdowed Poetry,
> Now thou art dead (Great Donne) one Elegie
> To crowne thy Hearse? Why yet dare we not trust
> Though with unkneaded dowe-bak't prose thy dust,
> Such as the unscisor'd Churchman from the flower
> Of fading Rhetorique, short liv'd as his houre,
> Dry as the sand that measures it, should lay
> Upon thy Ashes, on the funerall day?

Carew captures much of the spirit of Donne's achievement in his reference to "the flame/ Of thy brave Soule, that shot such heat and light,/ As burnt our earth, and made our darknesse bright." The disparate images that follow, related to the themes of gardening, the payment of debts, mining, and harvesting, are fused into a whole through the logical coherence of Carew's comments on Donne's genius and originality. Even here, however, Carew shows his allegiance to a dual tradition, concluding with a Jonsonian epitaph:

> Here lies a King, that rul'd as hee thought fit
> The universall Monarchy of wit;
> Here lie two Flamens, and both those, the best,
> Apollo's first, at last, the true Gods priest.

Carew's contrasting styles could scarcely be seen more clearly than by comparing the poem on Donne with the simple "Epitaph on the Lady Mary Villers," a lyric much like many of Jonson's elegies:

> This little Vault, this narrow roome,
> Of Love, and Beautie is the tombe;
> The dawning beame that 'gan to cleare
> Our clouded skie, lyes darkned here,
> For ever set to us, by death
> Sent to enflame the world beneath;
> 'Twas but a bud, yet did containe
> More sweetnesse then shall spring againe
> A budding starre that might have growne
> Into a Sun, when it had blowne
> This hopefull beautie, did create
> New life in Loves declining state;
> But now his Empire ends, and we
> From fire, and wounding darts are free:
> His brand, his bow, let no man feare
> The flames, the arrowes, all lye here.

Carew here draws skillfully on the classical tradition for the reference to Cupid and for the brevity and conciseness of his form. His handling of the tetrameter line is, throughout his works, masterful, and he achieves an elegiac spirit almost as moving in its simplicity as Jonson's epitaph on "Elizabeth, L. H.": "Under-neath this stone doth lye/ As much beautie, as could dye."

In addition to the love songs and elegies that make up the majority of Carew's poems, he wrote several long verse epistles, modeled on those of Horace and Jonson's imitations of them. These works foreshadow the long reflective poems of the neoclassic age; written in heroic couplets, they are meditative, philosophical, and occasionally satirical, essentially conversations in verse. In one of these epistles, addressed "To Ben Jonson, upon Occasion of his Ode of Defiance annext to his Play of the New Inne," Carew mildly and sympathetically chides his aging master for allowing the strictures of contemporary critics to move him; although Jonson may have created all his works, like children, with equal love, onlookers "may distinguish of their sexe, and place":

Let others glut on the extorted praise
Of vulgar breath, trust thou to after dayes:
Thy labour'd workes shall live, when Time devoures
Th' abortive off-spring of their hastie houres.
Thou art not of their ranke, the quarrell lyes
Within thine own Virge, then let this suffice,
The wiser world doth greater Thee confesse
Then all men else, then Thy selfe onely lesse.

The epistle to Aurelian Townshend, a minor poet who had addressed to Carew verses requesting him to write an elegy on the recently deceased king of Sweden, Gustavus Adolphus, a powerful military commander, gives interesting insight into Carew's sense of his function as a poet. He is no chronicler of heroic deeds:

But these are subjects proper to our clyme
Tourneyes, Masques, Theaters, better become
Our Halcyon dayes; what though the German Drum
Bellow for freedome and revenge, the noyse
Concernes not us, nor should divert our joyes.

Revels and pastoral poetry are the most suitable for him and Townshend, not the chronicles of heroes; he seems to have had no sense that the "halcyon dayes" were soon to draw to a bloody close.

Carew's epistles cover a variety of subjects. As a court poet he often wrote verses welcoming courtiers who had returned from abroad, congratulating members of the royal family on their birthdays or on the births of their children, and commending the plays and poems of his friends as they appeared before the public. His style varied with the subject matter, shifting from Jonsonian clarity and straightforwardness to the intricate vocabulary of the followers of Donne. The latter mode predominates in lines such as the following, from the epistle "To my worthy friend Master George Sands, on his translation of the Psalmes":

I Presse not to the Quire, nor dare I greet
The holy place with my unhallowed feet;
My unwasht Muse, Pollutes not things Divine,
Nor mingles her prophaner notes with thine;
Here, humbly at the porch she listning stayes,
And with glad eares sucks in thy sacred layes.

Carew's most extended work is his masque, *Coelum Britannicum*, presented at Whitehall in 1634. The intellectual content of this work far surpasses that of the other Caroline masques, in which theme and dialogue were generally sacrificed to elaborate dances and complex stage effects. For the subject of the masque and for the content of most of the prose passages Carew drew on the work of the late sixteenth century Italian philosopher Giordano Bruno. The plot concerns a revolution on Mount Olympus; the gods have been so moved by the virtue of the English monarchs that they have resolved to reform, and all the constellations, which represent the old morality, have been banished from the sky. Momus and Mercury, given the task of choosing worthy figures to replace them, listen to the claims of several bizarre figures: Wealth, Poverty, Fortune, and Pleasure. Each of these professes to be the most influential force in determining human actions. The masque ends with an elaborate pageant glorifying the virtues of King Charles and Henrietta Maria; the monarch and his courtiers, dressed as British heroes, take their places in the heavens as the new constellations.

Carew was probably the ablest of all the Cavalier poets. He shows, in flashes, an intellectual depth and a control of language that suggest his potential greatness. His poetic output was limited, however, partly by his own preference for the exciting life of the court and partly by the poetic fashions of his day. He seems to have lacked that spark of genius that can transform conventions and the techniques of others into great original work.

Further Reading

Barbour, Reid. "'Wee, of th' adult'rate mixture not complaine': Thomas Carew and Poetic Hybridity." *John Donne Journal* 7, no. 1 (1988): 92-113. Examines such characteristic qualities of Carew's poetry as doubts about the value of lyric love poems, ambivalence about investing the poet's personality in enduring matters such as letters, and attempts to find a form to accommodate and synthesize these ambivalences. Shows precedents for these tendencies and traces them in several of Carew's poems.

Corns, Thomas N., ed. *The Cambridge Companion to English Poetry, Donne to Marvell*. New York: Cambridge University Press, 1993. Collection of essays includes examinations of common characteristics of sixteenth and seventeenth century poetry, such as its treatment of politics, religion, and gender. Also addressed are the works of individual poets, including Corns's essay "Thomas Carew, Sir John Suckling, and Richard Lovelace."

Doelman, James. "The Statues in Carew's *To G. N., From Wrest*: Other Possibilities." *English Language Notes* 43, no. 2 (December, 2005): 47-50. Provides a contextual analysis of the poem.

Low, Anthony. "Thomas Carew: Patronage, Family, and New-Model Love." In *Renaissance Discourses of Desire*, edited by Claude J. Summers and Ted-Larry Pebworth. Columbia: University of Missouri Press, 1993. Discusses the unconventional absence of Petrarchism in Carew's love poetry. Traces Carew's life circumstances and demonstrates that his failure to secure traditional patronage forced him into rebellion and a reworking of conceptions of love in economic terms.

Parker, Michael P. "Diamond's Dust: Carew, King, and the Legacy of Donne." In *The Eagle and the Dove: Reassessing John Donne*, edited by Claude J. Summers and Ted-Larry Pebworth. Columbia: University of Missouri Press, 1986. Focuses on Carew's elegy on John Donne, exploring how succeeding generations of poets reconciled the two sides of Donne's personality. Follows Carew's argument in his elegy and shows that Carew synthesizes Donne's biography through paradox using Donne's own poetic methods.

Ray, Robert H. "The Admiration of Sir Philip Sidney by Lovelace and Carew: New Seventeenth-Century Allusions." *ANQ* 18, no. 1 (Winter, 2005): 18-21. Describes the influence of Sir Philip Sidney on the poetry of Carew and Richard Lovelace.

Sadler, Lynn. *Thomas Carew*. Boston: Twayne, 1979. Offers a good basic introduction to all aspects of Carew's life and writings. Tackles the problem of categorizing Carew and focuses on the secular nature of the poems. Includes close readings of individual poems.

Semler, L. E. *The English Mannerist Poets and the Visual Arts*. Madison, N.J.: Fairleigh Dickinson University Press, 1998. Explores the relationship between the English mannerist poets and the visual arts in England and the Continent, establishing common characteristics of style. Chapter 4 is devoted to an analysis of Carew's poetry.

Poetry of Clare

Author: John Clare (1793-1864)
First published: 1820-1835; includes *Poems Descriptive of Rural Life and Scenery*, 1820; *The Village Minstrel, and Other Poems*, 1821; *The Shepherd's Calendar*, 1827; *The Rural Muse*, 1835
Type of work: Poetry

The curve of John Clare's life—country-born and country-raised, enjoying literary success in London until the late 1820's, ending his days in a madhouse—is important to appreciate in any reading of his poetry. Clare's roots in the language and customs of the English countryside, more specifically of the little village of Helpstone on the borders of the Lincolnshire Fens, are immediately evident in his earlier poems, as are his extremely delicate perceptions, the totalism of a sensibility nearly always hovering on the edge either of ecstasy or of despair.

Less evident are Clare's strong literary affiliations with the James Thomson of *The Seasons* (1730, 1744, 1746), the William Wordsworth of the *Ode*, and the Lord Byron of *Childe Harold's Pilgrimage* (1812-1818). With Robert Burns, Clare is one of the finest of the "original geniuses" of the late eighteenth and early nineteenth centuries, and he wrote in a vein more authentic and serious than was then in vogue. His own Northamptonshire version of the conserving myth of the countryside, eloquently expressed in his lament

for the loss of Swordy Fell by the enclosures of the 1820's, is in the line of Thomas Gray and Wordsworth and points directly to the writings of William Barnes and Thomas Hardy later in the nineteenth century.

Clare's provincialism, his distance from the literary fashions of his early adulthood, permitted him to mine his slender gift deeply. Again and again he returns to the themes, the moral and technical elements that are present in his earliest poems. The same subjects are to him always new and pressing: the importance of place, the loss of childhood innocence, the destruction of the countryside, absence in love, the poet as nature's spokesperson. There is an uncomplicated resting in nostalgic description rather than a thrusting and exploratory meditation; there is no Wordsworthian straining after the philosophical poem, and Clare's successes are therefore more limited but purer than those of Wordsworth.

Clare's ordinary medium is the loosened heroic couplet, the informal ballad stanza, and the simple quatrain of the later Augustans, and he is not above using the "poetic diction" that Wordsworth explicitly rejected. Clare's originality was not one of perspective or technique so much as it was the focusing of a single-minded intensity upon the problems and perceptions of people living in the country. The "ecstasy" Clare so often alludes to explains much in the tone of his poems on nature and on human love, but it is also directly related to a personal instability, the delicacy or fragility that led to the madness he himself had been anticipating.

Clare begins one of his best poems thus: "Hail, humble Helpstone. . . . Unletter'd spot! unhead in poet's song." The peculiarly Romantic celebration of the local and unique is here, but also a sense that the obscure village may be taken as standing for hundreds of others like it, places finally being encroached upon by wealth and civilization. The enclosure of common forage lands and the leveling of woodlands are concerns even as early as this poem of 1809: "How oft I've sigh'd at alterations made,/ To see the woodman's cruel axe employ'd/ A tree beaheaded, or bush destroy'd."

The resulting conviction that nature is itself somehow threatened accounts for some of the loving anxiousness in Clare's descriptions of both landscape and village life. One may take for an instance the fine stanza from "Summer Images."

> To note on hedgrow baulks, in moisture spent,
> The jetty snail creep from the mossy thorn,
> With earnest heed and tremulous intent,
> Frail brother of the morn,
> That from the tiny bent's dew-misted leaves
> Withdraws his timid horn,
> And fearful vision weaves.

The descriptive vignette, complete in a stanza, is characteristic. Clare is a cataloger, a poet who, with an evocative title ("Morning," "Autumn") or a generalizing opening, launches a poem organized mainly into a progression of instances. "Noon" begins multiplying instances and images with the second line of the poem.

> All how silent and how still;
> Nothing heard but yonder mill:
> While the dazzled eye surveys
> All around a liquid blaze;
> And amid the scorching gleams,
> If we earnest look, it seems
> As if crooked bits of glass
> Seemed repeatedly to pass. . . .
> Not a twig is seen to shake,
> Nor the smallest bent to quake.

"Liquid blaze," though obviously a piece of poetic diction, is nevertheless a small triumph of authenticity. In line with this effect is Clare's inclination to relate human moods to the four seasons. One remembers his comment that the first poetry that genuinely moved him was Thomson's *The Seasons*. Perhaps the finest of his nature poems is "Autumn," written in the unrhymed stanza of William Collins's "Ode to Evening."

> Soon must I view thee as a pleasant dream
> Droop faintly, and so reckon for thine end,
> As sad the winds sink low
> In dirges for their queen;
> While in the moment of their weary pause,
> To cheer thy bankrupt pomp, the willing lark
> Starts from his shielding clod,
> Snatching sweet scraps of song.

Here as elsewhere there are comparisons made between nature and human nature. This analogy works both ways; sometimes there are such phrases as "wind-enamoured aspen" ("Summer Images"). At other times childhood and virginity find images in the blooming of trees or flowers: "Young Jenny blooming in her womanhood/ That hides from day like lilies while in bud." In the poems of Clare's madness, when he writes of the impossibility of recovering his childhood, or of repossessing the unblemished love of his first sweetheart, Mary Joyce, he unconsciously connects his loss with the moods of the natural world. He longs "for scenes, where man hath never trod," where he can "sleep as I in childhood sweetly slept,/ Untroubling, and untroubled where I lie,/ The grass below—above the vaulted sky."

In such poems as "The Village Minstrel," "To the Rural Muse," "Pastoral Poesy," and "The Progress of Rhyme," Clare sets forth the naïve poetics that informs all his lyric utterance. He engages in a radical but fruitful confusion of the process of writing and the observation of natural phenomena: "Wordsworth I love, his books are like the fields" ("To Wordsworth") and "True poesy is not in words,/ But images that thoughts express," and observation affords a "language that is ever green. . . . As hawthorn blossoms, soon as seen,/ Give May to every heart" ("Pastoral Poesy"). It is one indication of Clare's provinciality that he meant these lines quite literally.

An important result of this assumption about the nature and function of poetry is Clare's accuracy of image and phrase. Where the local English is most apt, he will use it, though the effect is idiosyncratic: "—And never choose/ The little sinky foss,/ Streaking the moors whence spared/ water spews/ From pudges fringed with moss."

No animal, insect, or scene is too insignificant to bear description: "I see. . . . I see" is one of Clare's most habitual phrases, and when he writes of "shower-be dimpled sandy lanes," "smoke-tanned chimney tops," or "broad old cesspools" that "glittered in the sun," he is bringing new veridical images into English poetry. In "Eternity of Nature," Clare praises the power behind nature by a marvelously convincing collection of the ways the number five recurs in the phenomena of the world: "So trailing bindweed, with its pinky cup,/ Five leaves of paler hue go streaking up;/ And many a bird, too, keeps the rule alive,/ Laying five eggs, nor more nor less than five."

John Keats thought that Clare was too descriptive, that the images from nature tend in his poetry to remain instances rather than being integrated with sentiment and meditation. The judgment is correct as far as it goes; Clare had visual accuracy, but his descriptive success must be matched against the larger enterprise of Wordsworth, who risked his poetry itself to make it a moral and teaching medium. In Wordsworth and Keats, observation leads more quickly to meditation than in Clare, a poet who does not explore the more symbolic uses of the natural image.

Clare is best known for lyric poetry that nevertheless poses serious questions about life and death and eternity. His longer works have many of the same qualities of observation to recommend them. "The Village Minstrel" and "Childe Harold" are both autobiographical, both charged with the same kind of visual acuity one finds in the shorter poems. One gets from these two poems some sense of what the "Eden" of Clare's humble childhood was like in a poor agricultural community. Clare himself never tires of emphasizing that it was a genuine community; this is the burden of the excellent poem on the labors and customs of a country village presented in *The Shepherd's Calendar*. Here, Clare describes the work, the sport, the violence, and the frank sexuality of provincial farm communities in the early nineteenth century. The honesty of his genre scenes, like the impetuous couplets of the poem, stand in vivid contrast to *The Shepheardes Calender* (1579) of Edmund Spenser.

Clare's "Poems Written in Madness" remain to be described, yet there is no way to describe them in terms or categories other than those used above to discuss poems written before his institutionalization for madness. The superb poems from this period—"To Wordsworth," "Written in a Thunderstorm," "I've Wandered Many a Weary Mile," "I Am," "Hesperus"—represent only an unconscious focusing on the elements of despair and absence already conveyed earlier in Clare's work.

Further Reading

Barrell, John. *The Idea of Landscape and the Sense of Place, 1730-1840: An Approach to the Poetry of John Clare.* New York: Cambridge University Press, 1972. Convincingly places Clare in social and cultural context, with a focus on the poet's love of place and landscape. Barrell's book is the study from which all further Clare criticism proceeds.

Bate, Jonathan. *John Clare: A Biography.* New York: Farrar, Straus, and Giroux, 2003. A detailed biography that sympathetically recounts the events of Clare's often tragic life.

Chirico, Paul. *John Clare and the Imagination of the Reader.* New York: Palgrave Macmillan, 2007. Analyzes the broad range of Clare's poetry, focusing on his literary influences, his comments about contemporary culture, and his obsession with posterity.

Clare, Johanne. *John Clare and the Bounds of Circumstance.* Montreal: McGill-Queen's University Press, 1987. This study of Clare's interest in the localities around him is less sentimental about his politics than most commentaries. Also provides excellent readings of individual poems.

Haughton, Hugh, Adam Phillips, and Geoffrey Summerfield. *John Clare in Context.* New York: Cambridge University Press, 1994. Commissioned to celebrate the bicentennial of Clare's birth, this wide-ranging collection of essays on Clare display various postmodern critical perspectives. Includes essays by such critics as Seamus Heaney, John Lucas, and Nicholas Birns. Also contains an extensive annotated bibliography.

Lucas, John. *England and Englishness: Ideas of Nationhood in English Poetry, 1688-1900.* Iowa City: University of Iowa Press, 1990. Examines Clare's representation of the idea of England in comparison with those of several other poets. Also discusses Clare's depiction of nature and his inner mental state.

Sychrava, Juliet. *Schiller to Derrida: Idealism in Aesthetics.* New York: Cambridge University Press, 1989. A convincing defense of Clare's poetic method as opposed to the dominant Romantic tradition of aesthetics represented by William Wordsworth.

Vardy, Alan D. *John Clare, Politics, and Poetry.* New York: Palgrave Macmillan, 2003. Challenges the traditional view that Clare was a helpless victim of personal and professional disasters. Vardy depicts the poet as being fully involved in his literary career and in the social and political issues of his time.

Poetry of du Bellay

Author: Joachim du Bellay (1522-1560)

First published: 1549-1559; includes *L'Olive*, 1549;
Vers Lyriques, 1549; *Recueil de poésies*, 1549; *La
Musagnoeomachie*, 1550; *XIII Sonnets de l'honnête
amour*, 1552; *Les Antiquités de Rome*, 1558 (partial
translation, 1591, as *Ruines of Rome*); *Les Regrets*,
1558 (*The Regrets*, 1984); *Poemata*, 1558; *Le Poète
courtisan*, 1559

Type of work: Poetry

Orphaned early in his short life, Angevin nobleman Joachim du Bellay wrote some of the finest elegiac and satiric poetry in the French language, although much of it was imitated or simply translated from ancient Greek, Roman, and Italian sources. While studying works from those traditions with the Hellenist Jean Dorat at the latter's Collège de Coqueret, de Bellay and his friends Pierre de Ronsard and Jean-Antoine de Baïf founded the group of seven writers later known as the Pléiade, borrowing the name from a famous school of ancient Greek poets in Alexandria. The group's name referred to the seven daughters of Atlas in Greek mythology, transformed into a constellation of stars. The Pléiade became the most famous French poetic school between the medieval Troubadours and the nineteenth century Romantics.

Fearing that he and his friends would be overshadowed by Thomas Sébillet, who advocated a radical renewal of French language and literature in his *Art Poétique* (1548), the ambitious du Bellay rushed into print with a similar program in his polemical essay *La Défense et illustration de la langue française* (1549; *The Defence and Illustration of the French Language*, 1939). At the time, French was still considered an inferior language to Latin, which was used widely in the Catholic Church and for instruction in universities. Du Bellay advocated revitalizing the French language by reviving archaic words, inventing new words, and imitating what he considered the most prestigious literary forms, such as satire as well as the Italian sonnet (Petrarch) and the Latin epic (Vergil), ode (Horace), and elegy (Ovid). These would replace the medieval French *ballades*, *lais*, *virelais*, *rondeaux*, and *chansons*, with their playful, personal, and often comical subjects.

During the first half of the sixteenth century, humanist scholars had used their study of ancient languages to retranslate the Bible and to call many teachings of the Catholic Church into question. Some poets, such as Clément Marot and Marguerite de Navarre, sympathized with the Huguenots (Protestants), although without leaving the Church. The

Pléiade poets, however, remained loyal Catholics. Their poetry compartmentalizes pagan and Christian mythology and imagery, often placing them together without feeling any doctrinal contradiction. In their popularized Neoplatonism, they represented the idealized lady to whom their poems were dedicated as the window that offered a glimpse of ideal beauty and perfection, without intending to solicit sexual favors or advocate adultery. Thus, they continued the word-games of medieval courtly love.

To illustrate the renewed French literature and language he had recommended in his essay, du Bellay published *L'Olive*, a cycle of fifty sonnets, of which more than half were of neo-Petrarchan inspiration. Fifteen years earlier, the poets Clément Marot and Mellin de Saint-Gelais had introduced the sonnet (a fourteen-line poem with a fixed rhyme scheme, typically *abba*, *abba*, *ccd*, *ede*) to France, but du Bellay was the first to introduce a cycle of sonnets focused on a single love object. (The poems to Lesbia of the ancient Roman Catullus, and the fourteenth century French poet Guillaume de Machaut's *Le Voir Dit*—although not sonnets—were among other precursors.) Despite its predominantly literary inspiration and its frequent Petrarchan antitheses, the world of *L'Olive* richly and sensuously blends mythological references, notations of color and sound, nature images, and intellectual subtlety. The title refers to a (probably imaginary) woman; to the wisdom of the goddess Athena (the olive was her tree); and to du Bellay's main model, Petrarch, who had made the laurel tree famous by celebrating a woman named Laura. Published together with *L'Olive* were the *Vers Lyriques*. Here, du Bellay seems to achieve a more personal tone. Typical topics are the rapid flight of time and the fragility of all worldly goods.

An expanded edition of *L'Olive*, with sixty-five additional sonnets, appeared in 1550. Here the poet turns to the Christian religion to seek and find solace for the loss of his lady. At this moment, Petrarchism becomes transformed by a fervent Platonism, as in the famous sonnet 113. The poet is liberated from the problems of time and earthly beauty by the soul's winged ascent to re-experience (*reconnaître*) the eternal ideas of Beauty, Goodness, and Truth. A striking example of du Bellay's syncretism (the blending of diverse religions) appears in sonnet 114 of *L'Olive*, where Platonic terms infiltrate a text from Saint Paul's Epistle to the Romans.

Unexpectedly, du Bellay's second cousin, Cardinal Jean du Bellay, summoned him to go to Rome as the cardinal's private secretary. The young poet was thrilled by the idea of living in a city whose civilization had so inspired him. Because the cardinal was the French king's main ambassador to Rome, which was then the center not only of Catholic power but also of French political efforts to dominate its great rival Spain, du Bellay no doubt dreamed of playing an influential role in history. Instead, he found himself used as a household manager and errand boy. He also was disgusted by the venality, sexual license, and political corruption of the highest Church officials of the time. He could not safely publish such reactions until he returned to France, but then, in 1558, his two poetic masterpieces, both sonnet cycles, appeared: *Les Antiquités de Rome* and *The Regrets*.

The first, *Les Antiquités de Rome*, celebrates and laments the vanished glories of ancient Roman civilization; the ruins of Rome are compared to fallen giants vanquished by the gods. The second, *The Regrets*, virulently satirizes the corruption of the modern Papacy and dramatizes his own bitter disillusionment. Both reintroduce the alexandrine (twelve-syllable) verse into French, where it would dominate poetry until the early twentieth century and theater until late in the nineteenth century.

The Regrets, a collection of 191 sonnets, contains du Bellay's greatest elegiac and satirical poetry, mature and original. Its purpose was to ease the sorrow of his exile and, by an act of poetic creation, to forget his unpleasant, demanding job and his misfortunes such as loneliness and worsening deafness. However, this attempt often failed, as sonnet 6 reveals:

> Alas, where is my scorn for Fortune's blows?
> Where courage to master adversity,
> My noble wish for immortality,
> And inspiration no commoner knows?
> Where the sweet joys of a sheltering night
> When, free to frolic with the Muses' band
> On the green carpet of a hidden strand
> I led their dances beneath the moon's light?
> Cruel Fortune has overmastered me:
> Now my heart that used to be proud and free
> Is wracked by a thousand regrets and pain.

> Posthumous fame no longer comes to mind;
> Inspiration I can no longer find,
> And the Muses, estranged, flee in disdain.

This poem displays many characteristic features of du Bellay's style. It is quite impersonal, despite the frequent use of the first-person singular. Characters other than the poet are often conventional figures from pagan mythology (Fortune, the Muses). The statements are nearly all negations, which express loss, suffering, and confusion. However, one could construct no coherent biography from the feelings expressed, and no precise landscape from the vague, stock details (night, the bank of a stream, the moon). Du Bellay's tone is usually intensely self-conscious and, often, as here, he paradoxically writes a poem about being unable to find anything to write because he is so deeply depressed. Both personally and historically, in his world the past was always better than the present, where there is no hope. He consistently expresses a flagrantly elitist attitude—Horace's "odi profanum vulgus et arceo" (I detest and shun the common herd)—but finds no energy except in memories, anger, disgust at others, and in the formal rigor of his word structures.

Du Bellay frequently develops the message of a sonnet in the last line, often through irony, causing the reader's imagination to yield in silence to the creative impulse it has received. Antithesis, however, is the usual instrument of du Bellay's wit. It appears as a procedure of composition as well as a device of style. The sonnet itself is an antithetical form, and the subject matter of du Bellay's poetry lends itself to antithetical treatment. Thus in sonnet 6 he contrasts his past life and poetic manner in the quatrains to his present in the tercets. The great myth that does dominate the poems is, of course, that of the exile: Ulysses or Jason, or both together, as in the famous sonnet 31:

> Happy Ulysses who ploughed the seaways
> Or that one who captured the Golden Fleece
> Before returning home to live in peace,
> Wise, with his relatives for all his days.
> Oh when shall I see my village of yore
> With smoking chimneys, never to depart?
> When shall I see my gardens, ranged with art,
> Which are a kingdom to me, and much more?
> I find more joy in my ancestral home
> Than in the haughty palaces of Rome:
> To their proud marble, French slate I prefer.
> I love our Loire more than Tiber's renown;
> Than the Palatine hill, our little town;
> And love sweet Anjou more than Rome's salt air.

Typically for du Bellay, the mythological references clash ironically with their context. Jason, who won the Golden Fleece, lost his children when his abandoned wife Medea killed them for revenge. Both Jason and Ulysses were seafaring conquerors, but the sonnet's last line unfavorably compares Rome's ocean air (connoting military domination of the seas and the empire) to the little freshwater (*eau douce*) streams of du Bellay's village, Liré.

In 1557, du Bellay returned to France to flattering acclaim but also legal difficulties, which, with increasing illness, embittered his last three years. *Le Poète courtisan*, a kind of satirical last will and testament, appeared in 1559, offering ironic advice to the would-be court poet on how to succeed where he himself had failed. In it, du Bellay antithetically takes up again the arguments of *The Defence and Illustration of the French Language*. He then died suddenly on January 1, 1560. The judgment of posterity, however, sees in du Bellay one of France's greatest satiric and lyric poets, second only to Ronsard in his own age and an uncontested master of the sonnet. His innovations helped found modern French poetry.

Revised by Laurence M. Porter

Further Reading

Du Bellay, Joachim. *"The Regrets," with "The Antiquities of Rome," "Three Latin Elegies," and "The Defense and Enrichment of the French Language."* Edited and translated by Richard Helgerson. Philadelphia: University of Pennsylvania Press, 2006. A bilingual edition, with plain prose translations of du Bellay's major works, as well as copious notes, a bibliography, and useful indexes. The excellent introduction is the best starting point for studies of du Bellay.

Katz, Richard A. *The Ordered Text: The Sonnet Sequences of du Bellay.* New York: Peter Lang, 1985. Carefully brings to light the intricate structures of du Bellay's major collections of poems (*L'Olive, Les Regrets, Les Antiquités de Rome*), which all blend elegy (lament), satire (ironic personal attacks), and encomium (praise of influential or potential patrons). The poet's mixed admiration and envy of his close friend Pierre de Ronsard emerges starkly.

Keating, L. Clark. *Joachim du Bellay.* New York: Twayne, 1971. Thoughtful, original, and sensitive in relating du Bellay's biography and inner life to the literature, philosophy, religion, and politics of his times. Outlines and analyzes the major works.

Shapiro, Norman R., and Hope Glidden, eds. *Lyrics of the French Renaissance: Marot, du Bellay, Ronsard.* New Haven, Conn.: Yale University Press, 2002. English versions by Shapiro, introduction by Glidden, notes by Glidden and Shapiro. Shapiro's translations of some 150 poems by du Bellay and his contemporaries faithfully imitate the form of the originals and capture English equivalents of sixteenth century French expressions. The introduction surveys French Renaissance verse; detailed notes accompany some poems.

Poetry of George

Author: Stefan George (1868-1933)

First published: 1890-1928; includes *Hymnen,* 1890 (*Odes,* 1949); *Pilgerfahrten,* 1891 (*Pilgrimages,* 1949); *Algabal,* 1892 (English translation, 1949); *Die Bücher der Hirten und Preisgedichte, der Sagen und Sänge, und der hängenden Gärten,* 1895 (*The Books of Eclogues and Eulogies, of Legends and Lays, and of the Hanging Gardens,* 1949); *Das Jahr der Seele,* 1897 (*The Year of the Soul,* 1949); *Der Teppich des Lebens und die Lieder von Traum und Tod, mit einem Vorspiel,* 1899 (*Prelude, the Tapestry of Life, and The Songs of Dream and of Death,* 1949); *Die Fibel,* 1901 (*The Primer,* 1949); *Der siebente Ring,* 1907 (*The Seventh Ring,* 1949); *Der Stern des Bundes,* 1914 (*The Star of the Covenant,* 1949); *Das neue Reich,* 1928 (*The Kingdom Come,* 1949)

Type of work: Poetry

Stefan George was probably the strongest defender in Germany of the art for art's sake thesis, and his sense of the aesthetic was strong enough to lead him to write his first poems in an invented language, a *lingua romana* similar to Spanish. He disregarded the German rule of grammar that calls for capitalization of all nouns. The resulting loss in reading speed was a most desired effect for the author because he wanted his readers to note that individual words were artistic instruments that may evoke as many, or more, emotions as the colors of a painter's palette. For many years, he printed his books privately, and they were not offered to the public until 1899.

In 1890, George published his first series of poems. With the title of the first poem, "Initiation," he indicates his awareness of his radical departure from the literary mainstream and of his poetry's limited appeal to an audience used to naturalism: "The river calls! Defiant reeds unfurl/ Their slender banners to the languid breeze/ And check the coaxing ripples as they swirl/ To mossy shores in tender galaxies."

The author surrounded himself with a small treasured circle of devoted friends. Most of his works carry dedications; that of his next work, *Pilgrimages*, was written for the Austrian poet Hugo von Hofmannsthal, although that friendship, as the poem anticipates, never matured: "Then I journeyed forth/ And became a stranger,/ And I sought for some one/ To share my mournfulness,/ And there was no one."

In *Hymns* and *Pilgrimages*, George illuminates the conflict between his poetic ideals and the baseness of everyday life. For his next work he used earlier historical periods and Asia as times and places for escape from the unpleasant realities of the present. *Algabal*, written in Paris in 1892, is his personal interpretation of a Roman emperor who moves in a world of time-removed serenity and passionate feelings. George's sense of remoteness, however, never excluded his knowledge of the "mystical body of Christ" inherited from his Catholic childhood in a small town in the German Rhineland: "For I, the one, comprise the multitude."

The Books of Eclogues and Eulogies, of Legends and Lays, and of the Hanging Gardens indicates a turn toward tranquillity; the wanderer once in desperate search for beauty finds it in his own backyard.

> Struck with amazement, as though we were
>   entering a region
> Frostbound when last we had seen it, yet now
>   full of flowers,
> We, who felt old and sorrowful, gazed at
>   each other,
> And our reflections were fused in the river
>   below us.

The Year of the Soul, probably George's best-known book, indicates that the author no longer needed to search for remote backgrounds; an old park is sufficient for the description of images symbolizing the principles of nature and love. Beginning with autumn, the seasons of the year are portrayed, with the exception of the overworked season of spring. The poet invites an unseen friend: "Come to the park they say is dead, and you/ Will see the glint of smiling shores beyond,/ Pure clouds with rifts of unexpected blue/ Diffuse a light on patterned path and pond." In *The Year of the Soul* the lonely prophet speaks again: "The word of seers is not for common sharing."

In 1899, George published *Prelude, The Tapestry of Life, The Songs of Dream and of Death*; each of the main sections contains twenty-four poems, and especially in *The Tapestry of Life*, a poet's picture book, George employs the impressionistic power of words. In the prelude, the poet recollects his struggles: "When pale with zeal, I searched for hidden store. . . ." He almost regrets that his stormy period has ended: "Give me the solemn breath that never failed,/ Give me the fire again that makes us young,/ On which the wings of childhood rose among/ The fumes our earliest offerings exhaled." *The Songs of Dream and of Death* is dedicated to persons or occasions in the poet's life; the sequence ends with a forceful description of everlasting conflict: "All this whirls, tears and pounds, flames and flies,/ Until late in the night-vaulted skies/ They are joined to a bright jewelled beam:/ Fame and glow, pain and bliss, death and dream."

By the time George published *The Seventh Ring* in 1907, a decisive influence had entered his life, the partial fulfillment of his poetic vision. This was his encounter with a young man whom he called Maximin. To George, this youth was the embodiment of a dream and temporarily—Maximin died very young—an end to loneliness. The poet describes the appearance of Maximin: "softened by the mobility and vague sadness that centuries of Christian civilization have wrought in the faces of the people . . . youth in that unbroken fullness and purity that can still move mountains." When Maximin died, George considered his death in the light of a mystical, almost religious event.

> The forest shivers.
> In vain it clothed itself in leaves of spring,
> The field your foot made consecrate is numb
> And cold without the sun you bring.
> The fragile blades on hilly pastures quiver,
> For now you never come.
>
> . . . .
> You also were elect, so do not mourn

For all the days which unfulfillment sheathed.
Praise to your city where a god was born,
Praise to your time in which a god has breathed!

George's next work, *The Star of the Covenant*, a book of a thousand verses, also deals with the significance of Maximin. Some of the poems are not rhymed, but a strong rhythmic flow is present at all times: "You took away the pain of inner schism,/ You, who were fusion made incarnate, bringing/ The two extremes together: light and frenzy!" The poet pleads again for a spiritual life and complains that the German people do not listen to their prophets, one being Friedrich Nietzsche, who, according to George, delivered his message "With such insistence that his throat was cracked./ And you? The shrewd or dull, the false or true,/ You acted as if nothing had occurred." This collection ends with a chorus declaiming that the power to lead a spiritual life is available.

In 1928, George published his last volume, *The Kingdom Come*, in which he remembers the rich literary inheritance of Johann Wolfgang von Goethe and Friedrich Hölderlin. The book also contains a poetic prophecy about war, which had been written during World War I and seems to anticipate the horrors of the next world conflict: "You shall not cheer. No rise will mark the end,/ But only downfalls, many and inglorious./ Monsters of lead and iron, tubes and rods/ Escape their maker's hand and rage unruly."

In "Secret Germany," George expresses abhorrence for the regime and pleads that traditional German values be retained. From then on he wrote no more poetry, and after refusing to become identified with Adolf Hitler's Germany, he died in self-imposed exile in Switzerland in 1933.

During George's lifetime, his poetry appealed to only a small readership, though many were influenced by his translations of the French poets Stéphane Mallarmé, Charles Baudelaire, and Arthur Rimbaud. Those who were his admirers recognized in him a high priest of German literature, a writer who appeared at a time when the ideals of Goethe were still venerated but poetic expression was in danger of being suffocated by excessive romanticism and sentimentality. Under the poet's leadership, a George Circle was founded, which promoted the idea of transforming life to mystical heights by way of art rather than through scientific positivism.

George made the German language an instrument of art, and as a poet he carried Germany's classical tradition into the twentieth century. His inventiveness with the German language makes any translation effort a most difficult undertaking, but the 1949 translations by Olga Marx and Ernst Morwitz succeed in conveying much of George's intensity of feeling into English.

Further Reading

Antosik, Stanley J. *The Question of Elites: An Essay on the Cultural Elitism of Nietzsche, George, and Hesse*. Las Vegas, Nev.: Peter Lang, 1978. An intelligent reappraisal of a dominant aspect of early twentieth century literature.

Bennett, Edwin Keppel. *Stefan George*. New Haven, Conn.: Yale University Press, 1954. An interpretive study that appeared as part of a series on modern European literature and thought. Neither partisan nor judgmental, the appraisal is discriminating and concisely presented. Includes a bibliography.

George, Stefan. *The Works of Stefan George*. Translated by Olga Marx and Ernst Morwitz. 1949. Rev. ed. Chapel Hill: University of North Carolina Press, 1974. An enlarged and newly edited version of the original English translations of George's works. Offers many changes within poems, as well as additional translations intended to give a representative survey of George's earliest poems.

Metzger, Michael M., and Erika A. Metzger. *Stefan George*. New York: Twayne, 1972. A general introduction to the poet, presenting both a biographical sketch and an interpretation of his principal works.

Norton, Robert E. *Secret Germany: Stefan George and His Circle*. Ithaca, N.Y.: Cornell University Press, 2002. Biography focusing on the last three decades of George's life, when he was the center of a group of historians, philosophers, poets, and others who believed they represented the "real" but "secret" Germany and opposed the bourgeois social values of the Weimar Republic.

Rieckmann, Jens, ed. *A Companion to the Works of Stefan George*. Rochester, N.Y.: Camden House, 2005. Collection of essays, including discussions of George's poetics, early works, concepts of love and gay rights, and the essay "George, Nietzsche, and Nazism."

Strathausen, Carsten. *The Look of Things: Poetry and Vision Around 1900*. Chapel Hill: University of North Carolina Press, 2003. Analyzes the relationship of philosophy and visual media to the poetry of George, Rainer Maria Rilke, and Hugo von Hofmannsthal. Argues that the three German-language poets used language as a way to compete aesthetically with photography and film.

Underwood, Von Edward. *A History That Includes the Self: Essays on the Poetry of Stefan George, Hugo von Hofmannsthal, William Carlos Williams, and Wallace Stevens*. New York: Garland, 1988. A collection of comparative and interpretive essays. Includes a bibliography.

Poetry of Laforgue

Author: Jules Laforgue (1860-1887)
First published: 1885-1903; includes *Les Complaintes*,
     1885; *L'Imitation de Notre-Dame la Lune*, 1886; *Les
     Derniers Vers de Jules Laforgue*, 1890; *Le Sanglot
     de la terre*, 1903 (English translation, 1956, as
     Selected Writings of Jules Laforgue; 1958, as *Poems
     of Jules Laforgue*; 1984, as *Selected Poems*)
Type of work: Poetry

Although Jules Laforgue's span of creative activity was tragically brief (about nine years), his poetry attests a prolific and versatile innovator. His artistic evolution carried him from the traditional Alexandrines and somewhat oratorical poems of the posthumous *Le Sanglot de la terre*, written between 1878 and 1882, to experimentation with the rhythm and mood of *chansons populaires* in *Les Complaintes* and, finally, to culmination in *Les Derniers Vers de Jules Laforgue*. Here Laforgue made frequent use of free verse and of what he himself described as psychology in dream form presented in melodic and rhythmic patterns of verse.

"Funeral March for the Death of the Earth," the most celebrated of the poems in *Le Sanglot de la terre*, reveals a young poet who is not afraid to indulge in an uninhibited display of his personal views and to capitulate to a rather bleak pessimism concerning the state of the universe. The poet's cries of despair as he bombastically depicts the horrors of civilization and the corpse of the earth are rarely muted, as they are in succeeding works. Certain lines ("The nocturnal silence of echoless calm,/ Floats, an immense and solitary wreck") are reminiscent of Charles Baudelaire, the precursor of Symbolist poetry whose spell and sphere of influence were ubiquitous in the late nineteenth century.

One of the most distinctive qualities of Laforgue's own personal manner is effective in *Les Complaintes*: The poet cultivates a witty and mocking detachment as an antidote to the blunt expression of personal feelings. The theme of death recurs often in Laforgue's poetry, but it is not personified as a sinister figure in "Complaint About Forgetting the Dead"; Laforguian irony changes death into the "good gravedigger" who scratches at the door. If you refuse to welcome him,

> If you can't be polite,
> He'll come (but not in spite)
> and drag you by your feet
> Into some moonlit night!

The "complaints," named for a folk-song style that the poet imitates, also reveal a flair for inventing humorous anecdotes and dialogues couched in colloquial language; a case in point is the "Complaint of the Outraged Husband," an amusing conversation in verse form between an irate husband, who insists he saw his wife flirting with an officer in church, and his wife, who maintains with injured innocence that she was piously conversing with a "life-size Christ."

A predilection for creating a cast of characters and for dramatizing experience remains a permanent characteristic of Laforgue's style; it reappears most notably in 1886 in the form of a verse drama titled *Le Concile féerique* (*The Faerie Council*). This work, which again demonstrates the poet's preference for depersonalized expression of his sentiments, places onstage the Gentleman, who bemoans the indifference of the cosmos and the tedium of existence, and the Lady, who offers her charms as a cure for his ennui. The subject is typically Laforguian: Love is painted as lacking in glamour, as being somewhat sordid, but it is still an acceptable escape from the disenchanting realities of the world. The structure of this verse drama, as of many of Laforgue's poems, presents an ironic commentary on experience, since a certain frame of mind is developed in the course of the drama and then negated at the end. The earth is round "like a pot of stew," and we are mired in its banalities, but, since this is all human beings can possess, acceptance of one's lot is preferable to some sort of impassioned and futile revolt ("Why don't you see that that is truly our Earth!/ And all there is! and the rest is nothing but tax/ About which you might just as well relax!"). Gaiety and disdain are the prevailing moods of Laforgue, and he prefers these to bitterness and melancholy.

Perhaps the most startling and engaging product of Laforgue's imagination is to be found in the collection titled *L'Imitation de Notre-Dame la Lune*. This work contains a gallery of "choirboys of the Moon," all of whom are named Pierrot. These bizarre individuals prefer lunar landscapes because the moon seems to symbolize aspiration to some absolute, whether it be savoring the love of an ideal and idealized female or giving in to the temptation of suicide and blissful nothingness. However, the thirst for self-extinction inevitably ends with an antithetical declaration of a prosaic determination to enjoy the present moment: "—Of course! the Absolute's rights are nil/ As long as the Truth consists of living."

Clowns are a favorite source of inspiration for modern painters and poets, and few are more individualized and appealing than the Pierrots of Laforgue. They are uniformly white except for a black skullcap and a scarlet mouth:

> It's, on a stiff neck emerging thus
> From similarly starchèd lace,
> A callow under cold-cream face
> Like hydrocephalic asparagus.
>
> The eyes are downed in opium
> Of universal clemency,
> The mouth of a clown bewitches
> Like a peculiar geranium.

It is worth noting that Ezra Pound was struck by the phrase "like hydrocephalic asparagus" and, in general, by Laforgue's frequent reliance on a scientific lexicon to revivify patterns of poetic expression. In this domain, also, the French poet was an important innovator.

The Pierrots, who "feed on the absolute, and sometimes on vegetables, too," are distinguished not only by their acute awareness of death and by their refusal to seek solace and protection from their fate but also by the inexplicable spell they cast over the opposite sex. They rhapsodize extravagantly when they talk of love, but they speak "with toneless voices." As amusing embodiments of contradictory elements, they offer another example of Laforguian irony. In addition, the portraits of these "dandies of the Moon" permit Laforgue to assume an imaginary identity and expound behind a mask a blasé and mocking view of love, life, and death.

Laforgue was one of the first poets in the nineteenth century to exploit successfully the possibilities of the free-verse form. "Solo by Moonlight" in *Les Derniers Vers de Jules Laforgue* is an excellent illustration of his talent for molding the length of the verse line to conform to the flow of thought and the association of images: The poet is stretched out on top of a stagecoach moving rapidly through a moonlit countryside, and his composure, as well as his body, is jolted, for he remembers a promising love that ended in misunderstanding. The rhythm and mood are partially created by Laforgue's use of lines of radically different length. At the same time, the poem is infused with a dreamlike atmosphere;

impressions are nebulous, and the woman is only briefly glimpsed and partially understood as the poet attempts to recall the past. The theme of frustrated love is purposely left ambiguous and contributes to the evocation of psychology in dream form. A kind of paralysis engendered by boredom and a vague malaise prevented the poet from declaring himself; a simple gesture would have elicited a warm response in the woman, but "Ennui was keeping me exiled,/ Ennui which came from everything. So."

Familiar themes recur in *Les Derniers Vers de Jules Laforgue*. "The Coming Winter" is a poem on autumn that suggests encroaching deterioration and imminent death. Startling verbal juxtapositions help avert the dangers of overstatement and sentimentalism ("Rust gnaws the kilometric spleens/ Of telegraph wires on highways no one passes"), and Laforgue's sense of humor remains very much in evidence, as in "Oh! the turns in the highways,/ And without the wandering Little Red Riding Hood."

Critics have frequently noted the debt that many French writers of imposing stature owe to Laforgue's original handling of irony, versification, imagery, and colloquial language. At the same time, along with Paul Verlaine, Laforgue inspired composers as different as Arnold Schoenberg, Darius Milhaud, and Jacques Ibert. He also had a profound influence on the poetry of T. S. Eliot, Ezra Pound, and Hart Crane.

Further Reading

Arkell, David. *Looking for Laforgue: An Informal Biography*. New York: Persea Books, 1979. Accessible biography traces elements of Laforgue's poetry to specific events in his life. Includes translations of many of Laforgue's letters, providing insight into his personal relationships and creative evolution. Includes illustrations.

Collie, Michael. *Jules Laforgue*. London: Athlone Press, 1977. Brief volume offers a well-constructed introduction to Laforgue and his poetry. Includes sections on the poetry and its influence on later writers, a brief critical analysis by Collie, and select appraisals by other critics.

Everdell, William R. "Whitman, Rimbaud, and Jules Laforgue: Poems Without Meter, 1886." In *The First Moderns: Profiles in the Origins of Twentieth-Century Thought*. Chicago: University of Chicago Press, 1997. Argues that the three nineteenth century poets laid the groundwork for the modernist poetry of the twentieth century. Discusses Laforgue's life and literary influences, his literary career, and the characteristics of his poetry.

Holmes, Anne. "'De nouveaux rhythmes': The Verse of Laforgue's 'Solo de Lune.'" *French Studies* 62, no. 2 (April, 2008): 162-172. Analyzes the poem in the light of the Symbolists' claim that their free verse was inspired by music. Examines the poem's double narrative and contrapuntal structure and its use of musical features, describing how Laforgue's desire to connect music, Impressionist painting, and free verse influenced the poem's structure and detail.

_____. *Jules Laforgue and Poetic Innovation*. New York: Oxford University Press, 1993. Excellent, exhaustive study is divided into sections on Laforgue's collections of poetry. Focuses primarily on *Derniers Vers* but provides ample information about all of the poetry, including its effects on later poets and its place within literary discourse.

Laforgue, Jules. *Poems of Jules Laforgue*. Translated and introduced by Peter Dale. Rev. ed. London: Anvil Press Po-

etry, 2001. Dale, himself a poet, provides new English translations of Laforgue's poems accompanied by an introduction that discusses Laforgue's work and influence.

Ramsey, Warren. *Jules Laforgue and the Ironic Inheritance*. New York: Oxford University Press, 1953. Enduring study of Laforgue examines his aesthetics and his poetry. Includes chapters on Laforgue's influence on T. S. Eliot, Ezra Pound, and Hart Crane.

_____, ed. *Jules Laforgue: Essays on a Poet's Life and Work*. Carbondale: Southern Illinois University Press, 1969. Collection of twelve essays includes biographical information, analyses of the poetry, and discussions of Laforgue in relation to his contemporaries and literary heirs in France and the United States.

Poetry of Machado

Author: Antonio Machado (1875-1939)
First published: 1907-1926; includes *Soledades, galerías, y otros poemas*, 1907 (*Solitudes, Galleries, and Other Poems*, 1987); *Campos de Castilla*, 1912 (*The Castilian Camp*, 1982); *Nuevas canciones*, 1924; *De un cancionero apócrifo*, 1926
Type of work: Poetry

The spiritual crisis brought about in Spain by the loss of its last overseas possessions in Spanish America in 1898 found expression through the works of the Spanish writers of the Generation of '98. Pessimism, analysis of the past, desire for change, and consciousness of history are reflected in productions of Spanish writers of that time.

Spain had actually been suffering a prolonged frustration in its national goals. Most of Spain's American colonies—discovered, explored, conquered, acculturated, and exploited by the mother country—had obtained their independence during the first quarter of the nineteenth century. A relatively small portion of the old Spanish Empire remained. When Cuba and Puerto Rico gained their freedom, Spain lost all its political links with the American continent. Four centuries of Spanish rule and influence in the Americas had ended.

A strong reaction appeared among the Spanish intelligentsia. Spain was obliged to set new goals, examine its traditions, and reexamine its political life. Philosophers, fiction writers, and essayists put together their efforts to arouse the

soul of their country and make it open its eyes to reality and the future. It could be thought that this generation had no place for poets, who are often unconcerned with national affairs. Antonio Machado, however, who is the best poet of the Generation of '98, fully shared the intellectual and emotional attitude of his age. The development of his themes and his poetic perspective began in the critical years following the last breath of the Spanish Empire. From his first poems Machado shows the concerns of his poetry. He is, in all his books, the poet of time, of melancholy memories, of death, and of concern for his country. He would die in exile.

Perhaps no other Spanish-speaking poet has written so much about the phenomenon of time. For him, poetry is the essential method by which one may communicate with his or her time. Poetry is a way of bridging time and obtaining permanent, intemporal results. In other words, poetry for him is the result of inner, personal experience, in contact with his world, expressed not only by way of ideas, but mainly by way of intuition, with the intention of giving to such experiences a universal value.

Few writers have felt the burden of time as Machado did. A philosopher and poet, he went deep into the analysis of its essence both as a metaphysical entity and as a reality affecting human life. He did not theorize about it; through poetry he tried to grasp its meaning and to present its pathetic impact upon the individual.

Among his preferred ways of meeting time and interpreting his own life, Machado finds in daydreams a fit instrument. For Machado, poetry is also a daydream; life is a permanent attitude of watchful vision with open eyes. Readers can frequently discover in his poetry an ecstatic mood. Rather than recalling his memories, he used to dream of them. For him the true interior life was that of dreams and, conversely, dreams were the best way of knowing his inward being.

These dreams are not the substance of the subconscious, nor are they expressed in a super-realistic manner. They are simply the manifestation of yesterday that presses upon the poet, causing him to live his life again in recollection. In this way they are made present and converted into poetic forms. Time is the span between birth and death. For Machado, who was reared in an educational environment devoid of religious training, death is only a limit, a state of absolute finiteness, rather than the last act of human life or the beginning of a different one. Since nobody can boast of having experienced death, its apprehension is only a concept, the object of belief, not of knowledge. At the same time, death is always possible. As a result of death's constant imminence, Machado experiences the anguish of death but meets it with a stoic resignation. In his poetry there is neither the cry of rebelliousness nor belief in the immortality of the soul. Sometimes death appears as something connatural with the poet—a companion. The presence of death is sometimes so sharp that Machado suddenly thinks that his end is imminent, but he is appeased by the hope of living more days until he may see the bright morning of death.

"Spain aches me," was the poignant cry of Miguel de Unamuno y Jugo, one of the writers of the Generation of '98. It was an attitude shared by all his contemporaries. That generation of Spaniards took as their own the collective problems of their country. These problems were the consequence of many years of national life without collective values and endeavors. Machado devoted his pen to a poetic dissection of his country. *The Castilian Camp* is his contribution to the most pungent question of his generation: the past and future of Spain.

A doubled Spain appears in this book: the "official" and the "authentic" Spain. For Machado, the two Spains have been living divorced for many years. The "official" has created a Spain of tradition, laziness, individualism, and presumptions. The "authentic" is the Spain of the people, who dream and fight and think and live after their own ideals of honesty, hard work, and patriotism.

Castile is, for the writers of this generation, the heart and symbol of Spain, because it has played a special role in Spanish life for many years. Machado chooses this region and tries to find in it both the constructive and destructive forces that have molded the Spanish soul. The landscape of his vision is chiefly that of Soria, where he spent some important years of his life and where he met his wife, who died a few years later. He remembers his childhood in Seville, merry and colorful, in contrast to a less happy youth in the Castilian plateau.

The Castilian Camp abounds in strong, pessimistic poems, written mainly in the most traditional meters of Spanish poetry: the Alexandrine and the octosyllabic. Machado speaks of poor people, ancient warriors, barren fields, familiar tragedies, and the painful remembrance of his dead wife.

In "The Land of Alvargonzalez," the longest poem in the book, Machado depicts the tragedy of a rural family. The poet, in bitter, popular, and lyric *romanzas*, tells a story of envy and murder. The father is killed by his older sons; his farm, which they inherit, becomes arid; and when Miguel, the last born of the brothers, returns rich from the New World, he buys the farm from his brothers. The land flourishes, and his brothers, repentant of their sin, plunge into the Black Lagoon.

The Castilian landscape is frequently associated with his wife, Leonor, dead at the age of seventeen in Soria. This only true love was born, met the poet, married him, and died in the Castilian land. Machado imagines going with her, enjoying the scenery, though the consciousness of her death makes him melancholy. Machado never gave profound expression of religious origin. His education, based on the principles of secularization of thought and the philosophy of positivism, was not concerned with the relationship between divinity and humanity. There is an agnostic attitude in most of his books. His interpellations to God are vague and made among dreams.

In Machado's poetry some preference is made toward the metaphysical treatment of love. For him, love begins as an abrupt increment of the vital energy, yet with nothing tangible that needs attention. It is like the explosion of spring, an attitude of being escorted by an impersonal and merely suggested companion. A second step in love comes later when a man encounters a real woman, but then, paradoxically, anguish and waste of life plague the lover because in spite of his efforts he cannot yield himself totally to the loved one. When she disappears from the immediate circle of the lover, oblivion comes. Finally, she becomes only a subject of reminiscence and poetry.

Time, the past, dreams, death, love, and the nation are the eternal questions of human life. Poets and philosophers have tried to find some answer to them. Machado, poet and philosopher, made an attempt to find an explanation of himself and his world in a given time and space. He did not succeed, and he did not expect to, but he left the deep, beautiful, tentative testimony of one who thinks that he is only a traveler in this world, condemned to the yoke of time and to obtaining at best a glimpse of life's mysteries.

Further Reading

Cobb, Carl W. *Antonio Machado*. New York: Twayne, 1971. An excellent starting point for the discussion of Machado's poetry. Contains a useful chronology of the poet's life and works, a good bibliography, and critical analyses of the major poems.

Diaz-Plaja, Guillermo. *A History of Spanish Literature*. Edited and translated by Hugh A. Harter. New York: New York University Press, 1971. A necessary and interesting introduction not only to Machado's poetry but also to the famous literary and philosophical group to which he belonged, the Generation of '98. Highlights the poet's use of its themes and preoccupations.

Johnston, Philip G. *The Power of Paradox in the Work of Spanish Poet Antonio Machado, 1875-1939*. Lewiston, N.Y.: E. Mellen Press, 2002. Johnston's study focuses on two types of paradox: the ambiguities and contradictions in Machado's work and Machado's use of paradox as a figure of speech and rhetorical device.

Krogh, Kevin. *The Landscape Poetry of Antonio Machado: A Dialogical Study of "Campos de Castilla."* Lewiston, N.Y.: E. Mellen Press, 2001. Examines how the landscape in this collection of poetry is either a "protagonist or coprotagonist with man in the human experience."

Young, Howard Thomas. *The Victorious Expression: A Study of Four Contemporary Poets*. Madison: University of Wisconsin Press, 1964. In this intricate analysis, the themes, structures, and leitmotifs of Machado's poetry are juxtaposed and contrasted with those of three of his contemporaries.

Poetry of Mörike

Author: Eduard Mörike (1804-1875)
First published: 1838-1846; includes *Gedichte*, 1838 (*Poems*, 1959); *Idylle vom Bodensee: Oder, Fischer Martin und die Glockendiebe*, 1846
Type of work: Poetry

Since the Romantic period was, among other things, a revolt against the Age of Reason, it is frequently asserted that the Romantics were sentimental eccentrics. Eduard Mörike cannot be classified as such. He was a sensitive dreamer, a skillful poet, but above all a poet of simplicity. A contemporary critic called him "a human being in nightgown and soft slippers." Although purists of the Romantic period praise Friedrich Hölderlin, Mörike was able to appeal to a larger public. Many of his poems became folk songs and the basis of folklore during his lifetime. Johannes Brahms, Franz Schumann, and Hugo Wolf set some of his poems to music, and most of these works are still to be heard in concert halls all over the world. Mörike was a master of classical meters, but he abhorred strict theoretical principles in his work. D. F. Strauss, his famous theologian contemporary, said of Mörike, "Thanks to his work, nobody can sell us rhetoric for poetry." Describing the poet's intuitive creativity, he stated that "Mörike takes a handful of earth, squeezes it ever so little, and a little bird flies out."

Mörike made full use of the wealth of inflections that the German language offers. Some critics, however, object to a lack of composition in his poems. Frequently, past, present, and future are interwoven without proper sequence. Mörike himself was suspicious of a purely academic approach. In an epigram, he replied to his German critics: "You can see in his poems that he can express himself in Latin." He was a representative of the Schwaebische Dichterschule (Swabian school), which had formed around poet Ludwig Uhland. Heinrich Heine, who detested the lack of cosmopolitan ambitions, attacked the school with satirical comments. Mörike always remained a native son, and some of his poems are written in Swabian dialect. He did not leave Swabia except for a few excursions into Bavaria, Tyrol, and Switzerland, and he disregarded the problematic speculations of his time, which caused Johann Wolfgang von Goethe to examine all aspects of nineteenth century knowledge and which made Hölderlin seek refuge in the idealistic world of Greece. Goethe tried to explore the unexplorable, while Mörike maintained a childlike vision and radiated in his poems an adoration of life without torturing his mind with a multitude of question marks. This attitude is demonstrated in his most frequently quoted poem, "Prayer":

> Lord, send what pleaseth Thee!
> Let it be weal or woe;
> Thy hands give both, and so
> Either contenteth me.
> But, Lord, whichever
> Thou giv'st, pain or pleasure,
> O do not drench me!
> In sweet mid-measure Lieth true plenty.

A prose translation of the same poem may serve to illustrate the simple choice of words that could not be employed in a poetical translation:

> Lord, send what you will
> Love or sorrow
> I am happy
> That both flow from your hand.
> Do not overload me
> With joy
> Or with sorrow
> In the middle lies sweet contentment.

Mörike, the seventh child in a family of thirteen, was born in 1804, the son of a medical doctor. A student of theology, he entered the Lower Seminary at Urach and continued his studies at the Higher Seminary. Although he came to dislike theological study, he nevertheless became a pastor in the small Swabian village of Kleversulzbach, chiefly because his mother felt that the ministry was the proper profession for any educated man. His father had died early, and his mother came from a vicar's family. An attempt in 1828 to establish himself as writer and editor had failed. He admitted feeling

"like a tethered goat" when he started his pastoral duties, and he preferred to write poetry instead of sermons. Frequently he had to borrow his Sunday sermons from a colleague. In 1838 he published his first volume, *Poems*. His attitude toward his parishioners is described in "A Parson's Experience":

> Fortunately my peasants like a "sharp sermon." What happens is that on Saturday evening after eleven o'clock they creep into my garden and steal my lettuce and on Sunday in the morning service they expect the vinegar for it. But I make the ending gentle: they get the oil.

After nine years, in 1843, Mörike resigned from his position as pastor for reasons of ill health. The major reason was his desire to be free from his pastoral duties. His happiest time arrived when he obtained a position as a professor of literature in a girls' high school. A one-hour teaching assignment each week left sufficient time for writing poetry, and the girls enjoyed being lectured on poetry by a real poet. He even earned an honorary doctor's degree, and the queen attended one of his lectures. His major diversions from his literary work were his delightful drawings, which showed again his ability to create something without strenuous effort. His drawings, issued as a separate volume, have only recently found a larger audience.

Mörike married in 1851, but eventually he and his wife separated. He had also had an unhappy experience with the opposite sex in his student days, when he fell in love with a beautiful young woman who had a doubtful reputation and who failed to remain faithful to him. Five poems with the title "Peregrina" describe his joy and sorrow in love. The cycle ends with the following words:

> Could I forsake such beauty? The old bliss
> Returns, and seems yet sweeter than before.
> O come! My arms have waited long for this.
> But at the look she gives my heart grows sore.
> Hatred and love are mingled in her kiss.
> She turns away, and will return no more.

Another love affair, which resulted in an engagement, was called off three years later. Retelling his experience, Mörike again demonstrates his ability to evoke deep feelings with simple words:

> Fare you well—you could not guess
> What a pang the words imparted,
> For you spoke with cheerful face,

Going on your way light-hearted.
Fare you well—time and again
Since that day these words I've spoken,
Never weary of the pain,
Though my heart as oft was broken.

In spite of unfortunate love affairs and an unhappy marriage, Mörike never lost his serenity, which was based on a sincere belief in the goodness of his creator and his place in God's creation. In his most famous prose piece, "Mozart auf der Reise nach Prag" ("Mozart on a Voyage to Prague"), he inserted a poem, usually titled "O Soul, Remember," which indicates his sense of tranquillity while speaking about the ever-present reality of death:

A sapling springs, who knows
Where, in the forest;
A rosebush, who can say
Within what garden?
Chosen already both—
O soul, remember—
To root upon your grave
And to grow there.

Like most Romantics, Mörike used nature as his major source of inspiration. When he was a curate, he was found resting in the grass of the churchyard while the honor of the Sunday sermon was given to young assistants. Restful poems such as "Withdrawal" were the result of such leisure:

Let me go, world, let me go!
Come no more with gifts to woo me!
Leave this heart of mine, now, to me,
With its joy and with its woe!

In his adoration of nature he also refrained from the emotional eccentricities that can be noted in the work of his contemporaries. He described his impressions in simple rhymes, which found their way into numerous poetry collections, children's books, and schoolbooks. "September Morning" falls into this category:

The world's at rest still, sun not through,
Forest and field lie dreaming:
But soon now, when the veil drops, you
Will see the sky's unmisted blue;
Lusty with autumn and subdued,
The world in warm gold swimming.

Many love poems, free of affectation, also flowed easily from Mörike's pen. "Question and Answer" is typical:

Whence, you ask me, did the demon
Love gain entrance to my heart?
Why was not long since his venom
Wrenched out boldly with the dart?

Mörike's poems are not the products of tense creative effort by candlelight in an attic (a setting used by most Romantic painters of the era to depict poets). In all of his poems the element of spontaneity is apparent. Nothing sounds labored or contrived. One of his poems, written in bed on a morning, is "The Sisters," now a well-known Brahms duet. The popular love poem "Fair Rohtraut" was started when he saw the name in a dictionary:

Then they rode home without a word, Rohtraut,
Fair Rohtraut;
The lad's heart sang though he made no sound:
If you were queen and today were crowned,
It would not grieve me!
You thousand leaves of the forest wist
That I Fair Rohtraut's mouth have kissed!
—Quiet, quiet, my heart!

It is not surprising that Mörike's deep love of nature and his childlike purity of imagination made him also an outstanding teller of fairy tales and writer of ballads. The mythical world of ghosts and elves comes alive in the "Song of the Elves" and "The Ghosts at Mummeisee."

In spite of his marriage to a Roman Catholic, the poet never showed an inclination to become a member of any church after he left his pastoral assignment. He was under the influence of his friend D. F. Strauss, who wrote the most unorthodox biography of Jesus of this time. That Mörike admired the ritual of the Catholic Church is evident, however, in his poem "Holy Week."

Following his separation from his wife in 1873, he lived in several places and at spas, residence made possible by financial help from his friends. He died in 1875, and on his deathbed he was reconciled with his wife.

The simplicity of Mörike's poems made many of them popular during his lifetime, yet at the same time this quality prevented proper recognition of his art by many of his fellow Romantics. In spite of his unsophisticated writings, no critic ever accused Mörike of being trivial. If the test of time is considered the most valid gauge of the value of a poet's work, Mörike easily has passed the test, and he will probably remain a popular poet for generations to come. Gottfried Keller, a contemporary Swiss poet and novelist, said after Mörike's death, "He died like the departure of a quiet mountain spirit . . . like a beautiful day in June. If his death does not bring him closer to the people—it is only the people's fault."

Further Reading

Adams, Jeffrey, ed. *Mörike's Muses: Critical Essays on Eduard Mörike*. Columbia, S.C.: Camden House, 1990. Ten scholarly essays provide textual and thematic analysis of Mörike's poetry; a number suggest sources for the poet's inspiration and comment on the psychological dimensions of his creative drive.

Mare, Margaret. *Eduard Mörike: The Man and the Poet*. 1957. Reprint. Westport, Conn.: Greenwood Press, 1973. Detailed, comprehensive biography interweaves analysis of the poetry into Mörike's life story. Quotations from the works are presented in the original German.

Rennert, Hal H. *Eduard Mörike's Reading and the Reconstruction of His Extant Library*. New York: Peter Lang, 1985. Focuses on the poet's reading to show how other writers influenced the development of Mörike's poetry and how his works reflect his debt to his literary masters.

Slessarev, Helga. *Eduard Mörike*. New York: Twayne, 1970. Sketches the poet's life and reviews the major works, providing textual analysis and concentrated examination of poetic form in Mörike's lyrics. Includes an assessment of Mörike's appeal to modern-day readers.

Stern, J. P. *Idylls and Realities: Studies in Nineteenth-Century German Literature*. New York: Frederick Ungar, 1971. Includes a chapter on Mörike that describes his accomplishments as a lyricist, claiming the poet "excels at showing man in contact with the natural world." Explicates a number of the poems.

Ulrich, Martin Karl. *Eduard Mörike Among Friends and "False Prophets": The Synthesia of Literature, Music, and Art*. New York: Peter Lang, 1996. Examines the images in Mörike's poetry, his novella about Wolfgang Amadeus Mozart, and the Mörike poems that Hugo Wolf and other composers set to music.

Youens, Susan. *Hugo Wolf and His Mörike Songs*. New York: Cambridge University Press, 2000. Examines the collaboration between Mörike and Wolf, a Viennese composer who set fifty-three of Mörike's poems to music. Describes how the two men had different ideas about the arts and how Wolf's own experiences and ideas are reflected in the songs that resulted from the collaboration.

Poetry of Skelton

Author: John Skelton (c. 1460-1529)
First published: 1568, as *Pithy, Pleasaunt, and Profitable Workes of Maister Skelton, Poet Laureate*
Type of work: Poetry

To place John Skelton in a convenient niche in literary history is difficult, but it is even more difficult to find an appropriate artistic designation for the work of this early Tudor poet. Nearer in time to the writing of Sir Thomas Wyatt or Henry Howard, earl of Surrey, Skelton is much nearer in his style to the writing of the medieval Latinists.

Despite being called a Humanist scholar, Skelton did not have much in common with the Humanists and even indulged in some feuding with them. While the Humanists (a group of scholars, associated with Desiderius Erasmus, whose intellectual focus was on the human rather than the divine) were reviving an interest in the classical Greek and Latin writers and using them for examples, Skelton continued to copy the style of fourteenth and fifteenth century writ-

ers. What he had in common with the Humanists, however, was an interest in the world and in people as they are.

"The Bouge of Court" is typical of the medieval tradition in several ways. It uses rhyme royal to tell a dream allegory, relies heavily on personification and the use of court terms, and has the usual astronomical opening and closing apology. The prologue begins with allusions to the sun, the moon, and Mars. The narrator wishes he could write, but being warned by Ignorance not to try, he lies down and dreams of going aboard a ship, *The Bouge of Court*, which is owned by Sans Peer and captained by Fortune. The narrator, who reveals that he is called Drede, is first accosted and frightened by Danger, the chief gentlewoman of Sans Peer. Before Drede can flee, he is soothed by Desire, who persuades him to stay aboard.

After this introduction comes the main body of the poem, which consists of conversation between Drede and seven of the passengers, Skelton's representations of the seven deadly sins. Drede first describes the approaching figure in unforgettable detail; then, as the figure speaks, an even sharper focus of his personality is achieved. The seven passengers are named Favel or Flattery, Suspect, Harvy Hafter, Disdain, Riot, Dissimulation, and Deceit. Harvy Hafter is Skelton's most colorful creation in the poem, and he is still around.

> But as I stood musing in my mind,
> Harvy Hafter came leaping, light as lynde.
> Upon his breast he bare a versing-box,
> His throat was clear, and lustily could fayne.
> Methought his gown was all furréd with fox,
> And ever he sang, '*Sith I am nothing plain . . .*'
> To keep him from picking it was a great pain:
> He gazed on me with goatish beard;
> Whan I looked on him, my purse was half afeard.

Thus, Harvy Hafter is the typical confidence man, always optimistic, always ready to dispel all doubts and fears with pat answers and stale jokes.

After talking with these seven characters, Drede fears for his life and jumps overboard. The leap and hitting the water awaken him, and he seizes his pen and records his dream. In the final stanza, his apology, he states that what he has recorded is only a dream, but sometimes even dreams contain truth.

> I would therewith no man were miscontent,
> Beseeching you that shall it see or read
> In every point to be indifferent,
> Sith all in substance of slumbring cloth proceed.
> I will not say it is matter indeed,
> But yet oft-time such dreams be found true.
> Now construe ye what is the residue!

Though this poem is typical of the medieval tradition, its importance lies in how it deviates from the tradition: Its difference is Skelton's contribution. His characters are certainly types, as in a dream allegory they must be, but they are more than the mere pictured figures of medieval writing. They are highly individualized characters, as shown by Harvy Hafter's description, and they are characterized not only by description but also by their own speech. Furthermore, Skelton's setting is more concrete than is usual in the medieval tradition.

The allegory depicts the life at court as Skelton saw it. The highest achievement of the courtier was to be recognized by the king and to maintain his favor, no matter what the means. Those who attained his favor were openly praised but privately scorned and envied by the others. Thus, if one succeeded, he failed to maintain the true friendship of his fellow courtiers, for flattery, jealousy, disdain, suspicion, and other feelings all joined forces to destroy such friendship. To Skelton, the irony of such a life was that gaining the attention of the king was accomplished purely by chance. Since this kind of court life was demeaning, in Skelton's view, he attacked it.

Another of Skelton's early poems that shows the poet still working in the medieval tradition is "Philip Sparrow." Following a medieval point of view, Skelton wrote this poem in the short-lined couplets, tercets, and quatrains now known as Skeltonic verse. This poem is Skelton's most playful and most popular work; in it, readers see the poet in a mood in which he casts dignity and restraint aside and indulges himself in a bit of fantasy. He describes the activities of the bird, its death, and its funeral. It is a long and rather loose poem that can be broken into three distinct parts.

The first part, which takes over half of the 1,382 lines in the poem, is a dramatic monologue with Jane Scroop as narrator telling of her Philip Sparrow. Through her, Skelton gives the reader his appraisal of Geoffrey Chaucer, John Gower, and John Lydgate, and uses the opportunity to display his wide reading in Greek and Latin. He parodies the funeral mass by having the whole host of birds chant over the dead body of Philip Sparrow. The most delightful lines are those in which Jane talks of her pet.

> It had a velvet cap,
> And would sit upon my lap,
> And seek after small wormes,
> And sometimes white bread-crumbes;
> And many times and oft
> Between my breastes soft
> It woulde lie and rest;
> It was proper and prest.
>
> Sometime he would gasp
> When he saw a wasp;
> A fly or a gnat,
> He would fly at that;
> And prettily would he pant
> When he saw an ant.
> Lord, how he would pry
> After the butterfly!

In the second part of the poem, "The Commendacione," Skelton commends and defends Jane Scroop as the composer of the first section. He also spends much time reporting "the goodly sort/ Of her features clear," and ends each section of the "Commendacione" with a refrain: "For this most goodly floure,/ This blossom of fresh colour,/ So Jupiter me succour,/ She flourisheth new and new/ In beauty and virtue." The third part of the poem, the "Addition," was clearly added after the other two had been written. It is an answer to the critics of the poem and a protest against their criticism.

"The Tunning of Elinour Rumming," more than all the other poems together, has earned for Skelton the title of scurrilous or, as from Alexander Pope, "beastly." It is Skelton's most notorious work. The first part of the poem introduces the host, Elinour. Then follow seven sections of various scenes in a tavern. This study of the Tudor lower classes is extremely realistic. To show the stench and squalor of the bar, Skelton eliminates no details, no matter how crude or coarse. Still, there is a vitality in the realism of the scene, and the impression—no matter how unpleasant it may be to some, though to others it may be only humorous—is an unforgettable one. For example,

> Maud Ruggy thither skippéd:
> She was ugly hippéd,
> And ugly thick lippéd,
> Like an onion sided,
> Like tan leather hided.
> She had her so guided
> Between the cup and the wall
> That she was there withal
> Into a palsy fall;
> With that her head shakéd,
> And her handes quakéd,
> One's head would have achéd
> To see her nakéd.

Even Skelton decides he has gone too far in his description of the tawdry existence: "I have written too much/ Of this mad mumming/ Of Elinour Rumming."

Like many others after him, Skelton excuses himself for his descent by saying that he has written the poem to show others how to escape from such a fall. The gusto of the representation shows a familiarity with the subject that is unexpected in such a scholar and churchman.

Perhaps Skelton's most puzzling work is "Speak, Parrot." There are several reasons for the vagueness of the poem, which has been called unintelligible. In the first place, there is strong evidence to suggest that the work is a collection of many poems written at various times. Although some of the poems are even dated, the method Skelton used to date them is not conventional, so that any attempt to decipher these dates is mostly guesswork. Another reason for the vagueness is that Skelton thought that to protect himself from charges of treason he had to veil his allusions to topical incidents in allegorical language. He uses the book of Judges for many terms of this language. Present knowledge of particular events of the day also cloud an intelligible interpretation. Finally, the device Skelton uses as framework for "Speak, Parrot" compounds the vagueness. He puts the whole narration into the mouth of a parrot who relates the poem in no particular chronological sequence, and at times the parrot speaks only gibberish.

In this poem Skelton still relies on the medieval use of allegory, and the verse form is basically rhyme royal. Except in these particulars, he is much farther from the medieval tradition in this poem than he is in, for example, "The Bouge of Court." Since Skelton went to such pains to conceal his message, his targets must have been powerful and the events well known; and members of the court probably had little trouble understanding just what Skelton was writing about. Still, by having the parrot speak, he was able to deny any treasonous charges.

With "Colin Clout" comes Skelton's complete severance from the medieval tradition. He abandons the dream structures for one narrator, personification and allegory for direct statement, and rhyme royal for Skeltonic verse. His use of Colin Clout as narrator is fortunate, for Colin simply repeats what he hears during his travels: "Thus I, Colin Clout,/ As I go about,/ And wandering as I walk/ I hear the people talk." Thus, he cannot vouch for the truthfulness of what he hears, nor can he be blamed for his crudeness. This flexible framework also allows him to repeat in any order what he has heard, and this order, or lack of it, is sometimes frustrating.

One of Skelton's attacks in the poem is against the conflict between church and state. He is on the side of the Catholic Church, but, like Erasmus, he takes a humanistic viewpoint. He argues that the Church should be independent, not parasitic on the state; that the selling of salvation leads to total disorganization of the Church; and that the clergy are ignorant, mainly because of the careless selection of priests. All of this leads the laity to distrust the clergy. As Erasmus does in his writings, Skelton calls upon the Church to cleanse itself, to carry out reform from within. He is not calling for a change in doctrine, but rather asks that the old doctrines be more closely followed. His bitterness is directed against those who are defiling the sacraments of the Church and those who allow this defiling. Thus, the focus of the attack is Cardinal Wolsey, who, in Skelton's opinion, is the epitome of the sacrifice of the interests of the Church to those of the state. The power of the poem lies not in the bitterness of the invective, but in the appeals for reform.

"Why Come Ye Not to Court?" is Skelton's third and most direct indictment against Wolsey. Like "Speak, Parrot" and "Colin Clout," this poem lacks any basic organization, and the lines tumble one upon another with a seeming lack of order. Furthermore, there is no chronological order to the events referred to in the work. This loose structure might lead one to assume that the poem was composed in pieces at various times.

Skelton does not use allegorical language or biblical terms to describe Wolsey but rather speaks of him plainly as the cardinal or "red hat." The cardinal is in complete control of the kingdom, so the situation is bad, because Wolsey is concerned only with money and lavish living.

> We have cast up our war,
> And made a worthy truce
> With, 'gup level suse!'
> Our money madly lent,
> and more madly spent:
> . . . .
> With crowns of gold emblazéd
> They make him so amazéd
> And his eyen so dazéd
> That he ne see can
> To know God nor man!
> . . . .
> *Why come ye not to court?*
> To which court?
> To the kingés court,
> Or to Hampton Court?
> *Nay, to the kingés court.*
> The kingés court
> Should have the excellence,
> But Hampton Court
> Hath the preéminence.

One of Skelton's last poems, and one of his longest, is "The Garland of Laurel." Strangely enough, it is dedicated to Wolsey; therefore, some degree of reconciliation must have taken place, for Skelton died while living in the protection of the Church. Once more the poet reverts to his medieval tradition of the dream allegory, using mostly rhyme royal to tell how the garland of laurel has come to be placed on his head. A long procession of poets, headed by Gower, Lydgate, and Chaucer, come to Skelton. He agrees to carry on in the tradition and places the garland on his own head. "The Garland of Laurel" is in one respect the most remarkable poem in all literature, for no other poet has ever written sixteen hundred lines to honor him- or herself.

Had Skelton given more time and energy to developing his lyrical poetry, he might be better known today, for he did have a definite gift for shaping verse. There are, however, only a few poems as evidence; unfortunately, Skelton did not spend much time or effort on lyrics. Some of his better ones are "Woefully arrayed," "The Manner of the World Nowadays," "Womanhood, Wanton, ye want," and "My Darling Dear, my Daisy Flower."

Skelton is not an imitator of those who went before him, nor is he a founder of any style or school much copied by those who came after him. True, he did write in the medieval tradition, but not entirely, and he is better in those poems in which he does not follow the tradition. He had some imitators of his style in his day, but they made no significant contribution to literature. Thus, Skelton is unique. He was a poet following the medieval tradition while the other scholars were heralding England's Renaissance, yet a poet creating his own particular style; a tender poet capable of the warm humor of "Philip Sparrow"; a realistic poet capable of the crude grossness of "The Tunning of Elinour Rumming"; a religious poet, loving his Church yet calling for its inner reformation; a secular poet knowledgeable in the ways of the world; and most of all, a courageous poet who spoke his mind to the powerful and pursued his individual artistic gifts.

Further Reading

Carlson, David R., ed. *John Skelton and Early Modern Culture: Papers Honoring Robert S. Kinsman.* Tempe: Arizona Center for Medieval and Renaissance Studies, 2008. Papers in this collection examine Skelton and the royal court, his English poems in manuscript and print, the lyrics of *The Garlande of Laurell* from manuscript to print, and his work in relationship to other writers of his era.

Carpenter, Nan Cooke. *John Skelton.* New York: Twayne, 1967. An excellent introductory volume. Places Skelton in the intellectual, political, and artistic settings of his times.

Cooney, Helen. "Skelton's *Bowge of Court* and the Crisis of Allegory in Late-Medieval England." In *Nation, Court, and Culture: New Essays on Fifteenth-Century English Poetry.* Dublin: Four Courts Press, 2001. Collection of essays reappraising the political and aesthetic importance of fifteenth century English poetry. The contributors maintain that England in this period was about to experience radical and irrevocable change, and they analyze how Skelton and other poets respond to these developments.

Fish, Stanley. *John Skelton's Poetry*. New Haven, Conn.: Yale University Press, 1965. A closely reasoned work giving special attention to the composition and techniques of Skelton's verse. "Speak, Parrot" is extensively analyzed.

Griffiths, Jane. *John Skelton and Poetic Authority: Defining the Liberty to Speak*. New York: Oxford University Press, 2006. An analysis of Skelton's writings, linking his poetic theory to his work as a writer and translator and reassessing his place in English literature.

Heiserman, Arthur Ray. *Skelton and Satire*. Chicago: University of Chicago Press, 1961. Views Skelton and his poetry in terms of the traditions of medieval satire, particularly in his use of conventional rhetorical figures and allegory. Considers Skelton to be a traditional figure in the English literature of his time.

Kinney, Arthur F. *John Skelton, Priest as Poet: Seasons of Discovery*. Chapel Hill: University of North Carolina Press, 1987. Disputes the contentions that Skelton was primarily an early Renaissance Humanist, a typically medieval satirist, and an idiosyncratic poet. In the place of these views, Kinney advances the thesis that Skelton was foremost a priest, whose verses were concerned with moral and religious themes and ideas.

Pollet, Maurice. *John Skelton: Poet of Tudor England*. Translated by John Warrington. Cranbury, N.J.: Bucknell University Press, 1971. Useful in placing Skelton within the political context of his times. Offers helpful insights about how Skelton's poetics were shaped by his politics.

Poetry of Traherne

Author: Thomas Traherne (c. 1637-1674)
First published: 1699, 1903, 1910; includes *A Serious and Patheticall Contemplation of the Mercies of God*, 1699; *The Poetical Works of Thomas Traherne*, 1903; *Traherne's Poems of Felicity*, 1910
Type of work: Poetry

Thomas Traherne was one of the last seventeenth century inheritors of the Metaphysical tradition of religious poetry, developed to its height by John Donne and George Herbert, who drew of every aspect of the world around them to express their faith and their longing for closer communion with God. Much of their complexity of thought and their awareness of the essentially paradoxical nature of the Christian religion was lost on Traherne, whose concepts and style were much simpler and less compact than theirs. The greatest differences between Traherne and his predecessors undoubtedly resulted from his radically different theology. Both Donne and Herbert struggled with a strong sense of sin, a feeling of human unworthiness, and as a consequence of this realization they had an equally overwhelming perception of the miraculous, outreaching mercy of God.

Traherne, who was closer in spirit to the great Romantic poets William Blake and William Wordsworth than to his own contemporaries, wrote out of a deep conviction of innate human innocence. Original sin forms no part of his faith, though he was conscious, intellectually if not emotionally, of human corruption, which he felt was derived from the world's emphasis on materialism. Evil comes from human greed; gold, silver, and jewels are symbols not of beauty but of temptation and of that avarice that perverts youthful joy in the creation. Nature, not wealth, is for Traherne the greatest of human possessions. Those who are inheritors of the light of the stars and the fruitful soil can desire no more.

Just as Donne's complex metaphorical language reflects his equally involved theology, so Traherne's brief stanzas echo the essential simplicity of his vision. His lyrics have been compared to Blake's *Songs of Innocence* (1789), though he never achieved the sustained control of the later poet. Both his form and his devotional tone are perhaps closest to the less impassioned poems of Herbert, who may have inspired him to experiment with a wide variety of verse forms, not always successfully. Traherne's work is characterized by lines of striking loveliness in the middle of uninspired, wordy mediocrity. His limitations in his religious thought are partly responsible for those of his poetry: a narrowness of vision, a lack of awareness of many significant sides of life, and a tendency to repetitiveness. He never really mastered the poetic control of Donne, of Herbert, or even of Henry Vaughan, another late Metaphysical poet with mystical tendencies, who shared Traherne's propensity for unevenness in his writing. This problem can be clearly seen in a lyric that begins with an unusual and striking vision of "new worlds beneath the water." The intensity of the opening is dissipated by the weakness of the end of the stanza.

> I saw new worlds beneath the water lie,
>   New people; yea, another sky
>   And sun, which seen by day
>   Might things more clear display.
>   Just such another
>   Of late my brother
> Did in his travel see, and saw by night
>   A much more strange and wondrous sight;
> Nor could the world exhibit such another
>   So great a sight, but in a brother.

Dominant themes in Traherne's poetry include the innocence of childhood, when human eyes look upon everything with delight and wonder, the glories of the natural world, and the corruptions of the commerce-directed society of the time. Perhaps the best known and most skillful treatment of these characteristic themes comes in "Wonder," a rather ecstatic statement of the poet's childhood reaction to the world around him.

> How like an Angel came I down!
>   How Bright are all Things here!
> When first among his Works I did appear
>   O how their GLORY me did Crown?
> The World resembled his Eternitie,
>   In which my Soul did Walk;
> And every Thing that I did see,
>   Did with me talk.

Like Wordsworth, Traherne suggests a kind of platonic preexistence, when human souls were united with God. Children retain some of this divine luster until greed gradually wears it away. Though Wordsworth could not have known Traherne's poems, since they were lost until late in the nineteenth century, his *Ode* has surprising echoes of a poem called "News," in which Traherne ponders his early sense that there was a world of bliss beyond the one he saw. Unlike Wordsworth, however, Traherne finds the creation not a consolation for the loss of heavenly bliss, but this bliss itself.

> But little did the infant dream
> That all the treasures of the world were by,
>   And that himself was so the cream
> And crown of all which round about did lie.
>   Yet thus it was! The gem,
>   The diadem,
>   The ring enclosing all
> That stood upon this earthen ball,
>   The heav'nly eye,
>   Much wider than the sky,
> Wherein they all included were,
> The love, the soul, that was the king
> Made to possess them, did appear
>   A very little thing.

In another poem, "The Apostasy," distinguished by a complex, well-handled stanza form, Traherne comments at greater length on his childish appreciation of the natural world, when he seemed to dwell in Eden before the fall.

>   As Eve
>   I did believe
>   Myself in Eden set,
> Affecting neither gold nor ermined crowns,
>   Nor aught else that I need forget;
> No mud did foul my limpid streams,
> No mist eclipsed my sun with frowns;
>   Set off with heav'nly beams,
> My joys were meadows, fields, and towns.

Temptation entered his paradise with "those little, new-invented things, fine lace and silks . . . or worldly pelf that us destroys." His own fall was gradual, but he, like all other humans, was corrupted, separated, finally made "a stranger to the shining skies."

Traherne's poetry has a pervasive quality of innocence and purity; even when he speaks of corruption, he seems to be living in an incorruptible world himself, and he preserved a child's "uncomplex" awareness of existence. Both his language and his images reflect these characteristics. They are expanded, not compressed; a poet of mood, rather than of ideas, Traherne built much of his effect through repetition and restatement, deriving images from the preceding ones, finding new examples to express the same idea, as he does in the following stanza:

A globe of earth is better far
Than if it were a globe of gold; a star
Much brighter than a precious stone;
The sun more glorious than a costly throne—
His warming beam,
A living stream
Of liquid pearl, that from a spring
Waters the earth, is a most precious thing.

Traherne's fondness for the exclamatory tone is especially evident in a little verse appropriately entitled "The Rapture," which conveys that joy in existence that is part of so much of his poetry, especially that about childhood: "Sweet infancy!/ O heavenly fire! O sacred light!/ How fair and bright!/ How great am I,/ Whom the whole world doth magnify!"

The poet does have other voices. In "Insatiableness," a poem faintly reminiscent of Herbert's "The Pulley," in which God is seen withholding the gift of rest from humans that "weariness" may turn them back toward the Deity, Traherne restates in three successive stanzas the impossibility of satisfying the "busy, vast, inquiring soul" of humans. His conclusion differs from Herbert's; this restless spirit is, finally, proof of the existence of God: "Sure there's a God, (for else there's no delight,) One infinite."

One of the most unusual of Traherne's poems is "A Serious and Curious Night Meditation," where he deals with a theme he rarely touches on—death as a physical process, rather than as a spiritual reunion with God. Some of the images have the harsh, almost macabre realism of the true Metaphysical poets like Donne and Andrew Marvell.

What is my Fathers House! and what am I!
My fathers House is Earth; where I must lie:
And I a worm, no man; that fits no room,
Till like a worm, I crawl into my Tomb.

Even here there is a suggestion of the awareness of beauty that is characteristic of Traherne, in the lines "Whilst, at my window, pretty Birds do Ring my Knell, and with their Notes my Obit sing." The conclusion is a weaker version of Donne's triumphant affirmation in his sonnet, "Death Be Not Proud": "Sleep is Cousin-german unto Death:/ Sleep and Death differ, no more, than a Carcass/ And a skeleton." Therefore, since he sleeps peacefully in his bed, he has no reason to fear death.

Traherne's formula for "felicity," a term that recurs frequently in both his poetry and in his fine prose work, the *Centuries of Meditations* (wr. c. 1657-1661, pb. 1908), is effectively summarized in "The Recovery." Here he presents his conviction that human pleasure is God's reward: "Our blessedness to see/ Is even to the Deity/ A Beatific vision." Humans see God's glory in his works and worship him through their joy.

All gold and silver is but empty dross.
Rubies and sapphires are but loss,
The very sun and stars and seas
Far less His spirit please:
One voluntary act of love
Far more delightful to His soul doth prove
And is above all these as far as love.

Traherne's own joy in the works of God is perhaps the most memorable quality of his poetry; his exuberant praise of nature and the innocence of childhood is for the reader, at least, temporarily infectious. There is, however, a sameness about his work, a lack of variety in his ideas and in his vocabulary, which makes it difficult to read many of his poems at a sitting without feeling the sweetness and the smoothness rather oppressive. When even evil is described in terms of gold and silver, rubies and sapphires, words that have inevitably been associated with beauty rather than with corruption, the reader eventually begins to long for a single harsh phrase or metaphor of real ugliness. However, notwithstanding all his limitations, Traherne deserves a place of respect among the poets of his century for expressing, often very beautifully and appropriately, his own unique view of life and the way to human happiness.

Further Reading

Blevins, Jacob, ed. *Re-reading Thomas Traherne: A Collection of New Critical Essays*. Tempe: Arizona Center for Medieval and Renaissance Studies, 2007. Discussions of Traherne and the laws of property, his use of "curious" visual language, and the quest for prelapsarian speech in his writings and those of his contemporaries.

Cefalu, Paul. "Infinite Love and the Limits of Neo-Scholasticism in the Prose and Poetry of Thomas Traherne." In *English Renaissance Literature and Contemporary Theory: Sublime Objects of Theology*. New York: Palgrave Macmillan, 2007. Applies modern philosophy and critical theory to analyze seventeenth century English devotional poetry by Traherne and other writers. Focuses on the writers' depictions of the relationship of God to the poems' subjects.

Clements, A. L. *The Mystical Poetry of Thomas Traherne*. Cambridge, Mass.: Harvard University Press, 1969. A comprehensive study of Traherne's poetic technique, themes, symbolism, and diction. Discusses the poems contained in the Dobell manuscript, one of the major sources of Traherne's poetry, as an interrelated sequence in the Christian contemplative tradition of writing. Includes appendixes on Traherne and Renaissance poetic theory and practice, and on the mystical tradition.

Day, Malcolm M. *Thomas Traherne*. Boston: Twayne, 1982. A useful introduction to the Traherne canon, with a short chapter on the two most important manuscripts of Traherne's poetry, the Dobell and the Burney manuscripts. Includes a Traherne chronology and a short life history.

Reid, David. *The Metaphysical Poets*. Harlow, England: Longman, 2000. Chapter 6 focuses on Traherne, discussing his poetry of deprivation and transcendence and interpreting his work from the perspective of Metaphysical poetry.

Stewart, Stanley. *The Expanded Voice: The Art of Thomas Traherne*. San Marino, Calif.: Huntington Library, 1970. Contains two insightful, highly detailed chapters on Traherne's poetry. Stewart believes that Traherne's poetic craftsmanship has been underappreciated, an oversight he rectifies.

Poetry of Vaughan

Author: Henry Vaughan (1622-1695)
First published: 1646-1678; includes *Poems*, 1646; *Olor Iscanus*, 1651; *Silex Scintillans*, part 1 (1650), part 2 (1655); *Thalia Rediviva*, 1678
Type of work: Poetry

Henry Vaughan is best known as a religious poet, a follower of the metaphysical tradition of John Donne and George Herbert, and a precursor of William Wordsworth in his interest in the ideas of the seventeenth century Platonists. The Platonist philosophers emphasized humanity's innate good, the innocent wisdom of childhood, and the possibility of mystical union with God. Like Donne, Vaughan turned to religious poetry relatively late in his career; he was a law student in London, and his first volume of verse, *Poems*, reveals his close reading of the popular court poets of the age of Charles I.

A number of Vaughan's early poems are love lyrics addressed to Amoret, probably an imaginary lady. They show little originality, though they are competent, pleasant, polished works. Even at this stage in his development Vaughan was a skillful metrist, able to create many different effects through a variety of verse forms. His sentiments and images are typical of the age; his passion is strictly "platonic." It is the lady's soul he loves, though he complains that she is as heartless and unyielding as the ladies addressed by the other Cavalier poets. Cupid, the cruel god of love, plays a major part in many of Vaughan's lyrics, as he does in the works of writers like Ben Jonson and Thomas Randolph, to whom the poet acknowledges his debt.

There are, among the imitative and undistinguished lines of these poems, flashes of that gift of language that makes some of Vaughan's later lyrics rank high among the verses of his century.

> If, Amoret, that glorious Eye,
>   In the first birth of light,
>   And death of Night,
> Had with those elder fires you spy
>   Scatter'd so high
>   Received form, and sight;
> We might suspect in the vast Ring,
>   Amidst these golden glories,
>   And fierie stories;
> Whether the Sun had been the King,
>   And guide of Day,
>   Or your brighter eye should sway.

The comparison of the lady's brightness to that of the sun is commonplace, but the poet's vision of the night sky is his own.

Poems included, in addition to the typically Carolinian love lyrics, an amusing description of London night life that ended with a drinking song and a translation of Juvenal's tenth satire. Vaughan's translation reads smoothly, but it suffers greatly by comparison with Samuel Johnson's "The Vanity of Human Wishes," an adaptation of the same Latin poem. Though both English poets used iambic pentameter rhyming couplets, Vaughan's extended verse paragraphs have little of the pointed conciseness that the eighteenth century poet gave to the form. Satire was, in any case, quite foreign to Vaughan's temperament, and he wisely turned his attention to other subjects in his later works.

Most of the poems in *Olor Iscanus* were written in the mid-1640's; they also show the influence of poets of the preceding generation. Most of the poems are epistles to Vaughan's acquaintances on a variety of occasions: the publication of a volume of plays, an invitation to dinner, or the marriage of friends. The influence of Ben Jonson's poetry is clear in these works, as well as in the two elegies on Vaughan's friends who met their deaths in war. There are echoes of Jonson's famous poem on the death of Sir Henry Morison in "An Elegy on the Death of Mr. R. W. slain in the late unfortunate differences at Routon Heath, near Chester."

> Though in so short a span
> His riper thoughts had purchas'd more of man
> Than all those worthless livers, which yet quick,
> Have quite outgone their own Arithmetick.
> He seiz'd perfections, and without a dull
> And mossy gray possess'd a solid skull.

Vaughan's limitations as an elegiac poet are clear when one compares the following lines from Jonson on a similar subject:

> It is not growing like a tree
> In bulk doth make man better be;
> Or standing long an oak, three hundred year,
> To fall a log at last, dry, bald, and sere;
> A lily of a day
> Is Fairer far in May,
> Although it fall and die that night,
> It was the plant and flower of light.
> In small proportions we just beauties see;
> And in short measures, life may perfect be.

One of the most pleasant poems in *Olor Iscanus* is the one addressed "To the River Isca," from which the volume takes its name. This pastoral, reflective lyric, filled with the traditional images of "gentle swains," "beauteous nymphs," and "bubbling springs and gliding streams," promises fame to the river through the poetry it inspired in Vaughan.

Had Vaughan's career ended with *Olor Iscanus*, he would probably have ranked with the very minor Cavalier poets.

However, some event, or combination of events, perhaps the death of a beloved younger brother, brought about his religious conversion, and he found his true poetic voice in the works that appeared in the first part of *Silex Scintillans*. Vaughan's debt to Herbert is evident in many of the poems; he followed Herbert's example in experimenting with various stanza forms and unusual patterns of syntax. Vaughan's "Sundays," like Herbert's "Prayer," consists exclusively of phrases describing the title word.

> Bright shadows of true Rest! some shoots of bliss,
> Heaven once a week;
> The next world's gladness prepossessed in this;
> A day to seek;
> Eternity in time; the steps by which
> We Climb above all ages; Lamps that light
> Man through his heap of dark days; and the rich,
> And full redemption of the whole weeks flight.

A number of Vaughan's themes also seem to have been drawn from Herbert's poetry, among them the ceremonies of the Church, the celebration of important days in the Christian year, and the constantly emphasized relationship of human repentance and God's grace. What stands out as uniquely Vaughan's is the sense of innocence and joy that pervades much of his work. Although at some times he seems strongly aware of sin and the need for penitence, at others his Platonism seems to obliterate his consciousness of evil and he writes simple, joyous lyrics like the following:

> My Soul, there is a Country
> Far beyond the stars,
> Where stands a winged Sentry
> All skillful in the wars,
> There above noise, and danger
> Sweet peace sits crown'd with smiles,
> And one born in a Manger
> Commands the Beauteous files,
> He is thy gracious friend,
> And (O my Soul awake!)
> Did in pure love descend
> To die here for thy sake.

A poem often discussed in connection with Wordsworth's immortality ode is "The Retreat," in which Vaughan's Platonism is particularly evident. He refers to the glorious vision of God he preserved in his childhood and to his closeness to nature, which seemed to take him back to that heaven he inhabited before his birth.

Happy those early dayes! when I
Shin'd in my Angel-infancy.
Before I understood this place
Appointed for my second race,
Or taught my soul to fancy ought
But a white, Celestial thought,
When yet I had not walked above
A mile, or two, from my first love,
And looking back (at that short space,)
Could see a glimpse of his bright-face;
When on some gilded Cloud, or flower
My gazing soul would dwell an hour,
And in those weaker glories spy
Some shadows of eternity.

Some of Vaughan's other poems are far less sanguine about the human condition. "The World," whose opening lines, "I saw Eternity the other night like a great Ring of pure and endless light," are among the poet's most famous, pictures human beings as greedy and self-seeking: "the darksome statesman hung with weights and woe," "the fearful miser on a heap of rust," "the downright Epicure." The poet comments on the folly of those who reject salvation, who "prefer dark night before true light."

Another theme that seems to have fascinated Vaughan was the relationship of body and soul. Unlike the medieval poets who presented two forces pulling in opposite directions, the soul toward God and the body toward the gratification of physical desires, Vaughan sees them as harmonious, concerned chiefly about that period of separation between death and the resurrection. In "Resurrection and Immortality," the soul reassures the body, as if it were a frightened child, that all will be well.

Like some spruce Bride,
Shall one day rise, and cloth'd with shining light
All pure, and bright
Re-marry to the soul, for 'tis most plain
Thou [the body] only fall'st to be refin'd again.

It is difficult to pinpoint characteristic images in Vaughan's poetry as a whole, for he varies his language with his theme. However, his use of light, brightness, the sun, and the stars to reflect his sense of the glory of God is especially memorable. There is a particularly interesting variation on this typically Platonic use of light in the poem entitled "Night."

There is in God (some say)
A deep, but dazzling darkness; As men here

Say it is late and dusky, because they
See not all clear;
O for that night! where I in him
Might live invisible and dim.

Vaughan makes effective use of commonplace images in a number of his poems. He builds one around the analogy between the root, lying dormant in the ground before it can appear clothed in new loveliness in the spring, and the buried body, preparing in death for the resurrection. In "Man," he describes the human condition in the language of weaving.

He knocks at all doors, strays and roams,
Nay hath not so much wit as some stones have
Which in the darkest nights point to their homes,
By some hid sense their Maker gave;
Man is the shuttle, to whose winding quest
And passage through these looms
God order'd motion, but ordain'd no rest.

Vaughan never entirely abandoned the poetic diction of some of the poems in *Olor Iscanus*, and his last volume, *Thalia Rediviva*, contains several works approaching the neoclassical manner of Edmund Waller and Sir John Denham. It should be noted, however, that many of these "late" poems were actually written many years before their publication, before Vaughan had done his best work.

Vaughan's religious poems are seldom brilliant throughout; he was a writer whose genius showed itself more fully in single fine lines than in sustained thoughts. However, his ability to convey a sense of personal feeling in his meditations, which sometimes reflect his moods of ecstasy, sometimes his melancholy view of humanity's rejection of salvation, makes his works moving in their entirety. His natural bent seems to have been more toward an exalted, visionary state than toward depression, for it is in the poems describing his joy that he is generally at his best. His sense of sin and struggle seems more often imitative of Herbert's poetry than drawn from his own feelings. Vaughan's work provides an interesting bridge between the intense struggle for personal faith that fills the poetry of Donne and Herbert and the ecstatic paeans of Richard Crashaw and Thomas Traherne.

Further Reading

Dickson, Donald R., and Holly Faith Nelson, eds. *Of Paradise and Light: Essays on Henry Vaughan and John Milton in Honor of Alan Rudrum*. Newark: University of Delaware Press, 2004. The essays analyze some of Vaughan's collections and individual poems, including *Silex scintil-*

lans, *Olar Iscanus*, "The Mount of Olives," and "The Search."

Durr, R. A. *On the Mystical Poetry of Henry Vaughan*. Cambridge, Mass.: Harvard University Press, 1962. Sees Vaughan's poetry as a realization and celebration of a mystical experience. Looks at major metaphors and gives a close reading of several poems.

Hutchinson, F. E. *Henry Vaughan: A Life and Interpretation*. Oxford, England: Clarendon Press, 1947. Uses private letters, poetry, and Vaughan's other writings to record the major events of Vaughan's life, the poet's Welsh roots, and his intellectual development.

Martz, Louis L. "Henry Vaughan: The Caves of Memory." In *The Paradise Within: Studies in Vaughan, Traherne, and Milton*. New Haven, Conn.: Yale University Press, 1964. Sees the influence of George Herbert in Vaughan's poetry and considers many themes and images reflective of Vaughan's spiritual and intellectual development.

Post, Jonathan F. S. "Henry Vaughan." In *The Cambridge Companion to English Poetry, Donne to Marvell*, edited by Thomas N. Corns. New York: Cambridge University Press, 1993. Most of the fourteen essays focus on the work of individual poets, including Post's article about Vaughan. Other essays provide context for these poets' works by discussing politics, religion, gender, genre, and tradition in the early seventeenth century.

Simmonds, James D. *Masques of God: Form and Theme in the Poetry of Henry Vaughan*. Pittsburgh, Pa.: University of Pittsburgh Press, 1972. Seeks to correct previous misunderstandings of Vaughan's work. Sees in Vaughan's poetry an organic development in close touch with human experience and marked by humor, a playful spirit, and a lively awareness of the world.

Sullivan, Ceri. *The Rhetoric of the Conscience in Donne, Herbert, and Vaughan*. New York: Oxford University Press, 2008. Compares the work of three Metaphysical poets—Vaughan, John Donne, and George Herbert. Focuses on their depiction of the conscience, which they see as only party under their control.

Young, R. V. *Doctrine and Devotion in Seventeenth-Century Poetry: Studies in Donne, Herbert, Crashaw, and Vaughan*. Rochester, N.Y.: D. S. Brewer, 2000. Young takes exception to other critics, who view seventeenth century devotional poetry from the perspective of Protestant theology and postmodern theory. He demonstrates how the ideas and poetic devices in the English poets' work also are evident in the Catholic poetry of France and Spain and the theology of Saint Augustine and Thomas Aquinas.

Poetry of Verlaine

Author: Paul Verlaine (1844-1896)

First published: 1866-1977; includes *Poèmes saturniens*, 1866; *Fêtes galantes*, 1869 (*Galant Parties*, 1912); *La Bonne Chanson*, 1870; *Romances sans paroles*, 1874 (*Romances Without Words*, 1921); *Sagesse*, 1881; *Jadis et naguère*, 1884; *Amour*, 1888; *Parallèlement*, 1889, 1894 (English translation, 1939); *Bonheur*, 1891; *Chansons pour elle*, 1891; *Femmes*, 1891 (English translation, 1977); *Liturgies intimes*, 1892; *Élégies*, 1893; *Odes et son honneur*, 1893; *Dans les limbes*, 1894; *Épigrammes*, 1894; *Chair, dernière poésies*, 1896; *Invectives*, 1896 (English translation, 1939); *Hombres*, 1903 (English translation, 1977); *Selected Poems*, 1948; *Femmes/Hombres*, 1977 (includes English translation of *Femmes* and *Hombres*).

Type of work: Poetry

The importance of literary groups or schools has always seemed greater in France than in England or the United States, and much of French literary history can best be understood through the reaction of one school against another. After the great wave of Romanticism in the 1830's and 1840's, a counterwave was inevitable. This originated in the group known as the Parnassians, which first made itself known in 1866 and was led by Charles Marie René Leconte de Lisle and continued by José-Maria de Heredia.

The members of the school had two objectives. They wanted the reformation of the loose metrical methods of the disciples of Victor Hugo and Alphonse de Lamartine and a return to something like the traditional strictness of French prosody. More important, they were reacting against the excessive subjectivity and emotionalism of Romantics like Alfred de Musset, who exploited his famous love affair with novelist George Sand in his verse. Poetry, according to the Parnassians, should aim at an "abstract beauty" and avoid the cultivation of "private sorrows and their lamentation"; it should be cold and aloof, purely objective. In the famous "Elephants" (1862) by de Lisle, for example, the great beasts solemnly march across the desert of red sand and as solemnly disappear; "and the desert resumes its immobility." As James Elroy Flecker, one of the group's few English disciples, wrote, Parnassians considered it abhorrent "to overlay fine work with gross and irrelevant egoism," as Hugo had done; had the movement existed in England, Alfred, Lord Tennyson "would never have published 'Locksley Hall.'"

It was in this spirit that Paul Verlaine wrote his early poems. He was, however, never a thoroughgoing Parnassian; occasionally, as in "A Dahlia" (1866), he achieved something of the desired objectivity, but even in his first volume there were hints of the much more characteristic manner that was to develop three years later in *Fêtes galantes*. In such a poem as "Classic Walpurgis Night" (1866), with its description of the "correct, ridiculous, and charming" garden designed by André Le Nôtre, there is a distinct foreshadowing of the eighteenth century fantasies of his subsequent volume. Also included in this first book is what became one of his most famous poems, "Autumn Song," one of those almost wordless little songs associated with his later manner.

The publication, between 1857 and 1875, of three books by Edmond de Goncourt and Jules de Goncourt on various aspects of life and art during the eighteenth century marked another sharp break with the Romantics. As had happened earlier in England, the French Romantics had turned violently against the preceding century, detesting what they considered to be its coldness and artificiality. However, as a result of this latest turn of the wheel of taste, this very artificiality became the eighteenth century's greatest charm; some writers were fascinated by the brilliant, stately society that their grandfathers had overthrown.

Verlaine's *Fêtes galantes*—probably his best-known book outside France—belongs to this pattern; in it, as Holbrook Jackson said, "Watteau became literature." It is an evocation of the world of François Boucher and Jean-Honoré Fragonard, with its formal gardens, silks, fluttering of fans, and tinkling of mandolins in the eternal twilight or moonlight, while abbés, female shepherds, and others stroll along paths beside the fountains. Stylistically, most of its twenty-two poems are still indebted to the Parnassian style, but some of the poems in the volume also mark Verlaine's first flirtation with symbolism.

Structurally, *Fêtes galantes* can be divided into two large sections of ten poems and twelve poems, respectively. The first group of poems is largely written in a Parnassian-influenced style and concludes with "Skating," a colossal, sixty-four-line poem that contrasts sharply with the shorter poems that comprise the rest of the collection. Most of the poems are written in traditional Parnassian forms: quatrains with traditional rhyme schemes, such as *rimes croisées* (*abab*) and *rimes embrasées* (*abba*); and *sizains* (six-line stanzas with a rhyme scheme of *aabccb*). "Seashells" even reprises the Renaissance fixed form of the villanelle. Other poems— particularly in the second half of the collection—are more progressive, however, foreshadowing favored forms of the Symbolists: "Sailing" is in a *tercet monorime* (*aaa*, *bbb*), and "Lovers' Chat" is written in blank-verse couplets.

Although the title *Fêtes galantes* directly refers to the eighteenth century painting style of Jean-Antoine Watteau, Verlaine uses this theme merely as a starting point, expanding upon it throughout his collection. For instance, moonlight was not explored by Watteau or his contemporary painters, but moonlight becomes the main theme in three of Verlaine's *Fêtes galantes* poems, as the collection *Poetry of Paul Verlaine* is best known: "Moonlight," "Puppets," and "Mandolin." In "Le faune," readers enter a scene not from an eighteenth century *Fêtes galantes* painting; rather, readers glimpse two lovers who have wandered away from the festivities. To Verlaine, the original subject is no longer the subject of interest.

In some of the *Fêtes galantes* poems, Verlaine also introduces metaphor and ambiguity, indicating the beginning of his more mature Symbolist phase. In the opening poem, "Claire de lune," the traditional Watteauesque scenery becomes a metaphor for the human soul itself: "Your soul is a landscape which maskers and bergamasks charm." In the final poem, "Colloque sentimental," Verlaine presents two ghostly figures to the reader. In an obtuse dialogue, they pose questions to one another that are not answered with any sort of clarity or certainty. Even the genders of the two ghosts cannot be gleaned from Verlaine's words. Shrouded in an atmosphere of mystery, it could be justified that Verlaine's symbolist period begins with poems like these.

Indeed, Verlaine's chief literary significance lies in his connection with the Symbolist movement, which began as an unconscious protest against what has been called the Spartan creed of the Parnassians and which had links with the work of the Impressionist painters. Arthur Symons, who knew many of the writers involved and who translated a few of Verlaine's pieces, called the whole body of late nineteenth century French literature the Decadent movement, which he then divided into impressionism and Symbolism. It is difficult and perhaps unnecessary to make a distinction between the two. According to Symons, impressionism gives the truth "of the visible world to the eyes that see it," and Symbolism gives "the truth of spiritual things to the spiritual vision." Still, Symons cited Verlaine's *Romances sans paroles*, the book that is usually considered the beginning of the poet's Symbolist period, as an example of impressionism.

It was the effort of the Symbolists to see through outward appearances to inward reality by trying to express "the secret affinities of things with one's soul." It is generally thought that the germ of this point of view is to be found in Charles Baudelaire's poem "Correspondences" (1857). Baudelaire saw nature as a "forest of symbols," in which "perfumes, colors, and sounds answer one another." This perspective leads to poetry in which the subject becomes unimportant or disappears altogether. The meaning of the poem is of no more significance than it is in a musical composition. The following remark by nineteenth century critic Walter Pater is frequently quoted in this connection:

All art constantly aspires towards the condition of music; and the perfection of poetry seems to depend in part on a certain suppression of mere subject, so that the meaning reaches readers through ways not distinctly traceable by the understanding.

Verlaine, in his "The Art of Poetry," said "Music before everything." He also declared, "no color, only the nuance," for it is this nuance that weds "the dream to the dream." His later poems became almost literally songs without words, in which the content consists only of half hints and vague suggestions.

In France, this kind of poetry led to the work of Stéphane Mallarmé, who composed poems filled with symbols within symbols, in which hardly a word is meant to be taken in its

customary sense; the French claim that his verse is better understood by those not French. In England, Verlaine was much admired by the "minor" poets of the 1890's, several of whom—among them Symons, John Gray, and Ernest Dowson—translated some of his poems. It is certainly possible to see his influence, or that of his school, on some of the early poems of William Butler Yeats as well.

Although Verlaine experienced a religious conversion that found expression in many of the poems in *Sagesse*, his life was a tragic one. He has been called a modern François Villon. Almost everyone who wrote about Verlaine has referred to his childlike qualities. François Coppée said,

Alas, like a child he was without any defense, and life wounded him often and cruelly. Suffering, though, is the ransom paid by genius, and this word can be uttered in speaking of Verlaine, for his name will always awaken the memory of an absolutely new poetry which, in French literature, has acquired the importance of a discovery.

Revised by Matthew Hoch

Further Reading

Adam, Antoine. *The Art of Paul Verlaine*. Translated by Carl Morse. New York: New York University Press, 1963. A dated but classic psychological study of Verlaine's works. Provides considerable analysis of his oeuvre in the context of his times.

Balakian, Anna. *The Symbolist Movement: A Critical Appraisal*. New York: New York University Press, 1977. Explores Verlaine's role in the European Symbolist movement. Proposes that the *Fêtes galantes* poems, with their suggestive emotional nuance, musicality, and attentiveness to color, mark the inception of Verlaine's Symbolist poetry.

Carter, A. E. *Paul Verlaine*. New York: Twayne, 1971. Provides a chronological overview of Verlaine's life and works. Concludes that melancholy and alienation reside beneath the musicality and light manner of the poetry.

Holmes, Anne. "Finding a Language: Verlaine and Laforgue." *French Studies* 50, no. 3 (July, 1996). Examines the poetry of Verlaine and Jules Laforgue, discussing their quests for an authentic language, their similar poetic expression, and their use of dialogue.

Lepelletier, Edmond. *Paul Verlaine: His Life—His Work.* 1909. Reprint. Translated by E. M. Lang. Whitefish, Mont.: Kessinger, 2006. An intimate look at Verlaine through the eyes of a close friend. Part of Kessinger's Rare Reprints series.

Taylor-Horrex, Susan. *Verlaine, "Fêtes galantes," and "Romances sans paroles."* London: Grant & Cutler, 1988. Analyzes individual poems as well as prominent themes unifying the collections. Emphasizes the coherence of the collections as landscapes of the soul and cites the concepts of love and passivity as being primary to the poetry. Discusses several possible sources of influence.

Whidden, Seth Adam. *Leaving Parnassus: The Lyric Subject in Verlaine and Rimbaud*. New York: Rodopi, 2007. Discusses the "crisis of the lyric subject" in nineteenth century French poetry, which was dominated by the lyric. Describes how Verlaine and Arthur Rimbaud rebelled against the stringent rules of their predecessors to create a radical new poetry.

Point Counter Point

Author: Aldous Huxley (1894-1963)
First published: 1928
Type of work: Novel
Type of plot: Social realism
Time of plot: 1920's
Locale: England

Principal characters:
PHILIP QUARLES, a novelist
ELINOR, his wife
SIDNEY, his father
RACHEL, his mother
JOHN BIDLAKE, Elinor's father
MRS. BIDLAKE, her mother
LITTLE PHILIP, Philip and Elinor's son
DENIS BURLAP, the editor of *The Literary World*
BEATRICE GILRAY, his mistress
SPANDRELL, a cynic
EVERARD WEBLEY, a disciple of force
WALTER BIDLAKE, Elinor's brother
MARJORIE CARLING, Walter's mistress
LUCY TANTAMOUNT, the woman with whom Walter is infatuated
MARK RAMPION, an artist

The Story:

Walter Bidlake has been living with a married woman named Marjorie Carling for a year and a half, and he is growing tired of her. He feels tied to her by a moral obligation but oppressed by her attempts to possess him; she has rejected his proposal that they live together as close friends but leading independent lives. In any case, it is too late for that now, because Marjorie is pregnant. Her jealousy toward his latest infatuation, Lucy Tantamount, pricks Walter's conscience, and he is angry with himself for making Marjorie unhappy by going to a party at Tantamount House without her.

Elinor and Philip Quarles travel abroad, leaving little Philip behind under the care of a governess and his grandmother, Mrs. Bidlake. Philip is a novelist, and his life consists of jotting down in his notebook incidents and thoughts that might make material for his next novel. His mind is turned inward, introspective, and his self-centered interests give him little time for emotional experience. Elinor wishes that he would love her as much as she loves him, but she resigns herself to the unhappy dilemma of being loved as much as Philip could possibly love any woman.

Denis Burlap, editor of *The Literary World*, flatters himself with the just conceit that although his magazine is not a financial success, it at least contributes to the intellectual life of his time. Walter, one of his chief contributors, asks for more pay; Burlap hedges until Walter feels ashamed of his demands. Burlap is attracted to Beatrice Gilray, a pathetic figure who has feared the very touch of a man ever since she had been attacked by her uncle while riding in a taxicab. Burlap hopes eventually to seduce Beatrice. Meanwhile, they are living together. Also part of this social set is Spandrell, an indolent son of a doting mother who supports him, and Everard Webley, a friend of Elinor and the leader of a conservative militaristic group called the British Freemen.

Philip's father, Sidney Quarles, pretends that he is writing a long history, but he has not progressed much beyond the purchase of office equipment. His wife, Rachel, assumes the burden of managing their affairs and patiently endures Sidney's whims and mild flirtations. Now it is apparently someone in London, for Sidney makes frequent trips to the British Museum to gather material for his history. The young woman appears one day at the Quarleses' country house and in loud and furious tones informs Sidney that she is pregnant. When Rachel appears, Sidney quietly leaves the room. Rachel settles the affair quietly.

Marjorie continues to arouse Walter's pity and cause him to regret his association with Lucy Tantamount, particularly because Lucy is not much interested in Walter. She becomes tired of London and leaves for Paris. When Elinor and Philip return from abroad, they find their son faring well under the care of his governess and his grandmother. John Bidlake learns that he is dying of cancer and returns to his wife's home. He has become a cantankerous patient and treats little Philip alternately with kindness and harshness.

Since Lucy is in Paris, Philip is able to persuade Walter to take Marjorie to the Quarles home in the country in the hope that this will lead to some sort of reconciliation. Rachel Quarles begins to like Marjorie, and the pregnant woman becomes more cheerful in the new environment. Shortly after she and Walter arrive at the Quarles estate, Walter receives a letter from Lucy in Paris, telling him that she has found a new lover who seduced her in a shabby Parisian studio. With her newly acquired contentment, Marjorie feels sympathy for Walter, who is crestfallen at Lucy's rejection.

Everard Webley has long been in love with Elinor. Sometimes she wonders whether Philip will care if she leaves for another man, and she decides that it will be Philip's own fault if she turns to Everard. She feels that a breach is forming between herself and Philip, but she cannot arouse his attention to make him realize what is happening. She arranges a rendezvous with Everard.

Behind the scenes of lovemaking and unfaithfulness lurks the political enmity between Spandrell and Everard. Elinor Quarles is home alone awaiting Everard's call when Spandrell and a telegram arrive simultaneously. The telegram informs Elinor that little Philip is ill and urges her to come to her father's home. Elinor asks Spandrell to wait and tell Everard that she cannot keep her appointment with him. Spandrell agrees. When Everard arrives at Elinor's home, Spandrell attacks him and kills him. Spandrell lugs the dead body into a car and drives away. Later that evening, he meets Philip and tells him his son is ill.

Philip arrives at the Bidlake estate the next day in time to hear the doctor say that young Philip has meningitis. Elinor stays by the child's side for days, waiting for the crisis to pass. One night, the sick boy opens his eyes and tells his parents that he is hungry. They are overjoyed at his apparent recovery; later that night, he dies suddenly. As they had done in the past, Elinor and Philip escape by going abroad.

For a long while, the Webley murder baffles the police. Despairing of ever escaping from his meaningless existence, Spandrell sends the British Freemen a note stating that Everard's murderer, armed, will be found at a certain address at a certain hour. On their arrival, the Freemen find Spandrell pointing a gun at them. They shoot him.

Burlap is the only happy man among these sensualists and intellectuals. One night, he and Beatrice pretend they are children and splash merrily while taking their bath together.

Critical Evaluation:

Aldous Huxley was one of the most intellectual writers of the twentieth century. Classically educated, he was interested in a wide range of subjects, and his novels are primarily vehicles to present his intellectual and philosophical views. In *Point Counter Point*, he describes such books as novels of ideas.

Beyond being a structurally and thematically complex novel, *Point Counter Point* is a harsh, insightful portrait of London society in the 1920's. D. H. Lawrence once praised it by saying that if the public truly understood Huxley's message, they would be banning it rather than his own *Lady Chatterley's Lover* (1928). Not only a novel of ideas, *Point Counter Point* is also a roman à clef, in which the characters are thinly veiled portraits, or in this case caricatures of real people. Rampion is Huxley's version of Lawrence, while Philip Quarles represents Huxley himself.

Huxley reveals the novel's structure, as well as its theme, in the title. In music, "counterpoint" refers to notes added to the main melody, or the point, to create a second melody that combines with the first in an intended relationship. Philip Quarles, in his notebooks on writing, explains his desire to musicalize fiction. To do this, he thinks an author should "show several people falling in love or dying or praying in different ways." This describes Huxley's structure. Parallel relationships abound in the novel. Situations are introduced and later reappear with different characters. With this method, Huxley examines the central relationships in human lives: those between lovers, between parents and children, and between humans and God. The harmony sought in musical counterpoint rarely appears in this novel, however, for the society he presents lacks balance. This lack, in combination with the characters' inability to combine feelings and intellect, passion and reason, lies at the novel's core.

The very first scene sets the tone as Marjorie pleads with her lover, Walter, to stay, while at the same time she is too refined to make a scene. Clearly it would be better both for her and for the relationship if she would act on her feelings, but she is unable to do so. When Walter leaves to pursue the shallow, sadistic Lucy Tantamount, he knows he is behaving badly; indeed, he has spent his entire life trying to avoid imitating his father's jolly careless sensuality but is unable to stop himself.

This first triangle is contrasted with the relationship between Philip and Elinor Quarles. Elinor loves Philip, but he is too intellectual to respond to her with feeling and has instead withdrawn into a dispassionate, analytical state where Elinor is unable to reach him. While they are in India, a full Moon reminds Elinor of evenings spent together in Hertfordshire when they were first in love. Although Philip understands what she means when she talks of the moon, he engages her in a debate about logic because he is unhappy about being interrupted. Discussing his feelings makes him uncomfortable and threatens his remote, frigid silence. Philip, like Walter, is fully aware of the flaws in his nature and wishes to respond differently, yet he, too, is unable to make the effort necessary to change. Elinor is driven into pursuing a relationship with Webley simply because he possesses the emotion Philip lacks. Almost all of the male-female relationships in the novel are similarly damaged.

Huxley also explores parent-child relationships and their later effect on adult behavior. While Philip and Elinor travel around the world, they entrust their young son to a nursemaid and the boy's grandmother. Even when they return, they are not really a part of his life. When he is ill, both Philip and Elinor resent being called to his bedside. Elinor comments that nature never intended her to have children. The most painful parent-child relationship exists between Spandrell and his mother. He can pinpoint one moment in his life, when he was fifteen years old and watching his mother as they skied in Europe, as the dividing line between the innocent happiness of his youth and the utter cynicism and contempt he now feels. After his mother married the arrogant General Knoyle, Spandrell deliberately started making the worst possible choices in everything. "He was spiting her, spiting himself, spiting God." Again the lack of balance is clear.

Religion intrudes to some extent, but it is seen in most cases as promoting unnatural, rather than harmonious, behavior. Throughout their marriage, Marjorie's husband, a drunken preacher, uses religion to torment her. Huxley criticizes saints and ascetics as unnatural. Rampion contemptuously describes Saint Francis of Assisi licking the sores of lepers not to help the lepers in any way but only to degrade himself. It is Spandrell, the degenerate cynic, who most desperately searches for God yet cannot change. Rampion finds him refusing "to be a man . . . either a daemon or a dead angel."

All but two of the central characters in the novel—the artist Rampion and his wife, May—are missing balance. Rampion provides the counterpoint as the voice of balance and reason. Lawrence found his fictionalized self, "a boring gas bag." Although he illustrates balance, it is only in the early idyllic courtship scenes that Rampion does anything but pontificate. In fact, there is a good deal of satire in the presentation. However, it is clear that Huxley intends him to be the novel's central figure, since he provides a touchstone for the other characters in the story who seek his advice and approval.

"Critical Evaluation" by Mary Mahony

Further Reading

Baker, Robert. *The Dark Historic Page: Social Satire and Historicism in the Novels of Aldous Huxley, 1921-1939.* Madison: University of Wisconsin Press, 1982. Presents four of the novel's main contrapuntal plot lines, which are centered on relationships with parents, lovers, death, and God. Argues that Spandrell is central to each of these plot lines.

Barfoot, C. C., ed. *Aldous Huxley: Between East and West.* New York: Rodopi, 2001. Collection of essays, including analyses of the themes of science and modernity in Huxley's interwar novels, utopian themes in his work, his views of nature, and his use of psychedelic drugs and mescaline.

Bedford, Sybille. *Aldous Huxley: A Biography.* New York: Alfred A. Knopf, 1973. Detailed biography based primarily on oral sources that traces Huxley's intellectual and moral development from early childhood on. Presents a fascinating insight into the Huxley family. Discusses the novel's theme, characterization, and critical reaction.

Bowering, Peter. *Aldous Huxley: A Study of the Major Novels.* New York: Oxford University Press, 1969. Presents Huxley as a novelist of ideas who uses minimal plot and character development to focus on theme and satire. Discusses Huxley's relationship with D. H. Lawrence and its influence on the themes and ideas in *Point Counter Point.*

Meckier, Jerome. *Aldous Huxley: Modern Satirical Novelist of Ideas—A Collection of Essays.* Edited by Peter Firchow and Bernfried Nugel. London: Global, 2006. This collection of Meckier's essays written from 1966 through 2005 includes two discussions of *Point Counter*

Point: "Quarles Among the Monkeys: Huxley's Zoological Novels" and "Philip Quarles's Passage to India: Jesting Pilate, *Point Counter Point*, and Bloomsbury."

_____. *Aldous Huxley: Satire and Structure*. London: Chatto & Windus, 1969. An excellent introductory source that isolates major themes of *Point Counter Point* and provides the clearest overview of its structure. Includes an analysis of Rampion's central role and of his ruthless assessments of other characters, as well as the use of models for many characters.

_____, ed. *Critical Essays on Aldous Huxley*. New York: G. K. Hall, 1996. Includes thoughtful essays on Huxley's oeuvre, including several pieces interpreting *Point Counter Point*.

Murray, Nicholas. *Aldous Huxley: A Biography*. New York: St. Martin's Press, 2003. Murray's 500-plus-page biography and intellectual history is a wide-ranging survey of Huxley's writing and his social, personal, and political life. Covers Huxley's early satirical writing, his peace activism, his close relations and friendships with Hollywood filmmakers and other intellectuals, and his fascination with spirituality and mysticism. Illustrations, bibliography, and index.

Nance, Guinevera A. *Aldous Huxley*. New York: Continuum, 1988. A clear introductory work that discusses Huxley's intellectual development and his detached, reflective presentation of a society without balance. Analyzes the characters, parallel story lines, and recurring themes of *Point Counter Point*.

The Poisonwood Bible

Author: Barbara Kingsolver (1955-   )
First published: 1998
Type of work: Novel
Type of plot: Political allegory
Time of plot: 1959 to 1980's
Locale: Kilanga, the Belgian Congo; Bethlehem, Georgia

Principal characters:
NATHAN PRICE, a Christian missionary
ORLEANNA PRICE, his wife
RACHEL,
LEAH,
ADAH, and
RUTH MAY, their daughters
MAMA BEKWA TATABA, a housekeeper for the Price family
BROTHER FYNTAN FOWLES, a missionary
ANATOLE NGEMBA, a village teacher
EEBEN AXELROOT, a bush pilot

The Story:

The Price family, in 1959, journeys to the Belgian Congo from their home in Bethlehem, Georgia, as Christian missionaries. The Reverend Nathan Price and his family, loosely affiliated with Southern Baptist sponsors, arrive at the village of Kilanga with no understanding of what they will face. They know nothing of their living conditions or the types of challenges they will encounter as Nathan preaches his spiritual message.

Orleanna, Nathan's wife, and their daughters Rachel (fifteen years old), Leah and Adah (twelve-year-old twins), and Ruth May (six years old), tend to their authoritarian father, who sees himself as the guide, guardian, and absolute ruler of his family of females. Their sole duty is to make Nathan's life in Kilanga tolerable by creating his meals and keeping his home. He liberally hands down advice and often-cruel, even sadistic, punishment, forcing the girls to, among other things, copy long passages of Scripture to make amends for their sins or hitting them or their mother when they displease him. He is a figure to be feared, and his only connection to his family is relaying the condemnations of an angry God for giving in to human weakness.

Each daughter has her own perspective on Africa, Nathan, and the family's mission. Rachel, longing only for a sweet-sixteen party, abhors the heat and dirt of the Congo, not to mention its distance from the United States. She has nowhere to go, no friends, and no interest in what is around her except as it furthers her desire to feel pretty or act more grown up. Leah, thoughtful and longing for righteousness, tries hard to win Nathan's approval and blessing. Imperfect Adah, suffering from hemiplegia (paralysis of half the body), carries on a consistent internal monologue but restricts her speech to palindromes; she also limps when she walks. Ruth May takes in the world around her with characteristically childlike attention to details, including facts about her family and the games and language of the village children. She inadvertently reveals her father's character by remarking on his nastiness and dislikes.

Orleanna complies with Nathan's demands as well as she can in a kitchen where her Betty Crocker cake mixes only serve to highlight the distance she and her family are from the United States or any other modern world. She tries to learn something about the local ways of managing food from Mama Bekwa Tataba, the family's housekeeper. Each day Orleanna faces the taxing work of building fires, hauling water, preparing as-fresh-as-possible food, and presenting a decent meal at noon. The laundry and other housekeeping chores, even with Tataba's help, prove daunting, and Orleanna begins to lose her stamina along with her faith in the rightness of her and Nathan's calling.

Nathan disdains help of any kind, including advice about how to set out plants to protect them from floods and how to speak the local language. Instead, he makes a fool of himself. Ignoring Mama Tataba's gardening habits, Nathan loses all his plants in a deluge. Perhaps his most arrogant offense is his refusal to use a translator and thereby mispronounce the words of the Kikongo language. His faulty pronunciation assures his congregation that Jesus is love, and that Jesus will make them itch like poison, as does the poisonwood tree. Thinking he is proclaiming God's love, Nathan completely undermines his message. Tragically, and none the wiser, he smugly boasts of his ability to talk to the Congolese in their own tongue.

As a final blow to his credibility and ability to reach anyone in the village, Nathan insists on baptizing children in a crocodile-infested river. This rite terrifies them with images of death and impending doom—several local children have recently disappeared, snatched by crocodiles in the same river. Similar missteps and a patronizing attitude foster miscommunication and damage Nathan's relations with the villagers.

Brother Fyntan Fowles tries to help Nathan with his mission, but Nathan disdains him because he has married a Congolese woman and lives a kind of itinerant life. Fowles has given up both the form and message of Western Christianity in an attempt to do some good for the people who trust him.

Anatole Ngemba, the village teacher, is a regular part of the Price home as a tutor for the girls. With him they tackle academics; perhaps as important, they learn from him the history of the freedom movement in pre-independence Congo. Leah quickly figures out he can be trusted. They become fast friends.

Orleanna wilts under the pressure of the grueling daily work she must complete just to survive in the often-hostile landscape and climate, and the girls fall into their habitual roles. Rachel complains and seeks a way to be a "normal" teenager, somehow, in a place she despises. Adah keeps her own counsel but thinks constantly about the foolishness and cruelty of her father's approach to life and faith. Leah slowly comes to grips with her father's faltering role as a worthy authority figure as well as her own growing sense of morality. Ruth May plays with the village children and bonds with them without pretense.

Ruth May is bitten by a green mamba snake. Confusion about what had happened to her makes it impossible for anyone to act quickly enough to save her life. She dies, and Orleanna descends into a nightmare of grief and longing. She faces the loss of her daughter and then finally admits Nathan's overbearing cruelty against the family and his manipulation. She no longer feels obligated to her husband.

The Congo is thrust into chaos during its movement for independence from Belgium, marking the end of colonial domination for an entire people and also the collapse of Nathan's patriarchal dominance. Orleanna abandons him, placing all her trust in her abilities to survive and save her remaining children. In the flight to freedom, Rachel flies off with Eeben Axelroot, a bush pilot, to begin her life with him in Africa; they soon marry. Orleanna manages to leave the Congo with Adah, and Leah marries Anatole and supports his resistance to the newly corrupt regime.

Nathan, years after his family had left him and had established lives of their own, wanders like a crazy man, rambling and alienating everyone he encounters. He dies alone, burning to death in a freakish accident while villagers stand by, reluctant to intervene. His death is a just finale to his brutish behavior toward his wife and daughters and toward the Congolese he tried to intimidate into accepting Christianity.

Orleanna, with Adah, resides in the United States, leading a quiet life of musings, grief, and regret. She comes to terms with the course her life has taken, and she develops a way to forgive herself and continue living. She finds solace in the land and plants. Adah devotes herself to medical research that is focused on problems endemic to Africa.

Critical Evaluation:

Most critics consider *The Poisonwood Bible* to be Barbara Kingsolver's most ambitious and serious work. The book's narrative develops out of Kingsolver's conviction that life is political on all levels. Her other novels showcase social or political wrongs on a small scale. *The Poisonwood Bible* is global in its perspective and involves matters of faith, cultural negation, colonial power, psychological and physical domestic abuse, and American interference in the internal workings of a nation neither cared about nor really understood by these same Americans. All these themes intersect in the lives of one family from Bethlehem, Georgia, who arrive in Africa with a misguided sense of their importance and mission.

Critics agree on the political commentary in the novel, but they differ in their assessments of how significant that commentary is in the end. To highlight how Kingsolver uses her characters to generate ideas about the colonial presence of Westerners in Africa, it will be helpful to consider the members of the Price family, and the story's male characters, individually. In addition to furthering the plot, each character contributes a perspective that suggests wider implications for the story as a whole.

The four Price girls represent a range of responses to life in Africa. The self-centered approach of Rachel, the eldest daughter, leads her to exploit every circumstance or person to make her own life more palatable, that is, less African. Her never-ending sense of entitlement, along with her manipulative and forceful behavior, sets her up as a symbol of colonial power. She marries repeatedly to further her cause, using men the way the United States used the Congolese to further its own cause during the Congo's struggle for independence. At novel's end, Rachel owns a hotel in South Africa that serves a white clientele only. Her racist life typifies the colonial practice of taking care of the privileged classes, making a profit, and disdaining the country and people who make that profit possible.

Well-intentioned Leah is an American who is ready and able to appreciate the Congo's language, customs, and people. Her sense of mission never overwhelms her ability to absorb Congolese life or her willingness to understand the world she is discovering. Leah remains in Africa, married to Anatole Ngemba, a teacher. With his extended family and their own sons they struggle to survive in an economy riddled with corruption and the effects of long-term poverty. Anatole is politically active and is in and out of jail, his existence precarious. Congo struggles with internal divisions and reels under the influence of the self-serving U.S. government, which sponsors the country's dictatorship in exchange for certain natural resources. Leah "lives" Africa in a way her father never could, or would. Her route to redemption features grassroots political activity based on what is best for the Afri-

can people and not on what is best for politicians, governments, or religious zealots.

Leah's twin, Adah, physically disabled and unable to communicate well with others, acts as a type of underground conscience for the book. She rarely speaks out in the story, but her cryptic musings about the Price family's interactions with each other and with the members of the village "congregation" call Nathan's godliness into question—and call into question his ability to parent with compassion and wisdom. Adah's thoughts and palindromic utterances condemn the presence of the Prices in Africa, calling attention to the hypocrisy, cruelty, and irrelevance of Nathan's message and actions. Ultimately, Adah finds her voice and becomes a physician devoted to the study of viruses prevalent on the African continent. Her path to wholeness emerges as she makes important discoveries about the Ebola virus and AIDS/HIV. Science helps her frame a philosophy of life that incorporates not only her own past but also the past of Africa and its environment, the past of medicine, and the history of medical research.

The twins present two types of moral force: Leah's politically active life keeps her directly involved with the fate of Congo. Adah's medical work contributes substantially, but more obliquely than Leah's activity, to the quality of life on the African continent. The twins represent the determination of Westerners to contribute to Africa and its peoples in positive ways.

The very young Ruth May becomes a symbol for the effects of uncompromising domination on those unable to resist. She exemplifies the most openhearted and naïve white presence in the novel. Her death shows dramatically that the ill-prepared can be struck down by forces they do not understand. Her presence typifies those who enter Africa naïvely, learn some local "culture," such as games and language, and yet show no real concern or disdain for the social forces around them. Ruth May represents those who can be felled by forces they, or their elders, fail to comprehend. By making Ruth May a youngster, Kingsolver has heightened the poignancy of the child's death. Ruth May, a casualty of her father's calling, may be the single exception to Leah's comment that "We have in this story the ignorant, but no innocents."

Orleanna, caring for her household, becomes complicit in Nathan's outrageous and harmful dealings with his family and the village congregation because she fails to stand up to him—and fails to do so until it is too late for Ruth May. None of Orleanna's methods of coping or finding meaning in life transfers to her life in Africa, where her appeasing ways shore up nothing but Nathan's autocratic behavior. Her leaving him marks the start of a new life, one defined by self-determination rather than obedience. Her survival in the United States illustrates the ability of the self-aware to save themselves even after great trauma. The resilience of thinking women is a recurring Kingsolver theme.

The men in *The Poisonwood Bible* also display Western ways of thinking about Africa. Nathan's hard-hearted pursuit of righteousness makes him an overbearing husband, father, and pastor—an authority figure inspiring fear and mockery, not respect or allegiance. He views Africans as children, incapable of subtlety or self-help. On the other hand, Brother Fowles's respect for African ways allies him with Leah and Adah as a character devoted to positive change in the Congo. He is the better person, and Nathan, their father, is the enemy.

Eeben Axelroot is a white South African-born bush pilot. His exploitive behavior springs from his sense of entitlement and an understanding of the power he can wield. The self-serving use of his talents brings him money and influence in a limited sphere. He is worse than Nathan because he exploits with intention. Nathan exploits from a platform of moral righteousness, blind to the Congolese society he seeks to redeem. Rachel marries Eeben to escape the fate of being her father's daughter and living in dirt and chaos. Eeben is the first of Rachel's husbands, all of whom end up supporting white privilege at the expense of Africans. Rachel embraces this materialistic philosophy, which makes her worse than Nathan; she exploits without even the pretense of faith's moral underpinnings.

Themes spotlighting the morality of the Western missionary, the nature of goodness, and the trauma of political upheaval and colonial hubris weave throughout *The Poisonwood Bible*. Some critics find that the lens of the Price family is too limiting, that the novel is too domestic for serious consideration as a text dealing with political destiny the interference of the U.S. government in the Congo's internal affairs. Other critics read the novel in the context of Kingsolver's political activism and, thereby, understand her intent.

This novel took Kingsolver fifteen years to complete, much of that time devoted to collecting material and mulling over the deeper issues. Kingsolver wrote other books while moving toward the epic scope of this story, a cautionary tale about the trespasses of Western governments in the Congo and about America's role in the tragedies that ensued.

Karen Arnold

Further Reading

DeMarr, Mary Jean. *Barbara Kingsolver: A Critical Companion*. Westport, Conn.: Greenwood Press, 1999. This study is a detailed overview of Kingsolver's works, through the late 1990's. The chapter on *The Poisonwood Bible* concentrates on various approaches to the novel, with detailed analyses of plots, characters, and genre readings. Also includes the chapter "Politics and Genres."

Demory, Pamela A. "Into the Heart of Light: Barbara Kingsolver Rereads *Heart of Darkness*." *Conradians* 34, no. 3 (Fall, 2002): 181-195. An insightful comparison of *The Poisonwood Bible* and Joseph Conrad's *Heart of Darkness* (1902).

Koza, Kimberly A. "The Africa of Two Western Women Writers: Barbara Kingsolver and Margaret Laurence." *Critique: Studies in Contemporary Literature* 44, no. 3 (Spring, 2003): 284-295. Careful look at how *The Poisonwood Bible* characterizes complex African issues through the eyes of the Price family women. Includes a comparison to Margaret Laurence's books and methods.

Oonibene, Elaine R. "The Missionary Position: Barbara Kingsolver's *The Poisonwood Bible*." *College Literature* 30, no. 3 (Summer, 2003): 19-23. A discussion of colonial and postcolonial excesses of Western nations that use religious rhetoric to justify the ways they intervene in and rearrange the cultures of African nations, the Congo in this case.

Snodgrass, Mary Ellen. *Barbara Kingsolver: A Literary Companion*. Jefferson, N.C.: McFarland, 2004. Alphabetical entries include analyses of characters, dates, historical figures and events, allusions, literary motifs, and themes from Kingsolver's work. An excellent resource for studies of Kingsolver.

York, R. A. *The Extension of Life: Fiction and History in the American Novel*. Madison, N.J.: Fairleigh Dickinson University Press, 2003. York examines the "complementary tendencies" in the fiction of American writers, including Kingsolver, to document history while balancing creativity, to be true to facts while maintaining "self-conscious fabulation." Also examines works by Joyce Carol Oates, Bernard Malamud, Saul Bellow, Truman Capote, Toni Morrison, Jane Smiley, and others.

Pollyanna

Author: Eleanor H. Porter (1868-1920)
First published: 1913
Type of work: Novel
Type of plot: Sentimental
Time of plot: Early twentieth century
Locale: Beldingsville, Vermont

Principal characters:
MISS POLLY HARRINGTON, a stern unmarried woman
POLLYANNA WHITTIER, Miss Polly's orphaned eleven-year-old niece
NANCY, Miss Polly's servant
OLD TOM, Miss Polly's gardener
JIMMY BEAN, a ten-year-old orphan boy
MR. JOHN PENDLETON, a wealthy citizen of the town
DR. CHILTON, a local physician

The Story:

As Miss Polly Harrington tells her servant Nancy to prepare an attic room for the arrival of her orphaned eleven-year-old niece, Pollyanna, it is clear that Miss Polly is not fond of children. Pollyanna's mother—Miss Polly's sister—died years ago, but Miss Polly still thinks disapprovingly of her sister's marriage. Rejecting a proposal from a wealthy local man, Miss Polly's sister instead fell in love with a humble young minister, married him, and moved west. Now, the minister, Pollyanna's father, has died too, and Pollyanna is coming to live with dutiful Aunt Polly.

Good-hearted Nancy readies the room for Pollyanna and complains about Miss Polly's prickly ways to Old Tom, the gardener. Old Tom reveals that Miss Polly's sour demeanor began after an unhappy love affair, and the man she loved still lives in town. Nancy is eager to learn the man's identity, but Old Tom refuses to give away the secret.

Miss Polly sends Nancy to the train station to meet Pollyanna instead of going herself. The attic room proves hot and uncomfortable, and Miss Polly punishes Pollyanna for climbing out the window. In each case, Pollyanna assumes the best motives of Miss Polly and finds a way to be glad about her situation.

Pollyanna then explains what she calls the "Glad Game" to Nancy. It began when her father asked for supplies for his missionary efforts, including a doll for Pollyanna. The churchwomen sending the supplies had no doll and sent a pair of crutches instead. Her father explained to the disappointed Pollyanna that the game involved always finding something to be glad about; the crutches could be a source of gladness for Pollyanna and her father because they could be glad that they did not need them. Nancy begins to play the Glad Game in her own life. Pollyanna is unable to tell Aunt Polly about the Glad Game, however, because Aunt Polly, still holding old grudges, refuses to let Pollyanna mention her father.

Pollyanna's cheerful ways begin to win over the neighborhood. She delivers delicacies to the invalid Mrs. Snow, arranging her hair and inspiring her to take a renewed interest in life. Pollyanna even begins greeting a bad-tempered man she sees on the street. Nancy tells Pollyanna that the man is John Pendleton, a wealthy and reclusive gentleman.

Although Aunt Polly refuses to hear about the Glad Game, Pollyanna uses it to find ways to be glad about her poor attic room. Pollyanna's innocent gladness shames Aunt Polly into giving her a more comfortable room downstairs. Pollyanna also innocently assumes that Aunt Polly will be glad to take in a forlorn kitten and a stray dog and persuades her to do so. Pollyanna then comes across the bedraggled orphan Jimmy Bean. Pollyanna is sure Aunt Polly will be glad to take him in as well, but Aunt Polly rejects him and loses her temper.

Pollyanna comes up with a new plan to help Jimmy Bean, appealing to the Ladies' Aid society at the church. However, she finds that the society's members are more interested in helping children in India than those in town because helping Indian children will earn them a prominent place in the society's annual report.

Out for a walk, Pollyanna comes across John Pendleton, who has fallen and broken his leg. She runs to his house and phones for his doctor, Dr. Chilton. While they wait, she talks to Pendleton and says that she can see that he is not as gruff on the inside as he is outside. She stays to comfort him until Dr. Chilton and rescuers arrive.

That week, Pollyanna asks Aunt Polly if, instead of taking calf's-foot jelly to Mrs. Snow, she can take it to another invalid. Aunt Polly agrees but grows angry when she learns that the recipient is John Pendleton. Finally, she relents on the condition that Pollyanna does not let Pendleton think that the jelly came from Aunt Polly. Pollyanna takes the jelly to Pendleton, who is startled to learn that she is Aunt Polly's niece. Pollyanna is careful to tell Pendleton that Aunt Polly did not send the jelly, which causes amusement from him and later horror from Aunt Polly.

Pollyanna persuades Aunt Polly to let her arrange her aunt's hair and drape a pretty shawl over her shoulders, but Aunt Polly is furious when Dr. Chilton catches a glimpse of her. He has come to ask Pollyanna to help cheer up Pendleton. After she returns, Pollyanna mentions her conversation with Pendleton to Nancy: Pendleton told Pollyanna that she reminded him of something he wants to forget. Nancy, who has read many sensational romances, guesses that Pendleton was Aunt Polly's tragic lover.

Pendleton is so inspired by Pollyanna that he asks her if he can adopt her. Pollyanna unwittingly assumes that he means to marry Aunt Polly and is overjoyed. Pendleton reveals, however, that he was never Aunt Polly's suitor. He was in love with Pollyanna's mother and was devastated when she married another man. Embittered, he has only started to recover after encountering Pollyanna's bright spirits.

Learning that Aunt Polly has been worried about her, Pollyanna is happy to hear that she cares for her. She tells Pendleton that she cannot live with him but suggests he adopt Jimmy Bean. She also cheers up the town minister, the Reverend Paul Ford, who is discouraged by parish difficulties. She tells him that her father found eight hundred passages about rejoicing in the Bible, and the reverend decides to preach more positive sermons.

Dr. Chilton reveals to Pollyana that he has his own lost love. Later, crossing a road, Pollyanna is hit by a car. She is badly hurt, and the household is consumed with worry. Pendleton comes to visit her, which leads Old Tom to tell Nancy about Pendleton. After Pendleton had been rejected by Aunt Polly's sister, town gossips spread the rumor that Aunt Polly was chasing after him. This rumor caused an estrangement that only Pollyanna has begun to heal. Pendleton reveals to Aunt Polly that he wanted to adopt Pollyanna and that Pollyanna chose to stay with Aunt Polly.

Pollyanna remains ill and unable to walk, and Aunt Polly insists on calling in a specialist rather than Dr. Chilton. Pollyanna overhears that she may never be able to walk again and is devastated. She laments that she finds it too hard to play the Glad Game now. Pendleton tells her that he has decided to adopt Jimmy Bean. A flood of others tell Aunt Polly how their lives have been changed by playing the Glad Game. Aunt Polly is puzzled, so finally Nancy describes the Glad Game to her. So many people testify that they have benefited from the Glad Game that Pollyanna begins to find things to be glad about again.

As the weeks pass and Pollyanna remains an invalid, Dr.

Chilton tells Pendleton that he wishes he could see Pollyanna. He thinks he knows of a cure, but his relationship with Aunt Polly is too awkward for him to be consulted. It is actually Dr. Chilton who is Aunt Polly's estranged lover. Jimmy Bean overhears the conversation and goes to Aunt Polly himself. When she hears that Dr. Chilton might have a cure, she sends for him immediately.

Pollyanna is sent to a hospital. She writes a letter to Aunt Polly and "Uncle Tom" Chilton, telling them that she has already been able to take her first steps. She is delighed that Aunt Polly and Dr. Chilton were married at her bedside, and she is finding ways to be glad about losing the ability to walk for a while, because now she appreciates it so much more.

Critical Evaluation:

Pollyanna was an immediate success, remaining on the best-seller list for two years, and it has never been out of print. Its popularity inspired Eleanor H. Porter to write a sequel, *Pollyanna Grows Up* (1915). In the sequel, Pollyanna moves to Boston to help cheer up an unhappy woman and befriends a range of people, including Jamie, a boy in a wheelchair. She continues to play and teach the Glad Game, which continues to change the lives of those who practice it. By the end of the book, Pollyanna is a young lady courted by both Jamie and the grown-up and more sophisticated Jimmy Bean.

After Porter's death, her publisher commissioned further *Pollyanna* books from Harriet Lummis Smith and, later, Elizabeth Borton. The novels continued Porter's tradition of portraying Pollyanna and her Glad Game transforming people's outlooks. The sequels by later writers have not proven as enduring as Porter's own *Pollyanna* books.

In 1920, *Pollyanna* was adapted into a film starring Mary Pickford, as well as a stage play. In 1960, the Walt Disney Studios released another film adaptation starring Hayley Mills. A third *Pollyanna* was released in 2003 with Georgina Terry as Pollyanna.

Pollyanna fits squarely into the tradition of late nineteeth and early twentieth century American girls' novels such as Kate Douglas Wiggin's *Rebecca of Sunnybrook Farm* (1903), L. M. Montgomery's *Anne of Green Gables* (1908), and Frances Hodgson Burnett's *The Secret Garden* (serial, 1910; book, 1911). In each novel, a plucky orphan comes to live with a sour, unmarried older person or persons and wins over her caretaker and her community with her good humor and optimism. The end of each book sees the orphan having formed her household into a real family. *Pollyanna* is unique among these novels, though, in containing its own specific formula for coping with misfortune, the Glad Game. Although the Glad Game is the book's prescription for difficult times, Pollyanna herself also reforms her elders by innocently assuming the best motivations behind their often selfish actions, thereby shaming or inspiring them into better behavior.

In the years after the books were published, Glad Game clubs sprang up across the country. There are still a number of Web sites about the Glad Game, amounting to an informal movement of Glad Game practicioners. *Pollyanna* is unique among classic girls' books in leaving a legacy that is more psychological than literary. It is also notable for being the most sentimental of classic American girls' books and has been derided as having a mawkish, simplistic view of life. The word "pollyanna" has come into English as a term to describe an excessively or annoyingly cheerful person.

Martha Bayless

Further Reading

Griswold, Jerry. *Audacious Kids: Coming of Age in America's Classic Children's Books.* New York: Oxford University Press, 1992. A book for specialists, outlining a Freudian reading of *Pollyanna.* Analyzes the books in terms of Freud's ideas of the stages of child development, concluding that *Pollyanna* is full of oedipal conflict and that Pollyanna herself is a manipulative character.

Levine, Murray. "Pollyanna and the Glad Game: A Potential Contribution to Positive Psychology." *Journal of Positive Psychology* 2, no. 4 (2007): 219-227. Discusses the potential of the Glad Game to provide a model for psychological processes.

Mills, Alice. "Pollyanna and the Not So Glad Game." *Children's Literature* 27 (1999): 87-104. A psychotherapist examines the use and limitations of the Glad Game in *Pollyanna* and its many sequels, concluding that the Glad Game is not always the best choice of response.

Sanders, Joe Sutliff. "Spinning Sympathy: Orphan Girl Novels and the Sentimental Tradition." *Children's Literature Association Quarterly* 33, no. 1 (2008): 41-61. Situates *Pollyanna* among other classic girls' books that focus on sympathy and sentiment.

Seelye, John. *Jane Eyre's American Daughters—From "The Wide, Wide World" to "Anne of Green Gables": A Study of Marginalized Maidens and What They Mean.* Newark: University of Delaware Press, 2005. Discusses classic girls' novels; includes a chapter on *Pollyanna* and its debt to books such as Burnett's *Little Lord Fauntleroy* (serial, 1885; book, 1886).

Polyeucte

Author: Pierre Corneille (1606-1684)
First produced: 1642; first published, 1643 (English translation, 1655)
Type of work: Drama
Type of plot: Tragedy
Time of plot: 250 C.E.
Locale: Melitene, Armenia

Principal characters:
FÉLIX, Roman governor of Armenia
PAULINE, his daughter
POLYEUCTE, his son-in-law, an Armenian nobleman
NÉARQUE, Polyeucte's friend
STRATONICE, Pauline's friend
ALBIN, Félix's friend
SÉVÈRE, a Roman warrior, in love with Pauline

The Story:

Pauline, daughter of Félix, the Roman governor in Melitene, has been married fourteen days to Polyeucte, an Armenian nobleman. Terrified by dreams that seem to portend her husband's death, she vainly seeks to delay his departure on a secret mission, the nature of which is known only to his friend, Néarque. She relates her fears to her friend, Stratonice, and tells her of her earlier love for Sévère, a Roman of high birth whom her father would not allow her to marry because of Sévère's lack of fortune. When Emperor Decie had appointed Félix governor of Armenia, she had accompanied him and dutifully married an Armenian nobleman of her father's selection. Meanwhile, they had heard that Sévère had met a hero's death while aiding the emperor in battle against the Persians. According to the report, the young Roman's body has never been found.

Pauline has dreamed that Sévère is not dead, but rather threatens her husband's life; that a band of impious Christians had thrown Polyeucte at the feet of Sévère, and that she,

Pauline, crying out for aid from her father, has seen Sévère raise a dagger to pierce Polyeucte's breast. Her fears are further stirred when her father approaches and says that Sévère is alive and is at that moment entering the city. It seems that the king of Persia, struck by Sévère's gallantry, had reclaimed the body from the battlefield to gain the Roman an honorable burial. Miraculously, life had been restored to Sévère and the Persians had sent him to Rome in exchange for royal prisoners. Thereafter, his greater deeds in war had bound him closer to the emperor, who had sent him to Armenia to proclaim the good news of his victories and to make sacrifices of thanksgiving to the gods.

His love for Pauline is what really brings Sévère to Armenia. Sévère, informed by his servant that Pauline is married, decides that life is not worth living and that he would rather die in battle. First, however, he will see Pauline. When they meet, she tells him that if hers alone had been the choice she would, despite his poverty, have chosen him. She is married, however, and she will remain loyal to the husband whom she has learned to love. Pauline and Sévère say farewell to each other, he ready to die in battle, she to pray for him in secret.

Polyeucte returns from his mission, on which he had been secretly baptized a Christian. Ordered by a messenger from Félix to attend the sacrifices in the temple, he and Néarque plan to defy the idolatry of the worshipers there. Pauline tells him of Sévère's visit but adds that she had obtained his promise not to see her again. Stratonice, a witness at the temple sacrifices, hurries to Pauline with the news that Polyeucte has become a Christian, a traitor to the Roman gods. He has mocked the sacred mysteries and, with Néarque, declared that their god alone is the almighty king of earth and heaven. This defilement, Félix declares, would cost Néarque his life, but he hopes Polyeucte might come to his senses and recant after witnessing the punishment and death of his friend.

When Albin, the friend of Félix, brings news that Néarque is dead, he adds that Polyeucte had witnessed his execution undismayed. Pauline, reminding her father that Polyeucte is his choice and that in marrying him she had but fulfilled her filial duty, begs him to spare his life. Félix, fearing the thunderbolts of his gods and Sévère as well, refuses to listen when Albin urges that Polyeucte's sentence be left to the emperor. Besides, he is tempted by the thought that Polyeucte's death would allow Sévère to wed his daughter and thus he would gain for himself a far more powerful protector than he now has. Meanwhile, Pauline visits Polyeucte in jail with the plea that if he must worship his chosen god he should do so silently and secretly, and thus give Félix grounds for mercy. To her importunings Polyeucte replies that he is done with mortal ties, that he loves her, but loves his God more.

Polyeucte calls for Sévère and tells him that even as his wedding had parted the true love of Sévère and Pauline, so now by dying he hopes to bring them happily together. He hopes also that they will die Christians. Declaring himself ready for death, he is marched off by his guards. Sévère is amazed at this example of magnanimity, but his hopes are shattered when Pauline tells him she could never marry him, that it would stain her honor to wed anyone who, even innocently, had brought Polyeucte to his sad fate. She begs him, however, to try to save her husband from the death her father has ordered. He consents, if for no other reason than to prove to Pauline that he could equal her in nobility and thus be worthy of her.

Félix, although he regards this intervention on behalf of a rival as a trick to expose him to the full strength of the emperor's wrath, makes one last effort to sway his son-in-law. He tells Polyeucte that only on Sévère's account has he publicly taken his rigid stand and that he himself will adopt Christianity if Polyeucte will only pretend to follow the old gods until after Sévère has left the city. Polyeucte refuses. Angered, Félix said he will avenge his gods and himself. When Pauline enters, Polyeucte commands her to wed Sévère or die with him as a Christian.

Again, Pauline pleads for Polyeucte's life, and again, Félix is moved to make another attempt to persuade Polyeucte to abjure his new faith, but to no avail. Bidding farewell to Pauline, Polyeucte is marched out to death by Félix's order. Pauline rushes out after him, lamenting that she, too, will die if he were to die. Félix orders Albin to deter her but issues his order too late; Pauline sees her husband executed. Seeing him die, she feels that his death has unsealed her own eyes, acting as a divine visitation of grace. She declares herself a Christian, ready for death.

Sévère upbraids Félix for Polyeucte's death and threatens retaliation. Félix, suddenly yielding to a strange feeling that overcomes him, declares that his son-in-law's death has made him a Christian. This sudden conversion strikes Sévère as miraculous. He orders Félix to retain his position of authority, and promises to use all his persuasion to urge Emperor Decie to revoke his cruel commands and to let all worship the gods of their choice without fear of punishment.

Critical Evaluation:

Polyeucte, although a favorite of the general public in Pierre Corneille's time, was not considered his best play. Modern criticism, however, has revised this judgment. Despite the play's somewhat improbable plot, climaxed by miraculous conversions, it holds for today's public particular religious interest, since it deals with the working of divine grace in the human soul. It is, however, the strong delineation of the main characters that has won for this work its present acclaim.

Ever since *Polyeucte*'s initial performance, critics have wondered what Corneille meant when he called the play "a Christian tragedy." Corneille was a practicing Catholic who was educated by Jesuits. He translated religious works such as *The Imitation of Christ* (1486), a work traditionally attributed to Saint Thomas à Kempis, into French. No serious critic has ever questioned the sincerity of Corneille's commitment to Christianity. For the title character in *Polyeucte* there is no conflict. Although he loves his wife, Pauline, he understands clearly that he would lose his immortal soul if he were to renounce Christianity to save his life. When he married Pauline, he was still a pagan, but afterward he received the gift of faith and was converted to Christianity, a religion then persecuted throughout the Roman Empire. He respects the temporal authority of his father-in-law Félix, who is the Roman governor of Armenia, but Polyeucte realizes that he owes a higher allegiance to God than he does to the Roman Empire. Certain critics have suggested that *Polyeucte* can be viewed as a tragedy for its other three principal characters, namely Félix, Pauline, and the Roman nobleman Sévère, but it is necessary to stress the major differences among these three characters.

Until his totally unexpected conversion announced in the final scene of the fifth act, Félix acts in a petty and insensitive manner. Félix is from Rome, and he considers himself superior to the Armenians whom he governs. Before her marriage to Polyeucte, Pauline had been attracted to Sévère, but she willingly acceded to her father's request when he arranged her marriage to Polyeucte. Félix thought that Polyeucte would have a more promising political career than Sévère, but things turned out differently. Polyeucte never developed any interest in political intrigue, and Sévère's military valor brought him to the attention of influential people in Rome, and he quickly became a trusted confidant of Emperor Decie. Pauline loves and respects her husband, who is a decent and kind man. Félix is, however, insensitive to his daughter's feelings for her husband, and he regrets bitterly that he chose the wrong husband for her. When he learns from Sévère that the Roman emperor Decie, who reigned for just two years (249-251), demands that all Roman governors enforce Roman laws that required a sentence of death for people found practicing Christianity, Félix does not hesitate. He is more afraid of losing his political position than worried about saving the life of his son-in-law. Félix also acts in a rather sadistic manner. In a vain effort to persuade Polyeucte to renounce Christianity, he forces his son-in-law to watch the execution

of his friend and fellow Christian Néarque, but his martyrdom serves only to reinforce Polyeucte's commitment to Christianity. Why should he fear death? He believes that his martyrdom will guarantee his spending eternity in heaven.

For Félix and Polyeucte no tragic conflict exists, but this is not necessarily the case for Sévère and Pauline. Their passion for each other was profound, and they would have gotten married had Félix not chosen Polyeucte to marry Pauline. Pauline and Sévère are, however, responsible adults, and they both resist temptation. Neither wants to commit adultery. Although her confidant, Stratonice, and her father tell her repeatedly that Néarque had "seduced" Polyeucte into converting to the hated religion of Christianity, Pauline still loves her husband and respects his judgment.

The most emotionally charged scene in *Polyeucte* is act 4, scene 3, which takes place in Polyeucte's prison cell. Pauline tells her husband that his desire for martyrdom means that he has rejected her after she had sacrificed everything for him. Polyeucte assures her that he still loves her so much that he wants to lead her to Christianity so that she can also be saved. She is baffled by his arguments, which she describes as a "strange blindness." Sévère is equally mystified by the behavior of Christians who willingly sacrifice their lives and even pray for those who condemn them to death. At the end of the fourth act, Sévère speaks of his intention of defending Polyeucte and other Christians who have been sentenced to death.

Also, there is a tragic misunderstanding between Sévère and Félix. Félix assumes that Sévère will have him dismissed from his position if he appears weak by requesting clemency for his son-in-law or if he does not enforce Decie's cruel and unjust laws against Christians by ordering the execution of Polyeucte. Félix does not realize that Sévère believes that certain laws are so unconscionable that one's conscience requires one to resist them. Félix acts hastily and orders Polyeucte's execution before Sévère has an opportunity to reverse this unjust decision.

The martyrdom of Polyeucte produces extraordinary changes in the other three major characters. Félix and Polyeucte receive the divine grace of faith and announce their conversions to Sévère, who spares them both and expresses a fervent wish that the persecution of Christians will soon end. *Polyeucte* does not truly express a tragic vision of the world, but it does illustrate Corneille's extraordinary skill in creating heroic characters whose actions are so admirable and exemplary that they provoke unexpected moral changes in others.

"Critical Evaluation" by Edmund J. Campion

Further Reading

Abraham, Claude. *Pierre Corneille*. New York: Twayne, 1972. An excellent introduction to Corneille's plays that includes an annotated bibliography of important critical studies. Discusses the meaning of divine grace and the extraordinary evolution of Pauline.

Ekstein, Nina. *Corneille's Irony*. Charlottesville, Va.: Rookwood Press, 2007. A detailed examination of the use of irony in Corneille's plays, describing the different types of irony he employs and how each functions in specific plays.

Harwood-Gordon, Sharon. *The Poetic Style of Corneille's Tragedies: An Aesthetic Interpretation*. Lewiston, N.Y.: Edwin Mellen Press, 1989. Examines the rhetorical brilliance of key speeches in *Polyeucte* and other tragedies by Corneille. Explores the emotional and religious arguments that should cause audience members not to question the sincerity of Pauline's conversion to Christianity.

Longstaffe, Moya. *Metamorphoses of Passion and the Heroic in French Literature: Corneille, Stendhal, Claudel*. Lewiston, N.Y.: Edwin Mellen Press, 1999. Maintains that the works of Corneille, Paul Claudel, and Stendhal share a common aspiration for human dignity. Compares the writers' treatments of the ideal of the heroic and the relationship between men and women.

Margitic, Milorad R. *Cornelian Power Games: Variations on a Theme in Pierre Corneille's Theatre from "Mélite" to "Polyeucte."* Tübingen, Germany: Narr, 2002. Analyzes Corneille's first twelve plays, including *Polyeucte*, showing how each demonstrates a particular strategy of power. Margitic concludes that Corneille's universe is a highly manipulative and political place and his characters are complex and changing.

Muratore, Mary Jo. *The Evolution of the Cornelian Heroine*. Potomac, Md.: Studia Humanitatis, 1982. Examines the differences between idealistic heroines, such as Pauline, and unsympathetic female characters, including Cleopatra and Medea. Questions the sincerity of Pauline's religious conversion after her husband's martyrdom.

Nelson, Robert J. *Corneille: His Heroes and Their Worlds*. Philadelphia: University of Pennsylvania Press, 1963. Explores the evolving nature of heroism for Corneille's male characters. Discusses the political and psychological opposition between Polyeucte and Sévère.

Pocock, Gordon. *Corneille and Racine: Problems of Tragic Form*. New York: Cambridge University Press, 1973. Analyzes the formal structure of *Polyeucte* and explores the problematic nature of the conversion of Pauline and Félix after Polyeucte's execution. Examines the rhetorical effectiveness of key speeches in the tragedy.

Poly-Olbion

Author: Michael Drayton (1563-1631)
First published: 1612, part 1; 1622, part 2
Type of work: Poetry

The complete title of Michael Drayton's long topographical poem is *Poly-Olbion: Or, A Chorographicall Description of Tracts, Rivers, Mountaines, Forests, and other Parts of this renowned Isle of Great Britaine, With intermixture of the most Remarquable Stories, Antiquities, Wonders, Rarityes, Pleasures, and Commodities of the same, Digested in a Poem*. Quite a bit of digesting is entailed, especially when a title page note continues, "With a Table added, for direction to those occurrences of Story and Antiquitie, whereunto the Course of the Volume easily leades not." This table is Drayton's extensive index to the proper names in the poem, and it is printed separately in volume 5 of the standard edition. The poem's title derives from the Greek *poly*, meaning

"many," and Albion, a name for England that is related to the Greek word for "happy."

Drayton's opus comprises thirty songs—as he calls his poems—eighteen in part 1 and twelve in part 2, each preceded by a summary "argument" of twelve to twenty lines in rhymed iambic tetrameter. Each song celebrates the natural beauties and historic events of a particular region of Great Britain and is accompanied by an impressionistic map of that area. Although songs 22 and 24 go on for 1,638 and 1,320 lines, respectively, most of the songs are between 450 and 500 lines in length; the rhymed Alexandrines, or lines of iambic hexameter, are divided frequently by caesuras and split almost evenly between end-stopped and enjambed. Allusions to British history and classical myth abound, and personification becomes a reliable narrative device, notably in the pretense that it is Drayton's muse who is speaking. The term "chorography," which is no longer used, in Drayton's time commonly specified writings about topography, and several classical models of the genre were available to Drayton. Among many influences on Drayton, the Renaissance historian and antiquarian William Camden organized his *Brittania* (1596) by counties, as Drayton organizes this work. Part 1 of *Poly-Olbion* is dedicated to Prince Henry, son of the reigning British monarch, James I.

The frontispiece to *Poly-Olbion*, an engraving by William Hole, presents an elaborate tangle of allegorical meanings. Great Britain is personified as a woman seated within a triumphal arch. Britain holds in her right hand a scepter that signifies her power, and in her left an overflowing cornucopia symbolizes the richness of her land. The open sea behind Britain teems with ships that suggest the sea power Great Britain enjoyed under Elizabeth I, and indeed it is hard not to see the dead queen in the personified Britain. The soft folds of Britain's clothing are adorned with the peaks and valleys appropriate to a topographical poem. On the four corners of the arch appear statues of Great Britain's four conquerors: Brute, or Brutus, the legendary nephew of Aeneas; Julius Caesar; the Saxon Hengist, who conquered the land in 449; and William the Conqueror, who led the Norman triumph at Hastings in 1066, and from whom King James I traced his descent. These figures form a loose historical framework for part 1 of the poem.

Summed up broadly, Drayton's poem depicts the pre-Anglo Saxon period as the source of Great Britain's distinctive culture. The Romans and the Saxon hordes of Hengist contributed their own unique elements—for example, the Anglo Saxons brought the Christian influence—but the Normans despoiled the land by oppressing its conquered people. It is significant that, considering that part 1 appeared in the middle of James I's reign (from 1603 to 1625), Drayton concludes his short poem explicating the frontispiece with these lines: "Divorst from Him [the Roman], the *Saxon sable Horse,*/ Borne by sterne *Hengist*, wins her [Britain]: but through force/ Garding the *Norman Leopards bath'd in Gules,*/ She chang'd hir Love to Him, whose Line yet rules."

Each song in part 1 is followed by "illustrations," or several pages of dense notes expanding on the historical backgrounds and meanings of individual lines. The author of these notes was John Selden, a learned scholar and friend of Drayton, who explained his mission as illuminating "What the Verse oft, with allusion, as supposing a full knowing Reader, lets slip; or in winding steps of Personating Fictions

(as some times) so infolds, that suddaine conceipt cannot abstract a Forme of the clothed Truth." The erudition of Selden's annotations can exhaust the unwary reader, especially one who ventures into the marginal glosses, speckled with Greek and Latin, that offer clarifying refinements on the illustrations themselves.

In the rather peevish "To the General Reader" prefacing part 1, Drayton complains of a "great disadvantage" against him in "this lunatique Age." He is referring to poems that are "wholly deduc't to Chambers," "kept in Cabinets," and circulated only "by Transcription." He inveighs against coterie poetry, the property of small elitist groups. This fashion works against a poet such as Drayton, who writes with a nationalist bias and hopes for a large public audience. He grumbles that his "unusuall tract may perhaps seeme difficult, to the female Sex; yea, and I feare, to some that think themselves not meanly learned." These cabinet poets are reviled in song 21 for "Inforcing things in Verse for Poesie unfit,/ Mere filthy stuffe, that breakes out of the sores of wit." Drayton was the first to introduce this distinction between public and private verse, now a commonplace in the literary history of the period.

In condemning coterie verse, Drayton asserted the value, going back to Aristotle's *Poetics* (c. 334-323 B.C.E.), of nemesis, or imitation, in art. He pleads in song 21 for smooth lines that flow "like swelling *Euphrates*" and states that poets are like painters in expressing things "neerest to the life." The power of the poet's art resembles that of Orpheus, who charmed the trees and rocks and led them "T' imbrace a civill life, by his inticing Layes." This theory assumes a serious civic role for the poet, a responsibility the frustrated Drayton feels has been thwarted by the cabinet poets.

Poly-Olbion has a prominent historical context and reveals some strong prejudices. For instance, Drayton had studied Welsh historians and apparently accepted their claim that the Welsh were descended from the Trojans and were the first inhabitants of Great Britain. Song 1 includes a long account of how "Noble Brutus" and his Trojan cohorts arrived in Cornwall and fought the "monstrous Giants" there. In Drayton's telling, Cornwall received its name from the Trojan Corineus, who wrestled the huge Gogmagog and threw him into the sea. This account exemplifies Drayton's fanciful blending of legend with topography.

Drayton's confidence that Great Britain had its counterparts for everything that the Greeks and Romans had leads him in song 10 to praise the historicity of the stories about Great Britain's Trojan ancestors. Throughout *Poly-Olbion*, aspects of British life are validated by their superiority to classical antecedents, as in these lines from song 7 in which the Golden Fleece is bested: "*Lug* little *Oney* first, then *Arro* in doth take [describing the confluence of three rivers],/ At *Lemster*, for her Wooll whose Staple doth excell,/ And seemes to over-match the golden *Phrygian* fell." Guy of Warwick ("The Knight through all the world renown'd for Chivalrie" in song 12) becomes a virtual Hercules through the magnificence of his accomplishments.

The legends traditionally associated with Bath, Avon, and Avalon enrich the hymns to various rivers and streams that make up song 3. The centerpiece of the song becomes the Arthurian material, such as "great Arthurs Tombe" and "holy Joseph's grave." The monastery at Glastonbury reflects "our great fathers pompe, devotion and their skill." This passage moves Selden in his illustrations to recite the story that Henry II ordered the local abbot, Henry of Blois, to dig up Arthur's body, which was duly found in a wooden coffin. It is a mark of Selden's dutifulness that he observes of the wood in this coffin, "*Girald* saith Oken, *Leland* thinks Alder."

Renaissance poets frequently pondered the mysteries of time and change, and this fondness for the mutability theme intersects in song 3 with Drayton's fascination with Stonehenge. For Drayton, the "Dull heape" stands as a memorial to some grand past now lost to time. Drayton's personified "mightie Mount" of Wansdike "doth complaine" to Stonehenge in these lines: "Ill did those mightie men to trust thee with their storie,/ That hast forgot their names, who rear'd thee for their glorie:/ For all their wondrous cost, thou that hast serv'd them so,/ What tis to trust to Tombes, by thee we easely know." Humanity can take no solace in monuments, and thus it becomes imperative for the artist—the poet, such as Drayton—to preserve the memory of a long and grand tradition.

Drayton returns to this theme in part 2, dedicated to Prince Charles, but the work begins on a bilious note. In his brief preface to part 2, "To Any That Will Read It," Drayton laments that when he began his "Herculean labour" he was hopeful of its success, "But it hath fallen out otherwise." He blames the "barbarous Ignorance" of British readers and the greedy stationers who are eager to market their "beastly and abominable Trash." With his voice rising to a screech, Drayton curses that small number who take pride in their benightedness: "For these, since they delight in their folly, I wish it may be hereditary from them to their posteritie, that their children may bee beg'd for Fooles to the fifth Generation, untill it may be beyond the memory of man to know that there was ever any other of their Families."

The bitterness in these lines anticipates the hints of pessimism in part 2. *Poly-Olbion* ends with Drayton contemplating a mysterious grouping of "Stones seventie seven" formed in a ring. He complains sadly, "The victories for which these

Trophies were begun,/ From darke oblivion thou, O Time, shouldst have protected." In the final line of his work, his Herculean toil has picked up a new adjective and become "This strange *Herculean* toyle," as if perhaps even he himself cannot decide exactly what he has wrought in these 14,454 lines supplemented by the equally heroic toil of Selden in his illustrations to part 1.

"Critical Evaluation" by Frank Day

Further Reading

Brink, Jean R. *Michael Drayton Revisited*. Boston: Twayne, 1990. Revisionist study of Drayton's work is influenced by the new historicism. Attributes to Drayton more influence on literary theory than previously acknowledged. Spells out the humanist and antiquarian sources of *Poly-Olbion*.

Drayton, Michael. *Poly-Olbion*. Vols. 4 and 5 in *The Works of Michael Drayton*, edited by J. William Hebel. Oxford, England: Basil Blackwell, 1961. Standard edition of Drayton's poem includes excellent editorial notes and a bibliography in volume 5. Glosses and typography in the large volume 4 capture a feeling for the original text.

Galbraith, David Ian. *Architectonics of Imitation in Spenser, Daniel, and Drayton*. Toronto: University of Toronto Press, 2000. Examines *Poly-Olbion* and two other poems of the English Renaissance—Edmund Spenser's *The Faerie Queene* (1590, 1596) and Samuel Daniel's *Civil Wars* (1595). Discusses how the three poets "enter into a dialogue" with the poets of ancient Rome, as well as with writers of their own era, in order to negotiate a boundary between poetry and history.

Lyne, Raphael. *Ovid's Changing Worlds: English Metamorphoses, 1567-1632*. New York: Oxford University Press, 2001. Examines *Poly-Olbion* and three other English Renaissance poems to describe how Drayton and the other writers adapted the works of Ovid. Demonstrates how Drayton and his contemporaries created an English literary language at the same time they imitated classical poetry.

McEachern, Claire. *The Poetics of English Nationhood, 1590-1612*. New York: Cambridge University Press, 1996. Examines the creation of English national identity through an analysis of how the concept of nationality was expressed in *Poly-Olbion* and other works of the period.

Richmond, Velma Bourgeois. *The Legend of Guy of Warwick*. New York: Garland, 1996. Meticulously traces the evolution of the legend from its antecedents to its reception and adaptation in the twentieth century, analyzing the various texts in which the legend has been recounted. Includes discussion of Drayton's version of the legend in *Poly-Olbion*.

The Ponder Heart

Author: Eudora Welty (1909-2001)
First published: 1954
Type of work: Novella
Type of plot: Regional
Time of plot: Early 1950's
Locale: Clay, Mississippi

Principal characters:
MISS EDNA EARLE PONDER, the proprietor of a small family hotel
UNCLE DANIEL PONDER, her generous uncle
BONNIE DEE PEACOCK PONDER, his "trial" wife

The Story:

Uncle Daniel, who is rich as Croesus and correspondingly generous, is not very bright, but he looks impressive and neat as a pin. He invariably wears spotless white suits and a red bow tie and carries a huge Stetson hat just swept off his head. Kept under his father's thumb until he was mature, he was for a long time unable to be as generous as his nature dictates. He gave Edna Earle the hotel she runs, but his father was glad to get rid of it. The cattle and fields he gave away were easily retrieved. People like Uncle Daniel because he is always giving something away, even if it is only small change, but he always feels alone.

After his father's death, Uncle Daniel becomes Edna Earle's responsibility. She feels fairly safe about his giving things away as long as he is unconcerned about money. His father had always given him an allowance of three dollars a week, and she continues the practice with no objection from Uncle Daniel because he is happy to have a little change in his pocket. His desire to give things to people makes a wonderful topic for Edna Earle to discuss with the traveling salesmen who stay in her hotel. Stories of Uncle Daniel involve the whole town and most of the surrounding countryside.

One day, Uncle Daniel escapes Edna Earle long enough to take a new salesgirl at the five-and-dime as his second bride. Edna Earle had been rather reticent about his first wife, who left him, though there seemed to be no rancor on either side. Since Uncle Daniel assures her that his second wife is just "on trial," Edna Earle has to sit back and see what happens. Bonnie Dee Peacock Ponder holds Uncle Daniel enthralled for five years before she disappears. He always claims she looked good enough to eat and that she could cut his hair better than anyone had ever done before.

Edna Earle tells this story of the Ponder heart to prepare her listener, a traveling salesman guest in her hotel, for the change in Uncle Daniel since the salesman had last seen him. As she describes Uncle Daniel, his married life, and his most recent experiences, Edna Earle's own situation becomes clear. The last respectable member of a disintegrating family, she is conscious of her dignity and jealous of the position she wishes for Uncle Daniel. She feels responsible for making things run, whether it be Uncle Daniel's life or the rummage sale every week for the poor people in town. She wants things to run her way, however, and does not refrain from demanding her way with the servants, lawyers, shopkeepers, or even the judge. Though she deplores the fact that the town is no longer on a through route, she actually loves it. She despises the Peacock family, but she does her duty by them because Uncle Daniel married one of them. Edna Earle's monologue covers the hunt for Bonnie Dee, Bonnie Dee's return, her turning Uncle Daniel out of his own house, her wholesale purchase of useless things (like the washing machine she put on the front porch before the house was wired for electricity), her sudden death, and the trial of Uncle Daniel for her murder.

As a bribe to bring Bonnie Dee back home after she had disappeared, Edna Earle promised Uncle Daniel that Bonnie Dee would get an allowance. No one had thought to give her one during her five-year "trial" marriage. Uncle Daniel reacts slowly to the thought of money. Not until the day of the trial does he think of the wealth he has in the bank. Apparently, it is a whim that day that prompts him to go to the bank early, when the only clerk there is someone who has never been warned not to give money to Uncle Daniel. He withdraws every cent he has, pads his pockets with the money, and goes to his trial.

Uncle Daniel's murder trial brings together the whole town and all of Bonnie Dee's huge family from the country. Edna Earle and the lawyer she has hired do not intend to let Uncle Daniel speak in his own defense. They rely too much on his previous obedience, however, and neglect to take into account the feelings he will naturally have at being, for once, the focal point in a big situation. Uncle Daniel listens carefully to all the witnesses and then, without warning, takes over the trial. Throwing money right and left, pressing bills upon all the people, he immediately convinces the jury of his innocence and even softens the hearts of Bonnie Dee's family. Afterward, however, he is more alone than ever. People still do not understand him, and now he has nothing more to give them.

Critical Evaluation:

If the origin of comedy is in the disruption of routine and logical or rational expectation without the result of genuine pain, then *The Ponder Heart* is a comic masterpiece. The world Eudora Welty creates in the small town of Clay, Mississippi, in the early 1950's is peopled by characters for whom reason and logical predictability appear to be the exception rather than the rule. The punch line, after all, is that one of the characters dies not by being smothered by her estranged husband or from a fright-induced heart attack but from laughing.

At the center of the novella, which is narrated in a dramatic monologue to the reader—"you," a stranded guest at the Beulah Hotel three days after the famous trial—is Uncle Daniel Ponder, who has the mind of a child and is unable to deal with the world rationally. Lovable in his imbecility, Uncle Daniel spends most of his time giving things away. When, however, Grandpa Ponder attempts to commit Uncle Daniel to an asylum, the tables are turned and Grandpa ends up being detained while Uncle Daniel, then in his fifties, promptly marries Bonnie Dee Peacock, a girl of seventeen who works at the dime store.

Incongruities of all sorts show up throughout the novella, not only in how the characters behave but also in what they say. Edna Earle Ponder, who narrates the events in a torrent of clichés and colloquialisms, is master of the non sequitur. The comic centerpiece of the novella is the trial. The occasion is founded on the assumption that justice derives rationally from motivation and evidence, but in a case in which the coroner is blind and the only motive for the supposed murder appears to be love, it can be expected that justice will have little to do with reason.

As the title implies, the main theme of the novella concerns the heart, or love. The doctor has described Bonnie Dee's death as heart failure, "death by misadventure," but, as Edna Earle describes it, the prosecuting attorney, Dorris Gladney, scratching his head and pretending to think, thereupon asks the double-edged question, "What makes the heart fail?" The real mystery is not whether Uncle Daniel did or did not murder his childish, materialistic wife but why love fails.

Ironically, the character who seems most capable of universal and selfless love is Uncle Daniel, but society first commits him to an asylum and then accuses him of murder. The question arises whether Uncle Daniel's benevolent and loving nature is itself the object of ridicule, for he has only the slightest grasp on reality. His "fond and loving heart" is bent on an array of women, beginning with a motorcyclist, Intrepid Elsie Fleming, at the county fair, but, as Edna Earle

says, he was in his forties "before we ever dreamed that such a thing as love flittered through his mind." Welty's choice of the word "mind" here may be significant.

Grandpa Ponder arranges a marriage for Uncle Daniel with the widow Miss Teacake Magee, but that lasts only two months because the noise of her heels unnerves her new husband. His love for Bonnie Dee, who stays with him for five and a half years before leaving for no apparent reason, has as much to do with her willingness to cut his hair as anything else. For her part, Bonnie Dee appears to love only "things," and her return to Uncle Daniel is obviously in response to that portion of Edna Earle's poem in the newspaper that mentions "retroactive allowance." Although Uncle Daniel does feel her loss, he is quite willing to transfer his affections to her sister, but when he gives away all his money at the climax of the trial, he has nothing to offer that she wants.

The most important character in the novella is the narrator, Edna Earle, who understands the claims of both the head and the heart and who has set aside her own craving for romantic love in order to care for her family. The last of the Ponders, and the best embodiment in the novella of Christian charity, she describes herself as "the go-between . . . between my family and the world." The closest she comes to a self-indulgent romantic love is her affection for a traveling salesman named Ovid Springer; Welty's choice of first name, an obvious reference to the Augustan poet noted for his erotic love poems, appears to be ironic, for Springer shows no romantic inclination toward Edna Earle.

Edna Earle frequently comments on love, but her observations are usually buried in such a variety of contexts that they are easily overlooked. When Grandpa Ponder tells her about his plan to "fork up a good wife" for Uncle Daniel, she informs the guest, "The heart's a remarkable thing, if you ask me." She does not, however, let on to Grandpa Ponder that she herself might wish to be married. Commenting on Uncle Daniel's inability to understand money, Edna Earle says, "The riches were all off in the clouds somewhere—like true love is, I guess, like a castle in the sky." Although she is speaking of her uncle, her own wistfulness is apparent. When she attempts to bring Bonnie Dee and her uncle together after she sets up at the Ponder place outside town and leaves Uncle Daniel at the Beulah Hotel, Edna Earle comments, "I don't know if you can measure love at all." She adds, "There's a lot of it. . . . Love! There's always somebody wants it."

At the end of the novella, however, there appear to be no takers for the Ponders' immense love. No longer wealthy, they have been alienated from the town, for the citizens of Clay feel guilty over having accepted Uncle Daniel's last extravagant cash giveaway. Some critics have pointed out that the future belongs to the proud but worthless Peacocks, whereas the Ponders, whose name suggests thoughtfulness and something weighty or substantial in character, are left standing alone.

"Critical Evaluation" by Ron McFarland

Further Reading

Bloom, Harold, ed. *Eudora Welty.* Updated ed. New York: Chelsea House, 2007. Collection of essays presents analysis of Welty's work, including pieces by writers Robert Penn Warren and Elizabeth Bowen. Includes discussions of Welty's sense of place and her transformation of the public, the private, and the political. "The Strategy of Edna Earle Ponder," by Marilyn Arnold, focuses on *The Ponder Heart.*

Carson, Barbara Harrell. "In the Heart of Clay: Eudora Welty's *The Ponder Heart.*" *American Literature* 59 (December, 1987): 609-625. Excellent study describes Edna Earle as a "dynamic balancer of reason and feeling," both of which are essential to human nature, and Uncle Daniel as an irrational man of feeling, too much out of touch with reality to be capable of genuine love.

Cornell, Brenda G. "Ambiguous Necessity: A Study of *The Ponder Heart.*" In *Eudora Welty: Critical Essays*, edited by Peggy Whitman Prenshaw. Jackson: University Press of Mississippi, 1979. Examines the shortcomings of the 1956 stage adaptation of the novella, particularly with respect to the depiction of Edna Earle. Demonstrates how Welty's use of irony and paradox helps sustain the premise that life is full of mystery.

Idol, John L., Jr. "Edna Earle Ponder's Good Country People." In *The Critical Response to Eudora Welty's Fiction*, edited by Laurie Champion. Westport, Conn.: Green-

wood Press, 1994. Comments on the conflict in the novella between town and country, with Edna Earle representing the town. Includes a review of the novella and notes differences between the original work and the 1956 Broadway stage adaptation.

Kreyling, Michael. *Eudora Welty's Achievement of Order.* Baton Rouge: Louisiana State University Press, 1980. Includes a chapter that focuses on the "adjoining terror" that connects *The Ponder Heart* with serious comedy. Describes Edna Earle as Apollonian in her concern for knowledge and order, and Uncle Daniel as Dionysian in his spontaneity.

_____. *Understanding Eudora Welty.* Columbia: University of South Carolina Press, 1999. Examines Welty's work and summarizes its critical reception, including the opinions of the New Critics and feminist reviewers. Chapter 6 is devoted to an analysis of *The Ponder Heart.*

Marrs, Suzanne. *Eudora Welty: A Biography.* Orlando, Fla.: Harcourt, 2005. Literary biography by a friend of Welty provides insight into the author's life and writings and serves to refute some popular conceptions about her.

_____. *One Writer's Imagination: The Fiction of Eudora Welty.* Baton Rouge: Louisiana State University Press, 2002. Combination of critical analysis and memoir discusses the effects of close personal relationships and of social and political events on Welty's imagination and writing.

Thornton, Naoko Fuwa. "A Hilarious Destruction: The Glory of *The Ponder Heart.*" In *Strange Felicity: Eudora Welty's Subtexts on Fiction and Society.* Westport, Conn.: Praeger, 2003. Examines two kinds of metafiction in Welty's major works: literary issues, such as language, readership, and authorship, and the social subtexts below the surface of the works.

Poor Folk

Author: Fyodor Dostoevski (1821-1881)
First published: Bednye lyudi, 1846 (English translation, 1887)
Type of work: Novel
Type of plot: Impressionistic realism
Time of plot: Nineteenth century
Locale: St. Petersburg, Russia

Principal characters:
MAKAR DIEVUSHKIN, a destitute government clerk
BARBARA DOBROSELOVA, his friend
POKROVSKI, a young tutor
THE ELDER POKROVSKI, the tutor's father
BWIKOV, a wealthy landowner

The Story:

Makar Dievushkin, an impoverished government clerk, lives in an alcove in a rooming-house kitchen. Even though his accommodations are unpleasant, he consoles himself that he can see from his window the windows of Barbara Dobroselova, an unhappy young woman whom he supports in her shabby rooms across the street. Makar and Barbara carry on a written correspondence; occasionally, they walk together when Barbara feels well. Makar, poor but honorable, maintains the gravest dignity in his relationship and in his correspondence with Barbara. In their poverty and loneliness, each has warm sympathy and understanding for the other.

Among the boarders in the house where Makar lives is a public relations man of literary pretensions whose style Makar greatly admires. Makar also knows a former government clerk, Gorshkov, and his family of four. Gorshkov lost his job through a legal suit and is deeply in debt to the homely, shrewish landlady. Across the street, Barbara's cousin Sasha appears for the purpose of resolving a difference that has long existed between the cousins. Sasha questions Barbara's acceptance of Makar's charity.

Meanwhile, Makar sends gifts to Barbara and becomes poorer with each passing day. He pawns his uniform and, in his poverty, becomes the butt of jokes. Barbara, protesting somewhat weakly his sacrifices for her, sends him, in return, her life story, which she has written. The story reveals that Barbara is the daughter of the steward of a prince in the province of Tula. Her family moved to St. Petersburg when she was twelve years old. She did not like the city, and she detested the boarding school she attended. When Barbara was fourteen years old, her father died, leaving Barbara and her consumptive mother debt-ridden. Creditors took all of their possessions, and Barbara and her mother moved to the house of a distant relative, Anna Thedorovna, whose source of income was a mystery to them. There Barbara, with her orphan cousin Sasha, was tutored by a sick young student, Pokrovski, who was intelligent but irritable. The young girls teased Pokrovski remorselessly. Barbara, however, soon regretted her behavior and vowed to redeem herself in his eyes.

Pokrovski was visited from time to time by his father, a wizened, obsequious little man who worshiped his son. The old man was inquisitive and talkative, so Pokrovski limited the number of his visits to two a week. Old Pokrovski would do anything for his son. Barbara outgrew the tutoring, but she still had not redeemed herself with Pokrovski. Bent upon reading widely, she sneaked into his room and accidentally upset his bookshelf. Pokrovski entered, and while he and Barbara were replacing the books, they realized that they were in love.

As Pokrovski's birthday approached, Barbara joined forces with the elder Pokrovski to buy the young tutor the works of Pushkin; they would give the set to him together. At the birthday party, Barbara magnanimously let the doting old father give the books to his son. Pokrovski died soon afterward. Grief apparently weakened the old man's mind; he took his son's books and, following the funeral procession on foot, dropped a pathetic trail of books in the mud of the streets leading to the cemetery.

As the friendship between Makar and Barbara continues, Barbara becomes concerned about Makar's indulgences in her behalf, which he cannot afford. She urges him to get himself a decent uniform.

At the rooming house, Makar, utterly destitute, feels deep pity for Gorshkov in his poverty. He sends Barbara a volume of the writings of the public relations man, but Barbara declares the book is trash. When the possibility of her becoming a governess in a wealthy household presents itself to Barbara, Makar, despite his own poverty, proudly tells her that he can continue to care for her.

Hearing that Barbara has been insulted by an importunate suitor, Makar gets drunk and is brought home by the police. In desperation, he borrows money everywhere, even from Barbara. His penury seems to affect his mind. Meanwhile, the friendship between Makar and Barbara has become a source of laughter among the other boarders. Makar even suspects the public relations man of maliciously gossiping in civil service circles about Makar's having been brought home by the police. He fears for his reputation, which is all that he has left. Barbara invites him to live with her and her cook, Thedora; she urges him to stop borrowing money and to stop copying the public relations man's style in his letters.

A lecherous old man, sent by Anna Thedorovna, calls on Barbara. After Barbara and Thedora get rid of him, Barbara, in alarm, tells Makar that she has to move immediately. Lack of money, however, prevents her from doing so. Makar approaches a rich usurer, but he is refused a loan because he can offer no security. Everything goes wrong. Makar's position at the rooming house becomes impossible. Barbara burns her hand and cannot earn the little money she has been earning by sewing. She sends Makar some money, and he spends it on liquor. Even in his abject condition, however, Makar gives coins to Gorshkov that he might feed his family.

Makar makes a mistake in his official work and is ordered to appear before his superior, who is so affected at the sight of Makar's wretched person that he gives the poor clerk one hundred rubles and takes his hand. These gestures save Makar physically and morally. He regains his self-respect and faces life with a new vigor. All begins to go well for him at the office and at the rooming house.

Bwikov, a wealthy landowner who once courted Barbara and then deserted her in her misfortune, arrives in St. Petersburg and offers her money, which she refuses. Gorshkov, meanwhile, is officially absolved of guilt in a case involving misappropriation of funds and is awarded substantial monetary damages. Moved deeply by his newfound freedom and solvency, the man breaks in mind and body and dies of shock.

Bwikov returns to Barbara and offers marriage to atone for his previous desertion. He plans to take her to his country estate for her health. After much debate, Barbara and Makar agree that she must marry Bwikov. Makar cannot help remarking, however, that Bwikov would probably be happier married to a certain merchant's daughter in Moscow.

Barbara, preparing excitedly for a magnificent wedding, employs Makar to run countless petty errands for her. Makar plans to move into Barbara's rooms after she moves out and to retain Thedora as his cook. It saddens him to think of Barbara's leaving him, even though she is going to become the lady of a great estate. In a last letter, he implores her to stay but admits that his passionate turns of phrase are to some extent only a literary exercise.

Critical Evaluation:

"Honor and glory to the young poet whose Muse loves people in garrets and basements and tells the inhabitants of gilded palaces: 'look, they are also men, they are also your brethren.'" With these words, the great critic Vissarion Belinsky hailed the arrival of Fyodor Dostoevski on the Russian literary scene. *Poor Folk*, Dostoevski's first published work, appeared serially in 1846 in a literary periodical, *Recueil de Saint Petersbourg*. In this work, Dostoevski established a theme, the miseries of Russia's downtrodden masses, from which he never wandered far during his literary career. In the epistolary novel *Poor Folk*, however, one can detect a sly humor that never appeared again in his work. Indeed, the already somewhat morbid and sick artist could hardly have seen anything but black despair in life after his sojourn in Siberia, to which he was exiled in 1849 for revolutionary political activities.

Poor Folk is a remarkably perceptive account of the multifarious humiliations that torment the poor. In depicting the victimized and the eccentric, Dostoevski proved himself the equal of Charles Dickens, by whom he was much influenced. His portrayal of life in "garrets and basements" is entirely devoid of sentimentality; both the dignity and the wretchedness of Makar and Barbara come to light simultaneously.

Makar's persistent generosity is what finally distinguishes

him, while a poetic sensitivity to life ennobles Barbara. Both characters maintain these virtues in the face of impossible circumstances. To support Barbara, Makar must accept the chaos and stench of the three-to-a-room boardinghouse, where the walls are "so greasy that your hand sticks when you lean against them." His increasing poverty turns the smallest economic reversal into disaster. The deterioration of his wardrobe is humiliating, yet it deepens his sympathy for those in similar straits. His aroused compassion for other victims induces him not only to give Gorshkov twenty kopecks but also to add sugar to the poor man's tea. As her response to Pokrovski's father shows, Barbara is also capable of great generosity, but more impressive are her lyrical descriptions of her childhood and her feeling for nature. Despite Makar's literary pretensions, Barbara is by far the superior stylist, although she never boasts about her talent.

Dostoevski's main characters, however, are far from perfect human beings. Makar's love for Barbara is tainted by a desire to extract gratitude and praise from her. Barbara, in turn, reveals a shocking capacity for transforming Makar into her servant once she becomes engaged to the rich Bwikov. Both are too involved in their private dreamworlds and are excessively preoccupied with their reputations. Dostoevski suggests that these faults, however, must be seen partially as exaggerated attempts to maintain a modicum of dignity in an uncomprehending world. When one is absolutely vulnerable, one must create certain defenses; as Makar explains, "Poor people are touchy—that's in the nature of things."

Further Reading

Breger, Louis. *Dostoevsky: The Author as Psychoanalyst.* New York: New York University Press, 1989. Provides biographical information as well as discussion of the symbols (and their associations) in Dostoevski's novels. Includes a chapter on *Poor Folk*.

Jackson, Robert Louis. *Dostoevsky's Quest for Form: A Study of His Philosophy of Art.* 2d ed. Bloomington, Ind.: Physsardt, 1978. Considers the contradiction between Dostoevski's working aesthetic and his higher aesthetic of true beauty. A mature and helpful study for the serious Dostoevski reader.

Leatherbarrow, William J. *Fedor Dostoevsky.* Boston: Twayne, 1981. Provides an excellent guide for the study of Dostoevski's writing, with commentary on *Poor Folk* and other early works. Includes a biographical sketch and a chronology of the events of Dostoevski's life.

_____, ed. *The Cambridge Companion to Dostoevskii.* New York: Cambridge University Press, 2006. Collection of essays examines the author's life and works, discussing such topics as his relationship to Russian folk heritage and his attitudes toward money, the intelligentsia, psychology, religion, the family, and science.

McReynolds, Susan. *Redemption and the Merchant God: Dostoevsky's Economy of Salvation and Antisemitism.* Evanston, Ill.: Northwestern University Press, 2008. Asserts that readers cannot fully understand Dostoevski's writings without understanding his obsession with the Jews. Analyzes the elements of anti-Semitism in his works as well as his views on the Crucifixion, the Resurrection, morality, and other aspects of Christian doctrine. Chapter 5 is devoted to a discussion of *Poor Folk.*

Scanlan, James P. *Dostoevsky the Thinker: A Philosophical Study.* Ithaca, N.Y.: Cornell University Press, 2002. Draws on Dostoevski's novels, essays, letters, and notebooks to provide a comprehensive account of his philosophy, examining the weaknesses as well as the strengths of his ideas. Concludes that Dostoevski's thought was shaped by anthropocentrism and the struggle to define the very essence of humanity.

Straus, Nina Pelikan. *Dostoevsky and the Woman Question: Rereadings at the End of a Century.* New York: St. Martin's Press, 1994. Argues that Dostoevski's compulsion to depict men's cruelties to women is an important part of his vision and his metaphysics. Maintains that Dostoevski attacked masculine notions of autonomy and that his works evolved toward "the death of the patriarchy."

Poor Richard's Almanack

Author: Benjamin Franklin (1706-1790)
First published: 1732-1757
Type of work: History and philosophy

Benjamin Franklin circulated the annual *Poor Richard's Almanack* with great success in prerevolutionary Philadelphia. He boasted in his autobiography that the almanac eventually reached ten thousand readers, a remarkable feat in a city with a population of approximately fifteen thousand people. Franklin had published short pieces using pseudonyms such as Silence Dogood, but the pseudonym Richard Saunders or, as he would come to be known, Poor Richard, became one of Franklin's favorites during his early career as a printer.

In Franklin's time, the almanac served not only as a valuable source of information about the weather but also as a form of entertainment. Franklin's effort to both inform and entertain is evident from the beginning of *Poor Richard's Almanack*, but his emphasis changed over time. As Franklin grew older and became involved in civic improvements in Philadelphia, the desire to offer useful advice began to overshadow the humor found in earlier issues of the almanac.

Beginning with the 1733 issue and continuing to the issue of 1739, one can identify a number of similarities. Each issue begins with a short essay of introduction, signed by Richard Saunders (with one exception), followed by monthly poems and several maxims. The issues close with some additional material, most often a report on eclipses that Franklin sometimes uses for humorous purposes. One can detect Franklin's struggle to make the almanac stand out from its competitors in the market: For example, he makes use of a hoax concerning the death of a rival, Titan Leeds, even having Leeds return from the dead to write a ghostly letter replying to disbelievers. Problems in mathematics and mysteriously worded prophecies provide diversions for the reader as well. Many of these elements are presented in the form of what today might by called cliffhangers, with the promise of further revelations in subsequent issues.

The format of the introductory essay, monthly poems and maxims, and a variety of closing material is used in issues published after 1739. Although Franklin varies the presentations somewhat, the basic structure of the almanac remains the same.

The monthly poems, which usually deliver some moral point, as well as the maxims, made *Poor Richard's Almanack* famous. Many well-known quotations from Franklin come in the form of his maxims. They all share the characteristic of being short, and are often playfully worded. The maxims, which cover a variety of topics, consistently advocate, for example, moderation and temperance in the consumption of food and spirits (with frequent warnings against drunkenness). His advice on money encourages the reader to work hard, save money, and live simply; however, he also frequently warns against seeking wealth for its own sake and against being miserly.

Franklin's maxims also reflect the gender and religious prejudices of his day. His maxims on courtship and marriage elevate women to importance, but only in terms of married life, the keeping of a household, and obedience to husbands. Similarly jarring to modern ears are Franklin's occasional anti-Catholic references, accusing one rival of conversion to Catholicism as a means of turning public opinion against the writer. Franklin's Protestantism led him to praise both Martin Luther and John Calvin in his 1749 issue, although his chief praise for both men focuses on their moderation and temperance, not on their religious doctrines.

Most interesting, given Franklin's later political career, is his general avoidance of colonial politics, including Pennsylvania's role as a proprietary colony (an issue he would later address as a representative to London) and the British king's power over the colonies. For the most part, Franklin advises readers to stay out of politics, and the most criticism he levels at monarchy, if one could call it criticism, is to remind the reader of the king's humanity.

By 1739, the tone of the almanac begins to change. Franklin occasionally inserts brief essays of advice, and nearly every issue between 1740 and 1746 ends with a brief essay or poem attacking lawyers and the courts. Franklin's closings occasionally include brief essays on living a long life or on how to discover the best amount of meat and drink to consume. In 1743, he offers instruction on how to make wine, and in 1745 he instructs on how to pick out the planets from the stars. He even laments the death of a rival printer, Jacob Taylor, in 1747.

The death of Taylor, in fact, had prompted an important change in the almanac. Franklin announces in his introductory essay to the 1748 issue that he plans to improve the contents of future issues in honor of Taylor. Prior to 1748, each issue had averaged about twenty-four pages, but the improved almanac, he says, will now feature thirty-six pages of material. Into these pages, Franklin pours a series of essays designed to "improve" the reader rather than merely entertain. While the humor of the earlier issues does not disappear, a tone of seriousness begins to dominate the post-1748 issues. Franklin includes essays on topics such as getting rich (1748), the best use of time (1751), the change in calendar ordered by the king (1752), hymns to the creator (1753), the movement of the earth (1753), protecting a house from lightning (1753), and the clergy (1755). For a short time, Franklin

even features information on everyday events, such as births and deaths, breaking the pattern of having only poems and maxims. He began this practice in 1748 but ended it by 1751.

The final issues of the almanac reflect this new seriousness most dramatically. The 1756 issue includes short essays covering topics such as curing heartburn and burns on the skin as well as good conversation, expenses, good health, honest labor, temperance, simple living, adjusting to hardship, honor, and industry. A similar list follows in 1757, an issue that includes a lengthy opening essay on setting up a sundial and a closing essay on comets. These two issues—1756 and 1757—are the lengthiest in the series.

The final issue of *Poor Richard's Almanack* stands apart from all the others. Franklin had constructed the issue as a culmination of his work: It begins with a lengthy essay relating a story concerning a sermon on self-improvement. In the essay, Franklin collects the variety of maxims on work and frugality that appear in earlier issues of the almanac and concludes that hard work, along with heavenly intervention, will lead to success. This popular essay has since been reprinted under the title "The Way to Wealth."

Franklin's legacy as a statesman and visionary could have obscured the significance of *Poor Richard's Almanack*, but the almanac's enduring appeal is based partly on its still-relevant maxims and its still-relevant evocations of what today are called middle-class values. Franklin's own affection for the moderation that runs through the maxims characterizes his later career, sometimes to the frustration of his political friends. Modern business texts still refer to Franklin's advice for wisdom, and some critics have argued that Franklin gave early expression to American pragmatism and, thus, to much of the work of philosophers William James and John Dewey.

David Smailes

Further Reading

Baida, Peter. *Poor Richard's Legacy: American Business Values from Benjamin Franklin to Donald Trump*. New York: HarperCollins, 1991. Baida traces the ongoing legacy of Franklin's advice on thrift and honesty, finding that American business practices have dramatically departed from those presented in *Poor Richard's Almanack*.

Cullen, J. P. "Benjamin Franklin: 'The Glory of America.'" *American History Illustrated* 6, no. 1 (1971): 40-47. Cullen's description of Franklin's early years as a printer is a valuable resource both for understanding Franklin's ideas and for tracing his early development.

Isaacson, Walter. *Benjamin Franklin: An American Life.*

New York: Simon & Schuster, 2003. An excellent biography of Franklin, with a lengthy description of the circumstances in which the almanac was written and published. Makes a strong case for Franklin's pragmatism as well.

Lipton, Christina, "Two Texts Told Twice: Poor Richard, Poor Yorick, and the Case of the Word's Return." *Early American Literature* 40, no. 3 (Fall, 2005): 471-499. Lipton traces the continued interest in the final essay of the almanac. Argues that Franklin's desire to be taken seriously in the essay may have been undermined by the form of the almanac itself.

Warner, Michael. "Franklin and the Letters of the Republic." *Representations* 16 (Autumn, 1986): 110-130. Warner gives an academic critique of Franklin's arguments in the almanac, with analysis of his language. For advanced readers.

Poor White

Author: Sherwood Anderson (1876-1941)
First published: 1920
Type of work: Novel
Type of plot: Psychological realism
Time of plot: 1866-1900
Locale: Missouri and Ohio

Principal characters:
HUGH McVEY, an inventor and manufacturer
SARAH SHEPARD, his foster mother
STEVE HUNTER, his partner
TOM BUTTERWORTH, his father-in-law
CLARA BUTTERWORTH, his wife

The Story:

Born in 1866, Hugh McVey grew up in a small Missouri town as the motherless child of a drunken father. Spending his days lounging and dreaming on the banks of the Mississippi River, Hugh had no formal education, learned few manners, and became very lazy. The railroad comes to town in 1880 when Hugh is fourteen years old, and he gets a job as a factotum at the station, loading baggage and sweeping the platform. Hugh receives little pay but gets to live with his boss, Henry Shepard, and his wife, Sarah. The childless couple treat Hugh as their own son, providing him with shelter, food, new clothes, and affection. Soon Sarah begins to educate him. Sarah, who is from New England, always preserves her memory of quiet Eastern villages and large industrial cities. Determined to educate Hugh, she lavishes on him the discipline and affection she would have given her own child.

The situation is difficult, at first, for both of them, but Sarah Shepard is a determined woman. She teaches Hugh to read, to write, and to wonder about the world beyond the little town. She instills within him the belief that his family had been of no account, and he grows to have a revulsion toward the poor white farmers and workers. Sarah always holds out before him the promise of the East, the progress and growth of that region. Gradually, Hugh begins to win his fight against natural indolence and to adjust himself to his new way of life. When the Shepards leave town, Hugh, then nineteen years old, is appointed station agent for the railroad.

Hugh keeps the job for a year. During that time, the dream of Eastern cities grew more and more vivid for Hugh. When his father dies, Hugh gives up his job and travels east, working wherever he can. Always lonely, always apart from people, he feels an impenetrable wall between himself and the rest of the world. He keeps on the journey, through Illinois, Indiana, and then Ohio.

Hugh is twenty-three years old when he settles down in Ohio. By accident, he gets the job of telegraph operator, just a mile from the town of Bidwell. There he lives alone, a familiar and puzzling figure to the people of the town. The rumor begins to spread that he is an inventor working on a new device. Others suggest that he is looking over the town for a possible factory site. Hugh is doing neither as yet. Then, during his walks around the farmlands, he becomes fascinated by the motions of the farmers planting their seeds and their crops. Slowly there grows in his mind an idea for a crop-setting machine that would save the labor of the farmers and their families.

Steve Hunter, who has just come back from school in Buffalo, is another dreamer. He dreams of being a manufacturer, the wealthiest in Bidwell. He succeeds in convincing the town's important people that Hugh is his man, and that he is working on an invention that will make them both rich. He persuades them to invest in a new company that would build a factory and promote Hugh's invention. Steve goes to see

Hugh, who has completed the blueprint for a plant-setting machine. The two young men come to an agreement.

A skilled woodworker makes models of the machine, and the machine itself is finally constructed in an old building carefully guarded from the curious. When the machine fails to work, Hugh invents another, his mind more and more pre-occupied with the planning of devices and machines. A factory is then built, and many workers are hired. Bidwell's industrialization begins.

What is happening in Bidwell is the same growth of industrialism that is changing the entire structure of the United States. It is a period of transition. Bidwell, being a small town, feels the effects of the new development keenly. Workers become part of the community, in which there had been only farmers and merchants.

Joe Wainsworth, the harness maker, loses his life savings to Hugh's invention. An independent man, a craftsman, he comes to resent the factory, the very idea of the machine. People come into his shop less often. They are buying the machine-made harness. Joe becomes a broken man. His employee, Jim Gibson, a spiritual bully, really runs the business, and Joe submits meekly.

Meanwhile, Clara Butterworth, daughter of a wealthy farmer, returns to Bidwell after three years at the university in Columbus. She, too, is lonely and unhappy. She sees that the old Bidwell is gone, that her father, Tom Butterworth, is wealthier than before, and that the growth of the town is primarily the result of the efforts of one person, Hugh McVey. A week after she meets Hugh, he walks up to the farm and asks her to marry him. They elope and are married that night. The marriage is not consummated for several days, however, because Hugh, fearing he is not good enough for Clara, cannot bring himself to approach her.

For four years, they live together in a strange, strained relationship. During those four years, Joe's fury against Steve, against the new age of industry that had taken his savings, increases. One day, he hears Jim Gibson brag about his stocking factory-made harnesses in the shop. That night, Joe kills Jim Gibson. Fleeing from the scene, he meets Steve and shoots him, but not fatally.

Clara, Hugh, and Tom are returning from a drive in the family's first automobile when they learn what had happened. Two men have captured Joe, and when they try to put him into the automobile to take him back to town, Joe jumps toward Hugh and sinks his fingers into his neck. It is Clara who breaks his grip upon her husband. Somehow the incident brings Hugh and Clara closer together.

Hugh's career as an inventor no longer satisfies him. Joe's attack has unnerved him and made him doubt the worth of his

work. It does not matter so much that someone in Iowa invented a machine exactly like his, and he does not intend to dispute the rights of the Iowan.

Clara is pregnant. She tells him of the child one night as they stand listening to the noises of the farm and the snoring of the hired hand. As they walk into the house side by side, the factory whistles blow in the night. Hugh hardly hears them. The dark midwestern nights, men and women, the land itself—the full, deep life current will go on in spite of factories and machines.

Critical Evaluation:

In Sherwood Anderson's *Poor White*, Hugh McVey's life stands as an allegory for a young, war-shocked nation struggling to ride a massive wave of industrialization. Born near the end of the American Civil War, McVey is at the peak of his inventing career in the late 1890's and early twentieth century. Celebrations of technology were common in those years, as for example when Henry Adams philosophizes about the Gallery of Machines in "The Dynamo and the Virgin" chapter of *The Education of Henry Adams* (1907). During the late nineteenth century, factory smokestacks could be seen across the Midwest as industrialism came to small towns. By the end of *Poor White*, Bidwell is an industrial town with factories surrounded by fields of cheap housing. New workers (strangers and recent immigrants) have flooded the town. The tide of industrialization has moved forward.

As Bidwell grows, individuals must shed their preindustrial ways of life and adapt to new roles in society. Hugh, the daydreamer, becomes an inventor; Tom Butterworth, the gentleman farmer, becomes an investor; and young farmhands from across the county become millworkers. Even mentally disabled Allie Mulberry, a woodworker, builds models of McVey's inventions. Individuals who do not adapt cannot survive. Joe Wainsworth, the local harness maker, who refuses to sell or repair factory-made harnesses, becomes an example when his assistant, Jim Gibson, pushes him around, takes control of the business, and hangs eighteen manufactured harnesses on the shop wall. Joe reacts like an animal struggling to delay his extinction. Pushed to the breaking point by Jim's bragging, he slits his assistant's throat and shreds the new harnesses into a pile on the shop floor.

Growth of industry in the Midwest was not an abstract phenomenon for Anderson, who in 1906 served as president (in title only) of United Factories Company, a mail-order business in Cleveland, Ohio. He was fired after only one year when the company lost thousands of dollars in a lawsuit involving faulty incubators. The machines had been contracted for sale before the manufacturer knew whether they would work. A similar situation happens in *Poor White* when Steve and Tom conspire to market one of Hugh's pieces of farm machinery that they suspect will never work. In 1907, Anderson moved to Elyria, Ohio, and became the true president of a company that by 1911 manufactured nearly all conceivable types of roofing and painting materials. Like Steve, Anderson was a businessperson, an entrepreneur who organized and profited from other people's inventions and resources. Specializing in public relations, Anderson was well acquainted with (and sometimes practiced) less-than-honest advertising tactics and business dealings. These experiences are reflected in *Poor White*.

The characters in *Poor White* come alive with intricate, often grotesque detail, such as the extended sketch of a rich lawyer's widow (Jane Orange), who is caught stealing eggs and has yolk running down her legs after a clerk hits the pocket where the eggs are hidden. Critics often discuss *Poor White* as a form of American bildungsroman, and Hugh as a post-Civil War Huck Finn.

The hero of Mark Twain's *Adventures of Huckleberry Finn* (1884) tells readers at the end of the novel, "I reckon I got to light out for the Territory ahead of the rest, because Aunt Sally she's going to adopt me and sivilize me, and I can't stand it." With the closing of the American frontier, young men and women across the country began to look to science and technology as the new territory where they could stake a claim and make their mark. Getting "sivilized" is what happens to young Hugh, who has no West to run to, and who until age fourteen has spent his time lazing on the banks of the Mississippi beside his father's dilapidated shack. Sarah Shepard, like Huck's Aunt Polly, nurtures Hugh with strong New England values, and the boy resists. The momentum of industrialization drags the indolent young man forward. Although successful in manufacturing, he laments his lowly roots at the end of chapter 14: "By struggle and work he had conquered the dreams but could not conquer his ancestry, nor change the fact that he was at bottom poor white trash." Entrepreneurs find they must always struggle against such determinism.

The only fully developed character besides Hugh is Clara Butterworth, whose sexual awakening surfaces in flirtations with farmhands and in a brief relationship with a schoolteacher. Concerned about Clara's virtue and worried that she has been associating too much with lower classes, Tom sends his daughter away to college in Columbus to become a lady and perhaps meet a suitable husband. At college, however, Clara meets Kate Chancellor, a lesbian classmate who rejects the limitations of marriage and plans to become a doctor. Kate teaches Clara to question society's traditional expecta-

tions. Clara, rather than becoming ladylike, acts to control her life and decide with whom, if anyone, she will share it. Industrialization takes families away from the farm and allows women greater options.

As a chronicle of industrialization, *Poor White* is related to business novels such as William Dean Howells's *The Rise of Silas Lapham* (1885) and Frank Norris's *The Pit* (1903). Hugh's inventions recall the numerous patents filed by Sam Hamilton in John Steinbeck's *East of Eden* (1952). With the appearance of a socialist agitator at the end of the novel, Anderson foreshadows another stage of industrial development—in the Progressive Era, workers renewed the fight for fair wages and safe factory conditions. Agitators appear in similar but more prominent roles in political social-protest fiction such as Upton Sinclair's *The Jungle* (1906) and John Steinbeck's *In Dubious Battle* (1936). Although not the great American novel, *Poor White* is a significant literary account of America's industrial coming-of-age.

"Critical Evaluation" by Geralyn Strecker

Further Reading

Anderson, David D. *Sherwood Anderson: An Introduction and Interpretation*. New York: Barnes & Noble, 1967. Discusses Hugh McVey in terms of industrialism's effect on the individual. Characterizes the struggle in Bidwell as one of people trying to maintain their humanity in the face of industrialism. Explains how Anderson shifts from seeing industry as the source of evil to accepting its potential for good.

Bassett, John Earl. "Literary Success." In *Sherwood Anderson: An American Career*. Selinsgrove, Pa.: Susquehanna University Press, 2006. Bassett's overview of Anderson's life, career, and works includes a chapter focusing on Anderson's early successes, including *Poor White*.

Gelfant, Blanche Housman. *The American City Novel*. Norman: University of Oklahoma Press, 1954. Characterizes *Poor White* as "a novel of becoming," in which the changing town, growing with industrialism, plays a role parallel to that of Hugh McVey. The town and the person illustrate the process of social change.

Miller, Donald L. "The Industrial Age, 1865 to 1917." *American Heritage* 55, no. 6 (November-December, 2004): 42-45. Miller discusses *Poor White* as a reflection of national concerns about the Industrial Revolution.

Rideout, Walter B. *Sherwood Anderson: A Writer in America*. 2 vols. Madison: University of Wisconsin Press, 2006-2007. A comprehensive, two-volume, updated account of Anderson's life and work.

Taylor, Welford Dunaway. *Sherwood Anderson*. New York: Frederick Ungar, 1977. Asserts that *Poor White's* strengths outweigh its weaknesses. Characterizes the narrative as moving from "vagueness to definiteness." Taylor's book, however, displays stereotypes of the working classes.

Townsend, Kim. *Sherwood Anderson*. Boston: Houghton Mifflin, 1987. Compares Hugh McVey and Sarah Shepard to Huck Finn and Aunt Polly in Mark Twain's *Adventures of Huckleberry Finn*. Offers a reading of Hugh's haunting of the cabbage field while inventing the planting machine.

The Poorhouse Fair

Author: John Updike (1932-2009)
First published: 1959
Type of work: Novel
Type of plot: Social satire
Time of plot: 1980's
Locale: New Jersey

Principal characters:
JOHN HOOK,
BILLY GREGG,
GEORGE LUCAS, and
MARTHA LUCAS, residents of the Diamond County Home for the Aged
STEPHEN CONNER, the home's prefect
BUDDY, his assistant
TED, a teenage delivery boy

The Story:

At the Diamond County Home for the Aged it is the day of the annual fair, when the elderly men and women set up stands and sell such homemade products as quilts, candy, and peach-stone carvings to visitors from nearby communities. This year, the great day gets off to a bad start. Two of the home's residents, or inmates—John Hook, a ninety-four-year-old former schoolteacher, and Billy Gregg, a seventy-year-old retired electrician—discover that the home's porch chairs have had name tags attached, and hereafter each inmate is to occupy only the chair assigned to him or her. This latest action by Mr. Conner, the prefect of the institution, provides an opportunity for protest.

Misunderstandings and misadventures add to Conner's burden of do-gooding humanitarianism. When Gregg introduces a diseased stray cat onto the grounds, Conner orders Buddy, the prefect's adoring assistant, to shoot the animal. Ted, a teenage truck driver, knocks down part of a stone wall while delivering cases of Pepsi-Cola for the fair. A pet parakeet belonging to Martha Lucas, the wife of George Lucas, a former real estate salesman, gets loose in the infirmary. When rain threatens to ruin the fair, the inmates take refuge in the community sitting room, where Hook and Conner argue the ideals of an older America of faith and idealism against the theories of scientific determinism and social perfectibility.

Hook, a gentle, meditative man, looks back to the days of William Howard Taft, a period when Americans had greater political freedom (despite economic uncertainty), pride of craftsmanship, and, in times of private or public calamity, trust in God. Filled with that sense of satisfaction that is time's final gift to the old, he has faith in the possible virtue of humanity. Hook believes that this quality of virtue redeems the human animal's capacity for folly and evil because such virtue brings humanity close to the idea of God.

In contrast, in Conner's brave new world there is no more place for God than there is for error. Fanatical in his belief in progress, order, hygiene, and the elimination of superstition and pain, Conner possesses the inhuman energy of a machine. The truth is that he does not think of the home's residents as people; they are his charges, and it is his job to confer on them the good they often cannot understand and sometimes do not want. In his view, all of life should be regulated and institutionalized, as passionless as the antics of tomorrow's adolescents, who satisfy their emotional needs by undressing and then staring in curiosity but without desire at one another's nude bodies. Conner is a citizen of a planned society, and the institution is his calling.

The tensions of the day finally break when the inmates turn on Conner and stone him with the rubble from the damaged wall. Then the skies clear, and the fair is held after all, but under circumstances that allow the old people to save some remnants of their pride and self-respect. Asking only the bread of understanding, they have been offered the cold stone of charity, and they have rejected it along with a world they never made.

Critical Evaluation:

John Updike's *The Poorhouse Fair* is one of the more striking debuts by a novelist in the history of American letters. It was widely noticed but only cautiously appreciated by many prominent critics when it was published in the same year as Updike's first collection of short fiction (*The Same Door*, 1959) and one year after his earliest volume, the poetry in *The Carpentered Hen, and Other Tame Creatures*. Most commentators found some element in the book to praise, emphasizing the poetic use of language, the critique of rational social engineering, or the somewhat (for its time) unconventional structure. There was a degree of consensus that Updike had not been entirely successful in connecting all of the prominent features of the novel. Within the context of his prolific work during the following decades, it is clear that Updike, in this debut novel, was presenting some of the most important themes that informed his writing from its inception. Each element of the novel is operating in service to fundamental themes.

Updike was twenty-seven when *The Poorhouse Fair* was written, and the novel's strongest, most passionately expressive sections are tributes to a rich cultural legacy he obtained from his neighbors in rural Pennsylvania. The central character, John Hook, is very affectionately drawn from Updike's maternal grandfather, John Hoyer. Updike's approach to Hook's characterization is a meditative exploration of the mind and soul of a man whose admirable qualities are vanishing into the emptiness of a technological wasteland. Updike later recollected, in his memoir *Self-Consciousness* (1989), that "the family I grew up in was old-fashioned," with an old-fashioned notion about "trying to do the right thing"; he recalled his grandfather quoting proverbs "in a clear and elocutionary voice." The Hoyers, Updike declared proudly, "had become peaceful, reasonable people who valued civilization," and Hook's generally positive outlook stems from a belief in a just American society and the conviction that God, the creator of the universe, is manifest in the world. This religious foundation, which Updike saw as a complement to, rather than a foreign element in, the life of the mind, was an integral part of his Lutheran heritage, what he called "my deepest and most fruitful self." At Oxford and at Harvard, he found himself removed from the verities of his rural Pennsylvania community and came to think of his Christianity as "battered and vestigial." The character of Stephen Conner is not just a critique of the bloodless, ultrarational social scientists who were emerging in the late 1950's—he is also an expression of Updike's own doubts about the consolations of the religious tradition.

The narrative advance of *The Poorhouse Fair* is literally suspended while Hook and Conner are engaged in a debate about the existence of God. Some critics have asserted that Conner is a target of Updike's satire, but Updike claimed in a 1968 interview that "once I'd set Conner in motion I did to the best of my ability try to love him." Accordingly, Updike gives Conner the most powerful of modern arguments against the existence of God, and Hook is somewhat shaken by Conner's points, since he is himself a practitioner of intellectual discourse. It is significant, however, that Conner is not comforted by his own assertions, whereas Hook is able to regain his composure because he has evidence sufficiently strong to overcome the logic of Conner's ideas. The debate sets the terms of the argument: Conner's rational humanism, constructed on the creed that "prized a useful over a pleasant life," versus Hook's instinctive responses to the natural phenomena of the universe and the unruly, endlessly interesting flow of human society. For Updike, the poetry is the proof of Hook's argument.

From the beginning of his career, Updike was often dismissed as a writer whose command of language disguised his lack of anything to say. A much more discerning judgment recognizes that, as Donald Greiner puts it, Updike "lavishes so much care on his prose that its very intensity approaches poetry." In *The Poorhouse Fair*, Updike depends on the power of language to make Hook's delight in the intricate details of landscape and skyscape not only plausible but also inspiring. Updike's own joy is palpable in the evocative descriptions of terrain, storm, appetite, song, and the celebratory carnival that concludes the novel. In a sense, the beauty of his writing is his own testament to God's creation. As other residents join Hook in envisioning a heavenly realm, Updike's idea of earth as a tantalizing reflection of "the giant, cosmic other" gains credence through the eloquence of their descriptions.

The community within the poorhouse, in spite of its tensions and disagreements, is another analogue of a heavenly place. Updike later remarked that "an illusion of eternal comfort reposes in clubbiness," and *The Poorhouse Fair* is designed as a fond return to the town of Shillington (which is also the setting for *Olinger Stories: A Selection*, 1964), a location that Updike remembered with "furtive" love years later and that stood for a time in his life when the outside world had not yet intruded on a young boy's idea of his own destiny. The visitors from the town to the fair, and the residents of the home themselves, are patterned on the society in which Updike grew up and are all part of a picture of a way of life that even in 1959 Updike feared was being overwhelmed by the tendencies toward the controlled and the mundane that Conner stands for.

The philosophical position that Updike affirms in *The Poorhouse Fair* is almost classically traditional, but some of the techniques he employs are conspicuously contemporary. He later mentioned that he thought of this work as an anti-novel in the mode of modernist European fiction. His shifting narrative focus, including a surreal dream-vision of a heavily medicated patient and an extended passage of unidentified voices mixed in short stretches of dialogue, has confused some critics. Also daunting is the very open-ended conclusion in which Hook, the avatar of an earlier time, looks onward into an unknown future, still carrying the obligations of conscience and concern that speak for the best of human intentions.

"Critical Evaluation" by Leon Lewis

Further Reading

Detweiler, Robert. *John Updike*. Rev. ed. Boston: Twayne, 1984. Offers an excellent introductory survey of Updike's work through 1983, with biographical information and analyses of individual works. The chapter on *The Poorhouse Fair* briefly covers the novel's setting and its use of language, characters, and themes.

Greiner, Donald J. *John Updike's Novels*. Athens: Ohio University Press, 1984. Examination of Updike's long fiction includes a chapter that discusses the origins of *The Poorhouse Fair*, drawing on Updike's introduction to the revised edition of 1977.

Hamilton, Alice, and Kenneth Hamilton. *The Elements of John Updike*. Grand Rapids, Mich.: Wm. B. Eerdmans, 1970. Provides detailed discussion of the theological dimensions of *The Poorhouse Fair*, noting and explaining the religious allusions and symbols that appear in the novel.

Newman, Judie. *John Updike*. New York: St. Martin's Press, 1988. Compares Updike's 1968 novel *Couples* with *The Poorhouse Fair* in a chapter that considers both books in the context of American society at the times they were written. Includes informative discussion of Updike's uses of metaphor.

Pritchard, William H. *Updike: America's Man of Letters*. South Royalton, Vt.: Steerforth Press, 2000. Presents a chronological survey and analysis of Updike's work. Chapter 1, "Fresh Fruits," includes a discussion of *The Poorhouse Fair*.

Schiff, James A. *John Updike Revisited*. New York: Twayne, 1998. Endeavors to understand Updike's entire oeuvre, putting individual works in context for the reader. Provides commentary on works that have largely been ignored by the public as well as books that have received little critical attention. Chapter 2 includes a critical analysis of *The Poorhouse Fair*.

Updike, John. *Self-Consciousness: Memoirs*. New York: Alfred A. Knopf, 1989. In the essay "On Being a Self Forever," Updike discusses his position on religion at length, covering many of the issues he examines in *The Poorhouse Fair*.

Vargo, Edward P. *Rainstorms and Fire: Ritual in the Novels of John Updike*. Port Washington, N.Y.: Kennikat Press, 1973. Includes a chapter on *The Poorhouse Fair* that focuses on how rituals and celebrations are used as means of expressing a religious vision.

Porgy

Author: DuBose Heyward (1885-1940)
First published: 1925
Type of work: Novel
Type of plot: Regional
Time of plot: Early twentieth century
Locale: Charleston, South Carolina

Principal characters:
PORGY, a disabled African American beggar
CROWN, a stevedore, or dockworker
BESS, Crown's lover

The Story:

Before the American Civil War, Catfish Row had been the fine mansion of a wealthy white family. By the early twentieth century, it was home for a community of poor African American families, descendants of former slaves. Porgy, a disabled beggar, inhabits a ground-floor room. No one knows his age, and his large, powerful hands are in strange contrast to his frail body. Porgy's neighbor, Peter, transports him to and from his begging each day in his wagon.

Porgy's single vice is gambling—throwing dice with friends in the courtyard of Catfish Row. One evening in April, Robbins, the husband of Serena and father of three children, is killed by the traveling stevedore Crown, whom he had accused of cheating at dice. When police investigate, no one offers testimony, so the police take Peter into custody, hoping he will provide information. While Peter is in jail for ten days, the horse and wagon that he had been buying on contract are repossessed, and Porgy loses his only means of transportation.

By May, Porgy is destitute and has to find another means of getting downtown. His new emancipation comes when he builds a "chariot"—a goat-pulled, two-wheeled, toilet-soap crate. He no longer has to remain at one stand all day, but can now roam at will and take in more money. In June, Crown's lover, Bess, comes to Catfish Row. Maria, who operates a kitchen in the building, gives her food. Bess then goes to live with Porgy and becomes a new woman, giving up drugs and alcohol. Happier than ever, Porgy wins often at gambling, so his friends get suspicious.

One day, a dandy, Sportin' Life, comes to town and gives Bess cocaine. She is arrested for disorderly conduct. Porgy tries to pay her fine, but when the judge sees the beggar, to whom he had often given dimes, with ten dollars, he becomes enraged, takes the money, and sentences Bess to ten days in a filthy, overcrowded prison, where she gets seriously ill with fever. With the help of Maria and other women in Catfish Row, Porgy nurses Bess back to health.

At the Sons and Daughters of Repent Ye Saith the Lord picnic on Kittiwar Island, Bess is accosted by Crown, who had been hiding on the island. He takes her to his hut and sexually assaults her, but at the end of the day, he lets her return to Porgy, promising that he will take her back in the fall, when cotton shipments will provide stevedoring work in Savannah.

One day in September, the Mosquito Fleet of fishing boats celebrates a record-breaking catch. As they prepare to go out the next morning, Catfish Row resident Clara futilely warns her husband, Jake, not to go out in his boat that day. Soon after the fleet leaves the pier, warning bells chime and the hurricane flag rises over the customhouse. After an ominous calm, a hurricane strikes the city. Water, driven by the shrieking wind, rises above the seawall, crosses the street, and invades the ground floor of Catfish Row, where forty frightened residents huddle in the great second-story ballroom. During a lull in the storm, Clara sees the wreck of her husband's boat near the wharf, leaves her baby with Bess, and goes out into the flood. A few minutes later, she is over-

whelmed in the storm's sudden return. The hurricane claims several Catfish Row fishermen. Bess and Porgy adopt Clara's baby.

In October, drays loaded with heavy bales of cotton come rumbling down the street. Catfish Row boils with excitement, for stevedoring jobs and money will bring prosperity. The cotton, however, means disaster to Porgy. He asks Bess whether she is his lover, or Crown's lover. His, she answers, unless Crown seizes her again as he did at the picnic. If that happens, she cannot answer for herself. Porgy assures her that he will not let Crown take her away from him.

Crown returns to Catfish Row and, despite warnings from Maria, stalks Bess. When Crown breaks into Porgy and Bess's room one midnight, Porgy stabs him. The next day, the body is found in the river near Catfish Row. Again, residents give police no information, and the community sighs in relief when the officers leave without arresting anyone. A buzzard that had fed upon Crown's body lights on the parapet above Porgy's room, forecasting doom.

Asked to identify Crown's body at the morgue, Porgy flees in his goat-cart, hotly pursued by a patrol wagon. Passersby laugh at the ridiculously one-sided race. Porgy is caught at the edge of town but is no longer needed, because someone else has identified the body. Porgy is jailed for five days for contempt of court. Without witnesses or evidence, the police declare Crown was killed at the hands of a person or persons unknown.

When Porgy returns from jail and finds Serena holding Jake and Clara's orphan baby, he suspects the worst. Neighbors tell him that some stevedores had gotten Bess drunk and taken her off to Savannah. Porgy knows she will never return. Serena adopts the baby. For one summer, Porgy experienced brief glimpses of happiness, but by fall, he is left again a solitary beggar.

Critical Evaluation:

It is important to remember when reading *Porgy* that DuBose Heyward came from the white aristocracy of Charleston, South Carolina. The Heywards came to America in the late seventeenth century, and Thomas Heyward signed the Declaration of Independence. Although Heyward had the family name, he did not share its wealth. He was two years old when his father died, and his mother took in sewing to meet expenses. At the age of nine, he sold newspapers, at the age of fourteen he worked in a hardware store, and at twenty he became a steamship checker, working among black stevedores. Venturing in insurance and real estate, at twenty-three years of age he reclaimed some black tenements in Charleston and eventually gained financial stability.

Heyward's hardships were not all economic, however. He contracted polio at the age of eighteen and typhoid at twenty, and he suffered attacks of pleurisy at twenty-one and thirty-two years of age. All of these experiences influenced *Porgy*. Self-educated to a great degree, Heyward read much of James Fenimore Cooper and Charles Dickens. His first one-act play was produced in 1913. In 1920, he turned to poetry, helped found the Poetry Society of South Carolina, and became involved with writers from across the United States at the MacDowell Colony in New Hampshire, where he met playwright Dorothy Hartzell Kuhns, whom he married in 1923. One of Heyward's literary goals was to disprove H. L. Mencken's charge that no good literature was produced south of the Potomac River.

Heyward wrote *Porgy*, his first novel, after reading about a disabled man who had been pursued in his goat-cart by police. First published in 1925, *Porgy* received overwhelmingly favorable responses from critics and general readers. Kuhns and Heyward developed the plot into a play in 1927, and Heyward later collaborated with George and Ira Gershwin in creating *Porgy and Bess*, the first American opera with primarily black characters, which premiered on Broadway on October 10, 1935. The novel, play, and opera share similar plots and characters, but Heyward's literary skill is best displayed in the novel, *Porgy*.

Changing fate is the novel's major theme. Catfish Row illustrates the altered fate of Charleston's white aristocracy: The once great mansion is now a tenement for poor African American families. In its courtyard, residents wager on dice, outcomes determined by fate, not skill. Characters in *Porgy* have neither good luck nor bad; instead, their luck is subject to change without notice. Early in the novel, Serena enjoys her comfortable position as a well-paid servant in a kind, wealthy family. She and her husband are well-off compared to their neighbors; however, their fate changes when Robbins is killed after accusing Crown of using loaded dice. The fishermen of Catfish Row suffer a brutal twist of fate when they drown at sea during a hurricane on the day after a record catch.

Fate's influence is developed extensively in Porgy's character. At the beginning of the novel, he is content, but he loses his lifeline when Peter is arrested. Nearly destitute, Porgy attempts to take fate into his own hands by creating his "second emancipation" in the form of a goat-cart. Life improves when he meets Bess, and the couple hopes to live happily ever after; however, fate, in the guises of disease and the white legal system, ensures that their happiness does not last. Even Porgy's good fortune winning at dice brings about suspicion from neighbors and contributes to his downfall.

Porgy's decay suggests another theme in the novel—that of a crumbled or crumbling Eden. The novel's action takes place between April and October, symbolizing the shift from spring to fall, birth to death, hope to despair, innocence to experience. Catfish Row's inhabitants face constant temptation, but rather than one great fall, they experience periodic falls. Bess faces serpent-like temptations in Sportin' Life, cocaine, and Crown. Just before encountering Crown on Kittiwar Island, Bess sees a snake but is not harmed—that is, until Crown tempts her to sin. Connected to the crumbling Eden theme is the deliberate contrast between barren white society (felled by the Civil War and economic devastation during Reconstruction) and the hopeful black community. Heyward makes many subtle comparisons between sterile white Christianity and the vitality of faith among Catfish Row residents. He also contrasts white medicine, which always seems to lead black patients to death and anatomy laboratories, with the black community's blend of superstition and herbal medicine. Even justice has color distinctions. The white police officers, lawyers, and judges believe wrongful deeds must be punished at any cost, even if innocents must suffer, as shown by Peter's arrest after the first murder. Catfish Row residents do not betray their neighbors to police, but deliver justice within their community; for example, Porgy kills Crown.

Community is the key to survival in Catfish Row. The building originally housed one family, with space for individuals to isolate themselves from one another in private chambers; conversely, privacy cannot exist in the tenement, where several members of a large family often share a single room. "Family" is broadly defined in this community. When Serena cannot afford to bury Robbins, neighbors contribute to his "saucer burial"—people drop money into a saucer on the corpse's chest until the funeral expenses are met. Similarly, Bess and Porgy think nothing of adopting Clara's baby after the hurricane.

In theme and style, *Porgy* reflects several early twentieth century literary trends. It is an example of realism in its abundant use of detail, local color in its use of vernacular and local customs, naturalism in its candid details of hopeless poverty, and Southern romance in its gothic elements and melodrama. Hence, *Porgy* has been compared with William Faulkner's fiction. In genre, this novel, which includes poetry and is written in vignettes (scenes that suggest drama), can be compared to generically heterogeneous works such as Jean Toomer's *Cane* (1923). Although Heyward wrote several novels, plays, and poems, *Porgy* is considered his only literary success.

Geralyn Strecker

Further Reading

Alpert, Hollis. *The Life and Times of "Porgy and Bess": The Story of an American Classic*. New York: Alfred A. Knopf, 1990. Traces the history of *Porgy* from Heyward's novel to the 1935 Broadway premiere of the opera *Porgy and Bess*. Includes illustrations from several productions of the opera.

Durham, Frank. *DuBose Heyward: The Man Who Wrote "Porgy."* Port Washington, N.Y.: Kennikat Press, 1965. Focuses primarily on the novel *Porgy* and its stage versions. Ignores the author's other works, however, but offers valuable background to *Porgy*'s creation and reception.

_____. "The Reputed Demises of Uncle Tom: Or, The Treatment of the Negro in Fiction by White Southern Authors in the 1920's." *Southern Literary Review* 2, no. 2 (Spring, 1970): 26-50. Discusses *Porgy* in relation to African American characters in literary history: from primitive portrayals in abolition literature, to the plantation myth of the black man as folk figure type during Reconstruction, to the New Negro after World War I.

Hutchisson, James M. *DuBose Heyward: A Charleston Gentleman and the World of "Porgy and Bess."* Jackson: University Press of Mississippi, 2000. In this critical biography, Hutchisson argues that *Porgy* was the first major Southern novel to portray African Americans without condescension; he describes how Heyward overcame ra-

cial and social restrictions to depict the humanity of black people.

_____. "Professional Authorship in the Charleston Renaissance: The Career of DuBose Heyward." In *Renaissance in Charleston: Art and Life in the Carolina Low Country, 1900-1940*, edited by James M. Hutchisson and Harlan Greene. Athens: University of Georgia Press, 2003. An overview of Heyward's career, placed within the social and historical context of Charleston, South Carolina, during the city's cultural renaissance.

Rhodes, Chip. "Primitive Desires and the Desire for the Primitive: DuBose Heyward and Nella Larsen." In *Structures of the Jazz Age: Mass Culture, Progressive Education, and Racial Discourse in American Modernism*. London: Verso, 1998. Analyzes Heyward's work as part of the cult of primitivism that attained popularity in the United States in the 1920's.

_____. "Writing up the New Negro: The Construction of Consumer Desire in the Twenties." *Journal of American Studies* 28, no. 2 (August, 1994): 191-207. Discusses desire in *Porgy* in context with other works of Southern literature. Describes Catfish Row as a place in limbo between slavery and freedom.

Slavick, William H. *DuBose Heyward*. Boston: Twayne, 1981. Critical biography provides extensive discussion of the novel *Porgy*, as well as Heyward's other fiction, poetry, and drama.

Portnoy's Complaint

Author: Philip Roth (1933-)
First published: 1969
Type of work: Novel
Type of plot: Bildungsroman
Time of plot: Mid-twentieth century
Locale: Newark, New Jersey

Principal characters:
ALEXANDER PORTNOY, the protagonist
SOPHIE PORTNOY, his mother
JACK PORTNOY, his father
MARY JANE REED, the Monkey
KAY CAMPBELL, the Pumpkin
SARAH ABBOTT MAULSBY, the Pilgrim
NAOMI, an Israeli soldier

The Story:

Alexander Portnoy has a very difficult childhood and young adulthood growing up in a lower-middle-class Jewish family in Newark, New Jersey. Part of his problem is his emotionally overcharged home environment; another part is the conflict between his desire to be a dutiful son and his wish to enjoy life to the utmost as a fully assimilated American. As

a result he becomes highly neurotic and seeks therapy from a psychiatrist, Dr. Spielvogel, to whom he recounts his experiences.

Portnoy's mother, Sophie, is an overbearing woman (a stereotypical "Jewish momma") who torments Alex with demands he hardly knows how to fulfill. His poor, constipated father, Jack, is no help at all in containing Sophie's dictatorial control of the household. Neither is Alex's sister, Hannah, who plays only a shadowy role in Alex's descriptions of the family. For example, throughout his boyhood and into later life, Portnoy could never understand what it was that he did as a little boy that made his mother lock him outside their apartment door. What crime had he committed? Try as he would to please her, at least once a month he finds himself locked outside, vainly hammering on the door and pleading to be allowed back inside.

As he enters puberty, Portnoy's sex drive goes into high gear. Some of the most hilarious occasions he recalls for his psychiatrist involve masturbation and an early, futile attempt to have sex with a local teenager, Bubbles Girardi, that ends with his ejaculation into his own eye. He then has the fantasy of becoming blind and returning home with a seeing-eye dog, which his mother would not permit in the house. In this episode Portnoy shows how the melodrama he repeatedly experiences at home influences his rich fantasy life as well. Whether it is polio season or Alex indulging himself by eating french fries with his friend, Melvin Weiner, anything and everything becomes an occasion for hysteria and melodrama in the Portnoy household.

Although fantasy is a large part of his life, Portnoy's "adventures" are real enough. As a college student, he takes up with Kay Campbell, whom he nicknames the Pumpkin because of her complexion and physique but who is otherwise an "exemplary" person. She represents for Portnoy the liberal, high-minded, worthy Protestant female he thinks he will someday marry. When he goes home with her to Iowa for Thanksgiving, he finds her family to be as different from his own as could possibly be imagined. The Campbells never raise their voices, and their dinner table is a model of decorum. Portnoy is so thrilled to be their "weekend guest" that he can only reply with a polite "thank you" to anything anyone says; he even speaks thus to inanimate objects, including a chair he accidentally bumps into.

The college romance with Kay ends when Alex casually suggests that when they get married Kay could convert to Judaism, and she indicates that she will not do so—not that Alex is a seriously observant Jew: Following his Bar Mitzvah, he stubbornly refuses to attend even High Holiday services, the pleas of his family notwithstanding. Alex's attraction to gentile women, shiksas, however, is a recurring part of his problems of adjustment. After the Pumpkin and college, he takes up with Sarah Abbott Maulsby, the Pilgrim, so-called because of her family origins. That romance ends when Alex realizes he could never marry the "beautiful and adoring girl" because their backgrounds, even the expres-

sions they use, are so different. Moreover, Portnoy recognizes that a major part of Sarah's attraction—and the attraction of others like her—is not her self but her heritage, which he is desperately and vainly trying to assimilate into his own—or to take revenge upon because he could not.

Things seem somewhat different with Mary Jane Reed, the Monkey, a nickname she acquired after she ate a banana while another couple had intercourse. A New York model, Mary Jane was born and reared in the hills of West Virginia. Although she seems to satisfy Portnoy's grandest sexual fantasies and encourage others, he still regards her as essentially an uneducated hillbilly, which in important respects she is. By this time Portnoy has an important job as the assistant commissioner for human opportunity in New York, and unknown to many, his private life and his professional life are at odds with each other. As Alex tries to educate Mary Jane, she falls deeply in love with him, regarding him as her "breakthrough" to a new and different kind of life from the one she has hitherto led. She nicknames him Breakie, and for a brief while—as when they spend a weekend in a quaint New England village inn—he fantasizes that they might indeed become a couple. Afterward, however, during a trip to Europe, when they have sex together with a Roman prostitute, they quarrel bitterly, and the affair comes to an abrupt halt.

Continuing his trip alone, Alex goes to Israel, where he gets his serious comeuppance. Trying to seduce a very attractive sabra in her army uniform, he is physically and emotionally humiliated by her. Naomi is having none of it—none of Alex's coarse sexual advances, none of his "ghetto humor" or his self-deprecating, self-mocking attitude, and especially none of the corrupt values he had developed by living in the diaspora. To her, he is an utter schlemiel, as indeed he is without fully realizing it.

After all this, Alex finally undertakes an extended series of sessions on Dr. Spielvogel's couch, from where he tells his tales of self-pity and self-torture. The novel ends with the ironic (and now famous) words, "So [said the doctor]. Now vee may perhaps to begin."

Critical Evaluation:

Often grouped with two other accomplished Jewish American writers, Saul Bellow and Bernard Malamud, Philip Roth is actually as different from each of them as they are from each other. Their intellectual outlooks as well as their sense of humor are by no means similar; and if Bellow's favorite milieu is Chicago and Malamud's is New York, Roth's is Newark, New Jersey, in the 1930's and 1940's, where, like Alexander Portnoy, he grew up. Because of this association, many critics mistakenly have taken Portnoy's experiences to be Roth's—an event he fictionalizes in a later novel called *Zuckerman Unbound* (1981). The reader is warned, therefore, not to confuse fiction with biography, which Roth supplies in *The Facts: A Novelist's Autobiography* (1988).

The major conflict that Portnoy endures and that Roth suggests characterizes many young Jewish American men of his generation is described in the preliminary matter to the novel, where "Portnoy's Complaint" is given a dictionary definition. The conflict involves "strongly felt ethical and altruistic impulses" that are constantly at war with "extreme sexual longings, often of a perverse nature." Try as he may, Portnoy cannot shake off his Jewish ethical heritage for a life of unrestrained libidinous satisfaction. In Freudian terms, he is the victim of an unrelenting battle between the reality principle and the pleasure principle, the alter ego and the id, in which his poor ego emerges invariably battered and bewildered. Though much of the novel is humorous, for Portnoy what is happening to him is a very serious matter. As he cries out to Dr. Spielvogel, he is living in the middle of a Jewish joke—he is the son in a Jewish joke—but for him *"it ain't no joke."*

In many ways, *Portnoy's Complaint* brings the confessional novel to its logical and absurd conclusion. A tour de force that has won favor with many readers and critics (like *Goodbye, Columbus* [1959] it was made into a film), it has also been attacked by observant Jews as a travesty of Jewish life in America, and by feminists as offering demeaning, even vicious portraits of women. Roth's defense (as it was for his earlier stories in *Goodbye, Columbus*, which won for him the National Book Award in 1960) is that he is a writer who writes out of his own experience to explore the depths of human nature and human experience—not to provide palliatives or propaganda for any cause or causes. As for Portnoy's use of obscene language throughout the novel, Roth explained that he used it in the novel not so much for its realism as for a vehicle to demonstrate Portnoy's passion to be "saved"—saved from himself and from the conflict that was wearing him out. In this sense, *Portnoy's Complaint* is like Erica Jong's *Fear of Flying* (1973), often mistaken as a piece of feminist pornography instead of the serious novel about a woman's struggle to find herself that underlies all the sex and language to which many have objected.

Indeed, Roth's linguistic versatility is one of the major accomplishments of the novel, which one critic has described as "the high comedy of style," deriving from "the same contrast between innocence and experience which shapes the action, a contrast exemplified in incongruities between language and subject." Another accomplishment is Roth's adap-

tation of the stand-up comic's *spritz*, or spray of words that evokes gales of laughter from audiences by its remarkable energy and momentum. Moreover, Roth has a superb ear for the cadences and idioms of actual speech, which he deftly varies from character to character so that the novel never loses its fascination, whether Portnoy is a child bewildered by his parents or an adult trying to reason with Mary Jane Reed or an emotional wreck appealing for help from his psychiatrist Dr. Spielvogel. Roth's use of metaphorical language rivals in its way what Southern agrarian writers have achieved in theirs. Yet the novel's lasting importance remains its tragicomic portrait of someone growing up Jewish in an urban environment in mid-twentieth century America.

Jay L. Halio

Further Reading

Bloom, Harold, ed. *Philip Roth's "Portnoy's Complaint."* Philadelphia: Chelsea House, 2004. Collection of essays analyzing the novel, with discussions of Roth's psychoanalysts, the portrayal of the Jewish mother in the novel and in American popular culture, the novel's depiction of and rebellion against Jewishness, and Roth and the American unconscious.

Brauner, David. "'Getting in Your Retaliation First': Narrative Strategies in *Portnoy's Complaint*." In *Philip Roth: New Perspectives on an American Author*, edited by Derek Parker Royal. Westport, Conn.: Praeger, 2005. Discusses numerous aspects of the novel, including its innovative form and content, its use of Freudian psychoanalytical theories, and the ways in which it revolutionized Jewish American literature.

Cohen, Sarah Blacher. "Philip Roth's Would-Be Patriarchs and Their *Shikses* and Shrews." *Studies in American Jewish Literature* 1 (Spring, 1975): 16-23. Reprinted in *Critical Essays on Philip Roth*, edited by Sanford Pinsker. Boston: G. K. Hall, 1982. Examines the women in several of Roth's novels, including *Portnoy's Complaint*. Describes how Roth's "petulant" young men typically blame their "Yiddishe mommes" for their problems and powerlessness.

Grebstein, Sheldon. "The Comic Anatomy of *Portnoy's Complaint*." In *Comic Relief: Humor in Contemporary American Literature*, edited by Sarah Blacher Cohen. Urbana: University of Illinois Press, 1978. An excellent essay on Roth's "stand-up" humor, as developed from professional comedians, such as Henny Youngman and others.

Guttmann, Allen. *The Jewish Writer in America: Assimila-*

tion and the Crisis of Identity. New York: Oxford University Press, 1971. Contains an essay, "Philip Roth and the Rabbis," that shows Roth's sensitivity to the problems of assimilation in the United States.

Halio, Jay L. *Philip Roth Revisited.* New York: Twayne, 1992. The chapter "The Comedy of Excess" treats various aspects of Roth's comic mastery in *Portnoy's Complaint.* It also comments on the underlying humanity of

Mary Jane Reed, or the Monkey, as Portnoy, who fails to recognize her humanity, derisively nicknames her.

Parrish, Timothy, ed. *The Cambridge Companion to Philip Roth.* New York: Cambridge University Press, 2007. Collection of essays discussing, among other subjects, Roth and ethnic identity, postmodernism, the Holocaust, Israel, and gender. The references to *Portnoy's Complaint* are listed in the index.

Il porto sepolto

Author: Giuseppe Ungaretti (1888-1970)
First published: 1916 (partial translation, 1990, in *The Buried Harbour: Selected Poems of Guiseppe Ungaretti*)
Type of work: Poetry

Giuseppe Ungaretti's *Il porto sepolto* (the buried harbor) came out of the peculiar circumstances of World War I; Ungaretti had volunteered in May of 1915 to join the Italian military. Each of the thirty-three poems of this, Ungaretti's first volume, is tagged with the date and place of composition. Two of the poems were written in December, 1915, and twenty-eight were composed between April, 1916, and September, 1916. They are for the most part placed within the volume in chronological order. Thematically, the collection explores solitude and the various ways in which human beings try to bridge the spaces between themselves and others. It shows the heights to which human aspiration can ascend, even out of the depths of trench warfare.

Il porto sepolto forms one of three parts of a larger collection, *Allegria di naufragi* (1919; the joy of shipwrecks). The "harbor" that is "buried" is most likely the harbor off Pharos at Alexandria, Egypt, the city of Ungaretti's youth. The harbor become mythic for Ungaretti. Like the legendary lost city of Atlantis, the harbor is so far below the surface, and so legendary, that it represents the unfathomable depths of the human psyche as well as the height of the most intense consciousness. It is to him, he writes, "the mirage of Italy"; it represents that part of one's early life that is submerged in the subconscious "or in the intense heat of the mirage."

The human condition of separateness and the striving of the human mind and spirit to overcome that condition is addressed in the poem titled "Pilgrimage." In it, the poet refers

to himself as "Ungaretti/ man of pain," who gains courage from illusion. This statement is paradoxical: The first stanza shows the individual in the trenches in war, "in these bowels/ of rubble" where "hour on hour" the poet-soldier has "dragged" his "carcass/ worn away by mud/ like a sole." Ungaretti's illusion is the illusion of light beyond those pathetic, degrading, and dehumanizing—because disconnecting—conditions. He writes, "Beyond/ a searchlight/ sets a sea/ into the fog," showing his illusion to be the possibility of order, of light, of form rather than chaos, of purification (the sea) instead of putrefaction ("bowels of rubble"). Toward the close of the poem, the faculty of the imagination is shown to lift the human spirit above the physical and psychological depths of the trenches: From the trenches, the poet perceives the essential similarity and the ultimate connectedness of things and seeks to communicate that vision in his poetry. The title "Pilgrimage" indicates more than a mere journey; it is a religious journey from the physicality of despair into the open air of spiritual aspiration.

Ungaretti was rooted in more than one literary and philosophical tradition, and he derives imagery from Italian and other Western cultures, from Asian literary traditions, and from the modern world. His images and symbols evoke thereby a curious admixture of resonances, often concerned with the search for identity. Such a theme is explored in "In Memoriam," written on September 30, 1916, at Locvizza. This funereal and contemplative poem concerns Mohammad Sheab, a friend of Ungaretti from his days at a French school in Alexandria and with whom he later attended school in Paris. Ungaretti perceived Sheab, an Arab, and himself as individuals estranged from their roots, and on this estrangement Ungaretti blames the suicide of Sheab, "Descendent/ of emirs of nomads," who changes his name from Mohammad to Marcel, who cannot remember how to live with Arab culture, and who takes his own life at 5 Rue des Carmes, to be buried in Ivry. In contrast, Ungaretti, the soldier-poet, finds his connection to Italy and to the Italian people.

The fact that Ungaretti was a man of both Asian and Western cultures, that he was fluent in at least three languages and was a writer in three literary traditions, becomes apparent again in "Phase," in which he describes the depths of love as being in the "eye/ of thousandth-and-one night," clearly an allusion to the famous collection of tales known as *The Arabian Nights' Entertainments* or *The Thousand and One Nights*. He mixes the Eastern image of the "deserted garden" with the Western myth of the dove descending. In "June," he writes of the end of an evening of lovemaking, comparing the way in which "the sky is shut" to the concurrent movement of "the jasmine" "in my African land."

"Rivers," written at Cotici, August 16, 1916, opens with the poet holding on to a "crippled tree" that is alone in a ravine and that has as a quality "the laziness of a circus/ before or after the performance." If this were the traditional symbol of a tree of life, it would come to represent a life "crippled," "*mutilato*"—a life made dysfunctional through having been made the object of harm. The tree seems to be emblematic of human anguish. While the "circus" might appear to be lazy specifically when the performance is not on, it may also represent social instability and disorder. The poet-soldier, in repose, then watches the clouds pass in front of the moon, and the following morning he rests "like a relic." In writing of the rivers, he establishes a stark setting and places himself first in Bedouin culture as "a pliant fiber/ of the universe." He writes of the Serchio, to which his ancestry is connected; of the Nile, which witnessed the growth of the young man; and of the Seine, where his identity was "remingled and remade" and where he gained self-knowledge. After separating things in order to examine them in the harsh glare of the desert light, he resolves and modulates through a visual paradox: Night falls, and he writes, "now my life seems to me/ a corolla/ of shadows."

In the middle of the series, the poem "Leavetaking" expresses Ungaretti's poetics. In eight lines that run in fluid movement, he writes of poetry as "the world humanity/ one's own life/ flowering from the word"—and the reader envisions the most abstract expression, "the world humanity," quickly transformed into concreteness through a special kind of metaphor: Flowers come out of words, and the flowers, and the words, and the action of the flowers coming from the words, all express life. Each word has the power to so impress one that, as Ungaretti describes it, "it is dug into my life/ like an abyss." He tells readers to read every word and to let every word pour out its full complex of meanings. It is with this advice from the poet that the reader can approach the poetry. Ungaretti's verse cannot be read quickly; rather, it must be allowed to unfold itself word by word. The reader must allow the poet to re-create in him or her the poet's experience or perception. Ungaretti does not relate experience but re-creates it, and to enter into that re-creation is the reader's challenge. Everything in Ungaretti's poetry depends not on the narrative line but on each word.

Il porto sepolto marks such a dramatic break from the Italian poetry of the nineteenth century that Ungaretti has been seen as the first modern Italian poet. In "Morning," written at Santa Maria La Longa, he writes a poem of two lines: "Immensity/ illumines me." This work typifies the intensity and the sparseness of diction that characterize Ungaretti's work.

Ungaretti himself described the intent of *Il porto sepolto*: Although clearly written by a soldier, it does not praise war and heroic glory. Rather, it is a cry for human connection, for brotherhood in the face of suffering. Participating in the waging of war paradoxically heightened Ungaretti's vision of the essential integrity of all things in the cosmos and affirmed for him the possibility that the virtue of brotherly love can sustain a very fragile humanity in the face of cataclysm. He expresses the tenuousness of life during war in "Soldiers" and of human communication in "Brothers" by comparing both to leaves on the verge of falling from trees. He closes "Brothers" with the image of "man facing his fragility," although facing it along with, and sustained by, his "brothers." "Watch" displays Ungaretti's paradox that through contemplating loss and death so often, he is actually engaging in a poetry of life. As he holds his dead, "massacred comrade," he is moved by the image of death to speak; not even in love letters has he himself "held/ so/ fast to life" as he does in physically holding his dead friend.

The dominant contrast in Ungaretti is physical place: the desert, through which one roams alone, with only the memory of the promised land. It is the calling of poetry, according to Ungaretti, to redeem humanity, to make real the promised land. It is the possibility of poetry to help humanity become pure and attain its own perfection, to overcome its own anguish, to be in harmony with the universe.

The settings of Ungaretti's poetry are often stark, elemental, although peopled with the subjects of the poems. He plays with the senses, often accomplishing difficult things with great agility, such as the verbal re-creation of sound. For example, in "Pleasure," he compares the feeling of remorse after a day's pleasure to the haunting sound of "a dog's bark/ lost in the/ desert." Similarly, in "Solitude," he writes that the sound of his own voice in anguish can "wound/ like lightning bolts/ the faint bell/ of the sky."

Ungaretti faced the challenge of an Italian poet of his time, either to write in or not write in literary Italian. He chose to pare down his language so far that he thought he might reach the essence of each word and each line, and, in fact, he put much work into revision for poetic compression and for the concentration of perception. It was Ungaretti's belief that to break through into a new era of poetry in Italian, he would have to be intensely introspective, able to perceive his existence as part of a greater whole, and unequivocally able to express the consciousness of his own conscience. This, Ungaretti accomplished.

Donna Berliner

Further Reading

Auster, Paul. "Man of Pain." *The New York Review of Books*, April 29, 1976. Offers a good introduction to Ungaretti's poetry for the general reader.

Brose, Margaret. "Metaphor and Simile in Giuseppe Ungaretti's *L'Allegria*." *Lingua e Stile* (March, 1976): 43-73. Discusses Ungaretti's adaptations of Symbolist techniques as well as his use of other aesthetic and stylistic devices.

Cary, Joseph. *Three Modern Italian Poets: Saba, Ungaretti, Montale*. 2d ed. Chicago: University of Chicago Press, 1993. Includes an introductory chapter that provides accessible background information. Chapter on Ungaretti traces his career from his early days through his later poetry of anguish.

Frisardi, Andrew. "Giuseppe Ungaretti and the Image of Desolation." *Hudson Review* 60, no. 1 (Spring, 2002): 75-89. Examines Ungaretti's reputation as a poet, analyzing some of his work and placing him within the Italian poetic tradition. This issue of *Hudson Review* also contains some of Ungaretti's poems.

Jones, Frederic J. *Giuseppe Ungaretti: Poet and Critic*. Edinburgh: Edinburgh University Press, 1977. Provides biographical information before examining Ungaretti's perspective and discussing his work in terms of his connections to Alexandria, Paris, and Italy.

Pickering-Iazzi, Robin. "Alexandria Revisited: Colonialism and the Egyptian Works of Enrico Pea and Giuseppe Ungaretti." In *A Place in the Sun: Africa in Italian Colonial Culture from Post-Unification to the Present*, edited by Patrizia Palumbo. Berkeley: University of California Press, 2003. Focuses on the two poets' lives in Alexandria, Egypt, and how their experiences there are reflected in their work. Includes discussion of *Il porto sepolto*.

Ungaretti, Giuseppe. *The Buried Harbour: Selected Poems of Giuseppe Ungaretti*. Canberra, A.C.T.: Leros Press, 1990. Offers excellent English translations of selections from *Il porto sepolto*.

The Portrait of a Lady

Author: Henry James (1843-1916)
First published: 1880-1881, serial; 1881, book
Type of work: Novel
Type of plot: Psychological realism
Time of plot: c. 1875
Locale: England, France, and Italy

Principal characters:
ISABEL ARCHER, an American heir
GILBERT OSMOND, her husband
RALPH TOUCHETT, her cousin
MADAME MERLE, her friend and Osmond's former mistress
PANSY OSMOND, Osmond's daughter
LORD WARBURTON, Isabel's English suitor
CASPAR GOODWOOD, Isabel's American suitor
HENRIETTA STACKPOLE, an American newspaper correspondent and Isabel's friend

The Story:

Upon the death of her father, Isabel Archer had been visited by her aunt, Mrs. Touchett, who considers her so attractive that she decides to give her the advantage of a more cosmopolitan experience. Isabel is quickly carried off to Europe so she might see something of the world of culture and fashion. On the day the two women arrive at the Touchett home in England, Isabel's sickly young cousin, Ralph Touchett, and his father are taking tea in the garden with their friend, Lord Warburton. The young nobleman, who had just been confessing his boredom with life, is much taken with the American girl's grace and lively manner.

Isabel had barely settled at Gardencourt, her aunt's home, when she received a letter from an American friend, Henrietta Stackpole, a journalist who is writing a series of articles on the sights of Europe. At Ralph's invitation, Henrietta comes to Gardencourt to visit Isabel and obtain material for her writing. Soon after Henrietta's arrival, Isabel hears from another American friend and a would-be suitor, Caspar Goodwood, who had followed her abroad and learned her whereabouts from Henrietta. Isabel, irritated by his aggressiveness, decides not to answer his letter.

On the day Isabel receives the letter from Goodwood, Lord Warburton proposes to her. Not wishing to seem indifferent to the honor of his proposal, she asks for time to consider it, but she decides finally that she will not be able to marry the young Englishman because she wishes to see considerably more of the world before she marries. She is also afraid that marriage to Warburton, although he is a model of kindness and thoughtfulness, might prove stifling.

Because Isabel had not seen London on her journey with Mrs. Touchett and since it is on Henrietta Stackpole's itinerary, the two young women, accompanied by Ralph Touchett, visit the capital. Henrietta soon makes the acquaintance of a Mr. Bantling, who begins to squire her around. When Caspar Goodwood visits Isabel at her hotel, she again refuses him, though when he persists, she agrees that he could ask for her hand again in two years.

While the party is in London, a telegram comes from Gardencourt, informing them that old Mr. Touchett is seriously ill of gout and his wife much alarmed. Isabel and Ralph leave on the afternoon train. Henrietta remains under the escort of her new friend.

During the time Mr. Touchett lay dying and his family is preoccupied, Isabel spends a great deal of time with Madame Merle, an old friend of Mrs. Touchett, who had come to Gardencourt to spend a few days. She and Isabel are thrown together a great deal and exchange many confidences. Isabel admires the older woman for her ability to amuse herself, for her skill at needlework, painting, and the piano, and for her ability to accommodate herself to any social situation. For her part, Madame Merle speaks enviously of Isabel's youth and intelligence and laments the life that has left her, at middle age, a widow with no children and no visible success in life.

Isabel's uncle dies, leaving her, at his son's instigation, half of his fortune. Ralph, impressed with his young cousin's brilliance, had persuaded his father that she should be given the opportunity to fly as far and as high as she might. Ralph knows he cannot live long because of his pulmonary illness, and his own legacy is enough to let him live in comfort.

As quickly as she can, Mrs. Touchett sells her London house and takes Isabel to Paris with her. Ralph goes south for the winter to preserve what is left of his health. In Paris, the new heir is introduced to many of her aunt's friends among American expatriates, but she is not impressed. She thinks their indolent lives worthy only of contempt. Meanwhile, Henrietta and Mr. Bantling have arrived in Paris, and Isabel spends much time with them and Edward Rosier, another dilettante living on the income from his inheritance. She had known Rosier when they were children and had been traveling abroad with her father. Rosier explains to Isabel that he cannot return to his own country because there is no occupation there worthy of a gentleman.

In February, Mrs. Touchett and her niece visit the Palazzo Crescentini, the Touchett house in Florence. They stop on the way to see Ralph, who is staying in San Remo. In Florence they are joined once more by Madame Merle. Unknown to Isabel or her aunt, Madame Merle also visits her friend Gilbert Osmond, another American who lives in voluntary exile outside Florence with his art collection and his young convent-bred daughter, Pansy. Madame Merle tells Osmond of Isabel's arrival in Florence, saying that as the heir to a fortune, Isabel would be a valuable addition to Osmond's collection.

The heir who had already rejected two worthy suitors does not refuse the third. Isabel is quickly captivated by the charm of the sheltered life Gilbert Osmond has created for himself. Her friends are against the match. Henrietta Stackpole is inclined to favor Caspar Goodwood and convinced that Osmond is interested only in Isabel's money, as is Isabel's aunt. Mrs. Touchett has requested Madame Merle, the good friend of both parties, to discover the state of their affections; she is convinced that Madame Merle could have prevented the match. Ralph Touchett is disappointed that his cousin should have fallen from her flight so quickly. Caspar Goodwood, learning of Isabel's intended marriage when he revisits her after the passage of the two years agreed upon, cannot persuade her to reconsider her step. Isabel is indignant when he comments that she does not even know her intended husband's antecedents.

After they marry, Isabel and Osmond establish their home in Rome, in a setting completely expressive of Osmond's tastes. Before three years pass, Isabel begins to realize that her friends were not completely wrong in their objections to her marriage. Osmond's exquisite taste has made their home one of the most popular in Rome, but his ceaseless effort to press his wife into a mold, to make her a reflection of his own ideas, has not made their marriage one of the happiest.

Osmond succeeds in destroying a romance between Pansy and Edward Rosier, who had visited the girl's stepmother and found the daughter attractive. Osmond does not succeed, however, in contracting the match he desires between Pansy and Lord Warburton. Warburton finds Pansy as pleasing as Isabel had once been, but he dropped his suit when he saw that the girl's affections lay with Rosier.

Ralph Touchett, his health growing steadily worse, gives up his wanderings on the Continent and returns to Gardencourt to die. When Isabel receives a telegram from his mother telling her that Ralph would like to see her before his death, she feels it her duty to go to Gardencourt at once. Osmond reacts to her wish as if it were a personal insult. He expects that his wife would want to remain at his side and that she would not disobey any wish of his. He also makes it plain that he dislikes Ralph.

In a state of turmoil after that conversation with her husband, Isabel meets the Countess Gemini, Osmond's sister. The countess, who is visiting the Osmonds, sees how matters lay between her brother and Isabel. An honest soul, she feels more sympathy for her sister-in-law than for her brother. To comfort Isabel, she tells her the story of Gilbert's past. After his first wife had died, he and Madame Merle had had an affair for six or seven years. During that time, Madame Merle, who was then a widow, had a child, Pansy. Changing his residence, Osmond was able to pretend to his new circle of friends that the original Mrs. Osmond had died in giving birth to the child.

With this news fresh in her mind and still determined to go to England, Isabel stops to say goodbye to Pansy, who is staying in a convent where her father had sent her to get over her affair with Rosier. There she also meets Madame Merle, who with her keen intuition immediately perceives that Isabel knows her secret. When she remarks that Isabel need never see her again, that she will go to America, Isabel is certain Madame Merle will also find in America much to her own advantage.

Isabel arrives in England in time to see her cousin before his death. She stays on briefly at Gardencourt after the funeral, long enough to bid goodbye to Lord Warburton, who has come to offer condolences to her aunt and to reject a third offer from Caspar Goodwood, who knows of her marital problems. When she leaves to start her journey back to Italy, Isabel knows that her first duty is not toward herself but to put her house in order.

Critical Evaluation:

The Portrait of a Lady, usually regarded as the major achievement of Henry James's early period of fiction writing, is also recognized to be one of literature's great novels. In it, James shows that he has learned well from two European masters of the novel. Ivan Turgenev taught him how to use a single character who shapes the work and is seen throughout in relationship to the other characters, and from George Eliot he had learned the importance of a tight structure and a form that develops logically out of the given materials. He advances in *The Portrait of a Lady* beyond Eliot in minimizing his own authorial comments and analysis and permitting his heroine to be seen through her own tardily awakening self-realization, as well as through the consciousness of the men and women who are closest to her. Thus his "portrait" of a lady is one that grows slowly, stroke by stroke, with each new touch bringing out highlights and shadows until at the end of the novel Isabel Archer stands revealed as a woman whose experiences of excitement, joy, pain, and knowledge have given her an enduring beauty and dignity.

Isabel is one of James's finest creations and one of the most memorable women in the history of the novel. A number of sources have been suggested for her. She may have been partly drawn from James's cousin, Mary "Minny" Temple, whom he was later to immortalize as Milly Theale in *The Wings of the Dove* (1902). Isabel has also been compared to two of Eliot's heroines, Dorothea Brooke in *Middlemarch* (1871-1872) and Gwendolen Harleth in *Daniel Deronda* (1876); to Diana Belfield in an early romantic tale by James entitled "Longstaff's Marriage"; to Bathsheba Everdene in Thomas Hardy's *Far from the Madding Crowd* (1874); and even to James himself, some of whose early experiences closely parallel those of Isabel.

While James may have drawn from both real and fictional people in portraying Isabel, she possesses her own identity, having grown, as James later wrote in his preface to the novel, from his "conception of a certain young woman affronting her destiny." He visualized her as "an intelligent but presumptuous girl" who was nevertheless "complex" and who would be offered a series of opportunities for free choice in confronting that destiny. Because of her presumption in believing that she knew more about herself and the world than she actually did, Isabel made mistakes, including the tragic error of misjudging Gilbert Osmond's nature. Her intelligence, however, though insufficient to save her from suffering, enabled her to achieve a moral triumph in the end.

Of the four men in Isabel's life, three love her and one uses her innocence to gain for himself what he would not otherwise have had. She refuses to marry Lord Warburton because, though he offers her a great fortune, a title, an entry into English society, and an agreeable and entertaining personality, she believes she can do better. She turns down the equally wealthy Caspar Goodwood because she finds him stiff and is frightened by his aggressiveness. Her cousin, Ralph Touchett, does not propose because he does not wish her to be tied to a man who daily faces death. She does not even suspect the extent of his love and adoration until she learns of it just as death takes him from her, which almost overwhelms her. She accepts Osmond because she is deceived by his calculated charm and because she believes that he deserves what she can offer him: a fortune that will make it possible for him to live in idleness but surrounded by the objects of the culture she believes he represents, and a mother's love and care for his supposedly motherless daughter. Half of the novel is given over to Isabel's living with, adjusting to, and finally triumphing over that disastrous choice.

In his preface, James uses an architectural figure to describe *The Portrait of a Lady*. He says the "large building" of the novel "came to be a square and spacious house." Much of what occurs in the novel occurs in or near a series of houses, each of which relates significantly to Isabel or to other characters. The action begins at Gardencourt, the tudor English country house of Daniel Touchett that Isabel finds more beautiful than anything she has ever seen. The charm of the house is enhanced by its age and natural setting beside the Thames above London. It contrasts greatly with the "old house at Albany, a large, square, double house" belonging to her grandmother, which Isabel in her childhood had found romantic and in which she had indulged in dreams stimulated by her reading.

Mrs. Touchett's taking Isabel from the Albany house to Gardencourt is a first step in her plan to "introduce her to the world." When Isabel visits Lockleigh, Lord Warburton's home, she sees it from the gardens as resembling "a castle in a legend," though inside it has been modernized. She does not view it as a home for herself, or its titled owner as her husband, despite the many advantages of both. The front of Osmond's house in Florence is "imposing" but of "a somewhat uncommunicative character," a "mask." It symbolizes Os-

mond, behind whose mask Isabel does not see until after she is married to him. The last of the houses in *The Portrait of a Lady* is the Palazzo Roccanera, the Roman home of the Osmonds, which James first describes as "a kind of domestic fortress . . . which smelt of historic deeds, of crime and craft and violence." When Isabel later broods over it during her night-long meditation in chapter 42, it is "the house of darkness, the house of dumbness, the house of suffocation."

Isabel is first seen at Gardencourt on her visit with Mrs. Touchett, and it is here that she turns down the first of three proposals of marriage. It is fitting that she should be last seen here with each of the three men who have loved her. Asserting the independence on which she has so long prided herself, she has defied her imperious husband by going to England to see the dying Ralph, whose last words tell her that if she is now hated by Osmond, she has been adored by her cousin. In a brief conversation with Lord Warburton after Ralph's death, Isabel turns down an invitation to visit him and his sisters at Lockleigh. Shortly afterward, a scene from six years earlier is reversed: Then she had sat on a rustic bench at Gardencourt and looked up from reading Goodwood's letter (in which he writes that he will come to England and propose to her) to see and hear Warburton preparing to propose. Now Goodwood surprises her by appearing just after she has dismissed Warburton.

There follows the one sexually passionate scene in the novel. In it Isabel has "an immense desire to appear to resist" the force of Goodwood's argument that she should leave Osmond and turn to him. She pleads with streaming tears, "As you love me, as you pity me, leave me alone!" Defying her plea, Goodwood kisses her, but he possesses her for a moment only. Immediately after, she flees into the house and then to Rome, as Goodwood learns in the brief scene in London with Henrietta Stackpole that closes the novel. James leaves the reader to conclude that Isabel's love for Pansy Osmond has principally determined her decision to continue enduring a marriage that she had freely—though so ignorantly and foolishly—chosen.

"Critical Evaluation" by Henderson Kincheloe

Further Reading

Coulson, Victoria. *Henry James, Women, and Realism*. New York: Cambridge University Press, 2007. Examines James's important friendships with three women: his sister, Alice James, and the novelists Constance Fenimore Woolson and Edith Wharton. These three writers and James shared what Coulson describes as an "ambivalent realism," or a cultural ambivalence about gender identity, and she examines how this idea is manifest in James's works, including *The Portrait of a Lady.*

Flannery, Denis. *Henry James: A Certain Illusion.* Brookfield, Vt.: Ashgate, 2000. An analysis of the concept of illusion in James's works, including *The Portrait of a Lady.*

Freedman, Jonathan, ed. *The Cambridge Companion to Henry James.* New York: Cambridge University Press, 1998. A collection of essays that provides extensive information on James's life and literary influences and describes his works and their characters. Robert Weisbuch's essay "Henry James and the Idea of Evil" devotes several pages to a discussion of *The Portrait of a Lady.*

Grover, Philip. *Henry James and the French Novel: A Study in Inspiration.* New York: Barnes & Noble, 1973. Analyzes James's works up to and including *The Portrait of a Lady.* Tries to show the ways in which James was influenced by Honoré de Balzac, Gustave Flaubert, and the French art-for-art's-sake movement. Compares the themes and subjects of French writers with those of James.

Kelley, Cornelia Pulsifer. *The Early Development of Henry James.* Rev. ed. Urbana: University of Illinois Press, 1965. Traces the development of the Jamesian novel from *Roderick Hudson* (1876) through *The Portrait of a Lady.* Examines French influences on James but also claims that the two novelists who influenced James most significantly were Ivan Turgenev and George Eliot, whose influence can be seen best in *The Portrait of a Lady.*

Kirschke, James J. *Henry James and Impressionism.* Troy, N.Y.: Whitston Press, 1981. Traces impressionist influences on James and claims that impressionism is the key to comprehending the modernist movement in literature and the pictorial arts.

Kress, Jill M. *The Figure of Consciousness: William James, Henry James, and Edith Wharton.* New York: Routledge, 2002. Focuses on James's metaphorical descriptions of consciousness in *The Portrait of a Lady* as a means of depicting gender, social class, the self, and knowledge.

Matthiessen, F. O. *Henry James: The Major Phase.* 1944. Reprint. New York: Oxford University Press, 1981. Written by one of the foremost critics of American literature, this classic study examines James's expatriatism and the paradox that although James had cut himself off from the United States, his novels deeply searched the American consciousness.

Pippin, Robert B. *Henry James and Modern Moral Life.* New York: Cambridge University Press, 2000. A look at the moral message James sought to convey through his writings. Pippin interprets several of James's works, including *The Portrait of a Lady.*

Portrait of the Artist as a Young Dog

Author: Dylan Thomas (1914-1953)
First published: 1940
Type of work: Short fiction

Posthumous biographical studies of Dylan Thomas record a change in appreciation that was long overdue. During his lifetime, Thomas was regarded in the United States as a great English poet and reciter, but only after his death did his work—which includes poetry, fiction, dramas, essays, and impressionistic sketches—come to be regarded as a multifaceted whole. Representative of this reassessment was the growing respect accorded his first collection of short stories, which is also a mock-autobiography, that Thomas titled in imitation of James Joyce's *A Portrait of the Artist as a Young Man* (1916).

If his critics are right in concluding that most of Thomas's best poetry was written in Swansea before he left Wales for London at the age of twenty, it may also be suggested that this collection of short stories, *Portrait of the Artist as a Young Dog*, set in Swansea and environs, laid the foundations for much of the work that was to follow. "One Warm Saturday," the final story in the collection, seems to anticipate the events of Thomas's next book of prose, the unfinished novel *Adventures in the Skin Trade* (1955), which uses the same surrealistic style. In both the story and the novel, the ever-pursued eludes capture by the hero as reality dissolves around him. In fact, this may well be the underlying theme of the entire collection *Portrait of the Artist as a Young Dog.*

The relationship of these stories to the Thomas canon, however, is not entirely straightforward. *Adventures in the*

Skin Trade was the first prose work; Thomas called it his "Welsh book." It was commissioned by a London publisher, and the first chapter appeared in the periodical *Wales* in 1937. The previous year, Richard Church had suggested that Thomas write some autobiographical prose tales. After his marriage in July, 1937, Thomas took up this project but set to work in a very different style. He first produced "A Visit to Grandpa's," in which the surrealism is muted and the lyrical tone sustained by the young narrator; this story, standing second in *Portrait of the Artist as a Young Dog*, became Thomas's favorite broadcast and reading material. The most interesting feature of the new style of story is the rapid succession of apparently logical but often haphazardly related events, the whole ending in a diminuendo that seems anticlimactic. The intention of the play of events on the diminutive observer is to record, by means of an episode that largely concerns or happens to others, a stage in the observer's growth, that is, in his development as a "young dog."

The development of the Thomas found in the collection into the "young dog" of the final tales is related to the development of the real Thomas as a writer. This is seen principally in his use of autobiographical material for prose, poetry, and drama. Thomas delivered the typescript of *Portrait of the Artist as a Young Dog* to his publisher, in lieu of the "Welsh book," in December, 1939. Nine days later, talking to Richard Hughes, he remarked that the people of Laugharne, where he was then living, needed a play of their own. This remark is usually recognized as the origin of *Under Milk Wood*, which was first broadcast as a radio drama in 1954. Some years earlier, Thomas had toyed with the notion of doing another imitation of Joyce, a sort of Welsh *Ulysses* that would cover twenty-four hours in the life of a Welsh village. The notion of imitating Joyce and the suggestions of Church and Hughes coalesced with his development of a distinct prose style (instead of a prose extension of his verse, as in *Adventures in the Skin Trade*) and resulted in his best-known prose and drama. The autobiographical base is common to both works and to his poetry.

Fern Hill and Ann Jones stood as models to Gorsehill and Auntie Ann of the first story, "The Peaches," and also to the poems "Fern Hill" and "Ann Jones." The fourth story, "The Fight," is a version of Thomas's first meeting with Daniel Jones, the Welsh composer, when they were boys in Swansea. Trevor Hughes, his first genuine admirer, became the central character of the eighth story, "Who Do You Wish Was with Us?" and some of Thomas's experiences on the *South Wales Daily Post* are recorded in four of the stories, especially the last two.

Although composed of short stories, the book is given a sense of direction by careful ordering of the sequence and by repeated and cumulative details inside the stories. The ten stories fall into three periods of life: childhood, boyhood, and young adulthood. The central character is called Dylan Thomas, and although this fact is not stressed in every story, it is obliquely indicated in most. Some characters reappear in more than one tale, including his cousin, Gwilym Jones, and his older colleagues in journalism. The chief cohesive factor in the collection, however, is not the central character so much as that each story celebrates a visit or an excursion either within the provincial town or just beyond it. The town and its environs becomes a character in the book, elaborated in the names of its houses, its shops and pubs, and its weather, which ranges from the warmth of summer evenings on the beach to wet wintry nights. The locales of the stories, like the seasons of the year, change from story to story and help create the image of the region as a setting for the gallery of minor characters who dominate each story. The hero remains, as he says in "Just Like Little Dogs," a lonely and late-night observer of the odd doings of the townsfolk. The landmarks of the locale become associated with the stories of chance or temporary acquaintances met on his excursions. As is certainly true of *Under Milk Wood* (1953), these stories too generally imply that every person has a skeleton in his or her kitchen cupboard.

That skeleton is generally a private vice that is not too vicious and may be both comic and pathetic. From the first three stories, "The Peaches," "A Visit to Grandpa's," and "Patricia, Edith, and Arnold," readers learn that Dylan's Uncle Jim is drinking his pigs away; Cousin Gwilym has his own makeshift chapel and rehearses his coming ministry there; Grandfather Dan dreams he is driving a team of demon horses and has delusions about being buried; the Thomas family's maid, Patricia, is involved with the sweetheart of the maid next door. In the next pair of stories, "The Fight" and "Extraordinary Little Cough," the pains and pleasures of boyhood begin to affect the hero, chiefly in finding a soul mate, a fellow artist. He also encounters the horror of viciousness in his companions. The remainder of the stories deal with young adulthood and are varied in subject and treatment—from the recital of a tale told to the narrator to the final story in which the narrator for the first time becomes the protagonist, although an ineffectual one. Most of the stories include an episode set at night, and it seems a pity that the best of Thomas's night stories, the ghostly "The Followers," could not have been included in the collection.

The stories are arranged in roughly chronological order, culminating in "One Warm Saturday" and "Old Garbo," which show Thomas's inner way of escape from his hometown as reality disappears in a wash of beer and a montage of what-might-have-been. In real life, Thomas took to London and to drink as a way to get out of Swansea; by the time he arrived in London, he had already discovered how to blur the concrete outlines of provincial life and make its values jump. He was to do this best in *Under Milk Wood*. There is another possible explanation for his ability to see events under the conditions of dream, and that is his Welshness; there is a hint of that in the story "Where Tawe Flows," titled after the "Great Welsh Novel" that a character named Mr. Thomas and three older friends are writing in weekly installments. Mr. Thomas is about to leave for London and a career as a freelance journalist. The novel is supposed to be a study of provincial life, but the collaborators are only at the second chapter. Readers do not hear Mr. Thomas's contribution because he has spent the week writing the story of a dead governess who turned into a vampire when a cat jumped over her at the moment of her death. One of the foursome offers, instead, the biography of a character named Mary, an account supposed to be realistic but as fantastic as anything the real Thomas ever wrote.

Portrait of the Artist as a Young Dog collects the tensions of provincial life to the breaking point, as does Joyce's *A Portrait of the Artist as a Young Man*. At the end of both books, the hero breaks from home and the style becomes distinctly broken. The increasingly nonrealistic style at the end of both books, a formal expression of the protagonists' whirling thoughts, could be somehow symptomatic of the breaking of ties with Dublin (Joyce) and Swansea (Thomas). In both books, but more obviously in Joyce, the break is long prepared in the tensions as they mount from a highly imaginative childhood through the pains of adolescence to the frustrations of university study or journalism on a provincial daily. The tensions are so strong that they expel their subjects far from their place of origin. If readers want to know why Joyce died in Zurich, Switzerland, or Thomas in New York, the answer is in their own autobiographies of provincial life.

Further Reading

Davies, Peter. *Student Guide to Dylan Thomas*. London: Greenwich Exchange, 2005. Biographical and critical study of Thomas. Disagrees with critics who charge that Thomas's poetry is merely a "careless outpouring of incoherent feeling," demonstrating how he was a dedicated craftsman who struggled to make his works communicate.

Goodby, John, and Chris Wigginton, eds. *Dylan Thomas*. New York: Palgrave, 2001. Collection of essays, including discussions of Thomas and women, Welsh contexts in his poetry, and his depiction of "radical morbidity." References to *Portrait of the Artist as a Young Dog* are listed in the index.

Korg, Jacob. *Dylan Thomas*. Rev. ed. New York: Twayne, 1992. Argues that although the tone of the stories is generally comic, the personal futility and inadequacy of the characters produces irony. Individuals come to recognize a shared sense of loss.

Lycett, Andrew. *Dylan Thomas: A New Life*. Woodstock, N.Y.: Overlook Press, 2005. A candid biography, featuring a wealth of detail about Thomas's life. Examines the contradiction between the man who lived like the devil and the poet who wrote like an angel.

Peach, Linden. *The Prose Writing of Dylan Thomas*. New York: Barnes & Noble, 1988. Shows Thomas shedding his fears of the darker side of sexuality, not so much condemning people for their idiosyncrasies as recording those characteristics with fascination.

Pratt, Annis. "Dylan Thomas's Prose." In *Dylan Thomas: A Collection of Critical Essays*, edited by C. Brian Cox. Englewood Cliffs, N.J.: Prentice-Hall, 1966. Demonstrates how Thomas turned away from the tumultuous psychic drama of his early prose and moved from those inward concerns to a confrontation with the events of the social world. Asserts that in *Portrait of the Artist as a Young Dog* and subsequent work he speaks through a mask.

Seib, Kenneth. "*Portrait of the Artist as a Young Dog*: Dylan's *Dubliners*." In *Critical Essays on Dylan Thomas*, selected by Georg Gaston. Boston: G. K. Hall, 1989. Concludes that Thomas sought to do for the Welsh what Joyce did for the Irish: write a chapter of their moral history and allow them to view themselves through his eyes. The stories are linked by repetitive theme and metaphor.

A Portrait of the Artist as a Young Man

Author: James Joyce (1882-1941)
First published: 1914-1915, serial; 1916, book
Type of work: Novel
Type of plot: Bildungsroman
Time of plot: 1882-1903
Locale: Ireland

Principal characters:
STEPHEN DEDALUS, an Irish student
SIMON DEDALUS, his father
EMMA, his friend

The Story:

When Stephen Dedalus goes to school for the first time, his last name soon gets him into trouble. It sounds too Latin, and the boys tease him about it. The other boys see that he is sensitive and shy, and they begin to bully him. School is filled with unfortunate incidents for Stephen. He is happy when he gets sick and is put in the infirmary away from the other boys. Just before the Christmas holidays, and again in the infirmary, he worries about dying and death. As he lay on the bed thinking, he hears the news of Charles Stewart Parnell's death. The death of the great Irish leader is the first date he remembers—October 6, 1891.

At home during vacation time, he learns more of Parnell. Stephen's father, Simon Dedalus, worships the dead man's memory and defends him on every count. Stephen's aunt, Dante Riordan, despised Parnell as a heretic and a rabble-rouser. The fierce arguments that they get into every day burn themselves into Stephen's memory. He worships his father, and his father says that Parnell had tried to free Ireland, to rid it of the priests who were ruining the country. Dante insists that the opposite is true. A violent defender of the priests, she levels every kind of abuse against Simon and his ideas. The disagreement between them becomes a problem that, in due time, Stephen will have to solve for himself.

Returning to school after the holidays, Stephen gets in trouble with Father Dolan, one of the administrators of the church school he attends. Stephen has broken his glasses, and he cannot study until a new pair arrives. Father Dolan sees that Stephen is not working, and thinking that his excuse about the glasses is false, he beats the boy's hands. For once, the rest of the boys are on Stephen's side, and they urge him to complain to the head of the school. With fear and trembling, Stephen goes to the headmaster and presents his case. The head understands and promises to speak to Father Dolan about the matter. When Stephen tells the boys about his conversation, they hoist him in their arms like a victorious fighter and call him a hero.

Afterward, life is much easier for Stephen. Only one unfortunate incident marks the term. In the spirit of fun, one of his professors announces in class that Stephen has expressed heresy in one of his essays. Stephen quickly changes the offending phrase and hopes that the mistake will be forgotten. After class, however, several of the boys accuse him not only of being a heretic but also of liking Lord Byron, whom they consider an immoral man and therefore no good as a poet. In replying to their charges, Stephen has his first real encounter with the problems of art and morality. They are to follow him throughout his life.

On a trip to Cork with his father, Stephen is forced to listen to the often-told tales of his father's youth. They visit the places his father had loved as a boy. Each night, Stephen is forced to cover up his father's drunkenness and sentimental outbursts. The trip is an education in everything Stephen dislikes. At the end of the school year, Stephen wins several prizes. He buys presents for everyone, starts to redo his room, and begins an ill-fated loan service. As long as the money lasts, life is wonderful. One night, when his money is almost gone, he is enticed into a house by a woman wearing a long pink gown. He learns what love is at age sixteen.

Not until the school holds a retreat in honor of Saint Francis Xavier does Stephen realize how deeply conscious he is of the sins he has committed with women. The sermons of the priests about heaven and hell, especially about hell, eat into his mind. At night, his dreams are of nothing but the eternal torture that he feels he must endure after death. He cannot bear to make confession in school. At last, he goes into the city to a church where he is unknown. There he opens his unhappy mind and heart to an understanding and wise old priest, who advises him and comforts his soul. After the confession, Stephen promises to sin no more, and he feels sure that he will keep his promise. For a time, Stephen's life follows a model course. He studies Thomas Aquinas and Aristotle and wins acclaim from his teachers. One day, the director of the school calls Stephen into his office; after a long conversation, he asks him if he had ever thought of joining the order of the Jesuits. Stephen is deeply flattered. Priesthood becomes his life's goal.

When Stephen enters the university, however, a change comes over his thinking. He begins to doubt, and the longer he studies, the more confused and doubtful he becomes. His problems draw him closer to two of his fellow students, Davin and Lynch, and farther away from Emma, a girl for whom he had felt affection since childhood. He discusses his ideas about beauty and the working of the mind with Davin and Lynch. Stephen will not sign a petition for world peace, winning the enmity of many of the fellows. They call him antisocial and egotistic. Finally, neither the peace movement, the Irish Revival, nor the Church itself could claim his support.

Davin is the first to question Stephen about his ideas. When he suggests to Stephen that Ireland should come first in everything, Stephen answers that to him Ireland is an old sow that ate her offspring.

One day, Stephen meets Emma at a carnival, and she asks him why he had stopped coming by to see her. He answers that he had been born to be a monk. When Emma says that she thinks him a heretic instead of a monk, his last link with Ireland seems to be broken. At least he is not afraid to be alone. If he wants to find and to understand beauty, he has to leave Ireland, where there is nothing in which he believes. His friend's prayers, asking that he return to the faith, go unanswered. Stephen gathers his belongings, packs, and leaves Ireland, intending never to return. He does intend to write a book someday that will make clear his views on Ireland and the Irish.

Critical Evaluation:

A Portrait of the Artist as a Young Man by James Joyce is possibly the greatest example in the English language of the bildungsroman, a novel tracing the physical, mental, and spiritual growth and education of a young person. Other examples of this genre range from Gustave Flaubert's *L'Éducation sentimentale* (1869; *A Sentimental Education*, 1898) to D. H. Lawrence's *Sons and Lovers* (1913). Published in book form in 1916, *A Portrait of the Artist as a Young Man* stands stylistically between the fusion of highly condensed naturalism and Symbolism found in his *Dubliners* (1914) and the elaborate mythological structure, interior monologues, and stream-of-consciousness style of his *Ulysses* (1922). There is a consistent concern for entrapment, isolation, and rebellion from home, Church, and nation in all three of these works.

A Portrait of the Artist as a Young Man is autobiographical, but in the final analysis, the variants from, rather than the parallels with, Joyce's own life are of the greater artistic significance. The events of Stephen Dedalus's life are taken from the lives of Joyce, his brother, Stanislaus, and his friend, Byrne, covering the period between 1885 and 1902. The book begins with the earliest memories of his childhood, recounted in childlike language, and ends when Stephen is twenty-two years old with his decision to leave his native Dublin in search of artistic development to forge the conscience of his race. In the intervening years, like Joyce, Stephen attends the Jesuit Clongowes Wood School, which he must leave because of family financial difficulties; attends a day school in Dublin; has his first sexual experience; has his first religious crisis; and finally attends University College, where he decides on his vocation as a writer. The dedication to pure art involves for Stephen, and Joyce, a rejection of the claims on him of duty to family, to the Catholic Church, and to Irish nationalism, either of the political type or of the literary type espoused by the writers of the Irish Renaissance.

In his characterization of Stephen, however, Joyce eliminates much of himself: his sense of humor and love of sport, his graduation from the university before leaving Dublin, his desire to attend medical school in France, his deep concern for his mother's health and affection for his father, and the lifelong liaison he established with Nora Barnacle, who left Ireland with Joyce in 1904. The effect of these omissions is to make a narrower, more isolated character of Stephen than Joyce himself.

On one level, *A Portrait of the Artist as a Young Man* is an initiation story in which an innocent, idealistic youth with a sense of trust in his elders is brought slowly to the recognition that this is a flawed, imperfect world, characterized by injustice and disharmony. Stephen finds this fact at home, at school, at church, in relationships with women and friends, and in the past and present history of his nation. His pride, however, prevents him from seeing any shortcomings in himself. In the second portion of the novel, he becomes involved in the excesses of carnal lust; in the third portion, in the excesses of penitent piety, which also eventually disgust him. In the fourth section, in which he assumes Lucifer's motto, I Will Not Serve—although he sees himself as a pagan worshiper of beauty—he becomes involved in excessive intellectual pride. In the final portion of the novel, Stephen develops his aesthetic theory of the epiphany—the sudden revelation of truth and beauty—through the artistic goals of "wholeness, harmony, and radiance." Therefore, his final flight from his actual home—family, Church, nation—is still part of an almost adolescent rejection of the imperfections of this world and an attempt to replace it with the perfection of form, justice, and harmony of artistic creation.

Stephen Dedalus's very name is chosen to underline his character. His first name links him to Saint Stephen, the first martyr to Christianity; Dedalus sees himself as a martyr, willing to give up all to the services of art. His last name is famous from classical antiquity. It was Daedalus, the Athenian exile, who designed the great caste for King Minos of Crete and later designed the famous labyrinth in which the monstrous Minotaur was kept captive. Later, longing to return to his own land but imprisoned in his labyrinth, Daedalus invented wings for himself and his son, Icarus, to fly from the labyrinth. Stephen, the artist, sees Dublin as the labyrinth from which he must fly to become the great artificer Daedalus was. It is important to remember, however, that Daedalus's son, Icarus, ignored his father's instructions on how to use the wings; because of pride and the desire to exceed, he flew too close to the sun, and his wings melted. He plunged into the ocean and drowned. It is only later, in *Ulysses*, that Stephen recognizes himself as "lap-winged Icarus" rather than as Daedalus.

Joyce's technical skill is obvious in the series of interwoven recurrent symbols of the novel. The rose, for example, which is associated with women, chivalric love, and creativity, appears throughout the novel. In addition, water is found in almost every chapter of the novel: It can be the water that drowns and brings death; it can also be the water that gives life, symbolic of renewal as in baptism and the final choice of escape by sea.

The central themes of *A Portrait of the Artist as a Young Man*—alienation, isolation, rejection, betrayal, the Fall, the search for the father—are developed with amazing virtuosity. This development is the second, following *Dubliners*, of the four major parts in Joyce's cyclical treatment of the life of humans that moves, as the great medieval cyclical plays, from Fall to Redemption, from isolation and alienation to acceptance. Joyce's analysis of the human condition and of the relationship of art to life is later developed in *Ulysses* and *Finnegans Wake* (1939).

Joyce has emphasized the importance of the word "young" in the title of this work, and his conclusion, in the form of Stephen's diary illustrating Stephen's own perceptions, words, and style, forces the reader to become more objective and detached in his or her judgment of Stephen. The reader realizes that all of Stephen's previous epiphanies have failed and recognizes in these final pages the human complexity of Stephen's important triumph in escaping from the nets of Ireland; the reader, however, also realizes that Stephen's triumph is complicated by important losses and sacrifices.

"Critical Evaluation" by Ann E. Reynolds

Further Reading

Brown, Richard. *James Joyce and Sexuality.* New York: Cambridge University Press, 1985. An analysis of the political implications in Joyce's works, especially in marriage and other intimate relationships.

_____, ed. *A Companion to James Joyce.* Malden, Mass.: Blackwell, 2008. Collection of essays, many of which focus on the worldwide influence of Joyce's work, with specific analysis of his impact upon the literature of Ireland, Germany, Japan, India, New Zealand, and France. The essay "Desire, Freedom, and Confessional Culture in *A Portrait of the Artist as a Young Man*" examines this novel.

Bulson, Eric. *The Cambridge Introduction to James Joyce.* New York: Cambridge University Press, 2006. Introductory overview of Joyce's life and work, placing them within the context of Joyce as a modernist, journalist, translator, lecturer, and lover. Chapter 3 analyzes five of Joyce's works, including *A Portrait of the Artist as a Young Man*, while chapter 4 chronicles his works' critical reception from 1914 through 2005.

Ellman, Richard. *James Joyce.* 2d ed. New York: Oxford University Press, 1982. Widely considered the finest literary biography of the twentieth century. Contains extensive discussion and analysis of Joyce's life and works. Highly recommended.

Joyce, James. *A Portrait of the Artist as a Young Man: Authoritative Text, Backgrounds and Contexts, Criticism.* Edited by John Paul Riquelme, text edited by Hans Walter Gabler with Walter Hettche. New York: W. W. Norton, 2007. In addition to the text of the novel, critical essays place the work in its cultural and literary context. One essay describes the novel's structural form and twelve essays provide various interpretations of the work.

McCabe, Colin. *James Joyce and the Revolution of the Word.* New York: Barnes & Noble, 1979. A poststructuralist interpretation of the novel that points out the difficulties of establishing any secure critical reading of the book.

Pierce, David. *Reading Joyce.* New York: Pearson Longman, 2008. Pierce, a longtime teacher and scholar of Joyce, provides a framework to Joyce's work. One chapter examines *A Portrait of the Artist as a Young Man*.

Scholes, Robert, and Richard M. Kain, eds. *The Workshop of Dedalus: James Joyce and the Raw Materials for "A Portrait of the Artist as a Young Man."* Evanston, Ill.: Northwestern University Press, 1965. Still one of the best source studies available on the novel. Includes notebooks, fragments of the manuscript, and biographical information to help readers understand the contexts in which the novel was created.

Wollaeger, Mark A., ed. *James Joyce's "A Portrait of the Artist as a Young Man": A Casebook.* New York: Oxford University Press, 2003. Collection of essays providing various interpretations of the novel, including discussions of Stephen's diary, Joyce's depiction of women, and a comparison of the novel to Homer's *Odyssey* (725 B.C.E.).

The Possessed

Author: Fyodor Dostoevski (1821-1881)
First published: Besy, 1871-1872 (English translation, 1913)
Type of work: Novel
Type of plot: Psychological realism
Time of plot: Mid-nineteenth century
Locale: Russia

Principal characters:
STEPAN VERHOVENSKY, a provincial patriot and mild progressive
PYOTR, his nihilist son
VARVARA STAVROGIN, a provincial lady and Stepan's employer
NIKOLAY, her son
MARYA, Nikolay's wife
SHATOV, the independent son of one of Varvara's serfs
ALEXEI KIRILLOV, a construction engineer

The Story:

Stepan Verhovensky, a self-styled progressive patriot and erstwhile university lecturer, is at loose ends in a provincial Russian town until Varvara Stavrogin hires him to tutor her only son, Nikolay Stavrogin. Stepan's radicalism, which is largely a pose, shocks Varvara, but the two become friends. Varvara's husband dies, and Stepan looks forward to marrying his friend. They travel together to St. Petersburg, where they move in daringly radical circles. After attempting without success to start a literary journal, they leave St. Petersburg, Varvara returning to the province and Stepan, in an attempt to assert his independence, going to Berlin. After four months in Germany, Stepan, realizing that he is in Varvara's thrall emotionally and financially, returns to the province to be near her.

Stepan becomes the leader of a small group that meets to discuss progressive ideas. The group includes Shatov, the independent son of one of Varvara's serfs, a liberal named Virginsky, and Liputin, a man who makes everyone's business his business. Nikolay, whom Stepan had introduced to progressivism, goes on to school in St. Petersburg and from there into the army as an officer. He resigns his commission, however, returns to St. Petersburg, and lives in the slums. When he returns home, at Varvara's request, he insults the members of Stepan's group. He bites the ear of the provincial governor during an interview with that dignitary. Everyone concludes that he is mentally unbalanced, and Nikolay is committed to bed. Three months later, apparently recovered, he apologizes for his actions and again leaves the province.

Some months later, Varvara is invited to visit a childhood friend in Switzerland, where Nikolay is paying court to her friend's daughter, Lizaveta. Before the party returns to Russia, Lizaveta and Nikolay break their engagement because Nikolay is interested in Dasha, Varvara's servant woman. In Switzerland, Nikolay and Stepan's son, Pyotr, meet and find themselves in sympathy on political matters.

A new governor, von Lembke, comes to the provinces. Stepan is lost without Varvara, and he visibly deteriorates during her absence. Varvara arranges for Dasha, who is the sister of Shatov and twenty years old, to marry Stepan, who is fifty-three years old. Dasha submits passively to her mistress's wishes, and Stepan reluctantly consents to the marriage, but he balks when he discovers from a member of his group that he is being used to cover up Nikolay's relations with the girl.

New arrivals in the province include Captain Lebyadkin and his disabled sister, Marya. One day, Marya attracts the attention of Varvara in front of the cathedral, whereupon Varvara takes Marya home with her. She learns that Nikolay had known the Lebyadkins in St. Petersburg. Pyotr assures Varvara, who is suspicious, that Nikolay and Marya Lebyadkin are not married.

Using his personal charm and representing himself as a mysterious revolutionary agent returned from exile, Pyotr begins to dominate Stepan's liberal friends and becomes, for his own scheming purposes, the protégé of Yulia, the governor's wife. Nikolay at first follows Pyotr in his political activities but then turns against the revolutionary movement and warns Shatov that Pyotr's group is plotting to kill Shatov because of information he possesses. Nikolay confesses to Shatov that on a bet he had married Marya Lebyadkin in St. Petersburg.

As a result of a duel between Nikolay and a local aristocrat who hates him, a duel in which Nikolay emerges victorious without killing his opponent, Nikolay becomes a local hero. He continues to be intimate with Dasha, and Lizaveta has meanwhile announced her engagement to another man. Pyotr sows seeds of dissension among all classes in the town. He discloses von Lembke's possession of a collection of radical manifestos; he causes a break between Stepan and Varvara; and he secretly incites the working people to rebel against their masters.

Yulia leads the leaders of the town in preparations for a grand fete. Pyotr, seeing in the fete the opportunity to bring chaos into the orderly community, causes friction between von Lembke, who is an inept governor, and Yulia, who actually governs the province through her salon. At a meeting of the revolutionary group, despair and confusion prevail until Pyotr welds it together with mysterious talk of orders from higher revolutionary leaders. He talks of many other such groups engaged in similar activities. Shatov, who attends the meeting, denounces Pyotr as a spy and a scoundrel and walks out. Pyotr discloses to Nikolay his nihilistic beliefs and proposes that Nikolay be brought forward as the Pretender after the revolution is accomplished.

Blum, von Lembke's secretary, raids Stepan's quarters and confiscates all of Stepan's private papers, among them some political manifestos. Stepan goes to the governor to demand his rights under the law and witnesses in front of the governor's mansion how dissident workers who had been quietly demonstrating for redress of their grievances are lashed into turmoil. Von Lembke appeases Stepan by saying that the raid on his room is a mistake.

The fete is doomed from the start. Many agitators without tickets are admitted. Liputin reads a comic and seditious poem. Karmazinov, a great novelist, makes a fool of himself by recalling the follies of his youth. Stepan insults the agitators by championing the higher culture. When an unidentified agitator rises to speak, the afternoon session becomes a bedlam, so that it is doubtful whether the ball will be able to take place that night. Abetted by Pyotr, Nikolay and Lizaveta elope in the afternoon to the country house of Varvara.

The ball is not canceled, but not many of the landowners of the town or countryside appear. Drunkenness and brawling soon reduce the ball to a rout, and the evening comes to a sorry end when fire is discovered raging through some houses along the river. Captain Lebyadkin, Marya, and their servant are discovered murdered in their house, which remained unburned in the path of the fire. When Pyotr informs Nikolay of the murders, Nikolay confesses that he had known of the possibility that violence would take place but that he had done nothing to prevent it. Horrified, Lizaveta leaves to see the murdered pair; she is beaten to death by the enraged townspeople because of her connections with Nikolay. Nikolay leaves town quickly and quietly.

When the revolutionary group meets again, they all mistrust one another. Pyotr explains to them that Fedka, a former convict, had murdered the Lebyadkins for robbery, but he fails to mention that Nikolay had all but paid Fedka to commit the crime. He warns the group against Shatov and says that a fanatic named Alexei Kirillov had agreed to cover up

the proposed murder of Shatov. Fedka denounces Pyotr as an atheistic scoundrel; Fedka is later found dead on a road outside the town.

Marie, Shatov's wife, returns to the town. The couple had been separated for three years; Marie is ill and pregnant. When she begins her labor, Shatov procures Virginsky's wife as midwife. The couple is reconciled after Marie gives birth to a baby boy, for the child serves to make Shatov happy once more. He leaves his wife and baby alone to keep an appointment with the revolutionary group made for the purpose of separating himself from the plotters. Pyotr attacks then shoots and kills him, then weights his body with stones and throws it into a pond. After the murder, Pyotr goes to Kirillov to get his promised confession for the murder of Shatov. Kirillov, who is Shatov's neighbor and who had seen Shatov's happiness at the return of his wife, at first refuses to sign, but Pyotr finally prevails on him to put his name to the false confession. Then, morally bound to end his life, Kirillov shoots himself. Pyotr leaves the province.

Stepan, meanwhile, leaves town to seek a new life. He wanders for a time among peasants and at last becomes dangerously ill. Varvara meets up with him, and the two friends are reconciled before the old scholar dies. Varvara disowns her son. Marie and the baby die of exposure and neglect after Shatov fails to return home. One of the radical group breaks down and confesses to the violence that had been committed in the town at the instigation of Pyotr. Liputin escapes to St. Petersburg, where he is apprehended in a drunken stupor in a brothel.

Nikolay writes to Dasha, the servant, suggesting that the two of them go to Switzerland and begin a new life. Before Dasha could pack her things, however, Nikolay returns home secretly and hangs himself in his room.

Critical Evaluation:

Fyodor Dostoevski was nearly fifty years old when the final version of *The Possessed* appeared. Because of his poverty, he had been forced to write the book first in serial form for a Moscow literary review. Many readers thought the novel raged so wildly against liberalism and atheistic socialism that they concluded the once progressive author must have become a reactionary. Dostoevski himself lent credibility to this notion by his public statements. In a famous letter to Alexander III, Dostoevski characterized *The Possessed* as a historical study of the perverse radicalism that results when the intelligentsia detaches itself from the Russian people. In another letter, he proclaimed, "He who loses his people and his nationality loses his faith in his country and in God. This is the theme of my novel."

Given the nature of Dostoevski's personal history, a movement toward conservatism would not have been illogical. An aristocrat by birth, Dostoevski had involved himself deeply in the Petrashevski Circle, a St. Petersburg discussion group interested in utopian socialism. Part of this group formed a clandestine revolutionary cadre, and Dostoevski was arrested for his participation in the conspiracy. There followed a mock execution, four years of imprisonment, and another four years of enforced service as a private in the Siberian army. Although he was freed in 1858, Dostoevski remained under surveillance and his right to publish was always in jeopardy. He thus had every inducement to prove to government censors his fidelity to the regime and its principles.

The Possessed is not a reactionary novel, nor does Dostoevski in the book defend the institutions of monarchy, aristocracy, or censorship. He upholds Russian orthodoxy in a way that suggests a theocratic challenge to the status quo. His exaltation of the peasantry constitutes no defense of capitalism or imperialism. While appearing to embrace Russian nationalism, he presents an image of small-town culture that is anything but approving. His portrait of the ruling class is as devastating as any essay on the subject by Karl Marx or Friedrich Engels.

Dostoevski's critique of radical political ideas proceeds from a basis other than that of extremist conservatism. The key to that basis is partially revealed in Shatov's statement that half-truth is uniquely despotic. *The Possessed* is at once a criticism of a variety of political and philosophical half-truths and a searching toward a principle of wholeness, a truth that has the capacity to reunite and compose the fragmented human psyche, the divided social and political order, and the shattered relationship with God. Dostoevski does not describe that truth, believing the truth too mysterious and grand to be expressed in human language. Rather, he points to it by showing the defects and incompleteness in positions that pretend to be the truth.

It is through the enigmatic character of Nikolay Stavrogin that Dostoevski most fully carries out his quest for wholeness, for Nikolay has embraced and discarded all the philosophies that Dostoevski deems inadequate. As a result, Nikolay is the embodiment of pure negativity and pure emptiness. He is also pure evil, more evil still than Pyotr, who at least has his absolute devotion to Nikolay as the ruling principle in his life. From Stepan Verhovensky, Nikolay learns skepticism and the tolerant principles of "higher liberalism." In St. Petersburg, he advances to utopian socialism and a more passionate faith in the possibility of salvation through science. The elitism and shallow rationalism of this faith cause

Nikolay to take up messianic Russian populism. After he is led beyond this stage to an investigation of orthodox theology, he finds himself unable to commit to the Christian faith and perpetrates the hideous crime he later confesses to Father Tihon.

At each step in his development, Nikolay trains disciples who propagate his teachings and carry them to their logical extremes. Pyotr belongs partly to Nikolay's socialist period, while Shatov embraces the populist creed and Alexei Kirillov elaborates the themes of the theological phase. In Pyotr, socialist criticism of traditional society has produced a monomaniacal fascination with the revolutionary destruction and violence by which a new order is to emerge. Modeling this character after the infamous Russian terrorist Sergey Nechayev, Dostoevski suggests that Pyotr is the natural outcome of socialism's faith in the power of reason to establish absolute values. Shigolov's rational defense of a socialist tyranny shows how thoroughly rational structures rely on nonrational premises. For Pyotr, the absence of rational certainties means that all behavior is permissible and all social orders are equally valid. He chooses to fight for a society based on the hunger of human beings for submission, their fear of death, their longing for a messiah. Like Niccolò Machiavelli, Pyotr decides that only by founding society on the most wretched aspects of human nature can anything really lasting and dependable be built. As his messiah, Pyotr has chosen Nikolay, whose awe-inspiring and arbitrary will could be the source of order in a new society.

Kirillov elevates Pyotr Verhovensky's fascination with strength of will into a theological principle. Kirillov is not content with the limited transcendence of the determinism of nature. He aspires to the total freedom of God. Paradoxically, this freedom can be achieved only through suicide, that act that overcomes the natural fear of death by which God keeps human beings in thrall. Not until all people are prepared at every moment to commit suicide can humanity take full responsibility for its own destiny. The great drawback in Kirillov's view is that it causes him to suppress his feelings of love and relatedness to his fellow human beings. Shatov's nationalistic theology is an attempt to do justice to these feelings. Rebelling against Kirillov's isolated quest for godhood, Shatov wishes to achieve the same goal by submerging himself in the life of a "God-bearing people." Yet Shatov's creed remains abstract and sentimental until Marie returns and provides him with a real person to love.

The birth of Marie's child, together with Stepan's "discovery" of the Russian people, are the symbols by which Dostoevski reveals his own answer to Nikolay. The child is for Shatov an unimaginable act of grace. Significantly,

Kirillov experiences a sudden serenity and a confirmation of his mystical insight that "everything is good." For Dostoevski, the source of this grace is God, who brings exquisite order to the most corrupted human situations. Shatov's rapturous love stands in utter contradiction to Nikolay's empty indifference. Because the child's real father is Nikolay, Shatov's love is all the more wondrous. Nikolay's final inability to respond to Lizaveta's love is the logical result of his long struggle to free himself of the dependency on his family, his people, and his church. He boasts that he does not need anyone; from that claim comes spiritual and moral death. All that Nikolay has touched, including Shatov, is dead in the end.

The magnificence of Dostoevski's artistry is nowhere more apparent than in the conclusion to *The Possessed*, for he does not embody his great theme—human wholeness through human dependence—in a titanic character like Nikolay or Kirillov but in the all-too-human Stepan. This quixotic buffoon, who is both laughable and pitiable, ultimately attains the dignity he seeks. He himself is surprised by it all, for it comes in a way he least expected it: through an encounter with his people, reunion with Varvara, and the administration of the sacrament.

"Critical Evaluation" by Leslie E. Gerber

Further Reading

Holquist, Michael. *Dostoevsky and the Novel*. Princeton, N.J.: Princeton University Press, 1977. An examination of Dostoevski's works as studies in the problem of self-identification. Holquist's discussion of *The Possessed* highlights Nikolay Stavrogin's struggle to resist group pressures and to assert himself as an individual.

Ivanov, Viacheslav. *Freedom and the Tragic Life: A Study in Dostoevsky*. New York: Noonday Press, 1971. An investigation into the religious and mythical foundations of Dostoevski's work. Ivanov argues that *The Possessed* depicts in symbolic forms the relationship between the powers of evil and the daring human spirit.

Leatherbarrow, W. J., ed. *The Cambridge Companion to Dostoevskii*. New York: Cambridge University Press, 2006. Collection of essays that examine the author's life and works, discussing his relationship to Russian folk heritage, money, the intelligentsia, psychology, religion, the family, and science, among other topics. Includes a chronology and a bibliography.

_____. *Dostoevsky's "The Devils": A Critical Companion*. Evanston, Ill.: Northwestern University Press, 1999.

Essays place *The Possessed* (referred to here as *The Devils*) within the context of Dostoevski's life and work and contemporary Russian thought and politics; others discuss the book's narrator, narrative techniques, and characters. Also contains excerpts of Dostoevski's correspondence regarding the novel.

Miller, Robin Feuer. *Dostoevsky's Unfinished Journey*. New Haven, Conn.: Yale University Press, 2007. Miller examines Dostoevski's works from numerous perspectives, analyzing the themes of conversion and healing in his fiction and questioning his literary influence. *The Possessed* is examined in chapter 5.

Mochul'skii, Konstantin. *Dostoevsky: His Life and Work*. Translated by Michael A. Minihan. Princeton, N.J.: Princeton University Press, 1967. A detailed analytical discussion of the evolution of Dostoevski's art. Examines the ways in which *The Possessed* emerged from two different preliminary projects and describes the central ideological and spiritual themes of the work.

Peace, Richard. *Dostoyevsky: An Examination of the Major Novels*. New York: Cambridge University Press, 1971. Includes two chapters on *The Possessed*, in which Peace discusses the historical background for the novel and analyzes the significant interrelationships among the main characters. Concludes that the secondary figures serve to highlight the tragic situation of the central protagonist.

Scanlan, James P. *Dostoevsky the Thinker: A Philosophical Study*. Ithaca, N.Y.: Cornell University Press, 2002. Analyzes Dostoevski's novels, essays, letters, and notebooks to provide a comprehensive account of his philosophy, examining the weaknesses as well as the strengths of Dostoevski's ideas. Concludes that Dostoevski's thought was shaped by anthropocentrism—a struggle to define the very essence of humanity.

Straus, Nina Pelikan. *Dostoevsky and the Woman Question: Rereadings at the End of a Century*. New York: St. Martin's Press, 1994. Straus argues that Dostoevski's compulsion to depict men's cruelties to women is an important part of his vision and his metaphysics. She maintains that Dostoevski attacks masculine notions of autonomy and that his works evolve toward "the death of the patriarchy." Chapter 5 examines *The Possessed*.

Williams, Rowan. *Dostoevsky: Language, Faith, and Fiction*. Waco, Tex.: Baylor University Press, 2008. Examines the speech, fiction, metaphor, and iconography in four novels, including *The Possessed*. Williams maintains that the style and goals of Dostoevski's fiction are inseparable from his religious commitments.

Possession

Author: A. S. Byatt (Antonia Susan Drabble, 1936-   )
First published: 1990
Type of work: Novel
Type of plot: Historical realism
Time of plot: September, 1986, to October, 1987
Locale: England and France

Principal characters:
RANDOLPH HENRY ASH, an English Victorian poet
CHRISTABEL LA MOTTE, an English Victorian poet
ROLAND MICHELL, a research assistant and Ash scholar
JAMES BLACKADDER, an Ash scholar
ELLEN BEST ASH, Randolph's wife
MAUD BAILEY, a scholar and a relative of La Motte
LEONORA STERN, an American La Motte scholar and a friend of Maud
BLANCHE GLOVER, La Motte's lover
MORTIMER CROPPER, an American Ash scholar
VAL, Roland's girlfriend
FERGUS WOLFF, a colleague of Maud and Roland

The Story:

In September of 1986, twenty-nine-year-old Roland Michell is sitting in the basement of the London Library examining a book owned by Victorian poet Randolph Henry Ash. Roland's job is to provide research material on Ash for his adviser, Dr. James Blackadder, but his dissertation is on Ash's poems and he is hopeful of finding out something new about Ash. Roland is a part-time research assistant funded by Blackadder's Ash Factory, but is unhappy with his meager earnings and his unsatisfying personal life. Opening the book of poems, Roland sees two letters fall out, revealing the first clues in a mystery that will change Roland's life.

Roland, intimately familiar with all the known details of Ash's life, is immediately drawn to the letters, which are addressed to an unknown woman. The subject matter of the letters is completely foreign to Roland, who sees not only that they have never been published but also, more important, that they have never even been seen by anyone other than Ash. The letters present the literary opportunity of a lifetime.

Ash had written love poetry, and he often wrote about romantic love. A woman named Embla was Ash's muse and the inspiration for much of his work. Ash scholars have debated fiercely who Embla really was. The conventional nature of Ash's life seems to suggest that Embla was a figment of his imagination; the only woman in Ash's life was his wife, Ellen, but the fierce love described in Ash's poetry did not fit their tepid marital devotion. For Roland, the letters suggest that Embla was a real woman. He decides, not without some twinges of guilt, to take the letters and research their meaning himself.

Roland returns home to the dingy basement apartment that he shares with his girlfriend, Val, and wonders if he will ever escape from its fetid reek of failure and cat urine. Although Roland and Val had fallen in love over romantic poems and heady critical debates, the harsh reality of academic life—the A-Levels and Firsts—exposed a troubling insecurity in Val. While Roland does well in his studies, Val, paradoxically, falters. The final blow comes when she fails her final exams. She takes a job as a secretary, but her financial support of Roland comes with a price: He must not only tolerate her disappointment with her life but also her ridicule of his inability to do better. He tells her now about the letters, but Val is completely disinterested in Roland's find.

Initial research on the setting described in Ash's letters leads Roland to tentatively identify Embla as Christabel La Motte, a poet and a contemporary of Ash. Roland is unfamiliar with La Motte's life or works, but he happens to run into a colleague, Fergus Wolff, who advises him to consult with Dr. Maud Bailey. Maud is not only a distant relation of La Motte but also an expert on her poetry. Maud also is well-known in feminist circles and is the keeper of the archive of La Motte's manuscripts at Lincoln University.

Maud turns out to be beautiful, but she is cold and distant with Roland. He discovers that she is, in fact, La Motte's great-great-great niece and that Lincoln University's archive had originally belonged to her great-great-grandmother Maia Thomasina "May" Bailey. Maud reads Roland's letters and wonders also how they fit into the lives of the conventional Ash and the whimsical La Motte. Maud had assumed that La Motte was lesbian, not only because she had never married but also because she had been known to have had a lesbian relationship with Blanche Glover, an artist. Maud suggests that a trip to her family home in Lincolnshire might prove to be a source of new information about Ash and La Motte.

Maud and Roland keep the purpose of their travels secret, not only because of the legal ramifications of Roland's initial theft but also because both have become aware of the movements of a well-funded American professor, Dr. Mortimer Cropper, who has offered a great deal of money for the purchase of Ash manuscripts and memorabilia. He also would be more than happy to steal the academic fruits of Roland's and Maud's work.

The trip to the Bailey home reveals a hidden store of Ash's letters to La Motte, and of letters that La Motte had sent to Ash. The intimacy Roland and Maud had seen only in brief references had been, in actuality, a full-fledged love affair. While Ash's love for La Motte had inspired him to write most of his greatest poems, La Motte's passion for Ash had taken away the freedom she previously enjoyed in her life. She had broken up with Ash and unexpectedly left England. Her departure drove her other lover, Blanche, to suicide.

Deeply inspired by the romance of Ash and La Motte, Roland and Maud begin to realize their feelings for each other. Neither has ever really felt as fully accepted and valued by their respective lovers as they now do with each other. It seems only natural, then, that together they seek to know the whole story of Ash and La Motte.

Dr. Leonora Stern, another La Motte scholar, provides some of the answers Roland and Maud seek; Leonora had received a letter from a young French La Motte scholar who had found a journal written by a young cousin of La Motte. When Roland and Maud track down the journal, they discover that La Motte had, in fact, been pregnant and had gone to Brittany to give birth to her illegitimate child. What remains a mystery, however, is what La Motte did with the child. Not knowing where else to look, Roland and Maud inspect Ellen Ash's journal, which reveals that she kept La Motte from seeing Ash on his deathbed. She also wrote that when Ash had died, she had placed certain letters and artifacts from La Motte in his grave to prevent them from becoming public knowledge.

The scholars' make a final journey to Ash's grave, during a fierce rainstorm, to discover the truth: Maud's great-great-grandmother May was not La Motte's niece, but her daughter by Ash. Ellen Ash's fear of sexual intercourse kept her from consummating her marriage with Ash, and Ash could not consequently resist the lure of passion offered by the sensual La Motte. Maud is the descendent of both poets and, being legally the owner of both Ash and La Motte's personal effects, is able to foil Cropper's schemes and guarantee Roland that he, as well as any future scholar, will be able to do ground-breaking critical research on Ash and La Motte. Roland will never again have to live a life defined by failure.

Critical Evaluation:

Possession is a quirky novel that splices scenes of the slow-paced love affair of two academic researchers with letters and poems highlighting a much more consuming passion between two Victorian poets. A. S. Byatt has said that she was initially inspired to write *Possession* by two different impulses.

The first impulse occurred after Byatt had a chance conversation with a Samuel Taylor Coleridge scholar in the basement of the British Museum. Byatt, impressed with the depth of the woman's knowledge, had wondered if Coleridge himself had "possessed" the woman and compelled her to devote so much of her life to him. The second impulse happened much later, when Byatt was teaching a course on Robert Browning at University College in London. The relationship between Browning and Elizabeth Barrett (later Barrett Browning) was fascinating to her, and she wished she could write an account of the affair that would make it seem as immediate as a modern-day romance. Concerns about the legal aspects of addressing the lives of the Brownings discouraged her briefly, but Byatt could not suppress her desire to write a truly literary romance entirely.

Each of Byatt's fictional characters is a pastiche of many different Victorian poets; Randolph Henry Ash reminds the reader of poets William Wordsworth, Coleridge, and John Keats. His wife, Ellen Best Ash, is a dutiful domestic like Dorothy Wordsworth and poet Emily Dickinson. His lover, Christabel La Motte, reminds one of writers Christina Rossetti and Elizabeth Barrett Browning.

Thematically, the novel analyzes the many ways in which possession (desire) can affect the behavior of otherwise rational men and women. One of the more obvious definitions of unhealthy possession, the concept of obsessively seeking ownership of something, appears early in the novel and becomes a secondary plot that adds urgency to the characters' actions. The American Ash scholar, Mortimer Cropper, wants to literally possess everything related to the life of his literary hero, Ash. A generous endowment by his university provides the excuse he needs to not only purchase but also steal historical artifacts from unwary owners. Roland Michell and Maud Bailey are painfully aware throughout their time together that their joint investigations must be kept secret lest Cropper discover the documents' owners and use his considerable wealth to purchase their findings for himself.

The word "possession" has other meanings for Byatt. She examines the obsessive qualities inherent in sexual relationships—the possession of a beloved by a pursuing lover. Fergus Wolff and Leonora Stern provide standard representations of heterosexual and homosexual sexual voracity. However, beyond the idea of sexual possession of the living is Byatt's idea that one can become obsessed and seek, through reading private letters, poems, and diaries, to vicariously possess even someone who is long dead. James Blackadder, whose sexuality has been sublimated into his all-encompassing career, has substituted research for an actual relationship. Blackadder has been working on his edition of the complete works of Ash since 1951, wanting to possess some basic, inherent truth in his study of Ash's life and reduce complex problems into predictable facts.

Possession also suggests that a man and a woman can become so emotionally caught up in the development of another couple's love affair that they themselves fall in love as if possessed by the spirits of the lovers. Roland and Maud share a common disgust with sex and sexuality at the beginning of *Possession*. Their attachment is, for the most part, based on an unspoken agreement to enjoy each other solely on intellectual and spiritual grounds. Although they are both obsessed with the passion they see in the letters and poems of Ash and La Motte, vicariously living the passionate love affair, they can distance themselves from any uncomfortable feelings by objectifying their pursuit; it is "just" research. On the other hand, it is directly through Roland's and Maud's research that they, themselves, fall in love and allow themselves to possess one another.

Julia M. Meyers

Further Reading

Alfer, Alexa, and Michael J. Noble, eds. *Essays on the Fiction of A. S. Byatt*. Westport, Conn.: Greenwood Press, 2001. For the advanced student of Byatt. This volume includes at least one essay on each of her major works (two on *Possession*). Includes an index and a select bibliography.

Burgess, Catherine. *A. S. Byatt's "Possession": A Reader's Guide*. New York: Continuum, 2002. A clear and comprehensive introduction to the novel, including sections on Byatt, background reading, and critical commentary.

Fountain, J. Stephen. "Ashes to Ashes: Kristeva's Jouissance, Altizer's Apocalypse, Byatt's *Possession*, and 'The Dream of the Rood.'" *Literature and Theology* 8, no. 2 (1994): 193-208. Fountain analyzes metaphors of death, sexual release, and rebirth in the selected works. Examines Byatt's skillful reworking of classical myth as it might have been interpreted and used by Victorian sensibilities.

Giobbi, Giuliana. "Sisters Beware of Sisters: Sisterhood as a Literary Motif in Jane Austen, A. S. Byatt, and I. Bossi Fedrigotti." *Journal of European Studies* 22 (September, 1992): 32-41. Giobbi presents a particularly interesting analysis of *Possession*'s apparent distrust of feminine love.

Holmes, Frederick M. "The Historical Imagination and the Victorian Past: A. S. Byatt's *Possession*." *English Studies in Canada* 20, no. 3 (1994): 319-334. Questions Byatt's characterization of Victorian poets and analyzes to what extent historical truth must be changed to satisfy the requirements of modern fiction.

Hotho Jackson, Sabine. "Literary History in Literature: An Aspect of the Contemporary Novel." *Moderna Sprak* 86, no. 2 (1992): 113-119. Not many critical works focus on a novel's attempt to describe the academic pursuit of knowledge. This essay examines how Byatt portrays the creation of a critical text.

Kelly, Kathleen Coyne. *A. S. Byatt*. New York: Twayne, 1996. Part of a well-established series of introductions to literary figures, this volume includes a chronology, an annotated bibliography, a biographical sketch, and a commentary on Byatt's individual works.

Reynolds, Margaret, and Jonathan Noakes. *A. S. Byatt: The Essential Guide*. New York: Random House, 2004. Provides a close reading of Byatt's novels, including *Possession*; a well-developed interview with Byatt; and a thorough discussion of her themes and techniques.

Webb, Caroline. "History Through Metaphor: Woolf's *Orlando* and Byatt's *Possession: A Romance*." In *Virginia Woolf: Emerging Perspectives*, edited by Mark Hussey and Vara Neverow. New York: Pace University Press, 1994. A fascinating comparison of Woolf's and Byatt's use of metaphor as a way to explain complex philosophical truths. Argues that the best way to understand the philosophy that shapes a generation of thinkers is to examine their use of language.

The Postman Always Rings Twice

Author: James M. Cain (1892-1977)
First published: 1934
Type of work: Novel
Type of plot: Psychological realism
Time of plot: 1933
Locale: Southern California

Principal characters:
FRANK CHAMBERS, a young drifter
CORA PAPADAKIS, the young wife of a restaurant-tavern owner
NICK PAPADAKIS, Cora's husband, and the proprietor of the Twin Oaks Tavern
KATZ, Frank's lawyer

The Story:

For years, Frank Chambers has been in trouble with the law, drifting back and forth through California and always looking for a con or a dollar. When he comes to Nick Papadakis's restaurant, he sees the same old dreams invested in a tiny hash house just like all the restaurants down the road. The one difference is that this hash house contains Cora, a svelte, beautiful, sensuous woman who had married her Greek husband to get out of an even worse life as a waitress in Los Angeles. She had won a beauty contest in the Midwest and taken a bus to California. Finding her prospects to be nonexistent, she married a man who at least had the advantage of owning property.

The attraction between Cora and Frank is almost instantaneous, and before Frank is there a week, the two sleep together. Cora is the one who first proposes getting rid of her husband so she and Frank can run away. Frank plans to have Cora bludgeon her husband while he is in the bath. Immediately afterward, Frank is to climb a ladder into the bathroom and remove the body. From the beginning things go wrong. A passing motorcycle officer stops to chat with Frank and probably sees the ladder. Then, just when Cora hits her husband, all the lights in the restaurant go out, which is noticed by the officer as he leaves. Frank rushes in to find Cora standing in the bathroom and her husband splashing around in the water. Quickly, they patch him up and call an ambulance. They have no idea what happened to the lights. Eventually, Nick is taken to a hospital, where Frank, Cora, and several police officers watch him, no one sure what he will say. When he wakes up, he says something about slipping in the shower. The motorcycle officer is suspicious and accompanies Frank and Cora back to the restaurant to see what had happened to the fuse box. They find a dead cat there, obviously electrocuted.

Frank and Cora enjoy each other's company while Nick is in the hospital, but when he returns one week later he tells Cora that he wants a son. She is appalled by the prospect and turns to Frank again. She tries to tempt him by promising that they can take over the restaurant once her husband is dead, but Frank is impatient to be on the road.

The second attempt at killing Nick is complex. Nick acquires tickets to a Santa Barbara street fair, to which he invites Frank and Cora. They stay in a hotel for the weekend and then head back. Cora drives because her husband is drunk and Frank is pretending to be drunk. On the way to Ventura, south of Santa Barbara, Nick passes out. Cora stops the car and she and Frank get out. Frank gets back into the car and sends it over an embankment. He tries to get out in time but is not successful. The car crashes, killing Nick and leading to a broken leg for Frank.

Frank and Cora are both charged with murder. A jail guard furnishes Frank with the name of a good lawyer—named Katz—after the police persuade Frank to sign a document saying that Cora had killed Nick and had been planning to kill him as well. This document turns them against each other, but Katz devises a scenario in which Cora, alone, will be considered guilty of the murder. Katz had read the details of a life-and-accident policy that Nick had taken out right after his "accident" in the bathtub. Because Frank had been a "guest" in the car, Katz argues that he has the right to collect the full ten thousand dollars of the policy. Katz figures that the jury would be sympathetic toward Cora and that the manslaughter with which she is charged would be treated as a technicality. As a result, Frank is acquitted and Cora is given six months in jail, with three months suspended. Katz charges them five thousand dollars for his services.

Cora goes briefly to jail, and Frank goes to Mexico, where he meets another woman. Cora learns of this affair, and after she is released from jail, she presents Frank with proof of his infidelity. Cora, however, wants to improve the restaurant, with Frank, and make it a success. Frank wants nothing to do with it.

In an attempt at reconciliation (by this time Frank knows that Cora is pregnant), Frank and Cora go to the beach. Cora has sudden cramping, so Frank carries her to the car. On the way to the hospital, Frank tries to pass a truck and collides with an abutment. Turned around in his seat, Frank can hear the dripping of Cora's blood on the hood of the car. She had been thrown through the windshield and was killed instantly.

A jury quickly convicts Frank of murder for the purpose of collecting on Cora's life insurance and the restaurant and property. Nothing Katz could say this time makes any difference. Frank writes the story from death row.

"The Story" by John Jacob

Critical Evaluation:

Three related genres that developed in the United States during the 1930's were the hard-boiled private detective novel, which departed from the genteel English novel of detection; the proletarian novel, which derived from European naturalism and American realism; and the tough-guy novel, which derived from both of those strands. Dashiell Hammett's *The Maltese Falcon* (1929) and Raymond Chandler's *The Big Sleep* (1939) are perhaps the best-known examples of the private detective novel. B. Traven's *The Death Ship* (1934) is a good example of the proletarian novel, and Horace McCoy's *They Shoot Horses, Don't They?* (1935) belongs to the minor classics of tough-guy novels. These and novels like them expressed the mood of American society during the Depression, and they influenced motion pictures, affected the tone and attitude of more serious writers, and inspired some European novelists during the 1940's. The quintessence of these genres is represented by James M. Cain's *The Postman Always Rings Twice*.

Although Frank Chambers, the twenty-four-year-old narrator of Cain's novel, belongs to that legion of unemployed who became tramps of the road, hoboes of the rails, and migrant workers, Cain is not deliberately interested in depicting the social ills of his time; if there is an attack on conditions that produced a man like Frank, it is only implicit. Frank is an easygoing fellow, remarkably free of bitterness, even when given cause; although he commits murder and pistol whips a blackmailer, he is not willfully vicious. A spontaneous creature of action whose psychological nature readily accommodates ambivalent attitudes, he can be fond of Nick Papadakis and weep at his funeral after having seduced Cora and twice attempted to kill Nick.

Although this novel is concerned, as are many of Cain's novels, with murder and other forms of violence, it cannot be classified as a detective tale. Cain, like the readers he has in mind, is fascinated by the intricacies of civil and insurance law, but he is primarily interested in presenting an inside view of the criminal act. However, Frank is no gangster and Cora no moll; they are not far removed in status or aspiration from the average person who reads the book.

Frank and Cora lie down in the great American dreamed of the 1920's, only to wake up in the 1930's in a living nightmare. Only a lurid decade could have produced such a lurid relationship and such a lurid tale. When they meet at Nick's Twin Oaks Tavern on a highway outside Los Angeles, Frank has just been thrown off a truck, having sneaked into the back for a ride up the coast from Tijuana, and Cora is washing dishes in the restaurant. To demonstrate the deep passion of their encounter, Cain has them meet on page 5, make love on page 15, and decide to murder the obese, middle-aged Greek on page 23. Sharing the dream of getting drunk and making love without hiding, they go on what Cain calls "the Love-Rack." He regards the concept of "the wish that comes true" as a terrifying thing. This terror becomes palpable as soon as Frank and Cora believe they have gotten away with murder and have acquired money, property, and freedom.

In the background, however, each has another dream, which mocks the shared realization of the immediate wish. Cora came to Hollywood from a small town in Iowa bemused by the dream many girls and young women of the 1930's cherished: to become a film star. She failed, and Nick rescued her from a hash house. Basically, her values are middle-class, and above all she wants respectability, even if murder is the prerequisite. An anachronism in the age of technology, though he has a certain skill as a garage mechanic, Frank desires to be always on the move, compelled by something of the spirit of the open road that Walt Whitman celebrated. For a moment, but only for a moment, he shares this romantic, idyllic vision with Cora. After the failure of their first attempt to murder Nick, they set out together for a life of wandering. In the criminal affair of these lovers, these deliberate outsiders, two central dreams of the American experience—unrestrained mobility and respectable sedentariness—and two views of the American landscape—the open road and the mortgaged house—collide. As the dreams finally betray them, they begin to turn on each other, for basically what Frank wants is Cora, the sexual dynamo, and what Cora wants is an instrument to be used to gain her ends—money and respectability.

Although the novel's larger thematic dimensions exist in the background, as a kind of fable of the American experience, giving it a lasting value in literature, Cain is more immediately concerned with the lovers and with the action that results from their wish. This action keeps in motion certain elements that almost guarantee the reader's interest: illicit love; murder; the smell of tainted money; sexual violence that verges on the abnormal; and the strong characterizations of such men as district attorney Sackett, eccentric lawyer Katz, and Madge Allen, who takes Frank to South America to capture jaguars.

What fascinates serious readers of literature is Cain's technique for manipulating reader response. Not only does he almost automatically achieve certain thematic ironies inherent in his raw material, but the ironies of action are stunningly executed. Frank cons Nick out of a free meal, for example, but the con backfires when Nick cons Frank into staying on to operate the service station, a situation that eventually leaves three people dead.

Cain's structural techniques are impressive. Each development, each scene, is controlled, and inherent in each episode is the inevitability of the next. Everything is kept strictly to the essentials; the characters exist only for the immediate action; there is almost no exposition as such. Cain is the acknowledged master of pace. Violence and sexual passion are thrust forward at a rate that is itself part of the reader's vicarious experience. Contributing to this sense of pace is the swift rhythm of the dialogue, which also manages to keep certain undercurrents flowing. Frank's character justifies the economy of style, the nerve-end adherence to the spine of the action. Albert Camus modeled the style of *L'Étranger* (1942; *The Stranger*, 1946) on Cain's novel and cut his character Meursault to the pattern of Frank.

Cain has written what has been called a pure novel, for his deliberate intentions go no further than the immediate experience, brief as a motion picture is, as unified in its impression as a poem usually is. Though Frank writes his story on the eve of his execution, Cain does not even suggest the simplest moral, that crime does not pay. An intense experience, which a man tells in such a way as to make it, briefly, the reader's experience, it is its own reason for being.

Further Reading

Ahnebrink, Lars. *Beginnings of Naturalism in American Fiction*. New York: Russell & Russell, 1961. A useful introductory overview of Cain and his works that includes criticism of *The Postman Always Rings Twice*.

Cain, James M. *The Complete Novels*. New York: Wings Books, 1994. Contains critical commentary and a comparison of *The Postman Always Rings Twice* with Cain's other novels.

Hoopes, Roy. *Cain*. New York: Holt, Rinehart and Winston, 1982. This comprehensive biography is divided into four chronological parts, covering different periods in Cain's life. Includes an afterword on Cain as a journalist. Supplemented by extensive source notes, a list of Cain's publications, a filmography, and an index.

Madden, David. *Cain's Craft*. Metuchen, N.J.: Scarecrow Press, 1985. One of Cain's earliest academic champions explores the author's literary techniques. Compares some of Cain's works to novels by other writers, and addresses the ways in which Cain's books have been adapted to the screen.

Marling, William. *The American Roman Noir: Hammett, Cain, and Chandler*. Athens: University of Georgia Press, 1995. Links the hard-boiled detective writing of Cain, Dashiell Hammett, and Raymond Chandler to contemporary economic and technological changes. Marling considers these writers as pioneers of an aesthetic for the postindustrial age. Includes a fourteen-page analysis of *The Postman Always Rings Twice*.

Nyman, Jopi. *Hard-Boiled Fiction and Dark Romanticism*. New York: Peter Lang, 1998. Examines the fiction of Cain, Dashiell Hammett, Ernest Hemingway, and Horace McCoy. Nyman maintains that the romanticism and pathos in these authors' works reflects their nostalgia for a lost world of individualism and true adulthood.

Oates, Joyce Carol. "Man Under Sentence of Death: The Novels of James M. Cain." In *Tough Guy Writers of the Thirties*, edited by David Madden. Carbondale: Southern Illinois University Press, 1968. A brief but wide-ranging essay by a noted American novelist that approaches Cain's novels as significant for the light they throw on his relationship with the American audience of the 1930's and 1940's.

Shaw, Patrick W. *The Modern American Novel of Violence*. Troy, N.Y.: Whitson, 2000. Shaw's analysis of violence in American novels includes an examination of *The Postman Always Rings Twice*. Shaw concludes that in writing what he calls a sadistic novel, Cain created a "sardonic, unencumbered narrative style that proved more influential than the story it conveyed."

Wilson, Edmund. "The Boys in the Back Room." In *Classics and Commercials*. New York: Farrar, Straus and Giroux, 1950. Personal essay by an astute social and cultural commentator groups Cain with John Steinbeck, John O'Hara, William Saroyan, and others in the 1930's and 1940's who were influenced by Ernest Hemingway. Wilson considers Cain to be the best of these writers.

The Pot of Gold

Author: Plautus (c. 254-184 B.C.E.)
First produced: Aulularia, 200-191 B.C.E. (English
 translation, 1767)
Type of work: Drama
Type of plot: Comedy
Time of plot: Second century B.C.E.
Locale: Athens

Principal characters:
EUCLIO, a miser
PHAEDRIA, his daughter
MEGADORUS, Euclio's rich neighbor, who wishes to marry
 Phaedria
EUNOMIA, Megadorus's sister
LYCONIDES, Eunomia's son, in love with Phaedria
STAPHYLA, a slave belonging to Euclio

The Story:

The grandfather of Euclio, an Athenian miser, entrusted a pot of gold to his household deity after burying the pot in the hearth. The god, angered in turn at Euclio's grandfather, his father, and Euclio himself, has kept the secret of the treasure from all, until finally the daughter of Euclio, Phaedria, has endeared herself to the god. In an effort to help the young woman, the deity shows Euclio where the gold is hidden, so that the miser, by using the money as a dowry, might marry his daughter to Lyconides, the young man who has seduced her.

Euclio, miserly and distrustful by nature, is thrown into a feverish excitement by the discovery of the gold. He fears that someone will learn of its existence and either steal it or trick him out of it. After carefully hiding the gold in his house once more, he is afraid that even his old female slave, Staphyla, might learn of its whereabouts. Staphyla becomes worried about her master's strange behavior and about the fact that her young mistress is pregnant.

Meanwhile, Megadorus, a wealthy neighbor and uncle of Lyconides, plans to marry Euclio's daughter himself, and he enlists the aid of his sister Eunomia in his suit. Megadorus declares that he is so pleased with Phaedria's character that he will marry her without a dowry, which is contrary to the Athenian custom.

Seeing Euclio in the street, Megadorus goes to ask the old miser for his daughter's hand in marriage. Euclio, distrustful because of his newfound gold, thinks that Megadorus is in reality plotting to take the gold from him, but Megadorus assures him that all he wants is to marry Phaedria, with or without a dowry; he even offers to pay the expenses of the wedding. On these terms Euclio agrees to marry his daughter to Megadorus. After Megadorus leaves, however, Euclio cannot convince himself that the prospective bridegroom is not after the pot of gold.

Euclio informs Staphyla of the proposed marriage, which is to take place that same day. Staphyla knows that after Phaedria is married she will no longer be able to conceal her pregnancy, but she has little time to worry. Soon a caterer, bringing cooks, entertainers, and food, arrives at Euclio's house to prepare the wedding feast. Megadorus has hired the caterer as he has promised.

Returning from the marketplace with incense and flowers to place on the altar of his household god, Euclio is horrified to see all the strangers bustling about his house, for he immediately suspects that they are seeking his pot of gold. In a fury of apprehension, Euclio first drives all the caterer's people from the house and then removes his pot of gold from its hiding place. Only after he has removed it from the house does he tell them to return to their work.

Euclio decides to take the gold and hide it in the nearby temple of Faith. On the way there, he meets Megadorus, who asks Euclio to join him in drinking a bottle or two of wine. Euclio refuses, suspecting that Megadorus wants to get him drunk and then steal the pot of gold. Going on to the temple of Faith, Euclio hides the money. Although he does not know it, a slave belonging to Lyconides, the young man who has violated Euclio's daughter, observes where Euclio places the money. The slave is just taking the money from its hiding place when Euclio, rushing back to see if it is still safe, prevents the theft.

In a further effort to find a safe hiding place for his gold, Euclio takes it to the grove of Silvanus. Lyconides' slave, anxious to please his master and to repay Euclio for the beating he just received for trying to steal the gold, watches Euclio and sees where he hides the gold in the grove.

In the meantime, Lyconides, having learned of Megadorus's plans to marry Phaedria, goes to Eunomia, his mother, and tells her that he himself wants to marry the young woman. Pressed by Eunomia for his reasons, Lyconides reveals that he violated Phaedria while he was drunk and he now wishes to make amends by marrying her. Even as they speak, the excitement among the women in Euclio's house tells Eunomia and Lyconides that Phaedria's baby has been born. Eunomia agrees to help her son.

Lyconides goes to Euclio to tell him of his guilt in violating the miser's daughter. He finds Euclio greatly upset, for the miser has just discovered the theft of his gold from the grove. Lyconides believes that Euclio is angry with him because he fathered Phaedria's child, and Euclio thinks that the crime to which Lyconides is confessing is the theft of the gold. Finally, the young man convinces Euclio that he did not steal the miser's gold. He then tells Euclio about his violation of Phaedria and about the birth of the child. Megadorus has, in the meantime, renounced his claim to Phaedria. Euclio, who had been looking forward to the marriage of his daughter to the rich Megadorus, feels that he has been utterly betrayed by the world.

After Euclio and Lyconides part, the slave appears and tells Lyconides about the pot of gold he has stolen. Lyconides insists that the slave bring the gold to him. After a lengthy argument, the slave reluctantly obeys; he hates to think that the gold will be returned to the miserly Euclio.

After the slave brings him the gold, Lyconides goes to Euclio's house and returns the treasure. The miser is so happy to have the pot of gold once more in his hands that he readily agrees to a marriage between his daughter and Lyconides, in spite of the fact that Lyconides violated Phaedria and caused her to bear a child out of wedlock. Strangely enough, after the wedding Euclio has a change of heart and gives the entire pot of gold to the newly wedded couple.

Critical Evaluation:

The Pot of Gold is an example of Plautus's dramaturgy at its best. The plot has two strands of action: Euclio's frantic attempts to keep his pot of gold safe from thieves and Phaedria's offers of marriage on the very day she gives birth to Lyconides' illegitimate baby. The two lines of action are skillfully interwoven, the dramatic pace is swift and purposeful, and each scene arises from the last with no digressions. This farce also exhibits Plautus's verbal exuberance—his punning, his comic alliteration, his idiomatic language, his metrical variety, and his keen sense of timing—to good effect. Few playwrights of that era knew how to handle a joke with such deftness. Merely reading Plautus's plays—especially in translation—can be tiresome, however. It is necessary to visualize the action taking place on a stage to get some idea of Plautus's ability.

Plautine drama was quite similar to nineteenth and twentieth century musical comedy in that it used song and dance

as part of the action, it was best presented by actors with considerable theatrical experience, and the plays were based on adapted works. Plautus borrowed heavily from the Greek writers of the New Comedy, and it is often conjectured that *The Pot of Gold* was taken from a play by Menander, although it is impossible to determine which one. The miser has been a stock figure of farce almost from the genre's inception.

The text of *The Pot of Gold* is no longer complete, as the conclusion is missing. On the basis of the two "Arguments" summarizing the plot—verses that preface the play, added by later Roman editors—the ending can, however, be reconstructed.

The main interest of this play lies in the character of Euclio. Three generations of poverty, hard toil, and thrift have had their effects on his personality. Euclio is so miserly that the neighbor's servants make jokes about his stinginess, and when he uncovers a pot of gold in his house, his only thought is to keep it from being stolen. The gold acts as a curse for him. It makes him suspicious of every kind word, every good deed, and every person entering or leaving his house. He even suspects that the cooks are using a rooster to locate his gold. He acts like a madman in his apprehension, distractedly dashing in and out of his home. The gold is a burden that cuts him off from everyone. He does not realize that his daughter is pregnant, learning of the pregnancy only after she has given birth. Such a person invites the very thing that he or she fears.

Ironically, in trying to find the safest hiding place of all, Euclio unwittingly gives himself away and the gold is stolen—an event that only increases his frenzy. In the best scene in the play, when Lyconides tries to tell him that he drunkenly made love to Phaedria, Euclio is so preoccupied with the theft that he thinks Lyconides is confessing to having taken the gold. Even when he learns of Phaedria's pregnancy and the birth of her child, these are minor concerns to him. Clearly, something dramatic must take place to induce the change of heart in Euclio that causes him to realize that his daughter could use the gold as a dowry. What happens to transform Euclio is part of the play's missing conclusion.

The subplot in which Phaedria is at last married off to a man who loves her seems perfunctory, but it ties in nicely with Euclio's obsession. Megadorus is elderly, rich, innocent of Phaedria's condition, and willing to take her without a dowry. He sends his cooks to prepare the wedding feast at Euclio's house, which prompts Euclio to remove the gold. After it is stolen, Lyconides becomes the instrument by which it is returned, which establishes him as the successful suitor. Presumably, Megadorus withdrew his offer of marriage when he learned that Phaedria was not a virgin. From the beginning of the play, one knows that Megadorus is simply the playwright's means of getting Lyconides to propose.

Like most Plautine comedies, this play had considerable influence on European drama. Seventeenth century versions of Plautus's play include works by Ben Jonson, Molière, and Thomas Shadwell. Henry Fielding's *The Miser* (pr., pb. 1733) was also based in part on the Plautine comedy. Certainly the finest re-creation of Euclio was Molière's Harpagon in *L'Avare* (pr. 1668; *The Miser*, 1672).

"Critical Evaluation" by James Weigel, Jr.

Further Reading

Anderson, William S. *Barbarian Play: Plautus' Roman Comedy*. Toronto: University of Toronto Press, 1993. Important critical study focuses on Plautus's plotting techniques. The chapter "Comic Language, Metre, and Staging" explains why Euclio, who is often called Plautus's best comic villain, dominates the stage.

Arnott, W. Geoffrey. *Menander, Plautus, Terence*. New York: Oxford University Press, 1975. Disagrees with the prevailing interpretations of the character of Euclio, asserting that they ignore the climate of the age in which the play was written. Argues that Plautus's genius is evident in the subtle techniques he uses to bring Euclio to life.

Fraenkel, Eduard. *Plautine Elements in Plautus*. Translated by Tomas Drevikovsky and Frances Muecke. New York: Oxford University Press, 2007. In the first English translation of a German study initially published in 1922, Fraenkel, an influential twentieth century classicist, provides an analytic overview of Plautus's plays, including their motifs of transformation and identification, mythological material, and dialogue.

Hunter, R. L. *The New Comedy of Greece and Rome*. New York: Cambridge University Press, 1985. Well-organized work discusses topics ranging from matters of form to thematic and didactic considerations. The final chapter examines how Plautus altered his source material to make Euclio a more complex character.

Leigh, Matthew. *Comedy and the Rise of Rome*. New York: Oxford University Press, 2004. Analyzes the comedies of Plautus and Terence, placing them within the context of political and economic conditions in Rome during the third and second centuries B.C.E. Discusses how audiences of that time responded to these comedies.

Segal, Erich. *Roman Laughter: The Comedy of Plautus*. Cambridge, Mass.: Harvard University Press, 1968. Valuable study of Plautus's work addresses the social and cultural contexts in which the plays were written and originally performed and comments on their appeal to Roman audiences. Euclio is discussed at length in the chapter "Puritans, Principles, Pleasures."

_____, ed. *Oxford Readings in Menander, Plautus, and Terence*. New York: Oxford University Press, 2001. Includes essays on Plautus and the public stage, the response of Plautus's audience, and traditions, theatrical improvisation, and mastery of comic language in his plays. David Konstan's essay "*Aulularia*: City-State and Individual" analyzes *The Pot of Gold*.

Power

Author: Lion Feuchtwanger (1884-1958)
First published: Jud Süss, 1925 (English translation, 1926)
Type of work: Novel
Type of plot: Historical
Time of plot: Mid-eighteenth century
Locale: Germany

Principal characters:
JOSEF SÜSS OPPENHEIMER, a court favorite
RABBI GABRIEL, his uncle
NAEMI, Gabriel's daughter
KARL ALEXANDER, a duke
MARIE AUGUSTE, a duchess
WEISSENSEE, a politician
MAGDALEN SIBYLLE, his daughter
THE COUNTESS
ISAAC LANDAUER, her financial agent

The Story:

All of Prussia rejoices, and European courts lose their best topic of scandal when Duke Eberhard Ludwig breaks with the countess who had been his mistress and returns to his wife to beget another heir to the throne. The countess had been his mistress for thirty years, bleeding the country with her extravagant demands for wealth and jewels. Ludwig had been too vain, however, to remain her lover when she grew fat and middle-aged.

The countess sends for Isaac Landauer, the wealthy international banker who is her financial agent. Unable to advise her as to the means by which she could keep her hold on the duke, he offers to liquidate her possessions and send them to another province. The countess, who has a strong belief in black magic, nevertheless insists that Landauer bring to her the Wandering Jew to help cast a spell on Ludwig.

Landauer visits his young friend, Joseph Süss Oppenheimer, and offers half of what his dealings with the countess will bring him if the young man will aid Landauer in the countess's scheme. The so-called Wandering Jew is an uncle of Süss, Rabbi Gabriel, whose melancholy demeanor and mystic ways had caused people to think that he is the legendary Wandering Jew. Süss considers the offer. It is tempting, but for some unknown reason the young man is half afraid of his uncle, whose presence always instills in his nephew a feeling of inferiority. Furthermore, Rabbi Gabriel is rearing motherless, fourteen-year-old Naemi, the daughter whom Süss wishes to conceal from the rest of the world. At last, however, he sends for Rabbi Gabriel.

Penniless Prince Karl Alexander comes to Wildbad in hopes of gaining the grant of a substantial income from the duke. Süss, discovering the poverty of the prince, makes himself the financial adviser of the destitute nobleman. Although Landauer warns him that Karl Alexander is a poor risk, Süss continues his association with the prince merely because he hopes to ingratiate himself with the nobility. Half in gratitude, half in jest, the prince grants Süss admission to his levees.

On his arrival in Wildbad, Rabbi Gabriel tells Süss that he intends to bring Naemi to his nephew. Landauer, however, no longer needs Gabriel to help carry out the countess's scheme, and the rabbi returns to his home. The countess had been banished from the duchy, taking with her the money procured by Landauer.

Süss becomes the favorite of Prince Karl Alexander. To Wildbad also comes Prince Anselm Franz of Thurn and Taxis and his daughter, Princess Marie Auguste. Their mission is to urge Karl Alexander to marry the princess and turn Catholic. Angry because the duke has refused to give him a pension, the prince consents.

Duke Eberhard Ludwig dies suddenly, and Karl Alexander, now a Catholic, inherits the duchy. Süss becomes a court favorite, appointed by the new duchess to be keeper of her privy purse. Although Jews are forbidden to live in the duchy, the people have to acknowledge that the duke should be allowed his private court Jew.

Rabbi Gabriel had bought a little white house where he lives with Naemi and a servant. For three days, while the uncle is away, Süss goes to Hirsau to visit his daughter. Then he returns to his duke. Since Karl Alexander's succession, Süss has slyly directed him in measures that are resulting in a complete control of Swabia by the duke himself. The constitution and the parliament are powerless. Great noblemen have been ruined. Although his income is enormous, Süss refrains from holding any office. Süss has picked one former cabinet member, Weissensee, as president of the Ecclesiastical Council. One night he gives a party to which Weissensee brings his daughter, Magdalen Sibylle. Süss, noting the duke's attentiveness toward Weissensee's daughter, entices her into his bedroom, where the duke follows. After this evening, the duke sends gifts to Magdalen Sibylle, his declared mistress, and Weissensee is promoted to a high office. Weissensee hates Süss and secretly hopes to bring the favorite into disfavor at court. Learning that Süss has a daughter, he plans to place the Jew in the same position that Süss had placed him on the night Karl Alexander had taken Magdalen Sibylle.

The murder of a child revives the old legend that Jews had sacrificed a Christian child at the Passover feast, and a Jew, Reb Jecheskel Seligmann, is arrested for the crime. Pressure is put on Süss to use his power to save the innocent man, but he refuses because of the danger to his position at court. Then Rabbi Gabriel sends word to Süss that Naemi has heard rumors of his wickedness. At last, Süss decides that he will help the arrested man. In rescuing Seligmann, he feels anew his power as the court Jew. Soon afterward, at the request of Rabbi Gabriel, he visits his mother. He learns from her that his real father had been a great Christian marshal in the German army. Confused, Süss finally decides that he is a Jew and will remain so.

Convinced at last that Süss is a swindler, the duke threatens to dismiss and dishonor him, but when Süss offers his own fortune in exchange for proof of any financial trickery, the duke changes his mind and roars his anger at the enemies of Süss. Realizing that the favorite now has more power than ever, Weissensee continues to plot his revenge. Arranging for the duke to spend some time at his home in Hirsau while Rabbi Gabriel is not at home, Weissensee takes the duke to Süss's daughter. With visions of a heavenly rescue, the quiet, lonely child climbs to the roof of the house to escape from her attacker. She falls from the roof to her death.

Outwardly, Süss professes forgiveness toward the duke, but he pockets more and more funds from the ducal treasury. His personality alters. Instead of ingratiating himself at court, he criticizes and ridicules his acquaintances. Filling the duke's head with dreams of conquest, Süss inveigles him into leading a new military coup. At the same time, he plans the duke's destruction. While Karl Alexander lays dying at the scene of his defeat, Süss rains over his head a torrent of pent-up abuse. His enemies order his arrest.

For many months, the case against Süss drags on. Finally, he is put into a stinking, rat-infested hole, where every day the authorities goad him for a confession, but he remains stubbornly alive and sane. Sentenced to hang, he assails the court with icy, cutting words. He could have freed himself by declaring his Christian birth, but he had kept silent. On the day of the hanging Süss dies with the name Adonai, the Hebrew name for God, on his lips, and the word is echoed by all the Jews gathered to watch him die.

Critical Evaluation:

The main theme of *Power* is anti-Semitism. The central thought that Lion Feuchtwanger wishes to communicate in the novel is that no Jew can ever be safe, whether or not he or she trusts the political and social system, and whether or not he or she achieves power in that system. In the end, Feuchtwanger says, the Jew will be murdered—and there will only be other Jews to mourn his or her passing.

Feuchtwanger was an important literary figure in pre-World War II Germany who was forced to flee the Nazis. He was a friend of playwright Bertolt Brecht and was at the center of much of the significant literary activity of the Weimar Republic. The flavor of the cultural life of Weimar is evident in *Power*. The density of the prose; the brutality; the sensuality and perversion; and the breakdown of values, minds, and political institutions have all been taken by Feuchtwanger and transposed to eighteenth century Germany, where they become the perfect medium for tracing the development of anti-Semitism.

In the 1920's, when *Power* was first published, anti-Semitism had not yet reached genocidal proportions. There were a few groups, right-wing nationalists for the most part, who denounced the Jews as the cause of Germany's defeat in World War I; but at the same time, there were still Jews in positions of prominence in German social, cultural, and political life. It is to Feuchtwanger's special credit that he had the historical and dramatic insight to understand the embryonic stirrings of homicidal racism in Europe and especially in Germany and to develop this theme in a novel. Additionally, the use of a minority group as a scapegoat, and the casual indifference (or outright collaboration) of officialdom in the violence committed against that group, are phenomena that retain their significance for the contemporary reader. *Power* is incredibly and horribly prophetic.

Further Reading

Dollinger, Roland. "Lion Feuchtwanger's Historical Novels of the Weimar Republic." In *German Novelists of the Weimar Republic: Intersections of Literature and Politics*, edited by Karl Leydecker. Rochester, N.Y.: Camden House, 2006. Feuchtwanger is one of twelve German writers whose work is analyzed in this study of Weimar Republic literature. The essays focus on the authors' response to the political, social, and economic instability of the era.

Kahn, Lothar. *Insight and Action: The Life and Work of Lion Feuchtwanger.* Madison, N.J.: Fairleigh Dickinson University Press, 1975. A definitive and thorough biography. Provides many insights into the milieu in which Feuchtwanger worked and a great deal of discussion about *Power*.

Laqueur, Walter. "Central European Writers as a Social Force." *Partisan Review* 59, no. 4 (1992): 639-665. Describes Feuchtwanger's trip to the Soviet Union in 1936. Feuchtwanger regarded the Soviet Union as a bulwark against fascism.

Mauthner, Martin. *German Writers in French Exile, 1933-1940.* London: Vallentine Mitchell, 2007. Recounts what happened to Feuchtwanger and other German writers and intellectuals who fled the Nazis and settled in the south of France, where they tried to alert Western Europe and the United States to the dangers of Nazism.

The Power and the Glory

Author: Graham Greene (1904-1991)
First published: 1940
Type of work: Novel
Type of plot: Psychological realism
Time of plot: 1930's
Locale: Mexico

Principal characters:
THE PRIEST, a fugitive priest
MARCÍA, the mother of his child
FATHER JOSÉ, a renegade priest
LIEUTENANT OF POLICE
POOR MESTIZO

The Story:

In a state in Mexico, the Catholic Church has been outlawed and the priests driven underground on threat of being executed. After several months, the governor's office announces that one priest is still moving from village to village carrying on the work of the Church by administering the sacraments and saying Mass. A young lieutenant of police, an ardent revolutionist and an anticlerical, persuades his chief to let him search for the priest, who, as the authorities see it, is guilty of treason.

Two photographs are pasted up together in the police station. One is the picture of a fugitive American bank robber who has killed several police officers in Texas; the other is that of the priest. No one notices the irony, least of all the young lieutenant, who is far more interested in arresting the clergyman. At the same time that the officer is receiving permission to make a search for the priest, the priest is in the village; he has come there to get aboard a boat that will take him to the city of Vera Cruz and to safety.

Before the priest can board the boat, word comes to him that an Indian woman is dying several miles inland. True to his calling, the priest mounts a mule and sets out to administer the last rites to the dying woman, although he realizes that he might not find another ship to carry him to safety. There is one other priest in the vicinity, Father José. Father José, however, had been cowardly enough to renounce the Church, even to the point of taking a wife, a shrewish old woman. The authorities pay no attention to him at all, for they think, in Father José's case correctly, that a priest who has renounced his vows is a detriment and a shame to the Church.

After completing his mission, the priest returns to the coast, where he spends the night in a banana warehouse. The English manager on the plantation allows him to hide there. The following day, he sets out on muleback for the interior, hoping to find refuge from the police and from the revolutionary party of Red Shirts. As he travels, he thinks of his own past and of himself as a poor example of the priesthood. The priest is a whiskey priest, a cleric who would do almost anything for a drink of spirits. In addition, he has in a moment

of weakness fathered a child by a woman in an inland village. Although he considers himself a weak man and a poor priest, he is still determined to carry on the work of the Church as long as he can, not because he wants to be a martyr but because he knows nothing else to do.

After twelve hours of travel, he reaches the village where his onetime mistress and his child live. The woman takes him in overnight, and the following morning he says a Mass for the villagers. Before he can escape, the police enter the village. Marcía claims him as her husband, and his child, a girl seven years old, names him as her father. In that manner, because of his earlier sins, he escapes. Meanwhile, the police decide on a new tactic in uncovering the fugitive. As they pass through each village, they take a hostage. When a certain length of time passes without the apprehension of the priest, a hostage is shot. In this way, the lieutenant of police in charge of the hunt hopes to persuade the people to betray their priest. After the police leave the village without discovering him, the priest mounts his mule and continues on his way. He travels northward in an effort to escape the police and, if possible, to make his way temporarily into another state.

Some hours after leaving the village, the priest meets with a mestizo who joins him. Before long, the mestizo discovers that the priest is the one being sought by police. He promises that, as a good Catholic, he will not betray the secret, but the priest is afraid that the promised reward of seven hundred pesos will be too much of a temptation for the poor man.

When they reach a town, however, it is the priest's own weakness that puts him into the hands of the police. He has to have some liquor, the sale of which is against the law. He manages to buy some illegally, but his possession of the contraband is discovered by one of the revolutionary Red Shirts, who come after him. The priest is tracked down by a posse, caught, and placed in jail. Fortunately, he is not recognized by the police, but since he has no money, he is kept in jail to work out the fine.

The lieutenant of police, who is searching feverishly for him, unknowingly does the priest a good turn. Seeing the ragged old man working about the jail, the lieutenant stops to talk with him. The priest claims to be a vagrant who has no home of his own. The lieutenant feels sorry for the old fellow, releases him, and gives him a present of five pesos. The priest leaves town and starts out across the country to find a place of temporary safety. After traveling for some time, he meets an Indian woman who can speak only a few words of Spanish. She manages to make him understand that something is wrong with her child. He goes with her and finds that the baby has been shot; his immediate guess is that the American bandit had done the deed.

After performing rites over the child, the priest continues his flight. He eventually makes his way into the next state, where he is given sanctuary by a German plantation owner. After resting a few days, he plans to go to a city and present his problems to his bishop. Before he can leave, however, he is found by the mestizo, who says that the American bandit, a Catholic, is dying and needs the priest. The priest answers the call, although he is sure he is being led into a trap. The bandit is really dying, but he lay in the state from which the priest had just escaped. Police are with him, waiting for the priest's appearance.

Immediately after the bandit's death, the police close in and capture the priest. Taken back to the capital of the state and tried for treason, he is found guilty and sentenced to be shot. The lieutenant of police, who feels somewhat sorry for the old priest, tries to persuade the renegade Father José to hear the priest's last confession, but Father José, who fears the authorities, refuses. The priest is led out and shot without the benefit of the Church's grace. Nevertheless, the lieutenant of police has not succeeded in removing the Church's influence; on the evening of the day on which the priest died, another priest secretly makes his way into the town where the execution had taken place.

Critical Evaluation:

The Power and the Glory is one of the most powerful of Graham Greene's novels, and many critics consider it his finest. The story arose from Greene's journey through Tabasco and Chiapas in 1938. President Plutarco Elías Calles, in the name of revolution, had closed the churches and exiled and murdered priests and practicing Catholics. In Greene's journalistic account of his visit, *The Lawless Roads* (1938), he describes characters and settings that reappear and form the basis of his novel.

The theme of the hunted man establishes an exciting and nightmarish atmosphere to this novel and makes it a thriller.

Greene has, moreover, created characters who are at once human and symbolic. The priest and the lieutenant embody the extreme dualism in the human spirit: godliness versus godlessness, love versus hatred, spirituality versus materialism, concern for the individual versus concern for the state. After the lieutenant captures the priest, Greene provides an extended dialogue between these two figures that forms a disputation that lies at the heart of his parable of good and evil.

The lieutenant is the antithesis of the priest, but ironically his obsession with the hunt and with the task of eradicating all traces of Catholicism from his country leads him to live a life that is ironically priestlike. His simple lodgings, for example, are described as "comfortless as a prison or a monastic cell." Like the priest, he has an abiding concern for the children and the suffering poor.

The priest, who has endured pain, anxiety, and guilt for years, recognizes in his suffering the purposeful presence of God's love: "It might even look like—hate. It would be enough to scare us—God's love." This philosophic insight is hard won. The priest is keenly aware of his weakness and failure as a man and as a priest. An alcoholic, a scandalous priest with an illegitimate child, a man terrified of pain and death, he harbors no illusions about himself. It is, in fact, his self-knowledge that raises him to the level of the heroic.

When he is in prison for possessing brandy, he tells one of the pious inmates who thinks he is a martyr, "My children, you must never think the holy martyrs are like me. . . . I am a whisky priest." Unlike Father José, however, who has married and accepted the life of a grotesque buffoon, mocked by the children, the whisky priest is redeemed by his keen sense of responsibility for his sins and for the suffering he has brought upon others. His purgatory is in Mexico, in his years of flight, and especially in the torment of his own conscience.

He accepts his loss of peace in the belief that the only reason God denies him rest is so "he could still be of use in saving a soul, his or another's." After he sees his daughter, Brigida, his love and sense of responsibility for this child and her blighted innocence overwhelm him. An illegitimate child with the hunted alcoholic priest as her father, she appears to have lost her innocence prematurely and has little hope for joy in the world. Through her—and, ironically, through the sin out of which she was conceived—he finds his salvation. He knows that the love he feels for his daughter should encompass every soul in the world, but "all the fear and the wish to save [are] concentrated unjustly on the one child." His final recognition that sainthood is the most important destiny for a Christian suggests that he has achieved a form of saintly martyrdom himself.

The lieutenant, on the other hand, is a diminished figure at the end of the novel. For one thing, once the obsession with the hunt has been satisfied, "He felt without a purpose, as if life had drained out of the world." The child Luis, who earlier had admired him, now hates him, suggesting the lieutenant's and the state's failure to win the sympathy of the youth through violent social revolution.

In the providential plan of the novel, the lieutenant's hunt for and persecution of the priest turns the priest into a martyr in the eyes of the people. The lieutenant hates the rich and loves the poor, he says, but he cannot understand or tolerate pain. He wants to let his heart speak "at the end of a gun," if necessary, to bring about a social utopia.

To be sure, the whisky priest is a Greene saint, not a Saint Francis or a Saint Anthony whose life shines in the legends of selfless, charitable actions. Greene undercuts any sentimentality in his hero. The daughter he prays and dies for is doomed: "The world was in her heart already, like the small spot of decay in a fruit." His final prayer is spoken with brandy on his lips. It is the priest's humanity, however, that Greene celebrates, in contrast with the abstract compulsion of the lieutenant "who cared only for things like the state, the republic."

The novel concludes with a mysterious stranger knocking at the door of Luis' home. The stranger identifies himself as a priest, and Luis "put his lips to his hand before the other could give himself a name." The fugitive Church, the reader is thus assured, continues to be a vital presence in Mexico and will survive the oppression. Greene's fable of the conflict between spirituality and materialism, between the individual and the state, between love and hatred, comes full circle. Like the phoenix, the Catholic Church rises out of the ashes of its martyrs to challenge desperate measures of a godless state.

"Critical Evaluation" by Richard Kelly

Further Reading

Allott, Kenneth, and Miriam Farris. *The Art of Graham Greene*. New York: Russell, 1963. An invaluable study of Greene as an author whose obsessions shaped the themes and characters of his fiction. Such obsessive themes as betrayal, the fear of failure, and the hunted man illuminate Allot and Farris's reading of *The Power and the Glory*.

Bergonzi, Bernard. *A Study in Greene: Graham Greene and the Art of the Novel*. New York: Oxford University Press, 2006. Bergonzi examines Greene's novels, analyzing their language, structure, and recurring motifs. Argues that Greene's earliest work was his best, *Brighton Rock* was his masterpiece, and his novels published after the 1950's showed a marked decline in his abilities. Chapter 5 includes a discussion of *The Power and the Glory*.

Bosco, Mark. *Graham Greene's Catholic Imagination*. New York: Oxford University Press, 2005. Focuses on the elements of Catholic doctrine in Greene's novels. Bosco contradicts many critics, who maintain these elements are present in Greene's early novels only, demonstrating how the writer's religious faith is a pervasive aspect in all of his work.

DeVitis, A. A. *Graham Greene*. Boston: Twayne, 1986. A fine introductory study of Greene's major novels with a sensitive reading of Greene's Catholicism and how it influences his fiction. More than a dozen pages are dedicated to *The Power and the Glory*.

Kelly, Richard. *Graham Greene*. New York: Frederick Ungar, 1984. Provides a brief biography of the author, followed by analyses of his novels, thrillers, short fiction, and plays. Extends one critic's argument that Greene's creativity was obsessional, examining Greene's later writings.

Land, Stephen K. *The Human Imperative: A Study of the Novels of Graham Greene*. New York: AMS Press, 2008. A chronological consideration of all of Greene's work, demonstrating the common themes and character types in his novels and other fiction. Charts Greene's development as a writer.

Roston, Murray. *Graham Greene's Narrative Strategies: A Study of the Major Novels*. New York: Palgrave Macmillan, 2006. Roston focuses on seven novels, including *The Power and the Glory*, to describe the narrative strategies Greene uses to deflect readers' hostility toward his advocacy of Catholicism and to create heroic characters at a time when the traditional hero was no longer a credible protagonist.

Sherry, Norman. *The Life of Graham Greene*. 3 vols. New York: Viking Press, 1989-2004. This biography is a comprehensive and authoritative account of Greene's life, written with complete access to his papers and the full cooperation of family, friends, and the novelist himself. Includes a generous collection of photographs, a bibliography, and an index.

Zabel, Morton Dauwen. "Graham Greene: The Best and the Worst." In *Craft and Character in Modern Fiction*. New York: Viking Press, 1957. Despite the many volumes of critical material on Greene, this piece still ranks at the top for its perceptive critical insights into Greene's fictional world.

The Power of Darkness

Author: Leo Tolstoy (1828-1910)
First produced: Vlast tmy: Ili, "Kogotok uvyaz, vsey
 ptichke propast," 1888; first published, 1887 (English
 translation, 1888)
Type of work: Drama
Type of plot: Domestic tragedy
Time of plot: Nineteenth century
Locale: Russia

Principal characters:
NIKITA AKIMITCH TCHILIKIN, a laborer
ANISYA, his mistress
PETER IGNÁTITCH, Anisya's husband, a well-to-do peasant
MATRYONA, Nikita's mother
AKIM, Nikita's father
AKOULINA, Peter's daughter by his first marriage
MARINA, an orphan girl

The Story:

Peter Ignátitch, a well-to-do peasant, is forty-two years old and sickly. His second wife, Anisya, is only thirty-two years old. Still feeling young, she starts an affair with Nikita Akimitch Tchilikin, their hired man. Peter considers Nikita a loafer and thinks of dismissing him. As he is explaining his intention to Anisya, they learn that Nikita is talking about getting married and leaving their farm. Anisya complains to Peter that Nikita's departure will leave her with more work than she can handle.

When Anisya and Nikita are alone, he tells her that in spite of his marriage plans he will always come back to her. Anisya threatens to do violence to herself if Nikita leaves, adding that when her husband dies, Nikita could marry her and become master of the farm. Nikita declares, however, that he is satisfied with his lot. Matryona, Nikita's mother, comes in and says that Nikita's marriage is his father's plan, not her own, and that he need not worry about it. She then asks Nikita to leave the room.

Left alone with Matryona, Anisya confesses her love for Nikita. Matryona, who says that she has known of their affair all along, gives Anisya some poison and advises her to bury her husband before spring; she suggests also that Nikita will make a good master on the farm. Concerning the marriage, she explains that Nikita had an affair with Marina, an orphan girl, and that when Akim, his father, learned about it he had insisted that Nikita marry her. Matryona suggests that they talk the matter over with Peter, who is Nikita's master. Having explained the situation, Matryona again urges Anisya to use the poison on Peter, who is near death anyway.

At that point Peter and Akim come in, discussing Nikita's proposed marriage. Peter seems to approve of the match until Matryona tells him that Marina is promiscuous and so has no claim on Nikita. To determine the truth of this charge, Peter sends for Nikita, who falsely swears that there had been nothing between him and Marina. As a result, the marriage is called off. Marina visits Nikita and pleads her love, saying

that she has always been faithful to him, but Nikita sends her away, saying that he is no longer interested in her.

Six months later, Anisya and Matryona are worried because Peter is about to die but has not told anyone where his money pouch is hidden. Anisya tells Matryona that she has put the poison into Peter's tea. As they stand talking in the courtyard, Peter appears on the porch of his house, sees Nikita, who is happening by, and asks his forgiveness, a formal request made by the dying. Nikita is temporarily struck with remorse. Matryona, who then helps Peter back into the house, discovers that the money pouch is hanging by a cord around the sick man's neck. Anisya goes into the house and comes out again with the money pouch, which she gives to Nikita. She then returns to the house, only to reappear a short time later, wailing a formal lament for Peter, who has just died.

Nine months after Peter's death, Nikita, who has married Anisya and become the master of the farm, grows tired of his wife and begins an affair with Akoulina, Peter's daughter by his first marriage. Anisya is afraid to say anything for fear that her murder of Peter will be discovered.

In the following autumn, Matryona arranges a marriage for Akoulina, who has become pregnant by Nikita. Matryona tells the father of the suitor that Akoulina herself cannot be seen because she is sickly; at that moment, in fact, Akoulina is delivering her child in the barn. Nikita cannot decide what to do about the child, but Anisya gives him a spade and tells him to dig a hole in the cellar. Nikita balks at the suggestion, feeling that he is not to blame for all his troubles. Anisya, happy that she can force Nikita into sharing her own guilt, tells him that he is already guilty because he knows that she had poisoned Peter and because he had accepted Peter's money pouch. At last, Nikita goes to the cellar and digs the hole.

When Anisya brings the baby to him, covered with rags, Nikita is horrified to discover that the infant is still alive. Anisya and Matryona push Nikita into the cellar, where he murders the baby. Nikita reappears in a frenzy, threatening to kill his mother and claiming that he can still hear the baby whimpering. He then goes off to forget his troubles in drink.

Some time later, Akoulina's wedding feast is held at Nikita's farm. Nikita sees Marina, who has been able to marry respectably and who is now a wedding guest. Alone and troubled, he tells Marina that his only happiness has been with her. Distraught, Marina leaves Nikita to himself. Then Matryona and Anisya arrive to tell him that the bridal pair awaits his formal blessing. Feeling that it will be impossible to give his blessing, Nikita thinks of committing suicide until Mitrich, a drunken former soldier, appears and begins to talk of his experiences, concluding with the thought that a person should never be afraid of anyone. With this thought in mind, Nikita decides to join the wedding feast.

When Nikita appears before the guests, he is holding Akim by the hand. Suddenly, instead of blessing the bridal pair, he falls on his knees before his father. Proclaiming that he is guilty and wishes to make his confession, he begs forgiveness of Marina, whom he has misused, and of Akoulina, saying that he had poisoned Peter. Akoulina says that she knows who poisoned her father, yet a police officer, who happens to be a guest at the wedding, wants to arrest Nikita immediately. Akim prevents him by saying that his son must attend to God's business first. Nikita then confesses that he had seduced Akoulina and murdered her child. Finally, turning again to his father, Nikita asks for his forgiveness. Akim tells him that God will forgive him and show him mercy. Nikita is then bound and led away.

Critical Evaluation:

Leo Tolstoy came to playwriting relatively late in his career, after he had completed his prose masterpieces *Voyna i mir* (1865-1869; *War and Peace*, 1886) and *Anna Karenina* (1875-1877; English translation, 1886) and at a time when his religious conversion prompted him to view his writing in moralistic, rather than artistic, terms. Hence, the works of this period are heavily didactic and lack much of the balance, scope, and humanity of this previous efforts. Nevertheless, *The Power of Darkness* is a potent realistic play, one of the most intense and moving dramas of the period, and perhaps the outstanding realistic play of the pre-Chekhovian Russian theater.

Although there was no direct influence, *The Power of Darkness* resembles the powerful naturalistic dramas that were, at that time, rejuvenating Western theater. As in a typical naturalistic play, *The Power of Darkness* shows a group of weak, ordinary people who, after committing petty crimes out of greed, sexual jealousy, and self-deception, find themselves caught up by forces they cannot understand or control,

driven to further, greater crimes, and ultimately destroyed by the momentum of the evil they had so thoughtlessly unloosed. Small sins automatically lead to bigger ones; lesser crimes require more extreme deeds to maintain concealment; casual observers or passive accomplices are drawn into active conspiracy. Each evil deed, the participants believe, will be the last one and the one to lead them, finally, to happiness. Instead, the opposite is the case; they bind themselves tighter and tighter in a suffocating net of their own making.

Tolstoy's chronicling of this disintegration is fascinating in its realistic accuracy. Even in the middle of their depravity, the characters retain a certain sympathy; they are trapped and drawn to their destruction almost unconsciously. The catalyst is Nikita's mother, Matryona, the one character who seems consciously and deliberately evil, and she is one of the most fascinating creations of the modern stage. She plays on the others and seems to enjoy intrigue for its own sake. She is the consummate hypocrite, acting the role of pious matron while engineering diabolical schemes. As Peter dies, for example, from the poison she had supplied, Matryona offers him religious consolation.

However, if in the process of disintegration and self-destruction described in *The Power of Darkness* it resembles naturalistic plays, its resolution is quite different. To the naturalists, human beings are the helpless victims of biological and economic circumstances. Naturalistic plays and novels were intended to illustrate that hopeless situation in the face of an impersonal scientific universe. Tolstoy's vision was quite the opposite. To him, the power of darkness was more than balanced by the power of light, and his play is, above all, not a story of damnation but of redemption.

The focus of redemption is on Nikita. From the beginning of the play his sin is clearly the product of arrogance and sensuality, rather than any positive inclination to evil. When circumstances force him to the most vicious of the crimes, the murder of the baby, he is too weak to withstand the pressure of his mother, and he commits the act in a half-conscious frenzy. Immediately he is overwhelmed by guilt and remorse. He hears the breaking bones, the cries of the dying child, and seems on the edge of madness—but he is not granted that escape. He prepares to commit suicide, but that, too, is denied him.

Nikita's insight comes when, in the middle of his suicide attempt, he is accosted by the drunken laborer Mitritch, who tells him a parable about the devil's power, concluding with the words, "when you begin to be afraid of people, then the devil, with his cloven hoof, will snatch you up right away and stick you wherever he wants to."

Nikita thus realizes that his descent into evil comes from

his fear of the opinion of others and his own foolish desire for transient material pleasures. Shorn of that fear he gains his resolve and goes to the wedding party to confess. He accepts all of the blame for the crimes, which is, in a spiritual sense, true, even though the other conspirators are responsible for the crimes as well. Despite the magnitude of his guilt, however, he is redeemed.

Further Reading

Benson, Ruth Crego. *Women in Tolstoy: The Ideal and the Erotic*. Urbana: University of Illinois Press, 1973. Provocative feminist criticism concentrates on Tolstoy's changing vision of the role and importance of family life. Suggests that he struggled most of his life with a dichotomous view of women, regarding them in strictly black-and-white terms, as saints or sinners, and analyzes the female characters in the major and several minor works in terms of such a double view.

De Courcel, Martine. *Tolstoy: The Ultimate Reconciliation*. Translated by Peter Levi. New York: Charles Scribner's Sons, 1988. A long and thorough discussion of Tolstoy's life and work, the public and critical reception of *The Power of Darkness*, and the events of Tolstoy's life when he wrote the play and the time immediately following it.

Donskov, Andrew. "Tolstoy's Use of Proverbs in *The Power of Darkness*." In *Proverbs in Russian Literature: From Catherine the Great to Alexander Solzhenitsyn*, edited by Kevin J. McKenna. Burlington: University of Vermont Press, 1998. Examines how Tolstoy incorporated proverbs, sayings, and bits of folk wisdom in *The Power of Darkness*.

McLean, Hugh. *In Quest of Tolstoy*. Boston: Academic Studies Press, 2008. McLean, a longtime Tolstoy scholar, compiled this collection of essays that examine Tolstoy's writings and ideas and assess his influence on other writers and thinkers. Includes discussions of the young Tolstoy and women as well as Tolstoy's thinking about Jesus, Charles Darwin, Ernest Hemingway, and Maxim Gorky.

Noyes, George Rapall. *Tolstoy*. Mineola, N.Y.: Dover, 1968. Connects the many works of Tolstoy and refers to biographical information pertinent to understanding his writings. Explains the theme of conversion in *The Power of Darkness* and the dramatic differences between this play and Tolstoy's novels.

Orwin, Donna Tussig, ed. The *Cambridge Companion to Tolstoy*. New York: Cambridge University Press, 2002. Collection of essays, including discussions of Tolstoy as a writer of popular literature, the development of his style and themes, his aesthetics, and his reception in the twentieth century. References to *The Power of Darkness* are listed in the index.

Simmons, Ernest J. *Introduction to Tolstoy's Writings*. Chicago: University of Chicago Press, 1968. Discusses all the works of Tolstoy that have proved to have enduring significance. Devotes a chapter to Tolstoy's dramatic writings, examining the literary devices and theatrical production of *The Power of Darkness*.

Troyat, Henri. *Tolstoy*. Translated by Nancy Amphoux. 1967. New ed. New York: Grove Press, 2001. Provides biographical information concerning the time when Tolstoy wrote *The Power of Darkness* and his intentions for the play. Includes many illustrations.

Pragmatism
A New Name for Some Old Ways of Thinking

Author: William James (1842-1910)
First published: 1907
Type of work: Philosophy

William James's *Pragmatism* is likely the most illuminating and entertaining account of pragmatism ever composed. It is, however, more than a popular exposition prepared for the academic audiences of the Lowell Institute and Columbia University during the winter of 1906-1907. It is historic philosophy in the making. Although profoundly influenced by Charles Sanders Peirce, who invented the basic statement and name of pragmatism, James was an independent thinker with a creative direction of his own.

Peirce's essay "How to Make Our Ideas Clear" (1878) introduced the pragmatic notion that ideas are clarified by considering what would be expected in the way of experience if certain actions were to be carried out. The concept of the "sensible effects" of an object is the extent of the human conception of the objects, according to Peirce. His clear, radical, entertaining essay appeared in *Popular Science Monthly*, but professional philosophers were not interested in theory advanced by a mathematician, particularly when the theory went against the prevailing idealism of American philosophers. It was not until James revived the idea in 1898 with a talk on "Philosophical Conceptions and Practical Results" that pragmatic philosophy began to stir up controversy. With his lectures on meaning and truth that were published under the titles *Pragmatism* and *The Meaning of Truth*, the former in 1907 and the latter in 1909, James brought pragmatism into the forefront of American thought.

In his first lecture on "The Present Dilemma in Philosophy," James distinguished between the temperamentally "tender-minded" and "tough-minded." The former inclines toward a philosophy that is rational, religious, dogmatic, idealistic, and optimistic, the latter toward a philosophy that is empirical, irreligious, skeptical, materialistic, and pessimistic. James went on to state his conviction that philosophy can satisfy both temperaments by becoming pragmatic.

James's lecture on the pragmatic method begins with one of the most entertaining anecdotes in philosophical discourse. James describes a discussion by a group of philosophers on the question, Does a man go around a squirrel that is on a tree trunk if the squirrel keeps moving on the tree to keep the trunk always between himself and the man? Some of the philosophers claimed that the man did not go around the squirrel, while others claimed that he did. James settled the matter by saying, "Which party is right depends on what you practically mean by 'going round' the squirrel." It could be said that the man goes around the squirrel since he passes from the north of the squirrel to the east, south, and west of the squirrel. On the other hand, the man could be said not to go around the squirrel since he is never able to get on the various sides of the squirrel itself. "Make the distinction," James said, "and there is no occasion for any further dispute."

James then applied the method to a number of perennial philosophical problems, but only after a careful exposition of the meaning of pragmatism. He described the pragmatic method as a way of interpreting ideas by discovering their practical consequences, that is, the difference the truth of the idea would make in human experience. He asks, "What difference would it practically make to anyone if this notion rather than that notion were true?" and he replies, "If no practical difference whatever can be traced, then the alternatives mean practically the same thing, and all dispute is idle."

In his lecture, James argued that the pragmatic method was not new: Socrates, Aristotle, John Locke, George Berkeley, and David Hume had used it. What was new was the explicit formulation of the method and a new faith in its power. Pragmatism is to be understood, however, not as a set of grand theories but as a method that turns attention away from first principles and absolutes toward facts, consequences, and results in human experience.

A bare declaration would hardly have been enough to make pragmatism famous. James devoted a considerable part of his lectures to brief examples of the application of the pragmatic method. He cited with approval Berkeley's analysis of matter as being made up of sensations. Sensations, he said, "are the cash-value of the term. The difference matter makes to us by truly being is that we then get such sensations." Similarly, James claimed, Locke applied the pragmatic method when he discovered that unless "spirit" is defined as consciousness, the term means nothing.

Is materialism or theism true? Is the universe simply matter acting and interacting, or is God involved? James considers this problem pragmatically and reaches a curious result. As far as the past is concerned, he says, it makes no difference. If rival theories are meant to explain what is the case and if it makes no difference which theory is true, then the theories do not differ in meaning. If one considers the difference now and in the future, however, the case is different: "Materialism means simply the denial that the moral order is eternal. . . . Spiritualism means the affirmation of an eternal moral order and the letting loose of hope."

To this kind of analysis some critics have answered with the charge that James is one of the "tender-minded" philosophers he chastised in his earlier lectures. Yet throughout the course of this series of lectures and in subsequent books, James continued to use pragmatism as a way of combining the tough and tender temperaments. He extended the use of the term "difference" so that the meaning of an idea or term was no longer to be understood merely in terms of sense experiences, as Peirce had urged, but also in terms of passionate differences, of effects upon human hopes and fears. The essays in *Pragmatism* show this liberalizing tendency hard at work.

The temperate tone of James's suggestions concerning the religious hypothesis is clear in one of his later lectures in the book. In "Pragmatism and Religion," he writes that "Pragmatism has to postpone dogmatic answer, for we do not yet know certainly which type of religion is going to work best in the long run." He states again that the tough-minded can be satisfied with "the hurly-burly of the sensible facts of nature," and that the tender-minded can take up a monistic form of religion; but those who mix temperaments, as James does, prefer a religious synthesis that is moralistic and pluralistic and allows for human development and creativity in various directions.

Pragmatism is important not only as a clear statement of the pragmatic method and as an illustration of its application to certain central problems but also as an introductory exposition of James's pragmatic theory of truth. His ideas were developed more fully two years later in *The Meaning of Truth*.

Beginning with the common notion that truth is a property of ideas that agree with reality, James asked what was meant by the term "agreement." He decided that the conception of truth as a static relation between an idea and reality was in error, that pragmatic analysis shows that true ideas are those that can be verified, and that an idea is said to be verified when it leads usefully to an anticipated conclusion. Because verification is a process, it becomes appropriate to say that truth "happens to" an idea, and that an idea "becomes true" and "is made true by events." A revealing summary statement is the following: "'The true,' to put it very briefly, is only the expedient in the way of our thinking, just as 'the right' is only the expedient in the way of our behaving."

The ambiguity of James's account, an ambiguity he did not succeed in removing, allows extremes of interpretation. On the one hand, a reader might take the tender-minded route, something in the manner of James himself, and argue that all kinds of beliefs about God, freedom, and immortality are true insofar as they lead people usefully in the course of their lives. Tough-minded readers, on the other hand, might be inclined to agree with James that an idea is true if the expectations in terms of which the idea makes sense are expectations that would be met, if one acted—but they might reject James's suggestions that this means that a great many ideas that would ordinarily be regarded as doubtful "become true" when they satisfy the emotional needs of a believer.

One difficulty with which James was forced to deal resulted, it might be argued, not from his idea of truth as the "workableness" of an idea but from his inadequate analyses of the meanings of certain terms such as "God," "freedom," and "design." James maintained that, pragmatically speaking, these terms all meant the same thing, that is, the presence of "promise" in the world. If this were so, then it would be plausible to suppose that the idea that the world is promising would be true if it were shown to have worked out. If, however, James's analysis is mistaken, if "God" means more than the possibility of things working out for the better, then James's claim that beliefs about God are true if they work loses its plausibility. Whatever its philosophic faults, *Pragmatism* offers readers the rare experience of confronting first-rate ideas by way of a clear and entertaining, even informal, style.

Further Reading:

Barzun, Jacques. *A Stroll with William James*. New York: Harper & Row, 1983. Barzun instructively discusses important subtleties surrounding the terms "pragmatism" and "pragmatic" in this readable introduction to James's intellectual world.

Bauerlein, Mark. *The Pragmatic Mind: Explorations in the Psychology of Belief*. Durham, N.C.: Duke University Press, 1997. A helpful treatment of James's views on claims about truth and on the relationships among belief, consciousness, the human will, and knowledge.

Cotkin, George. *William James, Public Philosopher*. Baltimore: Johns Hopkins University Press, 1990. Cotkin explores the social and political context in which James worked and draws out James's contributions to the important debates of his day, as well as the lasting implications of his work.

Gale, Richard M. *The Philosophy of William James: An Introduction*. New York: Cambridge University Press, 2005. An overview of two aspects of James's philosophy: his Promethean pragmatism and his anti-Promethean mysticism. This edition is a revision of Gale's earlier book *The Divided Self of William James* (1999).

Menand, Louis. *The Metaphysical Club*. New York: Farrar, Straus and Giroux, 2001. Menand's Pulitzer Prize-winning book examines how James, Oliver Wendell Holmes, Charles Sanders Peirce, and John Dewey developed a philosophy of pragmatism after the American Civil War. Menand argues that the four thinkers "were more responsible than any other group for moving American thought into the modern world."

Myers, Gerald E. *William James: His Life and Thought*. New Haven, Conn.: Yale University Press, 1986. A well-written, carefully researched, comprehensive study of James's life and ideas.

Olin, Doris, ed. *William James: "Pragmatism" in Focus*. London: Routledge & Kegan Paul, 1992. Essentially a casebook, in which the complete text of *Pragmatism* is presented together with Olin's succinct introduction and six discussions, including philosophical commentaries by G. E. Moore and Bertrand Russell.

Perry, Ralph Barton. *The Thought and Character of William James*. Nashville, Tenn.: Vanderbilt University Press, 1996. A reprint of a classic by a well-respected philosopher, this book contains valuable discussions about James's life and work.

Putnam, Ruth Anna, ed. *The Cambridge Companion to William James*. New York: Cambridge University Press, 1997. Significant essays by well-qualified James scholars, who interpret and assess a wide range of topics and problems in his philosophy and his theories of psychology.

Simon, Linda. *Genuine Reality: A Life of William James*. New York: Harcourt, Brace, 1998. A worthwhile account of James's life and his pioneering work in both psychology and philosophy.

Suckiel, Ellen Kappy. *Heaven's Champion: William James's Philosophy of Religion*. Notre Dame, Ind.: University of Notre Dame Press, 1996. A study of the themes and lasting significance of James's philosophy and its emphasis on religion.

Taylor, Eugene. *William James on Consciousness Beyond the Margin*. Princeton, N.J.: Princeton University Press, 1996. Explores James's interests in and theories about human consciousness, psychology, religious experience, and other forms of experience.

The Prairie
A Tale

Author: James Fenimore Cooper (1789-1851)
First published: 1827
Type of work: Novel
Type of plot: Adventure
Time of plot: 1804
Locale: Great Plains of the United States

Principal characters:
NATTY "TRAPPER" BUMPPO, an eighty-seven-year-old frontiersman
ISHMAEL BUSH, a squatter who is traveling with his possessions and family to the prairie
ESTHER BUSH, his burdened wife, and mother of their fourteen children
ELLEN WADE, niece of Esther's deceased first husband
ABIRAM WHITE, Esther's brother
OBED BATTIUS, a physician-naturalist
PAUL HOVER, a bee hunter betrothed to Ellen
DUNCAN MIDDLETON, a U.S. Army captain
INEZ MIDDLETON, his wife, and daughter of a wealthy Louisiana landowner
HARD-HEART, a Pawnee chief, and Trapper's adopted son

The Story:

Shortly after the time of the Louisiana Purchase, Ishmael Bush, his wife, Esther, and their children travel westward from the Mississippi River. Their wagon train includes their fourteen sons and daughters; Esther's niece, Ellen Wade; Esther's brother, Abiram White; and Dr. Obed Battius, a physician and naturalist. While searching for a place to camp one evening, the group meets old Trapper (Natty Bumppo) and his dog, Hector. The trapper directs them to a nearby stream for a campsite.

After night falls, Trapper discovers Ellen in a secret meeting with her lover, Paul Hover, a wandering bee hunter. A band of Sioux Indians captures the three, but they manage to escape. The raiders steal all the horses and cattle from Ishmael's caravan. Unable to proceed across the prairie, the group occupies a naturally fortified hilltop shown to them by Trapper.

A week later, Hover, Trapper, and Battius gather around Trapper's campsite. Soon, a young stranger who introduces himself as Captain Duncan Middleton of the U.S. Army, joins them. Middleton is the grandson of Trapper's old friends, Major Duncan Heyward and Alice Munro-Heyward; Trapper had known the Heywards in the days of the French and Indian Wars. Middleton is looking for his wife, Inez, whom Abiram White, Esther's brother, has been holding captive since shortly after her marriage. Paul, Trapper, and Battius agree to help Middleton rescue Inez.

Ishmael and his sons leave their camp to hunt buffalo. In the evening, they return with meat. However, Asa, the oldest son, is missing. In the morning, the entire family sets out to search for Asa. They find his dead body in a thicket; one of Trapper's bullets had entered his back. The Bush family buries Asa and returns to camp, only to find that both Ellen and Inez are gone.

The young women, who have been rescued by Middleton and his friends, are making their escape across the prairie when a meeting with the Pawnee warrior Hard-Heart interrupts their journey. After the warrior gallops away on his horse, the travelers find themselves in the path of a stampeding herd of buffalo. At the last moment, the braying of Battius's donkey saves the group from being trampled to death; the donkey's strange cry had caused the herd to turn aside.

The band of Sioux that held Trapper, Paul, and Ellen captive continues pursuing the bison herd. The warriors now take Middleton's party captive. About the same time, Ishmael and his sons, who are searching for Inez and Ellen, approach on foot. The Sioux remount and give horses to their captives so that they all can ride to Ishmael's camp while Ishmael and his sons are away. During the Indian raid on the camp, Trapper helps his friends escape on horseback.

The escapees ride as far as possible before making camp for the night; in the morning, the runaways find that the Sioux have followed them and have set fire to the prairie to drive them into the open. Trapper rescues the fugitives by burning off the nearby prairie, thereby preventing the larger fire from reaching them.

As the deserters depart, they meet Hard-Heart again. From him, they learn that the Sioux and Ishmael's family have joined forces to search for them. Because Hard-Heart and the little band have a common enemy in the Sioux, Hard-Heart agrees to take them to his Pawnee village for protection.

The fugitives decide to cross a nearby river. As they reach the far bank, the Sioux appear on the opposite shore. That night, the fugitives are still free, but a snowfall makes it impossible for them to escape without being tracked. The Sioux capture them and take them to the Sioux village. The captors place the women in the lodge of the Sioux chief and tightly bind Hard-Heart, Paul, and Middleton. Trapper, because of his age, is not bound, but he declines to leave his friends. Using Trapper as an interpreter, the Sioux chief asks Inez to be his wife. Ishmael asks the chief to give him Inez, Ellen, and Trapper as they had previously agreed. When the chief refuses, Ishmael departs angrily.

Many Sioux clamor to torture Hard-Heart to death, and a council convenes to decide Hard-Heart's fate. An old warrior steps forward and declares that he wishes to make the Paw-

nee his adopted son, but Hard-Heart refuses to join the Sioux tribe. The Sioux begin to torture their captives, but Hard-Heart manages escape and joins a war party of his own Pawnee, who arrive on the scene.

Leaving the women to guard the prisoners, the Sioux men prepare to fight the Pawnee. The braves of the two tribes gather on the opposite banks of a river, but neither side dares to make the first move. Hard-Heart challenges the Sioux chief to single combat. Meanwhile, Trapper helps the rest of the captives to escape. Shortly after, however, Ishmael captures them once again. Hard-Heart prevails against the Sioux chief, and his warriors put the remaining Sioux warriors to flight in the subsequent battle.

The next morning, Ishmael holds a court of justice to deal with his captives. He realizes his mistake in carrying Inez away from her husband and allows the couple their freedom. He gives Ellen her choice of remaining with his family or going with Paul. She chooses to go with her lover. Ishmael gives Dr. Battius his freedom because he does not think that the scientist is worth the bother. Finally, Trapper comes up for judgment.

Ishmael still believes that Trapper shot and killed his son, Asa, but Trapper reveals that Abiram had fired the shot. Abiram confesses his crime and then faints. Ishmael is reluctant to pronounce judgment on his brother-in-law, but he believes it his duty to do so. That evening, he gives Abiram the choice of starving to death or hanging himself. Late that night, Ishmael and Esther return to find Abiram hanging. They bury him and continue on their way to the settlement.

Middleton, Paul, and the young women invite Trapper to return to the settlement with them; by remaining with them he would be taken care of in his last days. Trapper refuses their invitation and decides instead to remain in the Pawnee village with Hard-Heart.

One year later, Middleton's duties as an Army officer bring him near the Pawnee village, where he visits Trapper. The old frontiersman appears near death, but Trapper revives sufficiently to greet his old friend. By sundown, however, Trapper seems to be breathing his last breaths. As the sun sinks beneath the horizon, he makes one last tremendous effort, rises to his feet with the help of his friends, and utters a loud and firm "here" before falling back dead into the arms of his friends.

Critical Evaluation:

James Fenimore Cooper's *The Prairie* is the third of five historical novels to appear in his Leatherstocking series. The name Leatherstocking comes from the nickname settlers gave to the character Natty Bumppo (Trapper). Even though

The Prairie is not the last of Cooper's Leatherstocking tales to appear in print, it is the concluding saga of the five books of the series.

The setting of *The Prairie* is essential to the plot. Cooper sets this historical novel in 1804 in the Great Plains, a symbol for a place of peace. Natty Bumppo carries the nickname Trapper in *The Prairie* and the names Deerslayer, Pathfinder, and Hawkeye in other Cooper novels. In *The Prairie*, Trapper is traveling west to escape civilization and to find his ideal life in unsettled territory—real or imagined.

The structure of the plot of *The Prairie* is progressive: One must read the entire book or story to find the answers to the questions raised. The order of the plot first appears chronological and appears to foreshadow the destruction civilization may bring to the land, the animals, and the people. Like the series itself, however, this novel is not strictly chronological. Because the series employs flashbacks and is not sequentially written or published, the reader cannot be sure that a story's "ending" is actually an ending.

As important as the plot and setting may be, the characters make the book memorable and vivid for the reader. Cooper uses many devices to make his characters round, or fully developed. His initial description of Trapper indicates to the reader that the frontiersman will be vital to the volume: "a human form appeared.... The figure was colossal.... The effect of such a spectacle was instantaneous and powerful."

Certain resemblances are evident between the characters and character relationships in *The Last of the Mohicans: A Narrative of 1757* (1826) and those in *The Prairie*. The genteel Captain Duncan Middleton of *The Prairie* is a grandson of Duncan Heyward and Alice Munro-Heyward of *The Last of the Mohicans*. Trapper's love for his adopted son, Hard-Heart, parallels his feeling for young Uncas. The enmity of Hard-Heart and Mahtoree, a Teton Sioux chief, in *The Prairie* is as fierce as that of Uncas and Magua in *The Last of the Mohicans*; the two feuds end differently, however.

The speech of the characters is revealing in *The Prairie*. The main character, Trapper, is the most verbose; his words make up about one-third of the instances of discourse in the book. It is he who translates the speech of others and who presents a commentary on what he sees and hears. Trapper often warns about the harm that people can cause to the land and its inhabitants; he attributes much of this destruction to their "morals" and "their wickedness and their pride," but "chiefly [to] their waste." Cooper's prediction of future environmental destruction leads many readers to call his work apocalyptic fiction.

Trapper's most memorable line is his last. Supported by friends, he rises from his death bed to utter one word: "here."

This final declaration has many interpretations: He is answering a roll call, asking for this place to be his final resting place, declaring he will die here. Throughout *The Prairie*, the pompous Dr. Obed Battius, in contrast to Trapper, provides book knowledge but also comic relief. He claims to have found a new species: *Vespertilio Horribilis, Americanus*. The new species, however, turns out to be his own mule, Asinus.

The picaresque (journey) theme is primary in *The Prairie*. All the characters are traveling. Eighty-seven-year-old Trapper is moving toward the setting sun, a metaphor for the end of the trail, for the demise of a way of life, for the encroaching land development, and for his rapidly approaching death. Once a virile hunter, scout, and frontiersman, and an expert marksman, he is trying to rediscover lost peace and quiet in the Great Plains. He now traps game for his survival; he is a somewhat tragic figure in his perhaps futile search, in his failing health, and in the isolation he endures in his quest.

The Prairie, set in 1804 and published in 1827, repeats two important themes from Cooper's earlier Leatherstocking tales: *The Pioneers: Or, The Sources of the Susquehanna* (1823) and *The Last of the Mohicans*. All three of these books warn against the wasting of America's natural resources, the demise of American Indians, and radically changing the face of America. In *The Pioneers*, Trapper condemns the wasteful cutting and burning of trees, the slaughter of passenger pigeons, and the seining, or netting, of fish left to rot on the lakeshore. In *The Prairie*, Trapper mourns the disappearance of the beauty of the wilderness and fears the "vanishing American."

Cooper also employs symbolism in *The Prairie*. He uses the axe to signify the destruction both of the environment and of Trapper's satisfaction; the axe, therefore, represents evil. The denuded land and the sound of the axe are the causes of Trapper's journey to find a refuge. To Trapper, the forest represents a sacred place facing destruction; he cautions that a destructive, "accursed band of choppers and loggers" will follow. Cooper conveys his new environmental message. The first actions of Ishmael's sons upon reaching their campsite are to place the axe from the East against the prairie in the West, to claim control, and to begin felling the cottonwood trees. The squatter Ishmael begins to seize the land and the people about him and to claim them as his own. Cooper describes the Bush family as "indolent, lounging, and inert as usual."

Other symbols appear in *The Prairie*. The Sioux are described as "treacherous serpents" and "beasts." The Sioux, in turn, describe the settlers with the following warning: "Where a Pale-face comes, a Red-man cannot stay. The land is too small. They are always hungry. See, they are here already!" Cooper, however, depicts Hard-Heart, a Pawnee, as the innocent, "noble savage."

Cooper frequently uses animal metaphors. Esther, for example, compares Asa's hunger to that of a bear. Ishmael, at one point, shakes himself as a lion might do. Cooper depicts Abiram as being as nimble as a grasshopper. The doctor seems to run his course like a trained hound. Paul Hover uses his practical knowledge of insects as a bee hunter and later as a legislator who is a keeper of people.

Trapper prepares for death by bequeathing his goods to Hard-Heart instead of to Middleton, thereby indicating his dislike of the actions of the settlers and of the Army. Interestingly, this is the second will and testament that Cooper mentions for Trapper. In *The Deerslayer: Or, The First War-Path, a Tale* (1841), Trapper declares a second will for the series but a first will in Trapper's/Deerslayer's life. He declares in this revoked will that his goods should go to Hist-oh-Hist, who is engaged to marry Chingachgook. Perhaps Cooper now values families over individuals and gives increased importance to women in this later work.

Another important element of *The Prairie* is its authenticity. Though the book is fiction, the characters, plot, and setting are believable. The actions and the speech of the people are realistic for the setting.

Revised by Anita Price Davis

Further Reading

Brotherston, Gordon. "*The Prairie* and Cooper's Invention of the West." In *James Fenimore Cooper: New Critical Essays*, edited by Robert Clark. Totowa, N.J.: Barnes & Noble, 1986. Defines *The Prairie* as "the most distinctive if not the best written" of Cooper's novels about American Indians. Explores the lasting historical and cultural images that Cooper helped create.

Franklin, Wayne. *James Fenimore Cooper: The Early Years*. New Haven, Conn.: Yale University Press, 2007. A detailed and scholarly biography of Cooper. This 700-plus-page volume explores Cooper's early years, from his birth in 1789 to 1826, the year before *The Prairie* was published.

Krauthammer, Anna. *The Representation of the Savage in James Fenimore Cooper and Herman Melville*. New York: Peter Lang, 2008. Focuses on Cooper's (and Herman Melville's) creations of American Indian, African American, and other non-European characters, including Natty Bumppo in *The Prairie*. Discusses how readers perceive these characters as "savages," both noble and ignoble.

Newman, Russell T. *The Gentleman in the Garden: The Influential Landscape in the Works of James Fenimore Cooper*. Lanham, Md.: Lexington Books, 2003. Discusses the importance of landscape in Cooper's novels, focusing on the land's relation to social standing. A "a creative and insightful exploration of the pioneer aesthetic" of Cooper.

Person, Leland S., ed. *A Historical Guide to James Fenimore Cooper*. New York: Oxford University Press, 2007. Collection of essays, including a brief biography of Cooper by Wayne Franklin and a survey of Cooper scholarship and criticism. See particularly "Cooper's Leatherstocking Conversations: Identity, Friendship, and Democracy in the New Nation" by Dana D. Nelson. Features an illustrated chronology of Cooper's life and important nineteenth century events.

Rans, Geoffrey. *Cooper's Leather-Stocking Novels: A Secular Reading*. Chapel Hill: University of North Carolina Press, 1991. References in the section "The Uses of Memory" suggest how *The Prairie* employs selective memory of its past, particularly of its past injustices, to move forward.

Wegener, Signe O. *James Fenimore Cooper Versus the Cult of Domesticity: Progressive Themes of Femininity and Family in the Novels*. Jefferson, N.C.: McFarland, 2005. Examines Cooper's reaction to and treatment of America's cultural values, particularly those that shaped the private and public lives of individuals, between 1820 and 1860. Details Cooper's inclusion of women as an integral part of his plot lines.

White, Craig. *Student Companion to James Fenimore Cooper*. Westport, Conn.: Greenwood Press, 2006. A guide written especially for students, covering Cooper's life and career. Includes examination of *The Prairie*. Part of the Student Companions to Classic Writers series.

The Praise of Folly

Author: Desiderius Erasmus (1466?-1536)
First published: Moriæ Encomium, 1511 (English
    translation, 1549)
Type of work: Criticism and satire

Considered by many to be the founder of modern letters, Desiderius Erasmus spent a lifetime producing some of the most important scholarly works of the early Renaissance. Ironically, *The Praise of Folly*, written as an amusement, became the most enduring of his contributions to Western literature. Erasmus himself never thought highly of this work, yet it is the one for which he is best remembered. He wrote it in approximately seven days in 1509, while he was recovering from an illness at the home of his English friend, Thomas More. It was not until two years after its writing that he had the book secretly printed in France. More than forty editions of *The Praise of Folly* appeared in the author's lifetime. The work caused Erasmus considerable trouble; his portraits of the clergy did little to endear him to the hierarchy of the Roman Catholic Church, and for years the volume was banned as anti-Catholic. Nevertheless, the treatise has passed into the canon of Western literature, ranking as one of the premier examples of satiric writing in European letters.

The Praise of Folly makes use of one of the oldest forms of rhetorical discourse: the encomium. In a mock encomium, Erasmus makes use of the satirical devices of one of the world's most influential satirists, Lucian, to poke gentle fun at the tradition of praising great people and great ideas. Putting words of wisdom in the mouth of Folly, Erasmus highlights the paradoxical relationship between conventional wisdom and the religious dimensions of human life. Like all great satirists, Erasmus focuses on specific targets (especially the clergy of his own day), but his general aim is to tell his readers something about universal human nature. Beneath his carefully constructed argument, Erasmus echoes the biblical lesson that, in the eyes of the world, it is truly folly to adopt the Christian lifestyle; in that folly, however, lies real wisdom.

Although written centuries ago, *The Praise of Folly* is still an effective analytic examination of humankind's abilities and vanities. It not only gives the modern reader an idea of the struggle of the Humanists in their effort to rid the world of the conventions and forms of the Middle Ages but also provides insight into continuing problems of life. As the result of this work and several others, Erasmus became one of the most popular men of letters of his time and, consequently,

one of the most influential. He was of prime importance in the spread of Humanism through the northern part of Europe and was instrumental in many aspects of both the Reformation and the later phase of the Renaissance. Everything he did was to aid humankind in tearing away the veils of foolish traditions and customs, so that people could find the road back to the true God and their true selves.

The form itself is an immediate indication of the type of work that the book is to be. Written as a parody of a classical oration, the essay sets Folly as the orator. Her subject is society, and she quickly becomes a many-sided symbol that stands for all that is natural in people, all of their misdirected efforts, and all of their attempts to get the wrong things out of life. She discusses the problem of wisdom and tells how it can be united with action to gain success in a world of folly; she is concerned with the way in which reason and simple Christian advice can be presented to humankind; she wonders what Christian Humanists can do for themselves and the world. Parody, irony, and satire are used throughout the essay to show people what they do and what they should do. No one is spared. Neither king nor prince, pope nor priest, aristocrat nor worker escapes the indignation that Erasmus feels toward society.

At the beginning of her oration, Folly declares that she is giving a eulogy for herself, and she justifies the impertinence by saying that she knows herself better than anyone else and that no one else will do it for her. Her father, she says, is Plutus, the real father of all people and gods, and she was born out of his passion for Youth. Significantly, her birth took place in the Fortunate Isles, and she lists among her followers Drunkenness, Ignorance, Self-love, Flattery, Forgetfulness, Laziness, Pleasure, Madness, Sensuality, Intemperance, and Sound Sleep—all of whom help her to gain control of all things.

It is Folly, for instance, who leads people to marriage and the conception of life, thus prolonging this life that is so foolish. It is Pleasure, one of her followers, who makes life bearable at all. It is Forgetfulness who makes youth such a carefree time, and who restores this same characteristic to old age, thereby bringing about a second childhood. By throwing off care and avoiding wisdom, one can achieve perpetual youth.

Folly goes on to say that she is the source of all that is pleasurable in life. People will never be completely divorced from Folly, because they are ruled more by passion than by reason, and the two most ruling passions are anger and lust. One of the chief sources of men's pleasure, of course, is women, who are even more subject to folly than are men. Men's coarser looks are a result of the infection of wisdom.

Friendship also derives from Folly because it makes people ignore the faults and defects of others. Marriage itself is held together with compromise, infatuation, and duplicity. Without Folly, people could not get along with each other; they would soon begin to hate themselves and everything would seem sordid and loathsome.

Folly praises herself under the guise of Prudence, because she allows humans to have firsthand experience with the world. She frees people from the shame and fear that cloud their minds and inhibit their actions, thus preventing real experience. Thanks to Prudence, people go along with the crowd, which is Folly. It is Folly who has caused all the great achievements of humanity; wisdom and learning are no great help. Everything that a person does is motivated by self-love, vainglory, flattery, or other followers of Folly.

To lead such a life of folly, error, and ignorance is to be human; it is to express one's true nature. All other forms of life are content with limitations, but humans are vainly ambitious. Those who are most ignorant are the happiest; those who are most deluded are those who delight in telling lies. For an example, one might consider the priests—those who propose to gain happiness by relying on magic charms and prayers, saints and particular rites. There is no happiness without Folly, because all emotions belong to Folly, and happiness depends on expressing one's human nature, which is full of folly.

Among the most foolish people, therefore, are those who try to deny their true nature and find happiness through the Christian religion. Folly proves that this religion has more to do with her nature than with wisdom by showing that children, women, old people, and fools take more delight in it than do others. It is they who are always nearest the altars. In the way that Christianity is most often taught and practiced, humans must deny their true nature by disdaining life and preferring death. One must overlook injuries, avoid pleasure, and feast on hunger, vigils, tears, and labors. One must give up and scorn all physical pleasures, or at least take them more lightly than spiritual pleasures.

Folly is at her most serious when she says that this is the most foolish way, and the only sure way, to true happiness. Only by forgetting the body and everything physical can a person approach this goal. People must give themselves up

completely to the spiritual aspects of life to achieve it. Few are able to accomplish this task completely enough while in this world to approach an experience that, she says, is close to madness. This madness, in turn, is similar to the heavenly joys that one will experience after death when the spirit has completely left the body.

Further Reading

Augustijn, Cornelis. *Erasmus: His Life, Works, and Influence*. Translated by J. C. Grayson. Buffalo, N.Y.: University of Toronto Press, 1991. Originally published in Dutch in 1986, this book reevaluates Erasmus's life, works, and significance.

Erasmus. *The Praise of Folly*. Translated with an introduction and commentary by Clarence H. Miller, afterword by William H. Gass. New Haven, Conn.: Yale University Press, 2003. In addition to a new translation of *The Praise of Folly*, this volume's introduction examines both the humanistic and theological aspects of Erasmus's philosophy as exemplified by this work. Gass, an American novelist and essayist, provides a humorous afterword in which he considers the meanings of folly and offers his own interpretation of the work.

Halkin, Léon-E. *Erasmus: A Critical Biography*. Translated by John Tonkin. Cambridge, Mass.: Blackwell, 1994. Analyzes many different levels of meaning in *The Praise of Folly* and describes Erasmus's contrast between worldly wisdom and Christian folly. Contains an excellent biographical guide for research on Erasmus.

Kaiser, Walter. *Praisers of Folly: Erasmus, Rabelais, and Shakespeare*. Cambridge, Mass.: Harvard University Press, 1963. Examines *The Praise of Folly* within the Renaissance tradition of the mock encomium. Also contains solid comments on representations of folly by William Shakespeare and François Rabelais.

Phillips, Margaret Mann. *Erasmus and the Northern Renaissance*. Rev. ed. Totowa, N.J.: Rowman & Littlefield, 1981. Clear introduction to the life and career of Erasmus by an Erasmus scholar. Contains an excellent analysis of the religious dimension of *The Praise of Folly*.

Rummel, Erika. *Erasmus*. London: Continuum, 2004. Discusses Erasmus's ideas on education, piety, the social order, and epistemology.

Tracy, James D. *Erasmus of the Low Countries*. Berkeley: University of California Press, 1997. An intellectual biography that discusses how Erasmus used his writings to bring moral and religious renewal to Christian society. Includes the chapters "The Ideal of Christian Civility" and "Between Wisdom and Folly."

Praisesong for the Widow

Author: Paule Marshall (1929-   )
First published: 1983
Type of work: Novel
Type of plot: Psychological realism
Time of plot: 1920's, 1940's, and mid-1970's
Locale: New York, Grenada, and Carriacou

Principal characters:
AVATARA "AVEY" JOHNSON, a middle-age woman
THOMASINA and CLARICE, her traveling companions
JEROME "JAY" JOHNSON, her late husband
LEBERT JOSEPH, an old shopkeeper in Grenada
ROSALIE PARVAY, Joseph's daughter
AUNT CUNEY, Avey's great-aunt

The Story:

Avey Johnson, a sixty-four-year-old African American woman, now single, is packing her bags. She is aboard the cruise ship *Bianca Pride* with her friends Thomasina and Clarice, and she has decided in the middle of the night to leave the cruise and fly home to New York. Three nights earlier, Avey had a dream about her great-aunt Cuney, with whom she used to spend summers as a child on Tatem Island off the South Carolina coast. In the dream, Aunt Cuney called Avey to follow her down the path they used to walk together in Tatem, down to the shore where Aunt Cuney would tell the story of a group of Igbo slaves who walked across the water back to Africa. Since the dream, Avey has felt bloated and unsettled.

After quarreling with her friends about her hasty decision, Avey spends the morning trying to avoid the other passengers, but she cannot find a place to be alone. Finally, the ship docks at Grenada, and she gets off with her six suitcases and hatbox. She quickly realizes that she has not thought through her plans for getting home. She has assumed that it would be easy to get a cab to the airport and to get a flight home, but instead she finds herself on a crowded wharf with cobblestone streets, crowds of people speaking a patois she cannot understand, and no vehicles or guides in sight. The people crowding the wharf seem to be locals, dressed up and carrying overnight bags and wrapped presents and boarding an assortment of old wooden cargo ships. Finally, she finds a taxi driver and learns that the one daily flight to New York has already left. As the driver takes her to a large tourist hotel, he explains that the locals are taking their annual excursion to Carriacou Island, a trip he has never understood.

Avey begins to remember her early years with her late husband, Jay, and then hears his voice, challenging her for wasting money on the unfinished cruise. The couple had lived on Halsey Street in Brooklyn, New York. Jay, as Avey moves back to the past, is a hard-working man, dedicated to providing for his family; he works two or three jobs at a time

and had completed an accounting degree, but no white men will hire him. Avey does clerical work and is raising three daughters. There is love in the home—for awhile. Jay comes home in the evenings and plays jazz or blues records, and the two dance and make love. As time goes on and life gets harder, Jay becomes exhausted and Avey becomes suspicious and shrill. A dramatic argument one night almost separates them forever. Although they stay together, they never recapture their passion for each other. Gradually, though, Jay succeeds with his own accounting business, and the family is able to buy a house in the wealthy suburb of North White Plains.

Avey enjoys her new prosperity but sometimes longs for the early years with Jay. He never plays records any more or dances in the living room. He had shaved off the moustache he used to be vain about, and he begins to make disparaging comments about other African Americans and what he sees as their frivolous, unproductive ways. Now in the present moment, Avey, in her hotel room in Grenada, mourns for all she has lost, crying herself to sleep.

Avey wakes up and decides to take a walk before her flight. As she walks farther down the deserted beach she feels her mood lighten. Finally, she realizes she has walked too far in the heat and finds shelter from the sun in a little rum shop. The old man who runs it, Lebert Joseph, can tell immediately that Avey is troubled. He describes the importance of the Carriacou excursion, during which the people visit their families, remember their ancestors, and hold a big drum dance. He is concerned because Avey cannot even name the nation of her ancestors, and that his own grandchildren in New York have never participated in the big drum dance. He sings to her, gives her a glass of fresh coconut water, and persuades her to delay her flight and go with him to Carriacou.

Avey boards one of the old sloops and is seated with a group of old women. She remembers the trip she used to take down to Aunt Cuney's home every summer, and she remembers a fiery sermon one Easter Sunday. Suddenly, she becomes violently ill, vomiting and losing control of her bowels. The other women embrace her and help her lie down.

Avey wakes up in a bedroom in the home of Rosalie, Joseph's daughter, and she is gently bathed and massaged by Rosalie and her maid. Joseph has stayed awake all night watching her, feeling guilty that he encouraged her to make the trip. Avey decides to fly back to Grenada, which means staying another day. That night, she attends the big drum dance. As she listens to the singing and watches each group dance its ancestral dance, she recognizes some of the steps of the "Carriacou Tramp" from a dance she witnessed as a child in Tatem. She joins the dance. The next morning, she flies home, determined that she will fix up Aunt Cuney's place and teach her grandchildren the old stories.

Critical Evaluation:

Paule Marshall is considered one of the most important of the African American women novelists who reached broad popular and critical success beginning in the 1960's. An American writer whose parents were born on the island of Barbados in the Caribbean, Marshall created a body of work about Caribbean immigrants and their descendants that anticipated the work of later Caribbean American writers, such as Jamaica Kincaid and Edwidge Danticat. Marshall was awarded a MacArthur Foundation genius grant in 1992.

Marshall's semiautobiographical first novel, *Brown Girl, Brownstones* (1959), was groundbreaking for featuring a female protagonist from a black immigrant family. The novel introduces a theme that would continue to be important in Marshall's fiction: African Americans maintaining and honoring ties to the Caribbean and to Africa. In *Praisesong for the Widow*, the third of Marshall's novels, she lends voice to a middle-age upper-middle-class African American woman. As the novel opens, the main character, Avatara "Avey" Johnson, is on a cruise through the Caribbean on a ship named *Bianca Pride* ("white pride"); with her six suitcases and a hatbox and her mainly white shipmates, she is as far away as she could be from the poverty, struggle, and joy she knew as a young wife in Brooklyn.

As a child, Avey spent summers with her Aunt Cuney on Tatem Island, off the coast of South Carolina, and heard again and again stories of the slaves who landed there in captivity. Newly married, she lives in Brooklyn with her husband, Jay, and finds a spiritual connection with her heritage in the music of Duke Ellington, Count Basie, and Ma Rainey and in the poetry of Langston Hughes, Paul Lawrence Dunbar, and Gwendolyn Brooks. However, as Avey and Jay turn their focus more and more to material success,

they lose all cultural connection. They stop listening to Jay's jazz and blues records, stop going to Harlem to see friends and go to shows, and stop making their annual trips to Tatem. Avey is barely aware of the Civil Rights movement, although her daughter Marion participates in demonstrations and tries to encourage her mother to visit Ghana or Brazil instead of taking a cruise on the *Bianca Pride*.

Avey's journey to Carriacou and to her forgotten heritage takes place in four stages, represented by the novel's four parts. In "Runagate" (which means "renegade" or "vagabond"), Avey breaks away from her two traveling companions and leaves the cruise. The section's title comes from a poem by African American poet Robert Hayden called "Runagate, Runagate," about the Underground Railroad. In "Sleeper's Wake," Avey remembers her early years with Jay, the desperation that nearly tore them apart, and their twelve-year climb toward financial success. The section title is metaphorical, not literal—in fact, the section ends with Avey falling asleep after a long period of weeping and raging over all that she and Jay lost in their pursuit of material comfort. It is Avey's sleeping memories that have awakened.

The title of the third section, "Lavé Tête" ("washing the head," or a vessel for washing one's hair), also is ironic or metaphoric: The section ends not with a physical bathing but with Avey soiling herself with vomit and diarrhea. Her spiritual cleansing begins in this section, however, as she meets Lebert Joseph, drinks his offering of coconut milk, admits that she is empty and lost, and agrees to accompany him on the Carriacou excursion. An important part of the cleansing that is to come happens during the tumultuous boat ride to Carriacou, when in Avey's dreams she reaches back before her own childhood to the experiences of slaves making the horrific journey from Africa. Finally, in "The Beg Pardon," she is bathed by Rosalie and Milda and also attends the big drum dance. During the ceremony, she reconnects with her forgotten past and experiences a darkness she has not seen since her childhood in Tatem; participates in the Beg Pardon, a community prayer on behalf of those present and all the far-flung people of the African diaspora; and finds that somehow she remembers the steps of a dance she has never danced before. In these four stages, Avey reconnects with her cultural heritage, and with her forgotten self.

The novel is structured to follow a nonlinear path, echoing the confusion Avey experiences during the four days of her journey. It features frequent flashbacks and dreams, quotes but does not translate words and phrases in the local patois, and depicts in striking detail Avey's physical feelings of nausea, dizziness, bloatedness, and emptiness. All of these techniques throw the reader off balance, making it difficult at times to know immediately what is happening. Avey's transformation comes unexpectedly, when she is not looking for change. By creating an unpredictable fictional world for her readers, Marshall creates the possibility that they, too, will make unexpected connections.

Cynthia A. Bily

Further Reading

Anatol, Giselle Liza. "Caribbean Migration, Ex-Isles, and the New World Novel." In *The Cambridge Companion to the African American Novel*, edited by Maryemma Graham. New York: Cambridge University Press, 2004. Examines the works of Paule Marshall and Haitian American writer Edwidge Danticat as literary representations of the dynamics between African diasporic populations in the United States.

Benjamin, Shanna Greene. "Weaving the Web of Reintegration: Locating Aunt Nancy in *Praisesong for the Widow*." *MELUS* 30, no. 1 (Spring, 2005): 49-67. Examines the influence of folk stories about Aunt Nancy, the American version of the half-woman, half-spider trickster of West African tales.

Coser, Stelamaris. "From the Natives' Point of View: The Ethnographic Novels of Paule Marshall." In *Bridging the Americas: The Literature of Paule Marshall, Toni Morrison, and Gayl Jones*. Philadelphia: Temple University Press, 1994. An accessible overview of the novel. Focuses on the Caribbean as the place midway between Africa and New York for Avey and for Marshall, the place where history and the future are intertwined.

DeLamotte, Eugenia C. "Voice, Spirit, Materiality, and the Road to Freedom: Third World Feminism in *Praisesong for the Widow*." In *Places of Silence, Journeys of Freedom: The Fiction of Paule Marshall*. Philadelphia: University of Pennsylvania Press, 1998. Focuses on American materialism as an outgrowth of American racism, separating Avey from her spiritual and sensual hungers.

Denniston, Dorothy Hamer. "Recognition and Recovery: Diasporan Connections in *Praisesong for the Widow*." In *The Fiction of Paule Marshall: Reconstructions of History, Culture, and Gender*. Knoxville: University of Tennessee Press, 1995. An analysis of African American and Caribbean cultural elements—music, poetry, dance—that reflect the wholeness Avey sacrifices for materialism, but ultimately reclaims.

Gnage, Marie Foster. "Reconfiguring Self: A Matter of Place in Selected Novels by Paule Marshall." In *Middle Passages and the Healing Place of History: Migration and Identity in Black Women's Literature*, edited by Elizabeth Brown-Guillory. Columbus: Ohio State University Press, 2006. Focuses on Marshall's treatment of women on their journeys to selfhood, examining how those journeys cause or shape their migrations. Novels discussed include *Praisesong for the Widow*.

Pettis, Joyce. "The Journey Completed: Spiritual Regeneration in *Praisesong for the Widow*." In *Toward Wholeness in Paule Marshall's Fiction*. Charlottesville: University Press of Virginia, 1995. Pettis sees Marshall as an explorer on a journey toward a new spiritual vision, with *Praisesong for the Widow* as the author's only novel whose protagonist realizes this goal.

Rogers, Susan. "Embodying Cultural Memory in Paule Marshall's *Praisesong for the Widow*." *African American Review* 34, no. 1 (Spring, 2000): 77-93. Explores the idea, suggested by the novel, that Avey's Africanness is an authentic part of her identity, while being an American is not. Also examines the significance of Avey's return to the United States after her reawakening.

Smith, Maria T. *African Religious Influences on Three Black Women Novelists: The Aesthetics of Vodun—Zora Neale Hurston, Simone Schwarz-Bart, and Paule Marshall*. Lewiston, N.Y.: Edwin Mellen Press, 2007. Examines the ways in which Marshall's *Praisesong for the Widow* alludes to the vodun, or Voodoo, pantheon and ancestor veneration that recognizes the interconnectedness of all living things but also functions as a source of cultural resistance.

A Prayer for Owen Meany

Author: John Irving (1942-   )
First published: 1989
Type of work: Novel
Type of plot: Bildungsroman
Time of plot: 1940's-1980's
Locale: New Hampshire; Arizona; Toronto, Ontario,
    Canada

Principal characters:
OWEN MEANY, a boy and man with a squeaky voice and
    very small stature
JOHNNY WHEELWRIGHT, the narrator, Owen's best friend
TABITHA WHEELWRIGHT NEEDHAM, Johnny's mother
DAN NEEDHAM, Tabitha's husband, a teacher
HESTER, Johnny's cousin and Owen's girlfriend
HARRIET WHEELWRIGHT, Johnny's aristocratic
    grandmother
RANDY WHITE, school headmaster
REVEREND LEWIS MERRILL, Congregational minister
DICK JARVITS, a deranged killer

The Story:

Johnny and Owen are best friends growing up in Gravesend, New Hampshire. Johnny resides in a lively household with his wealthy and outspoken grandmother Harriet, his pretty unwed mother Tabitha, visiting rambunctious cousins, and servants. Owen has a crush on Tabitha and likes to put clothes on her dressmaker's dummy. Johnny's grandmother financially supports Owen, and the two conduct a running commentary about television programs and world events.

Owen's father owns a granite quarry, and his mother is a recluse. In a good-natured game, Johnny and other children in their Sunday school class lift tiny Owen up in the air and pass him around above their heads. Owen and Johnny speculate about who Johnny's biological father could be. Dan, a suitor for Tabitha's hand, brings Johnny the gift of a stuffed armadillo, and both boys cherish it. Dan and Tabitha marry, giving Johnny a wonderful father figure. Dan is a teacher and also directs the town's amateur plays.

Owen is small but possesses exceptional intellect and wisdom. He presides over ceremonies such as the funeral for a neighbor's dog and shows precocious understanding of world events. He wins over Johnny's cousins, becoming the pack leader. Females are particularly attracted to Owen, always wanting to touch him. Owen expresses great dislike for the Catholic Church, a view he learned from his parents.

In a terrible accident, Owen hits a foul ball at a baseball game that strikes Johnny's mother and kills her. The ball disappears, and the boys come to believe that it will lead them to Johnny's biological father. Owen and Johnny comfort each other after the death with an exchange of valued objects: the stuffed armadillo and baseball cards. Owen takes possession of the dressmaker's dummy to save Dan and Johnny from further sadness.

The boys attend the private Gravesend Academy, where Owen is an academic star. He writes opinion columns in the school newspaper as "The Voice." His strong beliefs enrage the controlling and mean-spirited headmaster, Randy White. At the end of his senior year, Owen is dismissed for making fake draft cards on the school's copying machine. Owen pulls a prank on the headmaster: Using his granite-quarry skills, Owen hauls a headless, armless religious statue to the school stage and bolts it in place just before a student body meeting.

Though still tiny, teenaged Owen matures earlier than Johnny. He drives a car, smokes, dates girls, and develops muscles working in the granite quarry. He begins a serious romantic relationship with Johnny's headstrong cousin Hester. Owen develops a fervent religious faith and the ability to predict the future. He tries to convince Johnny that he, too, should believe in God. Owen believes that he is God's instrument, and that he will do something heroic then die. Owen has a dream in which he saves Asian children and is comforted by a nun before he dies. He pictures his own gravestone with the words "1LT PAUL O MEANY, JR." and expects to die in the Vietnam War.

While still in high school, the boys go to Boston hoping to learn the identity of Johnny's biological father. They are unsuccessful but learn that Tabitha took singing lessons there and sang in a supper club wearing a red dress. Throughout their youth and young adulthood, the friends practice "the shot" on the basketball court, in which Johnny lifts Owen so that he can slam-dunk the ball in three seconds.

Johnny and Owen attend the University of New Hampshire, where Johnny develops as a scholar. Owen is an average student but excels in Reserve Officers' Training Corps

(ROTC) courses. He graduates then joins the Adjutant General's Corps in Arizona, where he is assigned to be a body escort. Johnny goes on to graduate school, where Owen helps him start his thesis on Thomas Hardy. When Johnny gets orders to report for a preinduction physical, Owen helps him avoid being drafted by cutting off his index finger with a diamond granite saw.

Owen arranges for Johnny to be with him on the day he expects to die, July 8, 1968. They are on a body escort assignment in Phoenix. Owen cannot understand how the predicted Asian children and nuns could appear there, but at the airport they spot Vietnamese orphaned refugees and nuns disembarking from a plane. Owen and Johnny help the little boys use a restroom in the terminal. Owen yells after seeing an angry and deranged teenager, Dick Jarvits, hurl a hand grenade to Johnny. The children obey Owen's command to lie down because of his distinctive voice. Johnny passes the grenade to Owen while lifting him to a high window where it explodes, killing Owen but leaving everyone else uninjured.

Many revelations follow Owen's death. Johnny visits Owen's parents, where he obtains Owen's diary. Mr. Meany tells Johnny that Owen was a virgin birth. Several Catholic churches refused to accept this account by Mr. and Mrs. Meany, leading to their dislike of Catholicism. Mr. Meany shows Johnny a gravestone that Owen made for himself during his last visit, with the date already marked. Johnny learns that the four-year delay in Dan and Tabitha's marriage was to satisfy his biological father, who demanded that Tabitha accept this delay in exchange for his promise never to identify himself to Johnny.

Owen's ghost visits Johnny twice. The first visitation occurs when Johnny visits Reverend Merrill to discuss plans for Owen's funeral. He urges Merrill to believe in miracles, but the faithless Merrill cannot. Suddenly, Merrill's voice changes to Owen's voice and says to look in a desk drawer. Merrill pulls open the drawer, and the fated baseball rolls out. Merrill admits that he is Johnny's father. Seeing Tabitha wave to him at the baseball game, Merrill momentarily prayed that she would die. Her death caused him to lose his faith.

Johnny is disappointed to learn his father's identity. To teach Merrill a lesson, Johnny dresses the dressmaker's dummy in his mother's red dress and places it outside Merrill's church office. Johnny throws the baseball through the church window. When Merrill comes outside, he sees the dummy and believes it is Tabitha's ghost. The incident causes him to regain his religious faith.

In the second visitation, Johnny nearly falls down darkened basement stairs. He feels Owen's hand grab him and

hears Owen's voice say that he need not be afraid. Both Hester and Johnny are affected by Owen for the rest of their lives. Hester takes part in antiwar protests, performs as a folk singer, and later becomes a successful rock star. Following a suggestion made by Owen, Johnny moves to Canada, where he finds work as a teacher at Bishop Strachan and joins the Anglican Church. He often says a prayer for Owen Meany, especially one asking angels to guide Owen to heaven.

Critical Evaluation:

John Irving had published five novels, including the best-selling *The World According to Garp* (1978), when he released *A Prayer for Owen Meany* in 1989. The novel also became a best seller and a favorite of Irving's fans. Irving disowned a 1998 film adaption, *Simon Birch*, demanding that character names be changed to distance the project from his work.

A Prayer for Owen Meany shares common themes with Irving's other books, including the setting of a boy's boarding school, absent or missing parents, and a fatal accident. Irving uses the repeated motif of an armless figure in the novel: The armadillo's claws have been removed, the Mary Magdalene statue's arms have been severed, Owen cuts off John's finger, and Owen's arms are blown away in the explosion. As with many of Irving's main characters, Owen embodies multiple symbolic identities: He is at times a Christ figure, a martyr, a prophet, and a toy. His small size contrasts with his emotional and spiritual stature, emphasizing that he is a larger-than-life hero.

Irving uses two primary characters: Johnny, who narrates the story of their youth and young adulthood, and Owen, who teaches Johnny about life and faith through his words and deeds. Irving prints all Owen's words in capital letters, a device that calls attention to Owen's precocious thoughts while reminding readers of his unusual, squeaky voice and tiny stature. The story follows a fairly linear chronological sequence, except for the many inserted short references to Johnny Wheelwright in the 1980's reflecting back upon Owen's lasting influences on him.

The story poses multiple mysteries to be solved, and eventually all the solutions are revealed. Readers discover what happened to the baseball, the identity of Johnny's father, the reason that Owen's parents dislike Catholicism, the purpose of Owen's unusual voice, and the role of the dunk shot the boys practice endlessly. Owen's funeral service brings closure to the story, as most of the novel's characters reappear in the pews.

Irving has been greatly influenced by Charles Dickens, Kurt Vonnegut, and Günter Grass. Like them, he displays a vivid imagination and addresses moral issues. Irving has commented on his appreciation of Dickens and in particular of the author's willingness to be sentimental. Irving uses repeated phrases that sum up characters' strong reactions, such as "Hester the Molester" and "made for television." In common with other Irving novels, *A Prayer for Owen Meany* features many scenes that combine high tragedy with high comedy. An example is the funeral of Tabitha Wheelwright, who was killed by an errant baseball. Those in attendance wince at the repeated crack of a bat coming from a baseball game taking place just outside the window. Irving is a very funny writer, and frequently the laughter comes in the absence of tragedy, such as during the nativity play in which Owen plays the Christ child or a school prank involving Dr. Dolder's Volkswagen.

Irving's personal animosity toward many national policies is revealed through Owen's pronouncements about the Vietnam War and the Iran-Contra affair. The story presents a long causal chain of damage resulting directly and indirectly from the Vietnam conflict. The adult Johnny Wheelwright, narrating from Toronto, follows these with similar stinging critiques of U.S. government policies. In other novels, Irving penned polemics on subjects including abortion and racism.

An overarching theme of Irving's novel is the importance of small, close groupings such as families and small towns, "the gemeinschaft." Readers come to know and love the Wheelwright family, the Gravesend Academy community, and Johnny's circle of friends in Toronto. The book depicts many gatherings of these closely knit groups, such as funerals, a wedding, dramatic presentations, and the morning meetings at Gravesend Academy.

Not all critics have admired Irving's works. Some have found his plots vulgar and his characters "too cute." His fantastic plots have been seen by some critics as evidence that the author has "sold out" to a mass readership. Irving has answered these criticisms by pointing out that real life has many fantastic happenings: Terrible accidents and violent deaths really do happen. Improbable people are elected to high office and implement irrational national policies. He hopes his readers will gain insight and understanding from his work.

Irving's goal is authentic writing with vivid, believable language. An example is the poignant scene at Owen's funeral, where Reverend Merrill's fingers move with the fervor of his Bible readings while a beam of sunlight passes through the broken church window and lights the medal for heroism lying on Owen's flag-draped casket. Irving wants his novels to be accessible and entertaining to large numbers of people. He hopes to console readers who have experienced life's tragedies by helping them develop a positive spirit.

Nancy Conn Terjesen

Further Reading

Bloom, Harold, ed. *John Irving*. Broomall, Pa.: Chelsea House, 2001. Collection of twelve essays on the author's work from a variety of critical perspectives, with many references to *A Prayer for Owen Meany*.

Campbell, Josie P. *John Irving: A Critical Companion*. Westport, Conn.: Greenwood Press, 1998. Analysis and overview of Irving's work by an English professor who specializes in folklore. Includes a chapter on *A Prayer for Owen Meany*, as well as an extensive bibliography.

Davis, Todd F., and Kenneth Womack. *A Critical Response to John Irving*. Westport, Conn.: Praeger, 2004. This criticism of the postmodernist writings of Irving includes a chapter on *A Prayer for Owen Meany*.

Harter, Carol C., and James R. Thompson. *John Irving*. Boston: Twayne, 1986. Devotes a chapter to each of Irving's first six novels, showing the writer's development in both style and subject matter leading up to *A Prayer for Owen Meany*.

Reilly, Edward C. *Understanding John Irving*. Columbia: University of South Carolina Press, 1991. Examines seven novels, including *A Prayer for Owen Meany*. Heavily researched; looks at literary techniques, characters, and themes in comparing novels.

Shostak, Debra. "Plot as Repetition: John Irving's Narrative Experiments." *Critique* 27, no. 1 (Fall, 1995): 51-70. Examines repeated motifs in Irving's works and the reaction of readers to those motifs.

Preface to Shakespeare

Author: Samuel Johnson (1709-1784)
First published: 1765
Type of work: Literary criticism

Samuel Johnson's preface to *The Plays of William Shakespeare* has long been considered a classic document of English literary criticism. In it Johnson sets forth his editorial principles and gives an appreciative analysis of the "excellences" and "defects" of the work of the great Elizabethan dramatist. Many of his points have become fundamental tenets of modern criticism; others give greater insight into Johnson's prejudices than into Shakespeare's genius. The resonant prose of the preface adds authority to the views of its author.

Perhaps no other document exhibits the character of eighteenth century literary criticism better than what is commonly known as Johnson's *Preface to Shakespeare*. Written after Johnson had spent nine years laboring to produce an edition of Shakespeare's plays, the *Preface to Shakespeare* is characterized by sweeping generalizations about the dramatist's work and by stunning pronouncements about its merits, judgments that elevated Shakespeare to the top spot among European writers of any century. At times, Johnson displays the tendency of his contemporaries to fault Shakespeare for his propensity for wordplay and for ignoring the demands for poetic justice in his plays; readers of subsequent generations have found these criticisms to reflect the inadequacies of the critic more than they do those of the dramatist. What sets Johnson's work apart from that of his contemporaries, however, is the immense learning that lies beneath so many of his judgments; he consistently displays his familiarity with the texts, and his generalizations are rooted in specific passages from the dramas. Further, Johnson is the first among the great Shakespeare critics to stress the playwright's sound understanding of human nature. Johnson's focus on character analysis initiated a critical trend that would be dominant in Shakespeare criticism (in fact, all of dramatic criticism) for more than a century and would lead to the great work of critics such as Samuel Taylor Coleridge, Charles Lamb, and A. C. Bradley.

The significance of the *Preface to Shakespeare*, however, goes beyond its contributions to Shakespeare scholarship. First, it is the most significant practical application of a critical principle that Johnson espoused consistently and that has become a staple of the practice since: comparison. His systematic attempt to measure Shakespeare against others, both classical and contemporary, became the model. Second, the *Preface to Shakespeare* exemplifies Johnson's belief that good criticism can be produced only after good scholarship has been practiced. The critic who wishes to judge an author's originality or an author's contributions to the tradition must first practice sound literary reading and research in order to understand what has been borrowed and what has been invented.

Characteristically, Johnson makes his Shakespeare criticism the foundation for general statements about people, nature, and literature. He is a true classicist in his concern with the universal rather than with the particular; the highest praise he can bestow upon Shakespeare is to say that his plays are "just representations of general nature." The dramatist has relied upon his knowledge of human nature, rather than on bizarre effects, for his success. "The pleasures of sudden wonder are soon exhausted, and the mind can only repose on the stability of truth," Johnson concludes. It is for this reason that Shakespeare has outlived his century and reached the point at which his works can be judged solely on their own merits, without the interference of personal interests and prejudices that make criticism of one's contemporaries difficult.

Johnson feels that the readers of his time can often understand the universality of Shakespeare's vision better than the audiences of Elizabethan England could, for the intervening centuries have freed the plays of their topicality. The characters in the plays are not limited by time or nationality; they are, rather, "the genuine progeny of common humanity, such as the world will always supply, and observation will always find."

Implicitly criticizing earlier editors of Shakespeare, who had dotted their pages with asterisks marking particularly fine passages, Johnson contends that the greatness of the plays lies primarily in their total effect, in the naturalness of the action, the dialogue, and the characterization. Again and again Johnson stresses the same point: "This, therefore, is the praise of Shakespeare, that his drama is the mirror of life." The playwright's personages are drawn from the world familiar to everyone: "Shakespeare has no heroes; his scenes are occupied only by men, who act and speak as the reader thinks that he should himself have spoken or acted on the same occasion."

That Shakespeare wrote "contrary to the rules of criticism" is, for Johnson, not a problem. Aside from the fact that Aristotle's rules were not widely known during Shakespeare's time, Johnson notes, "There is always an appeal open from criticism to nature." Life itself justifies the mingling of comedy and tragedy on the stage; together they exhibit "the real state of sublunary nature, which partakes of good and evil, joy and sorrow, mingled with endless variety of proportion and innumerable modes of combination."

While Johnson is aware of Shakespeare's skills in both comedy and tragedy, he suggests that the playwright's natural forte was the former: "In tragedy he is always struggling after some occasion to be comick; but in comedy he seems to repose, or to luxuriate, as in a mode of thinking congenial to his nature." Johnson later criticizes some of the plays' tragic speeches as bombast, forced, unnatural emotion, and he complains that all too often scenes of pathos are marred by "idle conceits," those inspiring terror and pity by "sudden frigidity." The critic later confesses, however, that in spite of these flaws one finds one's mind seized more strongly by Shakespeare's tragedies than by those of any other writer.

Johnson praises Shakespeare's language as that of the "common intercourse of life," used among those who speak only to be understood, without ambition or elegance. One of Johnson's most stringent objections to Shakespeare's work arises from Johnson's strong conviction that literature is, or should be, essentially didactic. He is disturbed by Shakespeare's disregard of poetic justice. Johnson, convinced that a writer should show the virtuous rewarded and the evil punished, asserts that Shakespeare, by ignoring this premise, "sacrifices virtue to convenience." In Johnson's eyes, the fact that in life evil often triumphs over good is no excuse: "It is always a writer's duty to make the world better."

Shakespeare's careless plotting and his "disregard for distinctions of time and place" are also noted as flaws: "We need not wonder to find Hector quoting Aristotle, when we see the loves of Theseus and Hippolyta combined with the Gothick mythology of fairies." Although Johnson dislikes Shakespeare's often coarse language, he is willing to concede that that fault, at least, might have rested with the indelicacy of the ladies and gentlemen at the courts of Elizabeth I and James I rather than with the playwright. These minor "errors" are far less irritating to Johnson than Shakespeare's use of puns: "A quibble was to him the fatal Cleopatra for which he lost the world, and was content to lose it." Puns, being language's form of disorderly conduct, disturbed Johnson's neoclassical understanding.

Johnson's contemporaries often condemned Shakespeare for his lack of attention to the Aristotelian unities of time,

place, and action, which were assiduously observed by the French classical dramatists and their English imitators. Johnson notes that Shakespeare observed the principle of unity of action in giving each of his plays a beginning, a middle, and an end, and in developing his plots by cause and effect. Moreover, Johnson sees no harm in Shakespeare's failure in most cases to limit his action to one place and one day. Most strict neoclassical critics maintained that such limitations of time and space are necessary for dramatic credibility, but Johnson finds this assertion ridiculous, for every member of the audience knows that all drama is illusion: "He that can take the stage at one time for the palace of the Ptolemies, may take it in half an hour for the promontory of Actium. Delusion, if delusion be admitted, has no certain limitation." Real dramatic credibility comes from the validity of the emotions presented: "The reflection that strikes the heart is not, that the evils before us are real evils, but that they are evils to which we ourselves may be exposed."

Anticipating the historical critics of the nineteenth and twentieth centuries, Johnson assesses some of the aspects of Elizabethan England that probably influenced Shakespeare. He stresses the fact that the dramatist was in many ways a pioneer, for he had few truly outstanding English works of drama or poetry on which to build. Shakespeare's complicated plots can be traced to the popularity of the elaborate pastoral romances read by his audiences and occasionally used as sources for the plays.

Johnson does not emphasize Shakespeare's learning, noting that the playwright could have read in translation the classical works he mentions. Shakespeare's greatest knowledge came not from books, but from life: "Mankind was not then to be studied in the closet; he that would know the world, was under the necessity of gleaning his own remarks, by mingling as he could in its business and amusements."

Concluding his general commentary, Johnson summarizes Shakespeare's gifts to English literature:

> The form, the characters, the language, and the shows of the English drama are his. . . . To him we must ascribe the praise, unless Spenser may divide it with him, of having first discovered to how much smoothness and harmony the English language could be softened.

In the remainder of the *Preface to Shakespeare*, Johnson delineates his editorial standards, rejecting the temptation to follow the practices of his predecessors, who had emended—essentially rewritten—the plays where they could not understand or did not like what they found in the earliest texts of Shakespeare's works. Johnson followed Alexander Pope in basing his edition on the original quarto versions of the plays and on the first folio, and he states that he attempted to leave them as nearly as possible as he found them. His explanatory notes offer not only his own ideas but also the views of earlier critics. He quotes others to refute them more often than to praise them, believing that "the first care of the builder of a new system, is to demolish the fabrics which are standing."

In a final exhortation to the reader, Johnson places his efforts in perspective; notes are often necessary, but they are necessary evils. The reader who has not yet experienced Shakespeare's genius must first ignore the editor's aids and simply read for "the highest pleasure that the drama can give." Johnson's modesty is in itself a tribute to Shakespeare; his whole task as editor and critic was to make the great plays more accessible to the public, and his criticism still gives valuable insights to the modern lover of Shakespeare.

Further Reading

Clingham, Greg. *Johnson, Writing, and Memory*. New York: Cambridge University Press, 2002. Examines Johnson's writing and places it within the context of eighteenth century ideas about literature, history, fiction, and law, discussing the challenges that these ideas pose to twentieth and twenty-first century critical theory.

_____, ed. *The Cambridge Companion to Samuel Johnson*. New York: Cambridge University Press, 1997. Collection of essays includes discussions of Johnson and the arts of conversation, poetry, and the essay as well as examination of his political views. The *Preface to Shakespeare* is discussed in Philip Smallwood's essay "Shakespeare: Johnson's Poet of Nature."

Hart, Kevin. *Samuel Johnson and the Culture of Property*. New York: Cambridge University Press, 1999. Examines Johnson's literary legacy and reputation and analyzes the works of those biographers and critics who helped create the "Age of Johnson." Asserts that James Boswell's famous biography turned Johnson into a public monument.

Johnson, Samuel. *Johnson's "Preface to Shakespeare": A Facsimile of the 1778 Edition with Introduction and Commentary by P. J. Smallwood*. Edited by P. J. Smallwood. Bristol, England: Bristol Classical Press, 1985. Especially informative volume offers the full text of the *Preface to Shakespeare* along with extensive commentary by the editor aimed at elucidating every detail of Johnson's work.

Martin, Peter. *Samuel Johnson: A Biography*. Cambridge, Mass.: Harvard University Press, 2008. Provides a psychological profile of Johnson, focusing on aspects of his personality and life that are not covered in Boswell's biography, such as Johnson's insecurities, bouts of deep depression, and self-doubt.

Parker, G. F. *Johnson's Shakespeare*. New York: Oxford University Press, 1989. Contradicts the opinions of scholars who argue that Johnson's interpretation of William Shakespeare has been superseded by subsequent critiques; explains why Johnson's opinion that Shakespeare was "the poet of nature" remains a radical viewpoint.

Stock, R. D. *Samuel Johnson and Neoclassical Dramatic Theory: The Intellectual Context of the "Preface to Shakespeare."* Lincoln: University of Nebraska Press, 1973. Offers a lengthy, detailed review of the critical context that Johnson inherited and concludes with a close look at the *Preface to Shakespeare*.

Tomarken, Edward. *A History of the Commentary on Selected Writings of Samuel Johnson*. Columbia, S.C.: Camden House, 1994. Provides an informative survey of what critics have said of Johnson's Shakespeare criticism. Argues that Johnson's work is a model of criticism that continues to offer valuable instruction.

Prejudices

Author: H. L. Mencken (1880-1956)
First published: 1919-1927
Type of work: Essays

During the 1920's, few literary events were so eagerly awaited in the United States as the appearance of a new volume of H. L. Mencken's *Prejudices*. A wide range of people enjoyed the spectacle of the Sage of Baltimore, as he was called, pulling yet another popular idol down from its pedestal. Mencken's iconoclasm was accomplished with so much gusto and with such vigorous and picturesque language as to enchant a whole generation grown weary of the solemnity of much American writing. Indeed, the decade badly needed an iconoclast, for what later became almost exclusively thought of as the Jazz Age was also the era of the Ku Klux Klan and the Anti-Saloon League, of Babbittry and boosterism.

Mencken's essays in these volumes can be divided into two categories: literary criticism and criticism of the contemporary American scene. Literary criticism Mencken defines as a "catalytic process" in which the critic serves as the catalyst. As a critic, however, Mencken derived mainly from James Huneker, whom he admired enormously and had known personally. Huneker had been familiar with Continental writers, then not too well known in the United States, and his criticism was essentially impressionistic, often couched in breezy, epigrammatic language. Mencken carried certain of these characteristics much further; indeed, his verbal acrobatics became his hallmark. His was a racy, pungent style very effective for the "debunking" then so popular and deliberately calculated to drive conservative readers into frenzies.

Mencken's chief target, of which he never tired, was the Puritan tradition in American literature with its consequent timidity, stuffiness, and narrow-mindedness. As he saw it, the Puritan was afraid of aesthetic emotion and thus could neither create nor enjoy art. This fear had inhibited American literature, he claimed, and had made American criticism timid and conventional. Further, criticism had fallen into the hands of the professors, and there was nothing—not even a prohibition agent—that Mencken detested so much as the average American university professor. Hence, he heaped scorn on such men as Paul Elmer More, Irving Babbitt, Stuart P. Sherman, and William Lyon Phelps for years.

It is ironic that the critical writings of some of these academics have withstood the passage of time more successfully than have those of Mencken. For though less a geographical provincial than they, he was more provincial in time and was interested mainly in the contemporary. Of the older native writers, he really admired only Edgar Allan Poe, Mark Twain, and Walt Whitman—the nonconformists. Even among the progressives of his age his preferences were curiously limited. He had great regard for Joseph Conrad and Theodore Dreiser, but he overlooked much of the talent that was budding during the 1920's. That he should have overpraised some of his contemporaries, James Branch Cabell, for example, or Dreiser, should not be held against him; few critics are sufficiently detached to escape this fault. Dreiser was an important writer but not the "colossal phenomenon" that Mencken called him.

Mencken's greatest failure as a critic was his blindness to poetry. In the third series of *Prejudices* he includes an essay,

"The Poet and His Art," a study so full of false assumptions, logical fallacies, and plain misstatements of fact as to be an embarrassing legacy for a critic to have left behind him. Because Dante's theology was unacceptable to Mencken, he therefore judged that Dante could not really have believed what he wrote; according to Mencken, *The Divine Comedy* (c. 1320) was a satire on the Christian doctrine of heaven and hell.

The essays dealing with the national scene are written in the same slashing manner and naturally infuriated far more readers, since Mencken here attacks people, institutions, and ideas familiar to everyone. Many of these pieces retain little significance in later times, for they deal with situations reserved for that particular decade. Yet some of them are valid still: "The Sahara of the Bozart" (second series) is in some ways almost as true of the South today as it was in 1920; his comments on the farmer ("The Husbandman," fourth series) are even more appropriate, and his dissections of such eminent figures as Theodore Roosevelt and Thorstein Veblen are still funny.

Of Americans in general, Mencken had a low opinion, considering them a mongrel people incapable of high spiritual aspiration. His opinion of democracy was equally low. It was, he felt, merely a scheme to con the have-nots in their unending battle with the haves. The inferiority of Americans Mencken attributed to the lack of a genuine aristocracy and to Puritanism. Without an aristocracy, there could be no real leadership in America, and the vacuum would inevitably be filled by politicians, whom he detested. Nor did he have any faith in reform or reformers.

As for Puritanism, Mencken believed that it had always been the dominant force in American history and had left Americans the narrow-minded victims of religious bigotry. The predominance during the 1920's of the more extreme forms of religious fundamentalism gave some support to his argument. In his attacks on religion, however, he made the mistake of throwing the baby out with the bath water. Because he himself was a complete skeptic, he could not believe that there could be intelligent and yet sincere Christians.

Mencken's enemies were always urging him, in anguished tones, to leave the United States if he found it so distasteful. His reply was that nowhere else could so much entertainment be had so cheaply. According to his calculations, it cost him personally only eighty cents a year to maintain Warren Harding in the White House. Where could a better show be found for the money? In spite of his exaggerations, crudities, and often bad taste, Mencken performed a valuable service as a national gadfly, and his cynical wit provided the sting at just the right historic moment.

Further Reading

Fitzpatrick, Vincent. *H. L. Mencken.* New York: Continuum, 1989. Reprint. Mercer, Ga.: Mercer University Press, 2004. Assesses Mencken's influence on American life and letters through the presentation of significant relationships and battles. Notes Mencken's intent in *Prejudices* to attack cherished beliefs and stir up his fellow Americans.

Geismar, Maxwell. *The Last of the Provincials: The American Novel, 1915-1925.* Boston: Houghton Mifflin, 1949. Views Mencken as the dominant literary voice of the 1920's, supporting the conquest of American values of older rural life. Concludes that *Prejudices* reflects his efforts to champion the new economic order of industrialization over Puritan conscience and the reaches of the American hinterland.

Kazin, Alfred. *On Native Grounds: An Interpretation of Modern American Prose Literature.* 1942. New ed. San Diego, Calif.: Harcourt Brace, 1995. Classic treatment of the emergence of modern American literature. Considers Mencken's capacity for imposing his skepticism on a new generation. Argues that Mencken is the perfect illustration of America's passage into the second half of the twentieth century.

Lippman, Walter. "H. L. Mencken." *Saturday Review of Literature* (December 11, 1926): 413-415. One of the earliest and most astute assessments of Mencken's ideas. Insists that Mencken's effectiveness lies in his ability to alter prejudices. Sees Mencken as a personal force overwhelmingly preoccupied with popular culture working for the liberty of an ideal democracy.

Rodgers, Marion Elizabeth. *Mencken: The American Iconoclast.* New York: Oxford University Press, 2006. Comprehensive, meticulously researched portrait of Mencken. Includes information about the creation and reception of *Prejudices.*

Teachout, Terry. *The Skeptic: A Life of H. L. Mencken.* New York: HarperCollins, 2002. Concise but thorough biography that discusses how Mencken's work helped shape American social attitudes.

Williams, W. H. A. *H. L. Mencken.* Boston: Twayne, 1977. A chronological study of Mencken's life, focusing on the development of his ideas and the way he draws on them throughout his criticism. Evaluates Mencken's social criticism in the 1920's and concludes that his involvement with the struggle between the rural and the urban, as shown in *Prejudices,* was his major theme of the decade.

_____. *H. L. Mencken Revisited.* New York: Twayne, 1998. Williams's revision of his 1977 study includes two decades of new scholarship on Mencken to provide a more up-to-date overview of the writer's life and work. Chronicles the development of Mencken's ideas, examines the major themes of his work, and discusses his opinions about American society.

The Prelude
Or, The Growth of a Poet's Mind

Author: William Wordsworth (1770-1850)
First published: 1850
Type of work: Poetry

The Prelude, which was not published until shortly after William Wordsworth's death in 1850, was planned as the introductory section of a long autobiographical and philosophical poem that was never finished, titled *The Recluse.* In that ambitious work, Wordsworth intended to trace in blank verse the development of his views on humanity, society, and nature. Of the projected three parts, only the second, *The Excursion* (1814), written between 1799 and 1805, was completed and published. The important "Friend" to whom the poem is addressed is Samuel Taylor Coleridge.

Wordsworth strongly advocated the use of poetry for the expression of individual emotions and insights. *The Prelude* contains many fine passages that illustrate the clarity and force of his use of language to provide both a precise description of nature and a grasp of its meaning. Although the poem contains long prosaic stretches, it also conveys a sense of the calm beauty and power of nature that distinguishes Words-worth's verse.

The work begins with an account of the poet's childhood in the English Lake District. With many digressions addressed to nature and its power, wisdom, and infusing spirit, the poet describes the influence of nature on his solitary childhood. Some of the sense of awe and pleasure that he found in nature, as well as some of his clearest and most penetrating uses of diction, is evident in the passage in which he describes how he found a boat in a cave, unchained the boat, and rowed out into the center of a lake:

> Lustily
> I dipped my oars into the silent lake,
> And, as I rose upon the stroke, my boat
> Went heaving through the water like a swan;
> When, from behind that craggy steep till then
> The horizon's bound, a huge peak, black and huge,
> As if with voluntary power instinct
> Upreared its head. I struck and struck again,
> And growing still in stature the grim shape
> Towered up between me and the stars, and still,
> For so it seemed, with purpose of its own
> And measured motion like a living thing,
> Strode after me.

The image of the peak is invested with such simplicity and power that it is transformed into a force conveying both terror and beauty to the guilty boy who has stolen a ride in a boat.

The poet speaks of his youthful love of freedom and liberty, which he enjoyed in rambles through the woods and on mountain paths where he did not feel fettered by the claims of society and schoolwork. He makes sure to reassure the reader, however, that he was outwardly docile and obedient, keeping his rebellion and sense of freedom in the realm of the spirit. This combination of outward calm and inward rebellion helps explain Wordsworth's ability to control highly individualistic thought in calm, dignified, unostentatious verse forms and diction. Wordsworth does not use the speech of the common people; indeed, his speech is often abstract, speculative, and pervaded with a sense of the mystery and meaning of nature. At its best, however, Wordsworth's diction has a dignity and calm control, a lack of pretense, through which the force of his inner meaning gently radiates.

Wordsworth describes his journey through Cambridge, telling of experiences there and discussing the fact that he neither was nor cared to be a scholar. Despite his studies, he continues to concentrate inwardly on the spirit of things, the power of nature, and the impetus nature gives to his feelings.

At this point, Wordsworth begins to speculate on the differences between reason and emotion or passion, equating reason with scholars and emotion with his own apprehension of the world of nature:

> But all the meditations of mankind,
> Yea, all the adamantine holds of truth
> By reason built, or passion, which itself
> Is highest reason in a soul sublime.

Throughout the poem, Wordsworth makes the distinction between reason and passion, and he attributes an ultimate sterility to the quality of reason while glorifying the element of passion or imagination.

Wordsworth tells of traveling to the Alps after leaving Cambridge. The mountains there reminded him of the mountains familiar to him from his childhood, and he felt again and even more keenly that the majesty and awe of the scenery found reflection in his spirit. He begins, more strongly, to feel his kinship with nature and juxtaposes that with a description of his life among the crowds and industries of London after his return from Europe. He describes how, dissatisfied with life in London, he traveled to France during the early stages of the French Revolution. In this section he expresses his feeling that he has not cared for human beings sufficiently—in his devotion to nature, he has neglected his feeling for his fellow creatures. Recalling his early love for freedom and liberty and adding his new conviction of the importance of political liberty, Wordsworth became strongly attracted to the cause of the French Revolution, feeling, as he says in *The Prelude*, that he was tied emotionally and spiritually to the popular struggle against the monarchy. He became disillusioned, however, by the bloodiness of the war and by the popular ingratitude and refusal to acknowledge the heroes who championed the Revolution's cause with greatest fervor and sincerity. He began to feel that blood had poisoned the cause of liberty in France, and he returned to England.

Disillusioned and alone, he sought to bring meaning back into his life. The penultimate section of *The Prelude* is titled "Imagination and Taste, How Impaired and Restored." At that period of his life he turned back to nature, finding there not solace alone but a sense of law and order lacking in human society. He began to realize the difference in scale between nature and people and the range and effect of nature in comparison to the tiny ineffectuality of human beings. Sections of resolution in the poem frequently include passages such as the following interpolation in the midst of a narrative section:

> O Soul of Nature! that, by laws divine
> Sustained and governed, still dost overflow
> With an impassioned life, what feeble ones
> Walk on this earth!

In Wordsworth's view, nature provides not only awe and spiritual impetus for human beings but also order, rules of conduct, and the means of molding human behavior. In the final sections of the poem, he uses nature as the authority for his new morality and assumes a much more overtly moral tone. He didactically advocates the importance of faith and obedience and of not relying on unaided human reason. Whereas in the poem's earlier sections he praises emotion and freedom in opposition to rational restraint, here the poet praises the restraint of faith and spirit in opposition to rational license. This change is illustrative of a change in Wordsworth's career, from the poet advocating the simple joy and freedom of nature to the sage defending abstract and conventional truths. His attitude becomes clear in the following passage from the conclusion of the poem:

> But, the dawn beginning now
> To re-appear, 'twas proved that not in vain
> I had been taught to reverence a Power
> That is the visible quality and shape
> And image of right reason; that matures
> Her processes by steadfast laws; gives birth
> To no impatient or fallacious hopes,
> No heat of passion or excessive zeal,
> No vain conceits; provokes to no quick turns
> Of self-applauding intellect; but trains
> To meekness, and exalts by humble faith.

The Prelude documents Wordsworth's changing attitudes toward nature and human beings while at the same time reflecting the different characteristics of his diction and poetic power. No other single poem expresses his reverence for nature with such power and simplicity. *The Prelude* is truly a monument to Wordsworth's career, his evolving ideas, and his transforming use of poetry.

Further Reading

Bloom, Harold, ed. *William Wordsworth's "The Prelude."* New York: Chelsea House, 1986. Collection of essays provides analyses of *The Prelude* as well as an informative editor's introduction and a chronology of the events of Wordsworth's life.

Fry, Paul H. *Wordsworth and the Poetry of What We Are.* New Haven, Conn.: Yale University Press, 2008. Argues that underneath the themes of transcendence and love of nature in Wordsworth's poetry is a basic insight: "The poet is most astonished not that the world he experiences has any particular qualities or significance, but rather that it simply exists." Asserts that this astonishment is what makes Wordsworth's poetry original. Includes discussion of *The Prelude*.

Gill, Stephen, ed. *The Cambridge Companion to Wordsworth.* New York: Cambridge University Press, 2003. Collection of essays includes discussion of such topics as the shape of Wordsworth's poetic career, his craft, and gender and domesticity in his work. *The Prelude* is addressed in Lucy Newlyn's essay "The Noble Living and the Noble Dead: Community in *The Prelude*."

_____. *William Wordsworth's "The Prelude": A Casebook.* New York: Oxford University Press, 2006. Collection of essays provides numerous analyses and interpretations of the poem, including discussions of Wordsworth's conception of *The Prelude*, Wordsworth and the lyric voice, and the presence of Samuel Taylor Coleridge in the poem.

Jarvis, Simon. *Wordsworth's Philosophic Song.* New York: Cambridge University Press, 2007. Argues that Wordsworth's desire to create "philosophic song" is essential to his greatness as a poet. Describes how his combination of poetry and philosophy changed the way English poetry was written. Includes discussion of *The Prelude*.

Lindenberger, Herbert. *On Wordsworth's "Prelude."* 1963. Reprint. Westport, Conn.: Greenwood Press, 1976. Examines the success of *The Prelude* and discusses how Wordsworth was able to find a style of language and organization to encompass his poem's personal history and prophetic utterance.

Noyes, Russell. *William Wordsworth.* Updated by John O. Hayden. Boston: Twayne, 1991. Provides an overview of Wordsworth's life and works. Chapter 4, which addresses *The Prelude*, notes that the poem is an idealization, not a factual rendering, of the poet's life.

Wordsworth, William. *"The Prelude," 1799, 1805, 1850.* Edited by Jonathan Wordsworth, M. H. Abrams, and Stephen Gill. New York: W. W. Norton, 1979. Contains the text of the poem, excerpts from sixteen sources of contemporary reaction to the work, and seven modern critical essays. Includes a chronology of Wordsworth's life.

Preludes for Memnon

Author: Conrad Aiken (1889-1973)
First published: 1931
Type of work: Poetry

Conrad Aiken produced a remarkable variety of works, encompassing many different literary genres, among them short stories, novels, literary criticism, and a fascinating stream-of-conscious autobiographical essay. Any one of these works would mark him an important literary figure in the twentieth century. His greatest literary accomplishment, however, emerges in his poetry.

For many reasons, Aiken has been largely neglected by the academic and critical establishments. A quiet individual and extremely personal writer, he never fit conveniently into any particular poetic movement. Unlike such poets of his time as E. E. Cummings, he was not interested in challenging poetic form and line; he did not use poetry as a means of social comment, as did W. H. Auden and Stephen Spender, nor was he a Symbolist in the tradition of T. S. Eliot and William Butler Yeats. Aiken is a more traditional poet; in many ways, he is a descendant of the Romantic movement. He built on the traditional form, using elements from a variety of styles to form his personal poetic search for meaning.

Aiken's poetry challenges the imagination by presenting complex images and ideas that are not always readily accessible to the reader. Although his language is elegant and expressive, he seldom uses sustained descriptions to illustrate a theme. For the most part, his poetry is reflective rather than dramatic. Metaphors appear, are dropped, and reappear almost at random. This is particularly true in *Preludes for Memnon*. This series of sixty-three poems, taken together with its companion work *Time in the Rock* (1936), forms the core of Aiken's most mature work and contains the central themes and ideas in his writing. It is a series of meditations, images to greet the day. None of the individual poems is given an individual title, and there is no theme that builds from one poem to another. Instead, each poem deals with a separate song or search for attitude. Each explores a new theme or presents a different reflection on an old theme.

The title figure, Memnon, is the son of Tithonus, a mortal, grandson of the king of Troy and Eos, the goddess of the dawn. After the death of Hector, Troy's greatest warrior, Memnon attempts to avenge him but is slain by Achilles. Eos's grief at the loss of her son is so great that Zeus, moved to pity, makes Memnon immortal. The name Memnon is also connected with a seventy-foot column in Alexandria dedicated to Amenhotep III. In 27 B.C.E., the column was partly destroyed by an earthquake; it remained standing, but the earthquake had produced an unusual phenomenon in the column: When the sun's rays first touched it each dawn, musical sounds resembling harp strings could be heard. These were interpreted as Memnon greeting his mother, the dawn.

Aiken's concern is with the individual's search for identity. In a preface, written in 1965, to the joint publication of *Preludes for Memnon* and *Time in the Rock*, Aiken states the dilemma that inspired the poems. At a time when Sigmund Freud, Albert Einstein, Charles Darwin, and Friedrich Nietzsche had redefined the world and the old religions, philosophy, ethics, language, and poetry were no longer able to answer the questions raised by science and mathematics, Aiken wanted to explore ways in which human beings could search for belief. For Aiken, it was vital that people search both inside the self and outside, in the world. The first prelude begins with a discussion of winter, the reality in nature, and the symbolic meaning of winter in the soul.

> Winter is there, outside, is here in me:
> Drapes the planets with snow, deepens the ice
>   on the moon,
> Darkens the darkness that was already darkness.
> The mind too has its snows, its slippery paths,
> Walls bayoneted with ice, leaves ice-encased.

As the poem continues, Aiken introduces other motifs, which recur repeatedly at random places throughout the collection: the void; chaos; memory, which here appears as a juggler balancing the colored balls of inconsequential human action and thoughts; the distorting mirror; silence. Aiken ends by describing the angelic and demoniac wings that conjure the echo of the abyss, of death. With the poem's final line, Aiken reminds his reader, "And this is you."

This prelude provides no simple picture; it is, rather, part of Aiken's attempt to define the complex and shifting realities in human identity. Because Aiken believed that identity lies within human consciousness, his poetry explores that world. It is a place of ever-changing focuses, new ideas, contradictory thoughts. Paradox is central to many of the preludes. Aiken presents the contrasts between growth and dying, birth and death, winter and summer, silence and sound. Understanding these contrasts provides the only way to establish identity or, indeed, to protect the soul in a changing, impermanent universe.

Critics often turn to Aiken's own life to explain his fascination with identity and paradox. In *Ushant* (1952), his autobiographical essay, Aiken recalls the tragic event that shaped his life and psyche forever. When he was eleven years old, his father had killed his mother and then shot himself; having heard the shot, Aiken had gone to their room and discovered them. With this tragedy, he wrote later, he lost his parents physically but found himself tied to them forever. After their death, his brothers were sent to live with family in Georgia, while he was sent alone to be raised by relatives in New England.

Aiken became interested in Freud and his theories, feeling he must continually search for self-understanding, balance, and harmony. He always remained aware of the dark side of existence, in both humans and nature; yet he also saw hope, and his poems examine these differing aspects of human nature, together and separately.

A major theme, symbol, and controlling device in Aiken's poetry is music. The idea of a prelude or introduction provides a key to the poems as individual examinations of meaning that resemble Memnon's morning greetings to his mother. Music imposes order on sound, and Aiken uses the imagery of music in many ways. Prelude 4 begins with the image of music springing out of silence to bring delight. Such joy does not always last, and prelude 5 describes symbols of despair, things broken and spilled while "the string snaps, and the music stops." Prelude 9 equates beauty and music, and prelude 21 compares human lives to a series of notes: Daily, people rise to the first simple note and by evening the chord breaks and is silent.

Time, too, is the subject of many preludes. Prelude 28, for example, begins with the clock announcing that time has come, and it continues to remind of the passage of time, of days coming and going; in conclusion, the heart ticks like the clock. Prelude 19 is a reminder that, if one were to watch long enough, the cycle of existence could be seen to repeat itself over and over again.

Many poems face directly the paradox in human beings and nature. Prelude 13 introduces a question Aiken poses several times: How is it possible to find a beginning or an ending, when no such thing exists in nature? In the continuum of time, what enables an individual to point to a moment and say with certainty, yes, this is where something started or ended? Prelude 27 provides another study in the contrast and flux that exists in the world. Nothing remains; even love turns to other emotions. Still, Aiken presents the reverse: Out of decay, a daffodil will grow. Aiken frequently reverses ideas to express paradox, as in prelude 50: "The world is intricate, and we are nothing./ The world is nothing: we are intricate./ Alas, how simple to invert the world/ Inverting phrases." The poem goes on to explore the ambiguous nature of human beings, capable of believing two disparate ideas, feeling two contradictory emotions at the same time. Prelude 49 reinforces the conflicts in human nature: People kill both what they hate and what they love; what distinguishes the two is that they kill what they love slowly and with far more subtlety.

In many poems, language, even poetry itself, is the subject. Aiken, whose choice of words is thoughtful and precise, laments the failure of language. Prelude 5 discusses symbol and its imperfect ability to convey thought. For him, each symbol is both more and less than it appears on the page. A symbol, he declares, is as transient as the ghost of a thought. Prelude 28 reinforces the imprecision of words that seem precise, requesting the reader to take someone else's words and change the meaning that person intended the words to have. This poem centers on the effect of inherited words. When people accept foreign definitions, they become slaves to meanings from other people's consciousness. Parents and ancestors hand down words that reflect their identity, which may be quite different from the reality that their descendants experienced.

Ultimately, Aiken's poetry deals with the human need to deal with the contradictions and despair of the world. Individuals must use their own words, find an identity, discover balance. This is an ongoing task, a cycle without end; human beings must, as prelude 42 states, be forever vigilant, exploring their consciousness, redefining themselves, renewing their identity, "Then say: I was a part of nature's plan:/ Knew her cold heart, for I was consciousness:/ Came first to hate her, and at last to bless;/ Believed in her; doubted; believed again."

Mary Mahony

Further Reading

Aiken, Conrad. *Ushant: An Essay*. New York: Oxford University Press, 1971. Aiken's autobiographical essay of more than three hundred pages provides enormous insight into his perspectives on writing and on life in general. An important introductory source to help readers understand the complex imagery in Aiken's poetry. Originally published in 1952.

Butscher, Edward. *Conrad Aiken: Poet of White Horse Vale.* Athens: University of Georgia Press, 1988. A psycho-biography that covers Aiken's childhood in Georgia and Massachusetts, his years at Harvard University, and his friendships and involvements with other poets, including T. S. Eliot, Ezra Pound, and Amy Lowell. Also analyzes and traces the development of Aiken's literary works.

Cowley, Malcolm. "Conrad Aiken: From Savannah to Emerson." In *New England Writers and Writing*, edited by Donald W. Faulkner. Hanover, N.H.: University Press of New England, 1996. This essay discussing Aiken's work and its relation to New England is part of a collection that analyzes nineteenth and twentieth centuries authors from the New England region.

Marten, Harry. *The Art of Knowing: The Poetry and Prose of Conrad Aiken.* Columbia: University of Missouri Press, 1988. Discusses the organization of the *Preludes for Memnon*, including Aiken's views on consciousness, identity, and the change and flow in the life cycle. Analyzes poetic line and style.

Martin, Jay. *Conrad Aiken: A Life of His Art.* Princeton, N.J.: Princeton University Press, 1962. Traces Aiken's critical reputation and his development as a poet. Provides clear analysis of Aiken's style and themes, finding the *Preludes for Memnon* the central defining work of his career.

Spivey, Ted, and Arthur Waterman, eds. *Conrad Aiken: A Priest of Consciousness.* New York: AMS Press, 1989. An excellent collection of essays that provide clear insights into Aiken's work. Individual essays examine Aiken's views on consciousness and language; essays on the *Preludes for Memnon* discuss metapoetics and provide a contextual reading of several poems.

The Pretenders

Author: Ludovico Ariosto (1474-1533)
First produced: I suppositi, 1509; first published, 1509 (English translation, 1566)
Type of work: Drama
Type of plot: Farce
Time of plot: c. 1500
Locale: Ferrara, Italy

Principal characters:
DULIPPO, posing as a servant, actually Erostrato
EROSTRATO, posing as a student, actually Dulippo
POLINESTA, a young lady of Ferrara
DAMON, a wealthy merchant, her father
CLEANDRO, an ancient doctor of law, her suitor
A SIENESE, posing as Erostrato's father
FILOGONO, a wealthy Sicilian merchant, father of Erostrato
PASIFILO, a meddlesome parasite
BALIA, Polinesta's nurse

The Story:

Balia, nurse to beautiful young Polinesta, expresses concern about her mistress's practice of sleeping with her father's servant, Dulippo. Polinesta reproves Balia, reminding her that it is she who first gave Dulippo access to Polinesta's bedroom. Polinesta also reassures Balia by explaining that Dulippo is, in reality, not a servant, but Erostrato, the son of a wealthy Sicilian merchant. Having come to Ferrara to pursue his studies, he fell in love with Polinesta upon his arrival. Consequently, he has taken the name of his servant Dulippo and has secured employment in the house of his beloved's father. Meanwhile, the true Dulippo has assumed the identity of Erostrato and occupies the house next door.

This affair has been going on for two years, but now it is being complicated by the fact that Cleandro, a doddering old doctor of law, has become a suitor for Polinesta's hand,

tempting her father with an offer of two thousand ducats. The real Erostrato is attempting to forestall him by having the false Erostrato ask for her hand, too, and by having him meet Cleandro's offer.

The old doctor arrives in the company of his ever-hungry parasite, Pasifilo, and the two ladies retire. Cleandro's eyesight is so bad that he cannot tell who they are. Under Pasifilo's prodding, Cleandro boasts that he will go to any price to secure Polinesta. He has, he claims, amassed a fortune of ten thousand ducats during the time he has lived in Ferrara, and he boasts that this is the second fortune he has made. The first he lost at the fall of Otranto twenty years before. That loss, he recalls sadly, was nothing to the loss of his five-year-old son, captured by the Turks during the battle.

After Cleandro has gone, the false Dulippo appears to invite Pasifilo to dinner. The false Erostrato confronts the false Dulippo with bad news: Damon, Polinesta's father, doubts Erostrato's ability to match Cleandro's offer for his daughter. The two connivers agree that they must devise some ruse to convince the grasping merchant of their ability to pay.

The false Dulippo, to alienate Cleandro and Pasifilo, tells the old doctor that Pasifilo has insulted Cleandro, illustrating the insults in an extremely comic way. After Cleandro leaves, enraged, the false Erostrato arrives, this time with good news. He has met a foolish Sienese gentleman whom he has frightened with the claim that all visitors from Siena are persecuted in Ferrara. The Sienese has sought protection by agreeing to pose as Erostrato's father. He will meet any sum that Cleandro can offer.

The trick is never played. Damon has overheard Balia quarreling with a servant over the propriety of Polinesta's conduct and has learned of his daughter's two-year affair. Dulippo and Balia are thrown into Damon's private dungeon. Damon, aware of the extralegal nature of this procedure, swears the servant to secrecy, but, unknown to him, Pasifilo, who had been sleeping off an attack of indigestion in the stables nearby, had awakened in time to overhear everything.

Meanwhile, to complicate matters further, Filogono, Erostrato's true father, has arrived from Sicily. He had written asking Erostrato to return home, but his pleas were ignored, so he has decided to come in person for his son. He is conducted to Erostrato's house by a local innkeeper. The false Erostrato sees him in time, however, and attempts to hide.

A hilarious bit of byplay follows in which the Sienese, aided by Erostrato's servants, and Filogono, assisted by his servants, both claim to be Erostrato's father. Finally Filogono espies the false Erostrato, whom he knows as his servant Dulippo, and calls on him to substantiate his claim. He is confounded when the real Dulippo declares that he is Erostrato, that the Sienese is Filogono of Sicily, and that the old man is an impostor or mad. Certain that Dulippo has done away with his son, Filogono goes off to seek aid from the authorities.

Pasifilo arrives to cadge a dinner from Erostrato. Concerned over the affair with Filogono, for he really loves the old man who has been a father to him, the false Erostrato asks Pasifilo if he has seen Dulippo, and Pasifilo tells him the whole story of the discovery and imprisonment. Afraid that the ruse has gone too far, the servant rushes off to confess all to Filogono, leaving Pasifilo, to the latter's delight, in charge of the dinner.

Filogono returns with the lawyer he has retained—old Cleandro. He explains how his trusted servant, whom he had

saved from the Turks twenty years before, has betrayed him. On hearing this story, Cleandro closely questions Filogono about the boy. To Cleandro's delight, the real Dulippo turns out to be the old man's long-lost son.

Next comes Damon. Polinesta has revealed the whole truth of her affair, and he has rushed out to check up on her claim that his servant is actually the wealthy and highborn Erostrato. Finally, the false Erostrato returns to make his confession, and all the entanglements are straightened out. The true Erostrato is released and united with his mistress, whom his father promises to procure as his bride—thereby pacifying Damon. Cleandro renounces his claim on Polinesta; he had wanted a wife only to produce an heir and now he has one in the true Dulippo. Even Cleandro and Pasifilo are reconciled, and Pasifilo is given a permanent invitation to dine at Cleandro's house.

Critical Evaluation:

Ludovico Ariosto, best known for his epic poem masterpiece *Orlando furioso* (1516, 1521, 1532; English translation, 1591), wrote many other works. His four comedies include *The Pretenders*. There are two basic versions of *The Pretenders*: The first was a prose edition, produced in Ferrara in 1509 and enacted in the ducal palace, and the second was reworked in verse and performed ten years later in Rome for Pope Leo X. The story and action of both versions are the same, but the second, versified one is more developed. The dialogue is more intricate at times, and central figures have more depth.

Comedy emerged in the late fifteenth and early sixteenth centuries as a major form of dramatic literature in Italy, and Ariosto was a crucial element in its popularity and in its influence on literature in other European countries. *The Pretenders* was written and debuted not only in a thriving, leading center of Italian theater but also at the theater's zenith.

Ariosto was a poet and humanist employed in the service of several members of the politically dominant Este family in Ferrara during the early sixteenth century. In addition to his administrative duties, he found time for study and composition. The works that resulted were written for his courtly audience, and, because of his ties with the court, his works were also performed publicly. His minor works include his comedies, and he quickly earned a reputation as a skilled composer who was able not only to provide entertainment but also to incorporate into his plays his acquaintance with Renaissance humanistic studies of classical (ancient) literature.

Ariosto's reflection of classical Roman literature is known as erudite comedy; it is a style based on the poet's familiarity with and conscious imitation of ancient works. *The Pretend-*

ers mirrors a story used by the ancient Roman playwright Plautus in his *Menaechmi* (pr. second century B.C.E.; English translation, 1595). The action in both plays involves mistaken identities and humorous situations, and, eventually, all players become aware of the true identities of one another—which results in a happy resolution of the confused situation. Ariosto also drew on Plautus's other plays and on the works of another Roman author, Terence, for formation of some of the characters and incidents in *The Pretenders*.

Italian critics have tended to dismiss erudite comedy as an artificial, unimaginative imitation of Roman comedies with no true appeal of its own as literature; however, the Renaissance Italian comics did not seek to create a new, innovative form of drama. Ariosto and other Renaissance litterateurs drew upon their humanistic studies of antiquity, and their audiences recognized their borrowings from the works of the ancient authors. *The Pretenders*, like other contemporary Italian comedies, however, also accomplished other aims. *The Pretenders* furthered the evolution of Italian as a literary language and reflects Ariosto's historical situation. The comedy is set in his own city, in his own time, and with stereotypical characters that the audience would have readily recognized. Above all, the play is designed as earthy, ribald, pleasing entertainment.

In contrast with earlier humanistic playwrights who adopted classical figures or settings for their plays—Poliziano, for example, in *Orfeo* (pr. 1480; English translation, 1879)—Ariosto and other erudite comic writers adhered to the structure of classical plays while setting them in contemporary situations. The plays of Plautus and Terence follow a pattern of five acts; this pattern was considered a rule to be followed absolutely. Ariosto followed this rule, but some of the individual scenes do not advance the action; these scenes were inserted for their own sake.

Ancient authors and commentators held to a tripartite development—three basic stages—for the unfolding of a play, and Ariosto followed that strategy. Acts 1 and 2 present the general predicament of the central figures. The audience learns that Erostrato and Dulippo have exchanged identities and why they have done so. Acts 3 and 4 introduce complications, incidents that arise from the characters' intentional confusion of identities—but the complications were not anticipated by the characters. The intensified efforts of Cleandro as a suitor for Polinesta and the arrival of the true Filogono are examples of these complications. Act 5 resolves the situation, but it does so in a way that surpasses the original contrivances; for example, the revelation of Dulippo as Cleandro's lost son provides an extra twist to the circumstances. Everyone is left happy.

Ariosto's audience would have expected that the mistaken identities of the play's characters would lead to farcical situations. There are also other typical elements of erudite comedy in *The Pretenders*: servants who outwit nobles, parasites who do duty for patrons and thereby advance the action, figures who talk in asides to the playgoers, persons who arrive unexpectedly and so might unravel the scheme, and persons lost long ago whose identities, in the play's denouement, are revealed. Sixteenth century audiences would have enjoyed the amusement of distinct moments caused by all these features, but they would also have eagerly awaited the incidents that contained complications and especially the twist in the resolution. The forms of the comedy would have been unpredictable; therefore, although the essential style of Renaissance comedies, and *The Pretenders* in particular, is fundamentally formulaic, the playwright had substantial opportunity to manipulate the specific situation to the enjoyment of his audience.

Contemporary life has a crucial role in the play. Regardless of the ancient Roman inspiration for the plot, the setting is entirely Italian, with references to specific geographic and political features of the society of Ferrara. Discussion of the invasion of the Italian peninsula by the Turks decades earlier reinforces the contemporary setting and explains an incident crucial to the successful resolution of the plot—the loss of the young Dulippo in the course of the Turkish incursion. Ariosto also reflects Italy's heritage of vernacular literature. The story of Erostrato, a rich noble youth who disguises himself as a servant in order to enjoy being with his desired love, comes from Giovanni Boccaccio's *Decameron: O, Prencipe Galeotto* (1349-1351; *The Decameron*, 1620), which helped to establish the Italian language as a vehicle for serious literature in the fourteenth century.

"Critical Evaluation" by Alan Cottrell

Further Reading

Ariosto, Ludovico. *The Comedies of Ariosto*. Translated by Edmond M. Beame and Leonard G. Sbrocchi. Chicago: University of Chicago Press, 1975. Presents very enjoyable English translations of Ariosto's four comedies, including *The Pretenders*, with informative accompanying notes and brief analysis. The introduction situates Ariosto in his literary heritage, describes the historical circumstances of Renaissance Ferrara, and discusses various themes and rhetorical devices that Ariosto employed in his comedies.

Beecher, Donald, ed. *Renaissance Comedy: The Italian Masters*. Vol. 1. Toronto: University of Toronto Press, 2008.

First volume of a projected two-volume reassessment of Italian Renaissance comedy includes a full English translation of *The Pretenders*. Beecher's introduction, "Erudite Comedy in Renaissance Italy," describes the characteristics of Italian Renaissance comedy and recounts performance histories of the plays.

Bianchi, Stefano. "The Theatre of Ariosto." In *Ariosto Today: Contemporary Perspectives*, edited by Donald Beecher, Massimo Ciavolella, and Roberto Fedi. Toronto: University of Toronto Press, 2003. Examination of Ariosto's plays is included in a collection of essays covering various aspects of the writer's works.

Griffin, Robert. *Ludovico Ariosto*. New York: Twayne, 1974. Critical study of Ariosto includes a chapter devoted to

consideration of his minor works, including *The Pretenders* and other satires and lyrics.

Orr, David. *Italian Renaissance Drama in England Before 1625: The Influence of Erudita Tragedy, Comedy, and Pastoral on Elizabethan and Jacobean Drama*. Chapel Hill: University of North Carolina Press, 1970. Discussion of the general influence of Italian drama on English drama during the Renaissance includes evaluation of a 1566 English translation of *The Pretenders*.

Radcliff-Umstead, Douglas. *The Birth of Modern Comedy in Renaissance Italy*. Chicago: University of Chicago Press, 1969. Explains the importance of interpreting Italian Renaissance comedy according to its historical setting.

Pride and Prejudice

Author: Jane Austen (1775-1817)
First published: 1813
Type of work: Novel
Type of plot: Domestic realism
Time of plot: Early nineteenth century
Locale: Rural England

Principal characters:
MR. BENNET, the father of five daughters
MRS. BENNET, his wife
JANE BENNET, the oldest daughter and the family beauty
ELIZABETH BENNET, her father's favorite
MARY,
CATHERINE (KITTY), and
LYDIA BENNET, the younger sisters
MR. BINGLEY, an eligible bachelor
CAROLINE BINGLEY, his sister
MR. DARCY, Bingley's friend
MR. COLLINS, a vicar
LADY CATHERINE DE BOURGH, Darcy's aunt and Collins's patron

The Story:

The chief business of Mrs. Bennet's life is to find suitable husbands for her five daughters. Consequently, she is elated when she hears that nearby Netherfield Park has been let to a Mr. Bingley, a gentleman from the north of England. Gossip reports him to be a rich and eligible young bachelor. Mr. Bingley's first public appearance in the neighborhood is at a ball. With him are his two sisters, the husband of the older, and Mr. Darcy, Bingley's friend.

Bingley is an immediate success in local society, and he and Jane, the oldest Bennet daughter, a pretty girl of sweet and gentle disposition, are attracted to each other at once. His friend, Darcy, however, seems cold and extremely proud and

creates a bad impression. In particular, he insults Elizabeth Bennet, a girl of spirit and intelligence and her father's favorite, by refusing to dance with her when she is sitting down for lack of a partner; he says in her hearing that he is in no mood to prefer young ladies slighted by other men. On later occasions, however, he begins to admire Elizabeth in spite of himself, and at one party she has the satisfaction of refusing him a dance.

Jane's romance with Bingley flourishes quietly, aided by family calls, dinners, and balls. His sisters pretend great fondness for Jane, who believes them completely sincere. Elizabeth is more critical and discerning; she suspects them of hypocrisy, and quite rightly, for they make great fun of Jane's relations, especially her vulgar, garrulous mother and her two ill-bred officer-mad younger sisters. Miss Caroline Bingley, who is eager to marry Darcy and shrewdly aware of his growing admiration for Elizabeth, is especially loud in her ridicule of the Bennet family. Elizabeth herself becomes Caroline's particular target when she walks three miles through muddy pastures to visit Jane when she falls ill at Netherfield Park. Until Jane is able to be moved home, Elizabeth stays to nurse her. During her visit, Elizabeth receives enough attention from Darcy to make Caroline Bingley long sincerely for Jane's recovery. Her fears are not ill-founded. Darcy admits to himself that he would be in some danger from the charm of Elizabeth, if it were not for her inferior family connections.

Elizabeth acquires a new admirer in Mr. Collins, a ridiculously pompous clergyman and a distant cousin of the Bennets, who will someday inherit Mr. Bennet's property because that gentleman has no male heir. Mr. Collins's patron, Lady Catherine de Bourgh, urged him to marry, and he, always obsequiously obedient to her wishes, hastens to comply. Thinking to alleviate the hardship caused the Bennet sisters by the entail that gave their father's property to him, Mr. Collins proposes to Elizabeth. Much to her mother's displeasure and her father's relief, she firmly and promptly rejects him. He almost immediately transfers his affections to Elizabeth's best friend, Charlotte Lucas, who, being twenty-seven years old and somewhat homely, accepts at once.

During Mr. Collins's visit and on one of their many walks to Meryton, the younger Bennet sisters, Kitty and Lydia, meet a delightful young officer, Mr. Wickham, who is stationed with the regiment there. Outwardly charming, he becomes a favorite among all the ladies, including Elizabeth. She is willing to believe the story that he had been cheated out of an inheritance left to him by Darcy's father, who had been his godfather. Her belief in Darcy's arrogant and grasping nature deepens when Wickham does not come to a ball given by the Bingleys, a dance at which Darcy is present.

Soon after the ball, the entire Bingley party suddenly leaves Netherfield Park. They depart with no intention of returning, as Caroline writes Jane in a short farewell note, in which she hints that Bingley might soon become engaged to Darcy's sister. Jane believes that her friend, Caroline, is trying gently to tell her that her brother loves elsewhere and that she must cease to hope. Elizabeth, however, is sure of a plot by Darcy and Caroline to separate Bingley and Jane. She persuades Jane that Bingley does love her and that he will return to Hertfordshire before the winter is over. Jane almost believes her, until she receives a letter from Caroline assuring her that they are all settled in London for the winter. Even after Jane tells her this news, Elizabeth remains convinced of Bingley's affection for her sister and deplores the lack of resolution that makes him putty in the hands of his scheming friend.

About that time, Mrs. Bennet's sister, Mrs. Gardiner, an amiable and intelligent woman with a great deal of affection for her two oldest nieces, arrives for a Christmas visit. She suggests to the Bennets that Jane return to London with her for a rest and change of scene and—so it is understood between Mrs. Gardiner and Elizabeth—to renew her acquaintance with Bingley. Elizabeth is not hopeful for the success of the plan and points out that proud Darcy would never let his friend call on Jane in the unfashionable London street on which the Gardiners live. Jane accepts the invitation, however, and she and Mrs. Gardiner set out for London.

The time draws near for the wedding of Elizabeth's friend Charlotte Lucas, who asks Elizabeth to visit her in Kent. Despite feeling that there can be little pleasure in such a visit, Elizabeth promises to do so. She does not approve of Charlotte's marrying simply for the sake of an establishment, and since she does not sympathize with her friend's decision, she thinks their days of real intimacy are over. As March approaches, however, she finds herself eager to see her friend, and she sets out with pleasure on the journey with Charlotte's father and sister. On their way, the party stops in London to see the Gardiners and Jane. Elizabeth finds her sister well and outwardly serene; she had not seen Bingley and his sisters had paid only one call. Elizabeth is sure Bingley had not been told of Jane's presence in London and blames Darcy for keeping it from him.

Soon after arriving at the Collins's home, the whole party is honored, as Mr. Collins repeatedly assures them, by a dinner invitation from Lady Catherine de Bourgh. Elizabeth finds her to be a haughty, ill-mannered woman, and her daughter thin, sickly, and shy. Lady Catherine is extremely fond of inquiring into the affairs of others and giving them unsolicited advice. Elizabeth turns off her meddling questions with cool indirectness and sees from the effect that she is probably the first who has ever dared do so.

Soon after Elizabeth's arrival, Darcy comes to visit his aunt and cousin. He calls frequently at the parsonage, and he and Elizabeth resume their conversational fencing matches, which culminate in a sudden and unexpected proposal of marriage; he couches his proposal, however, in such proud, even unwilling, terms that Elizabeth not only refuses him but is able to do so indignantly. When he requests her reason for her emphatic rejection, she mentions his part in separating Bingley and Jane, as well as his mistreatment of Wickham, whereupon he leaves abruptly. The next day, he brings a long letter in which he answers her charges. He does not deny his part in separating Jane and Bingley but gives as his reasons the improprieties of Mrs. Bennet and her younger daughters and also his sincere belief that Jane does not love Bingley. As for his alleged mistreatment of Wickham, he writes that he has in reality acted most generously toward Wickham, who is an unprincipled liar, and has repaid his kindness by attempting to elope with Darcy's young sister. At first incensed at the tone of the letter, Elizabeth is gradually forced to acknowledge the justice of some of what he wrote; she regrets having judged him so harshly but is relieved not to see him again before returning home.

There, she finds her younger sisters clamoring to go to Brighton, where the regiment formerly stationed at Meryton had been ordered. When an invitation comes to Lydia from a young officer's wife, Lydia is allowed to accept it over Elizabeth's protests. Elizabeth is asked by the Gardiners to go with them on a tour that will take them into Derbyshire, Darcy's home county. She accepts, reasoning that she is not very likely to meet Darcy merely by going into his county. While they are there, however, Mrs. Gardiner decides they should visit Pemberley, Darcy's home. Elizabeth makes several excuses, but her aunt insists. Only when she learns that the Darcy family is not in residence does Elizabeth consent to go along.

At Pemberley, an unexpected and embarrassing meeting takes place between Elizabeth and Darcy. He is more polite than Elizabeth has ever known him to be, and he asks permission for his sister to call upon her. The call is duly paid and returned, but the pleasant intercourse between the Darcys and Elizabeth's party is suddenly cut short when a letter from Jane informs Elizabeth that Lydia has run away with Wickham. Elizabeth tells Darcy what had happened, and she and the Gardiners leave for home at once. After several days, the runaway couple is located and a marriage arranged between them. When Lydia comes home as heedless as ever, she tells Elizabeth that Darcy had attended her wedding. Suspecting the truth, Elizabeth learns from Mrs. Gardiner that it was indeed Darcy who brought about the marriage by giving Wickham money.

Soon after Lydia and Wickham leave, Bingley returns to Netherfield Park, accompanied by Darcy. Elizabeth, now much more favorably inclined toward him, hopes his coming means that he still loves her, but he gives no sign. Bingley and Jane, on the other hand, are still obviously in love with each other, and they soon became engaged, to the great satisfaction of Mrs. Bennet. Soon afterward, Lady Catherine pays the Bennets an unexpected call. She hears rumors that Darcy is engaged to Elizabeth. Hoping to marry her own daughter to Darcy, she had come to order Elizabeth not to accept the proposal. The spirited girl is not to be intimidated by the bullying Lady Catherine and coolly refuses to promise not to marry Darcy, even though she is regretfully far from certain that she will have the opportunity to do so again. However, she does not have long to wonder.

Lady Catherine, unluckily for her own purpose, repeats to Darcy the substance of her conversation with Elizabeth, and he knows Elizabeth well enough to surmise that her feelings toward him must have greatly changed. He immediately returns to Netherfield Park, and he and Elizabeth became engaged. Pride has been humbled and prejudice dissolved.

Critical Evaluation:

In 1813, her thirty-eighth year, Jane Austen published her second novel *Pride and Prejudice*. She had begun this work in 1796, when she was twenty-one years old, calling it "First Impressions." It had so delighted her family that her father had tried, without success, to have it published. Eventually, Austen put it aside, probably not to return to it until her first published novel, *Sense and Sensibility*, appeared in 1811. "First Impressions" is no longer extant, but it was presumably radically rewritten, because *Pride and Prejudice* is in no way an apprenticeship novel but a completely mature work. *Pride and Prejudice* continues to be the author's most popular novel, perhaps because readers share Darcy's admiration for the "liveliness" of Elizabeth Bennet's mind.

The original title, "First Impressions," focuses on the initial errors of judgment out of which the story develops, whereas the title *Pride and Prejudice*, besides suggesting the kind of antithetical topic that delighted rationalistic eighteenth century readers, indicates the central conflicts that characterized the relationships between Elizabeth and Darcy, and between Jane Bennet and Bingley.

As in all of Austen's novels, individual conflicts are defined and resolved within a rigidly delimited social context, in which relationships are determined by wealth and rank. The oft-quoted opening sentence establishes the societal values that underlie the main conflict: "It is a truth universally acknowledged, that a single man in possession of a good fortune, must be in want of a wife." Mr. and Mrs. Bennet's opening dialogue concerning the eligible Bingley explores this truth. Devoid of individuality, Mrs. Bennet is nevertheless well attuned to society's edicts. Mr. Bennet, an individualist to the point of eccentricity, represents neither personal conviction nor social conviction, and he views with equal indifference Bingley's right to his own reason for settling there and society's right to see him primarily as a potential husband. Having repudiated society, Mr. Bennet cannot take seriously either the claims of the individual or the social order.

As the central character, Elizabeth, her father's favorite and her mother's least favorite child, must come to terms with the conflicting values implicit in her parents' antithetical characters. She is like her father in her scorn of society's conventional judgments, but she champions the concept of individual merit independent of money and rank. She is, indeed, prejudiced against the prejudices of society. From this premise, she attacks Darcy's pride, assuming that it derives from the causes that Charlotte Lucas identifies: "with family, fortune, everything in his favour . . . he has a right to be proud."

Flaunting her contempt for money, Elizabeth indignantly spurns Charlotte's advice that Jane ought to make a calculated play for Bingley's affections. She loftily argues, while under the spell of Wickham's charm, that young people who are truly in love should be unconcerned about financial standing. As a champion of the individual, Elizabeth prides herself on her discriminating judgment and boasts that she is a student of character. Significantly, it is Darcy who warns her against prejudiced conclusions, reminding her that her experience is quite limited. Darcy is not simply the representative of a society that primarily values wealth and consequence—as Elizabeth initially views him—but also a citizen of a larger society than the village to which Elizabeth has been confined by circumstance. Consequently, it is only when she begins to move into Darcy's world that she can judge with true discrimination both individual merit and the dictates of the society that she has rejected. Fundamentally honest, she revises her conclusions as new experiences warrant, and in the case of Darcy and Wickham she ends up radically altering her opinion.

More significant than the obviously ironic reversals, however, is the growing revelation of Elizabeth's unconscious commitment to society. Her original condemnation of Darcy's pride coincides with the verdict of Meryton society. Moreover, she shares society's regard for wealth. Even while denying the importance of Wickham's poverty, she countenances his pursuit of the ugly Miss King's fortune, discerning her own inconsistency only after she learns of his bad character. Most revealing, when Lydia Bennet runs off with Wickham, Elizabeth instinctively understands the judgment of society when she laments that Wickham would never marry a woman without money.

Almost unconsciously, Elizabeth acknowledges a connection between wealth and human values at the crucial moment when she first looks upon Pemberley, the Darcy estate. She is not entirely joking when she tells Jane that her love for Darcy began when she first saw his beautiful estate. Elizabeth's experiences, especially her discoveries of the well-ordered Pemberley and Darcy's tactful generosity to Lydia and Wickham, lead her to differentiate between Charlotte's theory that family and fortune bestow a "*right* to be proud" and Darcy's position that the intelligent person does not indulge in false pride. Darcy's pride is real, but it is regulated by responsibility. Unlike his aunt, Lady Catherine de Bourgh, who relishes the distinction of rank, he disapproves less of the Bennets' undistinguished family and fortune than of the lack of propriety displayed by most of the family. Therefore, Elizabeth scarcely overstates her case when, at the end, she assures her father that Darcy has no improper pride.

Elizabeth begins by rejecting the values and restraints of society as they are represented by such people as her mother, the Lucases, Miss Bingley, and Lady Catherine. Instead, she initially upholds the claims of the individual, which are elsewhere represented only by her whimsical father. By the end of the novel, the heart of her conflict appears in the contrast between her father and Darcy. She loves her father and has tried to overlook his lack of decorum in conjugal matters, but she has been forced to see that his freedom is really irresponsibility, the essential cause of Jane's misery as well as Lydia's amorality. The implicit comparison between Mr. Bennet's and Darcy's approach to matrimony illustrates their different methods of dealing with society's restraints. Unrestrained by society, having been captivated by the inferior Mrs. Bennet's youth and beauty, Mr. Bennet consulted only his personal desires and made a disastrous marriage. Darcy, in contrast, defies society only when he has made certain that Elizabeth is a woman worthy of his love and lifetime devotion.

When Elizabeth confronts Lady Catherine, her words are declarative not of absolute defiance of society but of the selective freedom that is her compromise and very similar to Darcy's: "I am only resolved to act in that manner, which will, in my own opinion, constitute my happiness, without reference to you, or to any person so wholly unconnected with me." Austen does not falsify the compromise. If Elizabeth dares with impunity to defy the society of Rosings, Longbourne, and Meryton, she does so only because Darcy is exactly the man for her and, further, because she can anticipate "with delight . . . the time when they should be removed from society so little pleasing to either, to all the comfort and elegance . . . at Pemberley." In a sense, her marriage to Darcy is a triumph of the individual over society; but, paradoxically, Elizabeth achieves her most genuine conquest of pride and prejudice only after she accepts the full social value of her judgment that "to be mistress of Pemberley might be something!"

Granting the full force of the snobbery, the exploitation, the inhumanity of all the evils that diminish the human spirit and are inherent in a materialistic society, the novel clearly confirms the cynical "truth" of the opening sentence. At the same time, without evading the degree of Elizabeth's capitulation to society, it affirms the vitality and the independent life that is possible, at least to an Elizabeth Bennet. *Pride and Prejudice*, like its title, offers deceptively simple antitheses that yield up the complexity of life itself.

"Critical Evaluation" by Catherine E. Moore

Further Reading

Austen, Jane. *Pride and Prejudice: An Authoritative Text, Backgrounds and Sources, Criticism.* 3d ed. Edited by Donald Gray. New York: Norton, 2001. In addition to an annotated text of the novel, this edition contains biographical portraits of the author written by Austen's family members and biographers, seventeen letters written by Austen, and eighteen critical essays by nineteenth and twentieth century writers.

Bloom, Harold, ed. *Elizabeth Bennet.* Philadelphia: Chelsea House, 2004. Collection of essays about Austen's best-known fictional creation, including discussions of Elizabeth's humiliation and wit, the use of irony in *Pride and Prejudice*, and a note on Austen written by C. S. Lewis.

_____. *Jane Austen's "Pride and Prejudice."* Updated ed. New York: Bloom's Literary Criticism, 2007. Collection of critical essays about the novel, including pieces examining Elizabeth's pastoral world, the stylistic influences for the novel, and "Jane Austen and Elizabeth Bennett: The Limits of Irony."

Crusie, Jennifer, and Glenn Yeffeth, eds. *Flirting with "Pride and Prejudice": Fresh Perspectives on the Original Chick-Lit Masterpiece.* Dallas, Tex.: BenBella Books, 2005. Collection of essays by twenty-first century romance writers, who view *Pride and Prejudice* as the prototype for the modern "chick-lit" novel. The contributors explore numerous aspects of the novel, including Austen's social commentary, film adaptations of *Pride and Prejudice*, the character of Mr. Darcy, and Austen in the twenty-first century.

Gillie, Christopher. *A Preface to Austen.* Rev. ed. New York: Longman, 2000. An invaluable guide that includes useful background material and brief discussions of Austen's novels. A reference section contains notes on people and places of importance, maps, and explanations of numerous words used in the works. Amply illustrated. Annotated bibliography.

Halperin, John, ed. *Jane Austen: Bicentenary Essays.* New York: Cambridge University Press, 1975. A collection of essays on various aspects of Austen's work. An excellent chapter by Robert B. Heilman explains how the title *Pride and Prejudice* defines the theme and the structure of the novel. In another essay, Karl Kroeber suggests some reasons for the work's lasting popularity.

Honan, Park. *Jane Austen: Her Life.* Rev. ed. London: MAX, 2007. A detailed biography that depicts Austen's life and work and provides a portrait of England and the age. The chapter on *Pride and Prejudice* focuses on the novel's reflection of a changing society in which economics, social class, and character all affect individual happiness.

Howe, Florence, ed. *Tradition and the Talents of Women.* Urbana: University of Illinois Press, 1991. Feminist criticism of various writers. An essay by Jen Ferguson Carr notes that although both Mrs. Bennet and Elizabeth are excluded from power in a male-dominated society, only the daughter is intelligent enough to use language to "dissociate herself from her devalued position."

Kirkham, Margaret. *Jane Austen, Feminism, and Fiction.* Brighton, England: Harvester Press, 1983. Although Elizabeth is the most appealing of Austen's heroines, the novelist herself had misgivings about *Pride and Prejudice*, probably because its light-hearted ending depends upon Elizabeth's losing her integrity. Concludes with a helpful summary of the critical tradition.

Moler, Kenneth L. *"Pride and Prejudice": A Study in Artistic Economy.* Boston: Twayne, 1989. Intended as a student's companion to the novel, a useful book for the first-time reader of Austen. Includes a historical context and critical reception of the novel. Also examines the themes of moral blindness and self-knowledge, art, and nature, as well as Austen's use of symbolism, language, and literary allusion.

Smith, LeRoy W. *Jane Austen and the Drama of Woman.* New York: St. Martin's Press, 1983. In *Pride and Prejudice*, Austen shows the ideal marriage as depending upon overcoming the institution's "threat to selfhood." Unlike most women of her period, Elizabeth insists both on choosing her own husband and on retaining her intellectual and emotional independence.

Sulloway, Alison G. *Jane Austen and the Province of Womanhood.* Philadelphia: University of Pennsylvania Press, 1989. Reminding readers that nineteenth century men had "rights" and women had "duties," this author examines the various areas in which women function in Austen's novels. Sulloway's approach is original and perceptive.

The Prime of Miss Jean Brodie

Author: Muriel Spark (1918-2006)
First published: 1961
Type of work: Novel
Type of plot: Satire
Time of plot: 1930-late 1950's
Locale: Edinburgh, Scotland

Principal characters:
JEAN BRODIE, English and history teacher at the Marcia
   Blaine School for Girls
MONICA DOUGLAS,
ROSE STANLEY,
EUNICE GARDINER,
SANDY STRANGER,
JENNY GRAY, and
MARY MACGREGOR, her students, Miss Brodie's "crème de
   la crème"
JOYCE EMILY HAMMOND, a student killed in the Spanish
   Civil War
MISS MACKAY, the school's headmistress
GORDON LOWTHER, the singing teacher
TEDDY LLOYD, the art master, who lost an arm in World
   War I
MISS LOCKHART, a science teacher
ALISON and ELLEN KERR, sewing teachers
HUGH CARRUTHERS, Miss Brodie's fiancée, who was
   killed at the Battle of Flanders in 1918

The Story:

Miss Jean Brodie has six favorite pupils at the Marcia Blaine School for Girls in Edinburgh: Monica Douglas, famous for math; Rose Stanley, famous for sex; Eunice Gardiner, famous for gymnastics; Jenny Gray, famous for her grace; Mary Macgregor, famously stupid; and Sandy Stranger, famous for articulation and notorious for her small eyes. The girls stand just outside the school, talking awkwardly with a small group of boys. They are sixteen and have been under Miss Brodie's influence since they were ten. Miss Brodie approaches the group, dismisses the boys, and asks the girls to dinner so they can discuss the administration's newest plan to force her resignation.

Mary, at the time of her death in a hotel fire twelve years later, will remember these years with Miss Brodie as the happiest of her life. At Sandy's tenth birthday party, she and Jenny Gray write adventure tales using as raw material Miss Brodie's memories of her fiancée, Hugh Carruthers, a scholar who was killed at Flanders in World War I (1914-1918). Such reminiscences often replace the English and history lessons Miss Brodie is supposed to impart.

Although the girls are fascinated by their science teacher, Miss Lockhart, Miss Brodie insists that art takes precedence over science. Miss Brodie's first protégé, Eunice Gardiner, is an accomplished gymnast who will become a nurse and

marry a doctor. Years later, Eunice will remember to put flowers on Miss Brodie's grave while recalling that one of their set betrayed her.

Miss Brodie takes the girls walking through Edinburgh to see the cultural sites. She dismisses the unemployment lines, claiming that Benito Mussolini (1883-1945), one of the fascist European leaders responsible for World War II (1939-1945), has eliminated such problems in Italy. Miss Brodie complains that her headmistress Miss Mackay would have her fill the girls with knowledge, but she insists that her own method of education is to summon forth that which is already in the pupil's soul. Ironically, she does not realize that Sandy is busily imagining adventures with the hero of Robert Louis Stevenson's *Kidnapped: Being Memoirs of the Adventures of David Balfour in the Year 1751* (1886), contemplating the true nature of passion, and reflecting that the girls form a sort of fascist army themselves.

Miss Brodie opens the year's second term with the girls by describing her Italian holiday. Her own Roman profile deeply impresses Sandy, as the teacher admires the military might and the poetic legacy of the Italians. Later that year, Monica claims to have seen Miss Brodie being kissed by the art master, Teddy Lloyd, a married Catholic veteran of World War I. While the girls try to decide if Monica's story could be true, Miss Brodie goes out on sick leave and Gordon Lowther, the singing master, takes a vacation.

Years later, Sandy will meet Miss Brodie at the Braid Hills Hotel, where she will confirm the truth of these affairs. During their conversation, Sandy will reflect on her betrayal of the older woman, but when Miss Mackay tries to pump the eleven-year-old girls for information, they are unable to assist her, since they know nothing definite. Toward the end of the term, Jenny is accosted by an exhibitionist, but Sandy begs her not to tell Miss Brodie because she is reluctant to engage with her in any real sexual details. As the spring progresses, Miss Brodie begins to embellish the story of her love affair with Hugh with details about Lloyd and Lowther, providing rich material for the girls' own fantasies.

Soon enough, the girls begin Senior division, away from Miss Brodie, but they refuse to succumb to the school's enforced spirit of competition. They thus create a new house that meets every Saturday with Miss Brodie for tea. While Jenny and Sandy teach Miss Brodie Greek and accidentally reveal that Lloyd has begun painting Rose, she shows them how she keeps house for the wealthy and single Lowther.

Sandy visits with the Lloyds and is surprised both when Teddy kisses her and when she discovers that all of his portraits of Rose resemble Miss Brodie—an economical artistic method also employed by Miss Brodie herself when shaping her life story. For the summer holiday, Miss Brodie plans to visit Germany and compare German Nazi dictator Adolf Hitler (1889-1945) to Mussolini. She also makes plans for what she hopes will be a fantastic love affair between Lloyd and Rose, but Sandy sleeps with him instead. Miss Brodie is almost equally surprised by Lowther's engagement to Miss Lockhart.

The Marcia Blaine School briefly hosts a new student, Joyce Emily Hammond, but she runs away to fight in the Spanish Civil War at Miss Brodie's suggestion and is killed. After graduation, Sandy advises Miss Mackay to pursue her quarry on political grounds, so Miss Brodie is fired in 1939 for her fascist leanings. Years later, Sandy becomes Sister Helena and receives visitors to her cloister in admiration of her treatise, "The Transfiguration of the Commonplace." When asked about her influences, she names only one: "a Miss Jean Brodie in her prime."

Critical Evaluation:

Muriel Spark was a poet for many years before she became a novelist, and her prose has been praised for its compressed, lyrical style. *The Prime of Miss Jean Brodie* describes a time period and a character, rather than developing an intricate plot. The novel is narrated objectively in the third person omniscient perspective; still, most of the story is told from Sandy's point of view. She has a vivid imagination and often carries on dialogue, writes letters, or conceives of action sequences while Miss Brodie is teaching, thereby further diluting the narrative trajectory.

Despite the novel's anticlimactic revelations, Spark keeps her readers interested by anchoring descriptions to specific actions that develop key themes, while withholding information central to those actions. For example, one Saturday afternoon when they are in Senior division, Sandy and Jenny are invited to take tea with Miss Brodie at Lowther's wealthy estate. The purpose of the episode is to characterize the couple's relationship during what was for the times a rather torrid love affair. For a reader, the single day becomes the centerpiece in a narrative web that includes all the characters who have reason to betray the teacher, as well as the possible means they might employ to do so. None of the characters is confirmed as the betrayer, and the episode concludes with a simple domestic musing by Miss Brodie. The musing forms a prime example of how each of their commonplace lives will be transfigured by the impending world war, the aftermath of which is not directly addressed in the text.

Early in her career, Spark tended to distance herself from her Scottish heritage. She once wrote,

> Edinburgh is the place that I, a constitutional exile, am essentially exiled from. . . . It was Edinburgh that bred within me the conditions of exiledom.

Still, Spark uses this elemental locale as the setting for her novel. Additionally, she makes Miss Brodie a quintessential Scot by specifying that she is descended from Deacon William Brodie (1741-1788), a businessman and thief who was hanged on a gallows he himself had designed. Brodie's antagonist, Sandy Stranger, is part English, and her different heritage is marked by both her clean articulation and her family's high-toned restrictions on the excursions she may make. The Scottish Miss Brodie may instruct the girls in taste and culture, but she is ultimately too romantic to survive in the modern world, while Sandy's rational approach proves politically effective, if ruthless.

The Scottish allegory necessarily involves questions of religion with which Spark herself wrestled before converting to Catholicism. Sandy is a "stranger" to both the city of Edinburgh and its Calvinistic doctrines. At one point, she reflects that her teacher's admiration for the Italians, as well as her passion for beauty, make her a natural candidate for Catholicism. Instead, Miss Brodie denounces the Church as too superstitious and chooses a democratic participation in

Scotland's range of religious traditions, from the Anglican Church to the Zionist. This spectrum includes Presbyterianism, heavily influenced by John Calvin's (1509-1564) theory of predestination. Calvin taught that each individual's fate in the afterlife is decided by God at birth and that no amount of religious devotion can influence His decision. This fatalistic attitude is the factor that most alienates Sandy from the town in which she lives. The idea that her destiny is predetermined either by God or by Miss Brodie is repugnant to the young student and ultimately forces her to rebel.

In speaking of her own conversion, Spark claims to have been "put off a long time by individual Catholics," and her characters reflect this general tendency. Sandy, the future nun, is judgmental and querulous, while Teddy Lloyd, the Catholic art master, seduces the schoolchildren he teaches and is unfaithful to his wife in their own home. Still, the novel tends to uphold a Catholic worldview, specifically in its portrayal of the transformative power of God's grace and the absolute free will of humanity. What Sandy rebels against and what readers also are trained to abhor is Brodie's predestinatory claims, which are depicted as a barrier to ethical development and personal contentedness. Sandy's treatise can thus be read as an ironic commentary on her own betrayal of her teacher, as well as an uplifting meditation on the possibilities offered by Catholicism.

Central to the novel is the question of free will, a question with religious, philosophical, and artistic implications. Spark claims that her religion gives her a stable worldview from which she can construct a literary theory and technique and thus provide shape to her fiction. Many postmodern authors resist the description of their role as that of a God-like figure who unfairly, perhaps unethically, creates a world, manipulates its inhabitants, and then leaves it open for interpretation. Such authors have exposed this fictional construct in order to comment on the ethical responsibilities of people in power, both political and religious. Spark is no exception. Miss Brodie and Sandy each attempt to shape a life other than their own in ways that are possibly within moral and ethical bounds but that still violate the principles of free will and individual expression. For that, they are judged both despicable and sympathetic.

L. Michelle Baker

Further Reading

Bold, Alan, ed. *Muriel Spark: An Odd Capacity for Vision.* Totowa, N.J.: Barnes & Noble, 1984. A thematically oriented collection that addresses Spark's insistence on free will and her Scottish heritage, as well as analyzing Spark's output as a critic, a poet, and an author of short fiction.

Cheyette, Bryan. *Muriel Spark.* Horndon, England: Northcote House/British Council, 2000. Offers a chronology of Spark's work and accomplishments. Discusses her place within British literature as a Catholic writer, particularly the question of her centrality or marginality.

Hart, Francis Russell. *The Scottish Novel: From Smollett to Spark.* Cambridge, Mass.: Harvard University Press, 1978. Hart's survey includes only one, relatively short section on Spark that nevertheless defines an important historic aspect of her work.

Hynes, Joseph, ed. *Critical Essays on Muriel Spark.* New York: G. K. Hall, 1992. A valuable collection of significant primary and secondary sources, including interviews and reviews, most notably a 1963 "House of Fiction" interview by Frank Kermode that originally appeared in the *Partisan Review* and is often referenced by other critics.

Kemp, Peter. *Muriel Spark.* New York: Barnes & Noble, 1975. Important analysis of Spark's place in the contemporary British canon.

McQuillan, Martin, ed. *Theorizing Muriel Spark: Gender, Race, Deconstruction.* New York: Palgrave, 2002. Collection of essays that interpret Spark through critical, theoretical lenses that she often resisted but that the complexity of her work demands. Includes two reviews of Spark's novels by the eminent feminist critic Hélène Cixous, as well as an interview of Spark conducted by the editor.

Malkoff, Karl. *Muriel Spark.* New York: Columbia University Press, 1968. Provides a short, accessible overview of the biographical and critical context for Spark's work, as well as a summary and critical discussion of her novels.

Modern Fiction Studies 54, no. 3 (Fall, 2008). A special Muriel Spark issue, providing the first major set of critical analyses to be published after her death in 2006.

Stanford, Derek. *Muriel Spark: A Biographical and Critical Study.* Fontwell, England: Centaur Press, 1963. An early but influential study of Spark's life and work.

Whittaker, Ruth. *The Faith and Fiction of Muriel Spark.* New York: St. Martin's Press, 1982. Places Spark between realism and experimentalism by virtue of the religious attitude that pervades her work without making it too polemical.

The Prince

Author: Niccolò Machiavelli (1469-1527)
First published: Il principe, 1532 (English translation, 1640)
Type of work: Politics

The Prince is the book that gives meaning to the adjective Machiavellian. The book is an ingenious and fascinating study of the art of practical politics, composed by a man who never rose higher than the position of secretary to the second chancery in Florence. The success of *The Prince* can be attributed partly to Niccolò Machiavelli's wit and partly to his having known some of the most clever and powerful rogues of the Renaissance. His model for the "prince" was Cesare Borgia, who used all means of conquest, including murder, to achieve and hold political power.

Machiavelli never pretended that his book was a guide to the virtuous. On the other hand, he did not set out to prescribe the way to wickedness. He meant his account to be a practical guide to political power and, through a combination of experience, logic, and imagination, he constructed one of the most intriguing handbooks of Western civilization: a primer for princes.

In beginning a discussion concerned with the manners and attitudes of a prince—that is, a ruler of a state—Machiavelli writes,

> Since . . . it has been my intention to write something which may be of use to the understanding reader, it has seemed wiser to me to follow the real truth of the matter rather than what we imagine it to be. For imagination has created many principalities and republics that have never been seen or known to have any real existence, for how we live is so different from how we ought to live that he who studies what ought to be done rather than what is done will learn the way to his downfall rather than to his preservation.

This passage makes it clear that Machiavelli intends to explain how successful politicians really work rather than how they ought to work.

The Prince begins with a one-paragraph chapter that illustrates Machiavelli's logical approach to the problem of advising prospective princes. He claims that all states are either republics or monarchies. Monarchies are either hereditary or new. New monarchies are either entirely new or acquired. Acquired states have either been dominated by a prince or been free; they are acquired either by a prince's own arms or by those of others; and they fall to him either by fortune or because of his own character and ability. Having outlined this inclusive logical bifurcation, Machiavelli first discusses the problems connected with governing a hereditary monarchy, then discusses mixed monarchies.

In each case, as he develops his argument, Machiavelli considers the logical alternatives, and what should be done in each case if the prince is to acquire and hold power. In writing of mixed monarchies, for example, he points out that acquired states are either culturally similar to the conquering state or not, and then considers each possibility. If the acquired state is culturally similar, it is no problem to keep it; but if the acquired state is different in its customs, laws, or language, then there is a problem to be solved. One solution might be to have the ruler go to the acquired territory and live there. As an example, Machiavelli refers to the presence of the Turkish ruler in Greece.

Another possible solution to the problems resulting when an acquired territory differs culturally from the conquering state is the establishment of colonies. Colonies are inexpensive to acquire and maintain, he argues, because the land is acquired from a few landowners of the conquered territory, leading to few complaints. Such a plan is preferable to maintaining soldiers, for policing a new state not only is expensive but also offends the citizens being policed.

Thus, by the device of considering logical alternatives, Machiavelli uses his limited experience to build a guide to power. What he says, although refreshing in its direct approach to the hard facts of practical politics, is not entirely fanciful or naïve. Not only did Machiavelli, through his diplomatic missions, come to know intimately such leaders as Louis XII, Julius II, Maximilian, and Borgia, he also used his time to advantage, noting political tricks that actually worked and building up his store of psychological truths.

It is doubtful that any ruler or rebel ever succeeded simply by following Machiavelli to the letter, but it may well be that some political coups have been the result of inspiration from *The Prince.* (Shortly after Fidel Castro's overthrow of the government in Cuba in 1959, a newspaper account reported that among the books on Castro's revolutionary reading list was *The Prince.*)

What is inspiring for the politically ambitious in *The*

Prince is not the substance but the attitude, not the prescription but the unabashed, calculating, and aggressive air with which the author analyzes the means to power. For the reader without political ambition, *The Prince* is a sometimes amusing and sometimes frightening reminder of the realities of political fortune. For example, Machiavelli writes that one who helps a prince to power is bound to fall him- or herself, because he (or she) has contributed to the success either by his cleverness or by his power, and no prince can tolerate the existence of either in another person close to him.

Machiavelli considers this question: Why did the kingdom of Darius, occupied by Alexander the Great, not rebel after Alexander's death? The answer is that monarchies are governed either by a prince and his staff, or by a prince and a number of barons. A monarchy controlled by the prince through his representatives is difficult to conquer, because the entire staff owes its existence to the prince and is, consequently, loyal. Once such a monarchy is captured, however, power is easily maintained. So it was in Alexander's case. On the other hand, a nation like the France of Machiavelli's day is ruled by a king and barons. The barons are princes of a sort over their portions of the state, and they maintain control over their subjects. It is easier to conquer such a state, because there are always unhappy barons willing to join a movement to overthrow the king. Once conquered, however, such a state is difficult to hold because the barons may regroup and overthrow the new prince.

Sometimes power is acquired through crime, Machiavelli admits, and he cites a violent example: the murder of Giovanni Fogliani of Fermo by his nephew, Oliverotto. Machiavelli advises that the cruelty necessary to attain power be kept to a minimum and not be continued, for the purely practical reason that the prince will lose power otherwise. The best thing to do, Machiavelli says, is to commit one's acts of cruelty all at once, not over an extended period.

This cold practicality is echoed in such injunctions as those to the effect that if one cannot afford to be generous, then one must accept with indifference the name of miser; it is safer to be feared than to be loved, if one must choose; a prince need not have a morally worthwhile character, but he must appear to have it; if a prince's military support is good, he will always have good friends; to keep power one must be careful not to be hated by the people; it is always wiser for a prince to be a true friend or a true enemy than to be neutral; a prince should never listen to advice unless he asks for it; and it is better to be bold than cautious.

Machiavelli's prime examples are Francesco Sforza and Borgia, particularly the latter. The author writes that he is always able to find examples for his points by referring to the deeds of Borgia. Considering the value of using auxiliary arms, the military force of another state, Machiavelli refers to Borgia's unfortunate experience with auxiliaries in the capture of Romagna. Finding the auxiliaries untrustworthy, Borgia turned to mercenaries, but they were no better, so he finally used only his own troops. Machiavelli's conclusion in regard to auxiliary troops is that "If any one . . . wants to make sure of not winning he will avail himself of troops such as these."

After reviewing Borgia's rise to power (with the remark that "I could not suggest better precepts to a new prince than the examples of Cesare's actions"), Machiavelli concludes that

> I can find nothing with which to reproach him, rather it seems that I ought to point him out as an example . . . to all those who have risen to power by fortune or by the arms of others.

This praise follows a description of such acts as Borgia's killing of as many of the hapless lords he had despoiled "as he could lay hands on."

Machiavelli praises the actions of other leaders, such as Sforza and Popes Alexander VI and Julius II, but only Borgia wins unqualified praise. Sforza, for example, is recognized as having become duke of Milan "by the proper means and through his own ability," but later on he is criticized because of a castle he built when he should have been trying to win the goodwill of the people.

The Prince concludes with a plea to the Medici family to free Italy from the "barbarians" who ruled the republic of Florence and kept Italy in bondage. Machiavelli makes a plea for liberation, expresses his disappointment that Borgia is not available because of a turn of fortune, and closes with the capitalized cry that "this barbarian occupation stinks in the nostrils of all of us." Unfortunately for the author, his plea to the Medici family did him no good, and he died with the republic still in power. Perhaps he himself was not bold enough; perhaps he was not cruel enough. In any case, he left behind a work to be used by any leader who is willing to be both.

Further Reading

Bernard, John D. *Why Machiavelli Matters: A Guide to Citizenship in a Democracy.* Westport, Conn.: Praeger, 2009. Examines Machiavelli's political philosophy as expressed in *The Prince* and other works. Describes the many character traits he believes are required of a citizen, including masculinity, boldness, and self-esteem.

Bondanella, Peter E. *Machiavelli and the Art of Renaissance History*. Detroit, Mich.: Wayne State University Press, 1973. This astute study constitutes a chronological survey of Machiavelli's development as a literary stylist. Focuses on the compositional techniques he employed in depicting the character and conduct of heroic personages. Lacks a formal bibliography, but there are copious endnotes for each chapter.

Garver, Eugene. "*The Prince*: A Neglected Rhetorical Classic." In *Machiavelli and the History of Prudence*. Madison: University of Wisconsin Press, 1987. Asserts that *The Prince* should be studied as a work of rhetoric as well as from nonliterary standpoints. Reveals rhetorical principles found in *The Prince* and shows how they contribute to Renaissance rhetoric.

Grant, Ruth Weissbourd. *Hypocrisy and Integrity: Machiavelli, Rousseau, and the Ethics of Politics*. Chicago: University of Chicago Press, 1997. This work challenges the usual standards for political ethics and sheds light on Machiavelli's argument for the necessity of hypocrisy. Grant interprets the writings of Machiavelli as "prohypocrite" and the writings of Jean-Jacques Rousseau as "antihypocrite," and balances them in a conceptual framework encompassing the moral limits of compromise and integrity in political behavior.

King, Ross. *Machiavelli: Philosopher of Power*. New York: Atlas Books/HarperCollins, 2007. Concise but comprehensive biography, recounting the events of Machiavelli's life. Places Machiavelli in the political and social contexts of Renaissance Italy and also discusses his writings.

Parel, Anthony. "*The Prince*." In *The Machiavellian Cosmos*. New Haven, Conn.: Yale University Press, 1992. Emphasizes Machiavelli's combination of virtue and fortune in relationship to principalities. Discusses how *The Prince* uses that relationship to explain past and present principalities with logical consequences of power and glory.

Pitkin, Hanna Fenichel. *Fortune Is a Woman: Gender and Politics in the Thought of Niccolò Machiavelli*. Berkeley: University of California Press, 1984. This pioneering study of gender as a factor in political theory depicts Machiavelli as a misogynist authoritarian. Particularly useful in clarifying the manner in which Machiavelli employs the concepts of *fortuna* and *virtù*. Text is extensively annotated and supplemented by a detailed index and a useful bibliography.

Rudowski, Victor. *The Prince: A Historical Critique*. New York: Twayne, 1992. Puts *The Prince* in historical context. Defines terms and identifies individuals in *The Prince*. Presents the impact of the book on European monarchs for several centuries. Examines the initial critical reception of Machiavelli's masterpiece.

Sullivan, Vickie B. *Machiavelli's Three Romes: Religion, Human Liberty, and Politics Reformed*. De Kalb: Northern Illinois University Press, 1996. Drawing on Machiavelli's writings from *The Florentine History, The Prince*, and *Discourses on the First Ten Books of Titus Livius*, the author provides a unique and important study of Machiavelli's political thought. Offers a new understanding of Machiavelli's religious views, maintaining that he uses both pagan and Christian elements in his political philosophy.

Viroli, Maurizio. *Niccolò Machiavelli: A Biography of Machiavelli*. New York: Farrar Straus & Giroux, 2000. A brief general-interest biography of Machiavelli focusing primarily on his career as a diplomat and as a secretary with the Republic of Florence, but also on his life as a writer.

The Prince and the Pauper

Author: Mark Twain (1835-1910)
First published: 1881
Type of work: Novel
Type of plot: Social satire and historical
Time of plot: Early sixteenth century, primarily 1547
Locale: England

Principal characters:
TOM CANTY, a street beggar
JOHN CANTY, his father
EDWARD, the Prince of Wales, who becomes King Edward VI
MILES HENDON, a disinherited knight
HUGH HENDON, his brother
FATHER ANDREW, a priest
HUGO, a thief

The Story:

Tom Canty and Prince Edward are born in London on the same day. Tom, however, is unwanted, and Edward has been long awaited. While the prince lies robed in silks, Tom grows up in the filth of Offal Court. As a small child, Tom is forced by his father to beg during the day and is beaten by him at night. Gathering a ragtag court of street urchins around him, Tom often pretends that he is a prince. Father Andrew, a priest who lives in Tom's house, teaches Tom to read.

One day, hoping to see Prince Edward of England, Tom visits the royal precincts, but when he approaches too near, he is cuffed by a guard and ordered away. Edward, who has witnessed the incident, protects Tom and takes the young beggar into the palace. There, in the privacy of Edward's chamber, Tom confesses his longing to be a prince. When the two boys exchange garments, they discover that they are identical in appearance. Before they can switch clothes again, Edward is mistaken for the beggar boy and thrown out of the palace. He wanders helplessly in the streets, mocked by people whom he approaches with pleas that they pay homage to him as their rightful prince.

In the palace, it is thought that the prince has gone mad because he can recall none of the royal matters that he is supposed to know. King Henry VIII issues an edict that no one should discuss the royal lapse of memory, and Edward's half-sister, Princess Elizabeth (later Queen Elizabeth I); his cousin Lady Jane Grey; and his whipping boy, Sir Humphrey Marlowe, kindly try to aid the supposed prince, who by this time is too frightened to confess that he is Tom Canty, a beggar dressed in the prince's clothing.

While he had been ill, King Henry VIII had given the great seal of the kingdom to Prince Edward for safekeeping. Henry now demands the return of his seal, but Tom reports that he does not know where it is.

The Prince of Wales is still wandering the streets as a homeless waif when King Henry dies. Edward is found by John Canty, Tom's father, and brought to Offal Court, but during the wild celebration of the ascension to the throne of the prince of Wales, Edward escapes from his supposed father. Again tormented by crowds who laugh at his protests that he is the king of England, Edward is rescued by Miles Hendon, a disinherited knight and the son of a baronet. Thinking Edward is mad, Miles pities the little boy and pretends to pay him the homage due to a monarch.

Miles had loved a girl named Edith, who was coveted by Miles's brother, Hugh. Hugh had gained his father's confidence by trickery, and Miles had been turned from home. Edward declares that Miles has suffered unjustly and promises the adventurer any boon he might ask. Recalling the story of De Courcy, who, given a similar opportunity by King John, had requested that he and all of his descendants might be permitted to wear hats in the presence of the king of England, Miles wisely asks that he be permitted to sit in Edward's presence, for the young king has been ordering Miles about like a personal servant.

Meanwhile, having had the role of king of England thrust upon him, Tom is slowly learning to conduct himself royally. Because his attendants thought him mad, he is able to be honest about his lack of training and his failure to recall events that would have been familiar to Edward. At the same time, his gradual improvement offers hope that his derangement is only temporary.

John Canty lures Edward from Miles's protection and takes the boy to Southwark to join a pack of thieves there. Still vainly declaring himself king, Edward again becomes the center of ridicule. One of the thieves, Hugo, undertakes to teach Edward the tricks of his trade. Making his escape, Edward wanders to a farmhouse, where a kind woman, pitying the poor, insane beggar boy who declares himself king of England, feeds him. Edward wanders on to the hut of a hermit who accepts Edward's claim to royalty. In turn, the hermit, who indeed is mad, reveals to Edward that he is an archangel. While Edward sleeps, the hermit broods over the wrongs done him by King Henry. Believing Edward to be the king, as he has claimed, the hermit plans to murder him. He manages to tie up the boy while he sleeps. John and Hugo, following the trail of the escaped waif, rescue him and force him to rejoin the band of rogues. Again he is compelled to aid Hugo in his dishonest trade. At last, Miles finds the boy and saves him.

Miles and Edward then proceed to Hendon Hall to claim his heritage and to claim Edith for a wife. When they arrive at their destination, they find that Miles's father is dead and that Hugh, married to Edith, is now master of Hendon Hall. Only five of the old servants are still living, and all of them, in addition to Hugh and Edith, pretend not to recognize Miles. Denounced as a pretender, Miles is sentenced to the stocks, where the abuse showered upon him by the mob so enrages Edward that he protests loudly. When the guards decide to whip the boy, Miles offers to bear the flogging instead. Grateful to his friend, Edward dubs Miles an earl, which only makes the imprisoned man sorrow for the boy's relapse into insanity. Upon Miles's release from the stocks, the two set out for London, where they arrive on the day before the coronation of Tom Canty as King Edward VI.

In regal splendor, enjoying the adulation of his subjects, but recognized for who he really is by his mother, Tom rides through the streets of London toward Westminster Abbey. There, just as the crown is about to be set on his head, a voice rings out demanding that the ceremony cease, and the real king, clothed in rags, steps forth. As the guards move to seize the troublemaker, Tom, recognizing Edward, orders them to halt. The Lord Protector cuts through the confusion by asking the ragged king to locate the great seal that had been lost since King Henry's death. Edward, after an initial mistake, manages to remember where he had placed the seal before leaving Tom the day he was expelled from the palace. Tom admits that he had innocently used the seal to crack nuts.

Miles, when brought before the rightful King Edward, exercises his privilege of sitting in the king's presence. At first, he had doubted that the waif was really the king, but when Edward orders his outraged guards to permit that disrespectful act, Miles knows that his young friend had not been insane after all. Edward confirms Miles's title of earl and strips Hugh of his titles and land. After Hugh dies, Miles marries Edith, who had refused to acknowledge Miles's identity because Hugh had threatened to kill Miles.

Made Edward's royal ward, Tom has Edward's promise that he and his family would be honored for the rest of their lives. Edward rights many of the wrongs he had encountered during his adventures. John Canty, whom he had wanted to hang, is never heard from again.

Critical Evaluation:

The Prince and the Pauper is Mark Twain's first attempt at writing historical fiction. Stylistically, the novel is very different from *The Adventures of Tom Sawyer* (1876) and *Adventures of Huckleberry Finn* (1884). It combines his fascination with Europe's romantic past with his natural bent for satirizing the injustices and social conventions of his own age. He was to do the same later, to far better effect, in *A Connecticut Yankee in King Arthur's Court* (1889) and, with less success, in *Personal Recollections of Joan of Arc* (1896).

In *The Prince and the Pauper*, Twain begins by challenging authority, but in the end, he submits to it. In *A Connecticut Yankee in King Arthur's Court*, he also challenges authority. The earlier book is also more optimistic, because it reflects Twain's belief in progress.

Although twenty-first century readers think of *The Adventures of Tom Sawyer* and *Adventures of Huckleberry Finn* as children's books, *The Prince and the Pauper* is the only novel Twain ever wrote specifically for children, especially his two young daughters. He aims the other two books at general audiences of all ages. Except for Lewis Carroll's *Alice's Adventures in Wonderland* (1865), children's literature was very didactic up to this time, and contemporary reviewers did

not know what to make of it. Carroll and Twain introduced the then-radical concept that children's literature should be entertaining, which is one reason why their books are still being read in the twenty-first century.

One recurring theme in the children's literature of the nineteenth century was children's obedience—or lack of—to authority; books in which children obey authority figures always have happy endings, and those books in which children disobey have unhappy ones (if these characters lived long enough). Twain mercilessly parodies these stories with "Story of the Bad Little Boy" (1865) and "The Story of the Good Little Boy" (1875), in which exactly the opposite happens: the good-boy story has an unhappy ending, and the bad-boy story has a happy ending.

In *The Prince and the Pauper*, Tom Canty is much better off if he stays away from his abusive, alcoholic, controlling father, who is both a thief and a murderer. Twain was one of the first authors of children's literature to recognize the concept of parental abuse and to make the father the principal villain of the story. However, Twain had been quite naïve to think that Tom would not have been affected. By this time, Tom would have suffered significant psychological damage, even if he were able to avoid the cycle of the children of abuse becoming abusive parents themselves. In Twain's defense, the psychology of abuse was not well understood during his lifetime.

Twain begins to contrast and compare Edward and Tom as early as the novel's opening paragraph. They are born on the same day, but Tom is poor and not wanted by his parents; Edward is incredibly wealthy and is much desired by his parents and his country. Edward dreams about being free, and Tom wonders what it would be like to be a prince. After they inadvertently exchange places, Tom has an easier time of it, because from his reading and tutoring by the kindly Father Andrew he has a rough idea of what it means to be a prince and is willing to ask Humphrey Marlow, Prince Edward's whipping boy, for help. Tom's intelligence and sense of fairness lead him to make humane decisions. Edward is used to being protected and to having his commands obeyed instantly, so he has a rude awakening when he finds himself in danger and when no one pays attention to his orders. Except for Miles Hendon, all react with laughter.

In this novel, Twain employs many themes and devices, which he learned so expertly as a teller of tall tales. These themes and devices include tongue-in-cheek irony, ridiculous understatement, exaggeration, coincidence, and exchange of identities. He also uses the occasion to underscore some of the social follies, hypocrisies, and injustices of his own age without actually having to attack them directly, a technique he later uses in *A Connecticut Yankee in King Arthur's Court*. He does this by treating the social and legal conventions of Tudor England satirically, trusting that his readers will recognize the parallels with their own respective times. In one chapter, "In Prison," religious intolerance is the target. It is a chapter in which two women who have befriended Edward and Miles are burned at the stake because they are Anabaptists. Tom Canty, as king, labors to change laws that are unduly harsh or blatantly unjust, and Edward learns of the unnecessary cruelty of prisons at first hand, as well as the nature of poverty. By becoming a better person, he will become a better king. Both Tom and Edward are innocents who, like Joan of Arc in Twain's later book, fight for justice.

Twain's major criticism of society, both in Tudor times and in his own, is the mistake of gauging a person's true worth based on that person's outward appearance, that is, by judging them, for example, strictly by the clothes they wear. Edward and Tom are not identical twins, so it seems that the premise that no one, except for Tom's mother, would recognize their true identities would be difficult for an adult reader to accept. In addition, the chain of coincidences that lead to Edward's and Tom's predicaments is quite implausible. However, Twain executes his premises so masterfully in this intricately plotted novel that even an adult reader is more than willing to suspend disbelief.

Another premise of the novel is that anyone can be a king, just as Tom, given the opportunity, quickly learns to be a good one. It is an easy assumption to accept, because it is prodemocratic. However, Twain does establish that Tom was able to read both English and Latin before he made the switch with Edward. Tom and Edward are equally intelligent and virtuous young boys, though born to different worlds. Chance and circumstances alone determine much of an individual's outward behavior and appearance. In the context of the nature/nurture controversy, Twain's belief is that a person's environment, more so than their ancestry, or genes, determines their character. Twain does not let Tom keep the throne; he restores Edward, who is, by the end of the novel, much more qualified to be king. Edward's adventure had been a kind of moral training, and he becomes a better king for it.

Miles Hendon, a minor noble, is the one character most like the traditional protagonist in heroic fiction; in a more conventional story, he would be the central character. When Edward meets him, Miles is on a quest to claim his inheritance and be united with his true love. He is warmhearted, sympathetic, kind, and loyal, and he interrupts his quest to help Edward, a purely selfless act given that he does not be-lieve that Edward really is the Prince of Wales and that he will never be rewarded for his actions. Later in the novel, Miles accepts the lashes meant for Edward, and in prison, he makes sure the boy gets more food than himself, still believing Edward to be a commoner. Still, it is these actions that ultimately allow him to fulfill his quest.

In his novel, Twain provides footnotes and incorporates passages from major histories of England, including David Hume's *History of England* (1754), Leigh Hunt's *The Town: Its Memorable Characters and Events* (1848), John Timbs's *Curiosities of London* (1855), and J. Hammond Trumbull's *The True-Blue Laws of Connecticut and New Haven* (1876). This feature of *The Prince and the Pauper* helps to minimize its occasional anachronisms. For instance, a reference is made to a plumber, although there had been no such trade in the sixteenth century. Twain also had spent time checking the settings for his novel when he visited England in 1879.

"Critical Evaluation" by Thomas R. Feller

Further Reading

Baetzhold, Howard G. *Mark Twain and John Bull*. Bloomington: Indiana University Press, 1970. Includes a twenty-page chapter documenting Twain's British sources for historical details in *The Prince and the Pauper*.

Camfield, Gregg. *The Oxford Companion to Mark Twain*. New York: Oxford University Press, 2003. Collection of about three hundred original essays on individual works, themes, characters, languages, and other subjects that interested Twain. Includes an appendix on researching Twain, which lists useful secondary sources, and an annotated bibliography of novels, plays, poems, and other writings by Twain.

Cummings, Sherwood. *Mark Twain and Science: Adventures of a Mind*. Baton Rouge: Louisiana State University Press, 1988. Examines the often overlooked influence of Twain's reading of French history on many details in *The Prince and the Pauper*. Summarizes the novel's flaws, but notes that an important theme in the work is the power of training.

Emerson, Everett. *Mark Twain: A Literary Life*. Philadelphia: University of Pennsylvania Press, 2000. A complete revision of Emerson's *The Authentic Mark Twain* (1984), this masterful study traces the development of Twain's writing against the events in his life and provides illuminating discussions of many individual works.

Morris, Linda A. "*The Adventures of Tom Sawyer* and *The Prince and the Pauper* as Juvenile Literature." In *A Companion to Mark Twain*, edited by Peter Messent and Louis

J. Budd. Malden, Mass.: Blackwell, 2005. Analyzes the two novels for young readers, noting similarities and differences between the works.

Rasmussen, R. Kent. *Bloom's How to Write About Mark Twain*. New York: Bloom's Literary Criticism, 2008. Designed for students, this volume contains a chapter offering clear guidelines on how to write essays on literature, a chapter on writing about Twain, and chapters providing specific advice on individual works, including *The Prince and the Pauper.*

_____. *Critical Companion to Mark Twain: A Literary Reference to His Life and Work.* 2 vols. New York: Facts On File, 2007. A revised and significantly expanded edition of Rasmussen's *Mark Twain A to Z* (1995), with alphabetically arranged entries about the plots, characters, places, and other subjects relating to Twain's writings and life. Features extended analytical essays on Twain's major works, an expanded and fully annotated bibliography of books about Twain, and a glossary explaining unusual words in Twain's vocabulary.

The Prince of Homburg

Author: Heinrich von Kleist (1777-1811)
First produced: Prinz Friedrich von Homburg, 1821; first published, 1821 (English translation, 1875)
Type of work: Drama
Type of plot: Historical
Time of plot: 1675
Locale: Prussia

Principal characters:
FREDERICK WILLIAM, the elector of Brandenburg
THE ELECTRESS
PRINCESS NATALIE OF ORANGE, the niece of the elector
FIELD MARSHAL DORFLING
PRINCE FREDERICK ARTHUR OF HOMBURG
COLONEL KOTTWITZ, a member of the regiment of the princess of Orange
COUNT HOHENZOLLERN, a member of the elector's suite

The Story:

After three days spent heading a cavalry charge in pursuit of the Swedes, Prince Frederick Arthur of Homburg has returned to Fehrbellin. Exhausted and battle-weary, the prince falls into a dreamlike sleep, weaving a laurel wreath as he half dozes. The elector of Brandenburg, Frederick William, is informed by Count Hohenzollern of the prince's strange condition, and the elector, the electress, and their niece, Princess Natalie, arrive in the garden where the prince is sleeping. The elector takes the wreath from the prince, entwines it in his neck chain, and gives it to Natalie. They back away as the somnambulistic prince follows, murmuring incoherently, and as they retreat inside, the prince snatches a glove from Natalie's hand. When the prince awakes, he tells Count Hohenzollern about the occurrence, which he thinks was a dream. Hohenzollern reproves him for his romantic fantasies and urges him to make ready for the coming battle with the Swedes.

The field marshal of Brandenburg dictates the orders of battle to his officers, but the prince, who is to play an important role in the battle, is absorbed in his own thoughts. Hoping to remember from whom he obtained the glove he has found in his possession, he wears it in his collar. The electress

and Natalie are present, and plans are being formed to send them to a place of safety. As the field marshal reaches the section of the orders that pertains to the prince, Natalie, preparing to depart, suddenly realizes that she has but one glove. The prince, who loves Natalie, quickly becomes aware that he holds the missing glove. In order to be sure it is hers, he drops it on the floor in front of him to see if Natalie will claim it. When she does, the prince, in a fit of ecstasy, fails to hear his battle orders clearly, though his mission is to be a key one.

The battlefield of Fehrbellin resounds with cannon, and the elector's forces are sure of victory. As the rout of the Swedes becomes apparent, the prince precipitately gives orders to advance. His colleagues make an effort to dissuade him from this impetuous action, and they insist that he hear the order of battle again, for he is supposed to remain in his position until a particular signal is given. However, the prince rebukes Kottwitz, an elderly colonel, for lack of fervor, and Kottwitz, rather than appear unpatriotic, joins the prince in the advance.

The electress and Natalie have paused during their journey to safety at a house in a nearby village, where news reaches them that the elector has died in battle; both he and his great white horse are reported to have been killed during the bombardment. The prince seeks out the women and takes the opportunity to tell the distraught Natalie of his love for her and to offer her his protection. The elector was her only relative, and now that he is dead she is alone in the world.

The elector is not dead, however. He had changed horses with one of his officers, and that officer, astride the white horse, was mistakenly identified as the elector. The same messenger who brings word that the elector is still alive also brings news of further cause for rejoicing: The war is over for the time being, and the elector has returned to Berlin.

It is apparent to the elector that Prince Frederick ignored the battle order, and, although terms for peace with the Swedes are being discussed, the strong military spirit of the elector prompts him to punish the prince for failing to follow orders. The prince is sentenced to die and is placed in prison to await the day of his execution. He is, however, given permission to visit the electress, and he seeks clemency through her. She is touched by his plea, as is Natalie, who throws herself at the feet of the elector to beg for the prince's life. Given Natalie's plea and the fact that the officers of the elector's army have circulated a petition asking that the prince's life be spared, the elector at last agrees to pardon him.

Natalie takes the letter of pardon from the elector to the prince's cell. In the letter, the elector specifies that the prince's sword will be returned to him if the young man thinks the elector has been unjust in his sentence. The prince thereupon refuses the pardon, for his military training and nationalistic spirit prompt him to realize that the sentence is just.

The officers of the army visit the elector to plead on the prince's behalf. Count Hohenzollern makes the strongest case, noting that had the elector not deceived the young prince by snatching the laurel wreath and entwining it with his neck chain, the prince would not have felt an uncontrollable destiny forcing him into battle. It was therefore the elector's own fault that the prince's mind was clouded by what he thought was a vision foretelling valorous deeds. The elector counters by blaming Count Hohenzollern himself for the whole affair, for he was the one who led the elector to the sleeping prince.

When the prince appears before the assembled officers and the elector, he is ready to die; nevertheless, he makes such a strong plea to the elector that he is able to save himself. In the meantime, peace with Gustaf Karl of Sweden has been effected through the promise of Natalie's hand in marriage to a Swedish nobleman. The prince begs the elector to revoke the agreement and attack the Swedes instead. The elector, ordering his troops to resume battle, tears up the death warrant.

Prince Frederick Arthur is hailed as the hero of the field of Fehrbellin.

Critical Evaluation:

Heinrich von Kleist's last play, *The Prince of Homburg*, is a work of contrast—between the heart, feelings, and spontaneous, intuitive action on one hand and the head, reflection, and rational thinking on the other. Dream and reality operate simultaneously. In thus incorporating the tension of opposites, this play reflects the Kleistian mind. In his personal life, Kleist was constantly tortured by such demands of the bourgeois life as having a career, earning a livelihood, and creating a name for himself. His quest for knowledge or absolute truth did not permit him to accept the trodden path. Even the notion of absolute truth failed to provide him comfort, for he saw flaws there, too. Alienated from the world and disenchanted with the existing order of religion, politics, and literature, he often contemplated ending his life, and at the age of thirty-four he did so.

The two main protagonists in *The Prince of Homburg* are by nature utterly different. The prince is a young man incapable of reflection, and he lets his heart rule his mind. The elector of Brandenburg, the sovereign, is a mature man who considers the autonomy of rules to be just. For him, the state needs the submission of its citizens: All sacrifices in the name of the state are justified. Conversely, individuality for the elector is synonymous with anarchy. The prince is an individual led by his feelings. When he impetuously advances, thus failing to follow the elector's orders, it becomes clear that he does not possess the necessary calm and mature judgment of a military commander. Some critics have analyzed the play's opposition between the individual and the state and concluded that the resolution is synonymous with the victory of one over the other. Others have interpreted the elector's softening toward the prince and the prince's acceptance of his death sentence as a compromise.

The elector, in his Prussian belief in obedience to authority, cannot tolerate disobedience. It takes the prince a while to realize that he must lose his life for leading his country to victory against the Swedish army at Fehrbellin. At the thought of his impending death the prince loses all sense of dignity. In portraying the weak prince groveling at the feet of the electress and begging his beloved Natalie to approach the elector for his pardon, Kleist brilliantly captures the humanness in the prince. He thereby also mocks the sublime portrayals of death in the dramas of antiquity, for in reality death is invariably accompanied by fear. Kleist does not present the prince as the embodiment of valor who can sacrifice himself for the sake of the state. He even forsakes his love for Natalie, assuming, though wrongly so, that the elector may take a more severe view of his situation once he knows that the prince is the hindrance to the plan to marry Natalie to the king of Sweden.

Instead of emphasizing the feminine characteristics of the two women in the play, Kleist focuses more on their ability to take control of the situation. In act 1, scene 1, when Hohenzollern leads the elector, his wife, and Natalie to the garden where the prince of Homburg sits bareheaded with his shirt open at the throat in a somnambulistic state weaving a laurel wreath, the electress is the only one to express sympathy regarding his condition. She interrupts Hohenzollern and her husband and recommends that they try to help him instead of making fun of him. Later, when the prince has sunk into the depths of despair, Natalie makes a compelling argument for the prince. She cleverly conveys to the elector that he has the power to grant the prince mercy and that his refusal to do so would be inhumane. She appeals to his emotions when she says that he will not be able to enjoy Prussia's victory if it is gained at the cost of a friend's life. By the last scene of the play, when Natalie crowns the prince with a laurel wreath and announces his pardon, the prince has lost his composure and dignity so thoroughly that he faints. Natalie, with compassion and understanding, exclaims, "Heavens—killed with joy!"

Upon recovering, the prince cannot believe that his crowning and pardon are really taking place. As in the first scene, where his somnambulistic state is responsible for his confused state of mind, in the resolution of the play too it seems as if he cannot distinguish between reality and dream. To his question, "No, it's a dream! Do say—is it a dream?" the mature veteran of war Colonel Kottwitz answers, "A dream, what else?" The prince has felt the proximity of death and knows now that life is transitory. Only one thing is certain, and that is death. In the midst of the joyful occasion, he asks the seemingly naïve but in fact profound question about the dreamlike quality of life. Colonel Kottwitz displays his understanding of the hidden meaning in his question when he agrees that life is a mere dream. Kleist thus ends his play with a reference to life's being a preparation for death. When military officers shout about war while preparing for battle, they are at the same time preparing for their end.

"Critical Evaluation" by Vibha Bakshi Gokhale

Further Reading

Doctorow, E. L. Foreword to *Plays*, by Heinrich von Kleist, edited by Walter Hinderer. New York: Continuum, 1982. Examines the paradoxical nature of Kleist's plays. Suggests that the main theme of *The Prince of Homburg* is not the victory of the state over the individual but the existential angst of the individual.

Fischer, Bernd, ed. *A Companion to the Works of Heinrich von Kleist*. Columbia, S.C.: Camden House, 2003. Collection of essays analyzes various aspects of Kleist's work, including its themes of death, violence, and revenge and its challenge to Enlightenment humanism.

Fordham, Kim. *Trials and Tribunals in the Dramas of Heinrich von Kleist*. New York: Peter Lang, 2007. Focuses on the various sorts of trials that occur in *The Prince of Homburg* and Kleist's other plays, demonstrating how powerful people manipulate these proceedings, seeking not truth and justice but their own versions of order.

Greenberg, Martin. Introduction to *Five Plays*, by Heinrich von Kleist. New Haven, Conn.: Yale University Press, 1988. Presents a brilliant discussion of the duality inherent in *The Prince of Homburg*.

Griffiths, Elystan. *Political Change and Human Emancipation in the Works of Heinrich von Kleist*. Rochester, N.Y.: Camden House, 2005. Discusses how Kleist's works offered responses to four major political and philosophical issues in late eighteenth and early nineteenth century Prussia: the relationship of national culture to the state, education and social reform, the theory and practice of war, and the administration and delivery of justice.

Maass, Joachim. *Kleist: A Biography*. Translated by Ralph Manheim. New York: Farrar, Straus and Giroux, 1983. Written in an anecdotal style with a sense of humor, this biography makes for a light reading. The chapter on *The Prince of Homburg* points out the influence of Kleist's own emotional and psychological makeup on the characters he created.

Reeve, William C. *Kleist on Stage, 1804-1987*. Montreal: McGill-Queen's University Press, 1993. Excellent resource on the history of the production of Kleist's various plays. The chapter on *The Prince of Homburg* describes its reception when first staged in 1821 as well as how the play was received through the 1980's, including the enthusiasm it generated during the Nazi era.

The Princess
A Medley

Author: Alfred, Lord Tennyson (1809-1892)
First published: 1847
Type of work: Poetry

Principal characters:
THE POET
SIR WALTER VIVIAN, owner of an English country estate
WALTER VIVIAN, the heir of the estate
LILIA, Walter's sister
RALPH, a friend of Walter and the poet-narrator
PRINCE OF THE NORTHERN KINGDOM
THE KING, his father
PRINCESS IDA, principal of a women's college
KING GAMA, her father, king of the southern kingdom
ARAC, her brother
LADY PSYCHE and LADY BLANCHE, tutors
AGLAIA, the daughter of Psyche
MELISSA, the daughter of Blanche
CYRIL and FLORIAN, two friends of the prince

The Poem:

Prologue. The poet and three college companions join their friend Walter Vivian on his father's estate. Sir Walter Vivian has opened his grounds to the nearby village and a neighboring educational institute, of which he is patron. A number of mechanical inventions are on display. A book of family history relating the courage of a female ancestor inspires Lilia, Walter's sister, to speak out for women's rights, particularly to higher education. Walter mentions how at college the friends tell chain stories to pass away the time; Lilia suggests that they tell such a story now. Walter agrees and decides that Lilia will be the heroine—"grand, epic, homicidal"—and the poet, who will begin the story, the hero. Each of the seven people in the group, which includes a maiden aunt, who shares Lilia's views, will narrate part of the story.

Part 1. A country is divided into a southern and a northern kingdom. The young prince learns that the princess to whom he was once betrothed as a child now rejects him and wishes to "live alone/ Among her women" in a castle set aside for a women's college just over the border in the southern kingdom. He begs his father to be allowed to investigate her refusal, but the warlike king, believing a binding treaty is being broken, replies that they will settle the dispute by war. Driven by an inner conviction, the prince rides off to the southern kingdom, accompanied by his two friends Cyril and Florian. At a town near the castle, the prince obtains women's clothes for Cyril, Florian, and himself, and they enter the col-

lege disguised, despite the gates stating that any man shall enter on pain of death. The prince bears a letter of introduction from King Gama, the princess's father, whom he has earlier met.

Part 2. The college porter leads the disguised males to Princess Ida, who greets them as new students and explains the rules to them: For three years they must not correspond with home, leave the boundaries of the college grounds, or converse with men. Ida tells them they must give up their conventional thinking and work for the freedom of women. She seems surprised when the newcomers extravagantly praise the prince, her former suitor. The men next encounter Florian's recently widowed sister, Psyche, Ida's favorite tutor. They admire Aglaia, Psyche's daughter, while Psyche lectures them on feminist history. When Psyche recognizes her brother and the others beneath their disguises, she nearly betrays them, but her natural affection overcomes her duty to Ida. Melissa, the daughter of Ida's other tutor, Blanche, also learns their identity but refuses to reveal their secret.

Part 3. Ida invites the newcomers to go on a geological field trip with her. The prince acts as his own mock-ambassador in trying to acquaint Ida with his passion for her and with her unnatural attitude toward men; he alludes to her missing "what every woman counts her due,/ 'Love, children, happiness.'" Ida reiterates her dedication to her ideals, claiming that while children may die, "great deeds" cannot.

Part 4. A maid sings "Tears, Idle Tears," but Ida remains

unmoved by the expressed sentiment of love. The prince replies with his song, "O Swallow," but Ida spurns his "mere love poem," saying she admires only art addressed to great ends. At this point, Cyril, half-drunk, sings a bawdy song that discloses their true identity. The women flee in panic, and Ida in her haste falls into the river. The prince rescues her but is captured by her retinue.

Part 5. The prince and his companions, whom the princess has released out of gratitude, are expelled and stumble into the camp of the prince's father. He has taken King Gama as a hostage to force the issue of the marriage. They argue about how to win Ida's hand; the king being in favor of attacking, but Gama and the prince suggesting peaceful means. Taunted as a coward by Ida's brother Arac, the prince agrees to a tournament, with fifty knights on either side. He fights bravely but is defeated, and falls into a deep coma.

Part 6. Ida in her triumph sings "Our enemies have fallen," then opens the castle as a hospital for the wounded. Her insistence on ascetic withdrawal and her unnatural contempt for men remain evident. After gazing on the wounded prince, however, she begs the king to allow her to care for him. She embraces Psyche, whom she has dismissed as a traitor, and restores Aglaia to her. Over Blanche's objections, Ida disbands the college until peace is restored.

Part 7. The palace becomes a hospital where the young women with sufficient training nurse the wounded. Ida is heartsick because her ideals have been frustrated, but she finds peace in aiding the wounded men. As she tends the prince as he lies in his delirious state, she begins to love him and, casting off her falser self, kisses him. That rouses him from his coma, and he fall into a blissful sleep. That night, he awakens to find her reading the poems "Now Sleeps the Crimson Petal" and "Come Down, O Maid." In the second poem, love is described as being of the valley, not of the mountain heights where Ida's idealism has carried her.

Ida admits her lack of humility and her desire to achieve power rather than truth, yet she continues to regret the collapse of her idealistic plans to help women achieve status. The prince, who respects her idealism, replies that they would work together for her goal. He tells her that women are not "undevelopt" men and that they should join with man in love; from this union, the man gains "sweetness" and "moral height," the woman "mental breadth" without losing "the childlike in the larger mind." Either gender alone is "half itself," and together in marriage each "fulfils/ Defect in each." The prince attributes his rebirth into a better life to Ida.

Conclusion. At Sir Walter's estate, the gates are due to close. Walter is praised as an enlightened benefactor, and the storytellers are thoughtful as they disperse.

Critical Evaluation:

After the success of *Poems* (1842), Alfred, Lord Tennyson's friends and reviewers encouraged him to address a theme of modern life. Tennyson settled on what might be called the woman question—that is, the role of education for women and their place in society—and wrote *The Princess.* As early as 1839, Tennyson had been interested in women's education, which provides the theme and core of the poem. Using the Victorian notion of women's proper rights and duties within a separate sphere, Tennyson attempts to enlarge on the social theme. The poem predates both the opening of higher education to women in England and the entry of middle-class women into the nursing profession, a move inspired by Florence Nightingale. To that extent, the poem is both topical and prophetic.

For all its intellectual ideas and the seriousness with which Tennyson treats them, however, *The Princess* reveals the poet's inability to dramatize a poem whose social themes deeply touch him. The poet reverts to a mock archaic style that is at once evasive in its playfulness and deprecatory in its whimsicality. There is a stylistic conflict between the beautiful lyrics and the often quite banal narrative blank verse. The conflict suggests, on the one hand, the embarrassed romanticism of suppressed sexual desire, and on the other hand, a self-consciousness arising from Victorian gender typing and sexism. Both *The Princess*'s prologue and its conclusion are unpretentious in their naïve idyllic tone. The message is clear: universal harmony between classes and genders, between humankind and science and nature, and between all creation and "the Heaven of Heavens."

Revisions to the original 1848 poem take some of the emphasis off the rather awkward treatment of feminist aspirations for learning. A subplot is introduced of a curse on the prince's family, a curse of seizures. More important, Tennyson added six more songs to the original five lyrics. Many of these songs gained a popularity of their own, especially "Tears, Idle Tears" and "Now Sleeps the Crimson Petal," both being set to music and sung as individual compositions. The additional six songs have, it would seem, only a tenuous link to the narrative, but they give more credence to the poem's subtitle, *A Medley.*

Ostensibly, then, Tennyson's main concern seems to be the principal characters discovering and accepting gender roles that will liberate them and enhance the lives of their own genders. However, more modern readings see this concern in a more subordinate role; the real theme is the characters discovering their own sexual natures. The issue of women's rights and the romantic love story both climax in the prince's long conciliatory speech to Princess Ida in part 7:

The woman's cause is man's; they rise or sink
Together . . .
For woman is not undevelopt man,
But diverse. Could we make her as the man,
Sweet Love was slain; his dearest bond is this,
Not like to like, but like in difference.

It is argued in some modern readings, however, that the question of feminism here is being carried beyond the social sphere into psychosexual terms. The story might be characterized as one that traces the complementary movements of the princess toward "true" femininity and of the prince toward "true" masculinity. This sort of reading might help to explain Tennyson's embarrassment or his conflicted tonalities, and also might explain the additional material and give a greater unity to the understanding of the poem.

In part 1, the prince is described as being "like a girl." He and his friends, Cyril and Florian, are arrayed in female garb. To the prince's taunting foes, it is a case of "like to like." To the prince's father, it is simply a matter of effeminacy. These views oversimplify the prince. He reveals to the princess that he is not homosexual nor a "scorner of [her] sex/ But venerator." Such veneration has led him to attempt to win Princess Ida by disguising rather than asserting his sexuality. The prince's devotion to women is not generalized; he is devoted to one—his mother. As psychoanalyst Carl Jung theorized, this female image, the anima, is subsequently identified with other women, in this case Princess Ida, to whom the prince had been "proxy wedded" in childhood. Women, to the prince, are unassailable paragons.

The barrier to love is in Ida. She denies her femininity as much as the prince conceals his masculinity. Jung contends that the anima produces moods (the prince's seizures) and the animus—the masculine element in women—produces opinions, to which the princess clings. Against this opinionated female mind, instinct prevails. After the prince is wounded in a fight, Princess Ida moves into her true element and begins to accept a part of her own nature that she had repressed, thus approaching selfhood. She tells her followers to lift up their natures. Eventually, she is kissed by the prince. After this taste of passion, Ida loses her contempt for conventionalized love poems; her reading the erotic "Now Sleeps the Crimson Petal" demonstrates her acceptance of and response to a different sort of love poetry.

The prince's move toward selfhood requires that he cast off the crude self embodied in his father—the "manly man" his father wishes his son to become. As the prince reveals his full nature, he seems inclined to grant woman hers. He reminds his father that women have as many differences as do men, acknowledging in woman a wholeness lacking in "the piebald miscellany, man." The prince's tribute to distinctive womanhood in part 7 shows his progress from veneration of women to genuine appreciation.

The poem is a series of oppositions wherein the prince and the princess, in taking possession of each other and their selfhoods, represent a unity and wholeness. The prince tells Ida that "either sex alone/ Is half itself." They look to a time when "The man [will] be more of woman, she of man." This ideal is the reward of accepting sexuality instead of rejecting it. In *The Princess*, Tennyson, thus, takes a positive if somewhat culturally inhibited view toward sex. When viewed falsely, it separates man and woman. The prince expects that his marriage to Ida will "accomplish thou my manhood and thyself," affirming their relationship as neither degrading idol worship nor a jealousy-ridden contest but as a mutual enterprise for self-knowledge and fulfillment.

At the time of its publication, the poem was labeled trivial, incongruous, and in poor taste. Later readings of the poem, however, show that Tennyson anticipated Jungian analysis and the coming of a day when women would be the social equals of men. Its failure as a cohesive poetic statement can be explained both in terms of Tennyson's inner conflicted sexuality and also in terms of the cultural tensions in gender theory in mid-Victorian culture.

"Critical Evaluation" by Thomas D. Petitjean, Jr.;
revised by David Barratt

Further Reading

Bailey, Albert Edward. *Notes on the Literary Aspects of Tennyson's "Princess."* 1897. Reprint. Folcroft, Pa.: Folcroft Library Editions, 1973. A book-length study of the literary aspects of Tennyson's *The Princess*, written at a time when the values of the Victorians were being harshly assessed and revamped. Useful in comparing the sentimentality of the Victorians with Bailey's more secular age.

Barton, Anna. *Tennyson's Name: Identity and Responsibility in the Poetry of Alfred, Lord Tennyson.* Burlington, Vt.: Ashgate, 2008. Traces the development of Tennyson's poetry, focusing on his reaction to the increasing importance of "brand names" in Victorian culture. Argues that Tennyson had a strong sense of his professional identity and the ethics of literature, which led him to establish a "responsible" poetry.

Bloom, Harold, ed. *Alfred, Lord Tennyson.* Edgemont, Pa.: Chelsea House, 1985. A collection of twentieth century essays that demonstrate how Tennyson voiced the doubts, beliefs, and clouded hopes of a generation of men and women faced with secularism, political turmoil, industrialization, and the woman question.

Hall, Donald E. "The Anti-Feminist Ideology of Tennyson's *The Princess*." *Modern Language Studies* 21 (Fall, 1991): 49-62. Argues that Tennyson's poem, while purporting to be a solution to the woman question, is essentially anti-feminist in its approach to this topic.

Hood, James W. *Divining Desire: Tennyson and the Poetics of Transcendence*. Brookfield, Vt.: Ashgate, 2000. An analysis of Tennyson's poetry, focusing on his attempt to depict desire in a divine fashion. Argues that "Tennyson's poems, his characters, and his speakers employ erotic devotion and artistic creation as the means by which to approximate the transcendence that constitutes their ultimate goal." Chapter 3 is devoted to an examination of *The Princess*.

Mazzeno, Laurence W. *Alfred Tennyson: The Critical Legacy*. Rochester, N.Y.: Camden House, 2004. Traces the critical reception of Tennyson's work, from the opinions of his contemporaries to those at the end of the twentieth century. Charts how his work has been both reviled and revived since his death, discusses his reputation among poststructuralists, and provides a twenty-first century prospectus.

Sedgwick, Eve Kosofsky. "Tennyson's *Princess*: One Bride for Seven Brothers." In *Critical Essays on Alfred, Lord Tennyson*, edited by Herbert F. Tucker. New York: Maxwell Macmillan International, 1993. A reading of *The Princess* based on Sedgwick's specialized gender- and feminist-based critical approach.

The Princess Casamassima

Author: Henry James (1843-1916)
First published: 1885-1886, serial; 1886, book
Type of work: Novel
Type of plot: Social realism
Time of plot: Late nineteenth century
Locale: London

Principal characters:
HYACINTH ROBINSON, an orphan, apprenticed bookbinder, and revolutionary
AMANDA PYNSENT, the dressmaker who raised Hyacinth
PRINCESS CASAMASSIMA, an Italian princess with "modern" ideas
ANASTASIUS VETCH, a musician and a friend of Miss Pynsent
PAUL MUNIMENT, the chemist who leads Hyacinth into revolutionary work
LADY AURORA LANGRISH, a noblewoman who works for the good of the poor
MILLICENT HENNING, Hyacinth's childhood playmate

The Story:

Florentine Vivier, a French dressmaker, gives birth to an illegitimate son and accuses an Englishman, Lord Frederick Purvis, of being the boy's father. When Lord Frederick and his family refuse to recognize the baby, Florentine stabs Lord Frederick to death, a crime for which she receives the maximum prison sentence; she entrusts her son, whom she calls Hyacinth Robinson, to Miss Amanda Pynsent, a poor dressmaker, who raises the boy without telling him the unfortunate circumstances surrounding his birth.

Years later, Mrs. Bowerbank, a prison matron, visits Miss Pynsent to tell her that Florentine is dying in the prison hospital and had asked to see her son, now ten years of age. Miss Pynsent consults Mr. Vetch, a violinist in a Bloomsbury theater, who is her closest friend. On his advice, she takes Hyacinth to the prison but does not tell him at first that the woman is his mother. The grim prison frightens him, and at first his mother speaks only in French, saying that she fears he is ashamed of her. She embraces him pitifully before the matron bustles the visitors away.

During the following years, the rowdy family of Millicent Henning, Hyacinth's childhood friend, is ejected from their quarters next to Miss Pynsent's shop in Lomax Place. When

Mr. Vetch has a copy of Lord Bacon's *Essays* bound as a gift for Hyacinth, he meets the master bookbinder Eustache Poupin, who had been exiled from France after the Commune of 1871. Mr. Vetch learns that he and Poupin have a common bond of hate for the existing social and political fabric. Poupin secures an apprenticeship for Hyacinth with Crookenden's bookbindery and teaches him French and socialism.

Millicent Henning, grown to a bold, handsome young woman, unexpectedly appears in Lomax Place to renew her friendship with Hyacinth. Poupin introduces Hyacinth to a chemist and revolutionary named Paul Muniment, who takes him to visit his disabled sister, Rose Muniment. There they meet Lady Aurora Langrish, who devotes her time to caring for the poor and who admires Paul a great deal. She is a spinster much neglected by her large and wealthy family. Paul leads Hyacinth more deeply into revolutionary activity. Hyacinth has meanwhile looked up the newspaper reports of his mother's trial, and he considers himself the aggrieved son of Lord Frederick.

Mr. Vetch gets tickets for Hyacinth to take Millicent to see the play, *The Pearl of Paraguay*. Captain Godfrey Sholto, whom Hyacinth had met at a revolutionists' discussion group at The Sun and Moon public house, comes from his box at the theater to invite Hyacinth to meet the Princess Casamassima and her old companion, Madame Grandoni.

Prince Casamassima tries to see the princess to beg her to return to him, but she refuses to see him. As the prince leaves her house, he sees Hyacinth ushered in, at the princess's invitation, to tea. Later, Hyacinth binds a copy of Tennyson poems as a gift for the princess, but when he tries to deliver his gift, he learns that she had left London for a series of visits in the country. Hyacinth encounters Captain Sholto in a bar and, as Sholto hurries him strangely along, they encounter Millicent. Hyacinth suspects that Millicent had arranged to meet Sholto.

Paul announces at a meeting at The Sun and Moon that the revolutionary organizer Hoffendahl, who had spent twelve years in Prussian prisons, is in London. When Hyacinth declares his readiness to give his life for the cause, Paul takes him to see Hoffendahl. There he swears an oath to perform an act of violence whenever Hoffendahl should send the order.

Meanwhile, the princess invites Hyacinth to stay at her country house, Medley. The princess is extremely pleasant, and Hyacinth stays on in the country. One day, Captain Sholto rides up to Hyacinth as he is walking on the estate and asks Hyacinth to obtain an invitation to dinner for him. Clearly, Hyacinth has replaced Sholto as the princess's favorite.

Hyacinth returns from Medley to find Miss Pynsent dying. In her will, she leaves a small sum of money to him. Mr. Vetch adds to this sum and advises Hyacinth to travel on the Continent. On his return, he hears that the princess had sold all her beautiful furnishings, had moved to a tawdry, lower-middle-class house in Madeira Crescent, and had become friendly with Paul, who is now deeply involved in revolutionary activities. In the meantime, Hyacinth's own contact with wealth and leisure had made life seem more valuable and the society that produces and appreciates art more tolerable.

After the prince follows the princess and observes her going out with Paul, he demands that Madame Grandoni tell him what she is doing. As the prince leaves Madame Grandoni, he meets Hyacinth. While they are walking away from the house, they see Paul and the princess return and enter together. Madame Grandoni abandons the princess, and the prince writes to Paul saying that he would send no more money to his wife.

At Poupin's, Hyacinth finds the German worker Schinkel with sealed orders for him. He is to go to a grand party and there assassinate a duke. Mr. Vetch tries to keep Hyacinth from doing some desperate action. Hyacinth goes to the store where Millicent works, only to find her talking to Captain Sholto. The princess, going to Hyacinth's room, finds Schinkel waiting. She demands that he break in. Inside, they find that Hyacinth had shot himself in the heart.

Critical Evaluation:

The Princess Casamassima represents an attempt by Henry James, who had made his reputation as a novelist of the upper classes, to capture the full spectrum of modern urban life. He continues to depict the life of the idle rich in the figure of the prince, but his characters the princess and Lady Aurora agree that the rich have a responsibility to use their wealth toward some useful end.

In this novel, James made a significant addition to his previous spectrum of characters with a gallery of striving working-class figures: the sublime figure of Millicent Henning, who claws her way out of Lomax Place to the relative affluence of the West End shops; Anastasius Vetch, who makes the grand gesture of forgiving a debt of about seventeen pounds; and the hero of the book, Hyacinth Robinson, a journeyman bookbinder with a commitment to revolutionary socialism. James also examines the sick and the dispossessed in the figure of the disabled woman, Rose Muniment, whose greatest treasure is a bed jacket given her by Lady Aurora. Finally, James depicts the shadowy figures of the revolutionary anarchists, whose goal, or so they claim, is nothing less than the total destruction of all these social classes.

The all-pervading irony of James's novel, however, is that none of these figures is quite what each claims. The princess plays at revolution because she is bored with her empty upper-class life, and her only real commitment is a monetary one. Yet her money buys her neither worthwhile deeds nor true involvement in the making of policy. Hyacinth begins his career caring deeply about society and committed to the need for revolution, but once he has been exposed to the princess's wealth and the beauty of fine material objects, he no longer wants to destroy the rich but merely to reallocate their wealth. As he comes to realize, there is "nothing more terrible than to find yourself face to face with your obligation and to feel at the same time the spirit originally prompting it dead within you."

Even the minor figures are false to themselves and their stated ideals. Lady Aurora continues to minister to Rose Muniment mainly because she is devotedly in love with Rose's brother, Paul Muniment; in his turn, Paul uses the revolutionary cause to pad his own pockets and further his personal ambitions. The only character who remains true to herself is Millicent Henning, and she does so out of shallowness, not nobility; she entrusts her fate to capitalist society, never looking ahead to the day when her beauty will fade and her modeling talents will no longer be in demand.

James could write *The Princess Casamassima* because he himself, as an American and a writer, was an outsider gazing in at the riches of the upper classes. As James says in his 1904 preface to the novel, "I had only to conceive his watching the same public show I had watched myself." Yet where Hyacinth never becomes more than a spectator of the princess's wealth and freedom, James succeeded in penetrating the great mansions and in becoming a figure in demand; between October, 1878, and June, 1879, he was invited to dinner more than one hundred times. Hyacinth, on the other hand, binds books in beautifully tooled leather, but he cannot write, publish, or market them. Similarly, when the princess gives up her beautiful West End mansion and moves to the dreary reaches of Madeira Crescent, the reader is asked to admire the noble sacrifice she has made of all her beautiful possessions; nevertheless, James notes, she still uses only the finest tea.

As usual in a novel by James, the battle lines are ultimately drawn not according to social class or geographic background but according to psychological type. It may be impossible to declare that Hyacinth is a successful individual, but it is clear that he is a caring and loyal one. Neither Hyacinth nor the narrator ever decides whether the princess's revolutionary ardor is "superficial or profound," but her attachment to Hyacinth justifies our sympathy for her. Conversely, Paul seems attached to no one but himself; his cold ambition makes him the villain in the reader's eyes, even though he never commits any crime. Morality is always tied to personal honor for James.

James's greatest accomplishment is his creation of a shadowy underground world of incipient violence, hidden by fog, darkness, and obscurity from the everyday perceptions of the middle and upper classes. Although James lacked any direct knowledge of the revolutionary movement, he blended contemporary newspaper accounts, recent fiction, and his own experience as an outsider in creating a world of idealistic yet deeply disaffected individuals in search of a dramatic event that could change their lives and the world in which they live. In the late Victorian period, when accuracy was a major criterion in art, James was criticized for his lack of concrete detail in describing his socialists and anarchists, but this position eroded with time. As conditions change, some works of art that are firmly rooted in their time and place become irrelevant to later times. Works such as *The Princess Casamassima*, however, remain vital and relevant far beyond the time of their creation.

This novel's vitality is largely the result of James's contrast between a public world of cabs, public bars, West End shops, and country estates and an immense underworld that carries on "in silence, in darkness" and along "invisible, impalpable wires." James's vision of reality is closely attuned to the complex world of later times, as people continued to feel abused, even manipulated, by faceless forces beyond their control.

"Critical Evaluation" by Hartley S. Spatt

Further Reading

Bell, Millicent. *Meaning in Henry James*. Cambridge, Mass.: Harvard University Press, 1991. Bell focuses on James's belief that a novel is "about nothing so much as its own coming-into-being." Chapter 4 discusses the conflict in *The Princess Casamassima* between naturalism and impressionism.

Coulson, Victoria. *Henry James, Women, and Realism*. New York: Cambridge University Press, 2007. Examines James's important friendships with three women: his sister Alice James and the novelists Constance Fenimore Woolson and Edith Wharton. James shared with them what Coulson describes as an "ambivalent realism," or a cultural ambivalence about gender identity, and she examines how this idea is manifest in James's works, including *The Princess Casamassima*.

Freedman, Jonathan, ed. *The Cambridge Companion to*

Henry James. New York: Cambridge University Press, 1998. A collection of essays examining James's life and literary influences and describing his works and the characters in them.

Jacobson, Jacob. *Queer Desire in Henry James: The Politics of Erotics in "The Bostonians" and "The Princess Casamassima."* New York: Peter Lang, 2000. Analyzes the depiction of homoerotic, or same-gender, desire in what Jacobson argues are James's "most deliberately queer novels": *The Princess Casamassima* and *The Bostonians.*

Johnson, Warren. "'Hyacinth Robinson' or *The Princess Casamassima?" Texas Studies in Literature and Language* 28, no. 3 (Fall, 1986): 296-323. Johnson maintains that both Hyacinth and the princess are masks for James, who investigates their fates to test his own freedom; the novel was named for the princess, and not for Hyacinth, because readers "prefer her knowledge to Hyacinth's example."

Jolly, Roslyn. *Henry James: History, Narrative, Fiction.* New York: Oxford University Press, 1993. Jolly discusses *The Princess Casamassima* as a novel in which James tries to unite history and fiction; the main conflict for both Hyacinth and the princess is the fight between their personal visions of the future and the social constraints on those visions.

Seltzer, Mark. *Henry James and the Art of Power.* Ithaca, N.Y.: Cornell University Press, 1984. Seltzer applies to James's work the ideas of Michel Foucault on power and subterfuge. In chapter 1, *The Princess Casamassima* is used to link naturalism with the novelist's "will to power."

Stevens, Hugh. *Henry James and Sexuality.* New York: Cambridge University Press, 1998. A study of sexuality as it presents itself in James's work, including discussions of homosexuality and gender roles. Chapter 5 examines "queer plotting" in *The Princess Casamassima.*

Tilley, Wesley H. *The Background of "The Princess Casamassima."* Gainesville: University Press of Florida, 1961. Tilley traces the sources of James's knowledge of anarchism to articles in *The Times* of London and finds models for Millicent, Muniment, and Hoffendahl in actual subjects of news reports during the 1870's and 1880's.

The Princess of Clèves

Author: Madame de La Fayette (1634-1693)
First published: La Princesse de Clèves, 1678 (English translation, 1679)
Type of work: Novel
Type of plot: Love
Time of plot: Sixteenth century
Locale: France

Principal characters:
PRINCESS DE CLÈVES, née Chartres, a beautiful young noblewoman
PRINCE DE CLÈVES, her husband
MADAME DE CHARTRES, her mother
DUKE DE NEMOURS, in love with the princess
VIDAME DE CHARTRES, the uncle of the princess
QUEEN DAUPHINE, Mary, Queen of Scots, and a friend of the princess

The Story:

The court of Henry II of France is filled with many intrigues, as much of the heart as of anything else. The court itself is divided into several groups. One group is partial to the queen, who is at odds with Henry because he chooses to be guided in his personal life and in his government by Diane de Poitiers, the duchess of Valentinois, who had been his father's mistress and is now a grandmother in her own right. A second group is that which surrounds the duchess of Valentinois. A third group is that which has as its center Princess Mary, wife of the dauphin, the beautiful and brilliant young woman who is also queen of Scotland.

Into this scene of rivalry comes Madame de Chartres, with her very beautiful daughter, to be married to a nobleman with a rank as high as possible; Madame de Chartres hopes even for a prince of royal blood. Unfortunately for the mother's hopes, the intrigues of the court keep her from arranging a match so brilliant or advantageous. A marriage with either monsieur de Monpensier, the chevalier de Guise, or the Prince de Clèves seems the best that could be made, and there are obstacles to a marriage with either of those, as Madame de Chartres discovers. Each of the groups at the court is afraid that such a marriage would upset the status of the powers as they stand.

Finally, arrangements are made for a marriage to the Prince de Clèves. The gentleman, however, is perturbed by the attitude of his bride. He loves her greatly, and she seems to love him dutifully but without the abandon for which he wishes. He tries to be satisfied when she tells him that she will do her best to love him, but that she feels no real passion for him or any man. The marriage is celebrated in grand style, and a fine dinner party, attended by the king and queen, is given at the Louvre.

For many months no one at the court, where extramarital attachments are the rule rather than the exception, dare to say anything about the young wife. Thanks to her mother's solicitude and her own lack of passion where men are concerned, the Princess de Clèves keeps a spotless reputation. Her mother, who soon is on her deathbed, knows from various conferences with the princess—unusual conferences for a married woman to have with her mother, for in reality they are confessions—that the princess has no inclinations to stray from her marital vows.

One evening, however, a court ball is given in honor of one of the king's daughters, whose marriage is pending. A late arrival at the ball is the duke de Nemours, the most handsome and gallant courtier in France. At his entrance, the Princess de Clèves, who had never seen the duke before, is ordered by the king to dance with him.

Queen Elizabeth of England has taken an interest in the duke de Nemours and has expressed the wish that the young man would visit her court, but the duke remains where he can be near the Princess de Clèves. Even the repeated requests of the French king, who sees in Nemours a possible consort for Queen Elizabeth, cannot remove the duke from her side. Meanwhile, the Princess de Clèves does everything she can to conceal her love for the duke from everyone, even from her lover himself. She is determined to remain a faithful and dutiful wife.

One day, while the princess and the duke are in the apartments of the Queen Dauphine, the princess sees Nemours steal a miniature portrait of her. Although she has ample opportunity, the princess says nothing to stop him from taking her picture. Sometime later, the duke is injured by a horse in a tournament, and several people note the look of distress on the face of the Princess de Clèves. The court is beginning to realize that love is blossoming between the two.

As soon as she realizes what is happening in her heart, the Princess de Clèves goes to her husband and asks him to take her away from Paris for a time. They go to an estate in the country. While there, the princess confesses to her husband that she is falling in love with someone. Admiring her candor, he promises to help her overcome the passion. Although she refuses to name the man she loves, the Prince de Clèves guesses that it is one of three men, a trio that includes the duke de Nemours, but he has no proof. Although neither knows it, while the princess is confessing her love, de Nemours is hiding so close to them that he can overhear what is said.

Months go by, and gradually, despite her efforts to keep away from him, the princess indicates to her husband that the duke de Nemours is the man she loves. The prince is torn by jealousy, but his wife's confession and her obvious efforts to curb her love prevent him from taking any action in the matter. His only recourse is to accuse her at intervals of not being fair to him in loving another.

The strain becomes too much for the Princess de Clèves, and she asks her husband's permission to retire to a country estate near Paris. He yields graciously but sends one of his own retainers to make sure of her conduct while she is away. The retainer returns to report that twice, at night, the duke de Nemours had entered the garden where the princess was; the retainer does not know and so cannot report that his mistress had refused to see the man who loves her.

After the retainer has made his report, the prince falls ill of a fever. When the princess returns, she is unable to convince him that she has not been unfaithful, even though he wants to believe her. Rather than stand in the way of her happiness, he languishes and dies.

Some months after her husband's death, the duke de Nemours prevails upon the princess's uncle, the vidame de Chartres, to intercede for him with the princess. The uncle agrees and arranges for an interview between the two. At this time, the princess tells the duke that, in spite of her love for him, she could never marry him. Soon afterward, she retires to her estate in the Pyrenees. She falls gravely ill there and, during her recuperation, experiences a religious conversion. She spends six months of each year praying in a convent and the remaining six months doing charitable work in her parish. Several years later she dies, although she is still quite young.

Critical Evaluation:

Although critics have disagreed sharply about the ending of this novel as well as the novel's mother-daughter relationship, the contrasts between appearance and reality, and the meaning of the various representations of love, almost all scholars agree that *The Princess of Clèves* was the first profound psychological novel written in France. The many different narrative techniques employed by Madame de La Fayette and the changing perspectives lead readers to reach wildly diverse interpretations of the work.

La Fayette includes in this novel several stories told by various characters. These stories illustrate in a subtle manner the feelings of her central characters. In the second of the four parts of *The Princess of Clèves*, Marie Stuart, who was married to King Francis II of France and later became Mary, Queen of Scots, speaks about the tragic death of Anne Boleyn, the mother of Queen Elizabeth I, whom the duke de Nemours had considered marrying. Marie Stuart attributes the beheading of Boleyn to the irrational jealousy of her husband Henry VIII, who had falsely suspected her of marital infidelity. Marie Stuart suggests that, in addition to being excessively violent, Henry VIII was a hypocrite because it was he and not Boleyn who had committed adultery. Soon after her execution at the Tower of London, he married Jane Seymour. His adulterous affair must have begun before Boleyn's execution.

At first glance, this story seems to have little to do with the plot of *The Princess of Clèves*, but when one rereads this novel, one comes to see a similarity between this and the Prince de Clèves's unjustified jealousy directed against his wife. Moreover, Henry VIII's obvious infidelity and hypocrisy lead one to believe that the Prince de Clèves and the duke de Nemours probably both had mistresses, although they demanded absolute fidelity from the princess, who had, in fact, remained faithful to her marriage vows. These and other stories in this novel subtly but effectively help one to understand that the Prince de Clèves and the duke de Nemours may not necessarily be as sympathetic as the courtiers believe them to be. Appearance and reality are often quite different in *The Princess of Clèves*. Although these inserted stories serve to illustrate the moral weakness and the bad faith of the two leading male characters in this novel, many critics have tended to downplay the importance of these stories because the stories are incompatible with the traditional view of the Prince de Clèves and the duke de Nemours as basically sympathetic characters and not as victimizers of the Princess de Clèves.

Another technique La Fayette used well in this novel is her descriptions of scenes from the point of view of several different characters. Excellent examples of this narrative technique can be found in the descriptions of the courtship and wedding of the princess and her decision to retire permanently from the royal court near the end of this novel. Each character reveals part of what actually happened, and readers must decide on their own what each scene means for them and the fictional characters.

The preparations for the wedding of Mademoiselle de Chartres to the Prince de Clèves illustrate nicely La Fayette's skill in presenting several different perspectives. The Prince de Clèves and Madame de Chartres are eagerly making plans for an elaborate palace wedding reception. For them, this was to be a glorious social event, but Mademoiselle de Chartres approaches this wedding with a complete lack of enthusiasm. She feels betrayed by her mother, who wants to force her to marry a man for whom the sixteen-year-old princess "felt no particular attraction." She tells the prince that she will agree to marry him if both Madame de Chartres and he insist, but she points out to him that she could never love him, although she intends to remain faithful to her marriage vows out of respect for herself and because of her desire not to risk her immortal soul by committing the mortal sin of adultery. Readers admire her honesty, but they suspect that the wedding reception was not an especially joyous experience for the new couple. The Princess de Clèves views this arranged marriage as yet another example of the exploitation of women by insensitive men such as her husband.

Another example of La Fayette's skill in using this narrative technique can be found at the end of the novel when the Princess de Clèves, whose husband has just died, decides to leave the royal court to seek inner peace on her country estate in the Pyrenees. Once the duke de Nemours realizes that she would probably never return to Paris, he asks numerous influential people at the royal court, including the queen herself and the princess's uncle, the vidame de Chartres, to write to her in an effort to persuade her of the foolishness of her decision to abandon courtly pleasures for what he and many literary critics considered a boring existence in a small and remote country village. While she is staying at her country estate, the young widow falls gravely ill, and the narrator suggests that this close brush with death has caused the princess to "see the things of this life differently from the way they appear when one is in good health." La Fayette is perhaps suggesting that the princess is preparing herself spiritually for the next life, whereas those still at the royal court are indifferent to such thoughts. Her behavior is incomprehensible to superficial characters such as the duke de Nemours, but it makes perfect sense if one concludes that she experienced a spiritual conversion shortly before her death.

La Fayette ends this psychological novel with the following comment on the title character: "Her life, which was quite short, left inimitable examples of virtue." This is a very sensible interpretation for readers who agree with the narrator, but it seems utter madness to readers who share the duke de Nemours's belief that no intelligent person would ever want to leave the apparent splendor of a royal court. Ever since its first publication in 1678, *The Princess of Clèves* has remained a marvelously ambiguous novel whose meanings for readers depend on those characters with whom they identify.

"Critical Evaluation" by Edmund J. Campion

Further Reading

Beasley, Faith, and Katherine Ann Jensen, eds. *Approaches to Teaching Lafayette's "The Princess of Clèves."* New York: Modern Language Association of America, 1998. Provides useful background material and analysis for students. Places La Fayette's novel within the context of the French novel and of seventeenth century French history, and discusses the themes, structure, treatment of masculinity, and other topics.

DeJean, Joan. *Tender Geographies: Women and the Origins of the Novel in France.* New York: Columbia University Press, 1991. The extensive chapter "Lafayette and the Generation of 1660-1689" places *The Princess of Clèves* in a broad historical context and situates it with regard to politics and to other French women writers of the period.

François, Anne-Lise. "L'Aveu sans suite: Love's Open Secret in Lafayette's *La Princesse de Clèves*." In *Open Secrets: The Literature of Uncounted Experience.* Stanford, Calif.: Stanford University Press, 2008. François describes La Fayette's novel as a work of "uncounted experience," or literature in which "nothing happens" because the characters reject modernist pressures for self-actualization and self-denial.

Green, Anne. *Privileged Anonymity: The Writings of Madame de Lafayette.* Oxford, England: Legenda, 1996. Green analyzes La Fayette's novels and nonfiction from the perspective of gender studies. She argues that La Fayette was conflicted about being a woman and an author and she expresses these feelings in her depiction of sexual relationships.

Haig, Stirling. *Madame de La Fayette.* New York: Twayne, 1970. Contains a very thoughtful overview of Madame de La Fayette's career as a novelist. Haig describes well her place in the development of the historical novel as a genre in seventeenth century France.

Henry, Patrick, ed. *An Inimitable Example: The Case for "La Princesse de Clèves."* Washington, D.C.: Catholic University of America Press, 1992. Includes twelve excellent essays that provide feminist, sociocritical, psychological, and religious interpretations of this novel. Contains a thorough bibliography of critical studies on *The Princess of Clèves.*

Miller, Nancy K. *Subject to Change: Reading Feminist Writing.* New York: Columbia University Press, 1988. This book reprints Miller's seminal article "Emphasis Added: Plots and Plausibilities in Women's Fiction." Miller takes up the question of verisimilitude ("plausibility") to offer a new interpretation of the princess's choice as an act of desire rather than renunciation.

Paulson, Michael G. *Facets of a Princess: Multiple Readings of Madame de la Fayette's "La Princesse de Cleves."* New York: Peter Lang, 1998. Paulson brings a multifaceted approach to his examination of La Fayette's novel, analyzing the book from political, historical, feminist, and religious perspectives. Includes bibliographical references.

Racevskis, Roland. "Time and Information in and Around *La Princesse de Cleves*: Anteriority, Communication, Interiority." In *Time and Ways of Knowing Under Louis XIV: Molière, Sévigné, Lafayette.* Lewisburg, Pa.: Bucknell University Press, 2003. Racevskis analyzes the representation of time in La Fayette's novel as part of this study of how the then-new technology of clocks and timepieces was reflected in seventeenth century French literature.

Tiefenbrun, Susan W. *A Structural Stylistic Analysis of "La Princesse de Cleves."* The Hague, the Netherlands: Mouton, 1976. Contains an excellent study of the formal structure of the novel. Tiefenbrun clearly explains the complicated relationships among the princess, her husband, and the duke de Nemours.

Principia

Author: Sir Isaac Newton (1642/1643-1727)
First published: Philosophiae Naturalis Principia
   Mathematica, 1687 (English translation, 1729, as
   Mathematical Principles of Natural Philosophy)
Type of work: Science and philosophy

One of the most influential books in history is Sir Isaac Newton's *Principia.* Published in 1687, the book immediately led to intellectual controversy among the scientists and philosophers of the day, including Gottfried Wilhelm Leibniz, Robert Hooke, and John Flamsteed, who felt it necessary to argue with many of the propositions and conclusions Newton advances. These arguments give at least as much testimony to the importance of *Principia* as they undermine its theories. Newton's book remained the principal document in the field of physics for two hundred years.

Newton's work in physics has never been supplanted or debunked; relativity and other discoveries of the twentieth century are modifications and additions to his scientific discoveries rather than replacements. The philosophical implications of relativity and other discoveries of the twentieth century, however, are radically different from the philosophical implications of Newton's discoveries. During the eighteenth century and after, Newton's masterpiece also was a highly revered work of philosophy. Newton became one of the most honored figures in Western culture, one of the first formulators of scientific method, and the person whose work formed the basis for scientific study and application of principles. Physics, as a field of theory and knowledge, did not exist before Newton's work.

Newton's preface to the *Principia* announces that he is interested in the laws of mathematics as a means of discovering nature, or getting at philosophical truth. He thinks that mathematics is not a pure, abstract system, but rather a human and rational means for discovering the principles of the universe, for making a kind of universal order out of the disparate experience of the senses. In fact, he believes in this function of mathematics so strongly that, in the body of the *Principia*, every experiment or demonstration is concluded with a scholium. Each scholium is a short essay giving the philosophical implications or the speculative use of the mathematical or physical principle just demonstrated. Thus, Newton's book is a philosophical as well as a scientific work.

After the preface, Newton supplies a series of definitions for such terms as "motion," "force," and "quantity," terms necessary for even an elementary understanding of his work.

These definitions are still standard among students of physics. Newton thereupon states his famous three axioms or laws of motion. These axioms are still relevant in any account of physical forces in the everyday world; relativity comes into play to a significant extent at the level of the atom and at speeds at or near the speed of light. Newton states these laws as axioms on which his whole account of the universe rests.

The first axiom states that a body remains in its existing state of motion or rest unless acted upon by an outside force. This is also known as the law of inertia. The second axiom states that the change in motion of a body is proportional, in precise mathematical terms, to the force applied to it. This is known as the law of acceleration. The third axiom states that for every action there is an equal and opposite reaction. Newton could not prove these axioms universally; rather, these principles are what best explain the various facts and data that people find in physical phenomena around them. The axioms, like the definitions, are necessary beginnings, points that must be accepted in order that all physical data can make rational sense. The axioms have six corollaries, propositions that can be established from the axioms and that can be used in turn to establish other propositions.

In the first book of the *Principia*, Newton deals with the motion of bodies. To simplify and explain his theories, in the first book he confines his observations and proofs to bodies moving in a vacuum. He begins with the more purely mathematical: establishing ratios (demonstrating the logic of the number system), determining the vectors of forces, tracing and proving how bodies move in various arcs, parabolas, and ellipses. For all these geometric demonstrations he gives mathematical proof by inventing and proving his equations and by making frequent reference to his many diagrammatic figures. He also develops and proves equations dealing with the ascent and descent of bodies, again confining his work to bodies in a vacuum. He also devises a mathematical explanation for the oscillations of a pendulum. Finally, at the end of the first book, Newton deals with the attractions of bodies for one another, setting up equations to demonstrate this necessary and universal principle of attraction and repulsion. In addition to defining the terms of physics, the basic laws of physics, and the mathematics to describe the laws of motion, Newton "discovers" gravity.

In the second book, Newton deals with the motion of bodies in resisting mediums. The nature of resisting mediums, such as water or air, make his proofs become more intricate and complicated. Newton usually attempts to simplify his demonstrations by assuming that the medium is constant. These experiments allow Newton to calculate and, more important, to explain the resistance of substances such as water and air to the motion of bodies passing through them. He gives further demonstrations of motion, analyzing some of the problems dealt with in his first book. He brings up, for example, the oscillations of the pendulum and charts the equations for the motion of a pendulum through air. His consideration of the resistance to bodies allows Newton to present and demonstrate the solution to other problems in the physical universe. In this section, dealing with means of determining the density and compression of fluids, he develops equations to explain the behavior of fluids: the density they offer as resistance and the force they exert when compressed. This work on fluids permits Newton to establish his equations to determine the velocity of waves.

Newton calls his third book the "System of the World," his specific intention in this book being to develop the philosophical principles that he believes follow directly from his mathematical proofs and his experimentation. He begins the book by stating his rules for accurate reasoning, based on his belief that there are no superfluous causes in nature. Each cause that one can talk of sensibly has direct effects, which one is able to observe and subdue to order with mathematical and rational equipment. In other words, Newton believes that the simplicity of the design of the universe is a basic rule; causes are never extraneous. Causes are the basis for observable and frequently calculable phenomena.

Another significant rule is Newton's belief that all conclusions are based on induction. One reasons from the observable facts and always needs to refer one's conclusions or theories to observable facts. In this complete devotion to scientific method, there is the necessity of constant application of all of the data to the theory. Newton fully realizes, therefore, that theories might well have to be altered to provide explanations for data that challenge the theory. Post-Newtonian physics would not have surprised Newton, for he had always acknowledged that scientific theories could be no more than the best conclusions available from the data at hand at the moment the conclusion was made. Thus, Newton makes his significant contribution to the scientific method, which is a basis for the many discoveries made since his time.

The third book sets forth Newton's mathematical demonstrations of the periodic times and movements of the planets. Again, he derives many new equations to demonstrate, with accuracy, the movements of the planets and to correlate this knowledge with the system of time on Earth. He also proves that gravity applies to all bodies and calculates the ratio of gravity. Much of the third section is devoted to lunar motion, establishing equations and calculating, in terms of time, the various changing relationships between the moon and the earth. These matters lead Newton into consideration of the effect of the sun and the moon on the waters of the earth, and he devises means of measuring the tides. He also computes the times and ranges of recurrent comets. Newton thereby provides practical applications for his theories and mathematics.

In a long, final "Scholium" designed to tie the extensive parts of the *Principia* together, Newton develops the basis for his belief in God. He asserts that such a perfect, and perfectly simple, system must have, as its ultimate or final cause, a perfect, and perfectly simple, Being. This Being must embody all the intelligence, the rationality, the perfection, of the system itself. Newton views God as this ultimate principle, not as a personal God or a larger edition of a human being. Firm in his devotion to his principle, he answers, in later editions of the *Principia*, charges of atheism brought against his system. This principle, the final cause, is the originator of the whole Newtonian universe, the perfectly rational origin of all the laws, mathematics, and reason that people can use to develop and describe the meaningful pattern in the universe. God, the perfect Being, having set this vast plan in constant motion, is constantly at hand to make sure the universe does not run down.

This concept of God became, during the eighteenth century, one of the principal concepts held by intellectuals. The religion of Deism, of viewing God as the perpetrator and final cause of a complete, perfect, mechanistic universe, is derived from Newton's thorough and systematic explanation.

As science and as philosophy, the *Principia* is one of humanity's great achievements. The book vastly increased the store of human knowledge and derived a sound and rational basis for making conclusions about the physical universe. In addition, Newton illustrates and defines the method by which people may continue to test his observations, develops a new and important area for the human intellect, and establishes a metaphysical system that governed the thought and scientific investigation of the world's leading intellects for more than a century.

Further Reading

Chandrasekhar, S. *Newton's "Principia" for the Common Reader*. New York: Oxford University Press, 1995. Chandrasekhar, an eminent mathematical astrophysicist, provides an accessible explanation of and commentary on Newton's famous work.

Christianson, Gale E. *In the Presence of the Creator: Isaac Newton and His Times*. New York: Free Press, 1984. This very readable biography places Newton's life in the context of the scientific revolution.

Cohen, I. Bernard. *Introduction to Newton's "Principia."* Cambridge, Mass.: Harvard University Press, 1971. A massive work of scholarship. Presents the background to the publishing of the variorum edition of Newton's influential book. Itemizes revisions and corrections in the various editions and translations. Surveys the early reviews. Includes a comprehensive bibliography.

Cohen, I. Bernard, and George E. Smith, eds. *The Cambridge Companion to Newton*. New York: Cambridge University Press, 2002. Collection of essays, including discussions of Newton's concepts of force, mass, gravitation, celestial mechanics, optics, and mathematics. An essay by George E. Smith examines the methodology of *Principia*.

De Gandt, Francois. *Force and Geometry in Newton's "Principia."* Translated by Curtis Wilson. Princeton, N.J.: Princeton University Press, 1995. An introduction to Newton's *Principia*.

Dobbs, Betty Jo Teeter. *The Janus Faces of Genius: The Role of Alchemy in Newton's Thought*. New York: Cambridge University Press, 1992. Dobbs argues that Newton's primary goal was to establish a unified system that includes both natural and divine principles. Special attention is given to alchemy.

Fauvel, John, et al., eds. *Let Newton Be!* New York: Oxford University Press, 1988. Twelve articles explicate the modern and historical contexts of Newton's work. John Roche's accessible overview is an excellent starting point for students new to Newton's difficult work.

Gjertsen, Derek. *The Newton Handbook*. London: Routledge & Kegan Paul, 1986. Provides a wealth of information, including a chronology and discussion of the origin and production of the work, and an assessment of the difficulty of the work. The contents and central arguments of the *Principia* are usefully summarized.

Gleick, James. *Isaac Newton*. New York: Pantheon, 2003. Gleick ventures into well-trodden territory with yet another biography of Newton, but he reveals Newton's seemingly contradictory passions for both the mysterious, such as alchemy, and that which is considered not-so-mysterious, such as rational thinking. Includes illustrations and an index.

Stayer, Marcia Sweet. *Newton's Dream*. Kingston, Ont.: McGill-Queens University Press, 1988. Marks the tercentenary of Newton's seminal work. Examines the work's enduring impact. The title essay by physics Nobel laureate Steven Weinberg is especially lucid.

Westfall, Richard S. *Never at Rest: A Biography of Isaac Newton*. New York: Cambridge University Press, 1980. Westfall's lengthy biography presents Newton's scientific discoveries in the context of his life. Includes a valuable bibliographical essay and an appendix.

Principia Ethica

Author: G. E. Moore (1873-1958)
First published: 1903
Type of work: Philosophy

A philosopher in the analytic tradition, G. E. Moore believed that clear questions solve philosophical problems. In *Principia Ethica*, he poses three questions:

(1) What ought to exist for its own sake?
(2) What actions should one perform?
(3) What is the nature of the evidence to prove or disprove ethical propositions?

Moore believes that the answer to the first question is self-evident. To ascertain the answer to the second question, causal truths must be used as evidence. Moore's goal is to establish a scientific (that is, a practical) ethics.

Moore asserts that "pleasure" is not definable in terms of "good." This is the case because "good" is a primitive term. That is, it is indefinable. For example, "green" may be defined as a combination of "yellow" and "blue." However, "yellow," as the name of a primary color, has no definition other than itself. "Yellow" and "blue" are primitives.

Ordinary-language philosophy distinguishes good or value as a means from goods in themselves, or intrinsic values. Goods as means cause or produce intrinsic values. Intrinsic values, like primitives, are simply good by definition.

Moore asserts that any action must produce a predictable effect. Since the human mind can predict only tenuously, however, people must work with uncertainty under varying conditions. They would have to know all results of a given action in order to determine with certainty whether a decision is productive of more good than evil. Moreover, they would have to know all the outcomes of all possible alternative decisions. Such knowledge is impossible. Therefore, ethical reasoning necessarily proceeds with uncertainties: A certain ethical proposition is inherently false. By contrast, a statement referring to generally good effects, rather than making an absolute assertion of goodness, may be true for a limited time.

Statements about intrinsic goods are different since they do not rely on predictions. An intrinsic good, or a good in itself, exists regardless of the contingencies and uncertainties of the world around it. For Moore, then, ethical inquiry differentiates between goodness in itself and goodness as a result. To decide what to do in a given situation, a person relies on an analysis of both intrinsic good and resulting good. The best course of action is the one that will lead to the greatest sum of intrinsic value. One must weigh the intrinsic good of an action, the intrinsic good of its results, the intrinsic good of the results of those results, and the goods and evils involved in all possible alternative actions and their resulting causal chains.

The union of all parts of actions (their causes, conditions, and results) forms what Moore calls an "organic whole." For example, Menenius Agrippa's allegory of body parts that all complain about the lazy stomach at the center illustrates an organic whole. Parts of a picture have a similar relationship of reciprocity. The parts are of a whole and share its nature. Organic wholes may be understood as wholes that have intrinsic values greater than the sums of the values of their respective parts.

Moore discusses naturalistic ethics. Generally, ethics includes nature. Nature he defines as all phenomena that are taken by physics, biology, and psychology as their proper objects of study. Naturalism assigns to any given thing or event the quality of being either natural (normal) or unnatural (abnormal). As such, Moore believes, it offers no reasons for ethical principles. Instead, it deceives people with false ethical principles.

Since "good" is not definable and nature offers no guidelines, Moore insists, one must begin ethical inquiry with an open mind. Objects of nature may be good, but goodness is not a natural property. Feelings are natural, but goodness is not a feeling. Considering goodness as a feeling commits the naturalistic fallacy, which is an illogical crossover from nature into nonnature. This fallacy often involves confusing "is" and "ought."

Living "naturally," Moore asserts, renders ethics obsolete since all actions in the world are natural. For example, though health is good, disease, too, is natural. Evolution also cannot set a standard for how one ought to live. Evolution ethics, derived from Charles Darwin's concept of natural selection, classifies "higher" and "lower" races or groups. If this reasoning were correct, the cockroach, which may survive humanity after a collapse of an ecosystem, would be a "higher" species than humanity. Whether a surviving species is "higher" or "lower" than another is an open question. For this reason, Darwin did not combine his theory with the questionable assumption of evolution as progress. Forces of nature cannot set standards for moral thinkers.

Moore evaluates the hedonistic view that "nothing is good but pleasure." Hedonism is an all-or-nothing doctrine. It rejects the notion that pleasure is just one good of several. Hedonists think that things are good only if they lead to pleasure as an outcome. Moore rejects such valuation as a basis for ethics.

John Stuart Mill observed that the fact that people desire something is proof that that thing is desirable. However, the proposition that one ought to desire a thing because one does desire that thing is another example of the naturalistic fallacy. Moore allows that the proposition "pleasure alone is good as an end" may still be intuitively true, if and only if intuitions are consistent. When Mill distinguishes between "qualities of pleasures," however, he must admit that intuitions are not universal. Therefore, pleasure—which relies on intuitions—cannot be the only good since pleasures vary in terms of their goodness.

Moore also rejects egoism. Egoism is a way of asserting the importance of one's own happiness. Its secondary effect is to create a generally happy society as all pursue this good. In ordinary parlance, egoists serve their own interests or their own good. Egoism holds that each person's happiness is the sole good. Each person values different good things, however, so the highest good consists of many different goods. A universal good cannot be both universal and relative simultaneously. Adding "for him" or "for her" to account for differences in taste or desire produces confusions in ethical theory. In other words, a consistent theory cannot simultaneously value a single person's happiness as sole good and value the aggregate of all persons' happiness as the sole good, because "sole good" in each case refers to a different entity, a different good.

Moore reviews the theories of the Greek Stoic philosophers, as well as those of Baruch Spinoza, Immanuel Kant, Georg Wilhelm Friedrich Hegel, and Hegel's followers. He labels them all as metaphysical ethicists. Metaphysicians make claims of knowledge about objects that are suprasensible. Metaphysical ethicists consider nature as perfect moral entity (Stoics), or as absolute substance in harmony with the intellectual love of God (Spinoza), or as the realm of law as such (Kant), or as the material substance of reality, which is coming through human history to develop and know itself (Hegel). These systems all commit the naturalistic fallacy since they all advocate the "good" as an attribute of a super-reality beyond that which is empirically knowable. If the Christian heaven and hell, for example, have greater reality than the here and now, then ethics from the Christian perspective is meaningless and pointless because ethics can only affect temporal reality. If some good exists in temporal reality, then eternal reality cannot be the sole good.

Next, Moore discusses what one should do. People need reasons for their ethical decisions, so they need a very clear meaning of "good." Causal knowledge is also necessary for ethical judgments; such knowledge must include all possible alternatives and all conceivable effects. Such certainty is practically impossible, so certainty in ethical decisions is impossible. Likely alternatives and likely results, thus, must suffice. "Likely alternatives" are those that occur to a person. Another alternative may be best, but it may not occur to the person and thus cannot be considered.

Some rules for Moore do approach certainty, such as a rule against murder if one values life, a rule against theft if one values property, a rule in support of industry if one values the acquisition of property, a rule in support of temperance if one values health sufficient for the acquisition of property, or a rule in support of promise-keeping if one values exchanges in the acquisition of property. Thus, preserving life and acquiring property are universals of ethics. Chastity, on the other hand, is not a universal since a society without conjugal jealousy or paternal affection is conceivable. Of all duties, crimes, and sins, an individual must be able to perform or avoid them, because choice is an inherent feature of ethics. Moreover, performing or avoiding moral actions must generally produce better or worse results, respectively, and those results must be so predictable as to appear universal.

Since reliable prognostication is impossible, a binding analysis of exceptions to rules is also impossible. Such exceptions may be known, but not their conditions. Breaking a rule may encourage others to break the rule also if they see a spurious analogy without comparable moral clarity. Thus, Moore asserts, one should adhere to custom even where custom is bad, although an individual's understanding may become great enough to justify breaking rules. If that action inspires others and if the rule broken is truly bad, then the overall effect will be a good one. An individual's own analysis of probable outcomes should generally take precedence over any rules, but only when the individual accepts that by breaking rules he or she risks sanctions.

Moore lists the following moral rules:

(1) A lesser good is proper for an individual if she cannot see the greater one.
(2) A good closer to self and loved ones is of greater importance.
(3) Temporally near goods are generally better than distant ones.
(4) Duty is that which produces the best possible outcome.
(5) Everything must be either part of the universal good or else not good at all; no third alternative ("good for me") exists.

Moore agrees with Aristotle's "habitual disposition" as a definition of "virtue." However, to consider a virtue to be an intrinsic good, one should have to demonstrate its good results. Therefore, virtues are not intrinsic goods. Christians, for example, will see virtue as a sole good and see it rewarded by heaven. Thus, heaven is a greater good, containing happiness. Happiness is a good yet greater than heaven alone. All these goods claim a logically impossible sole-good status. Acting habitually does not constitute virtue.

The ideal is the best state conceivable. Heaven and utopias, for example, would be such states. To attain a heavenly or utopian ideal, Moore believes, one must compare goods to arrive at the best possible combination in an organic whole. Two construction errors are likely in making this determination: First, one may isolate goods that serve as means and stock the ideal setting with such goods. This would render the ideal worthless, since it would lack intrinsic value. Second, one may neglect the principle of organic unity by rejecting a part that seems to have no intrinsic value. Doing so would destroy the organic whole.

Knowledge of the highest good adds value, although knowledge itself is value neutral. Theoretically, God's perfection outdoes that of any human, but the love of God is inferior to human love if God does not exist. With relationships among people, mental beauty adds to the appreciation.

Purely material existence does not have as great a value as do mental events. Both together offer an organic whole; neither is irrelevant.

Evil is similar. The addition of true belief to a positive evil constitutes a worse evil than a purely imagined evil. A "mixed" evil might be an imagined evil that is contemplated. Thus, a tragedy (an imagined evil that is contemplated) can be productive of an overall good. However, delighting in evil by taking pleasure from the pain of others enhances its vileness. Meanwhile, a true belief in the existence of a good or beautiful object or person that one hates will enhance through one's hatred the badness of this organic whole. An erroneous judgment, by contrast, may lessen the badness of the organic whole.

Pain appears to be a far greater evil than pleasure is a good. If pleasure enhances an evil state—if a criminal contemplates with joy the pain of victims, for example—the resultant organic whole is worse than it would be without this pleasure. If pain enhances an evil state—if the criminal feels the pain of remorse or receives punishment—the resultant organic whole may be improved by that pain. Retributive punishments consist of wickedness (the criminal act) and pain (the penalty). Targeting existing evil adds greater value to the world. Punishing existing evil meliorates it.

Moore is aware that his remarks in his final chapter on the ideal are inconclusive and affected by his feelings. If pain, evil, pleasure, and good were all of equal status, calculations such as Jeremy Bentham's hedonic calculus would make ethical analysis much easier. The simple scale of dolors and hedons used by Bentham is turned by Moore into an analytic enterprise of great complexity, as far beyond Bentham's work as a modern passenger jet is beyond the initial flier invented by the Wright Brothers. Moore is to be lauded for the great precision of his analytic approach.

Reinhold Schlieper

Further Reading

Altman, Andrew. "Breathing Life into a Dead Argument: G. E. Moore and the Open Question." *Philosophical Studies* 117, no. 3 (February, 2004): 395. Moore's reference to an open question when he talks about the good as property. Altman deals in depth with the logical possibilities of this concept.

Baldwin, Thomas. "The Indefinability of Good." *Journal of Value Inquiry* 37, no. 3 (2003): 313. Develops Moore's idea that "good" is indefinable and has no more basic components, drawing a useful distinction between Moore's metaethical analysis and his moral points.

Bateman, Bradley W. "G. E. Moore and J. M. Keynes: A Missing Chapter in the History of the Expected Utility Model." *American Economic Review* 78, no. 5 (December, 1988): 1098. Moore's reasoning contains some ambivalence about rules to follow and about a rugged autonomy in ethical deciding. Bateman's essay focuses on some of these ambivalences. British economist J. M. Keynes is seen as a disciple of Moore.

Frankena, William. "The Naturalistic Fallacy." *Mind* 48 (1939): 464-477. Well-established work that is foundational to the Moore criticism that followed.

Rugina, Anghel N. "Toward a New *Principia Ethica*: The Third Revolution in Ethics." *International Journal of Social Economics* 25, no. 5 (1998): 755. Sees Moore's work as an ethics that complements traditional views and that does not break with traditional ethics. Lauds Moore for producing the fundamental principles of a new scientific approach to ethical thinking.

Shook, J. R. "Themes from G. E. Moore: New Essays in Epistemology and Ethics." *Choice* 46, no. 2 (October, 2008): 313. Points out properly that Moore leaves more questions than he answers.

Principia Mathematica

Authors: Bertrand Russell (1872-1970) and Alfred
   North Whitehead (1861-1947)
First published: 1910-1913
Type of work: Philosophy

The *Principia Mathematica* of Bertrand Russell and Alfred North Whitehead is an attempt to analyze the roots of mathematics in the language of logic. The new notation of symbolic logic, which is derived from Guiseppe Peano and had its origins in the work of Gottlob Frege, is the vehicle for this task.

Russell and Whitehead begin with the functions of propositions, in which letters such as p or q stand for logical propositions such as "Socrates is a man" or "Socrates is mortal." These functions include the following:

- the contradictory function "−(p • −p)," read as "not (p and not p)" and meaning that it is false to assert both a statement and its denial
- the logical sum "p v q," read as "p or q" and meaning that exactly one of the two propositions is true
- the logical product "p • q," read as "p and q" and meaning that both of the propositions are true
- the implicative function "p > q," read as "p implies q" and meaning that if p is true, then q must also be true
- the function "−p v q," read as "not p or q" and meaning that either p is false or q is true, but not both

The standard symbol is used for equivalence: "p q" (meaning that p and q are either both true or both false). Truth value is denoted by either "T" for true or "F" for false. A less customary symbol is the assertion sign "⊢," as in "⊢ p > ⊢ q," which means "we assert p; thus, we assert q." In other words, if the first statement is asserted as true, then the second statement must be asserted as true also—the standard form of modus ponens in greatly abbreviated notation.

Russell and Whitehead's notation follows Peano's notation, using dots instead of parentheses or brackets. One primitive propositional rule, for example, is the law of tautology. In the notation of the *Principia Mathematica*, this formula is expressed as " ⊢: p. ≡ .p • p," or 'we assert that any statement is equivalent to the logical product of the same statement.' In slightly more customary notation, this would read " ⊢ [p ≡ (p • p)]." Since the dots stand for bracket notation and for the logical product, the notation is a bit intuitively challenging. Most of the *Principia Mathematica*'s two thou-

sand pages are expressed in symbolic notation, with additional operators added chapter by chapter.

The *Principia Mathematica* seeks to avoid paradoxes by redefining sets and lists. Several of the paradoxes in need of resolution are general knowledge. For example, the statement "all generalizations are false" is a generalization. Thus, if it is true, then it must be false (because it asserts that all statements in a class of which it is a member are false). Similarly, if one posits a town called Mayberry, in which all barbers are male and the barber only shaves people who do not shave themselves, one creates an infinite regression, because the barber should only shave himself if he does not shave himself, and if he does shave himself then he should not shave himself.

One more example that dates back to ancient Greece is the liar's paradox: An Athenian comes to Sparta and reports "all Athenians are liars." If the statement is true, the Athenian must be lying, so the statement must be false. If the statement is false, it is consistent with what it says about Athenians and thus should be true.

The solution in all of these cases is a reflection about the nature of sets and subsets. For example, my family is a set. My two sons are a subset of that set. Statements also make up sets. There is the set of generalizations, for example. The apparent paradox involving generalizations arises when the statement "all generalizations are false" is considered to be part of the set of generalizations. In fact, the statement is part of a descriptive superset that includes the set of generalizations, plus an additional statement describing that set. Ignoring the limits of sets creates logical contradictions.

The same error applies to the other paradoxes as well. The barber is part of a superset whose subset is "men from Mayberry"; thus, he is not targeted by the statement. The Athenian likewise must be considered external to the set of Athenians described by his statement before that statement can be evaluated. Sets in mathematics and geometry can generate similar paradoxes. Avoiding these problematic characteristics of sets, supersets, and subsets by way of the "axiom of reducibility" is the purpose of the *Principia Mathematica*. Russell and Whitehead assert the axiom of reducibility as a smaller assumption than the assumption that there are classes. The axiom asserts that a predicative function can always replace classes; in other words, any mathematical class reduces to a logical predication.

Another generally known problem that the *Principia Mathematica* addresses is called "existential presupposition." Ordinary intuition indicates that if "John passed the examination" is true, then "John did not pass the examination" should be false—unless there are two different Johns. Where only one person is under consideration, one of the two statements should be true and the other should be false. If the world contained no people named "John" at all, problems would arise.

Russell and Whitehead explore this notion by speaking of kings. "The present king of England is bald" was a true statement in 1903. The subcontrary "The present king of England is not bald" was then false. However, "The present king of France is bald" and "the present king of France is not bald" would actually be both false statements, in 1903 as in the twenty-first century, because no present king of France exists. In other words, the subject of both propositions is the null set, a set without content. Set characteristics of the null set then produce a problem. The avoidance of classes altogether while becoming aware of ambiguities would avoid this problem.

The *Principia Mathematica* is not leisure reading. Russell himself is said to have quipped that he knew of only six people who had read it from cover to cover: three people from Poland and three from Texas. The notational formula employed by the work is difficult to follow without extensive notes and "cheat sheets." The *Principia Mathematica* helped Bertrand Russell gain his reputation as the father of analytical philosophy, particularly in combination with his association with Ludwig Wittgenstein, who is associated with the Vienna Circle and logical positivism. The *Principia Mathematica* is still a treasure trove of ideas yet to be developed.

Reinhold Schlieper

Further Reading

Goldstein, Laurence. "The Indefinability of 'One.'" *Journal of Philosophical Logic* 31 (2002): 29-42. Attempts to show that the reduction of all mathematics to a set of logical statements does not work.

Hylton, Peter, ed. *Propositions, Functions, and Analysis: Selected Essays on Russell's Philosophy.* New York: Oxford University Press, 2008. Collection of essays that shed light on Russell's general philosophical stances; provides a philosophical context for the *Principia Mathematica.*

Kripke, Saul. "Russell's Notion of Scope." *Mind* 114 (October, 2005): 1005-1037. Addresses scope ambiguities in statements with subjects that represent the null set, such as "The present king of France is bald."

Link, Godehard, ed. *One Hundred Years of Russell's Paradox.* New York: Walter de Gruyter, 2004. A collection of essays and conference papers of the International Munich Centenary Conference in 2001. The contributions all focus on Russell's paradox.

Monk, Ray, and Anthony Palmer, eds. *Bertrand Russell and the Origins of Analytical Philosophy.* London: Continuum International, 1996. This collection of essays focuses on the precursors to Russell in the traditions of analytical philosophy, specifically on Gottlob Frege's contributions.

Priest, Graham. "The Structure of the Paradoxes of Self-Reference." *Mind* 103 (January, 1994): 25. Reviews a selection of paradoxes and their solutions in slightly more technical language.

Proops, Ian. "Russell's Reasons for Logicism." *Journal of the History of Philosophy* 44, no. 2 (April, 2006): 267-292. Reviews historical aspects of Russell's philosophical development. The text is accessibly written and avoids highly technical language.

Soames, Scott. "No Class: Russell on Contextual Definition and the Elimination of Sets." *Philosophical Studies* 139 (2008): 213-218. Explains the intension and extension of propositional functions.

Sorel, Nancy Caldwell. "When Ludwig Wittgenstein Met Bertrand Russell." *The Independent*, August 19, 1995, p. 42. Amusing anecdote of the meeting between Russell and Wittgenstein.

Stevens, Graham. *The Russellian Origins of Analytical Philosophy: Bertrand Russell and the Unity of the Proposition.* New York: Routledge, 2005. Focuses on the historical development of analytical philosophy.

Principles of Political Economy

Author: John Stuart Mill (1806-1873)
First published: 1848
Type of work: Economics

John Stuart Mill's central concern in *Principles of Political Economy* is the production and distribution of wealth, which he defines as everything that serves human desires that is not provided gratuitously by nature. The most important elements in wealth are goods currently produced.

Production requires labor and appropriate natural objects. The labor devoted to a product is rewarded out of its sale proceeds, but before these sales are realized, advances to workers are required, which come from capital. Productive labor is what yields an increase in material wealth.

Capital consists of wealth used for productive activity. Capital provides the tools and materials needed to carry on production, as well as subsistence for the laborers while the production process is going on. The quantity of a nation's industry is limited by its stock of capital. Increased capital means increased ability to hire workers, and thus increased employment and output. The accumulation of capital results from saving. It is not from demand for commodities, but from capital, that demand for labor arises, although the demand for commodities determines in what productive activities workers can find employment.

Differences in the productivity of nations may arise from geographic factors such as climate and the fertility of soil. There are also important differences in labor quality: in physical vigor; in ability to persevere in pursuit of distant objectives; in skill, knowledge, and trustworthiness. Productivity is enhanced by legal and social institutions favoring security of person and property, and by effective cooperation as manifested in division of labor. As a result of greater specialization of workers and equipment, large-scale productive establishments are often more efficient than small ones.

The rate at which production grows depends on the rate of growth of labor, capital, and land, and on improvements in productive technique. Increases in population tend to raise the total quantity of production by increasing the labor supply but may, by increasing the number of consumers, keep down the living standards of the working class. Unless birth rates are limited, increases in population and labor supply must continually tend to force wages to low levels.

The rate at which capital increases, reflects the flow of saving, which depends on the level of income and the desire to accumulate rather than to consume. Willingness to save is encouraged when the expected profits of investment are high and when uncertainty and insecurity are at a minimum. Whether a society is progressive or backward depends in large degree on the level of saving it achieves.

The real limits to production growth arise from the limited quantity and limited productiveness of land. Cultivation of land is subject to diminishing returns—that is, increased application of labor and capital by any given proportion will increase total output only in some lesser proportion. Tendencies toward diminishing return can be counteracted by improvements in methods of production, but these are more likely to produce decreasing costs in industry than in agriculture. The pressure of population growth against diminishing returns is the principal cause of widespread poverty.

Although the laws of production are essentially physical, the principles of distribution are social; once the goods are produced, they can be distributed as people wish. An important determinant of income distribution is the nature and distribution of private property. Some critics find much fault with the institution of private property and propose socialist systems involving democratic management of productive operations and equal division of the product. Such schemes cannot be dismissed as impracticable. Some people might shirk their responsibilities to work, but this is also a serious defect of other property and wage arrangements. A communitarian society would have to guard against an excessive birthrate and might encounter problems in determining who should perform which tasks. Practices relating to private property have not conformed to the ideal of assuring to each person the fruits of his or her labor or abstinence. The best system will be one that is consistent with the greatest amount of human liberty and spontaneity.

The produce of society is divided among the three classes who provide productive agents: labor, capital, and land. Wages are determined by the proportion between population (supply) and capital (demand); thus high birthrates tend to inhibit increases in wage rates. Limitation of births by the working class would be promoted by the extension of education and by any sudden, rapid improvement in their condition.

The profits of the capitalist are the reward for abstinence, for risk-taking, and for the effort of superintendence. Profits arise from the fact that labor produces more than is required for its subsistence; workers depend on the relationship between the productivity of labor and the wage rate. The rent of land is determined by the demand for it (and its produce), the supply of land being fixed. Differences in rent reflect differences in productivity on lands of different quality. Growth of population and capital tends to increase rents as demand for food increases.

As economic systems expand through growth of labor and capital, the rate of profit tends to decline because higher food prices force up wage costs. The declining rate of profit may halt the increase of capital and produce a stationary state. This state of affairs would not necessarily be bad, provided no one were poor, and provided the unseemly struggle for wealth and power were replaced by more elevated pursuits. Social improvement would also result from improvement of the relationship between employer and worker, perhaps through profit sharing or through cooperatives of producers or consumers.

The value of any article comes from the amounts of other things for which it can be exchanged in the market. To possess value, an article must possess utility (be desired) and be subject to some difficulty of attainment. Value tends to that level at which the quantity that buyers will take (demand) is equal to the quantity that sellers will offer (supply). Since cost of production is a chief determinant of supply, value tends to equal cost (plus a normal profit for capital), unless monopoly conditions prevail. Although labor is the chief element of cost, capital must also be rewarded or it will not be forthcoming. The longer the waiting period between the application of labor and the emergence of the finished product, the greater the capital cost.

Money provides a common measure of value and facilitates specialization and exchange. Variations in the general price level tend to be proportional to changes in the quantity of money, or in its rapidity of circulation, assuming the quantity of goods remains unchanged. Since credit may serve as a substitute for actual money, it can also influence the level of prices. Expansion or contraction of credit, in such forms as promissory notes or bank deposits, are principal elements accounting for periodic commercial crises. A paper currency not convertible into precious metal is liable to depreciate through excessive issue.

Although the supply of any individual commodity may exceed the demand for it, it is not possible for the supply of all commodities to be excessive. Each person's willingness to work and produce reflects his or her desire to acquire goods for consumption or investment. In international exchanges, value depends not on the absolute levels of labor and capital required to produce an item, but on the comparative costs. A country may be able to import cloth more cheaply than to produce it, by paying for it with exports of another product in which its labor and capital are highly efficient, even though it could produce cloth with less labor and capital than the country from which it imports. Both participants in such trade tend to benefit from it, and total world output may be increased by the more efficient use of resources through specialization.

Should a country's imports be excessive in relation to its exports, it will tend to export gold and silver to pay the difference. The outflow of money will tend to reduce the price level in that country, and raise it elsewhere, until the trade imbalance is rectified. The proper functions of government extend, at the very least, to defining and determining the rights of property and contract, the rules of partnerships and corporations, the regulation of insolvency, the monetary system, and weights and measures. In addition, government activity may be necessary where the consumer cannot judge or achieve his or her own interest (for example, the education of children), or in cases in which each person's desire can be effectuated only if all conform (for example, limiting work hours). Government may undertake activities beneficial to the public, from which no private person could realize a profit (for example, providing lighthouses, or financing scientific research). Charity will be offered by private persons in any case, so it may be better to have it provided by the government so as to minimize possible harmful effects. Government should avoid activities based on fallacious doctrines: policies of tariff protection, price-fixing, restricting entry into a business or occupation, or prohibiting trade union activity.

Limitation of government activity is desirable to avoid undue enhancement of central power or the use of coercive authority in ways that infringe on important individual freedoms. Enlargement of government may also impair the efficiency of its operations. Taxation should be imposed so as to exact equal sacrifice from each person. This result could be achieved by an income tax that takes a fixed proportion of income beyond a minimum exemption. Taxation of inheritance and of unearned increases in land rent is highly desirable, but current saving should be excluded in calculating taxable income. There is a presumption in favor of laissez-faire; that is, the burden of proof is on those who favor extension of the role of government.

Although no longer a blueprint for specific economic reforms, Mill's *Principles of Political Economy* remains one of the most provocative, systematic statements of liberal political and economic thought in Western literature. Applying the principles of utilitarian philosophy to a study of the economic system in England, Mill explains why, in democratic societies, it is imperative for labor and management to share in decision making and participate as equals in determining the future of business. Mill is convinced that only such collective brainpower will guarantee that people receive fair treatment and that business will prosper.

Mill's stance is not pure socialism, however. He advocates a laissez-faire approach by government, so that the private sector bears chief responsibility for managing its own affairs. He insists, however, that individuals with superior education and insight—a cadre of "intellectual elite"—take responsibility for managing business affairs in such a way that the poor will benefit. As he does in all his writings, Mill emphasizes the necessity that corporations operate for the benefit of those employed by them as well as those who have invested in them or who manage business operations.

Throughout the *Principles of Political Economy*, Mill insists on recognition of the rights of individuals and the importance of allowing individuals certain liberties that permit them to achieve dignity and happiness. His approach may have been radical to contemporaries, most of whom believed that the right to make decisions in any business rested solely with those who invested in it and who stood to gain or lose financially from its success or failure. Nevertheless, Mill's farsighted analysis of the symbiotic relationship between workers and supervisors became the model for enlightened labor-management practices in modern Western-style businesses in the twentieth and twenty-first centuries.

Further Reading

Borchard, Ruth. *John Stuart Mill, the Man*. London: C. A. Watts, 1957. *Principles of Political Economy* is placed within the context of Mill's life. Discusses the work's ideas, reception, and relation to Mill's socialism.

Reeves, Richard. *John Stuart Mill: Victorian Firebrand*. London: Atlantic Books, 2007. Authoritative and well-received biography that recounts Mill's life, philosophy, and pursuit of truth and liberty for all.

Riley, Jonathan. "Mill's Political Economy: Ricardian Science and Liberal Utilitarian Art." In *The Cambridge Companion to Mill*, edited by John Skorupski. New York: Cambridge University Press, 1998. Riley discusses Mill's ideas about political economy, placing them within the context of Victorian economic theory.

Schwartz, Pedro. *The New Political Economy of J. S. Mill*. Durham, N.C.: Duke University Press, 1972. A comprehensive study of Mill's political economy, offering a detailed analysis of his theory of economic and social policy. A lengthy, if dated, bibliography provides an excellent guide for further study.

Varouxakis, Georgios, and P. J. Kelly. *John Stuart Mill, Thought and Influence: The Saint of Rationalism*. New York: Routledge, 2010. Examines Mill's "fate and reputation; his youthful political and intellectual activism; his views on the formation of character; [and] the development of his thought on logic." Also discusses his ideas on the environmental and on feminism.

The Prisoner of Zenda

Author: Anthony Hope (1863-1933)
First published: 1894
Type of work: Novel
Type of plot: Adventure
Time of plot: 1880's
Locale: Ruritania

Principal characters:
RUDOLF RASSENDYLL, an English gentleman
LADY ROSE BURLESDON, his sister-in-law
RUDOLF, king of Ruritania
MICHAEL, DUKE OF STRELSAU, King Rudolf's half brother
ANTOINETTE DE MAUBAN, Michael's beloved
PRINCESS FLAVIA, King Rudolf's fiancé
RUPERT HENTZAU, aide to Michael
FRITZ VON TARLENHEIM, a loyal subject of the king
COLONEL SAPT, another loyal subject

The Story:

To his sister-in-law, Lady Rose Burlesdon, Rudolf Rassendyll is a great disappointment. In the first place, he is twenty-nine years old and has no useful occupation. Second,

he bears such a striking resemblance to the Elphbergs, the ruling house of Ruritania, that for Rose he is a constant reminder of an old scandal in which her husband's family was involved. More than one hundred years before, a prince of the country of Ruritania had visited England and had become involved with the wife of one of the Rassendyll men. A child was born who had the red hair and the large, straight nose of the Elphbergs. Since that unfortunate event, five or six descendants of the English lady and the Ruritanian prince have had the characteristic nose and red hair of their royal ancestor. Rose finds Rudolf's red hair and large nose a disgrace for that reason.

Rassendyll himself, however, has no concern over his resemblance to the Ruritanian royal family. A new king is to be crowned in that country within a few weeks, and Rassendyll decides to travel to Ruritania for the coronation to get a closer view of his unclaimed relatives. Realizing that his brother and sister-in-law will try to prevent him from taking the journey if they know his plans, he tells them that he is going to take a tour of the Tyrol. After he leaves England, his first stop is Paris, where he learns something more about affairs in the country he is to visit. The new king, also called Rudolf, has a half brother, Michael, duke of Strelsau. Michael would have liked to become king, and it is hinted that he will try to prevent the coronation of Rudolf. Rassendyll also learns that there is a beautiful lady, Antoinette de Mauban, who loves Michael and has his favor. She, too, is traveling to Ruritania for the coronation.

When he reaches Ruritania and finds the capital city crowded, Rassendyll takes lodging in Zenda, a small town approximately fifty miles from the capital, and prepares to travel to the capital by train for the coronation. Zenda is part of Michael's domain; his hunting lodge is only a few miles from the inn where Rassendyll is staying. Rassendyll also learns that King Rudolf is a guest at his half brother's hunting lodge while waiting for the coronation. In addition, he hears more rumors of a plot against the king and talk that Black Michael, as he is called, plans to seize the throne.

As he passes the days before the scheduled coronation, Rassendyll takes a walk every day through the woods near Michael's hunting lodge. One day, near the lodge, he hears two men discussing his close resemblance to the king. The men introduce themselves as Fritz von Tarlenheim and Colonel Sapt, faithful friends of King Rudolf. While the three men talk, the king himself appears. The king has shaved his beard, but otherwise he and Rassendyll are identical in appearance. The king is pleased to meet his distant cousin and invites Rassendyll to the lodge; there the king drinks so much that Fritz and Sapt cannot wake him the next morning, the day of the coronation.

As the king sleeps in his stupor, Fritz and Sapt propose a daring plan to Rassendyll. They know that if the king does not appear for the coronation, Black Michael will seize the throne. Their plan is to shave Rassendyll's beard, dress him in the king's clothes, and have him crowned in the king's place. By the time the ceremonies are over, the king will have recovered and will be able to take his rightful place; no one will be the wiser. It is a dangerous gamble, for exposure could mean death, but Rassendyll agrees to take part in the plot.

Fritz and Sapt lock the king in the lodge's wine cellar and leave a servant to tell him of the plan when he awakes. Rassendyll, with Fritz and Sapt, then proceeds to the palace. With the two men to help him, he carries off the deception; he even convinces the Princess Flavia, who is betrothed to King Rudolf, that he is the real king. Playing the role of the king with Flavia is the most difficult part for Rassendyll, for he has to be gracious and yet not commit the king too far.

The success of the conspirators does not last long, however. When they return that night to the lodge, they find the servant they left behind murdered and the real king gone. Black Michael's men have worked well. Black Michael and his men know that the supposed king is an impostor, and Rassendyll, Fritz, and Sapt know that Black Michael has the real king. Neither group, however, dares call the other's hand. Rassendyll's only chance is to rescue the rightful king. Black Michael's intention is to kill both Rassendyll and the king and thus seize the throne and Princess Flavia for himself. Michael, with the help of his men, including the handsome Rupert Hentzau, attacks and almost kills Rassendyll many times. Once Rassendyll is saved by a warning from Antoinette de Mauban, for, although she loves Michael, she does not want to be a party to murder. Also, she does not want Michael to be successful, for his coup would mean his marriage to Flavia. Michael learns of Antoinette's aid to Rassendyll and holds her a semiprisoner in the hunting lodge where he has also hidden the king.

Playing the part of the king, Rassendyll is forced to spend a great deal of time with Flavia. He wants to tell her his real identity, but Fritz and Sapt appeal to his honor and persuade him that all will be ruined if Flavia finds out that he is not the true king.

Rassendyll, Fritz, and Sapt learn that King Rudolf is dying, and they know that they must take a daring chance to rescue him. They and part of the king's army attack the lodge; those not aware of Rassendyll's deception are told that Black Michael has imprisoned a friend of the king. A bloody battle takes place both outside and inside the lodge. Black Michael is killed and King Rudolf wounded before the rescue is completed.

When it becomes clear that the king will survive, Rassendyll realizes that his role in Ruritania is over. The king sends for him and thanks him for his brave work in saving the throne. Princess Flavia also sends for him. She has been told the whole story, but her only concern is to learn whether Rassendyll was speaking for himself or for the king when he told her of his love for her. He tells her that he will always love only her and begs her to go away with him. She loves him as well, but she is too honorable to leave her people and her king, and she remains in Ruritania, later to marry the king and rule with him.

Rassendyll leaves Ruritania and spends a few weeks in the Tyrol before returning to England. His sister-in-law, still trying to get him to lead a more useful life, arranges through a friend to get him a diplomatic post. When he learns the post is to be in Ruritania, he declines it. Rassendyll resumes his former idle life, with one break in his monotonous routine. Once each year, Fritz and Rassendyll meet in Dresden, and Fritz always brings with him a box for Rassendyll that contains a rose, a token from Flavia.

Critical Evaluation:

Despite its severe brevity and occasional plot weaknesses, *The Prisoner of Zenda* is among the most enduring of adventures. In part, the reasons for this are predictable. Mystery, intrigue, suspense, and love are integrated neatly in the tale. There is plenty of adventure, much of it framed as a conflict between evident good and evil, and there is a strong central character—Rudolf Rassendyll—to hold the book together. It is, therefore, a highly formulaic and popular story. It is also much more than that, however; in its touches of ethical ambiguity and its clever use of disguise (both thematic and dramatic), *The Prisoner of Zenda* takes up the complex matter of defining, then judging, humanity's moral nature.

Early branded a wastrel by his sister-in-law, Rassendyll in time proves his sincerity and honor. What he learns, simply, is value—a theme that Anthony Hope explores not only in his major character but also socially in his excoriations of kings and gentry. What the reader learns, as the sister-in-law does not, is the difference between real and apparent nobility. Readers come to judge Rassendyll not by his complexion or his attitude of indifference but by his courageous, constant actions. In the same way, his "kingliness" is evidenced not in borrowed robes and crowns but in a quality of spirit that cannot be counterfeited.

Nevertheless, Rassendyll's character is also qualified throughout the novel. He is genuinely tempted by the throne and by Flavia's attendant charms. Too often he ignores the questionable morality of his actions: once when he stabs a guard in the back and again when, madly vengeful, he destroys two of Black Michael's hirelings. With bold strokes, Hope defines Rassendyll's identity through two character foils—the dissipated real king (significantly, a namesake and distant relative) and the brash knave, Black Michael's henchman Rupert Hentzau. The former reinforces Rassendyll's worst qualities even as he illustrates, by contrast, the best. On the other hand, Hentzau appears at a glance to be thoroughly different from Rassendyll, yet Rassendyll's fascination with Hentzau's attractive evil clearly suggests an affinity between them. When Rassendyll spares his enemy and then later tries desperately to slay him, the psychological overtones are plain: Regretfully, he has let the evil in himself escape.

The themes of moral ambiguity ("If it were a sin may it be forgiven me," says Rudolf at one point) and political chicanery in the novel fit well with the idea of individual honor. What is one to gain by acting honorably in a world without principle? This is a penetrating question, especially toward the end of the adventure, when Rassendyll and Flavia must elect honorable self-sacrifice or selfish love. Their choice of the former, it seems, points out the novel's answer. The world becomes a measure better, and an individual a measure greater, only as there are those ready to prefer honor over happiness.

Further Reading

Goldsworthy, Vesna. "Prisoners of Zenda: The Imagined States of the Balkans." In *Inventing Ruritania: The Imperialism of the Imagination*. New Haven, Conn.: Yale University Press, 1998. Offers a postcolonial reading of the novel, describing how *The Prisoner of Zenda* and other nineteenth century novels, as well as twentieth century films, shaped Western perceptions of the Balkans, creating a "narrative colonization."

Mallet, Sir Charles Edward. *Anthony Hope and His Books: Being the Authorized Life of Sir Anthony Hope Hawkins*. Port Washington, N.Y.: Kennikat Press, 1968. Analyzes Hope's style of writing and examines the influence of Hope's life on *The Prisoner of Zenda*. Chronicles the instantaneous success of the book and its warm reception by authors such as Robert Louis Stevenson, Sir Arthur Quiller-Couch, and Andrew Lang. Also examines the book's sequel, *Rupert of Hentzau* (1898), and the adaptation of *The Prisoner of Zenda* for stage.

Orel, Harold. *The Historical Novel from Scott to Sabatini: Changing Attitudes Toward a Literary Genre, 1814-1920*. New York: St. Martin's Press, 1995. Provides an analysis of Hope's novel *Simon Dale* (1898), placing the writer's work within the larger context of the historical novel.

Putt, S. Gorley. "*The Prisoner of Zenda*: Anthony Hope and the Novel of Society." *Essays in Criticism* 6 (January, 1956): 38-59. Places *The Prisoner of Zenda* in its proper late-Victorian milieu. Unlike the aesthetic writers of the 1890's, Hope celebrates traditional values, such as honor, virtue, and sacrifice.

Wallace, Raymond P. "Cardboard Kingdoms." *San Jose Studies* 13, no. 2 (Spring, 1987): 23-34. Compares *The Prisoner of Zenda* to George Barr McCutcheon's Grau-

stark series and George Meredith's *Adventures of Harry Richmond* (1871). Considers how imaginary kingdoms and royalty were more appealing to late-Victorian readers than were realistic elements of the time.

Warner, Gerald. "Plumed Hats, Rapiers, and Heaving Bosoms." *The Spectator*, June 14, 2008. Presents a brief overview of the "swashbuckling novel," describing the reasons for the popularity of *The Prisoner of Zenda* and its sequel, *Rupert of Hentzau.*

The Private Life of the Master Race

Author: Bertolt Brecht (1898-1956)

First produced: 1938 (selected scenes in French); 1945, complete version (in English); first published (in English), 1944; in German, 1945, as *Furcht und Elend des dritten Reiches*

Type of work: Drama

Type of plot: Political realism

Time of plot: 1933-1938

Locale: Germany

Principal characters:

CITIZENS OF THE THIRD REICH

The Story:

It is 1933, and fear prevails when a husband and wife discuss the brutal treatment by police of their communist neighbor, whom the couple betrayed for listening to broadcasts from Russia. A storm trooper visits his girlfriend, a maid in the household of an affluent Berlin family. An unemployed worker arrives to repair the radio, and the storm trooper engages him in a discussion to ferret out his true opinion about the Nazi regime. To gain the worker's confidence, the storm trooper demonstrates how he exposes critics of the Nazis. Pretending to be sympathetic to complaints, the storm trooper surreptitiously marks critics with a chalk cross on their backs so that they can be easily identified and interrogated. After both the worker and the storm trooper leave, the maid expresses her grave concerns to the cook about her boyfriend's changed behavior; she no longer trusts him.

In a concentration camp, imprisoned Social Democrats and communists still quarrel about who is responsible for the Nazis' rise to power. However, they, as well as a pastor, show solidarity when faced with the demands of a guard. A radio reporter interviews workers at a factory but rudely interrupts them when they refer to insufficient sanitary facilities. Storm troopers deliver a coffin with the corpse of a worker to his

wife with a stern warning not to open the casket to prevent her from seeing his battered body. Scientists are forbidden to have contacts with Jewish colleagues; physicists at the University of Göttingen who have corresponded with the eminent Albert Einstein, a Jewish emigré, are terribly afraid that they may be found out.

It is 1935 in Frankfurt, and a prominent physician is experiencing problems at his clinic because his wife is Jewish; friends and neighbors are shunning the couple. To escape this intolerable situation, the wife has decided to leave for Amsterdam. After calling friends and relatives to ask them to look after things during her absence, she rehearses her speech explaining to her husband why she is leaving. However, when her husband returns, neither he nor she refers to the real reasons for her departure. Rather, they both pretend that she is going on a spring holiday. The fur coat she packs provides an indication of the truth.

A pathetically spineless judge in the city of Augsburg searches for the resolution of a complicated and well-publicized court case that will satisfy all parties involved and will not cost him his job. The interests of the three storm troopers, who had robbed a Jewish jeweler, the well-connected jeweler's Aryan partner, and the jeweler's landlord differ considerably and cannot be reconciled. The judge is eager to do whatever is expected of him, but none of his colleagues is able or willing to offer any sound advice, and the judge enters the courtroom with great trepidation.

In 1935 Cologne, a teacher and his wife are terribly afraid that their young son, who has overheard their conversation, will report his father's critical remarks about the Nazi regime to the leaders of his youth organization. Even though the son claims that he did not betray them, the parents are not sure whether to believe him and remain terror-stricken. Such fearful distrust is also evident when a worker, who has been released from a concentration camp, visits a husband and a wife who had shared his political convictions. Now they are very much in doubt whether they can still rely on him.

Even those who had supported Adolf Hitler before 1933 have become disillusioned. A butcher's loyalty is tested to the utmost when he is ordered to display cardboard hams, which look real, rather than the real product. As a sign of protest, he hangs himself in his shop window with a poster around his neck proclaiming that he had voted for Hitler.

Two bakers meet in prison. The first one has been sentenced because he had adulterated his bread, the second because he had refused to do so when shortages became more common. A working mother refuses to finance her teenage daughter's summer labor in the countryside under the auspices of the Hitler Youth. A farmer, despite orders not to feed his pigs because of grain shortages, defies the authorities. Storm troopers bring food and a small amount of money to an old lady as part of the winter aid organization's efforts to aid the elderly and the poor. When the old lady inadvertently reveals that her daughter, who is visiting her, has criticized the regime, the storm troopers take the daughter away.

It is now 1937, and in the city of Lübeck, a fisherman on his deathbed cannot buy a motor for his boat because motors are essential for the rearmament prior to the impending war. His son, a storm trooper, supports the rearmament and rejects the pastor's reference to the "Jewish" Sermon on the Mount.

Critical Evaluation:

Bertolt Brecht's *The Private Life of the Master Race* consists of seventeen scenes of various lengths and interspersed songs. These scenes are independent of each other in that no character appears more than once; they also take place in a variety of social milieus and in different German cities and regions. Still, the scenes are essentially arranged in chronological order from 1933, the year the Nazis came to power, to March, 1938, the date of the bloodless annexation of Austria.

In their totality, they do convey a sense of life under the Nazi dictatorship during the pre-World War II years.

Brecht had left Germany in February, 1933, shortly after the Nazis came to power; as a leftist playwright, he was no longer safe. During the first phase of his exile he lived in Denmark, where he wrote *The Private Life of the Master Race*. Brecht composed the individual scenes on the basis of newspaper accounts and eyewitness reports. The relatively precarious conditions of exile explain, in part, the rather unusual publication and production history. In 1938, increasing political tensions on the eve of World War II ended the planned publication in Prague of twenty-seven scenes.

Brecht arrived in the United States in 1941; Eric Bentley's translation of seventeen scenes—as *The Private Life of the Master Race*—was published in 1944. Although each of the scenes appears to be autonomous, they are related to each other via the overarching themes of fear and misery in Hitler's Germany. Moreover, their interrelation is emphasized by the quadruple appearance of a Panzer (actually, a tank rather than an armored troop-carrying truck) at the beginning and the end and between scenes. The Panzer carries German soldiers who do not correspond to the heroic image propagated by the Nazis; rather, their faces are white with fear. They act as a chorus and provide comments on the action; in this way, the connection between Hitler's preparations for war, which are referred to in various scenes, and World War II is established.

A number of scenes approach the length of one-act plays and seem to pertain to conventional drama rather than to Brecht's famed epic theater, which he defines in his notes to the opera *Aufstieg und Fall der Stadt Mahagonny* (pb. 1929, pr. 1930; *Rise and Fall of the City of Mahagonny*, 1957). Epic theater dispenses with the attempt to imitate life on stage, create suspense, and affect the emotions. Instead, it appeals to a new kind of spectator who follows the happenings unemotionally and critically and then draws his or her own conclusions as to which conditions presented on stage are in need of change.

Critics disagree somewhat as to the epic character of *The Private Life of the Master Race*. For instance, a scene such as "The Jewish Wife" appears—if one ignores the racial aspect—to conform to the pattern of a traditional middle-class drama. However, this scene represents a Brechtian "gest," that is, a combination of physical gesture and social attitude, as evidenced by the husband's initial protestations that his wife does not have to leave on account of his experiencing difficulties at work, followed by his admission that her supposedly brief sojourn abroad might be beneficial, and, finally, by his handing her the fur coat she does not need for an absence of short duration. The scenes in their entirety represent a number of typical responses to the challenges of life under Nazism that various individuals are forced to face.

There is, however, a noticeable difference between individual responses to life under Nazism. Whereas bourgeois intellectuals and professionals such as the physician, the physicists, and particularly the spineless judge—but also the extremely fearful teacher—seek to accommodate their new masters at almost all costs, the responses of the workers and even those of the members of the lower middle-class are markedly different. Apart from the call to resist in "Plebiscite," a scene that has been strategically placed at the end of *The Private Life of the Master Race*, there is little evidence of outright resistance against Hitler's regime—in part because the Nazis have incarcerated their political opponents in concentration camps or, as is evident from Brecht's biography, because they are living in exile.

Hitler's totalitarian regime has created an atmosphere of fear and misery that prevails even in the domestic realm. A particularly ghastly scene is "The Box," in which the wife of the slain worker follows the orders of the storm troopers not to open the coffin out of consideration for her brother who might suffer a similar fate if she disobeys the strict instructions. Hence, in view of the prevalence of fear, the various minor acts of resistance assume considerable significance; they clearly demonstrate the limits of the power the totalitarian regime can exert.

As a quasi-documentary record of the Nazi period in Germany, *The Private Life of the Master Race* and its more comprehensive version, *Fear and Misery of the Third Reich* (1983), continue to retain their relevance as an evocation of the conditions prevailing in prewar Nazi Germany. At the same time, these scenes may serve as a warning to not let such conditions prevail again.

"Critical Evaluation" by Siegfried Mews

Further Reading

Benjamin, Walter. *Understanding Brecht*. Translated by Anna Bostock. 1973. Reprint. London: Verso, 2003. An acutely insightful commentary by one of Brecht's contemporaries and fellow Germans, who in 1940 killed himself to avoid falling into the hands of the Gestapo. Includes an introduction by Stanley Mitchell.

Bentley, Eric. *The Brecht Commentaries, 1943-1980*. New York: Grove Press, 1981. Contains reviews and articles by Bentley, Brecht's principal American translator and champion. Includes an essay on *The Private Life of the Master Race*.

Esslin, Martin. *Brecht: A Choice of Evils*. 4th rev. ed. New York: Methuen, 1984. Esslin's influential study prepared the way for Brecht's acceptance in the West during the Cold War by separating the poet from the Marxist. Esslin also provides brief synopses of the plays.

Gillett, Robert, and Godela Weiss-Sussex, eds. *"Verwisch die Spuren!" Bertolt Brecht's Work and Legacy. A Reassessment*. New York: Rodopi, 2008. Included among the contributions is an essay by John and Ann White with an analysis of the epic elements, particularly songs, of the various versions of *Fear and Misery of the Third Reich*.

Hayman, Ronald. *Brecht: A Biography*. New York: Oxford University Press, 1983. More than one dozen references to *The Private Life of the Master Race* dot this large and detailed survey.

Lyon, James K. *Bertolt Brecht in America*. Princeton, N.J.: Princeton University Press, 1980. Lyon repeatedly refers to *The Private Life of the Master Race* and devotes a chapter to the 1945 off-Broadway production.

Thomson, Peter, and Glendyr Sacks, eds. *The Cambridge Companion to Brecht*. 2d ed. New York: Cambridge University Press, 2006. A collection of essays offering numerous interpretations of Brecht's work, including examinations of Brecht and cabaret, music, and stage design; his work with the Berliner Ensemble; and key terms of his theory and practice of theater.

Unwin, Stephen. *A Guide to the Plays of Bertolt Brecht*. London: Methuen, 2005. Contains analyses of many of Brecht's plays and discusses his theories of drama, his impact, and his legacy. Designed as an accessible introduction to Brecht for students, teachers, and general readers.

Private Lives

Author: Noël Coward (1899-1973)
First produced: 1930; first published, 1930
Type of work: Drama
Type of plot: Comedy of manners
Time of plot: 1930
Locale: France

Principal characters:
SIBYL CHASE, a bride
ELYOT CHASE, her husband
AMANDA PRYNNE, Elyot's first wife
VICTOR PRYNNE, her husband

The Story:

Sibyl Chase loves being married. She is as much in love with the idea of being a bride as she is with her husband, Elyot, and perhaps more so. On the first night of their honeymoon, Sibyl had gone into raptures over Elyot, but she did not forget, or let him forget, that she knew he had loved his first wife Amanda madly. She is now certain that the breakup of that marriage had been Amanda's fault and that she had been a mean-tempered and probably a wanton woman. When Sibyl tells him that she knows how to handle a husband, how to make him happy, Elyot fears that she means she knows how to manage a husband. He is a trifle disturbed.

Unknown at first to the Chases, Amanda is honeymooning at the same hotel with her new husband, Victor Prynne. Victor has much the same ideas about marriage as does Sibyl. He intends to take care of Amanda, to make her forget that dreadful brute to whom she had been married. The fact that Amanda never asked to be taken care of is unimportant. Victor will teach her to be a suitable wife.

When Amanda and Elyot see each other again, each wants to move out of the hotel before their respective mates knows about the presence of the other couple. Sibyl and Victor, however, who are not accustomed to making abrupt changes without reason, refuse to leave. Amanda and Elyot thereupon decides that they are not culpable when they talk together again and recall their happy times together. Both try for a time to avoid the issue uppermost in their hearts and minds, but at last Elyot breaks off the polite conversation to say that he still loves Amanda. They fall into each other's arms.

Amanda tries for a time to make them consider Sibyl and Victor, but Elyot easily convinces her that those two will suffer more if they all live a lie. After making plans to go to Paris, Amanda and Elyot leave without a word of explanation.

Because they had fought so violently and so often in their married days, Amanda makes Elyot promise that whenever they start to bicker they will use a password and each keep quiet for two minutes. In Amanda's flat in Paris, they are of-

ten forced into quick use of the magic password, for they are torn equally between love and hate. Amanda's conscience bothers her a little, but Elyot can easily soothe that nagging little voice with love, logic, or a flippant remark. Sorry that they had wasted five years of separation after their divorce, they agree to marry each other again as soon as Sibyl and Victor will divorce them. Elyot is annoyed when he learns that Amanda had spent those five years in having little affairs with various men, but he sees no reason for her being annoyed at his own transgressions.

Their quarrels occur over nonsensical things for the most part. At the root is often Amanda's concern for the moral questions involved in their past and present relationship. When Elyot brushes these aside with worldly and flippant comments, Amanda comes back to him more passionately than before.

The last explosion occurs when Amanda mentions a man of whom Elyot had always been jealous. Without knowing quite how the quarrel got out of hand, they find themselves throwing things at each other and slapping each other viciously. The magic password fails to work. As each slams into a different bedroom, neither is aware that Sibyl and Victor had come into the room at the height of the rumpus and settled themselves quietly on the sofa.

The next morning, Sibyl and Victor have a very sensible discussion concerning the situation of the night before. Sibyl weeps copiously, not so much from sorrow as from custom; it is the right thing for an injured wife to do. Each blames the other's mate for the sordid scene in Amanda's apartment. When Amanda and Elyot join them, they are very polite with each other and with Sibyl and Victor. At first the situation is like a morning call for coffee. When Amanda and Elyot admit that they are sorry, that it was all a mess and a mistake, Sibyl and Victor agree that the culprits are not contrite enough. Elyot, in particular, seems crass about the whole thing, particularly to Victor, who wants to thrash him. Elyot sees no use in heroics; he honestly admits that his flippancy is only an attempt to cover real embarrassment.

Initially, Amanda and Elyot refuse to speak to each other, but as Sibyl and Victor continue to be proper and to mouth little platitudes about morals and the sanctity of marriage, Elyot winks at Amanda. While the injured spouses make and reverse plans for divorces, the sinners pay less and less attention. At last, Sibyl and Victor begin to quarrel, each accusing the other of weakness in still loving such a wicked and worldly person as Amanda or Elyot. When Sibyl gives Victor a resounding slap, he in turn shakes her soundly. In the middle of the quarrel, Amanda and Elyot pick up their suitcases and tiptoe out the door together.

Critical Evaluation:

In the centuries since the life of William Shakespeare, probably the best British dramatists have been those who wrote comedies of manners, from the Restoration period, to Oscar Wilde at the end of the nineteenth century, to Noël Coward in the twentieth century. To paraphrase one critic, Coward actually wrote comedies of *bad* manners; when society's rules prove too stringent for his characters, they sulk, throw tantrums, become regressive, or go into denial. This may sound unpleasant, but Coward renders these reactions hilariously funny.

A professional actor by the age of twelve, Coward brought a sure sense of theater to his dramas, an informed ability to decide what lines, moves, and situations would prove most telling. He often acted in his own plays, and it was while playing the lead in *The Vortex* (written by Coward, and first produced in Hampstead, London, in 1924) that he won fame as both actor and writer. Later in life, he was successful as an actor in motion pictures as well as television shows.

Private Lives is vintage Coward. The situation is at once unlikely and provocative: Two newlywed couples honeymooning at the same hotel turn out to have a prior connection—one of the husbands used to be married to one of the wives. Elyot Chase and Amanda Prynne find the moonlight and their chance propinquity irresistible. All their romantic feelings for each other come flooding back, causing them to abandon their new mates. Such behavior is inexcusable by any measure of decency, but Coward wins some sympathy for the erring couple. To begin with, he makes their mates slightly unsympathetic—a bit doltish, a trifle too eager to please. By contrast, the dialogue only starts to crackle when Elyot and Amanda are alone together, and their witty duels are entertaining. The audience is encouraged to believe what Elyot and Amanda are inclined to believe, that they belong together and made a mistake in divorcing each other.

That said, it must be admitted that there are severe limitations to this play. Witty though they are, the characters are shallow people, with neither work nor aspirations to give them personality. The fact that they lead pampered lives in the shadow of World War I and the Great Depression without once referring to either of these giant catastrophes calls their creator's humanity into question. Elyot and Amanda are particularly selfish, self-indulgent, spoiled, and infantile, but Coward's heart appears to be with them. They cannot live without each other, but they cannot live with each other. Moreover, they cannot face these or any other facts for more than a few seconds without a drink, a cigarette, a quarrel, or a change of subject. They appear to have no parents to care for, neither do they have (or speak of having) children. So bleak are their lives, that some authorities have proclaimed Coward as a forerunner of Samuel Beckett and Harold Pinter. *Private Lives* is a far cry from Pinter's *The Dumb Waiter* (1959) or Beckett's *Waiting for Godot* (1952). Its characters are not waiting for anything—they are far too impatient.

Even so, they show us a truth of being human. Their attempts to make light of their lot point out their profound vulnerability. With nothing to count on except each other, there is nothing of which they can be sure. Although they long to be swept off their feet—for in the grip of an impulse, one can, however briefly, feel confident—at the same time, they do all they can to avoid losing their heads.

Perhaps the best passages in *Private Lives* are those where the characters walk a tightrope between sentimentality and cynicism, as in act 2, when Elyot and Amanda discuss their heartbreak and their longing for each other. Although the audience can be sure that this mood will not last long, it is just as certain that it will recur. Coward and his leading lady, Gertrude Lawrence, for whom these roles were created, were brilliant at skirting such issues, turning the English gift for understatement into a highly stylized comedic mode. To hear their recorded performance is to grasp how this delicate work could best be presented. There is a sense of the private that will not be violated, even in the casual and rather promiscuous world of *Private Lives*. What is admirable about these four characters has to do with their inviolability, which, try as they might, they cannot shed.

"Critical Evaluation" by David Bromige

Further Reading

Coward, Noël. *Noël Coward: Autobiography.* London: Methuen, 1999. Coward's two-volume autobiography, originally published in 1937 and 1954. In the first volume, Coward says of *Private Lives*, "As a complete play, it leaves a lot to be desired." The "secondary characters

[Sybil and Victor] . . . are little better than ninepins, lightly wooden, and only there to be repeatedly knocked down and stood up again." Declares that he wrote the play as a vehicle for himself and Gertrude Lawrence in the principal roles.

Hoare, Philip. *Noël Coward: A Biography.* New York: Simon & Schuster, 1995. A detailed biography discussing, among many other topics, Coward's family background, his drive to succeed, his devotion to his mother, his homosexuality, and how he transformed his life into his art.

Kaplan, Joel, and Sheila Stowell, eds. *Look Back in Pleasure: Noël Coward Reconsidered.* London: Methuen, 2000. Collection of essays and interviews assessing Coward's contribution to the British theater. Essays examine Coward's transformation of British comedy, Coward and effeminacy, and "Cowardice, Decadence, and the Contemporary Theatre." A roundtable of actors, directors, and other participants discusses the challenges of staging Coward's plays in the twenty-first century.

Lahr, John. *Coward the Playwright.* New York: Methuen, 1982. Reprint. Berkeley: University of California Press, 2002. A chronological study, with extended excerpts from individual plays. Notes that *Private Lives* is the first play Coward wrote after the advent of the Great Depression, and that the play catches the mood of dissolution: "a plotless play for purposeless people."

Levin, Milton. *Noël Coward.* New York: Twayne, 1968. Survey of Coward's body of work that neither idolizes nor condemns him. Includes sound comments on the structure and impact of *Private Lives.*

O'Connor, Sean. *Straight Acting: Popular Gay Drama from Wilde to Rattigan.* London: Cassell, 1998. Describes the influence of Oscar Wilde on Coward and other British gay male playwrights. Places these playwrights' lives and work within the context of twentieth century social history, describing the restrictions the writers endured in their personal lives and in their treatment of gay issues.

Tynan, Kenneth. *The Sound of Two Hands Clapping.* 1975. Reprint. New York: Da Capo Press, 1982. A witty book by one of Britain's foremost drama critics. The passages on Coward sum up much that the post-World War II generation found objectionable in his work.

The Problems of Philosophy

Author: Bertrand Russell (1872-1970)
First published: 1912
Type of work: Philosophy

Bertrand Russell's *The Problems of Philosophy* is an introduction to some of the central issues in metaphysics and epistemology. The work is still regarded as one of the best introductions to philosophy, and it is also historically significant as one of the first book-length examples of analytic philosophy, the type of philosophy founded by Russell, his Cambridge colleague G. E. Moore, and German mathematician Gottlob Frege.

Analytic philosophy is distinguished by its emphasis on clarity and the attempt to establish its conclusions by the strongest rational means possible. While the book deals with a number of philosophical issues, much of it is centered on the problem of the external world and the problem of a priori knowledge—that is, knowledge that in principle can be gained through thought alone, independent of empirical experience.

Russell begins by asking whether there is any knowledge that is so certain that no reasonable person can doubt it. While it may seem obvious that there is such knowledge, Russell shows that it is not easy to arrive at an adequate answer to this question. Take for example an ordinary table. It is usually taken for granted that sensory experience reveals what the table is like: that it is brown, smooth, rectangular, and so forth. This seeming obviousness, however, ignores, for example, that the table may not look uniformly brown. As a perceiver changes location, the color of the table will appear to change. The same is true for all of the properties of the table apprehended through sensory experience: They may seem stable, but they are in fact alterable based on the situation and attitude of a perceiver. While this fact is usually ignored in everyday life, it is vitally important to a philosopher trying to determine whether sensory experience yields genuine knowledge of the external world. Physical objects can appear to have incompatible properties: A table that appears to be smooth to the naked eye may appear to be rough when viewed under a microscope. However, Russell believes, physical objects cannot really have incompatible properties; thus, it seems to him that perception can reveal only how things appear and not how they really are.

Based on considerations such as these, many philosophers have adopted attitudes of either skepticism (the real world is unknowable) or idealism (the world is essentially mental). Russell argues that drawing either a skeptical or an idealist conclusion is not mandatory. His first step in this argument is to introduce the concept of sense data, or the things that are immediately known in sensation. Colors, sounds, smells, and so forth are examples of sense data. Russell is careful to distinguish sense data from sensation, which is the mental act of being aware of sense data. Without this distinction, there is a tendency to think that the only things that can be known or can exist are mental, and this tendency leads to either skepticism or idealism.

Russell next asks about the relation between sense data and mind-independent physical objects. While skeptical arguments may demonstrate that the existence of physical objects can be denied without contradiction, Russell argues that there are good reasons for thinking that such objects do exist. His argument begins with the fact that the patterns of sense data experienced by the mind are not totally chaotic but are, rather, relatively coherent. This fact requires an explanation, and, according to Russell, the best explanation is that the sense data are caused by the interaction of physical objects and a person's sense organs. This interaction ultimately causes the person to be aware of a particular pattern of sense data. Thus, since positing the existence of physical objects provides the best explanation for the patterns of sense data that are experienced by humans, it is reasonable to believe that there is an objective world of mind-independent physical objects.

Russell's important distinction between knowledge by acquaintance and knowledge by description can be used to explain the difference between the sorts of knowledge one has of sense data and physical objects. Sense data are known directly, immediately, and noninferentially; this type of knowledge Russell calls knowledge by acquaintance. Physical objects, on the other hand, are known by description. For example, a table is the cause of this particular cluster of sense data. Knowledge by acquaintance is extremely important for Russell's epistemology. He suggests that any proposition that a person can understand must be entirely composed of elements with which that person is acquainted. (That is, each element of a proposition must correspond to some sense datum or data that the person has personally experienced.)

Russell maintains that one may have knowledge of both things and truths. While some knowledge of truths is empirical, based on sense experience, knowledge of other truths is a priori. For example, knowledge of the necessarily true principles of logic and mathematics could not be based on experience because experience can only reveal how things are at a given moment, not how they must be.

Russell's solution to the problem of a priori knowledge involves the introduction of universals. A traditional metaphysical distinction exists between universals and particulars. Particulars are unique individual things. Thus, a specific red tomato would be an example of a particular. Particulars have properties that they can share with other particulars. For example, the red tomato shares the property of redness with a red cherry and the property of tomatoness with other tomatoes. The property red or redness is a universal—that is, a general, shareable feature exemplified by particular things. Russell's conception of universals is similar to Plato's. According to both philosophers, universals are abstract (not existing in space or time) and nonmental entities that are apprehended in pure thought. Russell maintains that universals are known by acquaintance.

Sense data and universals should not be confused. Seeing a red tomato involves the sensation of a red sense datum, which is a particular, but the sense datum exemplifies the universal redness, which can be shared by other particulars and which is known by reason, not the senses. One of Russell's innovations is that he emphasizes not only that there are monadic universals, such as redness or justice, but also that there are relational universals, such as those expressed by the phrases "north of" or "greater than."

Russell's argument that there are universals is based on a reductio ad absurdum: Rather than argue directly that universals exist, Russell attempts to show that the assumption that there are no universals implies an absurdity and must therefore be false. For there to be no universals, there would instead be only particular things with properties that merely resemble the properties of other particular things. If one assumes that this is the case, one must assume that two red things, a and b, do not share universal redness but only resemble each other. Similarly, two green things, c and d, would again only resemble each other without reference to a universal greenness. However, consider the relation of resemblance that holds between a and b and the one that holds between c and d. The assumption that everything is particular implies that these instances of resemblance are themselves particular and so only resemble each other. That is, there is no universal known as resemblance either, so the relationship between *a* and *b* is similar to, but not exactly the same as, the relationship between *c* and *d*. Thus, an infinite regress is being generated. The only way of blocking the regress is to acknowledge that the instances of resemblance are the same—that is, that the relation of resemblance is a universal. Thus, there must be at least one universal, the relation of resemblance. Having admitted the existence of one such universal, there is no reason not to admit the existence of others.

Believing that he has made the case that there are universals, Russell is now in a position to offer his solution to the problem of how a priori knowledge is possible. The basic idea is that a priori knowledge is explained in terms of the apprehension of relations between universals. Take the a priori proposition that nothing is entire red and entirely green at the same time. This seems necessarily true and knowable independently of experience; there is no need to examine all colored surfaces in the world to make sure that none are both red and green. By just reflecting on the universals redness and greenness, a philosopher may recognize the proposition as self-evidently true.

The Problems of Philosophy concludes with Russell's reflections on the limits of philosophical knowledge and the value of philosophy. Many philosophers have thought that a priori metaphysical reasoning can establish truths about the nature of reality as a whole. They have asserted, for example, that reality is essentially spiritual. Russell, as a founder of the analytic tradition in philosophy, has a more modest view regarding the scope of philosophical knowledge. This modesty is due to the higher standards of clarity and proof that one typically finds among analytic philosophers. Russell is quite skeptical of the claim that human reason, unaided by empirical investigation, can determine the ultimate nature or final truth about the world.

Regarding the value of philosophy, Russell asserts that this value does not lie in the definite knowledge that philosophy produces but rather in the effect it has on those who study it. Those who do not study philosophy, he believes, are imprisoned by the unexamined prejudices of their society. The study of philosophy allows one to examine critically these beliefs, to retain those that survive critical scrutiny, and to reject those that do not. Philosophy for Russell thus liberates those who study it.

David Haugen

Further Reading

Ayer, A. J. *Bertrand Russell*. New York: Viking Press, 1972. An interpretation of Russell's life and thought by a major British philosopher.

Daniel, David Mills, and Megan Daniel. *Briefly: Russell's "The Problems of Philosophy."* London: SCM Press, 2007. A concise monograph designed to introduce interested readers to all important features of Russell's treatise.

Grayling, A. C. *Russell*. New York: Oxford University Press, 1996. A general introduction to Russell's philosophy. Provides coverage of all aspects of Russell's thought, including logic, epistemology, metaphysics, and ethics.

Hylton, Peter. *Russell, Idealism, and the Emergence of Analytic Philosophy*. New York: Oxford University Press, 1990. An advanced treatment of the development of Russell's philosophy in the decade preceding the publication of *The Problems of Philosophy*.

Pears, D. F. *Bertrand Russell: A Collection of Critical Essays*. New York: Doubleday, 1972. An excellent collection of essays on Russell's philosophy by major philosophers and scholars, including several dealing with the doctrines and ideas of *The Problems of Philosophy*.

Russell, Bertrand. *My Philosophical Development*. 1959. Reprint. New York: Routledge, 1995. This philosophical autobiography puts the ideas of *The Problems of Philosophy* in the context of the nearly seventy years of Russell's work.

The Professor's House

Author: Willa Cather (1873-1947)
First published: 1925
Type of work: Novel
Type of plot: Psychological realism
Time of plot: A few years after World War I
Locale: Hamilton, near Lake Michigan

Principal characters:
GODFREY ST. PETER, a middle-aged teacher and historian
LILLIAN ST. PETER, his wife
ROSAMOND and KATHLEEN, their daughters
LOUIE MARCELLUS, Rosamond's husband
SCOTT MCGREGOR, Kathleen's husband
TOM OUTLAND, a former student at Hamilton
AUGUSTA, a seamstress

The Story:

The Oxford prize for history brings Professor Godfrey St. Peter not only a certain international reputation but also the sum of five thousand pounds. The five thousand pounds, in turn, helps the St. Peter family build a new house, into which the professor is frankly reluctant to move.

For half a lifetime, the attic of the old house has been his favorite spot—it was there that he had done his best writing, with his daughters' dress forms for his only company—and it is in this workroom that Augusta, the family sewing woman, finds him when she arrives to transfer the dress forms to the new house. To her astonishment, the professor declares quizzically that she cannot have them; he intends to retain the old house to preserve his workroom intact, and everything must be left as it is.

Nevertheless, the new house makes its own claims. That same evening the professor hosts a small dinner party for a visiting Englishman. The professor's daughters and their husbands are present, and during dinner, the conversation turns to the new country house being built by Rosamond and Louie. Louie explains to the visitor why the name Outland had been selected for the estate. Tom Outland had been a brilliant scientific student at Hamilton, as well as the professor's protégé. Before being killed in the war, he had been engaged to Rosamond. His will had left everything to her, including control of his revolutionary invention, the Outland vacuum. Later, Louie Marcellus married Rosamond and successfully marketed Tom's invention. The new house, Louie had concluded, would serve in some measure as a memorial to Outland.

Louie's lack of reserve visibly irritates the McGregors, and the professor maintains a cool silence. The next morning, his wife takes him to task for it. Lillian has been fiercely jealous of her husband's interest in Tom Outland. The professor finds himself reflecting that people who fall in love, and who go on being in love, always meet with something that suddenly or gradually makes a difference. Oddly enough, in the case of Lillian and her husband, it had seemed to be his pupil, Tom Outland.

More and more, the professor seeks the refuge of his study in the old house, where he can insulate himself against increasing family strain. Even there, however, there are interruptions. Once it is Rosamond, self-conscious about accepting all the benefits of the Outland invention. Her father refuses to share her good fortune but suggests that she aid cancer-ridden Professor Crane, who had collaborated with Tom in his experiments. Rosamond stiffens immediately, for outside the family, she recognizes no obligations.

Soon there is more evidence that the family is drifting apart. Kathleen confesses to her father her violent reaction to Rosamond's arrogance. It becomes known that Louie, attempting to join the Arts and Letters Club, had been blackballed by his brother-in-law. The professor is distressed by the rift between his daughters, both of whom he loves, although he has a special affection for Kathleen.

Louie's real fondness for the St. Peters is demonstrated when the time comes for the professor to fill a lecture date in Chicago. Louie and Rosamond, paying all bills, take them to Chicago, install them in a luxurious hotel suite, and tempt them with diversions. During a performance of *Mignon*, Lillian, softened by memories aroused by the opera, confirms the professor's impression that her resentment of Tom has affected their marriage.

Louie's next plan is even more elaborate: He and Rosamond will take the professor and Lillian to France for the summer. The professor loves France, but he recognizes the futility of trying to compromise his and Louie's ideas of a European vacation. He begs off, pleading the pressure of work, and eventually the others depart without him.

The professor moves back into the old house and luxuriates in independence. He decides to edit for publication Tom's youthful diary, and constantly he turns over in his mind the events in Tom's dramatic history. Years before, Tom had appeared on the professor's doorstep as a sunburned young man who was obviously unaccustomed to the ways of society. Tom wanted to go to college, although his only previous instruction had come from a priest in New Mexico. Interested and curious, the professor saw to it that Tom had a chance to make up his deficiencies and enter the university. The St. Peter house became the boy's second home, and the little girls were endlessly fascinated by his tales of the Southwest. To them, he confided that his parents had died during their wagon journey westward and that he had been adopted by a kindly worker on the Santa Fe Railroad.

Tom's diary is chiefly concerned with his strangest boyhood adventure. To regain his strength after an attack of pneumonia, he became a herd rider on the summer range. With him was his closest friend, Roddie Blake. On the range, Tom and Roddie were challenged by the nearness of the mysterious Blue Mesa, hitherto unclimbed and unexplored. They saved their wages and made plans; when their job was finished, they set out to conquer Blue Mesa.

They had made a striking discovery. In the remote canyons of the mesa are Indian rock villages, undisturbed for three hundred years and in a miraculous state of preservation. This gift of history had stirred Tom to a strong decision. His find should be presented to his country; the relics must not be exploited for profit. With Roddie's consent, he took six hundred dollars, boarded a train, and left for Washington. Weeks later he returned, worn out by red tape and indifference, only to learn that Roddie had finally weakened and sold the Indian treasures to a foreign scientist. In a climax of bitterness, he quarreled with Roddie. A year later, he walked into the professor's garden.

Recalling Tom has always brought the professor a kind of second youth. Tom is the type of person the professor had started out to be—vigorous, unspoiled, and ambitious. Marrying Lillian had brought happiness, nonetheless real for having now faded; but it has chained him as well, he feels, and diverted the true course of his life. Now, reviewing the past, the professor suddenly feels tired and old. At the news that the travelers will soon return, he feels he cannot again assume a family role that had become meaningless.

When Augusta comes for the keys to reopen the new house, she finds the professor lying unconscious on the floor of his den. Its one window had blown shut and the unvented gas stove had done the rest. Augusta sends for the doctor, and the professor is revived. His temporary release from consciousness had cleared his mind. He is ready not only to face his family but also himself and a problem that came too late for him to flee.

Critical Evaluation:

During her lifetime, Willa Cather was known primarily for her novels, notably *One of Ours* (1922), which won the Pulitzer Prize, and such classics of midwestern and Western life as *O Pioneers!* (1913), *My Ántonia* (1918), and *Death Comes for the Archbishop* (1927). However, later studies of her life and works have led critics to conclude that Cather deserves an even higher place in the annals of American literature than she has generally been given. They point not only to her influence on other writers, especially the help she gave those who were new and unknown during her years as an editor of *McClure's*, but also to the craftsmanship she displayed in hundreds of articles, reviews, and essays, as well as in her short stories, many of which appeared in national magazines noted for the high quality of their fiction.

Cather is no longer called a local color writer or a women's writer. Instead, critics have become ever more impressed with the depth of Cather's knowledge, as revealed in her subtle and effective allusions; with her technical virtuosity, anticipating the methods of modernism; and with her profound vision, which enabled her to identify the most troublesome issues of her time.

Although it is not among Cather's most famous novels, *The Professor's House* is one of her most interesting. The work is dominated by the character of the protagonist. Godfrey St. Peter is a rather unlikely hero, in that he is a middle-aged professor established in his profession but not famous outside his discipline, a married man without plans for an extramarital affair, and a father whose daughters are married and out of the house. His immediate problem, the move to a new house, would seem to be a purely domestic matter.

However, Cather soon makes it clear that there is much more at issue than a change of environment. The professor is caught between three worlds, and ill at ease in all of them. His movements among these worlds, in search of a home, constitute the real plot of the novel.

The world where the professor is happiest is the house where he spent the early days of his marriage. Everyone else moves out of the house, and the professor's first reaction to the change might be called denial. Arguing that he cannot work anywhere except in his little attic, the professor leases the house for an extended period. Thus, at least during working hours, he can pretend that nothing has changed. He can even pretend that the unseen empty rooms are inhabited by a loving wife and two young, innocent children. To the professor, the old house is the past, and as long as he remains in it, the past still exists.

The world that contains everything the professor loathes and fears is represented by the new house. It was purchased with his money, but the place has been taken over by Lillian. In the new house, Lillian is no longer the person the professor married; instead, she is as coldly materialistic as the era in which she is living. Lillian seems quite at ease with her daughters, especially the wealthy Rosamond, and enchanted with her sons-in-law, who remind her of her youth. However, whenever he enters this world, the professor finds himself plunged into despair. It is no wonder that as soon as Lillian leaves for Europe, he moves back into the old house.

The professor is also aware of the existence of a third world, Tom Outland's Blue Mesa. Though he has never actually been there, the professor still feels the call of the unspoiled villages that Tom described so vividly. Like Tom, the professor sees Blue Mesa as symbolizing nature and a life in harmony with nature, and with Tom, he grieves when it is pillaged. Since Outland's death, however, Blue Mesa has taken on some added meanings for the professor. Not only does it represent a past that was lived and lost by his alter ego, Tom, but it also symbolizes all that he himself has lost.

This interpretation of *The Professor's House* makes it clear why Cather constructed her novel as she did. The first long section establishes the nature of the two worlds between which the professor is expected to choose. Cather then brings Tom back to life, so that he can make the case for the third world, Blue Mesa. In the final section, however, the professor has to face the fact that two of his options are no longer available. The old house will not enable him to return to his "first" youth, nor can his memories of Tom and Blue Mesa take him back to his "second," lost youth. The possibilities before him are either escape into death or acceptance of the house and the corrupt, materialistic world.

By sending Augusta to save the professor, it may be argued that Cather could not answer her own question. Her professor never does decide whether death is worse than a joyless life. In later novels, however, such as *Death Comes for the Archbishop*, Cather is more optimistic. While she still sees greed as a major force in the modern world, she also believes that dedicated human beings could triumph over that greed. If there had been a sequel to *The Professor's House*, the professor might well have won.

"Critical Evaluation" by Rosemary M. Canfield Reisman

Further Reading

Bloom, Harold, ed. *Willa Cather*. New York: Chelsea House, 1985. A collection of essays about Cather. Two important and very different interpretations of *The Professor's House* appear in essays by David Daiches and E. K. Brown. A good place to start research on Cather.

De Roche, Linda. *Student Companion to Willa Cather*. Westport, Conn.: Greenwood Press, 2006. An introductory overview of Cather's life and work aimed at high school and college students and general readers. Discusses the character development, themes, and plots of six novels, with chapter 7 focusing on *The Professor's House*.

Leddy, Michael. "*The Professor's House*: The Sense of an Ending." *Studies in the Novel* 23 (Winter, 1991): 443-451. Leddy maintains that the novel's ending makes a valid, although vague, point. The professor's rediscovery of his boyhood home in Kansas points to a renewal or rebirth at the end of the story.

Lindermann, Marilee. *The Cambridge Companion to Willa Cather*. New York: Cambridge University Press, 2005. Thirteen essays, including those that examine Cather's politics, sexuality, and modernism. One of the essays focuses on *The Professor's House*.

Love, Glen A. "Place, Style, and Human Nature in Willa Cather's *The Professor's House*." In *Practical Ecocriticism: Literature, Biology, and the Environment*. Charlottesville: University of Virginia Press, 2003. Interprets the novel from the perspective of ecocriticism, or the application of ideas about ecology and the environment to literary works.

_____. "*The Professor's House*: Cather, Hemingway, and the Chastening of American Prose Style." *Western American Literature* 24 (February, 1990): 295-311. Love argues that Cather's writing style is closer to the modern style because of her economy and lack of emotion. Uses *The Professor's House* as an example of this prose style.

O'Brien, Sharon. *Willa Cather: The Emerging Voice*. New York: Oxford University Press, 1987. O'Brien maintains that the character of the professor in the novel is the alter ego of Cather.

Stout, Janis P., ed. *Willa Cather and Material Culture: Real-World Writing, Writing the Real World*. Tuscaloosa: University of Alabama Press, 2005. Essays examine the objects—or material culture—in Cather's life and the objects about which she wrote. Other topics include the symbolism of quilts as well as consumerism in "'An Orgy of Acquisition': The Female Consumer, Infidelity, and Commodity Culture in *A Lost Lady* and *The Professor's House*."

Trout, Steven. *Memorial Fictions: Willa Cather and the First World War*. Lincoln: University of Nebraska Press, 2002. Analyzes Cather's career and work during and after World War I, including a reappraisal of *The Professor's House*. Trout argues this novel is "haunted" by the presence of the war.

Prometheus Bound

Author: Aeschylus (525/524-456/455 B.C.E.)
First produced: Prometheus desmōtes, date unknown
    (English translation, 1777)
Type of work: Drama
Type of plot: Tragedy
Time of plot: Antiquity
Locale: A barren cliff in Scythia

Principal characters:
PROMETHEUS, a Titan
HEPHAESTUS, his kinsman and the god of fire
KRATOS, Might
BIA, Force
OCEANUS, the god of the sea
Io, the daughter of the river god Inachus
HERMES, the winged messenger of the gods

The Story:

Condemned by Zeus for giving fire to mortals, the Titan Prometheus is brought to a barren cliff in Scythia by Hephaestus, the god of fire, and two guards named Kratos and Bia. There he is to be bound to the jagged cliffs. Kratos and Bia are willing to obey Zeus's commands, but Hephaestus experiences pangs of sorrow and is reluctant to bind his kinsman to the storm-beaten cliff in that desolate region, where Prometheus will never again hear the voice or see the form of a human being. Hephaestus grieves that the Titan is doomed forever to be guardian of the desolate cliff, but he is powerless against the commands of Zeus. At last, he chains Prometheus to the cliff. He rivets Prometheus's arms beyond release, thrusts a wedge of adamant straight through his heart, and puts iron girths on both his sides with shackles around his legs. After Hephaestus and Bia depart, Kratos remains to hurl one last taunt at Prometheus, asking him what aid he expects humankind to offer their benefactor. The gods who gave Prometheus his name, which means Forethinker, were foolish, Kratos points out, for Prometheus requires a higher intelligence to do his thinking for him.

Alone and chained, Prometheus calls upon the winds, the waters, mother earth, and the sun to look on him and see how the gods torture a god. He admits that he will have to bear his lot as best he can because the power of fate is invincible, but he remains defiant. He has committed no crime, he insists; he has merely loved humankind. He remembers how the gods first conceived the plan to revolt against the rule of Kronos and seat Zeus on the throne. At first Prometheus did his best to bring about a reasonable peace between the ancient Titans and the gods. When he failed, to avoid further violence, he had placed himself on the side of Zeus, who through the counsel of Prometheus overthrew Kronos. Once on the throne, Zeus parceled out to the lesser gods their share of power, but he ignored mortals. His ultimate plan was to destroy them completely and create another race that would

cringe and be servile to Zeus's every word. Among all the gods, only Prometheus objected to this heartless proposal, and it was Prometheus's courage, his act alone, that had saved human beings from burial in the deepest black of Hades. It was he who had taught blind hope to spring within the hearts of mortals, and he had given them the gift of fire. He had understood the significance of these deeds—he had sinned willingly.

Oceanus, Prometheus's brother, comes to offer aid out of love and kinship, but he first offers Prometheus advice and preaches humility in the face of Zeus's wrath. Prometheus remains proud and defiant, and he refuses his brother's offer of help on the grounds that Oceanus himself would be punished were it discovered that he sympathizes with a rebel. Convinced by Prometheus's argument, Oceanus takes sorrowful leave of his brother.

Once more Prometheus recalls that human beings were creatures without language who had been ignorant of everything before Prometheus came and told them of the rising and setting of stars, of numbers, of letters, of the function of beasts of burden, of the utility of ships, of curing diseases, of happiness and lurking evil, and of methods to bring wealth in iron, silver, copper, and gold out of the earth. In spite of his torment, he rejoices that he had taught the arts to humankind.

Io, daughter of the river god Inachus, comes to the place where Prometheus is chained. Because Io is beloved by Zeus, Zeus's wife, Hera, had out of jealousy turned Io into a cow and set Argus, the hundred-eyed monster, to watch her. When Zeus had Argus put to death, Hera sent a gadfly to sting Io and drive her all over the earth. Prometheus prophesies her future wanderings to the end of the earth and says that the day will come when Zeus will restore her to human form and together they will conceive a son named Epaphus. Before Io leaves, Prometheus also names his own rescuer,

Hercules, who with his bow and arrow will kill the eagle devouring Prometheus's vital parts.

Hermes, Zeus's messenger, comes to see Prometheus and threatens him with more awful terrors at the hands of angry Zeus. Prometheus, still defiant, belittles Hermes' position among the gods and calls him a mere menial. Suddenly there is a turbulent rumbling of the earth, accompanied by lightning, thunder, and blasts of wind. Zeus shatters the rock with a thunderbolt and hurls Prometheus into an abysmal dungeon within the earth. Such is the terrible fate of the fire-bearer who defied the gods.

Critical Evaluation:

In several ways *Prometheus Bound* is something of a puzzle. The date of its first production is unknown, though it can probably be assumed to have come rather late in Aeschylus's career, possibly between 466 B.C.E. and 456 B.C.E., the year of his death. Because this is the only surviving play of the Aeschylean trilogy on Prometheus, it is also not known whether it was intended to be the first or second in the trilogy, though it is known that it was to be followed by *Prometheus Unbound*. *Prometheus Bound* is the one extant play by Aeschylus to deal directly with a metaphysical problem by means of supernatural characters, yet even the questions raised in the work remain unresolved. It is a mystery centering on a mystery.

The situation of the play is static: Prometheus is fastened to a Scythian crag for having enabled humankind to live when Zeus was intending to destroy the ephemeral humans. Once Hephaestus wedges and binds him down, Prometheus is immobile. Thereafter, the theatrical movement lies in his visitors—the chorus of nymphs, Oceanus, Io, and Hermes. Essentially this is a drama of ideas, and those ideas probe the nature of the cosmos. It is irrelevant that the characters are extinct Greek gods, for the issues that Aeschylus raises are eternal ones.

The Greeks loved a contest, and *Prometheus Bound* is about a contest of wills. On one side is Zeus, who is omnipotent in this world, while on the other is Prometheus, who has divine intelligence. Neither will give an inch, for each feels he is perfectly justified. Zeus rules by right of conquest, and Prometheus resists by right of moral superiority. On Zeus's side are Might and Force, the powers of compulsion and tyranny, but Prometheus has knowledge and prescience.

Zeus, inscrutable and majestic as he is, does not appear except through his agents who enforce his will. The drama begins and ends with the exercise of his power, which is used here simply to make Prometheus suffer. This power first binds Prometheus to a crag and finally envelops him in a cataclysm. Zeus has a fearsome capacity to inflict pain, not merely on Prometheus but on Io as well, and in both instances it is motivated by what he perceives as their disobedience. Prometheus opposed Zeus by giving human beings both fire and the skills needed to survive; Io resisted Zeus's love. Prometheus, being a Titan, had shown rebellion on the divine plane, while Io rebels on the human level. The price of their rebellion is written in their flesh, and both regard Zeus as their persecutor.

Aeschylus certainly disliked political tyranny, but it is a mistake to read this play merely as a parable of human inhumanity. The issues go far deeper, for Prometheus has omniscience and therefore knew what would come of his revolt. He made a great personal sacrifice when he supported humankind out of compassion. He is a savior and a tremendous hero, but his knowledge does not keep him from suffering like a mortal, nor does it make him accept his pain calmly. He knows why he suffers but defies his fate nevertheless, for he is convinced that he is right and Zeus wrong. Moreover, he claims that Zeus is not the ultimate power; indeed, he asserts that Zeus must submit to the Fates and the Furies.

Prometheus holds the winning hand in this play, for he possesses a secret that Zeus needs to retain his power. This knowledge is his only consolation in his torment. Every counsel to moderation or humility is vain, for Prometheus has no intention of giving up the joy of seeing Zeus humbled just to alleviate his own agony. This motivation comes through clearly in Prometheus's bitter dialogue with Hermes.

Prometheus is not only self-righteous and vengeful but also full of arrogant pride. He chooses his pain; perhaps he even deserves it. No one justifies Zeus, for he is beyond any notion of justice, but Prometheus exults in justifying himself to any divinity who will listen. Because of his services to humankind, the audience must feel compassion for him. He is an authentic tragic hero, arousing both pity and fear.

As a dramatic character, Io represents the human condition. The daughter of a god, she is shut out of her home by Zeus's command, given a bestial body, and made to run over the face of the earth in pain, stung by the ghost of many-eyed Argus (conscience). Only in the distant future will she and Zeus be reconciled.

The resolution of the Zeus-Prometheus conflict in Aeschylus's *Prometheus Unbound* can only be surmised. It is possible that Zeus gained in maturity after centuries of rule and decided to release the Titan, after which Prometheus may have given him the secret. Just as human beings evolved through the gifts of Prometheus into civilized creatures, Zeus may have changed and made his reign one of wisdom and force. It is hard to believe that Prometheus would alter unless such a change did come about in Zeus, but this is pure speculation. The debate between Prometheus and Zeus remains open. Aeschylus never solves this dilemma in the play; he merely shows it in the strongest dramatic terms. Tautly written, *Prometheus Bound* is profound precisely because it remains an enigma.

"Critical Evaluation" by James Weigel, Jr.

Further Reading

Goward, Barbara. *Telling Tragedy: Narrative Technique in Aeschylus, Sophocles, and Euripides*. London: Duckworth, 2004. Examination of ancient Greek drama includes a discussion of *Prometheus Bound*, devoting one chapter to a detailed analysis of the play's Io scene.

Grene, David. "Introduction to *Prometheus Bound*." In *Aeschylus: The Complete Greek Tragedies*, edited by David Grene and Richmond Lattimore. Vol. 1. Chicago: University of Chicago Press, 1969. Reviews eighteenth century criticism of *Prometheus Bound* and compares the work to Aristotle's *Poetics* (c. 334-323 B.C.E.). Discusses problems with the play, including its episodic plot, improbable and extravagant characters, and uncouth diction.

Kitto, H. D. F. *Greek Tragedy: A Literary Study*. London: Methuen, 1970. Places *Prometheus Bound* in the category of Old Tragedy. One chapter offers a detailed examination of the play.

_____. *Poiesis: Structure and Thought*. Berkeley: University of California Press, 1966. Discusses what is known as Farnall's dilemma: that Aeschylus was writing about Zeus in a derogatory sense and that the playwright should have been prosecuted for blasphemy. Because he was not, he could not have written *Prometheus Bound*.

Podlecki, Anthony J. *The Political Background of Aeschylean Tragedy*. Ann Arbor: University of Michigan Press, 1966. Discusses similarities between *Prometheus Bound* and Aeschylus's drama *Oresteia* (458 B.C.E.; English translation, 1777).

Stanford, William Bedell. *Aeschylus in His Style: A Study in Language and Personality*. Dublin: Dublin University Press, 1942. Discussion focuses on helping students better understand the language of Aeschylus. Notes that Aeschylus borrowed language in *Prometheus Bound* from two types of sources, one literary and the other colloquial.

Thomson, George. *Aeschylus and Athens: A Study in the Social Origins of Drama*. New York: Grosset & Dunlap, 1968. Presents history and interpretations of the myth of Prometheus; explains how this myth fits into *Prometheus Bound*.

West, M. L. "The Prometheus Trilogy." In *Aeschylus*, edited by Michael Lloyd. New York: Oxford University Press, 2007. Considers the problems of staging *Prometheus Bound*, attempts to reconstruct the trilogy that included this play, and argues that the trilogy dates back to 440 B.C.E.

Prometheus Unbound
A Lyrical Drama in Four Acts

Author: Percy Bysshe Shelley (1792-1822)
First published: 1820
Type of work: Poetry
Type of plot: Allegory
Time of plot: Antiquity
Locale: Asia

Principal characters:
PROMETHEUS, a Titan
EARTH, his mother
ASIA, Prometheus's wife
JUPITER, king of the gods
DEMOGORGON, supreme power, ruling the gods
MERCURY, messenger of the gods
HERAKLES, hero of virtue and strength
PANTHEA and IONE, the Oceanides

The Poem:

Prometheus, the benefactor of humankind, is bound to a rocky cliff by order of Jupiter, who is jealous of the Titan's power. Three thousand years of torture Prometheus suffers there, while an eagle continually eats at his heart and he is afflicted by heat, cold, and many other torments. Prometheus nevertheless continues to defy the power of Jupiter. At last

Prometheus asks Panthea and Ione, the two Oceanides, to repeat to him the curse he had pronounced upon Jupiter when Jupiter first began to torture him. Neither his mother Earth nor the Oceanides will answer him. At last the Phantasm of Jupiter appears and repeats the curse. When Prometheus hears the words, he repudiates them. Now that he has suffered tortures and finds that his spirit remains unconquered, he wishes pain to no living thing. Earth and the Oceanides mourn that the curse has been withdrawn, for they think that Jupiter has at last conquered Prometheus's spirit.

Then Mercury approaches with the Furies. Mercury tells the captive Prometheus that he will suffer even greater tortures if he does not reveal the secret that he alone knows—the future fate of Jupiter. Jupiter, afraid, wishes to avert catastrophe by learning the secret, and Mercury promises Prometheus that he will be released if he reveals it. Prometheus, however, refuses. He admits only that he knows Jupiter's reign will come to an end, that Jupiter will not be king of the gods for all eternity. Prometheus says that he is willing to suffer torture until Jupiter's reign ends. Although the Furies try to frighten him by describing the pains they can inflict, they know they have no power over his soul.

The Furies mock Prometheus and humankind, showing Prometheus visions of blood and despair on earth; they show him the Passion of Christ and humanity's disregard for Christ's message of love. Fear and hypocrisy rule; tyrants take the thrones of the world. A group of spirits appear and prophesy that Love will cure the ills of humankind. They prophesy also that Prometheus will be able to bring Love to earth and halt the reign of evil and grief. When the spirits have gone, Prometheus acknowledges the power of Love, for his love for Asia, his wife, has enabled him to suffer pain without surrendering.

While Asia, alone in a lovely valley, mourns for her lost husband, Panthea appears to tell of two dreams she has had. In one, she saw Prometheus released from bondage and all the world filled with sweetness. In the other dream she received only a command to follow. Just then the echoes in the valley break their silence, calling for Asia and Panthea to follow them. The listeners obey and follow the echoes to the realm of Demogorgon, the supreme power ruling the gods. They stop on a pinnacle of rock, but spirits beckon them down into Demogorgon's cave. There Demogorgon tells Asia and Panthea that he will answer any question they put to him. When they ask who made the living world, he replies that God created it. Then they ask who made pain and evil. Prometheus had given knowledge to humankind, but humankind had not eradicated evil with all the gifts of science. They ask whether Jupiter is the source of these ills, the evil master

over humanity. Demogorgon answers that nothing that serves evil can be master, for only eternal Love rules all.

Asia asks when Prometheus will gain his freedom and bring Love into the world to conquer Jupiter. Demogorgon then shows his guests the passage of the Hours. A dreadful Hour passes, marking Jupiter's fall; the next Hour is beautiful, marking Prometheus's release. Asia and Panthea accompany the Spirit of the Hour in her chariot and pass by Age, Manhood, Youth, Infancy, and Death into a new paradise.

Meanwhile, Jupiter, who has just married Thetis, celebrates his omnipotence over all but the human soul. Then Demogorgon appears and pronounces judgment on Jupiter. Jupiter cries for mercy, but his power is gone. He sinks downward through darkness and ruin. At the same time, Herakles approaches Prometheus. In the presence of Asia, Panthea, the Spirit of the Hour, and Earth, the captive is set free. Joyfully, Prometheus tells Asia how they will spend the rest of their days together with Love. Then he sends the Spirit of the Hour to announce his release to all humankind. He kisses Earth, and Love infuses all of her animal, vegetable, and mineral parts.

The Spirit of Earth later comes to the cave where Asia and Prometheus live and tells them of the transformation that has come over humankind. Anger, pride, insincerity, and all the other ills of humanity have passed away. The Spirit of the Hour reports other wonders that have taken place. Thrones are empty, and all human beings rule over themselves, free from guilt and pain. People are, however, still subject to chance, death, and mutability, without which they would oversoar their destined place in the world.

Later, in a vision, Panthea and Ione see how all the evil things of the world lay dead and decayed. Earth's happiness is boundless, and even the moon feels the beams of Love from Earth as snow melts on its bleak lunar mountains. Earth rejoices that hate, fear, and pain have left humankind forever. Humanity is now master of its fate and of all the secrets of Earth.

Critical Evaluation:

Prometheus Unbound glorifies the rebellious impulse toward freedom in the human spirit. The poem dramatizes and explains Percy Bysshe Shelley's philosophical and religious understanding, which was individual. *Prometheus Unbound* is Shelley's credo; the impulse to freedom and to rebel against authoritarian orthodoxy is one he valued highly. Shelley's beliefs typify Romanticism. As did such Romantic poets as William Blake, Lord Byron, and Samuel Taylor Coleridge, Shelley wrote of the freedom of the individual and of the primacy of the imagination. Institutions, social structures, and established belief were, in these poets' views, suspect. For them, evil lay in limitation imposed on the human spirit, which, when free, was good.

Shelley and other Romantic poets also at times did more than write about their beliefs. They were activists in the causes of liberty and reform of their times. Shelley, for example, favored vegetarianism, freedom for Ireland and for slaves, the abolition of monarchy and marriage, the overthrow of established religion, extension of voting rights, empowerment of the working class, and equality for women. He advocated these ideas in his writings, which in his time was a provocative and courageous act. While a student at Oxford he collaborated on a pamphlet titled *The Necessity of Atheism* (1811) and sent copies to all the college authorities and every bishop in the Church of England. He was expelled from the university as a result.

Prometheus Unbound is a play in verse in which the poetry takes precedence over the drama. This work could not easily be brought to the stage; the reader may best realize the drama of the conflicts of gods and allegorical figures with the imagination. From Prometheus's opening oration to the paeanlike ending, the reader is carried along with the delicacy, vivacity, thunder, or choric effect of the lines. The spacelessness of the work is its virtue, and its muted, ethereal effect is lyrically matchless. This work illustrates how well Shelley fashions not only his own invented lyric patterns but also the Pindaric ode, the fourteen-syllable line, the Spenserian stanza, couplets, and infinite variations of the Greek choral effects. Every conceivable meter can be detected; the inversions, the intricately developed rhythm patterns are numerous. A "lyrical flowering" seems an appropriate phrase for the entire work, perhaps Shelley's greatest.

Although Shelley wrote poetry that was intended to generate controversy, and did, his poetry is unmatched in its civilized, urbane, and elegant spirit. His work is still capable of offending those whose political or religious convictions are conservative. Perhaps for this reason, his verse is sometimes wrongly described as being strident or self-centered.

Prometheus Unbound uses the well-known Greek myth as a vehicle for Shelley's themes. The playwright Aeschylus's tragedy *Prometheus Bound* (fifth century B.C.E.) was known to Shelley, who could read Greek. In Aeschylus's version of the myth, Prometheus made humanity out of clay. Zeus, envious, retaliated by oppressing human beings and depriving them of fire. Prometheus stole fire from heaven and gave it to humans; he also taught the humans many arts. Aeschylus's play opens with Zeus's causing Prometheus to be chained to a rock for his rebellion and refusing to free him

until Prometheus agrees to reveal a secret prophecy with which he has been entrusted.

In the preface to *Prometheus Unbound*, Shelley points out that writers in ancient Greece felt free to revise myths as needed for their themes. Shelley states that it is not his purpose to restore the lost play *Prometheus Unbound*, which Aeschylus was supposed to have written after *Prometheus Bound*. Rather, Shelley intends in his play to create a new myth appropriate to Shelley's times. Shelley compares Prometheus with Satan, who, in Christian myth and in John Milton's *Paradise Lost* (1667, 1674), rebels (for many Romantics, heroically) against God. "Prometheus," Shelley argues, "is . . . the type of the highest perfection of moral and intellectual nature, impelled by the purest and the truest motives to the best and noblest ends."

"Critical Evaluation" by Dennis R. Dean

Further Reading

Baker, Carlos. *Shelley's Major Poetry: The Fabric of a Vision*. 1948. Reprint. Princeton, N.J.: Princeton University Press, 1973. Standard work provides an introductory survey of Shelley's most important poetic writings. Includes a chapter and an appendix on *Prometheus Unbound*.

Cameron, Kenneth Neill. *Shelley: The Golden Years*. Cambridge, Mass.: Harvard University Press, 1974. In part a biography, this survey of Shelley's work from 1814 to 1822 analyzes all of his important poetry and culminates with a two-chapter discussion of *Prometheus Unbound*.

Duffy, Cian. *Shelley and the Revolutionary Sublime*. New York: Cambridge University Press, 2005. Focuses on Shelley's fascination with sublime natural phenomena and how this interest influenced his writing and his ideas about political and social reform.

Frosch, Thomas R. *Shelley and the Romantic Imagination: A Psychological Study*. Newark: University of Delaware Press, 2007. Offers a psychoanalytic interpretation of some of Shelley's works, with five chapters devoted to a detailed analysis of the Prometheus myth in *Prometheus Unbound*. Examines Shelley's attempt to create images of ideal love and a human paradise.

Lewis, Linda M. *The Promethean Politics of Milton, Blake, and Shelley*. Columbia: University of Missouri Press, 1992. Focuses on the political elements of the Prometheus myth, describing how Shelley adapted Promethean figures and images to express his political ideas in *Prometheus Unbound*.

Morton, Timothy, ed. *The Cambridge Companion to Shelley*. New York: Cambridge University Press, 2006. Collection of essays addresses various aspects of Shelley's life and work, including Shelley as a lyricist, dramatist, story-teller, political poet, and translator. Includes discussion of *Prometheus Unbound*.

Wasserman, Earl R. *Shelley's "Prometheus Unbound": A*

Critical Reading. Baltimore: Johns Hopkins University Press, 1965. An example of close reading and profound thought, Wasserman's philosophical interpretation of *Prometheus Unbound* defends the poem's fundamental unity.

The Promised Land

Author: Henrik Pontoppidan (1857-1943)
First published: Det forjættede land, 1891-1895
    (English translation, 1896)
Type of work: Novel
Type of plot: Social criticism
Time of plot: Late nineteenth century
Locale: Denmark

Principal characters:
EMANUEL HANSTED, a clergyman and a reformer
HANSINE, his wife
MISS TONNESEN, his former fiancé
DR. HASSING, a physician

The Story:

Emanuel Hansted, the minister son of a wealthy Copenhagen couple, long ago left his hometown to take over a pastorate in the country. Somewhat of a reformer, he has become enthusiastic about the socialism rife in Europe in the second half of the nineteenth century, and to prove his fellowship with the peasants whom he serves, he has married a young peasant woman and has undertaken to farm the land on which his rectory is situated.

As the years have passed, Emanuel's wife, Hansine, has presented him with three children; his land, however, has repaid him only with debts. Although he tries experiment after experiment, Emanuel's fields do not produce enough to support his family. Stubbornly, Emanuel refuses to acknowledge that he is no farmer; he even continues to refuse any payment from his parishioners and gives away the money he receives for the benefit of the poor.

Despite Emanuel's sacrifices, and despite his never-flagging efforts to share their lives and his ties with them through marriage, the peasants do not accept him as one of them. The fact that he came among them as an outlander is too strong for them to forget, even in the times of stress that come when the newly formed People's Party of Denmark, representing chiefly the peasantry, tries to control the government in order to provide for the education of the masses and to improve the lot of the common people generally.

To the casual eye, Emanuel might seem to be a peasant, for he has nothing to do with the few gentry who live in the vicinity. He even distrusts the doctor, whom he has to call in oc-

casionally to treat a member of his family. Indeed, Emanuel summons Dr. Hassing only when an emergency arises. As for his family, Emanuel has put his father and his sister entirely out of his mind; he acknowledges as kin only his wife and children, who tie him to the peasantry.

One summer, all of nature and humankind seem determined to show that Emanuel is a misfit in the rural area he has adopted. His crops are even poorer than usual; nature refuses to send the weather he needs to produce successful yields in the fields he has planted with borrowed seed. In the capital, Copenhagen, the Conservative Party gains in strength and defeats the People's Party—first in small items, then in large. As the peasants lose their political power, the people of Emanuel's parish begin to look at him as one who belongs to the other side.

As if these problems were not enough, Emanuel's oldest child, a son, begins to suffer from an ear inflammation that has gone untended for two years. At last, upon Hansine's insistence, Emanuel sends for Dr. Hassing. The physician cannot believe that Emanuel has permitted the child's health to fall into such a dangerous state; Emanuel, on his part, does not seem to understand that the child is really ill. Failing to follow the doctor's advice, he treats his son as if he were well and healthy. The boy dies as a result of his father's failure to face reality.

Before long, Emanuel and Hansine begin to drift apart, for their son's death has exacerbated a barrier between them that has been years in the making. Hansine feels that her husband is unhappy, and she believes that he actually wants to escape from his dismal, unappreciative rural parish.

Quite by chance, while out walking alone to prepare his Sunday sermon, Emanuel comes upon Dr. Hassing and a small party of picnickers. Prevailed upon to join the group, he finds among them Miss Tonnesen, his former fiancé from Copenhagen. Emanuel walks back to Dr. Hassing's home with the picnickers and, because it is growing dark, remains for supper. The genteel conversation of the guests, the quiet wealth of the home, the very food on the table, the music after supper—all of these things remind Emanuel of what he lost when he refused Miss Tonnesen's love, rejected the family warmth of his parents' home, and turned instead toward the simple, rude life of the peasants. In the days following his evening at the doctor's home, he ridicules the people with whom he spent a few hours, but Hansine sees that he is merely trying to convince himself that he has chosen the right path in his life's work.

A few weeks later, Miss Tonnesen, who has traveled to the rural area to prove to herself that her former suitor has sunk beneath her, visits the rectory. Her father was formerly the rector of the parish, and under his care the rectory had been a place of beauty, both within and without. His daughter, seeing it for the first time in many years, is amazed to see how Emanuel has let it fall into disrepair. Only a few of the rooms, equipped with the barest of essentials, are in use. The gardens and lawns are overgrown; even the outbuildings and fields have gone years without proper care. Miss Tonnesen can scarcely believe that the man she loved could have permitted the grounds in his charge, and himself as well, to slip into the state in which she finds them.

Miss Tonnesen's visit bothers Hansine, who sees in the other woman all that her husband gave up when he married her instead of someone from his own social class. Even Hansine and Emanuel's children ask if they can go to Copenhagen to visit the beautiful lady. Emanuel himself realizes that Miss Tonnesen represents something he has lost but can still regain. He becomes dissatisfied with the peasantry, and his parishioners quickly sense his unrest. His farmworkers leave him when, angry because the rains have ruined any chance he had of harvesting a crop of rye, he accuses them of laziness.

The climax comes following the death of the director of the district high school. This man, as head of the institution, has done much for the peasants, and everyone in the region attends his funeral. After the funeral is over, an informal political meeting takes place. Emanuel, asked to address the meeting, speaks out against the sloth and narrow prejudices of the peasants. As he is speaking, a murmuring arises among

those present; he finally has to stop speaking when many in the crowd begin to shout insults and ridicule. As he slowly leaves the meeting, he hears the next speaker declare that the pastor should return to his own people.

Emanuel meets Hansine at the edge of the crowd, and slowly they start for home. On the way, Hansine tells Emanuel that he ought to return to Copenhagen and she to her former life. He sadly agrees. The children, it is decided, will go with their father. To Emanuel's delight, his father and sister write to him and ask him to return as soon as possible. As a result, one morning he and his remaining two children climb into a carriage and drive away as Hansine turns to walk to her parents' cottage.

Critical Evaluation:

Nobel Prize winner Henrik Pontoppidan attempts in *The Promised Land* to illustrate the conflicts that overtake human beings when they try to submerge their instincts to follow their intellectual beliefs. Emanuel Hansted is a complicated, tormented individual, divided between theory and instinct, duty and passion. He is not entirely sympathetic, but he is understandable and pitiable. A dreamer, he tries unsuccessfully to gain the confidence of the peasants but, despite his efforts to make himself one with the soil and the peasant life, his urban background ultimately betrays his ambitions.

Pontoppidan's novel reflects the class distinctions and the division between town and country folk in nineteenth century Denmark, at a time when the peasants were struggling for a greater voice in the affairs of that country. As in the case of so many European novels dealing with social problems, the characterization, the plot, and the events that take place are secondary to the social meaning and the tone of the work. As a result, the characters are types rather than individuals, and in a plot subordinate to theme the events depicted are not skillfully tied together. Quite obviously these items were relatively unimportant to the author; he was intent on creating a picture of the struggle between the People's Party and the Conservatives, and the effects of that struggle on individuals. Sympathetic to the less favored group, Pontoppidan, like so many problem novelists, tells only one side of the story; one result is that his upper-class characters, like those of the American novelist Theodore Dreiser, are often overdrawn.

Pontoppidan writes with a deceptively aloof, almost cold, style, but his characters are warm-blooded, many-faceted human beings. Hansine, Emanuel's wife, speaks little, but it is clear that she feels deeply. Emanuel married her because she is a peasant, because he felt that she would help him to forget his past, but gradually she comes to realize that they are wrong for each other. With great artistry, the author subtly suggests her feelings, implying much with few words. Her sacrifice at the end of the book is both inevitable and touching.

Emanuel's past in Copenhagen is revealed only in pieces, through allusions in conversation. His former relationship with the attractive, sophisticated Ragnhild Tonnesen is disclosed bit by bit; the reader discovers the realities behind the appearances slowly. This technique requires great control on the part of the author as the story builds with relentless inevitability to the emotional crisis at the heart of the book. Politics and religion play important parts in the novel, but primarily it is a story of human beings.

Emanuel had seen everything evil in the sophistication of his past life in the city and has made the mistake of seeing only good in the crude life of the peasants. He craves truth and justice, and he sees a moral earnestness in the peasants' faces that touches him deeply. So completely has he rejected the city and its ways, including science and progress, that he refuses to let a doctor see his son until it is too late to save the boy's life. There is a dormant power in the people, he believes, and he wants to be the one to awaken it. As one of the other characters comments, however, he only sacrifices himself—and his family—to his opinions. Niels, in contrast, is the exact opposite of Emanuel, a young, upwardly mobile peasant, writing for the local newspapers in his spare time, ambitious, hopeful for the future. Everywhere, signs of change are in the air, but Emanuel cannot understand where they are leading. His vague dreams and misplaced ideals only lead him astray. His doubts and struggles are vividly portrayed by the author in this important novel of the birth of the modern age in Denmark.

Further Reading

Gray, Charlotte Schiander. "From Opposition to Identification: The Social and Psychological Structure Behind Henrik Pontoppidan's Literary Development." *Scandinavian Studies* 51 (Summer, 1979): 273-284. Examines the character of Emanuel Hansted as a kind of negative parallel to the author, describing how Pontoppidan swerves away from Hansted's excessive idealism in his own authorial perspective.

Ingwersen, Niels. "The Crisis of the Modern Breakthrough." In *A History of Danish Literature*, edited by Sven H. Rossel. Lincoln: University of Nebraska Press, in cooperation with the American-Scandinavian Foundation, 1992. Contains a few pages summarizing Pontoppidan's life, literary career, and writings. Describes *The Promised Land* as one of his three major novels, all of which depict protagonists who fail to attain the promise of their youth.

Jones, W. Glyn. "Henrik Pontoppidan (1857-1943)." *Modern Language Review* 52, no. 3 (July, 1957): 576-583. Emphasizes Pontoppidan's interest in Danish history and politics, especially his relationship to the government of Jacob Brønnum Scavenius Estrup. Asserts that the novel is the author's moral judgment on the Danish nation.

Lebowitz, Naomi. "The World's Pontoppidan and His *Lykke Per.*" *Scandinavian Studies* 78, no. 1 (Spring, 2006): 43-70. Focuses on Pontoppidan's eight-volume novel *Lykke-Per* (1898-1904), which has never been translated into English. Describes how *Lykke-Per* is concerned with the problem of spiritual authority during the early years of Danish modernism; compares the novel's protagonist to Pontoppidan. Mentions *The Promised Land* and other works by Pontoppidan.

Madsen, Borge. "*The Promised Land.*" In *Scandinavian Studies*, edited by Carl F. Bayerschmidt and Erik J. Friis. Seattle: University of Washington Press, 1965. Focuses on the inner psychology of Emanuel Hansted, exploring the motivations behind his impracticality and the novel's ambivalent perspective toward the fantastic.

Mitchell, P. M. *Henrik Pontoppidan.* Boston: Twayne, 1979. Provides an excellent introduction to Pontoppidan's work. Discussion of *The Promised Land* emphasizes the novel's skepticism toward traditional Danish state and church structures.

Robertson, John George. "Henrik Pontopiddan." In *Essays and Addresses on Literature.* 1935. Reprint. Freeport, N.Y.: Books for Libraries Press, 1968. Explores *The Promised Land* as a manual for the disillusioned. Discusses the heavy influence of the works of Norwegian playwright Henrik Ibsen on Pontopiddan's work.

The Prophet

Author: Kahlil Gibran (1883-1931)
First published: 1923
Type of work: Poetry
Type of plot: Philosophical
Time of plot: Ielool, the month of reaping
Locale: Orphalese

Principal characters:
ALMUSTAFA, a mystic and prophet
ALMITRA, a seer

The Poem:

The Prophet, an old man named Almustafa, is about to board a ship that has arrived to take him back to his native land after twelve years among the people of the city of Orphalese. In these twelve years the people of the city have come to love and revere the Prophet for his wisdom and gentle spirit, and they gather in the great square before the temple and beseech him not to leave but to remain with them forever. As the multitude weeps and pleads, Almitra, the seer who had first befriended the Prophet on his arrival in the city, comes out of the sanctuary and asks him to speak to the people about life.

Almitra asks that he first speak of love, whereupon the Prophet admonishes the hushed audience to follow love when he beckons, even though he might wound as he caresses, might destroy dreams as he entices. For love, he says, demands complete commitment, a testing in the sacred fires, if one is to see into one's own heart and have knowledge of life's heart. The cowardly should cover themselves and flee from love, and those who can never be possessed by love can never know fulfillment.

The Prophet is then asked to speak of marriage, children, giving, eating and drinking, work, joy and sorrow, houses, clothes, buying and selling, and crime and punishment. In response to the latter request by a judge of the city, the Prophet speaks at length, pointing out that whereas the most righteous cannot rise above the highest that is in all people, so the weak and wicked cannot fall below the lowest in all people; therefore, people must condemn lightly, for they, the whole, are not entirely blameless for the evil done by one of their parts.

Then a lawyer in the crowd asks for comment on laws, an orator asks for a talk on freedom, and a woman priest asks for discussion on reason and passion. The Prophet compares reason to a ship's rudder and passion to its sails. Without both, a ship is useless. Without the rudder it will toss aimlessly, and without the sails it will lie becalmed like a wingless bird.

The Prophet then speaks of pain, teaching, friendship, talking, time, good and evil, prayer, pleasure, beauty—which he finds too elusive for definition—religion, death, and self-knowledge—wherein he likens the self to a limitless, immeasurable, sea. Of death he urges mature acceptance, for, like the brook and the lake, life and death are one.

By the time the Prophet has finished speaking, twilight has fallen. He goes straight to his ship and bids a final farewell to his followers. As the ship lifts anchor, the sorrowful crowd disperses until only Almitra remains upon the seawall, watching his ship recede into the dusk and remembering his promise to return in another way at another time.

Critical Evaluation:

Kahlil Gibran's *The Prophet* comprises twenty-seven poetic essays on various aspects of life, preceded by an introduction and followed by a farewell. In the farewell, the Prophet, newly born, promises to return to his people after a momentary rest upon the wind. Thus, the continuity of life is implied—the circle of birth, death, and rebirth.

The Prophet belongs to a unique group of works that include Edward FitzGerald's *The Rubáiyát of Omar Khayyám* (1859) and certain works of William Blake, to whom Gibran has been compared. FitzGerald's translation of *The Rubáiyát of Omar Khayyám* appeals especially to impressionable young adults: The poem had been bound in leather in a miniature edition and used as a prom favor at college dances.

Similarly, *The Prophet* owes much of its popularity to the young, who find in Gibran's poetry the elusive quality of sincerity. At the height of its popularity in the 1960's, *The Prophet* sold about five thousand copies per week. In large part because of personal recommendations rather than marketing, this best known of Gibran's seventeen published books (nine in Arabic and eight in English) has been published in more than twenty languages and has sold tens of millions of copies, making Gibran one of the most widely published poets, behind only William Shakespeare and Lao Tzu. The hardcover sales of this thin volume made Gibran the best-selling Arabic author of the twentieth century, a remarkable feat considering *The Prophet* is a book of poetry. *The Prophet* has sold more copies for publisher Alfred A. Knopf than any other book in the publisher's history.

Gibran intended *The Prophet* to be the first part of a trilogy—followed by *The Garden of the Prophet* and *The Death of the Prophet*. The second of this series was published posthumously (in 1933) and the third title was written by Jason Leen and released in 1979. Often compared to Friedrich Nietzsche's *Also sprach Zarathustra: Ein Buch für Alle und Keinen* (1883-1885; *Thus Spake Zarathustra*, 1896), another philosophical, prophetical work in which divine beings walk among humans and dispense wisdom, *The Prophet* has been interpreted as Gibran's longing to return to Lebanon. Penned after twelve years of living in New York City, Gibran views his absence from his homeland as an exile. The Prophet, Almustafa, also twelve years in exile, addresses the citizens of Orphalese, whom he has come to love and admire, much as Gibran admired his fellow Greenwich Village neighbors. Almitra likely was inspired by Mary Haskell, head of a Boston school who became Gibran's muse.

To understand the power of Gibran's words, it is necessary to know something of his life, of the agonies of remorse that burned within him, and of the loneliness of spirit that heightened his senses. Gibran was born in Bsharri, Lebanon (then a part of Ottoman Syria), the son of a poor shepherd family. When he was twelve years old, his mother took the family to the United States, to the city of Boston, hoping, like many immigrants of the day, to gain wealth quickly and then return to Lebanon. Gibran's easygoing father had remained in Lebanon to care for the family's small holdings. Soon the opportunities in the United States were apparent, and the mother decided that the sensitive Gibran must be educated. The older son and the two daughters joined the mother at unskilled labor to earn the money with which Gibran might gain an education. Within a few years, the family had been decimated by tuberculosis, and only Gibran and his sister, Marianna, remained. He never completely recovered from his grief and his sense of guilt for the deaths of his family members, who had, in a sense, died for him.

Bolstered by the loyalty and industry of Marianna, Gibran began to write and draw. He illustrated his own writings, as had Blake. Financial success was elusive, but Gibran gained a patron who encouraged him to go abroad for study. He spent two years in Paris, then returned to the United States and soon set up a studio in Greenwich Village, where he worked for the remainder of his life. He began to write and publish in the English language in 1918 with *The Madman*, and in 1923 he published his masterpiece, *The Prophet*.

Never out of print, *The Prophet* has consistently found readers, but critics have been less kind, calling the work long and tedious; it is, however, only twenty-thousand words. It is a work that seems destined to be embraced by its youthful readers and repelled by its older critics, for it is often criticized for dispensing simplistic wisdom in a mystical fashion that defies experience and common sense. The messages of *The Prophet* ring hollow with more jaded critics when they submit the verse to closer inspection.

Gibran's insistent subjectivity, shrouded in a religious-like mysticism, swirls the reader's mind toward the center of a vortex in which evil has been flung aside and in which the human soul stands revealed in all its nobility and goodness. However, from a more practical standpoint, critics have noted, for example, that Almustafa, an old man, stands in one spot from morning until night, delivering one sermon after another without pausing to rest himself or his audience.

Gibran's illustrations that accompany most of the poetry are often as striking as the words. Indeed, his works now hang in some of America's finest art museums. In addition to living in Boston and in New York City, Gibran spent two years in Paris and studied at the famed École des Beaux-Arts with French sculptor Auguste Rodin.

Always frail, Gibran was driven beyond endurance by an inner force that would not let him rest. Death from a liver ailment caused by years of alcoholism overtook him in 1931 in the full flower of his productivity. His body was returned to Lebanon and buried with great honors in the village of his birth.

Revised by Randy L. Abbott

Further Reading

Acocella, Joan. "Prophet Motive: The Kahlil Gibran Phenomenon." *The New Yorker*, January 7, 2008. An extensive biography of Gibran and an overview of his literary career. Critiques the poet's writings, including *The Prophet*. Describes how Gibran's literary idealism and sentimentality were popular with readers but caused contemporary writers and artists to ignore his work.

Bushrui, Suheil B., and Joe Jenkins. *Kahlil Gibran, Man and Poet: A New Biography*. Boston: Oneworld, 1999. A meticulously researched biography that provides updated information about Gibran's life and literary contributions. Includes illustrations of and by Gibran as well as notes and an extensive bibliography.

Gibran, Jean. *Kahlil Gibran: His Life and World*. Boston: New York Graphic Society, 1974. Rev. ed. New York: Interlink Books, 1998. This revised and updated work provides a general overview of Gibran's life and the influences that shaped his writings. General references to *The Prophet* are found throughout.

Hilu, Virginia, ed. *Beloved Prophet: The Love Letters of Kahlil Gibran and Mary Haskell, and Her Private Journal*. 1972. Reprint. New York: Knopf, 1985. More than six hundred letters and decades of journals were processed by the editor and arranged to present the romantic and spiritual relationship between Gibran, the young poet, and Mary Haskell, the older school teacher who became both his most trusted collaborator and his benefactor.

Nassar, Eugene Paul. "Cultural Discontinuity in the Works of Kahlil Gibran." *MELUS* 7, no. 2 (Summer, 1980): 21-36. Looks at Gibran's experiences of cultural alienation and how these became the theme of loneliness that recurs in his writings, including *The Prophet*. The authors compare this poem to works by William Blake, Walt Whitman, and others.

Waterfield, Robin. *Prophet: The Life and Times of Kahlil Gibran*. New York: St. Martin's Press, 1998. The biographer depicts Gibran as an unhappy man, who was at home neither in his native Arab culture nor in the United States. Assesses Gibran's influence on Arabic literature and New Age spirituality. Concludes that despite the poet's personal conflicts, Gibran produced a body of work that remains meaningful to readers.

Young, Barbara. *This Man from Lebanon: A Study of Kahlil Gibran*. 1945. Reprint. New York: Knopf, 1981. Young, a long-time secretary and confidant to Gibran, provides an intimate, behind-the scenes picture of Gibran's life and times. *The Prophet* is discussed as it relates to influential events and people in Gibran's life.

Prosas Profanas, and Other Poems

Author: Rubén Darío (1867-1916)
First published: Prosas profanas, y otros poemas, 1896
   (English translation, 1922)
Type of work: Poetry

Although Latin American literature has a long and honorable history, it was not until the end of the nineteenth century that it began to produce writers, especially poets, whose innovative techniques and technical mastery brought them worldwide recognition as significant and influential artists. Among this group, one of the first, and certainly one of the most important, was Rubén Darío, whose *Prosas Profanas* ("profane hymns") is among the most innovative and enduring works of Latin American verse. As a key part of Darío's complete writings—which are considerable, given the brief span of his life—*Prosas Profanas* is indicative of the scope, breadth, and power of his poetic achievements.

Born in Metapa, Nicaragua, in January, 1867, and christened Félix Rubén García Sarmiento, the poet began a lifetime of wandering at the age of fourteen. By the time he was nineteen Darío was living and studying in Chile, where he spent several years that were critical to his development as a writer; in Chile he absorbed the latest works by Central and South American authors as well as European authors. He later lived in Argentina, Spain, and France, where he edited an influential and innovative literary journal, *Mundial*, in Paris.

With the outbreak of World War I, Darío returned to live in Latin America. To relieve his considerable financial difficulties, he embarked on a strenuous lecturing tour that took him as far north as New York City, where he fell seriously ill. He returned home to Nicaragua, where he died on February 6, 1916, at the age of forty-nine.

At an early time during his travels, he had shortened his name to Rubén Darío. The Mexican writer Octavio Paz, among others, saw in this choice of names a deliberate attempt by the poet to link himself to the great literary and artistic traditions of the Middle East, uniting both Jewish (Ruben) and non-Jewish (Darius, king of Persia) heritages. Whatever the ultimate source or reason, his choice of name clearly indicates that Darío considered himself to be, like his poetry, original, but he also tacitly acknowledged his debt to the great creations and creators of the past.

Latin America had always maintained close cultural ties with Europe and prided itself on its transatlantic culture. This was especially true in artistic matters, including literary influences. After the middle of the nineteenth century, these European influences exerted a profound pressure on Latin American writers. The literary models of modernism and Symbolism, largely inspired by French examples, were especially important, and Darío's *Prosas Profanas* shows the considerable influence of both.

Modernism helped writers such as Darío break free of the conventions of earlier poetry. Modernism encouraged new and innovative uses of language, including the incorporation and adaptation of peasant or folk forms and the creation of new and individual poetic structures. In the hands of a writer such as Darío, modernism and the use of rhythm were more than poetic forms or devices. Modernism and rhythm became for him a way of looking at the world and seeing everything in it as mysteriously yet intimately connected. Darío believed that it was the poet alone who could express these connections, through the power of the art of poetry. For Darío, analogy was an exalted expression of the imagination.

Darío was also deeply influenced by the writings of authors such as Edgar Allan Poe and Walt Whitman, but his natural preference, reinforced by his readings of French poets such as Charles Baudelaire, was for the aristocratic refinement and symbolic mannerism of Poe rather than the democratic vistas and demotic cadences of Whitman. Darío's careful choice of words, his preference for sensuous and emotion-laden rhythmic patterns, and his refined and often rarefied subject matter all reveal his debt to Poe and to Poe's French admirers. Throughout *Prosas Profanas* the scenes and settings are of far-off and long-ago places, often aristocratic and courtly, with an emphasis on the artificial and the self-consciously theatrical.

The influences of modernism and Symbolism are especially notable in *Prosas Profanas*; the poems in this volume rely primarily on sensations and feelings rather than on ideas or logical progression. This is seen most clearly in the way that the various poems present the reader with a succession of different facets of human emotion. Darío, using his masterful command of language, symbolism, and analogy, moves smoothly from a frivolous tone to the hedonistic and on to the erotic, ending, finally, in a wistful, almost elegiac reflective fashion, affirming the presence and importance of beauty in human life while accepting beauty's momentary and perhaps illusory nature.

The poems in *Prosas Profanas* are linked through the feelings and emotions the various lyrics evoke rather than through the ideas they present. It seems to have been the poet's purpose to create in his readers an appreciation of the

awakening to a sense of pleasure, including sensual, even erotic pleasure—an experience that he had encountered in his own life. The poems attempt to capture those emotions through the use of allusive, symbolic language and settings. While there is in the poems certainly an acknowledgment that such pleasure is fleeting, there is also the insistence that pleasure is no less real for being transitory.

"It was a gentle air" is a representative poem expressing this sensibility. Set in a kingly court, perhaps "in the reign of Louis, King of France," perhaps a completely imaginary setting that never existed in reality, the poem tells in a dreamlike fashion of a time when courtiers and courtesans assumed various guises, sometimes of classical deities and at other times of simple shepherds and their lovers, yet all are equally artificial while remaining, in some paradoxical fashion, real. Throughout the poem there is a constant sense of the erotic, never quite openly stated but expressed in a subtle, hinted fashion. The power of the verse—and perhaps its true meaning—comes in its use of the sounds and resonances of the words and their rhythms as well as their references to lost golden ages. The French royal court before the Revolution and the mythical Arcadia are evoked as representative of times and places where beauty and pleasure were accorded their true and therefore dominant place in human life. Time and modern life have left this land behind, but the poems remember and, in a sense, re-create beauty and pleasure for the reader. In this fashion, lost beauty is revived, if only in the mind of the reader.

"Sonatina" continues the theme through the metaphor of the fairy tale. The sad princess sits in her tower, waiting for her prince to come and rescue her. She is like a butterfly, imprisoned in its cocoon and ready to awake. Already, in the distance, "the joyous knight who adores you unseen" is on his way. The poem is about the princess in the beautiful, tragic moment before her deliverance.

The poems "Blazon" and "The Swan" use the swan, that most typically poetic of birds, in subtly different fashions. In "Blazon," the "snow-white Olympic swan" is praised as the symbol and the inspiration of true poetry. The swan is, in a sense, both the poem and the poet, who makes art and who makes his or her life into a work of art: "the regal bird who, dying, rhymes the soul in his song." This power is heightened in "The Swan," where through the romantic power of art, the song of the swan—which was once heard only at its death—never ceases; instead of marking an end, the song signals "a new dawning and a new life."

"Symphony in Gray Major" is one of the key poems in *Prosas Profanas*. In an impressionistic fashion the poem presents a seaside scene where the sun, the waves, and an old sailor dozing and dreaming on the wharf merge into memories of other places and other times ("that distant land of mists"), which then return to blend into the present. "Symphony in Gray Major" is notable not for what it reveals but for what it suggests.

Prosas Profanas occupies a central position in Rubén Darío's works. It reveals an artist who is capable of exploring to the utmost the limits of language and imagery and who does so with wit, imagination, and a natural affection for the positive rhythms of human existence.

Michael Witkoski

Further Reading

Acereda, Alberto, and Rigoberto Guevara. *Modernism, Rubén Darío, and the Poetics of Despair.* Dallas, Tex.: University Press of America, 2004. Focuses on the element of despair in Darío's life and work, placing this depression within the context of nineteenth century philosophy, particularly the works of Arthur Schopenhauer.

Castro, Juan E. de. "Rubén Darío Visits Ricardo Palma: Tradition, Cosmopolitanism, and the Development of an Independent Latin American Literature." In *The Spaces of Latin American Literature: Tradition, Globalization, and Cultural Production.* New York: Palgrave Macmillan, 2008. Describes how Darío and other Latin American writers, artists, and intellectuals negotiated a relationship with Western culture. Demonstrates how the region's literature has roots in specific cultural, political, and economic conditions.

Gonzales-Gerth, Michael, and George D. Schade, eds. *Rubén Darío Centennial Studies.* Austin: University of Texas Press, 1970. Collection of essays considers various aspects of Darío's work and is especially informative regarding the extent of his knowledge of the works of other poets and their contributions.

Imbert, Enrique Anderson. "Rubén Darío." In *Latin American Writers*, edited by Carlos A. Sole. New York: Charles Scribner's Sons, 1989. Assesses Darío's writings both as an independent body of work and as an influence on Latin American literature in general. Argues convincingly that Darío's writings divide Latin American literature into "before" and "after" periods, and that therefore Darío is a major transitional figure.

Moreno, Cesar Fernandez, ed. *Latin America in Its Literature.* Translated by Mary G. Berg, edited by Ivan A. Schulman. New York: Holmes & Meier, 1980. Thematic study of the region's writers addresses Darío's literary contributions in a number of areas. Significant essays touching on Darío include "Ruptures of Tradition," "The Language of Literature," and "Social Functions of Literature." Excellent for placing Darío within his social, political, and cultural context.

Paz, Octavio. Introduction to *Selected Poems*, by Rubén Darío. Translated by Lysander Kemp. 1965. Reprint. Austin: University of Texas Press, 1988. A premier Latin American author presents an insightful and rewarding study of Darío, placing his work within the context of both Hispanic literature in particular and world literature in general.

Proserpine and Ceres

Author: Unknown
First published: Unknown
Type of work: Short fiction
Type of plot: Myth
Time of plot: Antiquity
Locale: The Mediterranean

Principal characters:
CERES, the goddess of fertility
PROSERPINE, her daughter
HADES, the king of the underworld
VENUS, the goddess of love
CUPID, her son
TRIPTOLEMUS, the builder of a temple to Ceres
ARETHUSA, a fountain nymph
ALPHEUS, a river god
DIANA, the goddess of the hunt
JUPITER, the king of the gods
MERCURY, a messenger of the gods

The Story:

One of the Titans, Typhoeus, long imprisoned for his part in the rebellion against Jupiter, lies in agony beneath Mount Aetna on the island of Sicily in the Mediterranean Sea. When Typhoeus groans and stirs, he shakes the sea and the island of Sicily so much that the god of the underworld, Hades, becomes frightened lest his kingdom be revealed to the light of day.

Rising to the upper world to make entrance to his kingdom, Hades is discovered by Venus, who orders her son Cupid to aim one of his love darts into the breast of Hades and so cause him to fall in love with Proserpine, daughter of Ceres, goddess of fertility. Proserpine went with her companions to gather flowers by the banks of a stream in the beautiful vale of Enna. There Hades, stricken by Cupid's dart, sees Proserpine, seizes her, and lashes his fiery horses to greater speed as he carries her away. In her fright the girl drops her apron, full of flowers she gathered. At the River Cyane, Hades strikes the earth with his scepter, causing a passageway to appear through which he drives his chariot and takes his captive to the underworld.

Ceres searches for her daughter everywhere. At last, sad and tired, she sits down to rest. A peasant and his daughter find her in her disguise as an old woman; they take pity on her and urge her to go with them to their rude home. When the three arrive at the house, they find that the peasant's only son, Triptolemus, is dying. Ceres first gathers some poppies. Then, kissing the child, she restores him to health. The happy family bids her to join them in their simple meal of honey, cream, apples, and curds. Ceres puts some of the poppy juice in the boy's milk. That night when he is sleeping, she places the child in the fire. The mother, awakening, seizes her child from the flames. Ceres assumes her proper form and tells the parents that it was her plan to make the boy immortal. Since the mother hindered that plan, she will instead teach him the use of the plow.

Then the goddess mother continues her search for Proserpine until she returns to Sicily. There, at the very spot Hades entered the underworld, she asks the river nymph if she saw anything of her daughter. Fearful of punishment, the river nymph refuses to tell what she saw but gave to Ceres the belt of Proserpine, which the girl lost in her struggles.

Ceres decides to take revenge upon the land, to deny it further gift of her favors so that herbage and grain will not grow. In an effort to save the land that Ceres is intent upon cursing, the fountain Arethusa tells the following story to Ceres. Arethusa was hunting in the forest, where she was formerly a woodland nymph. Finding a stream, she decided to bathe. As she sported in the water, the river god Alpheus began to call her. Frightened, the nymph ran, the god pursuing.

The goddess Diana, seeing her plight, changed Arethusa into a fountain that ran through the underworld and emerged in Sicily. While passing through the underworld, Arethusa saw Proserpine, now queen of the dead, sad at the separation from her mother but at the same time bearing the dignity and power of the bride of Hades. Ceres immediately demanded help from Jupiter, ruler of the gods. The king of the gods said that Proserpine should be allowed to return to the valley of Enna from which she was abducted only if in the underworld she took no food.

Mercury was sent to demand Proserpine for her mother. Proserpine, however, had eaten of a pomegranate. She had eaten only part of the fruit, however, so a compromise was made. Half of the time she was to pass with her mother and the rest with Hades. Ceres, happy over the return of Proserpine during one half of each year, caused the earth to be fertile again during the time Proserpine lived with her.

Ceres remembers her promise to the peasant boy, Triptolemus. She teaches him to plow and to plant seed, and he gathers with her all the valuable seeds of the earth. In gratitude the peasant's son builds a temple to Ceres in Eleusis where priests administer rites called the Eleusinian mysteries. Those rites surpass all other Greek religious celebrations. The mysteries involve, as does the story of Proserpine and Ceres, the cycle of death and growth.

Critical Evaluation:

This fertility myth seems to have Mycenaean (pre-Homeric) origins, but the earliest and in many ways the best version that survives is from the late seventh century B.C.E. in the Homeric hymn to Demeter, or Ceres. Demeter (either "earth mother" or "grain mother") and her daughter Persephone (corrupted by the Romans into Proserpina) were originally two aspects of one mythic personality: The mother was associated with the harvest, the daughter with the sprouting grain. The Greeks, fearfully avoiding mention of the daughter's name, called her simply Kore, that is, "grain" maiden. This practice of avoiding the actual name was usual with the powerful and mysterious chthonian (underworld) deities whom the Greeks wished not to risk offending.

The literary history of the myth is extensive, including two appearances in Ovid—*Metamorphoses* (c. 8 C.E.; English translation, 1567) and *Fasti* (c. 8 C.E.; English translation, 1859)—but there are only minor variations, such as where the rape occurred, who Triptolemus was, how many pomegranate seeds Proserpine ate, and how much of the year she remains with Hades. The above synopsis, which is a conflation of Ovid's accounts, differs from the Homeric hymn in the Triptolemus episode. In the hymn, Ceres' hosts, Celeus and Metanira, are not peasants but the rulers of Eleusis, near Athens. In her old age, Metanira gives birth to a child, Demophon, whom she gives to Ceres, disguised as Doso, to suckle. Triptolemus was one of Eleusis's youthful nobility and was among the first to participate in Ceres' mysteries, or secret rites, in the temple built by Celeus. The hymn also has Proserpine spend one-third of the year with her husband below the earth; this reflects a tripartite seasonal year of spring, summer, winter. Despite mention in the hymn that Proserpine emerges to the upperworld in the spring, reputable scholars argue that her four months' absence is associated with the summer-long storage of harvested grain in June. (The grain was put in jars in the cool earth till planting in the winter.) The traditional interpretation is that the fresh seed grain is planted in the winter and the maiden shoots emerge in the early spring.

The Eleusinian mysteries most closely resemble what one might call a universal religion. Its objective is preparation for eternal peace through understanding the mystery of cyclic growth. Although great numbers of Greek-speaking persons were initiated into the mysteries, little authoritative information about them survives. Clement of Alexandria, a convert to Christianity, reveals that votaries dramatized the myth of Ceres and Proserpine, fasted, handled sacred objects, and partook of the sacramental porridge of water, flour, and mint that Ceres was offered at Eleusis. The Lesser Mysteries were celebrated in Athens in the early spring; they consisted of prayers, purifications, and the like. The Great Mysteries were performed in September/October; nine days of grand procession from Athens to Eleusis and back featured numerous rituals, at the height of which priests and priestesses were consecrated. Certainly the mysteries relied heavily on symbolic ritual and mythic reenactment. The nine days of the Greater Mysteries correspond to the nine days of Ceres' fasting as she searched for her daughter; the pomegranate with its many "bloody" seeds symbolizes fertility; Proserpine's marriage to Hades metaphorically explains the mystery of fertilization and growth within the earth. It is even theorized that the secret dramas included ritualistic sexuality, imitating the *hieros gamos* ("sacred union") of the underworld deities that brings fertility to the fields. Such a ritual was common to a number of cults, and within the myth of Ceres herself is her union with her brother Jupiter, the sky god, which produces Proserpine.

The basic structure of the myth is simple: peaceful innocence, sudden violence, misguided revenge, and finally reconciliation; within this dramatic structure, the mythmakers have woven origins of the Eleusinian cult. Ovid's insertion of the Arethusa myth is forced, since it is merely preparation for its lengthier telling immediately following in *Metamorphoses*. There are also some excellent descriptive sequences: the gathering of flowers by Proserpine, the sudden dark violence of Hades, the awesome burning of Metanira's child in the fire. Finally, the characterizations of both in Ovid's versions and in the hymn are classic: Proserpine as the innocent virgin, carefully protected; Demeter, the doting mother; Hades, the lustful villain who creates trouble when he makes an unprecedented appearance in the upperworld; Jupiter, the supreme administrator and magistrate, who must act to prevent the extinction, through starvation, of humanity (the gods' sacrificers) and who must strike a compromise between forces of equal power. The resolution is no doubt necessary to explain why in other myths Proserpine seems quite at ease in her role as queen of the dead. It is likely that her character is a confusion of the witch goddess, Hecate, and a primitive earth goddess. In the underworld, she rules with authority. There she appears to the various heroes who descend to Hades, including Orpheus, Aeneas, and others; she is also the object of an attempted rape by Theseus and Pirithous. The most significant twentieth century adaptation of the myth is the musical drama *Persephone* (1934) by Igor Stravinsky and André Gide, in which the heroine willingly sacrifices herself to bring joy and youth to the gloomy realm below.

"Critical Evaluation" by E. N. Genovese

Further Reading

Agha-Jaffar, Tamara. *Demeter and Persephone: Lessons from a Myth.* Jefferson, N.C.: McFarland, 2002. Agha-Jaffar recounts the myth of Proserpine and Ceres, interpreting it from the perspectives of both mother and daughter. She analyzes the symbolism, subject of rape, the meaning of the underworld, and other aspects of the story to demonstrate its relevance to modern society.

Campbell, Joseph. *The Masks of God: Occidental Mythology.* New York: Viking Press, 1964. Campbell discusses the images and symbolism of the myth of Proserpine and Ceres.

Donovan, Josephine. *After the Fall: The Demeter-Persephone Myth in Wharton, Cather, and Glasgow.* University Park: Pennsylvania State University Press, 1989. Analyzes the fictional symbols of Proserpine and Ceres in works by three American women writers. Donovan examines the image of the mother-daughter relationship as it is revealed in these modern treatments.

Downing, Christine, ed. *The Long Journey Home: Re-vision-*

ing the Myth of Demeter and Persephone for Our Time. Boston: Shambhala, 1994. A collection of essays, prose, and poetry interpreting the myth from numerous perspectives, including twentieth century women's retellings of the story.

Frazer, James. *The Golden Bough: A Study in Magic and Religion.* New York: Macmillan, 1922. Analyzes the Eleusinian mysteries associated with Ceres and Proserpine. Shows their similarities to the Egyptian goddesses Isis and Osiris, the Syrian Ishtar, and other ancient deities. Includes some mention of human sacrifice associated with Proserpine's death.

Gimbutas, Marija. *The Language of the Goddess.* San Francisco: Harper & Row, 1989. Places Proserpine and Ceres in the context of their symbolic meaning: life-giving and fertility. Ceres is seen as the earth mother and appears as a pregnant woman in pottery and burial sites.

Graves, Robert. *The Greek Myths.* New York: Penguin Books, 1960. Reprint. Combined ed. New York: Penguin Books, 1992. A thorough retelling of the story of Ceres and Proserpine as corn goddesses. Proserpine is also connected with images of Aphrodite and Adonis. Graves claims that Proserpine is involved with the Eleusinian mysteries.

Pseudolus

Author: Plautus (c. 254-184 B.C.E.)
First produced: 191 B.C.E. (English translation, 1774)
Type of work: Drama
Type of plot: Comedy
Time of plot: Late third century B.C.E.
Locale: Athens

Principal characters:
SIMO, an old Athenian gentleman
CALIDORUS, his son
PSEUDOLUS, Simo's servant
BALLIO, a procurer, owner of Phoenicium
HARPAX, a messenger
SIMIA, a servant of one of Calidorus's friends
PHOENICIUM, a slave girl loved by Calidorus

The Story:

Pseudolus, a servant of the Athenian Simo, observes one day that his master's son Calidorus is deeply despondent about something. Questioning him on the matter, Pseudolus is given a letter from Phoenicium, a slave girl with whom Calidorus is in love. She has written that Ballio, her master, has sold her to a Macedonian military officer for the sum of twenty minae. However, the transaction is not yet complete; the officer has given Ballio fifteen minae to seal the bargain and has arranged that Phoenicium is to be delivered to a servant of his who will bring the remaining five minae and a letter bearing a seal to match the one the officer has made with his ring and left in Ballio's keeping. This servant is to arrive during the festival of Bacchus, now being celebrated. Calidorus is thoroughly upset by this news, for he has no money with which to buy Phoenicium and no prospect of acquiring any. Desperate, he appeals to the wily Pseudolus for help. With great self-confidence, the servant promises to trick Calidorus's father, Simo, out of the money.

Before any plan can be formulated, Ballio appears, cursing and beating some of his slaves. Calidorus and Pseudolus approach him and beg him to reconsider his bargain, pointing

out that Phoenicium has been promised to Calidorus as soon as the young man can find the money to pay for her. The unscrupulous Ballio remains unmoved and even taunts Calidorus for his poverty and his inability to get money from his father. Before they part, however, he craftily points out that today is the day on which the officer has agreed to send his final installment of the payment for Phoenicium and that if the promised money is not received, Ballio will be free to sell her to another bidder.

As Pseudolus is turning over various plans in his mind, he overhears Simo talking to a friend and learns that the old man has already heard of Calidorus's plight and has steeled himself in advance against any plea for money that his son might make. Finding his task thus complicated, Pseudolus steps forward and brazenly admits his commission, telling Simo that he intends to get the twenty minae from him and that Simo should consequently be on his guard. The slave also tells his master that he intends to trick Ballio out of the slave girl. Simo is skeptical, but Pseudolus finally goads him into promising to pay for the girl if Pseudolus is successful in getting her away from the procurer.

Soon afterward, Pseudolus is fortunate enough to overhear a newcomer identify himself as Harpax, the Macedonian captain's messenger, come to conclude the dealings for Phoenicium. Accosting the messenger, Pseudolus identifies himself as one of Ballio's servants and persuades Harpax to allow him to deliver the sealed letter that is to identify the rightful purchaser. Then he induces Harpax to go to an inn to rest from his journey until Pseudolus comes to get him. When the messenger has gone, Calidorus appears in the company of a friend, and in the conversation that follows, the latter agrees to lend five minae for the execution of Pseudolus's plot. He agrees, moreover, to allow his servant Simia to be used in the enterprise.

Once these arrangements are made, the three leave to conclude their preparations. Ballio appears in the company of a cook, and it becomes clear that it is the procurer's birthday and that he is preparing a feast for his customers. Before Ballio goes into his house, he discloses that Simo has met him in the marketplace and warned him to be on his guard against Pseudolus's plot.

Immediately after Ballio goes inside, Pseudolus appears with Simia. During their conversation, Simia reveals himself to be shrewd and wily, and in the ensuing confrontation with Ballio he proves as apt a dissembler as Pseudolus himself. When Ballio comes out of his house, Simia approaches him and asks directions to find the procurer. Ballio identifies himself, but, suspicious, he asks Simia the name of the man who sent him. For a moment, the eavesdropping Pseudolus is afraid that his plot has collapsed, for Simia has not been told the name of the Macedonian captain. Simia adroitly evades the trap, however, by pretending suspicion on his own part and refusing to give Ballio the sealed letter until the procurer has himself identified Phoenicium's purchaser. Ballio does so, receives the letter and the money, and releases Phoenicium into Simia's custody.

After Simia and Phoenicium have gone, Ballio, congratulating himself on having outwitted Pseudolus, chuckles at the prospect of the servant making his tardy effort to obtain the girl. When Simo appears, the procurer expresses his certainty that Pseudolus has been foiled and declares that he will give Simo twenty minae and relinquish his right to the girl as well if Pseudolus is successful in his plot.

At that moment Harpax enters, grumbling that Pseudolus has not come to get him as he had promised to do. Confronting Ballio, he learns the procurer's identity and sets about to close the bargain his master had made. Ballio, convinced that Harpax is in the employ of Pseudolus, does his best to humiliate the messenger, until Harpax mentions having given the sealed letter to a "servant" of Ballio. From the description,

Ballio realizes with chagrin that he has been thoroughly duped. Simo holds him to his word regarding the twenty minae and the relinquishment of his rights to Phoenicium, and Harpax, learning that the girl is no longer available, insists that Ballio return the fifteen minae the captain had already deposited.

Meanwhile, Pseudolus, Calidorus, and Phoenicium are celebrating their victory with wine. Pseudolus later meets Simo and demands the twenty minae that the old man owes him for having successfully tricked Ballio. As the money is not coming out of his own pocket, Simo turns it over with good grace. Pseudolus returns half the sum and takes his master off to drink to their good fortune.

Critical Evaluation:

Between the death of Aristophanes, the first Greek master of comedy, and the Roman Plautus, who has been described as the most successful comic poet in the ancient world, the Greek Menander created the New Comedy. Only one complete play by Menander is now extant, but most Roman comedies are known, from fragments and various accounts, to be imitations of Greek models. Only twenty of the approximately one hundred plays written by Plautus—who is also the first known professional playwright—remain.

Plautus was the first Latin author whose work has survived; he was very popular in Rome. His plays greatly influenced the comedies of William Shakespeare and Molière, and, as recently as the 1960's, an adaptation combining three of his plays, including *Pseudolus* (which literally means "the trickster"), achieved considerable success as a Broadway musical titled *A Funny Thing Happened on the Way to the Forum* (pr., pb. 1962), which was in turn adapted as a motion picture (1966).

Whereas some of Shakespeare's comedies have been described as being serious, dark, or even problem plays, the comedies of Plautus are almost always festive and playful. Performed at planting or harvest festivals, the plays offered Roman audiences an opportunity to free themselves temporarily from the confines of their society, which demanded strict adherence to law, filial obedience—fathers could legally execute their children—and pursuit of financial gain. Roman morality has been described as puritanical, and the institution of slavery was vital to Roman civilization. What the comedies offered was an inversion of these cultural values: The slave becomes master over his master, the son over his father, youth over age. In the comic world of Plautus, money and morality merely get in the way, and those who are committed to either are usually the villains.

Actually, the term "villain" is a bit severe to describe any of the characters in a play like *Pseudolus*. The pimp (in Latin, *leno*) Ballio is more a rascal than a villain. He is a blocking character—that is, he prevents the good characters, the slave Pseudolus and his master's son, Calidorus, from having a good time. "Having a good time" in this case means arranging for Calidorus to gain possession of his girlfriend, Phoenicium, before Ballio can sell her to a Macedonian officer with the nearly unpronounceable name of Polymachaeroplagides. (Roman audiences would probably have laughed over such awkward Greek names; this one roughly translates as "many swords at the side.") The officer himself never appears onstage, but his orderly, Harpax (the name means "snatcher" or "thief"), is there to be outwitted, along with nearly everyone else, by the clever Pseudolus.

To turn the world familiar to his Roman audience upside down, Plautus sets the play in Athens, although perhaps any city in Greece would have sufficed, given the Roman prejudice against Greeks. Far from being the homeland of rational thinking or of Platonic idealism, the stage in Athens is a place of frivolity and license. The fact that Greek slaves often served as tutors and that knowledge of Greek was prized among Roman aristocrats did not prevent Greeks from being the objects of ridicule. Whereas, however, Calidorus performs as a typically inept adolescent in love and out of money, and Ballio is greedy, irascible, and heartless, Pseudolus is presented as clever, witty, and loyal. Perhaps in this characterization Plautus is paying some tribute to the Greek mind.

The plot is simple and conventional, which is what the audience would have expected. Sincere romantic love would have been out of place, and it is appropriate that Calidorus's boyish passion for Phoenicium is conventionally erotic. His role as a spendthrift and, therefore, penniless son and his father Simo's role as a well-to-do and unsympathetic parent are conventional, as is the role of Ballio, the unlikable pimp who first appears onstage lashing his slaves. Similarly, the clever Pseudolus is conventionally likable. What makes the play work is the way Pseudolus outwits Ballio and at the same time manages to trick Simo into funding the adventure. Through a friend of Calidorus, Pseudolus acquires the services of Simia (the name means "monkey"), who masquerades as Harpax and proves equally clever when it comes to duping Ballio. Plautus also sets up a subplot involving a cook hired by Ballio for his birthday banquet; Plautus does not develop that plot, but the cook has some good moments in the play.

The range of comic characters and the thematic triumphs of slave over master, youth over age, and love (of a sort) over profit account for much of the appeal of this comedy. Some of the clever wordplay also translates well, as in an early scene when Calidorus and Pseudolus call Ballio such names

as "scoundrel" and "slime" only to hear him placidly agree with them. Throughout the play, Pseudolus likes to refer to his schemes in military terms because he sees himself leading his legions against Ballio and taking on Simo. Above all, the satisfaction granted to the audience in this play is that of watching an unpleasant person being outsmarted.

Pseudolus appears toward the end of the play highly intoxicated and in a mood to celebrate, and it is in keeping with the tone of the play that Simo cannot resist being proud of his slave's wily triumph, even though he himself has been shown up. Part of Pseudolus's victory lies in the fact that he is so brazen as to tell Simo from the first to be on the watch for him. Plautus thus asserts a kind of comic justice. In the spirit of inverted values and of distorted historical probabilities, Pseudolus insists that Simo join him in his drunken carouse. He then turns to those in the audience and invites them to the next performance.

"Critical Evaluation" by Ron McFarland

Further Reading

Fraenkel, Eduard. *Plautine Elements in Plautus*. Translated by Tomas Drevikovsky and Frances Muecke. New York: Oxford University Press, 2007. This is the first English translation of a German study initially published in 1922. Fraenkel, an influential twentieth century classicist, provides an analytic overview of Plautus's plays, including their motifs of transformation and identification, mythological material, dialogue, and the predominance of the slave's role.

Garton, Charles. "How Roscius Acted Ballio." In *Personal Aspects of the Roman Theatre*. Toronto: Hakkert, 1972. The most renowned actor of his day, Roscius, played Ballio in *Pseudolus* instead of the lead role of the title character. Garton discusses comments made by Cicero and examines the role and how the actor appeared on stage.

Leigh, Matthew. *Comedy and the Rise of Rome*. New York: Oxford University Press, 2004. Analyzes the comedies of Plautus and Terence, placing them within the context of political and economic conditions in Rome during the third and second centuries B.C.E. Discusses how audiences of that time responded to these comedies.

Plautus, Titus Maccius. *Pseudolus/Plautus*. Edited by M. M. Wilcock. Bristol, England: Bristol Classical Press, 1987. In addition to the Latin text accompanied by an introduction and commentary in English, this edition presents close plot analysis of the play.

Segal, Erich. *Roman Laughter: The Comedy of Plautus*.

Cambridge, Mass.: Harvard University Press, 1968. Valuable study of Plautus's work discusses the social and cultural contexts in which the plays were written and originally performed and comments on their appeal to Roman audiences.

_____, ed. *Oxford Readings in Menander, Plautus, and Terence*. New York: Oxford University Press, 2001. Includes essays on Plautus and the public stage, the response of Plautus's audience, and traditions, theatrical improvisation, and mastery of comic language in his plays. *Pseudolus* is analyzed by A. R. Sharrock in the essay "Art of Deceit: *Pseudolus* and the Nature of Reading."

Slater, Niall. *Plautus in Performance: The Theatre of the Mind*. 2d ed. Princeton, N.J.: Princeton University Press, 2000. The chapter on *Pseudolus* follows the evolution of Pseudolus's scheme, which he concocts as he goes along. Emphasizes the power of language through which Pseudolus, speaking for Plautus, constructs a metadrama (a play about making a play) by using theatrical metaphor and direct address to the audience.

Purgatory

Author: William Butler Yeats (1865-1939)
First produced: 1938; first published, 1939
Type of work: Drama
Type of plot: Fantasy
Time of plot: Early twentieth century
Locale: Ireland

Principal characters:
AN OLD MAN
A BOY, the Old Man's sixteen-year-old son

The Story:

An Old Man and his adolescent son stand before a ruined old house, behind which stands only one bare tree. The boy complains of long wandering carrying a heavy pack while having to listen to his father's talk. Ignoring the complaints, the Old Man instructs the boy to study the house, which once was the scene of camaraderie, storytelling, and jokes. He is now the only living person with such memories. Although the boy scoffs at these reminiscences as pointless, the Old Man continues with his moonlit reverie about the cloud-shadowed house. He had visited the site one year earlier when the tree was as bare as it is now. Fifty years earlier, before lightning had struck it, he had seen the tree at the height of its beauty, ennobled with luxuriantly green leaves just as the house had been luxurious with intellectual life.

At the Old Man's direction, the boy sets down his pack and stands in the ruined doorway, squinting to see the person the Old Man says is still inside. He sees no one. The floors, windows, and roof are gone; the only recognizable object is an eggshell that a jackdaw had dropped. Unbelievable to the boy is the Old Man's insistence that souls in Purgatory return regularly to reenact their still troubling former transgressions. Since they are dead, insists the Old Man, the souls can understand the consequences of their failings. Those who had been made to suffer from the soul's earthly actions might eventually offer forgiveness, but those whose transgressions were self-inflicted must render their own forgiveness or rely on God's mercy.

Disgusted, the boy tells the Old Man to tell his fantastic story to the jackdaws if he must but to leave him alone. Forcefully, the father commands his angry son to sit on a stone; the house belongs to the boy's grandmother and is where the Old Man was born. Caught by this revelation, the boy sits and listens to the Old Man's tale.

The Old Man's mother owned more than the house; her property extended as far as one could see. Kennels and stables had housed prize animals; one of her horses raced at Curragh, a nearby racetrack. There, she had met and quickly married a lowly groom; after this, her mother had never spoken to her again. The Old Man shares his grandmother's condemnation of his mother's impulsive passion. The boy disagrees, for the groom, his grandfather, had won both the woman and the wealth. Seeming not to hear the boy, the Old Man repeats his description of his mother's hasty mistake, that she had merely looked at the groom, then married him, but that she had never known her bridegroom's true character, for she died soon after in giving birth to her son, the Old Man. Thereafter, her husband had squandered all her wealth.

Exciting memories of the great house animate the Old Man: Military officers, members of Parliament, governors of foreign lands, and Irish patriotic heroes had lived or visited the house, loving the ancient trees and profuse flowers. Then the husband had laid the land waste, felled the trees, and ruined the house. "To kill a house," the Old Man curses, "I here declare a capital offense."

Ignoring the Old Man's bitterness, the boy envisions his father's grand childhood with its horses and fine clothes. Ignoring his son's covetousness, the Old Man sneers at his father's ignorance. The Old Man had been forbidden to attend school, so he had learned to read from a gamekeeper's wife and learned Latin from a priest. In the great library, fine old books were plentiful. What of that education had the Old Man passed on to him, the boy asks. Since the boy is only a bastard conceived in a ditch with a peddler's daughter, he receives only what is due his station, replies the Old Man.

When the Old Man was sixteen, his drunken father had burned down the great house, destroying all the treasures in it. The boy suddenly realizes that he, too, is sixteen years old. Tentatively, he asks if the rumor were true that the Old Man had killed his dissolute father in the burning house. The Old Man confesses that he had, but that because the body was charred he was never convicted. Threatened by his dead father's friends, however, he had disguised himself and fled, to return to his father's low station by becoming a wandering peddler. He boasts that he still uses the murder weapon to cut his dinner meat.

Suddenly, the Old Man hears hoofbeats and remembers that today is the anniversary of his mother's wedding night. Although the boy cannot see anything, the Old Man sees and describes a vision of a ghostly young woman, the Old Man's mother, inside the ruined house awaiting her husband's late return from a drinking spree. The spectral husband stables the horse, and the woman leads him to her bedroom. Entering the dream scene, the Old Man shouts in vain to his mother not to let his father touch her to beget him. Then he realizes that the scene must be repeated because his mother's remorse for her marriage was the cause of the reenactment.

While the Old Man is fantasizing, the boy tries to steal his inheritance from his father's bundle of money. Halting the boy, the Old Man justifies his stinginess by asserting that the boy is like his dissolute grandfather and would have squandered everything on drink. As they struggle for the money, the dream lights up a vision of the ghostly grandfather pouring whiskey. The boy threatens to continue the family murders by killing the Old Man, then pauses, horrified, when he, too, sees the Old Man's vision of the man and woman, his grandparents. Quickly, the Old Man repeatedly stabs and kills the boy, then sings a lullaby to the young corpse.

The vision fades and is replaced by moonlight on the bare tree. The Old Man assures his dead mother that his murderous act will finish the cycle of repeated scenes and that his killing his son will stop the family's generational pollution. He will now wander in distant lands, far from the nightmare. Then he hears approaching hoofbeats again and realizes that the nightmare is about to begin anew. Dejected, the Old Man pleads with God to rescue his mother from her cycle of remorse.

Critical Evaluation:

Written in 1938, *Purgatory* demonstrates William Butler Yeats's lifelong fascination with the connections between the present world and the past and future. In his last public appearance in August, 1938, on the occasion of the play's opening, the old Irish poet-dramatist told the audience that the drama expressed his beliefs about this world and the next. *Purgatory*, asserted Yeats, was symbolic, not allegorical. The plot does not represent a story in a real-world context.

To Yeats, geometric symbols of circles and conical gyres expressed the repetitious pattern of time, which incorporates past and present into future cycles. In *Purgatory*, the Old Man believes that souls in Purgatory bring the past into the present by reliving past transgressions. The repeated hoofbeats of his father's ghost approaching at the play's end indicate that the cycle will continue into the future also and that the Old Man's prayer for God to release his mother's soul from its recurrent dream clearly will not be granted.

Purgatory, like other Yeats plays—*Calvary* (1921), *The Resurrection* (1927), and *The Words upon the Windowpane* (1930)—explores possibilities of life after death, especially ritualistic death. Killing his father in the inferno the father had created resembles a ritual of punishment; killing his son, whom he identifies with the hated father, after watching his own begetting repeats the murder ritual. Many Yeats plays center on father/son relationships, especially those about the Irish mythic hero Cuchulain, who kills a young man before remorsefully learning that the victim was his own son.

The thought of his mother's life after death is agonizing for the Old Man. While he prays to relieve his mother's dream, he is evidently interested in his own relief as well. His anguish in watching sexual relations between his father and mother has obvious Oedipal ramifications. In the Greek tale, Oedipus vengefully kills his father, marries his mother, and fathers children. In this drama, too, the son appears to be jealous of his father's privilege; he cannot tear himself from the scene. He loathes the sight in the vision of his mother's lust and calls out to her not to let her husband touch her using the argument that they will beget the husband's murderer. He is fascinated with his ghost-mother's ability to experience sexual pleasure even while bringing on her own remorse.

Pleasure leading to destruction, and the interweaving of sex and death, is a familiar theme in Yeats's drama. Here, sexual culmination in the vision is directly followed by the boy's murder. Irony is evident when the boy is able to see the Old Man's vision only during the moment before he is killed, when he tries to stop the vision from repeating. Another common Yeats theme is the impossibility of lasting love, which resonates in the story of the mother's haste leading to betrayal and isolation from her bridegroom.

As in other Yeats pieces with simple plots involving violence, the narrative drive of *Purgatory* concentrates on an intensely dramatic moment, here the torturing vision. Stage directions are rare, as is characteristic of Yeats's verse plays; the reader must infer from the dialogue what action would actually be seen on stage. For example, the reader finds out about the boy's location and his subsequent attempt to steal solely from the dialogue itself, when the Old Man commands the boy to sit on the rock, and later to "Come back!/ And so you thought to slip away,/ My bag of money between your fingers." The play's quick resolution is also typical of Yeats's dramas, as is his combining art and religion in some of the symbolism. Yeats believed that the supernatural world met the natural through dreams, both pleasant and unpleasant.

The play has been variously interpreted. Among those who have studied it, some contend that underlying the play is Yeats's anger against a domineering, overly talkative, and emotionally undemonstrative father. In *Purgatory*, the Old Man never addresses the boy as his son; only once does the boy address him as "father," and that is when the Old Man is about to confess to having murdered his father. The boy challenges his father, just as the Old Man challenged his father; each ignores the other's concerns.

Some critics have attempted to interpret the play's symbols. The Old Man's knife can be thought to have Freudian implications; the eggshell might represent broken femaleness or cycles of birth and death. The bare tree, which inhabits many Yeats plays and often symbolizes seasonal rebirth, here might be thought to represent the mother's stripped wealth. Birds are ever-present in Yeats poetry and drama, often representing spiritual soaring; in *Purgatory*, a jackdaw has discarded from a nest, a site for births, the only sign of life in the ruined house, an eggshell. The nightmare cycles of *Purgatory* could be interpreted as symbolizing the political violence in Irish history, which Yeats often deplored in such works as the poem "September 1913." Certainly the ruined great house bears an unmistakable resemblance to Coole, Lady Gregory's ruined home where Yeats often lived during his most productive years. He often lamented the fall of the Irish aristocracy in his poetry.

The play never gained widespread popularity, perhaps because the symbols are not sufficiently defined. Undoubtedly, *Purgatory* is a disturbing work for its treatment of such human taboos as filicide, parricide, and a son's observation of sexual relations between his parents. Still, the play offers rich poetic imagery, impassioned characters, and intense dramatic climaxes, and it is permeated by themes that are evident in Yeats's entire oeuvre.

Nancy A. Macky

Further Reading

Bradley, Anthony. *William Butler Yeats*. New York: Frederick Ungar, 1979. A clearly written overview of Yeats's life, with a discussion of his accomplishments as a dramatist in the Irish context. Includes photographs of productions, including those of *Purgatory*. Part of the World Dramatists series.

Howes, Marjorie, and John Kelly, eds. *The Cambridge Companion to W. B. Yeats*. New York: Cambridge University Press, 2006. Collection of essays providing an overview of Yeats's work in all genres, including a discussion of Yeats and the drama.

Jeffares, A. Norman. *W. B. Yeats: A New Biography*. New York: Continuum, 2001. A thoroughly rewritten and updated version of Jeffares's 1949 work *W. B. Yeats: Man and Poet* by a noted Yeats scholar. This 2001 work incorporates newly found material on Yeats, and includes more than one hundred photographs and drawings.

_____, ed. *W. B. Yeats: The Critical Heritage*. Boston: Routledge & Kegan Paul, 1977. An excellent collection of contemporary critical comment on several Yeats plays, including a chapter on *Purgatory* and its relationship to other Yeats works.

Moore, John Rees. *Masks of Love and Death: Yeats as Dramatist*. Ithaca, N.Y.: Cornell University Press, 1971. Chapter 14 focuses on *Purgatory* as a dark view of fate taking vengeance on mean-spirited materialism.

Richman, David. *Passionate Action: Yeats's Mastery of Drama*. Newark: University of Delaware Press, 2000. Draws on Yeats's correspondence and the many drafts of his plays to chronicle his work as a playwright and theatrical producer.

Ure, Peter. *Yeats the Playwright: A Commentary on Character and Design in the Major Plays*. New York: Barnes & Noble, 1969. A thorough investigation of all of Yeats's major plays, showing the relationship of structure, theme, and character. Chapter 5, "From Grave to Cradle," includes a discussion of *Purgatory*.

Purple Dust

Author: Sean O'Casey (1880-1964)
First produced: 1944; first published, 1940
Type of work: Drama
Type of plot: Satire
Time of plot: 1940's
Locale: Clune na Geera, Ireland

Principal characters:
CYRIL POGES, a pompous English businessman
JACK O'KILLIGAIN, a foreman stonemason
BASIL STOKE, Poges's colleague
SOUHAUN, Poges's mistress
AVRIL, Stoke's mistress
THREE IRISH WORKMEN

The Story:

Three workmen are standing languidly in a large, gloomy room that once had been the living room of a ruined Elizabethan mansion. The three ponder the wisdom of two English gentlemen, Cyril Poges and Basil Stoke, in coming to live in such a decaying old house. Although the fresh paint had brightened things up a bit, it covers, for the most part, rotting wood. The sudden appearance of the sixty-five-year-old Poges and the serious Basil—who is in his thirties—followed by their mistresses, Souhaun and Avril, respectively, confirms the workmen's suspicions that the owners are slightly awry in their thinking. The group dances in, boisterously singing of the joys of country living. The handsome foreman, Jack O'Killigain, explains to the workmen that these are people who see historical loveliness in decaying ruins, and who take foolish delight in any locale with a story behind it. With the reappearance of the pretty Avril, Stokes's mistress, O'Killigain exerts his poetic Irish charm to entice her into a rendezvous later that night.

Poges, Basil, and Souhaun return from a walk in the fields. Poges and Basil talk excitedly about the glories of past history and its better times, much to the disgust of O'Killigain, who firmly believes that life in its present state is far more worth living. His philosophy is lost on the other two, who go about their comic business of hanging pictures and discovering aspects of country living—new business for them, but common enjoyment for the hardy Irish workmen.

Although Poges wants to forget the outside world and its ways, his reverie is constantly interrupted by prosaic occurrences: arguments with Basil and the women, altercations with his butler over men outside who wish to know if he desires roosters and hens, and interruptions by one of the workmen, who informs him of an excellent buy in a cow. Poges rages that he will get in touch with the department of agriculture. At Poges's displeasure over the disconnected telephone, another workman loses his temper. Poges hears himself scorned as a man who thinks that the glory of the world could be stuffed into a purse, a man who is patronizing toward the Irish, a mighty race a thousand years older than his own.

Basil and Avril leave for a horseback ride, in spite of warnings that Irish horses are true horses, instead of English animals. The predictions are accurate; a battered Basil appears shortly afterward and announces that his horse indeed had become wild and ungovernable, and that, when last seen, Avril was riding away quite naked with O'Killigain.

The next day brings a cold dawn. Though Poges and Basil had spent the night fully clothed, they had almost frozen to death in the old house, along with the rest of the household. Poges still tries to rationalize; the cold air will revitalize them and exhilarate them. Barney, the butler, and Cloyne, the maid, are disgusted with the whole situation; they think the place an unlighted dungeon. As Barney struggles to light a damp fire, Cloyne rushes back into the room to scream that there is a wild bull in the entrance hall. This announcement causes a great panic among the transplanted city dwellers. Basil reenters with a gun, then runs for his life as Poges roars for help and Cloyne faints. A workman saves them all by shooing out a harmless cow that had innocently wandered into the hallway.

Later, Poges thinks he has found a friend in the workman, who reminisces with him over glorious days in the past. Once again, Poges expresses his philosophy that all the greats had gone with their glory, their finery turned to purple dust, and that today's people are shallow by comparison. O'Killigain and another workman later transfix Poges, however, with their poetic stories of the glorious Irish past and the fight for independence (an event not blurred in the mists of distant time). Although Poges is momentarily surprised to find that these country workers have such depth, his spirit of English nationalism quickly asserts itself.

Poges's calamities continue. His next misadventure is with an oversized, heavy garden roller. Though his friends warn him, Poges persists in his efforts to operate the machine. The result is a wrecked wall, as Poges lets the roller get away from him to roll into and through the side of the house. Following closely on this incident, a terrified Basil shoots and kills the indolent cow that had earlier invaded the hallway.

An interview with the local canon lifts Poges's spirits when the churchman praises Poges for restoring a portion of the past to slow down the reckless speed of the present. As the workmen continue to bring in furniture, Souhaun almost succumbs to one of the workmen and his poetic charm. The moving into the room of a gilded desk-bureau proves to be another disaster. The top is first scarred by a workman's boot; then the bureau and the entrance are both damaged as the piece of furniture is pushed and pried through the door.

The wind is rising and storm clouds are brewing ominously, so the workmen are sent away, but not before O'Killigain and the workman entreat Avril and Souhaun to accompany them. The beautiful picture of Irish life conjured quickly by the men leaves the women quite unsettled, but Poges and Basil make great fun of the workmen's poetic proposals. As the day grows darker and the rain falls, Poges finds still other troubles; the postmaster arrives to complain about Poges's midnight phone calls to him. Suddenly the sound of a galloping horse is heard over the howl of the wind.

Warned that the river is rising, the terrified group in the darkened room make plans to climb to the roof before the house is flooded. Souhaun is nowhere to be found; she is with the workman on the galloping horse. O'Killigain, who had said that he would come for Avril when the river rose, appears as he had promised. Avril leaves, renouncing Basil as a gilded monkey. Basil runs for the roof and a defeated Poges follows slowly, longing for dear England.

Critical Evaluation:

In *Purple Dust*, Sean O'Casey returned to certain stylistic aspects of his earlier plays, including the mixture of moving poetry with extravagant comedy. Although the occasional poetic passages of the Irish workmen concerning their noble past are indeed beautiful, the emphasis of the play is on the profoundly comic situation of two stuffy Englishmen trying to adjust to the rigors of the bucolic life. O'Casey, as usual, is extolling the hardy Irish, and disapproves of those who cling to the past without partly looking to the future. When people venerate the past without a true sense of understanding and appreciation, as do Poges and Stoke, the result is especially disastrous.

Purple Dust may be O'Casey's funniest play. He begins with a potentially hilarious situation, the attempt by two Englishmen to restore an ancient, ramshackle Tudor mansion in the Irish countryside in the face of opposition from the local citizenry. To this beginning he adds a cast of broad, colorful, and sometimes poetic types, and utilizing a thin but completely functional plot line, presents a sequence of zany scenes that would have fit nicely into a Marx Brothers film.

Purple Dust has, however, some serious content. Eschewing the kind of abstract symbolism and forced rhetoric that damaged such earlier idea plays as *Within the Gates* (1933), *The Star Turns Red* (1940), and *Oak Leaves and Lavender: Or, A World on Wallpaper* (1946), O'Casey mixes comedy with message so adroitly in *Purple Dust* that he is able to present some strident satire and provocative ideas without losing any humor or theatrical effectiveness.

Cyril Poges and Basil Stoke are two brilliant comedic and satiric creations. Poges is the self-made man, the blustery pragmatic tycoon who has bullied his way to the top and believes he can impose his will on anyone and anything. At the same time, he senses his lack of depth and tries to compensate by consuming large amounts of culture; he fancies himself an instant expert on art, history, poetry, and literature because he has bought great quantities of it. Stoke, on the other hand, represents inherited wealth, position, and formal education. He considers himself a thinker and speaks in long, abstract, convoluted sentences that turn the simplest thing into a complex metaphysical problem. Their hilarious debate over the nature of a primrose is an example of the hilarious lunacy that O'Casey is able to inject into his satire.

Regardless of their differences, both men are embodiments of the British capitalist. Their various pretensions and blind spots set them up as perfect dupes for the canny rural Irish workmen. The chief symbol of the play is, of course, the absurd Tudor house that the two Englishmen mean to refurbish as a way of making a connection with the historical "grandeur" of the past (Tudor England restored in rural Ireland) as well as finding pastoral simplicity in the present. They add any object to the house that seems vaguely historical, regardless of its authenticity or its appropriateness—a "Jacobean" table, "Cambodian" bowl (from Woolworth's), a set of medieval armor, a "quattrocento" bureau—while at the same time denying themselves such "luxuries" as modern indoor plumbing and electricity on the grounds that they are historically inauthentic.

This "culture" soon turns to disaster—the bowls are smashed, the bureau is broken to pieces, and finally the house itself is submerged. Their dream of bucolic simplicity likewise turns into a nightmare; the animals keep them awake at night, a cow wanders into the house and they flee in terror from the "wild beast," and the gentle autumn rain grows into a flood that inundates them all.

O'Casey is not attacking tradition as such—only a false,

pretentious, and ignorant use of it. Opposed to the old English capitalists are the young Irish workers, and two of them, Jack O'Killigain and Philip O'Dempsey, articulate O'Casey's positive vision of humanity, tradition, and Ireland. Poges's ignorance of history is contrasted with O'Dempsey's profound grasp of his heroic historical and cultural background. He divorces himself from most of his contemporaries and aligns himself with the Irish heroes of the past. These visions are put into action when, as the flood waters start pouring in on Poges and Stoke, O'Killigain and O'Dempsey spirit the women, Avril and Souhaun, off to a mountain sanctuary. The survivors of the new flood will be the young, the passionate, and the Irish.

Further Reading

Benstock, Bernard. *Paycocks and Others: Sean O'Casey's World.* New York: Barnes & Noble, 1976. A comprehensive thematic survey of all of O'Casey's works. Establishes the place of *Purple Dust* in O'Casey's development and connects it to the rest of the playwright's output. Discusses the play's contributions to O'Casey's concept of the hero.

Kosok, Heinz. *O'Casey the Dramatist.* Translated by Heinz Kosok and Joseph T. Swann. New York: Barnes & Noble, 1985. The chapter on *Purple Dust* opens with a succinct treatment of the play's different texts. Concentrates on the interplay of satire, farce, and other comic elements in this play. Contains notes on various productions.

Krause, David. *Sean O'Casey: The Man and His Work.* New York: Macmillan, 1960. A comprehensive treatment of O'Casey from a biographical and critical point of view.

Argues that *Purple Dust* inaugurates the tone of O'Casey's later plays.

McDonald, Ronan. *Tragedy and Irish Literature: Synge, O'Casey, Beckett.* New York: Palgrave, 2002. Compares the work of three Irish playwrights, analyzing how their cultures of suffering, loss, and guilt are reflected in their dramas.

Murray, Christopher. *Sean O'Casey: Writer at Work—A Biography.* Montreal: McGill-Queen's University Press, 2004. Biography focusing on O'Casey's literary career, tracing the development of his writing from his early nationalist work to later socialist writings.

O'Casey, Sean. "Purple Dust in Their Eyes." In *Under a Colored Cap: Articles Merry and Mournful—With Comments and a Song.* New York: St. Martin's Press, 1963. O'Casey's critical response to reviews of the 1962 London production of *Purple Dust.* The essay considers the play's political aspects and argues for their relevance to the playwright's vision.

O'Riordan, John. *A Guide to O'Casey's Plays: From the Plough to the Stars.* New York: Macmillan, 1984. An exhaustive treatment of O'Casey's plays, covering all of the playwright's major and minor works, with notes on production histories. Assesses literary sources for *Purple Dust* and considers its intellectual underpinnings.

Stewart, Victoria. *About O'Casey: The Playwright and the Work.* New ed. New York: Faber & Faber, 2006. Describes the political and social conditions in Ireland that led to O'Casey's association with the Abbey Theatre and his subsequent literary career. Includes interviews with O'Casey and people who worked with him.

Pygmalion

Author: George Bernard Shaw (1856-1950)
First produced: 1913; first published, 1912
Type of work: Drama
Type of plot: Comedy
Time of plot: c. 1900
Locale: London

The Story:

Late one evening in the Covent Garden theater district of London, playgoers are attempting to summon taxicabs in the rain when a crowd gathers around an unkempt young woman selling flowers. The flower girl has been speaking in a very

Principal characters:
HENRY HIGGINS, a phonetician
ELIZA DOOLITTLE, a flower girl
ALFRED DOOLITTLE, her father, a dustman
COLONEL PICKERING, another phonetician
MRS. PEARCE, Higgins's housekeeper
FREDDY EYNSFORD HILL, a poor young gentleman

strong Cockney dialect, and a distinguished gentleman has been transcribing her speech into a notebook. The gentleman, Henry Higgins, is a professional phonetician who earns a handsome income teaching people how to change their lower- and middle-class accents so that they can pass as members of the upper class. Higgins amazes the crowd by using his analysis of individuals' accents to pinpoint where each of them lives. Appalled by the flower girl's lower-class dialect, Higgins boasts that in a matter of months he could teach her how to speak properly and pass as a duchess at an ambassador's garden party.

The next morning, in the drawing room and laboratory of Higgins's Wimpole Street residence, Higgins is showing Colonel Pickering his elaborate equipment for recording speech when the housekeeper, Mrs. Pearce, announces the arrival of the flower girl, Eliza Doolittle. Eliza wants to take lessons from Higgins so she can improve her speech and get a job as a clerk in a proper flower shop. Higgins is impressed by the percentage of her meager wealth that Eliza is willing to pay and accepts her as a student, making a wager with Pickering that in six months he can pass Eliza off as a duchess. Mrs. Pearce asks what is to become of Eliza when Higgins has finished his teaching, but Higgins dismisses the question as trivial. After Mrs. Pearce takes Eliza away so that the young woman can bathe, Pickering asks Higgins if his intentions toward Eliza are honorable; Higgins assures Pickering that he is a confirmed bachelor, determined not to let women into his life.

After helping Eliza into the bath, Mrs. Pearce reenters the drawing room to set down rules for Higgins's behavior while Eliza is staying in the house—proper dress and table manners and no swearing. Eliza's father, Alfred Doolittle, a dustman, or trash collector, arrives and attempts to extort money from Higgins. When Higgins insists that Doolittle take his daughter back immediately, he drives down Doolittle's price to a five-pound note. Higgins offers Doolittle ten pounds, but Doolittle refuses the extra five because he does not want to be tempted to save money. On his way out, Doolittle sees his daughter but does not immediately recognize her, as Eliza is clean and well dressed.

After a few months, the training has gone so well that Higgins decides to test Eliza by taking her to his mother's flat for a formal visit. He arrives first to prepare his mother, informing her that Eliza can converse on only two topics—the weather and everyone's health. Unfortunately, as Higgins is explaining the situation, three unexpected visitors are announced: Mrs. Eynsford Hill, her daughter Clara, and her son Freddy. Initially, Higgins is upset with the intrusion of the Eynsford Hills, but then he welcomes them as a greater challenge for Eliza's performance. When Eliza arrives she is exquisitely dressed and produces an impression of remarkable distinction and beauty. She begins conversing quite adeptly, but as she becomes more engaged in the conversation she slips back into some of her lower-class speech patterns. Higgins, however, is able to convince the Eynsford Hills that her speech is a new and fashionable way of speaking, the "new small talk," and they are convinced that she is a lady of high society; by the time Eliza leaves, Freddy has obviously fallen in love with her. After the Eynsford Hills leave, Higgins is exultant, but his mother asks him what is to be done with Eliza after the lessons are completed.

When the time comes for Eliza's performance at the ambassador's garden party, she succeeds splendidly. Afterward, Higgins and Pickering celebrate their triumph, talking of how glad they are that their work is over and complaining that they had ultimately become bored by the whole affair. Eliza, on the other hand, is brooding and silent. Higgins wonders out loud where his slippers are, and Eliza leaves the room and fetches them for him. Higgins and Pickering talk of the evening as if Eliza were not there, and as they are leaving for bed, Eliza throws Higgins's slippers after him, calling him a selfish brute. Now Eliza asks the question, "What's to become of me?"

That evening, Eliza leaves Higgins's flat to walk the streets of London, and by morning she has gone to stay with Higgins's mother. Later that morning, Higgins and Pickering, bewildered and worried about Eliza's disappearance, arrive at the mother's home. They are shortly followed by Eliza's father, who enters dressed like a gentleman, complaining that his life has been ruined because of Higgins. Higgins had written a joking letter to an American millionaire, and that letter has led to Alfred Doolittle's inheriting a huge sum of money. Now, Doolittle complains, everyone is begging money from him. His life is no longer impoverished, free, and simple.

Higgins's mother reveals that Eliza is upstairs, angered by the insensitivity and indifference Higgins has shown her. Mrs. Higgins asks Doolittle to step outside so that Eliza will not be shocked by his appearance when she comes downstairs. Eliza then enters and meets Higgins and Pickering as a refined lady, the transformation complete. Eliza explains that she has learned her nice manners from Pickering and that the real difference between a lady and a flower girl is not in how she behaves but in how she is treated.

Eliza's father reenters the room, and Eliza is surprised at how he looks. Doolittle reports that he is now a victim of middle-class morality and is on his way to his wedding. He invites everyone to come to the wedding, and Pickering and Mrs. Higgins leave to get ready, leaving Eliza and Higgins behind. Pickering has urged Eliza to return to live with him and Higgins, but in her last conversation with Higgins, Eliza has decided to leave Higgins forever. She claims that she is only looking for a little kindness and that she will marry

Freddy Eynsford Hill. She will earn her living as a teacher of phonetics, teaching others as she has been taught. Higgins is incensed but impressed with Eliza's spirit, and finally he sees her as more of an equal. As Eliza leaves, vowing never to see Higgins again, Higgins asserts confidently that she will return.

Critical Evaluation:

Throughout his career, George Bernard Shaw agitated for the reform of the vagaries of English spelling and pronunciation, but his assertion that *Pygmalion* was written to impress upon the public the importance of phoneticians is immaterial. *Pygmalion*, like all of Shaw's best plays, transcends its author's didactic intent. The play is performed and read not for Shaw's pet theories but for the laughter its plot and characters provoke.

The play is a modern adaptation of the Pygmalion myth (although some have claimed that it is a plagiarism of Tobias Smollett's *The Adventures of Peregrine Pickle*, 1751), in which the sculptor-king Pygmalion falls in love with Galatea, a creature of his own making, a statue that the goddess Aphrodite, pitying him, brings to life. The Pygmalion of Shaw's play turns up as Henry Higgins, a teacher of English speech; his Galatea is Eliza Doolittle, a Cockney flower girl whom Higgins transforms into a seeming English lady by teaching her to speak cultivated English. In the process of transforming a poor, uneducated girl into a lady, Higgins irrevocably changes a human life. By lifting Eliza above her own class and providing her with no more than the appurtenances of another, Higgins makes her unfit for both. On this change and Higgins's stubborn refusal to accept its reality and its consequences, Shaw builds his play.

From the beginning, when Higgins first observes her dialectal monstrosities, Eliza is characterized as a proud, stubborn girl, though educated only by the circumstances of her poverty and gutter environment. She has the courage to ask Higgins to make good his boast that he can pass her off as a duchess within a matter of months, and she calls on him and offers to pay him for elocution lessons that will enable her to work as a saleswoman in a flower shop. Like all the proud, she is also sensitive, and she tries to break off the interview when Higgins persists in treating her as his social inferior.

Higgins can best be understood in contrast to Colonel Pickering, his foil, who finances the transformation. As a fellow phonetician, Pickering approves of the project as a scientific experiment, but as a gentleman and a sensitive human being, he sympathizes with Eliza. It is Higgins's uproariously tragic flaw that he, like all of Shaw's heroes, is not a gentleman. He is brilliant and cultured, but he lacks manners

and refuses to learn or even affect any, believing himself to be superior to the conventions and civilities of polite society and preferring to treat everyone with bluntness and candor. He is, or so he thinks until Eliza leaves him, a self-sufficient man. When he discovers that she has made herself an indispensable part of his life, he goes to her and, in one of the most remarkable courtship scenes in the history of the theater, pleads with her to live with Pickering and himself as three dedicated bachelors. At the end of the play, he is confident that she will accept his unorthodox proposition, even when she bids him good-bye forever.

As a matter of fact, Shaw himself was never able to convince anyone that Eliza and Higgins did not marry and live happily ever after. The first producer of the play, Sir Herbert Beerbohm Tree, insisted on leaving the impression that the two were reconciled in the end as lovers, and this tradition has persisted. Enraged as always by any liberties taken with his work, Shaw wrote an essay that he attached to the play as a sequel in which he denounces sentimental interpretations of *Pygmalion*. He concedes that *Pygmalion* is a romance in that its heroine undergoes an almost miraculous change, but he argues that the logic of the characterization does not permit a conventional happy ending. Higgins is, after all, a god and Eliza only his creation; an abyss separates them. Furthermore, Shaw contends, their personalities, backgrounds, and philosophies are irreconcilable. Higgins is an inveterate bachelor and likely to remain so because he will never find a woman who can meet the standards he has set for ideal womanhood—those set by his mother. Eliza, on the other hand, being young and pretty, can always find a husband whose demands on a woman would not be impossible to meet. Therefore, Shaw insists, Eliza marries Freddy Eynsford Hill, a penniless but devoted young man who has only an insignificant role in the play. Stubbornly, Shaw does not even permit them the luxury of living happily ever after: They have financial problems that are gradually solved by their opening a flower shop subsidized by Colonel Pickering. Shaw's Pygmalion is too awe-inspiring for his Galatea ever to presume to love him.

Even with the addition of this unconventional ending to the play, *Pygmalion* would be highly atypical of Shavian drama were it not for the presence of Alfred Doolittle, Eliza's father. Through Doolittle, Shaw is able to indulge in economic and social moralizing, an ingredient with which Shaw could not dispense. Like Eliza, Doolittle undergoes a transformation as a result of Higgins's meddling, a transformation that in his case is, however, unpremeditated. Early in the play, Doolittle fascinates Higgins and Pickering with his successful attempt to capitalize on Eliza's good fortune. He literally charms Higgins out of five pounds by declaring himself an implacable foe of middle-class morality and insisting that he will use the money for a drunken spree. Delighted with the old scoundrel, Higgins mentions him in jest in a letter to a crackpot American millionaire, who subsequently bequeaths Doolittle a yearly allowance of three thousand pounds if he will lecture on morality. Thus this dustman becomes transformed into a lion of London society, and the reprobate becomes a victim of bourgeois morality. Although he appears only twice in the play, Doolittle is so vigorous and funny that he is almost as memorable a comic character as Higgins.

The play itself is memorable because of its vigor and fun, notwithstanding Shaw's protestations about its message. It is likely that Shaw insisted so strenuously on the serious intent of the play because he too realized that *Pygmalion* is his least serious and least didactic play. In 1956, *Pygmalion* was adapted into the Broadway musical *My Fair Lady*; the musical, with book and lyrics by Alan Jay Lerner and music by Frederick Loewe, was extremely successful, and several revivals have been produced since that time. A film version of *My Fair Lady*, starring Audrey Hepburn as Eliza and Rex Harrison as Higgins, was released in 1964.

"Critical Evaluation" by Terry Nienhuis

Further Reading

Berst, Charles A. *"Pygmalion": Shaw's Spin on Myth and Cinderella*. New York: Twayne, 1995. Excellent resource for students examines the literary and historical contexts of the play. Provides an intelligent and thorough interpretation, tracing Eliza's transformation into a woman and a lady. Focuses on Shaw's use of the Pygmalion myth and the Cinderella fairy tale.

Bloom, Harold, ed. *George Bernard Shaw's "Pygmalion."* New York: Chelsea House, 1988. Judiciously selected critical essays represent major interpretations of the play. In his introduction, Bloom argues that *Pygmalion* is Shaw's masterpiece. Excellent for students.

Dukore, Bernard F. *Shaw's Theater*. Gainesville: University Press of Florida, 2000. Focuses on the performance of Shaw's plays and how *Pygmalion* and other plays call attention to elements of the theater, such as the audience, characters directing other characters, and plays within plays. Includes a section titled "Bernard Shaw, Director," and another in which Shaw describes how a director should interpret *Pygmalion* for theatrical production.

Hornby, Richard. "Beyond the Verbal in *Pygmalion*." In *Shaw's Plays in Performance*, edited by Daniel Leary. University Park: Pennsylvania State University Press, 1983. Examines Shaw's stagecraft and the performance qualities inherent in the play as a script. Goes beyond "the purely verbal or literary" qualities of the play to show how the visual and aural elements convey meaning.

Huggett, Richard. *The Truth About "Pygmalion."* New York: Random House, 1969. Presents a fascinating narrative account of the original 1914 London production, which involved "three of the most monstrous egoists the theatre ever produced": actor Stella Campbell, who played Eliza; actor Sir Herbert Beerbohm Tree, who played Higgins; and Shaw himself.

Innes, Christopher, ed. *The Cambridge Companion to George Bernard Shaw*. New York: Cambridge University Press, 1998. Collection of scholarly essays examines Shaw's work, including discussions of Shaw's feminism, Shavian comedy's relation to the works of Oscar Wilde, Shaw's "discussion plays," and his influence on modern theater.

Pagliaro, Harold E. *Relations Between the Sexes in the Plays of George Bernard Shaw*. Lewiston, N.Y.: Edwin Mellen Press, 2004. Demonstrates how relationships between men and women are key elements in Shaw's plays. Notes the patterns in how Shaw depicts these relationships, including those between lovers destined by the "life force" to procreate and those between fathers and daughters and between mothers and sons. Also addresses Shaw's depictions of the sexuality of politically, intellectually, and emotionally strong men.

Reynolds, Jean. *"Pygmalion's" Wordplay: The Postmodern Shaw*. Gainesville: University Press of Florida, 1999. Argues that Shaw offers a critique of conventional language that foreshadows many of the ideas of Jacques Derrida and other postmodernist thinkers. Describes *Pygmalion* as a "Shavian creation myth" in which Henry Higgins transforms Eliza into a duchess just as Shaw reinvented himself as a larger-than-life personality.

Shaw, George Bernard. *George Bernard Shaw's Plays: "Mrs. Warren's Profession," "Pygmalion," "Man and Superman," "Major Barbara"—Contexts and Criticism*. 2d ed. Edited by Sandie Byrne. New York: W. W. Norton, 2002. In addition to an annotated text of *Pygmalion*, this volume contains critical essays and excerpts from books and reviews discussing Shaw's work generally and *Pygmalion* specifically.

Silver, Arnold. *Bernard Shaw: The Darker Side*. Stanford, Calif.: Stanford University Press, 1982. A major part of this challenging and unconventional book is a thorough and complex psychological interpretation of *Pygmalion* that shows Shaw working out intense personal conflicts. Fascinating material for more advanced students.

Q

Quartet in Autumn

Author: Barbara Pym (1913-1980)
First published: 1977
Type of work: Novel
Type of plot: Comedy of manners
Time of plot: 1970's
Locale: London

Principal characters:
EDWIN BRAITHWAITE, an office clerk
NORMAN, an office worker
LETTY CROWE, an office worker
MARCIA IVORY, an office worker
MARJORIE, Letty's longtime friend
FATHER GELLIBRAND, a parish Anglican priest
DAVID LYDELL, Marjorie's vicar
JANICE BRABNER, a volunteer social worker
MRS. POPE, Letty's landlady
KEN, Norman's brother-in-law
D. G. STRONG, Marcia's surgeon

The Story:

Four London coworkers in their sixties live quiet lives. Edwin Braithwaite, the only one of the quartet who had ever married, lives alone in Clapham Common in a semidetached house. His wife, Phyllis, had died, and his married daughter lives in another part of England, near Eastbourne.

Edwin devotes his free time to visiting churches. He is not particularly religious or even spiritual; rather, he enjoys the routine that the church calendar imposes. He serves on his local parochial church council and as master of ceremonies (an undefined position) of his parish church. Though he enjoys the company of his parish priest, Father Gellibrand, their conversation is limited to ecclesiastical subjects.

Norman, Edwin's coworker, rents a room in a house in Kilburn Park. His sister had married a man named Ken, a driving instructor. Edwin's sister dies, leaving Ken as Norman's only relative. The two have nothing in common. Norman hates cars so much that the sight of a damaged automobile delights him. He also dislikes the young, complains about inflation, and takes a dim view of life generally.

Sharing an office with Edwin and Norman are the fashion-conscious Letty Crowe and the fastidious Marcia Ivory. Letty was born in Malvern in 1914. In the late 1920's, she had moved to London to take a secretarial course and had met a woman named Marjorie, with whom she has remained in touch for more than forty years. Marjorie had married Brian, now deceased; she had tried to pair Letty with Brian's friend Stephen, but nothing came of this effort.

Letty now rents a room in the house of Miss Embrey, who has two other boarders: Marya from Hungary and Miss Alice Spurgeon. Letty is the only one of the office quartet who has traveled abroad extensively, taking her vacations with Marjorie. Letty expects to move into Marjorie's country cottage when she retires, but that plan goes awry when Marjorie becomes engaged to her local vicar, David Lydell.

Marcia lives alone in a semidetached house. She has had a mastectomy and had developed an infatuation with her surgeon, D. G. Strong. She even had traveled twice, just to look at his house. Fastidious about certain matters, Marcia maintains a collection of empty plastic bags arranged by size, and in her garden shed she keeps about one hundred empty United Dairy milk bottles, which she dusts periodically. The presence among the bottles of a County Dairies container, brought to her (full) by Letty, troubles Marcia deeply, until Marcia returns it to her coworker. Marcia, however, never dusts her furniture, and a hairball that her now-dead cat, Snowy, had coughed up long ago remains on the bedspread. A volunteer social worker, Janice Brabner, repeatedly visits and tries to lure Marcia to the social center, but Marcia rebuffs Janice.

One evening Miss Embrey invites her three boarders for coffee to announce that she has sold the house to Mr. Olatunde, a Nigerian priest; the tenants may remain if they choose. Letty is not certain whether she should move, but she finds the Olatundes and their parishioners, who hold services in the house, noisy. Though the men in the office think that Marcia should rent Letty a room, neither woman finds the prospect appealing. Edwin turns to the women of his church. Mrs. Pope, who lives in West Hampstead, agrees to take Letty as a boarder. Norman, in his typically pessimistic way, wonders how Letty will cope if Mrs. Pope, who is in her eighties, falls and needs assistance.

Letty and Marcia retire. To fill the time, Letty vainly tries to read serious books about the social sciences but finds them tedious. She then involves herself in church activities, which are not always satisfying. Her invitation to lunch with Marcia goes unanswered; then Marjorie comes to town to shop for her trousseau, and she wants to get together. Marjorie suggests that Letty move into a retirement home in Marjorie's village, a plan that displeases Letty. Eventually, she visits the place and notes that the director, Beth Doughty, serves all the vicar's favorite foods.

Despite Norman's objections, Edwin arranges a reunion lunch with the women. Norman unkindly remarks that Letty has gained weight, and that Marcia has not. Though Marcia's cupboards are filled with cans of food, she rarely opens any of the cans. At lunch with her former coworkers she orders only a cheese salad, and she barely touches that. She has stopped caring for her hair, and she appears oddly dressed at the luncheon. When the others ask about her recent activities, she remains secretive. In fact, there is little to report.

Norman visits Marcia at her house, but the two do not exchange words. Janice returns to the house just as Edwin and Father Gellibrand are visiting. The three find Marcia slumped over her kitchen table. The ambulance ride to the hospital fulfills one of Marcia's lifelong ambitions. Her weight upon admission is eighty-four pounds. During her brief hospitalization, Edwin brings her flowers, writing on the card that the flowers are from all three of her former office mates, though Letty has not contributed anything and Norman has begrudgingly given only fifty pence. Edwin also tells the receptionist that he is Marcia's next of kin. Marcia soon dies.

After Marcia's death, the drab lives of the others change. She had left her house to Norman, though he decides to sell it; the money gives him new options. Marjorie's vicar, David, leaves her for Beth; now Marjorie wants Letty to share her cottage. However, Letty is not certain she wants to leave London. She does take a day trip to see Marjorie, taking Edwin and Norman with her. There remains a slim hope that romance may still bloom.

Critical Evaluation:

Barbara Pym might have selected as the epigraph for *Quartet in Autumn* the epigraph from E. M. Forster's *How-*

ards End (1910), which reads "Only Connect." In what is arguably the bleakest of Pym's works, the novel depicts a world of anomie and isolation. The opening scene sets the novel's tone, as the four main characters visit the library, each at a different time. The library assistant does not notice them. Pym comments that if he had, he would have thought that the four somehow belonged together; yet they remain separate.

In large part, the quartet's isolation is self-imposed. Marcia's bequest of her house to Norman shows that she had harbored feelings for him. However, the only expression of emotion she allows herself is in making his coffee and in sharing the cost of an ironically named family-sized can of coffee. The one time Marcia is visited by Norman, she merely glares at him, not speaking and certainly not inviting him in. She rebuffs Letty's invitation to a lunch and hesitates to join her three coworkers for the reunion that Edwin had planned. Though she finally decides to attend the luncheon, she remains uncommunicative. Also, she will not allow her neighbors, or social worker Janice Brabner, to help her.

Marcia's coworkers are equally reclusive. The four never meet outside the office. Norman's and Letty's visit at Edwin's house for coffee before Marcia's cremation is the first time either has been inside his house. Edwin finds Letty a new place to live when he learns that she is unhappy with her new landlord, then dismisses her from his thoughts. Once, when he meets Letty at a religious service, he finds her greeting to be overly warm; he never goes back to that church. When he takes flowers to the hospital, he leaves them with the receptionist without trying to see Marcia. After spending Christmas with his daughter, Edwin escapes as quickly as he can.

Norman visits his brother-in-law, Ken, once, when Ken is hospitalized, but they barely converse then or at Christmas, when Norman briefly visits. Although Norman has no work the day the office reopens after the Christmas holiday, he refuses to attend a memorial service for a coworker; Letty and Marcia also do not attend. Only Edwin goes. Norman objects to Edwin's plans for a reunion lunch, fearing that the four will have nothing to say to each other. Letty refuses an invitation to dinner from the new owner of her living quarters, Mr. Olatunde, and she also avoids her new landlady, Mrs. Pope. Pym's decision to give the four coworkers no close relatives or even pets reflects their loneliness.

In her notebooks for the novel, Pym comments on the supposed social safety net that should help people like Letty and Marcia. However, as Pym observes, nets have holes through which people can fall. Early in the novel, Norman reads a newspaper account of a man who had died of hypothermia, an apt metaphor for the lack of human warmth available to the characters in the novel. On her way to work, Letty sees a woman slumped on a bench in the London subway; that woman, too, has fallen through the net of the welfare state.

Pym shows in the novel that those who should help those in need lack the compassion or knowledge to do so. Father Gellibrand hesitates to visit Marcia because she does not live in his parish. David Lydell visits his parishioners, but only to find the woman who will best cook his favorite foods. After Marcia and Letty retire, no one in their firm inquires about their financial situations. Janice repeatedly calls on Marcia, but never assists her. Instead, Janice repeats clichés to convince herself that she is making a difference. When Marcia refuses to let Janice into her house during her attempted first visit, Janice thinks that she has planted a seed, though her visit has changed nothing. When she is able to enter Marcia's house on the second visit, Janice stresses to herself not that she can finally help Marcia but that she has been able to gain access to Marcia's home, again; the social worker has not positively affected Marcia's life. The young medical resident who sees Marcia after her operation observes that she is thin but merely wonders whether all women her age are like that. A doctor tells Marcia to eat more, but then takes no further steps because she is the patient of another doctor, Dr. Strong.

Despite its elegiac tone, *Quartet in Autumn* remains comic in both situation and outcome. Rather than condemning the incompetence of those who should help, Pym treats them as figures of fun. The main characters, too, prove humorous rather than tragic. Marcia's exaggerated concern for her mismatched milk bottle, Edwin's flight from Letty's enthusiastic greeting, and Norman's delight at the sight of a wrecked car, give the idiosyncrasies a humorous turn. Even Marcia's collapse raises a smile, as Marcia is delighted to finally ride in an ambulance; she becomes disappointed, though, when the driver does not use the siren.

The women's situations mirror those of Pym. Like Marcia, Pym had a mastectomy. Like Letty, she had to find a new place to live when her sister sold their London house and moved to the country. Like both women, she retired from her job in 1974 and worried about her finances (she had published no books since 1961). Still, Pym could view her life, like those of her characters, with a detachment that invites smiles rather than tears.

Joseph Rosenblum

Further Reading

Allen, Orphia Jane. *Barbara Pym: Writing a Life*. Metuchen, N.J.: Scarecrow Press, 1994. An extremely useful volume for both beginning students and advanced scholars. Part 1 discusses Pym's life and work, part 2 analyzes her novels, part 3 examines different critical approaches to her work and presents a bibliographical essay, and part 4 provides a comprehensive primary and secondary bibliography.

Donato, Deborah. *Reading Barbara Pym*. Madison, N.J.: Fairleigh Dickinson University Press, 2005. Offers close readings of four of Pym's novels: *Quartet in Autumn*, *Some Tame Gazelle* (1950), *Excellent Women* (1952), and *Jane and Prudence* (1953). Pays particular attention to Pym's language.

Lenckos, Frauke Elisabeth, and Ellen J. Miller, eds. *"All This Reading": The Literary World of Barbara Pym*. Madison, N.J.: Fairleigh Dickinson University Press, 2003. A collection of essays that examines the roles of reading and libraries in Pym's work, including discussions of individual novels and of Pym's literary reputation. Includes an annotated bibliography of Pym criticism published from 1982 through 1998.

Nardin, Jane. *Barbara Pym*. Boston: Twayne, 1985. Provides an excellent introduction to Pym's life and career, noting the origins and development of her themes, character types, and style. Includes a chronology, notes, a bibliography of primary and secondary sources, and an index.

Rossen, Janice, ed. *Independent Women: The Function of Gender in the Novels of Barbara Pym*. New York: St. Martin's Press, 1988. A collection of ten essays that considers Pym's craftsmanship, the literary influences on her work, and her special use of language. The contributors use biographical, historical, and feminist approaches to explore Pym's unique creative process as it relates to events in her life. Includes notes and an index.

Salwak, Dale. *Barbara Pym: A Reference Guide*. Boston: G. K. Hall, 1991. A comprehensive chronologically arranged bibliography of writings about Pym for the period 1950 to 1990. Dated but still useful.

Wyatt-Brown, Anne M. *Barbara Pym: A Critical Biography*. Columbia: University of Missouri Press, 1992. Combines psychological and literary methodologies to assess Pym's life and works. Wyatt-Brown looks at Pym's diaries, letters, and manuscripts to show how she translated her experiences and observations into fiction.

Queen Mab
A Philosophical Poem, with Notes

Author: Percy Bysshe Shelley (1792-1822)
First published: 1813; revised, 1816, as *The Daemon of the World*
Type of work: Poetry
Type of plot: Didactic
Time of plot: Before, during, and after 1813
Locale: Earth and a palace in outer space

Principal characters:
IANTHE, a virtuous and beautiful young woman
MAB, the fairy queen
THE KING, an earthly tyrant
RELIGION, an old fiend
AHASUERUS, a phantom
HENRY, the man who loves Ianthe

The Poem:

Ianthe is sleeping, and when she awakes she will bring further joy to the person who is faithfully watching her. Mab, the fairy queen, descends to Ianthe's side in a chariot drawn by winged horses. With her translucent form glowing in the moonlight, Mab summons Ianthe's soul from the living body and invites the purely spiritual Ianthe to ascend with her in the chariot to receive the revelation that Ianthe's virtue has earned. While dawn nears, Mab and Ianthe rise in the magic chariot far above the earth, which eventually appears as only a tiny light in the starry vastness that forms the temple of the Spirit of Nature.

Ianthe gazes with special vision from the battlement of Mab's palace overlooking the harmonious universe, and she sees clearly the distant Earth as Mab shows her the ruins of the past and the destiny of human pride: Palmyra; the Pyramids; the site of the Temple in Jerusalem, where, says Mab, a bloodthirsty people worshiped their demon; Athens and Rome, where freedom once flourished; and the jungle-covered stones of Mesoamerican cities.

Ianthe thanks Mab for the insight into the past and says that humans will need no Heaven when they have a power to give joy to others that equals their will to do so. Turning Ianthe's attention to the present, Mab reveals a king who lives in a guarded palace standing amid the poor. For all his riches, the king is such a slave to vice that he cannot enjoy his meals or sleep peacefully. He and his courtiers have only a brief fame, but a virtuous person's fame endures because Nature works against monarchs and for citizens.

Mab depicts a calm winter night that turns into a stormy day followed by a night of battle that leaves soldiers dead and a city burned. War, says Mab, comes not from evil in human nature but from monarchs, clergymen, politicians, and commanders who blight even infants with their lies about Heaven, Hell, and God.

Mab portrays selfishness as religion's blighting twin and the source of a commerce through which the products of nature and artifice are sold instead of being given through the dictates of kindness to fulfill needs. Relying on gold, commerce leads to luxury for some and to poverty for others—poverty that stifles talent under the drudgery of the farm or factory. Selfishness corrupts sexual relationships and motivates both the clergyman and the soldier, but commerce based on money and pride will eventually yield to commerce based on goodness.

Grieved by the universal misery she has seen, Ianthe asks Mab whether hope exists, and Mab assures her that it does, for even in the worst times virtuous persons will speak truth and destroy falsehood. Old fiend Religion, Mab continues, has grown senile and is nearing death, to be mourned only by those whose pride depends upon him. Instead of the God that perverse humans have imagined, it is Necessity, the impersonal Spirit of Nature, which rules the universe and remains unchanged.

Ianthe remarks that, when she was a child, she had seen an atheist burned at the stake. Mab then echoes the atheist's statement that God does not exist, in the way most people have imagined, and proclaims that people have justified massacres worldwide in the name of their god.

Mab summons Ahasuerus, a phantom of erring imagination, whom Ianthe asks about God's existence. According to Ahasuerus, there is a God—hateful and powerful—who created the world and doomed all human souls to Hell until, responding to Moses' plea, he said he would send his son to die to save a few chosen ones, while millions still went to Hell. When the Incarnate God was on the cross, Ahasuerus summarized for him the slaughter carried out in God's name in Israel and, having mocked him, received his curse to wander Earth forever—to become the Wandering Jew. Continuing to address Ianthe, Ahasuerus tells of the crimes Christians have committed even against other Christians, and tells of his own defiance of divine tyranny. Eventually, Mab waves her wand, making him disappear into unreality.

Mab gladdens Ianthe by showing her the earthly paradise of the future, in which mild weather has transformed the poles, farms and groves cover what once was lifeless sand, lovely islands have risen like jewels in the formerly barren ocean, goats and vegetarian lions play together, and, amid health and peace and with passion and reason no longer at odds, human beings, also vegetarians, seek truth.

Mab presents the heavenly earth, which will gradually emerge. Old age will be vigorous and death gentle and hopeful. Sexual love will be free from legal tyranny, prostitution will be no more, and women will live in equality with men. Palaces, cathedrals, and prisons will be disappearing ruins. Perfection will come to Earth and humankind. When this vision of paradise ends, Mab praises Ianthe for her virtue, which raises her above a fear of death, and foretells that she will continue to strive against oppression. Finally, on Mab's chariot, Ianthe returns to Earth, where—her soul and her body joined again—she awakes to see her lover, Henry, kneeling at her side and sees the stars shining through the window.

Critical Evaluation:

Percy Bysshe Shelley's *Queen Mab* begins with French, Latin, and Greek epigraphs from, respectively, eighteenth century satirist Voltaire, first century B.C.E. poet Lucretius, and third century B.C.E. physicist Archimedes. After the epigraphs, which refer to crushing the infamous, eradicating superstition, and moving the world, respectively, Shelley includes a sixteen-line poem, "To Harriet *****," a work dedicated to Harriet Westbrook Shelley, his first wife, whom he praises as his inspiration.

Writing without rhyme, except for one accidental couplet, and often using blank verse (unrhymed iambic pentameter), Shelley finished *Queen Mab*, but not its notes, in February, 1813. By the end of June he had printed *Queen Mab* and its notes in a well-manufactured volume, possibly with the help of his publisher Thomas Hookham, who chose not to have his name on the work because he believed it violated the law forbidding blasphemy. Instead of actually publishing the volume, Shelley sent about 70 of the 250 printed copies to those he thought would like the theme, having first cut out his name and address as the printer and, in many instances, having also removed the short dedicatory poem. Despite the technically private distribution of *Queen Mab*, it had become so well known by 1817 that it figured in the Chancery Court's decision to deny Shelley the custody of his two children by his first wife, whom he had left in 1814 in favor of Mary Godwin and who had drowned herself in December, 1816.

To the poem itself, Shelley had attached seventeen endnotes, each devoted to a separate passage in the poem. Several of the notes are so long that they have footnotes themselves. The notes, which also feature the quotes of other authors—in Greek, Latin, French, and English—include topics such as astronomy, war, economics, Necessity, Christianity, time, and vegetarianism.

In 1815, parts of *Queen Mab* had appeared in the initial issue of *Theological Inquirer*, and in February, 1816, Shelley had published a significant revision of the first two cantos of *Queen Mab* as the long poem *The Daemon of the World*. However, *Queen Mab* did not reach the public in its entirety until 1821, when two pirated editions appeared. Afterward, despite legal danger, more unauthorized editions came out, including one (1832) small enough to fit into a pocket.

Popular with readers who sympathized with Shelley's ideas, *Queen Mab* became virtual scripture for Chartism, the influential British political reform movement that began in 1838. Friedrich Engels and Karl Marx noted the popularity of the poem among Chartists, and the work later influenced British Communists.

Shelley intended *Queen Mab* to subvert the British system of church and state. The name "Mab" was known to many readers in the early nineteenth century as that of the fairy who brings dreams, according to Mercutio in William Shakespeare's play *Romeo and Juliet* (pr. c. 1595-1596, pb. 1597), and as that of a figure like Mother Goose in volumes of children's stories published in the eighteenth century. Shelley chose the name because he thought it would cover his revolutionary message with innocence and would appeal to children of the aristocracy, whose parents, although they would not read the book, might find it superficially appealing not only because of its title but also because of its paper and binding.

Being well-read in classical and modern languages, Shelley formed his thoughts for *Queen Mab*, with its notes, from what he had gained from other authors, as well as from his experiences as the oldest son of a wealthy member of Parliament, and as a student, husband, and British subject. His unhappy relationship with his father, Timothy Shelley—whom he considered a hypocrite—and the tyranny he witnessed and suffered as a schoolboy—combined with his reading and his observation of society—made him a leftist eager to speak his mind, as he did in *Queen Mab*. Among his written sources for ideas were works by English reformer William Godwin (his second father-in-law) and the German-French materialist Paul-Henri Thiry, baron d'Holbach.

Queen Mab was influential in nineteenth century British politics, but the quality of the poem, despite the poet's erudition, is debatable. Some critics consider it a work of immaturity, but others consider it Shelley's first important poem. As an argument, the poem itself will seldom convince readers of its fairness unless they are already inclined to agree; even readers who see truth in Shelley's picture of British government in his time may see his picture of Christianity as severely distorted and his vision of an earthly paradise necessitated by the Spirit of Nature as a dream that Marxism proved a nightmare. Shelley himself never recanted his hatred of what he thought of as governmental, religious, and domestic despotism; but, in a letter written to a newspaper in 1821, he called *Queen Mab* a product of his youth that might inadvertently hurt the campaign for freedom.

Victor Lindsey

Further Reading

Bieri, James. *Percy Bysshe Shelley: A Biography*. 2 vols. Newark: University of Delaware Press, 2004-2005. Gives a detailed, psychologically probing account of Shelley's life. Discusses the first printing and early publication of *Queen Mab* and examines the part of the poem that led to the poet's loss of custody of his children.

Duffy, Cian. *Shelley and the Revolutionary Sublime*. New York: Cambridge University Press, 2005. Sees in *Queen Mab* an ideological conflict between peaceful and gradual change and violent revolution.

Miller, Christopher R. "Happily Ever After? The Necessity of Fairytale in *Queen Mab*." In *The Unfamiliar Shelley*, edited by Alan M. Weinberg and Timothy Webb. Burlington, Vt.: Ashgate, 2009. Argues that Shelley uses two fairytales in his poem to enhance his presentation of revolutionary ideas on politics and religion.

Shaaban, Bouthaina. "Shelley and the Chartists." In *Shelley: Poet and Legislator of the World*, edited by Betty T. Bennett and Stuart Curran. Baltimore: Johns Hopkins University Press, 1996. Demonstrates the popularity of Shelley's political poems within Chartism.

Shelley, Percy Bysshe. *Shelley: Poetical Works*. Edited by Thomas Hutchinson. New York: Oxford University Press, 1970. Places *Queen Mab* in the section "Juvenilia" but reproduces the whole poem along with editorial notes on the text, the poet's own notes (in thirty-four pages), and a long note by Mary Godwin Shelley, the poet's wife.

_____. *Shelley's Poetry and Prose: Authoritative Texts, Criticism*. 2d ed. Selected and edited by Donald H. Reiman and Neil Fraistat. New York: Norton, 2002. Includes an editorial introduction to *Queen Mab*, the poem itself, the editors' explanatory footnotes (with excerpts from Shelley's notes), scholarly essays, and a chronology of Shelley's life.

Silver, James P. "The Aesthetic of Utopia in Shelley's *Queen Mab*." In *A Brighter Morn: The Shelley Circle's Utopian Project*, edited by Darby Lewes. Lanham, Md.: Lexington Books, 2003. Contends that Henry, not Ianthe, has the utopian vision, a vision that hides his intent to seduce her.

Quentin Durward

Author: Sir Walter Scott (1771-1832)
First published: 1823
Type of work: Novel
Type of plot: Historical
Time of plot: 1468
Locale: France and Flanders

Principal characters:
QUENTIN DURWARD, a Scottish cadet
LUDOVIC LESLY or LE BALAFRÉ, his maternal uncle
ISABELLE, the countess of Croye, a servant, disguised as Jacqueline
LADY HAMELINE, her aunt
KING LOUIS XI, ruler of France
COUNT PHILIP DE CRÈVECŒUR, of Burgundy
CHARLES, the duke of Burgundy
WILLIAM DE LA MARCK, a Flemish outlaw
HAYRADDIN MAUGRABIN, a Bohemian

The Story:

When Quentin Durward, a young Scottish gentleman, approaches the ford of a small river near the castle of Plessisles-Tours, in France, he finds the river in flood. Two people watch him from the opposite bank. They are King Louis XI in his common disguise of Maître Pierre, a merchant, and Tristan l'Hermite, marshal of France. Quentin enters the flood and nearly drowns. Arriving on the other side and mistaking the king and his companion for a burgher and a butcher, he threatens the two with a drubbing because they did not warn him of the deep ford. Amused by Quentin's spirit and daring, Maître Pierre takes him to breakfast at a nearby inn to make amends. At the inn, Quentin meets a beautiful young peasant, Jacqueline, who actually is Isabelle, the countess of Croye. Quentin tries to learn why the merchant Maître Pierre acts so much like a noble. He sees many other things as well that arouse his curiosity but for which he finds no explanation.

Shortly afterward, Quentin meets Ludovic Lesly, known as Le Balafré, his maternal uncle, who is a member of King Louis's Scottish Archers. Le Balafré is exceedingly surprised to learn that Quentin can read and write, something that no other Durward or Lesly before him has been able to do.

Later, Quentin discovers the body of a man hanging from a tree. When he cuts the body down, he is seized by two officers of Tristan l'Hermite. They are about to hang Quentin for his deed when he asks of the crowd that has gathered if there is a good Christian among them who will inform Le Balafré of what is taking place. A Scottish Archer hears him and cuts his bonds. While Quentin and the man prepare to defend themselves from the mob, Le Balafré rides up with some of his men and takes command of the situation, haughtily insisting that Quentin is a member of the Scottish Archers and beyond the reach of the marshal's men. Quentin has not joined the guards as yet, but the lie saves his life. Le Balafré takes Quentin to see Lord Crawford, the commander of the guards, to enroll him. When the Scottish Archers are summoned to the royal presence, Quentin is amazed to see that Maître Pierre is King Louis.

Count Philip de Crèvecœur arrives at the castle to demand an audience with the king in the name of his master, the duke of Burgundy. When the king admits Crèvecœur, the messenger presents a list of wrongs and oppressions committed on the frontier for which the duke of Burgundy demands redress. The duke also requests that Louis cease his secret and underhanded dealings in the towns of Ghent, Liège, and Malines. Further, he requests that the king send back to Burgundy, under safeguard, the person of Isabelle, the countess of Croye; Isabelle is the duke's ward, and the duke accuses the king of harboring her in secret. Dissatisfied with the king's replies to these demands, Crèvecœur throws his gauntlet to the floor of the hall. Several of the king's attendants rush to pick it up and to accept the challenge it represents, but the king orders the bishop of Auxerre to lift the gauntlet and to remonstrate with Crèvecœur for thus declaring war between Burgundy and France. The king and his courtiers then leave to hunt wild boar.

During the hunt, Quentin Durward saves the king's life by spearing a wild boar after Louis has slipped and fallen before the infuriated beast. The king decides to reward Quentin with a special mission: He is ordered to stand guard in the room where the king is to entertain Crèvecœur and others; at a sign from the king, Quentin is to shoot the Burgundian. When the time comes, however, the king changes his mind and does not give the signal. The king then makes Quentin the personal bodyguard of Isabelle and her aunt, Lady Hameline, as they travel to seek the protection of the bishop of Liège.

En route to Liège, the party is assaulted by the Count de Dunois and the duke of Orleans. Quentin defends himself with great courage and receives timely help from Lord Crawford, who arrives with a body of Scottish Archers and takes both men prisoner. The party's guide on the second half of the journey is Hayraddin Maugrabin, a Bohemian; his brother was the man whom Quentin had cut down earlier. Nothing untoward occurs until the small party reaches Flanders. There Quentin discovers, by following Hayraddin, that a plot has been hatched to attack his party and carry off the women to William de la Marck, known as the Wild Boar of Ardennes. Quentin frustrates these plans by guiding the party up the left bank of the Maes instead of the right. They proceed safely to Liège, where Quentin gives the women over to the protection of the bishop at his castle of Schonwaldt. Four days later, William de la Marck attacks the castle and captures it during the night. Lady Hameline escapes. In the bishop's throne room in the castle, William de la Marck murders the churchman in front of his own episcopal throne. Aroused by the brutality of William, Quentin steps to the side of Carl Eberson, William's son, and places his dagger at the boy's throat; he threatens to kill the lad if William does not cease his butchery. In the ensuing confusion, Quentin finds Isabelle and takes her safely from the castle disguised as the daughter of the syndic of Liège. They are pursued by William's men but are rescued by a party under Count de Crèvecœur, who conducts them safely to the court of the duke of Burgundy at Peroune.

The king arrives at the castle of the duke of Burgundy, asserting the royal prerogative of visiting any of his vassals. Disregarding the laws of hospitality, the duke imprisons Louis and then holds a council to debate the difficulties between France and Burgundy. Hayraddin appears claiming to be a herald from William de la Marck, who has married the Lady Hameline. Toison d'Or, the duke's herald, however, unmasks Hayraddin, who has given himself away with his lack of knowledge of the science of heraldry. The duke releases Hayraddin and sets his fierce boar hounds on the Bohemian, but then he orders the dogs called off before they can tear

Hayraddin to shreds. The duke then orders that Hayraddin be hanged with the proper ceremony.

The king and the duke also debate the disposal of Isabelle's fortune and her hand in marriage, but she has fallen in love with Quentin and says that she prefers the cloister to any of their suggested alliances. The duke solves the problem, at least to his satisfaction, by declaring that Isabelle's hand will be given to the man who brings him the head of William de la Marck.

The king and the duke join forces to assault Liège. Their combined forces besiege the city but are forced to go into bivouac at nightfall. That night, William makes a foray but is driven back into the city. The next day, the forces of the king and the duke attack once more, make breaches in the wall, and pour into the city. Quentin comes face-to-face with William de la Marck, who rushes at him with all the fury of the wild boar for which he is named. Le Balafré stands by and roars out for fair play, indicating that this should be a duel of champions. At that moment, Quentin sees a woman being forcibly dragged along by a French soldier. When he turns to rescue her, Le Balafré attacks William and kills him.

Le Balafré is announced as the man who killed William de la Marck, but he gives most of the credit to Quentin's valiant behavior and defers to his nephew. While it is agreed that Quentin is responsible for William's death, there is still the problem of Quentin's lineage, which the duke questions. Lord Crawford, indignant, recites Quentin's pedigree and thereby proves his gentility. Without more ado, Quentin and Countess Isabelle are betrothed.

Critical Evaluation:

Quentin Durward appeared when Sir Walter Scott's career as a novelist was nearly a decade old. Although Scott was still signing his novels "By the Author of *Waverley*," his authorship was by no means unknown. The "Wizard of the North" touched the familiar formulas of his fiction with an undeniable magic. With *Waverley: Or, 'Tis Sixty Years Since* (1814), Scott had invented the historical novel, a new genre. This fictional treatment of the last of the Stuart uprisings in 1745, manifesting genuine insight into events "sixty years since," had been solidly founded on his knowledge of Scotland, its history, and its people. The author had perceived in the Jacobite-Hanoverian conflict the clash of two cultures at the very moment when the former was passing away forever and the other was just coming into being. He had made figures from history a part of his fiction, through them creating the tensions in which his fictitious characters were caught. This first novel established the pattern and theme for the serious historical novel, not only Scott's "Waverley novels"

but also the works of later writers such as James Fenimore Cooper.

Abounding in wealth and fame, his energies given also to public service, business, an estate in Scotland, an active social life, and other kinds of writing, Scott worked too hard and wrote too fast—one novel a year, sometimes two. With his tenth novel, *Ivanhoe* (1819), he sagaciously determined that his English reading public, after so many Scottish novels, would welcome a foray into English history. *Ivanhoe* became the talk of London, and his career gained new impetus. By 1823, however, his publisher, conscious of Scott's waning popularity, advised him to turn to other kinds of writing. The author, however, boldly moved into the foreign territory of fifteenth century France and once again created a literary sensation—the reception of his new novel in Paris rivaled that of *Ivanhoe* in London. After *Quentin Durward*, Scott was recognized as a great writer both at home and abroad.

Quentin Durward stands as a milestone in Scott's career rather than as a significant novel. His own remarks on the work contain casual apologies for his license with historical facts; some critics charge him with the worse fault of allowing superficial knowledge to make of *Quentin Durward* a mere costume romance rather than a serious historical novel. Others rate it simply as a good tale of adventure.

Nevertheless, *Quentin Durward* provides a good example of the conflict at the heart of Scott's best historical novels—the thematic clash between the old order and the new. The order that is passing away is the age of chivalry, with its feudal system and its chivalric code. The age that is coming into being takes its traits from the leader who, rather than the titular hero, is the central character of the novel—King Louis XI of France. Louis is the antithesis of the chivalric ideal. Honor is but a word to him; he studies the craft of dissimulation. His unceremonious manners express contempt rather than knightly humility. He exercises the virtues of generosity and courtesy only with ulterior motives. Crafty and false, committed to his own self-interest, he is a complete Machiavellian.

If Louis is the chief representative of the new age, no one is a genuine survivor of the old, despite noblemen who cling to a narrow concept of honor or imitate medieval splendor. Although Louis's principal rival, Charles of Burgundy, is his direct opposite, Charles is an inadequate symbol of chivalry. When Quentin says that he can win more honor under Charles's banner than under those of the king, Le Balafré counters with a description more accurate: "The Duke of Burgundy is a hot-brained, impetuous, pudding-headed, iron-ribbed dare-all." The decay of chivalry is epitomized in the hopelessness of Quentin's search for a leader who will keep his honor bright and is confirmed by his ultimate conclusion that none of these great leaders is any better than any other. During the dramatic episode at Charles's court, when the king, ironically, is prisoner of his own vassal, the court historian, Des Comines, reminds Louis—who knows better than anyone else—that strict interpretation of the feudal law is becoming outdated, while opportunity and power drive men to compromise and alter the old codes of chivalry.

Quentin Durward is the standard-bearer of the old order. Desiring to follow a man who will never avoid a battle and will keep a generous state, with tournaments and feasting and dancing with ladies, he lives on ideas of brave deeds and advancement. Quentin's ideals, however, are impossible from the start. His rootlessness is symptomatic of the dying culture he reveres. His only real ties are with the mercenary band of Scottish Archers. Their weatherbeaten leader, Lord Crawford, one of the last leaders of a brave band of Scottish lords and knights, as well as Quentin's kinsman, the hideously scarred, almost bestial Le Balafré, serve as evidence that the glorious past is irrevocably past.

Although Quentin is introduced as a simple and naïve youth, he is not a rare example of perfect chivalry. Equipped only with a rude mountain chivalry, he has his fair share of shrewdness and cunning. Far more politic than his experienced kinsman Le Balafré, this simple youth counsels Isabelle on the ways of telling half-truths with a skill that would credit Louis himself. Although it offends his dignity as a gentleman to accept money from a rich plebeian—ironically, King Louis disguised—Quentin immediately discerns that the simple maid of the little turret is far more attractive after she is revealed as Isabelle, the countess of Croye, a highborn heir. Presented by the king with an unpleasant crisis—an order to be prepared to kill the noble Crèvecœur from ambush—in which it would be "destruction in refusing, while his honor told him there would be disgrace in complying," Quentin chooses compliance.

As an emblem of the future, Quentin is neither as contemptible as his wily king nor as foolish as his older comrades deem him. The venerable Lord Crawford defends him well when he argues: "Quentin Durward is as much a gentleman as the king, only as the Spaniard says, not so rich. He is as noble as myself, and I am chief of my name." The youthful squire successfully endures the perilous journey, the chivalric testing of a man, bravely and skillfully evading the snares of the wicked, from the literal traps in and around Louis's castle to the treacherous ambush planned by the king and the more horrible fate threatening him during the sack of Schonwaldt. Therefore, only partially valid is Crèvecœur's ironic description of Quentin's trials as a pleasant journey full of heroic adventure and high hope. Crèvecœur's capitu-

lation at the end is more just: "But why should I grudge this youth his preferment? Since, after all, it is sense, firmness, and gallantry which have put him in possession of Wealth, Rank, and Beauty!"

In the characterization of both Quentin and Louis, Scott dramatizes the ambiguities that afflict a time of transition. Although Louis lacks any real sense of moral obligation, he nevertheless understands the interests of France and faithfully pursues them. Detested as too cautious and crafty, he nevertheless exhibits a coolness before the wrath of Charles that far outshines the brave deeds of arms that Quentin values. If Quentin too passively drifts into the service of Louis, he can summon courage enough to defy the king and principle enough to support the king in adversity—even at the cost of telling a little falsehood and the risk of sacrificing his life.

In this novel, as in others, Scott vividly depicts the various ways in which people cope with a world of changing values, where, as Crèvecœur's speech jocularly implies, sense and firmness have replaced gallantry, and wealth and rank have toppled beauty in the scale of things. It is this view of reality that seems most characteristic of the author: He is, like Quentin, most certainly a Romantic, idealizing the glories of a legendary time; but he understands the practical demands of a present reality and the value of a Louis or of a shrewd and brave youth such as Quentin Durward.

"Critical Evaluation" by Catherine E. Moore

Further Reading

Hart, Francis. *Scott's Novels: The Plotting of Historic Survival.* Charlottesville: University Press of Virginia, 1966. Provides excellent discussion of the historical background of Scott's works, allowing insight into the characters of Charles of Burgundy and Louis XI. Analyzes the theme of the importance of power in politics and raises questions about the difficult moral issues that accompany political allegiance.

Irvine, Robert P. "The State, the Domestic, and National Culture in the Waverley Novels." In *Enlightenment and Romance: Gender and Agency in Smollett and Scott.* New York: Peter Lang, 2000. Analyzes the fiction of Scott and Tobias Smollett within the context of the emergence of the social sciences and the dominance of novels written by female authors in the eighteenth century. Describes how Smollett and Scott adapted the feminine romance and the domestic novel to assert control over the narrative structure of their novels.

Johnson, Edgar. *Sir Walter Scott: The Great Unknown.* 2 vols. New York: Macmillan, 1970. Extensively researched biography explores Scott both as a man and as a writer. Provides a clear summary of the action in *Quentin Durward* and good analysis of the characters, themes, and setting, showing a society in which basic values have broken down, forcing the protagonist to fit into this corrupt world without losing his soul. An excellent introductory source.

Shaw, Harry E. *The Forms of Historical Fiction: Sir Walter Scott and His Successors.* Ithaca, N.Y.: Cornell University Press, 1983. Compares *Quentin Durward* to the other Waverley novels, discussing plot structure and noting that Scott described Louis XI as the novel's central character.

_____, ed. *Critical Essays on Sir Walter Scott: The Waverley Novels.* New York: G. K. Hall, 1996. Collection of essays published between 1858 and 1996 discusses Scott's series of novels. Includes journalist Walter Bagehot's 1858 article about the Waverley novels and discussions of such topics as Scott's rationalism, storytelling and subversion of the literary form in Scott's fiction, and what Scott's work meant to Victorian readers.

Sutherland, John. *The Life of Walter Scott: A Critical Biography.* New York: Blackwell, 1995. Describes Scott's research for a new setting for *Quentin Durward*, during which he studied maps of France. Compares details in the plot to incidents that occurred in Scott's private life.

Wagenknecht, Edward. *Sir Walter Scott.* New York: Continuum, 1991. Provides clear, detailed discussion of the political background of *Quentin Durward* as well as the novel's themes and characterization. Asserts that the title character is a realistic hero and that the characterization of James I is the finest in the novel.

The Quest for Certainty

Author: John Dewey (1859-1952)
First published: 1929
Type of work: Philosophy

John Dewey remains one of America's most influential philosophers, social reformers, and educators. His system of thought is part of an American school of pragmatism that began with Charles Sanders Peirce, grew with William James, and blossomed with Dewey. Pragmatism continues to influence American educators, philosophers, and social scientists.

Dewey's *A Quest for Certainty* is a collection of lectures, the Gifford Lectures, that Dewey delivered in 1929 at the University of Edinburgh, Scotland. James was one of the first Americans invited to deliver the Gifford Lectures, and he noted that American writers and philosophers had long listened to European scholars, but that this monologue became a dialogue when American pragmatists, such as James and Dewey, were invited to deliver the Gifford Lectures. Having just retired from full-time teaching at Columbia University, Dewey was seventy years old when he presented these eleven lectures. They represent Dewey's mature philosophy, his theory of knowledge.

Devoting the first three lectures to the failure of modern philosophy, Dewey demonstrates a need for pragmatism, a philosophy that can heal the schism created by modern thinkers between practice and theory. Dewey associates practice with experience, and experience is the realm of science, of the senses, and of common sense. Theory he associates with religion and philosophy, disciplines that dismiss experience and embrace abstraction. The separation of these two realms in modern times causes people to give prestige to the rational, religious, and philosophical as permanent, unsoiled, and absolute and to denigrate the practical as unreliable, physical, manual, and changing.

In his first lecture, "Escape from Peril," Dewey blames the present philosophical crisis on a long tradition of Western thinking going back to the Greeks. The Greeks began the quest for certainty, for permanent absolute answers to the ultimate questions in life. At first these answers were provided by religions, by references to gods as the ultimate cause and meaning of earthly experiences. Greek philosophers shifted this search for certainty from a religious quest to a rational quest, attempting to use reason to reach answers to questions such as What is truth? What exists? and What is justice? Dewey argues that so long as philosophers and theologians remain in the realm of pure, abstract thought, in a realm where they hope to find absolute, unchanging answers, they will fail to connect their theories to practical experience.

Dewey attacks this separation of theory and practice, arguing that philosophers were looking for absolutes that do not exist. Dewey develops a method of inquiry that replaces the "quest of absolute certainty by cognitive means" with the "search for security by practical means." He notes that the denigration of the practical realm, of sense experience, was easy in a society or culture in which religious beliefs were preeminent, but in modern societies the rise of science has challenged religion and philosophy, a challenge that philosophers have attempted to reconcile in numerous, flawed ways. When philosophers could no longer dismiss the findings of science, their preoccupation was the reconciliation of theory and practice, of religion and science, of essence and experience. To this end modern philosophers struggled to unify a world divided into the realm of the body and the realm of the spirit.

In his third lecture, "Conflict of Authorities," Dewey analyzes several modern attempts to reconcile these differences, arguing that each attempt ultimately privileges the abstract realm at the expense of human experience. Taking the philosophy of Baruch Spinoza as exemplifying idealism, Dewey explores how Spinoza's monism posits the physical realm as a means to the spiritual or ideal. Dewey then examines Immanuel Kant's influential solution of a division of pure reason and practical reason into two separate spheres, the one a realm of certainty, the other a realm of human activity and doubt. Dewey discusses Kant's solution as the most prevalent in modern times, and he attacks that solution as the theory that most clearly and destructively separates practice from experience. Finally, Dewey explores the dialectic idealism of Georg Wilhelm Friedrich Hegel, admiring Hegel's concern with the practical, the imperfect realm, but questioning Hegel's tendency toward seeking an ideal state of certainty. For Dewey, the danger in all modern philosophy is that method and content have been divided.

In lecture four, "The Art of Acceptance and the Art of Control," Dewey begins to outline his theory of inquiry, a method that will replace these failed modern ones, a theory of inquiry that he bases on the scientific method. Dewey asserts that this method is so common, so pervasive, and so obvious that philosophers have not recognized it or created a theory of knowledge around it. This theory of knowledge is based on scientific method. Dewey also asserts, as a caveat, that modern science too often views data as unrelated particulars divorced from human experience. To gain knowledge, however, people must advance a method that explains how they learn from experience. Experience is the only source of knowledge—for Dewey, experiences are what exist.

To prove that reason cannot operate independent of experience and that knowledge of the physical realm cannot exist independent of reason, Dewey considers the interconnection of mathematical principles and the world of experience, arguing that mathematical principles—ideas that come close to pure abstraction—only exist in the physical realm: "Mathematical space is not a kind of space distinct from so-called physical and empirical space, but is a name given to operations ideally or formally possible with respect to a thing having spacious qualities." To illustrate his method further, Dewey analyzes the analogy of a good doctor diagnosing a patient's illness, a technique that Dewey posits as exemplifying his epistemology.

Doctors have ideas and theories that they learned in school and from books, but this abstract knowledge is not enough—a good doctor must also have experience. When doctors see patients, they form hypotheses concerning the patients' illnesses, but the doctors must then perform experiments to confirm or reject these hypotheses. With each case and with each experience, the good doctor gains knowledge. Thus, experienced doctors form better hypotheses. Essential to this method is "the appreciation and use . . . of direct experience." At the core of Dewey's philosophy is his epistemology, his theory of how people know what they know. This theory has been labeled instrumental logic, but it is really a commonsense theory of scientific method. Dewey's theory relies on reflective experimentation.

In his ninth lecture, Dewey returns to the question of certainty and the method that should be employed in situations in which one is uncertain. Dewey states that uncertainty arises in new situations and that humans wish to quell the fear or doubt that arises in such situations. One may alleviate uncertainty quickly by retreating to an abstract realm. An example of this would be a person who, when in trouble, prays, hoping that the prayer will solve the problem. Humans want to eliminate uncertainty or fear quickly. Dewey argues against such methods. The intelligent person has a delayed reaction to uncertainty, a reaction that allows uncertainty to linger. People should experiment in an uncertain situation, and this is done by means of manipulation. By experimenting, people change their relationship to the situation that is creating fear and, perhaps, create a new situation from which they can learn.

In his tenth lecture, "The Construction of Good," Dewey extends his epistemology into an ethics by arguing that values are not absolutes that exist prior to and separate from a particular circumstance. The good arises from what one experiences in a specific situation, and this will change as conditions change. Again, method is essential to determine the good. People cannot separate the means from the end—this would be the same as separating practice from theory. People must know how and why something is good, and this consideration returns them to a particular situation, a particular problem. Dewey's epistemology draws on a commonsense means of knowing, and his ethics draws on a practical means of valuing. He believes that philosophers have spent too much time searching for the good in a permanent, transcendent realm, while most people find value in particular experiences.

Dewey ends *The Quest for Certainty* with the lecture, "The Copernican Revolution." Nicolaus Copernicus, relying on scientific experimentation, asserted that the sun, not the earth, was at the center of the solar system. Thus, he displaced the Ptolemaic notion that dominated the Middle Ages. Kant compared himself to Copernicus, saying that he created a revolution in philosophy as Copernicus created one in science, but Dewey maintains that Kant's philosophy in maintaining a realm of pure reason is Ptolemaic in that it places human beings and their quest of certainty at the center of the system. Dewey, on the other hand, sees himself and other American pragmatists performing a Copernican revolution by basing philosophy, education, and social theory on experience, and by privileging a method of inquiry that does not ignore human experience.

The Quest for Certainty is a significant work in that it presents the mature theory and method of an influential American philosopher. The lectures delineate his objection to previous philosophy, his own theory of inquiry, and his ethics. These lectures do not explore his authoritative theories of aesthetics, education, and politics. Dewey, in other works, extends his method of experimental inquiry into education, advocating experimentation as the way to knowledge. Dewey also argued that the active exchange of ideas that should occur in school could model the democratic process. A society based on his theories of education and democracy would form a community of free inquirers who test their ideas in a public forum, not in an abstract or isolated realm.

Roark Mulligan

Further Reading

Boisvert, Raymond D. *John Dewey: Rethinking Our Time.* Albany: State University of New York Press, 1998. Boisvert tracks the implications of Dewey's thought, demonstrating Dewey's significance for contemporary social and philosophical issues.

Burke, Tom. *Dewey's New Logic: A Reply to Russell.* Chicago: University of Chicago Press, 1994. Contrasts Dewey's instrumental logic with Bertrand Russell's more abstract theory of symbolic logic. In so doing, Burke elaborates on ideas raised in *The Quest for Certainty.*

Festenstein, Matthew. *Pragmatism and Political Theory: From Dewey to Rorty.* Chicago: University of Chicago Press, 1997. A careful and critical analysis that shows how pragmatism, including that of Dewey, has affected political theory and practice.

Hickman, Larry A., ed. *Reading Dewey: Interpretation for a Postmodern Generation.* Bloomington: Indiana University Press, 1998. Interpreters of Dewey's thought explore his continuing significance for postmodern inquiries into the nature of knowledge and ethics.

Hook, Sidney. *John Dewey: An Intellectual Portrait.* New York: John Day, 1939. Dated but still valuable, this work offers a sympathetic and thoughtful analysis of Dewey as a person and philosopher.

Kulp, Christopher B. *The End of Epistemology: Dewey and His Current Allies on the Spectator Theory of Knowledge.* Westport, Conn.: Greenwood Press, 1992. Explores Dewey's theory of knowledge, the same theory that is developed in *The Quest for Certainty.* Analyzes the relationship of Dewey's theory to that of later twentieth century philosophers.

Manicas, Peter T. *Rescuing Dewey: Essays in Pragmatic Naturalism.* Lanham, Md.: Lexington Books, 2008. Focuses on Dewey's rejection of established epistemological ideas and his creation of a new view of logic, which had important implications for psychology, the practice of democracy, and philosophy.

Rockefeller, Steven C. *John Dewey: Religious Faith and Democratic America.* New York: Columbia University Press, 1991. A detailed and important study of Dewey's life and thought, focusing on his views about religion and democracy.

Talisse, Robert B. *On Dewey: The Reconstruction of Philosophy.* Belmont, Calif.: Wadsworth, 2000. A brief introductory overview of Dewey's ideas about philosophy, experience, knowledge, and society. Designed for students and general readers seeking a basic understanding of Dewey's work.

Welchman, Jennifer. *Dewey's Ethical Thought.* Ithaca, N.Y.: Cornell University Press, 1995. A sympathetic but critical analysis of Dewey's moral philosophy and its implications.

Westbrook, Robert B. *John Dewey and American Democracy.* Ithaca, N.Y.: Cornell University Press, 1991. A readable and careful study of Dewey's influence on American culture and politics.

The Quest for Christa T.

Author: Christa Wolf (Christa Margarete Ihlenfeld,
  1929-   )
First published: Nachdenken über Christa T., 1968
  (English translation, 1970)
Type of work: Novel
Type of plot: Testimony
Time of plot: Fall, 1943, to summer, 1964
Locale: Mecklenburg, Leipzig, and Berlin, East
  Germany

Principal characters:
THE NARRATOR, reconstructs the life of her friend
  Christa T.
CHRISTA T., a proud and talented student
GÜNTER, a student who loves Christa T.
KOSTIA, a student who has poetical flirtations with
  Christa T.
JUSTUS, a veterinarian who marries Christa T.
BLASING, a friend of Christa T. and Justus

The Story:

The narrator, a schoolgirl, becomes fascinated with Christa T., who, while walking in the street one day with her classmates, suddenly makes a trumpet from a rolled-up newspaper and blows it. Such exhibitionism, without any apparent concern for approval, characterizes Christa T.'s elusive personality. A daring, independent tomboy, Christa T. seems a *Sternkind kein Herrnkind*, that is, a "star-child" with a special destiny but without any inherited, unearned social advantages. Her modest origins are underlined by her regional dialect, Plattdeutsch ("flatland German"), which has a simplified vocabulary and syntax (and heavy admixtures of Dutch and English). Speakers of standard High German consider the dialect a barbarous, primitive patois.

Christa T. and the narrator are separated for seven years by the evacuation of civilians fleeing the advancing Russian army in 1945 during the final year of World War II. Christa T. suffers a nervous breakdown. When she recovers, she decides to become a teacher. She writes compulsively throughout her life because she fears vanishing without a trace. Her posthumous papers are full of sketches for stories, and full of unfinished drafts. The young school principal from the next village loves her, but he is ultimately rejected by her. Christa T. loves children, but after three years of unvarying classroom routine, she decides to leave her family rather than succeed her father at his school.

As a university student at Leipzig in 1952, Christa T. reunites with the narrator but turns out to be a neglectful friend. Timid despite her bravado, and unmotivated, Christa T. drifts. She finds no value in her education. Her diaries and letters reveal her confused need for perfection, alternating with mild self-abasement. Günter, another student, loves her, but he is frustrated by her lack of commitment. She mistrusts propaganda that glorifies the new Socialist era, and she loves dead poets now forgotten. Her unrealistic expectations shape her attraction to the fickle, poetical Kostia, a fellow student.

She completes a successful dissertation on Theodor Storm, a kindred spirit and "predominantly lyrical" author with a "nervous sensibility." His "conflict between willing something and the inability to do it thrust him into a corner of life."

Christa T. returns to teaching secondary school in Berlin but becomes discouraged with her students' facile, cynical conformity to official Socialist doctrine. Her weary, cynical principal urges her to compromise to survive. Then a thuggish student, on a bet, bites off the head of a toad, an incident that further depresses Christa T.

In 1955, in her last six months in Berlin, Christa T. stops writing. Knowing that a Mecklenburg veterinarian, Justus, has fallen in love with her on sight during one of her visits to her family, she decides to call him. She drifts into an affair with him, becomes pregnant, and marries him in 1956. Her return to the country, where she seems to have abandoned her former ambitions, seems a loss to the narrator and friends who had expected great things of her. In the same year, the Soviet invasion of Hungary destroys any hope of a fellowship of communist nations under the benevolent leadership of the Soviet Union. Both the narrator and Christa T. feel bitterness at this "end of Utopia."

Despite parties and frequent visits from friends, Christa T. feels bored. She seduces a young forester to try to "feel alive." Her husband, Justus, learns about the affair and suffers, but stays with her nonetheless. Christa T. seeks some purpose in life by planning to build a new house overlooking a lake, in the middle of the dairy farms where Justus works. His work is successful, and he even helps to increase local milk production. Christa T.'s questions help him learn about the area. Despite developing cancer, she persists in her house project.

The narrator contrasts herself and Christa T.—members of the generation that lived through the war and the Soviet occupation—with the complacent, cynical younger generation. "Christa T.," the narrator says, "had the luck to be forced to create her identity at an age when one is passionate. With that as the standard, all other attractions are shallow."

Blasing, Christa T.'s and the narrator's skeptical writer friend, heightens their idealism by way of contrast: Christa T., he says, successfully uses her house designs as "a sort of instrument . . . to link herself more intimately with life." The narrator echos her friend's life-affirming motto, "When, if not now?"

Christa T. has developed an exceptional gift for nurturing all her friends without discrimination. During the narrator's last visit by the lake, Christa T. passes a red poppy to her through the window of the car. "It won't last, but you won't mind, will you?" This gesture makes a final, symbolic gift of self. Christa T. soon dies of her illness. The narrator reciprocates the gesture by speaking of Christa T. as she really was. She does so to ensure that her friend will be remembered not as always good or wise but as an irreplaceable source of value.

Critical Evaluation:

Christa Wolf believed that shared names reveal mysterious affinities. Consequently, she had felt a close connection with English writer Virginia Woolf. Christa, the first name of the protagonist of *The Quest for Christa T.*, suggests somehow that the protagonist resembles her author; her name also represents a hypothetical alternate life that Wolf herself might have lived under other circumstances. By creating Christa T., Wolf seeks an imaginative transcendence through self-realization as a writer. A 1965 passage collected in Wolf's *The Author's Dimension: Selected Essays* (1993) explains that

> The longing to produce a double, to express oneself, to pack several lives into this one, to be able to be in several places at once is, I believe, one of the most powerful and least [often considered] impulses behind writing.

Christa T. herself systematically collects life stories from local peasants, and she would have retold their stories had she survived her illness with cancer.

The *T* of Christa's never-revealed last name suggests the German words *Traum*, or "dream," and *Tee*, or "tea." *Traum* connotes an authorial creation and a possible destiny not experienced by the narrator, and *Tee* suggests the taste of Marcel Proust's madeleine cookie dipped in tea, which revives a flood of forgotten past impressions. The novel's introduction explains why the narrator compulsively wants to memorialize her (fictional) friend and reconstruct her inner life: Doing so is "for our sake. Because it seems we need her." Reading

this statement, one might think Christa T. offers an inspiring example of a flawed possible self who finally achieves self-realization despite uncertainty concerning her vocation and despite obscurity and adversity (dying young from cancer). Indeed, she has some talent as a writer, but never becomes well known. Later, however, the narrator flatly refutes this interpretation: "Just for once, I want to discover how it is and to tell it like it is: the unexemplary life, the life that can't be used as a model." How can readers reconcile these two contradictory attitudes?

Analyzing the fictional narrator as a character (Wolf explicitly said she had considered this narrator, as well as Christa T., an invention), it seems that as she matures, she overcomes her initial, naïve admiration for Christa T. but recuperates the friendship despite losing its illusions. Through Christa T., she learns the value of an ordinary life.

Wolf's desire to explore "the unexemplary life" appears to reflect her own transition from being both a fascist and a communist to having humanistic social values. Without anti-Semitic feelings, Wolf had participated in the Hitler Youth as an adolescent. Later, until the mid-1960's, she had tried to atone for her own and for German collective guilt for the Holocaust by dutifully writing Social Realist literature glorifying the ordinary worker. She did so according to the dictates of the East German Communist Party under Soviet domination. She deliberately and loyally remained in East Germany, although for a time it would have been easy for her to have escaped to West Germany. She did not acknowledge then that some people had remained in the East only through inertia and apathy, and that some flights to the West had been motivated by positive values. *The Quest for Christa T.*, however, reflects the author's fatigue with her role as official spokesperson of East German Socialist values.

Probably owing to censorship, publication of the novel had been delayed for a year, until 1968. The German Democratic Writers' Congress condemned the work for individualism and for infidelity to Socialist principles. Wolf's own publisher, the Mitteldeutsche Verlag, publicly denounced itself and repented for having published a book whose author seemed to confuse herself with her heroine and whose dominant tone was pessimistic. The publisher also repented for its humanistic rather than socialistic solution to life. Indeed, Christa T.'s struggle against cancer secretly represents the unmerited sufferings of peaceable, humanitarian Germans under fascism and then communism, and their intransigent inner resistance to these regimes.

Later, aggravating her "offense," Wolf published her best-known work, *Kindheitsmuster* (1976; *A Model Childhood*, 1980; also known as *Patterns of Childhood*, 1984), as a personal confession and a national expiation, reviving unwelcome memories of the national disgrace of fascism and attempting to explain but not justify how German citizens could have become or could have collaborated with Nazis. Already, in relation to its readership, *The Quest for Christa T.* had been intended to defeat the remnants of fascism in people's minds after it had been defeated militarily and to admit her own inextricable complicity with "the stormy, often cruel, shocking life of the times, which sometimes carries the writer along with it."

Christa T. surpassed her author in one important respect: She never succumbed to the pernicious euphoria of fascist or communist doctrine. She offers a model of (flawed) integrity that does not depend on doctrinal supports. This model returns in Wolf's later works.

Laurence M. Porter

Further Reading

Bunyan, Anita. "Christa Wolf." In *Landmarks in German Women's Writing*, edited by Hilary Brown. New York: Peter Lang, 2007. This chapter places Wolf's work within the context of her times and describes how being a woman has affected her writing and the reception of her works. Wolf is one of twelve German women writers discussed in this collection of essays.

Drees, Hajo. *A Comprehensive Interpretation of the Life and Work of Christa Wolf, Twentieth Century German Writer.* Lewiston, N.Y.: Edwin Mellen Press, 2002. An ambitious study of Wolf and her work that draws connections between her fiction and her life. Focuses on the manifestation of identity, socialization, and artistic expression in Wolf's work.

Finney, Gail. *Christa Wolf.* New York: Twayne, 1999. Provides a thorough introduction to Wolf's life and her works. Argues that Wolf's life and career are both distinctive and representative of those of other writers of her generation.

Fries, Marilyn Sibley, ed. *Responses to Christa Wolf: Critical Essays.* Detroit, Mich.: Wayne State University Press, 1989. A collection of twenty-one essays that were originally delivered at a special session on Christa Wolf held during the 1982 convention of the Modern Language Association of America. Includes a list of secondary articles and books and review articles on each of Wolf's books.

Porter, Laurence M. "Christa Wolf, Citizen of the World." In *Women's Vision in Western Literature: The Empathic Community.* Westport, Conn.: Praeger, 2005. Examines Wolf's perspective on Naziism. Part of a study of women writers who have imagined what Porter calls empathic and tolerant communities to deal with the threat, experience, and aftermath of war.

Resch, Margit. *Understanding Christa Wolf: Returning Home to a Foreign Land.* Columbia: University of South Carolina Press, 1997. Provides solid analyses of all of Wolf's major works up to 1990. Supplemented by an informative chronology, a list of selected articles in English, and an annotated bibliography of critical works.

The Quest of the Holy Grail

Author: Unknown
First published: c. 1300
Type of work: Short fiction
Type of plot: Arthurian romance
Time of plot: Early eighth century
Locale: England, France, and Wales

Principal characters:
JOSEPH OF ARIMATHEA, a disciple of Christ
MERLIN THE MAGICIAN, a wizard
KING ARTHUR, ruler of the Britons
PERCEVAL, son of Alein and seeker of the Grail
GAUVAIN or GAWAIN and HURGAINS, knights of the Round Table
THE FISHER KING

The Story:

Joseph of Arimathea is a disciple of Christ who, along with his colleague Nicodemus, attends the tomb of Christ. While washing the body of Christ, Joseph accidently opens a wound. To prevent Christ's blood from spilling, Joseph takes the Grail, the goblet from which Christ drank during the Last Supper, and collects the blood therein. He then hides the Grail in his house. The Jews, incensed upon hearing that he has taken the cup, imprison Joseph in a dark cell, but Nicodemus escapes. In the cell, Christ appears to Joseph with the vessel Joseph thought he had hidden. Christ gives Joseph the goblet with strict orders that only three persons are ever to gain possession of it. He does not, however, tell Joseph who those three persons are to be.

Hundreds of years later, the wizard Merlin, after choosing Arthur to become king of the Britons, arrives at the court of Britain and reveals the story of the Holy Grail. He explains the story of the three tables: one made by the Lord for the Last Supper, one by Joseph of Arimathea, and the last by his own hands. He states that the Grail was passed by Joseph to the rich Fisher King, an old, frail man whose mission was to await the coming of the purest knight in the world. To this knight he would pass the Grail and tell of its mighty power and secrets. Only then would the Fisher King's ailments and age be lifted. After his revelations, Merlin vanishes to far-away lands to await the reign of Arthur. Meanwhile, Alein le Gros is dying and is visited by the Holy Ghost, who tells him that his own father, Brons, lives in the islands of Ireland and possesses the Holy Grail. Alein is told that he will not be allowed to die until his son, Perceval, finds Brons and is taught the secrets of the Grail. First, however, Perceval has to go to the court of King Arthur and be taught the ways of chivalry and honor. He goes willingly and joyously.

One Easter, King Arthur decides to hold a tournament to honor the Round Table. Perceval, learning the ways of knighthood, wants no part of the tournament, but for the love of a woman, Aleine, niece of Sir Gawain, he agrees to fight. Aleine sends him a suit of red armor, and he enters the contest as an unknown, anonymous knight. He defeats all opponents and claims his right to sit at the Round Table. Arthur protests, but at the urging of others he gives in to the new knight. Before long, Perceval vows never to lie, to be pure, and to seek the Grail. Sir Gawain, Sagremors, Beduers, Hurgains, and Erec take the same vow, and all set forth on their quests.

Two days after beginning his quest for the Holy Grail, Perceval finds the body of the knight Hurganet, with a damsel weeping over it. Hurganet, she says, had saved her from a giant and had ridden with her into a tent. They were warned to run and not await the tent's master, who would surely kill them. The lord of the tent, Orgoillow Delandes, soon appeared, wearing red armor, and slew Hurganet. Upon hearing this story, Sir Perceval vows revenge for Hurganet's death and rides forth to the tent, where he also is warned about its master. Soon he is face-to-face with the knight of the tent; Perceval overcomes the knight and sends him to Arthur's court with the damsel.

Continuing his quest, Perceval comes to a fine castle. He enters but finds the castle uninhabited, with only a chess board for decoration. He makes an opening move on the chess board, and the opponent pieces begin to play against him. Three times he is checkmated. Angry at his defeat, he attempts to toss the chess pieces into the castle moat, but he is stopped by the entrance of a beautiful damsel. Overcome by her beauty, Perceval asks her for her love. She agrees to love him if he will capture the white stag of the wood. To this end, she lends him one hound and warns him to take care of the beast; he agrees. Perceval then chases and captures the stag, cuts off its head, and starts back to the castle. An old hag makes off with the hound, however, and vows not to return it to him until he goes to a certain grave and says, "Felon, he that put you there." After Perceval heeds the old lady's words, a knight in black armor appears on a black horse and challenges Perceval. Perceval soon overcomes the black knight, but while he is fighting a second man takes both the stag's head and the hound. Perceval follows the man but is unable to catch him.

Many feats follow. Perceval eventually arrives at his home and, with his niece, rides to the home of his uncle, a hermit, who tells him of the table, the Grail, and his destiny. He continues to wander for seven years, sending more than one hundred knights to King Arthur as prisoners. Finally, Perceval finds the Fisher King and is told the secrets of the Holy Grail, and all is well in Britain.

Critical Evaluation:

Among prose and poetry dedicated to the Grail, three distinct explanations for the Grail are provided: One work indicates that the Grail was the cup from which Christ drank at the Last Supper, one proposes that it was only used by Joseph of Arimathea to gather Jesus' blood, and the third is a combination of the two. Furthermore, the means by which the Grail is transferred from hand to hand, ultimately to Perceval, changes from account to account. This may well be a result of the antiquity of the stories, but the fact that the subject of the Holy Grail is found in only the most recent of Arthurian texts indicates yet another addition to the Christianization of King Arthur. The first historical references to King Arthur can be dated as far back as 548; the anonymously written *Quest of the Holy Grail* dates only as far back as c. 1300, long after the Christianization of Britain by Augustine. By this time, the great institutions of learning, primarily Cambridge, Oxford, and the University of Paris, were well established. This allowed scholars and writers better access to libraries and to their predecessors, such as Robert de Boron. Boron's poems were the primary sources for the anonymous poet of *The Quest of the Holy Grail.*

The poem displays an exaggerated and nostalgic conception of chivalry. The late Middle Ages, during which *The Quest of the Holy Grail* was written, saw little chivalry, few knights in armor, and even fewer heroes; thus the writers of the day looked to the past for great heroes. To these people, only Jesus himself, or a saint, could be a truly pure man. King Arthur had already been elevated to immortality over the centuries, so by logical extension his knights, among them Sir Perceval, himself added to the story by the French, became immortal heroes. According to this version, however, Perceval does not begin his quest as a holy or pure man. He deceives his way into Arthur's favor and, were it not for his father's purity, would have been cast into hell for taking his seat at the Round Table. It takes some time before Perceval vows to be chaste and never to kill again.

The fact that the story spends a great deal of time explaining the origin of the Holy Grail and its place in the ultimate plan of God indicates several possibilities regarding the background and intent of the author. First, it can be established that the author was Christian. By 1300, virtually all of Europe was ruled by the Roman Catholic Church, either directly or indirectly. England, however, was one of the nations most tolerant toward non-Christians. *The Quest of the Holy Grail* indicates that the author believed the Grail stories propagated by Robert de Boron, and although the real King Arthur would most certainly have been a pagan, he is referred to as a Christian who ruled his people by the grace of God. The concept of predestination is also reinforced throughout the story, as each character is led to his destiny by the Holy Ghost.

The Christian origin is obvious, but there is one possible pagan explanation for the Grail. Celtic folklore tells that a chalice, or grail, can be a symbol of sustenance, a vessel of life providing food, water, and even wine (which brings one closer to God). Thus it is the life-giver, and it is feminine. It is what Carl Jung called an archetypal symbol, part of the universal consciousness, understood by all persons of all cultures. Thus, although there are many possible explanations for the author's passion for the Grail stories, the influences of the time in which this work was written seem to have had the most effect on the author, and his understanding of the Joseph of Arimathea poem by Robert de Boron indicates an educated man with a good knowledge of French. The anonymous author may have been a priest or a monk. Whether the author was a priest, monk, or scholar, there is no denying the importance of *The Quest of the Holy Grail* as a literary work. Like all other Arthurian romances, it provided the British with a sense of history and national pride. It could even be said that these tales were not mere stories and poems; they were propaganda disseminated by either the throne or the Church to encourage the Christianizing of Britain. After all, once Perceval had retrieved the Grail and learned its secrets, all curses and plagues that had been placed upon pagan Britain were lifted for all time.

"Critical Evaluation" by Gordon Robert Maddison

Further Reading

Barber, Richard. *The Holy Grail: Imagination and Belief.* New York: Allen Lane, 2004. An expert in the Arthurian legends chronicles the history of stories about the Holy Grail from twelfth century romances to twenty-first century best sellers.

Griffin, Justin. *The Holy Grail: The Legend, the History, the Evidence.* Jefferson, N.C.: McFarland, 2001. Examines the historical events that gave rise to the Grail legend and the various theories of the Grail's identity. A useful introduction to the subject.

Nutt, Alfred. *Studies on the Legend of the Holy Grail.* New York: Cooper Square, 1965. Good resource for serious students of the subject focuses on the Celtic origins of the Grail legend.

Sinclair, Andrew. *The Grail: The Quest for a Legend.* Stroud, England: Sutton, 2007. Discusses the numerous adaptations of the Grail legend, from the myths of King Arthur to modern books such as those by Dan Brown to films such as the Indiana Jones adventures.

Weston, Jessie L. *The Quest of the Holy Grail.* New York: Barnes & Noble, 1964. This classic on the subject of the Grail was first published in 1913 but remains one of the clearest descriptions of the Grail cycle.

Wilhelm, James J., ed. *The Romance of Arthur: An Anthology of Medieval Texts in Translation.* New York: Garland, 1994. Critical edition includes some of the best translations of early Arthurian literature.

Quicksand

Author: Nella Larsen (1891-1964)
First published: 1928
Type of work: Novel
Type of plot: Psychological realism
Time of plot: Late 1920's
Locale: Southern and northern United States; Copenhagen, Denmark

Principal characters:
HELGA CRANE, a mixed-race teacher
JAMES VAYLE, her fiancé
DR. ROBERT ANDERSON, a teacher
PETER NILSSEN, Helga's benevolent uncle
KATRINA and POUL DAHL, her aunt and uncle in Copenhagen
JEANETTE HAYES-RORE, a lecturer on race relations
ANNE GREY, Hayes-Rore's elegant niece
AXEL OLSEN, a Danish portrait painter
REVEREND PLEASANT GREEN, an Alabama preacher

The Story:

Abandoned by her black father and held at bay by her white immigrant mother, Helga Crane is no stranger to the loneliness of an "unloved, unloving, and unhappy" childhood. Now her young adulthood has become just as troubled. Helga wants to flee the snobbery, drabness, and rigidity of Naxos, the school for black youth where she had taught for two listless years. She therefore breaks her engagement to the well-heeled black Atlantan James Vayle (much to the delight of his family, who considered her socially inferior) and gives notice of her resignation to her principal, Dr. Robert Anderson. This gentle young man was one of the few at that dour institution who could make Helga laugh and feel completely at ease. Yet when he complements her ladylike behavior, she assumes he is simply another social snob and departs at once.

In her new destination of Chicago, harsh reality withers Helga's excitement. What is meant to be a reunion with her uncle, Peter Nilssen, who had financed her studies, turns out to be a tense confrontation. He had remarried, and his new wife does not want to associate with Helga because of Helga's black parentage. Jobs, too, prove difficult to obtain unless the work is menial. At last, Helga secures temporary employment as a traveling companion for the civil rights activist and orator Jeanette Hayes-Rore.

Although the older woman's sobriety, plumpness, and haphazard grooming are the antitheses of Helga's enthusiasm, slimness, and impeccable style, the two become fast friends. Hayes-Rore becomes a confidante to the young woman, and she arranges for Helga to achieve another dream: to live and work in Harlem, the sophisticated black capital of the United States.

Helga lodges in New York with Anne Grey, Hayes-Rore's wealthy, widowed niece. Anne initiates Helga into her Harlem socialite's lifestyle of exclusive parties, expensive clothes, daring interracial romances, theater and gallery openings, servants, leisure, and excess. Working as a secretary by day, attending social and cultural events by night, Helga almost accomplishes the perfectly balanced, stimulating life that she had always craved. However, the allure of Harlem days and nights becomes clouded by the hypocrisy that belies Anne's pleasant demeanor. Anne spurns racial prejudice and social inequality; yet, she despises the music, dances, clothes, speech, and mannerisms associated with her own African American community. Helga's disillusionment with Anne is compounded by a replay of the old smothering restlessness and unhappiness, and a new wave of love for Dr. Anderson confuses her.

Helga flees America to visit relatives in Copenhagen. Overseas, people see her as an exotic curiosity. Her relatives, the Dahls, parade her around in outrageous outfits, elephantine jewelry, and peacock colors that reflect their own stereotypical assumptions about being *sorte*, the Danish word for "black." Soon, the dormant dissatisfaction flares; her aunt and uncle insist on making life decisions for her, and all the Danes are somewhat detached and cold because of her mixed-race identity.

Axel Olsen, a portrait painter, symbolizes all the behaviors that begin to frustrate Helga. He humiliates her by bombarding her with gifts of expensive clothes that caricature her as either an African savage or an Arab concubine. He insults her by courting her formally through her relatives. He infuriates her with his attitude that mingles desire and contempt for her ethnicity.

When Axel "insinuated marriage" to her, Helga learns

that her friend, Anne, had been betrothed to Dr. Anderson. Heartsick and lonely for black companions again, Helga refuses Olsen's proposal and returns to New York.

In Harlem, Helga sweeps away heartbreak in an undertow of parties and socializing. Vayle resurfaces at one summer party and again proposes to Helga. She laughs him aside. When she goes upstairs to repair a hem, Dr. Anderson belatedly confirms the love between them by giving her a kiss in secret. He later downplays the moment, however, leaving Helga devastated.

Helga soothes her mangled pride and unrequited passions in the church. Now married to the Reverend Pleasant Green, she moves to Alabama and immerses herself in an exhausting routine of charity work, Bible instruction, homemaking, and childbearing. This does not stave off the familiar restiveness and loneliness, however, which returns now accompanied by despair. As Helga nurses the temptation to abandon her marriage and children, she becomes pregnant with her fifth child.

Critical Evaluation:

Nella Larsen aligns herself with one of the agendas of the Harlem Renaissance: to expose the divergences and varieties among black artists' themes, styles, imaginative references, and politics. In her novels *Quicksand* and *Passing* (1929), the characters are distinctive. Instead of depicting the folksy, rural Southerners or the urban Northern wits who populate the works of African American writers Zora Neale Hurston, Langston Hughes, and Claude McKay, Larsen represents the black bourgeoisie in general and the female among this class in particular. Modernism's influence is apparent in her characters' interior reflections and in her technique, which combines abrupt and jagged sentences, condensed visual images, a potpourri of cultural references, and sketches of decadent and anonymous city life.

The title, *Quicksand*, alludes to the novel's theme of the gender- and race-specific pitfalls that have historically affected all African American women, regardless of skin complexion, social class, marital status, sexual orientation, regional affiliation, or education. Helga's quest for romantic love, her beauty, and her sexual freedom reject the extreme stereotyping of all black women as either hypersexed prostitutes or undesirable laboring machines. Yet, both whites and blacks pigeonhole her in one of these two categories. As she searches Chicago for employment, men of both races assume she is a prostitute and solicit her. Because shops and schools discriminate against her because of her skin color, she is hired instead as a domestic, reinforcing the stereotype of black women as mammies.

Helga is characterized from the novel's beginning by de-

tailed descriptions of her striking facial features, alluring skin, and impeccably tasteful attire, which includes shoes, blouses, dresses, scarves, hats, jewelry, handkerchiefs, purses, hair ornaments, and corsages. More than mirroring her moods, her attentive grooming and sophisticated, often inappropriate, fashions show Helga's determination to resist uniform definitions of womanhood. In Chicago, New York, and Copenhagen, she resists social pressures to suppress her unconventionality, spontaneity, imagination, and passion.

After her retreat from life into numb piety, the descriptions change. Once, fashion dominated her thoughts. Now, Helga focuses constantly on the ills of her body as it rebels against domestic labor, pastoral service, and unmitigated childbearing. The only description of Helga's garments refers to an old, unappealing nightgown, a remnant of her fashionable days. Larsen delineates Helga's body by nothing but brief comments about her starving, endlessly aching limbs. Helga's hair, always arranged in the past in glorious styles and decorated with flowers and combs, is now always in disarray, scattering on pillows or flying at angles. This artistic technique conveys the psychological death that ensues for women like Helga who are bound too tightly by domestic duties and social expectations.

Quicksand vocalizes the precautionary outcry among Harlem Renaissance artists and intellectuals, including Larsen, that the historical underpinnings of stereotypes come from deep within society and that black people's attitudes toward themselves have been globally and adversely affected by racist perspectives. Wherever Helga goes, her ethnicity is scrutinized and distorted. Ironically, Danish society appreciates variety and difference—in food, art, conversation, and languages. Yet, even the Danes are oblivious to varieties and differences among African Americans, as Helga learns when one person contends that all "Negroes were black and had woolly hair."

By the turn of the century, black churches and civic and benevolent organizations had launched an organized assault on "the race problem." This movement of self-help predicated that black people's advancement and full citizenship in American society depended upon education, labor, morality, discipline, thrift, respectability, and entrepreneurship. *Quicksand* thematically accuses this movement of having traded its visionary and innovative origins for elitism, self-hate, and orthodoxy. For instance, Naxos, where Helga is first employed, is but an anagram of "Saxon." It owes its existence, ironically, not to black entrepreneurs but to white philanthropists. It exemplifies, ironically, not the individualism and enterprise of Horatio Alger and Poor Richard but only frigid sameness and knee-jerk obedience.

Naxos's black students conform to the "formal calm" of European models of gender and behavior. The women wear muted pastels instead of bolder colors and prints. Both men and women attend sermons by paternalistic whites who exhort them to remain in a subordinate social position. Even among the faculty, the highest aspirations are to marry into the race's "good stock" and "first families," which also happen to constitute the race's fairest-skinned people.

Larsen's characterization of progressive blacks or race representatives extends this critique of the self-help movement. Unoriginal leaders such as Hayes-Rore rehash clichéd solutions. She virtually plagiarizes her speeches from the published works of foregone black leaders. Also, she, a "lemon-colored woman," fails to publicly address the taboos of adultery and rape that undergird national anxieties about race-mixing. Love itself is deadened by self-help when Vayle argues for marriage to Helga on the theory that the "better class" must bear children to advance the race.

Since enslavement, black politics and black religion have been intertwined. Such nineteenth century orators as David Walker, Maria Stewart, Frederick Douglass, and Sojourner Truth have argued for emancipation and enfranchisement by employing scriptural rationales. Evoking literal quicksand, Larsen relegates this combination of political and religious activism to bygone days. She uses images of unconsciousness, drowning, choking, and burial to present the sterility and passivity of black Christianity.

Christians are like zombies, drugged by impassioned worship and zealous calls to duty into abandoning individual will and personal responsibility. Their pastors' ulterior motives are ease and authority, and black women enable the bulk of this by abusing their bodies, limiting their social contacts, and neglecting their dreams. The Reverend Green resembles Hayes-Rore. With her, he shares hypocrisy and opportunism, especially as he flirts with the female membership right under the nose of his new wife, Helga.

In *Quicksand*, religion is thus a sibling to self-help and its perils. Both reflect what Larsen sees as a self-enslavement of African Americans. Both retard the very progress that the artists of the Harlem Renaissance espoused.

Barbara McCaskill

Further Reading

Ammons, Elizabeth. *Conflicting Stories: American Women Writers at the Turn into the Twentieth Century.* New York: Oxford University Press, 1991. Claims the ideas in *Quicksand* "declare their author's rebellion as an artist." Notes that in Helga, Larsen creates a character who re-fuses to act out the white fantasies she would be expected to perform. Compares Larsen with her contemporary Zora Neale Hurston.

Calloway, Licia Morrow. "Elite Rejection of Maternity in Nella Larsen's *Quicksand* and *Passing*." In *Black Family (Dys)function in Novels by Jessie Fauset, Nella Larsen, and Fannie Hurst.* New York: Peter Lang, 2003. Calloway analyzes Larsen's two novels, focusing on her depiction of maternity and her handling of the class pressures upon upward-aspiring African Americans.

Carby, Hazel V. *Reconstructing Womanhood: The Emergence of the Afro-American Woman Novelist.* New York: Oxford University Press, 1987. Treats Larsen's use of the mulatto figure as a "narrative device of mediation." Explores the interconnections of sexual, racial, and class identity, and makes the claim that Larsen offers no resolutions to the contradictions she raises in the novel.

Davis, Thadious M. *Nella Larsen, Novelist of the Harlem Renaissance: A Woman's Life Unveiled.* Baton Rouge: Louisiana State University Press, 1994. The definitive literary biography of Larsen. Considers the author's mixed motives for writing *Quicksand*, and argues that Helga enacts unresolved anger toward her disempowered and remote mother.

Hutchinson, George. In *Search of Nella Larsen: A Biography of the Color Line.* Cambridge, Mass.: Belknap Press of Harvard University Press, 2006. Examines Larsen's work, life, and place in social history, describing how she dealt with personal issues of racial identity and fear of abandonment in her novels. Chapter 13 focuses on *Quicksand*.

Kramer, Victor, ed. *The Harlem Renaissance Re-Examined.* New York: AMS Press, 1987. In the chapter "'A Lack Somewhere': Nella Larsen's *Quicksand* and the Harlem Renaissance," Lillie Howard argues that Helga's quests for materialism, the proper family, and acceptable expression of sexuality bespeak a fragmented self and a perpetual ambiguity about race that preclude her ability to take advantage of alternatives.

Kubitschek, Missy Dehn. *Claiming the Heritage: African-American Women Novelists and History.* Jackson: University Press of Mississippi, 1991. Kubitschek contends that as an immigrant white woman, Helga's mother's guidance of her daughter's black American woman's experiences would have been limited. Demonstrates Helga's internalization of racism and sexism, and highlights her multiple modes of repression.

McLendon, Jacquelyn Y. *The Politics of Color in the Fiction of Jessie Fauset and Nella Larsen.* Charlottesville: University of Virginia Press, 1995. A study of the theme of the "tragic mulatto" in the novels of Larsen and Fauset. Devotes a chapter to an analysis of *Quicksand*.

McDowell, Deborah E. Introduction to *Quicksand* and *Passing*, by Nella Larsen. New Brunswick, N.J.: Rutgers University Press, 1986. Extensive analysis of *Quicksand*. Deals with Larsen's exploration of female sexual fulfillment, and studies the novel's narrative strategy, which reflects the tension between sexual expression and repression.

Ransom, Portia Boulware. *Black Love and the Harlem Renaissance: The Novels of Nella Larsen, Jessie Redmon Fauset, and Zora Neale Hurston—An Essay in African American Literary Criticism.* Lewiston, N.Y.: Edwin Mellen Press, 2005. Examines how the three writers use their semibiographical fiction to focus on the tensions between black men and women who are trying to define themselves.

The Quiet American

Author: Graham Greene (1904-1991)
First published: 1955
Type of work: Novel
Type of plot: Tragedy
Time of plot: Early 1950's
Locale: Vietnam

Principal characters:
THOMAS FOWLER, an English newspaper correspondent
ALDEN PYLE, the quiet American, and an undercover agent in Vietnam
PHUONG, Fowler's mistress, and then Pyle's mistress
VIGOT, the French police chief investigating Pyle's murder

The Story:

Alden Pyle, an undercover U.S. agent, is found murdered in French Saigon. In the early 1950's, the French still controlled Vietnam as a colony, but they were beginning to lose control of the country to the communist revolutionaries. Pyle had come to investigate conditions and had befriended an English newspaper correspondent, Thomas Fowler. Vigot, the French police chief, orders Fowler and his former mistress, Phuong, to his office for questioning. Fowler is under suspicion because he is one of the last people to have seen Pyle alive, and Pyle had taken Phuong from Fowler.

Vigot interrogates Fowler, who proclaims not only his innocence but also his ignorance of what happened to Pyle. Phuong, who does not understand English, says nothing. After the interrogation, Fowler tells her that Pyle had been murdered. Her reaction is surprisingly mild, and she reveals almost nothing about her feelings. Fowler then goes over the sequence of events that led to Pyle's murder and Vigot's summons to police headquarters.

As the story goes, Pyle befriends Fowler during his first days in Saigon. Fowler is a reluctant companion. He dislikes Americans, especially ones like Pyle who seem on a mission to save the world. Pyle never admits to Fowler that he is a CIA agent—indeed no reference is made to the U.S. Central Intelligence Agency in the novel, except for Fowler's suggestion that Pyle might work for the U.S. Office of Strategic

Services (OSS). Established in World War II, the OSS was the precursor of the postwar CIA.

To Fowler, Pyle is an innocent who reads books on Vietnam but does not understand the reality of people's lives. Fowler believes that the Vietnamese should be left alone. He does not believe that their lives could be improved by Westerners. He considers himself a reporter without political commitments or opinions. He is an older man (not saying how much older) who disdains Pyle's idealism. Pyle wants to save Vietnam from communism. Fowler finds this attitude ridiculous and dangerous because it means Pyle would involve himself with the local Vietnamese anticommunist military, who seem to Fowler no more than gangsters. If the French were to lose Vietnam, it could not be saved by Americans looking for a "third force" (some group other than the communists or the French).

The third force is a theory Pyle had adopted from a book on Vietnam by York Harding. To Fowler, both Harding and Pyle ignored reality to pursue theory. Pyle even condones the terrorist acts of General Thé, an anticommunist thug. General Thé blew up a café, maiming men, women, and children. To Pyle, this atrocity was a mistake. He plans to straighten it out with the general. To Fowler, the atrocity proves that Pyle is doing great harm in spite of his good intentions.

On the personal level, Pyle takes Fowler's mistress away from him because Pyle believes that Phuong has to be saved. Pyle earnestly wants to know if Fowler loves Phuong and means to marry her. When Fowler admits he is using Phuong for his selfish pleasure, Pyle offers her marriage and a home in the United States, which she accepts.

In spite of their political and personal conflicts, Fowler finds it hard to reject Pyle. On a mission to observe the war in action, Fowler is injured and Pyle risks his own life to save him. Fowler knows that Pyle means well, and Pyle complicates Fowler's feelings about him by constantly saying he knows that Fowler is not nearly as cynical and selfish as he says.

Pyle's dangerous innocence and idealism so outrage Fowler that he decides he must thwart Pyle's plans to coordinate another terrorist act with General Thé. Fowler informs a communist agent of Pyle's plot. Thus, it is Fowler's own intervention in politics that leads to Pyle's death. Exactly how Pyle died and exactly who was responsible is never made clear. Fowler realizes, however, that Pyle's death is his doing, even though he had only wanted Pyle stopped, not murdered.

Phuong returns to Fowler after Pyle's death. Fowler also gets a cable from his wife announcing that she will give him a divorce. A happy Phuong goes to tell her sister that she is to be the "second Mrs. Fowlaire." Meanwhile, Fowler broods on Pyle's story. His last words reveal his guilt and his sense of responsibility for Pyle's murder: "Everything had gone right with me since he had died, but how I wished there existed someone to whom I could say that I was sorry."

Critical Evaluation:

The Quiet American is considered one of Graham Greene's major achievements. The story is told with great economy, superb characterization, and sophisticated irony. The plot resembles that of a mystery story. A crime has been committed. Who is the murderer? As in most mystery stories, as much needs to be learned about the victim as about the villain. What is learned, though, takes on political, moral, and religious significance. The story ends in mystery as well. Who exactly killed Pyle is not revealed, but the burden of the crime, like the burden of telling the story, is that of Fowler.

Fowler is a fascinating character and narrator because he simultaneously reveals and conceals so much about himself and his involvement in the story. On the one hand, he is openly contemptuous of Pyle. Like other Americans, Pyle is so obsessed with his mission to save the world that he does not register the reality around him. It is ludicrous for him to think that Phuong is an innocent he must rescue. She has stayed with Fowler because he offers her security. She leaves

Fowler for Pyle because he offers her even more wealth and protection. Pyle is shocked because Fowler says he is merely using Phuong for his own pleasure and because of his need to have a woman beside him to stave off loneliness. It never occurs to Pyle that Phuong has acted just as selfishly or that Pyle himself is using people.

On the other hand, Fowler is not entirely honest with himself. He claims to be disengaged, not only from politics but also from the sentiments of love Pyle professes. Yet Fowler's vehement rejection of Pyle's worldview and his passionate defense of the Vietnamese (who, he believes, should be allowed to worked out their own destiny, free of the French, the Americans, and any other intruding power) surely reveal anything but cynicism. In this respect, Pyle is right to see good in a person who claims to be without scruples.

Indeed, Pyle loses his life because of Fowler's moral outrage. Fowler is so revolted by the bombing atrocity at the café that he determines to put a stop to Pyle's activities. Fowler's passion is hardly consistent with his affectation of aloofness. Actually, he cares deeply about Phuong and about the Vietnamese. He believes in self-determination, which ironically is the ideology that Americans claim to support. Americans think they are supporting freedom by allying themselves with the anticommunists.

Thus, there are multiple ironies in *The Quiet American*. Fowler says he is a cynic, but he acts like a wounded idealist. Pyle says he is an idealist, but his trafficking with anticommunist thugs involves him in cynical and brutal plots. Phuong looks like a delicate, manipulable, and passive victim, and yet like many other Vietnamese, she is a survivor who plays one side against the other and bends with the political winds. Fowler declares to Vigot that he is not guilty and retells the story of his involvement with Fowler to absolve himself, yet he concludes by realizing that he is guilty.

The novel's title is ironic. In one sense, Pyle is quiet—even unassuming. He is not aggressive. He patiently questions Fowler about his tie to Phuong and even declares his love for her to Fowler before he courts her. Pyle is the opposite of loud, vulgar Americans such as his boss Joe, or the noisy American journalist Granger. In another sense, however, Pyle is anything but quiet. He stirs up Saigon with explosions; he turns Fowler's life into turmoil.

An even greater irony is that for all their differences, Fowler and Pyle are alike in their moral earnestness. Fowler is the sophisticated European who has learned not to wear his heart on his sleeve. He denies any form of selfless behavior. Pyle is a naïve American who is openhearted and believes he acts for the good of others. Yet both men cause great damage because they care about others. They are implicated in the evil that Fowler thinks he can elude and that Pyle thinks he can eliminate.

The political and moral divide between Fowler and Pyle is not as great as Fowler has supposed. His narrative ironically binds him to Pyle—a fate Fowler has consistently tried to avoid. The novel dramatizes Fowler's fate in the scene where he refuses to call Pyle by his first name. He also refuses to let Pyle call him Tom and insists on being called Thomas. No formalities can really separate the two men, however; Fowler's own narrative shows them to be twinned souls.

The religious basis of Greene's fiction has often been noted by his critics. He is a Catholic novelist who believes in the universality of human nature, that human beings cannot separate themselves from one another, and that all souls are alike in their propensity to sin. Although Fowler refers to himself several times as an atheist, Pyle refuses to believe him, saying the world does not make sense without a concept of God. Fowler retorts that the world does not make sense *with* a concept of God.

At the end of his narrative, however, Fowler is clearly seeking the solace of a higher power. He does not refer to God, but he mentions his good luck since Pyle has died. Phuong has returned to him; his wife has agreed to divorce him after initially indicating she would not. Everything seems to have fallen in place for a man worried about growing old and desiring the companionship of a younger woman. Yet Fowler is nevertheless disturbed. He tells Phuong he is sorry. She does not understand. To her, the telegram from Fowler's wife means that she will be happy. She does not know that Fowler needs to unburden himself. His story is part of his unburdening, but his last words reveal that he needs "someone else to whom I could say I was sorry." He has made a kind of confession; he has been unable to absolve himself of sin. His is a religious sentiment, a craving for a being to whom he wants himself to be accountable. He is on the verge of admitting his need for God.

Carl Rollyson

Further Reading

Bergonzi, Bernard. *A Study in Greene: Graham Greene and the Art of the Novel*. New York: Oxford University Press, 2006. Bergonzi examines all of Greene's novels, analyzing their language, structure, and recurring motifs. He argues that Greene's earliest work is his best, *Brighton Rock* is his masterpiece, and his novels published after the 1950's show a marked decline in his abilities. Chapter 7 includes a discussion of *The Quiet American*.

Bosco, Mark. *Graham Greene's Catholic Imagination*. New York: Oxford University Press, 2005. Focuses on the elements of Catholic doctrine in Greene's novels. Bosco contradicts many critics, who maintain these elements are present only in Greene's early novels, demonstrating how the writer's religious faith is a pervasive aspect in all of his work.

DeVitis, A. A. *Graham Greene*. Rev. ed. Boston: Twayne, 1986. Treats the novel as a transitional work, telling of Greene's experience in Indochina, his use of an unreliable narrator, and the novel's existentialism. Discusses the novel's links to Greene's religious fiction.

Gaston, Georg M. A. *The Pursuit of Salvation: A Critical Guide to the Novels of Graham Greene*. Troy, N.Y.: Whitston, 1984. Considers *The Quiet American* the most flawless novel Greene ever wrote but also one of his most controversial and misunderstood. Argues that critics have simplified the book's politics, and that the book's real issue is personal salvation.

Hoskins, Robert. *Graham Greene: An Approach to the Novels*. New York: Garland, 1999. An updated look at Greene's oeuvre with individual chapters providing analyses of several novels, including *The Quiet American*. Examines the protagonists of Greene's novels in the first and second phases of his career.

Land, Stephen K. *The Human Imperative: A Study of the Novels of Graham Greene*. New York: AMS Press, 2008. A chronological consideration of all of Greene's work, demonstrating the common themes and character types in his novels and other fiction. Charts Greene's development as a writer.

Sharrock, Roger. *Saints, Sinners, and Comedians: The Novels of Graham Greene*. Notre Dame, Ind.: University of Notre Dame Press, 1984. Compares the novel to Greene's earlier fiction and his treatments of real places with that of other great novelists. Analyzes Greene's political opinions, relates them to those of Fowler, and concludes that *The Quiet American* is Greene's most carefully constructed novel.

Quo Vadis
A Narrative of the Time of Nero

Author: Henryk Sienkiewicz (1846-1916)
First published: 1895-1896, serial; 1896, book (English translation, 1896)
Type of work: Novel
Type of plot: Historical
Time of plot: c. 64 C.E.
Locale: Rome

Principal characters:
VINICIUS, a young Roman patrician
LYGIA, a foreign princess whom Vinicius loves
PETRONIUS, Vinicius's uncle and an intimate friend of Nero
NERO, the Roman emperor
CHILO, a Greek sycophant
PETER, a leader of the Christians
TIGELLINUS, Petronius's enemy and Nero's friend

The Story:

When Vinicius returns to Rome after serving duty in the colonies, he calls on his uncle, Petronius, who is one of the most influential men in Rome. A friend of Emperor Nero, Petronius owns a beautiful home, choice slaves, and numerous objects of art. Petronius has no delusions about the emperor; he knows quite well that Nero is coarse, conceited, brutal, and thoroughly evil. Petronius is happy to see his handsome young nephew. Vinicius has fallen in love with Lygia, the daughter of a foreign king, now living with Aulus, Plautius, and Pomponia, and he asks his uncle to help him get Lygia as his concubine. Petronius speaks to Nero, and Lygia is ordered to be brought to the palace. Lygia's foster parents send with the young woman the giant Ursus, who is Lygia's devoted servant.

At a wild orgy in the palace, Vinicius attempts to make love to Lygia, but he does not succeed, owing to the watchfulness of Acte, who is a Christian and a former concubine of Nero. Lygia herself is a Christian, and she fears both the lust of Vinicius and that of the emperor himself. Then Acte receives information that Lygia is to be handed over to Vinicius. At the same time, the daughter of Empress Augusta dies, and the empress and her circle believe that Lygia bewitched the child. Alarmed at the dangers threatening Lygia, Acte and Ursus plan Lygia's escape.

That night, the servants of Vinicius arrive at the palace and lead Lygia away. Meanwhile, Vinicius waits at his house, where a great feast is to take place in honor of his success in securing Lygia. Lygia, however, never arrives, for on the way to his house Vinicius's servants are attacked by a group of Christians who are determined to free the young woman, their fellow Christian. Lygia's rescuers take her outside the city walls to live in a Christian colony.

Vinicius is furious when he learns what has happened. Petronius sends some of his own men to watch for Lygia at the gates of the city, and as the days pass Vinicius grows more and more upset. Finally, Chilo, a Greek who passes as a philosopher, offers to find Lygia—for a sufficient reward. By pretending to be a convert to Christianity, he learns where the Christians meet secretly. He and Vinicius, together with a giant named Croton, go to the meeting place and then follow Lygia to the house where she is staying. When they attempt to seize her, Ursus kills Croton, and Vinicius is injured during the fight. For a few days afterward he stays with the Christians, who take care of him. Lygia nurses him until she becomes aware that she is in love with the pagan patrician; when she realizes what her feelings are, she decides to leave his care to others rather than put herself in a position where she might succumb to temptation.

Vinicius heard the Christians speaking of their religious philosophy at their meeting, and while recuperating he is amazed by their goodness and their forgiveness. He hears their leader, Peter, talk of Christ and of Christ's miracles, and his mind becomes filled with odd and disturbing thoughts. He realizes that he must either hate or love the God who keeps Lygia from him. Strangely enough, Vinicius becomes convinced that he no longer has the desire to take Lygia by force. After he is well again, he maintains contact with the Christians, and at last, after he has accepted their faith, Lygia agrees to marry him.

In the meantime, Nero goes to Antium, where the nobleman Tigellinus plants in his mind the idea that he should burn Rome in order to write and sing a poem about the tremendous catastrophe. Accordingly, Nero sets fire to Rome, and almost all the city is destroyed. Vinicius rushes from Antium to save Lygia, but luckily she has already left the city.

After the fire, the people of Rome are angry about Nero's actions; rebellion is in the air. The empress and the Jews at court persuade Nero to blame the Christians for the fire.

Chilo, who has been befriended by the Christians, who have forgiven his abominable crimes, turns traitor. He gives the emperor all the information he has about the Christians and leads the emperor's guards to the hiding places of the sect. Cruel persecutions begin.

Petronius tries desperately to stop Nero and save Vinicius. Failing in his attempt, he knows that his own days are numbered. The Christians are first crammed into prisons and then brought into the arena for the entertainment of the populace. Virgins are raped by the gladiators and then fed to starving lions. Many Christians are crucified and burned alive. After Lygia is seized and imprisoned, Vinicius fails in an attempt to rescue her.

At last Lygia's turn comes to be led into the arena to amuse the brutal populace. She is stripped and tied to the back of a raging bull. When the bull is sent running into the arena, Ursus rushes forward and locks his strong arms around the animal. To the astonishment of all, the bull yields and dies. The people then demand that Lygia and Ursus be set free, and the emperor has to obey the public clamor. Petronius advises Vinicius that they should all leave the city, for Nero has ways of removing people who have offended him.

The persecutions continue, and as the spectacles in the arena grow more and more ghastly, the people at last begin to sicken of the bestial tortures. One of the Christians looks straight at Nero as he is dying and accuses the emperor of all his infamous crimes. As the Christian Glaucus is being burned alive, he looks toward Chilo, the Greek who betrayed the Christians. Glaucus, who earlier had been left for dead by Chilo, forgives the Greek for his past actions, which include his having caused Glaucus's wife and children to be sold into slavery. Moved by the dying man's mercy, Chilo cries out to the crowd in a loud voice that the Christians are innocent of the burning of Rome and that the guilty man is Nero. Despairing of his own fate, Chilo is on the point of complete collapse, but Paul of Tarsus takes him aside and assures him that Christ is merciful even to the worst of sinners. He then baptizes the Greek. When Chilo returns to his home, he is seized by the emperor's guards and led away to his death in the arena. Vinicius and Lygia escape to Sicily.

When Petronius hears that the emperor has ordered him to be killed, he invites some of the patricians to his house at Cumae, where he has gone with Nero and the court. There at a great feast he reads an attack against Nero, astounding everyone. Then he and Eunice, a slave who loves him, stretch out their arms to a physician, who opens their veins. While the party continues and the astonished guests look on, Petronius and Eunice bleed to death in each other's arms.

Nero returns to Rome. His subjects hate him more than ever, and a rebellion breaks out at last. Nero is informed that his death has been decreed, and he flees. With some of his slaves around him, he attempts to plunge a knife into his own throat, but he is too timid to complete the deed. As some soldiers approach to arrest him, a slave thrusts the fatal knife into his emperor's throat.

Critical Evaluation:

As it has become commonplace to assume that serious works of fiction cannot appeal to a wide readership, the enduring popularity of a novel with the general public can obscure its literary merits. Such has been the case with *Quo Vadis*, a work acclaimed by an early reviewer as "one of the great books of our day," subsequently translated into dozens of languages, and still in print more than a century after its initial publication. Henryk Sienkiewicz's deft handling of the central characters and focus on external action, coupled with his championing of traditional Christian values, have been both strengths and liabilities. While some have seen Henryk Sienkiewicz as a kind of prophet, revealing in his novel a way out of the moral morass that characterizes the modern era, others have dismissed *Quo Vadis* as propaganda that does little more than pander to popular sentiment by offering simplistic solutions to complex moral and social dilemmas.

To appreciate the literary merits of the novel, it may be helpful to understand the source of the novelist's inspiration for the work. During the nineteenth century, there emerged throughout Europe and the United States an interest in the civilizations of Greece and Rome, and writers found in the annals of classical societies fertile material for a number of popular works. Readers throughout the Western Hemisphere were treated to historical tales such as Edward Bulwer-Lytton's *The Last Days of Pompeii* (1834), John Henry Newman's *Callista: A Sketch of the Third Century* (1856), and Nicholas Wiseman's *Fabiola* (1854) in England (translated into Polish and widely read in Sienkiewicz's native land), and a number of Polish novels such as Józef Ignacy Kraszewski's many historical works. Sienkiewicz found a parallel between the moral chaos of his time and the history of Rome. The success of novels set in classical Rome convinced Sienkiewicz that the time was right for him to employ the history of Rome as a means of making a commentary on his own age and on timeless issues of human values.

Like all serious historical novelists, Sienkiewicz chose his materials carefully, so that the period he depicts is one in which a momentous historical crisis is imminent. The Rome of Nero was particularly decadent, and that period's growing popularity of Christianity as an antidote to the excesses of paganism is a matter of record. The novelist is careful to provide accurate historical details in his work, displaying his wide reading in the literature by classical figures and about life in ancient Rome. Like all good historical novelists, however, he is interested primarily in character and action rather than in setting. *Quo Vadis* is no mere period piece; rather, it is intended to demonstrate the conflict of values represented by the two great ideologies that dominated the Western world in the early centuries after the birth of Christ: Christianity and paganism as represented by the worship of the Romans, whose rule extended over much of what is now Europe and the Middle East.

Sienkiewicz reveals the conflict between these two opposing worldviews through a number of his central characters, both fictional and historical. The love story of Vinicius and Lygia provides the novelist an opportunity to dramatize the transforming power of Christianity, as readers see Vinicius move from lust for the attractive servant to a mature acceptance not only of his beloved but of her faith as well. The conflict of values is presented to readers most fully through the story of Petronius. This noble pagan is disgusted with the excesses he sees at Nero's court, and he is ready to see changes take place in Roman society. Nevertheless, he is not willing to give up easily what he finds good in his heritage. Possessing the Stoic virtues that characterize the best of the Romans, he never fully accepts the message of Christ; even at the end of the novel he retains enough of his pagan beliefs to commit suicide as a final gesture of defiance toward the emperor he has come to despise.

Petronius's story reveals that, far from being a simple propagandist for Christianity, Sienkiewicz remains faithful enough to the character he has created to allow him to die in a manner befitting a noble Roman. Petronius is far more than that, however, as numerous critics have observed. The protagonist has been described as the embodiment of nineteenth century values. This should not be surprising, since the aim of the novel is to point out the universality of Petronius's struggle against the forces of savagery, political despotism, and moral degeneracy. Like the distinguished gentlemen of Western Europe, he values moderation and personal dignity over political advancement. Additionally, Sienkiewicz complements his portrait of Petronius with depictions of several other admirable Romans, balancing the sadism of Nero and the excesses of those close to the emperor with scenes of men and women who lead dignified lives even though they have not yet been touched by Christianity. Sienkiewicz's message seems to be that the potential exists for people of goodwill in any age to withstand the evils of even the most corrupt society and maintain personal dignity, although often at great cost. Written at a time of great political chaos in his own country, and on the eve of a century when political and moral upheavals would become commonplace, *Quo Vadis* retains its didactic value for individuals looking for guidance in times of crisis.

"Critical Evaluation" by Laurence W. Mazzeno

Further Reading

Giergielewicz, Mieczyslaw. *Henryk Sienkiewicz.* 1968. Reprint. New York: Hippocrene Books, 1991. Good introductory volume offers a general survey of Sienkiewicz's achievements. A chapter on *Quo Vadis* discusses the novelist's adaptation of classical sources, his development of the idea of the fated dominance of Christianity, and his handling of plot and structure.

Kridl, Manfred. *A Survey of Polish Literature and Culture.* Translated by Olga Sherer-Virski. 1956. Reprint. New York: Columbia University Press, 1967. Discusses the novelist's techniques, which he repeats in many of his works, including *Quo Vadis.* Describes Sienkiewicz's use of history in this novel of ancient Rome.

Krżyanowski, Julian. *A History of Polish Literature.* Translated by Doris Ronowicz. Warsaw: PWN-Polish Scientific, 1978. Stresses the importance Sienkiewicz places on the accuracy of historical detail in his novels. Notes how he uses this approach successfully in *Quo Vadis.*

Lednicki, Waclaw. *Henryk Sienkiewicz: A Retrospective Synthesis.* The Hague, the Netherlands: Mouton, 1960. Provides an assessment of Sienkiewicz's career that gives readers a sense of the relative value of *Quo Vadis* to other works by the writer.

Miłosz, Czesław. *The History of Polish Literature.* 2d ed. Berkeley: University of California Press, 1983. Discusses Sienkiewicz in a chapter titled "Positivism." Notes the uneven quality of Sienkiewicz's fiction and argues that the novelist presents a simplistic portrait of the classical period in *Quo Vadis.*

Scodel, Ruth, and Anja Bettenworth. *Whither "Quo Vadis": Sienkiewicz's Novel in Film and Television.* Malden, Mass.: Wiley-Blackwell, 2009. Analyzes four films and a television version of *Quo Vadis,* describing how these adaptations modified the novel and its sources. Discusses the depictions of gender and ethnicity, politics, the Roman people, and religion in the adaptations, explaining how these portrayals reflect the historical and ideological concerns of the times in which the adaptations were produced.

R

The Rabbit Angstrom novels

Author: John Updike (1932-2009)
First published: 1960-1990; includes *Rabbit, Run*,
   1960; *Rabbit Redux*, 1971; *Rabbit Is Rich*, 1981;
   Rabbit at Rest, 1990
Type of work: Novels
Type of plot: Domestic realism
Time of plot: 1950's-1980's
Locale: Mt. Judge and Brewer, Pennsylvania; Florida

Principal characters:
HARRY "RABBIT" ANGSTROM, the main character, a former
   high-school basketball player
JANICE SPRINGER ANGSTROM, his wife, whose family owns
   a car dealership
NELSON ANGSTROM, son of Rabbit and Janice
REBECCA ANGSTROM, daughter of Rabbit and Janice,
   drowned in infancy
PRU ANGSTROM, Nelson's wife
CHARLIE STAVROS, a salesman for Springer Motors,
   Janice's lover
RUTH LEONARD, a prostitute, Harry's mistress
SKEETER, a black militant
JILL PENDLETON, a runaway flower child who is killed in a
   fire

The Story:

Rabbit, Run. Harry Angstrom, nicknamed Rabbit, was a high-school basketball star in Brewer, Pennsylvania. Rabbit does not go to college. Following a stint in the army, he marries Janice Springer, who is pregnant with his child. One day, Rabbit stops on his way home from work to play basketball with a group of young boys, remembering his days as a basketball star. After the excitement of the game, he returns to the reality of his dirty, cluttered apartment and a wife who is drinking too much. On a sudden impulse, Rabbit, feeling trapped by family responsibilities, gets in his car and heads south in an attempt to flee from the pressures that crowd his life. He gets as far as West Virginia and then turns back to Brewer. Still unwilling to return to his family, he seeks out his old coach, Marty Tothero, and through Tothero meets Ruth Leonard, a prostitute. Rabbit leaves his wife, who is pregnant with their second child, to move in with Ruth.

After Janice has the baby, Rebecca, Rabbit returns home, and they try to resume their life together. During a quarrel, Rabbit walks out on Janice and goes to Ruth's apartment. Janice gets drunk and while she is bathing Rebecca, she accidentally lets the baby drown. At the graveside, Rabbit shocks everyone by blaming Janice for the baby's death, saying, "You all keep acting as if I did it. I wasn't anywhere near. She's the one." After the funeral, he goes to Ruth's apartment and discovers that she is pregnant with his child. Again Rabbit runs.

Rabbit Redux. Rabbit, now thirty-six years of age, is no longer trying to run away from his problems. He works hard as a Linotypist in a local print shop, a job that ties him to events that take place in the summer of 1969: the Apollo moon shot, the race riots in York and Reading, and Ted Kennedy's problems following the Chappaquiddick drowning of Mary Jo Kopechne. Janice is working in her father's Toyota agency and having an affair with Charlie Stavros, one of the salesmen. Rabbit is laid off, and Janice moves in with Charlie. She leaves Rabbit to take care of Nelson.

Rabbit meets Jill, a rich, eighteen-year-old flower child who is running away from her family. She moves in with Rabbit, later bringing in Skeeter, a black Vietnam veteran who jumps bail on a drug-dealing charge. Skeeter tries to educate Rabbit on black history and radical politics as they smoke marijuana and argue about the morality of the Vietnam War. A fire destroys the house and, in spite of Nelson's heroic attempt to save her, Jill dies in the blaze. Janice leaves Charlie, and she and Rabbit reconcile.

Rabbit Is Rich. Rabbit, at forty-six years of age, is moderately wealthy, running the Springer family's Toyota dealership. He and Janice move into a new home and join the country club. Golf replaces basketball, and Rabbit gains weight. When Rabbit and Janice engage in wife-swapping on a vacation in the Caribbean, Rabbit is disappointed that he does not win Cindy, the woman who most attracts him. In the exchange, he draws Thelma, the wife of Ronnie Harrison, an old teammate of Rabbit. Rabbit continues the affair with Thelma when they all return to Brewer.

Rabbit takes a personal interest in the news, viewing oil prices and the decline of the dollar as they affect his Toyota business. An avid reader of *Consumer Reports*, Rabbit seems obsessed with financial news and investment advice. He invests in gold Krugerrands and spreads them over Janice's body, reveling in the sight and feel of the gold coins. Material wealth is at the center of Rabbit's life.

Although he is comfortable with his own lifestyle, Rabbit is disappointed in his son. Uncoordinated and lacking in athletic talent, Nelson possesses none of his father's grace. He is irresponsible, wrecking his father's car and failing to graduate from Kent State. Nelson returns to Brewer with Pru, his pregnant girlfriend, and the two are married. With the birth of Judy, Rabbit becomes a grandfather and reaffirms his belief in life.

Rabbit at Rest. Rabbit focuses on his heart trouble, Nelson's drug addiction, and Janice's new career. While Nelson, Pru, and their children, Judy and Roy, are visiting Rabbit and Janice in their Florida condo, Rabbit and Judy go sailing. When their sailboat capsizes, Rabbit struggles to get Judy safely to shore. In contrast to the tragedy of the drowning death of his daughter, Rabbit is able to save the child. The physical effort, however, puts added stress on Rabbit's heart. Rabbit and Janice return to Brewer, where Rabbit undergoes angioplasty. Janice enrolls in a real estate course, determined to have a career as a real estate agent. Nelson brings the family to the brink of financial disaster by stealing from the business to support his drug habit.

In Nelson's absence, Rabbit and Pru have a sexual encounter. When Nelson returns from the drug rehabilitation program, Pru confesses the transgression. Rather than face Janice and Nelson, Rabbit again takes flight, this time to the condo in Florida, where Janice stubbornly refuses to join him. In an attempt to live in a more healthy way, Rabbit begins walking. On one of his trips, he joins a group of young black men in a game of basketball. Exhilarated by the chal-

lenge, he returns to the neighborhood and plays a game of one-on-one with a young man. During the game, Rabbit drops to the ground with a massive heart attack. Janice and Nelson rush to the hospital in Florida, where Janice learns that Rabbit has no chance to live. Rabbit's last words are spoken to Nelson: He tells him that dying is not so bad.

Critical Evaluation:

A major contemporary American author, John Updike was awarded the Pulitzer Prize, the National Book Critics Circle Award, and the American Book Award for *Rabbit Is Rich*. Updike graduated from Harvard in 1954 and worked on the staff of *The New Yorker*. He published poems, short stories, essays, and book reviews in addition to several novels. The domestic life of the American middle class provides the major subject for those novels, as his characters struggle to find meaning and a sense of values in a changing world. *Rabbit, Run*, his second novel, begins the series of four novels that traces the life of Harry Angstrom, the former basketball star who searches for meaning beyond the confines of an unhappy marriage and the ordinary struggles of daily life. Each of the novels chronicles the history and culture of the decade before it was published, as it shows Rabbit's journey through middle age, prosperity, retirement, and death.

The image of the basketball court provides the frame for the series. In the first novel, the neighborhood basketball game reminds Rabbit of how much he misses the excitement of his high school years. This longing for something more in his life drives him to flee from his responsibilities. A similar game on a basketball court in Florida is the scene of the massive heart attack that leads to Rabbit's death.

The rabbit image is central to the novel. On the first page, Updike describes Harry's rabbitlike appearance with his broad white face, pale blue eyes, and "nervous flutter under his brief nose." Nervous blinks and quick movements on the basketball court add to the image of a rabbit. His desire to flee in the midst of trouble resembles a rabbit's instinct to run and hide. The first novel ends with more rabbit imagery as "he feels the wind on his ears" and with "a kind of sweet panic growing lighter and quicker and quieter, he runs." On his last trip in *Rabbit at Rest*, Rabbit, again running away from conflict, refers to the inside of his car as a cave.

Updike employs a number of devices to show the history of each decade and its effect on the main character. Rabbit's job as a typesetter for the Brewer newspaper links him to news events and provides him with an opportunity to comment on the events of the time. His arguments with Skeeter focus on the Vietnam War and race relations. In *Rabbit at Rest*, Rabbit, retired and lacking a purpose, spends hours watching television news and reading the newspaper, keeping up with current events. On his final trip from Brewer to Florida, Rabbit tours his old neighborhood, remembering stages of his life. On the road, as Rabbit listens to a golden oldies station on the radio, song lyrics remind him of the women and events in his life. News reports periodically interrupt the music, bringing news of Jim and Tammy Bakker, a bombing in Colombia, and the score of a Miami Dolphins-Philadelphia Eagles game.

The song lyrics show how Rabbit is seduced by the American dream. As Tony Bennett croons "Be My Love," Gogi Grant sings "The Wayward Wind," and Nat "King" Cole sings "Ramblin' Rose," Rabbit concentrates on the lyrics. He never liked Frank Sinatra's "foghorn" voice, preferring Elvis singing "Love Me Tender," or Ray Charles "dreaming of yesterdays." As Johnny Ray cries, "If your sweetheart sends a letter of good-bye," Rabbit remembers the "Dear John" letter that his first love, Mary Ann, sent him when he was in the army. Rabbit is the American dreamer, believing in the lyrics of the songs, always longing for something more. At the end of his life, Rabbit feels betrayed by the promise of the music that led him "down the garden path," a path that ends in disillusionment. Rabbit searches for meaning in his life until the end, and when death finally comes, he accepts it with grace.

"Critical Evaluation" by Judith Barton Williamson

Further Reading

Bailey, Peter J. *Rabbit (Un)Redeemed: The Drama of Belief in John Updike's Fiction.* Madison, N.J.: Fairleigh Dickinson University Press, 2006. Interprets the *Rabbit* saga as a fictionalized, spiritual autobiography in which Updike articulates his ethical and aesthetic ideas about the affirming capabilities of human perception and expression.

Boswell, Marshall. *John Updike's "Rabbit" Tetralogy: Mastered Irony in Motion.* Columbia: University of Missouri Press, 2001. Treats the four books as a single metanovel that provides a coherent expression of Updike's existential vision. Devotes a separate chapter to each novel.

Broer, Lawrence R., ed. *Rabbit Tales: Poetry and Politics in John Updike's "Rabbit" Novels.* Tuscaloosa: University of Alabama Press, 2000. Collection of twelve essays providing numerous interpretations of the novels, including discussions of sports, basketball, and "fortunate failure" in the tetralogy; the world of *Rabbit at Rest*; and "Rabbit Angstrom: John Updike's Ambiguous Pilgrim."

De Bellis, Jack, ed. *John Updike: The Critical Responses to the "Rabbit" Saga.* Westport, Conn.: Praeger, 2005. Reprints thirty-four reviews and critical essays about the four *Rabbit* novels and the novella *Rabbit Remembered*, treating them as both individual works and as an entire saga.

Doner, Dean. "Rabbit Angstrom's Unseen World." In *John Updike: A Collection of Critical Essays*, edited by David Thorburn and Howard Eiland. Englewood Cliffs, N.J.: Prentice-Hall, 1979. Compares *Rabbit, Run* to Updike's short story, "Ace in the Hole" (1959), whose protagonist was also a former high-school basketball star. Focuses on Rabbit's religious nature, observing that of all the people gathered at the baby's graveside, Rabbit is the only one who believes in God.

Greiner, Donald J. *John Updike's Novels.* Athens: Ohio University Press, 1984. Points out that Updike used three Rabbit novels to record the tone of a decade: religious speculation in *Rabbit, Run*, political concerns in *Rabbit Redux*, and economic practicalities in *Rabbit Is Rich*.

Newman, Judie. *John Updike.* New York: St. Martin's Press, 1988. One chapter, "The World of Work," deals with the major themes of the first three novels: work, technology, and sex.

Olster, Stacey, ed. *The Cambridge Companion to John Updike.* New York: Cambridge University Press, 2006. Collection of essays offering various interpretations of Updike's work, including discussions of Updike's depiction of race, ethnicity, women, and religion. Literary critic Donald J. Greiner examines "Updike, Rabbit, and the Myth of American Exceptionalism."

Schiff, James A. *John Updike Revisited.* New York: Twayne, 1998. Endeavors to understand Updike's entire body of work, putting individual works in context for the reader. Provides commentary on works that have largely been ignored by the public as well as books that have received little critical attention. Includes a critical analysis of the Rabbit Angstrom novels.

Uphaus, Suzanne Henning. *John Updike.* New York: Frederick Ungar, 1980. Discusses the religious images Updike used in *Rabbit, Run* to show the contradictions of Rabbit's character and the confusion and uncertainty of contemporary society. Argues that although the characters are portrayed realistically and convincingly, the historical emphasis of *Rabbit Redux* causes them to become agents of history.

Rabbit Boss

Author: Thomas Sanchez (1944-   )
First published: 1973
Type of work: Novel
Type of plot: Historical realism
Time of plot: 1846-1950's
Locale: Nevada and California

Principal characters:
RABBIT BOSS, chief of the Washo
GAYABUC, his son, later Rabbit Boss
PAINTED STICK, Gayabuc's wife
CAPTAIN REX, their son, latter Rabbit Boss
AYAS, Captain Rex's son, later Rabbit Boss
JOE BIRDSONG, the last Rabbit Boss

The Story:

In 1846, Gayabuc, the son of the powerful Rabbit Chief or Rabbit Boss of the Washo Indians, sets out on a hunting expedition in the middle of winter to obtain meat for his firstborn son's birth celebration. He encounters the Donner party, a group of whites who had been forced by starvation into cannibalism. Gayabuc returns to his family empty-handed and warns them about the white people who eat themselves. Gayabuc's father refuses to believe Gayabuc's account and asserts that Gayabuc had dreamed it. Painted Stick, Gayabuc's wife, believes that he came back without meat because he was forced to hunt in winter when game is scarce. Their son is born in winter because their first sexual union had occurred in spring, just before Painted Stick's first menstruation. Gayabuc and Painted Stick had violated Washo tradition by engaging in sexual relations before Painted Stick underwent the puberty ritual of the Dance of the Woman. The repercussions of their transgression culminated in Gayabuc's unlucky encounter at Donner Lake.

The cannibalism of the whites at Donner Lake continues to influence Gayabuc during the ensuing spring. Spring is the time that the Washos hunt the rabbits that provide their food and clothing. Gayabuc's father, the Rabbit Chief, is the leader of the hunt. Gayabuc believes that investigating the white invasion should take precedence over engaging in the hunt, but his father strongly disagrees. The men of the tribe vote and side with Gayabuc. The women and children conduct the hunt while the men explore the deserted white encampment. There they find animal traps they had never seen before. One of them contains a rabbit that was mangled by the trap, foreshadowing the eventual oppression of the Washos by the whites.

Gayabuc succeeds his father as Rabbit Chief. Gayabuc realizes that his shamanic role as chief hunter is vital to the survival of his people and to their way of life. During the spring hunt, Gayabuc dreams about the location of the prey. He knows that in his role as Rabbit Chief, his spiritual and moral powers are essential to the preservation of the tribe. Gayabuc notes, "All this I have dreamed. If I were dead, all this would not have been dreamed. . . . If I were dead, there would be no other to tell you this."

The disrupting influence of the whites becomes evident in the life of Captain Rex, the son of Gayabuc and Painted Stick. Captain Rex follows the old ways at first and inherits the position of Rabbit Chief. As the railroad encroaches on Washo land, however, the quality of life declines for the Washo. There are few rabbits to hunt, and the office of Rabbit Chief becomes obsolete. Captain Rex learns English from a white woman. As a result of his being bilingual, the white railroad workers employ him as a translator. Although the whites depend upon his bilingual abilities, the Washo people mistrust him. As a result of his cultural confusion, he becomes a drunkard, a petty thief, and a gambler.

Captain Rex's penchant for drink and gambling leads to a confrontation with the whites. Accused of stealing whiskey and horses, Captain Rex faces a lynch mob. John C. Luther, the Bummer, saves Rex from the mob because he falsely believes that Rex knows where to mine for gold. Luther organizes an expedition to search for the gold, with Captain Rex serving as a guide. Molly Moose, Luther's Washo mistress, accompanies them. When the group camps, the men rape Molly. They tie Rex to a tree to keep him from interfering.

Most of the men eventually leave the camp to find the gold. The men soon realize that Rex had given them misinformation, and they return to camp seeking vengeance. Molly cuts Rex's bonds, rescues him, and they flee. Molly becomes Captain Rex's wife, and the couple has a son, Ayas. In old age, Captain Rex, along with many of his tribe, contracts tuberculosis. He dies when the whites burn the Indian encampment to rid the area of the disease.

Ayas is raised by his grandmother, Painted Stick, for the first six years of his life. When she dies, he is taken in by the Dora family, who employs him as a farmworker. When they no longer need him, they give him to Abe Fixa, an elderly, blind dairyman. He becomes the boy's surrogate father and names him Bob. After Abe's death, Bob is placed in a government school for Indian children. An elderly Washo reveals to him his true name and heritage. Bob is subsequently kidnapped by a remnant of his tribe and taken to live with them in the mountains. He lives a traditional Washo life, but eventually leaves the camp because all the people are either dead or dying.

Bob travels east and works in the stockyards of Omaha, Nebraska. There he experiences the beginnings of a conversion to Christianity. He subsequently escapes the stockyards and joins two men on the road selling homemade whiskey. He becomes a medicine-show pitchman, selling the concoction to various Indian tribes. Bob makes his way back to California and gets a job on the Dixel ranch as a ranch hand and Rabbit Boss. By the 1920's, the Rabbit Boss is regarded more as an exterminator than a powerful shaman.

During his tenure at the Dixel ranch, Bob converts to Christianity. His fervor leads to his being known as Hallelujah Bob. He preaches the gospel to the Washo, although later in his life he follows the Ghost Dance religion. The Washo believe that it is not good for a man to live alone, and Medicine Maggie volunteers to live in his house. She becomes the mother of Sarah Dick and Joe Birdsong.

Joe Birdsong is the last of the Rabbit Bosses. Although Dixel views the job of Rabbit Boss in a pragmatic way, Joe still holds a reverence for the tradition underlying what had once been an exalted office. Joe also feels a deep attachment to the land that he inherited from his father. White developers try to force him to sell, and he refuses. To get him to turn the property over to them, the developers tell Joe that his title to the property is not binding because his father had not been a citizen when he gave the land to Joe.

Dixel informs Joe that he will no longer need a Rabbit Boss to conduct the spring extermination because he had bought a machine to kill the rabbits. In defiance of Dixel, Joe and Sarah Dick conduct the hunt. When Joe returns to his cabin after the hunt, Dixel's wife is there to warn him that her husband has been murdered and that the sheriff believes that Joe committed the crime. Joe escapes into the mountains and lives off the land for almost a year. During this time, he is accidentally shot in the leg by a group of deer hunters. The leg becomes infected, and the infection gradually spreads through his body. During the spring thaw, he reaches the shores of Donner Lake and dies from starvation and infection.

Critical Evaluation:

Rabbit Boss is Thomas Sanchez's first novel. Although Sanchez is not an American Indian, he was greatly influenced by his contact with American Indians when he attended a boys' boarding school for disadvantaged children. Sanchez chose to write about the Washo because he wished to demonstrate the cultural arrogance of the European Americans and the effect that their attitude of superiority had on Native American society.

The theme of cultural dichotomy is reinforced by characterization and language. For example, Gayabuc and Painted Stick are portrayed as Adam- and Eve-like figures. They have premarital intercourse, so they believe they have sinned against the ways of their people. Gayabuc's first encounter with the whites is somehow linked to this initial transgression, bringing further bad luck to the tribe. Their ensuing contact with the whites causes their expulsion from their land, which, in turn, adversely affects their traditions and ceremonies.

Captain Rex is probably the most tragic figure in the novel. He is caught between two cultures and is an outcast in both. At one point in the story, his clothing signifies his position. He appears wearing a pair of pants given to him by the white woman who taught him English, with a tattered rabbit blanket around his shoulders. The pants represent the "civilizing" influence of white culture; the worn blanket signifies the fading dignity and power of the Rabbit Chief.

Language is especially important in understanding the interrelations between whites and Indians and their cultural differences. The oral tradition in American Indian society is central in maintaining their cultural existence and identity. The importance of the oral tradition is underscored when Proud Dog first reveals to Bob his Indian identity. After Proud Dog dies, Bob and the children share stories from their different tribes. It is a way of affirming their identity as Indians and regaining a sense of pride that the whites had stripped from them.

Although language is a way for the Indians to affirm their cultural identity among themselves, it is also a means to differentiate themselves from the whites. After Gayabuc first witnesses the cannibalism of the Donner party, his father asks him what he saw and he answers, "Them." The Indians continually refer to the whites in the terms of "they," "their," and "them." The whites are the "other." They "eat of themselves," which is repulsive to the Washo and certainly uncivilized. The European Americans are referred to as White Ghosts or "the white burden." This latter phrase is also used to describe the snow of winter, which links the harshness of the season to the oppressiveness of the white society.

The portrayal of whites as cannibals in the first scene of the novel recurs throughout the book. To the Washo, cannibalism is abhorrent, because to eat a member of one's own species or one's totemic animal means a loss of power or "musege." The cannibalism of the Donner party foreshadows the environmental and social cannibalism that the whites perpetrate on the land and on the Washo. From a Washo point of view, it is ironic that even though the white people destroy the land and mistreat the Washo, their power only continues to grow as the Washo are reduced to a remnant of what they once were.

Pegge Bochynski

Further Reading

Gueder, P. A. "Language and Ethnic Interaction in *Rabbit Boss*: A Novel by Thomas Sanchez." In *Language and Ethnic Relations*, edited by Howard Giles and Bernard Saint-Jacques. Elmsford, N.Y.: Pergamon Press, 1979. Methodic discussion of the way language is used in the novel to reveal the disturbing interethnic relationship between the Washo Indians and the whites.

Marovitz, Sanford E. "The Entropic World of the Washo: Fatality and Self-Deception in *Rabbit Boss*." *Western American Literature* 19 (November, 1984): 219-230. Detailed analysis of the structure, themes, and characters of the novel, focusing on the desire of the Washo Indians to integrate their way of life into the dominant culture and how that desire precipitates their decline.

Sanchez, Thomas. "An Interview with Thomas Sanchez." Interview by Kay Bonetti. *Missouri Review* 14, no. 2 (1991): 77-95. An informative interview with Sanchez, in which he discusses the biographical and historical background that informs the plot of *Rabbit Boss*, particularly the influence of his family, his education, and the Vietnam War.

_____. "Telling History's Stories." Interview by Bridget Kinsella. *Publishers Weekly*, May 26, 2003. Sanchez talks about *Rabbit Boss*, his other novels, his family, and the importance of the city of San Francisco and the Golden Gate Bridge to his family and his upbringing.

_____. "The Visionary Imagination." *Melus* 3, no. 2 (1976): 2-5. Sanchez reveals his reasons for writing *Rabbit Boss*, the influence of American Indian thought on the structure of the novel, character motivation, and the contemporaneous political events that influenced the plot.

The Rainbow

Author: D. H. Lawrence (1885-1930)
First published: 1915
Type of work: Novel
Type of plot: Psychological realism
Time of plot: Nineteenth and early twentieth centuries
Locale: England

Principal characters:
TOM BRANGWEN, a farmer
LYDIA LENSKY, his wife
ANNA LENSKY, Lydia's child by her first husband
WILL BRANGWEN, Anna's husband
URSULA BRANGWEN, Anna and Will's daughter
ANTON SKREBENSKY, Ursula's lover

The Story:

Tom Brangwen is descended from a long line of small landholders who had owned Marsh Farm in Nottinghamshire for many generations. Tom is a man of the soil, and he lives alone on his farm with only an old woman, as company and as a housekeeper. Then a Polish widow, Lydia Lensky, becomes the housekeeper of the vicar of the local church. She brings her small daughter, Anna, with her. One evening a few months later, Tom finds the courage to present the widow with a bouquet of daffodils in the vicar's kitchen and to ask her to be his wife.

Judged by the standards of the world, their marriage is a satisfactory one. They have two sons, and Tom is kind to his stepdaughter. Knowing his stepdaughter, however, is easier for him than knowing Lydia. That they are of different nationalities, cultures, and even languages keeps them from ever becoming intellectually intimate with each other. There are times when one or both feels that their marriage is not what it should be and that they are not fulfilling the obligations imposed upon them by their marriage. On one occasion, Lydia even suggests to her husband that he needs another woman.

Little Anna is a haughty young girl who spends many hours imagining herself a great lady or even a queen. In her eighteenth year, a nephew of Tom comes to work in the lace factory in the nearby village of Ilkeston. He is only twenty years old, and the Brangwens at Marsh Farm look after him and make him welcome in their home.

Anna and young Will fall in love, with a naïve, touching affection for each other. When they soon announce to Tom and Lydia that they wish to be married, Tom leases a home for them in the village and gives them a present of twenty-five hundred pounds so they can manage financially, given Will's small salary.

The wedding is celebrated with rural pomp and hilarity. After the ceremony, the newly married couple spends two weeks alone in their cottage, ignoring the world and existing only for themselves. Anna is the first to come back to the world of reality. Her decision to give a tea party both bewilders and angers her husband, who has not yet realized that they cannot continue to live only for and by themselves. It takes him almost a lifetime to come to that realization.

Shortly after the marriage, Anna becomes pregnant, and the arrival of the child brings to Will the added shock that his wife is more a mother than she is a married lover. Each year, a new baby comes between Will and Anna. The oldest is Ursula, who remains her father's favorite. The love that Will wishes to give his wife is given to Ursula, for Anna refuses to have anything to do with him when she is expecting another child, and she is not happy unless she is pregnant.

In the second year of his marriage, Will tries to rebel. He meets a young woman at the theater and afterward takes her out for supper and a walk. After this incident, the intimate life of Will and Anna gains in passion, enough to carry Will through the daytime when he is not needed in the house until the night when he can rule his wife. Gradually, he becomes free in his own mind from Anna's domination.

Because Ursula is her father's favorite child, she is sent to high school, a rare privilege for a girl of her circumstances in the last decade of the nineteenth century. She drinks up knowledge in her study of Latin, French, and algebra. Before she finishes her studies, however, her academic interests are divided by her interest in a young man, the son of a Polish friend of her grandmother. Young, blond Anton Skrebensky, a lieutenant in the British army, is introduced in the Brangwen home, and during a month's leave, he falls in love with Ursula, who is already in love with him. On his next leave, however, he becomes afraid of her because her love is too possessive.

After finishing high school, Ursula takes an examination to enter the university. Even though she passes the exam, she decides to teach school for a time, for she wants to accumulate money to carry her through her education without being a burden to her parents. Anna and Will are furious when she

broaches the subject of leaving home. They compromise with her, however, by securing for her a position in a school in Ilkeston. Ursula spends two friendless, ill-paid, and thankless years teaching at the village elementary school. At the end of that time, she is more than ready to continue her education. She decides to become a botanist, for in botany she feels she is doing and learning for herself things that have an absolute truth.

One day, after the end of the Boer War, Ursula receives a letter from Anton, who writes that he wishes to see her again while he is in England on leave. Within a week, he arrives in Nottingham to visit her at school. Their love for each other is rekindled with greater intensity than they had known six years earlier. During the Easter holidays, they go away for a weekend at a hotel, where they pass as husband and wife. They travel to the Continent as soon as Ursula finishes classes for the summer. Anton increasingly presses for marriage, wanting Ursula to leave England with him when he returns to service in India, but she wants to return to college to earn her degree.

Ursula so neglects her studies during this time that she fails the final examinations for her degree. She studies all summer before taking them again, but fails again. Anton thereupon urges her to marry him immediately. In India, he insists, her degree will mean nothing anyway. One evening, at a house party, they realize that there is something wrong in their mating and that they cannot agree enough to make a successful marriage. They leave the party separately. A few weeks later, Anton leaves for India as the husband of his regimental commander's daughter.

Ursula then learns that she is pregnant. Not knowing that Anton is now married, she writes to him and promises to be a good wife if he still wishes to marry her. Before his answer comes from India, Ursula contracts pneumonia and loses the child. One day, as she is convalescing, she observes a rainbow in the sky. She hopes that it is the promise of better times to come.

Critical Evaluation:

Even while composing *The Rainbow*, D. H. Lawrence realized that neither the critics nor general readers would accept his novel. He wrote to Amy Lowell about the critical reception of a book of his short stories, telling her, "The critics really hate me. So they ought." It is a curious remark from any writer, but especially from one who was so intent on working a moral change in his readers.

Lawrence knew, however, not only that his fiction was "shocking" in its treatment of sexuality, particularly that of women—and it was to become more shocking yet—but that he also created character and experience that challenged the way the critics viewed the world. In his fiction, and this became fully apparent in *The Rainbow*, he dramatizes experience as dynamic, shifting, and elusive. For him, the world was neither stable, nor certain, nor finally rationally explicable; his vision undercuts all the preconceptions of the Edwardian critics. Their "hatred" of Lawrence's fiction was actually self-defense. When *The Rainbow* appeared during the first years of World War I, it seemed to validate Lawrence's argument against those who saw civilization as stable, knowable, and controllable.

One central question preoccupies Lawrence in *The Rainbow*: Is the self capable of expansion, of becoming an entity, of achieving freedom, especially in an age where the traditional supports of community, family, and religion have been weakened or eliminated? In Will and Anna Brangwen's generation, the first to enter the industrial world, the self does survive, though only minimally. If, unlike Tom and Lydia Brangwen, Will and Anna fail to create the "rainbow," an image of the fully realized self in passionate community, and if their love degenerates to lust, they at least endure. True freedom, however, is denied them.

For Ursula, Will and Anna's daughter and the novel's heroine, the question of freedom hardly pertains, at least at the beginning. It is simply a matter of her survival. Her vision of the "rainbow" at the end must be taken as a promise of freedom—and for many readers an unconvincing one—rather than as fulfillment. Nevertheless, it is a perception she earns by surviving both the inner and the outer terrors of her world.

The Rainbow is primarily a psychological novel, in which Lawrence is primarily concerned with states of feeling and being that exist below the level of history. Nevertheless, the social and political backgrounds are of utmost importance; indeed they are of central significance to an understanding of the question of self-realization. For if Lawrence explores the dialectic of the psyche, he does so in an understanding of the determining impact that history has on that psychological drama.

A novel of three generations, *The Rainbow*'s time span runs from 1840 to 1905. In the background, yet ever-present, are the major cultural changes of the age: the rapid expansion of industry, the diminution of arable land, the transformation of society from one based on the hamlet and town to a truly urban one, the breakdown of the nuclear family, and the spread of education. In short, Lawrence dramatizes the English revolution from a feudal to a democratic, capitalistic society. In the foreground of these radical changes are the relationships between Tom and Lydia, Will and Anna, and Ursula and Anton. As the novel moves in time from the middle of the nineteenth to the beginning of the twentieth century and in space from Ilkeston, Beldover, and Nottingham to London and Paris, what becomes increasingly apparent is that both relationships and the sanctity of the self are harder to sustain.

In the first generation, Tom and Lydia are firmly rooted in the earth. After an early crisis, their marriage flowers into a relationship of deep and lasting love, under whose influence their daughter, Anna, also grows. Nevertheless, though their life moves according to the rhythms of nature, it is limited by its pure physicality; it is fated, moreover, to be overwhelmed by other rhythms, those created by the motion of the piston. In fact, Tom himself is drowned when a canal bursts and floods his farm. The symbolic significance of his death—the rural life killed off by the industrial—is emphasized by its appearance at the structural midpoint of the novel.

The second generation, Anna and Will, move from the farm at Ilkeston first to the town of Beldover and finally to a major industrial city, Nottingham. Their escape from the limiting existence on the farm to the greater individual liberty of the town, however, exacts a great cost: Their love and marriage, although bountiful, fail to fulfill them. Because of their insistence on the self, they cannot make the deep connection that Tom and Lydia achieve. They are sustained by the rich fecundity of their marriage but are left without unity.

It is left to Ursula to carry out the quest that her parents abandoned: that search for the completely free self in unity. The forces confronting her, however, are even greater than those her parents faced. Not only is the new society, characterized by the machine, hostile to the individual, but it has successfully destroyed the community. Cut off as she is from the life of feeling and freed from the restraints imposed by the older society, Ursula wanders through London and Paris preyed on by all, especially by Anton, who would swallow her if she allowed him. Nevertheless, she survives as an independent self, aided by the strength she has inherited. However, Ursula has not discovered the necessary relationship to the whole spectrum of human life; this she can imagine only in her final vision of the "rainbow." It is precisely her vision, which was also Lawrence's, of human beings fully free, connected, and equal that challenged so effectively the worldview of his Edwardian readers and led to their uneasiness. Lawrence showed his critics that there was no hope for society based on what they themselves were.

"Critical Evaluation" by David L. Kubal

Further Reading

Bloom, Harold, ed. *D. H. Lawrence's "The Rainbow."* New York: Chelsea House, 1988. A collection of sophisticated critical essays, written from 1966 to 1984, covering Lawrence's Romanticism and the theological and psychological dimensions of *The Rainbow*. Includes an introduction, a chronology, a bibliography, and an index.

Burack, Charles Michael. *D. H. Lawrence's Language of Sacred Experience: The Transfiguration of the Reader.* New York: Palgrave Macmillan, 2005. Burack maintains that Lawrence structured *The Rainbow*, *Lady Chatterley's Lover*, *The Plumed Serpent*, and *Women in Love* as if they were religious initiation rites intended to evoke new spiritual experiences for their readers.

Cushman, Keith, and Earl G. Ingersoll, eds. *D. H. Lawrence: New Worlds.* Madison, N.J.: Fairleigh Dickinson University Press, 2003. Collection of essays that reinterpret Lawrence's work. Includes discussions of his influence on British fiction, the debate over his national identity, and analyses of several of his novels.

Day, Gary, and Libby Di Niro, eds. *"The Rainbow" and "Women in Love": D. H. Lawrence.* New York: Palgrave Macmillan, 2004. Features ten essays interpreting the two novels, including discussions of the politics of sexual liberation in both books, Lawrence and feminist psychoanalytic theory in *The Rainbow*, and historical change in *Women in Love*.

Fernihough, Anne, ed. *The Cambridge Companion to D. H. Lawrence.* New York: Cambridge University Press, 2001. Collection of essays interpreting Lawrence's work from various perspectives. Includes discussions of Lawrence and modernism, Lawrence in the 1920's, and the essay "Narrating Sexuality: *The Rainbow*" by Marianna Torgovnick.

Kinkead-Weekes, Mark, ed. *Twentieth Century Interpretations of "The Rainbow": A Collection of Critical Essays.* Englewood Cliffs, N.J.: Prentice-Hall, 1971. A collection of essays in four parts, one of which is on the interpretation of the three generations depicted in the novel. The concluding essay discusses the making of the novel. Includes a chronology.

Ryu, Doo-Sun. *D. H. Lawrence's "The Rainbow" and "Women in Love": A Critical Study.* New York: Peter Lang, 2005. Focuses on Lawrence's concept of "essential criticism" to analyze how he presents his ideas in both novels.

Sagar, Keith. *D. H. Lawrence: Life into Art.* New York: Viking Press, 1985. Concentrates on the process of Lawrence's writing as a creative artist. In a chapter on *The Rainbow*, entitled "New Heavens and Earth," Sagar focuses on the novel's genesis, as well as its critical reception and banning.

Wright, T. R. *D. H. Lawrence and the Bible.* New York: Cambridge University Press, 2000. Wright maintains that the Bible played a significant role in almost all of Lawrence's works, and he analyzes Lawrence's use of biblical allusions and themes. *The Rainbow* is discussed in chapter 6.

Raintree County

Author: Ross Lockridge, Jr. (1914-1948)
First published: 1948
Type of work: Novel
Type of plot: Historical realism
Time of plot: Late nineteenth century
Locale: Indiana, Tennessee, Georgia, Washington, D.C., and New York

Principal characters:
JOHN WICKLIFF SHAWNESSY, teacher, Civil War veteran, and longtime resident of Raintree County, Indiana
NELL GAITHER, a woman with whom he is in love
SUSANNA DRAKE, a visitor from the South who becomes John's first wife
ESTHER ROOT, John's student and later his second wife
GARWOOD B. JONES, John's boyhood friend and later a U.S. senator
JERUSALEM WEBSTER STILES, John's teacher and later his friend
FLASH PERKINS, fastest runner in Raintree County and later John's companion in the Civil War

The Story:

A big celebration is held in Raintree County, Indiana, on July 4, 1892. The birthday of the nation is noted with the usual parades and fireworks, and everyone is excited that Indiana senator Garwood Jones is returning to his hometown to make a speech. Among those who greet the senator is his old friend and rival John Wickliff Shawnessy, who once opposed Jones for political office and lost. As Shawnessy experiences the events of the day, his mind wanders back to other times.

Shawnessy remembers growing up in Raintree County, the son of T. D. Shawnessy, a physician and preacher, and Ellen Shawnessy, a wise and gentle woman. John's early life is haunted by the legend of the raintree, a magic tree with yellow flowers that is rumored to grow somewhere in the county. Most of the county is easy to travel over, so the most likely place for the fabulous raintree to be hidden is deep in a swamp at the end of a lake in the middle of the county. John vows that he will find the raintree some day. He also has another dream of writing a great epic that will encapsulate and explain not only Raintree County but also the American republic.

John's adolescence is affected by three people. Jerusalem Webster Stiles, known as the Perfessor, establishes an academy that young Johnny Shawnessy attends, along with his friends Garwood Jones and Nell Gaither. The Perfessor is only a few years older than his students, and he has a cynical, worldly-wise attitude that frequently puts him in conflict with his fellow citizens and occasions a debate with the more optimistic Shawnessy that lasts a lifetime. Garwood is a smoother self-promoter than the Perfessor; he knows how to manipulate people, telling them what they want to hear. Even as a youth he is well on his way to a successful career in politics. Nell Gaither is a spirited blond beauty with whom John is deeply in love. She loves him too, but each is too shy to approach the other. John and Nell communicate only through vague hints and inscriptions in books that they give each other. John's love for Nell is made permanent when he sees her naked, rising from the lake; Nell later reveals that she knew he was there that day.

The day of John's graduation from the Perfessor's academy is packed with excitement. When John has his graduation picture taken, he meets in the photographer's studio a beautiful visitor from the South, Susanna Drake. After the graduation ceremony, everyone goes to the lake, and John and Nell (who is apart for once from her usual escort, Garwood) are about to consummate their love for each other when they are interrupted by cries from their companions—a posse is hunting for the Perfessor, who has run off with the minister's wife. In fact, the couple missed their train, and the minister's wife has gone back home. Johnny finds the Perfessor and helps him to escape.

That same year, the Fourth of July celebration is enlivened by a race between John and Flash Perkins, a runner who has never been beaten. John's friends plan to fix the race by getting Flash drunk, but this scheme backfires when John gets drunk instead. He wins the race anyway, and once again everyone goes to the lake to picnic. His inhibitions loosened by drink, John makes love for the first time—with Susanna Drake.

Later Susanna tells John that she is pregnant, and he does the honorable thing and marries her. They take a trip to New Orleans, where John learns of Susanna's tragic past. Her mother had gone insane, and her father is rumored to have had an intimate relationship with a slave. All of these people died in a fire that destroyed the plantation house; only Susanna survived. Susanna is horrified by the possibility that she might be her father's child by the slave, and she is also worried that she might go mad like her mother. After they return to Raintree County, Susanna gives birth to a son, but soon her madness begins to assert itself, and Susanna burns down their house, killing their child. Hopelessly insane, she is sent back to the South.

Meanwhile, the Civil War has begun; because he had a family, John has not yet served in the Union Army. After Susanna is sent away, however, he becomes a soldier, meeting once again Flash Perkins and the Perfessor, who is a war correspondent. John and Flash are in the Battle of Chickamauga. Later, Flash is killed and John is wounded during General William T. Sherman's march through Georgia.

John recovers from his wounds in Washington, D.C., where he and the Perfessor witness the assassination of Abraham Lincoln. Back home, a false report leads people to believe that John is dead. After spending two years in New York with the Perfessor, John goes back to Raintree County after his mother's death. He discovers that Nell Gaither had married Garwood Jones and had died in childbirth. John runs against Garwood for a seat in Congress, but the people of the county are not ready to hear John's message of reconciliation with the South. John settles down to become the local schoolteacher, and after Susanna runs away from her keepers and is declared dead, he takes for his second wife one of his students, Esther Root. Esther's father disapproves of the marriage and refuses to see his daughter, even though John and Esther prosper and raise a family.

One event almost ruins John. A local preacher tries to attack him, saying that John has an illicit relationship with a local widow, but the Perfessor, in town for the celebration of

July 4, 1892, shows that it is actually the preacher who is guilty of adultery with one of the local women. The Perfessor, who was once run out of town by an angry minister, has the pleasure of revealing a minister as a hypocrite. As John returns from the Fourth of July celebration, he thinks of all of his life and the lives of his friends and his country as a great quest like quest one he started for the raintree long before.

Critical Evaluation:

Raintree County is a long and complex novel with an appeal to many audiences. In this work, Ross Lockridge, Jr., combines a historical novel, a gothic romance, and a love story. The technique, through which the events of the day of July 4, 1892, are interrupted by flashbacks and those flashbacks by further digressions, is that of the modern novel, with its insistence on the importance of psychological rather than chronological time. The overlay of Christian and pagan myths links the book to the great traditions of Western literature and philosophy. The forty years covered by the novel were a period of great strife leading to industrialization and territorial growth. The issue of slavery and the dual culture of the pre-Civil War United States led to the struggle that freed the slaves and settled the issue of the permanence of the Union. John Shawnessy is involved in this conflict on both political and personal levels. He participates in a political race and in Sherman's march to the sea, and he is a witness to Lincoln's assassination. The battle scenes are among the book's most vivid and memorable episodes.

The question of slavery also touches John's personal life. His first wife, Susanna, is bedeviled by the fear that she might be half black. In the racist society of the antebellum South, being half black was a worse fate than being insane. Susanna is not the child of her crazed legal mother but of her father's black mistress, but the realization that she is half black drives her insane anyway. John's relationship with Susanna and the creepy situations they encounter when they visit the South make up the part of the novel that resembles a grim gothic tragedy.

The three women in John's life also make the novel a love story, one that does not end, as most such stories do, in marriage or rejection. Instead, the love story lasts through all the years of John's life. John's most intense love is for the blond Nell Gaither, but the two are cut off from each other precisely because of this intensity and perhaps because of their familiarity with each other since childhood. When the dark-haired Susanna Drake arrives, the novelty of her beauty and behavior sweeps John off his feet. Susanna also uses trickery to capture John, playing on his sense of honor, something Nell is too principled to do. John and Nell love each other in part because of their shared sense of honor, but that very feature of their lives also makes them unable to connect as lovers. After the tumult of his early emotional life, John is at last able to find peace with his third love, Esther.

The use of the flashback technique, which blends all of John's experiences into recollections on July 4, 1892, is reminiscent of James Joyce's *Ulysses* (1922). Joyce packs all of his characters' lives, through memory and daydream, into one day, demonstrating that the past is not over but rather continues to be relived in the present. The last sentence of each chapter of *Raintree County* leads into the first sentence of the next chapter, even though the two sections may describe scenes that occur forty years apart, also suggesting the continuity of time. The flashback technique also allows Lockridge to maintain interest by generating suspense as he withholds several key events until the last hundred pages of the novel. The reader does not learn of Nell's death or how the Fourth of July race was won, for example, until late in the novel.

The mythic overlay gives the novel a universal quality that relates it to the heroic stories of literature. Many of the key scenes of *Raintree County* take place by the river that runs through Raintree County or in the dense swamp at the end of Paradise Lake. John strips to go swimming and sees Nell also naked there. Drunk, and stunned by Susanna's beauty, he makes love for the first time there. There also he obtains glimpses of the legendary raintree. The tree, the swamp, the forest around it, and the river all suggest the Garden of Eden.

The mysterious raintree, with its golden blossoms, is something that John sets out to find like a hero on a quest. To find the raintree would be to possess a power that no one else has; John wishes that he possessed the power to write the great epic that would explain his life and that of the nation. The raintree does not symbolize the tree of knowledge in the Bible, the eating of the fruit of which brought on sin and awareness of good and evil. Rather, it symbolizes the tree that is never mentioned in the biblical account, the tree of life. At the end of *Raintree County*, it seems that John has neither found the raintree nor written his great work, but he has found what the tree symbolizes. The novel's great story is John's own life and the lives of others whom he knew.

"Critical Evaluation" by Jim Baird

Further Reading

Blotner, Joseph L. "*Raintree County* Revisited." *Western Humanities Review* 10 (Winter, 1956): 57-64. Reassesses the novel favorably and places it in both Western and American literary traditions.

Erisman, Fred. "*Raintree County* and the Power of Place." *Markham Review* 8 (Winter, 1979): 36-40. Argues that much of the power of *Raintree County* derives from the tension between its contrasting urban and rural settings.

Greiner, Donald J. "Ross Lockridge and the Tragedy of *Raintree County*." *Critique* 20, no. 3 (April, 1979): 51-63. Identifies the author of the novel with the hero of the book and notes that both are on a quest. Shawnessy survives his failure to write a great epic, and Lockridge, who killed himself shortly after the book was published, was not able to accept that his epic was over.

Leggett, John. *Ross and Tom: Two American Tragedies*. Rev. ed. New York: Da Capo Press, 2000. Recounts the lives, literary careers, and suicides of Lockridge and Thomas Heggen, the author of *Mister Roberts* (1946).

Lockridge, Larry. *Shade of the Raintree: The Life and Death of Ross Lockridge, Jr., Author of "Raintree County."* New York: Viking Press, 1994. The definitive biography of the book's author, written by his son.

Madden, David, and Peggy Bach, eds. *Classics of Civil War Fiction*. 1991. Reprint. Tuscaloosa: University of Alabama Press, 2001. *Raintree County* is one of the fourteen works of Civil War fiction examined in this study. Includes an introduction that surveys the genre of Civil War literature and reassesses its place in American literary history.

White, Ray Lewis. "*Raintree County* and the Critics of '48." *MidAmerica* 11 (1984): 149-170. Assesses the first critical reception of the novel.

A Raisin in the Sun

Author: Lorraine Hansberry (1930-1965)
First produced: 1959; first published, 1959
Type of work: Drama
Type of plot: Family
Time of plot: 1950's
Locale: Chicago

Principal characters:
LENA YOUNGER, a retired domestic and the matriarch of an extended African American family
WALTER, her son
RUTH, Walter's wife
BENEATHA, Walter's sister
TRAVIS, Walter and Ruth's son
JOSEPH ASAGAI, a Nigerian student, Beneatha's suitor
GEORGE MURCHISON, a student, Beneatha's suitor
BOBO, Walter's friend
KARL LINDER, a representative of a suburban homeowners' association

The Story:

Walter Younger, Sr., known as Big Walter, has died, leaving his widow, Lena, with a life insurance policy worth ten thousand dollars. Lena wants to use the money as a down payment on a house in the suburbs so that her family can leave their crowded and shabby Chicago apartment. Lena's son, Walter, disgusted with his job as a rich white man's chauffeur, wants to invest the insurance money in a liquor store with two partners, Willy and Bobo. Beneatha, Walter's younger sister, a college student, wants to use part of the money to pay for medical school.

The family argues over how to spend the insurance money. Walter tells his sister to forget about medical school

and become a nurse or get married like other women. He appeals to his mother to give him the money so that he can pursue his dream of entrepreneurship and thereby improve the family's circumstances, but Lena is skeptical about investing in the liquor business. Beneatha and her mother also argue about religion. Lena maintains that Beneatha needs God's help to become a doctor, and Beneatha asserts that God has little to do with her educational achievements.

Lena informs Walter that his wife, Ruth, is pregnant and is considering terminating her pregnancy because she does not wish to add another family member to their crowded household. Lena encourages Walter to confront his wife and express his desire to have another child, but Walter storms out of the apartment in anger. As he leaves, Lena calls him a disgrace to his father's memory.

Beneatha is visited by two suitors, Joseph Asagai and George Murchison. Asagai, who has recently returned from his native Nigeria, brings Beneatha a traditional African gown and headdress and encourages her not to become an assimilationist Negro by forgetting her African heritage. George, the son of a well-to-do African American family, urges Beneatha to divorce herself from her heritage and not to take her studies too seriously.

Soon, Lena announces to her family that she has made a down payment on a single-family home in Clybourne Park, an all-white neighborhood. When he hears the news, Walter is outraged and accuses his mother of destroying his dream of owning his own business. He becomes deeply depressed; for three days, instead of going to work, he spends his time drinking heavily at a local tavern. Seeing her son's depression, Lena has a change of heart. She informs Walter that she put only thirty-five hundred dollars down on the house, and she gives him the rest, commanding him to deposit three thousand dollars of it in a bank account earmarked for Beneatha's medical school tuition and allowing him to invest the remainder as he sees fit.

Walter's mood changes dramatically when his mother gives him the money. He makes peace with his wife, and he excitedly tells his son, Travis, that he will make a business transaction that will make the family wealthy.

As the family members pack for the move to their new suburban home, Karl Linder, a representative of the Clybourne Park Improvement Association, visits and offers to buy the new home from them at a profit; his concern is with keeping a black family from integrating the all-white Clybourne Park neighborhood. Walter boldly expels Linder.

Immediately after Linder's departure, Walter's friend Bobo arrives, bringing the grim news that their business partner, Willy, has taken Bobo's and Walter's money and left town instead of using it to purchase the liquor store. Walter sadly informs his family that all $6,500 is lost, including the money that Walter was supposed to set aside for Beneatha's schooling. Lena beats her son for his irresponsible behavior.

Later, as the family unpacks, Walter calls Linder to inform him that they are ready to make a deal with him. Walter explains to his family that he intends to humble himself before Linder and agree to sell the family's new home for a profit. Hearing Walter's decision, Beneatha calls her brother a toothless rat.

When Linder arrives, however, Walter undergoes a profound change. Standing behind his son, he informs Linder that his family has decided to move into their new home in Clybourne Park. Walter speaks eloquently of his father's hard work and his family's pride. He proudly introduces Beneatha as a future doctor, and he introduces Travis as the sixth generation of Youngers in America. Linder leaves disappointed, and the Youngers begin packing again.

On moving day, Lena commands the moving men, and the Youngers begin carrying boxes out of the apartment. Beneatha announces that Asagai has proposed marriage, and Lena proudly tells Ruth that Walter has finally come into his manhood that day. Finally, Lena leaves her family's shabby apartment for the last time.

Critical Evaluation:

A Raisin in the Sun was the first play by an African American woman to be produced on Broadway. It enjoyed a successful run and won the New York Drama Critics' Circle Award. It has been staged many times by regional and university theaters since its first production in 1959, and it had a Broadway revival in 2004. It has been adapted for film three times: A 1961 version starred Sidney Poitier as Walter, an American Playhouse television production in 1989 featured Danny Glover in that role, and a 2008 television film starred Sean Combs.

Lorraine Hansberry's play confronts crucial issues that have faced African Americans: the fragmentation of the family, the black male's quest for manhood, and the problems of integration. Like Tennessee Williams's *The Glass Menagerie* (pr. 1944), Arthur Miller's *Death of a Salesman* (pr., pb. 1949), Eugene O'Neill's *Long Day's Journey into Night* (pr., pb. 1956), and other classic American plays, *A Raisin in the Sun* is fundamentally a family drama. Lena, the family matriarch, is attempting to keep her family together in difficult circumstances. She is the family's moral center, urging her children to end their quarreling, accept their responsibilities, and love and support each other. That the Youngers pull together in the closing scenes is more a credit to Lena than to her spirited but sometimes inconsiderate children, Walter and Beneatha. By allowing Lena to play this central role in the Younger family, Hansberry asserts the importance of the mother figure in the African American family.

An equally absorbing development in Hansberry's drama is Walter's quest for manhood. As the play opens, his father—Big Walter—has recently died, and Walter wants more than anything else to take his father's place as head of the family. Walter's job as a white man's chauffeur gives him a feeling of inferiority, and his wish to purchase a liquor store is an assertion of economic independence, a desire to provide for his family and live out his version of the American

Dream. Walter's selfishness and irresponsibility, however, prevent him from becoming the legitimate head of the family, and only in the end, when he vanquishes Linder and asserts his family's pride, is Walter able to achieve his manhood.

The play also confronts the problems of racial integration that African Americans faced throughout the twentieth century. As the play opens, the Youngers are trapped in a Chicago tenement, unable to break an invisible barrier that keeps them from the white suburban neighborhood. Linder's attempt to bribe the Youngers into observing the unwritten rules of northern segregation vividly illustrates the problems that even upwardly mobile black families had when they attempted to leave the inner city and move into the mainly white suburbs. Walter's decision not to sell out to Linder and the white neighbors he represents is an act of heroism and an act of protest. As the play ends, the Youngers assert their rights as American citizens by choosing to live where they please.

Hansberry's play is realistic in setting, characterization, and dialogue. In addition to confronting universal African American issues, it reflects the circumstances of African Americans in the 1950's, at the beginning of the Civil Rights movement. The doors of opportunity, if not wide open, had at least been unlocked for black Americans. Jackie Robinson had integrated baseball's major leagues, and the U.S. Supreme Court had outlawed school segregation. Hence Beneatha's dream of becoming a doctor is a realistic one, as is Walter's dream of becoming an entrepreneur.

These opportunities, however, create tensions and competition in the Younger family, dramatized by Walter's verbal battles with his mother and sister and Beneatha's arguments with her mother. Moreover, the elusiveness of these dreams creates frustration that leads to bitterness. The play's title comes from a line in a Langston Hughes poem: "What happens to a dream deferred?/ Does it dry up/ Like a raisin in the sun?" Although the play ends on a euphoric note, with the Youngers fulfilling the traditional American Dream of owning a home in the suburbs, there is no guarantee that their future will be trouble-free.

The play also captures the spirit of the budding feminist movement. Hansberry was the contemporary of feminist writers such as Adrienne Rich and Gloria Steinem, and the playwright reflects their dissatisfaction with traditional feminine roles in the post-World War II years. Beneatha's desire to become a physician, an occupation pursued by relatively few women in the 1950's, and her rejection of the conventional life she would lead as the wife of George Murchison suggest her rebellion against the conventions that kept women in the home or restricted to traditionally female occupations such as nursing and teaching. Beneatha's fascination with Asagai and her African heritage forecast the celebration of black Americans' African roots that would occur in the 1960's.

The success of *A Raisin in the Sun* opened theater doors to other African American dramatists such as James Baldwin, Amiri Baraka, Ed Bullins, and Ntozake Shange. Unfortunately, the promise suggested by Hansberry in *A Raisin in the Sun* was never completely fulfilled. She wrote a handful of plays after *A Raisin in the Sun*, but none received equal critical attention, and she died of cancer before her thirty-fifth birthday.

James Tackach

Further Reading

Abbotson, Susan C. W. "Lorraine Hansberry, *A Raisin in the Sun* (1959)." In *Masterpieces of Twentieth-Century American Drama*. Westport, Conn.: Greenwood Press, 2005. Critical overview provides biographical material about Hansberry and discussion of the play's plot, themes, characters, historical context, and critical reception.

Abramson, Doris. *Negro Playwrights in the American Theater: 1925-1959*. New York: Columbia University Press, 1969. This definitive work discusses the origins and development of the African American drama—its structure, themes, innovations, and impact—from its nineteenth century beginnings through Hansberry's work.

Carter, Steven R. *Hansberry's Drama: Commitment amid Complexity*. Urbana: University of Illinois Press, 1991. Presents a detailed study of Hansberry's entire body of work. Chapter 2 focuses on the stage version of *A Raisin in the Sun*, and the following chapter discusses the first two film versions as well as the hit musical adaptation, *Raisin*, that appeared in 1973.

Cheney, Anne. *Lorraine Hansberry*. Boston: Twayne, 1984. Generally complimentary biography cites both Paul Robeson, as political radical, and Langston Hughes, as poet of his people, as major influences on Hansberry. Also defends Hansberry's assimilationist views, which some African Americans criticized harshly.

Cho, Nancy. "'That Gentleman with Painfully Sympathetic Eyes—': Re-reading Lorraine Hansberry Through Tennessee Williams." In *The Influence of Tennessee Williams: Essays on Fifteen American Playwrights*, edited by Philip C. Kolin. Jefferson, N.C.: McFarland, 2008. Assesses how Hansberry's work was influenced by Williams's confessional style and choice of subject matter.

Hansberry, Lorraine. *To Be Young, Gifted, and Black*. Edited by Robert Nemiroff. Englewood Cliffs, N.J.: Prentice-Hall, 1969. Hansberry's husband and executor of her estate put together bits and pieces of her work—published and unpublished—including letters, autobiographical statements, and speeches, to give a clear picture of this extraordinary woman. The introduction, the affectionate essay "Sweet Lorraine," by James Baldwin, poignantly describes the playwright from 1957 until her untimely death in 1965.

Kappel, Lawrence, ed. *Readings on "A Raisin in the Sun."* San Diego, Calif.: Greenhaven Press, 2001. Resource designed for students presents analyses of the play from African American and feminist perspectives, examines the characters, discusses the universal themes in the work, and describes the forms and revisions it has undergone. Also contains a chronology of Hansberry's life and a discussion of the similarities between her life and the lives of the members of the Younger family.

Keyssar, Helene. *The Curtain and the Veil: Strategies in Black Drama.* New York: Burt Franklin, 1981. Critical study of African American drama focuses on the ambivalence of black playwrights. Devotes a full chapter to *A Raisin in the Sun*.

Wilkerson, Margaret. "Lorraine Hansberry: Artist, Activist, Feminist." In *Women and American Theatre*, edited by Helen Krich Chinoy and Linda Walsh Jenkins. Rev. 3d ed. New York: Theatre Communications Group, 2006. Stresses Hansberry's early awareness of the connection that exists between racism and sexism and argues that Hansberry understood and tried to dramatize the difference between Lena's notion of material advance for the family and Walter's crass materialism.

Ralph Roister Doister

Author: Nicholas Udall (1505?-1556)
First produced: c. 1552; first published, c. 1556
Type of work: Drama
Type of plot: Farce
Time of plot: Sixteenth century
Locale: England

Principal characters:
RALPH ROISTER DOISTER, a well-to-do, cowardly braggart
MATTHEW MERRYGREEKE, Roister Doister's hanger-on
DAME CHRISTIAN CUSTANCE, a well-to-do widow
GAWIN GOODLUCK, Dame Custance's fiancé
SYM SURESBY, Gawin Goodluck's friend

The Story:

Matthew Merrygreeke, a happy young rascal who likens himself to the grasshopper of the fable, often has fun and money at the expense of Ralph Roister Doister, a well-to-do, doltish young man who brags long and loud of his bravery but fails to act anything but the coward when called to action. In addition, Ralph Roister Doister imagines himself in love with every woman he meets, and he swears each time he falls in love that he cannot live without the woman who most lately catches his eye. One day, meeting Merrygreeke on the street, he asserts that he is now madly in love with Dame Christian Custance, a widow reported to be wealthy. She captivates Roister Doister when he sees her at supper. Merrygreeke, anxious to please the man he constantly gulls, agrees to help Roister Doister pursue his suit. He assures the foolish braggart that the widow is certain to accept him and that Roister Doister ought really to try to marry someone of higher station and greater fortune.

Merrygreeke goes for musicians to serenade Dame Custance, while Roister Doister waits in front of the widow's home. As he waits, three of the widow's servant women come from the house and talk and sing. When they notice Roister Doister, he comes up, talks to them, and tries to kiss them. After talking with them for a time, Roister Doister gives them a love letter to deliver to their mistress. He boasts that he wrote it himself.

Given the letter by her serving-woman, Dame Custance is furious. She reminds her servants that she is an honorable woman, affianced to Gawin Goodluck, who is for some months on a sea voyage. Dame Custance refuses to break the seal of the letter, much less read it. Meanwhile, to further his suit, Roister Doister sends his servant to the widow's house with some love gifts, a ring and a token in a cloth. The young servant, after some trouble, convinces the widow's serving-women to take the gifts to their mistress, even though she was angry at receiving the letter.

Handed the gifts, the widow becomes even angrier, lectures her servants on their conduct, and finally sends a boy to find the man who delivered the gifts to her house. Merrygreeke, after many a laugh over what happened during Roister Doister's suit, finally goes to Dame Custance and reveals his scheme for gulling Roister Doister. The widow says she would never marry such a doltish man, but she agrees to join in the fun at the braggart's expense. She goes so far as to read the letter he wrote her and says she will make a reply.

Rejoining Roister Doister, Merrygreeke listens to the suitor's woeful tale and then tells him in outrageous terms that the widow refused his suit, calls him vile names, and accuses him of cowardice. Roister Doister immediately vows that he will assault the widow's house with intent to kill her in combat, along with all her servants. Over Merrygreeke's protests, Roister Doister sets out to get his men together. Merrygreeke laughs and waits, knowing that the cowardly braggart will never carry out his vow.

When they arrive at the widow's house, Merrygreeke offers Roister Doister an excuse for not leading the assault. Instead, the braggart begins once more to woo the widow with music and song. He sends Merrygreeke to call the widow from her house. Dame Custance goes out to Roister Doister and repeats her refusal of his foolish proposal. Then she reads his letter aloud, and by rephrasing it and repunctuating it she makes the letter as insulting as Roister Doister meant it to be loving. The result thoroughly confuses the suitor, who vows it is not the letter he sent to her. After she leaves, Roister Doister sends for the scrivener who actually wrote the letter for him. The scrivener takes the letter, reads it correctly, and convinces Roister Doister that someone tricked him.

In the meantime Sym Suresby, friend of the widow's fiancé, arrives to tell Dame Custance that her affianced suitor, Gawin Goodluck, returned from his voyage and will be with her shortly. Suresby sees and hears enough of the conversation between the widow and Roister Doister to think that the widow is unfaithful to Goodluck. He goes off, leaving the widow furious at the tomfoolery of Roister Doister. When she chases Roister Doister off, he again vows to have revenge on the widow and her servants. Gathering his men, he approaches her house a second time.

The widow, meanwhile, goes to a trusted friend to enlist his support in getting rid of the troublesome Roister Doister, who threatens to ruin her approaching marriage to Goodluck. The friend consents to aid her. They also enlist Merrygreeke, who agrees to help them and at the same time pull more tricks at the expense of Roister Doister.

The foolish suitor and his men are routed by the widow with household utensils used as weapons. Having proved himself a coward as well as a fool, Roister Doister renounces his suit for the widow's hand. When Goodluck appears soon afterward, Dame Custance is able to assure him that the re-

ports he had from Sym Suresby are muddled and that she never broke her vows to him. She did, however, berate Suresby for not making certain of the truth before repeating what he heard.

Merrygreeke returns on behalf of Roister Doister and asks forgiveness of the widow and Goodluck. When he promises them that they would have much fun at Roister Doister's expense if they will but agree, they assent heartily and invite Merrygreeke and Roister Doister to have dinner with them that very day.

Critical Evaluation:

Ralph Roister Doister presents no problems of interpretation, but knowing its historical and literary contexts helps in imagining how it appeared to audiences in its own time. For example, it was written for performance by schoolboys, which explains why its language is clearer than that of *Gammer Gurton's Needle* (1566), another play written at about the same time. The author, Nicholas Udall, was a canon of St. George's Chapel, Windsor Castle, and *Ralph Roister Doister*, with its psalmody and mock requiem, was perhaps performed at Windsor Chapel as early as September, 1552, in front of an audience including the young King Edward VI.

Udall was a distinguished classical scholar, who studied at Corpus Christi College, Oxford, well known for its Humanistic studies. Udall, in fact, by the time he wrote *Ralph Roister Doister*, had translated the *Apophthegmes* and Latin commentaries on the New Testament by the Dutch scholar and Humanist Desiderius Erasmus. Udall's efforts as a classicist, as a scholar of Humanism, and as a teacher inform the theme, structure, and intent of his *Ralph Roister Doister*. The classical influence on *Ralph Roister Doister* comes largely from the Roman dramatist Terence, whose comedies were a feature of the medieval school curriculum. Terence's plays were praised for their comparative wholesomeness and for the excellence of their Latin. Udall's devotion to Terence appears in his *Floures for Latin Spekynge* (1534), which became a standard school textbook. The fourth century B.C.E. grammarian Donatus studied Terence and found in his plays certain principles that became fixed in the scholarship that Udall knew. The five-act structure that Udall uses in *Ralph Roister Doister*, for example, may have originated with Terence. The general familiarity of the educated of the time with Roman comedy may help explain why Renaissance comedies preceded tragedies.

The biggest debts in *Ralph Roister Doister* are to Plautus's *Miles Gloriosus* (pr. c. 205 B.C.E.; *The Braggart Soldier*, 1767) and Terence's *Eunuchus* (161 B.C.E.; *The Eunuch*,

1598). The *miles gloriosus* is the braggart soldier, the huffing, puffing windbag who is a parody of real military virtue. William Shakespeare's Falstaff is an example of this character type. Ralph Roister Doister appears as a parody of a parody. He is not by nature robust enough to look for women as a real roisterer would. Without the mischievous Matthew Merrygreeke to puff him up and urge him on, Ralph would hardly attempt as much as he does. He is silly and full of himself, however, and when he meets Dame Christian Custance he falls in love with her as quickly as he does with all others. He is something of a fool for love.

Ralph derives clearly from Plautus's braggart soldier, but the scheme that Merrygreeke involves him in comes straight out of Terence's *The Eunuch.* The subplot of that ancient comedy features a braggart, Thraso, who is egged on by the parasitical Gnatho (the inspiration for Merrygreeke) to court a faithful woman, who stays true to her absent lover. Thraso assaults the woman's house just as his descendant Ralph vows to assault the house of Dame Custance. In each case the blusterers collapse.

In *Ralph Roister Doister* it is not Terence's young Roman woman who is wooed but a redoubtable Christian widow whose name reveals her resistance to bold suitors. Dame Custance is capable of the kind of broad humor sometimes found in the morality plays and recalls Geoffrey Chaucer's Wife of Bath somewhat, but she hardly indulges in shocking coarseness. When Gawin Goodluck's friend, Sym Suresby, mistakenly suspects Dame Custance of betraying Goodluck, she compares herself to two famous heroines, the biblical Esther and Susanna of the Apocryphal story.

Merrygreeke owes something to the parasite Gnatho but also owes much to the figure of Vice from medieval morality plays. Vice would have been a familiar villain to Udall's audience. This stock character personifies human deviltry. He represents the world's corruption that has to be overcome, but it is impossible to ignore his genius for bawdiness and amusing shenanigans. Falstaff and Ben Jonson's Volpone are in this tradition; a truly evil villain such as Iago, however, is beyond the limits of such a character. A true monster is more likely to be found in a tragedy. Merrygreeke's ultimate harmlessness is implicit in the Prologue's assurance that "all scurrility we utterly refuse."

Writing for a cast of students, Udall would have been careful to create a work that was properly instructive. Delight comes to sweeten the instruction in the broad slapstick nonsense, such as the rout of Ralph and his followers by the widow armed with pots and pans, and instruction comes in the good-natured depiction of a virtuous woman complemented by a good man. Moreover, Roman themes and character types are well meshed with English materials. Such irreproachable citizens as Suresby and Tristram Trusty speak well of the morals of London's middle-class citizenry.

The meter of the play is a rhymed hexameter, but it does not scan well. In Udall's time, stress scansion was not yet fixed in practice, and the blank verse of Christopher Marlowe and Shakespeare was not to be used first until Thomas Sackville and Thomas Norton wrote *Gordoduc* (c. 1561). *Ralph Roister Doister* may seem primitive to today's readers, but it offers much to appreciate.

"Critical Evaluation" by Frank Day

Further Reading

Bevington, David M. *From "Mankind" to Marlowe: Growth of Structure in the Popular Drama of Tudor England.* Cambridge, Mass.: Harvard University Press, 1962. Discusses *Ralph Roister Doister* in one chapter, commenting on the casting, Matthew Merrygreeke's debt to the old Vice character, and the play's frequent allusions.

Downer, Alan S. *British Drama: A Handbook and Brief Chronicle.* East Norwalk, Conn.: Appleton-Century-Crofts, 1950. Explains the Roman influences on *Ralph Roister Doister,* discussing how Ralph represents the *miles gloriosus,* or braggart soldier. Stresses the moral intention of the author, assumed to be Udall.

Eaton, Walter Prichard. *The Drama in English.* New York: Charles Scribner's Sons, 1930. Begins with English drama's origins in the church and follows its progress into the market square. Chapters on the miracle plays, the moralities, and the interludes are followed by one titled "The First English Comedy—*Ralph Roister Doister.*"

Udall, Nicholas. *Nicholas Udall's "Roister Doister."* Edited with an introduction by G. Scheurweghs. Louvain, Belgium: Librairie Universitaire, C. Uystpruyst, 1939. The scholarly apparatus treats Udall's life and the play's sources. Copious notes elucidate vocabulary and other textual matters.

Whitworth, Charles Walters, ed. *Three Sixteenth-Century Comedies.* New York: W. W. Norton, 1984. An accessible modern paperback edition containing *Ralph Roister Doister.* A long introduction sets these works in historical context and footnotes facilitate reading.

Ramayana

Author: Vālmīki (fl. c. 500 B.C.E.)

First transcribed: Rāmāyaṇa, c. 500 B.C.E. (English translation, 1870-1874)

Type of work: Poetry

Type of plot: Epic

Time of plot: Antiquity

Locale: India

Principal characters:

RAMA, a prince and incarnation of Vishnu

SITA, his wife

LAKSHMAN, his brother and loyal follower

DASA-RATHA, his father, the king of the Kosalas

RAVAN, demon-king of Lanka (Sri Lanka)

KAIKEYI, one of King Dasa-ratha's wives and enemy of Rama

The Poem:

King Dasa-ratha of the Kosalas, who keeps his court at Ayodhya, has four sons, though not all by the same mother. According to legend, the god Vishnu, in answer to King Dasa-ratha's supplications, gave a divine liquor to all of the king's wives so that they might bring forth sons, each of whom is partly an incarnation of Vishnu. Of the sons, Rama is the handsomest and strongest of all, his mother having drunk more of the magic beverage than any of Dasa-ratha's other wives.

When Rama has grown to manhood he hears of Sita, the beautiful, talented, and virtuous daughter of King Janak and the earth mother. King Janak is the possessor of a wondrous bow, a mighty weapon that had belonged to the gods, and King Janak resolves that whoever can bend the bow shall have Sita for his wife. The king knows that no ordinary mortal can possibly accomplish the feat.

Rama and his brothers travel to the court of King Janak and are granted permission to try to draw the mighty bow. Rama bends the bow with ease; indeed, his strength is so great that the weapon snaps in two. King Janak promises that Sita shall be Rama's bride and that each of Rama's half brothers shall also have a noble bride from among the people of his kingdom.

Sita thus becomes the wife of Rama, and her sister Urmila marries Lakshman, Rama's favorite brother. Mandavi and Sruta-kriti, cousins of Sita, become the wives of Bharat and Satrughna, the other half brothers of Rama. When all return to Ayodhya, Dasa-ratha, fearing that rivalries among his children might create unhappiness and tragedy in his house, sends Bharat and Satrughna to live with their mothers' people.

Years pass, and King Dasa-ratha grows old. Wishing to have the time and opportunity to prepare himself for the next life, he proposes that Rama, his favorite son, should become regent. The king's council and the populace rejoice at the proposal, and plans are made to invest Rama with the regency and place him on the Kosala throne. Before the prepa-rations can been completed, however, Manthara, a maid to Queen Kaikeyi, one of King Dasa-ratha's wives, advises her mistress that Rama's succession to the throne should be prevented and that Bharat, Queen Kaikeyi's son, should become regent. The queen is influenced by this poor advice, and she remembers that her husband has promised her two boons. When King Dasa-ratha comes to her, she asks that he fulfill the boons by making Bharat regent and by sending Rama into exile for fourteen years. King Dasa-ratha is sad, but he has given his word and must honor his promises. A dutiful son, Rama accepts his father's decision and prepares to go into exile. He expects to go alone, but his wife, Sita, and his brother Lakshman prepare to go with him to share his lonely and uncomfortable life in the dismal Dandak forest. The Kosala people mourn his departure and accompany him on the first day of his journey away from Ayodhya.

Leaving his native country, Rama journeys south. He and his companions cross the Ganges and come to the hermitage of Bharad-vaja, a holy man. After visiting with him, they travel on to the hill of Chitrakuta, where stands the hermitage of Vālmīki, a learned and holy man. There they learn that King Dasa-ratha died the day after Rama's departure from Ayodhya, remembering in his hour of death a curse laid on him by a hermit whose son he had accidentally killed. Rama stays with Vālmīki for a time. In the meanwhile, Bharat returns to Ayodhya to become regent, as his mother has arranged. However, he recognizes Rama's claim to the throne and sets out on a journey to find Rama and ask him to become king of the Kosalas. He finds his brother, but Rama, having given his word, remains in exile as he has vowed to do. Bharat returns to Avodhya, where he places Rama's sandals on the throne as a symbol of Rama's right to the kingship.

In order that his kinsmen might not find him again, Rama leaves Vālmīki's hermitage, and after a long journey he establishes his own hermitage near the dwelling of Agastya, a holy and learned man. There Rama, Sita, and Lakshman live in peace until they are disturbed by a demon-maiden who is enamored of Rama. The demon-maiden, having been repulsed in her addresses by both Rama and Lakshman, seeks revenge. She goes to her brother, Ravan, demon-king of Lanka, and asks for his help. Ravan is a powerful being who through asceticism has achieved power even over the gods. His domination, according to legend, can be broken only by an alliance of humans and the monkey people.

Ravan sends a demon in the disguise of a deer to lead Rama astray while on a hunt. When Rama fails to return from hunting, Sita insists that Lakshman go to look for him. In the absence of the brothers, Sita is abducted by Ravan. Rama learns what has happened, and he allies himself with the monkey people in order to make war on the demons and win back his beloved wife. Hanuman, one of the leaders of the monkey people, finds Sita at Ravan's palace and leads Rama and the forces of the monkey people to Ceylon. There Ravan's city is besieged and many battles are fought, with combat between the great leaders of both sides and pitched battles between the forces of good and evil. Finally Ravan and his demon forces are defeated, Ravan is killed, and Sita is rescued and restored to her husband. Sita, who remained faithful to Rama throughout her captivity, proves in an ordeal by fire that she is still virtuous and worthy to be Rama's wife.

Rama, Sita, and Lakshman return in triumph to Ayodhya, where Rama is welcomed and becomes king of the Kosala people. Rumors spread, however, that Sita has not been faithful to her husband, until at last Rama sends his wife away. She goes to live at the hermitage of Vālmīki, and shortly after her arrival there, she gives birth to Rama's twin sons.

More years pass and the two sons grow up, tutored in their youth by the wise Vālmīki, who eventually takes his charges to Ayodhya. There Rama, recognizing them as his sons, sends for Sita and has her conducted to his court. Since her virtue has been in doubt, she is asked to offer a token to prove that she has been true to her marriage vows. The earth opens up, and out of a great chasm the earth mother herself rises up on her throne to speak on behalf of Sita and to take her to the land of the gods. Thus Sita is taken away from the husband and the others who have doubted her.

Critical Evaluation:

The story of Rama is one of the most popular tales among the people of India, where it holds great religious significance. The tale has been recounted for generations, and there are several versions of the story, but the main outlines remain the same, with Rama and Sita as the idealized versions of man and woman. To the Western reader the characters may appear to be human beings with supernatural powers, roughly equivalent to certain figures in Greek legend and myth, but to Hindus the characters of the *Ramayana* (the fortunes of Rama) are more than this; they are gods. Scholars disagree on which of the various versions of the *Ramayana* came first, and the problem of which parts are found in the original story and which are additions by later generations of storytellers will perhaps never be solved. The best approach for a general reader is probably to accept the story as it is told.

The *Ramayana* is one of two Hindu epics, the other being the earlier *Mahabharata*. Whereas the *Mahabharata* is a heroic (or folk) epic deriving from an oral tradition, the *Ramayana* is more nearly a literary epic, written in conscious imitation of the heroic tradition. Whatever the original may have been, the *Ramayana* has been altered many times by subsequent rewriting and critical revision. In its extant versions, the *Ramayana* contains about twenty-four thousand couplets (less than one-fourth the length of the *Mahabharata*) and is divided into seven books (the *Mahabharata* has eighteen books). Of the seven books of the *Ramayana*, the central story covers books 2 through 6; book 1 is introductory. Book 7 appears to be a species of appendix; it provides both epilogue to and critique of the preceding six books. It also provides instruction for the recital of the *Ramayana* by minstrels, in much the same way that medieval texts coach jongleurs in their repertoire and their performance. The *Ramayana*, like most Western epics and unlike the *Mahabharata*, has unity, which stems from its concentration on one main story.

One of the major themes in the central narrative of the *Ramayana* is the relationship between destiny and volition, with the consequent consideration of personal responsibility or the lack of it. The key questions ultimately revolve around the power of the gods, for the keeping of human promises hinges on belief in divine retribution. Hence King Dasa-ratha rescinds his proposal that Rama should succeed him as regent in order to honor his prior promise to Queen Kaikeyi. So, too, Rama dutifully accepts Bharat as regent and goes into exile, in deference to the king's expressed wishes (really, the gods' demands). Just as Rama accepts his fate, so also his brother Lakshman and his wife, Sita, accept theirs. Lakshman simply does his duty and perseveres, but Sita is subjected to the most stringent of tests. After being kidnapped by Ravan, she is called upon to prove her virtue. The trial is debilitating, and Sita is finally rescued by her earth mother. All of these claims on human endurance require intervention by the gods. The message of the *Ramayana* thus seems to be that human volition is subservient to divine will. The corollary also appears to establish the social order as subject to the divine order.

Closely allied to the theme of free will versus fate is the theme of duty. One aspect of this theme of duty is Rama's behavior, often cited as a model for emulation. Rama's submission to his father's decision, his acceptance of exile, and his fidelity to his promise to remain in exile all bespeak Rama's filial piety and deference to duty. This view of duty follows the pattern traditional for warriors, princes, and kings; as such, it is compatible with ideals presented in the *Mahabharata* as well as with Western ethical assumptions. The other, and more important, aspect of the theme of duty is less conventional in an epic, for this aspect concerns not wars and the affairs of state, the usual epic grist, but human love and domestic matters. This aspect of duty, then, deals with Sita's story, which, all things considered, forms the main plot line in the epic. Sita, like Rama, is held up as an exemplar of ideal behavior—for women. Her behavior is characterized by sweetness, tenderness, obedience, patient suffering, and, above all, faithfulness; her piety and self-sacrifice ultimately qualify her for relief from mortal travail by being reabsorbed into her earth mother. She endures all without complaint and thus becomes the model for the perfect woman, wife, and mother, her image of duty unalloyed.

The *Ramayana* also deals with typical Hindu motifs. There is, for example, the Brahman's curse that King Dasaratha remembers on his deathbed. Also, there is asceticism, as exemplified in Vālmīki's hermitage and in Rama's own abstemious life after he leaves Vālmīki's hermitage. In addition, this asceticism reflects another Hindu value: the emphasis on social order, which is manifested in the caste system. The orderly functioning of society, with all people acknowledging their proper places in it, is a high priority in the Hindu ethos. Furthermore, the concepts of truth and duty provide definitive guidelines for action. Truth and duty go hand in hand to create twin obligations for Dasa-ratha and Bharat as well as for Rama and Sita and every devout Hindu. The didactic elements of the *Ramayana* reinforce these typical Hindu motifs. Most explicitly, the teachings of Vālmīki convey the precepts, but the implicit message of the plot and of the human interaction conveys the ethical and moral substance even more clearly. The Hindu ideals of faith and conduct are thus both taught and demonstrated in the *Ramayana*.

In addition to the Hindu motifs, as well as the themes of duty and free will versus fate, the *Ramayana* presents an interesting juxtaposition of the natural and the supernatural. The central narrative begins with natural or "real-world" events: the political machinations at the court of King Dasaratha; the banishment of Rama, Sita, and Lakshman; and the death of King Dasa-ratha and the subsequent dilemma of Bharat when Rama refuses the throne. The next half of the narrative deals with the supernatural: the intrusion of the demon-maiden; the intervention of Ravan; the alliance with the monkey people; the real and allegorical battle between the forces of good and the forces of evil; and the earth mother's absorption of Sita. This combination of natural and supernatural worlds synthesizes the ethical and spiritual concerns of Hinduism, incorporating the concepts of fatalism and duty. Through this synthesis, the *Ramayana* goes beyond the confines of a national cultural epic to become part of the sacred literature of Hinduism. This religious perspective has made the *Ramayana* one of the best-known and best-loved works of literature in India.

"Critical Evaluation" by Joanne G. Kashdan

Further Reading

Bose, Mandakranta, ed. *The "Ramayana" Revisited.* New York: Oxford University Press, 2004. Collection of essays offers new interpretations of the *Ramayana*, focusing on the work's relationship to South Asian and Southeast Asian cultures. Topics addressed include how the epic has been adapted in works of twentieth century Bengali literature, in Javanese tales, and in Thai and Cambodian art. Also discussed are the depiction of gender and hierarchy in the work and the epic's narrative structure.

Brockington, John. *The Sanskrit Epics.* Boston: Brill, 1998. Analyzes the linguistic and stylistic elements of the *Ramayana* and the *Mahabharata*. Summarizes previous scholarship on the epics and places these works within the context of ancient Indian culture, examining their social, economic, political, and religious aspects.

Chakravarty, Bishnupada. *The Penguin Companion to the "Ramayana."* Translated by Debjani Banerjee. New Delhi: Penguin Books, 2006. Provides an overview and synopsis of the *Ramayana* and recounts and analyzes the epic, episode by episode. Examines the characters and describes how some embody virtues, such as filial loyalty and duty, while others symbolize vices, such as greed, lust, and pride.

Narayan, R. K. *The Ramayana: A Shortened Modern Prose Version of the Indian Epic.* New York: Viking Press, 1972. Easy-flowing translation by novelist Narayan, based on the Tamil poet Kamban's version of the original, provides enjoyable reading for all age groups. Includes a succinct epilogue that notes differences between the original Sanskrit version and the Tamil version.

Smith, H. Daniel, ed. *The Picturebook "Ramayana": An Illustrated Version of Vālmīki's Story.* Syracuse, N.Y.:

Maxwell School of Citizenship and Public Affairs, Syracuse University, 1981. Explains the basic plot of Rama's story in a summary preceding the illustrations, which are accompanied by verses from the *Ramayana*. Offers an accessible introduction to the epic for students.

Venkatesananda, Swami. *The Concise "Ramayana" of Vālmīki*. Albany: State University of New York Press, 1988. Condensed version of the epic is divided into seven chapters that describe Rama's life from his birth to his death. Very readable, with a simple narrative style and appropriate chapter intervals.

Vyas, Shantikumar Nanooram. *India in the "Ramayana" Age*. 1967. Reprint. Delhi: Atma Ram, 1988. Analyzes the social and cultural conditions in ancient India as portrayed in the *Ramayana*. Includes a chapter on the position of women in Indian society during this time.

Rameau's Nephew

Author: Denis Diderot (1713-1784)
First published: 1805; written 1761-1774; complete French edition, 1891 (English translation, 1897)
Type of work: Novel
Type of plot: Philosophical
Time of plot: 1761
Locale: Paris

Principal characters:
JEAN-FRANÇOIS RAMEAU, the nephew of the composer Jean-Philippe Rameau, also HE
DENIS DIDEROT, the author, also MYSELF

The Story:

Myself and He first discuss geniuses. Myself stresses their benefit to the larger society and future generations, but He berates them for personal flaws with which they harm themselves and those around them—they would be better off, He avers, amassing a fortune in business so they can live splendidly and pay buffoons such as him to make them laugh and procure girls for them. He concedes that He is vexed at lacking genius himself and declares that He would like to be someone else, on the chance of being one. He also remarks that He loves to hear discreditable things about geniuses—it lets him bear his mediocrity more easily.

At this point, He begins singing famous songs He wishes that He composed, and He details the good life that fame and fortune would afford him—a fine house, good food and wine, pretty women, a gaggle of flatterers, falling asleep with the gentle hum of praise in his ears. This alluring vision soon gives way to austere reality, however, for He was banished by his former patron. Rameau acknowledges that he himself is a foolish, lazy, impudent, greedy ne'er-do-well, but he adds that those with whom he lives like him precisely because of those qualities. He is their buffoon, their great greedy boob. In their mediocrity, they need someone to despise.

Myself advises Rameau either to apologize to his patron or to be courageous enough to be poor. That latter idea does not appeal to Rameau because there are so many wealthy fools to exploit. He admits self-contempt, but only for not making more lucrative use of his God-given talent for flattery, bootlicking, and seducing bourgeois daughters for his master.

Myself, distressed by these frank avowals of turpitude and perverted feelings, seeks to change the subject. Talk shifts to music (with mime of violin and keyboard) and education, but He discloses scams of the music tutoring trade and goes on to assert that such "idioms" are common to all professions and are the means by which restitution is achieved. Should He gain wealth, he would be happy to disperse it by gorging, gambling, wenching, and maintaining a whole troop of flatterers.

"You would certainly be doing honor to human nature," Myself dryly remarks. "Openly or no, most think as I do," He retorts. He dismisses patriotism (there are no countries, only tyrants and slaves), aiding friends (gratitude is a burden), even the devotion to the education of one's children. Myself, while admitting delight in sensual pleasures, says that even more he likes solving problems, reading good books, instructing his children, doing his duty. While he would give all to have written a great work, better still would be to rehabilitate the Huguenot Calas (Voltaire's great legal victory over Church and monarchy).

Rameau wants none of Myself's kind of happiness, finding it strange and rare (and adding that the virtuous are ill-humored). It is easier to follow one's natural vices, so congenial to French people and their little needs. Myself again suggests that He hurry back to his former patron, but He reveals a new motive: pride. He is quite willing to be abject, but at his pleasure, not under duress. He also tells more of the grim situation in "our house," which includes a grouchy master (the financier Bertin) and a mistress who is a stupid, second-rate actor growing fat, as well as fallen poets and despised musicians who form a mob of shameful toadies eager to tear down all that succeeds. He also details the faux pas—a brash quip about the hierarchy of freeloaders at Bertin's table—that led to his expulsion. The passage betrays that He wants both the benefits of being a parasite and the pleasure of feeling superior to his benefactors. Asked if he spreads malicious gossip about them, He replies that they should expect as much—would you blame a tiger that bites off a hand thrust into its cage? Asked why He is so open about his vices, He reveals that He wants admiration for sublimity in wickedness, and He describes in admiring detail a man who cleverly robbed and betrayed a Jew.

Again horrified, Myself shifts the subject to a lengthy discussion of French versus Italian new music, which elicits Rameau's most elaborate singing pantomime, a jumble of airs, emotions, and orchestral instruments. Startled chess players and passersby watch the spectacle of a man possessed. Myself wonders why a person so sensitive to refinements in music is so insensible to virtue, and he asks what Rameau wants for his own son. Rameau, a fatalistic and passive parent, hopes that the boy will learn the "golden art" of averting disgrace, shame, and the penalties of the law, but he seems unconcerned about giving his son direction. Myself observes that should the boy grow up uniting infant reasoning with adult passion, he might well strangle his father and sleep with his mother.

Asked why, for all his understanding of music, he never created a great work, Rameau blames his star, the low-grade people around him, and need, which forces him to take positions vis-à-vis his superiors. As He says, the needy man does not walk like the rest; he skips, twists, cringes, and crawls. While He contends that all must take positions, Myself declares that a philosopher such as Diogenes, who mastered his desires, does not. Rameau replies that he wants good food, bed, clothes, rest, and much else that he would rather owe to kindness than to toil. Myself insists that He overlooks the cost. Undeterred and uninstructed, He declares cheerfully that he who laughs last laughs best.

"The Story" by R. Craig Philips

Critical Evaluation:

Rameau's Nephew submits to no simple classification. Although the narrative is fictional, the characters are actual persons and the ideas they expound in the book probably closely resemble the opinions they actually held. There is the problem of deciding how much of Denis Diderot can be found in the character Rameau, and how much of Rameau in that of Diderot. In general, however, the Diderot in the book is a mild champion of traditional values whereas Rameau is a vivacious apologist for roguery. The brilliant turns of this satirical dialogue raise the suspicion that the author Diderot is delighted with the convention-defying attitudes of his friend Rameau; perhaps Diderot believes Rameau more than Rameau believes himself.

The dialogue is a satirical critique of manners and morals. It makes specific reference to prominent writers, musicians, politicians, critics, and other leading figures of eighteenth century France. Many of the comments are unkind, and some are painfully so—or would have been had the work been published at the time of its composition. Diderot saw to it, however, that his lively satire remained unpublished, not only because of its references to living persons but also because of a reluctance to stir up the censor and all those to whom Rameau's carefree morality might have proved unacceptable.

The character Rameau is marvelously wrought to suit Diderot's intention. Although Rameau is a fully drawn individual and convincing, as witty rogues in literature usually are, he is not simply one thing or another. On the contrary, Diderot states that Rameau is simultaneously his own opposite. Sometimes Rameau is thin, sometimes fat; sometimes he is filthy, sometimes powdered and curled. His physical vacillation is matched by vacillations of mood. Sometimes he is cheerful, sometimes depressed; sometimes he is courageous, sometimes timid to the point of being fearful. Rameau is a sensualist and a lover of wine and women, but his passionate defense of an egoistic hedonism is a sign of his need to apologize for his manner: His morality is a device to prop up his manner. Underneath Rameau's abandon can be perceived a poignant longing for depth and respectability.

Having created a character whose contrary traits reveal the human being in self-conflict—thus providing the motive for a discussion of morality—Diderot provides Rameau with a gentlemanly antagonist, the man of ideas, Diderot himself. Diderot's mild responses, ostensibly intended to counter Rameau's philosophy, actually, with the acuity of a Socrates, incite Rameau to a passionate defense of the sense-gratifying life of a social parasite.

Rameau, who contradicts himself within himself, and

Diderot, who contradicts Rameau, together bring out the difficulty of all moral problems and of morality itself. Human beings are neither merely intellectual nor merely sensual; their desire to understand is often in conflict with their desires, and their desires in conflict with one another. Consequently, no one moral rule or set of principles will do. To be a good person, one must have a kind of moral genius. For such a person, rules are instruments to be used only with ingenuity, and sometimes they need to be discarded altogether. People who are at war with themselves, or with another, as Rameau is with himself and with Diderot, may not be able to attain a just victory. Sometimes there is no such thing as the proper answer. For a good person, life is a creative struggle that must be judged as works of art are judged, without dogmatism and with respect for the impossible goals the human spirit sets for itself. Perhaps the theme of the dialogue is best understood dialectically: Without the restraint of reason and human consideration, the human being becomes something worse than a fool, but without attention to the fact of human appetites the moralist becomes something less than a human being.

Rameau is the fool and Diderot the moralist, but Rameau fancies himself as something of the classic fool, the darling of the courts, the discerning jester who makes the bitter truth palatable. In reality, he comes close to being a compromising sponger, a guest who is tolerated in great houses only because he is sometimes an amusing conversationalist. Although he comes close to being merely parasitical, he is saved by his own need for apology. A man who must speak to Diderot is already more than a professional guest.

The dialogue is presented against a background of chess. The narrator takes shelter in the Regency Café, where the finest chess players of Paris compete. When Rameau enters and engages Diderot in conversation, he begins a kind of verbal chess game that shows him to be a brilliant and an erratic player pitted against a slower but a cannier Diderot. Rameau's attitude is revealed at once when, in response to Diderot's expression of interest in the games, he speaks scornfully of the players—although they are the best in Paris. When Diderot remarks that Rameau forgives nothing but supreme genius, Rameau retorts that he has no use for mediocrity.

The dialogue must be read carefully for, to continue the chess metaphor, the moves are deceptive. Like Fyodor Dostoevski, Diderot appreciated the exceptional individual who stepped beyond the bounds of conventional morality; unlike Friedrich Nietzsche, he did not deify the immoralist. *Rameau's Nephew* is a skillful and satirical attempt to do justice to both the moralist and the animal in human beings.

Further Reading

Curran, Andrew. *Sublime Disorder: Physical Monstrosity in Diderot's Universe.* Oxford, England: Voltaire Foundation, 2001. Examines Diderot's fascination with anatomical monstrosity and analyzes how he represents the physically grotesque in his novels and other works. Includes bibliography and index.

Doolittle, James. *Rameau's Nephew: A Study of Diderot's "Second Satire."* Geneva: Librairie Droz, 1960. An insightful, reflective study of Diderot's most famous creative work. Relies heavily on the text itself and is free of the critical jargon and interpretive excesses of some later analyses.

Fellows, Otis. *Diderot.* Boston: Twayne, 1977. A sympathetic, clear introduction to Diderot's life and work. Relying heavily on earlier scholarship, Fellows reports varied interpretive views of Diderot's major writings.

Furbank, Philip Nicholas. *Diderot: A Critical Biography.* London: Martin Secker & Warburg, 1992. Emphasizes Diderot's literary works, particularly his fiction, and cites lengthy passages from his correspondence to clarify the issues that absorbed the philosopher. Furbank's interpretations make use of contemporary literary theory.

Goodden, Angelica. *Diderot and the Body.* Oxford, England: Legenda, 2001. A study of Diderot that focuses on his portrayal of the body. Examines Diderot's fiction and other works to describe his ideas about the relationship of the body to the mind, anatomy, ethical extensions of the body, sensuality, sexuality, and other concerns.

Rex, Walter E. *Diderot's Counterpoints: The Dynamics of Contrariety in His Major Works.* Oxford, England: Voltaire Foundation, 1998. Examines Diderot's works in relation to his era, including analysis of *Rameau's Nephew.* Includes bibliographical references and an index.

Villena-Alvarez, Juanita. *The Allegory of Literary Representation as Hybrid in Corneille's "L'Illusion comique," Diderot's "Le Neveu de Rameau," and Arrabal's "La Nuit est aussi un soleil."* New York: Peter Lang, 1997. Compares *Rameau's Nephew* to two other French works that Villena-Alvarez defines as "hybrid," or works containing elements of "differentiation, mutation, and creation."

Wilson, Arthur. *Diderot.* New York: Oxford University Press, 1972. A comprehensive study of Diderot, richly detailed and absorbing. Treats the man and his social world with assurance and subtle judgment. Describes Diderot's courage in going ahead with his *Encyclopédie* (1751-1772) even after others deserted the project.

The Rape of Lucrece

Author: William Shakespeare (1564-1616)
First published: 1594
Type of work: Poetry
Type of plot: Tragedy
Time of plot: 500 B.C.E.
Locale: Rome

Principal characters:
COLLATINE, a Roman general
LUCRECE, his wife
TARQUIN, Collatine's friend and son of the Roman king

The Poem:

At Ardea, where the Romans are fighting, two Roman leaders, Tarquin and Collatine, speak together one evening. Collatine describes his beautiful young wife, Lucrece, in such glowing terms that Tarquin's passions are aroused. The next morning, Tarquin leaves the Roman host and journeys to Collatium, where the unsuspecting Lucrece welcomes him as one of her husband's friends. As Tarquin tells her many tales of Collatine's prowess on the battlefield, he looks admiringly at Lucrece and decides that she is the most beautiful woman in Rome.

In the night, while the others of the household are asleep, Tarquin lays restless. Caught between desire for Lucrece and dread of being discovered, to the consequent loss of his honor, he wanders aimlessly about his chamber. On one hand, there is his position as a military man who should not be the slave of his emotions; on the other hand is his overwhelming desire. He fears the dreadful consequences that might be the result of his lustful deed. His disgrace would never be forgotten. Perhaps his own face would show the mark of his crimes and the advertisement linger on even after death. He thinks for a moment that he might try to woo Lucrece but decides that such a course would be to no avail. She is already married and is not mistress of her own desires. Again he considers the possible consequences of his deed.

At last, emotion conquers reason. As Tarquin makes his way to Lucrece's chamber, many petty annoyances deter him. The locks on the doors have to be forced; the threshold beneath the door grates under his footstep; the wind threatens to blow out his torch; he pricks his finger on a needle. Tarquin ignores these omens of disaster. In fact, he misconstrues them as forms of trial that only make his "prize" more worth winning.

When he reaches the chamber door, Tarquin begins to pray for success. Realizing, however, that heaven will not countenance his sin, he declares that Love and Fortune will henceforth be his gods. Entering the room, he gazes at Lucrece in sleep. When he reaches forward to touch her breast, she awakens with a cry of fear. He tells her that her beauty has captured his heart and that she must submit to his will. First he threatens Lucrece with force, telling her that if she refuses to submit to him, he will not only kill her but also dishonor her name. His intention is to murder one of her slaves, place him in her arms, and then swear that he killed them because he had seen Lucrece embracing the man. If she yields, however, he promises he will keep the whole affair secret. Lucrece begins to weep and pleads with Tarquin. For the sake of her hospitality, her husband's friendship, Tarquin's position as a warrior, he must pity her and refrain from this deed. Her tears only increase his lust. Tarquin smothers her cries with the bed linen while he rapes her.

Shame-ridden, Tarquin leaves Lucrece, who is horrified and revolted. She tears her nails and hopes the dawn will never come. In a desperate fury, she rails against the night; its darkness and secrecy have ruined her. She is afraid of the day, for surely her sin will be revealed. Still worse, through her fall, Collatine will be forever shamed. It is Opportunity that is at fault, she claims, working for the wicked and against the innocent. Time, the handmaiden of ugly Night, is hand-in-hand with Opportunity, but Time can work for Lucrece now. She implores Time to bring misery and pain to Tarquin. Exhausted from her emotional tirade, Lucrece falls back on her pillow. She longs for a suicide weapon; death alone could save her soul.

As the dawn breaks, she begins to consider her death. Not until she has told Collatine the complete details of her fall will she take the step, however, for Collatine must revenge her on Tarquin. Lucrece calls her maid and asks for pen and paper. Writing to Collatine, she asks him to return immediately. When she gives the messenger the letter, she imagines that he knows of her sin, for he gives her a sly, side glance. Surely everyone must know by now, she thinks. Her grief takes new channels. Studying a picture of the fall of Troy, she tries to find the face showing greatest grief. Hecuba, who gazes mournfully at Priam in his dying moments, seems the saddest. Lucrece grieves for those who died in the Trojan War, all because one man could not control his lust. Enraged, she tears the painting with her nails.

Collatine, returning home, finds Lucrece robed in black. With weeping and lamentations, she tells him of her shame, but without naming her violator. After she finishes, Collatine, driven half-mad by rage and grief, demands the name of the traitor. Before revealing it, Lucrece draws promises from the assembled soldiers that the loss of her honor would be avenged. Then, naming Tarquin, she draws a knife from her bosom and stabs herself.

Heartbroken, Collatine cries that he will kill himself as well, but Brutus, his friend, steps forward and argues that woe is no cure for woe; it is better to revenge Lucrece. The soldiers leave the palace to carry the bleeding body of Lucrece through Rome. The indignant citizens banish Tarquin and all his family.

Critical Evaluation:

The story of Tarquin's rape of Lucrece is an ancient Roman legend that has been presented in many versions, including in this poem by William Shakespeare. The Elizabethans were especially fond of this legend, so Shakespeare had numerous sources upon which to draw. Compared with his other writings, this poem is far more conventionally Elizabethan, yet its passages of great emotion and its consistently beautiful poetry rank it above other interpretations of the story known in his day.

The Rape of Lucrece was entered at the Stationers' Register on May 9, 1594. Like *Venus and Adonis* which had been published the previous year, it was finely printed by Richard Field and dedicated to the earl of Southampton. Both of these narrative poems had been written while the theaters were closed because of the plague, but these companion pieces are not the idle products of a dramatist during a period of forced inactivity. Rather, as the dedications and the care in publication indicate, they are efforts at what, in Shakespeare's day, was a more serious, more respectable type of composition than writing plays.

Longer and graver in tone than *Venus and Adonis*, *The Rape of Lucrece* was extremely popular, going through many editions, and was quoted frequently by contemporaries. The stern Gabriel Harvey, a Cambridge fellow and friend of Edmund Spenser, enthusiastically approved of the poem and paired it with *Hamlet, Prince of Denmark* (pr. c. 1600-1601, pb. 1603) for seriousness of intent. The poem may be the "graver labor" that Shakespeare promises Southampton in the dedication to *Venus and Adonis*. Whether or not Shakespeare intended to pair the poems, *The Rape of Lucrece* does provide a moralistic contrast to the view of love and sexuality expressed in the earlier poem.

The genre of *The Rape of Lucrece* is complaint, a form popular in the later Middle Ages and the Renaissance, and particularly in vogue in the late 1590's. Strictly speaking, the complaint is a monologue in which the speaker bewails his or her fate or the sad state of the world. Shakespeare, however, following the example of many contemporaries, took advantage of the possibilities for variety afforded by dialogue. The poem includes the long set speeches and significant digressions that had become associated with the complaint. The poetic style is the highly ornamented sort approved by sophisticated Elizabethan audiences.

The rhyme royal stanza may have been suggested by its traditional use in serious narrative or, more immediately, by Samuel Daniel's use of it in his popular *Complaint of Rosamond* (1592). *The Rape of Lucrece* shares with Daniel's poem the Elizabethan literary fascination with the distress of noble ladies. The poem is not sensual, except in the lushness of its imagery. The rape scene is attenuated by a grotesquely extended description of Lucrece's breasts, but the long, idealized description of the heroine is a rhetorical tour de force, not sexual stimulation. The theme of heroic chastity is always paramount, and readers are never distracted by action. Indeed, the prose "argument" that precedes the poem describes a story with enormous possibilities for action and adventure, but Shakespeare, consistent with his higher purpose, chooses to focus, reflectively and analytically, on the moral and psychological issues. Although the result is sometimes boring, there are occasional signs of Shakespeare's dramatic ability, especially in the exchanges before the rape.

The characters are static and stylized, but the revelation of the characters is skillfully done. As Tarquin's lust wrestles with his conscience, he is portrayed in an agony of indecision. The main medium of his internal conflict is the conventional theme of the antagonism of passion and reason. This section is a compendium of reflections on and rationalizations for the destructive power of lust. Tarquin thinks in terms of conventional images, but the contrasts and antitheses, as he is tossed back and forth between commonplaces, effectively represent his inner struggle. When Lucrece appeals to the very concerns that have bedeviled Tarquin, there is a dramatic poignancy that most of the rest of the poem lacks. After the rape, the change in Tarquin's thoughts from lust to guilt and shame is striking.

Lucrece's complaint is also wholly conventional in substance, but contrast and antithesis again give a vitality to her grief as she rationalizes her suicide as not the destruction of her soul but the only way to restore her honor. The imagistic alternations from day to night, clear to cloudy, reflect her anguish and the difficulty of her decision.

The poem's structure suggests that the exploration and decoration of conventional themes concerning lust and honor are the main intent. *The Rape of Lucrece* centers on the mental states and moral attitudes of the characters immediately before and after the crucial action. The rape is a premise for the reflections, the suicide a logical result. The set speeches are reinforced by free authorial moralizing. Significant digressions, like the long physical description of Lucrece and her extended apostrophe to Opportunity, further elaborate the main themes. The longest and most effective digression is Lucrece's contemplation of the Troy painting. The opportunities for finding correlatives are fully exploited. The city of Troy is apt, because it has been brought to destruction by a rape, and Paris is the perfect example of the selfishness of lust. Sinon, whose honest exterior belies his treachery, reminds Lucrece of the contrast between appearance and reality, nobility and baseness, that she had noted in Tarquin. The whole digression, which repeats by means of allusion, is ornamental rather than explanatory.

The severe paring of the plot further reveals Shakespeare's main concern. Collatine, the offended husband, appears only briefly, suffers silently, and does not even personally initiate the revenge; he does not intrude on the crucial issues. The bloodthirstiness of Lucrece's plea for revenge is another sign that elucidation of character is unimportant compared to the beautiful expression of moral imperatives. The revenge itself is, mysteriously, instigated by Brutus (an action that makes more sense in other versions of the tale) and is carried out perfunctorily in a few closing lines, because it is secondary to the themes of the poem.

Regardless of its moral earnestness and occasional tedium, *The Rape of Lucrece* is gorgeously ornamented with figures of speech, especially alliteration and assonance, and with figures of thought that please more for their brilliance of execution than their depth of conception. *The Rape of Lucrece* is, like *Venus and Adonis*, a rhetorical showpiece.

"Critical Evaluation" by Edward E. Foster

Further Reading

Breitenberg, Mark. "Publishing Chastity: Shakespeare's *The Rape of Lucrece*." In *Anxious Masculinity in Early Modern England*. New York: Cambridge University Press, 1996. Argues that the patriarchal culture of Elizabethan England engendered male sexual anxiety. Demonstrates how this masculine anxiety is reflected in Shakespeare's poem and other literature of the period.

Camino, Mercedes Maroto. *The Stage Am I: Raping Lucrece in Early Modern England*. Lewiston, N.Y.: E. Mellen Press, 1995. Examines how the rape of Lucrece was treated in Shakespeare's poem and in plays and other material created in early modern England. Describes how these works reflect contemporary ideas about gender and genre.

Cheney, Patrick, ed. *The Cambridge Companion to Shakespeare's Poetry*. New York: Cambridge University Press, 2007. Includes essays discussing Shakespeare and the development of English poetry; rhetoric, style, and form in his verse; the poetry in his plays; and his poetry as viewed from a twenty-first century perspective. "The Rape of Lucrece" by Catherine Belsey analyzes the poem.

Cousins, A. D. *Shakespeare's Sonnets and Narrative Poems*. New York: Longman, 2000. Chapter 2 focuses on *The Rape of Lucrece*. Discusses earlier versions of the story by Ovid, Livy, Giovanni Boccaccio, and Geoffrey Chaucer. Analyzes Shakespeare's adaptation of the tale.

Donaldson, Ian. *The Rapes of Lucretia: A Myth and Its Transformations*. 1982. New ed. Oxford, England: Clarendon Press, 2001. A thorough study of the Lucretia story in Western art and literature. Describes how Shakespeare's version of the story redirects the meaning of the myth to apply to late sixteenth century English culture.

Hyland, Peter. *An Introduction to Shakespeare's Poems*. New York: Palgrave Macmillan, 2003. Discusses the sources of Shakespeare's poetry. Analyzes *The Rape of Lucrece* and other nondramatic verse. Places Shakespeare's poetry within the context of the politics, values, and cultural tastes of Elizabethan England, arguing that he was a skeptical voice during this socially turbulent era.

Stimpson, Catharine R. "Shakespeare and the Soil of Rape." In *The Woman's Part: Feminist Criticism of Shakespeare*, edited by Carolyn Ruth Swift Lenz, Gayle Greene, and Carol Thomas Neely. Champaign: University of Illinois Press, 1980. Stimpson's essay on the theme of rape in Shakespeare's *The Rape of Lucrece* and other works is included in this excellent anthology of Shakespeare criticism written through the lens of feminist literary theory.

The Rape of the Lock

Author: Alexander Pope (1688-1744)
First published: 1712; expanded, 1714
Type of work: Poetry
Type of plot: Mock heroic
Time of plot: Early eighteenth century
Locale: London

Principal characters:
BELINDA, Miss Arabella Fermor
LORD PETRE, Belinda's suitor
THALESTRIS, Belinda's friend
ARIEL, a sprite
UMBRIEL, a gnome

The Poem:

At noon, when the sun is accustomed to awaken both lap dogs and lovers, Belinda is still asleep. She dreams that the sprite Ariel appears to whisper praises of her beauty in her ear. He says that he has been sent to protect her because something dreadful—what, he does not know—is about to befall her. He also warns her to beware of jealousy, pride, and, above all, men.

After Ariel vanishes, Shock, Belinda's lapdog, thinking that his mistress has slept long enough, awakens her with the lapping of his tongue. Rousing herself, Belinda spies a letter on her bed. After she reads it, she promptly forgets everything that Ariel told her, including the warning to beware of men.

Belinda, aided by her maid, Betty, begins her daily routine of grooming and dressing. Preening before her mirror, she is guilty of the pride against which Ariel cautioned her in her dream.

The sun, journeying across the sky, witnesses its brilliant rival, Belinda, boating on the Thames with her friends and suitors. All eyes are upon Belinda, and like a true coquette she smiles at her swains, but she favors no one more than another. Lord Petre, one of Belinda's suitors, admires a lock of her hair and vows that he will have it by fair means or foul. So set is he on getting the lock that, before the sun rose that morning, he built an altar to Love and threw on it all the trophies received from former sweethearts, meanwhile asking Love to give him soon the prize he wants and to let him keep it for a long time. Love, however, grants him only half his prayer.

Everyone except Ariel seems happy during the cruise on the Thames. The sprite summons his aides and reminds them that their duty is to watch over the fair Belinda, one sylph to guard her fan, another her watch, a third her favorite lock. Ariel himself is to guard Belinda's lapdog, Shock. Fifty sylphs are dispatched to watch over the maiden's petticoat, in order to protect her chastity. Any negligent sylphs, Ariel warns, will be punished severely.

After her cruise on the Thames, Belinda, accompanied by Lord Petre and the rest of the party, visits one of the palaces near London. There Belinda decides to play ombre, a Spanish card game, with two of her suitors, including Lord Petre. As she plays, invisible sylphs sit on her important cards to protect them.

Coffee is served after the game, and sylphs guard Belinda's dress to keep it from becoming spotted. The fumes from the coffee sharpen Lord Petre's wits to the point where he thinks of new stratagems for stealing Belinda's lock. One of his cronies hands him a pair of scissors. The sylphs, aware of Belinda's danger, attempt to warn her before Lord Petre can act, but as the maiden bends her head over her coffee cup, he clips the lock. Even Ariel is unable to warn Belinda in time.

At the rape of her lock, Belinda shrieks in horror. Lord Petre cries out in triumph. He praises the steel used in the scissors, comparing it with the metal of Greek swords that overcame the Trojans. Belinda's fury is as tempestuous as the rage of scornful virgins who have lost their charms. Ariel weeps bitterly and flies away.

Umbriel, a melancholy gnome, takes advantage of the human confusion and despair to fly down to the center of the earth to find the gloomy cave of Spleen, the queen of all bad tempers and the source of every detestable quality in human beings, including ill nature and affectation. Umbriel asks the queen to touch Belinda with chagrin, for he knows that if she is gloomy, melancholy and bad temper will spread to half the world. Spleen decides to grant Umbriel's request; she collects in a bag horrible noises such as those uttered by female lungs and tongues, and in a vial she puts tears, sorrows, and griefs. She gives both containers to Umbriel.

When the gnome returns to Belinda's world, he finds the young woman disheveled and dejected. Pouring the contents of the magic bag over her, Umbriel causes Belinda's wrath to be magnified many times. One of her friends, Thalestris, fans the flames of the maiden's anger by telling her that her honor is at stake and that behind her back her friends are talking about the rape of her lock. Thalestris then goes to her brother, Sir Plume, and demands that he confront Lord Petre and secure the return of the precious lock. Sir Plume considers the whole episode much magnified from little, but he does as his sister has asked. When he demands Belinda's lock, Lord Petre refuses to give up his prize.

Next Umbriel breaks the vial containing human sorrows, and Belinda is almost drowned in tears. She regrets the day that she ever entered society and also the day she learned to play ombre. She longs for simple country life. Suddenly she remembers, too late, that Ariel had warned her of impending evil.

In spite of Thalestris's pleas, Lord Petre is adamant about keeping the lock. Clarissa, another of Belinda's circle, wonders at the vanity of women and at the foolishness of men who fawn over them. Clarissa feels that both men and women need good sense, but in making her feelings known she exposes the tricks and deceits of women, causing Belinda to frown. Calling Clarissa a prude, Thalestris gathers her forces to battle with Belinda's enemies, including Clarissa and Lord Petre. Umbriel is delighted by this Homeric struggle of the teacups. Belinda pounces on Lord Petre, who is subdued when a pinch of snuff causes him to sneeze violently. She demands the lock, but it cannot be found. Some think that it has gone to the moon, where also go love letters and other tokens of tender passions. The muse of poetry sees the lock ascend to heaven and become a star.

Critical Evaluation:

The Rape of the Lock, generally considered the most popular of Alexander Pope's writings and the finest satirical poem in the English language, was written at the suggestion of John Caryll, Pope's friend, ostensibly to heal a family quarrel that resulted when an acquaintance of Pope, Lord Petre, playfully clipped a lock of hair from the head of Miss Arabella Fermor. Pope's larger purpose in writing the poem, however, was to ridicule the social vanity of his day and the importance attached to trifles.

When Robert Lord Petre cut off a lock of Arabella Fermor's hair one fateful day early in the eighteenth century, he did not know that the deed would gain fame, attracting attention over several centuries. What began as a trivial event in history turned, under the masterly guidance of Pope's literary hand, into one of the most famous poems in the English language and perhaps the most perfect example of burlesque in English. *The Rape of the Lock* was begun at Caryll's behest ("This verse, to Caryll, Muse! is due") in 1711; Pope spent about two weeks on it and produced a much shorter version

than the one he wrote two years later; more additions were made in 1717, when Pope developed the final draft of the poem as it now stands.

The poem uses the essentially trivial story of the stolen lock of hair as a vehicle for making some thoroughly mature and sophisticated comments on society and on women and men. Pope drew on his own classical background—he had translated Homer's *Iliad* (c. 750 B.C.E.; first English translation, 1611; Pope's translation, 1715-1720) and *Odyssey* (c. 725 B.C.E.; first English translation, 1614; Pope's translation, 1725-1726)—to combine epic literary conventions with his own keen, ironic sense of the values and societal structures shaping his age. The entire poem, divided into five cantos, is written in heroic couplets (pairs of rhymed iambic pentameter lines). Pope makes the most of this popular eighteenth century verse form, filling each line with balance, antithesis, bathos, allusions to serious epic poetry, and puns.

The literary genre of burlesque typically takes trivial subjects and elevates them to seemingly great importance; the effect is comic, and Pope manages an unbroken sense of amusement as he relates "What dire offense from amorous causes springs,/ What mighty contests rise from trivial things."

From the opening lines of the poem, suggestions of the epic tradition are clear. Pope knew well not only the *Iliad* and the *Odyssey* but also John Milton's *Paradise Lost* (1667, 1674). The narrator of *The Rape of the Lock* speaks like Homer, raising the epic question early in the poem: "Say what strange motive, goddess! could compel/ A well-bred lord t' assault a gentle belle?" Pope's elaborate description of Belinda's grooming rituals in canto 1 furthers comparison with the epic; it parodies the traditional epic passage describing a warrior's shield. Belinda's makeup routine is compared to the putting on of armor: "From each she nicely culls with curious toil,/ And decks the goddess with the glittering spoil."

The effect of Pope's use of epic conventions is humorous, but it also helps establish a double set of values in the poem, making the world of Belinda and Sir Plume at the same time trivial and significant. The poem rewards a reading that focuses on the seriousness of Belinda's activities and experience. The truth is, for a woman of her place and time, the unwanted cutting of a lock of hair was a serious matter. Epic conventions contribute to this double sense in each canto. The first canto is the epic dedication and invocation. The second is the conference of protective gods. The third details the games and the banquet. The fourth tells of the descent into the underworld. The fifth tells of heroic encounters and apotheosis. The overall result is that, although readers are presented with a basically silly situation, the poem has characters, such as Clarissa, who utter the always sensible virtues of the eighteenth century:

> Oh! if to dance all night, and dress all day,
> Charmed the smallpox, or chased old age away;
> Who would not scorn what housewife's cares produce,
> Or who would learn one earthly thing of use? . . .
> But since, alas, frail beauty must decay. . . .
> And she who scorns a man, must die a maid;
> What then remains but well our power to use,
> And keep good humor still what'er we lose?

Clarissa, in these lines from canto 5, expresses the norm of Pope's satire: the intelligent use of reason to control one's temperamental passions.

The heroic couplet merges perfectly with the epic devices in the poem, for as a verse form the heroic couplet naturally seems to express larger-than-life situations. It is, therefore, profoundly to Pope's credit that he successfully applies such a verse form to a subject that is anything but larger than life. Perhaps more than anyone else writing poetry in the eighteenth century, Pope demonstrates the flexibility of the heroic couplet. Shaped by his pen, it contains pithy aphorisms, social commentary, challenging puns, and delightful bathos (that is, the juxtaposition of the serious with the small, as in the line "wrapped in a gown for sickness and for show"). The key, if there is a key, to the classic popularity of *The Rape of the Lock* is the use of the heroic couplet to include—sometimes in great cataloged lists—those little, precise, and most revealing details about the age and the characters that peopled it. The opening lines of canto 3 illustrate Pope's expert use of detail. The passage describes court life at Hampton Court, outside London, and is a shrewd comment on the superficiality of the people there:

> Hither the heroes and the nymphs resort,
> To taste awhile the pleasures of a court;
> In various talks th' instructive hours they passed,
> Who gave the ball, or paid the visit last;
> One speaks the glory of the British queen,
> And one describes a charming Indian screen;
> A third interprets motions, looks, and eyes;
> At every word a reputation dies.
> Snuff, or the fan, supply each pause of chat,
> With singing, laughing, ogling, and all that.

The poet's criticism of such life is clear by the swift juxtaposition of Hampton Court life with a less pretty reality in the following lines:

> Meanwhile, declining from the noon of day,
> The sun obliquely shoots his burning ray;
> The hungry judges soon the sentence sign,
> And wretches hang that jurymen may dine.

Pope had a keen interest in the life of London's aristocracy, though he was always a critic of that life. A Catholic by birth, he was not always in favor with the Crown, but before the death of Queen Anne in 1714, he enjoyed meeting with a group of influential Tories. Sir Richard Steele and Joseph Addison, England's first newspaper editors, courted him on behalf of the Whig Party, but he refused to become its advocate.

Forbidden by law from living within several miles of London, Pope lived much of his adult life at Twickenham, a village on the Thames not too far from London but far enough. He transformed his dwelling there into an eighteenth century symbol with gardening and landscaping; he included vineyards, and the house had a temple and an obelisk to his mother's memory. During the 1720's he built his grotto, an underpass connecting the parts of his property under a dividing road. The grotto was a conversation piece; according to one contemporary, it had bits of mirror on the walls that reflected "all objects of the river, hills, woods, and boats, forming a moving picture in their visible radiations." For Pope, four feet, six inches tall and sick all his life, it was a symbol of the philosophical life and mind. Although he never married, his biographers have written that he felt a warm, if not always happy, affection for Martha and Teresa Blount, neighbors during his youth. Pope enjoyed great literary fame during his lifetime, and near the end of his life, when he entered a room, whispers of "Mr. Pope, Mr. Pope" would buzz among the occupants.

"Critical Evaluation" by Jean G. Marlowe

Further Reading

Baines, Paul. *Alexander Pope: A Sourcebook.* New York: Routledge, 2000. Provides biographical information and places Pope's life and work within historical and social context. Offers analysis of *The Rape of the Lock* and other works as well as critical commentary on Pope's poetry, politics, and depiction of gender issues.

Bloom, Harold, ed. *Alexander Pope's "The Rape of the Lock."* Edgemont, Pa.: Chelsea House, 1988. Collection of essays examines such topics as the poem's satirical intent, its social context, Pope's miniaturist tendencies, and the game of ombre.

Clark, Donald B. *Alexander Pope.* New York: Twayne, 1967. Provides in-depth analyses of several individual poems, including *The Rape of the Lock*. Includes pertinent historical, biographical, and philosophical information.

Goldsmith, Netta Murray. *Alexander Pope: The Evolution of a Poet*. Burlington, Vt.: Ashgate, 2002. Uses modern research on creativity to examine Pope's poetry in relation to that of his intellectual peers and to explain why he enjoyed spectacular success as a poet in his lifetime.

Grove, Robin. "Uniting Airy Substances: *The Rape of the Lock*, 1712-1736." In *The Art of Alexander Pope*, edited by Howard Erskine-Hill and Anne Smith. New York: Barnes & Noble, 1979. Focuses on Pope's revisions of *The Rape of the Lock*. Offers many insightful observations pertaining to Pope's aesthetic values.

Pollak, Ellen. "Rereading *The Rape of the Lock*: Pope and the Paradox of Female Power." *Studies in Eighteenth-Century Culture* 10 (1981): 429-444. Examines the poem from a feminist perspective and argues convincingly that the work is an allegory of the social and sexual initiation of a woman.

Rogers, Pat, ed. *The Cambridge Companion to Alexander Pope*. New York: Cambridge University Press, 2007. Collection of critical essays on various aspects of Pope's life and work contains several pieces about his poetry, including discussion of *The Rape of the Lock*. Topics addressed include Pope's depictions of gender, his attitudes toward money, and his involvement with the book trade.

Rappaccini's Daughter

Author: Nathaniel Hawthorne (1804-1864)
First published: 1844
Type of work: Short fiction
Type of plot: Allegory
Time of plot: Sixteenth or seventeenth century
Locale: Padua, Italy

Principal characters:
GIOVANNI GUASCONTI, an aspiring medical student
GIOCOMO RAPPACCINI, a brilliant, twisted scientist
BEATRICE, Rappaccini's daughter
PIETRO BAGLIONI, a gifted professor of medicine

The Story:

Giovanni Guasconti, a young man from Naples, comes to Padua to study medicine. He rents a gloomy room in a once noble house. The house was built by a defunct family, one of whose members was a character in Dante's *La divina commedia* (c. 1320; 3 volumes; *The Divine Comedy*, 1802), where he was portrayed as suffering in the Inferno. Giovanni's room looks down on a lush garden, centered on a still gurgling fountain and a shrub full of purple flowers. Lisabetta, the old woman who sets up the room, tells the young man that the garden belongs to the eminent scientist Giacomo Rappaccini.

Rappaccini, aging and scholarly, appears in the garden, intently studying the plants as if probing their essences. Wearing gloves to avoid contact, he does not sniff the flowers, reversing the approach people have brought to gardening since Adam and Eve. Approaching the luxuriant central plant, Rappaccini covers his nose and mouth with a mask, but these precautions prove inadequate. He backs off and, in the faltering voice of someone internally ill, calls his daughter Beatrice. She responds in a rich, sunny voice that strikes Giovanni as purple or crimson. As beautiful as a perfect day

or a blossom, splendidly garbed like the best of the flowers—to which she seems a sister—Beatrice helps her father. Her magnificence and healthy energy are held together by a wide belt called a virgin zone, commonly worn by maidens. Beatrice especially loves the central plant, which she says rewards her attention with kisses and perfume.

That night, Giovanni dreams of Beatrice and the flowers. Though obviously different, they seem very much the same in the dream, mysteriously dangerous. The dread night fades. Trapped as he is in Padua, Giovanni decides that the garden will serve to maintain his relationship to nature.

Armed with a letter of introduction, Giovanni pays a visit to his father's old friend Professor Pietro Baglioni at the medical school. When Baglioni hears the name of Giovanni's neighbor, he asserts that, though Rappaccini is as knowledgeable as any faculty member (with one possible exception), he is reprehensible: Science is more important to him than his patients, whom he uses experimentally. Rappaccini thinks all medicines fall into the realm of poisons produced by plants and that any cures he realizes are accidental products of his experiments. When Giovanni mentions

Beatrice, Baglioni avers that, educated by her father, she is most knowledgeable but not worth their attention. He tells Giovanni to finish drinking his Lacryma, and they part.

Chancing on a flower shop on his way home, Giovanni buys a bouquet. Looking down at Beatrice in the garden, he admires her beauty but is horrified when sap from a flower she plucks kills a lizard and again when Beatrice's breath kills an insect that flutters too close. Attracted, too, Giovanni throws Beatrice the bouquet. She graciously accepts it, but as she rushes off it appears to wilt. Beatrice, like her flowers, is attractive and dangerous.

Giovanni feels both love and horror. By chance, he meets Baglioni, whom he has been trying to avoid. While they are talking, Rappaccini passes. The scientists exchanges uncomfortable greetings, and, when Rappaccini is gone, Baglioni observes that the expression on Rappaccini's face revealed that Giovanni is the subject of an experiment. Insulted, Giovanni leaves, but Baglioni, valuing Giovanni as the son of an old friend, resolves to help him, thinking to use Beatrice to free him.

When Giovanni arrives home, Lisabetta tells him of a private entrance to the garden from their building. Giovanni gives her a gold coin, and she leads him to it. It occurs to him that Lisabetta may be part of an intrigue, but he enters anyway. The plants fascinate him. Many seem artificial, as if they were products of a depraved human intelligence. The few he recognizes as natural are poisonous.

While Giovanni is still looking around, Beatrice enters. She professes to know no more about plants than their beauty and odor. Rumors about her knowledge of science are untrue, she says. Though her breath smells sweet, Giovanni senses danger, but when he looks into her eyes he sees a splendid pure soul. They talk delightedly about Giovanni's home and family and become fast friends. Giovanni thinks to pluck a flower, but Beatrice catches back his hand. It is fatal to do so, she says. Later, Giovanni finds that where her fingers touched him he is painfully bruised. This discovery does not stop him from continuing to visit Beatrice. They love without touching.

Professor Baglioni visits Giovanni's room, chats awhile, and then tells him of an Indian prince who presented Alexander the Great with a beautiful woman. Alexander fell in love with her, but, nourished on poison, she was poison herself. Giovanni declares that the story is childish, but he is shaken. The professor notices an attractive but disagreeable odor in Giovanni's room. Shaken yet again, Giovanni asserts that Baglioni is imagining the smell. Baglioni recalls the odors with which Rappaccini tinctures his medicines and imagines that Beatrice uses them too.

Giovanni, acknowledging that Baglioni is trying to help, declares that Baglioni knows nothing of Beatrice. Undeterred, Baglioni states that both Rappaccini and Beatrice are poisonous. The Indian woman's fable has become a reality in the beautiful but deadly Beatrice, Baglioni says, and with Rappaccini now interested in Giovanni, the young medical student is in grave danger. Giovanni would like to dismiss the situation as a dream, but Baglioni, recognizing its reality, takes action: He gives Giovanni a silver vase that was created by the sculptor Benvenuto Cellini (1500-1571), declares that it contains an antidote to the poisons the notorious Borgia family used, and advises Giovanni to administer it to Beatrice. In love, Giovanni doubts his own observations of Beatrice's poisonous features. He only saw what he took to be evidence of these features from a distance. Resolved to test her at close range, he buys a fresh bouquet for her.

Before going down to the garden, Giovanni looks at himself in the mirror. His appearance is markedly improved, but, to his horror, the bouquet in his hand is wilting. Baglioni's comment about the odor in the room comes back to him. Is he himself becoming poisonous? When he tests himself by breathing on a spider, his breath kills it.

In the garden, Giovanni finds the formerly forbidding perfumes of the flowers delightful. He asks Beatrice about the origin of the purple flowering central plant and learns that she and it were born at the same time. In a way, they are twins. Rappaccini created both. The plant is the child of his mind, as Beatrice is the child of his body. She remarks on her loneliness before Heaven bestowed Giovanni upon her.

Horrified by his transformation, Giovanni accuses Beatrice of severing him from normal life. He hopes now that they can kiss, poison each other, and escape into death. Beatrice was unaware of her love's transformation. When he makes her aware of his condition, she realizes that it is the result of her father's work. Her body is poisonous, but her spirit is God's and desires love, which is its food.

Giovanni, unaware of the depth of the betrayal in his accusation against Beatrice, suggests that they can be cured and pursue normal lives together. He proposes that they drink Baglioni's antidote together to rid themselves of evil. Beatrice agrees to try the antidote, but she advises Giovanni to observe the effects of the antidote upon her before taking it himself. Even as she drinks, Rappaccini enters, delighted at the prospect of the two young lovers together. Giovanni's attraction to Beatrice and Rappaccini's work have transformed the young man into a fitting mate for his scientist's daughter. Beatrice, however, is dying as a result of drinking the antidote.

Beatrice asks her father why he doomed her as he did. Rappaccini avers that he made her invulnerable to enemies, but she tells him that she would have preferred to be loved rather than feared. At least now, she says, her poisonous body will die, releasing her spirit to the salubrious flowers in Eden. She bids Giovanni farewell, revealing the pain his verbal assault caused her. In the end, there was more poison in him than in her, but the ills he caused too shall pass. As Beatrice dies, Professor Baglioni upbraids Rappaccini for his destructive deeds.

Critical Evaluation:

"Rappaccini's Daughter," set in Italy, significantly combines the biblical Garden of Eden with Dante's medieval conception of Hell. Rappaccini's garden is an inverse of Eden, a heavenly hell. God's garden is positive, centered by a tree of life. Adam and Eve are expelled because they undertake to know good and evil. A plant of death centers Rappaccini's garden, the product of his quest to know more than humans should. The snake in this garden is the will to probe forbidden depths, including the human heart and the material world.

Aspiring to be the god of his garden, Rappaccini reverses God's creation. God created salubrious plants. Rappaccini creates poisonous ones. God created a male first, Adam, and—when the creatures around him proved inadequate— created Adam's female mate, Eve. Rappaccini creates a female first and—when the plants around her prove insufficient—undertakes to provide her with a male mate. What Rappaccini conceives of as an invaluable haven, safe because it is poisonous, is actually a hell of isolation to which he has condemned his child. He does not seek to rescue her from that hell, attempting instead to bring her happiness by supplying an equally poisonous companion.

Nathaniel Hawthorne's loose allegory is subtle. His characters, their feelings, and their perceptions have human qualities as well as figurative significance. Physically, Beatrice is an inverted Eve in a perverse Eden, a less effectual Beatrice than the one who leads Dante through Paradise, and there is an echo about her of Beatrice Cenci (1577-1599), who—with the help of her stepmother, brothers, and lover— effected the murder of the cruel father who imprisoned and abused her. Hawthorne's Beatrice is in her own right a sweet young woman trapped in an impossible situation. She hopes to share a heavenly relationship with Giovanni, but, though angelic, she is trapped in her father's ill-conceived hellish haven.

The allegorical aspects of the narrative do not impede readers from recognizing the characters' humanity. Giovanni is at the stage in life at which callow young men idealize the women who attract them physically. He thinks he is in love before he knows Beatrice, and, though their relationship blossoms, he is not above vicious verbal attacks that she correctly finds more poisonous than herself. Utterly decent, Beatrice is committed to making the best of an awful situation before she meets Giovanni. Some have suggested that she represents dangerous female sexuality, but her condition rules out physical contact. Like many innocent young women, she wants emotional and spiritual, not physical, love.

Even the story's brightest characters have limited understandings. Rappaccini myopically ignores the needs of others, imposing his sense of things on the people who fall under his control. Giovanni is subject to vicious rage. The well-meaning and accomplished Baglioni, for all his good intentions, is not quite adequate to the situation. He misunderstands Beatrice and intends to save Giovanni with her death, but the story ends with Giovanni still poisonous. Beatrice, too, is not quite up to the moment. Like Baglioni, she thinks to save Giovanni, but he remains trapped in the situation that her death allows her to escape. One can associate Rappaccini with the devil and think of Baglioni as a savior, but that oversimplifies the narrative. In their own ways, both men mean well and both fail. The story ends, but its horrific human situation continues. The affliction of poisonous evil within the human body, the result of a destructive impulse to alter nature, persists.

Self-consciousness about the manipulation of point of view had not yet gripped fiction writers when Hawthorne wrote, but he wonderfully limits his third-person narrative to Giovanni's perspective for the most part, with brief excursions into the wider perspective of a narrative voice that knows history and understands the limited visions of secondary characters such as Baglioni and Lisabetta. The language, too, is splendidly manipulated, with words serving multiple purposes. Lacryma, for example, is a white wine but also tears. "Rappaccini's Daughter" has tragic dimensions: The best intentions of the gifted humans in its pages pave paths to destruction.

Albert Wachtel

Further Reading

Bell, Millicent, ed. *New Essays on Hawthorne's Major Tales.* New York: Cambridge University Press, 1993. Carol M. Bensick's "World Lit Hawthorne: Or, Re-allegorizing 'Rappaccini's Daughter'" provides a thoughtful positive evaluation of the story, countering many attacks on the long-honored text as sexist or a cloaked treatment of an incestuous relationship.

Bloom, Harold, ed. *Nathaniel Hawthorne*. Philadelphia: Chelsea House, 2001. This critical anthology includes a section on "Rappaccini's Daughter," containing a plot summary, a list of characters, and essays discussing Beatrice, narrative red herrings, sources for Professor Baglioni, the representation of the relationship between the physical and spiritual worlds, and the story's Mexican genealogy.

Levin, Harry. *The Power of Blackness*. New York: Alfred A. Knopf, 1964. Examines the role of evil in the work of Hawthorne, Edgar Allan Poe, and Herman Melville.

McFarland, Phillip. *Hawthorne in Concord*. New York: Grove Press, 2004. This literary biography covers the period of Hawthorne's life during which he wrote "Rappaccini's Daughter."

Waggoner, Hyatt H. *Hawthorne: A Critical Study*. Cambridge, Mass.: Harvard University Press, 1955. Thoughtful, sensible analysis; a fine starting place.

Rasselas

Author: Samuel Johnson (1709-1784)
First published: 1759, as *The Prince of Abissinia: A Tale*
Type of work: Novel
Type of plot: Philosophical
Time of plot: Eighteenth century
Locale: Abyssinia and Cairo

Principal characters:
RASSELAS, prince of Abyssinia
NEKAYAH, his sister
PEKUAH, her maid
IMLAC, a poet

The Story:

It is the custom in Abyssinia for the sons and daughters of the emperor to be confined in a remote place until the order of succession to the throne is established. The spot in which Rasselas and his brothers and sisters are confined is a beautiful and fertile valley situated between high mountains. Everything needed for a luxurious life is present in the valley. Entertainers are brought in from the outside world to help the royal children pass the time pleasantly. These entertainers are never allowed to leave, for the outside world is not to know how the royal children live before they are called on to rule.

It is this perfection that causes Rasselas, in the twenty-sixth year of his life, to become melancholy and discontented. He is unhappy because he has everything to make him happy; he wants more than anything else to desire something that cannot be made available to him. When he talks of his longing with an old philosopher, he is told that he is foolish. The old man tells him of the misery and suffering of the people outside the valley and cautions him to be glad of his present situation. Rasselas, however, knows that he cannot be content until he sees the suffering of the world.

For many months, Rasselas ponders about his desire to escape from the valley. He takes no action, however, for the valley is carefully guarded and there is no chance for anyone to leave. Once he meets an inventor who promises to make some wings for him so that he can fly over the mountains, but the experiment is a failure. In his search for a way to escape, his labor is more mental than physical.

In the palace, there is a poet, Imlac, whose lines please Rasselas by their intelligence. Imlac also is tired of the perfect life in the valley, for in the past he traveled over much of the world. He observed the evil ways of humankind and learned that most wickedness stemmed from envy and jealousy. He noticed that people envy others with more worldly goods and oppress those who are weak. As he talks, Rasselas longs more than ever to see the world and its misery. Imlac tries to discourage him, for he believes that Rasselas will long for his present state if he ever sees the violence and treachery that abound in the lands beyond the mountains.

When Imlac realizes he cannot deter the prince, he agrees to join him in his attempt to leave the perfect state. Together the two men contrive to hew a path through the side of a mountain. When they are almost ready to leave, Rasselas sees his sister Nekayah watching them. She begs to accompany the travelers, for she also is bored with the valley and longs to see the rest of the world. She is Rasselas's favorite sister, so he gladly allows her and her maid, Pekuah, to join them.

The four make their way safely through the path in the

mountainside. They take enough jewels with them to supply them with money when they reach a city of trade. They are simply dressed, and no one recognizes them as royalty. In Cairo, they sell some of their jewels and rent a magnificent dwelling. They entertain great people and begin to learn the customs of people different from themselves. Their objective is to observe all possible manners and customs so that they can make their own choices about the kind of life each wants to pursue; but they find many drawbacks to every form of living.

Rasselas and Nekayah believe that it is necessary only to find the right pursuit to know perfect happiness and contentment. Imlac knows that few people live by choice, but rather by chance and the whims of fortune. Rasselas and Nekayah, however, believe that their chance birth at least gives them the advantage of being able to study all forms of living and thus to choose the one most suitable for them to pursue. So it is that the royal pair visit with persons of every station. They go into the courts and the fields. They visit sages of great fame and hermits who isolate themselves to meditate. Nowhere do they find a person completely happy and satisfied; everyone desires what another has, and all think their neighbors more fortunate than they are.

Only once does Rasselas find a happy man: a philosopher who preaches the doctrine of reason. He states that by reason, a person can conquer passions and disappointments and thus find true happiness. When Rasselas calls on the sage the following day, however, he finds the old man in a fit of despair. His daughter died in the night, and the reason that he urged others to use fails completely on the occasion of the philosopher's own grief.

Imlac and Nekayah spend long hours discussing the advantages of one kind of life over another. They question the state of marriage as compared with celibacy, and life at court as compared with pastoral pleasures, but at no time can they find satisfactory solutions for their questions. Nowhere can they find people living in happiness. Imlac suggests a visit to the pyramids so that they might learn of people of the past. While they are in a tomb, Pekuah is stolen by Arabs, and it is many months before she is returned to Nekayah. Pekuah tells her mistress that she spent some time in a monastery while she waited for her ransom, and she believes that the nuns found the one truly happy way of life.

Their search continues for a long period. Often they think they find a happy person, but always they find much sorrow in the life they think so serene. After a visit to the catacombs and a discourse on the soul, Nekayah decides that she will cease looking for happiness on earth and live so that she might find happiness in eternity.

The Nile floods the valley and confines them to their home for a time. The four friends discuss the ways of life that promise each the greatest happiness. Pekuah wishes to retire to a convent; Nekayah desires knowledge more than anything and wants to found a woman's college where she can both teach and learn; Rasselas thinks he wants a small kingdom where he can rule justly and wisely; Imlac says he will be content to drift through life, with no particular goal. All know their desires will never be fulfilled, and they begin to look forward to their return to the Abyssinian valley where everyone seems happy and there is nothing to desire.

Critical Evaluation:

According to his own statement, Samuel Johnson wrote *Rasselas* in the evenings of one week in 1759 to defray the expenses of his mother's funeral. Nevertheless, one should not assume either that the tale was completely spontaneous or that its mood was entirely determined by his mother's illness and death. Johnson had very likely been considering the subject for some time. His translation of Father Lobo's *A Voyage to Abyssinia* in 1735, Johnson's use of an Asian setting in his early play *Irene* (1749), and his employment of the device of the Asian apologue in several *Rambler* papers (which he edited from 1750-1752) all pointed the way. Furthermore, *Rambler* papers numbers 204 and 205 suggested part of the theme of *Rasselas* in telling how Seged, Lord of Ethiopia, decided to be happy for ten days by an act of will, and how this quest for pleasure was in vain. Even closer in theme is Johnson's finest poem, *The Vanity of Human Wishes* (1749).

The mood of *Rasselas* may seem to be predominantly gloomy, involving, if not cynicism, at least a tragic view of life. Still, it is possible to see in it some of the qualities of an ironic satire. The manuscript title of the book, *The Choice of Life*, is a key both to its plan and to its philosophy. Human nature being what it is, Johnson indicates, happiness can be only illusory, accidental, and ephemeral, existing more in hope than in reality, and, in the end, always being nothing when compared with life's miseries. Those who seek happiness through a choice of life are destined to end in failure. This reading of the story may seem simply pessimistic, but there is another aspect of it that recognizes the multifariousness of life, which resists and defeats facile theories about existence such as those of the young travelers in the novel. In this aspect there is opportunity for some comedy.

Johnson skillfully begins with the conventional conceit of a perfect bliss that exists in some earthly paradise. Rasselas, an Abyssinian prince, his sister, and two companions escape from what they come to regard as the boredom of the perfect life in the Happy Valley to set out on a search for true happiness in the outside world. They try all kinds of life: pleasure-loving society, solitude, the pastoral life, life of high and middle estates, public and private life. Although Rasselas holds that happiness is surely to be found, they find it nowhere. The simple life of the country dweller so praised by Jean-Jacques Rousseau and his followers is full of discontent. People with wealth and power cannot be happy, because they fear the loss of both. The hermit, unable to answer the question about the advantages of solitude, returns to civilization. The philosopher who preaches the philosophic systems of happiness succumbs to grief over the death of his daughter. A philosopher who thinks one can achieve happiness by "living according to nature" cannot explain what this phrase means. The abduction of the maid Pekuah enables Rasselas's sister, Nekayah, to learn that one "who has no one to love or to trust has little to hope." Pekuah reports on her return that the female "happy valley" of the harem is boring, because the women talk of nothing but the tediousness of life.

In the final chapter, all the travelers decide on an ideal vocation. Nevertheless, says the narrator, "they well knew that none could be obtained." So they resolve to return to Abyssinia. Such a return is not necessarily a defeat. All achieve a valuable education and lose their insularity. As one contemporary critic suggested, instead of ending in rationalistic despair, the four learned to ask important questions: What activity is most appropriate to humankind? What can best satisfy each person and fulfill his or her destiny?

Voltaire's *Candide: Ou, L'Optimisme* (1759; *Candide: Or, All for the Best*, 1759) and Johnson's *Rasselas* were published within two months of each other. Both attacked the fashionable optimism of their day. Candide begins in the best of all possible castles; Rasselas begins in the Happy Valley. Each has a philosopher friend—Pangloss and Imlac. Each sets out to explore the world, although for different reasons. Each is disillusioned. In contrast, Voltaire's wit is brilliant, slashing, and iconoclastic and is exerted on a tangible and vivid world. Johnson's wit is deliberate and speculative, balanced, measured, and conservative. His world is fanciful. If, like Thomas More in his *De Optimo Reipublicae Statu, deque Nova Insula Utopia* (1516; *Utopia*, 1551), Johnson chose to set his story in a non-Christian part of the world, he did so because he wished to deal with humanity on a purely naturalistic level and discuss basic issues without involving religious considerations that were too specific to his time. Johnson does not allow his deeply religious nature, however, so unlike Voltaire's skepticism, to go entirely unperceived. One does not forget, for example, that after Imlac's discus-

sion of the nature of the soul, Princess Nekayah is moved to insist that the choice of life is no longer so important as the choice of eternity.

To many readers, *Rasselas* has long seemed to be chiefly a series of essays, narrative and digressive, like those in the *Rambler*, loosely strung together with a narrative thread that could be described more nearly as plan than plot. Chapters such as "A Dissertation on the Art of Flying," "A Dissertation on Poetry," "A Disquisition upon Greatness," and "The Dangerous Prevalence of Imagination" can be lifted out of their context and almost stand independently as separate literary works. The characters are two-dimensional, and the dialogue is far from lifelike. In places, the style is so rhythmic and sonorous as to suggest poetry rather than prose. For these and other reasons, the right of the narrative to be called a novel has frequently been questioned.

More recent critics have suggested illuminating patterns in the structure of *Rasselas*. One useful suggestion is to regard the novel as having three sections or movements of sixteen chapters each, ending with a kind of coda. The first concerns the Happy Valley and the theme of the choice of life, centered on the restless prince and his determination to find happiness outside. The second section, in which the travelers make their comprehensive survey of humanity, is focused on Rasselas's experiments upon life and the discovery that no one fits his theory and possesses happiness. The section ends with Imlac's famous apostrophe to the pyramids. In the third section, the travelers, now no longer mere observers, find themselves actually involved in life as the victims of others. The chief incidents here are Pekuah's abduction and return, the encounter with the astronomer, the brief meeting with the disillusioned old man, the final visit to the catacombs, and the abandonment of the quest. To some critics, the coda, "A Conclusion in Which Nothing Is Concluded," is an aesthetic defect. In all fairness, however, it can probably be regarded as such only by those who would require Johnson to append more of a moral tag than he thought wise. The travelers' discoveries concerning life and the fallacy of their quest can be considered to have positive, rather than only negative, value and can be regarded as conclusion enough.

"Critical Evaluation" by Lodwick Hartley

Further Reading

Burke, John J., Jr., and Donald Kay, eds. *The Unknown Samuel Johnson*. Madison: University of Wisconsin Press, 1983. Offers new interpretations of *Rasselas*'s theme and meaning in light of Johnson's private life.

Clingham, Greg. *Johnson, Writing, and Memory*. New York:

Cambridge University Press, 2002. Clingham studies Johnson's writing, placing it within the context of eighteenth century ideas about literature, history, fiction, and law, and examines the challenges that these ideas pose to twentieth and twenty-first century critical theory.

_____, ed. *The Cambridge Companion to Samuel Johnson*. New York: Cambridge University Press, 1997. Collection of essays, including discussions of Johnson and the art of conversation, poetry, the essay, the condition of women, and politics. Also features Fred Parker's essay "The Skepticism of Johnson's *Rasselas*."

Curley, Thomas. "The Spiritual Journey Moralized in *Rasselas*." *Anglia* 91 (1973): 35-55. Generally positive review, focusing on the moral overtones of Johnson's choice-of-life ideology as it relates to the circumstances and actions of the travelers in *Rasselas*.

Ehrenpreis, Irvin. "*Rasselas* and Some Meanings of 'Structure' in Literary Criticism." *Novel* 14, no. 2 (Winter, 1981): 101-117. A rather disparaging view of Johnson's artistic abilities, noting the shallowness of his characters and the inconsistencies within the structure of *Rasselas*.

Hart, Kevin. *Samuel Johnson and the Culture of Property*. New York: Cambridge University Press, 1999. Hart examines Johnson's literary legacy and reputation. He contends that James Boswell's famous biography turned Johnson into a public monument, and he analyzes the works of other biographers and critics who helped create "The Age of Johnson."

Martin, Peter. *Samuel Johnson: A Biography*. Cambridge, Mass.: Harvard University Press, 2008. Provides a psychological profile of Johnson, focusing on the aspects of his personality and his life that were not covered in James Boswell's biography, such as Johnson's insecurities, bouts of deep depression, and self-doubt.

Nath, Prem, ed. *Fresh Reflections on Samuel Johnson: Essays in Criticism*. Troy, N.Y.: Whitston, 1987. Contains a broad range of critical essays dealing with Johnson's writings, with particular emphasis on its artistic nature. Useful for its opposing interpretations of theme and meaning in *Rasselas*.

Weinbrot, Howard D. *Aspects of Samuel Johnson: Essays on His Arts, Mind, Afterlife, and Politics*. Newark: University of Delaware Press, 2005. Contains sixteen essays by Weinbrot, a professor of English at the University of Wisconsin, which examine Johnson as prose writer, poet, lexicographer, historical figure, and literary and political thinker. Two of the essays examine various aspects of *Rasselas*.

The Razor's Edge

Author: W. Somerset Maugham (1874-1965)
First published: 1944
Type of work: Novel
Type of plot: Psychological realism
Time of plot: Early twentieth century
Locale: Chicago, Paris, and India

Principal characters:
LARRY DARRELL, restless former aviator
ISABEL BRADLEY, his fiancé
GRAY MATURIN, the man Isabel marries
ELLIOTT TEMPLETON, snobbish expatriate
SOPHIE MACDONALD, tragic victim of circumstances
SOMERSET MAUGHAM, narrator of the story

The Story:

Larry Darrell, a World War I aviator who sees his best friend killed, does his best to adjust to postwar life as a businessman in Chicago, but he cannot handle it. Everything seems too superficial and materialistic to this young man, whose encounters with the horrors of war had awakened in him a deep desire to probe the mysteries of life. Determined to discover meaning in life and in himself, he drops out of the Chicago business world of the 1920's and goes to India, where he spends five years in meditation and study. Eventually, he feels pulled back to the world he had known previously, but instead of returning to the United States, he goes to Europe. There he works as a common laborer, sometimes on a farm, sometimes in a mine, all the while getting closer to discovering the deeper meaning of life.

In the meantime, his former fiancé, Isabel Bradley, tired of waiting for him and impatient with behavior she cannot comprehend, marries Gray Maturin, an outgoing fellow and successful Chicago businessman. When the stock market crashes in 1929, Gray loses everything, and he and Isabel flee to Paris, where they are able to live more frugally on a modest inheritance. Isabel has never stopped loving Larry, and when the two cross paths in Paris, Isabel tries hard to get Larry to tell her just what had gone wrong. When he tries to explain his spiritual quest, she again does not understand and loses patience with him.

Two influential gentlemen figure importantly in the lives of Larry and Isabel. One is Elliott Templeton, a wealthy American who divides his time between Chicago and Paris, with regular visits to the French Riviera. Elliott is everything that Larry has come to disdain—selfish, snobbish, superficial. The other gentleman is Somerset Maugham (the narrator), a successful and widely traveled author who is a close friend of all concerned. For example, he is present when Sophie MacDonald, the debutante turned tramp, shows up at a café where he is dining one evening with Larry, Isabel, and Gray.

Sophie had been happily married and the mother of two when her husband and children were killed in a car crash that only she survived. Unable to cope with the loss and the grief, Sophie drifted to Paris, where she became an alcoholic and a prostitute. Now, Larry is terribly upset by her condition, and decides to do something about it. He gets her to stop drinking and even proposes marriage to her. When Isabel hears this, she is jealous and plans to stop the marriage. One day, she invites Sophie to stop by her apartment. Sophie arrives to encounter a scene of domestic bliss—a bitter reminder of everything she had lost. Isabel excuses herself to run the children to the dentist, promising to return shortly. She had left a bottle of what had once been Sophie's favorite liqueur in a conspicuous spot. The longer Sophie waits, the more agitated and depressed she becomes until, finally, she has one drink. It is not long before the bottle is empty, and when Isabel returns, Sophie is gone—for good. Eventually, her body is found washed ashore in Toulon, where she had returned to a life of alcohol, drugs, and sex.

Elliott Templeton died as he had lived, a snob. On his deathbed, he frets over not having received an invitation to a ball being given by a wealthy American "princess." When Maugham learns that Templeton is not on the guest list, he wangles an invitation and has it delivered. Templeton is delighted and relieved, and although he cannot attend, he takes great pleasure in sending his regrets, giving as his reason "a previous engagement with his Blessed Lord."

In Paris, Maugham has a long conversation with Isabel, during which she gives him a carefully edited version of the events of that fateful afternoon when Sophie had drunk the liqueur. Maugham accuses her of lying, and when she be-

comes angered, he insists that she had been responsible for Sophie's death. She then admits the whole scheme, but remains unrepentant, claiming that at least she had spared Larry a miserable marriage. Maugham then takes delight in telling her that Larry plans to return to the United States and work as a common laborer, whereupon Isabel bursts into tears, crying, "Now I really have lost him."

In the end, Larry does return to the United States, vowing to take a job in a garage or become a taxi driver. He has no desire for fame and is without ambition, an attitude Maugham says he respects but cannot entirely share.

Critical Evaluation:

W. Somerset Maugham took the title for this novel from a line in the *Katha-Upanishad* (c. 1000-c. 600 B.C.E.), an ancient book of Hindu wisdom: "The sharp edge of a razor is difficult to pass over: thus the wise say the path to Salvation is hard." In the late 1930's, Maugham traveled throughout India and spent considerable time in the presence of the renowned Indian sage and holy man Bhagavan. One of Bhagavan's disciples, and the probable source for the character Larry Darrell, was an American sailor who was on a quest for spiritual enlightenment. Maugham frankly admitted that he himself was unable to find complete satisfaction in the life of the spirit. He so respected the attempt on the part of others to abjure materialism in favor of inner peace, however, that he wrote *The Razor's Edge* in an attempt to articulate to himself the essence of his ambition.

Maugham starts the novel with the disclaimer that he has serious misgivings about in what direction the novel will go or if, in fact, it will even turn out to be a novel. By the end he has produced a novel; it was always Maugham's chief virtue as a writer that he could not help turning experience into first-class fiction. Fortunately, by adhering to the traditional novel form, Maugham is able to preserve the distance necessary to allow the characters to reveal themselves fully and to permit readers the freedom to make up their own minds. A comparison of two central characters, Larry Darrell and Elliott Templeton, will serve to illustrate this point.

Although these two men are worlds apart in character, they are presented with equal sympathy and objectivity. As a result, these opposites help unlock the mystery of each other's character. Templeton is vain and worldly, a hedonist and a snob who can only function in the right society and among expensive things. Darrell is selfless and otherworldly, a compassionate man who cares little for his own comfort or for the company of others, and he places no value on material things beyond necessity and function.

Maugham places himself somewhere between these two

men and tries to remain impartial. On one hand he finds Templeton's affectations charming and harmless and he appreciates Templeton's sophisticated tastes. On the other hand, he has an abiding respect for Darrell's pursuit of satisfying answers to ultimate questions. He knows that Templeton is shallow because he has never felt the need to look below the surface of life. Darrell has had shattering wartime experiences that will not let him rest until he can penetrate their meaning and understand what life is about. In the end, Maugham is quite frank about his own shortcomings on the spiritual side, for he admits that he is a product of Templeton's world and generation, and not those of Darrell.

The Razor's Edge was ahead of its time. It spoke more to the generation of the 1960's than it did to that of the 1940's, when it was written, or to that of the 1920's and 1930's, when it takes place. Much of its success is owing to Maugham's "detached involvement." Maugham is a character and a participant in his own book, much in the style of the New Journalism so popular in the 1960's. When Maugham gets the invitation for Templeton, he is simply stepping in where he has to in order to give the reader the clearest example possible of Templeton's pretentiousness. Similarly, when he confronts Isabel about Sophie and the bottle of liqueur, he is clearly interfering in his own story, but only he can get away with calling her a liar and forcing her to confess because he is an outsider who has nothing to lose. Finally, when he identifies Sophie's body, he is the only one who is able to salvage any dignity from such a sordid tragedy. Maugham's participation in the story gives it the authenticity of a factual account.

Maugham is one of the most underrated authors of the twentieth century. It is commonly admitted, even by those who admire him, that his main problem—other than that he was too popular—was that he writes too clearly. He is a born storyteller and a gentleman; he believes he owes the reader the best story he can tell in a manner most likely to please. One hundred pages into *The Razor's Edge*, Maugham begins a digression with the statement that to give the reader a moment's rest, he is starting upon a new section, but that he is only doing it for the reader's convenience. The preceding section had been a transcription of a conversation in which Larry had recounted his travels and revealed some of his most profound reflections. Realizing that the reader might need a respite from the weighty philosophizing, Maugham graciously interrupts the transcription at a point where he says a natural interruption occurred.

Maugham is one of the most frequently filmed writers, another strike against him in some quarters. *The Razor's Edge* was made into a highly successful film in 1946 and remade in 1984. Like all good novels, it can be read on several levels, ranging from a comedy of manners, to a social drama, to an intense search for religious revelation.

Thomas Whissen

Further Reading

Connolly, Cyril. "The Art of Being Good." In *The Condemned Playground—Essays: 1927-1944*. London: Routledge & Kegan Paul, 1945. Maugham is praised for his handling of major characters, especially his sensitive portrayal of Larry Darrell, and for his determination to use his narrative talents in the service of truth. Dated but still useful.

Cordell, Richard A. *Somerset Maugham: A Writer for All Seasons—A Biographical and Critical Study*. 2d ed. Bloomington: Indiana University Press, 1969. Includes a judicious commentary on *The Razor's Edge* as a novel worthy of the interest of discriminating readers.

Holden, Philip. "Transcending Sexuality: India and *The Razor's Edge*." In *Orienting Masculinity, Orienting Nation: W. Somerset Maugham's Exotic Fiction*. Westport, Conn.: Greenwood Press, 1996. Examines the themes of homosexuality, gender identity, and race relations in Maugham's works, including *The Razor's Edge*. Holden maintains that Maugham's writing shows a negotiation between two different masculine identities: the private gay man and the public writer.

Meyers, Jeffrey. *Somerset Maugham*. New York: Alfred A. Knopf, 2004. Meyers's biography emphasizes Maugham's "otherness," particularly his sexuality. Unlike other critics who have dismissed Maugham's work, Meyers defends him as a great writer who influenced authors such as George Orwell and V. S. Naipaul.

Rogal, Samuel J. *A Companion to the Characters in the Fiction and Drama of W. Somerset Maugham*. Westport, Conn.: Greenwood Press, 1996. An alphabetical listing of the characters in Maugham's fiction and drama. Each entry identifies the work in which a character appears and that character's role in a given work.

_____. *A William Somerset Maugham Encyclopedia*. Westport, Conn.: Greenwood Press, 1997. Alphabetically arranged entries on Maugham's writings, family members, friends, and settings, and the historical, cultural, social, and political issues associated with his life and work. Includes a bibliography and an index.

Weeks, Edward. "The Atlantic Bookshelf." *Atlantic Monthly*, May, 1944, 123-129. One of the few contemporary reviews to consider *The Razor's Edge* as being ahead of its time. Discusses the tension between "the urgent quest of youth and the cynical retreat of age." Dated but still relevant.

The Real Life of Sebastian Knight

Author: Vladimir Nabokov (1899-1977)
First published: 1941
Type of work: Novel
Type of plot: Parody
Time of plot: Early twentieth century
Locale: Russia, England, and France

Principal characters:
V., the narrator of the story and the biographer of Sebastian Knight
SEBASTIAN KNIGHT, V.'s half brother

The Story:

V. wants to write a biography of his deceased half brother, Sebastian Knight. Writing the book is V.'s act of homage, or commemoration, for Sebastian, whom he believes to be an unjustly forgotten novelist. V. has a rival, a Mr. Goodman, who had previously written a biography of Sebastian. V. objects to Goodman's book on the grounds that it is false, insensitive, and full of clichés in its portrayal of Sebastian and his unique genius.

The true reason for V.'s disgust with Goodman's biography, however, slowly emerges: jealousy. Goodman beat V. in writing the biography, and in the process, Goodman experienced what V. never had: four years of close contact with Sebastian. Goodman's book is commercially successful, and some of Sebastian's manuscripts had been left with him—which results in a lawsuit.

When V.'s attempts to gather information from several of Sebastian's friends and acquaintances prove unsuccessful, he, like Goodman, turns to Sebastian's novels for information. For his first novel, as a protest against the conventionality of second-rate authors, Sebastian wrote a parody of a detective novel titled *The Prismatic Bezel*. The secret of Sebastian's success with this novel is his use of formal innovation, and V. assimilates some of his half brother's techniques in his own biography. The heroes of Sebastian's detective novel are called "methods of composition" because Sebastian sought to convey a way of seeing a personality rather than the essence of a personality.

In his examination of Sebastian's next book, *Success*, V. notes that Sebastian elevates chance and coincidence into mystical, significant forces. The most significant element in *Success*, however, is the conjuror, who figures prominently in the work. This character makes an appearance in V.'s life in the form of a Mr. Silbermann, whom V. meets on a train. In V.'s search for a mysterious woman whom Sebastian had pursued just before he died, V. needs to obtain a list of the women who had stayed at the resort hotel that Sebastian visited the summer he met the woman. Silbermann expresses his sorrow for Sebastian's death, and he agrees to help V.; he produces the list, but he advises V. that the pursuit of the woman is pointless.

The rest of *The Real Life of Sebastian Knight* consists of a series of hints and guesses about various identities and suggestions about possibilities that the reader might entertain: that V. will successfully find his way through the maze of clues that obscure the identity of the woman Sebastian loved; that Sebastian's spirit will assist his half brother by easing V. into the evanescent world of a novelist's imaginings; and that V.'s obsession with his half brother will lead him into a nightmare world in which his goal recedes even as he seems to be drawing nearer. Another possibility is that the whole book could be a fictitious biography invented by Sebastian himself and populated by characters from all of his novels.

The main point of this exercise in the attempted recreation of another's life later becomes clear. At the point at which Sebastian's last novel ends, V. says that he feels as if he and his half brother are on the brink of some absolute truth— that Sebastian knew the "real truth" about death, and he was going to reveal it. The conclusion of Sebastian's novel anticipates the conclusion of V.'s biography; Sebastian announces that he has been granted a great truth. He had discovered the arbitrariness of the personality, and he conceived the book as the means by which this arbitrariness could best be conveyed. In Nabokov's novel, this moment of revelation is anticipated by a mock death scene in which V. rushes to the bedside of his dying half brother and listens from an adjoining room to the rhythm of Sebastian's breathing. The truth his brother is about to impart suddenly vanishes, and all that remains is the simpler truth, the human emotion of the love V. feels for him.

This profound rush of emotion turns out to be a ploy designed to trick those who, like V., are prone to sentimentality. When he leaves the room, V. learns that he has in fact, been visiting someone else and that Sebastian had died the night before. Life played another joke on V.

V. then announces that he himself is Sebastian Knight, and Nabokov's novel concludes with a vision of all the characters from Sebastian's life around him on a lighted stage. He is impersonating his half brother, and his act of sympathetic identification reaches a type of completion. These are not the closing remarks of the real Sebastian, who had all the while been pretending to be a nonexistent person. What V. does in the process of researching his biography is shape his own understanding of his subject; he locates that understanding on the edge of the ineffable. Unable to discover the contiguous, linear, horizontal narrative he seeks, he tells the story of his frustration, and in doing so creates the circular, vertical account that ends, not by announcing a truth, but by imparting an imaginative one.

Critical Evaluation:

Vladimir Nabokov explores the origins of creativity, the relationship of the artist to his or her work, and the nature of invented reality. A brilliant and controversial prose stylist, Nabokov entertains, inspires, and shocks his readers with his love of intellectual and verbal games. His technical genius, as well as the exuberance of his creative imagination, mark him as a major twentieth century author.

The Real Life of Sebastian Knight is a study of the complications that ensue when V. tries to sort out the details of the life of a person he hardly knows. The book reveals the complexities involved in any attempt to present a self in language—Nabokov's chief subject in the novel. By focusing on the conflation of life and art, by designing the reader's quest to mimic the quest of the narrator, Nabokov foregrounds the issues involved in making fiction.

Sebastian's "real life" is elusive; that is, the conventional means of reconstructing his life and writing his biography—interviewing friends and acquaintances, tracking down different accounts of relationships, and examining letters and documents—only lead to a series of comic dead ends in Nabokov's novel. Not only do fictional characters pop into existence out of nowhere, thereby disorienting the reader, but Nabokov further confuses readers by forcing them to ask continually, Who is speaking?

A major theme of Nabokov's novel is the theoretical and practical possibility of biography. V.'s warning to the reader to remember that what is told is shaped by the teller, reshaped by the listener, and concealed from both by the dead man of the tale suggests that Nabokov's conception of the relationship between a life and a biography is complex.

Nabokov's novel also is a detective story and a quest for self-knowledge. The title itself points in both these directions, and the clues that accumulate as the novel progresses lead the reader toward the identity of a man who has been recreated through the process of observing himself reflected in

a mirror. This mirror is actually many mirrors, since the narrator gets many glimpses of the identity of Sebastian, and of himself, from a variety of sources. In this respect, the characters of Nabokov's novel are similar to the characters in one of Sebastian's novels, *The Prismatic Bezel*. In *The Real Life of Sebastian Knight*, what the characters compose is Sebastian's real life; the reader's and the narrator's sense of that life depends in part on the accumulation of scattered bits of information and impressions the characters impart. Sebastian's life is, quite literally, composed, just as a painting or music is composed.

The image created, then, is not the person but, instead, others' idea of him, and that idea is always misleading because it is, of necessity, incomplete and external. Nabokov makes this a fundamental idea on which he bases the structure of his novel. Sebastian has no real life apart from the people who compose him, and to pay attention to the conceptions other people have of him is, in the end, to pay attention to Sebastian himself. In short, Nabokov seems to turn the fragmentary nature of perception into the very source of self-knowledge.

The source of the real life of Sebastian is his work, yet this work is a mask he wears over his own face. Anyone who tries to reconstruct Sebastian's real life, therefore, is doomed from the beginning to reconstruct the life of his mask, his imaginative life. Both men who attempt to accomplish this biographical reconstruction wear masks; what they write down will also be the life of a veil over reality, rather than reality itself. What the reader perceives, by the end of Nabokov's novel, is a composition that is at least twice removed from the facts; there is Sebastian, a masked Sebastian, and Sebastian's biographer with a mask on.

Readers are obliged to interpret Nabokov's novel on various levels simultaneously. At no time can they be certain what dimension has the familiar and comfortable solidarity of what is considered factual reality. The game consists chiefly in keeping alert enough to follow the shifting perceptions that characterize this kind of fiction; the danger is believing that one has found the "reality" promised by the narrator.

Like Sebastian himself, Nabokov uses the novel as a game, as a springboard to higher regions of intellectual activity. His purpose is to jar readers out of habitual modes of response to the world and lead them back into it with a fresh vision. Nabokov's primary concern is the reality of the imagination—that is, that reality cannot be conceived apart from the imagination. The act of perception involves both perceiver and perceived, and the knowledge gained from perception is a combination of the "facts"—the thing perceived—and the imagination, the frame of the mind of the perceiver. It is impossible to know anything as it is in itself; what people know is the idea of the thing itself. In this respect, everything wears a mask, and the very act of knowing is the act of being deceived. The narrator of Nabokov's novel says that he is Sebastian Knight, and yet this is to admit that he is a man whom he cannot know, except as he projects imaginative ideas of the individual. Self-knowledge is a curse when it is viewed in this way, and it is a kind of death. Only illusion—what one creates out of one's own imagination—seems to be real. *The Real Life of Sebastian Knight*, ends with the sentence "I am Sebastian, or Sebastian is I, or perhaps we both are someone whom neither of us knows."

Genevieve Slomski

Further Reading

Alexandrov, Vladimir E. *Nabokov's Otherworld*. Princeton, N.J.: Princeton University Press, 1991. Dismantles the widespread critical view that Nabokov is first and foremost a metaliterary writer. Suggests, instead, that an aesthetic rooted in his intuition of a transcendent realm is the basis of his art.

Boyd, Brian. *Vladimir Nabokov: The Russian Years* and *Vladimir Nabokov: The American Years*. 2 vols. Princeton, N.J.: Princeton University Press, 1990-1991. An essential biography, not only for its examination of Nabokov's life but also for its discussion of his life's relation to his art.

Connolly, Julian W. *The Cambridge Companion to Nabokov*. New York: Cambridge University Press, 2005. Collection of essays offering a concise introduction to Nabokov's life and writings. Some essays discuss Nabokov as a storyteller, a Russian writer, a modernist, and a poet, while others analyze the major Russian novels and Nabokov's transition to writing in English.

De la Durantaye, Leland. *Style Is Matter: The Moral Art of Vladimir Nabokov*. Ithaca, N.Y.: Cornell University Press, 2007. De la Durantaye focuses on *Lolita*, but also looks at some of Nabokov's other works, such as *The Real Life of Sebastian Knight*, to discuss the ethics of art in Nabokov's fiction. He maintains that although some readers find Nabokov to be cruel, his works contain a moral message—albeit one that is skillfully hidden in his texts.

Grayson, Jane, Arnold B. McMillin, and Priscilla Meyer, eds. *Nabokov's World: The Shape of Nabokov's World*. New York: Palgrave Macmillan, 2002.

_____. *Nabokov's World: Reading Nabokov*. New York: Palgrave Macmillan, 2002. A two-volume collection of essays written by an international group of Nabokov scholars. Includes discussions of intertextuality in Nabokov's works, the literary reception of his writings, and analyses of individual books. The second volume includes Priscilla Meyer's essay on *The Real Life of Sebastian Knight*.

Hyde, G. M. *Vladimir Nabokov: America's Russian Novelist*. Atlantic Highlands, N.J.: Humanities Press, 1977. Discusses Nabokov's novels as parodies of realism and parodies of themselves. Argues that the novels reveal the author's continuity with classic Russian literature, while also reevaluating that tradition.

Maddox, Lucy. *Nabokov's Novels in English*. Athens: University of Georgia Press, 1983. A thorough investigation of narrative structure, characterization, and theme in Nabokov's novels.

Rampton, David. *Vladimir Nabokov*. New York: St. Martin's Press, 1993. An insightful analysis of Nabokov's fiction. Discusses formal innovation, as well as theme and characterization. Includes a bibliography of primary and secondary works.

Roth, Phyllis A., comp. *Critical Essays on Vladimir Nabokov*. Boston: G. K. Hall, 1984. An excellent collection of essays on the play of language in Nabokov's works. Discusses the relationship between Nabokov's life and art. Includes an annotated bibliography.

Wood, Michael. *The Magician's Doubts: Nabokov and the Risks of Fiction*. Princeton, N.J.: Princeton University Press, 1995. Wood's close reading of Nabokov's texts shows the power and beauty of Nabokov's language and the subtlety of his art and uncovers the ethical and moral foundation of his work. Chapter 2 focuses on *The Real Life of Sebastian Knight*.

The Real Thing

Author: Tom Stoppard (Tomas Straussler, 1937-   )
First produced: 1982; first published, 1982
Type of work: Drama
Type of plot: Comic realism
Time of plot: 1980's
Locale: London

Principal characters:
HENRY, a playwright
CHARLOTTE, an actor, married to Henry
ANNIE, an actor, a social activist, and Henry's lover
MAX, an actor, married to Annie
BILLY, an actor
DEBBIE, Henry and Charlotte's daughter
BRODIE, a former soldier and a fledgling writer

The Story:

In a scene from Henry's play, Max is building a house of cards as Charlotte enters the room, just returning from a trip abroad. Max has been drinking, and soon he confronts Charlotte with her passport, which he had found while searching her room. He asks her about her lovers, but she is unwilling to talk about it. She leaves, but without her bag, in which Max finds a souvenir.

Charlotte is an actor married to Henry, a playwright. Max is an actor married to Annie, also an actor, who is involved in politics. Henry tells Charlotte that Max is on his way to the house, displeasing Charlotte.

Max arrives, and Henry says that Charlotte is out, though she arrives when Henry goes to get a bottle. Henry asks them about the performance the night before, and Charlotte starts poking fun at Henry and the play. Annie arrives with some groceries, and Henry discusses his picks for the radio program *Desert Island Discs*, which includes more pop standards than classical pieces.

Max and Charlotte go to the kitchen to prepare some vegetables and dip. Henry tells Annie that he loves her while she asks him to touch her. Max bursts in, having cut his finger, and interrupts the lovers. Henry gives him his handkerchief for the bleeding. After Max leaves the room, Henry and Annie debate telling their spouses about their affair. When Charlotte and Max return, they lace the conversation with hidden, intimate exchanges. Max returns Henry's handkerchief.

Annie is on her way to a rally to free Brodie, a former soldier who had been imprisoned for burning a wreath on the Tomb of the Unknown Soldier. Henry makes a joke about Brodie, angering Max. As Max and Charlotte leave the room, Annie says she will skip the rally so that she and Henry can meet.

Annie enters her house to find Max listening to Henry's broadcast. He confronts her with Henry's bloodied handkerchief, which he had found in their car. She admits her infidelity, and Max embraces her and weeps.

Annie is at Henry's house, telling him that she is unable to feel guilty for cheating on Max, who is frantically trying to contact her. Henry helps Annie memorize her lines for a production of August Strindberg's *Miss Julie*. Annie is planning on visiting Brodie, but becomes angry that Henry is not more jealous of her trips to see him. Henry assures her that he loves her, then leaves to pick up his seventeen-year-old daughter, Debbie.

Two years have elapsed. Henry and Annie are now married. She puts on an opera record that bores Henry. She asks him to read part of a play to her, a play that had been written by Brodie. Annie thinks the work would do well on television. She wants Henry to edit it, but he thinks it is badly written.

Annie accuses Henry of being an elitist. To illustrate a point about good writing, Henry uses a cricket bat. Cricket bats work so well because they are made to hit the ball far. Bad scripts are like pieces of wood trying to be cricket bats. To Henry, words have to be used properly. Annie says that she wants to appear in Brodie's play, then Henry asks her if she is in love with Brodie; she leaves the room angrily.

Annie is on a train to Glasgow, where she will be appearing in a production of John Ford's *'Tis Pity She's a Whore*. She is approached by an actor named Billy, who is also going to be in the play and who has read a copy of Brodie's script. Billy tells Annie that he will act in Brodie's play if she will too.

Henry is visiting Charlotte and Debbie, who is about to leave on a road trip with a young man. Debbie is cold toward her father, calling him by his first name and having a frank discussion with him about losing her virginity. After Charlotte leaves to take a bath, Debbie insults Henry's last play, *House of Cards*. Debbie leaves when Charlotte reenters the room. Henry and Charlotte have a talk about their marriage, and Charlotte admits she had nine lovers while they were married. She says marriage is more like a bargain than a commitment. Henry prefers to be a romantic idiot who believes in loyalty and devotion.

Annie and Billy are onstage, starring in *'Tis Pity She's a Whore*. At the end of one scene, they kiss, and it is clear that Annie is falling for Billy. Annie leaves for home to find Henry waiting for her. He asks her about her travel plans, having just returned from Glasgow. She begs him not to question her, but he persists. She tries to convince him that he should not care about whether she had an affair because she does not worry about him. Henry wants things messy and complicated, he explains. She tells him that Billy rode with her on the train, even though he had to be in Glasgow. She says she wants to go back to Glasgow to see his play, and Henry says he is going with her, though he changes his mind.

Annie and Billy are performing a scene from Brodie's teleplay, which is set on a train. Billy says the wrong line, and the scene halts. Annie and Billy exchange some tense, whispered words.

Henry has become the ghostwriter for Brodie's teleplay. As Annie is leaving for the studio, Billy calls. After she hangs up, she gets into an argument with Henry about their relationship. Henry has tried to remain passive about things, but he loves her too much. Annie explains that she had fallen in love with Billy unwillingly.

Brodie, in Henry and Annie's living room, is watching his teleplay. He says that he likes the original version of the script better. Brodie explains that rising military costs got him out of prison, as there had not been enough money to keep him there. Brodie acts ungrateful toward Henry, and they argue about the script. Annie joins in and berates Brodie's attempts to impress her. She smashes a bowl of dip in his face, and Brodie leaves.

Henry answers the phone; it is Max on the line, telling Henry that he is getting married. Annie kisses Henry as he talks on the phone, then turns off the lights and goes to the bedroom.

Critical Evaluation:

The Real Thing represents a key part of Tom Stoppard's ongoing interest in the nature of performance and theatricality. With its scenes of plays within the framework of the larger play, Stoppard, born Tomas Straussler, plays with the expectation and the perception of reality by both the characters and the audience. The play is also notable for being able to use this experimentation with a fairly conventional plot line. Stoppard confounds expectations by presenting a domestic dramatic narrative with the kind of theatrical experimentation seen in some of his earlier work, such as *The Real Inspector Hound* (pr., pb. 1968; one act).

The Real Thing also remains one of Stoppard's most popular and accessible works, with little of the historical and literary references that mark some of his other plays, such as *The Invention of Love* (pr., pb. 1997) and *The Coast of Utopia* (pr., pb. 2002). The emotional and possibly autobiographical nature of the play, with the main character being a playwright, also has been a source of interest for critics.

The central question of the play is reflected in the play's title. In the postmodern world, what is, if anything, the real thing? Characters grapple with commitment, responsibility, and prevailing moral codes in an effort to navigate a world in which meaning is relative. One of the chief institutions under examination is marriage. Henry and Charlotte have broken their matrimonial vows, but little weight is given to the vows, beyond their personal responsibility to each other. Charlotte even remarks that marriage is more like a bargain than a promise. Annie's devotion to Max is rather thin, and she is able to get over their relationship quickly, despite Max's protestations. In a conversation with his daughter Debbie, Henry talks about the mystery of sex while Debbie is frank and realistic about it.

The play also explores public responsibility through Annie's efforts to secure Brodie's release from prison. The motives behind her campaign are constantly in question. Annie's ambiguity also mirrors her unstable relationships, with both Max and Henry suffering the consequences of her infidelity. At times, Annie seems to value her campaign for Brodie more than her relationships with people. At other times, she shirks her civic and social responsibilities in favor of her latest fling. Her wavering represents the problem of instability presented by a postmodern world. However, Stoppard does not pass judgment, but leaves it up to the audience to critique his characters' actions.

The role of the artist is also under scrutiny. Henry is continuously dealing with conflicting roles of public artist and private aficionado. He agonizes about whether his list for *Desert Island Discs* is too pedestrian and is reluctant to discuss the science-fiction script that he is writing. However, he also worries about how he will be perceived if he works on a script that he believes to be poor—in the case of Brodie's teleplay. He and Annie debate the role of the writer and the nature of the artistic standards that Henry values. Annie also has to juggle her political work with her own acting career and has difficulty when trying to merge the two.

Henry also finds further difficulties in living both an artistic and a personal life. Annie teases him at one point about his inability to write realistic romantic scenes. Henry is able to live romance, but not write it. He is able to create alternate realities within his plays but is unable to ground his personal life in real, genuine commitment. The breakdown of his marriage to Charlotte results partly from his neglecting to take the marriage contract seriously, as evidenced by his affair with Annie.

At its heart, *The Real Thing* is an examination of theatricality, illusion, and reality. Most of the characters are involved in the theater and, therefore, make their living by creating illusions. This bleeds into their real lives when they start deceiving each other. Just as it is challenging for the audience to recognize whether a given scene is real or not, the characters have to discover whether their emotions, commitments, and promises are genuine. Stoppard's manipulation of theatricality highlights the question of genuineness for the audience and the reader.

David Coley

Further Reading

Corballis, Richard. *Stoppard: The Mystery and the Clockwork*. New York: Methuen, 1984. Corballis includes a look at Stoppard's exploration of himself in *The Real Thing* in this comprehensive survey of Stoppard's plays, both major and minor. Includes an appendix concerning adaptations of the plays.

Gussow, Mel. *Conversations with Stoppard*. New York: Limelight Editions, 1995. Gussow presents a collection of interviews with the playwright, covering a period of twenty-three years. Stoppard discusses the writing of *The Real Thing*, including his decision to make the main character, Henry, a playwright.

Harty, John, ed. *Tom Stoppard: A Casebook*. New York: Garland, 1988. This book brings together essays on Stoppard's major works, including one of his screenplays, *Brazil*. It includes two essays on *The Real Thing*, focusing on its comic style and its exploration of art and experience.

Hunter, Jim. *About Stoppard: The Playwright and the Work*. London: Faber & Faber, 2005. Presents a series of later interviews with Stoppard and with those who have staged his work. With a good introduction, this book places Stoppard's plays in context. An indispensable jargon-free guide.

Jenkins, Anthony. *The Theatre of Tom Stoppard*. 2d ed. New York: Cambridge University Press, 1990. Jenkins discusses each of Stoppard's plays through 1986, including a section on *The Real Thing*. Analyzes Stoppard's use of shifting realities and the emotional nature of the play, which contrasts with much of Stoppard's other work.

Rusinko, Susan. *Tom Stoppard*. Boston: Twayne, 1986. Rusinko looks at the whole of Stoppard's career, including his radio plays, television programs, and screenplays. She devotes a chapter to *The Real Thing*, which includes a discussion of Stoppard and dramatist-poet Harold Pinter.

Rebecca

Author: Daphne du Maurier (1907-1989)
First published: 1938
Type of work: Novel
Type of plot: Gothic
Time of plot: 1930's
Locale: England

Principal characters:
REBECCA DE WINTER, wife of Maxim de Winter
MAXIM DE WINTER, the owner of Manderley estate
MRS. DE WINTER, Maxim's new wife and the narrator
MRS. DANVERS, the housekeeper at Manderley
FRANK CRAWLEY, the estate manager of Manderley
JACK FAVELL, Rebecca's cousin
COLONEL JULYAN, a magistrate

The Story:

Manderley is gone. Since the fire had destroyed their home, Mr. and Mrs. de Winter have lived in a secluded hotel away from England. Occasionally, Mrs. de Winter recalls the circumstances that had brought Manderley and Maxim de Winter into her life.

A shy, sensitive orphan, Mrs. de Winter had been traveling about the Continent as companion to an overbearing American social climber, Mrs. Van Hopper. At Monte Carlo, Mrs. Van Hopper forced herself upon Maxim de Winter, owner of Manderley, one of the most famous estates in England. Before approaching him, Mrs. Van Hopper informed her companion that Mr. de Winter had been recovering from the shock of the tragic death of his wife, Rebecca, a few months previously.

During the following days, the young woman and Mr. de Winter become well acquainted; when Mrs. Van Hopper decides to return to America, Maxim de Winter unexpectedly proposes to her companion. Already deeply in love with him, the young woman accepts, and they are married shortly afterward.

After a long honeymoon in Italy and southern France, Mr. and Mrs. de Winter return to Manderley. Mrs. de Winter is extremely nervous, fearing that she will not fit into the life of a great estate like Manderley. The entire staff gathers to meet the new mistress. Mrs. Danvers, the housekeeper, who had been devoted to her former mistress, immediately begins to show her resentment toward the new Mrs. de Winter.

Gradually, Mrs. de Winter pieces together the story of Rebecca. She learns that Rebecca had been a beautiful, vivacious woman and a charming host. As Mrs. de Winter becomes acquainted with the relatives and friends of her husband, she becomes convinced that they find her lacking in those qualities that had made Rebecca so attractive and gracious. One day, she goes secretly to the closed rooms Rebecca had occupied. Everything is as Rebecca had left it before her fatal sail in her boat. Mrs. Danvers suddenly appears and forces her to view Rebecca's lovely clothes and other personal possessions.

When the bishop's wife suggests that the traditional Manderley dress ball be revived, Mr. de Winter gives his consent. Mrs. de Winter announces her intention of surprising them all with her costume. At Mrs. Danvers's suggestion, she plans to dress as an ancestor whose portrait hangs in the hall at Manderley; but as Mrs. de Winter descends the stairs that night, a silence falls over the guests, and her husband turns angrily away without speaking. Realizing that something is wrong, Mrs. de Winter returns to her room. Beatrice, Mr. de Winter's sister, goes to her immediately and explains that Rebecca had worn the identical costume to her last fancy dress ball. Again, Mrs. Danvers has humiliated her new mistress. Although Mrs. de Winter reappears at the ball in a simple dress, her husband does not speak to her all evening. Her belief that he has never ceased to love Rebecca becomes firmly established in her mind.

The next day, a steamer runs aground in the bay near Manderley. A diver is sent down to inspect the damaged steamer and discovers Rebecca's boat and in its cabin the remains of a human body. Mr. de Winter had previously identified the body of a woman found in the river as that of Rebecca.

Unable to keep silent any longer, Mr. de Winter tells his wife the whole story of Rebecca and her death. The world had believed their marriage a happy one, but Rebecca was an immoral woman, incapable of love. To avoid the scandal of a divorce, they make a bargain: Rebecca is to be outwardly the fitting mistress of Manderley, but she would be allowed to go to London periodically to visit her dissolute friends. All goes well until she begins to be careless, inviting her friends to Manderley and receiving them in the boathouse. Then she begins to plague Frank Crawley, the estate manager of Manderley, and Giles, Mr. de Winter's brother-in-law. After Frank and others had seen Rebecca's cousin, Jack Favell, at the boathouse with her, gossip ensued. One evening, Mr. de Winter follows her to the boathouse to tell her that their marriage is at an end. Rebecca taunts him; she suggests how difficult it would be to prove his case against her, and asserts that should she have a child it would bear his name and inherit Manderley. She assures him with a smile that she would be the perfect mother as she had been the perfect wife. She is still smiling when he shoots her. Then he puts her in the boat and sails out on the river. There he opens the seacocks, drills holes with a pike, and, leaving the boat to sink, rows back in the dinghy.

Mrs. de Winter is horrified, but at the same time, she feels a happiness she had not known before. Her husband loves her; he had never loved Rebecca. With that discovery, her personality changes. She assures her husband that she will guard his secret. A coroner's inquest is held, for the body in the boat is that of Rebecca. At the inquest, it is established that a storm could not have sunk the boat; evidence of a bolted door, the holes, and the open seacocks point to the verdict of suicide, determined by the coroner's jury.

Later that night, after the jury's verdict, a drunk Jack Favell appears at Manderley. Wildly expressing his love for Rebecca and revealing their intimate life, he tries to blackmail Mr. de Winter by threatening to prove that de Winter killed his wife. Mr. de Winter calls the magistrate, Colonel Julyan, to hear his case. Favell's theory is that Rebecca had asked her husband to free her so that she could marry Jack, and that de Winter, infuriated, had killed her.

From Rebecca's engagement book, it is learned that she had visited a Dr. Baker in London on the last day of her life. Colonel Julyan and Mr. and Mrs. de Winter, with Favell following in his car, drive to London to see Baker. On checking his records, the doctor finds that he had examined a Mrs. Danvers on the day in question. They realize that Rebecca had assumed the housekeeper's name. Baker explains that he had diagnosed Rebecca's ailment as cancer in an advanced stage. Colonel Julyan suggests that the matter be closed since the motive for suicide had been established.

Driving back to Manderley after leaving Colonel Julyan at his sister's home, Mr. de Winter tells his wife that he believes that Colonel Julyan had guessed the truth. He also realizes that Rebecca had intimated that she was pregnant because she had been sure that her husband would kill her; her last evil deed would be to ruin him and Manderley. Mr. de Winter telephones Frank from the inn where they had stopped for dinner, and the estate manager reports that Mrs. Danvers has disappeared. His news seems to upset Mr. de Winter. At two o'clock in the morning, they approach Manderley. Mrs. de Winter has been sleeping. Awaking, she thinks by the blaze of light that it is dawn. A moment later, she realizes that she is looking at Manderley, going up in flames.

Critical Evaluation:

For nearly four decades, Daphne du Maurier excited and terrified readers with some of the best suspense novels of the twentieth century. She is one of a small group of writers who, by their artistic ingenuity, has insight into character and situation, has technical virtuosity, and has the skill to elevate popular formula fiction into serious literature. There is no better example of her skill and power than her early suspense masterpiece, *Rebecca*.

The basic structure of *Rebecca* is what may be called the modern gothic romance, but du Maurier utilizes and transforms the rigid formula of this popular genre to create a very original and personal fiction. The unnamed narrator, at least for the first two-thirds of the novel, is the typical heroine of a gothic romance. Although her character is not deep, her qualities and desires are carefully chosen to provoke maximum interest and sympathy. Two narrative questions animate the rather leisurely early chapters of the novel: Can the heroine, an orphan with little training or worldly experience, adjust to the unfamiliar, demanding social role as mistress of Manderley? Can she win and keep the love of her passionately desired, but enigmatic, even sinister husband, Maxim de Winter? These two elements—Manderley, the isolated, beautiful, but ultimately threatening setting, and de Winter, the charming, handsome, rich, but moody and mysterious male love object—are essential in the genre.

After the de Winters set up residence at Manderley, these two questions lead to the dominating, almost spectral presence of Maxim's first wife, Rebecca. Her presence is made more threatening by Mrs. Danvers, the efficient, sinister, intimidating housekeeper, who still serves her original mistress, and by Jack Favell, Rebecca's crudely handsome, lascivious cousin. They, along with the gradual revelation that Rebecca's death was not accidental, give the novel that sense of growing menace that is so important to the gothic romance.

Approximately two-thirds of the way through the book,

however, du Maurier adds a special twist to the story that takes it out of the gothic romance category and establishes the book as a unique suspense thriller. Maxim finally breaks down and confesses to the heroine that Rebecca was "vicious, damnable, rotten through and through," and that he murdered her when she tormented him about a "son and heir" that was not his. Thereafter, the focus shifts from the heroine's mysterious danger to her husband's legal fate. Instead of fearing for the physical safety of the narrator, the reader is placed in the ironic position of rooting for the criminal to escape detection and punishment. Furthermore, the "villains"—Mrs. Danvers and Favell—become petty, pitiable creatures rather than seriously dangerous conspirators.

Importantly, the heroine is freed by this knowledge from Rebecca's onerous legacy. Knowing that Maxim loves and needs her, and faced with a threat that is real and specific rather than undefined and pervasive, she can deal with her situation in a direct, forceful way as an emotionally whole, self-confident woman. The heroine thus grows from a pretty household decoration to the mistress of Manderley, from a girl to a woman, and from a child bride to a mature wife. It is, finally, du Maurier's skill and sensitivity in describing her heroine's maturity in a manner that is psychologically believable and emotionally satisfying that qualifies *Rebecca* as a unique and serious work of art.

Further Reading

Auerbach, Nina. *Daphne du Maurier, Haunted Heiress*. Philadelphia: University of Pennsylvania Press, 1999. Auerbach discusses her literary passion for du Maurier and demonstrates how her work has been inaccurately categorized as romance fiction. The book includes a chapter on du Maurier's family, describing how her fiction was written in response to her male heritage.

Bakerman, Jane S., ed. *And Then There Were Nine . . . More Women of Mystery*. Bowling Green, Ohio: Bowling Green State University Popular Press, 1985. A collection of essays, including a chapter on du Maurier. Bakerman argues that in the writer's six "romantic suspense novels," including *Rebecca*, can be seen not only new uses of the gothic "formula" but also reflections of other literary traditions. Sees du Maurier as preeminent in her genre.

Beauman, Sally. "Rereading Rebecca." *The New Yorker*, November 8, 1993. Points out that the publication in 1993 of Margaret Forster's biography of du Maurier and of Susan Hill's *Mrs. de Winter*, a sequel to *Rebecca*, indicate the lasting importance of *Rebecca* in literary history. Beauman voices her surprise that feminist critics have not turned their attention to a work in which the narrator so clearly equates love with submission. A balanced and perceptive analysis.

Du Maurier, Daphne. *The Rebecca Notebook, and Other Memories.* Garden City, N.Y.: Doubleday, 1980. Examines the birth and adolescence of a novel. Contains all textual notes and personal commentary by the author. A comparison of this source and the final text is fascinating. Includes family anecdotes.

Forster, Margaret. *Daphne du Maurier: The Secret Life of the Renowned Storyteller.* New York: Doubleday, 1993. The first authorized biography of du Maurier. Using newly available source materials, Forster reveals du Maurier's lifelong ambivalence as to her sexual identity. She concludes that the novels permitted du Maurier to be psychologically, as well as financially, independent. Although it contains little critical analysis of the works, the volume is a useful addition to du Maurier scholarship.

Horner, Avril, and Sue Zlosnik. *Daphne du Maurier: Writing, Identity, and the Gothic Imagination.* New York: St. Martin's Press, 1998. An evaluation of du Maurier's fiction from historical, cultural, geographic, and female gothic literary perspectives. Chapter 4 is devoted to an analysis of *Rebecca*.

Kelly, Richard. *Daphne du Maurier.* Boston: Twayne, 1987. Discusses the notebook for *Rebecca*, as well as subsequent film and television versions of the novel. Includes commentary from periodicals and a list of all works in chronological order.

Shallcross, Martyn. *The Private World of Daphne du Maurier.* New York: St. Martin's Press, 1992. An insightful, sympathetic overview of the author by a close family friend. Includes many pictures and a chronological bibliography of the du Maurier canon.

Taylor, Helen, ed. *The Daphne du Maurier Companion.* London: Virago, 2007. Reprints introductions to du Maurier's novels and interviews with members of her family. Also includes newly commissioned essays on her works. Many of the essays discuss *Rebecca*.

The Recruiting Officer

Author: George Farquhar (1677/1678-1707)
First produced: 1706; first published, 1706
Type of work: Drama
Type of plot: Comedy
Time of plot: Early eighteenth century
Locale: Shrewsbury, England

Principal characters:
CAPTAIN PLUME, the recruiting officer, a gay blade
SYLVIA BALANCE, Captain Plume's fiancé
MR. WORTHY, Captain Plume's friend
MELINDA, Mr. Worthy's fiancé and cousin of Sylvia Balance
JUSTICE BALANCE, Sylvia's father
ROSE, the pretty young daughter of a farmer
SERGEANT KITE, Captain Plume's aide

The Story:

Captain Plume, commander of a company of grenadiers, and his aide, Sergeant Kite, arrive in Shrewsbury to enlist a number of recruits for Captain Plume's command. They have traveled to Shrewsbury because of success in gaining recruits in that city some months before and because of Captain Plume's amorous successes at the same time. Upon their arrival the pair are greeted with the news that a young woman who has just given birth has named Captain Plume as the baby's father. At the captain's request, Sergeant Kite marries the woman and goes on record as the father of the child. This is not the first time he has done as much for the captain; he has accumulated a list of six wives in the same manner.

Captain Plume also finds his good friend Mr. Worthy at Shrewsbury. Worthy had been a happy-go-lucky chap, much like Captain Plume, until his fiancé inherited a fortune. The young woman, Melinda, has taken on airs since becoming rich, and she has proceeded to make life miserable for Worthy. His latest grievance is that another officer on recruiting duty, one Captain Brazen, has apparently become a successful rival for Melinda's hand and fortune. Captain Plume asks Worthy about Melinda's cousin Sylvia Balance, whom the captain loves but cannot marry because his life is too uncertain and he has too little money. Worthy tells Captain Plume that Sylvia Balance still thinks very well of him.

While Worthy and Captain Plume are talking, Melinda

and Sylvia are having a conversation of their own, in which Sylvia tells her cousin that she is determined that the captain should not leave Shrewsbury alone. The two women quarrel, and after Sylvia's departure Melinda writes a letter to Sylvia's father in which she tells him that Captain Plume intends to dishonor Sylvia. That evening Captain Plume has dinner with Sylvia and her father, Justice Balance, who considers the captain a fine match for his daughter. During the evening, news comes from Germany by mail that Justice Balance's son and heir has died. Immediately Justice Balance revises his attitude toward Captain Plume, for he does not like to think of the captain as his daughter's husband if Sylvia is to inherit all of his fortune. Calling Sylvia into private conference, he tells her of the change in his attitude. Although the young woman is very much in love with the captain, she promises that she will not marry without her father's consent. Captain Plume leaves the house without learning what has happened, and a short time after his departure, Melinda's spiteful letter to Sylvia's father arrives. After reading the letter, Justice Balance, concerned with getting Sylvia away from the captain, immediately sends her by coach to one of his country estates.

When Worthy and Captain Plume learn of Sylvia's departure, they interpret the action erroneously: They think that she believes herself too good for the captain now that she is to inherit a fortune of two thousand pounds a year. The captain, claiming that he can get along fine without her, proceeds to go about his business of recruiting. While doing so, he meets Rose, the pretty young daughter of a farmer. Rose and he immediately fancy each other, and the captain goes so far as to give his half-promise that he will make the young woman his wife. In return, she helps him to add almost a dozen more recruits to his company, including her own brother and her former sweetheart.

One day Sylvia, disguised in some of her brother's clothes, returns to Shrewsbury, where she meets the two recruiting officers, Captain Plume and Captain Brazen, in the company of Melinda. When she tells them that she is Mr. Willful, a young man of good family who wishes to enlist, they both bid for the new recruit; Mr. Willful finally agrees to join Captain Plume's company. The captain is so pleased with young Mr. Willful that he proffers his friendship, even though the recruit is to be an enlisted man in the company.

Saying that he will be censured for entering the army voluntarily, the recruit asks Captain Plume to have him impressed into service by the provisions of the acts of Parliament. The captain agrees to do so. To help her deception, and to test the direction of Captain Plume's affections, Sylvia in her disguise also pretends to be in love with Rose.

Worthy's fiancé, meanwhile, goes to see a fortune-teller—actually Sergeant Kite in disguise. The fortune-teller tells Melinda that she will die unmarried if she lets a man who is to call on her at ten o'clock the following morning leave the country. Kite has also managed to secure a copy of her handwriting, which he shows her in an attempt to make her think the devil is his helper. Melinda is so impressed that she promises herself that she will follow the fortune-teller's advice.

Justice Balance decides that the best way to keep his daughter's honor and fortune from falling into the hands of Captain Plume is to provide the officer with the soldiers he needs, drafting them according to the provision made by Parliament. In order to do so, the justice opens his court and has the bailiff bring in a number of men who are eligible for the draft. Among the men is Sylvia in her disguise as Mr. Willful. Mr. Willful has been accused of having taken Rose as a common-law wife. In the courtroom Mr. Willful behaves impudently, and the justice decides to punish the brash young man by sending him off as a private in Captain Plume's company. Thus Sylvia tricks her father into sending her away with the captain. In fact, the justice orders Captain Plume not to discharge Mr. Willful for any reason.

After the hearing, Justice Balance goes to his home, where he learns that his daughter, dressed in her deceased brother's clothes, has disappeared from his country estate. The justice immediately realizes that he has been tricked, that the Mr. Willful whom he has sent off with Captain Plume is really Sylvia. He also thinks that Captain Plume has been a party to the deception. When the captain calls at the justice's home a short time later, however, it is soon apparent that he knew nothing of the scheme, for he agrees to discharge the new soldier at Justice Balance's request.

Mr. Willful is called in and unmasked as Sylvia. Then the justice, realizing how much his daughter loves the captain, gives them permission to marry. Immediately thereafter, Worthy and Melinda arrive to say that they have reached an agreement and are to be married shortly. Melinda also apologizes for the spiteful letter she sent to Justice Balance. Captain Plume, pleased at the prospect of the handsome fortune coming to him with his wife, announces that he is retiring from the army. He turns over all the recruits he has enlisted to Captain Brazen, who has been unsuccessful in finding any men for his company.

Critical Evaluation:

The Recruiting Officer is classified as a Restoration comedy, but that is something of a misnomer for several reasons. Restoration literature is usually understood to be British literature written between 1660 (the time of Charles II's ascent to the British throne, which had been vacant since the execution of his father, Charles I, in 1649) and 1700. It is convenient to classify works written in the last forty years of the seventeenth century with the word "Restoration," but additionally there is something distinctly different about much of the work of that period, particularly in drama. The recognizable characteristics of Restoration literature tend to slip over into the literature of the early eighteenth century. George Farquhar wrote *The Recruiting Officer* in 1705. He had, however, written plays as early as 1698, so there is some justification in calling him a Restoration playwright.

The play is best understood in comparison with more perfectly exemplary Restoration comedy. A Restoration comedy has a happy ending, usually one in which young men and women come together in matrimony or sincere pledges of marriage. It begins with males and females meeting, circling warily, engaging in the pleasures and pains of courtship (often harassed by concerned parents or social conventions), falling into short-lived quarrels, and finally coming together in mutual love. The Restoration comedy is, in short, something like life.

Restoration comedy also has its own conventions. These conventions arose from the expectations of the Restoration audience, which included the court of Charles II, who had lived in France and developed a taste for the sophisticated, risqué comedies of that country. He and his courtiers were the first patrons, financial supporters, and audience for the revived theater. They liked characters dressed as they were dressed, living in London, and living idealized, happy, upper-class lives. Male actors and, in a great development in English theater, female actors were expected to talk much in the manner of the court and with smart-set arrogance and high wit. Restoration audiences not only wanted the best-looking man to win the prettiest woman but also expected him to be the cleverest man on the stage, since intelligence and wittiness were the most admired qualities in the high society of the time. The contest between the leading man and contenders for that role was often played out in terms of intelligence. Intelligence, in turn, was often measured by characters' ability to deceive others and to use their sophistication to achieve their social goals, such as marriage and other moneymaking connections. Brazen, for instance, is a man who thinks he is witty, but he is really a dupe for both Plume and Worthy.

The Recruiting Officer is a second-stage comedy in the sense that the couples (often two couples work toward matrimony) have already gone through some initial phases of their relationships before the play begins. They are now in diffi-culty but still in love, and they must work their way through misunderstandings to achieve resolution. Plume is the smartest man on the stage. Worthy is also intelligent, and both of them are witty. The leading ladies in Restoration comedies are often quite as witty as their suitors and not reluctant to go after their men.

Restoration comic conventions run throughout the play. Sylvia's use of disguise is a common feature of Restoration comedy, for example. It is also an excuse to show off her figure. Fashion of the time allowed women to display their bosoms, but their voluminous dresses hid the rest of their bodies. Her disguise, therefore, was a bit risqué for the play's times. The play's mockery of old men is also a commonplace of Restoration comedy, and country folk in such plays are always fools. The play's placement in a province is uncommon, as London is the usual locale for these dramas.

This play, however, differs tonally from much Restoration comedy. The wit is brilliant, but it is less cruel than is typical in Restoration plays, and the innocent ignorance of country folk is not jeered at quite as rudely as might be considered usual. Advantage is taken of them, and the local magistrates turn a blind eye on the conduct of Plume and Kite, but the treatment seen in the play would not have seemed harsh to audiences aware of the difficulty of recruiting for the War of Spanish Succession, which had been going on for several years.

Plume, like most Restoration heroes (not to mention Charles II), has a questionable past, but he takes some care of his former conquests. He begins with an attempt to seduce Sylvia, but he learns to love her. Genuine feeling throughout the play culminates in engagements. Justice Balance, who approves of Plume initially, turns against him when Sylvia becomes his sole heir, but he is not so much punished for this as he is brought to his senses. A Restoration play might have given him, at least, a physical beating. All in all, the play is gentler than a typical Restoration comedy and less dismissive of flawed characters. In this way, it connects with the plays of the early eighteenth century, which were on their way to the sentimentality of late eighteenth century drama.

Some characters in the play are outside the romantic structure. Brazen is a marvelous grotesque. He is an example of sheer stupidity as a comic force. Sergeant Kite is a comic whirlwind. His fortune-teller is one of the finest pieces in the comic repertoire, and his comments on the way of the world provide an example of how these plays, seemingly trivial, are full of wisdom about human folly.

"Critical Evaluation" by Charles Pullen

Further Reading

Bull, John. *Vanbrugh and Farquhar.* New York: St. Martin's Press, 1998. Examines the work of Farquhar and Sir John Vanbrugh, whose plays appeared at the end of the period of post-Restoration comedy. Places Farquhar's plays within the context of his times and the history of theatrical production. Chapter 7 focuses on *The Recruiting Officer* and *The Beaux' Stratagem* (pr., pb. 1707).

Burns, Edward. *Restoration Comedy: Crises of Desire and Identity.* London: Macmillan, 1987. General study of Restoration comedy places emphasis on the use of disguise in the plays of the period.

Cunningham, John E. *Restoration Drama.* London: Evans Brothers, 1966. Discusses Farquhar in conjunction with the other masters of Restoration comedy.

Heard, Elisabeth J. *Experimentation on the English Stage, 1695-1708: The Career of George Farquhar.* Brookfield, Vt.: Pickering & Chatto, 2008. Examines how Farquhar and his contemporaries experimented with characters, plot lines, and dialogue to create a new type of English comedy. Chapter 4 discusses the success of these experiments in *The Recruiting Officer* and *The Beaux' Stratagem.*

Miner, Earl, ed. *Restoration Dramatists: A Collection of Critical Essays.* Englewood Cliffs, N.J.: Prentice-Hall, 1966. Excellent collection presents several different views of the period that shed light on how Farquhar's work is different from that of earlier Restoration writers.

Palmer, John. *The Comedy of Manners.* New York: Russell & Russell, 1962. Considers Restoration comic writers as part of the longer tradition of the comedy of manners. Includes a chapter on Farquhar.

Schneider, Ben Ross. *The Ethos of Restoration Comedy.* Champaign: University of Illinois Press, 1971. Places in historical perspective the issue of the morality of Restoration comedies, which has been a source of discussion since the 1690's.

The Rector of Justin

Author: Louis Auchincloss (1917-2010)
First published: 1964
Type of work: Novel
Type of plot: Narrative and novel of manners
Time of plot: 1879-1947
Locale: Massachusetts and New York City

Principal characters:
BRIAN ASPINWALL, an English instructor at the Justin Martyr school
THE REVEREND FRANCIS PRESCOTT, the school founder and rector
HARRIET WINSLOW, his wife
HORACE HAVISTOCK, his boyhood friend
DAVID GRISCAM, a lawyer and school board member
HARRIET KIDDER,
CORDELIA TURNBULL, and
EVELYN HOMANS, the Prescott daughters
CHARLEY STRONG, Cordelia's lover
JULES GRISCAM, David's son

The Story:

Brian Aspinwall, a graduate of Columbia and Oxford (Christ Church), accepts a position in 1939 to teach English at Justin Martyr, a residential school for boys located in rural Massachusetts. The school is still under the tutelage of its founder and headmaster, the Reverend Francis Prescott, who is, at the age of eighty, still a force to be reckoned with. Aspinwall is torn between returning to England to be part of the war raging in Europe and staying in the United States to study for the clergy, a calling he expresses some doubts about.

Although Aspinwall starts off rocky at Justin Martyr by not adequately disciplining his charges, the Reverend Prescott helps him out by demonstrating the proper way to dispense demerits and otherwise intimidate the boys in his house. He soon becomes a favorite of Mrs. Prescott—Harriet Winslow—the head's aristocratic wife, who is dying; she requests that Aspinwall read to her Henry James, an author not appreciated by her husband. Harriet, a grandniece of Ralph Waldo Emerson, the New England Transcendental philosopher, apparently was of great help to her husband during the school's early years. After her death, Aspinwall is made assistant to the headmaster to lessen his administrative duties as he enters the final year of his headmastership. It is in this capacity that Aspinwall decides to construct a biographical portrait of Prescott by collecting impressions of him from those who have known him through the years.

The first set of impressions comes from Horace Havistock's manuscript for his unfinished work "The Art of Friendship," and it provides the earliest memories of Prescott, who was Havistock's boyhood friend. Havistock and Prescott met at the residential boy's school St. Andrews in Dublin, New Hampshire, in 1876, and Prescott provided the less athletic and more effete Havistock with not only friendship but also protection from the bullying of the other boys. Later, Prescott founded his own school and based it on his experiences at St. Andrews, including his interactions with its headmaster, Dr. Howell. Prescott's Justin Martyr school became totally unlike St. Andrews, a place he abhorred.

After attending Balliol College, Oxford, Prescott goes to work for the Vanderbilt family's New York Central railroad in New York City. He joins the city's social world and falls in love with a rich young woman, Eliza Dean, daughter of a senator from the West. Fearing that she would not be the best partner for someone starting up a new school, Havistock persuades Eliza to give him up. After breaking off their engagement, Prescott leaves the business world and goes to Harvard Divinity School in a preparatory move toward founding a school for boys based on Christian principles. Later, Havistock is responsible for encouraging Prescott in his attachment to Harriet Winslow, a more suitable helpmeet for a schoolmaster.

Aspinwall's second source is the notes recorded by David Griscam, a wealthy New York lawyer, graduate of Justin Martyr, and now chair of the school's board of trustees. Griscam also had planned a biography of Prescott. Griscam's knowledge of Prescott spans the years from when he was a student and later when, as a member of the board of trustees, he persuaded his old friend to enlarge the modest school he had founded, thus doubling its size and considerably expanding the school's physical plant. The expansion created a loss of intimacy the smaller school provided, but it also enlarged the scope of Prescott's fame.

Aspinwall also receives information from Prescott's three daughters, Harriet Kidder, the eldest; Cordelia Turnbull, the youngest; and Evelyn Homans, the middle child. They provide an insider view of the great man, as Prescott was often called. Cordelia's perspective is perhaps the most revealing because her memories include a brief interlude with another

pupil, the disillusioned World War I veteran Charley Strong, whose religious life Prescott had saved while he visited him and Cordelia in Paris after the war, and just before Charley died of his wounds. Prescott even let Cordelia read the single chapter of Strong's memoirs, the rest of which he had destroyed. These various biographical sources conclude with the memoir of Jules Griscam, David's son, who had been thrown out of Justin, had failed at Harvard, and finally died an alcoholic suicide in the south of France. His expulsion and his subsequent life were both an affront to everything his father and Prescott stood for.

Aspinwall gathers multiple views of Prescott as minister, educator, and family man. The group portrait is supplemented by various journal entries from Aspinwall's diary, as he pieces together Prescott's past life and observes his present one, following him through the end of his active control of Justin Martyr to his death some years later. It is a composite portrait only loosely tied together by Aspinwall.

Critical Evaluation:

Louis Auchincloss made a career writing about the wealthy and privileged, often of New York City, who send their children to boarding schools like Justin Martyr before they move on to Ivy League universities and then to brokerage or law firms. Auchincloss was raised and educated similarly. His intimate acquaintance with the minute distinctions—social, political, and financial—that distinguish the upper classes gave him a privileged position in developing his fiction.

Although Auchincloss remained a practicing lawyer through most of his writing career, he managed to write dozens of novels, short stories, and nonfiction works, including a study of novelist Edith Wharton and a collection of her correspondence. The Wharton connection seems particularly appropriate given that Auchincloss's fiction, in many ways, continues Wharton's own portrayal of the rich of New York City.

Auchincloss denied any direct models for Justin Martyr and the Reverend Francis Prescott, though some speculation exists about the possible influence of his father's experience at the turn of the century at Groton School and this fictional portrait. Howland Auchincloss was a member of the 1904 class at Groton, a school founded in 1884 by the Reverend Endicott Peabody, a New England Puritan cleric who founded the school for boys and spent many years as its headmaster. Although it might only be tentative, *The Rector of Justin* does draw on the traditions of New England's segregated residential schools, to which the rich and connected have been sending their offspring since the mid-nineteenth century.

Auchincloss's novel is based on the cumulative impressions of several narrations interspersed with entries from English instructor Brian Aspinwall's diary. The effect is to create a portrait of Prescott, the rector of Justin, from multiple points of view, and to divide the narrative voice into several segments. It is a fictional technique Auchincloss used on more than one occasion, and it provided him with flexibility in fashioning his novels. It is like putting together a series of connected short stories. In this case the multiplicity provides a perfect literary device with which to develop the novel's portrait of the impact of Prescott on former pupils, family members, and professional acquaintances. In addition, Auchincloss's somewhat formal prose style also adds to the novel's authenticity: Its formality matches the character's turn-of-the-century sensibilities and their class positions.

The Rector of Justin is a social novel that captures the ethos of a period: It details the social, economic, and political specifics that make up the fabric of the characters' society. The life that Aspinwall puts together becomes a metaphor and reflects the broader times. Represented in the novel are the shifting values and cultural attitudes that mark the transition of the United States as a nation run by a traditional white, Anglo-Saxon, and Protestant establishment. This establishment had in one way or another been in control of the United states since its founding. Prescott's conventional values, shaped by a classical and elite education, represent the old family, old money Puritan establishment that becomes more and more challenged through the narrative. Money began to replace family, school, and class as determinants of value. A broader division of power also changed social and cultural values, as the country became more diverse; people of different ethnic and cultural backgrounds began to rise in prominence and power.

Near the end of the novel, when Prescott is becoming increasingly distanced from the school, one of the board members asks him about the origins of the school as a Protestant institution for boys of Anglo-Saxon descent. The board member comments on how the school is changing, expanding its admission policies by admitting boys of different ethnic and religious backgrounds. Prescott, at this point, no longer runs the school, but his opinions are still valued. By the end of the novel the religious beliefs and educational aspirations upon which the school was founded appear increasingly quaint, as the country has been battered by two world wars and a depression that have shifted ethical values.

The achievement of *The Rector of Justin* is the skill with which Auchincloss clothes these social changes in the pseudo-biography of Prescott, whose mind-set is largely trapped in the late nineteenth century. Aspinwall is the perfect narrator, as he, too, holds the same values but eventually undergoes some of the changes that Prescott avoids. However, there exists a sense of sadness in the declining importance of Prescott—his values and his patrician Puritan world. This nostalgia for a period gone by is echoed in much that Auchincloss wrote. In the end, the perspective of *The Rector of Justin* is as much nostalgic as it is critical in its survey of Prescott's life, career, and influence.

Charles L. P. Silet

Further Reading

Bryer, Jackson R. *Louis Auchincloss and His Critics: A Bibliographical Record.* Boston: G. K. Hall, 1977. This bibliographical record lists criticism about Auchincloss's writings and career. Dated but still helpful for its perspective.

Dahl, Christopher C. *Louis Auchincloss.* New York: Frederick Ungar, 1986. The first book-length study of Auchincloss's work. Examines his novels and stories and offers a balanced view of his accomplishments. Of special interest is the investigation of the boundaries between Auchincloss's fiction and fact, in which possible historical antecedents are noted for characters and plot.

Gelderman, Carol. *Louis Auchincloss: A Writer's Life.* 1993. Rev. ed. Columbia: University of South Carolina Press, 2007. A good biography that addresses the events and contradictions of Auchincloss's life and career. Includes photographs and an index.

Milne, Gordon. *The Sense of Society: A History of the American Novel of Manners.* Rutherford, N.J.: Fairleigh Dickinson University Press, 1977. This study provides an overview of the American novel of manners, with a chapter devoted to Auchincloss, in which his characterizations and prose style are examined.

Parsell, David B. *Louis Auchincloss.* Boston: Twayne, 1988. This book is another brief study of the author's life and writings.

Piket, Vincent. *Louis Auchincloss: The Growth of a Novelist.* New York: Macmillan, 1991. The study traces the development of Auchincloss as a writer.

The Red and the Black

Author: Stendhal (1783-1842)
First published: Le Rouge et le noir, 1830 (English
    translation, 1898)
Type of work: Novel
Type of plot: Psychological realism
Time of plot: Early nineteenth century
Locale: France

Principal characters:
JULIEN SOREL, an opportunist
MONSIEUR DE RÊNAL, the mayor of Verrières
MADAME DE RÊNAL, his wife
MATHILDE DE LA MOLE, Julien's mistress
FOUQUÉ, Julien's friend

The Story:

Julien Sorel is the son of a carpenter in the little town of Verrières, France. After Napoleon is defeated, Julien comes to believe that the church rather than the army is the way to power. Because of his assumed piety and his intelligence, Julien is appointed as tutor to the children of Monsieur de Rênal, the mayor of the village.

Madame de Rênal has done her duty all of her life. Although she is a good wife and a good mother, she has never been in love with her husband, who is coarse and hardly likely to inspire love in any woman. Madame de Rênal is immediately attracted to the pale young tutor and gradually falls in love with him. Julien, thinking it a duty he owes himself, makes love to her to gain power over her. He discovers after a time that he has actually fallen in love with Madame de Rênal.

Julien goes on a holiday to visit his friend, Fouqué, who tries to persuade Julien to go into the lumber business with him. Julien declines, for he enjoys his new life too much. His love affair with Madame de Rênal is, however, revealed to Monsieur de Rênal by an anonymous letter written by Monsieur Valenod, the local official in charge of the poorhouse. Valenod, who had become rich on graft, is jealous because Monsieur de Rênal had hired Julien as a tutor and because he himself had at one time made unsuccessful advances to Madame de Rênal.

Monsieur de Rênal agrees to send Julien to the seminary at Besançon, principally to keep him from becoming tutor at Monsieur Valenod's house. After Julien departs, Madame de Rênal is filled with remorse for her adultery and she becomes extremely religious.

Julien does not get on well at the seminary, for he finds it full of hypocrites. The students do not like him and fear his sharp intelligence. His only friend is the Abbé Pirard, a highly moral man. One day, Julien helps decorate the cathedral and by chance sees Madame de Rênal there. She faints, but he cannot help her because of his liturgical duties. The experience leaves him weak and shaken.

The Abbé Pirard loses his position at the seminary because he had supported the Marquis de La Mole, who is engaged in a lawsuit against Monsieur de Frilair, the vicar general of Besançon. When the Abbé Pirard leaves the seminary, the marquis obtains a living for him in Paris and hires Julien as his secretary.

Julien is thankful for his chance to leave the seminary. On his way to Paris, he calls secretly on Madame de Rênal. At first, conscious of her previous sin, she repulses his advances but then yields once again to his pleadings. Monsieur de Rênal becomes suspicious and decides to search his wife's room. Julien has to jump from the window to escape discovery, barely escaping with his life.

Finding Julien a good worker, the marquis entrusts him with many of the details of his business. Julien also is allowed to dine with the family and to mingle with the guests afterward. He finds the Marquise de La Mole to be extremely proud of her nobility. The daughter, Mathilde, seems to be of the same type, a reserved girl with beautiful eyes. The son, the Comte de La Mole, is an extremely polite and pleasant young man. Julien finds Parisian high society boring, however. No one is interested in discussing ideas.

Julien enjoys stealing volumes of Voltaire from the marquis' library and reading them in his room. He is astonished when he discovers that Mathilde is doing the same thing. Before long, they are spending much of their time together, although Julien is always conscious of his position as servant and sensitive to slights. Despite her pride, Mathilde falls in love with him because he is so different from the young men of her own class. After Julien spends two nights with her, Mathilde decides that it is degrading to be in love with a secretary. Her pride is an insult to Julien. Smarting, he plans to gain power over her and, consequently, over the household.

Meanwhile, the marquis entrusts Julien with a diplomatic mission on behalf of the nobility and clergy who want the monarchy reestablished. On this mission, Julien meets an old friend who advises him how to win Mathilde back, and upon his return he puts the plan into effect by beginning to pay court to a virtuous lady who is often a visitor in the de La Mole home. He begins a correspondence with her, all the while ignoring Mathilde, who thereupon realizes how much she loves him. She throws herself at his feet. Julien has won, but this time he does not let her gain the upper hand. As he continues to treat Mathilde coldly, her passion increases. In this way he maintains his power.

When Mathilde becomes pregnant, she is joyful, for she thinks Julien will now realize how much she cares for him. She had made the supreme sacrifice and would now have to marry Julien and give up her place in society. Julien, however, is not so happy about her pregnancy, for he fears the results of Mathilde telling her father.

At first, the marquis is furious. Eventually, he decides that the only way out of the difficulty is to make Julien rich and respectable. He gives Julien a fortune, a title, and a commission in the army. Overwhelmed with his new wealth and power, Julien scarcely gives a thought to Mathilde. Then the Marquis receives a letter from Madame de Rênal, whom Julien had suggested to the marquis for a character recommendation. Madame de Rênal is again filled with religious fervor; she reveals to the marquis the whole story of her relationship with Julien. The marquis thereupon retracts his permission to let Julien marry his daughter.

Julien's plans for glory and power are ruined. In a fit of rage, he rides to Verrières, where he finds Madame de Rênal at church. He fires two shots at her before he is arrested and taken off to prison. There he promptly admits his guilt, for he is ready to die. He got his revenge. Mathilde, who is still madly in love with Julien, arrives in Verrières and tries to bribe the jury. Fouqué arrives and begs Julien to try to escape, but Julien ignores the efforts of his friends to help.

Julien is tried, found guilty, and given the death sentence, even though his bullets had not killed Madame de Rênal. In fact, his action had only rekindled her passion for him. She visits him and begs him to appeal his sentence. The two are as much in love as they had ever been. When Monsieur de Rênal orders his wife to come home, Julien is left to his dreams of his one great love, Madame de Rênal. Mathilde only bores and angers him with her continued solicitude.

On the appointed day, Julien goes calmly to his death. The faithful Fouqué obtains the body so as to bury it in a cave in the mountains where Julien had once been fond of going to indulge in his daydreams of power. A famous ancestor of Mathilde had once been loved with an extreme passion. When that ancestor was executed, the woman had taken his severed head and buried it. Mathilde had always admired this family legend. After the funeral ceremony at the cave, she

now does the same for Julien, burying his head with her own hands. Later, she has the cave decorated with Italian marble. Madame de Rênal did not go to the funeral, but three days after Julien's death, she died while embracing her children.

Critical Evaluation:

Criticism of *The Red and the Black* might well begin with the novel's subtitle, *A Chronicle of 1830*. The thirty years of the nineteenth century that had elapsed at the time Stendhal wrote his novel divide rather neatly into two periods: the Napoleonic era, which ended with the Congress of Vienna in 1815, and the Bourbon Restoration, the restoration of the French monarchy, which extended from 1815 to 1830.

The first of these periods, dominated by Napoleon, is often associated with the "red" of Stendhal's title, red signifying, among other possibilities, military distinction (the means by which Napoleon began his rise to eminence) or revolution (the means by which the liberal bourgeoisie undertook to secure a measure of power). The second period, probably signified by Stendhal's "black," is associated with the clergy, who recaptured some of their former influence after 1815 and thus became a means to personal advancement, or reaction, political and social retrenchment by which the aristocracy undertook to recover their former dominance.

Julien Sorel, possessed of both ability and ambition, admires Napoleon in private, but he also knows that the former emperor is anathema to those who now hold power. His only escape from the coarse and limited world that seems to suit his father and brothers is through the exercise of learning. He has achieved a mastery of Latin, particularly of the New Testament, which he has practically memorized. When he becomes tutor to the Rênal children, he takes his first step toward the life he desires, but that step also requires him to assume a role similar to one played by minor clergy. Julien knows that there will be no further steps unless he is willing to practice a hypocrisy that, while not pervasive among all clergy, almost always characterizes those who hope to get on in life.

Julien's clerical advancement begins, ironically enough, in his illicit affair with Madame de Rênal. This affair, which Julien starts not out of passion but rather as a self-test of his resolve, becomes something serious and creates the necessity for sending the young man away to a seminary, where he further cultivates the hypocrisy necessary to achieve his goals. Though Julien recognizes and even honors the sincerity he occasionally discovers in a clergyman, his own goals have little to do with spiritual life. As he sees more of the world, he comes to realize that his ambition is larger than most of what the church can offer. What he finds attractive is not the liberal bourgeoisie, which might fit with his admiration of Napoleon, but the reactionary aristocracy, who may be shallow in their thinking but represent both the power and style to which he aspires.

Although Julien begins with attitudes that might be identified with Napoleonic liberalism, his belief in his own self-worth and in his right to a place among the aristocracy impels him toward the very structures of power and authority that had attempted to quell liberalism. One of the ironies of liberalism, in Stendhal's time and now, is that it tends to promote a democratization of style with which the Julien Sorels of the world have little sympathy. If the aristocracy resists free thought as something threatening to their privilege, they may nonetheless exercise their power in the protection of a style that continues to exert appeal.

All of this becomes clear to Julien after he leaves the seminary to assume duties as secretary to the Marquis de La Mole. He finds himself in the world he has coveted. When he discovers that he is not alone in reading Voltaire in secret, that Mathilde, the marquis' beautiful daughter, reads Voltaire also, it seems that he may be able to live among the rich and powerful while cultivating a freedom of thought that the rich and powerful consider seditious. When he begins a love affair with Mathilde, it seems that he may get everything he wants, especially after Mathilde becomes pregnant and the Marquis de La Mole decides to legitimize Julien by providing him with a title and a commission in the army. That commission would mean a final escape from black clerical clothing into a uniform that, if not red, is nevertheless still a military uniform worn by the privileged orders.

The Red and the Black may be read as a tragic novel. The collapse and subsequent end of Julien's life results, after all, from the very thing that was critical to his ascent, namely his success in passionate love, first with Madame de Rênal, then with Mathilde de La Mole. Though Julien is handsome in a pale, refined sort of way, he seems less driven by passion than many young men and makes use of his success in love only as a tool in the service of his ambition. The women who love him are sincere, however, and when he is exposed for his earlier affair by its object, Madame de Rênal, his response is to attempt to kill her. Stendhal, who was himself strongly attracted to women and had many love affairs, seems to indicate that passionate love must be fit into life's equations, especially among those who wish to live completely and despite the sometimes tragic results. The tragic moment in *The Red and the Black* comes with the hero's self-knowledge, when Julien realizes late in the story that he truly loves Madame de Rênal. *The Red and the Black* is a major novel of early nineteenth century France. Beyond being a chronicle of its own time, it is penetrating in its analysis of love and ambition and of the schemes, open or concealed, by which they are served.

"Critical Evaluation" by John Higby

Further Reading

Algazi, Lisa G. *Maternal Subjectivity in the Works of Stendhal.* Lewiston, N.Y.: Edwin Mellen Press, 2001. Examines Stendhal's depiction of maternal figures. Argues Stendhal was the first French writer to depict mothers as both maternal and sexual beings, challenging the traditional madonna/whore dichotomy.

Bloom, Harold, ed. *Stendhal.* New York: Chelsea House, 1989. A collection of essays by distinguished critics that address topics such as women in Stendhal's work, his use of autobiography, and his love plots. Includes an editor's introduction, a chronology of Stendhal's life, and a bibliography.

De la Motte, Dean, and Stirling Haig, eds. *Approaches to Teaching Stendhal's "The Red and the Black."* New York: Modern Language Association of America, 1999. Contains background information about the novel that is useful for students and general readers, as well as teachers. Includes essays discussing the historical background of *The Red and the Black*, the plot and the concept of freedom in the novel, the characters, the opening chapters, and the novel as a story of reading and writing.

Keates, Jonathan. *Stendhal.* 1994. New ed. New York: Carroll & Graf, 1997. A lucid and shrewd biography that emphasizes the events of Stendhal's life over analysis of his works. Includes a bibliography and an index.

Manzini, Francesco. *Stendhal's Parallel Lives.* New York: Peter Lang, 2004. Examines the influence of Plutarch's *Parallel Lives* on the biographical sketches and "imaginary biographies" in *The Red and the Black* and other works by Stendhal. Demonstrates how Stendhal compares his themes and the lives of his characters to one another.

Pearson, Roger. *Stendhal's Violin: A Novelist and His Reader.* New York: Oxford University Press, 1988. A long chapter entitled "Time and Imagination in *Le Rouge et le noir* (*The Red and the Black*)" is divided into subchapters that are partly self-contained and partly sequential.

Stendhal. *The Red and the Black: Authoritative Text, Context and Backgrounds, Criticism.* 2d ed. Edited by Susanna Lee, translated by Robert M. Adams. New York: W. W. Norton, 2008. In addition to the text of the novel, this book includes related writings by Stendhal and contemporary criticism of his novel. Nine additional essays provide numerous modern interpretations, including "In the Hotel de La Mole," Erich Auerbach's classic description of Stendhal's literary realism; a discussion of fathers and sons in the novel; and an analysis of madness in Stendhal's works. A map of 1830's France and political and literary chronologies place the book within the context of mid-nineteenth century French geography, history, and literature.

Talbot, Emile J. *Stendhal Revisited.* New York: Twayne, 1993. The chapter on *The Red and the Black*, subtitled "The Play of the Text," discusses the theme of playfulness in literature.

The Red Badge of Courage
An Episode of the American Civil War

Author: Stephen Crane (1871-1900)
First published: 1895
Type of work: Novel
Type of plot: Psychological realism
Time of plot: 1861-1865
Locale: A battlefield

Principal characters:
HENRY FLEMING, a young Army recruit
JIM CONKLIN, an Army veteran
WILSON, another Army veteran

The Story:

The tall soldier, Jim Conklin, and the loud soldier, Wilson, argue bitterly over the rumor that the troops are about to move. Henry Fleming is impatient to experience his first battle, and as he listens to the quarreling of the seasoned soldiers, he wonders if he will become frightened and run away under gunfire. He questions Wilson and Conklin, and each states that he will stand and fight no matter what happens.

Henry had come from a farm, where he had dreamed of battles and longed for Army life. His mother held him back at first. When she saw that her son was bored with the farm, she packed his woolen clothing and, with a warning that he must not associate with the wicked kind of men who were in the military camps, sent him off to join the Yankee troops.

One gray morning, Henry wakes up to find that his regiment is about to move. With a hazy feeling that death would be a relief from dull and meaningless marching, Henry is again disappointed. The troops make only another march. He begins to suspect that the generals are stupid fools, but the other men in his raw regiment scoff at his idea and tell him to shut up.

When the fighting suddenly begins, there is very little action in it for Henry. He lays on the ground with the other men and watches for signs of the enemy. Some of the men around him are wounded. He cannot see what is going on or what the battle is about. Then an attack comes. Immediately, Henry forgets all of his former confused thoughts, and he can only fire his rifle over and over; around him, men behave in their own strange individual manners as they are wounded. Henry feels a close comradeship with the men at his side—men who are firing at the enemy with him.

Suddenly the attack ends. To Henry, it seems strange that the sky above should still be blue after the guns had stopped firing. While the men are recovering from the attack, binding wounds, and gathering equipment, another surprise attack is launched from the enemy line. Unprepared and tired from the first round of fighting, the men retreat in panic. Henry, sharing their sudden terror, runs too.

When the fearful retreat ends, the fleeing men learn that the enemy had lost the battle. Now Henry feels a surge of guilt. Dreading to rejoin his companions, he flees into the forest. There he sees a squirrel run away from him in fright. The fleeing animal seems to vindicate in Henry's mind his own cowardly flight; he had acted according to nature, whose creatures run from danger. Then, seeing a dead man lying in a clearing, Henry hurries back into the retreating column of wounded men. Most are staggering along in helpless bewilderment, and some are being carried on stretchers. Henry realizes that he has no wound and that he does not belong in that group of staggering men. There is one pitiful-looking man, covered with dirt and blood, wandering about dazed and alone. Everyone is staring at him and avoiding him. When Henry approaches him, the young man sees that the soldier is

Conklin. He is horrified at the sight of the tall soldier. He tries to help Conklin, but with a wild motion of despair, Conklin falls to the ground dead. Once more Henry flees.

Henry's conscience is paining him. He wants to return to his regiment to finish the fight, but he thinks that his fellow soldiers will point to him as a deserter. He envies the dead men who are lying all about him. They are already heroes; he is a coward. Ahead he can hear the rumbling of artillery. As he nears the lines of his regiment, a retreating line of men breaks from the trees ahead of him. The men run fiercely, ignoring him or waving frantically at him as they shout something he cannot comprehend. He stands among the flying men, not knowing what to do. One man hits him on the head with the butt of a rifle.

Henry goes on carefully, the wound in his head paining him a great deal. He walks for a long while until he meets another soldier, who leads Henry back to his regiment. The first familiar man Henry meets is Wilson. Wilson, who had been a terrible braggart before the first battle, had given Henry a packet of letters to keep for him in case he were killed. Now, Henry feels superior to Wilson. If the man asks him where he has been, Henry will remind him of the letters. Lost is Henry's feeling of guilt; he feels superior now, his deeds of cowardice almost forgotten. No one knows that he had run off in terror. Wilson had changed. He no longer is the swaggering, boastful man who had annoyed Henry in the beginning. The men in the regiment wash Henry's wound and tell him to get some sleep.

The next morning, Wilson casually asks Henry for the letters. Half sorry that he has to yield them with no taunting remark, Henry returns the letters to his comrade. He feels sorry for Wilson's embarrassment. He feels himself a virtuous and heroic man. Another battle starts. This time, Henry holds his position doggedly and keeps firing his rifle without thinking. Once he falls down, and for a panicky moment he thinks that he has been shot, but he continues to fire his rifle blindly, loading and firing without even seeing the enemy. Finally, someone shouts to him that he must stop shooting, that the battle is over. Then, Henry looks up for the first time and sees that there are no enemy troops before him. Now he is a hero. Everyone stares at him when the lieutenant of the regiment compliments his fierce fighting. Henry realizes that he had behaved like a demon.

Wilson and Henry, off in the woods looking for water, overhear two officers discussing the coming battle. They say that Henry's regiment fights like mule drivers, but that they would have to be used anyway. Then one officer says that probably not many of the regiment will live through the day's fighting. Soon after the attack starts, the color-bearer is killed, and Henry takes up the flag, with Wilson at his side. Although the regiment fights bravely, one of the commanding officers of the Army says that the men had not gained the ground that they were expected to take. The same officer had complimented Henry for his courageous fighting. Henry begins to feel that he knows the measure of his own courage and endurance. His outfit fights one more engagement with the enemy. Henry is by this time a veteran, and the fighting holds less meaning for him than had the earlier battles. When it is over, he and Wilson march away with their victorious regiment.

Critical Evaluation:

The Red Badge of Courage, Stephen Crane's second novel (*Maggie: A Girl of the Streets* had appeared under a pseudonym in 1893) and his most famous work, has often been considered the first truly modern war novel. The war is the American Civil War, and the battle is presumed to be the one fought at Chancellorsville, though neither the war nor the battle is named in the novel. Further, there is no mention of Abraham Lincoln or the principal battle generals, Joseph Hooker (Union) and Robert E. Lee and Stonewall Jackson (Confederate). This is by design, since Crane was writing a different kind of war novel. He was not concerned with the causes of the war, the political and social implications of the prolonged and bloody conflict, the strategy and tactics of the commanding officers, or even the real outcome of the battle in which historically the combined losses were nearly thirty thousand men (including Jackson, mistakenly shot in darkness by one of his own men).

From beginning to end, the short novel focuses upon one Union Army volunteer. Though other characters enter the story and reappear intermittently, they are distinctly minor, and they are present primarily to show the relationship of Henry Fleming (usually called only "the youth") to one person, to a small group of soldiers, or to the complex war of which he is such an insignificant part. Much of the story takes the reader into Henry's consciousness. Readers share his boyish dreams of glory, his excitement in anticipating battle action, his fear of showing fear, his cowardice and flight, his inner justification of what he has done, his wish for a wound to symbolize a courage he has not shown, the ironic gaining of his false "red badge," his secret knowledge of the badge's origin, his "earning" the badge as he later fights fiercely and instinctively, his joy in musing on his own bravery and valiant actions, his anger at an officer who fails to appreciate his soldiers, and his final feeling that "the great death" is, after all, not a thing to be feared so much. Now, he tells himself, he is a man. In centering the story within the consciousness of an inexperienced youth caught in a war situation whose meaning and complexities he cannot understand, Crane anticipates Ford Madox Ford, Ernest Hemingway, and other later novelists.

Crane has been called a realist, a naturalist, an impressionist, and a Symbolist. He is all of these in *The Red Badge of Courage*. Though Crane had never seen a battle when he wrote the novel, he had read about them, had talked with veterans and had studied history under a Civil War general, and had imagined what it would be like to be a frightened young man facing violent death amid the confusion, noise, and turmoil of a conflict that had no clear meaning to him. Intuitively, he wrote so realistically that several early reviewers concluded that only an experienced soldier could have written the book. After Crane had later seen the Greeks and Turks fighting in 1897 (he was a journalist reporting the war), he told Joseph Conrad, "My picture of war was all right! I have found it as I imagined it."

Although naturalistic passages appear in the novel, Crane portrays in Henry not a helpless chip floating on the indifferent ocean of life but a youth sometimes impelled into action by society or by instinct yet also capable of consciously willed acts. Before the first skirmish, Henry wishes he could escape from his regiment and consider his plight: "there were iron laws of tradition and law on four sides. He was in a moving box." In the second skirmish, he runs "like a rabbit." When a squirrel in the forest flees after Henry throws a pinecone at him, Henry justifies his own flight: "There was the law, he said. Nature had given him a sign." He is not, however, content to look upon himself as on the squirrel's level. He feels guilt over his cowardice. When he carries the flag in the later skirmishes, he is not a terrified chicken or rabbit or squirrel but a young man motivated by pride, by a sense of belonging to a group, and by a determination to show his courage to an officer who had scornfully called the soldiers in his group "mule drivers."

From the beginning, critics have both admired and complained about Crane's impressionistic writing and his use of imagery and symbols in *The Red Badge of Courage*. Edward Garnett in 1898 called Crane "the chief impressionist of our day" and praised his "wonderful fervour and freshness of style." Conrad (himself an impressionist) was struck by Crane's "genuine verbal felicity, welding analysis and description in a continuous fascination of individual style," and Conrad saw Henry as "the symbol of all untried men." By contrast, one American critic in 1898 described the novel as "a mere riot of words" and condemned "the violent straining after effect" and the "absurd similes." Though H. G. Wells liked the book as a whole, he commented on "those chro-

matic splashes that at times deafen and confuse . . . those images that astonish rather than enlighten."

However, judging by the continuing popularity of *The Red Badge of Courage*, most readers are not repelled by Crane's repeated use of color—"blue demonstration," "red eyes," "red animal—war," "red sun"—or by his use of images—"dark shadows that moved like monsters," "the dragons were coming," guns that "belched and howled like brass devils guarding a gate." Only in a few passages does Crane indulge in "arty" writing—"the guns squatted in a row like savage chiefs. They argued with abrupt violence"—or drop into the pathetic fallacy—"The flag suddenly sank down as if dying. Its motion as it fell was a gesture of despair." Usually the impressionistic phrasing is appropriate to the scene or to the emotional state of Henry at a particular moment, as when, after he has fought heroically, the sun shines "now bright and gay in the blue, enameled sky." A brilliant work of the imagination, *The Red Badge of Courage* will endure as what Crane afterward wrote a friend he had intended it to be, "a psychological portrayal of fear."

"Critical Evaluation" by Henderson Kincheloe

Further Reading

Bloom, Harold, ed. *Stephen Crane's "The Red Badge of Courage."* New York: Bloom's Literary Criticism, 2007. In addition to a biographical sketch of Crane, list of characters, and plot summary and analysis, this volume contains several essays interpreting the novel. Includes discussions of Crane's form and style, Henry Fleming's initiation to war and manhood, the novel as a humanistic work of art, and the ideal and the actual in Fleming's war experience.

Cazemajou, Jean. "*The Red Badge of Courage*: The 'Religion of Peace' and the War Archetype." In *Stephen Crane in Transition: Centenary Essays*, edited by Joseph Katz. DeKalb: Northern Illinois University Press, 1972. Finds a balance in the novel between a metaphoric view of war as chaos and confusion, and a view of a world at peace. Maintains that war and peace function more as archetypes than as realities in the novel.

Johnson, Claudia D. *Understanding "The Red Badge of Courage": A Student Casebook to Issues, Sources, and Historical Documents*. Westport, Conn.: Greenwood Press, 1998. A companion to the novel that is particularly useful for students. Provides literary analysis and features primary and secondary source documents aimed at placing the novel within the context of the Civil War. Among the documents are firsthand accounts of the Battle of

Chancellorsville and other Civil War battles, memoirs, newspaper articles, and interviews.

LaFrance, Marston. *A Reading of Stephen Crane.* New York: Oxford University Press, 1971. LaFrance identifies Crane's genius not in creating literary naturalism, but rather in his psychological portrayal of Henry Fleming. Praises Crane's use of third-person limited point of view.

Mitchell, Lee Clark, ed. *New Essays on "The Red Badge of Courage."* New York: Cambridge University Press, 1986. Traces the novel's evolution, concluding that the original draft served as an outline to be expanded into the 1895 version. Identifies Crane's abstraction of the Civil War from its historical context as a distinctive contribution to American literature.

Monteiro, George. *Stephen Crane's Blue Badge of Courage.* Baton Rouge: Louisiana State University Press, 2000. A demonstration of the ironic role of temperance propaganda, in which Crane was immersed as a child, in the imagery and language of his darkest and best-known work.

Solomon, Eric. *Stephen Crane: From Parody to Realism.* Cambridge, Mass.: Harvard University Press, 1969. Credits Crane with countering a tradition of dashing heroes in war fiction by using parody and with giving the war novel a new form that became the model. Maintains that Crane selected his war stories for their value as fiction, creating rather than reliving war experiences.

Sorrentino, Paul, ed. *Stephen Crane Remembered.* Tuscaloosa: University of Alabama Press, 2006. Sorrentino brings together nearly one hundred documents from acquaintances of the novelist and poet for a revealing look at Crane's life and writings.

Wertheim, Stanley. *A Stephen Crane Encyclopedia.* Westport, Conn.: Greenwood Press, 1997. A thorough volume on Crane, with entries arranged alphabetically. Features articles about the full range of his work, his family and its influence upon him, the places he lived, his employers, the literary movement with which he is associated, and his characters, among other subjects.

Redburn
His First Voyage

Author: Herman Melville (1819-1891)
First published: 1849
Type of work: Novel
Type of plot: Bildungsroman
Time of plot: Mid-nineteenth century
Locale: New York, the Atlantic Ocean, and England

Principal characters:
WELLINGBOROUGH REDBURN, a young lad on his first voyage
CAPTAIN RIGA, the master of the *Highlander*
HARRY BOLTON, a young English prodigal

The Story:

Wellingborough Redburn's father dies, leaving his wife and children poorly provided for, although he had been a highly successful merchant and at one time a wealthy man. The young Redburn is in his middle teens, and he decides to take some of the burden off his mother by going to sea. Given an old gun and a hunting jacket by an older brother, Redburn leaves his home by the Hudson River and goes to New York to seek a berth on a ship.

A college friend of his older brother aids Redburn in finding a berth on a ship bound for Liverpool, England. Unfortunately, the friend had emphasized to the ship's crew that Redburn comes from a good family and has wealthy relatives; consequently, Captain Riga, master of the *Highlander*,

is able to hire the young lad for only three dollars a month. Having spent all his money and unable to get an advance on his wages, Redburn has to pawn his gun for a shirt and cap to wear aboard ship.

During his first few days out of port, Redburn believes he has made a dreadful mistake in going to sea. Redburn's fellow sailors jeer at him as a greenhorn. He makes many silly mistakes, becomes violently seasick, and discovers that he does not even have a spoon with which to take his portion of the food from the pots and pans. His coat proves inappropriate for life at sea; it shrinks after getting wet. His fellow crewmen find the odd coat amusing and give Redburn the nickname Buttons in derisive reference to the coat's many buttons. Most horrifying of all is the suicide of a sailor who dived over the side of the ship in a fit of delirium tremens.

As the thirty-day cruise to Liverpool from New York wears on, Redburn learns how to make himself useful and comfortable aboard the ship. When he goes aloft alone to release the topmost sails, he earns a little respect from his fellow seamen, although they never do, throughout the voyage, let him forget that he is still inexperienced and had signed on as a "boy." Redburn finds the sea fascinating in many ways; he also finds it terrifying, as when the *Highlander* had passed a derelict schooner on which three corpses were still bound to the railing.

For Redburn, one of the liveliest incidents of the voyage is the discovery of a little stowaway on board the *Highlander*. The small boy had been on board the vessel some months before, when his father had been a sailor signed on for a trip from Liverpool to New York. The father had since died, and the boy stowed himself away in an effort to return to England. Everyone on the ship, including the usually irascible Captain Riga, takes a liking to the homesick stowaway and make much of him.

Redburn has little in common with his fellow crew members, most of whom are rough fellows many years older than he. Through them, however, he receives an education quite different from that which he had been given in school. At first he tries to talk about church and good books to them, but he soon discovers that such conversation only irritates them into more than their usual profanity and obscenity. Redburn thinks that they are not really very bad men but that they had never had the chance to be good men. Most of all, he dislikes them because they look upon anyone who cannot follow the seaman's trade as a fool.

A long, low skyline in the distance is Redburn's first glimpse of Ireland. He meets his first European when an Irish fisherman hails the *Highlander* and asks for a line. After hauling fifteen or so fathoms of the line into his boat, the Irishman cuts the line, laughs, and sails away.

When the *Highlander* arrives at Liverpool, Redburn decides that the English city is not a great deal different from New York. Sailors and ships are the same everywhere, with a few notable exceptions. His trips into the city, away from the waterfront, and excursions into the Lancashire countryside convince him that he, as a foreigner, is not welcome. People distrust him because of his ragged clothing, and he has no money to purchase a new outfit, even though Captain Riga had advanced him three dollars, one month's pay, upon the ship's arrival in port.

Redburn's greatest disappointment comes when he tries to use for his excursions an old guidebook he had brought from his father's library. The guidebook, almost half a century old, is no longer reliable, for streets and structures it mentions are no longer in existence. Redburn feels that the whole world must have changed since his father's time; he sees in the unreliable guidebook a hint that as the years pass the habits and ideals of youth have to be charted anew. Each generation, he learns, has to make its own guidebook through the world.

While in Liverpool, Redburn meets Harry Bolton, a young Englishman of good family but a prodigal son. Bolton says that he had shipped on two voyages to the East Indies; now he wants to emigrate to America. With Redburn's help, Bolton is enrolled as a "boy" on the *Highlander* for its return trip to New York. The two boys, traveling on Bolton's money, make a quick excursion to London before the ship sails, but they are back in Liverpool within forty-eight hours. Redburn sees little of England beyond the port where he had arrived.

On the return trip to America, the ship carries a load of Irish emigrants. Redburn quickly feels sorry for them but, at the same time, superior to the miserable wretches crowded between the decks. The steerage passengers suffer a great deal during the voyage. Their quarters are cramped at best, and during heavy weather, they cannot remain on deck. For cooking they have a stove placed on one of the hatches, one stove for five hundred people. Worst of all, an epidemic of fever breaks out, killing many of the emigrants and one of the sailors.

Bolton has a miserable trip, and Redburn feels sorry for him, too. The English boy had lied in saying he had been at sea before. Bolton cannot bear to go aloft in the rigging, and he, in place of Redburn, becomes the butt of all the jokes and horseplay the crew devises.

After the ship reaches America, however, the voyage seems to both Redburn and Bolton to have been a good one. They discover that they really hate to leave the vessel that had been home to them for several weeks. Their nostalgia for the vessel, however, is soon dissipated by Captain Riga. The captain dismisses Redburn without pay because the lad had left his duties for one day while the ship was at Liverpool. The captain even tells Redburn that he owes the ship money for tools he had dropped into the sea. Bolton is given a dollar and a half for his work; the pittance makes him so angry that he throws it back on the captain's desk. The two boys then leave the ship, glad to be back on land once more.

Critical Evaluation:

Like most of Herman Melville's work, *Redburn* does not follow a conventional plot structure of complication, climax, and resolution, nor does the novel have characters who gradually develop and interact within a framework of interrelated events and circumstances. *Redburn* is a bildungsroman, a novel that deals with the development of a young protagonist moving from adolescence to maturity. *Redburn* is told by a first-person narrator who, in the course of his commentary, moves from innocence to experience.

At the outset, young Wellingborough Redburn's existence is protected, safe from the iniquities of the world outside village life. His enthusiasm to go to sea is the desire of postadolescence to move from the innocent state of childhood into the real world, to challenge that which adults have simultaneously idealized and, for as long as they could, withheld from children. The real world, however, proves to be a darker and more forbidding place than the naïve Redburn is prepared to enter. The rules of fair play and benevolence that have governed his childhood are greatly diminished, and in their place, Redburn finds little kindness and understanding; instead, he finds more than enough selfish indifference and pointless malevolence.

Melville places great emphasis on symbols to convey complex ideas. The glass ship, the moleskin shooting jacket, and the Liverpool guidebook all invite a variety of critical interpretations. As a child growing up in his father's house, Redburn was fascinated by a glass ship kept in a glass case. It is the basis of his great passion to go to sea, for he has grown up studying the minute detail of its glass spars and rigging and its glass figurine sailors earnestly plying their trade. The glass ship, although a strong stimulant for the imagination of an impressionable youth, suggests a fragile, tentative reality, like the imagined notion of a world one has not directly experienced. Having lived a sheltered life in his mother's home in the Hudson Valley, Redburn is as ill-prepared to undertake a genuine voyage upon the high seas as is the glass ship. Melville seems to suggest that people are more resilient than glass, and with the aid of luck and good fortune, people can withstand suffering and the mystery of what often seems a pointless universe.

The reality of the actual voyage is a harsh and brutal experience, one for which Redburn lacks both the psychological and practical necessities. On his departure, his older brother gives him two items: a fowling piece (a gun for hunting birds) and a cumbersome shooting jacket with large horn buttons, many pockets, and long skirts. Redburn has little money, however, and he has no idea of the basic necessities for his new undertaking. The gun is pawned at the first opportunity, perhaps suggesting that such a weapon is useless for the kinds of battles Redburn must now face. The jacket, however, has deeper symbolic implications, much like a similar article of clothing in *White-Jacket* (1850), the novel generally viewed

as Melville's sequel and companion piece to *Redburn*. The shooting jacket makes Redburn the object of derision by his fellow seafarers. The jacket earns him the nickname Buttons. As Redburn performs his seaman's tasks, he is repeatedly drenched by rain and seawater. Day by day the shooting jacket shrinks; the seams begin to widen to the point of splitting; and moving and working with the jacket on become increasingly difficult. The jacket has become the symbol of the world Redburn has left behind. One critic called the jacket an "obsessive emblem" of his lost gentility and social humiliation.

The concept of advancing to a new identity and breaking with the past is further enhanced by the incident of the Liverpool guidebook. Redburn brings with him the guidebook that his father had used on a visit to that same city fifty years earlier. The book on which Redburn—as a friendless stranger in a foreign city—had hoped to rely on, however, proves to be worthless. Following the map, he attempts to find Riddough's Hotel, the place where his father had stayed, but the hotel is a thing of the past, having been torn down decades earlier. New buildings now stand in its place, and its name is unknown to passersby. His father's Liverpool no longer exists in what Redburn now sadly realizes is a world marked by change, rather than constancy. Having hoped to follow in the comforting security of his father's footsteps, he knows now that he must chart his own course, as generations that follow him must do.

Melville surrounds Redburn with a collection of curious characters, few of them fully developed. For the most part, they seem close to caricature, primarily serving as foils for Redburn to offer observations regarding their moral shortcomings. The most compelling, however, is Jackson, the prototype of the tortured individual who would in various guises appear in Melville's later works. Jackson is the forerunner of Claggart in *Billy Budd, Foretopman* (1924), Babo in *Benito Cereno* (1856), and Ahab in *Moby Dick* (1851). Like them, he is a formidable leader—but he is also a tortured soul consumed by nihilism, believing in nothing and hating everything. For all his enmity, however, there is a curious paradox about Jackson; he is the Cain figure, the proud and forbidding outcast in whom, in spite of his wickedness, there is something pitiable and touching. *Redburn* is the first of Melville's novels to use the symbolic import of the sea as a backdrop for this kind of paradox and for the related, compelling subjects that troubled Melville most: the loss of innocence, the confrontation with evil, and the shifting ambiguities that connect innocence and evil.

"Critical Evaluation" by Richard Keenan

Further Reading

Bloom, Harold, ed. *Herman Melville*. New ed. New York: Bloom's Literary Criticism, 2008. Collection of critical essays analyzing Melville's work. Includes Stephen Mathewson's essay "'To Tell over Again the Story Just Told': The Composition of Melville's *Redburn*."

Branch, Watson G., ed. *Melville: The Critical Heritage*. London: Routledge & Kegan Paul, 1974. Contains contemporary reviews of *Redburn* in British and American periodicals; interesting for comparison with later Melville scholarship. *Redburn* was widely praised at its publication, but praised for its qualities as an adventure story rather than as serious fiction.

Bredahl, Carl A., Jr. *Melville's Angles of Vision*. Gainesville: University Press of Florida, 1972. Emphasizes Melville's concern with characters in their environment. Discusses Redburn as a first-person narrator adjusting to the psychological implications of life at sea.

Delbanco, Andrew. *Melville: His World and Work*. New York: Knopf, 2005. Delbanco's critically acclaimed biography places Melville in his time, with discussion about the debate over slavery and details of life in 1840's New York. Delbanco also discusses the significance of Melville's works at the time they were published and their reception into the twenty-first century.

Hillway, Tyrus. *Herman Melville*. Boston: Twayne, 1963. Excellent analysis of Melville's characterization, empha-

sizing how it improved since the publication of his earlier novels. Pays particular attention to the tragic contradictions in the character of Harry Bolton.

Kelley, Wyn. "'A Regular Story Founded on Striking Incidents': *Mardi*, *Redburn*, and *White-Jacket*." In *Herman Melville: An Introduction*. Malden, Mass.: Blackwell, 2008. Chronicles Melville's development as a writer, providing analyses of his works.

_____, ed. *A Companion to Herman Melville*. Malden, Mass.: Blackwell, 2006. Collection of thirty-five original essays aimed at twenty-first century readers of Melville's works. Includes discussions of Melville's travels; Melville and religion, slavery, and gender; and the Melville revival. Also includes the essay "Artist at Work: *Redburn*, *White-Jacket*, *Moby-Dick*, and *Pierre*" by Cindy Weinstein.

Kirby, David. *Herman Melville*. New York: Continuum, 1993. Examines the relationship between Melville's creative imagination and his life. Offers an engaging contrast between the fanciful *Mardi* and *Redburn*, which reveals Melville's personal experiences.

Rosenberry, Edward H. *Melville*. London: Routledge & Kegan Paul, 1979. Places particular emphasis on *Redburn* as an initiation novel in which personal experience is paramount in the development of the character of the mature adult. Rosenberry makes an interesting distinction between lust for life and a talent for living in *Redburn*.

Reflections in a Golden Eye

Author: Carson McCullers (1917-1967)
First published: 1941
Type of work: Novel
Type of plot: Psychological realism
Time of plot: 1930's
Locale: A military base in North Carolina

Principal characters:
PRIVATE ELLGEE WILLIAMS, an Army soldier
CAPTAIN WELDON PENDERTON, an ambitious Army officer
LEONORA PENDERTON, his wife
FIREBIRD, her horse
MAJOR MORRIS LANGDON, Leonora's lover
ALISON LANGDON, his sick wife
ANACLETO, her Filipino servant

The Story:

Seven characters are involved in a murder on a Southern U.S. Army post: "two officers, a soldier, two women, a Filipino, and a horse." The soldier is Private Ellgee Williams, a clean-living man who has neither friends nor enemies and is assigned to the stables because he is good with horses. One of the officers is Captain Weldon Penderton, who is married to Leonora Penderton. He knows that his wife has lovers, and he often becomes enamored of them. He asks for a soldier to be sent to clear some woods behind his house. The soldier is Private Williams, whom Penderton already dislikes because the young man had once spilled coffee on a new and expensive suit. Williams clears the woods thoroughly, cutting back a tree that Penderton did not want cut.

This evening, the Pendertons are expecting dinner guests, Major Morris Langdon and his wife, Alison. Major Langdon is Leonora Penderton's latest lover, and Captain Penderton is also interested in him. As they prepare for the guests, Penderton criticizes his wife for not wearing shoes, and she strips naked in front of him, making him furious. As she strips, Private Williams passes by the window and sees her.

Williams had never before seen a naked woman. His father, a Holiness preacher, reared him to believe that women carry deadly diseases. Therefore, Williams always avoids women. In fact, he has no real attachments to anyone. After he sees the scene between the Pendertons, he stays and watches their dinner party through the window. The next day, Private Williams is different. He is thinking of other times he had behaved spontaneously. There was the time he bought a cow his family did not need. There was the time he felt moved by the spirit at a revival, and the time he committed a crime. His enlistment in the Army had also been a spontaneous act. He knew he was about to do something unpredictable again.

For two weeks he observes the captain's house and its patterns. Then he goes to the windows and looks in, observing a blackjack game between Leonora and Major Langdon. Leonora cannot add the cards; she has to be told whether she wins or loses a game. Langdon asks his wife if she had seen her friend, Lieutenant Weincheck, that day. She replies that she had, and she and Leonora discuss the lieutenant's interest in art and music, an interest that Alison, but none of the rest of them, share.

Alison Langdon is ill, both physically and emotionally. She has a weak heart. Her husband's infidelity leaves her depressed and ailing. The death of their baby, Catherine, three years previously, had weakened her immensely. A few months before, Alison had snipped off her own nipples with a pair of gardening shears. She sits knitting, near tears, at the Pendertons's house as her husband plays cards with his lover. When she goes home, her husband stays to play another hand.

Major Langdon feels like an outsider in his own house. His baby had had a small deformity that made her repulsive to him. His wife and her houseboy, Anacleto, had taken care of the sick infant for eleven months. The baby's death had been a relief to the major but torture to his wife.

When the major returns home, Anacleto is dancing around, preparing a tray for Alison. Langdon is quite annoyed, and when Anacleto falls at the bottom of the stairs, the major mouths to him, "I-wish-you-had-bro-ken-your-neck."

Alison remembers discovering that her husband is having an affair with Leonora. She and Anacleto had driven up to the Langdons's house, realizing that Leonora and Langdon were there alone together in the dark.

Captain Penderton wants to hate Alison, but he cannot. She has once been witness to his stealing a silver spoon at a dinner party, one of only two times he had given in to a constant desire to be a thief.

Private Williams begins visiting the Pendertons's house at night and squatting by Leonora's bed to watch her sleep. After he touches a strand of her hair, he no longer fears that touching a woman could give him a fatal disease. One day, Captain Penderton goes to the stables and asks for his wife's horse, Firebird, which Williams saddles for him. Penderton, a mediocre horseman, has trouble handling Firebird. The horse reacts negatively to him and eventually throws him. Penderton takes a switch and beats the horse. He then realizes that a naked Williams had seen him. The private takes the horse back to the stables, and Penderton returns home on foot, arriving two hours late for a large dinner party he and his wife are hosting.

From that time forward, Penderton goes out of his way to see Williams. His feelings toward the private are almost obsessive, but they are also ambivalent, encompassing both love and hate.

After the party, Alison cannot sleep. Anacleto comes to her room and paints with watercolors while they talk. He stares into the fire and describes a peacock with one golden eye in which is reflected something he calls "tiny and. . . ." Mrs. Langdon finishes the description: "Grotesque."

Williams continues to visit Mrs. Penderton's room. He does not think much about his past, even about the time he stabbed an African American man in an argument over manure and hid the body in a quarry. He does, however, come to realize that Captain Penderton is following him.

One night, after Alison sees Williams sneak into the Pendertons's house, she leaves there to tell her friends about the intruder. Captain Penderton does not believe her, and word gets around that she has completely lost her mind. She then decides that she must leave her husband, so she and Anacleto pack and prepare to go. Major Langdon takes this as proof of her insanity and has her sent to an institution in Virginia, where, two days later, she dies of a heart attack. Anacleto leaves and is not heard from again. Langdon mourns his wife's death and spends even more time at home. Williams goes to the Penderton home for the seventh time. This time the captain sees him coming. He enters his wife's bedroom and shoots to death the man with whom he is obsessed.

Critical Evaluation:

Reflections in a Golden Eye was published one year after Carson McCullers's brilliant and well-received first novel, *The Heart Is a Lonely Hunter* (1940). The second work was often harshly criticized for dealing with morbid and depressing subjects, as well as for its grotesque characters. As evidence that McCullers was interested only in the darkest side of human nature, her detractors pointed to such incidents as in the novel as Alison Langdon's cutting off her nipples with gardening shears and Weldon Penderton's putting a purring kitten into a frozen mailbox.

Southern playwright Tennessee Williams, McCullers's friend, came to her defense. In an introduction to a later edition of the work, he explained that the world itself is full of morbidity and grotesqueness and that McCullers's novel encapsulates those qualities in a tiny space, thereby intensifying their effects.

Admirers of *Reflections in a Golden Eye* have also praised its economy. In 110 pages, McCullers paints thorough portraits of three characters: Captain Penderton, Private Williams, and Alison Langdon. Even characters who are less thoroughly drawn pique the reader's interest. This is especially true of the Filipino houseboy, Anacleto, who adores and emulates his mistress, even straining with her during labor. His dedication to her is both admirable and perverse.

Reflections in a Golden Eye explores the problems inherent in denying one's true nature and attempting too much to conform. Private Williams and Captain Penderton both try to deny their sexuality, resulting in one man's killing the other. The novel also shows what happens when a person fails to live up to his or her obligations to another. Major Langdon cannot be a true husband to Alison or a true father to his child; as a result, his wife becomes increasingly ill. Captain Penderton's inability to have a real relationship with his wife drives her to other men, again often causing pain to innocent people.

Setting the novel on an Army base intensifies the work's effect. Where people are expected to conform, nonconformity seems even more grotesque. As McCullers says, on the post, most men are expected to do no more than "follow the heels ahead of [them]." The people in this novel, however, are all out of step.

Reflections in a Golden Eye further illuminates one of McCullers's strongest themes: the effect of love on the lover. Major Langdon and Leonora Penderton have an affair; their love is requited, and they are the least interesting of the main characters. Langdon becomes sympathetic only after the death of his wife, when he wishes even that Anacleto were there so that he would have some daily reminder of Alison.

Captain Penderton, Alison, and Williams all love someone who cannot or will not love them in return. Penderton loves Williams; Williams loves Penderton's wife; and Mrs. Langdon loves her dead child. All are ultimately destroyed by their love. A related theme, also common with McCullers, is isolation. Almost everyone in the novel is in some way alone. Although the characters try to make connections, these attempts often result in further separation.

Respect for *Reflections in a Golden Eye* has increased with time. The short novel is now considered one of McCullers's masterpieces, although its grotesque characters, violent events, and unconventional sexuality continue to disturb readers.

M. Katherine Grimes

Further Reading

Carr, Virginia Spencer. *The Lonely Hunter: A Biography of Carson McCullers*. 1975. New ed. Athens: University of Georgia Press, 2003. This definitive biography of McCullers has numerous photographs and a good index. Discusses the circumstances surrounding the writing and publication of *Reflections in a Golden Eye*. Includes a new preface and a foreword by Tennessee Williams.

_____. *Understanding Carson McCullers*. 1990. New ed. Columbia: University of South Carolina Press, 2005. Argues that the characters in *Reflections in a Golden Eye* are grotesque. Describes characters and plot, giving a brief overview of contemporary reviews of the book. This edition of the book, originally published in 1990, includes updated scholarship about McCullers.

Clark, Beverly Lyon, and Melvin J. Friedman, eds. *Critical Essays on Carson McCullers*. New York: G. K. Hall, 1996. A collection of essays ranging from reviews of McCullers's major works, to tributes by such writers as Tennessee Williams and Kay Boyle, to critical analyses from a variety of perspectives.

Cook, Richard M. *Carson McCullers*. 1975. Reprint. New York: Frederick Ungar, 1984. Cook analyzes the main characters in *Reflections in a Golden Eye* and discusses the theme of isolation in the novel. Part of the Literature and Life series.

Gleeson-White, Sarah. *Strange Bodies: Gender and Identity in the Novels of Carson McCullers*. Tuscaloosa: University of Alabama Press, 2003. Gleeson-White analyzes McCullers's major novels, describing how their "grotesque" depictions of gender roles and sexuality provide the possibility of freedom and redemption for her characters. Chapter 2 analyzes *Reflections in a Golden Eye*.

McDowell, Margaret B. *Carson McCullers*. Boston: Twayne, 1980. Describes the novel's plot, then discusses its comic effects, the use of the gothic, its "fragmented vision of human existence," the motif of isolation, and its horror.

Savigneau, Josyane. *Carson McCullers: A Life*. Translated by Joan E. Howard. Boston: Houghton Mifflin, 2001. The McCullers estate granted Savigneau access to McCullers's unpublished papers, enabling her to obtain facts about her subject's life that were not available to previous biographers.

Whitt, Jan, ed. *Reflections in a Critical Eye: Essays on Carson McCullers*. Lanham, Md.: University Press of America, 2008. A collection of essays about McCullers's work, including discussions of lesbian desire in her novels and the topic of McCullers and the influence of alcohol on her life and writing.

Reflections on the Revolution in France

Author: Edmund Burke (1729-1797)
First published: 1790
Type of work: Politics

Edmund Burke was deeply involved in English public life as a Whig politician who served from 1765 to 1794 in Parliament. This experience convinced him that governments must respond to the practical needs of the peoples they govern and that political crises do not all yield to the same measures. When he saw what was unfolding in France in 1789 and 1790, Burke became alarmed that the revolutionaries were ignoring the wisdom achieved by long experience and that they were acting on assumptions that were contrary to human nature. *Reflections on the Revolution in France* was intended to warn the people of England against being caught up by the same enthusiasm for destructive change that Burke saw infecting the citizens of France.

The Reign of Terror had not yet begun when Burke took up his pen in 1790 (some would say it is foreseen in Burke's castigation of the revolutionaries), but in July, 1789, the Bastille had been taken and the Comitù des Recherches had been formed and given numerous repressive police powers. In August, the French National Assembly promulgated the *Declaration of the Rights of Man and Citizen*. Two months later, the king's family was transferred from Versailles to Paris. In November, the National Assembly appropriated the Catholic Church's property, which soon became the basis of a new paper currency known as *assignats*. The religious orders, excepting those concerned with charity or education, were shut down in February, 1790, and finally, in July, the hereditary nobility were stripped of their titles and perquisites. These were the drastic changes taking place in France as Burke wrote the *Reflections*.

In late 1789, a young French friend of Burke, Charles-Jean-François Depont, asked Burke for his thoughts on the recent events in France. After a first, short letter of response, Burke began again in earnest with the words "Dear Sir" and did not stop until he had written an entire book. In the *Reflections* he explains that he will "throw out" his thoughts and express his feelings "just as they arise in my mind, with very little attention to formal method." No chapter divisions or subheads appear in the work, only long, dense paragraphs packed with balanced statements and striking turns of phrase. Burke seizes a subject and wrings it dry, his tone frequently modulating between contempt and solemnity.

If his improvised style holds the reader with its rhetorical inventiveness, the substance of his account is often not to be trusted. His silly story of the mob's takeover of Versailles on October 6, 1789, which features the queen's servant being "cut down" by a "band of cruel ruffians and assassins," is a lurid fiction. This passage in particular was immediately ridiculed and hurt Burke's credibility. *Reflections on the Revolution in France* should not be read as history, however, but as a work of political theory that expresses a coherent point of view.

On November 4, 1789, in an area of London known as the Old Jewry, Dr. Richard Price, a dissenting minister, preached a fiery sermon praising the upheaval in France. Burke identifies (not quite verbatim) three fundamental rights that Price insisted the English people had acquired: "to choose our own governors," "to cashier them for misconduct," and "to frame a government for ourselves." Burke rejects this talk of "rights" and cites the Declaration of Right (the bill of rights written under William and Mary) as "the cornerstone of the constitution" and as the embodiment of the true principles of the Revolution of 1688.

The "Glorious Revolution" did not, Burke says, give people the lasting right to elect their own rulers but only the opportunity to resolve a crisis at that specific time. The British people were free to fill the throne only "upon the same grounds on which they might have wholly abolished their monarchy, and every other part of their constitution." In other words, the people had hardly any grounds, for a hereditary monarchy is rooted in British history. "An irregular, convulsive movement may be necessary to throw off an irregular, convulsive disease. But the course of succession is the healthy habit of the British constitution."

As for the second claim of the Revolution Society, the "right of cashiering their governors for *misconduct*," Burke focuses on the vagueness of the word "misconduct." No general principle of fundamental importance can be based on language so ill defined. The "virtual abdication" of King James II that resulted in the succession crisis was forced by specific charges of "nothing less than a design, confirmed by a multitude of illegal overt acts, to *subvert the Protestant church and state*" and of "having broken the *original contract* between king and people."

The third right that Burke accuses Price and his followers of advocating is the "right to form a government for ourselves." Burke dismisses this claim by appealing to a "uniform policy" stretching from the Magna Carta of 1215 to the Declaration of Right, a policy that reveals an "*entailed inheritance* derived to us from our forefathers . . . without any reference whatever to any other more general or prior right." Burke's discussion relies heavily on the bedrock assumption underlying his entire political theory, a conviction that the British system of law and government evolved from basic principles in nature itself. Indeed, *Reflections on the Revolution in France* can perhaps be understood as a long gloss on one magnificent, swelling sentence:

> Our political system is placed in a just correspondence and symmetry with the order of the world, and with the mode of existence decreed to a permanent body composed of transitory parts; wherein, by the dispensation of a stupendous wisdom, moulding together the great mysterious incorporation of the human race, the whole, at one time, is never old, or middle-aged, or young, but in a condition of unchangeable constancy, moves on through the varied tenour of perpetual decay, fall, renovation, and progression.

This sentence encapsulates Burke's political philosophy and his theology.

Burke's faith in a natural order of things approaches the conviction that whatever is, is right, simply because it is. If every human institution were not the best of its kind, then the institution would have evolved otherwise. This vision reflects an innate pragmatism that trusts no a priori judgments and leaves all arrangements to be forged in experience. Burke sneered at the French rationalists and especially at Jean-Jacques Rousseau. In "Letter to a Member of the National Assembly" (1791), in which he responds to questions about *Reflections on the Revolution in France*, Burke blisters Rousseau as "the great professor and founder of *the philosophy of vanity*" in England" and "the insane *Socrates* of the National Assembly." These philosophes and their rabble-rousing followers in England, Burke claims, inflame weak minds with their prating about "natural" rights that are mere abstractions too often born of greed and envy. They intend to abolish religion and to replace it with an education "founded in a knowledge of the physical wants of men; progressively carried to an enlightened self-interest, which, when well understood, they tell us will identify with an interest more enlarged and public."

Dr. Price and the other dissenting clergy represented in the Revolution Society applauded the National Assembly when it seized the property of the Catholic Church. As a defender of the sacredness of private property rights, Burke was horrified by the seizure, and he argues at length in *Reflections on the Revolution in France* that the corporate holdings of the Church should enjoy the same status as an individual's property. The dissidents who attack the Church forget its "duty to make a sure provision for the consolation of the feeble and the instruction of the ignorant" and seem to regard religion, "the great ruling principle of the moral and natural world, as a mere invention to keep the vulgar in obedience."

A third group whose perceived corruption Burke assails is the "stockjobbers," as he calls them, those individuals who put their own private economic interests above the nation's and seek to further those interests by exploiting the possibilities opened up by a dismantled Church economy. Among these, Burke targets speculators who fear for their investments because of the accumulating national debt, and many British readers must have been sensitive to that danger.

Prominent among the many enemies of the Church and the monarchy cited by Burke is a certain alienated personality that he describes as "discontented men of quality" who evince no love of country or of humankind. They fail "to love the little platoon we belong to in society" and "generally despise their own order," and they exhibit "a selfish and mischievous ambition" and "distempered passions." Had Burke lived to read Fyodor Dostoevski's *Besy* (1871-1872; *The Possessed*, 1913), he would have found in that novel's cankered nihilists precisely the sensibility to which he objected. His allegiance to the established Church extends to a sympathy for those Church members deprived of their rank and fortune. Speaking always of what is ideal, and well aware that many clergy betray that ideal, Burke defends the privileges accorded ecclesiastics, who, with the nobility, provide models to which the humble can aspire. As he says: "Some part of the wealth of the country is as usefully employed as it can be, in fomenting the luxury of individuals. It is the publick ornament. It is the publick consolation. It nourishes the publick hope."

Admitting to but a slight knowledge of the character of the French nobility, Burke argues that his lifetime study of "human nature" compensates for that deficiency. He ascribes to the French nobles a "high spirit" and "a delicate sense of honour." Their behavior toward the "inferior classes" appears good-natured and "more nearly approaching to familiarity" than the practice of their British counterparts. The fact that commoners who had achieved wealth did not enjoy adequate esteem in society Burke judges to be "one principal cause of the old nobility." Yet he considers the nobility and the established Church as the embodiment of the sacred principle of private property. "Nobility is a graceful ornament to the civil order. It is the Corinthian capital of polished society." The leveling instinct is therefore false to human nature. Holding these beliefs, then, it was natural for Burke to interpret the events in France as a threat to the foundations of a civil society in Britain.

Frank Day

Further Reading

Blakemore, Steven, ed. *Burke and the French Revolution.* Athens: University of Georgia Press, 1992. Collection of six essays written on the occasion of the bicentennial of the revolution includes comparison of the moral imaginations of Burke and Jean-Jacques Rousseau and examination of the "feminization" of *Reflections on the Revolution in France.*

Burke, Edmund. *Reflections on the Revolution in France.* Edited by Frank M. Turner. New Haven, Conn.: Yale University Press, 2003. In addition to the text of Burke's work, includes an informative editor's introduction and four essays analyzing various aspects of the book.

Chapman, Gerald. *Edmund Burke: The Practical Imagination.* Cambridge, Mass.: Harvard University Press, 1967. Presents sophisticated analysis of the *Reflections* and argues that Burke's absurd account of the events at Versailles led to a distortion of his position.

Hodson, Jane. *Language and Revolution in Burke, Wollstonecraft, Paine, and Godwin.* Burlington, Vt.: Ashgate, 2007. Analyzes *Reflections on the Revolution in France* and other works about the French Revolution to demonstrate how the writers use particular kinds of language to lend their texts greater authority.

Lock, F. P. *Burke's "Reflections on the Revolution in France."* London: Allen & Unwin, 1985. Offers authoritative commentary on the work and carefully explains the sequence of events that led to Burke's response to the revolution.

Mitchell, L. G. Introduction to *Reflections on the Revolution in France*, by Edmund Burke. New York: Oxford University Press, 1993. Concise and informative introduction appears in one of the most readily available paperback editions of *Reflections on the Revolution in France.*

Paine, Thomas. *Rights of Man.* 1791. Reprint. Edited by Henry Collins. Harmondsworth, England: Penguin Books, 1969. The famous response to Burke by the pamphleteer whose *Crisis* papers helped win the American Revolution.

Whale, John, ed. *Edmund Burke's "Reflections on the Revolution in France": New Interdisciplinary Essays.* New York: Manchester University Press, 2000. Collection includes discussion of the book's critical reception in the early 1790's as well as topics such as how Burke's work related to popular opinion and national identity.

The Reivers
A Reminiscence

Author: William Faulkner (1897-1962)
First published: 1962
Type of work: Novel
Type of plot: Psychological realism
Time of plot: May, 1905
Locale: Yoknapatawpha County, Mississippi; Memphis and Parsham, Tennessee

Principal characters:
LUCIUS PRIEST, the eleven-year-old narrator
BOON HOGGANBECK, a part-Chickasaw Indian and the poorest shot in the county
NED WILLIAM MCCASLIN, the Priests' coachman and a black member of the McCaslin and Priest families
LUCIUS QUINTUS PRIEST (BOSS), young Lucius's grandfather, a Jefferson banker, and owner of the stolen Winton Flyer
MISS SARAH, his wife
MAURY PRIEST, Lucius Quintus's son and Lucius's father
MISS ALISON, his wife
MISS REBA RIVERS, the madam of a Memphis brothel
EVERBE (MISS CORRIE) CORINTHIA, one of Miss Reba's girls and the beloved of Boon Hogganbeck
MR. BINFORD, Miss Reba's landlord and protector
MINNIE, Miss Reba's maid
OTIS, Miss Corrie's delinquent nephew from Arkansas
SAM CALDWELL, a railroad brakeman and Boon's rival
UNCLE PARSHAM HOOD, a dignified old black man who befriends young Lucius Priest
LYCURGUS BRIGGINS, his grandson
BUTCH LOVEMAIDEN, a brutal deputy sheriff
MCWILLIE, the rider of the racehorse Acheron
COLONEL LINSCOMB, Acheron's owner
MR. VAN TOSCH, the owner of Coppermine, the stolen racehorse renamed Lightning
BOBO BEAUCHAMP, Mr. van Tosch's stable boy and Ned William McCaslin's cousin
DELPHINE, Ned's wife and the Priests' cook

The Story:

In 1905, eleven-year-old Lucius Priest is on his way to Memphis with Boon Hogganbeck—a part-Chickasaw Indian man who is tough and faithful but completely unpredictable and unreliable and who is mad about machinery—and freeloading Ned William McCaslin, the Priests' black coachman and handyman. They are riding in the Winton Flyer owned by young Lucius's grandfather and "borrowed" for the excursion without his permission or knowledge. Lucius's grandfather, the president of a Jefferson bank and owner of the Winton Flyer, only the second automobile ever to be seen in the county, has gone to Louisiana to attend a funeral. Boon tempted the boy with the proposal that they drive the Winton Flyer to Memphis, and Lucius finally suc-

cumbed to the temptation. After considerable conniving, they set out, only to discover shortly afterward that Ned William McCaslin had hidden himself under a tarpaulin on the backseat.

Because of the condition of the roads, the truants are forced to make an overnight stop at Miss Ballenbaugh's, a small country store with a loft above it that holds mattresses for the convenience of fishermen and hunters. The next morning, after one of the breakfasts for which Miss Ballenbaugh is famous, they start out early and soon reach Hell Creek bottom, the deepest mud hole in all of Mississippi. There is no way around it—if they go in one direction, they will end up in Alabama, and if they go in the other, they will fall into the Mississippi River. The automobile becomes mired and remains stuck in the mud in spite of their labors with shovel, barbed wire, block and tackle, and piled branches. As they work, a barefoot redneck watches and waits on the porch of an unpainted cabin nearby, his two mules already harnessed in plow gear. When the boy and his companions give up in exasperation, this backwoods opportunist appears and pulls the car out of the slough, remarking that mud is one of the best crops in the region. Some stiff bargaining follows. Boon argues that six dollars is too much to pay for the job, all the more because one of his passengers is a boy and the other is black. The man answers that his mules are color-blind.

Eventually, they arrive in Memphis, but instead of going to the Gayoso Hotel, as Lucius is expecting (the McCaslins and the Priests always stay at the Gayoso because a distant member of both families had in Civil War times galloped into the hotel's lobby in an effort to capture a Yankee general), Boon drives his passengers to Miss Reba's brothel on Catalpa Street so that he can see Miss Corrie, one of Miss Reba's girls. That night, Ned, a reckless gambling man, trades the borrowed automobile for a stolen racehorse never known to run any better than second. Before the three can return to Jefferson, it is necessary for young Lucius to turn jockey and ride the stolen horse in a race against a better horse, Colonel Linscomb's Acheron.

Lucius also fights with Otis, a vicious boy who has slurred his aunt, Miss Corrie, and with this chivalric gesture Lucius restores the young woman's self-respect. Boon and Ned become involved in difficulties with the law, represented by a corrupt deputy sheriff named Butch Lovemaiden. It is discovered that Otis has stolen the gold tooth prized by Miss Reba's maid, Minnie. Boon finds that he has rivals for Miss Corrie's charms, and he has to fight them. As a result of these delays, Lucius is forced to assume a gentleman's responsibilities of courage and good conduct. He loses the innocence of childhood and is at times close to despair, but he realizes that to turn back would bring him shame.

Lucius survives his ordeal, but at considerable cost to his conscience and peace of mind. Grandfather Priest, who arrives to straighten everything out, has the final word on the boy's escapade. When Lucius asks how he can forget his folly and guilt, his grandfather tells him that he will not be able to, because nothing in life is ever forgotten or lost. When Lucius wants to know what he can do, his grandfather says that he must live with it. To the weeping boy's protests, the old man replies that a gentleman can live through anything because he must always accept the responsibility of his actions and the weight of their consequences. He concludes by telling Lucius to go wash his face: A gentleman may cry, but he washes his face afterward.

Critical Evaluation:

Subtitled *A Reminiscence*, *The Reivers*, for which William Faulkner posthumously received the 1963 Pulitzer Prize in fiction, begins on a note of action recalled in memory. About a fourth of the way through the novel, Faulkner finally begins one of his most engaging yarns, a tall tale whose idiom and spirit is reminiscent of a Huck Finn escapade brought forward in time. Its presence in *The Reivers* is less a matter of imitation than it is of a common source, for there is a sense in which Faulkner stands at the end of a literary tradition rather than, as many of his admirers claim, at the beginning of a new one. Through all of his writing runs a strain of broad folk humor and comic invention going back through Mark Twain to Augustus Baldwin Longstreet's *Georgia Scenes, Characters, Incidents, Etc. in the First Half Century of the Republic* (1835) and George Washington Harris's *Sut Lovingood's Yarns* (1867), and beyond them to the Davy Crockett almanacs and the anonymous masters of oral anecdote who flourished in the old Southwest.

Early Americans were by nature storytellers. The realities of frontier life and their own hard comic sense created a literature of tall men and tall deeds repeated in the trading post, the groggery, the rafters' camp, and wherever men met on the edge of the wilderness. These stories, shaped by a common experience and imagination, had a geography, a mythology, and a lingo of their own. Some were streaked with ballad sentiment, others with bawdy humor, but mostly these tales were comic elaborations of character, of fantastic misadventures in which the frontiersman dramatized himself with shrewd appraisal and salty enjoyment. Through these tales goes a ragtag procession of hunters, peddlers, horse traders, horse thieves, eagles, prophets, backwoods swains, land speculators, and settlers, creating a picture of the country and the times.

Faulkner's fictional Yoknapatawpha County lies, after all, in the same geographical belt as the Mississippi River and the Natchez Trace, and this is a region of history, folklore, and fantasy revealed in tall-story humor. This humor came into Faulkner's fiction as early as *Mosquitoes* (1927), in the account of Old Hickory's descendant who tried raising sheep in the Louisiana swamps and came to feel so much at home in the water that he turned into a shark. It contributes to effects of grotesque outrage and exaggeration in *As I Lay Dying* (1930), gives *Light in August* (1932) a warming pastoral glow, adds three episodes of pure comedy to *The Hamlet* (1940), and provides illuminating comment on the rise and fall of Flem Snopes. Faulkner's habit in the past, however, was to subordinate his racier effects to the more serious concerns of human mortality and the disorder of the moral universe. Not until he wrote *The Reivers* did he give free play to his talent for comedy of character and situation and, like Mark Twain in *Adventures of Huckleberry Finn* (1884), make it the master bias of structure and theme.

The Reivers also has other parallels with Twain's novel. One is the unmistakable flavor of a style derived from the drawled tones of reminiscence. In *Adventures of Huckleberry Finn*, this style is shaped to reveal habits of thought and feeling in art, a truly colloquial style marvelously tuned in pulse and improvisation and including the incorrectness of folk speech in its idiom. In *The Reivers*, this style is made to support both a burden of feeling within a boy's range of responses and an old man's accumulation of a lifetime's reflections. It is a style that can record sensory impressions with poetic finality.

Like *Adventures of Huckleberry Finn*, *The Reivers*, too, is a story of initiation, of innocence corrupted and evil exorcised. Both novels show the world through the eyes of childhood, an effective device that freshens experience and corrects judgment. Between the two novels there is this important difference, however: Huck is protected from the contamination of the shore by the earthy nonchalance of his own native shrewdness and resourcefulness; young Lucius Priest lives by the code of his class, the code of a gentleman, and he brings its values to the bordello and to the racetrack. The true test is not innocence itself but what lies behind the mask of innocence. Grandfather Priest claims that when adults speak of childish innocence, they really mean ignorance. Actually, children are neither innocent nor ignorant, in his opinion, for an eleven-year-old can envision any crime. If a child possesses innocence, it is probably lack of appetite, just as a child's ignorance may be a lack of opportunity or ability.

Under its surface of fantastic invention and tall-story humor, *The Reivers* is a moral fable in the Faulknerian manner, but its effect is different from that of the author's earlier, darker studies of manners and morals. In tragedy—and Faulkner was a great tragic artist—the human soul stands naked before a God who is not mocked. In comedy, it is not what is possible in humans that is revealed but what is probable in conduct or belief. Thus, in comedy, people are viewed in relation to some aspect of their society. In *The Reivers*— "reiver" is an old term for a plunderer or freebooter—a master of comedy is at work to show the testing of young Lucius Priest's code of gentlemanly behavior in a world of evasion and deceit, where it would be easier to run from responsibilities than to stand up and face them.

The triumph of *The Reivers* is in the manner of its telling. The novel presents the story of a boy, but the story is told by a man grown old and wise enough through the years of accumulated experience to look back on his adventure, relish it in all its qualities, and, at the same time, pass judgment on it. This judgment is never harsh. Lucius Priest, telling the story to his grandson, is revealed as a person of tolerance and understanding of much that is deeply and irrevocably ingrained in the eternal condition of humankind, and his point of view gives the novel added depth and dimension.

Among Faulkner's novels *The Reivers* is a minor work. Nevertheless, it is a good yarn in the tall-story tradition, skillfully told, comic in effect, and shrewd in its observation of manners, morals, politics, and human nature. More to the point, the novel broadens the reader's knowledge of Faulkner's legendary Mississippi county.

Further Reading

Brooks, Cleanth. *William Faulkner: The Yoknapatawpha Country*. New Haven, Conn.: Yale University Press, 1963. Excellent introduction to Faulkner's work contains separate chapters on his important novels, including *The Reivers*. Describes the plots and subtexts of the works; provides comparisons between the characters.

Towner, Theresa M. *The Cambridge Introduction to William Faulkner*. New York: Cambridge University Press, 2008. Accessible resource, aimed at students and general readers, provides detailed analyses of Faulkner's nineteen novels, discussion of his other works, and information about the critical reception for his fiction.

Vickery, Olga W. *The Novels of William Faulkner*. Rev. ed. 1964. Reprint. Baton Rouge: Louisiana State University Press, 1995. Provides a thorough examination of all of Faulkner's novels, summarizing Faulkner's technique, style, and themes as well as the encompassing philosophy that unifies his works.

Williams, David. *Faulkner's Women: The Myth and the Muse*. Montreal: McGill-Queen's University Press, 1977. Considers the women in Faulkner's novels from the perspective of psychoanalysis and Jungian archetypes. Includes a discussion of male and female characters in *The Reivers*.

Wittenberg, Judith Bryant. *Faulkner: The Transfiguration of Biography*. Lincoln: University of Nebraska Press, 1979. Biographical work draws on scenes from Faulkner's novels in examining the author's views on artists, family, and human responsibility. Discusses Lucius Priest of *The Reivers* as exemplary in his heroic conduct.

Relativity
The Special and the General Theory, Popular Exposition

Author: Albert Einstein (1879-1955)
*First published: Über die spezielle und die allgemeine
    Relativitätstheorie (Gemeinverständlich)*, 1917
    (English translation, 1920)
Type of work: Science

By 1916, Albert Einstein was a world-famous professor of physics at the University of Berlin, and he had seen several scientists and popularizers write books about his special theory of relativity, which he had first published in 1905. Other such books, published between 1913 and 1916, even included some of his preliminary ideas on the general theory of relativity. With the success of several of these popularizations, he knew that a large and willing audience was available to learn about the theories of relativity from the man who created them. Having spent the majority of his scientific career communicating with colleagues via journal articles that made heavy use of advanced mathematics, Einstein realized that he would need a different way to convey his discoveries to a lay readership. When, in the fall of 1915, he started thinking about how to make his ideas understandable to nonscientists, his work on the general theory of relativity was effectively complete, but his personal life was in turmoil, and all of this would play a role in the book's composition.

In 1914, Einstein had separated, not amicably, from his first wife Mileva and their two sons, but he was not formally divorced until 1919. During the interim, he formed an intimate relationship with his cousin Elsa Löwenthal, who had been married and had two teenaged daughters, Margot and Ilse. Einstein became friendly with the young girls, and in papers kept secret for many years scholars would later discover correspondence from Ilse in which she wrote that Einstein loved her "very much, perhaps more than any other man ever will," and that he was "prepared to marry" either her or her mother. After Einstein's marriage to Elsa in 1919, Margot and Ilse became his stepdaughters.

As Einstein wrote *Relativity*, he read aloud the completed pages to Margot, in the hope that if a teenager could understand his book then other nonscientists would as well. Scholars have compared surviving fragments of this manuscript with corrections in later editions and have detected the handwriting of Ilse. Einstein experienced some difficulty in getting started, but, driven by a desire to make his ideas widely understandable, he completed the manuscript by December, 1916. At the time, he told a friend that his presentation was so simple that a high school student could understand it, though he was unhappy with the book's style, which he characterized as "wooden." Nevertheless, German publishing house Vieweg in Braunschweig published *Relativity* in the spring of 1917, and it enjoyed rapid success. Several other German editions and many translations followed. Einstein sometimes added new prefaces to these translations, and he also made corrections and additions to both the German and the foreign versions. The book passed through fifteen German editions during Einstein's lifetime (though there was no fifteenth, and the last one, labeled the sixteenth, was published in 1954).

Einstein structured his book in three parts: The first part, comprising seventeen chapters, is on the special theory of relativity; the second, comprising twelve chapters, is on the general theory; the third, comprising three chapters, is titled "Considerations on the Universe as a Whole." Einstein warns readers that, despite the book's brevity, patience and willpower will be required to grasp the main ideas and their justifications. He first reviews the basic concepts of Euclidean geometry and Newtonian mechanics before beginning his treatment of special relativity in the sixth chapter, "The Apparent Incompatibility of the Law of Propagation of Light with the Principle of Relativity." Einstein had become aware of this incompatibility as a teenager, when he wondered what he would experience if he could travel as fast as a light wave. This thought experiment led to a dilemma that necessitated the abandonment of either the classical principle of relativity, which was based on the laws of motion discovered by Galileo and Sir Isaac Newton, or the classical laws of the propagation of light, based on the work of James Clerk Maxwell and others. Einstein discovered a way out of the dilemma by reasoning from two postulates of invariance: the constancy of light's speed in uniformly moving systems and the immutability of physical laws in such systems. In the next ten chapters, Einstein guides readers through some of the surprising consequences for scientists' understanding of space, time, simultaneity, mass, and energy when thought experiments are performed based on these two postulates.

A good example of this process involves Einstein's use of a moving train to deduce the relativity of simultaneity. He imagines a train passing an embankment: At the instant an observer in the middle of the train faces an observer on the embankment, lightning strikes the front and the back of the train. The observer on the train interprets this event as nonsimultaneous since he sees the flash from the front before the one from the back, whereas the observer on the embankment sees the flashes occurring simultaneously, since both flashes reach him at the same time. In this way, Einstein shows that Newton's idea of absolute simultaneity for all observers is wrong and that time does not have absolute significance but depends on the state of motion of the observer. Using similar reasoning, he shows that observers in different but uniformly moving systems will make dissimilar observations about an object's length and clock times. For example, moving clocks appear to run more slowly than clocks at rest, a phenomenon that came to be called "time dilation."

The most important and influential consequence of the special theory of relativity is Einstein's equation expressing the equivalence of mass and energy, which states that energy equals the mass of an object multiplied by the square of the speed of light. Because of the enormous size of light's speed, Einstein states that it is not yet possible to test this equation through experimentation, but with the development of advanced particle accelerators, Einstein would report in later editions that accelerations of subatomic particles confirmed his equation. Toward the end of his life, Einstein was distraught at the part his equation played in the development of the atomic bomb.

In part 2 of *Relativity*, Einstein confronts the much more demanding task of explaining general relativity to readers with modest mathematical backgrounds. What makes this theory "general" is its applicability to all systems, those moving nonuniformly as well as those moving uniformly. As he did in discussing the special theory, Einstein begins the second part of the book with a general principle—the equivalence of gravity and acceleration. During the decade between the publication of the two theories of relativity, Einstein had what he later called "the happiest thought of his life." He realized that a person falling from a building would have no experience of his weight.

In yet another thought experiment, Einstein analyzes what a person enclosed in a large box would experience if the box were resting on the Earth, and he compares that experience to the same person's experience if the box were being pulled by a rope in outer space. He concludes that the acceleration of the person toward the floor of the box is always of the same magnitude, whether the box is in a gravitational field or in an accelerated system. From this equivalence of gravity and acceleration, Einstein is able to ascertain some surprising consequences. For example, light rays travel curvilinearly in gravitational fields. This leads Einstein to urge physicists to test his idea during a solar eclipse (in later editions, he was able to report on the 1919 solar eclipse expeditions that successfully confirmed his predictions).

Most significant, the general theory of relativity explains something that Newton was never able to explain—the cause of gravity. For Einstein, matter is not contained in absolute space as Newton claimed; instead, matter modifies the space around it. This curved space then modifies the way that material objects behave. For example, the curvature of space around the Sun accounts for the elliptical motions of the planets. Einstein is even able to explain the anomalous behavior of the innermost planet of the solar system. Astronomers had observed that the point in Mercury's elliptical orbit nearest the Sun (the perihelion point) changes over time, something inexplicable in classical physics but accurately accounted for by general relativity.

In part 3 of *Relativity* Einstein analyzes such basic questions as whether the universe is finite or infinite, bounded or unbounded. He begins by explaining why Newton's conception of the stellar universe as a "finite island in the infinite ocean of space" is unsatisfactory, since the destiny of Newton's universe would be the systematic "impoverishment" of light and energy. The development of non-Euclidean geometries led to the discussion of spherical spaces that are finite but unbounded, and Einstein uses the two-dimensional surface of a sphere to give his readers an insight into the nature of three-dimensional spherical space. Beings existing on a sphere's surface discover that every line turns into a curve, which then leads to a recognition that this two-dimensional universe is finite but with no limits. Furthermore, these spherical-surface beings have no way of discovering whether they are in a finite or an infinite universe, because their "piece of the universe" is planar. Einstein uses the three-dimensional spherical analogue to this two-dimensional universe in his development of general relativity. He accepts astronomers' observations that matter in the universe is not distributed uniformly, leading him to conclude that the universe is "quasi-spherical" and finite. He concludes his book with the statement that his theory explains the connection between the "space-expanse" of the universe and the average density of matter in it.

Einstein's *Relativity* has an advantage over the many other popularizations of relativity theories produced during and after his life, since his book draws on the personal experiences that led him to formulate these theories. Reviewers have found his presentation of complex ideas clear and understandable, and his thought experiments have become standard in textbooks as well as other popular accounts. Historians of science have found Einstein's ongoing modifications and additions to his book helpful in understanding the evolution of his thinking about relativity, particularly its philosophical implications. In later editions, he shared with readers his skepticism about the new quantum mechanics, whose uncertainty principle challenged his profound belief in determinism. He famously said that God does not play dice with the universe. Despite many years of effort, Einstein was unable to successfully unify his general relativity and quantum mechanics, a task that continues to be the noble goal of many modern would-be Einsteins.

Robert J. Paradowski

Further Reading

Fölsing, Albrecht. *Albert Einstein: A Biography*. New York: Penguin Books, 1998. This massive and detailed work was praised on its first appearance in German and in its later English (abridged) version. Scientists and general readers have found his treatment of Einstein's life and work balanced and insightful. Extensive notes and bibliography, a helpful chronology, and an index.

Isaacson, Walter. *Einstein: His Life and Universe*. New York: Simon & Schuster, 2007. Isaacson, a former managing editor of *Time* magazine, uses many new documents in creating his portrait of "the complete Einstein"—scientist, humanist, husband, and father. The book, lauded by scientists and nonscientists, became a best seller. Notes to primary and secondary sources, brief biographies of the main characters, and an index.

Kox, A. J., Martin J. Klein, and Robert Schulmann, eds. *The Berlin Years: Writings, 1914-1917*. Vol. 6 in *The Collected Papers of Albert Einstein*. Princeton, N.J.: Princeton University Press, 1996. This volume of the ongoing protect to publish all of Einstein's extant writings contains the German text of his popularization of the special and general theories of relativity. The introductions and notes are in English, as is a softcover companion that contains English translations of all of the German writings of volume 6. Includes a section on literature cited, as well as an index of subjects and another of citations.

Levenson, Thomas. *Einstein in Berlin*. New York: Bantam Books, 2003. This biographical study of Einstein's life and work from 1914 to 1933 also contains much background material on the composition and publication of his popularization on relativity. Illustrated with photographs. Notes, bibliography, and index.

The Remains of the Day

Author: Kazuo Ishiguro (1954-   )
First published: 1989
Type of work: Novel
Type of plot: Psychological realism
Time of plot: 1922-1956
Locale: Southern England

Principal characters:
STEVENS, a butler at Darlington Hall
MISS KENTON, a housekeeper at Darlington Hall
WILLIAM STEVENS, Stevens's father
LORD DARLINGTON, the owner of Darlington Hall
REGINALD CARDINAL, a journalist, and Darlington's godson
MR. FARRADAY, a wealthy American and later owner of Darlington Hall
MR. LEWIS, a U.S. senator
HERR RIBBENTROP, a German ambassador
MONSIEUR DUPONT, a French dignitary

The Story:

Stevens is preparing to drive Mr. Farraday's Ford from Darlington Hall (near Oxford) to the West Country to meet with Miss Kenton, a former housekeeper at Darlington.

Stevens believes, on the basis of a recent letter from Miss Kenton, that she wants to return to her position at the mansion.

Stevens sets out on his drive, stopping the first night in Salisbury. As he travels, he engages in an introspective analysis of the concept of dignity. Recalling that his father, William Stevens, exemplified dignity, he remembers an event from thirty years earlier—seeing his father pacing the grounds in front of the summerhouse at Darlington Hall, carefully examining the ground.

It is spring, 1922, and Miss Kenton and William Stevens begin their employment at Darlington Hall. William falls while serving guests, months before an unofficial conference is to be held at Darlington. Representatives from Great Britain, the United States, Italy, Germany, and France will be assembling to discuss the punitive nature of the Treaty of Versailles. William's son reduces his father's official duties, at Lord Darlington's behest. As delegates begin arriving, the young Stevens is asked by Darlington to explain the facts of life to his godson, Reginald Cardinal. Cardinal, in turn, informs Stevens that he already has a clear understanding of the issue.

The assembled delegates believe that they must convince the French representative, Monsieur Dupont, that sanctions against Germany should be eased. As Stevens attends to Dupont's sore-covered feet, Stevens's father suffers another attack. Stevens overhears Mr. Lewis (the U.S. delegate) tell Dupont that the other delegates seek to manipulate Dupont. Stevens visits his bedridden father, who tells his son that he is proud of him; Stevens, though, is unable to respond with any emotion.

At the final dinner of the conference, Dupont rises to offer a toast, thanking Darlington, agreeing with the aims of the conference, and exposing Lewis's duplicity. Lewis responds, and dismisses the other delegates as gentlemen amateurs.

Miss Kenton informs Stevens that his father's health has taken a turn for the worse, but Stevens returns to his duties. Darlington asks Stevens if he has been crying. Stevens continues with his work, changing Dupont's bandages. Miss Kenton then tells Stevens that his father has died. Again, Stevens returns to his duties.

On his second day of traveling, Stevens recalls an event from earlier in the day. He had informed a local that he is employed at Darlington Hall, but he also denied having worked there when Lord Darlington was alive. Stevens is disturbed by his own deception, recalling that he had done the same thing a few months earlier with a visitor to Darlington Hall. He stays the night at an inn outside Taunton in Somerset. He goes to the bar and talks with some locals, but he soon realizes that he is unskilled in casual conversation.

Stevens remembers several unofficial meetings between a British lord, Halifax, and the German ambassador, Herr Ribbentrop, which occurred before World War II. Stevens supports the reportedly common view that Ribbentrop deceived many in Great Britain, and he believes, like many others, that Lord Darlington is a Nazi sympathizer and an anti-Semite. However, he defends Darlington because he had employed, over the years, many Jews.

Stevens insists that allegations of anti-Semitism against Darlington rest upon one episode in the early 1930's. Darlington had been encouraged by a female friend to order Stevens to fire two Jewish housemaids. Stevens had then told Miss Kenton of the situation, and she became so distraught that she considered resigning. Stevens also told Miss Kenton that people of their position are unqualified to understand such issues. Stevens, who recalls that Darlington had expressed remorse about his decision the following year, also tells Miss Kenton that he, too, had felt that the firings were wrong, upsetting Miss Kenton once again.

Stevens is staying the night at a private residence in Moscombe because he has run out of gasoline. He reflects upon his relationship with Miss Kenton, recalling an event twenty years earlier when Miss Kenton had brought flowers into his room. She had asked Stevens what he was reading, and he refused to reveal the title. She playfully wrestled the book from his hand, discovering that he had been reading a sentimental romance novel.

Stevens wants to reestablish a more professional relationship with Miss Kenton, and Miss Kenton begins to take all of her allotted days off to visit a male friend. Stevens puts an end to his evening meetings with Miss Kenton, a change that he considers to be a turning point.

Stevens, staying overnight in a private home, meets several neighbors who have dropped by. Mistaken for a wealthy gentleman, he tells them that he has had a role in international politics. One of the neighbors asserts that dignity is not exclusive to the wealthy. This debate reminds Stevens of an event that occurred in 1935, in which Darlington and several guests had questioned Stevens about current issues. Stevens had feigned ignorance, proving (in the minds of his inquisitors) that commoners have no role in political discourse. Darlington had apologized to Stevens the next morning, but in doing so also argued that democracy is outdated and that Germany and Italy have realized this fact. This memory unsettles Stevens, and he rejects any responsibility for Darlington's mistakes.

The next day of travel finds Stevens sitting in the dining hall of a hotel in Little Compton, Cornwall, waiting until it is time to meet Miss Kenton (who is now Mrs. Alice Benn). Stevens thinks about the events of the morning. One of the locals in Moscombe helps Stevens with the car he has been driving and asks him if, in fact, he is a manservant. Stevens confesses that he is the butler at Darlington Hall.

Stevens has been preoccupied with a particular memory—standing outside Miss Kenton's door as she cries inside her home. She had been crying not because of her aunt's death (as Stevens had previously thought) but because her friend had proposed marriage. Miss Kenton later tells Stevens that she had accepted the proposal, and Stevens offers congratulations.

Lord Darlington, Herr Ribbentrop, the British prime minister, and the British foreign secretary meet. Darlington's godson, Reginald Cardinal, who is also a journalist, arrives at Darlington Hall uninvited, having been tipped off about the secret meeting. Cardinal tells Stevens that the Nazis are manipulating Darlington, but Stevens refuses to question his employer's judgment. At the close of the evening, Stevens feels triumphant at having maintained his dignity during the trying events of the day.

On the sixth day of his travels, Stevens is in Weymouth, thinking about his meeting with Miss Kenton. He discovers that Miss Kenton is not on the verge of divorce, as he had assumed. He tells her that Cardinal had been killed in the war and that accusations against Lord Darlington about his alleged Nazi sympathies eventually broke him down. Stevens then asks Miss Kenton if her husband has mistreated her. She assures Stevens that he has not and that she has grown to love her husband. She confesses that she has often wondered what her life would have been like with Stevens. His heart breaks as he hears this. As evening falls, he realizes that he has wasted his life. He sits alone, thinking about the time that remains. He decides that he must improve his bantering skills—making conversation with light irony—so as to better serve Mr. Farraday, the new owner of Darlington Hall.

Critical Evaluation:

Kazuo Ishiguro's *The Remains of the Day*, his third novel, received the Booker Prize for Fiction in 1989. The novel represents a departure for Ishiguro, whose previous novels, *A Pale View of Hills* (1982) and *An Artist of the Floating World* (1986), are set in his native Japan. *The Remains of the Day* is Ishiguro's first novel set in his adopted country of England (to which his family moved when Ishiguro was five years old).

The narrative of *The Remains of the Day* is complex, leading to several questions. One question is, Does the story take place over six days in July, 1956, as Stevens drives through the south of England, or does the novel cover nearly forty years? The events of the past are all filtered through the memory of Stevens, and his memory sometimes proves faulty. Additionally, the novel crosses genres, displaying elements of tragedy, social realism, historical realism, social criticism, and fiction of manners. The filter of Stevens's memory makes the novel more a form of psychological realism than of any other category. The narrative takes the form of a diary, with Stevens recording his thoughts either at the close of each day or at breaks in his travels. This allows the reader to see changes in Stevens's thoughts on certain issues, and to see changes in his memories. The "diary" has an implicit reader, whom Stevens is addressing. He makes it clear several times that his reader is a servant, much like himself.

The novel's title, too, invites analysis. In the final chapter, a stranger tells Stevens that the evening is the best part of the day. Stevens, applying this thought to his own life, ponders what he should do with the remains of his own day. His question may be seen as alternatively hopeful and self-defeating, as he holds out hope for his future while also explicitly avoiding a thoughtful valuation of his past. This conundrum may be applied to British society as well. What should English identity become in an era in which the British Empire's global influence has declined or in which concepts of class are breaking down? The word "remains" can also be interpreted as referring to a corpse. With this double meaning comes the question, Who or what has died?

One episode in the novel serves as a sort of metaphor for much of the rest of the story—that is, when Stevens and Miss Kenton see Steven's father, William, carefully examining the grounds in front of the summerhouse as though he were searching for "some precious jewel" that he had dropped. Stevens's narrative itself, covering his memories of more than thirty years, could be considered a similar search, with Miss Kenton as the "jewel" that Stevens has allowed to slip through his fingers. Readers may even see the episode as a metaphor for the decline of the British Empire or the breakdown of the British class system.

Stevens's character provides the reader with a sort of cultural mirror for examining Great Britain during a period of drastic social change, when British ideas of class and national identity were undergoing significant shifts. In several interviews, Ishiguro has said that a butler like Stevens could be seen as representative of the general public, blindly serving unworthy masters.

The Remains of the Day, also, features themes that continue through all of Ishiguro's work: memory and suppressed memory. The reader must search for the ways in which Stevens practices careful self-deception. Only at the conclusion of the novel can Stevens no longer avoid the painful issues that his decisions (or lack thereof) have created in his life. Even so, in finally (if perhaps only temporarily) facing his failures, Stevens achieves a sort of painful dignity.

Marc Seals

Further Reading

Lewis, Barry. *Kazuo Ishiguro*. New York: Manchester University Press, 2000. A useful study of Ishiguro's life and work. Chapter 4, about *The Remains of the Day*, provides a careful and concise analysis of the character of Stevens and the symbolic implications of his characterization for British culture.

Parkes, Adam. *Kazuo Ishiguro's "The Remains of the Day": A Reader's Guide*. New York: Continuum, 2001. Presents a solid background on Ishiguro, an explication of the novel, a discussion of how the novel was critically received, and a discussion of the 1993 film adaptation.

Shaffer, Brian W. *Understanding Kazuo Ishiguro*. Columbia: University of South Carolina Press, 1998. The first full-length study of Ishiguro's work. This groundbreaking work explores Ishiguro's place in British literature in the context of his first three novels.

Shaffer, Brian W., and Cynthia F. Wong, eds. *Conversations with Kazuo Ishiguro*. Jackson: University Press of Mississippi, 2008. A collection of nineteen interviews with Ishiguro covering two decades. Most of these interviews offer valuable insights into Ishiguro's thoughts on *The Remains of the Day*.

Sim, Wai-chew. *Globalization and Dislocation in the Novels of Kazuo Ishiguro*. Lewiston, N.Y.: Edwin Mellen Press, 2006. Provides a perceptive look at the cosmopolitan aspects of Ishiguro's novels and the alienation of his female and male protagonists.

Wong, Cynthia. *Kazuo Ishiguro*. Tavistock, England: Northcote House/British Council, 2000. A concise and useful text that explores Ishiguro's work and his place in international literature, focusing on his use of memory.

Remembrance of Things Past

Author: Marcel Proust (1871-1922)

First published: À la recherche du temps perdu, 1913-1927 (English translation, 1922-1931, 1981); includes *Du côté de chez Swann*, 1913 (*Swann's Way*, 1922); *À l'ombre des jeunes filles en fleurs*, 1919 (*Within a Budding Grove*, 1924); *Le Côté de Guermantes*, 1920-1921 (*The Guermantes Way*, 1925); *Sodome et Gomorrhe*, 1922 (*Cities of the Plain*, 1927); *La Prisonnière*, 1925 (*The Captive*, 1929); *Albertine disparue*, 1925 (*The Sweet Cheat Gone*, 1930); *Le Temps retrouvé*, 1927 (*Time Regained*, 1931)

Type of work: Novels

Type of plot: Psychological realism

Time of plot: Late nineteenth and early twentieth centuries

Locale: France

Principal characters:

MARCEL, the narrator

MARCEL'S GRANDMOTHER, a kind and wise old woman

MONSIEUR SWANN, a wealthy broker and aesthete

MADAME SWANN, formerly a cocotte, Odette de Crecy

GILBERTE, their daughter and later Madame de Saint-Loup

MADAME DE VILLEPARISIS, friend of Marcel's grandmother

ROBERT DE SAINT-LOUP, her nephew and Marcel's friend

BARON DE CHARLUS, another nephew and a Gomorrite

MADAME VERDURIN, a vulgar social climber

PRINCE and PRINCESS DE GUERMANTES and DUKE and DUCHESS DE GUERMANTES, members of the old aristocracy

The Story:

All of his life Marcel finds it difficult to go to sleep at night. After he blows out the light, he lies quietly in the darkness and thinks of the book he had been reading, of an event in history, of some memory from the past. Sometimes he thinks of all the places in which he had slept—as a child in his great-aunt's house in the provincial town of Combray, in Balbec on a holiday with his grandmother, in the military town where his friend, Robert de Saint-Loup, had been stationed, in Paris, in Venice during a visit there with his mother.

He remembers always one night at Combray when he was a child: Monsieur Swann, a family friend, has come to dinner. Marcel is sent to bed early, and he lays awake for hours, nervous and unhappy until at last he hears Monsieur Swann leave. Then his mother comes upstairs to comfort him. For a long time, the memory of this night remains his chief recollection of Combray, where he spent a part of every summer with his grandparents and aunts. Years later, while drinking tea with his mother, the taste of a madeleine, or small sweet cake, suddenly brings back all the impressions of his old days at Combray.

Marcel remembers the two roads. One is Swann's way, a path that runs beside Monsieur Swann's park, where lilacs and hawthorns bloom. The other is the Guermantes way, along the river and past the château of the duke and duchess de Guermantes, the great family of Combray. He remembers the people he sees on his walks. There are familiar figures like the doctor and the priest. There is Monsieur Vinteuil, an old composer who died brokenhearted and shamed because of his daughter's friendship with a woman of bad reputation. There are the neighbors and friends of his grandparents. Most of all, he remembers Monsieur Swann, whose story he pieces together slowly from family conversations and village gossip.

Monsieur Swann is a wealthy Jew, accepted in rich and fashionable society. His wife is not received, however, for she is his former mistress, Odette de Crecy, a prostitute with the fair, haunting beauty of a Sandro Botticelli painting. Odette had first introduced Swann to the Verdurins, a common family that pretends to despise the polite world of the Guermantes. At an evening party given by Madame Verdurin, Swann hears a movement of Vinteuil's sonata and identifies his hopeless passion for Odette with that lovely music.

Swann's love is an unhappy affair. Tortured by jealousy, aware of the commonness and pettiness of the Verdurins, determined to forget his unfaithful mistress, he goes to Madame de Saint-Euverte's reception. There he hears Vinteuil's music again. Under its influence he decides, at whatever price, to marry Odette.

After their marriage, Swann drifts more and more into the bourgeois circle of the Verdurins. He travels alone to see his old friends in Combray and in the fashionable Faubourg Saint-Germain.

Many people think Marcel is both ridiculous and tragic. On his walks, Marcel sometimes sees Madame Swann and her daughter, Gilberte, in the park at Combray. Later, in Paris, he meets the little girl and becomes her playmate. That friendship, as they grow older, becomes an innocent love affair. Filled also with a schoolboyish passion for Madame Swann, Marcel goes to Swann's house as much to be in her company as in Gilberte's, but after a time, his pampered habits and brooding and neurasthenic nature begin to bore Gilberte. His pride hurt, he refuses to see her for many years.

Marcel's family begins to treat him as sickly. With his grandmother, he travels to Balbec, a seaside resort. There he meets Albertine, a girl to whom he is immediately attracted. He also meets Madame de Villeparisis, an old friend of his grandmother and a connection of the Guermantes family. Madame de Villeparisis introduces him to her two nephews, Robert de Saint-Loup and Baron de Charlus. Saint-Loup and Marcel become close friends. While visiting Saint-Loup in a nearby garrison town, Marcel meets his friend's mistress, a young Jewish actor named Rachel. Marcel is both fascinated and repelled by Baron de Charlus; he will not understand until later the baron's corrupt and depraved nature.

Through his friendship with Madame de Villeparisis and Saint-Loup, Marcel is introduced into the smart world of the Guermantes when he returns to Paris. One day, while he is walking with his grandmother, she suffers a stroke. The illness and death of that good and unselfish old woman makes him realize for the first time the empty worldliness of his smart and wealthy friends. For comfort he turns to Albertine, who stays with him in Paris while his family is away. Nevertheless, his desire to be humored and indulged in all of his whims, his suspicions of Albertine, and his petty jealousy finally force her to leave him and go back to Balbec. With her, he has been unhappy; without her, he is wretched. Then he learns that she has been accidentally killed in a fall from her horse. Later he receives a letter, written before her death, in which she promises to return to him.

More miserable than ever, Marcel tries to find diversion among his old friends. They are changing with the times. Swann is ill and soon to die. Gilberte had married Robert de Saint-Loup. Madame Verdurin, who had inherited a fortune, now entertains the old nobility. At one of her parties, Marcel hears a Vinteuil composition played by a musician named Morel, the nephew of a former servant and now a protégé of the notorious Baron de Charlus.

His health breaking down at last, Marcel spends the war years in a sanatorium. When he returns to Paris, he finds still greater changes. Robert de Saint-Loup had been killed in the war. Rachel, Saint-Loup's mistress, had become a famous actor. Swann also is dead, and his widow had remarried and is now a fashionable host who receives the Duchess de Guermantes. Prince de Guermantes, his fortune lost and his first wife dead, had married Madame Verdurin for her money. Baron de Charlus had grown senile.

Marcel goes to one last reception at the Princess de Guermantes' lavish house. There he meets the daughter of Gilberte de Saint-Loup; he realizes how time has passed, how old he has grown. In the Guermantes library, he happens to take down the novel by George Sand that his mother had read to him that remembered night in Combray, years before. Suddenly, in memory, he hears again the ringing of the bell that announces Monsieur Swann's departure and knows that it will echo in his mind forever. He sees then that everything in his own futile, wasted life dates from that long ago night in his childhood, and in that moment of self-revelation he sees also the ravages of time among all the people he had ever known.

Critical Evaluation:

Remembrance of Things Past is not a novel of traditional form. Symphonic in design, it unfolds without plot or crisis as the writer reveals in retrospect the motifs of his experience, holds them for thematic effect, and drops them, only to return to them once more in the processes of recurrence and change. This varied pattern of experience brings together a series of involved relationships through the imagination and observation of a narrator engaged in tracing with painstaking detail his perceptions of people and places as he himself grows from childhood to disillusioned middle age.

From the waking reverie in which he recalls the themes and characters of his novel to that closing paragraph with its slow, repeated echoes of the word "time," Marcel Proust's novel is great art distilled from memory itself, the structure determined entirely by moods and sensations evoked by the illusion of time passing, or seeming to pass, and time recurring, or seeming to recur.

In *Remembrance of Things Past*, Proust, together with Leo Tolstoy (*Voyna i mir*, 1865-1869; *War and Peace*, 1886), Fyodor Dostoevski (*Bratya Karamazovy*, 1879-1880; *The Brothers Karamazov*, 1912), Thomas Mann (*Die Geschichten Jaakobs*, 1933; *Joseph and His Brothers*, 1934), and James Joyce (*Ulysses*, 1922), transformed the novel from a linear account of events into a multidimensional art. The breakthrough was not into Freudian psychology, or existentialism, or scientific determinism, but into a realization that all things are, or may be, interwoven, bound by time, yet freed from time, open to every associational context.

What is reality? Certainly there is the reality of the sensory experience; yet any moment of sensory experience may have numerous successive or even simultaneous realities as it is relived in memory in different contexts, and perhaps the most significant reality—or realities—of a given act or moment may come long after the moment when the event first took place in time. Percy Shelley, in *A Defence of Poetry* (1840), said, "All things exist as they are perceived: at least in relation to the percipient." Things that may have seemed inconsequential at the moment of their occurrence may take on richly multifaceted meanings in relation to other events, other memories, other moments. The initial act is not as significant, not as real, as the perceptions of it which may come in new contexts. Reality, thus, is a context, made up of moods, of recollections joined by chance or design, sets of associations that have grown over the years. This concept of the notion of reality, one that had been taking shape with increased momentum since the Romantic movement, said Proust, opened the way to "those mysteries . . . the presentiment of which is the quality in life and art which moves us most deeply."

The elusive yet pervasively important nature of reality applies not only to events, such as the taste of the madeleine, but also to the absence of events, for the failure of Marcel's mother to give him his accustomed good-night kiss proved to be an occasion that memory would recall again and again in a variety of relationships. Thus reality can and inevitably for all people does sometimes include, if not indeed center on, the nonbeing of an event. That nonexistence can be placed in time and in successive times as surely as events that did happen; moreover "it"—that nothing where something might or should have been—may become a significant part of the contexts that, both in time and freed from time, constitute reality.

Such thematic variations and turns of thought have led some to identify Proust as a dilettante. Perhaps, in its literal sense, the term is justified, for his mind must have delighted in what, to the reader, may be unexpected turns of thought. In this he is most closely to be associated with Mann, whose consideration of time in the first volume of *Joseph and His Brothers* leads the reader into labyrinthine but essential paths; or whose speculations about the God-man relationship in volume 2, in the section headed "Abraham Discovers God," lead the reader down a dizzying path of whimsical yet serious thought. The fact remains, however, that Mann and Proust have opened doors of contemplation that modern readers cannot afford to ignore if they would increase their understanding of themselves, the world in which they live, and the tenuous nature of reality and of time.

What Proust does with time and reality he also does with character. Although he is a contemporary of Sigmund Freud, and although Freudian interpretation could be applied to some of his characters in part, Proust's concept of character is much too complex for reduction to the superego, the ego, the id, and the subconscious. Character, like reality, is a changing total context, not static and not a thing in itself to be held off and examined at arm's length. Baron de Charlus is at once a study of character in disintegration and a caricature, reduced in the end to a pitiable specimen, scarcely human. It is Marcel, however, the persona of the story, who is seen in most depth and frequently in tortured self-analysis. His character is seen in direct statements, in his comments about others and about situations, in what others say to him or the way they say it, even in descriptive passages that would at first glance not seem to relate to character at all. Mann said in the preface to his *The Magic Mountain* (1924), "Only the exhaustive can be truly interesting." Proust surely agreed. His detail is not of the catalog variety, however; it works cumulatively, developmentally, with the thematic progression of symphonic music.

Finally, the totality of the work is "the remembrance of things past," or as the title of the seventh and final volume has it, the past recaptured. To understand the work in its full richness, one must become and remain conscious of the author, isolated in his study, drawing upon his recollections and associating and reassociating moments, events, personalities (his own always central), both to recapture the past as it happened and to discover in it the transcendent reality that supersedes the time-bound moment of the initial occurrence. The total work is a story, a succession of stories, and a study of the life process, which, as one comes to understand it, must greatly enrich one's own sense of self and of the life one lives.

"Critical Evaluation" by Kenneth Oliver

Further Reading

Bales, Richard, ed. *The Cambridge Companion to Proust.* New York: Cambridge University Press, 2001. Collection of essays about *Remembrance of Things Past*, including discussions of the novel's birth and development, structure, and narrator; love, sex, and friendship in the novel; and French society from the belle époque to World War I.

Brown, Stephen Gilbert. *The Gardens of Desire: Marcel Proust and the Fugitive Sublime.* Albany: State University of New York Press, 2004. Brown provides a psychological critique of *Remembrance of Things Past*, applying theories by Sigmund Freud, Jacques Derrida, and Otto Rank to analyze the origins of the novel's creative impulse.

Cano, Christine M. *Proust's Deadline.* Urbana: University of Illinois Press, 2006. A history of the publication and reception of *Remembrance of Things Past*, including a discussion of how the later discovery of unpublished drafts touched off a debate about the novel's authenticity.

Carter, William C. *Marcel Proust: A Life.* New Haven, Conn.: Yale University Press, 2000. A meticulous account of Proust's life and literary career. Carter traces Proust's development as a writer, demonstrating how his earlier writings, including the abandoned novel *Jean Santeuil*, led him to create *Remembrance of Things Past.*

De Man, Paul. *Allegories of Reading: Figural Language in Rousseau, Nietzsche, Rilke, and Proust.* 1979. New ed. New Haven, Conn.: Yale University Press, 1982. Uses Proust to manifest the uncertainty of meaning by documenting the disjunction between grammar and rhetoric in the work.

Deleuze, Gilles. *Proust and Signs: The Complete Text.* Translated by Richard Howard. 1972. New ed. London: Athlone, 2000. Deleuze's landmark reading of Proust depicts the work as a search in which the disillusioned narrator learns to decode and discard the signs of worldliness and the signs of love, concluding that only the signs of art offer a kind of fulfillment that can withstand the corrosive force of time.

Genette, Gérard. "Proust Palimpsest" and "Proust and Indirect Language." In *Figures of Literary Discourse*, translated by Alan Sheridan. New York: Columbia University Press, 1982. Genette's classic analysis of Proust's use of figurative devices in general and of metaphor in particular.

Kristeva, Julia. *Proust and the Sense of Time.* Translated by Stephen Bann. New York: Columbia University Press, 1993. Kristeva's insightful reading is grounded in an investigation of the genesis of meaning. She traces the successive stages of subjectivity through which Proust's narrator passes.

Murphy, Michael. *Proust and America: The Influence of American Art, Culture, and Literature on "À la recherche du temps perdu."* Liverpool, England: Liverpool University Press, 2007. In this comparative study, Murphy interprets Proust's work within the context of American art, literature, and culture. Discusses Proust's reception of American authors Ralph Waldo Emerson and Edgar Allan Poe, as well as American neurologist George Beard's writings on neurasthenia and "American nervousness."

White, Edmund. *Marcel Proust.* New York: Viking Press, 1999. An excellent, updated, and concise biography of Proust. White, a gay literary critic and novelist, perceptively and honestly discusses, among other topics, Proust's homosexuality. Includes bibliographical references.

The Renaissance
Studies in Art and Poetry

Author: Walter Pater (1839-1894)
First published: 1873, as *Studies in the History of the Renaissance*; revised as *The Renaissance: Studies in Art and Poetry*, 1877, 1888, 1893
Type of work: Essays

In the preface to *The Renaissance*, Walter Pater writes, "The subjects of the following studies . . . touch what I think the chief points in that complex, many-sided movement." The subjects themselves are the French, Italian, and German writers, painters, and sculptors, ranging from the thirteenth to the eighteenth century, in whose lives and in whose works Pater finds represented the many sides, the divergent attitudes and aims, of the Renaissance.

Pater's method is impressionistic. The task of the aesthetic critic, he says, is first to realize distinctly the exact impression that a work of art makes upon him (or her), then to determine the source and conditions—the "virtue"—of that impression, and finally to express that virtue so that the impression it has made on him may be shared by others. *The Renaissance* is the record of the impressions induced in the refined sensibilities of Pater by the art he studied.

The Renaissance, for Pater, was "not merely the revival of classical antiquity which took place in the fifteenth century . . . but a whole complex movement, of which that revival of classical antiquity was but one element or symptom." Accordingly, in the first chapter, he finds the roots of the movement in twelfth and thirteenth century France, illustrated in two prose romances of that time, *Amis and Amile* and *Aucassin and Nicolette*. It is in their "spirit of rebellion and revolt against the moral and religious ideas of the time" that these tales prefigure that later "outbreak of the reason and the imagination," the high Renaissance of fifteenth century Italy.

One important part of that later Renaissance, according to Pater, was the effort made by fifteenth century Italian scholars "to reconcile Christianity with the religion of ancient Greece." Giovanni Pico della Mirandola typified that effort, in his writings as well as his life; he was "reconciled indeed to the new religion, but still [had] a tenderness for the earlier life." Lacking the historic sense, Pico and his contemporaries sought in vain, as Pater saw it, a reconciliation based on allegorical interpretations of religious belief: The "Renaissance of the fifteenth century was . . . great, rather by what it designed . . . than by what it actually achieved."

In discussing Sandro Botticelli, Pater acknowledges that he was a painter of secondary rank, not great as Michelangelo and Leonardo da Vinci were great. Nevertheless his work has a distinct quality, "the result of a blending in him of a sympathy for humanity in its uncertain condition . . . with his consciousness of the shadow upon it of the great things from which it shrinks." He is a forcible realist as well as a visionary painter. Part of his appeal to Pater is simply because "he has the freshness, the uncertain and diffident promise which belong to the earlier Renaissance"—that age that Pater called "perhaps the most interesting period in the history of the mind."

The chapter "Luca della Robbia" is as much about sculpture in general as it is about Luca. The limitation of sculpture, says Pater, is that it tends toward "a hard realism, a one-sided presentment of mere form." The Greeks countered this tendency by depicting the type rather than the individual, by purging the accidental until "their works came to be like some subtle extract or essence, or almost like pure thoughts or ideas." This sacrificed expression, however. Michelangelo, "with a genius spiritualized by the reverie of the middle age," offset the tendency of sculpture toward realism by "leaving nearly all his sculpture in a puzzling sort of incompleteness, which suggests rather than realizes actual form." Luca and other fifteenth century Tuscan sculptors achieved "a profound expressiveness" by working in low relief earthenware, the subtle delineation of line serving as the means of overcoming the special limitation of sculpture.

In "The Poetry of Michelangelo," Pater discusses not so much the poetry itself as his impressions of it. No one, says Pater, need be reminded of the strength of Michelangelo's work. There is, however, another and equally important quality of his work, and that Pater refers to variously as "charm," "sweetness," and "a lovely strangeness." It is in a "brooding spirit of life," achieved only through an idealization of life's "vehement sentiments," that this quality of sweetness resides. There were, says Pater, two traditions of the ideal that Michelangelo might have followed: that of Dante, who idealized the material world, and that of Platonism. It was the Platonic tradition that molded Michelangelo's verse: "Michelangelo is always pressing forward from the outward beauty . . . to apprehend the unseen beauty . . . that abstract form of beauty, about which the Platonists reason." Yet the influence of Dante is there, too, in the sentiment of imaginative love. To Pater, Michelangelo was "the last . . . of those on whom the peculiar sentiment of the Florence of Dante and Giotto descended: he is the consummate representative of the form that sentiment took in the fifteenth century." In this sentiment is another source of his "grave and temperate sweetness."

The fifteenth century witnessed two movements: the return to antiquity represented, says Pater, by Raphael and the return to nature represented by Leonardo da Vinci. In Leonardo the return to nature took on a special coloring, for his genius was composed not only of a desire for beauty but also of a curiosity that gave to his paintings "a type of subtle and curious grace." His landscapes, as in the background of his masterpiece, *La Gioconda*, partake of the "*bizarre of recherché.*" One of the most famous passages in the book is Pater's description of *La Gioconda*. Pater sees in the picture an archetypal woman: "All the thoughts and experience of the world have etched and moulded" her features.

In "The School of Giorgione" (which did not appear in the first edition of *The Renaissance*), Pater propounds his famous dictum that "All art constantly aspires towards the condition of music." The "condition of music" is a complete fusing, an interpenetration, of matter and form. The other arts achieve perfection in the degree that they approach or approximate this condition. Giorgione and others of the Venetian school are representative of the aspiration toward perfect identification of matter and form in their realization that "painting must be before all things decorative." Their subjects are from life, but "mere subject" is subordinated to pictorial design, so that matter is interpenetrated by form.

In the chapter on Joachim du Bellay, Pater turns from Italy to France, to the theories and the elegant verse of the *Pléiad*. Du Bellay wrote a tract in which he sought "to adjust the existing French culture to the rediscovered classical culture." In this tract, says Pater, the Renaissance became aware of itself as a systematic movement. The ambition of the *Pleiad* was to combine the "music of the measured, scanned verse of Latin and Greek poetry" with "the music of the rhymed, unscanned verse of Villon and the old French poets."

The longest chapter of *The Renaissance* is devoted to Johann Joachim Winckelmann, the German scholar of antiq-

uity. His importance, for Pater, is chiefly that he influenced Johann Wolfgang von Goethe, who "illustrates a union of the Romantic spirit . . . with Hellenism . . . that marriage . . . of which the art of the nineteenth century is the child." The Hellenic element, characterized by "breadth, centrality, with blitheness and repose," was made known to Goethe by Winckelmann, who consequently stands as a link between antiquity (and the Renaissance) and the post-Enlightenment world.

The most celebrated part of *The Renaissance*—and indeed of the author's entire body of writing—is the conclusion. Here, Pater utters the famous, and frequently misinterpreted, dicta "Not the fruit of experience, but experience itself, is the end" and "To burn always with this hard, gemlike flame, to maintain this ecstasy, is success in life." These statements must be seen in the context of Pater's conception of the nature of human existence.

For Pater, reality is human experience. It consists not in the objective, material world but in the impressions of color, odor, and texture which that world produces in the observer's mind. Each impression endures for but a single moment and then is gone. Life is made up of the succession of these momentary impressions, and life itself is brief.

Not to make the most of these moments, not to experience them fully, is to waste a lifetime. "What we have to do," says Pater, "is to be for ever curiously testing new opinions and courting new impressions." Given the brevity of human life and given as well the brevity of the very impressions that constitute human lives, "we shall hardly have time to make theories about the things we see and touch." Hence, "not the fruit of experience, but experience itself, is the end." This emphasis on experience also leads Pater to distinguish among kinds of experience. The highest kind, he says, is the great passions (themselves a kind of wisdom) gained from art. "For art comes to you proposing frankly to give nothing but the highest quality to your moments as they pass."

Pater omitted the conclusion from the second edition of the book, fearing "it might possibly mislead some of those young men into whose hands it might fall." Having explained his beliefs more fully in *Marius the Epicurean* (1885) and having altered the conclusion slightly, he restored it to later editions of *The Renaissance*.

In what may seem a curious irony, Pater stands with Matthew Arnold and John Ruskin as one of the great aesthetic critics of the nineteenth century. The seemingly radical differences between them—Pater pronouncing the primacy of art for art's sake, Ruskin and Arnold insisting on its moral value—tend to obscure some important similarities that offer insight into the ways the Victorians viewed the production and appreciation of art, poetry, and music. All are intent on close scrutiny of the work under examination; all emphasize the seriousness of purpose that great artists bring to their works, and all are convinced that the impact of art on humanity is profound.

Pater, however, stands on its head the famous Arnoldian dictum that the purpose of the viewer or reader is "to see the object as in itself it really is." Pater insists instead that the principal task of anyone who really wishes to appreciate art is "to know one's own impression of the object of art as it really is." The focus in *The Renaissance*, and in other writings by Pater, is on the significance of the individual impression made by art on the viewer or reader. For him, great art is not dependent on social or political context, and it does not exist principally to deliver a message or emphasize some moral dictum. Instead, art is essentially intended to stir the senses of those who partake in the aesthetic experience (reading a poem or novel, observing a painting or sculpture, listening to a musical composition).

Many of Pater's contemporaries found his approach disconcerting, especially his decoupling of art from the historical and political milieu in which it is produced. Nevertheless, Pater's influence can be seen distinctly in the late nineteenth century movement that is frequently, and unfortunately, labeled as "decadence," in which artists consciously attempted to divorce their works from the more mundane aspects of life. Oscar Wilde, Arthur Symons, and W. B. Yeats are the best among many of the generation whom Pater influenced. His insistence on looking closely at the art object to isolate and appreciate its beauty, rather than simply using it as a means for political or moral commentary, lies at the heart of one of the great critical movements of the twentieth century, New Criticism, whose proponents insist that great art is intrinsically worthwhile and that standards of judgment must rest on aesthetic rather than moral or political principles.

Further Reading

Brake, Laurel, Lesley Higgins, and Carolyn Williams, eds. *Walter Pater: Transparencies of Desire*. Greensboro, N.C.: ELT Press, 2002. Collection of essays, including discussions of Pater's entire body of work, Pater in the context of modernism, and Pater's reception outside England. Contains a bibliography and an index.

Buckler, William E., ed. Introduction to *Walter Pater: Three Major Texts*. New York: New York University Press, 1986. Examines *The Renaissance* and two other major

works by Pater in an effort to define and elucidate the writer's critical method.

Bullen, J. B. "The Historiography of Studies in the History of the Renaissance." In *Pater in the 1990's*, edited by Laurel Brake and Ian Small. Greensboro, N.C.: ELT Press, 1991. Analyzes Pater's method of writing *The Renaissance*, seeing the work ultimately as a revelation of Pater's vision of himself.

Crinkley, Richmond. *Walter Pater: Humanist*. Lexington: University Press of Kentucky, 1970. The first chapter discusses *The Renaissance* in relation to Pater's whole achievement as a critic and writer. Also examines a number of Pater's major ideas about the relationship between life and art.

Daley, Kenneth. *The Rescue of Romanticism: Walter Pater and John Ruskin*. Athens: Ohio University Press, 2001. Daley examines the relationship of the two prominent Victorian art critics, focusing on their different theories of Romanticism. He demonstrates how Pater's theory was a response to Ruskin, whom Pater considered a conservative thinker.

Donoghue, Denis. *Walter Pater: Lover of Strange Souls*. New York: Knopf, 1995. An exceptional biographical and critical source. Donoghue defines Pater as a precursor of modernism who influenced the later works of James Joyce, T. S. Eliot, Virginia Woolf, and other writers.

Pater, Walter. *The Renaissance: Studies in Art and Poetry—The 1893 Text*. Edited by Donald L. Hill. Berkeley: University of California Press, 1980. Pater's text is presented with scholarly thoroughness and care. Contains more than two hundred fifty pages of textual and explanatory notes.

Seiler, R. M., ed. *Walter Pater: The Critical Heritage*. 1980. New ed. New York: Routledge, 1995. Surveys the reception of *The Renaissance* by Pater's contemporaries and reviews Pater's critical reputation from 1895 to the 1970's. Included are seventeen reviews of *The Renaissance* that were published in the years immediately following its first appearance.

Shuter, William. *Rereading Walter Pater*. New York: Cambridge University Press, 1997. A reevaluation of Pater's writings. Shuter initially provides a conventional account of the texts in the order in which they were written; he then returns to the earlier books, demonstrating how the later work, paradoxically, offers an introduction to the earlier aesthetic rather than moral or political principles.

Renée Mauperin

Authors: Edmond de Goncourt (1822-1896) and Jules
de Goncourt (1830-1870)
First published: 1864 (English translation, 1888)
Type of work: Novel
Type of plot: Naturalism
Time of plot: Nineteenth century
Locale: France

Principal characters:
RENÉE MAUPERIN, a sensitive, talented girl in her late
teens
HENRI MAUPERIN, her brother
MADAME DAVARANDE, her sister
MONSIEUR MAUPERIN, Renée's father
MADAME MAUPERIN, his wife
NAOMI BOURJOT, Renée's friend and the fiancé of Henri
Mauperin
MADAME BOURJOT, her mother and the lover of Henri
Mauperin
MONSIEUR DENOISEL, a family friend of the Mauperins
DE VILLACOURT, the shabby heir of an old French family

The Story:

Renée Mauperin's father had served under the first Napoleon and battled for the liberal forces until he became a husband and father, when his new responsibilities forced him to return home. Since acquiring a family he has ceased being a scholar and political figure in order to pursue the more financially reliable career of sugar refiner. His wife, a very proper woman, wishes to see her children married well and respectably.

The two oldest of the Mauperins' offspring are model children, so well disciplined and quiet that they fail to excite their father's interest. Renée, however, the third child, born late in his life, has been a lively youngster from the beginning. She loves horses and action, is demonstrative in her affection, and has an artistic and spirited personality. While these qualities endear her to her father, they make her the bane of her mother's existence. The oldest daughter has dutifully married and become the respectable Madame Davarande, but Renée, now in her late teens, has already summarily dismissed a dozen suitors of good family and fortune and shows no inclination to accept any who come seeking her hand.

Almost as great a worry to Madame Mauperin is her son, Henri, on whom she dotes. Henri Mauperin is a political economist and a lawyer; he is also a cold and calculating fellow, though his mother, in her excessive love for him, fails to realize just how selfish he is. She thinks that he has never given a thought to marriage and chides him for his lack of interest. She feels that at the age of thirty he should have settled down.

Not knowing his plans, Madame Mauperin arranges to have Henri often in the company of Naomi Bourjot, the only daughter of a very rich family known to the Mauperins for many years. The only difficulty lies in convincing Naomi's father that Henri, who has no title, is a suitable match for his daughter. Henri himself, having realized that this is the greatest difficulty, has undertaken to gain the aid of Madame Bourjot in his suit for her daughter. His method of securing the mother's aid is to become her lover.

On the occasion of staging an amateur theatrical production, Naomi, Renée, and Henri find themselves in one another's company, although Naomi has had to be forced into the venture by her mother. Madame Bourjot had known that Henri wants to marry her daughter, but she has had no idea that he is really in love with the girl. Henri's portrayal of Naomi's lover onstage, however, reveals to Madame Bourjot the true state of his affections. Rather than lose him altogether, Madame Bourjot, as Henri has anticipated, resolves to help him win her daughter and the family fortune, although tearful and bitter scenes precede that decision. Urged on by Madame Bourjot, Naomi's father reluctantly consents to the marriage on the condition that Henri Mauperin acquire the government's permission to add "de Villacourt" to his name.

Naomi has meanwhile discovered that Henri and her mother have been lovers. She loves Henri and is much dismayed by this discovery; nevertheless, she has to go through with the marriage. Naomi's only consolation is to tell Renée what she has learned. Renée, horrified to learn of her brother's actions, confronts him with the story, and he curtly and angrily tells her that the affair is none of her business.

A short time later, when the antagonism between Renée

and her brother has been superficially smoothed over, she accompanies him to the government offices, where he receives permission to make the desired addition to his name. While waiting for him, she overhears two clerks saying that the real de Villacourt family has not really died out and that one member, a man, is still alive; the clerks even mention where he lives. Her knowledge gives Renée an opportunity for revenge on her brother, although she has no idea what might happen when she puts her plan into action. She takes a copy of the newspaper article announcing that the title "de Villacourt" is to be given to Henri Mauperin and sends it to the real de Villacourt, a villainous lout who immediately plans to kill the upstart who has dared to appropriate his title.

The real de Villacourt journeys to Paris and learns that, penniless as he is, he has no legal means to regain his title. He then goes to the apartment of Henri Mauperin and attempts to beat the young man. Henri, however, is no coward and challenges the man to a duel. The arrangements are made by Monsieur Denoisel, a friend of the Mauperin family for many years. He also serves as Henri's second in the affair. When the two men meet for the duel, Henri shoots de Villacourt and thinks that the duel is over, but de Villacourt is not fatally wounded. Calling Henri back, he shoots and kills him. Denoisel is given the unhappy duty of reporting Henri's untimely death to his family. To everyone's surprise, the one who seems to take the news hardest is Renée. She and her brother have never been close, so no one expects her to be so upset by his death.

One day, in conversation, Denoisel remarks that someone had sent the newspaper clipping to de Villacourt, and Renée, fearful that she has been discovered as the author of her brother's death, has a heart attack. For many months she lies ill, apparently with no desire to live; her realization that she has not revealed her guilt prevents her recovery. Her father calls in the best specialists he can find, but they only remark that her condition has been caused by some terrible shock. When told that she has recently lost a brother, they say that Henri's death is probably not the real cause of her illness.

Despite all efforts on her behalf, Renée Mauperin wastes away and finally dies. The tragedy of the Mauperins does not end there, however. They lose their third child, Madame Davarande, a few months afterward, when she dies in childbirth. Childless and alone, the elder Mauperins attempt to ease their grief and loneliness by traveling abroad.

Critical Evaluation:

Above all, Edmond and Jules de Goncourt valued truth in literature; in all of their novels, they attempted to find the truth of the subjects they chose. In this they were in the vanguard of a literary trend in the late nineteenth century known as naturalism, which reached its zenith in the works of Émile Zola. In *Renée Mauperin*, the Goncourts analyze with shrewdness and precision a particular segment of Parisian society. Viewing this world through the eyes of an intelligent and sensitive young woman, they depict the shallowness and pettiness of many of the self-satisfied people who dominate society and try to dominate her.

The book also describes the various conditions of women in mid-nineteenth century France. There is the impetuous young Renée, who as a child cuts Denoisel's hair and smokes her father's cigarette and who later struggles against the conventions imposed on young Parisian women in 1864. There is Madame Mauperin, with her passion for "symmetry" and her fairly ordinary habit of overvaluing her son and undervaluing her daughter. Two other typical types of the period are Madame Davarande, the society matron who is religious only because she believes that God is chic, and Madame Bourjot, an intelligent woman married to a shallow and petty fool. In this society, the authors seem to suggest, only a shallow person seems able to find contentment, and this seems particularly to be the case for women.

Many of the other characters, notably Renée's doting and scholarly father and the sophisticated and subtle Abbé Blampoix, are well drawn. The Goncourt brothers were not known for character analysis, but their characterization in this novel surpasses that in many of their other books. Renée's sudden admission of having inadvertently caused her brother's death is skillfully and devastatingly handled; the moment reveals complexities of Renée's character that up to that point had been only suggested.

The novel is filled with witty conversations that bring the era to life. The authors, aware of the value and interest of precise details, integrate them into the book through conversations and descriptions, often using them to delineate character. Frequently, conversations are used to suggest comments on society, as when a room full of talking people is described as "voices . . . all mingled together in the Babel: it was like the chirping of so many birds in a cage." It is this cage that Renée wants to escape, but ultimately this is possible only through her death.

The novelistic strength of the Goncourts lies in pure observation. Perhaps they are less broad in their accomplishments than the greatest nineteenth century novelists, but in their best books, such as *Renée Mauperin*, they combine a precise and vivid picture of the society they knew so well with a sympathetic and touching story and shrewd observations on human nature.

Further Reading

Ashley, Katherine. *Edmond de Goncourt and the Novel: Naturalism and Decadence*. Atlanta: Rodopi, 2005. Analyzes Edmond de Goncourt's four solo novels, arguing that these books deviate from the strict naturalistic style that characterizes the novels he wrote with his brother. Places Edmond's work within the larger context of late nineteenth century fin de siècle literature.

Baldick, Robert. *The Goncourts*. London: Bowes and Bowes, 1960. Very brief but excellent survey of the Goncourts' novels concentrates on biographical background but also provides some exploration of major themes in the works and aspects of literary style. Emphasizes the Goncourts' scorn of the bourgeoisie's lack of aesthetic sensibility.

Billy, André. *The Goncourt Brothers*. Translated by Margaret Shaw. London: A. Deutsch, 1960. Standard biography focuses on events in the lives of the brothers from which the novels emerged. Also provides examples of contemporary reaction to their novels.

Grant, Richard B. *The Goncourt Brothers*. New York: Twayne, 1972. Provides a solid survey of the life and works of Jules and Edmond de Goncourt. Integrates the lives of the authors with detailed stylistic and thematic analysis of their novels. The chapter on *Renée Mauperin* elaborates the brothers' political views and traces their derogatory commentary on bourgeois taste.

Heil, Elissa. *The Conflicting Discourses of the Drawing Room: Anthony Trollope and Edmond and Jules de Goncourt*. New York: Peter Lang, 1997. Focuses on the social discourses among characters in the Goncourts' *Renée Mauperin* and Trollope's *Barchester Towers* (1857), analyzing how the authors use these conversations to depict gender differences and other aspects of nineteenth century bourgeois society.

Nelson, Brian, ed. *Naturalism in the European Novel: New Critical Perspectives*. New York: Berg, 1992. Collection of essays by prominent scholars includes several important discussions of the Goncourts' role in the development of social documentary as a literary genre.

Silverman, Debora. *Art Nouveau in Fin-de-Siècle France: Politics, Psychology, and Style*. Berkeley: University of California Press, 1989. Discusses primarily the collecting habits and art criticism of the brothers Goncourt, but provides some valuable insight into their fictional works from a feminist perspective.

Representative Men
Seven Lectures

Author: Ralph Waldo Emerson (1803-1882)
First published: 1850
Type of work: Essays

Ralph Waldo Emerson's *Representative Men* was first presented as a course of lectures in Boston in the winter of 1845-1846 and later during his visit to England in 1847. The volume opens with a discussion of the uses of great thinkers and follows with six chapters on those who represent humanity in six aspects: Plato as philosopher, Emanuel Swedenborg as mystic, Michel Eyquem de Montaigne as skeptic, William Shakespeare as poet, Napoleon Bonaparte as man of the world, and Johann Wolfgang von Goethe as writer.

The book has often been mentioned in connection with Thomas Carlyle's *On Heroes, Hero-Worship, and the Heroic in History* (1841), but whereas Carlyle saw the hero as a divinely gifted individual above and apart from the common person, Emerson conceived of the "great man" as a lens through which people may see themselves. For Emerson the great man is one who through superior endowments "inhabits a higher sphere of thought, into which other men rise with labor and difficulty." Such individuals may give direct material or metaphysical aid, but more frequently they serve indirectly by the inspiration of their accomplishment of things and by their introduction of ideas. The great man does stirring deeds; he (or she) reveals knowledge and wisdom; he shows depths of emotion—and others resolve to emulate him. He accomplishes intellectual feats of memory, of abstract thought, of imaginative flights, and dull minds are brightened by his light. The true genius does not tyrannize; he liberates those who know him.

For Emerson, all humans are infinitely receptive in capacity; they need only the wise to rouse them, to clear their eyes and make them see, to feed and refresh them. Yet even the great man has limits of availability. People get from one what they can and pass on to another who can nourish mind or spirit or inform a dulled palate. As people are infinitely receptive, so are they eternally hungry; and as people find sustenance, through them the spirit of the world's great thinkers diffuses itself. Thus, through the ages the cumulative effect of great individuals is that they prepare the way for greater intellects.

Emerson views the representative philosopher Plato as an exhausting generalizer, a symbol of philosophy itself, a thinker whom people of all nations in all times recognize as kin to themselves. He absorbed the learning of his times, but Emerson sees in him a modern style and spirit identifying him with later ages as well. Plato honors the ideal, or laws of the mind, and fate, or the order of nature. Plato defines. He sees unity, or identity, on one hand and variety on the other. In him is found the idea (not original, it is true) of one deity in whom all things are absorbed. A balanced soul, Plato sees both the real and the ideal. He propounds the principle of absolute good, but he illustrates from the world around him. In this ability lies his power and charm. He is a great average man in whom others see their own dreams and thoughts. He acknowledges the ineffable and yet asserts that things are knowable; a lover of limits, he yet loves the illimitable. For Plato, virtue cannot be taught; it is divinely inspired. It is through Socrates that we learn much of Plato's philosophy, and to Emerson the older philosopher is a man of Franklin-like wisdom, a plain old uncle with great ears, an immense talker, a hard-headed humorist, an Aesop of the mob to whom the robed scholar Plato owed a great debt.

For Emerson the two principal defects of Plato as a philosopher are, first, that he is intellectual and therefore always literary, and second, that he has no system. He sees so much that he argues first on one side and then on another. Finally, says Emerson, the way to know Plato is to compare him, not with nature (an enigma now, as it was to Plato), but with others and to see that through the ages none has approached him.

Emerson would have preferred to discuss Jesus as the representative mystic, but to do so would have meant sailing into dangerous waters: The orthodox believers of the time would probably have objected to the inclusion of Jesus as a representative man. Emerson chose Swedenborg instead, but in reading this chapter of the book one gets the notion that Emerson was forcing himself to praise this eighteenth century mystic. Emerson remarks that this colossal soul, as he calls him, requires a long focal distance to be seen. Looking more closely, he finds in Swedenborg a style "lustrous with points and shooting spiculae of thought, and resembling one of those winter mornings when the air sparkles with crystals." He summarizes some of Swedenborg's leading ideas:

> the universality of each law in nature; the Platonic doctrine of the scale or degrees; the version or conversion of each into other, and so the correspondence of all the parts; the fine secret that little explains large, and large, little; the centrality of man in nature, and the connection that subsists throughout all things.

Emerson also quotes the following passage from Swedenborg's theology that must have appealed to the Unitarian Emerson:

> Man is a kind of very minute heaven, corresponding to the world of spirits and to heaven. Every particular idea of man, and every affection, yea, every smallest part of his affection, is an image and effigy of him. A spirit may be known from only a single thought. God is the grand old man.

When, however, Emerson comes to the Swedenborgian mystical view that each natural object has a definite symbolic value—as, a horse signifies carnal understanding; a tree, perception; the moon, faith—he rebels at its narrowness. As for Swedenborg's theological writings in general, Emerson complains of their immense and sandy diffuseness and their delirious incongruities. Emerson warns that such books as Swedenborg's treatise on love should be used with caution, and he suggests that a contemplative youth might read these mysteries of love and conscience once, and then throw them aside forever.

As Emerson continues his examination, he finds Swedenborg's heavens and hells dull, he objects to the theological determination of Swedenborg's mind and to the failure of Swedenborg in attaching himself "to the Christian symbol, instead of to the moral sentiment, which carries innumerable christianities, humanities, divinities, in its bosom." When Emerson imagines the impatient reader complaining, "What have I to do with jasper and sardonyx, beryl and chalcedony," and so on, Emerson's own writing awakes as from a semislumber, and one is reminded of his warning in "Self-Reliance" that when a person "claims to know and speak of God and carries you backward to the phraseology of some old moldered nation in another country, in another world, believe him not."

As Emerson perhaps felt relieved after having completed his lecture on Swedenborg, he surely must have anticipated with great pleasure his next on the skeptic Montaigne. He confesses to having had a love for the *Essais* (1580-1588; *The Essays*, 1603) since he was a young man. "It seemed to me," he says, "as if I had written the book, in some former life, so sincerely it spoke to my thought and experience." He is not repelled by Montaigne's grossness—his frank intimacy about himself—because the Frenchman is scrupulously honest in his confessions. As Emerson had found Swedenborg disagreeably wise and therefore repellent, he is in contrast drawn to Montaigne, whose motto *Que scais je?* was a constant reminder to the essayist to stick to the things he did know, such as his farm, his family, himself, and his likes and dislikes in food and friends.

Emerson is charmed by Montaigne's conversational style, his calm balance, and his stout solidity. The skeptic is not the impassioned patriot, the dogmatic adherent of creed or party. He is wary of an excess of belief, but he turns also from an excess of unbelief. He is content to say there are doubts. Yet for Emerson, when he turns from Montaigne the man to the skeptic in general whom he represents, the doubter is at base a person of belief. He believes in the moral design of the universe and that "it exists hospitably for the weal of souls." Thus, concludes Emerson, skepticism is finally dissolved in the moral sentiment that remains forever supreme. The skepticism is on the surface only; it questions specifics, but the skeptic can serenely view humankind's high ambitions defeated and the unequal distribution of power in the world because he believes that deity and moral law control the universe. Emerson himself was at bottom such a believer, though he had passed through his skeptical stage in life to arrive at his belief.

The discussion of Shakespeare as the representative poet begins with the comment, "Great men are more distinguished by range and extent than by originality." Shakespeare, like his fellow dramatists, used a mass of old plays with which to experiment. Building upon popular traditions, he was free to use his wide-ranging fancy and his imagination. Borrowing in all directions, he used what he borrowed with such art that it became his.

Emerson touches upon the mystery of Shakespeare's biography, mentioning the paucity of clear facts (only a few more have become known since the time when Emerson wrote), and then concluding, as have many of Shakespeare's readers, that his plays and his poetry give all the information that is really needed. In the sonnets readers find the lore of

friendship and of love. Through the characters of his plays people know Shakespeare because there is something of him in all of the characters.

The dramatic skill of Shakespeare is to Emerson less important than his poetry and philosophy and the broad expanse of his book of life, which pictured the men and women of his day and prefigured those of later ages. Shakespeare was inconceivably wise and made his characters as real as if they had lived in his home. His power to convert truth into music and verse makes him the exemplary poet. His music charms the ear and his sentence takes the mind. In his lines experience has been transformed into verse without a trace of egotism. One more royal trait of the poet Emerson finds in Shakespeare: His name suggests joy and emancipation to people's hearts. To Emerson, Shakespeare was master of the revels to humankind. It is this fact that Emerson regrets: The world's greatest poet used his genius for public amusement. As the poet was half-man in his role as entertainer, so the priests of old and of later days were half-men who took the joy and beauty out of life while they moralized and warned of the doom to come. Only in some future time, says Emerson, will there arise a poet-priest who may see, speak, and act with equal inspiration.

A frequently quoted remark of Emerson is that he liked people who could do things. His expansive praise of Napoleon in the opening pages of his portrayal of the Corsican as the representative man of the world is based upon his belief that Napoleon could and did do what others merely wanted to. Napoleon was idolized by common people because he was an uncommonly gifted common person. He succeeded through the virtues of punctuality, personal attention, courage, and thoroughness, qualities that others possess in lesser degrees. Emerson writes of Napoleon's reliance on his own sense and of his scorn of others' sense. To him, Napoleon is the agent or attorney of the middle class, with both the virtues and the vices of the people he represented. He was dishonest, stagy, unscrupulous, selfish, perfidious, and coarse. He was a cheat, a gossip, and when divested of his power and splendor he is seen to be an impostor and a rogue.

Emerson finds Napoleon the supreme democrat who illustrates in his career the three stages of the party: the democrat in youth, the conservative in later life, and the aristocrat at the end—a democrat ripe and gone to seed. Napoleon conducted an experiment in the use of the intellect without conscience. The experiment failed, however, because the French saw that they could not enjoy what Napoleon had gained for them. His colossal egotism drove him to more attempts at conquest, and so his followers deserted him. Yet Emerson asserts that it was not Napoleon's fault. He was defeated by the eternal law of humanity and of the world. Here, as before, Emerson sees the moral order in the universe. "Every experiment," he says, "by multitudes or by individuals, that has a selfish aim, will fail. . . . Only that good profits which we can taste with all doors open, and which serves all men."

Having considered Napoleon as a man of action who failed after having achieved enormous successes, Emerson turns to Goethe as the representative scholar or writer, one whose intellect moved in many directions and whose writings brought him fame as the greatest of German authors. Emerson calls him the soul of his century, one who clothed modern existence with poetry. Emerson, a lover of nature himself, remarks that Goethe said the best things about nature that ever were said.

Realizing the impossibility of analyzing the full range of Goethe's writings, Emerson chooses *Wilhelm Meisters Lehrjahre* (1795-1796; *Wilhelm Meister's Apprenticeship*, 1824) for rather brief comment. He describes it as provoking but also unsatisfactory, but though he has considerable praise for this novel in which a democrat becomes an aristocrat, readers do not really learn much about it. In fact, one feels that Emerson was struggling with a difficult subject in dealing with Goethe. One comment is worthy of noting, however, since it seems a reference to Emerson himself when he says that Goethe is "fragmentary; a writer of occasional poems and of an encyclopedia of sentences."

Among Emerson's works, *Representative Men* has received modest praise, and such chapters as those on Montaigne and Shakespeare have occasionally been reprinted. One of the aptest statements ever made about Emerson's book is that of Oliver Wendell Holmes, who wrote that Emerson "shows his own affinities and repulsions, and writes his own biography, no matter about whom or what he is talking."

Further Reading

Allen, Gay Wilson. *Waldo Emerson: A Biography.* New York: Viking Press, 1981. An excellent research tool. Addresses *Representative Men* in a thorough, accessible style. Pertinent and lucid discussion focuses on Emerson's thought as it is expressed in his choices of representative men. Makes reference to Emerson's journals and their value for understanding his texts.

Buell, Lawrence. *Emerson.* Cambridge, Mass.: Belknap Press, 2003. Revisits the life and work of America's first public intellectual on the occasion of Emerson's two-hundredth birthday. References to *Representative Men* are indexed.

Cameron, Kenneth Walter, ed. *Literary Comment in American Renaissance Newspapers: Fresh Discoveries Concerning Emerson, Thoreau, Alcott, and Transcendentalism.* Hartford, Conn.: Transcendental Books, 1977. Includes an evaluation of *Representative Men* published in the *New York Weekly Tribune* in 1850. Offers interesting insight into the work's strengths and weaknesses.

Carpenter, Frederic Ives. *Emerson Handbook.* New York: Hendricks House, 1967. A good research tool, providing background material to the ideas that shape Emerson's texts. Discusses Emerson's writing methods and style. Includes bibliographies.

Emerson, Ralph Waldo. *1820-24.* Vol. 1 in *Journals of Ralph Waldo Emerson*, edited by Ralph Waldo Emerson and Waldo Emerson Forbes. Boston: Houghton Mifflin, 1990. Some journal entries go back to Emerson's youth. In this volume, the young Emerson presents ideas that recur in *Representative Men*. Instills a deeper appreciation of Emerson's insights.

Lothstein, Arthur S., and Michael Brodrick, eds. *New Morning: Emerson in the Twenty-first Century.* Albany: State University of New York Press, 2008. Philosophers, poets, and literary critics, including Mark Strand, Gary Snyder, and Lawrence Buell, examine how Emerson's ideas about the environment, race, politics, spirituality, and other subjects remain relevant in the twenty-first century.

Porte, Joel. *Consciousness and Culture: Emerson and Thoreau Reviewed.* New Haven, Conn.: Yale University Press, 2004. Focuses on Emerson as a writer, analyzing the quality of his prose and the organization of his essays. References to *Representative Men* are indexed.

Porte, Joel, and Saundra Morris, eds. *The Cambridge Companion to Ralph Waldo Emerson.* New York: Cambridge University Press, 1999. Collection of essays in which contributors assess Emerson's writing, influence, and cultural significance. Chapter 4 examines Emerson as a lecturer.

Republic

Author: Plato (c. 427-347 B.C.E.)
First transcribed: Politeia, 388-366 B.C.E. (English
    translation, 1701)
Type of work: Philosophy
Time of plot: Fifth century B.C.E.
Locale: Piraeus, Greece

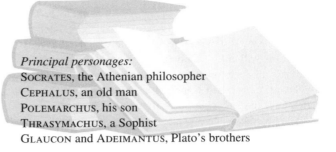

Principal personages:
SOCRATES, the Athenian philosopher
CEPHALUS, an old man
POLEMARCHUS, his son
THRASYMACHUS, a Sophist
GLAUCON and ADEIMANTUS, Plato's brothers

Republic is the first in a long line of works that are generally classified as Utopian literature. Although Plato is primarily interested in political issues, he is less concerned with mapping out a practical strategy for revamping current practices in the Greek city-states than he is in explaining the optimal ways in which people should be governed. Subscribing to what some commentators have described as an unashamedly elitist viewpoint, Plato makes it clear that some people are destined to rule, others to be ruled. Essentially antidemocratic, he concentrates on describing ways those who have the capacity to lead should be educated for their positions of great responsibility. Such an attitude no doubt seems alien and even threatening to modern readers, especially those in Western societies, where democracy in some form or other has been in favor for more than two hundred years. *Republic* may grate on the nerves of some who dislike Plato's concepts of social engineering and his distaste for artists. Others may feel his disdain for the masses links him with that most maligned of all political philosophers, Niccolò Machiavelli, whose advice is based on the notion that retaining power is the primary duty of those who rule.

One must remember, however, that Plato is at heart a philosopher. In *Republic*, he is interested in identifying the qualities of justice that should determine the governance of society. Undeterred by any popular sentiments for or against any particular political practice—Athens was a democracy during the years when Plato was writing his dialogues and teaching—the philosopher focuses on the ethical dimensions of leadership. He asks crucial questions: How ought one to govern, and how ought one be educated to serve in this significant social role? He is the first of the great political philosophers of the West.

Republic presents a fascinating defense of the author's conception of the ideal state and gives the most sustained and convincing portrait of Socrates as a critical and creative philosopher ever presented. Other dialogues featuring Socrates may be superior as studies of the personality and character of Socrates, but the *Republic* is unexcelled as an exhibition of

the famed Socratic method being brought to bear on such questions as "What is justice?" and "What kind of state would be most just?"

Although the constructive arguments of this dialogue come from the mouth of Socrates, it is safe to assume that much of the philosophy is Plato's. As a rough reading rule, one may say that the method is Socratic, but the content is provided by Plato himself. Among the ideas that are presented and defended in the *Republic* are the Platonic theory of ideas (the formal prototypes of all things, objective or intellectual), the Platonic conception of the nature and obligations of the philosopher, and the Platonic theory and criticism of poetry. The central concern of the author is with the idea of justice in the state.

The dialogue is a discussion between Socrates and various friends while they are in Piraeus for a festival. The discussion of justice is provoked by a remark made by an old man, Cephalus, to the effect that the principal advantage of being wealthy is that a man near death is able to repay what he owes to the gods and to people, and is thereby able to be just in the hope of achieving a happy afterlife. Socrates objects to this conception of justice, maintaining that whether persons should return what they have received depends on the circumstances. For example, a man who has received dangerous weapons from his friend while the friend was sane should not, if he is just, return those weapons if the friend, while mad, demands them.

Polemarchus amends the idea and declares that it is just to help one's friends and return to them what they are due, provided they are good and worthy of receiving the good. Enemies, on the other hand, should have harm done to them, for, as bad, that is what they are due. Socrates compels Polemarchus to admit that injuring anyone, even a wicked man, makes that person worse; and since no just person would ever sanction making others worse, justice must be something other than giving good to the good and bad to the bad.

Thrasymachus then proposes the theory that justice is whatever is to the interest of the stronger party. His idea is that justice is relative to the law, and the law is made by the stronger party according to his interests. In rebuttal, Socrates maneuvers Thrasymachus into saying that sometimes rulers make mistakes. If this is so, then sometimes the law is against their interests; when the law is against the interests of the stronger party, it is right to do what is not to the interest of the stronger party.

The secret of the Socratic method is evident from analysis of this argument. The term "interest" or "to the interest of" is ambiguous, sometimes meaning what one is interested in, what one wants, and at other times meaning what one could want if one were not in error. Examples in everyday life of such ambiguity are found in statements such as the following: "Although you want it, it is not really to your interest to have it." Socrates adroitly shifts from one sense of the expression to the other so that Thrasymachus apparently contradicts himself. In this indirect way Socrates makes it clear both to the "victim" and to the onlookers that the proponent of the claim—in this case, Thrasymachus—has not cleared it of all possibility of misinterpretation.

Socrates then goes on to say that justice must be relative to the needs of those who are served, not to the desires of those who serve them. The physician, for example, as physician, must make the health of the patient the primary concern if the physician is to be just. Socrates suggests that they might clarify their understanding of justice by considering a concrete case, such as the state: If by discussion they can come to understand what a state must be in order to be just, it might be possible for them to generalize and arrive at an idea of justice itself.

Beginning with an account of what a state would have to be in order to fulfill its functions as a state, Socrates then proceeds to develop the notion of an ideal state by asking what the relations of the various groups of citizens to each other should be. Every state needs three classes of citizens: the Guardians, who rule and advise the rest; the Auxiliaries, who provide military protection for the state; and the Workers, the providers of food, clothing, and other useful materials. In a just state these three classes of citizens function together, each class doing its own proper business without interfering with the tasks of the other classes.

Applying this idea to the individual, Socrates decides that just persons are those who give to each of their individual functions its proper task, relating the tasks to one another in a harmonious way. Just as the state has three distinct elements (the governing, the defending, and the producing bodies), so the individual person has three corresponding elements: the rational, the spirited, and the appetitive. By the "spirited" element, Plato means the passionate aspect of one's nature,

one's propensity to anger or other irrational emotions. His use of the term "anger" allows for what might be called righteous indignation, the passionate defense of reason against desire. The rational element is the discerning and calculating side of one's nature; it is what enables one to be wise and judicious. One's appetitive side is one's inclination to desire some things in preference to others.

A just person, then, is one who keeps all of these three elements doing their proper work, with the rational element in command. One is brave, says Socrates in the dialogue, if one's spirited element remains always in the service of reason. One is wise if one is governed by reason, for reason takes into account the welfare of the entire person, and one is temperate if the spirit and appetite work harmoniously under the guidance of reason.

In order to discover those citizens best suited to be Guardians, Socrates proposes that the ideal state educate all its citizens in music and gymnastics, continually observing them to decide upon the sort of occupation for which each would best be fitted. He also argues that the Guardians and Auxiliaries should have no private property, and that the members of each class should share a community of wives and children. These communal features of the ideal state have led many critics to dismiss Plato's construction as unacceptable. It is well to remember that in the dialogue Socrates tells his listeners that he is not concerned about the practicality of his state; the conception of the state is constructed merely to bring out the nature of justice.

In considering the education of the Guardians, Socrates builds the conception of the philosopher as the true aristocrat or rational thinker, the ideal ruler for the ideal state. The philosopher is a lover of wisdom, and the philosopher alone manages to keep appetite and spirit in harmony with reason. Consequently, the Guardians of the state should be educated as philosophers, supplementing their training in arithmetic, geometry, astronomy, and music with training in the philosophic skills of dialectic. The prospective Guardians should not be allowed to undertake philosophic education until they are old enough to take it seriously; such education should not be mere amusement. After his philosophic training the prospective Guardian should take part in the active life of his times, so that at fifty he can assume political power with some knowledge of the actual matters with which he shall be concerned.

In connection with his discussion of the philosopher, Socrates introduces his famous story of the cave. People are like prisoners in a cave, facing away from the light. Unable to see themselves or anyone else because they are shackled, they observe only the shadows of things on the wall in front of them, not realizing that the reality is something quite different from the shadows. The philosopher is like one who leaves the cave, comes to know things as they really are, and returns reluctantly to help the shackled ones, who think that shadows make up the true world.

The philosopher comes to know reality through a study of the ideas or forms of particular things. The world of experience is like the world of shadows, but the world of ideas is the true reality. For every class of objects there is an idea, a form shared by all particular items in that class of objects. Socrates uses the example of beds: There is an idea-bed, a form shared by all particular beds. One who studies only the individual beds made by carpenters, or only the pictures of beds made by artists, knows only copies of reality (and, in the case of the imitative artist, only copies of copies), but the philosopher, making the effort to learn the idea itself, comes closer to reality.

Socrates objects to poetry and art whenever they are imitative, which they usually are. Although he admits that some poetry can be inspiring in the patriotic training of the Guardians, he stresses the point that imitative art is corrupting because it is misleading. It represents physical things, which in turn are merely copies of the forms or ideas. Works of art are copies of physical things; hence, works of art are at least two steps removed from reality. Furthermore, the artist paints only a single aspect of a thing; hence, strictly speaking, art is three steps removed from reality. It is on this account, as well as because of the immoral effect of the poetic style of all but the most noble poets, that Socrates recommends that imitative poets be banned from the state.

The *Republic* closes with Socrates' reaffirmation of his conviction that only the just person is truly happy, for only one who is just harmonizes reason, appetite, and spirit by loving wisdom and the form of the good. The soul is immortal, he argues, because the soul's illness is injustice, and injustice does not destroy a soul. Since the soul cannot be destroyed by any illness other than its own, and its own cannot destroy it, it must be immortal. Socrates concludes by using a myth about life after death to show that the just and wise ones will prosper in this life and "during the journey of a thousand years."

Further Reading

Blackburn, Simon. *Plato's "Republic": A Biography*. New York: Atlantic Monthly Press, 2007. Describes the *Republic* as "the foodstuff of unintelligent fundamentalisms," arguing that Plato's view of a utopian government run by philosopher-kings may be partly responsible for Nazism, totalitarianism, and neoconservatism. Discusses the themes in the work that support this argument, such as its defense of the right of armies to conquer and colonize and its praise for a caste system.

Cropsey, Joseph. *Plato's World: Man's Place in the Cosmos*. Chicago: University of Chicago Press, 1995. Examines Plato's views on human nature, with particular attention to his political theories.

Ferrari, G. R. F., ed. *The Cambridge Companion to Plato's "Republic."* New York: Cambridge University Press, 2007. Collection of sixteen essays by Plato scholars provides a range of interpretations of the *Republic*, including discussions of the work's rhetoric, its place in Plato's philosophical thought, and its ideas about justice and virtue.

Hall, Robert W. *Plato*. London: Allen & Unwin, 1981. Presents an excellent discussion of Plato's political thought, most of it devoted to the *Republic*. Two chapters in particular, "Athenian Democracy" and "Plato's Political Heritage," help place Plato and his work within wider historical, cultural, and political contexts.

Howland, Jacob. *"The Republic": The Odyssey of Philosophy*. New York: Twayne, 1993. The ideal starting point for the study of the *Republic*. Provides a chapter that discusses the work's literary and historical contexts, a chronology of Plato's life and works, and a bibliography.

Klosko, George. *The Development of Plato's Political Theory*. 2d ed. New York: Oxford University Press, 2006. Examines the political concepts set forth in the *Republic* and Plato's other works, placing them in their social and historical context.

Pappas, Nikolas, ed. *Routledge Philosophy Guidebook to Plato and the "Republic."* New York: Routledge, 1995. Collection of informative essays is designed to clarify key Platonic concepts and theories for students.

Sayers, Sean. *Plato's "Republic": An Introduction*. Edinburgh: Edinburgh University Press, 2000. Provides clear explanations of Plato's theories and examines the significance of the work for the modern world.

Tuana, Nancy, ed. *Feminist Interpretations of Plato*. University Park: Pennsylvania State University Press, 1994. Scholarly essays evaluate Plato's understanding of gender issues and appraise his philosophy from the perspective of feminist theory.

White, Nicholas P. *A Companion to Plato's "Republic."* Indianapolis, Ind.: Hackett, 1979. Offers tremendously learned and cogent commentary based on a book-by-book summary of the *Republic*. The introductory chapters before the summary are especially helpful for students, as is the bibliography.

Requiem

Author: Anna Akhmatova (1889-1966)
First published: Rekviem, 1963 (English translation, 1964)
Type of work: Poetry

Anna Akhmatova was a prominent voice in Russian poetry for more than fifty years. When she died in 1966, she was hailed as one of the eminent poets of Russia, ranked with Aleksandr Blok, Boris Pasternak, and Osip Mandelstam. Her several collections attest the high quality of her craft. She drew attention to her poetry at the very start of her career, participating in a short-lived but eclectic group of poets called the Acmeists in the second decade of the twentieth century. She then struck her own path and, although she was frequently regarded with suspicion by Soviet authorities, she managed to retain the aura of brilliance and integrity until her last days.

It is generally agreed that her highest achievements are two cyclical poems, *Poema bez geroya* (1960; *A Poem Without a Hero*, 1973) and *Requiem*. Both are Akhmatova's poetic answers to the vicissitudes of life in Russia under communism and, because of that, their publication was delayed; *Requiem* first appeared abroad and was not published in Russia until many years later.

Requiem was written between 1935 and 1943, with a brief prose foreword added in 1957. Since its publication in Germany in 1963, it has been symbolic of both the suffering and silent defiance of the Russian people during the reign of terror perpetrated by Joseph Stalin and his henchmen. The poem is more than a protest against tyranny; it reflects the poet's personal tragedy. Her only son, Lev Gumilev, a prominent young scholar, was arrested on trumped-up charges and exiled to hard labor. Released during World War II, he was arrested again and released only in 1956. During his imprisonment, Akhmatova stood waiting in lines in front of the prison off and on for seventeen months, trying to learn the fate of her son and secure his release. Although *Requiem* is basically autobiographical, it should not be read purely as such, but primarily as any mother's grief. The poem itself is not as much a direct accusation of the inhumane treatment of the Soviet citizen, but a deeply felt outcry against the injustice done to all the children of Russia. Through her outcry, Akhmatova expresses a great love of and loyalty to Russia, and it is in this manner that one mother's grief and tragedy become a symbol of all of Russia, expressed in a perfect fusion of content and form.

Requiem opens with the brief prose introduction written in 1957, which places the poem in the fearful years of the secret police. She relates that, as she stood in line before the prison walls, an unknown woman asked, "Can you describe this?" "Yes, I can," Akhmatova replied. The first lines of the motto explain why she chose not to become an émigré: "No, not under a foreign heavenly dome,/ Not under the shield of foreign wings—/ I was with my people in those hours,/ There where, unhappily, my people were." These four lines are the best example of the style that follows—direct, precise, brief, and simple. They represent the full power of emotion that characterizes the entire poem.

In the opening poem, Akhmatova dedicates *Requiem* to all who suffered during the purges of the 1930's, those who waited before prison gates, wept upon hearing the sentences, and lived in the relentless fear of the powerless. Although the wind is still refreshing and the sunset beautiful, that beauty is lost on those in the vigil. The poet combines brief, contrasting sketches of the prison and Leningrad with the mood of the frightened, yet still hopeful, participants of the vigils. Recalling her friends from the two-year ordeal in 1940, she sends them her greetings, wherever they may be.

The spirit of the dedication is preserved in the introduction to the entire poem. Here she weeps for the "ranks of the condemned" and for the "innocent Rus'" (a poetic, endearing term for Russia) that "contorts under bloody boots and the tires of Black Marias" (black-painted prison vans). In these first two poems, Akhmatova is able to surmount personal grief and become a speaker for all who suffered with her, indeed for all victims of the country and perhaps all of humankind. In the following poems, she concentrates on her own grief as she observes the "stars of death" shining over her. In poem 1 (1935) she recalls how her son was taken away at dawn, the cold of icons on his lips and deadly sweat on his forehead. She likens herself to the wives who followed their husbands, army officers exiled to Siberia in the previous centuries. She deftly evokes the images of the Russian past, thus universalizing her personal misfortune.

In the next two poems, she feels the heavy burden of her situation, speaking in tones of self-pity. She evokes the stillness of the "quiet Don," an apparent sarcastic allusion to the novel *And Quiet Flows the Don* (1928) by Mikhail Sholokhov, a staunch supporter of Communist Party rule. She is ill and alone, with a husband (Nikolay Gumilev, who was killed by the Bolsheviks during the revolution) in his grave and their only son in prison. She pleads with them to pray for her, instead of the other way around. In poem 3, she even utters a denial of her plight, wishing that the nightmare would go away and the dark curtains cover the windows of her lightless room.

In poem 4, Akhmatova juxtaposes the past and the present. Addressing her own merry past, when she was loved and admired by her many friends, she sees herself now as only one of the three hundred standing in the vigil, her bitter tears hot enough to melt the winter ice, and under the crosses—a symbolic reference to their tragedy—while innocent lives are being snuffed out behind the prison walls.

The pervasive uncertainty of the times carries over into the next poem. The mother does not know what is to become of her son, or "who is a man and who is a beast," or how long the agony will last. In a funereal image of flowers and incense, there is again an allusion to death. In the dedication poem, it was first associated with stars, while now "a huge star/ threatens an impending death," a reference to the Communist emblem as well as to any natural phenomenon, for Akhmatova uses nature in conjunction with the certainty of death throughout the cycle. From poem 5 on, death becomes the most frequent image. Again there is a natural reference to white nights that speak of physical death in alluding to Akhmatova's son. More important and more moving is the depiction of mental death or madness and the need to kill memory ("One should again learn how to live"). Even in the middle of a bright summer day, the poet declares that she had foreboded a deserted house.

Poem 6, "To Death" (1939), expresses the poet's resignation to the inevitable and her death wish. She awaits death with indifference, not knowing only in what form it will come. There is a certain sense of deliverance: "I dimmed the light and open the door/ To you, so simple and beautiful." For the first time, she refers forebodingly to her son's exile to Siberia and to the horrible parting without saying goodbye: "The Yenisei is swirling,/ The Pole Star glittering. And the blue eyes/ I love are closing in the final horror."

The grief brings the mother close to madness in poem 9 (1940). In a reference to death, the "black valley" beckons, bereft of any memories of her son and allowing no consolation. Juxtaposing the images of nature with those of her son, she admits that the oncoming madness will not allow her to experience anything any more, "Not the dear coolness of his hands;/ Nor the waving shadows of lime-trees,/ Nor the distant whispering sound/ Of his parting words of consolation."

Perhaps the most dramatic poem of the cycle is "Crucifix-

ion" (1940-1943). Written during the war years, it underscores tersely the tragedy of Russia. By quoting Christ's biblical words to his mother, "Do not weep for Me, who am in the grave," the poet seems to liken her own grief, and by transference that of all Russian mothers, to that of the Mother of God. It is as if she searches for some meaning in her son's sacrifice, something such as the redemption of humankind, as in Christ's case. If so, the poem expresses some hope. There is also an afterthought of doubt that the sacrifice of her son would have any lasting meaning, hinted at in the closing lines: "And there where Mother stood silently/ no one even dared to look at her."

A two-part epilogue echoes the prose foreword in poetic form. Its main message is contained in a plea not to forget the ordeals she and her people have endured. As if sensing that she, too, may be guilty of this sin, she asks that, should a monument ever be erected to her, it should be there where she stood three hundred hours and where no door was opened for her. She sees herself as "the tortured mouth through which hundred million people cry." She reiterates that it was out of love and loyalty that she chose not to emigrate but rather to commemorate in some way these years and her people: "And I am praying not only for myself,/ But for all those who stood there with me/ In bitter cold, and in July heat,/ Under that blinding-red prison wall."

The contents of *Requiem* command most of the reader's attention, yet the poem displays stylistic excellence as well. In its combination of conventional and innovative verses, it is typical of the author's poetic craft. Brief personal sketches are spelled by contemplative verses, with skillful transitions from words of emotion to words of description, from the soul to nature, from feeling to fact. Through such mixture of facts and feeling, *Requiem* adds a human touch to history, serving as a steady reminder that a painful past should never be forgotten.

When Akhmatova was asked in an interview taken shortly before her death whether *Requiem* would ever be published in the Soviet Union, she replied, "What does it matter? Hundreds of thousands of people, most of whom had never even heard of me, have read it in transcript or handwritten copies." The events in Russia of the late 1980's and early 1990's proved Akhmatova right.

Vasa D. Mihailovich

Further Reading

Feinstein, Elaine. *Anna of All the Russias: The Life of Anna Akhmatova*. New York: Knopf, 2006. Feinstein's biography discusses Akhmatova's important poems, publishing some in new translations. A chapter is devoted to *Requiem*.

Haight, Amanda. *Anna Akhmatova: A Poetic Pilgrimage.* 1976. New ed. New York: Oxford University Press, 1990. An excellent study of Akhmatova's poems by one of the best authorities on her works. Part of the Oxford Lives series.

Harrington, Alexandra. *The Poetry of Anna Akhmatova: Living in Different Mirrors.* London: Anthem Press, 2006. An analysis of Akhmatova's poetry in its totality, tracing her development from a modernist to a postmodernist.

Hayward, Max. "Anna Akhmatova." In *Writers in Russia, 1917-1978.* San Diego, Calif.: Harcourt Brace Jovanovich, 1983. A fine biographical sketch of Akhmatova and discussion of the conditions under which she wrote her poems, including *Requiem*.

Leiter, Sharon. "The Terror and the War." In *Akhmatova's Petersburg.* Philadelphia: University of Pennsylvania Press, 1983. A review of Akhmatova's life in her beloved St. Petersburg and of political circumstances that provided the material for and led to the writing of *Requiem*.

Reeder, Roberta. *Anna Akhmatova: Poet and Prophet.* New York: St. Martin's Press, 1994. One of the most extensive books in English on Akhmatova, with scholarly discussion of all facets of her life and works. Discusses *Requiem* in detail, focusing on its artistic quality and the fascinating genesis of the poem created in the middle of the terror under which Akhmatova lived. A long, useful bibliography.

Rylkova, Galina. *The Archaeology of Anxiety: The Russian Silver Age and Its Legacy.* Pittsburgh, Pa.: University of Pittsburgh Press, 2007. Rylkova analyzes the work of Akhmatova and other writers, demonstrating how this literature reflects the social, political, and cultural anxiety that accompanied the Russian Revolution, civil war, and Joseph Stalin's terrorist government.

Thomas, D. M. Introduction to *Anna Akhmatova: "Requiem" and "Poem Without a Hero."* Translated by D. M. Thomas. London: Paul Elek, 1976. A brief but useful introduction to Akhmatova and her poems. Includes a cursory comparison with other translations of *Requiem*.

Requiem for a Nun

Author: William Faulkner (1897-1962)
First published: 1951
Type of work: Novel
Type of plot: Psychological realism
Time of plot: 1930's
Locale: Yoknapatawpha County, Mississippi

Principal characters:
MRS. GOWAN STEVENS (TEMPLE DRAKE), the mother of a murdered child
GOWAN STEVENS, her husband
GAVIN STEVENS, Gowan's uncle and Nancy's defense lawyer
NANCY MANNIGOE, the Stevens' nanny and a confessed murderer
GOVERNOR OF MISSISSIPPI
MR. TUBBS, the jailer of Jefferson

The Story:

The early settlers of what would later become Yoknapatawpha County founded the town of Jefferson to escape the "terrible freedom" of the wilderness. The town's courthouse evolved over time, from a wooden lean-to built on the old log jail to an imposing colonial Georgian building. The Georgian courthouse was designed in the nineteenth century by a French architect who had been imported by Colonel Sutpen to design his estate. The town grew around the courthouse, until it was burned to the ground by the invading Union troops during the Civil War. It was rebuilt during Reconstruction with the help of carpetbaggers, who remained afterward to prosper and eventually become part of the local community.

Now, on November 13, the courthouse is the scene of a sentencing hearing. Nancy Mannigoe is sentenced to death for killing the infant child of Mr. and Mrs. Gowan Stevens. In the presence of the Stevenses, as well as of Gavin Stevens—Nancy's defense attorney and the great-uncle of the slain infant—the judge orders that Nancy be hanged on March 13.

Later that evening, Gavin follows Gowan and his wife, Temple, back to their home, where they discuss Nancy's death sentence. Temple asks Gavin whether Nancy has confided in him and offered any excuse for the murder. Gowan brings in a tray containing a bottle of whiskey and three glasses. Before drinking the whiskey, Gowan states that he has not had a drink in eight years. The conversation continues, and Temple and Gowan discuss their plans to leave for California the next morning.

When Gowan briefly leaves the room, Temple anxiously asks Gavin what details Nancy has revealed about the night of the murder. Gavin states that Nancy's account of the tragic night has already been fully revealed. However, he tells Temple that he knows that an unknown man was present the night of the murder. When Gowan returns to the room and asks what Temple and Gavin are discussing, she says nothing. As Gowan drinks the whiskey, he tells Gavin that he had no say in avenging the death of his infant daughter because he is just the father of the victim and the court is concerned only with women and children.

Four months later, at 10:00 P.M. on March 11, Temple and Gavin meet again at the Stevenses' residence. Gowan has taken a sleeping pill and is sound asleep. In the living room, Temple tells Gavin why she and Gowan have coincidentally returned home from California two days before Nancy is to be hanged. Temple states that Nancy should be saved, especially since she has information that was not revealed during the trial. Even if this information is relevant to Nancy's conviction, however, Gavin does not see any feasible way to approach the court two days before Nancy's execution. Temple and Gavin decide that Nancy probably cannot be saved; however, he declares that they will go see the governor just for the sake of revealing the truth once and for all.

Later that evening, Temple discreetly telephones Gavin to make arrangements to visit the governor's mansion. While on the telephone, she notices some movement in the dark but does not give it any thought. After she disappears, Gowan enters the living room. He has heard Temple make arrangements to meet his uncle.

An interlude provides a thumbnail sketch of the history of Jackson, the capitol of Mississippi. It recounts how the capitol got its name and grew into a thriving railhead with a population of more than two hundred thousand.

At 2:00 A.M. on March 12, Gavin and Temple meet the governor of Mississippi in his office. Gavin persuades Temple to tell the governor the true story of her past and of its ef-fects on the murder of her infant daughter. Temple begins by asking the governor if he recalls the story surrounding the events in her life when she was a freshman in college. The governor states that he recalls her name, Temple Drake. Temple then changes the topic and recounts how she met Nancy Mannigoe, whom she describes as a "dope-fiend whore." Temple explains that she met Nancy after witnessing her being attacked by a white man. Nancy had approached the white man for two dollars he owed her for prostitution services.

Temple moves erratically back and forth as she recalls Nancy's past and explains why she and Gavin are speaking to the governor. The governor states that he remembers when Temple Drake disappeared after leaving the university on an evening more than eight years ago. The governor recalls that she finally reappeared as the star witness in the murder trial of her accused kidnapper. Temple recalls events during the time she was held hostage by Popeye Vitelli. While recalling her abduction and incarceration in a Memphis brothel, Temple admits to having been the lover of Alabama Red, a man who worked at the nightclub owned by Popeye. Temple continues to move back and forth between recounting her past and explaining the present circumstances involving Nancy. Gavin interrupts and states that Popeye murdered Alabama Red. Temple further reveals that she wrote incriminating letters to Alabama Red, which later landed in the hands of his brother, Pete, who used the letters to blackmail her.

At 9:30 P.M. on September 13, the night of the tragic murder, Temple and Pete are in Temple's private dressing room. Temple has decided to run away with Pete, even though Pete offers to burn the incriminating letters. After Nancy enters the room, Temple argues with her about taking the money and jewels with which she and Pete plan to escape. Nancy tries to persuade Temple not to leave with Pete. Temple, however, claims that she will never live down her scandalous past. Nancy condemns Temple for giving up and deciding to run out on her two children. Nancy states that she needs to go to the bathroom and warm the baby's bottle. Temple screams as she moves into the door of the nursery.

At 3:09 A.M. on March 12, Gowan is sitting in the governor's chair behind the desk in his office. At first, Temple does not realize that her husband is in the room. After she sees Gowan, they both discuss the past eight years of their marriage and the pain of attempting to live down her scandalous past and of trying to expiate Gowan's guilt for having abandoned her to Popeye's clutches. Temple, Gowan, and Gavin leave the governor's office without obtaining a stay of execution for Nancy.

During the Civil War, the North burned the town of Jefferson and gutted the courthouse. After the war and during Reconstruction, Jefferson was rebuilt exactly as it had been before the war. Although the county seat prospered into the twentieth century, lingering memories of the war and the past continue to shape the town and its inhabitants.

At 10:30 A.M. on March 12, Gavin and Temple visit Nancy in the jail just before her execution. They discuss human suffering and the need to believe in faith, even in the face of suffering. As Gowan and Temple prepare to leave, Temple declares that they are doomed.

Critical Evaluation:

Requiem for a Nun is William Faulkner's sequel to *Sanctuary* (1931), which first introduced Temple Drake. In *Sanctuary*, Faulkner provided the groundwork for Temple's subsequent feeling of inevitable doom, which is a result of her being abducted and raped with a corncob by a sexually impotent man, Popeye Vitelli. After the traumatic rape, Temple entered into a state of psychological dissociation and became Popeye's prostitute. Her sense of moral disconnect was further highlighted when she deliberately caused an innocent man to be executed. Not only did Temple impede justice, but she also sentenced herself to a hopeless future.

When she reappears in *Requiem for a Nun*, Temple is the reformed Mrs. Gowan Stevens, the mother of two children. One of her children is murdered because Temple fails to choose the present over the past. In *Requiem for a Nun*, Faulkner illustrates the psychological bondage that occurs when the human heart is in conflict with itself, which, according to Faulkner, "is only worth writing about."

Requiem for a Nun stands out in Faulkner's oeuvre for its unorthodox structure. The novel is divided into three acts, each of which begins with a prose section and continues with dramatic scenes. The prose sections fill in much of the information missing from Faulkner's other prose works about the history of Yoknapatawpha County. These sections also illustrate Faulkner's ideas about the function of memory in shaping a communal consciousness and in establishing a sense of place and belonging. The various scenes in each act convey the novel's present plot involving Temple and Nancy.

While the plot centers around the murder of the Stevens' infant child, Faulkner develops it through his characterization of Mrs. Gowan Stevens/Temple Drake. The dual-named character illustrates Faulkner's belief in the inevitable conflict of the human heart: Mrs. Gowan Stevens is a conventional wife and mother, while Temple Drake is the dark, sexual side of her personality. The integration of the two psyches represents the quest for moral and emotional redemption. Although her marriage to Gowan may have provided some ref-

uge, especially from a southern society that typically is not forgiving, Temple's new identity cannot suppress the hidden desires permeating her soul. However, her struggle and desire to find redemption and to become a whole, integrated individual is purchased at a great personal cost—complicity in the death of her own child.

Faulkner connects Temple's past to the murder after she confesses that she hired Nancy, not out of compassion for her fallen state as a "dope-fiend whore," but rather so that she could relive the dark side of her own nature with someone who had experienced a similar fate. By juxtaposing the morally bankrupt women, Faulkner explores the extent to which the lines of race and class are often blurred in southern society. He depicts Temple's realization of the sacrifice she has made when she states that not only is the past "never dead, it is not even past."

Recounting the past allows Temple to bring it into the present and resurrect the degradation that she needs to cope with her marital obligation. Ironically, Gowan married Temple out of a sense of obligation motivated by his own fear of failure and guilt. Temple's psychological journey over the course of the novel would arguably achieve a state of catharsis in most people. For Temple, though, it seems only to underscore her doomed fate, as she states that women will use any means necessary to protect themselves, even if it involves a child being used as a weapon. That she recalls the tragic night of her daughter's murder and is unable to shed any tears also illustrates Temple's emotional disconnection from her own motherhood.

Like many of Faulkner's works, *Requiem for a Nun* explores the nature of evil. The letters Temple wrote to Alabama Red detailed their sexual liaison. The letters remind Temple not only of her degradation but also of the pleasure she experienced in it, a pleasure she has for eight years sublimated in her marriage and in bearing her two children. Faulkner's description of this perverse yet liberating sexuality plays off against the conventionally tamed and sanctioned carnality that Temple experiences within the institution of her marriage to Gowan. Even that sexuality has its perverse side, since it is a reminder of Gowan's having abandoned Temple to Popeye. Temple and Gowan are, as she states at the conclusion of the novel, "doomed" to a life of recriminations and guilt, everlasting and ever-circling. As Temple explains on repeated occasions, one must be prepared to resist evil even before one knows how to identify it. Only through Nancy's acceptance of death and grace will Temple finally be able to discover a kind of peace in her own soul.

Charles L. P. Silet; revised by Theresa E. Dozier

Further Reading

Blotner, Joseph. *Faulkner: A Biography.* 2 vols. New York: Random House, 1974. A comprehensive biography of Faulkner that includes a historical discussion of his ancestors, his development as a writer, and the genesis of his work. An excellent beginning source.

Izard, Barbara, and Clara Hieronymous. *"Requiem for a Nun": Onstage and Off.* Nashville, Tenn.: Aurora, 1970. Traces the evolution of the text, its sources, the French adaptation by Albert Camus, and the performances of the dramatic portion of the novel in Germany, Greece, and Great Britain.

Polk, Noel. *Faulkner's "Requiem for a Nun": A Critical Study.* Bloomington: Indiana University Press, 1981. An exhaustive analysis of the novel that draws on the academic scholarship generated by the work and by Faulkner's career.

_____. *Requiem for a Nun: A Concordance to the Novel.* West Point, N.Y.: Faulkner Concordance Advisory Board, 1979. Written by a preeminent scholar of southern literature, this book establishes a critical tool of immense value to those who wish to examine the novel in depth and detail.

Ruppersburg, Hugh M. *Voice and Eye in Faulkner's Fiction.* Athens: University of Georgia Press, 1983. A fine, detailed, but easily accessible overall introduction to the study of the novel.

Towner, Theresa M. *The Cambridge Introduction to William Faulkner.* New York: Cambridge University Press, 2008. An accessible book aimed at students and general readers. Focusing on Faulkner's work, the book provides detailed analyses of his nineteen novels, discussion of his other works, and information about the critical reception for his fiction.

Watson, Jay. *Forensic Fictions: The Lawyer Figure in Faulkner.* Athens: University of Georgia Press, 1993. Chapter 5, "Maieutic Forensics: Or, *Requiem for a Nun* and the Talking Cure," focuses on the role of Gavin Stevens, Faulkner's quintessential lawyer.

Resurrection

Author: Leo Tolstoy (1828-1910)
First published: Voskreseniye, 1899 (English translation, 1899)
Type of work: Novel
Type of plot: Social realism
Time of plot: Late nineteenth century
Locale: Russia

Principal characters:
PRINCE DMITRI IVANOVITCH NEKHLUDOFF, a gentleman
KATERINA MASLOVA (KATUSHA), a prostitute
VALDEMAR SIMONSON and VERA DOUKHOVA, political prisoners

The Story:

Katerina Maslova, better known as Katusha, is being led out of prison to attend her trial for murder. Of illegitimate birth, she had been taken in by Sophia and Mary Ivanovna, well-to-do sisters who had cared for her and begun to educate her. When she turned sixteen, Katusha had been seduced by her guardians' nephew, Prince Dmitri Ivanovitch Nekhludoff. Learning that she was to become a mother, Katusha stayed with a village midwife until her child was born. The baby was taken to the foundling hospital, where it soon died, and Katusha, after a series of tribulations, became a prostitute. When she is twenty-six years old, she is accused of complicity in the murder of a Siberian merchant.

While Katusha is being led into court, Nekhludoff, her seducer, lays in bed considering his position. He had recently been having an affair with a married woman, even though he is almost engaged to marry Princess Mary Korchagin. He also thinks of having given away some of his lands to the peasants. Having arisen, Nekhludoff is reminded that he has to serve that day as a juror in the criminal court.

In court, Nekhludoff is astonished to see that the defendant is Katusha and that she is accused of having helped rob and poison the merchant from Siberia. The trial is disgusting because the officials are vain, stupid, and more concerned with formalities and their own self-interest than with a fair trial for the accused.

When Nekhludoff was a student at the university, he had spent his summers with his aunts, and it was there that he had first come to know and to like Katusha. He had given her books to read and had eventually fallen in love with her. When he next returned, three years later, military life had made him depraved and selfish, and he seduced her. On the following day, he had given her money and left for his regiment. When he returned after the war, he had learned that she had become pregnant and had gone away. Somewhat relieved, he had tried to forget her.

Now, at the trial, the sight of Katusha fills Nekhludoff with a mixture of loathing and pity. At first, he is afraid that his relation to her will be discovered, but Katusha does not recognize him, and gradually he begins to feel remorse for the life to which he has driven her. Because of a careless legalistic oversight by the jury, Katusha, though innocent, is sentenced to four years of hard labor in Siberia. Driven by his uneasy conscience, Nekhludoff goes to a lawyer to discuss the possibility of an appeal.

Later, when Nekhludoff is with the Korchagins, he realizes that their lives are empty and degenerate. He feels the need to cleanse his soul and decides that he will marry Katusha and give up his land.

When Nekhludoff goes to the prison and reveals his identity to Katusha, he is treated coldly by her. She also seems proud of her occupation as a prostitute, because it alone gives some meaning to her otherwise empty life. The next time he visits her, she behaves coarsely to him, and when he says that he wants to marry her, she becomes angry with him and returns to her cell.

On his next visit to the prison, Nekhludoff is told that Katusha cannot be seen because she had become drunk on vodka bought with money he had given her. Nekhludoff then sees Vera Doukhova, a revolutionist acquaintance who had sent him a note from the prison. He is surprised at the inordinate pride Vera takes in the sacrifices she has made for the revolutionary cause. Vera tells him that if he obtains a position for Katusha in the prison hospital, her situation will improve. Nekhludoff arranges to have Katusha transferred.

By this time, Nekhludoff is no longer enamored with the prospect of marrying Katusha. He is still determined to go through with his plan, however, and starts out on a journey to settle his estates in anticipation of his departure for Siberia. At Panovo, he sees the miserable conditions of the people. He sees Matrona Kharina, Katusha's aunt, and learns about the death of his child at the foundling hospital. He gives up his title to the land at Panovo and arranges for the peasants to have communal holdings in it, an act that brings him great joy.

Nekhludoff then goes to St. Petersburg. His chief reason is to appeal Katusha's case to the senate and to try to secure the release of Lydia Shoustova, an innocent prisoner who is Vera Doukhova's friend. In St. Petersburg, he moves within the aristocratic circle of his aunt, Katerina Ivanovna Tcharsky, who claims to be interested in evangelism but who has no pity for the unfortunate of the world. Nekhludoff sees various prominent people. The next day he learns that Lydia Shoustova has been released.

Katusha's case is put before the senate. Because one of the senators considers himself to be a Darwinian and thinks that Nekhludoff's morality in the case is disgusting, the girl's sentence is upheld. On the same day, Nekhludoff meets an old friend, Selenin, who is now a public prosecutor. He is an intelligent, honest man, but he had been drawn into the tangled web of "correct" society and its standards. Nekhludoff begins to see the same principle at work in all official circles: to condemn some who might be innocent to be assured of catching the truly guilty.

Back in Moscow, Nekhludoff visits Katusha to persuade her to sign a petition to the emperor. During his visit, he feels love taking hold of him once more. Katusha also loves Nekhludoff, but she feels that marriage to a woman like herself would be bad for him. While Nekhludoff is preparing for his journey to Siberia with Katusha, he begins to study and to think about the nature of criminal law. Although he begins to read much on the subject, he cannot find the answer to his desire to know by what right some people punish others. He also begins to feel that the only reasonable kinds of punishment are corporal and capital, which are both unfortunate and effective, whereas imprisonment is simply unfortunate.

On the long march to Siberia, Nekhludoff follows the prisoners and sees Katusha whenever possible. He also sees the horrible conditions of the exiles. Nekhludoff begins to feel a new love for Katusha, a love that includes tenderness and pity. He also learns to understand the point of view of the revolutionists, for Katusha had been allowed to travel with the political prisoners. One of these, Valdemar Simonson, falls in love with Katusha. He tells Nekhludoff that he wishes to marry Katusha but that she wants Nekhludoff to decide for her. Nekhludoff says that he would be pleased to know that Katusha is well cared for. When she learns of his answer, Katusha refuses to speak to Nekhludoff.

At a remote town in Eastern Siberia, Nekhludoff collects his mail and learns that Katusha's sentence to hard labor has been commuted to exile in a less remote region of Siberia. When he leaves to tell Katusha the news, he realizes how much he wants to have a family. Katusha says that she prefers to stay with Simonson; however, she refuses to say that she loves him. She tells Nekhludoff that he will have to live his own life.

Nekhludoff feels he is not needed any longer and that his affair with Katusha has ended. He sees that evil exists because those who try to correct it are themselves evil and that society has persevered, not because of systems of punishments, but because of human pity and love. He then realizes that the Sermon on the Mount could indeed be a practical law, and that night he begins his new life.

Critical Evaluation:

Resurrection is characteristic of Leo Tolstoy, one of Russia's foremost novelists, because of its rich visual record of people and settings and its deftness in presenting the vices of petty officialdom, the humor of small people who want to seem great, and the hollowness of ritualistic orthodoxy. Tolstoy was convinced that evil begins when people cease to listen to their conscience and become self-centered. The public theme of the novel revolves around the shortcomings of social organizations. The personal theme, which involves the need for forgiveness, takes a form characteristic of Tolstoy: human failure revealed by a sin committed in semi-ignorance, followed by a long and soul-strengthening atonement.

The greatest strength of *Resurrection* is in its penetrating exposure of an unjust social order. A secondary focus is on the personal level in the effect of Nekhludoff's philosophical and political conversion, specifically in his relationship with Katusha, without whom Nekhludoff's reawakening and self-sacrifice could not have occurred.

In his student days, Nekhludoff's social convictions were idealistic. He believed in perfectibility and rejected the principle of ownership of land by the elite. His idealism dimmed, however, after he entered military life, and he quickly abandoned all thoughts of perfection. He sacrificed both his relationship with Katusha and his own values to establish a public image that mirrored the standards of the aristocracy. It was not until his conscience was aroused at Katusha's trial ten years later that he questioned his life and, upon Katusha's conviction, dedicated himself to her rescue and to his spiritual atonement.

Nekhludoff thus came to view human nature as dualistic—animal and spiritual—and he struggled to negate the animal instincts that had led him to sin. He realized that he could deceive others, but not himself. Guided by an inner sense of righteousness, he set about to correct the wrong he had caused.

When Nekhludoff entered the world of prisoners and peasants, he began to realize the extent of the injustice of society. Among those who flocked to Nekhludoff for help were innocent people who had been incarcerated by error, political prisoners whose only crime was in holding differing opinions, and a crew of stonemasons imprisoned because of outdated visas.

Nekhludoff soon realized that social circumstance created criminals rather than the obverse: He rejected the concept of natural depravity based on individual or class characteristics. He further understood that the conditions that created powerlessness, poverty, hunger, sickness, and crime among the peasant classes were supported by the powerful to maintain the wealth of the privileged. Both government and science professed a desire to ameliorate these conditions but actually refused to consider the root of the problem. The only means of righting the situation, he found, was by returning the land to the people who worked it. Yet when Nekhludoff gave his land to the peasants, his wealthy friends and family grew concerned about his mental health, and the peasants eyed his offer with hostile suspicion.

Nekhludoff's exploration of the causes of injustice led him to ask the haunting question of whether truth is at work in the process of law. It was obvious to him that the law did not contain truth by decree or by the process of the courts, although such a notion was popularly accepted. The fact was, Nekhludoff concluded, that the purpose of the law was to uphold class interests and that those who carried out the law and those to whom the law catered were equally criminal with those upon whom the judgment of the law fell. The basic fallacy of the legal system was the belief that people have the power to judge one another. Evildoers cannot judge evildoers, Nekhludoff contended. The processes of judgment and punishment were not only harmful, cruel, and immoral but also ineffective. Justice, he decided, was not served by social systems. That society and order exist at all, despite the acts of both lawful and lawless criminals, is simply because people still pity and love one another.

In the course of the novel, Nekhludoff's resurrection is paralleled by Katusha's spiritual reawakening. At her first reunion with Nekhludoff after her conviction, she repressed her memories of youth and the pain of Nekhludoff's betrayal to the point of oblivion, for she had hardened herself to the necessities of survival as a prostitute. Nekhludoff realized that his sin against her was even greater than he had known, that Katusha had died and that another person called Maslova had taken her place. Although Nekhludoff assumed responsibility not only for Katusha's freedom but also for her spiritual renewal, his influence was only one of the factors that went into the emergence of the new Katusha. Katusha realized that Nekhludoff was again using her, but as he persisted in following her, old feelings for him reawakened. Ultimately, she sacrificed her love to save him from degradation, thus shouldering Nekhludoff's burden for the third time.

First she had suffered from his betrayal and from having his illegitimate child, then in allowing him to sacrifice himself for her, and finally in denying her love for him, by which means she released him from his pledge to marry her. Clearly, the novel's primary concern is Nekhludoff's resurrection.

The process of Nekhludoff's social reversal and spiritual regeneration is least convincing in his personal relationships. He shifts from victimizing Katusha to rescuing her, first taking advantage of her for his physical gratification and then using her to achieve his spiritual atonement. He remains the overlord whose decision precludes dialogue. He professes to see himself, like Jesus, not as the master but as the servant, but he is indeed a masterful servant. He imposes on Katusha the heavy burden of his self-sacrifice—his offer to marry her—without speaking a word of care or love. Nekhludoff's primary concern, it seems, is for the gratification resulting from humbling himself. Nekhludoff proclaims that he is dedicated to following God's will in his own conscience as far as he is able to do so and that in fulfilling such a commitment he will find peace and security.

The final, or perhaps first, genuine step in Nekhludoff's resurrection is the revelation of the truth in the gospel of Christianity. Accordingly, Nekhludoff recognizes that human beings' only duty is to fulfill these laws, but that they must do so without the guidance of the state church, which Nekhludoff judges to be as corrupt as the other institutions in society. Priests, for example, swear in witnesses at court proceedings with an air of self-importance but do not question whether justice is done. Ironically, prisoners corralled into prison chapels chant prayers for the powers that oppress them. Cynical, heretical priests lead their people farther into the darkness of superstition by telling them that "it is good for them." Nekhludoff's disgust for such hypocritical religion is as great as his disdain for his former life and all it represented, but it is his personal religious stance that propels him into a deep and revolutionary understanding of society and justice—an understanding that reflected Tolstoy's beliefs.

"Critical Evaluation" by Mary Peace Finley

Further Reading

Benson, Ruth Crego. *Women in Tolstoy: The Ideal and the Erotic.* Urbana: University of Illinois Press, 1973. Provocative feminist criticism concentrates on Tolstoy's changing vision of the role and importance of family life. Suggests that he struggled most of his life with a dichotomous view of women, regarding them in strictly black-and-white terms, as saints or sinners, and analyzes the female characters in his works in terms of such a double view.

De Courcel, Martine. *Tolstoy: The Ultimate Reconciliation.* Translated by Peter Levi. New York: Scribner's Sons, 1988. A thorough discussion of Tolstoy, touching on his important works. Describes the people and events in his life during the long and arduous writing of *Resurrection*, and includes an analysis of the novel.

McLean, Hugh. *In Quest of Tolstoy.* Boston: Academic Studies Press, 2008. McLean, a longtime Tolstoy scholar, compiled this collection of essays that examine Tolstoy's writings and ideas and assess his influence on other writers and thinkers. Includes discussions of the young Tolstoy and Tolstoy and women, as well as his thinking about Jesus, Charles Darwin, Ernest Hemingway, and Maxim Gorky.

Noyes, George Rapall. *Tolstoy.* 1918. Reprint. New York: Dover, 1968. Connects Tolstoy's many works with reference to biographical information that is pertinent to the understanding of his writings. Includes many of his published writings, diaries, and letters. Concludes that *Resurrection* is a novel of accessories, where the significance lies in gestures, mannerisms, and analysis of its characters' thoughts.

Orwin, Donna Tussig, ed. *The Cambridge Companion to Tolstoy.* New York: Cambridge University Press, 2002. Collection of essays, including discussions of Tolstoy as a writer of popular literature, the development of his style and themes, his aesthetics, and Tolstoy in the twentieth century. Tolstoy scholar Hugh McLean provides an analysis of *Resurrection*.

Rowe, William W. *Leo Tolstoy.* Boston: Twayne, 1986. Examines the historical facts from which Tolstoy derived *Resurrection*. Suggests the possible meanings and images of the novel. Includes biographical information, as well as discussions of several novels and stories.

Simmons, Ernest J. *Tolstoy.* London: Routledge & Kegan Paul, 1973. Focuses on Tolstoy as a major thinker of his time as well as a religious, social, and political reformer. Describes his childhood, his life as a writer, his motivation to write *Resurrection*, and the structure and intent of the novel.

Troyat, Henri. *Tolstoy.* Translated by Nancy Amphoux. 1967. New ed. New York: Grove Press, 2001. A thorough treatment of the author's life and work, with many illustrations. Gives a lengthy explanation of the conditions surrounding the writing of *Resurrection* and some explanation of the text.

The Return

Author: Walter de la Mare (1873-1956)
First published: 1910
Type of work: Novel
Type of plot: Ghost
Time of plot: Nineteenth century
Locale: England

Principal characters:
ARTHUR LAWFORD, a middle-aged Englishman
SHEILA, his wife
ALICE, their teenage daughter
THE REVEREND BETHANY, a rector
HERBERT HERBERT, a bookish recluse
GRISEL HERBERT, his sister

The Story:

Late one September evening, Arthur Lawford, who is recovering from an attack of influenza, is walking in an ancient churchyard. There he finds the grave of a man named Nicholas Sabathier, who killed himself in 1739. Suddenly tired, Lawford stops to rest and falls asleep. When he awakes, he feels very strange and quite recovered from his illness. He feels so well that he practically runs home.

Going to his room to dress for dinner, Lawford lights a candle and prepares to shave. He stops in horror when he sees in the mirror that his whole physical being has changed; he is now lean faced and dark, an entirely different person. The only thing that could have happened, he thinks, is that his nap in the churchyard changed him into someone else, perhaps the occupant of the grave, Sabathier. Still thankful that he retains his own mind, Lawford tries to think what to do. As he stands undecided, his wife comes to call him to dinner. When she enters the room, she is horrified. She refuses at first to believe that the person she sees is her husband, but in the end she is convinced.

The Lawfords call in the rector, the Reverend Bethany, who is also horrified. He is willing to believe, however, that something has happened to Lawford, and that the person he sees is not an impostor. The three decide to wait until a week has passed before doing anything drastic. Sheila Lawford refuses to stay with her husband at night; he seems too much a stranger to her in his new shape. She tries to get him to remain in his room, but he finds it necessary to go out in the evening. On one of his rambles at dusk, he meets an old woman who had been a school friend of his mother. She fails to recognize him in his new shape, even though he prompts her by telling her where she had known his mother. She does say that he looks somewhat like the late Mrs. Lawford.

On another of his rambles, this time back to the same churchyard, Lawford meets a strange man named Herbert Herbert. They talk over the grave of Nicholas Sabathier, and Lawford hints at his own history. Herbert seems interested and asks Lawford to come to tea the following day. When they shake hands to part, light falls on Lawford's face for the first time. As it does, Herbert is obviously startled by what he sees.

Lawford joins Herbert for tea the next day; the tea is served by Grisel Herbert, the host's sister. Herbert tells Lawford that his is the face of Nicholas Sabathier, whose picture is in a book that Herbert owns. The book also contains an autobiography of Sabathier, which reveals him as a man very fond of women. Grisel Herbert, seeing the look of fear on Lawford's face as he is leaving, runs after him with the book her brother mentioned. The two go for a walk, during which Lawford feels that he is wrestling with an alien spirit and winning out over it.

When Alice Lawford, Arthur and Sheila's daughter, returns home from school, she accidentally meets her father, and the shock of his appearance causes her to faint. Her mother tries to make her believe that the man she saw was someone else, a doctor, but Alice goes to her father in secret and tells him that she knows him and hopes all will turn out well in the end.

After several arguments with her changed husband, Sheila finally decides to go away for a few days, leaving Lawford alone in their big house to wrestle with his problem. Although he hopes to throw off the spirit that has taken possession of him, he fears that it might conquer him entirely.

Lonely after his wife has gone, Lawford turns to the Herberts, of whom neither the rector nor anyone else has previously heard. He spends several days and nights with his new friends, and he feels that he is getting better, that he is conquering whatever has taken hold of him. Grisel seems especially helpful.

One night, Lawford goes back to his house alone. There he has fearful dreams and once again has a spiritual battle with something he cannot name. The following day, he goes to see the Herberts, who take him on a picnic. The three walk many miles until, as they come over a hill, Lawford sees a village. The sight of the village awakens strange, horrible memories in him. He turns to Grisel and tells her that she knows what memories they are, and she makes no denial.

The next day, Grisel and Lawford go out together for a long walk, during which they reveal their mutual feeling that they had come to love each other in another life. It seems as if Nicholas Sabathier and a woman he loved are talking to each other through them. At last, Grisel tells Lawford that he is pursuing a dream that can never reach reality. They return to the Herberts' house, where Grisel tells her brother, who seems not in the least surprised, that Nicholas Sabathier has come to say good-bye for a while. They make their farewells, and Lawford, somewhat returning to himself, remarks that he never appreciated life before his strange adventure.

Lawford goes back to his own house and finds it locked. He lets himself in quietly and, standing in the hall, overhears a conversation that his wife is having with some friends she has entrusted with the secret of his change. The friends refuse to believe what has happened, in spite of what Sheila has seen, which one of them has also seen, plus the picture and account of Sabathier, which Sheila has found in the house. They advise her to have her husband placed in an asylum as mad or else put into prison as an impostor. When Sheila and her friends leave, Lawford remains, still silent, in the house.

That evening is the eve of St. Michael and All Angels, the same night on which Nicholas Sabathier killed himself in 1739. As he sits in the quiet house, Lawford feels himself returning to his original condition. Unexpectedly, he is visited by the old lady whom he had met on his walk, the woman who had known his mother at school. She has come to see him in order to assure herself that the man she met was not Lawford. This evening she immediately recognizes him as her school friend's son; he has almost no resemblance to the stranger who accosted her. As she is leaving, she makes some ambiguous remarks that lead Lawford to wonder if she has not, in some fashion, learned more than she has revealed. Nevertheless, he decides that he is sufficiently himself once more to write to his wife and let her know of the change. He sits down to write, but because of what he overheard earlier in the evening, he is unable to put into words what he wants to say. Fatigued, he falls asleep at the table.

As Lawford sleeps, the rector comes into the room, recognizes him as his own parishioner again, and sits down to watch over the sleeping man. Before long, the rector is also sound asleep.

Critical Evaluation:

The Return is among the earliest of Walter de la Mare's "ghost stories," and it contains many of the features that were to become intrinsic to his work in that vein—not least, of course, the ambiguity that requires the addition of quotation marks to the description. Although *The Return* uses an author-omniscient viewpoint rather than employing a possibly unreliable narrator (as many of de la Mare's later tales of this genre do), the question of what has happened to Arthur Lawford remains stubbornly unresolved and defiantly unresolvable.

The ending of the story is particularly revealing in this respect. Countless tales of surreal experience written in the previous century had been resolved by final awakenings, but de la Mare's story ends with both the protagonist and his observer falling asleep. Climactic awakenings implicitly condemn not only the particular supernatural intrusions of individual stories to the world of dreams but also all supernatural intrusion into people's everyday lives. De la Mare's reversal of the formula is no mere refusal of a cliché; it amounts to a claim that people's conscious lives are perpetually and inescapably shadowed by the supernatural—metaphorically, if not literally. Sleep can offer no release from this shadowing; at the beginning of the story, it is Lawford's lapse into sleep that facilitates the change that overtakes him. The text tells us nothing about the condition he will be in when—or if—he awakes from the slumber that overtakes him as he tries to write to his absent wife to explain that he has decided to "blunder on" within their unsatisfactory relationship.

It is difficult to say with certainty what actually happens in the course of the plot of *The Return*. Perhaps the soul of Nicholas Sabathier really does emerge from the suicide's grave to bid for possession of Lawford's body, only to fail on the anniversary of its previous retreat into oblivion. In that case, Lawford's spiritual battles really are the elements of a war of self-preservation. The main support for this thesis, however, is provided by the Herberts, whose own real existence seems to be a matter of some doubt; nor is the Herberts' support for a frankly supernatural explanation free of its own intrinsic ambiguities. Whether or not the Herberts inhabit the same world as Lawford's wife and her determinedly mundane friends, they are certainly not of that world. They represent a whole new world of possibilities into which Lawford might escape if only he has the will to do so, but it is a world that has problematic aspects of its own.

The alternative interpretation of Lawford's experience is that contemplation of the wrack and ruin of his life has combined with the symbol of Sabathier's gravestone to release something that has always been locked up within him: the man he might have been. Support for this view is provided by the fact that his convalescence gives him the sense that "behind all these past years, hidden as it were from his daily life, lay something not quite reckoned with." He reflects, morosely, that people all keep their crazy sides to themselves; this licenses the theory that what happens to him might be a brief liberation of his "crazy side," forcing a long-overdue reckoning that he is, in the end, incompetent to evaluate or follow through on.

If this is so, the story becomes a bleak meditation on the subject of impotence. Unlike Dr. Jekyll, who finds his other self so monstrous in appetite, inclination, and strength as to be uncontrollable once unleashed, poor Lawford surrenders his commitment to the "lawful" only to find his hidden self beset by uncertainties and confusions of its own. In the end, his metamorphosis is so tentative that there seems no prospect of his reaping the perverse rewards of reckless self-indulgence.

In *The Return*, Herbert calls attention to the significance of Sabathier's name, linking it to the hypothetical gatherings that witch-hunters called "sabbats" but suggesting that it might better be construed as a verb meaning "to bemuse or estrange with otherness." This is an appropriate description of what Lawford's possessor has done to him, and Lawford adopts it, speaking lightly to Grisel of the time "before I was Sabathiered."

In Lawford's conversations with Grisel, the notion of returning is incessantly invoked, but in several different ways. One return is that of "Nicholas Sabathier," whether that is an actual spirit from the historical past or merely a potential self that Arthur Lawford has put away and stifled. The more important return is that which Lawford decides to make in spite of the temptations that Grisel lays before him: the return that takes him back to his own house to overhear what he is, and will remain, in the estimation of the others. Herbert cannot understand why Lawford makes this choice, but Grisel can; she knows that love alone is not enough to sustain a relationship and that the demands of an unsatisfactory wife are always likely to prevail if there is a child to be considered.

When he wrote *The Return*, Walter de la Mare's life had recently undergone a considerable change. For nearly twenty years he had worked as a clerk for an oil company, but, at the age of thirty-six, he had been granted a Civil List pension that allowed him to retire to the country and devote himself entirely to writing. It is not unnatural, in such circumstances, that a man might find abundant time to contemplate what he had been, what he had become, and what he might henceforth make of himself; nor is it surprising that he might conclude that whatever he might once have made of himself, he was by now irrevocably confirmed in his own identity. However pusillanimous the last paragraph of the novel may seem, when

Bethany's response to the imagined "roar of Time's Winged Chariot hurrying near" is simply to go to sleep, it is certainly realistic. If the ambiguity of his subsequent work is any guide, de la Mare never quite made up his mind as to whether that kind of realism ought to be seen as an appalling kind of cowardice or as the quiet but triumphant heroism of common sense.

"Critical Evaluation" by Brian Stableford

Further Reading

Briggs, Julia. "On the Edge: Walter de la Mare." In *Night Visitors: The Rise and Fall of the English Ghost Story.* Winchester, Mass.: Faber & Faber, 1977. Offers a reverent account of de la Mare's ghost stories, drawing various comparisons between *The Return* and his short fiction.

Cavaliero, Glen. "Twilight Territories." In *The Supernatural and English Fiction.* New York: Oxford University Press, 1995. Chapter focuses on the works of Rudyard Kipling and de la Mare as part of a larger discussion of English authors' employment of elements of the supernatural in their fiction.

Clute, John. "Walter de la Mare." In *Supernatural Fiction Writers: Fantasy and Horror,* edited by Everett F. Bleiler. New York: Charles Scribner's Sons, 1985. Offers a sensitive discussion of de la Mare's ambiguous use of the supernatural. Gives more attention to *The Return* than most such essays, which often concentrate entirely on his short fiction.

McCrosson, Doris Ross. *Walter de la Mare.* New York: Twayne, 1966. Presents a compact but thorough account of de la Mare and his work. Chapter 8 is devoted to *The Return.*

Reid, Forrest. *Walter de la Mare: A Critical Study.* Winchester, Mass.: Faber & Faber, 1929. Early study of de la Mare's work was written when his reputation was at its height. Chapter 8 provides a detailed critique of *The Return* that is relatively uncolored by comparisons with de la Mare's later ghost stories.

Whistler, Theresa. *Imagination of the Heart: The Life of Walter de la Mare.* London: Duckworth, 1993. Biography examines de la Mare's life and work in much more detail than earlier attempts. *The Return* is set in its biographical context in chapter 8, which deals with the author's relationship with the poet Henry Newbolt, who was the prime mover in procuring de la Mare's Civil List pension.

The Return of the King

Author: J. R. R. Tolkien (1892-1973)
First published: 1955
Type of work: Novel
Type of plot: Epic
Time of plot: The Third Age in a remote legendary past
Locale: Middle-earth, chiefly Gondor, Mordor, and the
Shire

Principal characters:
FRODO BAGGINS, the Ring-bearer
SAMWISE GAMGEE (SAM), his loyal servant and the
temporary Ring-bearer
MERIADOC BRANDYBUCK (MERRY) and PEREGRIN TOOK
(PIPPIN), Frodo's cousins and the chief scourers of the
Shire
GANDALF (MITHRANDIR), a wizard and the White Rider
ARAGORN (ELESSAR), the returned king
ÉOMER, the nephew of King Théoden and his successor as
king of Rohan
ÉOWYN, Éomer's sister and a beautiful shield-maiden
DENETHOR, the steward of Gondor and the father of
Boromir and Faramir
FARAMIR, the hope of Gondor after Boromir's death
GOLLUM, a corrupted hobbit and once the owner of the
Ring
SARUMAN (SHARKEY), a traitor wizard and the corrupter of
the Shire
SAURON, the Dark Lord of Mordor

The Story:

Gandalf and Pippin ride on Shadowfax to the Realm of Gondor and are admitted to the presence of Denethor, steward of Gondor. Pippin tells of the heroic death of Boromir, Denethor's son, and swears allegiance to the kingly old man. Gandalf does not hinder this, although Pippin senses tension between Gandalf and Denethor. Beregond of the Guard gives Pippin the passwords and tells him how Gondor, closest of free lands to Mordor, bears the brunt of the Dark Lord's wrath.

After the departure of Gandalf, Théoden and his Riders, with Aragorn, Merry, Legolas, and Gimli, ride back to Dunharrow. They are joined by Rangers, Aragorn's kindred. Aragorn, sorely troubled, says that haste demands that he travel the Paths of the Dead. He has wrestled with the will of Sauron in his seeing stone, hoping to distract Sauron so that Frodo and Sam might fulfill their mission of destroying Sauron's Ring. Théoden's niece Éowyn begs Aragorn not to take the Paths of the Dead, from which none has returned, or to take her with him, but he refuses. Leading his company underground, he summons the ghosts of oathbreakers who failed to fight Sauron and who can have no peace until they keep the oath sworn to Aragorn's ancestor. They follow him, and wherever they pass, they spread terror.

Théoden and his nephew Éomer summon the Riders of

Rohan to answer Gondor's call for aid. Éowyn and Merry are denied a place among the combatants. When the Riders leave, a young warrior, Dernhelm, smuggles Merry with them under a cloak. The darkness that Sauron sends out to dismay his enemies conceals the movements of Rohan's Riders.

When Faramir, the younger son of Denethor, comes back from his outpost and reports his meeting with Frodo, Denethor is coldly furious that Faramir did not take the Ring by force. Boromir, he says, would have brought the Ring to his father. Gandalf replies that if Boromir had taken it, he would have fallen and replaced the Dark Lord only by becoming another Dark Lord, whom even his father would not have known.

Sauron's army, led by the chief of the Ringwraiths, attacks Gondor. Faramir returns to battle but is wounded by Ringwraiths. Despair seizes Denethor, who decides to burn himself and the unconscious but still living Faramir. Pippin seeks Gandalf to prevent this mad act. The hosts of Mordor batter down the gate, and the chief Ringwraith enters, confronted only by Gandalf. Horn blasts announce the arrival of Rohan, and the Ringwraith vanishes to return on his reptilian flying mount. Théoden's horse goes mad with fright and falls on his master. Sick with fear, Merry crawls behind the monster, but Dernhelm faces the Ringwraith. According to an old prophecy, no living man can destroy the Ringwraith, but Dernhelm is discovered to be Éowyn, not a man. She decapitates the Ringwraith's monstrous steed. Merry then thrusts from behind with his blade of Westernesse, and Éowyn strikes at the Ringwraith's head. Both are stunned, but the Ringwraith's empty cloak and armor collapse on the ground, and a shrill wail runs down the wind. Aragorn arrives in ships with reinforcements. The battle is won, but at great cost.

Denethor, thwarted by Beregond and Gandalf in his attempt to burn Faramir, burns himself, clutching his seeing stone, through which the will of Sauron entered Gondor. At Théoden's death, Éomer becomes king of Rohan. In the Houses of Healing, Aragorn treats Faramir, Éowyn, and Merry. Gandalf, Aragorn, and others march to the Black Gate of Mordor to distract Sauron yet again and keep his Eye from Frodo. At the Gate, Mordor's hordes attack them.

Meanwhile, Sam has made his way into Mordor to try to rescue Frodo. The orcs have fought over Frodo's mithril coat, and most of them are dead. Sam kills the lone guard and disguises Frodo and himself with orc armor. Nightmare days follow as they struggle across the ashen land toward Mount Doom, often escaping capture through seeming miracles, once being taken for orcs and forced to join them before escaping by a fortunate accident. As Sam carries the exhausted Frodo on his back, struggling toward Mount Doom and its restless fires, Gollum, who has been trailing them, leaps from a high rock and knocks Sam down. Gollum grapples with Frodo for the Ring, but Frodo flings him off and announces that if Gollum ever touches him again, he will be cast into the fire. Frodo moves on. Sam raises Sting, his dagger, to kill Gollum but cannot strike the wretched, repulsive creature. Gollum flees, and Sam follows Frodo into the fissure in the side of Mount Doom.

There, beside the Crack of Doom, with its fearful flames, Frodo puts on the Ring, and Sauron becomes aware of him. The Dark Lord calls his Ringwraiths from the battle. Gollum dashes past Sam and struggles with Frodo for the Ring, which he captures by biting off Frodo's finger. Dancing with joy, Gollum loses his balance and falls into the fire. The volcano erupts, the towers of Mordor disintegrate, and the Ringwraiths fly into the flames and are destroyed. The hosts of Mordor scatter like dust. The Captains of the West see a pall of smoke rise above Mordor, lean threateningly toward them, and then blow away. Gandalf and three great eagles pick up Frodo and Sam, who lie on an island of stone that is slowly being covered by molten lava, and bring them back for Aragorn's healing.

They are present at the crowning of Aragorn as King Elessar. Frodo takes the crown from Faramir, the steward of Gondor, and bears it to Gandalf, who crowns the king. Celeborn and Galadriel are there, and Elrond, with his two sons, brings his daughter Arwen Evenstar to marry Aragorn and become queen. King Éomer of Rohan then takes Théoden's body back to his country. He gives the hand of his sister Éowyn to Faramir, whom she has grown to love in the Houses of Healing.

The guests scatter—Legolas and Gimli to visit Fangorn, Celeborn and Galadriel to Lothlorien, Gandalf and the hobbits to Rivendell to visit Bilbo. Gandalf sends the four hobbits to the Shire after telling them they will find evil, which they can now remedy without help from him. In the Shire, Lotho Sackville-Baggins has set up a dictatorship, backed by the mysterious Sharkey. Merry and Pippin take charge of scouring the Shire with the help of other hobbits, who have needed only a leader. They kill or drive away the Boss's ruffians and learn that Sharkey is Saruman, whom Treebeard had released after Sauron's overthrow. Saruman tries to stab Frodo, but the mithril coat saves him again. Saruman and his henchman Wormtongue, who has murdered Lotho, are banished. Wormtongue hates Saruman and cuts his throat—when he does so, the wizard's body shrivels with rapid decay. Hobbits kill the fleeing Wormtongue.

Sam brings beauty back to the Shire, sprinkling over it the dust given him in Lothlorien by Galadriel. He marries Rosie Cotton, and they make a home in Bag End, looking after Frodo. Every year, Frodo's wounds trouble his body and his spirit until he joins Gandalf, Bilbo, Galadriel, and Elrond and sails away to the overseas haven of the elves. Thus ends the Third Age.

Critical Evaluation:

The Return of the King is the final volume of *The Lord of the Rings* (1955), J. R. R. Tolkien's epic fantasy of war between good and evil. Divided into two sections, *The Return of the King* carries the disparate narrative threads of the second volume in the trilogy, *The Two Towers* (1954), to their conclusions, drawing the War of the Ring to an ending that is at once happy and sad.

As in *The Two Towers*, the first portion (book 5) of *The Return of the King* is a sweeping view of a world at war. This section weaves together the experiences of several different heroes, large and small, each of whom must play a part to defeat the armies of the Dark Lord. By contrast, much of book 6 concentrates again on only three characters, the presence of each of whom is necessary for the destruction of the ruling Ring. The narrow focus of the Ring-bearer and his companions is united with the vast panorama of the world outside only after the Ring is gone. By employing this dual narrative style, Tolkien is able to address widely divergent questions regarding the ability of good to defeat evil.

The great battle of the War of the Ring takes place before the gates of Minas Tirith, chief city of Gondor. Throughout the story, Gondor has been portrayed as the essential fortress of the West, the most powerful defense against the triumph of evil. Although waning in strength, Gondor has remained true to the high vision of its founders, refusing to compromise with evil even as the days grow dark. It is, however, not enough. Sauron has marshaled armies so powerful that Lord Denethor, certain of the defeat of his city, goes mad.

Yet the day is saved. The gate of Minas Tirith is broken, and its armies quail in fear, but rescue comes from several sources. From the north, the Riders of Rohan attack with the dawn, dismaying the human allies of the Dark Lord. The Captain of Mordor is slain by a woman of Rohan and a hobbit of the Shire. Ships arrive from the south bearing Aragorn and his fellow Rangers of Westernesse. From the city ride the knights of Dol Amroth, leading the army of Gondor with renewed hope. The great wizard Gandalf does what he can to bring order to these events, but a power far stronger than even his subtle mind is at work. Together, this array of forces is just enough to defeat Sauron's first attack. Good has triumphed not because of the will or strength of any one warrior but because of the cooperation of all in a just cause. Each army suffers grievously, but the sufferings stand for nought in the face of defeating the great evil.

As the Captains of the West stand together to push the enemy to his last throw, the focus of the story shifts to Mordor, where three indomitable spirits make their way to Orodruin, the mountain of fire. Here is the same story etched in fine detail: Good triumphs not because of the heroic exploits of any one of them but because of the necessary contributions of all three.

Who is the hero of *The Lord of the Rings*? Frodo is the sacrificial martyr, dragging his body through the desert of Mordor while the Ring eats away at his mind. He must carry the Ring to the fire because no one else has the strength of will to do so. Frodo cannot make it, however, without Sam at his side, thinking of food and water, pointing the way, finally carrying his master up the side of the mountain. Only Frodo can take the Ring, but without Sam he would lie down in Mordor and die.

When they reach the fire, Frodo's will fails him at last. The Ring takes possession of his mind, spinning illusions of greatness and fending off its own destruction. Sam is helpless at this turn of events. He has brought his master to the mountain, but his master cannot fulfill the quest. Gollum has a last

part to play. Seizing the Ring in a last act of treachery and deceit, the maddened hobbit oversteps himself and falls into the fire with the Ring. Good comes of this final evil act, for the Ring is destroyed at last.

In both the War of Gondor and the final destruction of the Ring, good may be perceived as a force more powerful than any one individual, more powerful even than the actions of all the characters combined. The triumph of Gondor is achieved through the coordinated actions of many, a series of carefully timed events that no one person orchestrates. The Ring is destroyed because three vastly dissimilar hobbits are drawn to the fire, each with an essential part in the drama. Goodness is more than a quality within each individual; it is an active force guiding the actions of those who walk the earth, at times in spite of themselves.

In a lecture delivered in 1939, J. R. R. Tolkien argued that one of the essential ingredients of a successful fairy story is a happy ending. Whether *The Lord of the Rings* is successful in that regard is an open question. Certainly the forces representing good win a complete victory: Sauron and his minions are vanquished, the free peoples flourish, and Aragorn gains his crown. Yet there is an underlying element of change and loss. Their work finished, Elrond, Galadriel, and Gandalf must leave Middle-earth. Frodo and Bilbo, wounded by possession of the Ring, depart also. The younger hobbits become the recognized heroes of the Shire, while Sam Gamgee inherits all that might have come to Frodo. It is a bittersweet ending at best.

"Critical Evaluation" by Robert Kuhn McGregor

Further Reading

Curry, Patrick. *Defending Middle-earth: Tolkien, Myth, and Modernity.* 1997. Reprint. Boston: Houghton Mifflin, 2004. Examines the relevance of Tolkien's mythological world for modern readers. Focuses on three aspects of Tolkien's depiction of Middle-earth: its social and political structure, its nature and ecology, and its spirituality and ethics.

Dickerson, Matthew T., and Jonathan Evans. *Ents, Elves, and Eriador: The Environmental Vision of J. R. R. Tolkien.* Lexington: University Press of Kentucky, 2006. Discusses Tolkien's view of the natural world and environmental responsibility, arguing that the lifestyles of his fictional characters anticipate many of the tenets of modern environmentalism and agrarianism.

Drout, Michael D. C., ed. *J. R. R. Tolkien Encyclopedia: Scholarship and Critical Assessment.* New York: Routledge, 2007. Comprehensive reference work contains five hundred entries on a wide range of subjects related to Tolkien's writings and life. Topics covered include characters in Tolkien's fiction, the critical reception of his works, and adaptations of his writing to the screen and other media.

Giddings, Robert, ed. *J. R. R. Tolkien: This Far Land*. Totowa, N.J.: Barnes & Noble, 1983. Collection of essays covers varied topics, including Tolkien's use of humor, his depictions of female characters, and the narrative structure of his novels.

Isaacs, Neil D., and Rose A. Zimbardo, eds. *Tolkien: New Critical Perspectives*. Lexington: University Press of Kentucky, 1981. Offers an introduction to relatively early Tolkien criticism. Includes a chapter on Frodo as the old hero and Aragorn as the new, as well as a discussion of the combination of mythic and Christian elements in *The Return of the King*.

Lee, Stuart D., and Elizabeth Solopova. *The Keys of Middle-earth*. New York: Palgrave Macmillan, 2005. Interesting work provides information on Tolkien's medieval sources, featuring modern translations of the original texts.

Lobdell, Jared. *The Rise of Tolkienian Fantasy*. Chicago: Open Court, 2005. Examines Tolkien's fantasy fiction, discussing the writers who influenced him, the elements of his fantasy literature, and his literary heirs, including writers Ursula K. Le Guin, Stephen King, and J. K. Rowling.

Rosebury, Brian. *Tolkien: A Cultural Phenomenon*. 2d ed. New York: Palgrave Macmillan, 2003. Traces the development of Tolkien's writing over several decades, devoting a lengthy analysis to *The Lord of the Rings*. Also provides information on Tolkien scholarship and discusses director Peter Jackson's film adaptation of *The Lord of the Rings*.

The Return of the Native

Author: Thomas Hardy (1840-1928)
First published: 1878
Type of work: Novel
Type of plot: Tragedy
Time of plot: Mid-nineteenth century
Locale: Egdon Heath, in southern England

Principal characters:
DIGGORY VENN, a reddleman
DAMON WILDEVE, the proprietor of the Quiet Woman Inn
THOMASIN YEOBRIGHT, Wildeve's fiancé
MRS. YEOBRIGHT, Thomasin's guardian
CLYM YEOBRIGHT, Mrs. Yeobright's son
EUSTACIA VYE, a young woman who wants to escape the heath

The Story:

Egdon Heath is a gloomy wasteland in southern England. Against this majestic but solemn, brooding background, a small group of people are to work out their tragic drama in the impersonal presence of nature.

Guy Fawkes Day bonfires are glowing in the twilight as Diggory Venn, the reddleman, drives his van across the heath. Tired and ill, Thomasin Yeobright, the young girl whom Diggory loves, lies in the rear of his van. She had rejected his marriage proposal in order to marry Damon Wildeve, proprietor of the Quiet Woman Inn. Now, Diggory is carrying the girl to her home at Blooms-End. She had gone to marry Wildeve in a nearby town, but the ceremony did not take place because of an irregularity in the license. Shocked and shamed, Thomasin has asked her old sweetheart, Diggory, to take her home.

Mrs. Yeobright, Thomasin's aunt and guardian, hears the story from the reddleman. Concerned for the girl's welfare, she decides that the wedding should take place as soon as possible. Mrs. Yeobright has good cause to worry, for Wildeve's intentions are not wholly honorable. Later in the evening, after Wildeve has assured the Yeobrights, rather casually, that he intends to go through with his promise, his attention is turned to a bonfire blazing on Mistover Knap. There old Captain Vye lives with his beautiful granddaughter Eustacia. At dusk, Eustacia has started a fire on the heath as a signal to her lover, Wildeve, to come to her. Although he intends to break with Eustacia, he decides to obey her summons.

Meanwhile, Eustacia is waiting for Wildeve in the company of young Johnny Nunsuch. When Wildeve throws a pebble in the pond to announce his arrival, Eustacia tells Johnny to go home. The meeting between Wildeve and Eustacia is unsatisfactory for both. He complains that she gives him no peace, and she, in turn, resents his desertion. Meanwhile, Johnny Nunsuch, frightened by strange lights he has seen on the heath, returns to Mistover Knap to ask Eustacia to let her servant accompany him home, but he keeps silent when he comes upon Eustacia and Wildeve. Retracing his steps, he stumbles into a sandpit where the reddleman's van stands. Diggory learns from the boy of the meeting between Eustacia and Wildeve. Later, he overhears Eustacia declare her hatred of the heath to Wildeve, who asks her to run away with him to America. Her reply is vague, but the reddleman decides to see Eustacia without delay to beg her to let Thomasin have Wildeve.

Diggory's visit to Eustacia is fruitless. He then approaches Mrs. Yeobright, declares again his love for her niece, and offers to marry Thomasin. Mrs. Yeobright refuses the reddleman's offer because she feels that the girl should marry Wildeve. She confronts the innkeeper with vague references to another suitor, with the result that Wildeve's interest in Thomasin is awakened once more.

Shortly afterward, Mrs. Yeobright's son, Clym, returns from Paris, and a party to welcome him gives Eustacia the chance to view this stranger about whom she has heard so much. Uninvited, she goes to the party disguised as one of the mummers. Clym is fascinated by this interesting and mysterious young woman disguised as a man. Eustacia dreams of marrying Clym and going with him to Paris. She even breaks off with Wildeve, who, stung by her rejection, promptly marries Thomasin to spite Eustacia.

Clym Yeobright decides not to go back to France. Instead, he plans to open a school, although Mrs. Yeobright strongly opposes her son's decision. When Clym learns that Eustacia had been stabbed in church by a woman who thought that Eustacia was bewitching her children, his decision to educate the people of the heath is strengthened. Much against his mother's wishes, Clym visits Eustacia's home to ask her to teach in his school. Eustacia refuses because she hates the heath and the country peasants; as a result of his visit, however, Clym falls completely in love with the beautiful but heartless Eustacia.

Mrs. Yeobright blames Eustacia for Clym's wish to stay on the heath. When bitter feelings grow between mother and son, he decides to leave home. His marriage to Eustacia makes the break complete. Later, Mrs. Yeobright relents somewhat and gives a neighbor, Christian Cantle, a sum of money to be delivered in equal portions to Clym and Thomasin. Christian foolishly loses the money to Wildeve in a game of dice. Fortunately, Diggory wins the money from Wildeve; thinking that all of it belongs to Thomasin, he gives it to her. Mrs. Yeobright knows that Wildeve has duped Christian, but she does not know that the reddleman then won the money away from the innkeeper, and she mistakenly supposes that Wildeve has given the money to Eustacia. She meets with Eustacia and asks the girl if she has received any money from Wildeve. Eustacia is enraged by the question; in the course of her reply to Mrs. Yeobright's charge, she says that she would never have condescended to marry Clym had she known that she would have to remain on the heath. The two women part angrily.

Eustacia's unhappiness is increased by Clym's near blindness, a condition brought on by too much reading, for she fears that this means she will never get to Paris. When Clym becomes a woodcutter, Eustacia's feeling of degradation is complete. Bored with her life, she goes by herself one evening to a gypsy dance, where she accidentally meets Wildeve and again feels an attraction to him. The reddleman sees Eustacia and Wildeve together, tells Mrs. Yeobright of the meeting, and begs her to make peace with Eustacia for Clym's sake. She agrees to try.

Mrs. Yeobright's walk at noon across the hot, dry heath to see her son and daughter-in-law proves fatal. When she arrives in sight of Clym's house, she sees her son from a distance as he enters the front door. Then, while she rests on a knoll near the house, she sees another man entering, but she is too far away to recognize Wildeve. After resting for twenty minutes, Mrs. Yeobright walks on to Clym's cottage and knocks at the front door, but no one answers. Heartbroken by what she considers a rebuff by her own son, Mrs. Yeobright starts for home across the heath. Overcome by exhaustion and grief, she sits down to rest, and a poisonous adder bites her. She dies without knowing that inside her son's house Clym had been asleep, worn out by his morning's work. Eustacia did not go to the door because, as she later explains to her husband, she had thought he would answer the knock. The real reason for Eustacia's failure to go to the door was her fear of the consequences if Mrs. Yeobright found her with Wildeve.

Clym awakes with the decision to visit his mother. Starting out across the heath toward her house, he stumbles over her body. His grief is tempered by his bewilderment over the reason for her being on the heath at that time. When Clym discovers that Eustacia failed to let his mother enter the house and that Wildeve had been in the cottage, he orders Eustacia out of his house. She goes quietly because she feels in part responsible for Mrs. Yeobright's death.

Eustacia takes refuge in her grandfather's house, where a

faithful servant thwarts her in an attempt to commit suicide. In utter despair over her own wretched life and over the misery she has caused others, Eustacia turns to Wildeve, who has unexpectedly inherited eleven thousand pounds and who still wants her to run away with him. One night, she leaves her grandfather's house for a prearranged meeting with the innkeeper; in doing so, she fails to receive a letter of reconciliation that Thomasin has persuaded Clym to send to her. On her way to keep her rendezvous with Wildeve, she loses her way in the inky blackness of the heath and either falls accidentally or jumps into a small lake and drowns. Wildeve, who happens to be near the lake when she falls in, jumps in to try to save her and also drowns.

Originally, *The Return of the Native* ended with the deaths of Eustacia and Wildeve, but, in order to satisfy his romantic readers, Hardy made additions to the story in a later edition. In that version, the faithful Diggory marries Thomasin. Clym, unable to abolish ignorance and superstition on the heath by teaching, becomes an itinerant preacher.

Critical Evaluation:

Thomas Hardy was born in Dorset, England, on June 2, 1840. Although he attended several grammar schools and studied French at King's College London, Hardy had little formal education. Later, however, he read extensively in the Bible, the classics, and recent scientific publications. He was an architect's apprentice from 1856 to 1874 and later an ecclesiastical architect. During this time, he wrote poetry, which was not published until after he was a well-known novelist. His first novel, *Desperate Remedies*, was published in 1871. In 1872, he married Emma Gifford; after her death in 1912, he married Florence Dugdale. When storms of protest arose over the pessimism and the violation of strict Victorian sexual mores in his novels *Tess of the D'Urbervilles* (1891) and *Jude the Obscure* (1895), Hardy gave up writing long fiction but continued to write poetry. He died on January 11, 1928, and his ashes were placed in the Poets' Corner at Westminster Abbey. Among his best works are *Far from the Madding Crowd* (1874) and *The Return of the Native*.

In *The Return of the Native*, there is a strong conflict between nature or fate, represented by Egdon Heath, and human nature, represented by the characters in the novel, especially Eustacia. The title of the first chapter, "A Face on Which Time Makes but Little Impression," establishes the heath's role as much more significant than merely a setting for the action. The word "face" suggests that the heath assumes anthropomorphic proportions and becomes, in essence, a major character in the novel; somber and dark, "the

storm was its lover, and the wind its friend." While the characters struggle and become tired and disillusioned—or die—the heath remains indifferent and unchanged. The heath is a formidable foe; in fact, those who struggle against it—Eustacia, Wildeve, and Mrs. Yeobright—eventually die.

The heath, then, becomes a symbol of permanence. Other aspects of the setting become symbolic, and they also intensify the somber tone of the novel. Light and dark imagery is significant in that the dominance of dark imagery adds to the novel's pessimism. The bonfires on the heath provide small areas of light in the blackness of the night, yet the furze burns quickly and is soon extinguished, like the momentary happiness of Eustacia and Clym and the wild passion of Eustacia and Wildeve. The moon's eclipse on the night Clym proposes to Eustacia foreshadows the eclipse of their love. On the night of Eustacia's death, a violent storm echoes her violent emotions as she cries out against her fate.

Like his character Eustacia, Hardy often seems to blame fate for many of the catastrophes of life. Many critics believe that in this novel fate is completely dominant and that the characters are helpless victims of its malevolence. Such a view, however, seems inadequate. Admittedly, fate does play a significant role; for example, Eustacia accidentally meets Wildeve at the gypsy dance. Mrs. Yeobright just happens to choose an extremely hot day to visit Clym, just happens to arrive when Wildeve is there, and just happens to be bitten by an adder when she collapses from fatigue. Eustacia does not receive Clym's letter because her grandfather believes she is asleep. Much of the novel's tragedy, however, can be traced to the characters' motivations, decisions, and actions.

Mrs. Yeobright may seem victimized by Eustacia's failure to open the door to her, but one must remember that Mrs. Yeobright never accepts Eustacia and attempts to turn Clym against her. She feels socially superior to Eustacia, distrusts her because she is a free spirit, calls her lazy and irresponsible, and hints that she is behaving indiscreetly with Wildeve. In general, Mrs. Yeobright is jealous of Eustacia because she wants to keep Clym to herself. She refuses to attend Clym and Eustacia's wedding and later treats Eustacia in a condescending manner. She then harbors her grudge and keeps away from her son and his wife long enough for the gulf between them to widen greatly.

Clym, too, brings much of his trouble on himself. He is flattered by Eustacia's attention and passion for him but never really sees her as an individual totally different from himself. Without regard for her hatred of the heath and her longing for the excitement of Paris, he assumes that she will be a vital part of his teaching mission. After their marriage, he ignores her and devotes his time to his studies, which, perhaps, helps to bring about the physical blindness that becomes symbolic of his blindness to reality. Martyring himself as a furze cutter, he intensifies Eustacia's hatred for the heath and fails to see that his physical fatigue and his degrading work deal a crushing blow to his marriage. Even his desire to teach is selfish and unrealistic; he tries to escape from life's conflicts into an abstraction of truth, and he desires to impose his views on others. Clym's position at the end of the novel is ironic; as an itinerant preacher "less than thirty-three," he may suggest a Christ figure, but in his self-righteousness he fails to find the meaning of love.

Eustacia, who blames fate for her tragedy, is the novel's most ambiguous character; even the author seems to have ambivalent feelings toward her. She is an exciting, passionate "queen of the night" whose romanticism makes her long to be "loved to madness" by a man great enough to embody her dreams. Allowing her imagination to convince her that Clym can master this role, she marries him, hoping to manipulate him as she had manipulated Wildeve, and thus get to Paris. After her marriage, however, her liaison with Wildeve is at first innocent; only after Clym banishes her from his house does she agree to accept Wildeve's offer to help her leave the heath. Despite her desperation, Eustacia refuses to be humbled. Realizing that a lack of money will cause her to lose her honor for a man who is "not great enough" to meet her desires, she drowns herself to avoid humiliation. It is more believable that she dies willingly than that her death is an accident, because only in death does she seem to find peace.

Although Eustacia loses in her battle with the heath, her struggle proves that she is a strong, defiant character who is defeated partly by forces beyond her control and partly by her own refusal to give up her dream. Despite her selfishness and hauteur, her lively spirit gives life to the novel and makes her, in the end, its tragic but unforgettable heroine.

"Critical Evaluation" by Janet Wester

Further Reading

Bloom, Harold, ed. *Thomas Hardy's "The Return of the Native."* New York: Chelsea House, 1987. Collection of essays begins with an editor's introduction that addresses the relations of Arthur Schopenhauer and Percy Bysshe Shelley to Hardy and then discusses the "transformation" of Eustacia. Critical essays by D. H. Lawrence, Irving Howe, and others offer interpretations of the novel.

Daleski, H. M. *Thomas Hardy and Paradoxes of Love.* Columbia: University of Missouri Press, 1997. Examines the treatment of gender in Hardy's novels, defending the author from charges of sexism and maintaining that some

of Hardy's female characters are depicted sympathetically. Argues that Hardy is the premodern precursor of sexual failures and catastrophic ends.

Hardy, Thomas. *The Return of the Native.* Edited by James Gindin. New York: W. W. Norton, 1969. In addition to the text of the novel, this edition contains twelve of Hardy's poems and the portion of his autobiography related to the novel, five contemporary critiques, and fourteen later essays examining the characters, themes, and techniques of the novel.

Kramer, Dale, ed. *The Cambridge Companion to Thomas Hardy.* New York: Cambridge University Press, 1999. Provides an essential introduction to and general overview of all Hardy's work and specific demonstrations of Hardy's ideas and literary skills. Individual essays explore Hardy's biography, his aesthetics, and the impact on his work of developments in science, religion, and philosophy in the late nineteenth century. Jakob Lothe discusses *The Return of the Native* in "Variants on Genre: *The Return of the Native, The Mayor of Casterbridge, The Hand of Ethelberta.*"

Lawrence, D. H. "Study of Thomas Hardy." In *Selected Literary Criticism,* edited by Anthony Beal. New York: Viking Press, 1956. Early psychological study of Hardy's characters, published after Lawrence's death, focuses on what Clym and Eustacia desire. Explains why *The Return of the Native* is the "first tragic and important novel." Probes into the tragic effects of the heath on its inhabitants.

Mallett, Phillip, ed. *The Achievement of Thomas Hardy.* New York: St. Martin's Press, 2000. Collection of essays presents analyses of some of Hardy's novels and other works. Topics addressed include Hardy and nature, the architecture of Hardy, and the presence of the poet in his novels. Includes bibliography and index.

Millgate, Michael. *Thomas Hardy: A Biography Revisited.* New York: Oxford University Press, 2004. Biography enhances and replaces Millgate's 1982 biography, considered to be one of the best and most scholarly Hardy biographies available. Includes bibliography and index.

Page, Norman, ed. *Oxford Reader's Companion to Hardy.* New York: Oxford University Press, 2000. Contains three hundred alphabetically arranged entries on topics related to Hardy's life and works. Includes discussion of his family and friends, important places in his life and work, his influences, and critical approaches to his writings. Supplemented with a chronology of events in Hardy's life, lists of places and characters in his fiction, a glossary, and a bibliography.

Thomas, Brian. *"The Return of the Native": Saint George Defeated*. New York: Twayne, 1995. Analyzes the structure of the novel and argues that in this work Hardy anticipated the modernist obsession with structure. Also explores the role of pagan and Christian mythology in the novel, finding parallels to the legend of Saint George, the dragon slayer.

Tomalin, Claire. *Thomas Hardy*. New York: Penguin Books, 2007. Thorough and finely written biography by a respected Hardy scholar illuminates the novelist's efforts to indict the malice, neglect, and ignorance of his fellow human beings. Includes discussion of aspects of his life that are apparent in his literary works.

The Revenge of Bussy d'Ambois

Author: George Chapman (c. 1559-1634)
First produced: c. 1610; first published, 1613
Type of work: Drama
Type of plot: Tragedy
Time of plot: Sixteenth century
Locale: Paris

Principal characters:
CLERMONT D'AMBOIS, the brother of Bussy d'Ambois, a soldier of fortune recently murdered
BALIGNY, Clermont's brother-in-law
CHARLOTTE, Clermont's sister
MONTSURRY, Bussy's murderer
TAMYRA, his wife
DUC DE GUISE, close friend of Clermont
HENRY III, king of France
MAILLARD, Baligny's lieutenant

The Story:

Clermont d'Ambois has vowed to avenge the murder of his brother, Bussy. Although he doubts the virtue of repaying violence with violence, he has made a solemn promise to Bussy's ghost. His sister, Charlotte, unambiguous in her feelings, is impatient for immediate revenge, and her marriage to Baligny has been made under the stipulation that he, too, pledge himself to effect the death of Montsurry, Bussy's murderer. Tamyra, the wife of Montsurry and former mistress of Bussy, has returned to her husband, but she makes no secret of her hatred of him and her desire for his death. The design of these people is obstructed by the cowardly Montsurry, who has barricaded himself in his home.

Clermont, who insists on a fair duel and who will allow no one else to discharge his duty, has instructed Baligny to deliver his challenge. Baligny's entrance to Montsurry's home is accomplished with the help of a decadent nobleman, the Marquess Renel. Renel, visiting Montsurry on business, bribes the guards to admit Baligny. When Baligny enters, Montsurry is terrified and refuses to accept the proffered challenge. Baligny leaves the challenge with Tamyra, who promises to make her husband read it.

This plot is not the only one in which Baligny is involved. A treacherous man, he bases his actions on his belief that troubles for others mean blessings for himself. Wearing a different mask for every acquaintance, he is able to gain people's confidence and thus discover their dissatisfactions and sow the seeds of further discontent. In dealing with King Henry III, he expounds the doctrine that any evil done out of loyalty to a king is justified. Such a philosophy being agreeable to King Henry, Baligny has become his trusted agent. In talking to the duc de Guise, on the other hand, Baligny expresses the belief that conspiracy is sometimes defensible.

The principal object of jealousy in the court at this time is the Guise faction. King Henry is fearful and jealous of the increasing influence of the duc de Guise, and Baligny strives to increase his distrust. Guise's closest friend is Clermont d'Ambois, whom Guise not only admires but also endeavors to emulate. He sees in Clermont a valor equal to Bussy's and, more important, a profound knowledge of life. Clermont's principles of restraint, unworldliness, and stoic acceptance guide the actions of the powerful duke. Because of the close relationship between the two men, jealousy of Guise is often extended to include Clermont. Thus Baligny is able to convince King Henry of the advantage of getting rid of Clermont. He suggests that Clermont be invited to visit Cambrai, where, away from his friends at court, he can be arrested.

Baligny induces Clermont to go to Cambrai on the pretext that he will be reviewing a muster of the king's troops. In his conversation with Clermont, Baligny attempts to weaken Clermont's ties with Guise by criticizing the latter for his part in the St. Bartholomew's Day Massacre. The schemer's efforts are wasted on Clermont, who is convinced of Guise's virtue.

While Clermont is being entertained by his sister in Cambrai, he receives an anonymous letter informing him of the betrayal and of Baligny's complicity in it. Refusing to think evil of his sister's husband, he dismisses the letter as false. Charlotte, who can think of little but avenging Bussy's death, regards the message as an effort to enfeeble further Clermont's weak will in carrying out his duty.

Maillard, Baligny's lieutenant, has been instructed by the king to apprehend Clermont. When Maillard arrives at Charlotte's house, ostensibly for the purpose of accompanying Clermont on a tour, Clermont asks Maillard if he is charged to arrest Clermont. Maillard's obvious signs of guilt convince Clermont that his earlier suspicions about the journey were justified. Clermont offers to let Maillard take him peacefully, but Maillard denies that any intrigue is afoot. Although quite certain of the consequences, Clermont, with characteristic acceptance of fate, follows Maillard.

The plan is to take Clermont while he is reviewing the troops. Two soldiers disguised as lackeys are to lead him into an ambush, where several men will seize him. Clermont's strength exceeds the estimate of his attackers, however, and the disguised soldiers succeed only in unhorsing him. On foot, he easily beats them off and drives straight through the ambush. He runs until, exhausted, he falls to the ground and is captured.

Believing that outer circumstances have no power to touch the inner man without his will, Clermont accepts his capture with little concern. His only worry is that he will be unable to keep an appointment with his mistress, the countess of Cambrai, and his one request is that a message be sent to her. Other people, however, do not accept his internment with so much complacency. Upon receiving his message, the countess sends him jewels that she hopes he can use to effect his release and vows that she will cry until her eyes pour out. When the duc de Guise hears the news, he rushes to King Henry and speaks so passionately and eloquently of Clermont's virtues that the weak-willed king, unable to answer Guise, orders that Clermont be released.

After his release, Clermont goes to the home of the duc de Guise. There he again meets Bussy's ghost, who chides him for not yet having exacted revenge on Montsurry. Guise, who was implicated in Bussy's murder, feels that the ghost should

thunder threats against him, but Clermont asserts that the duke has fully compensated for his error. Guise is also worried about a plot against him; he believes that his efforts to propagate the Catholic cause are endangered. Clermont wants him to retire from his plans, but Guise regards withdrawal as an abandonment of France.

A plot is indeed threatening the duc de Guise; King Henry, with Baligny's encouragement, has ordered the duke's murder. The king, in addition to his long-standing jealousy of Guise, was angered when Guise forced his hand regarding Clermont. As the duke is on his way to visit the king, Henry's men step from behind a wall and kill him.

With the assistance of Tamyra, Clermont gains access to Montsurry's house. There he finds Charlotte, disguised as a man. She had planned to kill Montsurry herself but has been stopped by the ghost. When Clermont draws his sword, Montsurry at first refuses to defend himself; he does so only after Clermont offers to let Tamyra stab him. Although Montsurry at last gains sufficient courage to conduct himself courageously in the duel, Clermont succeeds in killing him.

Soon after Clermont has fulfilled his duty to his brother, he receives the news that the duc de Guise has been killed by the king's men. The death of his friend and patron is a severe blow to Clermont, whose life has been centered on his relationship with the powerful duke. Believing that his purpose in this world is destroyed, Clermont takes his own life.

Critical Evaluation:

The Revenge of Bussy d'Ambois is a portrait of George Chapman's ideal tragic hero. All other elements of the play are subordinated to the revelation of the character and philosophy of Clermont d'Ambois. Clermont, with his stoic idealism, is an interesting and compelling figure.

The title of Chapman's sequel to his tragedy *Bussy d'Ambois* (pr. 1604) might suggest that the play is but another of the many revenge tragedies or tragedies of blood that were popular in the last decades of Queen Elizabeth I's reign and the first years of her successor, James I. *The Revenge of Bussy d'Ambois* does contain elements of the traditional revenge tragedy: A good man has been murdered, his kinsman is sworn to avenge the murder, a scheming villain is guilty of the crime, and a ghost appears to encourage the revenge. Here, however, similarities end. Chapman has changed some key elements of the typical revenge tragedy: The delay in carrying out the act of revenge is not motivated by uncertainty, since the guilt of the villain is known by all; the stage remains remarkably free of bloodshed; and—most significant—the protagonist who must be the "scourge" to avenge the wrongful death of his brother seems too philosophical to take on the task. As a result, *The Revenge of Bussy d'Ambois* has often been compared unfavorably with such revenge tragedies as William Shakespeare's *Hamlet, Prince of Denmark* (pr. c. 1600-1601, pb. 1603) or Thomas Kyd's *The Spanish Tragedy* (pr. c. 1585-1589), or with the more sensational tragedies of blood such as John Ford's *'Tis Pity She's a Whore* (pr. 1629[?]-1633), plays that contain virtually all elements of their respective genres and bring the action to a final climax in which much blood is shed onstage as villain and hero meet their deaths.

Unquestionably, the play has structural and dramaturgical shortcomings. Most noticeable is Chapman's focus on rhetoric rather than action. Much of the dialogue of *The Revenge of Bussy d'Ambois* is little more than extended soliloquizing about the nature of humankind and the need for stoic acceptance of one's fate. The general knowledge that Montsurry has murdered Bussy lends little suspense to the drama; there is none of the tension created by Shakespeare in *Hamlet* over the guilt of the king and the complicity of the queen in the murder of the prince's father. Further, Montsurry's overt cowardice makes him an unworthy villain and cheapens the revenge Clermont seeks to gain by killing him. Many critics have chastised the playwright for simply pandering to popular sympathies for such dramas while remaining reticent to portray onstage the consequences of crime and punishment.

Such a reading does a disservice to Chapman. While *The Revenge of Bussy d'Ambois* makes use of some conventions of the genre, the play is a revenge tragedy only in a negative sense. That is, Chapman uses the elements of the genre as an ironic commentary on the inadequacy of the moral stance taken by those who celebrate revenge. Steeped as he was in the classical tradition, Chapman grafts onto the revenge drama the form of the classical tragedy, creating a portrait of the noble hero forced by circumstances to serve as a pawn of fate in carrying out an action that is reprehensible yet necessary in a society in which moral and political authority have become separated.

Central to Chapman's concept for this drama is the portrait he creates of his ideal hero, Clermont. Unlike other characters who carry out acts of violence to revenge the murders of those they love, Clermont is an ideal gentleman. He is a pillar of virtue, reluctant to act even though he knows his brother's murder should not go unpunished. His delay in carrying out his revenge comes not from calculation or from concern about the justice of his cause; in fact, he is hopeful that justice can be meted out through means other than the murder he is being encouraged to commit. Only when he is convinced that justice will not be served by those in power does he bring himself to act. Stoic by nature, he is willing to accept his fate; he does not rail against the forces of nature or against God, as other revengers tend to do. Like the true Stoic, he takes his own life when he determines there is no further purpose to be served by living.

A good portion of the drama is given over to characters who scheme to eliminate Clermont because they see him as a cancer in the realm of the French king. Led by Clermont's brother-in-law, Baligny, and abetted by courtiers allied against Clermont's patron, the duc de Guise, this faction manipulates the king against the protagonist, making it impossible for Bussy's murder to be avenged by lawful means. Clermont is able to act with dignity even when these forces overpower him and have him imprisoned; like the true Stoic, he is able to achieve inner peace by relying on the knowledge that he is blameless in any plots against the sovereign.

In many ways, Chapman's Clermont is closer to the tragic heroes of Greek and Roman dramas than he is to his Renaissance counterparts. The play itself is reminiscent of classical rather than Elizabethan drama in other ways as well. Although much violence is talked about, little is seen onstage; instead, declamation and argumentation replace action as the principal staples of Chapman's dramatic art. In plotting and in characterization, Chapman follows the lead of a much admired contemporary, Ben Jonson, whose adoption of classical principles is seen most clearly in *Sejanus His Fall* (pr. 1603), a play Chapman admired. Hence, in *The Revenge of Bussy d'Ambois* and in his other dramatic productions, Chapman furthers the integration of classical principles on the English stage.

"Critical Evaluation" by Laurence W. Mazzeno

Further Reading

Bertheau, Gilles. "George Chapman's French Tragedies: Or, Machiavelli Beyond the Mirror." In *Representing France and the French in Early Modern English Drama*, edited by Jean-Christophe Mayer. Newark: University of Delaware Press, 2008. Essay on Chapman's French tragedies is part of a collection that examines the role and significance of France in English Renaissance drama.

Bowers, Fredson. "The School of Kyd." In *Elizabethan Revenge Tragedy, 1587-1642.* Princeton, N.J.: Princeton University Press, 1940. Maintains that Chapman reverses the traditional pattern of the revenge tragedy in his sequel to *Bussy d'Ambois.* Explains how Chapman introduces the concept of virtue into the character of the revenger and makes him a respectable gentleman.

Braunmuller, A. R., and Michael Hattaway, eds. *The Cambridge Companion to English Renaissance Drama.* New

York: Cambridge University Press, 2003. Collection of essays examines many aspects of the English Renaissance drama. Includes discussion of Chapman's plays.

MacLure, Millar. *George Chapman: A Critical Study.* Toronto: University of Toronto Press, 1966. Focuses on Chapman's development of his tragic hero and discusses the playwright's abilities as a dramaturge. Briefly notes historical sources for the plot of *The Revenge of Bussy d'Ambois.*

Rees, Ennis. *The Tragedies of George Chapman: Renaissance Ethics in Action.* Cambridge, Mass.: Harvard University Press, 1954. Examines the political and ethical dimensions of Chapman's dramatic works. Highlights Chapman's careful depiction of contrasting qualities between Bussy and Clermont.

Spivack, Charlotte. *George Chapman.* New York: Twayne, 1967. Relates *The Revenge of Bussy d'Ambois* to revenge tragedies popular during the period. Comments on Chapman's handling of language and dramatic conventions.

Wieler, John William. *George Chapman: The Effect of Stoicism on His Tragedies.* New York: King's Crown Press, 1949. Explains how the drama reveals Chapman's interest in Stoicism and how that interest caused the playwright to change his attitude toward the character of Clermont, whom he eventually repudiates.

The Revenger's Tragedy

Author: Thomas Middleton (1580-1627)
First produced: 1606-1607; first published, 1607
Type of work: Drama
Type of plot: Tragedy
Time of plot: Renaissance
Locale: Italy

Principal characters:
VENDICE, the revenger, disguised as Piato
HIPPOLITO, his brother, also called Carlo
CASTIZA, their sister, object of Lussurioso's lust
GRATIANA, their mother, a widow
THE DUKE, the ruler of the principality
LUSSURIOSO, his legitimate son
SPURIO, his illegitimate son
THE DUCHESS, his recent bride
AMBITIOSO,
SUPERVACUO, and an
UNNAMED THIRD SON, the Duchess's sons by a previous marriage
ANTONIO, the Duke's final successor

The Story:

Vendice holds a skull in his hand. It is the skull of Gloriana, his late betrothed, who was poisoned by the Duke when she resisted his lecherous advances. Vendice watches as the Duke, accompanied by his new wife and his two sons, passes through the city. Combined with the hate provoked in Vendice by his fiancé's horrible murder is his outrage over the death of his father, caused by the same corrupt ruler. In addition, Vendice's brother reports that he has been asked by Lussurioso, the Duke's heir and a man as depraved as his father, to locate a pander. Vendice disguises himself as Piato, a pander, and is hired by Lussurioso, thereby gaining access to the ducal household.

The sons of the Duchess—the Duke's stepsons—are as corrupt as the Duke's sons. The Duchess's third son recently raped the wife of Antonio, who subsequently killed herself. When this son is brought to trial and sentenced, the Duke puts off the young man's execution and orders that he be kept in prison. His two older brothers promise to help him escape. Their mother, the Duchess, reveals her love for Spurio, the Duke's illegitimate son, who hates his father. Spurio accepts the Duchess's advances because adultery with his stepmother will avenge him on his father.

As Lussurioso's pander, Vendice is commissioned to set up an assignation between Lussurioso and Vendice's own sister, Castiza. Vendice is delighted when Castiza emphatically rejects Lussurioso's suit but is horrified when their mother tries to persuade her daughter to yield.

Having returned to the ducal palace, Vendice learns from

Hippolito that the Duchess and Spurio have been together and that they have an appointment for that very night. Vendice uses this information to deflect Lussurioso from his pursuit of Castiza. Ostensibly to protect his father's honor but actually to get rid of Spurio, his hated half brother, Lussurioso rushes to the Duke's bedchamber and attacks the man who is in bed with the Duchess. This man is not Spurio, however, but the Duke. The Duke, who is not seriously injured in the attack, orders Lussurioso taken to prison under sentence of death.

The Duchess's sons, eager to eliminate their stepbrothers, attempt to trick the Duke by seeming to ask for mercy for Lussurioso while depicting the heinousness of killing a ruler. The crafty Duke surprises them by granting their request to have Lussurioso executed. What they do not know is that Lussurioso has already been released through a prior order of the Duke. When they arrive at the prison and inform the jailer that it is the Duke's command that "their brother" is to die, the jailer, with only the Duchess's third son in custody, executes their younger brother.

Meanwhile, Vendice continues plotting. The Duke has commanded him, still disguised as Piato, to bring a woman to the Duke in some secluded spot. Knowing that the Duchess and Spurio are to meet in a particular lodge, Vendice selects this place and brings the skull of his betrothed, decked out in rich attire. On the mouth of the skull, he smears the same poison that the Duke used to kill her. The Duke is fooled into kissing the poisoned skull, and Vendice and Hippolito, who have been waiting, compel him to spend his dying moments watching his wife embrace his bastard son. Nine years after Gloriana's death, Vendice has gotten his revenge on the Duke for killing his beloved.

Before the meeting arranged by Vendice, the Duke had told others that he would be taking an undisclosed journey; hence no one knows where he has gone or makes any attempt to find him. Lussurioso, however, has resolved to get rid of Piato, whose information led to Lussurioso's imprisonment, and he orders Hippolito, whom he knows to have a brother unknown to the court, to bribe that brother to kill Piato. Vendice is thus in the strange position of being hired to murder himself. Vendice and Hippolito decide to dress the still-undiscovered body of the Duke in the clothes Vendice has worn in his disguise as Piato, believing that Piato will be assumed to have fled in the Duke's clothes. The brothers also decide to punish their mother because she urged their sister to yield to Lussurioso. They are so moved by her repentance, however, that they spare her life and return to the ducal palace to complete their plot.

The Duke's corpse, now dressed in the old clothes of Piato, is still lying in the lodge. The brothers plan to show the body to Lussurioso, tell him the manner of his father's death, and then kill him. However, Lussurioso does not arrive alone. Vendice and Hippolito are only able to point out the form of the supposed Piato lying on a couch, say he is drunk, and then stab him on Lussurioso's command. Discovering the true identity of the corpse, Lussurioso, pleased that his father's death makes him the new duke, gives three orders: to search for Piato, the suspected murderer; to hold revels in honor of his succession to the title; and to banish the Duchess.

The Duchess's two remaining sons resolve to murder the new duke. As Lussurioso and his nobles sit and argue over the ominous portent of a comet blazing in the sky, Vendice, Hippolito, and two other lords, in the fantastic costumes of masquers, enter and perform a dance. At its conclusion, they draw their swords and kill Lussurioso and his three companions.

The Duchess's sons, Ambitioso and Supervacuo, along with Spurio and a fourth noble, come into the hall dressed in similar costumes and bent on the same bloody errand. Finding Lussurioso and his companions already dead, the would-be murderers fall out among themselves. Ambitioso kills Supervacuo, and Spurio kills Ambitioso, only to be stabbed by the fourth noble. When Antonio and the guards rush in, they assume that the masquers they find there are the only murderers, but the surviving fourth noble convinces them otherwise. Lussurioso is not quite dead, and he undergoes the final agony of having the returning Vendice whisper in his ear the full account of his revenge.

The ducal line having been wiped out, Antonio is proclaimed ruler. Vendice cannot resist telling the new duke that he and his brother are the avengers, and Antonio orders them to be executed, asserting that the men who murdered the old duke and his family might well murder him. Vendice accepts his sentence calmly, saying it is time for him to die.

Critical Evaluation:

The Revenger's Tragedy appeared after the two most popular revenge plays in English Renaissance drama. Thomas Kyd's *The Spanish Tragedy* (pr. c. 1585-1589) was the first, and the second was William Shakespeare's *Hamlet, Prince of Denmark* (pr. c. 1600-1601, pb. 1603). Both of these plays would have been familiar to audiences and to playwrights of the time, including the likely author of *The Revenger's Tragedy*, Thomas Middleton. (For some time, it was believed that Cyril Tourneur was the play's author, but scholars now believe it was written by Middleton.) *The Revenger's Tragedy* might be called the perfect revenge play, but some exploration of why Vendice does not seem as real as Kyd's Hieronimo or Shakespeare's Hamlet is needed.

In *The Spanish Tragedy*, Hieronimo vows not to bury the body of his murdered son until he discovers the identities of his murderers. He tries to be just and not to act rashly. For this, Hieronimo is rebuked for his delay by Bel-Imperia, whose lover was killed by the same men. Hieronimo and Bel-Imperia kill the two murderers at a masque, and Bel-Imperia then kills herself. Hieronimo is somewhat unsatisfying as a revenger: He is neither unfeeling nor violent by nature. Sometimes he seems mad. As a killer, he lacks verve.

Hamlet is also an inept revenger. He spends a good part of the play attempting to verify the story told to him by his father's ghost. Hamlet's demeanor, like that of Hieronimo, can also be frustrating for an audience expecting a more exuberant killer.

There is no indication that Vendice experiences any kind of self-doubt. Rather, he presents himself as a most able revenger whose resolve never wavers. His brother, Hippolito, acts in unison with Vendice and shares Vendice's conviction that the Duke and his family are too corrupt to be saved. Presumably, Antonio, whose wife was raped by the Duchess's third son, would agree. Hippolito claims (in act 5, scene 2) that there are five hundred men who would assist in fighting this Duke. Vendice is consequently much less isolated than either Hieronimo or Hamlet.

Vendice initially appears as a bright young courtier, able even to argue his mother into persuading his sister to submit to Lussurioso's proposition. He then blames his mother for succumbing to his words and blames all women for tempting men. Vendice's sense of his own righteousness never falters. As is clear from Vendice's assertion (in act 3, scene 5) that a tragedy may be measured by the blood that flows and from his claim (in act 5, scene 3) that the death of the lustful is always good and that thunder indicates that heaven is pleased, he perceives himself as an agent of justice. Moreover, Vendice is didactic: He recites a catalog of the Duke's sins to him as the man is dying, and he reveals his own identity, for learning's sake, to Lussurioso as he is dying.

The Revenger's Tragedy is not a simple presentation of good versus evil. With the exception of Castiza, the characters show little evidence of good. None seems to have the capacity to celebrate beauty for its own sake or to experience the complexities of love for another. Vendice's hatred of vice is not countered by comparable love of any virtue other than sexual abstinence. Rather, the playwright presents blatant evil and an avenger whose identity rests solely on his extirpation of the evildoers.

In his last speech, Vendice asserts, "'Tis time to die when

we are ourselves our foes," but he remains pleased that he and his brother have murdered a rotten "nest of dukes." He is also smug in his awareness that he and Hippolito could have escaped unknown if they had wished. As he is taken out to be executed, Vendice displays an attitude that is essentially self-congratulatory.

There is much irony in this play. Vendice clearly has reason for revenge, but from act 3, scene 5, onward, his unflinching devotion to bloodshed renders him less and less sympathetic as it becomes increasingly clear that he believes he is divinely authorized. Few details are revealed about either Gloriana or Vendice's father, so Vendice's own personal history remains amorphous. Unlike Hamlet, Vendice does not care about having his story told after his death. In fact, whether he has a story of his own is in question. Vendice is ultimately a type. His unflagging hatred reduces him to the impersonal. With the righteousness of youth or of those obsessed, unburdened by self-doubt, Vendice is absolutely intent on eliminating every corrupt member of the royal household. Vendice's success as a revenger may satisfy an audience initially, but the play does not offer satisfaction to an audience's sense of ultimate justice.

Carol Bishop

Further Reading

Brucher, Richard T. "Fantasies of Violence: *Hamlet* and *The Revenger's Tragedy.*" *Studies in English Literature, 1500-1900* 211 (Spring, 1981): 257-270. Argues that as revenge tragedies, *The Revenger's Tragedy* and *Hamlet* are exactly opposite. Likens Vendice to Thomas Marlowe's Barabas or to Harry Callahan of the Dirty Harry films.

Coddon, Karin S. "'For Show or Useless Property': Necrophilia and *The Revenger's Tragedy.*" *English Literary History* 61 (Spring, 1994): 71-88. Offers historical information on attitudes toward and practices involving the dead. Argues that the skull of Gloriana functions as a symbol of female perfection and sinful female sexuality.

Corrigan, Brian Jay. "Middleton, *The Revenger's Tragedy*, and Crisis Literature." *Studies in English Literature, 1500-1900* 38, no. 2 (Spring, 1998): 281-295. Examines the question of the play's authorship, describing how it was long believed to be written by Cyril Tourneur but is now generally attributed to Thomas Middleton.

Finke, Laurie A. "Painting Women: Images of Femininity in Jacobean Tragedy." *Theatre Journal* 36 (October, 1984): 357-370. Argues that men idealize women's beauty to avoid the reality of death. Discusses how the painted woman is viewed with hostility in *The Revenger's Trag-*

edy, in John Webster's *The Duchess of Malfi* (pr. 1614), and in John Ford's *'Tis Pity She's a Whore* (pr. 1629[?]-1633).

McMillin, Scott. "Acting and Violence: *The Revenger's Tragedy* and Its Departures from *Hamlet*." *Studies in English Literature, 1500-1900* 24 (Spring, 1984): 275-291. Argues that *The Revenger's Tragedy* is about the theater and discusses the double identities with which it abounds.

Neill, Michael. "Death and *The Revenger's Tragedy*." In *Early Modern English Drama: A Critical Companion*, edited by Garrett A. Sullivan, Patrick Cheney, and Andrew Hadfield. New York: Oxford University Press, 2006. Es-

say on Middleton's play is part of a collection that examines individual plays of the period, addressing topics such as race, class, sexuality, social history, and the law.

Rist, Thomas. *Revenge Tragedy and the Drama of Commemoration in Reforming England*. Burlington, Vt.: Ashgate, 2008. Examines *The Revenger's Tragedy* and other works of the period, focusing on religious rituals related to the treatment of the dead.

White, Martin. *Middleton and Tourneur*. New York: St. Martin's Press, 1992. Reexamines plays by Tourneur and Thomas Middleton in the light of new information about their authorship.

The Revolt of the Masses

Author: José Ortega y Gasset (1883-1955)
First published: La rebelión de las masas, 1929
  (English translation, 1932)
Type of work: Essay

The Revolt of the Masses had its seeds in an earlier book by José Ortega y Gasset, *España invertebrada* (1922; *Invertebrate Spain,* 1937), in an article titled "Masas" (1926), and several lectures delivered in Argentina in 1928. As he wrote in a footnote to the title of the first chapter, "My purpose now is to collect and complete what I have already said, and so to produce an organic document concerning the most important fact of our time." In *The Revolt of the Masses,* Ortega y Gasset advocates a European confederation with judicial and political unity, an "integration, not a lamination," of nations, ultranational rather than international, where a new liberalism and a totalitarian form will each correct the excesses of the other. The resulting equilibrium, he promises, would produce a new faith.

Among the few Spanish authors of the modern era known beyond his national boundaries, Ortega y Gasset, a professor of metaphysics, a literary critic, and a journalist, also was a representative of the school that believes in the rule of an intellectual aristocracy or small group of superior minds, not the privileged caste of the old feudal nobility. Born in Madrid, Ortega y Gasset sought in Málaga the thorough training of a Jesuit college, then earned his doctorate in philosophy at the Central University of Madrid in 1904. Further study in Germany preceded his teaching career in Madrid. When Primo de Rivera y Orbaneja became dictator, overthrowing the monarchy, Ortega y Gasset, a critic of the mon-

archy, stopped teaching and began to write for the influential *El Sol.* In 1923, he founded the *Revista de Occidente,* the leading Spanish intellectual publication until 1936. The ascendancy of another dictator, Francisco Franco, led to Ortega y Gasset's leaving Spain. Ortega y Gasset traveled widely, lecturing in Buenos Aires, Paris, and the United States. Returning to Spain in 1945, he died in Madrid in 1955.

In the final paragraph to *The Revolt of the Masses,* Ortega y Gasset acknowledges that his contemporary situation results from basic defects in European culture, but he postpones any consideration of that problem, and so the work is incomplete. However, for the Buenos Aires edition of 1938, Ortega y Gasset added a prologue for French readers and an epilogue for English readers, in which he denies the accusation that his theme was the decadence of Spain since 1580. He is no pessimist. While he does look back, he insists that a return to the past is impossible. Stressing the advances and improvements of the twentieth century, he asserts that if anything superior is eventually evolved, it will be based on technical knowledge and liberal democracy.

Ortega y Gasset's main thesis is that among human beings there are two types of individuals: the excellent or superior man (or woman), who makes demands on himself, and the common man, who is content with who he is. The development and activities of these types are shown against the perspective of Western history. Greece and Rome evolved from rural communities and became cities. The ancients, concerned with their past, were unconscious of a future. Gradually the state came into existence, built in the Middle Ages by the feudal nobles. The state was relatively small. Ortega y Gasset quotes the economist Werner Sombart for the statement that Europe, from 700 to 1800, never had a population of more than 180 million people. Each state was directed by its superior individuals, without whom humanity would cease to preserve its essentials. The masses accepted higher authority and in general followed the orders of a select minority.

The first divergence came when the bourgeoisie adopted gunpowder, which the nobles never thought of using, and with it won battles against the nobility. Eventually a middle class took over the state and made it so powerful that "state intervention" has become a symbol of danger. What were once privileges became rights, even though the masses attack the institutions by which these rights are sanctioned.

During the nineteenth century the population of Europe rose to 460 million people and part of it overflowed to settle in the Americas. In Ortega y Gasset's view, however, those who look with astonishment at the rapid growth of the New World should turn their eyes to Europe, where the population increase had been even more spectacular. Friedrich Nietzsche foresaw a "flood tide of Nihilism rising." Actually, the world as it was organized during the nineteenth century automatically created a new type of person, provided with formidable appetites and powerful means of satisfying them. The nineteenth century left these new people to their own devices. Believing in direct action, they intervened violently in everything. Having been previously guided by others, these "barbarian products of modern civilization" determined to govern the world for and by themselves, and in their self-satisfaction, according to Ortega y Gasset, they now threatened the degeneration of human culture.

In tracing the development of the "mass man," Ortega y Gasset repeats his assertion that the civilization of the nineteenth century can be summed up under two headings: liberal democracy and technology. Modern technical advance represents the cooperation of capitalism and experimental science. The scientist is likely to become a mass man, a primitive, since he confines his knowledge to so small an area. There was a time, the author asserts, when people could be divided into the learned and the ignorant, but currently even those learned in science are frequently ignorant of the inner philosophy of the science they cultivate.

Ortega y Gasset discusses historians, or philologists, as he calls them, who turn their attention to sources instead of the future. The author does not believe in the absolute determin-

ism of history, because in his view the past does not tell people what to do, but what to avoid. Life has become greater in scope than ever before, presenting a greater array of choices. Circumstances offer a dilemma for the mass man to decide, but he has no concept of the future. In the Mediterranean countries, where the triumph of the masses made its greatest advance, the mass man lives for the moment, with no consideration for future existence.

Life has become worldwide in character, but time and space cannot be easily obliterated. The "purchasing power of life" has been broadened. People believe themselves capable of creation without knowing what to create. Power has brought insecurity. Liberal democracy based on technical knowledge is the highest type of public life yet known. The perfect organization of the nineteenth century gave the impression that it represented natural things, and therefore should belong to everybody; but all that it represents had earlier beginnings.

According to Ortega y Gasset, bolshevism and fascism are examples of retrogression in politics, because they handle rational elements in an antihistorical, even archaic, way. Consequently, the political hope of Europe lies in those who abhor archaic and primitive attitudes. Ortega y Gasset does not believe in the decadence of Europe, a legend begun by intellectuals who felt themselves stifled by their nationality and who longed to borrow from other literatures, or by politicians similarly motivated. If there should be a decadence among European nations, the result, he argues, would be the creation of a United States of Europe. There is no one else to "rule," by which Ortega y Gasset means "to control public opinion." New York and Moscow represent two sections of European order. Writing in 1929, Ortega y Gasset believed that Russia would need centuries before it could aspire to rule, but that it would never succeed if there was in Europe a political union with a new Western moral code and a new inspirational program of life.

In one important sense, the title of this work is misleading, in the light of recent history. The author is not referring to either actual revolt—*rebelión* is the Spanish word he uses—or to the Marxian proletarian revolution. What he had in mind was the mass man whose claim to the right to act is, in effect, a rebellion against his own destiny. Since that is what he, according to Ortega y Gasset, is doing at the present time, Ortega y Gasset considered his efforts to be a revolt of the masses.

Further Reading

Dobson, Andrew. *An Introduction to the Politics and Philosophy of José Ortega y Gasset*. New York: Cambridge University Press, 1989. An erudite, readable overview of Ortega y Gasset's political and philosophical background. Chapter 5, "*Nacionalización* and Decentralisation," and chapter 6, "Fascism?" are of particular interest to readers of *The Revolt of the Masses.*

Gonzalez, Pedro Blas. *Human Existence as Radical Reality: Ortega y Gasset's Philosophy of Subjectivity.* St. Paul, Minn.: Paragon House, 2005. Explains Ortega y Gasset's innovative philosophical concepts, focusing on his ideas about human subjectivity. Chapter 6, "*The Revolt of the Masses* and the Nature of Mass Culture," discusses this work.

_____. *Ortega's "The Revolt of the Masses" and the Triumph of the New Man.* New York: Algora, 2007. Explicates the ideas set forth in the book, including Ortega y Gasset's notions of mass man and noble man, subjectivity and mass culture, and mass man's existential revolt and the future of human freedom. Includes a glossary of terms used in *The Revolt of the Masses.*

Gray, Rockwell. *The Imperative of Modernity: An Intellectual Biography of José Ortega y Gasset.* Berkeley: University of California Press, 1989. A study of the intellectual evolution of Ortega y Gasset. Chapter 5, "The Level of the Times: 1929-1930," includes a discussion of the ideas in *The Revolt of the Masses*, arguing that the ideas are typical of European intellectuals during the period between the two world wars.

Lee, Donald C. "Ortega's Revolting Masses: A Reinterpretation." In *Ortega y Gasset Centennial.* Madrid: Ediciones José Porrúa Turanzas, 1985. Reevaluates Ortega's work more than fifty years after its initial publication and applies its propositions to the late twentieth century. Expands upon Ortega y Gasset's ideas about a united Europe.

Ouimette, Victor. *José Ortega y Gasset.* Boston: Twayne, 1982. Gives a succinct biography of Ortega y Gasset, including a synopsis of the social and political background of late nineteenth and early twentieth century Spain. Chapter 4, "Ratiovitalism," includes a subsection devoted to *The Revolt of the Masses.*

Raley, Harold C. *José Ortega y Gasset: Philosopher of European Unity.* Tuscaloosa: University of Alabama Press, 1971. A study of Ortega y Gasset's concept of European unity. The author considers this idea, an important one in *The Revolt of the Masses*, as integral to the development of the philosopher's body of works.

Reynard the Fox

Author: Unknown
First transcribed: c. 1175-1250 (English translation, 1481)
Type of work: Short fiction
Type of plot: Satire
Time of plot: Middle Ages
Locale: Europe

Principal characters:
REYNARD, the fox
NOBLE, the lion, king of beasts
ISENGRIM, the wolf
TIBERT, the cat
BRUIN, the bear
OTHER ANIMALS AND BIRDS

The Story:

When Noble, the great lion-king, holds court during the Feast of the Pentecost, all the animals tell the king of their grievances against Reynard the fox. The list of sins and crimes is almost as long as the list of animals present. First to complain is Isengrim the wolf, whose children have been made blind by the crafty fox. Panther tells how Reynard promised the hare that he would teach him his prayers, but when the hare stood in front of Reynard as he was instructed, Reynard grabbed him by the throat and tried to kill him. Reynard had approached Chanticleer the rooster disguised as a monk, saying that he would never eat flesh again, but when

Chanticleer relaxed his vigilance over his flock and believed the villain, Reynard grabbed Chanticleer's children and ate them.

So the complaints go on, with only Tibert the cat and Grimbard the brock (badger) speaking in Reynard's defense. These two remind the king of the crimes committed by the complainers, but the king is stern: Reynard must be brought to court to answer for his sins. Bruin the bear is sent to bring the culprit in. Bruin is strong and brave, and he promises the king that he will not be fooled by Reynard's knavery or flattering tongue.

When Bruin arrives at Reynard's castle and delivers the king's message, Reynard welcomes the bear and promises to accompany him back to court. In fact, Reynard says, he wishes they were already at court, for he has abstained from meat and eaten so much of a new food, called honeycombs, that his stomach is swollen and uncomfortable. Bruin falls into the trap and begs to be taken to the store of honey. Reynard pretends to be reluctant to delay their trip to court, but at last he agrees to show Bruin the honey. The wily fox leads Bruin into a trap in some tree trunks, where the poor bear is set upon by humans and beaten unmercifully. He escapes with his life and sadly makes his way back to court, mocked by the taunts of his betrayer.

Enraged at the insult to his personal messenger, the king sends Tibert the cat to tell Reynard to surrender himself at once, under penalty of death. Tibert, however, fares no better than Bruin. He is tricked into jumping into a net trap by the promise of a feast on mice and rats. He, too, escapes and returns to the court, no longer a defender of the traitorous Reynard. Next, the king sends Grimbard the brock to bring the fox in. He is also warmly received by Reynard, who promises to accompany him to court. This time the evil fox actually keeps his promise, confessing all of his sins to the brock as they journey.

At court, Reynard is confronted by all his accusers. One by one, they tell of his horrible crimes against them. Reynard defends himself against them all, saying that he is a loyal and true subject of the king and the object of many lies and deceits. The king is unmoved and sentences Reynard to death. On the gallows, the fox confesses his sins, saying that he is the more guilty because he did not steal from want, since money and jewels he has in great plenty. Hearing Reynard speak of his treasure, the greedy king wants it for himself, and he asks Reynard where the jewels are hidden. The fox says that he will gladly tell him the hiding place, for the treasure has been stolen in order to save the king's life. Crafty Reynard tells a story about a treasure that the other animals are going to use to depose the king and make Bruin the ruler in his place. In order to save the life of his sovereign, Reynard says, he has stolen the treasure from the traitors and now has it in his possession. The foolish king, believing the smooth liar, orders Reynard released from the gallows and made a favorite at court. Bruin the bear and Isengrim the wolf are arrested for high treason.

Reynard says that he himself cannot show the king the treasure because he has to make a pilgrimage to Rome to ask the pope to remove a curse from him. For his journey he is given the skin of the bear and the shoes of the wolf, leaving those two fellows in terrible pain. The king then puts his mail around Reynard's neck and a staff in his hand and sends him on his way. Kyward the hare and Bellin the ram accompany Reynard on the pilgrimage. They stop at the fox's castle to bid his wife good-bye, and there Reynard tricks the hare, kills him, and eats all but the head. He sends the hare's head back to the king with the ram, that stupid animal thinking he is carrying a letter for the monarch. The king is so furious when he sees the hare's head that he gives the ram and all of his lineage to the wolf and the bear to atone for the king's misjudgment of them.

Complaints against the fox again pour into the king's ear. At last he determines to lay siege to Reynard's castle until the culprit is captured—this time there will be no mercy. Grimbard the brock, however, hurries to the castle and warns Reynard of the plot. The crafty fellow sets out immediately for the court, where he will plead his case before the king. On the way, he again confesses to the brock that he is guilty of many sins, but he makes them seem mild in comparison with those of the animals now accusing him. To the king also he confesses that he has sinned, but he denies the worst of the crimes laid to his doing. His plea is that he would not have surrendered voluntarily had he been so guilty. His words are so moving that most of his accusers keep silent, fearing that the king will again believe Reynard and punish those who would condemn him. Only the wolf and the bear hold fast to their accusations. With the help of his aunt, the ape, Reynard once more excuses himself in the king's eyes and makes the monarch believe that it is the injured who are the guilty. Again Reynard talks of lost jewels of great value, jewels that he will search for and present to the king.

Only Isengrim the wolf will not accept Reynard's lies. He challenges the fox to a fight. Reynard would be hard put to fight with the wolf, except that Isengrim's feet are still sore from Reynard's taking of his shoes some time before. To help Reynard further, the ape shaves off the fox's fur and covers him with oil so that the wolf cannot get hold of him. Even so, Isengrim is on the way to defeating the fox when he listens to Reynard's promises of all the rewards Isengrim will receive if he lets Reynard go. At last the king stops the fight and orders all the animals to a great feast. There he forgives Reynard for all of his sins after taking the scamp's promise that he will commit no more crimes against his fellow animals. The king makes Reynard high bailiff of the country, thus setting him above all the others. From that time on, the mighty of the forest have bowed to the cunning of the weak.

Critical Evaluation:

Reynard the Fox is a beast fable, generally a satirical genre in which human follies are portrayed as belonging to animals. The underlying framework of this popular medieval literary form is a series of stories linked by common characters. In *Reynard the Fox*, the character of Reynard provides the connective thread. Most versions of *Reynard the Fox* are long, and the episodes are only vaguely related. In addition, the point of such beast fables is satire of the contemporary social and political scenes. *Reynard the Fox* satirizes the royal court, the judicial system, and many other aspects of medieval life.

The origins of the beast fable are still subject to scholarly debate. Some scholars maintain that this form derives from the oral folk tradition of storytelling, later formalized in writing by medieval monastic scribes. Others find precedents for the beast fable among the works of classical Latin authors. Both schools of thought have defensible positions, and both take their stands on the same set of facts, as many versions of stories such as those found in *Reynard the Fox*, one of the most important examples of this genre, are extant.

Some basic information emerges from the dispute. First, Ovid's *Metamorphoses* (c. 8 C.E.; English translation, 1567) contains stories similar to those in the *Reynard the Fox* series. Second, *Aesopea* (fourth century B.C.E.; *Aesop's Fables*, 1484) includes specific episodes that appear in *Reynard the Fox*. Limited access to such classical precedents in medieval times, however, renders arguments about the influence of these models moot. The earliest manifestations of *Reynard the Fox* are stories about the animosity between Reynard and his enemy, Isengrim the wolf. These stories may be derived from popular French, English, Dutch, Low German, and Latin folktales. They seem to have been initiated in the Low Countries, northern France, and northeastern Germany, although precedence cannot be definitely assigned. The earliest versions were in verse, although later versions appeared in prose.

A rather short poetic rendering of *Reynard the Fox* stories was done in medieval Latin by an eighth century cleric, Paulus Diaconus (Paul the Deacon), from Charlemagne's court. The basic Isengrim story—*Ysengrimus*—is attributed to Master Nivardus of Ghent, who wrote it in Latin about 1148. The evolution of vernacular versions is still open to question; some scholars claim priority for France, and others insist on Germanic primacy. The issue has not been resolved, but there is no question that twelfth and thirteenth century Flanders, western Germany, and northern France were fertile grounds for this literary form, especially for Reynard stories.

At approximately the same time that *Ysengrimus* was produced, there appeared in France a compilation called *Le Roman de Renart*, from the hands of several authors (many,

according to medieval custom, anonymous). This vernacular compilation deals mostly but not exclusively with stories of the protagonist Reynard facing his antagonist, Isengrim the wolf. The stories are usually arranged in chronological rather than in topical order; unfortunately, this arrangement tends to undermine the ideological impact of the stories. The didactic element is much stronger in the almost simultaneous (c. 1180) vernacular redaction of Heinrich der Glïchezäre.

Reynard the Fox appeared in Latin, French, German, Flemish, Dutch, and English versions—testimony to its popularity. It is evident, however, that questions about origins and the chronological order of various versions cannot be unequivocally answered with the information at hand. As is the case with much medieval history and literature, final answers must wait upon the discovery of further evidence. In the meantime, it is still possible to evaluate the extant material on its own terms, because *Reynard the Fox* evolved as the archetype of the beast fable. The central focus of the series concentrates on a single significant episode—Reynard's healing of the sick lion, in most versions—and other stories are spinoffs from this episode, all involving moralistic messages. The cast of animals varies from story to story and from version to version: Fox, lion, and wolf are constants; badger, bear, stag, rooster, cat, hare, camel, bear, ant, and others appear occasionally. The didactic factor is another constant, and for the temper of the times, it is a remarkably pragmatic one.

Indeed, the Reynard series is a lesson in ethics and morality. None of the animals is a paragon of virtue. All are vulnerable or corruptible or both; not even King Lion is exempt. They live in a world that recognizes no moral codes and where survival depends on wit and exploitation of others. Isengrim the wolf is doomed because he carries to extremes his penchant for besting everything and everybody. His compulsion is to surpass, and this compulsion blinds him to the necessary cooperation required for survival. By contrast, Reynard is pliable, adaptable, and fundamentally amoral. He survives because he is flexible. In the process, however, he becomes venal, power-hungry, and oblivious to humane values. Significantly, Geoffrey Chaucer's "Nun's Priest's Tale" (in *The Canterbury Tales*; 1387-1400) relates a Reynard story—the fox's attempt and failure to abduct the rooster Chanticleer—to demonstrate the weakness and the power of flattery. Reynard's tactics thus become an object lesson in compromised integrity.

Reynard is the ultimate opportunist, knowing no scruple. To be sure, Reynard is neither explicitly praised nor explicitly condemned in the context of medieval ethics or morality. Rather, he is held forth as an implicit example of what not to do. In this sense, the best didactic functions of the beast fable are upheld in *Reynard the Fox,* for it is the didactic element in such works that constitutes their intended benefit. Although scholarly disputes continue about the origins and the development of the beast fable, in the last analysis the more crucial point is the moral import of such stories. In this respect, *Reynard the Fox* succeeds.

"Critical Evaluation" by Joanne G. Kashdan

Further Reading

Bellon, Roger. "Trickery as an Element of the Character of Renart." *Forum for Modern Language Studies* 22, no. 1 (January, 1986): 34-52. Examines *Reynard the Fox* in terms of its use of archetypal elements of the medieval fable. Provides insight into the social significance of the trickster character.

Blake, N. F. "Reflections on William Caxton's *Reynard the Fox*." *Canadian Journal of Netherlandic Studies* 4, no. 1 (May, 1983): 69-76. Provides a thorough exploration of Caxton's translation of the medieval classic and discusses the work's place within the context of the Germanic literary tradition and the traditions of the folk narrative and the European fable.

Owen, D. D. R., trans., ed. *The Romance of "Reynard the Fox."* New York: Oxford University Press, 1994. In addition to the text of the work, the editor's notes and introduction offer a comprehensive overview of the fable, its history, its place in medieval art, and its revelations about medieval society.

Varty, Kenneth. "Animal Fable and Fabulous Animal." *Bestia: Yearbook of the Beast Fable Society* 3, no. 1 (May, 1991): 5-14. Discussion of European beast fables considers *Reynard the Fox* within its historical, aesthetic, and ideological context. Also considers the evolution of the animal in European folklore.

_____. *Reynard, Renart, Reinaert, and Other Foxes in Medieval England: The Iconographic Evidence—A Study of the Illustrating of Fox Lore and "Reynard the Fox" Stories in England During the Middle Ages, Followed by a Brief Survey of Their Fortunes in Post-Medieval Times.* Amsterdam: Amsterdam University Press, 1999. An authority on the Reynard tales presents evidence of the story in England prior to its translation by William Caxton. Uses many illustrations of Reynard and other foxes that were created in the medieval period in arguing that these fictional English animals descended from French and Dutch representations of Reynard. Includes more than two hundred illustrations.

_____, ed. *Reynard the Fox: Social Engagement and Cultural Metamorphoses in the Beast Epic from the Middle Ages to the Present.* New York: Berghahn Books, 2000. Collection of essays examines how the tale of Reynard has been retold in numerous countries and through various media. Describes how these legends reflect the cultural backgrounds of their tellers.

Rhadamistus and Zenobia

Author: Prosper Jolyot de Crébillon (1674-1762)
First produced: Rhadamiste et Zénobie, 1711; first published, 1711 (English translation, as *Zenobia,* 1768)
Type of work: Drama
Type of plot: Tragedy
Time of plot: c. 60 C.E.
Locale: Artanissa, Iberia

Principal characters:
RHADAMISTUS, the king of Armenia
ZENOBIA or ISMENIA, his wife
PHARASMANES, the king of Iberia, Rhadamistus's father
ARSAMES, Rhadamistus's brother
HIERO, the Armenian ambassador and Rhadamistus's confidant
MITHRANES, captain of the guards of Pharasmanes
HYDASPES, Pharasmanes's confidant
PHENICE, Zenobia's confidant

The Story:

Zenobia, wife of Rhadamistus, is the prisoner of Pharasmanes, the king of Iberia. When Phenice, her companion, attempts to persuade Zenobia that she should accept the love Pharasmanes offers her in the hope that she will become his queen, Zenobia, who has been using the name Ismenia, reveals that she cannot accept Pharasmanes because the king is her uncle and the father of Rhadamistus. Zenobia explains that her father, Mithridates, reared Rhadamistus as if the boy were his own son, but when Pharasmanes invaded the Armenian kingdom of Mithridates, Mithridates turned against Rhadamistus and refused to allow him to marry Zenobia as Rhadamistus had expected. Rhadamistus then attacked the kingdom of Mithridates and drove the king into exile. Zenobia, to protect her father, offered to wed Rhadamistus; only after the wedding did she learn that Rhadamistus had murdered her father. In a rage, Rhadamistus had then attacked his bride and thrown her into the river. He does not know that she was rescued; he believes her to be dead.

Zenobia ends her account by telling Phenice that Rhadamistus was later killed by his own father, who had been jealous of his son's rise to power. The most compelling reason against her marrying Pharasmanes, Zenobia tells Phenice, is that she is in love with Arsames, who is Rhadamistus's brother and Pharasmanes's son.

When Arsames arrives to see Zenobia after a campaign in Albania, he asks her whether she intends to marry Pharasmanes that day, as he has heard. He declares his love for her and his jealousy of his father. Zenobia assures him that she will not marry Pharasmanes, but she also declares that she can never consider marriage with Arsames. Arsames, who knows Zenobia only as Ismenia, is forced to accept her decision.

Pharasmanes appears and criticizes Arsames for returning to Iberia without permission. When Arsames declares that he has come in support of his father, to meet the invasion planned by Corbulo on behalf of Rome and Syria, Pharasmanes dismisses the excuse and forbids his son to profess love for Ismenia or ever to see her again. Pharasmanes, having dismissed Arsames, warns Zenobia that he will not tolerate her refusal of him. In desperation, Zenobia appeals to Phenice to tell the Roman ambassador of her plight.

Rhadamistus, however, still lives. Tortured by repentance, knowing himself to be the murderer of Zenobia's father, and believing himself to be the murderer of his wife, he arrives in Iberia as the representative of Rome and the Roman choice for king of Armenia. Rhadamistus tells his companion Hiero how he was wounded by Pharasmanes's soldiers and how Corbulo rescued him. Rhadamistus, vowing revenge on his father, has joined forces with Corbulo and has been appointed Roman ambassador. Hiero tells Rhadamistus that the Armenians, fearing Pharasmanes, hope to persuade Arsames to become their king.

Pharasmanes and the ambassador meet, and Rhadamistus tells Pharasmanes that the Roman emperor does not choose to have Pharasmanes become king of Armenia. Pharasmanes answers that Rome had better get its legions together, for he is determined to invade Armenia. He then supports his claim to the throne by referring to his brother, Mithridates, and to his son, Rhadamistus. Rhadamistus, who has managed to keep his identity hidden from his father, then angers Pharasmanes by declaring that the king should not expect to be heir to those he has murdered. Only Rhadamistus's status as ambassador keeps Pharasmanes from ordering him seized.

Arsames, not recognizing Rhadamistus, refuses to join with him in a revolt against Pharasmanes, but he urges the ambassador to take Ismenia from Iberia. Arsames also tells Rhadamistus of his love for Ismenia, which for some hidden reason she cannot return. Rhadamistus, who has no way of knowing that Ismenia and Zenobia are the same person, agrees to help Ismenia.

When Zenobia comes to Rhadamistus he recognizes her immediately, but only his outcry makes her realize that the ambassador is the husband who tried to murder her. Rhadamistus, throwing himself at her feet, blames himself for all his deeds, and Zenobia, partly from duty and partly from pity, forgives him his crimes.

Zenobia, who thinks herself guilty because of her love for Arsames, cannot wholly condemn Rhadamistus. When Arsames again tells her of his love, she reveals that Rhadamistus is alive and that he is her husband. Rhadamistus interrupts the conversation and gives way to angry jealousy when he learns that Zenobia has revealed his identity. Zenobia remonstrates with him, pointing out that she would never have admitted her love for Arsames had not Rhadamistus's anger prompted her. Rhadamistus, ashamed of his outburst, begs their forgiveness.

Pharasmanes, fearing that Arsames is in league with the Romans—for he has seen his son talking to the Roman ambassador—arrests Arsames and sends his soldiers to capture the envoy. His anger is further aroused when he observes that the ambassador has taken Ismenia with him. He pursues Rhadamistus and wounds him with his sword. Arsames's grief at this stirs Pharasmanes strangely; he feels that somehow he has done something terrible. Rhadamistus, dying, appears before Pharasmanes and, through a reference to Mithridates, makes his identity known to his father. Pharasmanes, realizing at last the fatal consequences of his jealousy and his lust for power, directs Arsames to take the Armenian throne. Sacrificing his own love for Zenobia as punishment for having killed his son, Pharasmanes relinquishes Zenobia to Arsames and tells the couple to flee from him lest his jealousy once again lead him to slay one of his own offspring.

Critical Evaluation:

Rhadamistus and Zenobia, for all its static presentation of background material in the first act, is successful at creating the tragic sense, the realization of the self-defeating character of human passion. Few members of a modern-day audience would tolerate Prosper Jolyot de Crébillon's play on the stage; it has many weaknesses, including lengthy expository passages, unmotivated antipathies, and an awkward and precipitous close. For readers, however, the play still offers passages of quiet force and power, and within the whole there are parts to be remembered.

Eighteenth century French tragedy became weighted down with philosophical speculations and undramatic, polemical material. Some dramas were nearly unactable, despite attempts to pour life into them with melodramatic horrors. Crébillon, in his attempts to startle and in his efforts to fill his plays with stately speeches, fits this pattern. Crébillon's tragedies were modeled after those of the Roman tragic writer Seneca and, like them, specialize in horror; however, Seneca's tragedies were meant only to be read, while Crébillon's plays were intended for the stage. Crébillon said that he aimed to move his audience to pity through terror, but his tragedies are at times merely sensational, depending less on psychological analysis than on violent and unnatural crimes.

Rhadamistus and Zenobia is considered Crébillon's finest play, although the plot is so complicated as to be almost incomprehensible. When it was first produced, it was greeted with tremendous respect and popularity. It was one of the most acted eighteenth century tragedies at the Comédie-Française, and Zenobia was considered one of the choice tragic roles for women in the eighteenth century French theater. This play and a few of Crébillon's other most successful works are considered to possess a vigor and passion unsurpassed in French classical drama, but even the playwright's admirers admit to a want of culture and a lack of care in his style and verse, although isolated passages are well done.

The subject of *Rhadamistus and Zenobia* has close analogies with Jean Racine's *Mithridate* (pr., pb. 1673; *Mithridates*, 1926). The heroine (disguised) is loved by a whole family, the members of which have been chiefly occupied with murdering her own family. There are swelling speeches and occasional inspiration, but the drama is melodramatic. In *Rhadamistus and Zenobia*, Crébillon keeps within the conventional form of tragedy, but his plot is a chaotic swirl of mistaken identities, recognitions, and tangled family relations. The audiences of his day thrilled, however, to the suspenseful story and the violence and terror it portrays.

In *Rhadamistus and Zenobia*, readers can see how much Crébillon resembles playwright Pierre Corneille, both in his defects and in his virtues as a dramatic poet. In Crébillon's attempt to make his diction energetic, he gives way to excess. He never possesses, even in this play, the polish of his enemy, Voltaire, although he achieves a rugged power beyond Voltaire. Crébillon does not fathom the heart of the human soul in this or any other of his plays, but he keeps alive the classical tradition, and his genius for inventing tense and tragic situations stimulated other writers. Voltaire himself used four of Crébillon's plots. Despite the play's shortcomings, the importance of *Rhadamistus and Zenobia* in the development of French drama cannot be denied.

Further Reading

Badir, Magdy Gabriel, and David J. Langdon. *Eighteenth-Century French Theatre: Aspects and Contexts*. Calgary: Departments of Romance Languages and Comparative Literature, University of Alberta, 1986. No contributions to this collection deal directly with *Rhadamistus and Zenobia*, but essays by Patrick Brady and David Trott provide context for Crébillon's work by describing the transformation of French tragedy after the death of Jean Racine in 1699.

Jourdain, Eleanor F. *Dramatic Theory and Practice in France, 1690-1808*. New York: Benjamin Blom, 1968. Includes an analysis of Crébillon's career and discusses his use of sentimentality and violence to move audiences.

Lancaster, Henry C. *Sunset: A History of Parisian Drama in the Last Years of Louis XIV, 1701-1715*. 1945. Reprint. Westport, Conn.: Greenwood Press, 1976. Historical study of the French theater includes an examination of Crébillon's skills as a tragic playwright in *Rhadamistus and Zenobia* and discussion of the psychological differences between the murderer Rhadamistus and the dignified Zenobia.

Tilley, Arthur. *The Decline of the Age of Louis XIV, 1687-1715*. New York: Barnes & Noble, 1968. Describes the evolution of French theater during the last part of Louis XIV's reign and explains clearly the historical importance of many neglected playwrights, including Crébillon.

Yarrow, P. J. *The Seventeenth Century, 1600-1715*. Vol. 2 in *A Literary History of France*, edited by Patrick Edward Charvet. New York: Barnes & Noble, 1967. Presents a clear historical overview of neoclassical French theater and literature from 1600 to 1715.

Rhinoceros

Author: Eugène Ionesco (1909-1994)
First produced: 1959; first published, 1959 (English translation, 1959)
Type of work: Drama
Type of plot: Absurdist
Time of plot: Indeterminate
Locale: A small provincial town in France

Principal characters:
BERENGER, the unheroic hero, unkempt and apathetic
JEAN, his friend, fastidious and self-confident
DAISY, Berenger's girlfriend, a secretary at the office where he works
THE WAITRESS
THE GROCER
THE GROCER'S WIFE
THE OLD GENTLEMAN
THE LOGICIAN
THE HOUSEWIFE
THE CAFÉ PROPRIETOR
MR. PAPILLON, Berenger's boss
DUDARD and BOTARD, fellow employees of Berenger
MRS. BOEUF, the wife of another employee
A FIREMAN
THE LITTLE OLD MAN
THE LITTLE OLD MAN'S WIFE

The Story:

In a square in a small provincial town, a large number of comic types pass by, chatting. Jean and Berenger converse across a table at a sidewalk café. Jean berates his unshaven friend for drinking too much. Berenger complains that his life is still unsettled. Jean, who proceeds to lecture Berenger about duty, tells him that he must get used to life as it is. Everything is interrupted by a rhinoceros, which thunders by immediately offstage. The townspeople are astounded and alarmed. Before long another rhinoceros gallops by, or perhaps it is the same one returning. The civic alarm is noticeably less acute the second time.

To the townspeople comes a startling revelation: The rhinoceroses are townspeople who underwent a strange metamorphosis. By the next day, the number of rhinoceroses is increasing. Berenger visits Jean, who turns into a rhinoceros. His voice becomes progressively hoarser and eventually unintelligible. His manner becomes aggressive and hostile toward humans. He makes periodic checks with the bathroom mirror, each time noting that his skin becomes greener and a bump on his head grows larger. During his last visit to the bathroom Jean's transformation is complete, and Berenger barely escapes being trampled. As Berenger flees the building, rhinoceros heads pop into view in doorways and windows; the lethargic Berenger goes into a state of panic.

Everyone in the town, except Berenger, changes into a

rhinoceros. Berenger seeks refuge in his room. For a time, before he is deserted by his last friend, Dudard, and by his fiancé, Daisy, Berenger tries to think of some way to combat a trend that he can see as only ominous. He decides to write to the newspapers, write a manifesto, or go to see the mayor, or his assistant if the mayor should be occupied at the time. Berenger's plans, ineffectual to begin with, are forgotten when, at the end, he is alone.

Berenger expresses his firm intention to remain a human being, to hold out no matter what. He begins to feel the terrible stress of utter isolation. He sees that he is in an intolerable, absurd position. He is not sure what language he is speaking. He becomes ashamed of his appearance and of his normal voice. He tries to become a rhinoceros, but he does not know how to effect the change. Then, either because he fails or perhaps because his courage reasserts itself, he declares that he will make a stand against the creatures. He is the last man left and he plans to remain a man; he will not give in.

Critical Evaluation:

Although Eugène Ionesco's style seemed quite startling to theatergoers when they first experienced his curious one-act plays in the early 1950's, by the time *Rhinoceros* opened in 1959 he had been recognized as one of France's preeminent dramatists. Early plays such as *La Cantatrice chauve* (1950; *The Bald Soprano*, 1956), *La Leçon* (1951; *The Lesson*, 1955), and *Les Chaises* (1952; *The Chairs*, 1958) had surprised critics and public alike. As the public became more familiar with Ionesco's dramas, they found that his unconventional use of theater conventions was at least consistent.

Gradually, in France and elsewhere, he and a number of other playwrights (including Samuel Beckett, Jean Genet, and Arthur Adamov) were identified as writing what eventually was called the Theater of the Absurd. Absurdist plays are characterized by a number of features. Their plots seem slight and their action appears to be almost arbitrary. Characters are usually one-dimensional, sketched out rather than fully drawn, and are often called by only a first or a last name or by their profession. Dialogue is frequently nonsensical, maintaining the form of actual language but lacking the communicative capacity usually associated with speech or writing. Absurdist playwrights emphasize the ways in which life becomes irrational and depict how easily ordinary existence can appear to be unintelligible. Isolated in a world that seems overwhelmingly chaotic and ridiculous, the protagonist in an absurdist play typically fights a losing battle in a minefield of strange, and occasionally hilarious, paradoxes.

A major difference between *Rhinoceros* and Ionesco's previous works is that this play is written for a large stage. It utilizes a good-sized cast and requires some stunning visual effects. The plays that came before were intended for smaller, more intimate theaters and tend to rely more upon the actors' performances. *Rhinoceros* received its French premiere at one of France's most prestigious playhouses, the Odéon in Paris, under the guidance of Jean-Louis Barrault, the great postwar actor-director. Moreover, the play went on to highly successful runs in London and in New York. *Rhinoceros*, not surprisingly therefore, is Ionesco's best-known play, and its production was the high point in his career. In France, Ionesco remains a highly regarded and often-produced dramatist, but his international reputation has diminished since the 1970's. His early work—those plays up to and including *Rhinoceros*—is what remains widely known.

Ionesco wrote and spoke about some of what had inspired him to write this play. Born in Romania, he left for France in 1938, around the time that many of his friends began to follow the Iron Guard movement—a Romanian fascist political organization, which during World War II allied itself with the Nazis. He began to notice how his friends, whom he had known for many years, seemed to have been as if infected by the movement's right-wing ideology, and he noticed how people with whose views he had once sympathized suddenly became monstrous to him. From his comments, one can eas-

ily connect his experience with the action of the play: the seeming invasion of the town by rhinos and the sudden change through which human beings are converted into beasts.

The play's implications extend beyond the playwright's own life, however. People in many different countries have been able to relate to the play. When, for example, *Rhinoceros* was first performed in Düsseldorf, Germany, the audiences immediately recognized the story because they lived through the period when the German people had succumbed to the Nazi Party and only a few had resisted. In a more immediate way, however, this play, written in French and intended for postwar French audiences, comments on how, after France was defeated by Germany in 1940 and then occupied by the German army until 1944, many French people were lured into sympathizing with the Nazis. Even though this play was not produced in France until 1960, the shame many French people felt about how some of their own citizens collaborated with the Germans remained very strong.

Rhinoceros has much to say about how people are often willing to follow the prevailing political scheme blindly. In conforming to the rhinos' ideology, the townspeople become themselves savage creatures. They lose their humanity, their individuality, their sense of self. Their identities, completely reshaped by their adherence to rhino values, are transformed by their desire to go along with the herd, to be just like everyone else, and to play it safe. The extent to which all the characters in the play, with the notable exception of Berenger, collaborate with the rhinoceroses makes them, in the end, no better than the thick-skinned beasts. In fact, the people become rhinos.

Ionesco goes beyond this political parable to explore the way through which the external affects the soul. The only person to emerge from the play as a fully developed character is Berenger, Ionesco's Everyman, who appears in several other of his plays. In Berenger's long final monologue, the playwright offers the audience a glimpse of how difficult it is for one person to stand alone against the political tide. Attracted to the notion of being one of the crowd and frightened by his lonely position as the very last human being on Earth, Berenger goes through a series of ambivalent reversals as he vows to fight to the end. He starts to feel doubt about how important it is to be a human being even as he valiantly tries to remain human.

Clearly, his decision to continue to resist seems sadly doomed. Perhaps what Ionesco wishes the audience to appreciate is the admirable effort of withstanding the forces of evil and the absurd struggle from which Berenger can never emerge as victor. This peculiarly contradictory pairing of victory and defeat makes Berenger an existential hero, whose courage derives not from any ultimate triumph but from his stoic acceptance of failure.

"Critical Evaluation" by Kenneth Krauss

Further Reading

Bloom, Harold, ed. *Eugene Ionesco*. Philadelphia: Chelsea House, 2003. Collection of essays providing critical interpretations of Ionesco's plays, including *Rhinoceros*.

Danner, G. Richard. "Bérenger's Defense of Humanity in *Rhinocéros*." *French Review: Journal of the American Association of the Teachers of French* 53, no. 2 (December, 1979): 207-214. An illuminating article that explores the beliefs of the main character of *Rhinoceros*. Danner finds a number of complexities in Berenger's struggle to maintain his own humanity and to justify that of others.

Esslin, Martin. *The Theatre of the Absurd*. 3d rev. ed. New York: Methuen, 2001. A good place to begin any research on Ionesco's plays. Examines how *Rhinoceros* connects with Ionesco's earlier works and suggests that this work, which on one level seems quite comprehensive, is in fact highly ambiguous.

Gaensbauer, Deborah B. *Eugène Ionesco Revisited*. New York: Twayne, 1996. Reevaluation of Ionesco's life and work published two years after his death. Gaensbauer analyzes all of the plays and Ionesco's other writings, and she concludes that each work was a piece in a long autobiography in which Ionesco sought to understand himself and humankind.

Haney, William S. "Eugene Ionesco's *Rhinoceros*: Defiance Versus Conformity." In *Integral Drama: Culture, Consciousness, and Identity*. New York: Rodopi, 2008. Analyzes the play from the perspective of Indian aesthetic theory and "consciousness studies." Describes how Berenger is able to attain a level of "ethical discernment" that transcends the "self-interested cravings" of the play's other characters.

Jacquart, Emmanuel. "Ionesco's Political Itinerary." In *The Dream and the Play: Ionesco's Theatrical Quest*, edited by Moshe Lazar. Malibu, Calif.: Undena, 1982. Ionesco's Everyman, Berenger, appears in several plays that characterize government and society as oppressive. This essay offers an interesting look at the political implications of *Rhinoceros*. Helpful to an understanding of the playwright's political views.

Lane, Nancy. *Understanding Eugène Ionesco*. Columbia: University of South Carolina Press, 1994. Although many have come to regard Ionesco's work as dated and limited, Lane sees his work as continuing to be both significant and relevant to the modern stage. Her discussion of *Rhinoceros* is guided by her belief that it is one of Ionesco's major plays.

Rigg, Patricia. "Ionesco's Berenger: Existential Philosopher or Philosophical Ironist?" *Modern Drama* 35, no. 4 (December, 1992): 538-551. A lucid examination of *Rhinoceros* and its main character. In trying to determine whether Berenger is an existential hero or an embodiment of paradox, Rigg manages to illuminate much of the philosophical background of the play.

The Rhymes

Author: Gustavo Adolfo Bécquer (1836-1870)
First published: Rimas, 1871 (English translation, 1891)
Type of work: Poetry

Appraised by many critics to be among the greatest love poets, Gustavo Adolfo Bécquer had not published any books before his death at age thirty-four. Although Bécquer had little money for his education because of the death of his parents when he was nine years old, he read voraciously and was writing odes by the time he was twelve. Bécquer obtained literary recognition when he was twenty-four with the beginning of the serial publication of *Cartas literarias a una mujer* (*Letters to an Unknown Woman*, 1924) in 1860 in the periodical *El Contemporáneo*. After Bécquer's death, his friends collected the poet's poems that had been printed in periodicals and published them in a book. The poems in *The Rhymes* represent the poet's major work.

Bécquer's poetry reflects a tendency toward Romanticism, a literary tendency advocated by the liberals upon their return to Spain in 1833 after the death of Fernando VII, who had exiled them. The desire of the Spanish people to depose this oppressive Bourbon monarch corresponded with their desire to free themselves from French classicism, which, as Spanish artists saw it, represented the point of view of the cultured elite of another country and restricted artists' freedom to compose works in their own styles. Romanticism directly opposes such classical restraints as using plots or subjects taken strictly from ancient sources and using formal language in a highly stylized format. Bécquer's poetry treats one of the themes characteristic of Romanticism: love. He shows the multiple facets of love: a longing for the ideal woman, disillusionment, and intense despair. Bécquer's poems expose the states of his soul as it wavers between light and darkness. His poems do not necessarily relate to real love affairs; Bécquer even indicates that he has mixed fact with fiction in his memory. Bécquer is so focused on love that he considers it an enigmatic power enlivening nature and permeating the universe.

The structure of *The Rhymes* reflects Bécquer's inner life. His work can be divided into sections that represent different spiritual states. Bécquer's work begins with his supreme attraction toward art in rhymes 1 through 8, in which he hopes to attain glory through the immortality of his creation. Rhyme 2 compares his spiritual state with a flickering light whose final spark may guide his footsteps to glory, and rhyme 7 refers to his underdeveloped talents; he, like Lazarus, is waiting for a voice to call him.

The next section, consisting of rhymes 9 to 12, reveals the vague foreshadowing of the proximity of love. Rhyme 9 portrays the image of the kisses that nature gives to her surroundings, such as the radiant clouds becoming purple and gold from the sun's kiss. Rhyme 11 is presented in the form of a dialogue; each of two women relates her attributes in the first-person singular, and the poet responds. Bécquer rejects the passionate dark-haired woman full of desires that transcend shame and the tender blond woman longing to make his dreams come true. He chooses the woman who is a fleeting phantom of light and mist. This phantasmic woman with whom Bécquer is enamored represents the feminine ideal of Romanticism, for she is not a physical being but a spiritual projection: a shadow, a phantom, or a dream. Bécquer thus embarks on an impossible quest for an inaccessible woman.

The next division, presented in rhymes 12 through 15, shows the poet's undefined feeling of love in the process of forming. In rhyme 12, Bécquer describes the physical features of the woman who so attracts him. Her eyes are as green as the sea, her cheeks are rose-colored, and her mouth is like rubies. Rhyme 15 emphasizes the powerful image of the woman's unavoidable eyes, which penetrate his soul.

The poet is then ready to declare his love in rhymes 16 through 24. His beloved appears like an image of a red flower asleep in the heart of the beloved; but upon inclining her head in times of sadness, she seems to him like a broken white lily. Bécquer links his concepts of love, flower, and sadness through his use of rhyme: *amor*, *flor*, and *dolor*. In rhyme 21, Bécquer defines the "you" of the poems, the woman, as poetry.

Rhymes 25 through 29 continue to express the poet's idealized love; at last he arrives at the perfect union of his soul with that of his beloved. Rhyme 24 completes this union through its image of two red tongues of fire growing close together and, upon kissing, forming a single flame. The exaltation of their love is continued in rhymes 25 through 29.

The idealized love begins to rupture in rhyme 30. This rupture, produced by pride and tears, results in the separation of the poet from his beloved, the two taking separate paths. Rhymes 31 through 36 show the effects of the broken love on the poet. He is dismayed, and his sadness leaves a permanent mark on his heart, producing a profound discouragement within his soul. He reveals his bitterness through his confusion of tears with laughter and pride with dignity. These distressing sentiments lead the poet to consider death for the first time; he fills his mind with melancholy memories of the past and, in rhyme 41, laments both his beloved's betrayal and her ingratitude.

Rhyme 42 accentuates the poet's complaint, indicating that even in his imagination he has not seen an abyss as deep as the heart of the woman who has betrayed him. Because the poet, reacting to his melancholy in frenzy, cannot silence the memory within his soul, he decides to let himself be carried away into the distant places that rhyme 52 suggests. After this delirious declaration, Bécquer becomes calm and delivers his best-known poem, rhyme 53, which begins "Volverán las oscuras golondrinas" (the dark swallows will return). The poet is saved by faith in his own love. Although the external manifestation of love (the faithful swallows, who return every year to the same nest) disappears, Bécquer will not be overcome by complete despair because his love is unchangeable. In the form of a symmetric ballad, the poem shows the future alternating with the past (the future year's return of the swallows recalls their past return and the poet's past love) and at the same time shows how the future cannot be the same as the past.

After this relatively optimistic poem, rhymes 54 and 55 disclose that Bécquer is inspired by memory and tears of repentance; rhymes 56 and 57 reveal the resurgence of the poet's loss of faith in love. The poet's skepticism is more ironic in rhymes 58 and 59, culminating in rhyme 60, in which evil deflowers the flowers of which Bécquer is fond. The next few poems demonstrate the poet's skeptical sentiments until his concentration on sadness and tears causes him to ponder death, and the final poems relate his yearning for the soul's infinite qualities, linking death with awakening.

The Rhymes reflects Romantic qualities of melancholy, passion, and yearning, but the poems in this collection also contain an element of ambiguity, signaling a new concept of poetry that was developing during the decade of the 1860's, when Bécquer was composing his poetry. Bécquer believed that poetry, like love, permeates every aspect of life and that the poet needs to suggest this idea to the reader. Hence, Bécquer's beloved in *The Rhymes* does not represent a person of flesh and blood; she appears as a symbol of the states of his soul. The poet's attempt to transmit to the reader the subtle nuances of his sentiments is reflected by his copious use of metaphors. As precise terms for the fleeting impressions that the poet wishes to discuss do not exist, he opts for the tools of poetry. Bécquer chooses his words and images for their imprecise emotional implications to suggest those feelings that cannot be directly designated.

Bécquer is one of those poets on whom the mantle of envisioning an innovative concept of poetry fell. Although at his death he seemed destined for obscurity, his poems have been widely read, imitated, and heralded as a high point of the Romantic era. Admiration for Bécquer's innovation and sympathy for his lamentable life give the reader additional reasons to appreciate his melodious, impassioned verses.

Linda Prewett Davis

Further Reading

Bell, Aubrey F. G. *Contemporary Spanish Literature*. New York: Russell & Russell, 1966. Briefly discusses Bécquer's poetic techniques. Shows how his poetry marks a transition from Romanticism to the modernist innovations of the twentieth century.

Brenan, Gerald. *The Literature of the Spanish People: From Roman Times to the Present Day*. 2d ed. New York: Cambridge University Press, 1976. Describes the characteristics of the poetry of the nineteenth century. Appraises the poetry of Bécquer and examines his place in Spanish literary history.

Bynum, B. Brant. *The Romantic Imagination in the Works of Gustavo Adolfo Bécquer*. Chapel Hill: University of North Carolina Press, 1993. Aptly explains how Bécquer utilizes Romantic techniques in *The Rhymes*. Includes an excellent list of consulted works.

Moss, Joyce, ed. *Spanish and Portuguese Literatures and Their Times: The Iberian Peninsula*. Vol. 5 in *World Literature and Its Times: Profiles of Notable Literary Works and the Historical Events That Influenced Them*. Detroit, Mich.: Gale Group, 2002. Reference work presents analyses of both *The Rhymes* and the Bécquer collection *The Infinite Passion* (1924).

Pattison, Walter T., and Donald W. Blezniek. *Representative Spanish Authors*. Vol. 2. New York: Oxford University Press, 1963. Concisely relates a brief history of Spanish literature in the nineteenth century and the tenets of Romanticism. Gives an excellent introduction to *The Rhymes*.

Turnbull, Eleanor L. *Ten Centuries of Spanish Poetry: An Anthology in English Verse with Original Texts, from the Eleventh Century to the Generation of 1898*. 1955. Reprint. Baltimore: Johns Hopkins University Press, 2002. Presents the Spanish and English texts of the best-known poems of Bécquer. Contains a brief but informative introduction to Bécquer's poetry by the renowned scholar Pedro Salinas.

Walters, D. Gareth. "Love Poetry." In *The Cambridge Introduction to Spanish Poetry*. New York: Cambridge University Press, 2002. Survey of poetry from Spain, Portugal, and Latin America is organized by genre; the section on love poetry discusses Bécquer's work.

Rhymes

Author: Petrarch (1304-1374)
First published: Rerum vulgarium fragmenta, 1470
  (English translation, 1879)
Type of work: Poetry

Of the 366 poems included in the collection that Petrarch made of his poetry, 317 are sonnets, 29 are canzoni, 9 are sestine, 7 are ballate, and 4 are madrigals. In giving the work the title *Rerum vulgarium fragmenta*, Petrarch called attention to the fact that the brief poems were written not in Latin but in the vernacular. The work also became known as *Rime* (*Rhymes*) and *Canzoniere.*

In considering the sonnets and songs of Petrarch, scholars invariably compare the poet with Dante, who also wrote in the vernacular Italian instead of Latin. Both these giants of Italian literature centered their poetry on a gracious lady suddenly discovered, idealized, and then praised throughout a lifetime. Dante wrote his *La vita nuova* (c. 1292; *Vita Nuova*, 1861; better known as *The New Life*) about Beatrice Portinari, whom he met when he was nine years old and she eight; he never stopped worshiping her as the ideal woman, and he continued to celebrate her in his poetry even after her death in 1290. Petrarch's ideal woman was Laura, possibly Laura de Noves, whom he first met on April 6, 1327, when he was in his twenty-second year. Laura died in 1348 from the plague.

Like Dante, Petrarch kept his passion at a distance—one might say at a poetic distance—from the woman who charmed him. In the works of both Dante and Petrarch, however, it is difficult to believe that the love was merely an excuse for the poetry; something of human passion, not just creative passion, burns in the poetry with a warmth that survives the centuries. It may be that this enduring emotion can be attributed to those distant ladies who set the poets to writing immortal poetry, but it is more reasonable to suppose that poetic genius worked in both cases to turn a sudden fancy into a lifelong poetic enterprise.

Critics have never ceased wondering who Laura may have been, and some question whether she actually existed. Even Petrarch's contemporaries were not certain, and some of them contended that the Laura of the poems was an invention, an ideal based on no model whatsoever. Petrarch denied the charge, pointing out that it would be madness to spend years writing hundreds of poems about an entirely imaginary woman. More significantly, the poems too deny the charge by the force of their feeling and imagery.

For both Dante and Petrarch the idealization process took them beyond earth to heaven. That is, the poetic figures of Beatrice and Laura are not merely ideal mortal, physical women but also spiritually significant, by their person and manner representing beings who symbolize the highest values the human soul can hope to attain. Dante made Beatrice an inspiration even in Paradise and used her as the central guiding figure of the second half of *La divina commedia* (c. 1320; *The Divine Comedy*, 1802). In writing of the painter Simon, Petrarch comments in poem 77:

> But certainly Simon saw paradise
> Wherein this gentle lady had her place;
> There he saw her and portrayed in such guise
> That is the witness here of her fair face.

Later, writing more explicitly of Laura after her death, Petrarch speaks of "Seeing her now on such intimate term/ With Him who in her life had her heart's right," and, in the same sonnet, 345, he concludes:

> For fairer than before, my inner eye
> Sees her soar up and with the angels fly
> At the feet of our own eternal Lord.

It has been traditional to divide Petrarch's sonnets and songs into two major parts, one including poems written while Laura was living and the other those written after her death. Poem 3 of the collection tells of the first meeting:

> It was the day when the sun's rays turned white
> Out of the pity it felt for its sire,
> When I was caught and taken by desire,
> For your fair eyes, my lady, held me quite.

In poem 5, Petrarch works the syllables of the name Laura into his verse in order to describe what happens when his sighs call her with the name that Love wrote on his heart: "Thus to LAUd and REvere teaches and vows/ The voice itself . . ." ("Così LAUdare e REverire insegna/La voce stessa . . .").

In poem 6 appears one of Petrarch's many puns on Laura's name, when he writes of Love as holding the bridle of his desire and thus being directed "Only to reach the laurel and its sour fruit . . ." ("Sol per venir al lauro . . ."). Again, in the following poem, he speaks of the "love of laurel." It was in part because of such puns that Petrarch was accused of inventing the character "Laura."

These plays with words were the least of Petrarch's accomplishments in the sonnet form. He was so adept at using the fourteen lines to express a complete idea or image with all its emotional correlate that poets have taken him as a model ever since. A full appreciation of Petrarch's work comes only from reading his poetry and sensing the beauty that results from his sensitive use of the sound and sense of language within the sonnet form. Although translation does not always succeed in reproducing the finely wrought rhythms of Petrarch's verse, the best has the great virtue of coming close to the form, sound, and even syntax of the original. Through such translation, even those who do not understand Italian can gain an appreciation of the original.

One of the advantages of Petrarch's having chosen to write in the tradition of love poetry is that he writes of his beloved from a poignant distance. In making Laura unobtainable, he secured her forever in his poetry. In poem 16, for example, he reminds his readers that he was never able to possess his Laura:

> A rain of bitter tears falls from my face
> And a tormenting wind blows with my sighs
> Whenever toward you I turn my eyes,
> Whose absence cuts me from the human race.

Much of Petrarch's poetry is concerned with the shortness of life, the inevitableness of death, and the end of all that is fair and young on earth, all matters that are related to Laura. Thus the poetry before her death has a great deal in common with the poetry written afterward. The greatest difference in the later works is that regret and speculation have now taken the place of fear for her loss. Before her death Petrarch amused himself with poetically metaphysical imagery by which he claimed that Laura would outshine stars and draw the angels to her, but after her death the poetic amusement is either absent or tempered by a sober recognition of the fact of death. If Laura is shown reverent respect by anyone in heaven, it is because of her spirit. In the following image from sonnet 127, later readers were reminded of John Donne:

> To count the constellations one by one
> And to pour in a goblet all the seas

> Was perhaps my intention when I took
> This small sheet to relate such mysteries.

Not all the poems are about Laura. Petrarch writes of Italy at war, of nature, of God and the love of God, of life and death, and of other matters of universal concern. Yet even these poems have a human dimension because they are fixed in the context of the Laura poetry. Perhaps it is because Petrarch had the heart and wit to be a love poet that he compels respect for his thoughts about universal matters as well.

After Laura's death, Petrarch wrote a sonnet of lament (poem 267), which begins, "Alas! the lovely face, the eyes that save/ Alas! the charming countenance and proud!" In the poem that followed, he asks, "What shall I do? What do you counsel, Love?/ It is now time to die./ And I have waited longer than I would./ My lady died and did my heart remove." The long lament ends:

> Flee the clearness, the green,
> Do not go near where there is song and laughter,
> Canzone, follow after
> Weeping: you are not fit for merry folk,
> A widow, without comfort, in black cloak.

Petrarch's lamentations gradually change character toward the end of the collection. Grief gives way to reflection, and reflection turns his thoughts to spiritual love—thus to the love of God. Laura becomes the symbol of what human beings should strive for, even though in life she was physically desirable as a woman. Because "Death quelled the sun wonted to overwhelm" him and "Dust is the one who was my chill and spark," Petrarch is able to write in sonnet 363, "From this I see my good" and "I find freedom at last, bitter and sweet/ And to the Lord whom I adore and greet,/ Who with his nod governs the holy things,/ I return, tired of life, and with life sated."

Further Reading

Bernardo, Aldo S. *Petrarch, Laura, and the "Triumphs."* Albany: State University of New York Press, 1974. Analyzes the poetic image of Laura from various perspectives. Devotes the first half of the book to Laura and the poems in *Rhymes*.

Braden, Gordon. *Petrarchan Love and the Continental Renaissance.* New Haven, Conn.: Yale University Press, 1999. Presents analysis of *Rhymes*, its poetic innovations, and its theme of an impossible object of desire. Describes the widespread influence of the poems, which from the mid-fifteenth through the early seventeenth centuries were imitated in every major language in western Europe and set the standard for love poetry.

Holmes, Olivia. *Assembling the Lyric Self: Authorship from Troubadour Song to Italian Poetry Book*. Minneapolis: University of Minnesota Press, 2000. Study of thirteenth and fourteenth century lyric poetry traces the transition from Provençal and Italian anthologies compiled by scribes to collections of works by single poets. Describes the attempts of individual poets, including Petrarch and Dante, to establish their authority in creating vernacular verse. The final chapter provides an analysis of *Rhymes*.

Jones, Frederic J. *The Structure of Petrarch's "Canzoniere": A Chronological, Psychological, and Stylistic Analysis*. Cambridge, England: D. S. Brewer, 1995. Focuses on the first and early part of *Rhymes*. Offers a study of the psychological evolution of Petrarch's work and the emotional ebb and flow of his relationship with Laura.

Mazzotta, Giuseppe. "The *Canzoniere* and the Language of the Self." In *Petrarch: Modern Critical Views*, edited by Harold Bloom. New York: Chelsea House, 1989. Emphasizes the importance of the poet's image of himself as being central to *Rhymes*.

Petrarch. *For Love of Laura: Poetry of Petrarch*. Translated by Marion Shore. Fayetteville: University of Arkansas Press, 1987. Excellent translation of selected poems in *Rhymes* captures the spirit of the collection's two major sections, which are rendered into the form of the English sonnet.

Sturm-Maddox, Sara. *Petrarch's Laurels*. University Park: Pennsylvania State University Press, 1992. Considers the fundamental issue of Petrarch's relating the laurel branch, symbol of poetic genius, with his ideal love, Laura. Shows how the poet connects the two in several of his works, but especially in *Rhymes*, and how he thereby creates the image of Laura.

Riceyman Steps

Author: Arnold Bennett (1867-1931)
First published: 1923
Type of work: Novel
Type of plot: Social realism
Time of plot: 1919
Locale: Riceyman Steps, London

Principal characters:
HENRY EARLFORWARD, a bookseller
VIOLET ARB, the owner of a nearby shop
ELSIE, the maid for both Earlforward and Mrs. Arb
JOE, Elsie's friend
DR. RASTE, a physician

The Story:

Henry Earlforward owns a bookstore left to him by his uncle, T. T. Riceyman. It is cluttered, dusty, and badly lit. Earlforward lives in a back room of the shop; the upstairs of the building is filled with old books. Elsie, his cleaning woman, comes into the shop one night. She tells Henry that she also works for Mrs. Violet Arb, who owns the confectioner's shop next door, and that Mrs. Arb has sent her for a cookbook. Henry finds one containing recipes for making substantial meals out of practically no food at all. A little later, Elsie returns and says that Mrs. Arb thanks him, but the book is too expensive.

Henry's curiosity is aroused, and he goes to Mrs. Arb's shop. Even though he marks down the price of the book, Mrs. Arb still refuses to buy it. Henry becomes more interested, for it is clear that Mrs. Arb is no spendthrift. The following Sunday, they go for a walk, and from then on, they are close

friends. Violet soon sells her shop and agrees to marry Henry. When Violet asks him about a wedding ring, he seems surprised, for he had supposed the one she already owns would do. He gets a file, saws off the ring, sells it, and buys another, all without really spending a penny. They are married one morning, and for a honeymoon spend the day in London.

They visit Madame Tussaud's Waxworks and the Chamber of Horrors. Henry, who had thought the wedding breakfast expensive enough, is distressed at being forced to spend more money. He wonders if he had been deceived, if Violet were not a spendthrift after all. He begins to complain about his lame foot. Violet is dismayed; she wants to see a motion picture. Henry cannot be persuaded to change his mind. He does not, he says, want a painful leg on his wedding day.

When they pass by the shop this same night, Henry thinks the place is on fire. It is glowing with light, and men are working inside. Violet explains that the men had been engaged to clean the dirty, cluttered shop. She had planned the work as her wedding gift to him, but he had spoiled the surprise by coming home before the men had finished their task. Henry shows Violet a safe that he had bought to safeguard her valuables and her money.

Violet soon discovers that miserly Henry will not light a fire, that he will not use electric light, and that he eats practically nothing. On their first morning together, she cooks an egg for him, but he refuses to eat it. Later, Elsie eats it in secret. At another time, Violet has Elsie cook steaks, but Henry will not touch them. There is an argument in which Violet calls him a miser who is starving her to death. He leaves the room, and his steak. That night, Elsie eats it.

When Violet discovers that Elsie has eaten the steak, another row ensues; but Elsie begins to eat more and more when nobody is there to observe her. She is half-starved in the miserly household. To stop Elsie's thefts of food, Henry goes to bed, calls Elsie to his room, announces he is seriously ill, and asks if she thinks it right to steal food while he lies dying. Elsie is glum and frightened.

A short time later, Henry actually becomes ill. In defiance of the Earlforwards, Elsie manages to get Dr. Raste to examine Henry. The doctor says that the sick man will have to go to the hospital. Then the doctor discovers that Violet also is ill. At first, Henry refuses to go, but Violet finally persuades him. When the doctor calls the next morning, it is Violet, however, who goes to the hospital. Henry stays at home in the care of Elsie.

In the meantime, Elsie is hoping for the return of Joe, her sweetheart. He had been employed by Dr. Raste, gotten sick, and then wandered off. Elsie is sure he will return some day.

One night, Elsie wants to send a boy to the hospital to inquire about Violet. When she asks Henry for sixpence for the messenger, he says she can go to the hospital herself. Not wanting to leave him, she picks up his keys, goes downstairs, and opens the safe. Amazed to find so much money there, she borrows sixpence and puts an IOU in its place. Then she dashes out to find a boy to carry her note. When she comes back, she finds Joe waiting for her. He is shabbily dressed and sick.

Elsie quietly carries Joe up to her room and takes care of him, taking pains so that Henry will not suspect his presence in the house. When Joe begins to improve, he tells her he had been in jail. Elsie does not care. She continues to take care of Henry and promises him that she will never desert him. The hospital informs them that Violet needs an operation. That night, Elsie goes next door to the confectioner's shop. Mrs.

Belrose, the wife of the new proprietor, telephones the hospital and is told that Violet died because her strength had been sapped through malnutrition.

Henry seems to take the news calmly enough, but he grows steadily worse. Dr. Raste returns to visit Henry and says that he must go to a hospital, but Henry refuses. Without Elsie's knowledge, Henry gets up and goes downstairs, where he discovers with dismay Elsie's appropriation of the sixpence. He sits down at his desk and begins to read his correspondence.

Elsie is in her room taking care of Joe. To the neighbors, the house seems quite dark. Accordingly, Mrs. Belrose insists that her husband go over to inquire about the sick man. He discovers Henry's body lying in the shop. A relative comes from London and sells the shop to Mr. Belrose. Joe recovers and returns to work for Dr. Raste. Elsie intends to marry Joe, so she also goes to work for Dr. Raste.

Critical Evaluation:

The word "Riceyman" rings throughout *Riceyman Steps*. The name is intimately associated with the family of Henry Earlforward, whose uncle, T. T. Riceyman, bequeathed the bookshop to Henry. The Riceyman Steps—that is, the steps that lead from the hurly-burly of King's Cross Road up to Riceyman Square—sit directly over the underground railway, which throbs with the passage of trains. These steps make Riceyman square into something of a stage setting, situated in the middle of Clerkenwell, a shabby neighborhood much loved by old Riceyman, who never tired of reciting how the original tunnel near Clerkenwell Green collapsed, in the spring of 1862. The three opening chapters that sketch this history set the stage for the drama that ensues.

Riceyman Steps tells two love stories, one dry and unsatisfying but a love story nevertheless, and the other tender and gratifying. Henry's marriage to Mrs. Violet Arb soon becomes little more than a struggle between two opposed sensibilities, with Violet yearning for something of the world's rich experiences as Henry suffocates her with his pathological acquisitiveness. Something clearly human and sexual, however, drives Henry to visit Violet's shop the first time. Her smile uplifts him, and he becomes "a little bit flurried." He admires her "fine movement" and his male vanity moves him to conceal his limp.

Things thus begin conventionally, although they do not exactly follow the usual account of a man's way with a maid (or widow, for that matter). The eccentric wooing that brings two lonely people together is presented with warmth. The two offer much to solace each other through their lives. The abbreviated honeymoon outing foretells what will go wrong.

The story is an ancient one: Once the man has preened and courted and won, he drops the pose of the lover and shows his true colors—and Henry's colors are extremely gray and drab. Violet's dream of marital happiness dissolves into a waking nightmare. Violet is an attractive character, lively, intelligent, and outgoing, and given half a chance she would make much of her life. She turns instead into the victim of fate, in the tradition of naturalism.

Various symbols help propel the narrative, among them light and fire, the wedding cake, and the safe. Henry cannot abide electric lights burning in his establishment, nor can he allow anyone to burn a candle. Fires consume fuel, and fuel costs money. So Henry, Violet, and Elsie live primitively in the cold darkness, as the two women yearn for light and warmth in their lives. Compared to the bookshop, the Belroses' establishment next door, taken over from Violet, positively blazes with a mad exuberance of electric lights. The brightness of the Belrose shop is an external sign of the human generosity and benign vision of life that reign within.

Food also means extravagance and, when Violet prepares the steak for Henry, his turning away from it indicates not only his stomach ailment but also his rejection of anything juicy and self-indulgent in life. The piece of wedding cake that the newlyweds eat seems to lead directly to Henry's illness, not literally but as a sign that anything so rich and foreign to his nature will poison him at some deep level. As their illnesses progress, Henry and Violet think back on the cake as a turning point in their lives.

Henry's safe looms up as a tangible, gross, heavy object embodying all of his parsimony. That he would leave his keys where Elsie could get them to unlock the safe is ironic. She does not steal from Henry, but his discovery that she had borrowed sixpence from the safe—to use in his service—bespeaks to him a monstrous betrayal. He dies, overcome by this last, bitter realization of fortune's power, and when the light burns on into the night over Henry's dead body, Mr. Belrose hurries across Riceyman Square to find an explanation.

The physical diseases that kill Henry and Violet complement the disorders that dominate their lives. A stomach cancer consumes Henry, destroying the body of a man described on the first page as "in the prime of life." It is not so much his stinginess that the cancer signifies, for he had been just as stingy before the cancer gripped him. Instead it is his stinginess with human feeling that drags him down. He abuses Violet and Elsie with his miserliness and his cruel oversight of their very ordinary behavior. In Violet's case, fibroid tumors strike her reproductive organs. Her life, already blighted by death and a constant hunger for something besides emotional and material penury, closes with an illness that mocks the barrenness of her existence. There is something spiteful about Arnold Bennett's choice of these fatal diseases, almost as if he as their creator were telling Henry and Violet that they must be punished appropriately for their failures in life.

Elsie and her Joe are the lovers whose story is tender and gratifying. Elsie, "a strongly-built wench," emerges as a kind of proletarian earth mother, gifted with practical competencies and a good heart that combine to see her through tough spots. Readers know it is a chancy thing, but with a little luck Elsie and Joe will make the most of their position with Dr. Raste.

Riceyman Steps succeeds because of its deft characterization of the miser. Henry is part of a literary tradition, the humors figure, someone dominated so completely by a single trait that he becomes an emblem of it. The narrative relentlessly tracks Henry's decay amid the gloom of his dingy shop, cluttered systematically by a merchant who knows his customers. Violet is the victim of Henry's meanness, and Elsie goes about caring and trying to do in the manner of a heroine left over from a Charles Dickens novel. The miser of Riceyman Steps achieves long literary life in dying miserably.

"Critical Evaluation" by Frank Day

Further Reading

Broomfield, Olga R. R. *Arnold Bennett*. Boston: Twayne, 1984. Contains a good overview of the life and works, a reliable bibliography of Bennett's publications, and a judicious selection and annotation of secondary sources. An excellent starting place to learn about Bennett.

Drabble, Margaret. *Arnold Bennett: A Biography*. 1974. Reprint. Boston: G. K. Hall, 1986. Drabble, a British novelist, draws from Bennett's journals and letters to focus on his background, childhood, and environment, all of which she ties to his literary works. Praises *Riceyman Steps* for its use of a London setting. Identifies F. Sommer Merryweather's *Lives and Anecdotes of Misers* (1850) as an important source for *Riceyman Steps*. Includes illustrations, an index, and a bibliography of Bennett's work.

Hepburn, James G. *The Art of Arnold Bennett*. 1963. Reprint. New York: Haskell House, 1973. Close analysis of Bennett's technique, symbols, images, and allegories. Hepburn praises *Riceyman Steps* as a "complex study of love and death."

Lucas, John. *Arnold Bennett: A Study of His Fiction*. New York: Methuen, 1974. Lucas admires Bennett's development of character in *Riceyman Steps* and his symbolism; he speculates on the possible psychosomatic origins of

Henry Earlforward's cancer. One of the best analyses of the novel.

McDonald, Peter D. "Playing the Field: Arnold Bennett as Novelist, Serialist, and Journalist." In *British Literary Culture and Publishing Practice, 1880-1914*. New York: Cambridge University Press, 1997. Examines the publishing careers of Bennett, Joseph Conrad, and Sir Arthur Conan Doyle to demonstrate the radical transformation of British literary culture in the years between 1880 and 1914.

Squillace, Robert. *Modernism, Modernity, and Arnold Bennett*. Lewisburg, Pa.: Bucknell University Press, 1997. Argues that Bennett saw more clearly than his contemporaries the emergence of the modern era, which transformed a male-dominated society to one open to all people regardless of class or gender. Detailed notes and a bibliography acknowledge the work of excellent Bennett scholars.

Stone, Donald. "The Art of Arnold Bennett: Transmutation and Empathy in *Anna of the Five Towns* and *Riceyman Steps*." In *Modernism Reconsidered*, edited by Robert Kiely. Cambridge, Mass.: Harvard University Press, 1983. A comparative study of Bennett's two novels in the context of twentieth century English literature. Includes bibliographic references.

Woolf, Virginia. "Mr. Bennett and Mrs. Brown." In *The Virginia Woolf Reader*, edited by Mitchell A. Leaska. Orlando, Fla.: Harcourt, 1984. A notorious attack on Bennett and his style, written in 1924 by perhaps the most famous member of the Bloomsbury group. Woolf argues that Bennett relies too much on external facts and physical descriptions in trying to create characters.

Richard II

Author: William Shakespeare (1564-1616)
First produced: c. 1595-1596; first published, 1600
Type of work: Drama
Type of plot: Historical
Time of plot: Fourteenth century
Locale: England

Principal characters:
RICHARD II, the king of England
JOHN OF GAUNT, the duke of Lancaster, Richard's uncle
EDMUND OF LANGLEY, the duke of York, another uncle of Richard
HENRY BOLINGBROKE, the duke of Hereford and the son of John of Gaunt
THE DUKE OF AUMERLE, son of the duke of York
THOMAS MOWBRAY, the duke of Norfolk
THE EARL OF NORTHUMBERLAND, a supporter of Bolingbroke

The Story:

During the reign of Richard II, the two young dukes Henry Bolingbroke and Thomas Mowbray quarrel bitterly, and the king finally summons them into his presence to settle their differences publicly. Although Bolingbroke is the eldest son of John of Gaunt, the duke of Lancaster, and therefore a cousin of the king, Richard is perfectly fair in his interview with the two men and shows neither any favoritism.

Bolingbroke accuses Mowbray, the duke of Norfolk, of mismanaging military funds and of helping to plot the murder of the dead duke of Gloucester, another of the king's uncles. Mowbray forcefully denies the charges. Richard decides that to settle the dispute the men should have a trial by combat at Coventry, and the court adjourns there to witness the tournament.

Richard, ever nervous and suspicious, grows uneasy as the contest begins. Suddenly, just after the beginning trumpet sounds, the king forbids that the combat take place. Instead, he banishes the two men from the country. Bolingbroke is to be exiled for six years and Mowbray for the rest of his life. At the same time, Richard demands that they promise they will never plot against him. Persisting in his accusations, Bolingbroke tries to persuade Mowbray to plead guilty to the charges before he leaves England. Mowbray, refusing to do so, warns Richard against Bolingbroke's cleverness.

Not long after his son is banished, John of Gaunt, duke of Lancaster, becomes ill and sends for Richard to give him advice. Although the duke of York points out to him that giving advice to Richard is too often a waste of time, John of Gaunt feels that perhaps the words of a dying man will be heeded where those of a living one would not. From his deathbed, he criticizes Richard for extravagance and for mishandling the public funds and impoverishing the nation. He warns Richard also that the kingdom will suffer for the monarch's selfishness.

Richard pays no attention to his uncle's advice, and after John of Gaunt dies, the king seizes his lands and wealth to back his Irish wars. The aged duke of York, another of Richard's uncles, attempts to dissuade him from his course, pointing out that Bolingbroke has influence among the people. York's fears are soon confirmed. Bolingbroke, hearing that his father's lands have been seized by the king's officers, uses the information as an excuse to terminate his banishment. Gathering together troops and supplies, he lands in the north of England, where he is joined by other dissatisfied lords, including Lord Ross, Lord Willoughby, the earl of Northumberland, and the earl's son, Henry Percy, known as Hotspur.

Richard, heedless of all warnings, has set off for Ireland to pursue his war, leaving his tottering kingdom in the hands of the weak duke of York, who is no match for the wily Bolingbroke. When the exiled traitor reaches Gloucestershire, the duke of York visits him at his camp. Caught between loyalty to Richard and despair over the bankrupt state of the country, York finally yields his troops to Bolingbroke. Richard, returning to England and expecting to find an army of Welshmen under his command, learns that after hearing false reports of his death they have gone over to Bolingbroke. Moreover, the strong men of his court—including the earl of Wiltshire, Bushy, and Green—have all been executed.

Destitute of friends and without an army, Richard takes refuge in Flint Castle. Bolingbroke, using his usurped titles and estates as his excuse, takes Richard prisoner and carries him to London. There Richard breaks down. He shows little interest in anything and spends his time philosophizing on his downfall. When he is brought before Bolingbroke and the cruel and unfeeling earl of Northumberland, Richard is forced to abdicate his throne and sign papers confessing his political crimes. Bolingbroke, assuming royal authority, orders Richard imprisoned in the Tower of London.

During a quarrel among the young dukes of the court, the bishop of Carlisle announces that Mowbray made a name for himself while fighting in the Holy Land and then retired to Venice, where he died. When Bolingbroke affects grief over the news, the bishop turns on him and denounces him for his

part in ousting Richard. Bolingbroke, armed with the legal documents he has collected to prove his rights, prepares to assume the throne as Henry IV. Richard predicts to the earl of Northumberland that Bolingbroke will soon come to distrust his old aide for his part in unseating a king. Soon after that, Richard is sent to the dungeons at Pomfret Castle, and his queen is banished to France.

At the duke of York's palace, the aging duke sorrowfully relates to his duchess the details of the coronation procession of Henry IV. When the duke discovers that his son, the duke of Aumerle, and other loyal followers of Richard are planning to assassinate Henry IV at Oxford, York immediately starts for the palace to warn the new monarch. The duchess, frantic at the thought of her son's danger, advises Aumerle to reach the palace ahead of his father, reveal his treachery to the king, and ask the royal pardon. She herself pleads for her son before the king and wins Aumerle's release.

Having punished the conspirators, Henry IV grows uneasy at the prospect of other treasonable activities, for while Richard lives there is always danger that he might be restored to power. Henry IV suggests casually to his faithful servant Sir Pierce Exton that he murder Richard at Pomfret. Exton's plan to carry out his king's wish is successful. In his dungeon, Richard is provoked to quarrel with his guard, and in the struggle that ensues the guard draws his sword and strikes down his unhappy prisoner. He then places Richard's body in a coffin, carries it to Windsor Castle, and there presents it to Henry IV. Distressed over the news of mounting insurrection in the country, King Henry pretends horror at the murder of Richard and vows to make a pilgrimage to the Holy Land to atone for the death of his fallen cousin.

Critical Evaluation:

Part of William Shakespeare's second tetralogy of historical plays (with *Henry IV, Part I*, pr. c. 1597-1598; *Henry IV, Part II*, pr. 1598; and *Henry V*, pr. c. 1598-1599), *Richard II* is also his second experiment in the *de casibus* genre of tragedy, dealing with the fall of an incompetent but not unsympathetic king. It is also part of the lyrical group of plays written between 1593 and 1596 in which Shakespeare's gradual transformation from poet to playwright can be traced. The sources of *Richard II* include the 1587 second edition of Raphael Holinshed's *Chronicles of England, Scotland, and Ireland* (1577); the chronicles of Jean Froissart and Edward Hall; George Ferrers and William Baldwin's *A Mirror for Magistrates* (1555); Samuel Daniel's verse epic on the War of the Roses, *The Civil Wars* (1595-1609); and a play by an unknown author titled *Thomas of Woodstock*.

The themes of the play are associated, in one way or another, with the question of sovereignty. Bolingbroke's challenge to Richard focuses on the divine right of kings and its historical basis and social implications. Connected with this is the matter of a subject's duty of passive obedience, especially as seen in the characters of Gaunt and York. Richard's arbitrariness in the opening scenes suggests the dangers of irresponsible despotism; throughout the play, Shakespeare follows Richard's thoughts and strange behavior and contrasts them with the caginess and certainty of Bolingbroke, whose thoughts are shown only translated into action; Richard thus becomes a study of the complex qualities of the ideal ruler. In this respect, the play reflects the Renaissance fascination with optimal behavior in various social roles, as seen, for example, in Niccolò Machiavelli's *Il principe* (1532; *The Prince*, 1640), Roger Ascham's *The Schoolmaster* (1570), and Sir Thomas Elyot's *The Boke Named the Governour* (1531). Shakespeare's psychological realism does not reach a falsely definitive conclusion, however; rather, the playwright creates a tragic aura of uncertainty around Richard, which makes him a most attractive character. In many ways, the play depicts not so much a contest for power as a struggle within Richard himself to adjust to his situation.

This is the first of Shakespeare's plays with a central figure who is an introspective, imaginative, and eloquent man. It is, therefore, not surprising that the work includes some of the author's finest lyrical passages. *Richard II* is in fact the only play Shakespeare wrote entirely in verse, a verse supported by a regal formality of design and manner and a profuse and delicate metaphorical base. Intricately interwoven throughout the play are image patterns centered on the eagle, the lion, the rose, the sun (which begins with Richard but moves to Bolingbroke), the state as theater, the earth as a neglected or well-tended garden, and the rise and fall of fortune's buckets. The complicated imagery illustrates the subconscious workings of Shakespeare's imagination that will enrich the great tragedies to follow. As Henry Morley said, the play is "full of passages that have floated out of their place in the drama to live in the minds of the people." These passages include Gaunt's great apostrophe to England in act 2, scene 1; York's description of "our two cousins coming into London"; Richard's prison soliloquy in act 5, scene 4; and his monologues on divine right and on the irony of kingship.

So poetic is Richard that critics speculate Shakespeare may have written the part for himself. Richard, the lover of music, spectacle, domestic courtesy, and dignified luxury, would be the ideal host to the courtier described by Baldassare Castiglione in *Il libro del cortegiano* (1528; *The Book of the Courtier*, 1561). His whimsical personality is balanced to great dramatic effect by his self-awareness. He seems fascinated with the contradictory flow of his own emotions, and this very fascination is a large part of his tragic flaw. Similarly, Richard's sensitivity is combined with a flair for self-dramatization that reveals only too clearly his ineptitude as a strong ruler. He plays to the wrong audience, seeking the approval of his court rather than that of the common people; he seems to shun the "vulgar crowd" in preference to the refined taste of a court that can appreciate his delicate character. The last three acts, in which Richard's charm as a man are emphasized, are obviously more central to the play's aesthetic than the first two, which reveal his weakness as a king. His sentimental vanity in the abdication scene is so effective that it was censored during Queen Elizabeth I's lifetime. The alternation of courage and despair in Richard's mind determines the rhythm of the play; as the English poet and literary critic Samuel Taylor Coleridge observed, "The play throughout is a history of the human mind."

When Richard speaks of "the unstooping firmness of my upright soul," we understand that he is compensating verbally for his inability to act. He insists on the sacramental nature of kingship, depending for his support on the formal, legal rituals associated with the throne; he is all ceremony and pathetically fatal pomp. Yet, from the outset, Richard contradicts even the logic of sovereign ceremony when he arbitrarily changes his decision and banishes the two opponents in the joust. Bolingbroke is quick to note the king's weakness and steps into the power vacuum it creates, for Bolingbroke is the consummate actor who can be all things to all men by seeming so. He is impressed by the kingly power Richard wields: "Four lagging winters and four wanton springs/ End in a word: such is the breath of kings." He likes what he sees and, in deciding to imitate it, surpasses Richard. Even when Bolingbroke is ceremonious, as when he bows his knee to Richard before the abdication, he is acting. The difference is that he knows the most effective audience. Richard laments that he has seen Bolingbroke's courtship of the common people: "How he did seem to dive into their hearts." He recognizes the actor in Bolingbroke and fears its power.

It is not coincidental that York compares the commoners to the fickle theater audience. As in so many of Shakespeare's plays, the theater itself becomes a central image; Richard's monologues are a stark contrast to Bolingbroke's speeches not only because they reveal internal states but also because they are narcissistically oriented. They reach inward, toward secrecy and communicative impotence; Bolingbroke speaks actively, reaching outward toward the audience he wishes to influence. His role can be compared usefully to that of Antony in Shakespeare's *Julius Caesar* (pr. c. 1599-1600, pb. 1623), Richard's to that of Brutus. The tension between the two styles of speaking, moreover, no doubt reflects the transformation in Shakespeare himself that will make the plays to follow more strikingly dramatic than sheerly poetic. The Bolingbroke of *Henry IV, Parts I* and *II*, is born in *Richard II*, his realistic, calculating, efficient, politically astute performance directly antithetical to Richard's impractical, mercurial, meditative, and inept behavior. Bolingbroke is an opportunist, favored by fortune. A man of action and of few words, Bolingbroke presents a clear alternative to Richard when the two men appear together. If Richard is the actor as prima donna, Bolingbroke is the actor as director.

"Critical Evaluation" by Kenneth John Atchity

Further Reading

Batson, Beatrice, ed. *Shakespeare's Second Historical Tetralogy: Some Christian Features.* West Cornwall, Conn.: Locust Hill Press, 2004. Collection of essays focuses on the Christian dimension of the second historical tetralogy and the Elizabethan worldview of religion. Includes a comparison of Shakespeare's histories and the Coventry mysteries as well as discussion of such themes in the plays as sons without fathers, loss, failure, denial, guilt, and expiation.

Calderwood, James L. "*Richard II*: Metadrama and the Fall of Speech." In *Shakespeare's History Plays: "Richard II" to "Henry V,"* edited by Graham Holderness. New York: St. Martin's Press, 1992. Focuses on the power of language in the play, examining the speeches of King Richard and his rival, Bolingbroke.

Evans, Gareth Lloyd. *The Upstart Crow: An Introduction to Shakespeare's Plays.* London: J. M. Dent and Sons, 1982. Offers a comprehensive discussion of the dramatic works of Shakespeare. Presents critical reviews of the plays along with discussions of sources and information on the circumstances surrounding the writing of the plays.

Farrell, Kirby, ed. *Critical Essays on Shakespeare's "Richard II."* New York: G. K. Hall, 1999. Collection of essays—originally published from the late 1960's through the late 1990's—challenges conventional interpretations of *Richard II*. Includes discussions of the realities of power, language and rebellion, and familial politics in the play as well as an examination of Elizabethan press censorship and a survey of the play's critical history.

Findlay, Alison. "Good Sometimes Queen: *Richard II*, Mary Stuart, and the Poetics of Queenship." In *Shakespeare's Histories and Counter-Histories*, edited by Dermot Cavanagh, Stuart Hampton-Rees, and Stephen Longstaffe. New York: Manchester University Press, 2006. Analyzes the diverse ways in which Shakespeare depicts both official and unofficial versions of history in his plays.

Lucas, John. *Shakespeare's Second Tetralogy: "Richard II"-"Henry V."* London: Greenwich Exchange, 2007. Focuses on the political issues generated by *Richard II* and the three other history plays in Shakespeare's second tetralogy. Notes that the plays were written when Elizabeth I's reign was coming to an end, and the questions they raise about the divinity of kings and the rights of their subjects reflect national uncertainty about the future of England.

Ribner, Irving. *The English History Play in the Age of Shakespeare.* Rev. ed. 1965. Reprint. London: Routledge, 2005. Discusses the development and sources of history plays in the Elizabethan era and assesses Shakespeare's contributions to the genre.

Spiekerman, Tim. *Shakespeare's Political Realism: The English History Plays.* Albany: State University of New York Press, 2001. Reexamines five of Shakespeare's history plays, including *Richard II*, with a focus on such political themes as ambition, legitimacy of rulership, and tradition. Argues that the playwright's view of politics continues to be relevant in the modern world.

Richard III

Author: William Shakespeare (1564-1616)
First produced: c. 1592-1593; first published, 1597
Type of work: Drama
Type of plot: Historical
Time of plot: Fifteenth century
Locale: England

Principal characters:
EDWARD IV, the king of England
RICHARD, his brother, the duke of Gloucester
GEORGE, his brother, the duke of Clarence
QUEEN ELIZABETH, wife of Edward IV
LADY ANNE, the widow of the son of Henry VI and later
    the wife of Richard III
QUEEN MARGARET, the widow of Henry VI
EDWARD, the Prince of Wales and son of Edward IV
RICHARD, the duke of York, another son of Edward IV
THE DUKE OF BUCKINGHAM, an accomplice of the duke of
    Gloucester
LORD HASTINGS, a supporter of Prince Edward
LORD STANLEY, the earl of Derby
SIR WILLIAM CATESBY, a court toady
HENRY TUDOR, the earl of Richmond and later King
    Henry VII

The Story:

After the conclusion of the wars between the houses of York and Lancaster, Edward IV is firmly restored to the throne. Before long, however, his treacherous brother Richard, the hunchbacked duke of Gloucester, resumes his plans for gaining the throne. Craftily he removes one obstacle in his path when he turns the king against the third brother, the duke of Clarence (whose given name is George) by telling the king of an ancient prophecy that his issue will be disinherited by one of the royal line whose name begins with the letter G. Clarence is immediately arrested and taken to the Tower. Richard goes to him, pretending sympathy, and advises him that the jealousy and hatred of Queen Elizabeth are responsible for his imprisonment. After promising to help his brother secure his freedom, Richard, as false in word as he is cruel in deed, gives orders that Clarence be stabbed in his cell and his body placed in a barrel of malmsey wine.

Hoping to make his position even stronger, Richard then makes plans to marry Lady Anne, the widow of Prince Edward, the former Prince of Wales whose father is the murdered Henry VI. Edward was slain by Richard and his brothers after the battles ended, and Lady Anne and Henry's widow, Queen Margaret, were the only remaining members of the once powerful House of Lancaster still living in England. Intercepting Lady Anne at the funeral procession of Henry VI, Richard attempts to woo her. Although she hates and fears her husband's murderer, she is persuaded to accept an engagement ring when Richard insists that it is for love of her that he murdered her husband.

Richard goes to the court, where Edward IV lies ill. There, he affects great sorrow and indignation over the news of the death of Clarence, thereby endearing himself to Lord Hastings and the duke of Buckingham, who were friends of Clarence. He insinuates that Queen Elizabeth and her followers turned the wrath of the king against Clarence, which brought about his death. Richard manages to convince everyone except Queen Margaret, who knows well what really happened. Openly accusing him, she attempts to warn Buckingham and the others against Richard, but they ignore her.

Edward IV, ailing and depressed, tries to make peace among the factions in his realm, but he dies before he can accomplish this end. His son, Prince Edward, is sent for from Ludlow to take his father's place. At the same time, Richard imprisons Lord Grey, Lord Rivers, and Lord Vaughan, who are followers and relatives of the queen, and has them executed.

Terrified, Queen Elizabeth seeks refuge for herself and her second son, the young duke of York, with the archbishop of Canterbury. When Richard hears of the queen's action, he pretends much concern over the welfare of his brother's children and sets himself up as their guardian. He manages to remove young York from the care of his mother and has him placed in the Tower along with Prince Edward. He announces that they are under his protection and that they will remain there only until Prince Edward is crowned.

Learning from Sir William Catesby, a court toady, that Lord Hastings is a loyal adherent of the young prince, Richard contrives to remove that influential nobleman from the court by summoning him to a meeting ostensibly called to discuss plans for the coronation of the new king. Although Lord Stanley warns Hastings that ill luck awaits him if he goes to the meeting, the trusting nobleman keeps his appointment with Richard in the Tower. There, on the basis of trumped-up evidence, Richard accuses Hastings of treason and orders his immediate execution. Richard and Buckingham then dress themselves in rusty old armor and pretend to the lord mayor that Hastings was plotting against them; the lord mayor is convinced by their false protestations that the execution is justified.

Richard plots to seize the throne for himself. Buckingham, supporting him, speaks in the Guildhall of the great immorality of the late King Edward and hints that both the king and his children are illegitimate. Shocked, a citizens' committee headed by the lord mayor approaches Richard and begs him to accept the crown. They find him in the company of two priests, with a prayer book in his hand. So impressed are they with his seeming piety, that they repeat their offer after he hypocritically refuses it. Pretending great reluctance, Richard finally accepts, after being urged by Buckingham, the lord mayor, and Catesby. Plans for an immediate coronation are made.

Lady Anne is interrupted during a visit to the Tower with Queen Elizabeth and the old duchess of York and ordered to Westminster to be crowned Richard's queen. The three women hear with horror that Richard has ascended the throne; they are all the more suspicious of him because they are prevented from seeing the young princes. Fearing the worst, they sorrow among themselves and foresee doom for the nation.

Soon after his coronation, Richard suggests to Buckingham that the two princes must be killed. When Buckingham balks at the order, Richard refuses to consider his request to be elevated to the earldom of Hereford. Proceeding alone to secure the safety of his position, he hires Sir James Tyrrel, a discontented nobleman, to smother the children in their sleep. To make his position still more secure, Richard plans to marry Elizabeth of York, his own niece and daughter of the deceased Edward IV. Spreading the news that Queen Anne is mortally ill, he has her secretly murdered. He removes any threat from Clarence's heirs by imprisoning his son and by arranging a marriage for the daughter that considerably lowers her social status.

None of these precautions, however, can stem the tide of threats that are beginning to endanger Richard. In Brittany, Henry Tudor, the earl of Richmond, gathers an army and invades the country. When news of Richmond's landing at Milford reaches London, Buckingham flees from Richard, whose cruelty and guilt are becoming apparent to even his closest friends and associates. Buckingham joins Richmond's forces, but shortly afterward Richard captures and executes him.

In a tremendous final battle, the armies of Richmond and Richard meet on Bosworth Field. There, on the night before the encounter, all the ghosts of Richard's victims appear to him in his sleep and prophesy his defeat. They also foretell the earl of Richmond's victory and success. The predictions hold true. The next day, Richard, fighting desperately, is slain in battle by Richmond, after crying out the offer of his ill-gotten kingdom for a horse, his own killed under him. The earl mounts the throne and marries Elizabeth of York, thus uniting the houses of York and Lancaster and ending the feud.

Critical Evaluation:

Richard III is the last of a series of four plays that began with the three parts of *Henry VI*. These plays, though not strictly speaking a tetralogy, trace the bloody conflicts between the houses of Lancaster and York and interpret the events leading up to the establishment of the Tudor dynasty. Despite Richard's painful experiences, the drama remains a history rather than a tragedy. Richard does not have the moral stature to be a tragic hero, who may murder, but only in violation of his own nature. Richard, by contrast, is a natural intriguer and murderer. Even as bloody a character as Macbeth contains within him an earlier, nobler, Macbeth. Richard is too intelligent and self-aware, and too much in control of himself and those around him, to raise any of the moral ambiguities or dilemmas that are necessary to tragedy. Nor does Richard achieve any transcendent understanding of his actions.

Richard is, nevertheless, the dominating figure in the play and a fascinating one. All the other characters pale before him. The play is primarily a series of encounters between him and the opponents who surround him. Because Richard is physically small and has a humpback, many commentators have suggested that his behavior is a compensation for his physical deformity. However, Richard is not a paranoid; everyone really does hate him. The deformity, a gross exaggeration of the historical reality, is more likely a physical representation of the grotesque shape of Richard's soul in a Renaissance world that took such correspondences seriously. In any case, Shakespeare created good theater by representing Richard as deformed, by which means his plots seem all the more grotesque.

Richard is also the master rhetorician in a play in which Shakespeare for the first time shows the full power of his language. Richard's speeches and the staccato exchanges among characters present the nervous energy that informs the more ambitious later plays. From his opening soliloquy, Richard fascinates not only with his language but also with his intelligence and candor. Until the very end, he is the stage manager of all that occurs. As a villain, he is unique in his total control and in the virtuosity of his performance. Even Iago pales before him, for Richard, in soliloquies and asides, explains to the audience exactly what he is going to do and then carries it off.

In his opening speech, it is immediately clear that Richard will preside if not eventually prevail. He reveals not only a self-confident awareness of his own physical limitations and intellectual superiority but also a disarming perception of his own evil and isolation. His honest villainy is more total than Iago's both in the way that he is able to convince every character that he is his only friend and in the full step-by-step disclosure of his intentions to the audience. Since everyone is against him, he almost generates involuntary sympathy.

Shakespeare's plot is the relentless working out of Richard's schemes as they lead to his final destruction. His first confrontation, with Anne, is a model of Richard's abilities: The exchange begins with Anne's heaping abuse on her husband's murderer and ends with Richard extracting from her a promise of marriage. Anne is overwhelmed more by the brilliance and the audacity of Richard's rhetorical wit than by the logic of his arguments. The audience, however, sees what an improbably brief time Richard needs to be successful. It is part of the definition of this villain that he can succeed in such a wildly improbable adventure. Richard is frequently shown using those who hate him for his own benefit, in a perverse gratification of his ostensible desire for power and his submerged desire to be loved. Only his mother is able to see through to the total corruption of his heart.

Richard sees the path to kingship as being simply a matter of ingratiating himself with the right people and of murdering all those who stand in his way. He contracts the murder of Clarence in the Tower amid a good bit of gallows humor, which sets the appropriately grim tone. Like a good Machiavel, he builds on past success and takes advantage of any fortuitous circumstances. He uses the death of Clarence to cast suspicion on Elizabeth and on her party and to get the support of Buckingham, and he seizes on the death of Edward IV to have the influential nobles imprisoned and killed. Most events happen at Richard's instigation, and others he deftly turns to his own advantage. He efficiently removes all near claims to the throne by lies, innuendoes, and direct, vigorous action.

So appealing is his virtuosity and so faithful is he in informing the audience of his plans, that Shakespeare is even able to arouse sympathy for him when the tide of opposition to him swells under the leadership of Richmond. Shakespeare neatly figures the balance of power by setting up the opposing camps on opposite sides of the stage. The ominous appearances of the ghosts, to Richmond as well as to Richard, portend that retribution is at hand. Although he is unnerved for the first time, Richard behaves with martial valor and struggles determinedly to the last. This last show of courage is the final complication of a consummate villain.

"Critical Evaluation" by Edward E. Foster

Further Reading

Day, Gillian. *King Richard III*. London: Arden Shakespeare in association with the Shakespeare Birthplace Trust, 2001. Analyzes how different directors, scenic designers, and actors have interpreted and adapted the play for productions mounted by the Royal Shakespeare Company since 1945. Includes photographs of company productions.

Farrell, Kirby. "Prophetic Behavior in Shakespeare's Histories." *Shakespeare Studies* 19 (1987): 17-40. Refers to historical prophecies in examining various kinds of prophecy in the play, both conscious and unconscious.

Hassel, R. Chris, Jr. *Songs of Death: Performance, Interpretation, and the Text of "Richard III."* Lincoln: University of Nebraska Press, 1987. Examines *Richard III* from various angles, including the theatrical and acting history of the play, the role of Providence, and the characters and their motives.

Lull, Janis. "Plantagenets, Lancastrians, Yorkists, and Tudors: *1-3 Henry VI, Richard III, Edward III*." In *The Cambridge Companion to Shakespeare's History Plays*, edited by Michael Hattaway. New York: Cambridge University Press, 2002. Describes *Richard III* as a "tragic pyramid" focusing on the rise and fall of a single protagonist: The action in the play rises to the peak of the pyramid, followed by the climax, crisis, and the falling action at the end.

Miner, Madonne M. "'Neither Mother, Wife, nor England's Queen': The Roles of Women in *Richard III*." In *William Shakespeare's "Richard III,"* edited by Harold Bloom. New York: Chelsea House, 1988. The three sections of the essay examine the depth of characterization given to the women and their interactions. Discusses the imagery of femaleness in the play.

Neill, Michael. "Shakespeare's Halle of Mirrors: Play, Politics, and Psychology in *Richard III*." In *William Shakespeare's "Richard III,"* edited by Harold Bloom. New York: Chelsea House, 1988. Examines the idea of theatricality in the play. Argues that Richard, like Hamlet, is an actor in the dramatic events that surround him.

Partee, Morriss Henry. *Childhood in Shakespeare's Plays.* New York: Peter Lang, 2006. Examines the depiction of the child characters in *Richard III* and some of Shakespeare's other plays. Challenges the idea that Shakespeare regarded children as small adults; demonstrates that he did not portray children as either unnaturally precocious or sentimentally innocent.

Prescott, Paul. *"Richard III": A Guide to the Text and Its Theatrical Life.* New York: Palgrave Macmillan, 2006. Handbook providing an overview of the play. Discusses its text, sources, early performances, cultural context, key productions and performances on stage and on film, and critical assessments.

Riders in the Chariot

Author: Patrick White (1912-1990)
First published: 1961
Type of work: Novel
Type of plot: Parable
Time of plot: Mid-twentieth century
Locale: Sarsaparilla, Sydney, Australia

Principal characters:
MRS. RUTH GODBOLD, a mother, wife, and washerwoman of good and simple heart
MORDECAI HIMMELFARB, a former professor of English and a Jewish immigrant
MISS MARY HARE, an elderly spinster and the owner of Xanadu
ALF DUBBO, an Aborigine painter
HARRY ROSETREE (born HAIM ROSENBAUM), a factory owner
MRS. JOLLEY, the gossiping, malicious, widowed housekeeper at Xanadu
MRS. FLACK, her friend and a woman of genteel malevolence
BLUE, Mrs. Flack's illegitimate son

The Story:

Three residents of Sarsaparilla, Australia, are dying: Alf Dubbo, an Aborigine painter; Miss Mary Hare, an aging spinster from a good family; and Mordecai Himmelfarb, an elderly Jewish immigrant, or "New Australian," working in a factory. Before their deaths, the three recall the events of their lives. Mary Hare is the last remnant of a distinguished old Australian settler family. Her estate, Xanadu, is deteriorating and is being rapidly encroached upon by the expanding middle-class suburb of Sarsaparilla. Miss Hare was once a beautiful young woman, but she frittered away her potential chances at happiness with her cousin Eustace and with other young men and has become an old maid living in her estate on drastically diminished revenues.

After the end of World War II, an English cousin resumes paying Miss Hare an allowance and she simultaneously finds herself in need of assistance with keeping her house in order. She engages a housekeeper, Mrs. Jolley. Mrs. Jolley enjoys discussing everything that happens at Xanadu with her friend Mrs. Fleck. Mrs. Jolley is a widow and has been rejected by her family as the probable murderess of her husband. Miss Hare soon learns to fear Mrs. Jolley's ordinariness and her spite. The two women develop an intense love-hate relationship.

Miss Hare recounts some of the details of her life to Mrs. Jolley: She grew up as the only, ugly, and unwanted daughter of English parents whose delusions of grandeur were reflected in the name of their house—Xanadu. She was nursed back to life from a serious illness by a local washerwoman, Mrs. Ruth Godbold. During her illness, she saw what she calls the "Chariot" and believes that she was therefore marked as a "rider"; she believes that Mrs. Godbold is a rider as well. She has fleeting encounters with two other riders: Dubbo and Himmelfarb. She also encounters Mrs. Flack, feeling her to be a palpable, malevolent presence.

Himmelfarb tells his story to Miss Hare when they meet by chance in the overgrown grounds of Xanadu. Himmelfarb comes from a wealthy German Jewish family that had the wherewithal and international connections to send him to university at Oxford, in England. There, he was traumatized when he caught a young woman with whom he had fallen in love, Catherine, having sexual relations with an Indian prince. Himmelfarb's father had converted to Catholicism to escape the stigma of being a Jew; his wish to assimilate into European society was such that he referred to his son Mordecai as "Martin." Both generations' illusions of escaping their Jewish identity—the father's through conversion, the son's through assimilation—were shattered with the rise of the Nazis and their anti-Semitic policies.

As the Nazis rose to power, Himmelfarb was sheltered for a time by old friends. When they, too, were taken by the Nazis, he gave himself up as a Jew and tried ineffectually to help his people while on the train to the gas chambers. Although he failed, he was miraculously delivered from the extermination camp and, half-blinded by the symbolic loss of his glasses, made his way to Israel, with the aid of many helping hands. Later, he rejected that haven and emigrated to Australia. Himmelfarb has had difficulty finding work and a context in Australia, partially because most ordinary Australians are biased against foreigners. He was steered in the direction of a Mr. Rosetree (originally Rosenbaum) for help. Rosetree treats Himmelfarb condescendingly and imperiously, because he thinks of himself as successfully assimilated into the Australian mainstream. However, Rosetree is in fact as rejected by British Australians as his subordinate. Himmelfarb has bought a run-down shack and has returned to the orthodox Jewish faith his father rejected. He works inconspicuously at Rosetree's bicycle factory but is never fully accepted by the working-class Australians who are his fellow laborers.

Himmelfarb strikes up an unlikely acquaintance with Miss Hare; after their chance meeting, she summons him to her house in the wake of the final departure of Mrs. Jolley. Miss Hare avows that she has no personal liking or concern for Himmelfarb, and she thinks of him rather categorically as "the Jew." She indicates to him, however, that she recognizes a kindred spiritual quality in him.

Alf Dubbo is a biracial Aborigine. Born in an Aborigine camp where his mother had been harbored, he was taken into the household of an Anglican priest, Timothy Calderon, from an early age. The priest sexually abused him, while he and his widowed sister, Mrs. Emily Pask, both encouraged Dubbo to pursue artistic and intellectual talents. When Mrs. Pask saw the experimental and explicit nature of Alf's paintings, however, she was horrified. Her discovery served as a prelude to her subsequent discovery that her brother was abusing the young boy, but when she caught her brother with Alf, she blamed the boy rather than her brother. Alf fled the house, eventually encountering a white woman, Mrs. Spice, to whom he disclosed his (fairly evident) Aboriginal ancestry. He later lodged with a prostitute named Hannah, who kept him on during the war and its attendant stresses, though she raised the rent.

Having internalized Mrs. Pask's dislike of Aborigines, Alf avoids contact with his fellow indigenous people, but he is still generally rejected by most whites. He holds himself aloof because of his artistic, visionary temperament. Eventually, Alf gets a job in Rosetree's factory, where he encounters Himmelfarb. When Himmelfarb realizes that he himself has no male friends, he looks in the direction of Alf Dubbo. Finding that Alf has read the Bible and is familiar with the Old Testament prophets, he cultivates a friendship.

Like Miss Hare, and Mrs. Godbold, Himmelfarb and Dubbo begin to sense their participation in the Chariot mystique. Together, these four seem to be the *tzaddikim*, or righteous, described in Jewish lore. Their interior, visionary quests comprise the *merkabah*, or chariot, referred to in the Old Testament book of Ezekiel.

Mrs. Flask's nephew, Blue, works in the factory along with Dubbo and Himmelfarb. He wins the lottery and is congratulated by his fellow workers, while Himmelfarb works on Passover—even though Rosetree, knowing Himmelfarb's revived Jewish piety, has excused him from working on the holy day. Worked up into a savage heat by the revelry, Blue and his workmates attack Himmelfarb, engaging in a parodic crucifixion in which Himmelfarb is mocked and humiliated. Leaving the factory for the last time, he immures himself in his shack and lights a fire that consumes the house. He is rescued by Miss Hare, who, with Mrs. Godbold, takes care of Himmelfarb until he dies on Easter Sunday; the two women give him a Christian burial.

Meanwhile, Mr. Rosetree hangs himself, ridden with shame because Himmelfarb's torment has revealed to him the moral consequences of trying to escape his Jewish identity. Following Himmelfarb's death, Miss Hare wanders away and is presumed dead. (Her cousin Eustace Cheugh, who once courted her, comes to dispose of the estate.) Dubbo dies of a tubercular hemorrhage after finishing a glorious final painting of the completed Chariot.

Mrs. Jolley has figured out Blue's true parentage, but Mrs. Flack knows that Mrs. Jolley's family has rejected her just as Blue has been rejected. The two widows live together in a hell of their own making. Only Mrs. Godbold is left with her family to watch brick bungalows gradually spreading over the site of Xanadu. On a visit to the real estate development, Mrs. Godbold achieves a perfect vision of the "riders in the chariot."

"The Story" revised by Nicholas Birns

Critical Evaluation:

Patrick White, who received the Nobel Prize in Literature in 1973, has created through *Riders in the Chariot* a striking parable—complex in its design and structure, yet altogether lucid in its meaning. Most often in White's novels, a single character acts as a visionary, grappling with life's mysteries and finally receiving illumination, usually through death or madness. In this novel, however, the stories of four prospective illuminati unfold individually then intertwine as they move toward their shared destiny as riders in the chariot. Their destiny is to glimpse life's great mystery, whose central force is love.

The seventeen chapters of the novel are organized in seven unequal parts to describe the events in and near the Australian town of Sarsaparilla, which White has fixed on as his recurrent locale. Parts 1 and 2 of the novel tell the past histories of Miss Hare and Himmelfarb; the fourth and fifth parts tell the stories of Mrs. Godbold and Alf Dubbo in less detail and at shorter length, a modification caused by the increasing pace of the plot in the later sections. In some ways, these characters form an unlikely quartet to embark on a mission of illumination: The four riders include the introverted offspring of decadent aristocracy, a Jewish refugee who has turned his back on religion, a tubercular Aboriginal painter who was seduced by a priest, and a local washerwoman whose husband deserted her and their six daughters. Nor is the setting one of grandeur: The action unfolds in the fictional Sarsaparilla, a dreary Australian suburb outside Sydney.

Superimposed on the stories of the four strange riders are those of other residents of White's imaginary suburb. Their drab surroundings are the symbols and teachings of world religion and Jungian philosophy. In spite of the apparent impossibility of the task White has set himself, *Riders in the Chariot* succeeds immensely as a narrative.

The novel's success rests primarily on its storytelling, which never lags. To explore the present actions of the four riders, the narrator relies on flashbacks, an unfashionable technique in contemporary writing. The most striking of these visits into the past is Mordecai Himmelfarb's story, beginning in his native Germany where he taught at a university, then moving into the Nazi period, when Himmelfarb and his wife were taken to a concentration camp, and finally progressing to Himmelfarb's miraculous escape, which brought him first to Israel then to Australia. For each of the other characters, there is a similar unfolding of the past: Mary's miserable childhood, Dubbo's unhappy experience in a white Christian household, and Mrs. Godbold's bleak life, first as a servant, then as a deserted wife taking in washing to support her daughters. The quality that dominates all of these past experiences is the absence of love. This absence is extreme when Himmelfarb faces Hitler's rise in Germany and a persistent feature of Dubbo's experience as a member of a colonized race. It manifests itself more subtly in the humiliation Mary suffers at the hands of her father, who dislikes her because she is ugly and awkward. In Mrs. Godbold's case, it is a matter of love turning into possessiveness.

Hate, which is a subtext of the novel, finally reveals itself completely through the book's most memorable scene, the mock crucifixion of Himmelfarb that takes place at the bicycle factory on Maundy Thursday of Passion Week. Led by Blue, a simple-minded and cruel man, the workers conduct the grisly rite: "The Jew had been hoisted as high as he was likely to go on the mutilated tree. . . . a burlesque. . . . what they suspected might be blasphemy. . . . The Jew hung." The onlookers relish the bleeding Jew, especially his one hand that looks as though it has been pierced. They laugh and spit water at him; one throws an orange but misses her target; a purple-haired old woman offers to buy Blue a drink as a reward for his cleverness. This may well be the most unpleasant passage in modern literature. The four illuminati are integrated into this pivotal scene—Dubbo is a stunned witness. Mrs. Godbold is at home ironing sheets thinking of how the women of the New Testament lovingly prepared such sheets to receive Christ's body after His crucifixion. Miss Hare is in her crumbling mansion watching "the marble shudder, the crack widen," which is suggestive of the quaking described in that original Crucifixion.

This scene has often been criticized as melodramatic, unlikely, or unmotivated. Regardless, it not only remains essential to the overall pattern of the novel but also demonstrates White's rare technique of consistently implanting idea into action. The hatred of the factory workers is directed toward immigrants to Australia after World War II, especially Jewish ones. This becomes evident when some of the onlookers shout: "Go home to Germany!" The painful events, which take place near the end of the novel, expand in meaning when considered as the climactic moment in the riders' movement toward the chariot and the truth within. To eliminate or to alter the crucifixion scene would be to unbalance the intricate structure of *Riders in the Chariot*, from a narrative and a thematic standpoint.

The antidote to hatred is love, to darkness is light, to death is life. As the complex story of the riders comes to an end, love, light, and life triumph. Such a conclusion might appear contradictory because only Mrs. Godbold survives. Mary Hare disappears into the night after Himmelfarb's death in the burning house. Alf Dubbo dies in his room, where "The sharp pain poured in crimson tones." Most often in White's novels, the visionary fails outwardly and can unravel life's mystery only in death or madness.

For a visionary to survive whole, as Mrs. Godbold does, is a rare occurrence, but Mrs. Godbold lacks the complexity of Himmelfarb, the European Jew; of Mary Hare, the daughter of sophisticates; or of Alf Dubbo, the gifted painter. That the washerwoman appears last, in a sense as the mediator for her more accomplished fellow riders, illustrates the novel's move from complexity to lucidity, its leap from condemnation to celebration. In spite of the novel's record of cruelty, cultural desolation, ignorance, and malevolence in all its forms, its ending tempers the bleak picture. Mrs. Godbold, trudging upward—if it is only up the hill toward the shed where she lives—has experienced a reconciling vision that redeems and heals: "She had her own vision of the Chariot. Even now, at the thought of it her very center was touched by the wings of love and charity."

"Critical Evaluation" by Robert L. Ross

Further Reading

Bliss, Carolyn. "*Riders in the Chariot*." In *Patrick White's Fiction*. New York: St. Martin's Press, 1986. Argues that the four protagonists, the "riders in the chariot," represent qualities that, if they were combined, "would produce a complete human being or society." Concludes that they reach wholeness through their "acceptance of failure."

Brady, Veronica. "God, History, and Patrick White." *Antipodes: A North American Journal of Australian Literature* 19, no. 2 (December, 2005): 172-176. Sees *Riders in the Chariot* as the pivotal unfolding of White's mature spiritual vision; reads White in a more ascetic and overtly Christian way than have previous studies of his work.

Chapman, Edgar L. "The Mandala Design of Patrick White's *Riders in the Chariot*." In *Critical Essays on Patrick White*, edited by Peter Wolfe. Boston: G. K. Hall, 1990. Examines the novel in the light of its mythological sources, including William Blake's visionary poetry, the biblical prophets, the apocalypse, the Jewish cabbalistic tradition, Jungian thought, and the mandala symbol. A complex and illuminating essay.

During, Simon. *Patrick White*. New York: Oxford University Press, 1996. Examines White's place in Australian history and culture, arguing that his work reflected the end of the country's colonial relationship with Great Britain. Analyzes the connection between White's homosexuality and his writing. The first treatment to stress the inescapability of the book's setting in suburbia.

Dutton, Geoffrey. "White's Triumphal Chariot." In *Critical Essays on Patrick White*, edited by Peter Wolfe. Boston: G. K. Hall, 1990. Admires the novel's scope, vision, language, and characterization. An excellent general introduction to the work.

Edgecombe, Rodney S. "*Riders in the Chariot*." In *Vision and Style in Patrick White: A Study of Four Novels*. Tuscaloosa: University of Alabama Press, 1989. A South African critic, Edgecombe analyzes each of the chariot's riders in detail, showing their roles in the elaborate allegory and their relationships with one another. Combines this discussion with an examination of the work's complex structure.

Hewill, Helen Verity. *Patrick White—Painter Manqué: Paintings, Painters, and Their Influence on His Writing*. Carlton, Vic.: Miegunyah Press, 2002. Describes how painting was a source of inspiration for White, discussing the influence of twentieth century Australian art and European modernist and romantic art upon his work.

McCann, Andrew. "The Ethics of Abjection: Patrick White's *Riders in the Chariot*." *Australian Literary Studies* 18, no. 2 (October, 1997): 145-155. Provides the first treatment of the novel influenced by postmodernism and cultural critique; focuses on the book's portrait of suburbia in the late modernist era.

Morley, Patricia. *The Mystery of Unity: Theme and Technique in the Novels of Patrick White*. Montreal: McGill-Queen's University Press, 1972. Remains an important and standard study. Places White's work in the mainstream of European writing and investigates how it employs the Western tradition along with archetypes that dominate Western literature. Helpful as a background for *Riders in the Chariot*.

Riders to the Sea

Author: John Millington Synge (1871-1909)
First produced: 1904; first published, 1903
Type of work: Drama
Type of plot: Tragedy
Time of plot: Late nineteenth century
Locale: Island off the west coast of Ireland

Principal characters:
MAURYA, an old woman
BARTLEY, her son
CATHLEEN, her elder daughter
NORA, her younger daughter

The Story:

Maurya, an old peasant woman, is worried about her son Michael. Her husband, her father-in-law, and four of her sons have been drowned in earlier sea accidents, leaving her with two sons, Michael and Bartley, and two daughters, Cathleen and Nora. Now Michael is missing at sea. As Maurya sleeps, Cathleen works at her spinning and makes a cake for Bartley, the younger of her two remaining brothers, to take on a trip. Bartley is planning to go to the horse fair on the mainland. Nora comes into the house with a bundle of clothes a priest has given her. The clothes, a shirt and a stocking, have been taken from the body of an unidentified young man found floating off the coast of Donegal to the north. Hearing their mother stir, Cathleen and Nora decide to hide the clothes. They plan to examine them later to see if they are Michael's before saying anything to Maurya.

Cathleen asks Nora if she asked the priest to urge Bartley not to sail in the stormy weather. Nora says that the priest told her to trust God not to leave Maurya without any sons. Cathleen climbs into the loft and hides the clothes. When she hears her mother getting up, she pretends she has been fetching turf for the kitchen fire. Maurya scolds her for wasting turf.

Maurya asks where Bartley is, and Nora tells her that he has gone to check on the boat schedule. Moments later, Bartley hurries into the room looking for a piece of rope to make a horse halter. His mother tries various arguments to stop Bartley from going to the horse fair. She tells him that he ought to leave the rope where it is because they might need it to lower Michael's coffin into his grave if he has drowned. When Bartley tells her it is expected to be a good fair, Maurya replies that a thousand horses cannot be worth as much as a son. Bartley continues with his plans anyway, knotting the rope into a horse halter and giving Cathleen last-minute instructions for looking after things during his absence. Bartley and Maurya leave, and Nora decides not to mention anything about the hidden clothing until Bartley returns safely.

When Maurya returns after seeing Bartley off, she sits by the fire and begins to moan and cry. Nora and Cathleen demand to know what is wrong, and she tells them that she has seen Bartley riding the red horse, with Michael, in fine clothes and new shoes, riding behind him on the gray pony. When she tried to call her blessing to them, her voice choked in her throat.

Shocked by her mother's words, Cathleen gives in and tells her that Michael has drowned. Maurya continues to speak as if to herself, recounting her losses one by one, as other old women come into the house, cross themselves, and kneel to pray. Cathleen hands Maurya the bit of Michael's clothing, and then Maurya knows it is true that he is dead.

They hear a sound outside and find that it is men carrying Bartley's wet body. The gray pony had knocked Bartley down in the surf, and he had been swept out with the tide and drowned. Now Maurya realizes the finality of her loss. She will never see Michael again, and Bartley, her last son, is also dead. She says there is nothing left to threaten her now. The men prepare to build a coffin for Bartley from the white boards Maurya had earlier gotten for Michael's burial. Maurya sprinkles the last of the holy water on Michael's clothes in final benediction and asks for God's blessing. She notes that no one can live forever and that one must be satisfied with a decent grave.

Critical Evaluation:

John Millington Synge is considered the greatest playwright of the Irish Literary Revival, a movement in Ireland associated with the poet William Butler Yeats and other Irish writers. This revival took place at the end of the nineteenth century and the beginning of the twentieth. Irish-born, Synge studied at Trinity College in Dublin and received a scholarship to study music. He traveled to the Continent and lived in Paris, where he taught English and began writing poetry. In Paris, in 1896, Synge met Yeats, a leading writer and one of the founders of the Abbey Theatre in Dublin, a theater dedicated to performing Irish plays. Yeats advised Synge to return to Ireland and take as a model for his writing the people of the Aran Islands off the west coast of Ireland.

Synge followed Yeats's advice. From this experience came Synge's book, *The Aran Islands* (1907), a travel memoir recounting island folklore and daily events in the lives of the local people. From this same material Synge took inspiration and material for his plays. Writing of actual events, Synge used expressions and speech patterns of the old-fashioned local dialect to give a poetic, particularly Irish quality to his drama. The Aran Islands are the inspiration for *Riders to the Sea*. The details regarding the drownings are realistic; drownings were not uncommon there, and all the adult men regularly went to sea. A young woman wonders if a drowned man whose body has been found is her missing brother. She puts together information about his clothing and an object found on him to confirm that the dead man must be her brother Mike. Synge weaves this and other material into the tragic story of Maurya, her two daughters, and the lost men of the family. In doing so he takes the story beyond the local to a mythic level.

Riders to the Sea begins with the image of the daughter Cathleen at her spinning wheel. Later, when Cathleen and Nora examine the clothing of the drowned man, trying to determine whether it is Michael's or not, Cathleen cuts the string that holds the bundle. Examining the stocking, Nora speaks of knitting, dropping and picking up stitches. These images of spinning, knitting, and cutting suggest the actions of the Fates, classical goddesses of destiny who determine the length of human life as they spin and cut the thread of life. Maurya's speech of resignation at the end of *Riders to the Sea* has been compared to the ending of a Greek tragedy, Sophocles' *Oidipous Tyrannos* (c. 429 B.C.E.; *Oedipus Tyrannus*, 1715), in which the chorus says that no mortal is happy until he has passed beyond life's pain. Maurya's vision of the dead Michael riding the gray horse as an omen of doom has a biblical flavor. It would be a mistake, however, to read Synge's allusions too strictly. Some of these images may have been suggested by other sources. Synge does not force such parallels; rather, he uses them to add color and a mythic scale.

Synge also uses images of sacraments. Water, often a sign of baptism and life, here takes away life, but the people have no choice but to turn to it for their living. The bread of life, a cake that is baking on the turf fire, goes uneaten by Bartley as he leaves without his mother's blessing. When she tries to correct this oversight he is already beyond her help.

Color images are also important. The few colors in the play stand out against a gray and stormy world. Nora speaks of "the green head" of land where the tide is turning and of the likelihood that Bartley will sail in spite of his mother's wishes. Later Cathleen refers to Bartley riding "over the green head" on his way to the boat. The rope that Bartley wants to use to tie the gray horse has been chewed on by the pig with the black feet. The boards the mother is saving for Michael's casket are white. The red mare and the gray pony are vivid images in an otherwise bleak landscape. Maurya cries out that when the black night falls she will not have a son left. When Nora tells of how Michael's body was found by two men rowing past the black cliffs to the north, the birds that fly over the sea where his body was found are described as "black hags." Maurya describes seeing the body of Patch, an older son, brought home dripping on a red sail. The women who come into the house to pray and mourn, like a tragic chorus, are wearing red petticoats, the color of the sail. Finally, Maurya says that Bartley will have a "fine coffin out of the white boards." Green, black, red, gray, and white create a pattern of life, death, and resignation.

The humble cottage in which the play is set is like an island itself, small and vulnerable in comparison to the large, dangerous world outside. The beauty of Synge's one-act play, which takes approximately half an hour to perform, is in its language and its simplicity. It presents the clear line of the tragedy itself, seen in its final hours. The players in this drama are not at fault for what happens to them. Instead, this is a tragedy of a fate that cannot be avoided and in the face of which there is no alternative but stoicism and acceptance.

Barbara Drake

Further Reading

Castle, Gregory. *Modernism and the Celtic Revival*. New York: Cambridge University Press, 2001. Analyzes how Synge and other Irish Revivalists employed techniques of anthropology to translate, reassemble, and edit material from Irish folk culture, using this material to combat British imperialism.

Gerstenberger, Donna. *John Millington Synge*. New York: Twayne, 1964. Excellent basic reference book on Synge devotes a chapter to *Riders to the Sea*. Points out that *Riders to the Sea* was the only one of Synge's plays that did not occasion angry outbursts from Irish audiences. Discusses imagery and the symbolic use of color in the play.

Gonzalez, Alexander G., ed. *Assessing the Achievement of J. M. Synge*. Westport, Conn.: Greenwood Press, 1996. Collection of fourteen original essays offers interpretations of Synge's dramatic works. "Tragic Self-Referral in *Riders to the Sea*," by Daniel Davy, focuses on this play.

Grene, Nicholas. *Synge: A Critical Study of the Plays*. New

York: Macmillan, 1975. Discusses Synge's Aran experience. Provides extensive discussion of *Riders to the Sea* and how it differs from Synge's other plays. Praises the economy of the play and delineates way in which props, such as the spinning wheel, the bread, the bundle, and the boards, are used for dramatic effect. Cautions against overemphasizing comparisons between the play and classical tragedy.

McDonald, Ronan. *Tragedy and Irish Literature: Synge, O'Casey, Beckett*. New York: Palgrave, 2002. Examines the work of Synge along with that of Sean O'Casey and Samuel Beckett, two other Irish playwrights. Describes how the Irish culture of suffering, loss, and guilt shaped their ideas of tragedy. Defines a peculiarly Irish form of tragedy by locating common themes and techniques in the playwrights' work.

Ritschel, Nelson O'Ceallaigh. *Synge and Irish Nationalism:*

The Precursor to Revolution. Westport, Conn.: Greenwood Press, 2002. Argues that Synge's plays are deeply rooted in ancient Irish literature and that the playwright's use of this material reflects his nationalist agenda.

Skelton, Robin. *J. M. Synge*. Cranbury, N.J.: Bucknell University Press, 1972. Offers a summary of Synge's background as well as analyses of his plays, including *Riders to the Sea*. Supplemented with a chronology of Synge's life and a bibliography.

_____. *The Writings of J. M. Synge*. Indianapolis: Bobbs-Merrill, 1971. Includes a chapter on *Riders to the Sea* that discusses the play's references to folklore and mythology.

Thornton, Weldon. *J. M. Synge and the Western Mind*. Gerrards Cross, England: Colin Smythe, 1979. Compares the views of a wide variety of critics and scholars on Synge. Provides an excellent introduction to what has been written about Synge's work.

The Right Stuff

Author: Tom Wolfe (1931-   )
First published: 1979
Type of work: New Journalism

The Right Stuff, Tom Wolfe's account of America's space program up to Project Mercury, evolved from his curiosity about the kind of person who was willing to sit on top of a thirty-six story container of explosives waiting for the fuse to be lit. His interest in these individuals—who they were, where they came from, and how they felt while perched atop twenty thousand pounds of liquid oxygen—fueled the research that resulted in this entertaining and enlightening look at America's astronauts. Wolfe explores the fraternity of fliers, the military lifestyle, the function of the press, and the nature of courage, providing the reader with an insightful journey into the heart of American culture. Although factual, the book allows itself liberties in the description of events and, for example, the re-creation of conversations or the thoughts that someone may have had.

Wolfe first discovers the "right stuff" among the close-knit group of military fighter and test pilots stationed at bleak air bases scattered around the United States in the late 1940's and early 1950's. He describes this "stuff" as

the ability to go up in a hurtling piece of machinery and . . . have the moxie, the reflexes, the experience, the coolness,

to pull it back in the last yawning moment—and then go up again *the next day*, and the next day, and every next day . . . and . . . do so in a cause that means something to thousands, to a people, to a nation, to humanity, to God.

This ability and willingness to "push the outside of the envelope" was the sole quality upon which the "True Brotherhood" of fliers judged themselves and each other. The right stuff determined, more surely than military rank, the fliers' status in the rigid hierarchy of flying.

Moving from one desolate outpost to another, these fliers aspired to assignments at the mecca of flying, Edwards Air Force Base, where pilots who had reached the pinnacle of their careers were stationed. In their quest to fly ever higher and faster in the most advanced American aeronautical technology available, the Edwards pilots risked their lives daily with the offhand calm that marked their breed, hoping to achieve what many considered impossible. The supreme impossible goal was reaching the speed of Mach 1, the sound barrier. The "most righteous of all the possessors of the right stuff," Chuck Yeager, while flying with two broken ribs, achieved the impossible, reaching Mach 1 on October 14,

1947. Yeager and his fellow pilots at Edwards, living what Wolfe termed the "Flying & Drinking and Drinking & Driving" lifestyle, continued achieving even greater speeds for the next decade, until a monumental shift in the direction of U.S. space exploration occurred.

On October 4, 1957, ten years minus ten days after Yeager broke the sound barrier, the Soviet Union sent *Sputnik I* into orbit. Panic followed the Soviets' first foray into space. It appeared to the people of the United States and their government that the control of the heavens was at stake, and an effort to launch an American into space, to close the gap with the Soviets, began immediately. After lengthy consideration about how to select the first American in space (at one point the field was to be open to any young male college graduate with experience in dangerous pursuits—mountain climbers, deep sea divers, skydivers, and the like), President Dwight D. Eisenhower ordered that the first astronauts be chosen from the ranks of military test pilots.

These pilots were not overwhelmingly eager at first to volunteer for this new program, uncertain as to whether it would represent a step up in status, or a leap into obscurity. The position of astronaut was unprecedented, and the fliers had to reach a consensus on where an astronaut would fit in their hierarchy. Many fliers argued that astronauts would be no better than passive lab animals, with little or no opportunity to exhibit the right stuff. Motivated largely by the fear of being left behind, the pilots volunteered in large numbers for the assignment, despite their misgivings. Those who decided to volunteer for Project Mercury very soon discovered a whole new set of assumptions at work in the space program. The seven finalists would not be chosen for their prowess as pilots, but rather for mental and physical stamina and adaptability. The rules were understood only by the doctors and scientists, who subjected the fliers to exhaustive and often humiliating examinations and tests, which made it abundantly clear that the fliers were merely lab rats in the brave new world of space exploration.

When the seven chosen—Alan Shepard, Virgil I. Grissom, John H. Glenn, Jr., M. Scott Carpenter, Walter M. Schirra, L. Gordon Cooper, and Donald K. Slayton—were presented to the press and the American public, not only was no mention made of their experience and qualifications as fliers, no one was really interested. The press asked about their wives and children, their religious affiliation, and their feelings of patriotism, not their stellar records as fighter jocks and test pilots. Determined to take a fitting tone and express the proper sentiment in a matter of serious national concern, the press (or, as Wolfe calls them, the Victorian Gentleman or Genteel Beast) played a major role in the

drama of the space race by portraying the astronauts as clean-cut, clean-living repositories of the highest moral virtues, whether or not the facts warranted such an interpretation. The press allowed no hint of the hard-drinking, hard-driving lifestyle of the astronauts to reach the American public, believing it their duty to provide "proper and fitting" images of America's newest heroes.

The press made instant heroes of the astronauts' wives as well, whose faces, airbrushed almost beyond recognition, appeared on the cover of *Life* magazine, which bought exclusive rights to their stories. The stories did not mention that Betty Grissom spent only a handful of days a year with her husband or that Gordon Cooper and his wife had been separated before he was chosen as an astronaut, because these facts did not fit conveniently with the required wholesome image. As test pilots' wives, the fear they endured while their husbands flew dangerous missions was private. As astronauts' wives, their anxiety not only became a public spectacle (as their homes were invaded by hordes of reporters), but it paled in comparison to the agony they suffered facing the idiotic and largely unanswerable questions of the press after the splashdown.

As the astronauts proceeded with their training they found themselves pitted against the establishment of the National Aeronautics and Space Administration (NASA), which wanted to use them only as experimental subjects, while they wanted at least some control over the operation of their capsules. Their job description evolved through continuing compromises with NASA concerning how much control they would be allowed over their flights, with the end result being that the astronauts were to be something between passengers and pilots. The astronauts lobbied for and got several changes in the design of the capsule, including a window, a hatch they could "blow," or open by explosives from the inside, an override control on re-entry, and other operational functions.

Although the public was led to believe all of the Mercury flights were successful, and all seven of the astronauts heroes, the astronauts themselves judged each other by their own standards as test pilots, and some were found wanting. Grissom, for example, apparently lost emotional control while waiting, floating in the middle of an ocean, to be picked up and blew his capsule's hatch prematurely, sinking the capsule and losing all of the valuable information recorded inside. Among themselves, the other six pilots believe he panicked and exhibited an alarming lack of the right stuff. Carpenter, who considered his orbital flight a great success, was considered less than successful by the others because he immersed himself in the in-flight science experiments assigned by NASA, at the expense of operational efficiency. Cooper probably exhibited the most impressive demonstration of the right stuff by actually falling asleep atop the rocket before his liftoff.

The unprecedented hero-worship that the Mercury astronauts inspired surprised no one so much as the astronauts themselves. Until their first meeting with the press, no one suspected the level of hysteria their existence would produce. They were great heroes before they donned a space suit or put a foot inside a capsule, worshiped for offering themselves up as sacrifices to the space race. Wolfe traces this phenomenon to an ancient element of warfare, the single-combat warrior. Hero-worship of the single-combat warrior was common in the pre-Christian world and the Middle Ages. Single-combat warfare pits each army's fiercest and most talented warrior against the other in lieu of a full flight between the entire armies. Sometimes this one-on-one fight settled the affair, with no full-scale fight taking place, and sometimes the result of the single combat was taken as an omen of what was to come, as an indication of which side was God's chosen in the fight. These single-combat warriors were treated as national heroes before they went into battle, much as the astronauts were treated as heroes before they were launched into space. According to Wolfe, the astronauts were the Cold War's single-combat warriors, offering to sit on top of the rockets to keep the Soviets from domination of the heavens.

Wolfe's distinctive style and narrative voice permeate *The Right Stuff*, setting a tone of high energy, enthusiasm, and humor. His use of exclamation points, italics, alliteration, and repetitive terms gives an almost cartoonlike feel to the narrative. This tone effectively offsets the bland, wholesome image of the astronauts promulgated by the press and NASA officials. This book provides one of the first glimpses behind the official propaganda of the space program and offers a fascinating insight into the history, technology, and personalities of one of the United States' most remarkable and ambitious enterprises.

Mary Virginia Davis

Further Reading

Blom, Mattias Bolkéus. "Reclaiming the Moral High Ground: Frontiers Old and New in Tom Wolfe's *The Right Stuff*." In *Stories of Old: The Imagined West and the Crisis of Historical Symbology in the 1970's*. Uppsala, Sweden: Uppsala University Library, 1999. Examines how Wolfe and other authors in the 1970's depicted the American frontier and the West through works that included atypical "frontier" tales.

McKeen, William. *Tom Wolfe*. New York: Twayne, 1995. Overview of Wolfe's life and career, with discussions of his journalism and his novels, including *The Right Stuff*. McKeen considers Wolfe the "great emancipator of journalism," the person who elevated journalism to the artistic level of the novel.

Ragen, Brian Abel. *Tom Wolfe: A Critical Companion*. Westport, Conn.: Greenwood Press, 2002. A compendium on Wolfe's life, assessing his place in contemporary literature and analyzing individual works. Chapter 6 is devoted to *The Right Stuff*.

Stokes, Lisa. "Tom Wolfe's Narratives as Stories of Growth." *Journal of American Culture* 14, no. 3 (1991): 19-24. Focuses on Wolfe's distinctive narrative voice and the relationship he establishes between his characters and narrator.

Stull, James N. "The Cultural Gamesmanship of Tom Wolfe." *Journal of American Culture* 14, no. 3 (1991): 25-30. Discusses Wolfe's use of arcane subcultures in his work and his exploration of status within these cultures, including the fraternity of pilots in *The Right Stuff*.

Weingarten, Marc. *The Gang That Wouldn't Write Straight: Wolfe, Thompson, Didion, and the New Journalism Revolution*. New York: Crown, 2005. Chronicles the rise of the New Journalism in the 1960's and 1970's, discussing the innovative writings of Wolfe, Hunter S. Thompson, Joan Didion, Normal Mailer, Truman Capote, and others.

Wolfe, Tom. "Literary Techniques of the Last Quarter of the Twentieth Century." In *The Writer's Craft: Hopwood Lectures, 1965-81*, edited by Robert A. Martin. Ann Arbor: University of Michigan Press, 1982. Discusses Wolfe's philosophy of writing and literature, which stresses the importance of reporting as a literary technique.

_____. "The *Rolling Stone* Interview: Tom Wolfe." In *Conversations with Tom Wolfe*, edited by Dorothy Scura. Jackson: University Press of Mississippi, 1990. Discusses the origins of *The Right Stuff*, revealing which astronauts agreed to be interviewed and how Wolfe came to discover the reality behind the hype. This book contains other informative interviews about *The Right Stuff*.

Right You Are (If You Think So)

Author: Luigi Pirandello (1867-1936)
First produced: Così è (se vi pare), 1917; first published,
 1918 (English translation, 1922)
Type of work: Drama
Type of plot: Parable
Time of plot: Early twentieth century
Locale: A small Italian town, the capital of a province

Principal characters:
LAMBERTO LAUDISI, an observer of human nature
PONZA, secretary to the provincial councillor
SIGNORA FROLA, his mother-in-law
SIGNORA PONZA, his wife
COMMENDATORE AGAZZI, a provincial councillor
AMALIA, his wife
DINA, their daughter
THE PREFECT
CENTURI, a police commissioner

The Story:

There is much talk in the small capital of an Italian province about the peculiar family arrangements of old Signora Frola and her daughter, the wife of Ponza, a newly appointed secretary to Commendatore Agazzi, the provincial councillor. Why is Signora Frola living by herself in a fine apartment next door to the Agazzis and not with her daughter and her son-in-law? Why are Ponza and his wife living in fifth-floor tenement rooms on the edge of town? Why does Ponza visit the old lady every evening and sometimes during the day, but always by himself? Why does Signora Frola never visit her daughter, and why does her daughter, whom no one except Ponza ever sees, never visit her? Why will the old lady not even permit Signora Agazzi and her daughter to pay a social call?

While the enigma is being discussed by Agazzi, his family, and several visitors in the Agazzi parlor, Signora Frola comes in to apologize for having refused to admit the Agazzis when they came calling and also to explain why she lives apart from her daughter. She does not want to interfere, she says, in the home life of her daughter and Ponza. She lives by herself, it is true, but she is not unhappy about it; she keeps in contact with her daughter, although there are no face-to-face visits.

Just after Signora Frola leaves the gathering in the parlor, Ponza—a fierce, nervous, sinister-looking man—comes in to explain about his poor mother-in-law. The truth is that she is mad, he says. Her daughter has been dead for four years, and he married again two years later. He has prevailed upon his second wife to humor the old woman by carrying on shouted conversations with her from a fifth-floor balcony and writing notes to be let down in a basket from the balcony to the old woman on the ground.

No sooner has Ponza gone than Signora Frola returns. Although the company at first denies it, she knows what Ponza has been telling them. The sad truth, however, is that he is the

mad one. The real truth, which she wishes she did not have to tell, is that when he married her young and innocent daughter he so frightened her with his passionate attentions that she had to be put into an institution for a while. When she finally returned, Ponza himself was in such a nervous state that he could not be convinced that she was his wife; she was prevailed upon to pretend that she is a second wife taking the place of the one he lost.

Before long, a plot is hatched to have Signora Frola and Ponza confront each other in the presence of Agazzi and the others in order that the truth might be uncovered. From the beginning of the gossipy, inquisitorial discussion, Lamberto Laudisi, the brother-in-law of Agazzi, has maintained that the private domestic lives of the Ponzas and Signora Frola are their own affair and should remain so. They are harming no one, and they are not seeking anyone's aid; they should be left alone. Laudisi is overruled, however. Agazzi leaves and comes back shortly to get some papers that he purposely left in his study so that he might bring Ponza back with him to get them. As they come in, Ponza hears a piano in the next room playing a tune that had been a favorite of his wife, Lena. Signora Frola is playing the piano; when she stops, her voice can be heard through the doorway. She is discussing her daughter's cherished melody in such a way as to suggest that Lena is still alive. When she confronts Ponza a moment later in the study, he furiously insists that Lena is dead, that he is now married to Julia, and that the piano that Lena used to play was smashed to pieces long ago.

While Ponza is shouting at her in a frenzy, Signora Frola occasionally glances about at the others in the room as if to call attention to his piteous state and to her forbearance in humoring him. After bursting into tears, Ponza suddenly orders her out of the room, and she soon leaves, also sobbing. When she has gone, Ponza immediately grows calm again and explains the reason for his actions. The old woman, he says, is so convinced of his madness that he has to pretend to be mad. Now he must go and see her. Laudisi, who had earlier insisted that truth is a relative thing and that what is one person's truth is not necessarily another's, laughs at the confusion of the Agazzis and their visitors. Now, he mocks, they have the truth they wanted.

Still the puzzle remains: Who is telling the truth and who is lying, either knowingly or unknowingly? Earlier, someone had suggested that documents, such as a marriage certificate for the second marriage or the letters that the second—or first—Signora Ponza wrote to the old woman, might be secured to prove who is right. One of those interested, Commissioner Centuri, arrives with some information that he has uncovered that might yet clear up the puzzle, but the information turns out to be as inconclusive as that already at hand.

A chance remark that Signora Ponza might as well be in another world, since no one has ever seen her, makes Laudisi wonder whether there really is a Signora Ponza. It is then suggested that Ponza go and get his wife so that she might be seen by everybody, to prove that she exists, and that she be questioned by the prefect in the presence of everyone so that the truth might be generally known. Ponza leaves after he has been assured that his wife and his mother-in-law will not be compelled to face each other. In his absence, the old woman returns to say that, since she cannot live her own life in peace, she will leave town and not come back. To pacify her, the prefect pretends to believe her version of the truth, although he earlier said he believed Ponza's. When Ponza returns with a heavily veiled woman dressed as if she were in deep mourning, he is shocked and angry to see his mother-in-law there, given that he had been assured that she would not be present. Signora Ponza, to quiet the clamor, asks Ponza to take the old woman away. Ponza and his mother-in-law go out weeping and with their arms about each other's waists.

Now the truth will finally come out: Signora Ponza will tell the entire group the whole truth. For the final time, however, the decision is left to each of her hearers. She is, it seems, the daughter of Signora Frola; she is also the second wife of Ponza; and, for herself, she is nobody. When the prefect insists that she must be one or the other of the two women, she answers that she is the person she is believed to be. Hearing that reply, Laudisi, saying that everybody now knows the truth, bursts out laughing.

Critical Evaluation:

Right You Are (If You Think So), which has been given varied English titles, may be Luigi Pirandello's most extreme statement on one of his favorite themes: the relativity of truth. Laudisi, who mocks the townspeople's determination

to pry out the secret of Signora Frola and the Ponzas, and who several times tries in vain to stop them, serves as the author's spokesman and the explicator of his theme. Despite the philosophical nature of the theme, the drama is an eminently actable one.

Pirandello sets up a situation in which the truth, as people are accustomed to verifying it, cannot be determined because of the inability to establish a single truth for all. An earthquake has destroyed the village from which the Ponza-Frola family came, dispersed or killed most of its inhabitants, and destroyed the official birth and death records. The author further indicates that even if factual evidence such as documents were to be found, a single truth acceptable to all could not be found because the documents would be interpreted differently by the various parties. This point, the theme of the play, is shown through the manner in which truth is perceived by various groups and characters within the play.

The first group consists of the townspeople (the Agazzi family and their friends). To them, truth is specific and concrete. It represents what one can see and feel, a decidedly empirical approach to reality. They assume that reality appears the same to all. It never occurs to them that they cannot find the truth because reality may appear differently to different people at different times. Thus they vacillate from belief in Ponza's version of the truth to belief in Signora Frola's version, depending on who is telling the tale.

For Ponza and Frola, truth is the illusion they have created in order to permit themselves to live. They have suffered a misfortune (exactly what it is, is never made clear), but they have created a truth that permits them to overcome their individual sorrow and continue to live. Their truth is based on love and consideration for each other. For this reason, Signora Ponza can state at the end of the play that she is "the daughter of Signora Frola . . . and the second wife of Signor Ponza." When the townspeople insist that she must be one or the other, she replies that she is "whom you believe me to be."

For Laudisi, truth is relative. He points out that one can never really know the truth about others, because each person perceives reality according to his or her own point of view. People perceive themselves in one way, but others perceive them differently. Which view is correct? Laudisi would suggest that all views are correct. Although the townspeople insist on a single reality that is the same for all, the mocking laughter of Laudisi that closes each act of the play would seem to indicate that finding the truth is impossible.

Pirandello called this play a parable, presumably about how one must respect the truths of others. When one person attempts to force other people to face "reality"—that is, his or her version of the truth—there is a danger of upsetting the delicate balance others have achieved in order to make their existence viable. Pirandello also suggests that one person's version of the truth is in no way more reliable or verifiable than anyone else's version.

Further Reading

Bassanese, Fiora A. *Understanding Luigi Pirandello*. Columbia: University of South Carolina Press, 1997. Offers an introduction to Pirandello's work, focusing largely on his thought and the relationship of his life to his work. Includes discussion of *Right You Are (If You Think So)*.

Bloom, Harold, ed. *Luigi Pirandello*. Philadelphia: Chelsea House, 2003. Collection of critical essays on Pirandello's work covers various topics, including analysis of *Right You Are (If You Think So)*.

Büdel, Oscar. *Pirandello*. New York: Hillary House, 1966. Presents an overview of the dramatist's achievements, organized thematically. Discusses *Right You Are (If You Think So)* as an example of Pirandello's extreme relativism and his use of humor to highlight the absurd plight of humanity.

Mariani, Umberto. "*Right You Are, If You Think You Are*: The Reality of Appearances." In *Living Masks: The Achievement of Pirandello*. Toronto: University of Toronto Press, 2008. Chapter examining *Right You Are (If You Think So)* is part of a larger work that focuses on the fundamental themes of Pirandello's plays and the aesthetic, technical, and critical problems associated with understanding and producing them.

Matthaei, Renate. *Luigi Pirandello*. Translated by Simon Young and Erika Young. New York: Frederick Ungar, 1973. Critical study of Pirandello's major plays examines *Right You Are (If You Think So)* as a social satire and reviews its critical reception in Europe and the United States.

Oliver, Roger W. *Dreams of Passion: The Theater of Luigi Pirandello*. New York: New York University Press, 1979. Reads *Right You Are (If You Think So)* and other Pirandello plays in light of the theory of the theater outlined in the playwright's essay *L'umorismo* (1908; *On Humour*, 1974).

Ragusa, Olga. *Luigi Pirandello: An Approach to His Theater*. Edinburgh: Edinburgh University Press, 1980. Shows how Pirandello's works illuminate the dramatist's vision of humankind and humanity's place in the world. Discusses *Right You Are (If You Think So)* as one of a group of plays published between 1916 and 1921 that share certain dramaturgic and thematic qualities.

Vittorini, Domenico. *The Drama of Luigi Pirandello*. 2d ed. New York: Russell & Russell, 1969. Examines Pirandello's works in light of the tradition of Italian theater. Asserts that the central idea of *Right You Are (If You Think So)* is that human beings are essentially subjective, and true social harmony can be achieved only if people accept others' points of view as being equally as valid as their own.

Rights of Man

Author: Thomas Paine (1737-1809)
First published: 1791, part 1; 1792, part 2
Type of work: Political philosophy

Thomas Paine, best known for his works *Common Sense* (1776) and *The American Crisis* (1776-1783), turns his attention to the French Revolution in *Rights of Man*. The book was written during a two-year period, during which Paine participated in the revolution as a member of the French National Assembly. *Rights of Man* comprises several books that transcend the revolution by examining the nature of human rights and the potential for nations to secure peace through the adoption of governments based on these rights. These discussions make the book an object of continuing interest.

Rights of Man is divided into two parts. Part 1 is chiefly a reply to an attack on the French Revolution made by British politician Edmund Burke in his work *Reflections on the Revolution in France* (1790). Part 2 presents a discussion of the principles of government, advocating the constitutional republic that the French Revolution had sought to establish.

Part 1, dedicated to U.S. president George Washington, presents a main essay after a brief preface. In the essay, Paine points out a number of errors made by Burke about the French Revolution. Paine's argument is somewhat disjointed, as he moves from point to point, replying to different parts of Burke's essay. Paine primarily describes the consequences of his fundamental disagreement with Burke on the origin of the English monarchy. Burke claims that England's Glorious

Revolution of 1688 bound future generations to obeying the hereditary monarchs that follow. Paine replies by arguing that the English monarchy began with the imposition of the monarchy by William the Conqueror in 1066, and that the decisions of previous generations cannot bind those that follow any more than the dead can control the actions of the living.

Although Burke focuses on the revolt against King Louis XVI, Paine argues that the French Revolution is against the despotism of the hereditary monarchy of the French government, not any particular monarch. Burke's error, Paine explains, leads Burke to ignore events like the fall of the Bastille, the infamous prison in Paris, and to exaggerate the violence accompanying the expedition to Versailles to force the king to Paris, events Paine details to claim that the revolution has, in fact, shown restraint in its use of force (later events of the revolution, such as the Terror, suggest Burke may have had a better sense of where the revolution was going).

Paine replies with what he argues are Burke's random observations on government, referring to concepts more systematically described in part 2. For example, Paine's concept of natural rights led to the formation of civil rights, which are limited to those natural rights one must exchange to achieve some goal by living with others. Paine concludes that civil governments are formed by making contracts between individuals, not governments, placing him outside the traditional thought of John Locke.

Paine's central point is that the French Revolution emerged from reason rather than force, and that reason has guided the principles of the new government. Paine includes as reasonable the French National Assembly's "Declaration of the Rights of Man and of the Citizen" (1789), noting that its first three principles are those of the revolution. These three principles are as follows: people are born free and equal, the end of political associations is to preserve rights, and the nation is the source of sovereignty and political authority. In this way, Paine argues the French system is in greater harmony with the principles of reason rather than with conquest. This argument is followed by a brief chapter on miscellaneous points of disagreement with Burke.

Paine's concluding chapter in part 1 summarizes his position in stark terms. He argues that the government of France had been founded on election and representation and is, therefore, through reason, accepted by its citizens. He also argues that the government of England, founded on hereditary succession, is a government that could only be accepted through ignorance. With remarkable foresight, Paine ends by predicting that if all nations controlled by hereditary monarchs would change their governments, those governments would no longer be driven by an excessive need for money.

This change would abolish war and establish a European congress, not unlike modern international organizations such as the United Nations.

Part 2 of *Rights of Man* was dedicated to Lafayette, who also had served in the National Assembly of France. After a brief preface, Paine begins with an introduction that describes the American Revolution as having been based on the principles of society and on human nature, both of which existed before any form of government. Paine writes that

> The mutual dependence and reciprocal interest which man has upon man, and all the parts of civilized community upon each other, create that great chain of connection which holds it together. The landholder, the farmer, the manufacturer, the merchant, the tradesman, and every occupation, prospers by the aid which each receives from the other, and from the whole. Common interest regulates their concerns, and forms their law; and the laws which common usage ordains, have a greater influence than the laws of government. In fine, society performs for itself almost everything which is ascribed to government.

Government becomes necessary only when individuals cannot satisfy all of their own wants: "No one man is capable, without the aid of society, of supplying his own wants, and those wants, acting upon every individual, impel the whole of them into society." Indeed, he continues, "Government is no farther necessary than to supply the few cases to which society and civilization are not conveniently competent." Furthermore, if a government seeks to exist only for itself and its own benefit, Paine argues, then that government becomes an imposition, often through excessive and unequal taxation.

Paine then draws a contrast been the old and new systems of government. The old system is characterized by hereditary monarchy, which bases its power on self-aggrandizement and relies on war to survive. The new system is characterized by representation and bases its power on the universal benefit of all. Given these systems, it is no wonder the new system rejects the old as an imposition upon humanity with no legitimate source of power. Furthermore, the old system is inadequate to meet the purposes for which government is created by increasing, not eliminating, conflict and instability. From this Paine argues representative governments are the most compatible with republics.

This leads Paine back to his argument on constitutionalism in part 1: People use their sovereignty to write constitutions to create and restrain governments. As he discusses some of the elements of a good constitution, however, Paine's weaknesses as a constitution-writer begin to show. For example, he advocates for a single, rather than bicameral, legislature, but ends up having to divide his legislature to preserve differences.

With these elements in place, Paine proceeds to the most ambitious part of his work: a description of how England can escape both war and the consequences of poverty through the new system of politics. By ending hereditary monarchies, the new system of government, with laws that end the surplus of money gathered by the government through unnecessarily large taxes, would reduce the level of conflict with other nations. Further, any surplus could be used to provide for the support of the poor and encourage the education of children. At the same time, this tax surplus would be used to care for the elderly and provide new employment.

Many of the arguments made by Paine in *Rights of Man* continue to resonate in politics. For example, Paine's argument that representative, democratic republics are less likely to engage in war is a widely debated concept in foreign policy circles and served as a key concept in the foreign policy of U.S. president George W. Bush. The desirability of what is today called a welfare state in Paine's concluding chapter continues to divide the spectrum of American politics. Finally, Paine's anticipation of international organizations dedicated to human rights and to ending conflict gives *Rights of Man* a contemporary importance.

David Smailes

Further Reading

Ayer, A. J. *Thomas Paine*. Chicago: University of Chicago Press, 1988. Ayer's work is a short, but valuable, resource for understanding Paine's thought. Gives both a historical context and a philosophical analysis of each of Paine's major works.

Conway, Moncure Daniel. *The Life of Thomas Paine*. 1892. Reprint. 2 vols. New York: Routledge/Thoemmes Press, 1996. The classic biography of Paine's life that remains one of the most complete accounts. An excellent resource for major events in Paine's career.

Hitchens, Christopher. *Thomas Paine's "Rights of Man": A Biography*. New York: Atlantic Monthly Press, 2006. Hitchens provides a general description of Paine's life and, from a contemporary political viewpoint, a lucid discussion of the main points in *Rights of Man*.

Kates, Gary. "From Liberalism to Radicalism: Tom Paine's *Rights of Man*." *Journal of the History of Ideas* 50, no. 4 (October-December, 1989): 569-587. Kates makes a strong case that Paine's ideas changed in *Rights of Man* between the more traditional liberal politics of part 1 and a more radical politics in part 2.

Keane, John. *Tom Paine: A Political Life*. 1995. New ed. New York: Grove Press, 2003. Keane's comprehensive biography of Paine pays particular attention to Paine's essays. A good beginning work for students unfamiliar with Paine's politics.

Walker, Thomas. "The Forgotten Prophet: Tom Paine's Cosmopolitanism and International Relations." *International Studies Quarterly* 44, no. 1 (March, 2000): 51-72. An excellent, if somewhat academic, description of Paine's concept of international peace based on the development of democratic republics.

The Rime of the Ancient Mariner

Author: Samuel Taylor Coleridge (1772-1834)
First published: 1798
Type of work: Poetry
Type of plot: Allegory
Time of plot: Late medieval period
Locale: High seas

Principal characters:
THE ANCIENT MARINER
A HERMIT
A WEDDING GUEST

The Poem:

Three young gallants on their way to a wedding are stopped by an old gray-headed sailor who detains one of them. The ancient Mariner holds with his gaze a young man whose next of kin is being married in the church nearby and forces him to listen, against his will, to the old seaman's tale. The ancient Mariner tells how his ship left the home port and sailed southward to the equator. In a storm the vessel was blown to polar regions of snow and ice. When an albatross flew out of the frozen silence, the crew hailed it as a good omen. The sailors made a pet of the albatross and regarded it as a fellow creature. One day the ancient Mariner killed the bird with his crossbow. The superstitious sailors believed bad luck would follow.

Fair winds blew the ship northward until it reached the equator, where it was suddenly becalmed and lay for days without moving. The thirsty seamen blamed the ancient Mariner and hung the dead albatross about his neck as a sign of his guilt.

In the distance a ship appeared, a skeleton ship that moved on the still sea where no wind blew. On its deck Death and Life-in-Death were casting dice for the crew and the ancient Mariner. As a result of the cast, Death won the two hundred crew members, who dropped dead one by one. As the soul of each dead sailor rushed by, the ancient Mariner was reminded of the sound of the rushing bolt of his crossbow when he shot the albatross. Life-in-Death won the ancient Mariner, who lived on to expiate his sins. Furthermore, the curse lived on in the eyes of the men who died accusing him. One night the ancient Mariner, observing the beauty of the water snakes around the ship, blessed these creatures in his heart. The spell was broken. The albatross fell from his neck into the sea.

At last the ancient Mariner was able to sleep. Rain fell to quench his thirst. The warped vessel began to move, and the bodies of the dead crew rose to resume their regular duties as the ship sailed quietly on, moved by a spirit toward the South Pole. The ancient Mariner fell into a trance. He awoke to behold his own country, the very port from which he set sail. Then the angelic spirits left the dead bodies of the crew and appeared in their own forms of light. Meanwhile, the pilot on the beach saw the lights, and he rowed out with his son and a holy Hermit to bring the ship in to harbor. Suddenly the ship sank, but the pilot pulled the ancient Mariner into his boat. Once ashore, the old man asked the Hermit to hear his confession and give him penance. The ancient Mariner tells the Wedding Guest that at times since that moment, the agony of the seaman's guilt returns and he has to tell the story of his voyage to one who must be taught love and reverence for all things God made and loved. The merry din of the wedding ceases, and the Wedding Guest returns home, a sadder and a wiser man.

Critical Evaluation:

Perhaps what is most strange about *The Rime of the Ancient Mariner* is not its uniqueness, which makes it seem strange, but its transparency. It is about what it says it is about. An epigraph, marginal glosses, and a moral at the end state the poem's ideas so clearly that one may try to second-

guess them. A reader may also argue that the poem succeeds in its stated aim—to teach lessons of the spirits, of guilt, of expiation, and of love for all of God's creations—and that the poem's oddity is instrumental in this success. Without the novelty of the tale, the ancient and simple lessons would be easier to ignore.

The epigraph by Thomas Burnet states that "[*f*]*acile credo*" (I believe with ease, or I may easily believe) there are many invisible beings in the universe. Burnet next points out that, while it is also easy to get bogged down in questions regarding such creatures, and therefore, implicitly, create an attitude of cynical skepticism, it is spiritually enriching to contemplate the invisible realm and thereby to imagine a greater and better world. Such thought gives one better perspective on the trivial concerns of daily life. Such contemplation, Burnet concludes, is not intended to lead away from truth. This epigraph may be interpreted, in the context of the poem, to state the following ideas: First, there is a spiritual realm, and its mysteries are to be respected although not fully understood. The Mariner makes the mistake of showing contempt for the spiritual world by killing what seems to be one of its representatives. Second, spiritual mysteries are wonderful, miraculous, and terrible. They can be described, but they are best understood emotionally rather than through analysis. When the Mariner "blessed them unaware" (part 4, line 285), his spiritual rebirth begins. Third, the marvels of the invisible can lead one to greater understanding. This is clear in the Mariner's case. Fourth, the marvels of the spiritual world are not intended to lead one away from truth. Perhaps to Burnet, truth meant doctrinal orthodoxy. To the Mariner, truth may mean, as Burnet says, avoiding extremes and telling day from night. In the Mariner's case, this means putting his hard-won knowledge to use in the world. He tells others what he learned. Perhaps to Coleridge, truth was the practice of his art, the creation of *The Rime of the Ancient Mariner*.

The Rime of the Ancient Mariner was published in the famous volume *Lyrical Ballads* (1798), a collaboration between Coleridge and William Wordsworth. The volume contains two kinds of poetry. In one type, as Coleridge would later write in chapter 14 of his *Biographia Literaria* (1817):

The incidents and agents were to be, in part at least, supernatural, and the excellence aimed at was to consist in the interesting of the affections by the dramatic truth of such emotions, as would naturally accompany such situations, supposing them real. . . . In this idea originated the plan of the *Lyrical Ballads*, in which it was agreed that my endeavors should be directed to persons and characters supernatural, or at least romantic; yet so as to transfer from our inward nature a human interest and a semblance of truth sufficient to procure for these shadows of imagination that willing suspension of disbelief which constitutes poetic faith. . . . With this view I wrote *The Ancient Mariner.*

Whether the faith be Christian, poetic, or pagan, *The Rime of the Ancient Mariner* is about, among other things, faith. For example, in part 1 of the poem, the albatross appears to guide, or seems to guide, the ship out of the ice, "As if it had been a Christian soul,/ We hailed it in God's name." A bird, after all, is not foreign to Christian symbolism. Coleridge hedges somewhat ("as if" and "supposing them real"), but this hedging is the test of faith. Readers may decide to take the poem literally, to accept it as a work of imagination that tells important spiritual truths, or to consider the poem simply a strange story of no consequence.

The quotation from Burnet (translated in most modern editions) should alert readers to the fact that Coleridge, who once planned to be a clergyman, is concerned in this poem with demonstrating the inadequacy of materialism and rationalism as interpretations of reality. Materialism is the belief that only matter and motion exist (as opposed to spiritual reality of any kind). Rationalism is the belief that reason is capable of comprehending the totality of nature. Although Coleridge was inconsistent as a philosopher, he regularly opposed both of these suppositions.

In a letter of December 31, 1796, for example, he opposed materialism and regarded himself as "a mere apparition—a naked Spirit!—And that Life is I myself I!" In January, 1798, he described himself as a committed defender of religion, regarding scientific discoveries of any kind as being important primarily for their theological revelations. In later years also, Coleridge would emerge as a significant religious teacher who always believed in a spiritual reality beyond the material one. *The Rime of the Ancient Mariner*, defying both reason and materialism, is something of a sermon on the sanctity of life, which in all its forms is a manifestation of the divine. It may be said that the poem argues, with perhaps deceptive simplicity and candor, that the laws that govern living things are not physical but moral and come from God.

Close reading of the poem can reveal how its spiritual themes, often discussed in reference to text not belonging to the poem, are developed. The poem's frame (the Mariner telling his story to the Wedding Guest), for example, may be examined in terms of Christian symbolism, the psychology of the reader (whose responses to the Mariner may be much like the guest's), and the creation of the willing suspension of disbelief. The Mariner's story follows a clear pattern of guilt, penance, expiation, and confession, and this pattern may be examined in terms of the flow of the narration and the uses of the irregular stanzas and of the glosses. Finally, what may be the poem's most memorable element—its descriptions of natural and supernatural phenomena—may be examined in terms of sheer poetic technique. In any case, *The Rime of the Ancient Mariner*'s uniqueness is indisputable, and its spiritual themes may be considered to be no less authentic for being stated clearly.

"Critical Evaluation" by Dennis R. Dean

Further Reading

Boulanger, James D., ed. *Twentieth Century Interpretations of "The Rime of the Ancient Mariner": A Collection of Critical Essays.* Englewood Cliffs, N.J.: Prentice-Hall, 1969. A useful collection of scholarly articles dealing with the poem, including an introduction that attempts to reconcile some of the differences of critical opinion.

Coleridge, Samuel Taylor. *The Annotated Ancient Mariner.* Edited by Martin Gardner. Illustrated by Gustave Doré. Cleveland, Ohio: World, 1967. Includes the last and the first versions of the poem, together with interpretive comments. Doré's illustrations remind readers how intensely visual the poem is.

_____. *"The Rime of the Ancient Mariner": Complete, Authoritative Texts of the 1798 and 1817 Versions with Biographical and Historical Contexts, Critical History, and Essays from Contemporary Critical Perspectives.* Edited by Paul H. Fry. Boston: Bedford/St. Martin's, 1999. In addition to the two versions of the poem, this volume contains six essays, five of which interpret the work from the perspectives of reader-response theory, Marxist, psychoanalytic, and deconstructionist criticism, and new historicism. The sixth essay suggests how these five approaches can be combined to offer another interpretation.

House, Humphry. *Coleridge: The Clark Lectures, 1951-52.* London: Hart-Davis, 1953. This book of fewer than 170 pages maintains its reputation as a sound introduction to the poet and his works. A thirty-page chapter on *The Rime of the Ancient Mariner* is sensible and straightforward.

Newlyn, Lucy, ed. *The Cambridge Companion to Coleridge.* New York: Cambridge University Press, 2002. Collection of essays discussing Coleridge's life and the genres, themes, and topics of his works. Chapter 3, "Slavery and Superstition in the Supernatural Poems" by Tim Fulford, includes analysis of *The Rime of the Ancient Mariner*; and other references to the poem are listed in the index.

Piper, H. W. *The Active Universe: Pantheism and the Concept of Imagination in the English Romantic Poets*. London: Athlone Press, 1962. Proposes the influence of various scientific and philosophical ideas upon Coleridge, with several chapters on the poet's intellectual development and one devoted entirely to *The Rime of the Ancient Mariner*.

Stevenson, Warren. A *Study of Coleridge's Three Great Poems—"Christabel," "Kubla Khan," and "The Rime of the Ancient Mariner."* Lewiston, N.Y.: Edwin Mellen Press, 2001. A revised and updated version of Stevenson's *Nimbus of Glory* (1983), including a new chapter entitled "The Case of the Missing Captain: Power Politics in *The Rime of the Ancient Mariner*." Stevenson also discusses the poem as "epic symbol" and assesses the influence of William Wordsworth's personality upon Coleridge's poetry.

The Ring and the Book

Author: Robert Browning (1812-1889)
First published: 1868-1869
Type of work: Poetry
Type of plot: Dramatic
Time of plot: Seventeenth century
Locale: Italy

Principal characters:
PIETRO COMPARINI, an aged Roman
VIOLANTE, Pietro's wife
POMPILIA, the Comparinis' adopted daughter
GUIDO FRANCESCHINI, Pompilia's husband
GIUSEPPE CAPONSACCHI, a priest

The Poem:

The first narrator in this series of dramatic monologues represents the voice of the poet himself. He relates how he found in a Florentine bookstall an old yellow book containing letters, accounts, and depositions relating to a 1698 Roman murder case. According to these documents, Count Guido Franceschini, descended from an ancient house of Aretine, married Pompilia Comparini, a beautiful teenaged Roman girl adopted at birth by an old couple, Pietro and Violante. Unhappy with her husband, the young wife fled back to Rome in the company of a young priest, Giuseppe Caponsacchi. Guido and four accomplices followed her, and on Christmas night Guido found his wife at her parents' home. He murdered the seventy-year-old couple and fatally wounded the seventeen-year-old Pompilia.

In a highly publicized, controversial month-long trial during which many testified on both sides, Guido and his friends were found guilty. They appealed to Pope Innocent XII, who upheld their conviction, and all five men were executed. Browning tells how he researched the case at the sites where it occurred. He discovered that the Italians were not interested in this bit of their own history, yet it came alive to him, and he subsequently wrote a work based on what he had learned. He compares the facts he found to bits of gold and his own imaginative powers to alloy that, mixed with the precious metal, "completes the incomplete" and enables the creation of a ring. This image is the source of Browning's title, *The Ring and the Book*.

The next narrator is an unnamed spokesperson for half of Rome, who recounts Pietro's and Violante's mutilated bodies being placed on exhibit in the church while Pompilia lies dying. This narrator describes the corpses with relish, and he disapproves of the couple's adoption of the low-born Pompilia, who was bought as an infant by Violante and passed off as her own offspring. He considers their murder as a rightful avengement of Guido's honor and compares Caponsacchi, Pompilia's protector, to a fox in the henhouse. He also draws a parallel between Caponsacchi and Lucifer, who tempted Eve to lure Adam to his downfall—just as the priest tempted Pompilia to lure Guido. In the narrator's eyes, Guido was cheated in his marriage because Pompilia's birth mother was a prostitute, rendering Pompilia ineligible to inherit the Comparini family fortunes. The narrator also hints that Pompilia's newborn son is Caponsacchi's. He scorns the involvement of the judiciary in the case, approving the "old way" of swift husbandly revenge upon wayward wives.

The next narrator is sympathetic to the murder victims, and he seeks to refute the previous narrator's condemnation. He agrees with his predecessor that the murders were caused by material greed, but he believes that the greed in question is that of Guido, who married Pompilia not only for her substantial dowry but also for her prospects of inheriting the Comparini riches. The narrator approves Violante's penitence in confessing that Pompilia was adopted, which resulted in a court's determining that Guido could keep her dowry but that Pompilia could not inherit the family fortunes. The decision caused Guido to feel robbed. He mistreated his wife, plotting to ruin her character and reputation by making false accusations against her and Caponsacchi and by forging letters from the illiterate Pompilia to her supposed lover. Guido also accused Pompilia of poisoning him. When Pompilia escaped to her parents' home, he hired four assassins to kill them all.

A lofty patrician next addresses the aristocrat-magistrate hearing the case, scorning the opinions of the rabble ventriloquized by the previous two narrators. The patrician sarcastically describes Violante's crime in adopting Pompilia as a craven way to ensure her and Pietro's financial future. He also blames Violante for secretly effecting the marriage between the thirteen-year-old Pompilia and the forty-six-year-old Guido in a conspiracy with the clergy. Because Guido is of noble blood, this narrator tends to side with him, and he also expresses biases against women, but he attempts to present all the facts and opinions of the case and then urges clemency for Guido.

Guido Franceschini himself speaks next, defending his actions. He lists the injustices he has suffered, denigrating Violante and Pietro as vulgar and grasping lowlifes. He does not admit to abusing Pompilia, only saying that the law requires wifely submission and that Pompilia should not expect love or romance. He declares that his wife is his to train or kill at his pleasure. Guido admits that he forged the love letters incriminating Pompilia and Caponsacchi, but he says the situation was all Pompilia's fault. He regrets being so lenient with her.

Guido feels entirely justified in his actions, characterizing himself as a martyr or victim and complaining that the humiliation he has borne has been worse than physical torture. Pompilia's child, he says, is Caponsacchi's, and he was only doing God's justice in killing the Comparinis, since it was Violante the "she-devil" who opened the door to all the troubles he experienced. He ends by saying that everyone other than himself has been lying; he has served the Church all his life and has done the court a favor by executing the law for them in killing his wife and her parents. He concludes by arguing that his life is useful to others, so it should not be taken.

Next to take the stand is Giuseppe Caponsacchi, the young priest who helped Pompilia escape from her husband. He is angry at being asked to relate the events of the case again, since, when he did so before, the court laughed at him and condemned him for meddling. He asks whether the court now recognizes the validity of "priestly interference" and says that, when he received the love letters from Pompilia, he

knew they were forged and refused them. One day, he received a genuine letter from Pompilia saying, in effect, "My husband hates me and his brother raped me. Take me to Rome, to my parents." He felt it was his duty to help her, so he agreed. The two travelers did not speak to each other on the road, but Guido overcame them and found the letters and stolen items he had planted on them. The two were imprisoned. Caponsacchi asks to see the dying Pompilia, affirms again that the letters were forged, and urges the court to deal with Guido.

Pompilia speaks. She is concerned about and grateful for her infant son, and she describes her life as a twelve-year-old bride, confused at her inability to please her husband. She tells of his cruel demands, his brother's debauchery, her maid's trickery, and of the archbishop's refusal to acquiesce to her pleas to be sent to a convent to escape them. She praises Caponsacchi for his kindness and bravery and consigns her soul to God.

Guido's lawyer, the procurator Dominus Hyacinthus de Archangelis, speaks next. He feels lucky to have gotten the case and says he will explain the murders, rather than denying that they took place or trying to pin Caponsacchi with the crimes. He claims that Guido's honor was besmirched, asserting that husbandly revenge is decent and proper. Even pagans killed adulteresses, the lawyer observes, and he compares Guido to the biblical Samson. Pompilia's parents were felons anyway, he says, while disposing of the various aggravations with which Guido has been charged. Archangelis concludes by saying that he is getting hungry and needs to finish up the case, which he rests on the cause of honor, asserting that the end justifies the means. He also pleads for Guido's four accomplices, because they are young and poor and only helped Guido out of friendship, as friends should do. These men have since admitted under torture that they meant to kill Guido for nonpayment of their assassins' fee. However, the lawyer says that Guido did not pay them because he did not want to sully his friends with filthy lucre.

Juris Doctor Johannes-Baptista Bottinius is supposedly a lawyer for the prosecution of Guido, but he expresses opinions that reveal his opposition to Pompilia and sympathy for the accused. He says Pompilia may have flirted, as women will, but at least she picked a well-born priest for her dalliance. He asserts that Pompilia wanted to get back at Guido by luring Caponsacchi, so she learned to read and write on the sly, pretending love for the priest so he would help her escape. Bottinius supposes that Pompilia kept Caponsacchi courageous with a few kisses and stole Guido's money because she needed it. What harm, he asks, if the priest fell in love and if the young bride lied and tricked her parents?

She should have trusted the angels, not the priest, whom Bottinius compares to Judas. Guido, he says, only came after his wife to persuade her to return. Meanwhile, Pompilia, feigning innocence, was wily in pretending death so she could tell her tale in court, and her child must be Caponsacchi's because she named it for him.

The pope issues a pronouncement. He condemns Guido, saying that Francheschini is as good as dead and needs to repent. He admits that he may be wrong, but asserts that God put him on Earth to judge, so any mistakes he makes are the fault of the Lord. The pope discourses on his burdens as a judge and characterizes Pompilia as pure and innocent.

The condemned Guido speaks again to the court, claiming that, if the pope were like Christ or Peter, he would pardon Guido. The accused man refuses to repent, despite the pope's declaration, asking what good it would do. Besides, he charges, the Church is corrupt. Personal pleasure and gain has always been the human creed, and Guido sees no reason to change that now. He again characterizes Pompilia's parents as fools and justifies his punishment of Pompilia by saying that she did not even pretend to respond to him.

The poet-narrator returns to sum up the case and conclude the tale. He notes that Pompilia died soon afterward, as did the pope himself. The fate of Pompilia's infant is unknown. The narrator quotes from the letter of a Roman observer, who described Guido's execution along with those of his accomplices, and who appears from his letter to have been jaded, refusing to assert that justice was served. Addressing the British public in presenting the finished "ring," the narrator comments that all human speech is flawed and that the truth is available only obliquely, through art.

"The Story" by Sally B. Palmer

Critical Evaluation:

The Ring and the Book reveals Robert Browning's deep perceptive and poetic powers at their greatest heights. Based on a murder trial that took place in the city of Florence in 1698, the poem attempts to probe the inner motivations of the people involved in this old, sordid tale of passion and crime. A series of dramatic characterizations and episodes carries readers to a magnificent conclusion. Pompilia and Caponsacchi are among Browning's most notable creations. Too long to be as widely read as Browning's briefer poems yet too masterful to be disregarded by any of his admirers, *The Ring and the Book* exhibits language of tremendous power.

Compared to William Shakespeare's greatest plays when it first appeared, *The Ring and the Book* put the final stamp of unqualified distinction on its author and confirmed his equal-

ity with Alfred, Lord Tennyson, the other giant of Victorian poetry. The Shakespearean comparison was a tribute to Browning's poetic range and to his capacity to dig deep into experience to raise up forms and people that were larger than life. John Keats thought Shakespeare divine because the bard could create both a depraved villain such as Iago and a virtuous heroine such as Imogen, each with equal dramatic power. Similarly, Browning was admired for the variety and complexity of his characters. In *Men and Women* (1855) Browning revealed his gift for penetrating character analysis in such brilliant dramatic monologues as "Fra Lippo Lippi" and "Andrea del Sarto." The joyous realism of Lippi—his relish for portraying things "just as they are"—contrasts sharply with the self-delusion of del Sarto, who betrays his talent and reputation for the sake of a worthless wife.

What Browning accomplished with individual monologues (his characteristic poetic form) became the basis for a cosmic view of human evil in *The Ring and the Book*. For four years, he worked on this ambitious project, and he published it at intervals from 1868 to 1869. The narrative poem consists of many long monologues, each expressing a different perspective upon the central action, Guido's murder of Pompilia and her parents. By reflecting each character in the thoughts of the others, Browning's monologues achieve dazzling effects in point of view and psychological revelation—despite the syntactical obscurity of much of the verse (Browning shares with the later Henry James a peculiar blend of impenetrable style and striking psychological insight).

The monologue form enables each character to speak his or her mind and to speculate on the thoughts and feelings of the others with a depth unavailable to the conventional drama. The effect evokes a juxtaposition of Shakespearean soliloquies—if such soliloquies could constitute a unified drama despite the absence of intervening dialogue and action. The analytical power of Browning's approach is reinforced by the variety of his characters. They are so divergent in temperament and nature that it is difficult to imagine them together in a conventional drama. The ruthless, sensual, and manic-depressive Guido alternates with the saintly but dangerously immature Pompilia; her venal and pathetic parents, petty in their thinking and vulnerable because of it; the worldly but impressionable priest, Caponsacchi; and the humanist pope. The pope must judge Guido and does so with a mixture of compassion and contempt that captures perfectly the realism and tough-minded spiritualism of the Renaissance Church.

The blend of people, values, and emotions that informs this poem is anticipated by the opening, in which the poet explains the title of his work. The "book" of the title is the Yellow Book, the old record of the story and trial that Browning found in a Florentine book stall. The "ring" is the result of mixing the raw gold of the Yellow Book with the alloy of Browning's art. In other words, the ring is the crafted result of the artist's sympathetic imagination—a power that penetrates the mysteries of experience with greater revelation than any other human effort. Browning's ring is also a symbol of the poem's circular reflection. It is a house of mirrors, in which the characters' several minds reflect on one another in the mind of a reader.

Browning's willingness to base a dramatic poem, full of what Matthew Arnold would have called high seriousness, on a sordid story of crime and mayhem stems largely from his conviction that anything representative of life as it truly is, is worthy of serious study. For Browning, the only absolute evil is the rejection of life. Anything that affirms life is finally good, even if human vileness is part of it. To recognize the existence of evil is not to condone it; Browning simply believed that an objective consideration of the vast range of evil in the world—from petty indifference to sadistic murder—only revealed ultimate moralities in bolder terms.

Elizabeth Barrett, Browning's wife, took issue with his insistence on the relevance of the sordid and the ugly to a moral art. She wanted him to omit his dramatic dialogues from the poem and speak only with his own voice. He insisted that his objective dramatizations, his dramatic monologues, were the best he had to give the world. He was right. Browning could put himself momentarily into someone else's psyche, and his ability to enter other people's minds enabled him to achieve states of perception beyond the mere self. What seemed an absence of identity or even of personal involvement on his part became finally a means to achieve a poetic understanding greater than that exemplified in the ardent subjectivity of his wife's poetry. Browning may have started off as an amoral dramatizer, but he ended as one of the major poet-teachers of his period.

The pope and his function in *The Ring and the Book* vindicate Browning's dramatic objectivity to his wife and all other Victorian critics. The pope is a spokesperson for Browning's hard-won ethical vision; he represents a projection of Browning's own power to sermonize and idealize in the very act of demonstrating the venality and terrifying corruptibility of the human soul. Browning, finally, is not a tragic writer. There is too much of a sometimes naïve robustness in him. Human flaws do not define his fate. On the contrary, Browning saw in the very imperfection of life the seeds of God's power. Browning, like John Milton, sought to justify the ways of God. People must strive to know all they can, as does

the pope in his soul-searching effort to comprehend Guido's crime, but the pope's limited understanding is part of God's design. In passing judgment on Guido, the pope realizes that his own moral vision is being tested and shaped: "All to the very end is trial in life." For some, this means anxiety and alienation. For Browning, it merely marks off the arena of human experience.

"Critical Evaluation" by Peter A. Brier

Further Reading

Ackerman, Michael. "Monstrous Men: Violence and Masculinity in Robert Browning's *The Ring and the Book*." In *Horrifying Sex: Essays on Sexual Difference in Gothic Literature*, edited by Ruth Bienstock Anolik. Jefferson, N.C.: McFarland, 2007. Discusses violence and male monsters in relationship to patriarchy, in a needed revision of the poem from the vantage of modern gender sensibilities.

Altick, Richard D., and James F. Loucks II. *Browning's Roman Murder Story: A Reading of "The Ring and the Book."* Chicago: University of Chicago Press, 1968. An intensive study of the work's artistry, as well as its treatment of religious themes, such as the infallibility of the pope.

Browning, Robert. *The Complete Works of Robert Browning, with Variant Readings and Annotations*. Edited by Roma King, Jr. Athens: Ohio University Press, 1985. Professor King's variorum edition contains extensive and invaluable notes.

_____. *Robert Browning's Poetry: Authoritative Texts, Criticism*. Selected and edited by James F. Loucks and Andrew M. Stauffer. 2d ed. New York: W. W. Norton, 2007. In addition to a selection of Browning's poetry, this volume contains essays about his work written by nineteenth and twentieth century poets, writers, and critics, including John Ruskin, Gerard Manley Hopkins, Thomas Carlyle, William Morris, and Oscar Wilde.

Hair, Donald S. "'For How Else Know We Save by Worth of Word?' *The Ring and the Book*." In *Robert Browning's Language*. Toronto, Ont.: University of Toronto Press, 1999. Examines the nature and use of words and syntax in Browning's poetry.

Hawlin, Stefan. *The Complete Critical Guide to Robert Browning*. New York: Routledge, 2002. This student sourcebook contains information about Browning's life and times, as well as discussion and criticism of his work. The chapter on *The Ring and the Book* focuses on moral considerations, Pompilia, and Caponsacchi.

Kennedy, Richard S., and Donald S. Hair. *The Dramatic Imagination of Robert Browning: A Literary Life*. Columbia: University of Missouri Press, 2007. A literary biography, recounting the events of Browning's life, placing it within the context of its times, and offering critical commentary on his poetry. Chapter 29, "Fathers, Sons, Books," includes information about *The Ring and the Book*.

King, Roma, Jr. *The Focusing Artifice: The Poetry of Robert Browning*. Athens: Ohio University Press, 1968. Traces the development of Browning's art, focusing on the aesthetic devices Browning uses to examine morality and values.

Rigg, Patricia Diane. *Robert Browning's Romantic Irony in "The Ring and the Book."* Madison, N.J.: Fairleigh Dickinson University Press, 1999. Demonstrates how Browning uses "romantic irony" to simultaneously subvert and reveal the truth.

Sassian, David. "The Ritual in 'The Novel in *The Ring and the Book*': Browning, Henry James, Eric Gans." *Victorian Poetry* 46, no. 3 (Fall, 2008): 233-247. Discusses consecration, ring symbolism, dramatic conventions, and violence in the poem.

Struve, Laua. "'This Is No Way to Tell a Story': Robert Browning's Attack on the Law in *The Ring and the Book*." *Law and Literature* 20, no. 3 (Fall, 2008): 423-443. Examines Browning's technique of multiple narration in relationship to the legal system as construed by Jeremy Bentham.

Sullivan, Mary Rose. *Browning's Voices in "The Ring and the Book": A Study of Method and Meaning*. Toronto, Ont.: University of Toronto Press, 1969. Examines how Browning uses narrative to create meaning.

Thompson, N. S. "Robert Browning's *The Ring and the Book*." In *British Writers: Classics*. Vol. 2. Edited by Jay Parini. New York: Scribner's, 2004. A chapter summarizing Browning's poem and its themes.

Tucker, Herbert. *Epic: Britain's Heroic Muse, 1790-1910*. New York: Oxford University Press, 2008. Analyzes Browning's work as an epic, in context with other nineteenth century epic poems.

Rip Van Winkle

Author: Washington Irving (1783-1859)
First published: 1819-1820
Type of work: Short fiction
Type of plot: Tall tale
Time of plot: Eighteenth century
Locale: New York State

Principal characters:
RIP VAN WINKLE, a henpecked husband
DAME VAN WINKLE, his wife

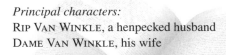

The Story:

Along the reaches of the Hudson River, not far from the Catskill Mountains, there is a small, Dutch town. The mountains overshadow the town, and there are times when the good Dutch burghers can see a hood of clouds hanging over the crests of the hills. In this small town lives a man named Rip Van Winkle. He is beloved by all his neighbors, by children, and by animals, but his life at home is made miserable by his shrewish wife. Though he is willing to help anyone else at any odd job that might be necessary, he is incapable of keeping his own house and farm in repair. He is descended from an old and good Dutch family, but he has none of the fine Dutch traits of thrift and energy.

Rip spends a great deal of his time at the village inn, under the sign of King George III, until his wife chases him from there. When this happens, he takes his gun and his dog, Wolf, and heads for the hills. Wolf is as happy as Rip is to get away from home. When Dame Van Winkle berates the two of them, Rip raises his eyes silently to heaven, but Wolf tucks his tail between his legs and slinks out of the house.

One fine day in autumn, Rip and Wolf walk high into the Catskills while hunting squirrels. As evening comes on, the two sit down to rest before heading for home. After they rise again and start down the mountainside, Rip hears his name called. A short, square little man with a grizzled beard is calling to Rip, asking him to help carry a keg of liquor. The little man is dressed in antique Dutch clothes. Although he accepts Rip's help in carrying the keg, he carries on no conversation. As they ascend the mountain, Rip hears noises that sound like claps of thunder. When they reach a sort of natural amphitheater near the top, Rip sees a band of little men, dressed and bearded like his companion, playing ninepins. One stout old gentleman, who seems to be the leader, wears a laced doublet and a high-crowned hat with a feather.

The little men are no more companionable than the first one has been, and Rip feels somewhat depressed. Because they seem to enjoy the liquor from the keg, Rip tastes it a few times while they are absorbed in their game. Then he falls into a deep sleep.

On waking, Rip looks in vain for the stout old gentleman and his companions. When he reaches for his gun, he finds that it is rusted. His dog does not answer his call. He tries to find the amphitheater where the little men were playing, but the way is blocked by a rushing stream.

The people Rip sees as he walks into town are all strangers to him. After many of them stroke their chins upon looking at him, Rip unconsciously strokes his own and finds that his beard has grown a foot long. The town itself looks different. At first, Rip thinks that the liquor from the keg has addled his head, for he has a hard time finding his own house. When he does locate it at last, he finds it in a state of decay. Even the sign over the inn has been changed to one carrying the name of General Washington. The men who are gathered under the sign talk gibberish to him, and they accuse him of trying to stir up trouble by coming armed to an election. When he is finally able to inquire into the whereabouts of his old friends, he is told that men by those names have moved away or have been dead for twenty years.

Finally, an eager young woman pushes through the crowd to look at Rip. Her voice starts a train of thought, and he asks her who she is and who her father is. When she claims to be Rip Van Winkle's daughter Judith, Rip asks after her mother. When Judith tells him that her mother died after breaking a blood vessel in a fit of anger at a Yankee peddler, Rip identifies himself as Judith's father.

Although an old woman claims that she recognizes him, the men at the inn only winked at his story until an old man, a descendant of the village historian, vouches for Rip's tale. He assures the men that he has it as a fact from his historian ancestor that Hendrick Hudson and his crew come to the mountains every twenty years to visit the scene of their exploits, and that the old historian has seen the crew in antique Dutch garb playing at ninepins, just as Rip has related.

Rip spends the rest of his life happily telling his story at the inn until everyone knows it by heart. Ever afterward, when the inhabitants of the village hear thunder in the Catskills, they say that Hendrick Hudson and his crew are playing ninepins, and many a henpecked husband wishes in vain for a drink of Rip Van Winkle's quieting brew.

Critical Evaluation:

As children, many readers have been told some version of the story of Rip Van Winkle before they ever get around to reading Washington Irving's tale. Moreover, a number of theatrical adaptations have made the basic elements of the story familiar to many who have never read it. As a consequence, the story comes across as one without an author, a product of the folk imagination, and there is much in the genesis of the tale that reinforces this impression. In these circumstances, it is altogether too easy to overlook the art involved in Irving's telling of his tale, especially given that it would be difficult to find anywhere in American literature a more compelling example of an art that conceals art.

"Rip Van Winkle" first appeared in Irving's collection *The Sketch Book of Geoffrey Crayon, Gent.* (1819-1820). Much of the content of this book, the first by an American to enjoy a transatlantic reputation, focuses on subject matter derived from Irving's stay in England, to which he had sailed in 1815. It expresses an attitude toward England, announced as that of Geoffrey Crayon, Irving's persona, that is often critical and sometimes melancholy. In this context, the American qualities of "Rip Van Winkle," set in the time of the revolution that established the independent United States of America where previously there had been only British colonies, make themselves emphatically felt.

Irving places the tale in a second context as well. The story was found, we are told, among the papers of Diedrich Knickerbocker. Knickerbocker is, of course, one of Irving's earlier creations, the fictional author of Diedrich Knickerbocker's *A History of New York from the Beginning of the World to the End of the Dutch Dynasties* (1809), Irving's first masterpiece. How the papers of Diedrich Knickerbocker came into the possession of Geoffrey Crayon is never explained. Two personae, Geoffrey Crayon and Diedrich Knickerbocker, separate Irving, the actual author, from the work; the separation encourages in the reader an air of ironic detachment toward the story Irving tells. It may also constitute a sort of authorial self-effacement, a disappearance of the author behind his work. It is ironic that this success results in a diminished sense of the author's accomplishment.

The actual source of the story is a German folktale; it is Irving's genius that resets the story in America and in history. The twenty years that Rip sleeps are not merely an arbitrary period, suggesting simply a long time, as is common in folktales. Rather, they are the twenty years during which the American nation was born in revolution. Rip himself is also historically situated. At the beginning of the story, he is a loyal subject of England's King George III. As his name suggests, however, he is descended from the Dutch settlers who preceded the English in the area that became New York. Before that, the Dutch the area was inhabited by American Indians. They are present in the story only as figures in the tales Rip tells to frighten and amuse the children of the village. History has pushed them to the margins, to dwell with the witches and ghosts who otherwise populate Rip's yarns, yet they remain in memory and imagination.

Irving thus suggests a multiplicity of historical layers beyond the surface of his tale. Even the most fantastic element, the apparition of Hendrick Hudson and his crew playing at ninepins, recalls the importance of Dutch exploration in American history. The background to the dynamic of history is provided by the Catskills, emblematic on this occasion of the American landscape, the theater in which the acts of the historical drama are played out. The latest (and not the last) act of this drama is the age to which Rip awakens. His awakening leads swiftly to a crisis of identity: He no longer knows who he is.

In his confusion, as he begs someone to identify him to himself, Rip articulates a version of one of the central questions of classic American literature: What are these new beings called Americans? Do they represent a new beginning in human history? Or is the change from British colonist to American citizen as superficial as the coat of paint that transforms the George III inn into the George Washington inn? In fusing the materials of a German folktale with the stuff of American history, Irving encourages in his readers an ironic reflection on just such questions.

Part of the art of this story, then, rests in the mastery of touch that allows Irving to bring into play such complexities of time and place while maintaining without rupture a surface of unruffled urbanity and humor. A mastery of narrative craft is at work here as well. The story opens on a panorama of the geographical setting. The passages in the Catskills, including Rip's encounter with the little men, are developed in more tightly focused, scenic terms. Viewpoint becomes strictly limited as the story moves to Rip's discovery, through his observation of the reactions of others, of his long beard. This prepares the reader for the inspired confusion of election day in the village as perceived by a befuddled old man who thinks he is coming home. "Rip Van Winkle" is a marvel in its author's manipulation of point of view.

"Critical Evaluation" by W. P. Kenney

Further Reading

Bowden, Mary Weatherspoon. *Washington Irving*. Boston: Twayne, 1981. Offers a general introduction to Irving's work. Emphasizes the integrity of *The Sketch Book of Geoffrey Crayon, Gent.*, in which "Rip Van Winkle" first appeared, and suggests that Irving's greatest literary accomplishment is his style. Includes a chronology of the events of Irving's life.

Burstein, Andrew. *The Original Knickerbocker: The Life of Washington Irving*. New York: Basic Books, 2007. Critical biography situates Irving's work within its social and political context, describing how Irving created an American literature. Argues that "Rip Van Winkle" symbolizes the youthful charm and energy of nineteenth century America. Includes photographs.

Ferguson, Robert A. "'Rip Van Winkle' and the Generational Divide in American Culture." *Early American Literature* 40, no. 3 (November, 2005): 529-544. Focuses on the techniques Irving uses to depict the "terrifying facts" of the life cycle.

Hedges, William L. *Washington Irving: An American Study, 1802-1832*. Baltimore: Johns Hopkins University Press, 1965. Asserts that Irving reached an intellectual dead end by 1825, but observes that in his greatest works, including "Rip Van Winkle," Irving stands as an important forerunner in style to Nathaniel Hawthorne and Henry James and in narrative and thematic concerns to Edgar Allan Poe and Herman Melville.

Jones, Brian Jay. *Washington Irving: An American Original*. New York: Arcade, 2008. Chronicles Irving's life and literary career, giving Irving credit for being the first American to make a living as a writer.

Myers, Andrew B., ed. *A Century of Commentary on the Works of Washington Irving, 1860-1974*. New York: Sleepy Hollow Restorations, 1976. Collection of essays provides a representative sampling of critical writing about Irving over a period of more than one hundred years, beginning shortly after the author's death in 1859.

Roth, Martin. *Comedy and America: The Lost World of Washington Irving*. Port Washington, N.Y.: Kennikat Press, 1976. Argues that "Rip Van Winkle" is one of the few exceptions to a decline in Irving's work that was already under way by the time he wrote *The Sketch Book of Geoffrey Crayon, Gent.*

Rubin-Dorsky, Jeffrey. *Adrift in the Old World: The Psychological Pilgrimage of Washington Irving*. Chicago: University of Chicago Press, 1988. Emphasizes the "Americanness" of Irving, the way he was shaped by, and came to identify himself with, his country and its particular heritage. Demonstrates how "Rip Van Winkle" reenacts Americans' doubts about identity and their fantasies of escape.

The Rise of Silas Lapham

Author: William Dean Howells (1837-1920)
First published: 1885
Type of work: Novel
Type of plot: Domestic realism
Time of plot: Nineteenth century
Locale: New England

Principal characters:
SILAS LAPHAM, a self-made manufacturer
MRS. LAPHAM, his wife
PENELOPE and IRENE, their daughters
TOM COREY, the Laphams's friend
ROGERS, Mr. Lapham's former partner

The Story:

Silas Lapham is being interviewed for a Boston paper. The journalist is secretly mocking Lapham's way of life, but Lapham is content with his success and pays little attention to his interviewer as he proudly exhibits a photograph of his two daughters and his wife. He tells how he had been brought up in a large family and had gone West with his brothers, how he had returned, bought a stage route, married the village schoolteacher, and finally hit upon the idea of making paint from a mineral his father had discovered on his farm. The story of his success is a story of determination and hard work. During the American Civil War, his wife kept the paint works going, and after the war, he had taken a man named Rogers as a partner for a short time.

After the interview, Lapham and his wife drive out to see the site of a house they are building in a more fashionable part of Boston. Although both look with pride upon the place soon to be their residence, they pretend not to want the house at all. They merely suggest the new home would be a greater advantage for Penelope and Irene when their friends visit. Neither Penelope nor Irene anticipates their coming change of living with great joy. They think the present house is more convenient for the horse cars. Secretly, both realize that their parents are awkward in social life, and they themselves have not been brought up to feel comfortable in the presence of people whose families had been accustomed to wealth for generations.

One day, as Mr. and Mrs. Lapham are dismounting from their carriage, Lapham's former partner appears unexpectedly. Rogers had provided money to help get the business started, but Lapham had eventually bought Rogers out. Lapham insists that what he had done had merely been good business, but Mrs. Lapham maintains that she never felt quite right about what had happened to Rogers. Seeing him again takes all the happiness out of her plans for the new house.

The next time the family ventures out to visit the partly completed house, Irene is surprised by the arrival of Tom Corey, a young man who had shown some interest in her. Immediately, Mr. Lapham begins to dominate the occasion, and

by his bragging he greatly embarrasses his daughters. That evening, young Corey talks to his father, Bromfield Corey, who does not agree with his son's easy acceptance of the Laphams but does not object when his son announces his intention of applying for a position in Lapham's firm.

Young Corey visits Lapham in his office to ask for a job. Lapham is so pleased that he invites Corey to go with him to Nantasket, where Mrs. Lapham and the girls are expecting Lapham for the weekend. At the Nantasket cottage, the girls and their mother cannot understand why young Corey is visiting for the weekend. They had thought Lapham's bragging would have kept him away forever.

That evening, Lapham discusses Corey with his wife. Mrs. Lapham contends that Corey is interested not in the paint or the paint business but in Irene. Mr. Lapham says that if the young man is not interested in the paint he will never get a chance to be interested in Irene. When Lapham says he intends to give the young man a chance, Mrs. Lapham warns him that he is playing with a situation that is bound to bring trouble. Corey's mother is concerned when she hears about her son's new employment. She admits she would not object if he makes a fortune from the paint business, but she does not want him to fall in love with either of the Lapham girls.

After Corey enters Lapham's employ, he is invited frequently to the Lapham home, for Irene is beginning to fall in love with him. Bromfield Corey grows more and more curious about the Laphams. He decides that he will encourage his wife to give a dinner for them in the autumn. The cost of the new house worries Mrs. Lapham, and she asks her husband to stop his lavish spending. She learns that he had given a substantial loan to Rogers, his former partner.

When Mrs. Corey returns from Bar Harbor, she debates a long time about giving a dinner party for the Laphams. In the first place, the Laphams are newcomers. On the other hand, she wants to give public recognition of the new connection between her son and the Lapham family. She finally decides to give a formal dinner early in the season, before her more prominent friends return to the city.

On the night of the dinner, the Laphams try to appear at ease. Penelope had refused to attend, thus causing her mother considerable embarrassment. Lapham watches the other men carefully, feeling sure that he has not made too many social blunders. The next day, however, he is not so sure, for he had taken too much wine at dinner.

At the office, Lapham finds Corey and mentions with embarrassment his behavior of the night before. He offers Corey his liberty to seek another job, a position among gentlemen, but Corey refuses to go, saying that Lapham's tipsy talk had been only an unfortunate accident. When they part, Corey insists that Lapham's conduct had been proper and entertaining. That night, feeling that he had actually patronized Lapham, Corey resolves to go to his employer and apologize. Lapham is out, but Penelope receives Corey. At the end of a long talk, he stammeringly confesses his love for her. In great confusion, he leaves without waiting to speak to Lapham.

The next day, Mrs. Lapham informs her husband that Corey had been coming to see Penelope all the time. She can only imagine what the shock will do to Irene. They feel, however, that Penelope would never permit Corey to become her suitor, for Penelope is convinced that he belongs to Irene, who is informed of the situation by her mother that evening. Irene immediately carries to her sister's room every memento of Corey's attentions that she possesses. After a few days, Lapham takes her to his boyhood village in Vermont. Corey calls on the Laphams to present his explanation, saying that he had cared for Penelope all the time. Penelope refuses to give him any satisfaction. She says she owes more to her sister's hurt feelings.

At the same time, Lapham's finances are troubling him greatly. People who owe him money are unable to pay, and his own creditors are pressing him. Lapham determines to take a trip West to inspect some mills held as security for his loan to Rogers. When he returns, he is even more concerned. Rogers had drawn him into a trap with his securities, for a railroad controlled the value of the property. Lapham decides it will be necessary to sell the new house unfinished. Learning of Lapham's difficulties, Corey offers to lend his employer thirty thousand dollars, but Lapham rejects the offer.

Lapham's affairs take a turn for the worse. An added blow is the destruction of the unfinished Back Bay house. Wandering through the house one night, he decided to test one of the chimneys. He made a fire from blocks and shavings that the workmen had left scattered about. He had left the house thinking the fire had burned out. That night the house burned to the ground. The insurance policy had expired a week before.

Determined to raise money by selling everything, Lapham visits his competitors who are working on a new mineral paint. They are willing to merge with him if he can raise money to help develop their plant. While he is trying to secure a loan, he learns from Rogers that some English gentlemen are interested in buying the property that Rogers had put up as security and that Lapham had thought valueless. Lapham refuses to sell the mills, however, because he believes a sale would be unethical as long as the railroad controlled their value.

Lapham asks for time to think over the proposition. Shortly afterward, the railroad forces him to sell the mills at a ruinous figure. Lapham feels that his honesty, which had kept him from selling the property to the Englishmen, had been unjustly abused. Rogers claims that Lapham had made it impossible for him to recover his losses. Lapham is now ruined, for he cannot raise capital to merge with the rival paint firm.

Corey is determined to marry Penelope in spite of her father's impending ruin. He does marry her after Lapham goes into bankruptcy, and his family accepts her for their own sake as well as for his. Irene, who returns from Vermont as soon as she hears of her father's troubles, is pleased with her sister's happiness. Lapham manages to save a part of his fortune, but more important to him is the belief that he had acted honestly in all his business dealings.

Critical Evaluation:

William Dean Howells, a prolific though never a brilliant writer, attempted to deal conscientiously with the everyday experiences of rather ordinary people. By presenting character and situation in a straightforward manner, he wrote novels characterized chiefly by their moral atmosphere and authentic domestic realism.

The reputation of Howells suffered much from the charge of many critics that his scope was too limited to satisfy the requirements of complexity demanded by sophisticated twentieth century readers. It is argued that his insights into social existence, for example, were based on tenets from a past age that no longer applied; the lack of intense passions and obsessions in the novels, as well as Howells's failure to explore in depth such areas as human sexuality and capacity for violence, are cited as evidence. Similarly, *The Rise of Silas Lapham*—the author's most popular work and in many ways his masterpiece—has been adversely judged by some on the grounds that its plot is too slender to support the weight of its own implications. To support such charges, however, is either to misunderstand the nature of Howells's moral vision of life, or to overlook its depth and breadth, universality, and applicability to all times and places.

Howells believed in people's interdependence with one another; he viewed each person's life as inextricably caught up with the lives of others, thus creating the web of interrelationships that forms societies. Such a belief meant that, for Howells, personal moral lives and social lives were fused; there was no such thing as a purely individual moral act, whether good or evil, since each personal act had its inevitable consequences in the interpersonal or social realm. This in turn led to the morally pragmatic stance that the proper course of action can often be chosen on the basis of which course will result in the most good for the greatest number of people.

This utilitarian viewpoint is reflected in such concepts as the economy-of-pain principle, propounded by Howells through the character of David Sewell in the scene from *The Rise of Silas Lapham* in which Silas and his wife seek the minister's advice concerning the love complication between their two daughters and Tom Corey. He tells them that in such a situation, for which no one is to blame, the best solution is the one that will cause suffering to the fewest number of people. In this case, therefore, Penelope would be wrong to sacrifice Tom to Irene, which would make all three persons suffer miserably; she should marry him herself, which would result in the great happiness of two people and the temporary hurt of only one.

Underlying this moral outlook are three basic assumptions: that all aspects of human life, including the social, are infused with moral purpose, thus making society an extremely precious commodity; that the preservation of society depends on human beings overcoming their destructive passions with reason; and that the function of art reveals the superiority of the civilized and reasoning side of human nature over the primitive and ignorant side. Howells's first assumption was shared by most people in his age, but it was his fervent espousal of the last proposition that placed him at the philosophical head of a group of writers whose aim it was to reveal the morality of life through the use of realism in their fiction. However, Howells abhorred sermonizing, and he attacked the didactic element in writing whenever he encountered it.

This seeming paradox is cleared up, however, when one examines more closely Howells's theory of literature. What he objected to was not the presence of moral purpose in a work but rather any attempt by an author to force artificially his or her set of beliefs into a fictional structure without regard to the organic dictates of the work itself.

When Howells was asked to summarize explicitly his theory of the moral purpose of literature, he began by identifying three progressively worse stages of "immorality" often practiced in fiction. The first involves the obscuring of the reader's judgment through indulgence of his or her "gross appetite for the marvelous"; the second, the elevation of passion over principles; and the third (and most pernicious), the presentation of characters who commit serious sins but are left unpunished by the penalties that follow such sins in the real world. The true function of the writer, Howells argued, is first to reject any absolute standard of morality and then to portray lives of characters in honest and careful detail; as the characters meet each new situation in their everyday lives, and as they are faced with decisions over what is right and what is wrong, they will respond as people do in life. Sometimes they will act in morally responsible ways and will be rewarded, if not with worldly success, with inner peace; at other times, they will commit wrongs and will suffer the inevitable consequences. Thus, Howells believed, all the author need do is describe reality truthfully, and the morality of life will become apparent through the narrative as naturally as it does in life.

Howells carried out his theory to near perfection in *The Rise of Silas Lapham*. This novel tells the story of a man who has been led astray from the true values in life by the corrupting influence of wealth. The action centers around Silas Lapham's fall into financial ruin, which turns out to be his salvation and his rise (hence the title) back into a morally healthy state. The plot is organic, reflecting the theme of the novel and growing out of the main character's growth. The beginning and end are linked masterfully, while the midway point in the story—the dinner party given by the Coreys—serves to pull together the threads spun out until then, suspending them momentarily for the reader's contemplation, and then directing them toward their climax and natural conclusion. In his interview with Bartley Hubbard at the opening of the novel, Silas is seen in all the glory of his material success: He is proud of his rise from humble beginnings, of his newly acquired social position, and of the new house he is just starting to build. The house becomes a symbol of Silas's fortunes; destined to be a magnificent mansion, it rises quickly until its construction is slowed down because of lack of funds. In the end, it is accidently burned to the ground. The destruction of the house represents Silas's rebirth, since his moral regeneration can only occur after he has been stripped of the false trappings of materialism. In his talk with Sewell at the end, Silas's transformation is set in dramatic contrast to his initial appearance in the Bartley interview: He has grown humble and honest, and his bragging has been replaced by sincerity.

Lapham has been able to reach this new stage of awareness by progressing through a series of moral tests, culminating in the legal, but morally dishonest, deal urged on him by Rogers and the Englishmen; when he refuses to participate, both his financial ruin and his personal salvation are secured. He has painfully but steadily moved from the easiest stages of redemption—acts of unselfishness and generosity on a personal, one-to-one basis—through a wider area of commitment to people in large groups, and has finally reached the highest, most difficult level of good action. This level involves an individual's commitment to the social body as a whole, to the welfare not of a personally known individual or group but of all human beings of a larger society.

Howells's efforts to uncover the underlying morality of all human action by focusing on the commonplace and familiar in his fiction reached a pinnacle in *The Rise of Silas Lapham*, but he was not fully conscious of the nature of his achievement until a year after the novel's publication. It was in 1886 that he began reading the works of Leo Tolstoy. His exposure to the Russian novelist was like a religious experience, and he wrote, "What I had instinctively known before, I now knew rationally." Following this illumination of his own motives and absorbing concerns as an artist, Howells was able to sum up the vision that had inspired not only *The Rise of Silas Lapham* but all of his other work: "Morality penetrates all things, it is the soul of all things."

"Critical Evaluation" by Nancy G. Ballard

Further Reading

Abeln, Paul. *William Dean Howells and the Ends of Realism.* New York: Routledge, 2004. Abeln analyzes Howells's fiction, providing a close look at his late works to demonstrate that Howells's writing is as significant in the American literary tradition as that of his better-regarded contemporaries, Henry James and Mark Twain.

Carrington, George C. *The Immense Complex Drama: The World and Art of the Howells Novel.* Columbus: Ohio State University Press, 1966. A classic study that remains influential in the field. Analyzes *The Rise of Silas Lapham* in relation to Howells's other novels. Considers theme, subject, technique, and form.

Eby, Clare Virginia. "Compromise and Complicity in *The Rise of Silas Lapham.*" *American Literary Realism, 1870-1910* 24, no. 1 (Fall, 1991): 39-53. Analyzes the use of class, privilege, and the businessperson in *The Rise of Silas Lapham*. Argues that in his depiction of the conflict between the Coreys and the Laphams, Howells advocates greater flexibility and compromise between class groups.

Goodman, Susan, and Carl Dawson. *William Dean Howells: A Writer's Life.* Berkeley: University of California Press, 2005. A broad and compelling biography providing a comprehensive account of Howells's life and work. Among other topics, the biographers discuss Howells's friendships with and support of contemporary writers and his significance in American letters. Includes illustrations.

Johnson, Joel A. *Beyond Practical Virtue: A Defense of Liberal Democracy Through Literature.* Columbia: University of Missouri Press, 2007. Examines the relationship between liberal democracy and the individual in works by Howells and other nineteenth century American writers

Pease, Donald E., ed. *New Essays on "The Rise of Silas Lapham."* New York: Cambridge University Press, 1991. A stimulating collection of essays on the novel. Includes topics ranging from Howells's treatment of the middle class and suffering under capitalism to a reexamination of realism and Howells's acquaintance with Mark Twain.

Stratman, Gregory J. *Speaking for Howells: Charting the Dean's Career Through the Language of His Characters.* Lanham, Md.: University Press of America, 2001. Analyzes Howells's interest in language, focusing on the language of his characters and his use of literary dialect. Argues that Howells's language perspective demonstrates how his career moved in a circular path, from Romanticism to realism and back to Romanticism

Thompson, Graham. "The Business of Sexuality in *The Rise of Silas Lapham.*" In *Male Sexuality Under Surveillance: The Office in American Literature.* Iowa City: University of Iowa Press, 2003. Thompson analyzes Howells's novel and other American literature to examine the depiction of male sexuality in the business world.

Vanderbilt, Kermit. *The Achievement of William Dean Howells: A Reinterpretation.* Princeton, N.J.: Princeton University Press, 1968. The chapter on *The Rise of Silas Lapham* examines revisions of the novel and personal letters to show Howells's concern with social eruption, class, and ethnicity in Boston during the Gilded Age.

The Rising of the Moon

Author: Lady Augusta Gregory (1852-1932)
First produced: 1907; first published, 1905
Type of work: Drama
Type of plot: Protest
Time of plot: Early twentieth century
Locale: Ireland

Principal characters:
SERGEANT, an older police officer
POLICEMAN X, Sergeant's assistant
POLICEMAN B, Sergeant's assistant
A RAGGED MAN, a ballad singer

The Story:

On a moonlit night on an Irish wharf, three Irish police officers in the service of the occupying English government paste up wanted posters for a clever escaped political criminal. Convinced that the escaped rebel might creep to the water's edge to be rescued by sea, they all hope to capture him for the hundred-pound reward and perhaps even a promotion. The Sergeant sends his two younger assistants with their only lantern to post more flyers around town while, uneasily, he keeps watch at the water's edge.

A man in rags tries to slip past the Sergeant, explaining that he merely wants to sell some songs to incoming sailors. The Ragged Man identifies himself as Jimmy Walsh, a ballad singer. When the man heads toward the steps to the water, the Sergeant stops him, insisting that Jimmy leave by way of town. Trying to interest the officer in his songs, the man sings a few ballads to the protesting Sergeant, who wants only to keep the area clear so he can catch the fleeing prisoner if he appears. The Sergeant orders the man to leave the area immediately.

The Ragged Man pretends to start toward town but stops to comment on the face on the poster, saying that he knows the man well. Interested, the Sergeant changes his mind about sending the Ragged Man away and insists that the stranger stay to furnish more information about the fugitive. The Ragged Man describes a dark, dangerous, muscular man who is an expert with many weapons, then he hints at previous murders of police officers on moonlit nights exactly like the present one.

Frightened, the Sergeant gladly accepts the Ragged Man's offer to stay with him on the wharf to help look for the escaped murderer. Sitting back-to-back on a barrel in order to have full view of the dock area, the two men smoke pipes together to calm the Sergeant's nerves. The Sergeant confesses that police work is difficult, especially for family men, because the officers spend long hours on dangerous missions. Accompanying the Sergeant's lament, the Ragged Man starts to sing a traditional sentimental song about lovers

and the beautiful Irish countryside. Then he begins a nationalistic ballad about a legendary oppressed old Irishwoman named Granuaile. The Sergeant stops him, protesting that it is inappropriate to sing about Irish oppression when political tempers are flaring between Ireland and England. His ragged companion replies that he is only singing the song to keep his spirits up during their dangerous and lonely watch; he then grabs his chest as if the forbidden singing is necessary to calm his frightened heart. When the pitying Sergeant allows him to continue his ballad, the man again sings about the fabled Irish martyr Granuaile, but this time he inserts the wrong lyrics. The Sergeant immediately corrects him and sings the proper line, revealing his knowledge of a rebel song even though he is supposed to be loyal to the English rulers.

The Ragged Man slyly begins to probe the Sergeant's memories of former days when, as a young man, the Sergeant lovingly sang several traditional Irish ballads, including "Granuaile." Confidentially, the Sergeant admits that he has sung every patriotic ballad the Ragged Man names. The man suggests that the Sergeant and the fugitive perhaps share the same youthful memories; in fact, the escaped prisoner might even have been among the Sergeant's close friends in their younger days. When the Sergeant admits the possibility, the man describes a hypothetical scene in which the Sergeant joins in with those former singing friends to free Ireland. Therefore, the Ragged Man concludes, it might have been fated that the Sergeant would be the pursued instead of the pursuer.

Caught up in the hypothetical scenario, the Sergeant muses that if he had made different choices—not going into the police force, not marrying and having children—he and the fugitive could well have exchanged roles. The possibility becomes so real for him that he begins to confuse his own identity with that of the escapee and imagines himself stealthily trying to escape, violently shooting or assaulting police officers. He is startled out of his reverie by a sound from the water; he suspects that the rescuers have at last arrived to carry away the fugitive.

The Ragged Man contends that the Sergeant in the past sympathized with the Irish nationalists and not with the law he currently represents. In fact, he suggests that the Sergeant still doubts the choice he made for the English law and against "the people." Boldly singing the rebel tune "The Rising of the Moon" as a signal to the rescuers on the water and ripping off his hat and wig, Jimmy, the ballad singer, reveals that he is in fact the fugitive himself, the man with a hundred-pound reward on his head.

Startled and struggling with his previously suppressed sympathies for the rebels, the Sergeant threatens to arrest the escapee and collect the reward when his younger police companions approach. He protests that his own rebel sentiments are buried in the past. Hiding from the nearing officers behind the barrel seat the two men so recently shared, the fugitive calls on the Sergeant's love for Ireland to keep his presence secret. Quickly hiding the fugitive's wig and hat behind him, the Sergeant denies to his subordinates that he has seen anyone. When the officers insist that they stay to aid their superior on his dangerous watch, the Sergeant gruffly rejects their noisy offers and sends them away with their lantern.

The escaped rebel gratefully retrieves his disguise and promises to return the favor when, "at the Rising of the Moon," the roles of oppressor and oppressed are inevitably reversed. Quickly, he slips into the rescue boat and is gone. Left musing alone on the moonlit wharf, the Sergeant thinks of the lost reward and wonders if he has been a great fool.

Critical Evaluation:

Lady Augusta Gregory's contribution to the Irish Literary Renaissance was twofold: cofounding the Abbey Theatre with William Butler Yeats and writing what became the Abbey's most popular plays, including *The Rising of the Moon*. Most of her drama featured Irish peasants and was not overtly political; she insisted that she was not promoting political rebellion with this play. Nevertheless, in 1907, when the play was first performed, many Irish knew the popular old ballad "The Rising of the Moon," in which the ascending moon is a signal for "rising," or rebellion. Lady Gregory's sympathies were with the people of Ireland. She was, however, adamantly against violence. She sympathized with Irish calls for independence from English rule, but she chose not to join the more strident Irish voices. Her chosen form of political statement was to highlight Irish language and customs. She was convinced that if the English saw the true Gaelic soul, they would sympathize with the desire of the

Irish to rule themselves. In this play, the rebel's cleverness is depicted, not his crimes.

As in other Gregory plays, the dialogue evokes native Irish rhythms and lore. The Ragged Man and the Sergeant share Irish speech and knowledge of old sentimental and patriotic songs, a feature of nearly all Gregory plays. Granuaile, the bound and wailing old woman in the song the Ragged Man sings, is a symbol for suffering Ireland. The line the Ragged Man leaves out and that the Sergeant furnishes is the most agonizing of all: "Her gown she wore was stained with gore." This reference to Irish martyrs would not have been lost on Lady Gregory's audience. In fact, when reviewers suspected that the play was a patriotic statement even though Lady Gregory denied it, the Dublin police force took back the uniforms it had previously lent to the drama company as costumes.

In *The Rising of the Moon*, moonlight plays an important role. Having given their only lantern to his deputies, the Sergeant is at a disadvantage in the dim moonlight. He cannot see clearly. Also, the dimness helps the Ragged Man enhance his frightening stories of the rebel's past violence to police officers. The moonlight inspires the Sergeant's reveries and weakens his sense of duty to the British authorities. At the end, when the Sergeant refuses the lantern, he is left alone in the moonlight puzzling over his identity—as an upholder of the law or as an Irish sympathizer.

The fugitive's cleverness precedes his entrance onstage, as the police officers recall that he is the head of the rebel organization and that he probably won sympathy and assistance from his jailers. This foreshadows the rest of the play. The Ragged Man cleverly wins sympathy from his would-be captor. He sets his trap for the Sergeant's heart once it is clear that the officer will not let him pass to the water. First, he sings "Johnny Hart," a romantic song about two lovers forbidden to marry. The sad song creates a melancholy mood and convinces the officer that the man is, indeed, a balladeer. Next, he intrigues the Sergeant into needing him by saying that he knows the escapee personally.

Craftily, the man paints a deadly picture of the powerful fugitive to frighten the Sergeant into wanting company. Then he shows sympathy for the Sergeant's weariness and suggests they share a seat on the barrel. As they sit back-to-back, the Sergeant cannot compare the man's face to that on the poster, but their bodies share space and a friendly pipe. The man pretends to be so frightened that he needs to sing a forbidden Irish political ballad, then tricks the Sergeant into revealing his knowledge of the patriotic song. He springs the trap with his assertion that the Sergeant himself harbored Irish sympathies years before and constructs a scenario of the

Sergeant's being part of a rebel group had fate not intervened. Caught, the Sergeant admits the possibility. Startled by the arriving rescue boat, however, he snaps into his uniformed role and acts as protector of the law.

As his fellow officers approach with the lantern the Sergeant must choose between his admitted rebel sympathies and his official duty, which promises rewards. Refusing the lantern and sending the other men away to protect the escaping fugitive, the Sergeant is unsure that he has made the right choice after all. He loses money, promotion, and recognition for himself and his family. The audience is left with admiration for the Ragged Man's successful strategy as well as sympathy for the officer who had two legitimate but conflicting loyalties. The brief play voices its author's political message: concern for the human dimensions of a complicated conflict.

Nancy A. Macky

Further Reading

Adams, Hazard. *Lady Gregory*. Lewisburg, Pa.: Bucknell University Press, 1973. Brief, insightful guide to Lady Gregory's various writings contains a biographical sketch and a chapter on each of the main areas of her work, including her plays. Includes chronology and brief bibliography.

Coxhead, Elizabeth. *Lady Gregory: A Literary Portrait*. London: Secker and Warburg, 1966. Uses a biographical approach in examining Lady Gregory's writings, discussing her literary and cultural relations with other leading figures in the Irish Literary Revival.

Gregory, Lady Augusta. *Lady Gregory: Interviews and Rec-ollections*. Edited by E. H. Mikhail. London: Macmillan, 1977. Selection of excerpts from memoirs, newspaper articles, and other contemporary sources provides a composite portrait of Lady Gregory's public life and her private life at her celebrated home at Coole Park. Includes some of her remarks about the early, controversial history of the Abbey Theatre.

Hill, Judith. *Lady Gregory: An Irish Life*. Stroud, England: Sutton, 2005. Comprehensive biography aims to explore Gregory's life and work in their own right, and not within the shadow of her friend William Butler Yeats.

Kohfeldt, Mary Lou. *Lady Gregory: The Woman Behind the Irish Renaissance*. New York: Athenaeum, 1985. Presents a full account of Lady Gregory's life and times, using archival material to broaden the picture of her youth, though the main emphasis remains on her public work on behalf of the arts in Ireland.

Pethica, James. "Lady Gregory's Abbey Theatre Drama: Ireland Real and Ideal." In *The Cambridge Companion to Twentieth-Century Irish Drama*, edited by Shaun Richards. New York: Cambridge University Press, 2004. Focuses on Gregory's involvement with the Abbey Theatre.

Saddlemyer, Ann, and Colin Smythe, eds. *Lady Gregory: Fifty Years After*. Totowa, N.J.: Barnes & Noble, 1987. Substantial collection of essays presents comprehensive scholarly treatment of Lady Gregory's life and times, with considerable material pertinent to an evaluation of the overall cultural significance of her contribution to Irish literature.

Tóibín, Colm. *Lady Gregory's Toothbrush*. Dublin: Lilliput, 2002. An acclaimed Irish novelist recounts the events of Gregory's life and discusses her writing.

Rites of Passage

Author: William Golding (1911-1993)
First published: 1980
Type of work: Novel
Type of plot: Symbolic realism
Time of plot: Early nineteenth century
Locale: On a ship in the Atlantic Ocean

Principal characters:
EDMUND TALBOT, a young gentleman taking up his first government appointment
THE REVEREND ROBERT JAMES COLLEY, a young Anglican clergyman taking up his first appointment
CAPTAIN ANDERSON, captain of the ship taking Talbot and a group of emigrants to Australia
LIEUTENANT SUMMERS, the ship's first lieutenant, who has risen from the ranks
LIEUTENANT DEVEREL, the second lieutenant, who is from the same class as Talbot
LIEUTENANT CUMBERSHUM, the third lieutenant
WHEELER, the servant assigned to Talbot and some of the higher-class passengers
BILLY ROGERS, one of the crew, a handsome young sailor
MR. BROCKLEBANK, a drunken painter and emigrant
ZENOBIA BROCKLEBANK, supposedly his daughter
MISS GRANHAM, a governess, daughter of a cathedral dignitary
MR. PRETTIMAN, an atheist and revolutionary

The Story:

Edmund Talbot writes a journal for his unnamed godfather and patron as he travels to Australia. His godfather has procured for Talbot an appointment as deputy to the governor of one of the new Australian colonies being settled. In return, the godfather has asked his godson to keep the journal so that he can revisit his own youth in his godson's adventures. Talbot is very full of the influence of his godfather in government circles and of his own position as the highest-ranking aristocrat aboard the ship. His is also very self-conscious of his own writing style, knowing his words will be read by his godfather, who presumably can continue to influence his career. Talbot particularly delights in learning the nautical jargon used by the sailors and showing off this knowledge in the journal.

At first, Talbot is overwhelmed by the ship's stink and crowded quarters. He describes his cabin as a "hutch," but, as the voyage begins, seasickness keeps him in it, as it does most of the middle-class, or "better sort of," passengers. When he emerges from his cabin, Talbot begins to meet the ship's officers—the lieutenants and midshipmen—as well as the middle-class passengers, all of whom are emigrants. He does not immediately meet the steerage passengers or the crew, who live in the forward part of the ship. Demarcation lines exist everywhere, but one demarcation Talbot fails to

notice is the approach to the captain. He believes he can introduce himself to the captain any time he wishes, though his servant Wheeler and Lieutenant Summers try to hint otherwise. When he attempts to do this, he is reminded by Captain Anderson that he should have read the "Captain's Orders," which expressly forbid approach to the captain except at the captain's invitation.

One of the last passengers to emerge from seasickness is a young clergyman named James Colley. Colley seems gauche and awkward, and Talbot judges him immediately as coming from a lower class. In the absence of a chaplain, however, Colley takes on himself the responsibility of arranging a Sunday service. Like Talbot, he fails to notice the ban on approaching the captain, but he is told off in a much more insulting way than Talbot was. Talbot decides to take it on himself to confront the captain and get a Sunday service organized, not because he is religious, but in an attempt to assert his superiority.

The service takes place, with a few of the lower-class passengers being allowed to join the better class and the ship's officers. Talbot finds Colley enormously embarrassing at the service, as Colley seems to be fooled by Zenobia Brocklebank, who acts both young and pious when she is clearly neither. Colley also looks on Talbot's efforts as a sign of Talbot's own piety and good breeding, when again it has been neither. His obsequious behavior toward Talbot mocks Talbot's own behavior toward his godfather.

Talbot perceives Zenobia's sexual availability, as do several other men. She is prepared to use her favors to gain help for her "father" when they land in Australia. In the meanwhile, Colley confronts the captain again in an effort to take his religious duties to the rest of the ship and to regain the prestige of the church. As Anderson is known to be anti-clerical, Colley never has a chance of success, and he finds himself banished from the upper decks. He does not fully understand where he is and is not allowed to go and so restricts himself unduly, losing contact with most of the passengers and becoming isolated. Talbot avoids Colley too.

When the ship is to cross the equator, the traditional rite of "Crossing the Line" is enacted. Talbot and Colley are both ignorant of this ritual. Talbot takes the opportunity to have sexual intercourse, or "commerce," with Zenobia, while Colley is hauled out of his cabin and subjected to a humiliating series of ordeals by the crew. The captain turns a blind eye to the procedure, which everyone witnesses except Talbot.

Colley again confronts Anderson about his treatment. The captain is forced to apologize and even agrees to allow Colley to speak to the crew in order to reprove them, although Lieutenant Summers realizes the danger of this plan. Summers asks for the men to be issued some rum in order to pacify them before Colley appears. Colley goes into the forward part of the ship and disappears from the sight of the other passengers. Strange sounds are heard of cheering, jeering, and applause. Finally, Summers warns the captain to stop whatever is going on and fires a gun to reinstate nautical authority. One of the sailors appears carrying Colley, obviously very drunk, to his cabin, from which he fails to reemerge.

Talbot goes in to try to rouse Colley from his unconscious state and finds a long letter the reverend has been writing to his sister in England. Others also try to rouse Colley, but he fails to respond. After a number of days, it is determined that he has, at some point, died. Later, Talbot realizes that the cause of his death must have been shame. The captain holds a brief inquest involving Talbot and Summers. When it emerges that homosexual acts were committed, Anderson decides to cover up the incident and declares that Colley died of a "low fever." Colley is then buried at sea. At the same time, Wheeler mysteriously disappears, but nothing is made of his supposed death.

Talbot reads Colley's letter. In it, he discovers a parallel narrative to that of his own journal, and he realizes a quite different perspective. He realizes, too, that Colley's sister will have to be told a complete set of lies about her brother's death. The narrative finishes with Talbot having filled his journal and the passengers turning to amateur dramatics to pass the remaining time until they reach Australia.

Critical Evaluation:

Although *Rites of Passage* was written as a stand-alone novel, William Golding wrote two sequels to it, bringing a conclusion to the characters' voyage to Australia. The three completed volumes were issued in 1991 as a trilogy titled *To the Ends of the Earth: A Sea Trilogy*. The trilogy can be seen as a bildungsroman tracing Edmund Talbot's growth from an insensitive and brash young gentleman into someone with a deepened moral sensitivity, in a committed love relationship, and without the support of a patron to give him the illusion of power.

Rites of Passage hints at such a development, but it is better to see it symbolically. Golding's own experiences as a sailor during World War II and his subsequent interest in old sailing ships give the story sufficient authenticity to stand as a realist historical novel, set during a period of lull in the Napoleonic Wars. In the light of Golding's earlier novels, however, it is easy to see the symbolism of the journey, of the structure of the ship, and of the events that occur aboard it.

The "rites" of the title might appear to be birth, marriage (or at least the engagement between Prettiman and Miss Granham), and death, but the plot leads readers to see the rites as those to do with crossing the equator that lead to Colley's death. These rites are shocking in that the ship has hitherto seemed an ordered and tightly disciplined society with a due sense of rank and status. Suddenly primordial forces emerge that scapegoat one man and sacrifice him through punishment and humiliation. No one seems able to prevent this from happening, certainly not Captain Anderson, who dislikes clergymen anyway, or Talbot, who is busy about his own amorous agenda.

The rites of the crossing pick up on Golding's first novel, *Lord of the Flies* (1954), in which civilization breaks down among a group of boys and they are soon committing bestial acts against one another. Golding's vision of a "heart of darkness" lying just beneath the surface of humanity is his central literary vision. The novel then raises the question of who can take responsibility for this darkness and the actions that arise from it.

At first, it seems as if Talbot, having read Colley's letter, has sufficient moral anger to force some account to be given by the captain. However, he is too ignorant of what has happened and too inexperienced to withstand Anderson's determination to whitewash the whole affair. What is entered into the ship's log is what is important. Talbot enters into his journal what has actually happened, but his account ceases to have any moral force, as Talbot realizes that he is implicated in Colley's isolation. He too mocked Colley, just as the crew did.

Only Summers emerges with any credit, though he also is complicit with the inquest finding. Talbot begins to learn through preferring Summers to the educated and upper-class Deverel (a name rather like 'Little Devil') that class is no substitute for moral integrity. Of all the confrontations that occur in the novel, Summers's confrontation of Talbot, in which he insists that status brings responsibility as well as power, is the bravest and most significant.

This incident is followed by Colley's confrontations with Anderson. The latter confrontations are essentially disinterested in that Colley is defending the honor of his faith in the face of Anderson's hatred of it. Colley's letter reveals other Christian virtues, such as a willingness to forgive his enemies and patience in the face of massive provocation. This technique of revealing a parallel and second perspective on the events of the narrative produces irony and an educative tool for Talbot. By contrast, Talbot's confrontations with Anderson are all rooted in the desire for power.

The theme of playacting quickly emerges in the novel as a central one. Talbot is aware of people playing their allotted roles or putting on appearances. He is aware that he too plays a role and certainly plays for power under the rules of the class-structured society he is used to. At the end of the novel, the passengers are planning to put on a play, thereby diverting themselves from having to consider Colley's death.

Golding does not suggest that all roleplaying is wrong. Anderson's power play is essential for the good management of the ship, though Golding suggests authority should not be confused with moral leadership. Colley's need to play the role of the chaplain is what his vows demand of him, and he demonstrates a real integrity as he tries to fulfil them. In this "ship of fools," the "holy fool" stands out. Talbot's development, readers may sense, will lie in whether he can separate the false moves of his own power play (such as threatening his patron's power) from the right moves of securing justice as the one person with enough social status to do so.

The ship itself is also symbolic, with its unplumbed and stinking depths, a symbol of the subconscious that in other novels is symbolized by cellars or foundations. The ship can be seen as a miniature society journeying to a new place. In medieval allegory, the "ship of fools" satirizes the failings of society. *Rites of Passage* won the Man Booker Prize for 1980, marking public recognition of Golding's return to novel writing after a twelve-year gap.

David Barratt

Further Reading

Crompton, Don, and Julia Briggs, eds. *A View from the Spire: William Golding's Later Novels.* New York: Basil Blackwell, 1985. Puts the novel in the context of the trilogy as a whole, as well as Golding's later developments as a novelist.

Dickson, L. L. *The Modern Allegories of William Golding.* Tampa: University of Southern Florida Press, 1990. Focuses on Golding's language and symbolism, especially his use of the quest motif. Golding as a modern allegorist is the main topic. Personal interviews with Golding are included.

Kinkead-Weekes, Mark, and Ian Gregor. *William Golding: A Critical Study of the Novels.* 3d rev. ed. London: Faber, 2002. This long-standing introduction to Golding's work has now been revised to include all of his novels.

Redpath, Phillip. *William Golding: A Structural Reading of his Fiction.* Lanham, Md.: Rowman and Littlefield, 1986. Golding's carefully designed structures are the key focus of this study.

Tiger, Virginia. *William Golding: The Unmoved Target.* London: Marion Boyars, 2003. Explores Golding's themes of human destiny and vision. Includes conversations with Golding himself. The link between structure and content is especially explored.

The Rivals

Author: Richard Brinsley Sheridan (1751-1816)
First produced: 1775; first published, 1775
Type of work: Drama
Type of plot: Comedy of manners
Time of plot: Eighteenth century
Locale: Bath, England

Principal characters:
CAPTAIN JACK ABSOLUTE or ENSIGN BEVERLEY, a young
    officer
SIR ANTHONY ABSOLUTE, his father
FAULKLAND, Jack's friend
BOB ACRES, a country squire
SIR LUCIUS O'TRIGGER, a fiery Irishman
LYDIA LANGUISH, an heir
MRS. MALAPROP, her aunt
JULIA MELVILLE, her cousin

The Story:

To beautiful and wealthy young Lydia Languish, who has been brought up on romantic novels, the only lover worth considering is one whose position in life is in complete contrast to her own. To this end she has fallen in love with a penniless young ensign named Beverley. To this same Beverley, her aunt, Mrs. Malaprop, raises serious objections. Her antipathy to young Mr. Beverley is partly aroused by letters that the ensign has written to Lydia, letters in which he has made uncomplimentary references to her aunt's age and appearance. Mrs. Malaprop has had some moments of extreme discomfiture as she has wondered whether she does resemble the she-dragon to which Beverley has compared her.

Mrs. Malaprop herself has fallen hopelessly in love with a quixotic Irishman named Sir Lucius O'Trigger, who presumably returns her affection. Sir Lucius, who has never seen Mrs. Malaprop, has been hoodwinked by a maidservant into believing that the romantic creature with whom he has been exchanging love letters is Lydia.

The situation is further complicated by the fact that Beverley is in reality young Captain Jack Absolute, the son of Sir Anthony Absolute, and as wealthy and aristocratic as Lydia herself. Jack very early sensed that he would get nowhere if he wooed the romantic Lydia in his own person, and so he assumed a character more nearly resembling the heroes of the novels that Lydia enjoys.

Jack's friend Faulkland has not fared any better than Jack in his own romantic pursuit of Lydia's cousin, Julia Melville. In fact, it might be thought that he has fared worse, for, unlike Jack, he is forever placing imaginary obstacles between himself and his beloved. Whenever they are separated, Faulkland imagines all kinds of horrible catastrophes that might have befallen her, and when he finds that she is alive and well he torments himself with the thought that she cannot be in love and remain so happy. At last Jack loses patience with his friend's ridiculous behavior, and even Julia becomes a little tired of her lover's unfounded jealousy.

Jack's curious love tangle reaches a crisis when Sir Anthony Absolute informs his son that he has selected the woman for him to marry, threatening that if Jack refuses, he will cut the young man off without a penny. Not having the faintest idea as to the identity of the woman his father has picked out for him, and conjuring up pictures of some homely heir his father intends to force on him against his will, Jack rebels. He declares that, whatever the consequences, he will have nothing to do with the woman his father has chosen.

Having been quite a connoisseur of pretty women in his youth, and being not exactly immune to their charms in his old age, Sir Anthony Absolute is not a man who would saddle his son with an unattractive wife. He has made an agreement with Mrs. Malaprop for the bestowal of her niece's hand upon his son. Mrs. Malaprop, in turn, is only too glad to save Lydia from a foolish marriage to Beverley. When Jack refuses to marry anyone not of his own choosing, Sir Anthony flies into a rage and insists that the marriage take place regardless of what the lady might be like.

By chance, however, Jack discovers that the woman Sir Anthony has selected as his bride is Lydia Languish, the same woman he has been wooing as Ensign Beverley. He immediately assures his father that he will be willing to marry anyone his father might choose. Sir Anthony, not used to such tractability on Jack's part, becomes suspicious and a little worried. He nevertheless makes arrangements for his son to meet the bride-to-be, thus placing Jack in a neat dilemma. Jack realizes that Lydia will have none of him as Sir Anthony Absolute's son. Finally, the supposed Ensign Beverley pretends to Lydia that in order to gain access to her aunt's house, he will be forced to pose as Jack Absolute.

Lydia has another suitor in the person of Bob Acres, a wealthy country squire and a neighbor of Sir Anthony, who has ambitions to become a man-about-town. Before Sir Anthony proposed his son as a husband for her niece, Mrs. Malaprop had favored Bob Acres as a likely candidate for Lydia's hand. When Acres discovers he has a rival in Ensign Beverley, he is disheartened. Encouraged by his friend Sir Lucius O'Trigger, he challenges Beverley to a duel. Never having seen young Beverley, he is forced to give the challenge to the ensign's friend, Jack Absolute, to deliver.

The great crisis in Jack's love affairs comes when he is forced to face Lydia in the company of his father. With his true identity revealed, Lydia's dreams of a romantic elopement with a penniless ensign vanish, and she dismisses Jack from her life forever. Chagrined by his abrupt dismissal, Jack accepts with positive gusto another challenge to a duel from Sir Lucius O'Trigger. Sir Lucius names the place as King's Mead Fields at six o'clock that very evening, when he has an appointment to act as a second to his friend, Acres, in a duel with a certain Ensign Beverley.

When Lydia learns that Jack has involved himself in a duel on her account, he becomes a different person in her eyes, and she hurries with her aunt to King's Mead Fields in an effort to halt the duel. Meanwhile, Sir Lucius O'Trigger has alarmed Acres with his bloodthirsty stories of dueling, so that when Acres recognizes his opponent as his old friend Jack Absolute, he heaves a sigh of relief.

With the arrival of Lydia and Mrs. Malaprop, the whole situation is quickly explained. Sir Lucius, much to his chagrin, is forced to realize that the writer of tender love letters to whom he has addressed his own impassioned correspondence is not Lydia but Mrs. Malaprop. Faulkland is content to accept Julia's love for the wholehearted thing it is. Lydia at last sees Ensign Beverley and Jack Absolute as the same person with whom she is in love. Bob Acres, happy because he will not be forced to fight a duel with anyone, ordered fiddles and entertainment for all in the fashionable parlors of Bath.

Critical Evaluation:

Together with that other masterpiece of late eighteenth century comedy, Oliver Goldsmith's *She Stoops to Conquer: Or, The Mistakes of a Night* (pr., pb. 1773), Richard Brinsley Sheridan's *The Rivals* represents a successful reclaiming of the essential spirit of English comedy. Too long subject to "the goddess of the woeful countenance—the sentimental muse" (as Sheridan addresses her in his prologue to *The Rivals*), English comedy had forgotten its boisterous heritage; a theater nurtured in the rich buffoonery of a Falstaff and the satirical malice of a Volpone had dissipated its energies in moralizing and saccharine "genteel" comedies. Although reluctant to return, and perhaps incapable of returning, to the

cynicism of Restoration comedy, Sheridan was anxious to rescue the healthy psychological realism traditional not only to English comedy but also, ever since Geoffrey Chaucer, to English literature generally. Sentiment was a French value. Sheridan's insistence on steering a middle course between sentiment and wit, between morality and reality, puts him at the center of the English literary tradition.

At the heart of all comedy is the ridicule of affectation. People may not all be fools, but all are, at times, foolish. Sheridan exploits the inevitable tendency in people to be foolish, regardless of their accomplishments in life. He does not resort to flat or stock characters, amusing only because they represent totally unrealistic or exaggerated foibles. His people are always human, and their foolishness often makes them more so.

Despite the stock-character aspect of their names (Absolute, Languish, and Malaprop), these characters are all larger than the epithets. Captain Absolute may be absolute about refusing his father's choice in a wife, but he is forced into a profound relativity when he has to be two people at the same time. When Absolute is at last revealed as having masqueraded as Beverley, he is, in any case, no longer absolute. Lydia Languish is ridiculed for languishing over sentimental novels, but she overcomes her foolishness when she refuses, finally, to languish in wounded pride for being duped by her Beverley.

Mrs. Malaprop's name was coined by Sheridan from the French *malapropos*, which means "not to the purpose." The word "malapropism" entered the English language in honor of Sheridan's character, and her abuses of the language are still hilarious. Sheridan, however, does not reduce Mrs. Malaprop to the one affectation of commanding a vocabulary that she does not, in truth, command. Her speaking "not to the purpose" is only symptomatic of a much deeper affectation; she is not to the purpose. Mrs. Malaprop favors the wrong suitor, Acres, for Lydia; she presumes, incorrectly, that the letters Sir Lucius O'Trigger has been writing are intended for her when they are in fact directed to Lydia; and, finally, at the end of the play, she blames her own willful and deluded misconceptions on the opposite sex. She is *malapropos* in more than diction; it is her human condition. Sheridan is careful not to pickle her in the brine of absolute ridicule. In her weakness lie the seeds of her vitality; by refusing to adhere "to the purpose" of her age and limited intellect, she achieves a touching transcendence that seems to turn the heart of Sir Anthony at play's end. There is hope for her.

Sheridan's fascination with human weakness led him to create a character that many critics feel is at odds with his avowed purpose in the play, which is essentially a broad attack on the sentimental in literature and life. The character in question is Faulkland. On the surface, it is clear that Faulkland's excessive concern with the pitch and nuance of his feelings for Julia, and hers for him, is so laden with anxiety that it is meant to be ridiculous. As such, Sheridan must have intended Faulkland's misplaced sentiment in life to complement Lydia Languish's misplaced sentiment in art. Lydia models her love-in-life on the sentimental romances she has read, and Faulkland constantly measures his relationship with Julia against an unrealistic idea of bliss in an imperfect world. Lydia's sentimental values are wrecked by the empirical fact that the man she loves turns out not to be the penniless Ensign Beverley but the rich and titled Captain Absolute. What sentimental art had decreed acceptable—the poor but dashing suitor—turns out to be the thing reality withholds. The revenge of life on a superficial idea of art is absolute. In Faulkland's case, the comic exposure is not as brilliant. As one critic has noted, while Sheridan laughs at Faulkland, he also identifies with his tortured sensibility.

Faulkland's constant anxiety is too serious a thing to dismiss categorically with laughter. His doubt is of the kind that a true awareness of reality implies. He may seem ridiculous in questioning his Julia's right to be healthy and happy in his absence, but his anxiety over the authenticity, as well as sincerity, of her love is the fate of his kind of mind.

Almost as if Sheridan senses that Faulkland does not completely succeed as an attack on the sentimental, the playwright creates another character in whom those anxieties are clearly absurd—namely, Acres. Acres's cowardice is finally ridiculous because it is dehumanizing; he is less a person for falling prey to O'Trigger's theatrical overdramatizing of dueling. Faulkland's anxiety, although uncalled for, is finally metaphysical; Acres's is completely venial and selfish.

Sheridan wrote this play at the age of twenty-three. It is a work of youthful genius and, together with *The School for Scandal* (pr. 1777), easily confirms his reputation as the outstanding dramatist of the eighteenth century. In Sheridan's work the wit of Restoration comedy and the best of sentimental comedy—its gift for feeling characterization—come to full fruition.

"Critical Evaluation" by Peter A. Brier

Further Reading

Auburn, Mark. *Sheridan's Comedies: Their Contexts and Achievements.* Lincoln: University of Nebraska Press, 1977. Treats Sheridan's comedies as excellent examples of the comic aesthetic. Discusses *The Rivals* as a practical play, designed to appeal to a specific audience and attempting no innovations or departures from popular stage practice.

Browne, Kevin Thomas. *Richard Brinsley Sheridan and Britain's School for Scandal: Interpreting His Theater Through Its Eighteenth-Century Social Context.* Lewiston, N.Y.: Edwin Mellen Press, 2006. Refutes criticism that Sheridan's plays are all style and no substance; argues that his plays depict how people from different social classes negotiate issues of British identity such as money, gender, class, morality, and language. Chapter 3 is devoted to *The Rivals.*

Mikhail, E. H. *Sheridan: Interviews and Recollections.* New York: St. Martin's Press, 1989. Biographical work draws on the writings of those who knew Sheridan. Includes contemporary accounts of *The Rivals* and opinions of the play from Sheridan's friends, relatives, and other contemporaries. Shows the range of opinion that accompanied the initial run of the play and reveals the nature of Sheridan's audience.

Morwood, James. *The Life and Works of Richard Brinsley Sheridan.* Edinburgh: Scottish Academic Press, 1985. Includes a section on *The Rivals* that comments on Sheridan's use of autobiographical allusions, his revisions of the play after opening night, and his debt to William Shakespeare. Discusses the two plots and their equation of moral judgment with common sense.

Morwood, James, and David Crane, eds. *Sheridan Studies.* New York: Cambridge University Press, 1995. Collection of essays about Sheridan's theatrical and political careers includes discussions of theater in the age of David Garrick and Sheridan, Sheridan's use of language, and the challenges of producing his plays.

O'Toole, Fintan. *A Traitor's Kiss: The Life of Richard Brinsley Sheridan.* London: Granta, 1997. Biography focuses on Sheridan's relationship to his native Ireland. Draws connections between Sheridan's life and his plays and provides a detailed examination of his political career.

Sherwin, Oscar. *Uncorking Old Sherry: The Life and Times of Richard Brinsley Sheridan.* New York: Twayne, 1960. Presents a chapter on *The Rivals* that covers the play's production history, including its initial failure and the revisions that Sheridan made that led to its later success. Includes a brief discussion of the play's effect on Sheridan's career as a playwright and theater manager.

Worth, Katharine. *Sheridan and Goldsmith.* New York: St. Martin's Press, 1992. Treats Sheridan and Oliver Goldsmith as two Irish dramatists whose works are firmly rooted in the eighteenth century English theater. Discusses *The Rivals* in the context of the pantomime tradition.

The Road

Author: Cormac McCarthy (1933-   )
First published: 2006
Type of work: Novel
Type of plot: Dystopian
Time of plot: Early twenty-first century
Locale: Probably the eastern United States

Principal characters:
THE MAN, a father
THE BOY, the man's son
THE MAN'S WIFE
ELY, an old man on the road
OTHER UNNAMED TRAVELERS ON THE ROAD

The Story:

An undisclosed cataclysmic event has obliterated all but a few scattered forms of life on Earth. These are largely human predators, who carve a brutal, inhuman existence from the remnants of the old world. A few dogs, mere sacks of bones, remain in the wasted world, but other creatures—birds, insects, and fish—have disappeared entirely. There are scant remnants of fungi, but the landscape for the most part is a vast, cold ruin of dust and ash.

About ten years after the cataclysm, a man and his son journey toward the eastern coast, ostensibly in an attempt to escape the oncoming Appalachian winter. The man's wife—and the boy's mother—committed suicide soon after the boy's birth. Only one season, nuclear winter, persists in this postapocalyptic world, and the man and the boy continually struggle against varying intensities of bitter cold throughout their trek.

Rain and snow mix with ash and toxic particulates that permanently shroud the sky; the biosphere has changed, and the few remaining people wear masks to reduce the torments of the diseased air they must breathe. Towns, cities, and all manner of human-made structures remain only as heaps of cinders and ashes.

The earth's devastation occurred quickly; the man recalls that the clocks stopped at 1:17 A.M. With the end of human civilization came the end of the earth's resources. The world is now filled with blood cults and marauders, who exist among the corpses and waste. Most remaining humans are members of roving bands of cannibals, and all manner of goodness and grace have ostensibly come an end.

Although the story follows the father and son as they travel the road, the man's recollections and dream visions are interspersed throughout the narrative. He dreams of an uncle and of his dead wife, and he wonders what place these images have in this bleak and cold world of abominations beyond human imaginings. Humans in this world are so desperate that they procreate to survive: In one scene, the father and son happen upon a charred human infant on a spit.

The man has a gun with two bullets, and he instructs his son that, if need be, the boy must use a bullet on himself. The man is protector, nurturer, and caregiver to his son. Indeed, he has survived solely for the boy's sake. The man shepherds and instructs his son because he knows that within the boy lies the possibility of human goodness, but the man is dying, and along the journey he often coughs up blood.

The road is dangerous, and the boy and the man walk, half-starved, pushing an old shopping cart filled with the few bits of food, tools, and clothing they possess. They live in constant peril of encountering other survivors who literally and metaphorically evince the unnatural landscape. The father and son refer to themselves as the "good guys," and they talk often about a fire that they carry within. The words are like mantras, and the father reminds the boy of them several times after encounters with the remnants of cannibalistic campers along the road. The father also tells the boy that good guys are lucky, and this often proves to be the case: On the road, the two chance upon morel mushrooms, rotten apples, an unopened can of soda, drops of gasoline or water that they siphon, and an undiscovered underground bunker full of boxes of food and drink.

Several times, the boy ceases to speak for a while as a result of the horrors he witnesses. Early in the novel, the two encounter a dazed man who has been struck by lightning. Later, they meet another old man who says his name is Ely and who talks to the father about the absence of God. The boy is much friendlier toward the old man than is his father. The boy, and all that he may represent, may be the only hope in this chaotic new world.

The man begins to cough more blood. The two travelers set up camp for the last time, and the father tells his son that he must go on alone. The following day, the boy wakens to find his father dead. He sits by the body of his dead father until a man appears on the road. Frightened at first, the boy trusts that the man is a good guy and so goes with him. There are others with the man, a woman and at least two children, and the woman talks to the boy about God. The final lines of the novel speak of brook trout in streams that once were.

Critical Evaluation:

The Road, Cormac McCarthy's tenth novel, was awarded the Pulitzer Prize in fiction in 2007. The postapocalyptic work ostensibly marked a thematic shift in McCarthy's corpus. His first novels—*The Orchard Keeper* (1965), *Outer Dark* (1968), *Child of God* (1973), and *Suttree* (1979), set in the mountains of Tennessee—are often broadly classified as Southern Gothic. A later set of novels began with *Blood Meridian: Or, The Evening Redness in the West* (1985) and continued through *The Border Trilogy* (1999; includes *All the Pretty Horses*, 1992, *The Crossing*, 1994, and *Cities of the Plain*, 1998) and *No Country for Old Men* (2005). These novels explore decidedly Western themes and terrains. Physical landscapes are of primary importance to McCarthy, often suggesting the interiority and moral compass of his main characters. *The Road* marked McCarthy's literary return to the southeast and explores themes, motifs, and concerns posed throughout the McCarthy canon.

In 2007, Oprah Winfrey selected *The Road* for Oprah's Book Club, heightening favorable mainstream reactions to the novel. Significantly, *The Road* was the first McCarthy novel to receive both popular and academic appreciation. The book's language is sparse yet poetic and philosophically motivated, and the text is composed not of chapters but of discrete, punctuated paragraphs that mirror the movements of the father and son on their journey.

The Road employs a third-person narration that is generally omniscient but that often lapses into a limited third-person perspective to develop the father's internal despair. Stylistically resembling *Suttree* and *The Crossing*, the hinge novel of *The Border Trilogy*, *The Road* employs the narrative shifts that emphasize the protagonist's moral compass, as well as the metaphorical nature of the titular road. The father and son journey, but their quest to reach the coast reveals a spirituality that supersedes the tangible. The man often sobs as he watches the boy sleep, but his sorrow is not about death: "He wasn't sure what it was about but he thought it was about beauty or about goodness." The father continually resurrects the rites he believes once brought beauty and grace to the world.

Born after the apocalypse, the boy has no memory of ceremonies and privileges of the previous world. At one point, the man realizes that he is like an alien to the boy, "a being from a planet that no longer existed." Throughout the novel, the man evokes the forms of his vanished world as he struggles to imbue his son with a sense of the lost civilization. Although the narrative often highlights the father's agnostic crisis and the man exhibits the ego necessary for his own survival, he ruminates on the loss of the world and the humanity

he once shared. As the father contemplates his complicity, moral and otherwise, in the devastation of the world, so do readers. The man tells the boy that he was appointed by God to care for him. Unlike the father, however, the boy exhibits no ego but only the altruism required for the survival of a species. The boy practices hope in a hopeless world; he appears to know no other way.

There is a mythic quality to all of McCarthy's works, and in *The Road* the ultimate challenge of humanity's cosmic insignificance is found in the fire spoken of by the man and the boy. As the man lies dying, he tells his son that the fire is real and that the boy must assume responsibility for it. "It's inside you. It was always there. I can see it," the man says. The man's journey has ended, as readers have come to know that it must. The woman who appears to instruct and love the boy after the father's death also reminds readers that, although keeping alive the memory of human kindness may be difficult in a seemingly forever-barren landscape of ash and human horrors, the fire of humanity—the breath of God—yet remains to kindle their hearts. The fire, in the end, burns strong, and it illuminates the boy. The man sees the light, which moves with the boy, all around him. Significantly, although the boy survives, it is the father whose vision readers share.

Regardless of the many charred bodies, ghastly horrors, evils, and vanished ethics of the human race that *The Road* portrays, the novel evinces an ambiguous hope in the possibility that goodness lies buried deep within the human frame. The forms are gone, but love can yet evoke that which can be known beyond language. This attitude makes *The Road* a profound and poignant work. There is a fearless wisdom in McCarthy's speculations. The novel invokes a fierce vision, but it is a vision wrought by shreds of optimism and the rules of redemption. *The Road*, despite the emptiness it ostensibly professes, nonetheless brims with a penetrating insight that obliges readers to reckon with the uneasy precariousness of what it means to be human. The collapse of the world is secondary to the collapse of all that is humane.

Cordelia E. Barrera

Further Reading

Bloom, Harold, ed. *Cormac McCarthy.* 2d ed. New York: Bloom's Literary Criticism, 2009. Collection of essays by leading scholars of McCarthy, several of which focus on space and landscape in his work. Includes a comprehensive introduction by Bloom. Essays in the first (2001) edition of the collection place McCarthy's work within a broader Southern canon that includes Flannery O'Connor and William Faulkner.

Cant, John. *Cormac McCarthy and the Myth of American Exceptionalism.* New York: Routledge, 2008. An excellent study that deconstructs the mythic forms surrounding American exceptionalism and grand narratives found throughout the McCarthy canon. Appendix 2 focuses on *The Road.*

_____, ed. *The Cormac McCarthy Journal* 6 (Autumn, 2008). This journal is published once a year by the Cormac McCarthy Society. Volume 6 is devoted to critical interpretations of *The Road* and features twelve essays. Contains the keynote address of the McCarthy Society 2007 conference in Knoxville, Tennessee, titled "The Road Home."

Greenwood, Willard P. *Reading Cormac McCarthy.* Santa Barbara, Calif.: Greenwood Press, 2009. Part of a series entitled "The Pop Lit Book Club," this volume is aimed at general readers. Focuses on McCarthy's works, characters, themes, and contexts and relates these to current events and popular culture. Includes sidebars, questions, prompts for discussion by students and book clubs.

Lilley, James D., ed. *Cormac McCarthy: New Directions.* Albuquerque: University of New Mexico Press, 2002. Twelve essays and an editor's introduction that develop the theme of storytelling and witnessing in the McCarthy canon.

Lincoln, Kenneth. *Cormac McCarthy: American Canticles.* New York: Palgrave Macmillan, 2009. Focusing on McCarthy's male protagonists and themes of regeneration through violence, this book provides thorough, accessible plot summaries of McCarthy's novels, play, and screenplay. Chapter 14 is devoted to *The Road.*

Wallach, Rick, ed. *Myth, Legend, Dust: Critical Responses to Cormac McCarthy.* New York: Manchester University Press, 2000. An invaluable source containing twenty-six essays by noted McCarthy scholars. Essays address the unity of the McCarthy canon and are divided into the Appalachian novels and the Southwestern novels.

Roan Stallion

Author: Robinson Jeffers (1887-1962)
First published: 1925
Type of work: Poetry
Type of plot: Symbolism
Time of plot: 1920's
Locale: Carmel coast, California

Principal characters:
CALIFORNIA, a farm wife
JOHNNY, her husband
CHRISTINE, their daughter

The Poem:

California is the daughter of a Scottish father and a Spanish and Indian mother. From her mother she has inherited a dark beauty and a passionate nature. When she is still very young, she marries a farmer named Johnny; by the time she is twenty-one, her features are already beginning to show the marks of hard work.

Johnny spends much of his time away from the farm, drinking and gambling. One evening, he brings home a splendid roan stallion he has won. It is shortly before Christmas, and California, pleased with his good fortune, decides to go in to town to buy some Christmas presents for their young daughter, Christine. Johnny delays her departure in the morning so that it is quite late before she can hitch their old mare to the buggy and set out for Monterey.

By nightfall, when she is ready to return home, a heavy rainstorm has started. The water is high when she reaches the ford, and before trying to cross in the darkness, she lashes the gifts she has bought around her body, hoping this will keep them dry. The mare refuses to cross the swollen stream and flounders back to shore. California soothes the mare and tries once more to guide her across the ford, but the animal is too frightened. Desperate, California prays for light. Suddenly, the heavens light up brilliantly and she sees in them the face of a child over whom angels are hovering. The mare, startled by the light, scrambles back to shore. Sobbing, California climbs out of the buggy, fastens the presents securely to her back, and mounts the horse. By the light of the heavens she is able to guide the mare across the stream and reach home safely.

California thinks that she hates the roan stallion, but she cannot stop thinking about the magnificent beast. When she tells young Christine of the miraculous light at the ford and describes the birth of Christ, she can hardly restrain herself from identifying the stallion with the deity. She knows that outside, Johnny is mating the stallion with a neighbor's mare.

That evening, Johnny goes down the valley to the home of a neighbor. After Christine falls asleep, California steals out to the stable, where she leans against the fence, listening to the far-off cries of coyotes and watching the moon rise over the hill. Once before, she thinks, she has seen God. If she were to ride to the top of the hill, perhaps she might do so again. She hurries down to the corral where the stallion is kept, and the horse hears her as she approaches. She caresses his flanks, wishing that nature had not made it impossible for him to possess her. Then she springs up onto his back and revels in the feel of his muscles as he gallops up the hillside. At the top they halt, and she dismounts and tethers the stallion lightly to a tree. Overwhelmed by his majesty and her desire, she throws herself at his feet.

The following night, California cannot bear the thought of being with Johnny. He has brought home some wine and, half drunk, orders her to drink some. Revolted at the thought of the night ahead, California steals to the door, opens it, and flees. Excited by the prospect of a chase, Johnny calls to his dog to help him. When California hears them approaching, she crawls under the fence into the corral, the dog close behind her. The stallion is frightened by the snarling, snapping dog, and when Johnny climbs into the corral, the fierce stallion tramples him.

Christine is awakened by the noise, and, frightened to be alone in the house, she makes her way to the corral. When she sees her injured father, she runs back to the house for the rifle. California takes the gun from her and shoots the dog. While she watches, the stallion strikes again at Johnny, killing him. Then, prompted by a remnant of fidelity to the human race, she raises the rifle and shoots the stallion. She feels as if she has killed God.

Critical Evaluation:

With the publication of *Roan Stallion* in 1925, Robinson Jeffers finally achieved recognition and financial reward. In a literary career that spanned forty-two years, from *Flagons and Apples* (1912) to *Hungerfield, and Other Poems* (1954), the poet reached the height of his popularity in the early 1930's. Jeffers, the son of a minister, had been educated in the classics, and many of his poems draw upon biblical and classical sources. His treatment of these sources is, however, extremely unconventional. He does not avoid topics of violence and sexual abnormality, but the center of his vision is at once religious (though not in the ordinary sense) and philosophical. His poetry, marked by dramatic power, has been called both "romantic" and "naturalistic." Certainly, nature figures prominently in Jeffers's thinking and in his works.

Roan Stallion, the shortest of Jeffers's long poems, combines elements of myth, Christianity, and the poet's own philosophy to produce a work that many consider one of his best. The story of the poem draws on those Egyptian and Greek myths in which a mortal falls in love with a powerful beast. In *Roan Stallion*, a woman falls in love with a magnificent horse that she comes to identify with God. Unlike the situation in traditional myth, however, here the union of woman and horse/god does not produce gods or demigods; rather, it leads to a heightened psychological awareness on the part of the woman. *Roan Stallion* is to some extent the story of California's initiation and journey toward identity.

At the beginning of the poem, the woman California stands "at the turn of the road," symbolic of the journey she is about to undertake. Throughout, she is opposed to her degenerate husband, Johnny. As the diminutive form of his name implies, Johnny has never become an adult; brutish and domineering, he spends much of his time gambling and drinking. He has no appreciation of his wife other than as an object for sex; indeed, he once gambles her away to another man for two nights. Johnny also has no appreciation for the majesty of the stallion, which he thinks of merely as a commodity for his use.

California, as her name implies, is "of the earth," and her name is also suggestive of the American West, a land of freedom and possibility. She is connected with the forces of nature, has a profound love for her daughter, Christine, and is aware of a spiritual plane. It is this connectedness that places California far above Johnny. California's prayers when she is trying to ford the stream are answered with a vision of the Christ child and light; she also sees angels with "birds' heads, hawks' heads." Although this combination of Christian and pagan elements disconcerted some of Jeffers's readers when the poem first appeared, it is consistent with Jeffers's pantheistic theme that the universe is a single organism and that there is a holiness in nature that can transcend the human sphere.

Unlike her husband, California comes to view the stallion as a pure embodiment of the natural world—he is beautiful and free, the "exultant strength of the world." The stallion also represents a pure, unadulterated male force that is superior to the human male in this poem, a theme somewhat similar to the one developed by the English novelist, short-story writer, and poet D. H. Lawrence in his novella *St. Mawr*, which was published in the same year as *Roan Stallion*.

Roan Stallion is an unrhymed narrative poem divided

chronologically into three main sections. The first takes place on Christmas Eve and consists of California's journey to Monterey and back to bring presents to her daughter Christine. On this journey, California experiences the vision, is symbolically baptized in the swollen stream, identifies with the mare, Dora, and in a daydream envisions a dangerous water-stallion whose sexual force has the power to crush her.

The second episode begins in springtime, symbolic of fertility and rebirth, and involves California's ride with the stallion to the hilltop. Though California is first afraid of being thrown or trampled, she ends up lying under the stallion's hooves in an act of submission and worship. This section of the poem is complicated by the intrusion of two verses that amplify the narrative in much the same way a Greek chorus does. These verses reinforce Jeffers's philosophical creed. The first intrusion occurs near the beginning of the second episode, right after Johnny has left for the night, and begins with the line that came to be used to explain Jeffers's philosophy of "inhumanism": "Humanity is the mould to break away from . . ./ The Atom to be split." The second intrusion occurs at the end of the second episode, while California is lying under the stallion's hooves. Both mystical and surreal, this verse elaborates on myth, religion, and the nature of human consciousness. Lying at the feet of the godlike stallion, California becomes the human race itself wedded to pure nature. The hilltop is appropriately likened to Calvary, since it is here that California completely dies to her old self and undergoes a transformation.

The third and final section of the poem occurs the following evening and includes the stallion's death at California's hands. Significantly, California's previous apathy toward her husband has turned to hate, exemplifying her new awareness of herself and her environment. With the powerful ending, Jeffers implies that California is human and loyal to humanity. Because the stallion has killed a human being, however insignificant that human being may have been, the animal must die. This fact, Jeffers seems to imply, is both tragic and inevitable.

In an alternative interpretation, California could be seen to have been initiated through the stallion from innocence into a profound knowing. Though California once believed that the stallion might kill her, it is she who at the end wields the godlike power of death. Symbolically, the stallion's sacrifice and death in spring indicate a return to mother earth and the process of regeneration for California. Knowing love, knowing God, and knowing suffering and death, California now also knows what it is to be truly human.

"Critical Evaluation" by Candace E. Andrews

Further Reading

Brophy, Robert J. *Robinson Jeffers: Myth, Ritual, and Symbol in His Narrative Poems.* Cleveland: Case Western Reserve University Press, 1973. Presents analysis of *Roan Stallion* that equates California with a marelike earth goddess, Johnny with a doomed year-spirit beast, Christine with a solstice-child, the stallion with a Poseidon-like steed of God, and California's dream with a Christian-pagan conflation lighted by natural dynamism.

_____, ed. *Robinson Jeffers: Dimensions of a Poet.* New York: Fordham University Press, 1995. Collection of essays offers various interpretations of Jeffers's poetry. Topics addressed include Jeffers's uses of history, the female archetype in his work, and his relationship to Carmel and Big Sur, California. An essay devoted to the poem is titled "*Roan Stallion* and the Narrative of Nature."

Coffin, Arthur B. *Robinson Jeffers: Poet of Inhumanism.* Madison: University of Wisconsin Press, 1971. Traces Jeffers's ideological advance toward inhumanism, noting *Roan Stallion* as a work of primary importance. Observes how the poem's heroine temporarily frees herself from accustomed social behavior by shedding human attributes, seeing God's eminence in a horse, and letting it kill her contemptible husband.

Everson, William. *The Excesses of God: Robinson Jeffers as a Religious Figure.* Stanford, Calif.: Stanford University Press, 1988. Contends that Jeffers, habitually combining paganism and mysticism, regards the religious aspect of sex as a primordial force, a supernatural wrath, and an analogy of divine life. Demonstrates how he dramatizes this belief in *Roan Stallion.*

McClintock, Scott. "The Poetics of Fission in Robinson Jeffers." *CLIO: A Journal of Literature, History, and the Philosophy of History* 37, no. 2 (Spring, 2008): 171-191. Analyzes the transformation of Jeffers's poetics from a metaphysical philosophy of inhumanism to his use of more violent imagery influenced by the development of nuclear weapons during the Cold War.

Nolte, William H. *Rock and Hawk: Robinson Jeffers and the Romantic Agony.* Athens: University of Georgia Press, 1978. Interprets the figure of California in *Roan Stallion* as enacting an unwilled, unconscious, beautiful microcosmic recapitulation of one of the several dark, macrocosmic myths ruling humanity.

Squires, Radcliffe. *The Loyalties of Robinson Jeffers.* Ann Arbor: University of Michigan Press, 1956. Divides Jeffers's poetry into diffuse, sagalike works and classically unified shorter poems. In the first category, Jeffers explores the ramifications of sinning. In the second category, best exemplified by *Roan Stallion*, he espouses breaking free of life as the solution to problems occasioned by sin.

Zaller, Robert, ed. *Centennial Essays for Robinson Jeffers.* Newark: University of Delaware Press, 1991. Collection of nine essays offers analyses of Jeffers's work, including pieces by poets William Everson and Czesław Miłosz.

Rob Roy

Author: Sir Walter Scott (1771-1832)
First published: 1817
Type of work: Novel
Type of plot: Historical
Time of plot: 1715
Locale: Northumberland, England; Glasgow, Scotland

Principal characters:
WILLIAM OSBALDISTONE, a man employed by the firm of Osbaldistone and Tresham
FRANK OSBALDISTONE, his son
SIR HILDEBRAND OSBALDISTONE, Frank's uncle
RASHLEIGH OSBALDISTONE, his son
SIR FREDERICK VERNON, a Jacobite
DIANA VERNON, his daughter
ROB ROY (MACGREGOR CAMPBELL), a Scottish outlaw

The Story:

Frank Osbaldistone is recalled from France, where his father had sent him to learn the family's mercantile business. Disappointed in his son's progress, the father angrily orders the young man to Osbaldistone Hall, home of his uncle, Sir Hildebrand Osbaldistone, in northern England. His father gives him fifty guineas for expenses and instructions to learn who among Sir Hildebrand's sons will accept a position in the trading house of Osbaldistone and Tresham.

On the road, Frank falls in with a traveler named Morris, who is carrying a large sum of money in a portmanteau strapped to his saddle. That evening, they stop at the Black Bear Inn in the town of Darlington, where they are joined at dinner by a Scotsman named Mr. Campbell, who is really Rob Roy, the Scottish outlaw. The next morning, Campbell and Morris leave together. At a secluded spot along the road, the men are halted and a highwayman robs Morris of his saddlebag. Meanwhile, Frank rides toward Osbaldistone Hall. As he nears the rambling old mansion, he sees that a fox hunt is in progress and meets Diana Vernon, Sir Hildebrand's niece. The outspoken Diana tells Frank that all of his cousins are mixtures in varying proportions of sot, gamekeeper, bully, horse jockey, and fool. Rashleigh, she says, is the most dangerous of the lot, for he maintains a private tyranny over everyone with whom he comes in contact. It is Rashleigh, however, who is prevailed upon to accept Frank's vacant position at Osbaldistone and Tresham.

Frank and his cousins dislike one another. One night,

while drinking with the family, Frank becomes enraged at Rashleigh's speech and actions and strikes him. Rashleigh never forgets the blow, although to all intents and purposes he and Frank declare themselves friends after their anger has cooled.

Shortly after Frank's arrival at Osbaldistone Hall, he is accused of highway robbery. He goes at once to Squire Inglewood's court to defend himself and to confront his accuser, who turns out to be Morris. Rob Roy, however, appears at the squire's court of justice and forces Morris to confess that Frank is not the man who robbed him.

When Rashleigh departs to go into business with Frank's father, Frank becomes Diana's tutor. Their association develops into deep affection on both sides, a mutual attraction marred only by the fact that Diana is a Catholic and Frank a Presbyterian.

One day, Frank receives a letter from his father's partner, Mr. Tresham. The letter informs him that his father has gone to the Continent on business, leaving Rashleigh in charge; Rashleigh, however, has gone to Scotland, where he is reportedly involved in a scheme to embezzle funds from Osbaldistone and Tresham.

Frank, accompanied by Andrew Fairservice, Sir Hildebrand's gardener, sets off for Glasgow in an attempt to frustrate Rashleigh's plans. Arriving in the city on Sunday, they go to church. As Frank stands listening to the preacher, a voice behind him whispers that he is in danger and that he should not look back at his informant. The mysterious messenger asks Frank to meet him on the bridge at midnight. Frank keeps the tryst and follows the man to the Tolbooth prison. There he finds his father's chief clerk, Mr. Owen, who has been arrested and thrown into prison at the instigation of MacVittie and MacFin, Glasgow traders who do business with his father. Frank learns that Campbell is his mysterious informant and guide, and, for the first time, he realizes that Campbell and Rob Roy are one and the same.

Shortly thereafter, Frank sees Morris, MacVittie, and Rashleigh talking together. He follows them, and, when Morris and MacVittie depart, Frank confronts Rashleigh and demands an explanation of his behavior. As their argument grows more heated, swords are drawn, but the duel is broken up by Rob Roy, who cries shame at them because they are men of the same blood. Rob Roy considers both men his friends. Frank also learns that his father's funds were mixed up with a Jacobite uprising in which Sir Hildebrand was one of the plotters. He suspects that Rashleigh robbed Morris based on information supplied by Rob Roy.

Frank and Andrew are arrested by an officer on their way to meet Rob Roy, and the officer who searches Frank discovers a note that Rob Roy had written to him. On the road, the company is attacked by Scotsmen under the direction of Helen, Rob Roy's wife, who captures or kills all the soldiers. Helen, a bloodthirsty woman, orders that Morris, who has fallen into the hands of the Highlanders, be put to death. In the meantime, Rob Roy too is captured, but he makes his escape when one of his captors rides close to him and surreptitiously cuts his bonds. Rob Roy then throws himself from his horse into the river and swims to safety before his guards can overtake him.

With a Highland uprising threatening, Frank thinks he has seen Diana for the last time, but he meets her soon afterward riding through a wood in the company of her father, Sir Frederick Vernon, a political exile. Diana gives Frank a packet of papers that Rashleigh has been forced to give up; they are notes to the credit of Osbaldistone and Tresham. Frank's father's fortune is safe.

In the Jacobite revolt of 1715, Rashleigh becomes a turncoat and joins the forces of King George. At the beginning of the revolt, Sir Hildebrand had made his will, listing the order in which his sons are to inherit to his lands. Because Rashleigh has betrayed the Stuart cause, Sir Hildebrand substitutes Frank's name for that of Rashleigh in the will. Sir Hildebrand is later captured by the royal forces and imprisoned at Newgate, where he dies. His four sons also die from various causes, and Frank inherits all the lands and properties that belonged to Sir Hildebrand. When Frank goes to Osbaldistone Hall to take over, Rashleigh shows up with a warrant for Diana and her father; but he is killed in a fight with Rob Roy. Frank becomes the lord of Osbaldistone Hall. At first, Frank's father does not like the idea of his son's marrying a Papist, but in the end he relents and gives his permission, and Frank and Diana are married.

Critical Evaluation:

Rob Roy, which captures the raging cultural and religious debates of the early eighteenth century, is considered one of Sir Walter Scott's Waverley novels because it too employs the technique the author first used in his *Waverley: Or, 'Tis Sixty Years Since* (1814), that of using historical fact within a novelistic setting. To read this novel profitably, it is important to get a sense of the history that frames its characters and events. *Rob Roy* is set in northern England and in Scotland at the time of "the fifteener." This was an attempted invasion in 1715 by the son of James II, whose Catholic family line was ousted in the so-called Glorious Revolution of 1688. His two daughters, Mary and Anne, were allowed to finish the Stuart legacy, which ended with the accession of King George I in 1714. James II's son was known as the Old Pretender, and by some Jacobites as James III. Those who supported the newly crowned King George were known as Royalists, and those who were for the Stuart family line were known as Jacobites because they were supporters of the Old Pretender, James III. That name was used because the names James and Jacob have the same linguistic root. It is important to keep these lineages and names in mind while reading *Rob Roy*.

After the Act of Union with Scotland in 1707, Scotland became a subordinate part of Great Britain, a position it was not happy to assume. The vast majority of people in the south of England solidly supported George I, but in the north, and especially among the Highland clans of Scotland, there was much support for the Stuart line and fervid anti-English sentiment. One reason for this is that both the Stuarts and the Highlanders were nominally Catholic, and they were able to establish lasting ties while the Stuarts were trying to remain in power during the Civil War. Memory of this loyalty was so strong that as late as 1745 the son of the Old Pretender tried one last invasion, again by way of Scotland, to place himself on the throne. It failed, but the attempt shows the great cultural differences between Scotland and England. These cultural differences lie at the heart of *Rob Roy*.

Rob Roy, or Robert MacGregor, was a historical figure who became an outlaw as a result of political intrigue and shifts in cultural values. He was also a Jacobite. At times a cattle thief and always at the fringes of the law, he skirmished and raided his way along the Scotland-England border and was seen as a sort of Robin Hood. The relation between this historical character and the one in the novel is important, for it marks Scott's attempt to combine authentic or true history with fictive romance. Indeed, Rob Roy was already the stuff of legend, and Scott was able to make use of this popular fascination and combine it with the more realistic elements of law and culture. The result was one of the groundbreaking novels in literary history.

Scott's melding of the romance and historical genres is an important contribution to the history of the novel as well as a fascinating element within *Rob Roy* itself. At the time Scott wrote *Rob Roy*, it was popularly assumed that the novel genre was dominated by women and what was considered feminine "romance" discourse. Scott began to change this not only by creating strong male and female characters but also by interfusing historical elements and those of chivalric romance. This combination of what most people considered opposing traditions began a new development in the history of the novel.

The figure of Rob Roy in Scott's novel is interesting not only because he is an outlaw but also because at many times his lawlessness is more legitimate than the laws wielded by the state. Rob Roy's ultimate contribution in the novel, killing Rashleigh after he tries to serve a warrant for Diana, aids in establishing Frank as the legitimate lord of Osbaldistone Hall. Furthermore, his apparently irresponsible and lawless act creates a marriage that transcends the limits of the anti-Catholic and anti-Protestant cultures that threaten to destroy the union between Frank and Diana. Rob Roy's actions in the novel show the ambivalence of power as it is wielded by the government, and they show that the correct use of power and law cannot be fully claimed by the state alone. *Rob Roy* also shows that the normal conventions of society do not prove to be useful and valid at all times. Even Frank's father realizes this. When he allows the marriage to take place, the novel shows that it is possible for people to transcend the given prejudices of any culture.

The epistolary structure of *Rob Roy* is on the surface rather traditional, following in a long line of novels that includes Samuel Richardson's *Clarissa: Or, The History of a Young Lady* (1747-1748) and Madame de Staël's *Delphine* (1802; English translation, 1803). Mary Wollstonecraft Shelley's *Frankenstein: Or, The Modern Prometheus* (1818), which was published the same year as *Rob Roy*, also has a similar format. Much has been made of the fragmentary style of these novels, but it must be kept in mind that these authors assumed they were telling the complete story and that nothing was left out or incomplete. However, a more verifiable

antitraditional element in *Rob Roy* is its emphasis on things that many people considered real.

Rob Roy centers on legalistic elements such as wills, courts, and other things with which a trained lawyer such as Scott would have been familiar. In fact, Scott was interested in reforming many of the law practices at the time, and it has been argued that the legalistic elements in this novel are a part of this agenda. *Rob Roy* also centers on religious and ethnic issues that, just seventy-five years earlier, were considered too inflammatory to discuss openly. All these elements combine to create a novel that was quite revolutionary for its time and continued to demand attention in subsequent times. Its analysis of power, ethnicity, culture, and the proper use of law speaks powerfully to any century.

"Critical Evaluation" by James Aaron Stanger

Further Reading

Anderson, James. *Sir Walter Scott and History*. Edinburgh: Edina, 1981. Presents Scott as an innovator in the historical novel who possessed the ability to delve into the embers of the Jacobite and Scottish/English conflicts of the eighteenth century.

Beiderwell, Bruce John. *Power and Punishment in Scott's Novels*. Athens: University of Georgia Press, 1992. Takes a Foucauldian approach in examining Scott's representations of the shifting structures of state power and punishment. Argues that *Rob Roy* represents the uses and misuses of power as well as Scott's ambivalence about paradigms of punishment and state discipline.

D'Arcy, Julian Meldon. *Subversive Scott: The Waverley Novels and Scottish Nationalism*. Reykjavík, Iceland: Vigdís Finnbogadóttir Institute of Foreign Languages, University of Iceland, 2005. Demonstrates how the novels contain dissonant elements, undetected manifestations of Scottish nationalism, and criticism of the United Kingdom and its imperial policy. Chapter 6 examines *Rob Roy*.

Ferris, Ina. *The Achievement of Literary Authority: Gender, History, and the Waverley Novels*. Ithaca, N.Y.: Cornell University Press, 1991. Revisionist history argues that the Waverley novels inscribed masculinist rhetoric and authority within the then female-dominated genre of the historical novel. Discusses how the feminine voice remained in Scott's writings and illuminates the role of gender in *Rob Roy*, accounting for Diana as a strong character.

Irvine, Robert P. "*Rob Roy* and Two Versions of Modernity: As Political Economy and as Polite Discourse." In *Enlightenment and Romance: Gender and Agency in Smol-*

lett and Scott. New York: Peter Lang, 2000. Analyzes the fiction of Scott and Tobias Smollett within the context of the emergence of the social sciences and the dominance of novels written by women in the eighteenth century. Describes how the authors adapted the feminine romance and the domestic novel to assert control over the narrative structure of their novels.

Lincoln, Andrew. *Walter Scott and Modernity*. Edinburgh: Edinburgh University Press, 2007. Examines Scott's novels and poems and asserts that these were not works of nostalgia; instead, Scott used the past as a means of exploring modernist moral, political, and social issues. Includes discussion of *Rob Roy*.

Murray, W. H. *Rob Roy MacGregor: His Life and Times*. Glasgow: R. Drew, 1982. Excellent biography of the historical figure details his part in the confusing and constantly shifting loyalties and political currents that existed in Scotland in the early eighteenth century. Portrays MacGregor as a Scottish Robin Hood.

Robertson, Fiona. *Legitimate Histories: Scott, Gothic, and the Authorities of Fiction*. New York: Oxford University Press, 1994. Analyzes Scott's Waverley novels within the context of eighteenth and nineteenth century gothic literature and examines the novels' critical reception. Devotes a chapter to *Rob Roy*.

Shaw, Harry E., ed. *Critical Essays on Sir Walter Scott: The Waverley Novels*. New York: G. K. Hall, 1996. Collection of essays published between 1858 and 1996 about Scott's series of novels includes journalist Walter Bagehot's 1858 article about the Waverley novels as well as discussions of Scott's rationalism, the subversion of the literary form in his fiction, and what his work meant to Victorian readers.

Sutherland, John. *The Life of Walter Scott: A Critical Biography*. New York: Blackwell, 1995. Authoritative biography on Scott provides insight into how his life and identity as a Scotsman helped influence his creation of such heroes as Rob Roy.

The Robe

Author: Lloyd C. Douglas (1877-1951)
First published: 1942
Type of work: Novel
Type of plot: Historical
Time of plot: c. 32-37 C.E.
Locale: Rome, Minoa, Jerusalem, and Greece

Principal characters:
JESUS, the crucified founder of a new religion
MARCELLUS LUCAN GALLIO, the crucifier of Jesus, who wins Jesus's robe
MARCUS LUCAN GALLIO, Marcellus Gallio's father
LUCIA GALLIO, Gallio's fifteen-year-old daughter
ADELPHOS DEMETRIUS, Marcellus's Corinthian slave and friend, who is an admirer of Theodosia Eupolis
PRINCE GAIUS, suitor who tries to force himself on Lucia and later Diana; a possible heir to the Roman throne
GAIUS CAESAR AUGUSTUS GERMANICUS (CALIGULA), third Roman emperor (37-41 C.E.) and Prince Gaius's nephew
TIBERIUS JULIUS CAESAR AUGUSTUS, second Roman emperor, 14-37 C.E.
DIANA ASINIAN, Tiberius's step-granddaughter
QUINTUS, Prince Gaius's personal foot soldier
PONTIUS PILATE, a local magistrate who "washes his hands" of Jesus' crucifixion
JUSTUS, Marcellus's guide in retracing the steps of Jesus
STEPHANOS (STEPHEN), a martyr stoned circa 33 C.E.
GEORGE EUPOLIS, Greek innkeeper who houses Marcellus and Demetrius
THEODOSIA EUPOLIS, his daughter

The Story:

Early on the morning following the Military Tribune Banquet, Marcellus Lucan Gallio tells his sister Lucia that he was drunk the night before and laughed outright at the tribute to Prince Gaius, who may be emperor someday. Lucia fears Gaius's revenge; she admits she has previously rejected Gaius's attempts to make love to her. In addition, Senator Gallio, their father, has recently criticized Gaius openly.

Marcellus receives orders to serve in Minoa, an undesirable port city in Southern Palestine. His Corinthian slave Adelphos Demetrius accompanies him. In Minoa, Marcellus receives new orders to take his troops to Jerusalem to ensure peace during Passover. The Roman government and the Sanhedrin (the legislative body of the Jewish temple) worry about the teacher Jesus, who has been drawing crowds and drove the money changers from the temple.

Jesus is seized by the Romans. Demetrius makes eye contact with Jesus as the soldiers push the abused man past him. Demetrius feels peace after the experience. The tormented Jesus goes before High Priest Caiaphas and the Sanhedrin. Pontius Pilate literally washes his hands of the matter and sends Jesus to the ruler who settles Galilean affairs, Herod Agrippa. Herod sentences the prophet to death by crucifixion.

Marcellus must oversee the cruelty inflicted upon Jesus. He heeds Centurion Paulos's advice to drink in order to endure overseeing the punishment. Marcellus even casts lots and wins Jesus' robe at the foot of the cross. Once Marcellus recovers his sobriety, he realizes what he has done. He asks Demetrius to dispose of the robe.

Marcellus goes to Pontius Pilate's banquet hall and charges Pilate with unfairness. At the banquet, Centurion Paulos asks to see the robe. Demetrius brings it to him, gaining peace from its touch. Marcellus dons the robe at Paulos's request and loses his mind at its touch. Marcellus becomes ill, and he and Demetrius return to Rome.

Senator Gallio suggests that Demetrius and Marcellus go to Athens to stay at George Eupolis's inn. An Athenian weaver named Benjamin repairs the robe and teaches the men more about Jesus. Emperor Tiberius sends new orders to Marcellus by Quintus, Gaius's personal soldier. When Quintus insults Eupolis's daughter, Demetrius attacks Quintus and wounds him severely.

Demetrius flees on the ship *Vetris* to Palestine and develops a plan to reunite with Marcellus later. Captain Fulvius protects Demetrius, who had once rescued the captain from an attacking slave. Once in Palestine, Demetrius works with Benyosef, a weaver. Demetrius learns the trade. He learns to read Aramaic; receives baptism from Peter, the Big Fisherman; and meets Matthais and Barsabas Justus, two replacements for the disciple Judas who betrayed Jesus.

Justus serves as a guide for Marcellus, who has orders from Tiberius to retrace Jesus' route, to gather information on Jesus, and to share the information with the emperor. Marcellus becomes a Christian. Along the roadsides, the two travelers begin to see the secret symbol of the Christians: a drawing of a fish. The Greek word for fish in an acronym of the phrase "Jesus Christ, Son of God, Savior." The fish symbol enables Christians to communicate secretly their belief in Jesus as the Savior.

Justus and Marcellus meet the crippled girl Miriam, whom Jesus endowed with a gift of song, and the boy Jonathan (Justus's grandson), whom Jesus healed. They learn from each of them. They visit Tamar, a widow whose looms were destroyed after she tried to weave on the Sabbath to earn money. The carpenter Jesus repaired her looms. She repairs the robe for Marcellus.

On his travels, Marcellus hears of Jesus's admonition to pay adequately and of Jesus's miracles of healing, calming the sea, and changing water to wine. Marcellus learns of the tax collector Zaccheus whom Jesus treated with respect, of a boy whose fish and loaves fed a multitude, of the fig-keeper and disciple Nathanael Bartholomew, of Lydia, who was healed by touching Jesus' robe, of those who encountered Jesus after the resurrection, and of the Good Samaritan. Marcellus learns that Pontius Pilate has gone to Crete because his mental condition has worsened since the crucifixion.

Demetrius receives a summons to appear before Paulos to explain what he did to Quintus. Paulos releases Demetrius. Marcellus sees the dangers in being Christian: Peter faces arrest because of his preaching, but he begins to heal others. Marcellus witnesses the martyrdom of Stephen. When he returns to Rome and to his family, he finds that his love Diana and the Emperor Tiberius are in Capri; he must go there to report to Tiberius and to see Diana.

Marcellus tells Diana of his new devotion to Jesus. She says she still loves him but does not yet understand his religion. The emperor calls Marcellus a fool when he hears what Marcellus has to say. Tiberius tells Marcellus to renounce Jesus the next day. If he does so, the emperor will give Marcellus Diana's hand in marriage. However, Tiberius gives Diana a different account. He tells Diana that he has sworn to Marcellus that Diana will be forced to marry Gaius if Marcellus does not give up his new religion.

Tiberius asks to see the robe at their meeting the next day. When Demetrius brings the garment, Tiberius refuses to touch it and sends Marcellus away on the *Augustus*; he orders Demetrius to serve as Diana's bodyguard. When night comes, Marcellus swims ashore with the robe and his money. He secures a job in Arpino as a scribe with Appius Kaeso and shares his newfound religion with others, both rich and poor. He finds that the story of Jesus changes lives.

Demetrius begins to spend his every spare moment plaiting hemp into rope. Every night, he takes a boat trip. He never explains his actions, but others become accustomed to his routine.

On Capri, changes are occurring. Price Gaius dies from poisoning. Emperor Tiberius's health fails quickly. Before his death, he asks that Gaius's nephew and namesake, Gaius Caesar Augustus Germanicus (Caligula) assume the throne. To indicate his whereabouts to Demetrius in Capri, Marcellus sends him a melon from Arpino and carves a fish on it. Marcellus continues to teach and preach. He even delivers Jesus' Beatitudes to his followers.

Demetrius continues to serve as a bodyguard. He observes Caligula making inappropriate advances to Diana and insists that Diana escape that night. Using the long rope he has woven, she must descend a rock cliff to his boat. While she is descending the cliff, two figures begin to pull her upward, so she lets go of the rope and falls into the water. Demetrius pulls into the boat and takes her to Greece.

On his way back to Rome, Demetrius receives severe wounds from three cavalrymen. His old friend Marcipor goes to the catacombs and calls Marcellus and Peter to Demetrius's side. Peter heals Demetrius. Marcellus's father secures Demetrius's passage to Greece, where he and Theodosia reunite. Diana—now the wife of Marcellus—and the Senator both attend Caligula's banquet. Salome, the daughter of Herod, discloses to the group that John the Baptist has been beheaded.

Caligula brings Marcellus to the banquet and orders him to renounce his new religion or face death. Marcellus refuses. Diana asks to die with Marcellus and professes to be a Christian. Hand in hand, the husband and wife walk to the palace's archery field. On their way out the door, Diana passes the robe to Marcipor for the Big Fisherman.

Critical Evaluation:

Lloyd C. Douglas has written that *The Robe* resulted from a question asked by Hazel McCann, an Ohio department-store clerk; McCann asked what had become of Jesus' robe. Douglas expanded the Gospel narratives to offer a possible answer and to create a Christian novel with human interest and romance. Douglas did not tie the events with a particular Christian sect.

Central to *The Robe* is the Jewish carpenter Jesus, the owner of the titular garment. A main fictional character is Marcellus Gallio, the Roman soldier who crucifies Jesus, wins Jesus' robe, and retraces Jesus' journeys. *The Robe* follows Marcellus's travels in the first century C.E. and depicts what Marcellus hears and sees as he explores the life of Jesus. Diverse people who encountered Jesus tell of their experiences throughout the novel; the story thus emerges from many different viewpoints, demonstrating the stylistic device of limited omniscience.

Douglas accurately depicts the historical sequence of Roman rulers during the first century. He portrays many of the events in the life of Jesus, the miracles, and the places Jesus visited in nonsequential order as Marcellus discovers them through his travels. Douglas provides neither a contents page nor an index to enable readers to locate a character, a place, or an event in the volume. The diction and the dialect of the characters are not suggestive of first century Rome. The sentence structure and Douglas's choice of words seem more evocative of 1942 than of 32 C.E.

Although many reviewers criticized the novel as merely escapist fiction, the sales of the book indicate its popularity. The novel was adapted into a 1953 epic film, the first film ever to be released in CinemaScope (an anamorphic lens technology used to create wide-screen films). The epic renewed public interest in the book.

Douglas uses open denouement in *The Robe*. Diana and Marcellus pass through a door and presumably move toward their deaths; Diana passes the robe to Marcipor with the instruction that it is for Peter. This open ending allowed Douglas to write a 1948 sequel, *The Big Fisherman*, Douglas's last novel. The motion picture industry also took advantage of the open ending of *The Robe* and produced two sequels: *Demetrius and the Gladiators* (1954) and *The Big Fisherman* (1959). Although some critics referred to these movies as "sword and sandal" pictures, the box office successes of the films indicated their popularity with the public.

Anita Price Davis

Further Reading

Dawson, Virginia Douglas, and Betty Douglas Wilson. *The Shape of Sunday: An Intimate Biography of Lloyd C. Douglas*. Boston: Houghton Mifflin, 1952. This account of Douglas's life is the work of two of his daughters. They share memories, letters, interviews, photographs, and clippings of and about their father.

Douglas, Lloyd C. *Time to Remember*. Boston: Houghton Mifflin, 1951. Douglas's autobiography begins with a notation that he was sick, crippled with arthritis, and bedfast at the time he was writing. The chronological volume begins with Douglas's birth and extends into his college years. He intended to write a second volutme but died before he could complete it, motivating his daughters to write *The Shape of Sunday.*

Fessenden, Tracy. *Culture and Redemption: Religion, the Secular, and American Literature.* Princeton, N.J.: Princeton University Press, 2007. Traces the history of representations of Christianity and deployments of Christian ideology in American literature, from colonial texts through the twentieth century.

Robert Elsmere

Author: Mary Augusta Ward (1851-1920)
First published: 1888
Type of work: Novel
Type of plot: Social realism
Time of plot: 1882-1886
Locale: Westmoreland, Oxford, Surrey, and London, England

Principal characters:
ROBERT ELSMERE, a clergyman
CATHERINE LEYBURN ELSMERE, his wife
ROSE LEYBURN, her sister
EDWARD LANGHAM, Robert's Oxford tutor
HENRY GREY, an Oxford don
SQUIRE WENDOVER, a landowner and scholar
HUGH FLAXMAN, Rose's suitor

The Story:

Catherine, Agnes, and Rose Leyburn, sisters living in a remote valley in Westmoreland, in England's Lake District, learn of the imminent arrival of Robert Elsmere, a young Anglican clergyman coming to visit his uncle and aunt before he assumes responsibility for a parish in southern England. Once he meets the Leyburns, Robert is quickly drawn to Catherine's seriousness and spirituality. Catherine resists her own attraction to Robert, having promised her deceased father to remain in Westmoreland and devote herself to her mother and sisters and to preserving the centrality of religion in their lives. Rose, a talented violinist, is already trying to break away to study music, but Catherine thinks music frivolous. Catherine is grateful when Robert persuades her to treat Rose's interests more sympathetically, but she feels she has to break off her relationship with him. She tells him that she cannot desert her family and had resolves to continue her life in Westmoreland. Her resolve is shaken when her mother, learning of her interest in Robert from Robert's matchmaking aunt, assures Catherine that she would be pleased with the match. Catherine feels her life's purpose is undermined. On a stormy evening, she attends the deathbed of a woman who bore an illegitimate child. Robert follows her and persuades her to marry him, promising that together they can live a life dedicated to God and to helping others.

This promise bears out as the Elsmeres enthusiastically embark on their work with Robert's new parishioners at Murewell, in Surrey. At the end of their first year, though, Catherine is troubled by Rose's interest in the disillusioned Edward Langham, a man with no sympathy for religious belief. Langham and Rose hope briefly that she might rouse him from the despair of his solitary, empty life, but Langham, believing himself unable to change, departs suddenly. Rose is embarrassed to have shown her interest in him.

A more serious crisis develops when Robert becomes friendly with Squire Wendover, the local large landowner and a scholar famous for his skeptical views of Christianity. Robert pursues his own study of history with the help of Wendover's library, and together they discuss nineteenth century German philosophy and historical research. Although Robert hopes his faith will be strong enough to withstand modern scholarship, he concludes that it compellingly refutes traditional beliefs in miracles, the Resurrection, and the divinity of Christ. He maintains a deep religious commitment to Jesus' life as an ethical model, but the loss of other orthodox beliefs is wrenchingly painful. Some other Anglican clergymen are able to doubt privately yet continue their lives of church service, but Robert knows this will be impossible for him. Not only does he have to end his ministry in Murewell, he is terrified that his changed faith will mean an irreparable breach with Catherine.

Robert goes to Oxford to ask the advice of Mr. Grey, an Oxford don he admired when he was a student, and someone whose religious beliefs are close to those Robert now holds. The understanding Grey advises Robert immediately to seek Catherine's help. When he does so, Catherine almost breaks down: Robert's loss of faith is incomprehensible to her. She tells Robert that she will continue to love and support him, but the distance between them grows.

In London, Robert finds a socially useful role in the slums of the East End. Here, he lectures and discusses his new beliefs with skeptical but interested artisans, with whom he founds a new church, the New Brotherhood of Christ. Because Catherine refuses any contact with this work, the rift between them widens and their unhappiness in their life together intensifies.

Meanwhile, musical study in Germany develops Rose's artistry. Taken up by socially prominent friends of Squire Wendover, she attracts the interest of the aristocratic Hugh Flaxman. Flaxman becomes fascinated with Robert's East End projects and gives financial support to the New Brotherhood. During this time, Rose is also seeing Langham, who is unable to stay away from her. Once again their relationship deepens and they declare their love, but the next morning, Langham writes Rose that his nature makes marriage impossible. Rose decides that her love for him was an immature romantic illusion. Her sense of propriety makes it difficult for her to accept a new lover, however, and when Flaxman, after waiting patiently, proposes to her, she asks him to wait six more months.

The Elsmeres' marriage regains its strength after advances from the amoral Madame de Netteville make Robert face his estrangement from Catherine and after Flaxman gives Catherine a moving account of Robert's experience with the New Brotherhood. Catherine is finally able to agree that Robert's beliefs, though she thinks them wrong, are still fundamentally religious. Robert's health, never strong, breaks under the strain of his work. Told that he will soon die from tuberculosis, he and Catherine go to Algiers in the hope that warm air will prolong his life. Rose and Flaxman join them and are there when he dies. After Rose and Flaxman marry, Catherine continues to attend an Anglican church but also works for the New Brotherhood, which thrives.

Critical Evaluation:

Mary Ward's *Robert Elsmere* was the most popular novel of its time in England and in the United States. It was widely read and discussed and became the subject of innumerable sermons. Its author had interesting family connections, as she was the niece of the eminent Victorian essayist and

poet Matthew Arnold and the granddaughter of Dr. Thomas Arnold, the famous headmaster of Rugby School. *Robert Elsmere* aroused more interest among readers, however, than Matthew Arnold's writing ever had. William Gladstone, Britain's former prime minister, called it "eminently an off-spring of the time" and wrote a much-quoted critique of its treatment of orthodox Christianity. *Robert Elsmere*, Ward's second novel, launched her career as one of the most successful novelists of the late Victorian era. By the early twentieth century, though, she came to be seen as the epitome of everything a younger generation of writers wanted to reject in their Victorian heritage, particularly given her role as a leader in the battle against women's suffrage. After World War I, her work sank into obscurity.

Of her Victorian predecessors, Ward said she greatly preferred Charlotte Brontë to George Eliot. There are several references to Brontë in *Robert Elsmere*, but in form, style, and themes the book is actually much closer to Eliot's novels. It resembles Eliot in its organization into seven books, in the central role that ideas play in the characters' lives, in its moral earnestness and preoccupation with problems of vocation, and in the detail with which it represents the changes taking place in nineteenth century society. Like many earlier Victorian novels, *Robert Elsmere* also owes a debt to Romantic poetry. The novel's first section includes lyrical descriptions of the Lake District landscape celebrated in William Wordsworth's poems, and Elsmere and Catherine Leyburn quote Wordsworth to each other.

The novel's central subjects are Elsmere's spiritual crisis and his marriage. Ward makes Elsmere a receptor of major developments in Victorian thought, including Charles Darwin's theory of evolution and German historical study and biblical "higher criticism"—the effort by nineteenth century scholars to establish the historical contexts in which the Bible was written. Ward dramatizes the moral and psychological bankruptcy many Victorians feared would be the consequence of this new thought by making its leading representative in the novel the arrogant Squire Wendover, whom she portrays as emotionally starved and isolated, living only for scholarship, deeply in need of the companionship he finds with Elsmere but also trying ruthlessly to coerce Elsmere into accepting his own skeptical beliefs. As a balance for Wendover, Ward gives Elsmere a more satisfying mentor, the Oxford don Henry Grey, who combines a skeptical rejection of Christian belief in miracles with a humanitarian commitment to social service. Grey, whom Ward based on the philosopher T. H. Green, is a model whose life inspires Elsmere in his final phase as the founder of a new workers' church, the New Brotherhood of Christ.

Ward dramatizes the emotional agony of Victorian religious doubt through her study of the Elsmeres' marriage as a complex relationship of two people who share many values and a strong mutual love but come from very different social worlds. These differences are defined not by social class—they are both children of university-educated professional fathers—but by relationships to cultural change. Following his early upbringing by an open-minded mother who encourages his curiosity in many directions, Robert is exposed to theological disputes and other modern trends during his student days at Oxford. This background is in contrast with Catherine's much narrower education, sheltered by a clergyman father who moves his family back to his native Westmoreland because he is determined to protect his family from the influences of an increasingly secular world. Although Robert falls in love with Catherine partly because of her saintlike spiritual dedication, and though they share a reformist dedication to improving the lives of the poor, their differences in temperament and social experience threaten to destroy their marriage when Catherine refuses even to try to comprehend Robert's altered religious views.

Robert Elsmere's preoccupation with its era's pull toward the fin de siècle is also apparent in the novel's subplot centered on Catherine's sister Rose. Whereas the older sister identifies with their father's resistance to the modern, the musically gifted Rose is a rebellious free spirit. At the beginning of the novel, she seems destined to emerge from adolescence as a late nineteenth century New Woman who will challenge conventional expectations about female propriety and find a profession and a life in the cosmopolitan world of the arts. The possibilities of a musical career for Rose fade, though, as she becomes one more Victorian heroine moving through a courtship plot in which her most important action is choosing the right husband. The wrong husband, significantly, is the bored aesthete Edward Langham, whose cynicism makes him like Squire Wendover, an embodiment of the emptiness of excessive modernity. The right husband, Hugh Flaxman, who, though politically progressive, scornfully labels Langham an *enfant du siècle*, is older and wiser than Rose and the nephew to a duke. One of Ward's friends was the novelist Henry James, who wrote to her that he wished she had made Rose "serious, deeply so, in her own line, as Catherine, for instance, is serious in hers." A few years later, Ward followed his advice when she created the New Woman heroine of another popular novel, *Marcella* (1894).

Anne Howells

Further Reading

Boughton, Gillian E. "Dr. Arnold's Granddaughter: Mary Augusta Ward." In *The Child Writer from Austen to Woolf*, edited by Christine Alexander and Juliet McMaster. New York: Cambridge University Press, 2005. Discusses Ward's childhood writings and how they led to her adult work. Provides biographical details about Ward.

Colby, Vineta. *The Singular Anomaly: Women Novelists of the Nineteenth Century*. New York: New York University Press, 1970. Colby, who sees Ward as a flawed novelist but a reliable documentarian of her times, discusses at some length *Robert Elsmere* and the reasons for its popularity.

Lewis, Linda M. "Mary Augusta Ward's Literary Portraits of the Artist as Medusa." In *Women's Literary Creativity and the Female Body*, edited by Diane Long Hoeveler and Donna Decker Schuster. New York: Palgrave Macmillan, 2007. Analyzes the significance of gender in Ward's writing, devoting several pages to a discussion of *Robert Elsmere*.

Peterson, William S. *Victorian Heretic: Mrs. Humphry Ward's "Robert Elsmere."* Leicester, England: Leicester University Press, 1976. Situates *Robert Elsmere* in its biographical, literary, and historical contexts and describes its publication history and critical reception.

Smith, Esther Marian Greenwell. *Mrs. Humphry Ward*. Boston: Twayne, 1980. Reviews changes in Ward's reputation as a novelist, summarizes comments by other late twentieth century critics, and argues for the continuing relevance of *Robert Elsmere*'s religious issues.

Sutherland, John. *Mrs. Humphry Ward: Eminent Victorian, Pre-eminent Edwardian*. New York: Oxford University Press, 1990. One of the best available biographies of Ward, a sympathetic account of her life and a richly detailed analysis of the changing social contexts in which she wrote. Describes her struggles with the composition and revision of *Robert Elsmere*, which Sutherland thinks is not her best novel.

Sutton-Ramspeck, Beth. *Raising the Dust: The Literary Housekeeping of Mary Ward, Sarah Grand, and Charlotte Perkins Gilman*. Athens: Ohio University Press, 2004. Describes how the three women authors rejected the aestheticism and modernism of the late Victorian era in favor of a more practical, mundane literature. Focuses on the authors' use of housekeeping as a symbol for the individual's responsibility in both the domestic and the public spheres.

Wilt, Judith. "*Robert Elsmere*: The Englishman as Heretic." In *Behind Her Times: Transition England in the Novels of*

Mary Arnold Ward. Charlottesville: University of Virginia Press, 2005. Examination of Ward's novels, demonstrating how her works provide a transition between the Romantic literature of Victorian England and the latter realism of the modernist movement.

Wolff, Robert Lee. *Gains and Losses: Novels of Faith and Doubt in Victorian England.* New York: Garland, 1977. The introductory chapter of this study usefully summarizes religious developments in England since the Reformation. The chapter on Ward includes an extensive description of *Robert Elsmere*, which Wolff, a historian, calls "the climactic Victorian novel of religious doubt."

Robin Hood's Adventures

Author: Unknown
First published: c. 1490
Type of work: Novel
Type of plot: Adventure
Time of plot: Thirteenth century
Locale: England

Principal characters:
ROBIN HOOD, earl of Huntingdon
LITTLE JOHN,
FRIAR TUCK,
WILL SCARLET,
A TINKER, and
A COOK, the members of the band of merry men
THE SHERIFF OF NOTTINGHAM
SIR RICHARD OF THE LEA, Robin Hood's friend

The Story:

Before he becomes an outlaw, Robin Hood is the rightful earl of Huntingdon. The times are corrupt, however, and Robin's father is dispossessed of his estates. Young Robin is driven into Sherwood Forest, where he protests social injustice by organizing a band of outlaws to prey on the rich to give to the poor.

Robin Hood's career as an outlaw begins when he is on his way to a shooting match in Nottingham. Some of the king's foresters meet him in Sherwood Forest and mock his youth. One of the foresters wagers that Robin cannot slay a deer, so Robin kills one to win the bet. The penalty for killing one of the king's stags, however, is death. The foresters give chase, and Robin is forced to hide in the forest. There he meets other landless, hunted men and becomes their leader.

While seeking adventure one day, Robin encounters a tall stranger at a bridge, and the stranger tumbles him into the stream. Robin then calls to his band of merry men, and together they soon overcome the stranger. A shooting match is then held between Robin and the stranger; Robin wins the match, and the stranger good-naturedly acknowledges defeat and joins Robin's band. The outlaws call him Little John because he is so big.

The Sheriff of Nottingham, angered because Robin Hood flouts the sheriff's authority, issues a warrant for the outlaw's arrest. A tinker carries the warrant into the forest, where he meets Robin but fails to recognize the fugitive because Robin is disguised. Robin takes the tinker to the Blue Boar Inn, gets him drunk, and steals the warrant. Later, the tinker meets Robin in the forest and fights with him. Robin wins the bout, and the tinker happily joins the other men in Robin's band.

The Sheriff of Nottingham grows more and more enraged by Robin's boldness. When the king rebukes him for not capturing the outlaw, the sheriff devises another plan. Knowing that Robin Hood prides himself on his skill in archery, the sheriff proclaims a shooting match in Nottingham Tower, hoping to catch Robin and his men. They outwit him, however, for they enter the match in disguise. As a tattered stranger, Robin is awarded the golden arrow given to the winner of the match. After he returns to Sherwood Forest, he sends the sheriff a note of thanks for the prize, an act that infuriates the sheriff even more.

The band of outlaws lies low in the forest for a time, and then Robin Hood sends one of his men to learn the sheriff's next plan. When the man is captured, Robin and the others set out to rescue him. As the man is being dragged forth in a cart to be hanged, Little John leaps into the cart and cuts the prisoner's bonds. The other outlaws then run from their hiding places and overcome the sheriff's men.

Next, Robin Hood buys some meat and takes it to Nottingham to sell to the poor at half price. Disguised as a butcher, he is thought by most people to be either a foolish peasant or a wealthy nobleman in disguise. When Robin offers to sell the sheriff a herd of cattle at a ridiculously low price, the sheriff gleefully accepts. Robin then takes the sheriff to Sherwood Forest, where he takes his money and then shows him the king's deer, telling him that there stands his herd.

As a lark, Little John goes to the fair at Nottingham Tower, where he treats all the people to food and drink. While there, he is asked to enter the sheriff's service because of his great size. Little John agrees, thinking that such employment might be fun. He finds life in the sheriff's household so pleasant that he stays six months, but gradually he grows bored. He starts to treat the steward in an arrogant manner, and the steward calls the cook to fight Little John. Both men, however, have eaten such a huge meal before the fight that neither can win. Finally, they decide to stop because they do not really dislike each other. Little John then persuades the cook to join Robin's band of merry men.

On another day, Robin Hood and his men go out to find Friar Tuck of Fountain Dale, supposedly a rich curate. Spying a strange monk singing and feasting beside a brook, Robin joins him. When Robin wishes to go across the water, he persuades the man to carry him on his back. On the return trip the monk, who is in reality Friar Tuck, dumps Robin into the water. After another great fight, with Robin the victor, the friar joyfully joins the outlaw band.

The queen, who has heard of Robin Hood's prowess and is fascinated by stories told about him and his men, invites Robin to London. In an attempt to outwit the king, she proposes an archery match at which she will put up three archers against his best three. If her team wins, the king is to issue a pardon of forty days to certain prisoners. The king accepts the wager. The queen's archers are Robin Hood, Little John, and Will Scarlet, all in disguise. Naturally, the outlaws win, although Will Scarlet is bested in his match. When the king learns that the queen's archers are Robin Hood and two of his men, he is angry, and the outlaws escape capture only with the queen's help. The others return safely to Sherwood Forest, but Robin Hood meets with many dangerous adventures as he makes his way back. During his journey he encounters Sir Richard of the Lea, a knight whom he had once aided, and Sir Richard advises him to return to London and throw himself on the queen's mercy. He does so, and the queen persuades the king to give Robin safe escort back to Sherwood Forest and to pay the wager of the shooting match.

Returning from the Crusades, King Richard the Lion-Hearted decides to seek out Robin Hood and his outlaw band. With six others, all disguised as friars, Richard encounters Robin and his men and bests them. Richard then reveals himself and pardons Robin and his men. He also restores Robin to his rightful honors as the earl of Huntingdon.

On a visit to Sherwood Forest several years later, Robin Hood becomes so homesick for his old life that he gives up his title and returns to live with the outlaws. His action infuriates John, the new king, and the Sheriff of Nottingham. They send their men to capture the outlaws, and during the fighting the sheriff is killed. Robin, ill and much depressed by this bloodshed, goes to Kirkley Abbey, where his cousin is prioress, to be bled. The prioress is a treacherous woman, and she has him bled too long, so that he lies dying. At last Little John, having pulled down bolts and bars to get to Robin, reaches his leader's bedside. As Robin lies dying in Little John's arms, he asks for his bow and arrows and says that he wishes to be buried wherever his arrow falls; he then shoots an arrow through the window of the priory. Little John marks its flight, and Robin is buried beneath the ancient oak that was his last target. His merry men disband after his death, but the stories of their brave deeds and the prowess of Robin Hood live on.

Critical Evaluation:

Robin Hood's Adventures is one of the best-loved stories of all time. It has many elements that make for entertaining reading: romance, adventure, the stage of history, and lofty characters. As a work of prose fiction, however, it is quite unusual in one respect: Comparatively few have actually read the book, whereas millions have heard the Robin Hood stories. Those who have not read the original have nevertheless come to know and love the characters of the Robin Hood legend through countless versions of the story in prose, fireside tales, motion pictures, and television programs.

The Robin Hood story goes back well into the Middle Ages. Legends developed about a "good" outlaw who protected and supported the poor while he stole from the rich. Early legends, however, did not center on one bandit. There appear to have been several similar heroes of this type who eventually coalesced into the character of Robin Hood, earl of Huntingdon, as he appears in this story. Whether or not the prototypes of Robin Hood were real, as some historians believe them to have been, is a moot point. It is the legend and not the reality of the story that has excited people for centuries.

Although the first recorded reference to Robin Hood occurs in the writings of the Scottish historian John of Fordun, who died in approximately 1384, the first known compilation of prose and poetry of the Robin Hood legend came in 1490 with the publication of the *Lytel Geste of Robin Hood*, by Wynkyn de Worde, a noted British printer. If there had been records for best sellers in those days, certainly this tale would have been high on the list. It proved so popular that the same version appeared again several decades later and has been reprinted and retold for centuries. It was used as a basis for works of later novelists such as Sir Walter Scott in *Ivanhoe* (1819) and more recently provided material for motion picture and television adaptations.

One may also measure its popularity by considering that playing Robin Hood is a fantasy game that remains popular with children. To the English especially, Robin Hood is a great hero. He and King Arthur are the most revered characters in British legends, and their popularity continues to thrive throughout the world.

Although *Robin Hood's Adventures* may not be classed as one of the great works of world literature, it is so entertaining that it may be read with delight over and over again. Readers can forgive a lack of character analysis when they are able to feel as if they are riding through Sherwood Forest by Robin Hood's side, engaging in adventures that are noble in spirit and yet full of mischief.

The story line of the tale is quite simple: The underdog, Robin Hood, fights oppression and injustice, in the form of the Sheriff of Nottingham and Prince John, to protect the poor and rally them around the good, but absent, King Richard I. Robin Hood represents an early attempt to personify *noblesse oblige*. He is a highborn man who helps the unfortunate. He does not condescend in his assistance, however, because he lives and works among the poor in Sherwood Forest. By contrast, Prince John is a powerful, oppressive leader. Persecuting Robin Hood, he inadvertently encourages Robin's followers. King Richard, Prince John's brother, represents the colorful "good king" who is away fighting in the Holy Land during the Third Crusade.

The narrative of Robin Hood makes for entertaining reading, but it is quite far removed from historical fact. As the legends grew about Robin Hood, the actual historical events surrounding the reigns of Richard and John became blurred. In reality, Richard was rarely seen in England after he became king. He preferred traveling and fighting in other countries. John was not a particularly good leader, but he was perhaps more unlucky than bad. He had the unfortunate habit of losing English territories to the French, and for this reason he became very unpopular, which contributed to his bad reputation down through the centuries. The possibility of real Robin Hood-type bandits existing in the period surrounding the signing of the Magna Carta may be admitted, but the legend has been expanded so much that historical accuracy is not an element of the Robin Hood story. The Robin Hood story is a folktale, the kind of literature that is re-created from generation to generation, responding to such basic human needs as justice and having fun. Readers of *Robin Hood's Adventures* should bear in mind that the tale is not historically accurate.

History aside, the book's adventures can be appreciated by almost anyone. Its characterizations, however, are weak; they are too black-and-white to be true reflections of life. One should realize, however, that English literature in the fifteenth century had not developed the novel. Literature was largely based on characters and events already familiar to readers: types, mythology, history, legend. The artistic goal of faithfulness to the shadings and complexities of good and evil in real people did not exist then. Readers should approach *Robin Hood's Adventures* as they would approach motion pictures that are made with no greater, and no lesser, intent than entertainment.

"Critical Evaluation" by Patricia Ann King

Further Reading

The Ballad of Robin Hood. Sung by Anthony Quayle. Lyre by Desmond Dupré. Caedmon TC 1177, 1963. The Robin Hood ballads were intended to be sung, not read. Many of them seem banal until they are heard in Quayle and Dupré's excellent renditions.

Dixon-Kennedy, Mike. *The Robin Hood Handbook: The Outlaw in History, Myth, and Legend*. Stroud, England: Sutton, 2006. Provides information about the characters, places, people, and background of the Robin Hood legend, drawing on the many different adaptations of the story, including poems, ballads, films, novels, and folklore.

Dobson, R. B., and John Taylor, comps. *Rymes of Robyn Hood: An Introduction to the English Outlaw*. Pittsburgh, Pa.: University of Pittsburgh Press, 1976. Invaluable resource for the study of Robin Hood collects the very best of the medieval and early modern versions of the Robin Hood story into one volume. Contains an excellent introduction describing the history and development of the legend.

Holt, J. C. *Robin Hood*. Rev. and enlarged ed. London: Thames & Hudson, 1989. Highly readable book discusses at length the various claims for the existence of an actual historical Robin Hood.

Keen, Maurice. *The Outlaws of Medieval Legend*. Rev. ed. London: Routledge & Kegan Paul, 1987. Gives the historical context for the medieval legend of Robin Hood by relating it to the stories of other outlaws. Examines the social causes of the rise of such legends.

Phillips, Helen, ed. *Robin Hood: Medieval and Post-Medieval*. Dublin: Four Courts Press, 2005. Collection of essays examines both the historical character of Robin

Hood and literature about the character, including works by Ben Jonson, Charlotte Brontë, and Alfred Noyes.

Pollard, A. J. *The First Robin Hood: The Early Stories in Historical Context, 1400-1550*. New York: Routledge, 2004. Interprets the earliest stories and ballads about Robin Hood, placing them within the economic, political, and social context of fifteenth and early sixteenth century England.

Robinson Crusoe

Author: Daniel Defoe (1660-1731)

First published: 1719, as *The Life and Strange Surprizing Adventures of Robinson Crusoe, of York, Mariner, Written by Himself*

Type of work: Novel

Type of plot: Adventure

Time of plot: 1651-1705

Locale: An island off the coast of South America and the Several Seas

Principal characters:

ROBINSON CRUSOE, a castaway

FRIDAY, his faithful servant

The Story:

Robinson Crusoe is the son of a middle-class English family. Although his father desires that he go into business and live a quiet life, the young man has such longing for the sea that he finds it impossible to remain at home. He takes his first voyage without his parents' knowledge. The ship is caught in a great storm, and Crusoe is so violently ill and so greatly afraid that he vows never to leave land again should he be so fortunate as to escape death.

When he lands safely, however, he finds his old longing still unsatisfied, and he engages as a trader, shipping first for the coast of Africa. The ship on which he sails is captured by a Turkish pirate vessel, and he is carried as a prisoner into Sallee, a Moorish port. There he becomes a slave. His life is unbearable, and at the first opportunity he escapes in a small boat. He is then rescued by a Portuguese freighter and carried safely to Brazil, where he buys a small plantation and begins the life of a planter.

When another English planter suggests that they make a voyage to Africa for a cargo of slaves, Crusoe once more gives in to his longing for the sea. This voyage is destined to bring him his greatest adventure of all, for the ship breaks apart on a reef near an island off the coast of South America. Of all the crew and passengers, only Crusoe survives, the waves washing him ashore. He takes stock of his situation

and finds that the island seems to be completely uninhabited, with no sign of wild beasts. In an attempt to make his castaway life as comfortable as possible, he constructs a raft and sails it to the broken ship to gather food, ammunition, water, wine, clothing, tools, sailcloth, and lumber.

He sets up a sailcloth tent on the side of a small hill and encircles his refuge with tall, sharp stakes; he enters his shelter by means of a ladder that he draws up after him. Into this area he brings all the goods he has salvaged, being particularly careful with the gunpowder. His next concern is his food supply. Finding little food from the ship that has not been ruined by rats or water, he eats sparingly during his first days on the island. Among the things Crusoe has brought from the ship are a quill and ink, and before long he begins to keep a journal. When he considers the good and evil of his situation, he finds that he has much for which to thank God.

He begins to make his shelter permanent. Behind his tent he finds a small cave, which he enlarges and braces. With crude tools, he makes a table and a chair, some shelves, and a rack for his guns. He spends many months on the work, all the time able to feed himself with wildfowl and other small game. He also finds several springs that keep him supplied with drinking water.

For the next twenty-four years, he spends his life in much the same way as in his first days after the shipwreck. He explores the island and builds what he is pleased to call his summer home on the other side. He is able to grow corn, barley, and rice, carefully saving the new kernels each year until he has enough to plant a small field. He learns to grind these grains to make meal and bakes coarse bread. He catches and tames wild goats to supply his larder and parrots for companionship. He makes better furniture and improves his cave, making it even safer from intruders, whom he still fears, although he has seen no sign of any living thing larger than small game, fowl, and goats. He also has time to read carefully the three Bibles he retrieved from the ship. At a devotional period each morning and night, he never fails to thank God for delivering him from the sea.

In the middle of Crusoe's twenty-fourth year on the island, an incident occurs that alters his way of living. About a year and a half previously, he had observed some savages who had apparently paddled over from another island. They had come in the night and gorged themselves on some other savages, obviously prisoners. Crusoe had found the bones and the torn flesh the next morning and had since been terrified that the cannibals might return and find him. Finally, a band of savages does return. While they prepare for their gruesome feast, Crusoe shoots some of them and frightens the others away. Able to rescue one of the prisoners, he at last has human companionship. He names the man Friday after the day of his rescue, and Friday becomes his faithful servant and friend.

Over the course of time, Crusoe is able to teach Friday to speak English. Friday tells him that seventeen white men are prisoners on the island from which he had come. Although Friday reports that the men are well treated, Crusoe has a great desire to go to them, thinking that together they might find some way to return to the civilized world. He and Friday build a canoe and prepare to sail to the other island, but before they are ready for their trip, another group of savages comes to their island with more prisoners. Crusoe discovers that one of the prisoners is a white man and manages to save him. He also rescues another savage, an old man who turns out to be Friday's father; there is great joy at the reunion of father and son. Crusoe cares for the old man and the white man, who is a Spaniard, one of the seventeen of whom Friday had spoken. A hostile tribe has captured Friday's island, and now the white men are no longer safe.

Crusoe dispatches the Spaniard and Friday's father to the neighboring island to try to rescue the white men. While waiting for their return, Crusoe sees an English ship one day at anchor near shore. Soon he finds the captain of the ship and two others, who have been set ashore by a mutinous crew. Crusoe, Friday, and the three seamen are able to retake the ship, and Crusoe is at last delivered from the island. He dislikes leaving before the Spaniard and Friday's father return, and he determines to go back to the island some day and see how they had fared. Five of the mutinous crew choose to remain on the island rather than be returned to England to be hanged. Crusoe and Friday then sail to England. Crusoe returns to his homeland after an absence of thirty-five years, arriving there, a stranger and unknown, in June of 1687.

His adventures are not over, however. When he visits his old home, he finds that his parents have died, as have all of his family but two sisters and the two children of one of his brothers. Having no reason to remain in England, he goes with Friday to Lisbon to inquire about his plantation. There he learns that friends have saved the income of his estate for him and that he is now worth about five thousand pounds sterling. Satisfied with this accounting, Crusoe and Friday return to England, where Crusoe marries and had three children.

After his wife dies, Crusoe sails again in 1695 as a private trader on a ship captained by his nephew and bound for the East Indies and China. The ship puts in at his castaway island, where he finds that the Spaniards and the English mutineers have taken native wives from a nearby island; consequently, the population is greatly increased. Crusoe is pleased with his little group and holds a feast for them. He also presents them with gifts from the ship.

After Crusoe has satisfied himself that the island colony is well cared for, he and Friday sail away. On their way to Brazil, savages attack their ship, and Friday is killed. From Brazil, Crusoe travels around the Cape of Good Hope and on to the coast of China. At one port, after the sailors on his ship take part in a massacre, Crusoe lectures them so severely that the crew members force the captain, Crusoe's nephew, to set him ashore in China, as they can no longer tolerate his preaching. There Crusoe joins a caravan that takes him into Siberia. At last, he reaches England again. Having spent the greater part of fifty-four years away from his homeland, he is finally glad to live out his life there in peace and in preparation for that longer journey from which he will never return.

Critical Evaluation:

The Life and Strange Surprizing Adventures of Robinson Crusoe, of York, Mariner, Written by Himself, as Daniel Defoe entitled his novel, is read as eagerly today as it was when it was first published. An exotic novel of travel and adventure, *Robinson Crusoe* functions primarily as Defoe's defense of his bourgeois Protestantism. Crusoe's adventures—

the shipwrecks, his life as a planter in South America, and his years of isolation on the island—provide an apt context for his polemic. A political dissenter and pamphleteer, Defoe saw as his enemies the Tory aristocrats whose royalism in government and religion blocked the aspirations of the middle class. Like Jonathan Swift in *Gulliver's Travels* (1726), Defoe in this novel presents a religiously and politically corrupt England. Both authors were intent on bringing about a moral revolution, and each uses his hero as an exemplum. Gulliver, however, represents a moral failure, whereas Crusoe's adventures reveal his spiritual conversion, a return to the ethics and religion of his father. As one critic has said of *Robinson Crusoe*:

> We read it . . . to follow with meticulous interest and constant self-identification the hero's success in building up, step by step, out of whatever material came to hand, a physical and moral replica of the world he had left behind him. If *Robinson Crusoe* is an adventure story, it is also a moral tale, a commercial accounting and a Puritan fable.

Significantly, Crusoe's origins are in northern England, in York, where he was born in the early part of the seventeenth century and where his father had made a fortune in trade. He belongs to the solid middle class, the class that was gaining political power during the early eighteenth century, when Defoe published his book. Crusoe's father is an apologist for the mercantile, Puritan ethic, which he tries without success to instill in his son. As Crusoe says, "Mine was the middle state," which his father

> had found by long experience was the best state in the world, the most suited to human happiness, not exposed to the miseries and hardships, the labour and sufferings of the mechanick part of mankind, and not embarrassed with the pride, luxury, ambition and envy of the upper part of mankind.

Its virtues and blessings were those of "temperance, moderation, quietness, health [and] society."

His father's philosophy, which is designed to buy a man happiness and pleasure in both this life and the next, nevertheless fails to persuade the young Crusoe, who finds nothing but boredom in the comforts of the middle class. He longs to go to sea, to follow a way of life that represents the antithesis of his father's. He seeks the extremes of sensation and danger, preferring to live on the periphery rather than in the middle, where all is secure. Crusoe's decision to become a sailor is an act of adolescent rebellion, yet it is also very much in the

tradition of Puritan individualism. Not content with the wisdom of his class, the young man feels it is necessary to test himself and to discover himself and his own ethic.

Even after the first stage in his adventures, which culminates in Crusoe's gaining a modest fortune in South America, he refuses to settle down. Intent on his own "inclination," as he says, he leaves his plantation and once again takes up the uncertain life of sea trade. It is at this point in the narrative that Crusoe is shipwrecked and abandoned on a tropical island without any hope of rescue.

Crusoe's first response to his isolation and the prospect of living the rest of his life alone is one of despair. He has, however, a strong survival instinct, and courageously he sets about the task of staying alive and eventually of creating a humane, comfortable society. One of the first things he does is to mark time, to make a calendar. Despite all of his efforts to continue his own life and environment, he falls ill, and it is at this point that he realizes his complete vulnerability, his absolute aloneness in the universe. Stripped of all his illusions, limited by necessity to one small place, Crusoe is thrown back upon himself and confronted by an immense emptiness. He asks desperately: "What is this earth and sea of which I have seen so much? Whence is it produced? And what am I and all the other creatures, wild and tame, human and brutal? Whence are we?"

All of these questions predate Crusoe's religious conversion, the central and most significant event of the novel. His answer to the questions is that all creation comes from God and that the state of all creation, including his own, is an expression of the will of God. Upon this act of faith he rebuilds not only his own life but also his own miniature society, which reflects in its simplicity, moderation, and comfort the philosophy his father had taught. Furthermore, his faith brings him to an acceptance of his own life and station, an acceptance that he was never able to make before: "I acquiesced in the dispositions of Providence, which I began now to own and to believe ordered everything for the best." Later, after two years on the island, he says,

> It is now that I began sensibly to feel how much more happy this life I now led was, with all its miserable circumstances, than the wicked, cursed, abominable life I led all the past part of my days; and now I changed both my sorrows and my joys; my very desires altered, my affections changed their gusts, and my delights were perfectly new from what they were at my first coming.

Once he is able to answer the overwhelming question of the novel—"Whence are we?"—the rest of the narrative and

Crusoe's adventures justify, to his aristocrat readers, his religious faith and the middle-class Puritan ethic. Apart from this justification, there also remains the glorification of the self-reliant and self-directing man. This was a man unfamiliar to Defoe's readers, a new man beginning to appear on the fringes of the power structure and about to demand his place in a society that was evolving toward a new political structure that became recognized as middle-class democracy.

"Critical Evaluation" by David L. Kubal

Further Reading

Damrosch, Leopold, Jr. *God's Plot and Man's Stories*. Chicago: University of Chicago Press, 1985. Devotes a chapter to *Robinson Crusoe*, which is examined largely within the context of Puritan doctrine. Provides a first-rate and highly recommended discussion of the work.

Defoe, Daniel. *Robinson Crusoe*. Edited by Michael Shinagel. New York: W. W. Norton, 1994. This edition constitutes a perfect beginner's guide to Defoe's great novel. In addition to an authoritative text of *Robinson Crusoe*, provides selections from twentieth century criticism, a bibliography, and a set of useful contextual materials.

Novak, Maximillian E. *Daniel Defoe: Master of Fictions—His Life and Ideas*. New York: Oxford University Press, 2001. Comprehensive biographical study by a leading Defoe scholar places Defoe's work within the context of the events of his life. Includes analysis of *Robinson Crusoe*, *Moll Flanders*, and other novels as well as discussion of Defoe's works in other genres.

Novak, Maximillian E., and Carl Fisher, eds. *Approaches to Teaching Defoe's "Robinson Crusoe."* New York: Modern Language Association of America, 2005. Offers advice for teaching the novel in various courses and settings and also presents a brief biography of Defoe, information about the book's critical reception, and essays discussing the book as international text, travel book, and castaway narrative. Other essays examine such topics as myths of modern individualism in the works of Defoe and other writers and the representation of masculinity and eighteenth century racial ideology in *Robinson Crusoe*.

Richetti, John J. *Life of Daniel Defoe: A Critical Biography*. Malden, Mass.: Blackwell, 2005. Provides a thorough look at Defoe's writing within the context of his life and opinions, including analysis of his fiction and political and religious journalism. Focuses on Defoe's distinctive literary style.

_____, ed. *The Cambridge Companion to Daniel Defoe*. New York: Cambridge University Press, 2008. Collection of essays includes analyses of Defoe's political and religious journalism as well as examinations of such topics as money and character in his fiction and Defoe as a narrative innovator. Includes a chapter devoted to *Robinson Crusoe*.

Rogers, Pat. *Robinson Crusoe*. London: Allen & Unwin, 1979. Rich resource for the study of Defoe's most famous work provides, among many other useful materials, a brief account of Defoe's life, a full bibliography, and two appendixes containing pre-*Robinson Crusoe* accounts of the life of Alexander Selkirk, the castaway who inspired Defoe's fictional character.

Spaas, Lieve, and Brian Stimpson, eds. *"Robinson Crusoe": Myths and Metamorphoses*. New York: St. Martin's Press, 1996. Collection of essays explores many aspects of the seminal novel. Topics addressed include Crusoe's women, cannibalism, and the novel within the context of eighteenth century history. Several essays focus on how other writers and filmmakers have adapted Defoe's novel for their own works.

Watt, Ian. *The Rise of the Novel: Studies in Defoe, Richardson, and Fielding*. 2d ed. Berkeley: University of California Press, 2001. First published in 1957, Watt's study remains, in spite of numerous challenges, one of the key works in the field of early English fiction. Devotes a long and fascinating chapter to *Robinson Crusoe*.

West, Richard. *Daniel Defoe: The Life and Strange, Surprising Adventures*. New York: Carroll and Graf, 1998. Covers all aspects of Defoe's life and work: the journalist, novelist, satirist, newsman, and pamphleteer as well as the tradesman, soldier, and spy. Written with considerable flair by a journalist and historian of wide-ranging experience.

The Rocking-Horse Winner

Author: D. H. Lawrence (1885-1930)
First published: 1926
Type of work: Short fiction
Type of plot: Psychological realism
Time of plot: Mid-1920's
Locale: London and Hampshire, England

Principal characters:
PAUL, a young boy approaching adolescence
HESTER, his mother
OSCAR CRESSWELL, his uncle
BASSETT, the family's gardener, Cresswell's batman during
    World War I
JOAN, Paul's sister
PAUL'S FATHER

The Story:

In a London suburb in the mid-1920's, a woman who maintains what most people would regard as quite a comfortable manner of living in a well-furnished house with several retainers is convinced that she has "no luck." Hester is beautiful and youthful, but her husband has not succeeded in advancing beyond a routine position in the city, and her children can sense that, in spite of the attention and care she offers them, she does not really love them. She herself is deeply troubled by what she feels is a "hard little place"at the center of her being that prevents her from loving anybody.

Hester's son Paul, a very sensitive boy who adores her and who is her favorite among the three children, understands on an instinctual level that his mother is not happy. He is on the threshold of adolescence, eager and energetic, and becoming increasingly curious about the ways of the adult world. Paul inquires as to why the family does not own a car but must take taxis or borrow the car of Hester's brother Oscar Cresswell. Hester tells Paul that his father has "no luck." Paul does not fully understand what this statement means, but his mother suggests that it is inextricably connected to money and, in the case of their family, its insufficiency.

While Paul and the other children are not familiar with the economics of their household, they have a grasp of the ways in which their mother's concerns have permeated every aspect of their lives. The house itself seems to echo Hester's conviction that *"There must be more money."* Paul ponders the problem, and, while he is taking an imaginative ride on his treasured toy rocking horse, he makes a kind of abstracted connection between the condition of consciousness he develops amid the rhythms of the ride and an entrance into another realm where some secrets of the universe are revealed to him. He becomes convinced that his beloved toy can carry him to a solution to his mother's unhappiness and, since money is at the core of the problem, enable him to provide what is missing in the household.

Paul's uncle Oscar, whom he admires and who loves him like a son, asks him the name of his horse. Paul is not entirely

sure what to say, since he has begun to think of his horse with the names of the champion racers of the day. Paul has learned these names from conversations with Bassett, the family's young gardener, a devoted turf fancier who was Oscar's batman (or personal aide) during World War I. Oscar is fascinated by Paul's account and is startled to find that Paul and Bassett have been placing winning bets on the horses whose names Paul chooses for his toy. They have already accumulated a private account of some substance, and Cresswell becomes a sort of senior partner to their enterprise, encouraging Paul by taking him on his first visit to an actual racetrack. The boy is enthralled by the setting, his eyes becoming like "blue fire."

Not all of Paul's picks have been winners, but when he has said that he was absolutely sure about a horse, he has never been wrong. Cresswell is somewhat unsettled by the large sums that are accumulating, but Paul explains that he must continue his endeavors since he is so anxious to make his mother happy and to stop "the house whispers like people laughing at you behind your back." Still, although the racetrack winnings have made more money available to the household, the increase in funds seems to have led to an implicit demand for ever greater sums. Paul's mother becomes concerned about her son's overwrought behavior and plans to send him away from the house to the sea coast, but Paul insists that he must stay—to be close to his rocking horse—until after the running of the Derby. He intends to put all of their winnings on one last bet in an attempt to finally amass enough money to quiet the whispers of discontent and distress.

Two nights before the Derby, Paul's parents are at a party when his mother is struck by an instinctual feeling of anxiety about her son. When she rushes home, she finds him in his room, in a frenzy of motion on the rocking horse. "It's Malabar," Paul shouts as he falls off the horse and descends into a semiconscious state. His uncle and Bassett, although worried about Paul, place a winning bet on Malabar that pays at fourteen to one. For three days, Paul remains in critical condition, reviving momentarily when Basset tells him the horse has won to proudly proclaim to his mother that he has brought luck to the house. However, he then lapses back into a coma and dies during the night. In a summary of the situation, Cresswell observes that the family has gained a fortune and lost a son, but that perhaps it is for the best considering the degree to which Paul drove himself in his efforts to give his mother what she lacked.

Critical Evaluation:

Three of D. H. Lawrence's most important themes are prominent in "The Rocking-Horse Winner": the corroding effects of acquisitive behavior on English society, the requirement for a truly loving relationship to achieve happiness and fulfillment, and the existence of forces in the natural world that humans might access if they were not limited by social and cultural conventions. These themes structure and inform the narrative, intertwining so that the presentation and development of each theme is connected to the others. Taken together, they offer a view of the philosophical positions that Lawrence worked toward in his most memorable writing.

Lawrence's father was a coal miner. He made an adequate living, but his wife had aspirations to a more comfortable and refined social setting. Lawrence himself was more concerned with aesthetic and romantic matters than with monetary ones, but as he began to write about British society he became increasingly displeased with what he felt was an economic system that placed an emphasis on things that he felt were not crucial for human well-being. As he wrote in *Apocalypse* (1931), "What we want is to destroy our false, inorganic connections, especially those related to money," a sentiment similar to many others that he expressed throughout his life. The advent of World War I forced Lawrence and his wife, who was of German descent, to move away from the Cornwall coast. Lawrence was living at the time primarily on borrowed funds and, in the words of his wife, was "a walking phenomenon of suspended fury." In addition, as he became a professional author, dependent on the income his writing produced, he was increasingly involved in negotiations regarding remuneration for his work.

Lawrence wrote "The Rocking-Horse Winner" for a collection of ghost stories being compiled by Lady Cynthia Asquith (who was partially the basis for Hester's character). He was paid fifteen pounds for the story's English publication rights and fifty pounds for the American rights. To put this payment in perspective, Virginia Woolf in her 1929 "A Room of One's Own" recommended a sum of five hundred pounds as minimal to secure an artist's independence. The sums that Paul's sure winners return, then, are far beyond what would be required to sustain an upper-middle-class family, and enough to place a family within the reaches of "real money," if not fabulous wealth. The family's final winnings of more than eighty thousand pounds would be equivalent to several million pounds in the twenty-first century.

Lawrence chose these impressive sums, far beyond what most of his readers could even contemplate, to demonstrate the futility of seeking ever-larger amounts of money in a futile quest for the elusive satisfaction of being rich. The corrosive effects of such a quest are strikingly illustrated by the ultimate sacrifice that Paul makes. The sacrifice is particularly pathetic, since the love he hopes to give his mother cannot be measured in monetary terms. Paul's death is an indictment of the social circle in London to which Lawrence was peripherally linked as he became a nationally known author. It represents an expression of what critic Sandra Gilbert has called Lawrence's revulsion at "the city's staleness, its walking dead, its mechanised ugliness."

A preoccupation with money was emblematic in Lawrence's eyes of the obstacles that prevented a man and a woman from joining in a harmonious partnership built on a mutual understanding of each other's needs. This utopian goal, which Lawrence recognized as difficult and relatively rarely achieved, was one of the central subjects of his work, and in his finest stories he examines and celebrates both the difficulties a couple has in reaching this goal and the ways in which it might become possible.

In "The Rocking-Horse Winner," Paul's parents are so completely alienated from each other that the "love" Hester seeks is, unsurprisingly, transferred to her children, especially her only son. This transference is drawn as a parallel to Lawrence's own relationship with his mother, who was disappointed to a degree in her marriage, which joined two people of dissimilar sensibilities. Lawrence explored the close relationship between Paul Morrell and his mother in his novel *Sons and Lovers* (1913), and he wrote to a friend shortly after his mother's death "We have loved each other almost with a husband and wife love, as well as filal and maternal," a reflection of the deep emotion that Lawrence felt.

Hester "married for love, and the love turned to dust." Paul's father, unnamed, is disdainfully depicted as an absent figure, remote and cold. He is not only unsatisfactory as a male mentor (the role filled by Uncle Oscar, who addresses Paul as "son," and augmented by Bassett, a kind of surrogate older brother) but also a failure as a man. In a complete dismissal, he is described by Hester as one who is "very unlucky" and by the narrator as one "who *never* would be able to do anything worth doing." Paul's father works in "some office" and his only words in the text are "I don't know," spoken stonily, when Hester asks what Malabar means.

As Paul approaches adolescence, his evolving sense of himself as a young man has been severely distorted by the psychic distress he feels in his home, where the unspoken phrase *"There must be more money"* represents an animistic projection of the psychological condition of the family. The love that Paul desires and that his mother needs is unavailable in the traditional family fashion, leading Paul to undertake his desperate efforts to change the situation.

Lawrence had a degree of disdain for what is regarded as purely rational analysis and maintained a belief in a kind of mystic power in the universe. He expressed this attitude in *Apocalypse*, where he wrote "We ought to dance with rapture that we should be alive and in the flesh, and part of the living incarnate cosmos." Paul's rides on his rocking horse are both a literal and a symbolic version of this dance, as he attempts to join the flow of energy that will reveal the mysteries of the universe. Lawrence's vivid descriptions of Paul's rides have an autoerotic component, but they are much more than a youth's distortions of emerging sexuality. Paul follows an instinctual aspect of his being, the "blood-consciousness" that Lawrence thought was a part of primal man, lost to the civilized citizens of England, and an element of male virility that could only be realized in a proper relationship with a woman. The fact that Paul's demise is attributed to his need to "force" his horse to take him to "where there was luck" suggests the well-meant but misguided way that Paul seeks access to illumination. His death is a cautionary comment on the misdi-rection of the life force as a consequence of social constraints that Lawrence railed against throughout his writing life.

Leon Lewis

Further Reading

Cowan, James C. *D. H. Lawrence: Self and Sexuality.* Columbus: Ohio State University Press, 2002. A sensible examination of the complex nature of Lawrence's considerations of sexual behavior in his work.

Kearney, Martin F. *Major Short Stories of D. H. Lawrence: A Handbook.* New York: Garland, 1998. "The Rocking-Horse Winner" is one of six Lawrence stories treated here. Each one receives comprehensive discussion, including an account of the history of its composition and publication, as well as critical analysis.

Poplawski, Paul, ed. *Writing the Body in D. H. Lawrence: Essays on Language, Representation, and Sexuality.* Westport, Conn.: Greenwood Press, 2001. An uneven but often enlightening series of essays on some of Lawrence's central concerns, tending toward theoretical considerations of Lawrence's writing.

Reeve, N. H. *Reading Late Lawrence.* New York: Palgrave Macmillan, 2004. Especially incisive discussions of Lawrence's later works of fiction.

Worthen, John. *D. H. Lawrence: The Life of an Outsider.* Berkeley, Calif.: Counterpoint, 2005. An informative, knowledgeable account of Lawrence's life by the author of the first volume of an acclaimed three-book Cambridge University Press biography.

Roderick Hudson

Author: Henry James (1843-1916)
First published: 1876
Type of work: Novel
Type of plot: Psychological realism
Time of plot: 1870's
Locale: Rome, Florence, and Switzerland

Principal characters:
RODERICK HUDSON, a young American sculptor
ROWLAND MALLET, a young, wealthy art patron
MRS. LIGHT, a vain and silly widow
CHRISTINA LIGHT, her beautiful daughter
THE CAVALIERE GIACOSA, Mrs. Light's companion
PRINCE CASAMASSIMA, Christina's husband
SAM SINGLETON, an American painter
HUDSON, Roderick's insipid mother
MARY GARLAND, Roderick's American fiancé

The Story:

Rowland Mallet, expecting to sail for Europe in September, visits his cousin Cecilia in Northampton, Massachusetts. He is an idle bachelor, having inherited money, and he feels that he is leading a useless life. Having a passion for art, he is interested to learn of a young sculptor who lives in the town, Roderick Hudson. On meeting the intense, impetuous

Roderick and seeing proof of his talent, Rowland offers to subsidize the young artist for a period of study in Rome and gains the assent of Roderick's widowed mother. At a farewell picnic, Rowland has a last talk with Mary Garland, a distant cousin of Mrs. Hudson, who has been visiting in Northampton. Rowland realizes that he will not see her again for perhaps three years. In their brief acquaintance, she has come to mean a great deal to him, but on the Atlantic voyage, Roderick Hudson tells Rowland that he is engaged to Mary.

In Rome that autumn, as Rowland expected, Roderick responds to the stimulus provided by the art treasures of the city. He assimilates experiences readily and becomes eager to create masterpieces of his own. Rowland is pleased with his role as patron and nourisher of talent. One day, while Rowland sits with Roderick while he sketches in the Villa Ludovisi, the two companions observe a trio of passersby—a shabbily dressed man, a middle-aged woman, and a young woman with blue eyes, dusky hair, and perfect features. Roderick is enraptured by the young woman and yearns to model her, but they do not stop.

Rowland begins to introduce Roderick into society, and the young and handsome sculptor, attractively impertinent and strident, becomes a favorite. He spends his days hard at work and his nights in Roman drawing rooms. His first work, a life-size Adam, draws admirers to his studio. Among them are another sculptor, Gloriani, and a young American painter, Sam Singleton. Gloriani is skeptical of Roderick's staying power, but Singleton is an uncritical worshiper. Roderick frequently grows lyrical about his own brilliant future.

The onset of summer, however, brings Roderick to an impasse; his exuberance and inspiration depart. Rowland prescribes for him a change of scenery, and the two leave Rome to ramble northward. Roderick desires to spend most of the summer alone, and Rowland returns to England. After a month with no word from Roderick, Rowland dispatches a letter. The reply is unsettling; Roderick has been gambling and is heavily in debt. When the two friends meet in Geneva, Roderick admits debauchery but feels no remorse. He has learned that he is susceptible to the beauty and mystery of women.

Back in Rome, Roderick is discontented and works only in fits and starts. Then, one day, the couple and the beautiful young woman whom he had observed in the Ludovisi gardens burst into his studio. Madame Light and her daughter, Christina, along with the Cavaliere Giacosa, have come to see the rising young sculptor and his works. Roderick insists that he must sculpt a bust of Christina.

Mrs. Light is a vain, silly widow. She has picked up the old Cavaliere in her European ramblings and now lives solely to marry Christina to a fortune. During the winter, Roderick works on his bust of Christina, whose beauty is supplemented by wit, will, and education. He becomes enamored of her, and Rowland fears the young woman's influence on his friend. To Rowland she seems selfish and vicious, a complex person who demands worship. Meanwhile, Christina's mother is becoming established in Roman society, and Roderick takes a commission from an American snob to create in marble the ideal of Intellectual Refinement.

The old Cavaliere confides in Rowland that Roderick will find his love unrequited, as Mrs. Light is determined that Christina marry a man of wealth and position. Though Rowland and Christina dislike each other, they achieve a certain understanding. Christina confesses to him that she despises her own egotism and longs for someone to free her from herself.

Roderick's adoration of Christina continues, and in an effort to cool the relationship, Rowland informs Christina of Roderick's engagement. Roderick's subsequent anger reveals something to Rowland: His friend lacks a feeling heart; he does not care about hurting Mary. Rowland feels that his faith in Roderick's potential has been foolish—the artistic temperament is amoral.

Winter brings a new personage on the scene: Prince Casamassima is seen with the Light entourage. He is Mrs. Light's choice for Christina.

Rowland encounters Christina at various places in Rome, and their exchange of frank confidences continues. Rowland asks her to leave Roderick alone. Christina seems to desire Rowland's respect, but when she leaves Rome briefly, Roderick follows.

Despite Roderick's interlude of riotous living in Naples, Rowland's fondness for him is undiminished. Even when the sculptor stops working on Intellectual Refinement, Rowland tries to understand.

Christina's engagement to Prince Casamassima is announced, but Roderick continues his pursuit. Rowland admits himself disgusted with people. His good deed has turned sour; Mrs. Hudson and Mary Garland will be hurt to learn the truth about Roderick. Rowland's thoughts keep going back to Mary.

Hoping to save the situation, Rowland sends for Mrs. Hudson and Mary. When they arrive, Roderick greets Mary in a state of drunkenness. Rowland finds her even more attractive than he had before.

Although Christina's wedding date is set for June, Roderick's infatuation continues. Rowland is astonished to learn from Madame Grandoni that his own love for Mary Garland is perfectly evident to others. Then Christina breaks off her engagement to the prince, and Roderick isolates himself in his quarters for a week to contemplate this good fortune. Mrs. Light summons Rowland to talk sense to Christina. Meanwhile, Mrs. Hudson and Mary, still unaware of the complex situation, suffer in silence.

Rowland unwillingly converses with Christina. Although Prince Casamassima's money does not excite her, she refuses to accept Roderick's proposal of marriage. Three days later, Christina and the prince are suddenly and privately married. Simultaneously, a secret comes out: Mrs. Light's lover, the Cavaliere, is Christina's real father. Christina has married quickly because of her fear that such a scandal could cause the prince to break with her.

Roderick, angry, disappointed, and miserable, is ready to leave Rome. He places himself entirely in Rowland's hands. Rowland agrees when Roderick confesses to his mother and Mary that he is a failure. Mrs. Hudson is appalled to learn that the uncompleted Intellectual Refinement was a five-thousand-dollar commission.

Throughout the dreary, idle summer, Rowland vaguely hopes that Roderick can still pull himself together. In the meantime, Rowland finds that he admires Mary more and more. In the fall, they travel to Switzerland. It is clear that Roderick's perceptions of beauty are as acute as ever, but he is unable to do anything constructive.

Rowland presses the point with Roderick about his engagement to Mary. Roderick admits that Mary does not interest him, but he does not break the engagement. Roderick sees no point in Rowland's desire to keep his own admiration for Mary a secret.

In one of their daily rambles, Roderick and Rowland encounter the Prince and Princess Casamassima. Christina detests her husband, and Roderick, previously petulant and unforgiving of her, turns to pursuit again. The next day, he asks Rowland for one thousand francs so that he can meet Christina at Interlaken. Rowland, at the end of his patience, refuses the request, but Roderick gets some money from Mary. He chides Rowland for moralizing, but Rowland admits his love for Mary.

Roderick then disappears. A spectacular mountain thunderstorm arises in the afternoon, and by dawn the next day he has not returned. Sam Singleton, who has been diligently sketching all the while Roderick has idled, stops in for a visit, and he and Rowland go to look for Roderick. They find his body beneath a high cliff three hours' walk from the inn. He had fallen, apparently, on his way to Interlaken.

Mrs. Hudson and Mary Garland go back to Northampton. Rowland, with his inexhaustible patience, frequently calls on Mary.

Critical Evaluation:

Roderick Hudson is Henry James's first novel. It came after many short stories, through which James had developed not only his technical skills but also many of his thematic interests. It might be said that James was interested in three themes: the problem of young men or women who need help to express themselves fully as human beings; the problem of young Americans, whom he saw as needing the experience of European society, traditions, and institutions; and money, particularly how money can be used to help promising individuals fulfill themselves.

James's belief in the civilizing effects of Europe on young Americans must be understood in the context of the time. He wrote at the end of the nineteenth century and the beginning of the twentieth, when the United States was a less confident country than it later became. His enthusiasm for what Europe could do to polish an American (intellectually, artistically, socially, and psychologically) must be understood in conjunction with a caveat: Such an encounter could sometimes do harm, particularly since the European ethos was not without flaws that the innocent American might not be able to resist.

This novel manifests, in simpler ways than James's later works, many of these ideas. It is a tale of a young man—Roderick Hudson—of artistic promise who needs the experience of the great world of European art and who, at least initially, proves able to profit from his experience. He learns to express himself with considerable promise. He seems personally flawed, proud of his gift, but arrogantly unconcerned about how precious it is and how susceptible he is to the distractions of pleasure, which is readily at hand in the moneyed circles in which Rowland places him. He is sometimes unable and sometimes unwilling to distinguish between the valuable aspects of European experience and its destructive temptations.

When Christina Light comes along, Roderick is unable to believe that his love can be resisted. He understands little of the least attractive powers of money and social position. He comes to Rome as an innocent, blessed with talent that others envy but lacking the self-discipline of the artist or the moral strength of his friend Rowland Mallet, who thinks that he can protect Roderick from his lack of character and from a world wiser, older, and more corrupt than he can imagine. It must also be said that Roderick is at some considerable fault, particularly in his self-absorption and self-pity and in his cruel lack of interest in how his conduct affects others. Europe is not responsible for his selfishness. He seems to have no concern for proving worthy of Rowland's help, which goes far beyond financial support, and his treatment of his mother and Mary Garland can hardly be blamed on the evils of European high society. He is a spoiled, arrogant young man who sadly throws away an artistic gift that lesser artists of his acquaintance in Rome look upon with yearning. Talent, James seems to be saying, will not protect one from a lack of character.

This is a good novel with which to begin an exploration of the works of Henry James, but readers new to James need to understand certain oddities about his work. James is not much interested in complicated plot or adventurous incident. He is interested in character, particularly a young American character of promise meeting the temptations of European high life. On top of that, he is strongly inclined toward the use of two technical devices that can cause difficulty for readers who are used to fast-moving stories. He likes his characters to talk at length and with fineness of thought about their problems. He gives them the capacity for subtle expression and often a muted wittiness that can be missed by those who read too quickly. He extends this minuteness of expression to his narrative third-person voice, which is allowed, usually within a limited set of parameters, to penetrate the minds of his characters. What James seems to be suggesting is that if his characters could express themselves with the fineness and high intelligence that his narrative voice possesses, they would thus define themselves. Realistic credibility, in short, gives way to depth and subtlety of expression. The secret of this novel, and of James's novels that followed it, is the artistic pleasure not in what happens but in how the problems, mainly moral, are considered by the characters and by the narrator, who is always the most perceptive voice in the novel. It is not simply a matter of what happens; it is equally a matter of how what happens is experienced by all involved.

The conclusion of Roderick Hudson is somewhat banal, but tonally it has a wry and anticlimactic air about it that suggested at the time it was published that James was not going to be an easy novelist or, indeed, a particularly popular one. The real power of the book is not in its ending but in its contemplation of how people make messes of their lives while attempting to do the opposite.

"Critical Evaluation" by Charles Pullen

Further Reading

Anderson, Charles R. *Person, Place, and Thing in Henry James's Novels*. Durham, N.C.: Duke University Press, 1977. Examines the connections between James's novels and other novels of the nineteenth century. A chapter on *Roderick Hudson* refers to James's life in Rome and discusses how the characters relate to one another.

Edel, Leon. *Henry James: A Life*. New York: Harper & Row, 1985. Valuable biographical study includes discussion of James's work, with substantial comment on *Roderick Hudson*.

Freedman, Jonathan, ed. *The Cambridge Companion to Henry James*. New York: Cambridge University Press, 1998. Collection of essays provides extensive information on James's life and literary influences in addition to describing his works and the characters in them.

Graham, Kenneth. *Henry James, a Literary Life*. New York: St. Martin's Press, 1996. Critical overview of James's most important writings offers information on his career as a novelist in the United States, England, and continental Europe. Places James within the literary and intellectual climate of his time.

Lane, Christopher. "The Impossibility of Seduction in James's *Roderick Hudson* and *The Tragic Muse*." In *Mapping Male Sexuality: Nineteenth-Century England*, edited by Jay Losey, Elizabeth J. Dell, and William D. Brewer. Madison, N.J.: Fairleigh Dickinson University Press, 2000. Examines the dynamics of male friendship in the two novels.

Lee, Brian. *The Novels of Henry James: A Study of Culture and Consciousness*. London: Edward Arnold, 1978. Examination of James's work focuses on the relationship of culture to the individual. Includes a chapter on *Roderick Hudson* that discusses James's enthusiasm for European culture.

McCormack, Peggy. *The Rule of Money: Gender, Class, and Exchange Economics in the Fiction of Henry James*. Ann Arbor: University of Michigan Press, 1990. Discusses how James's characters learn to adjust to the rules of the game in their society. Useful for understanding the mores and practices of a departed era.

Person, Leland S. *Henry James and the Suspense of Masculinity*. Philadelphia: University of Pennsylvania Press, 2003. Examines several of James's works, including *Roderick Hudson*, to describe how he challenged traditional concepts of heterosexual masculinity, depicting characters with alternate sexual and gender identities.

Stevens, Hugh. *Henry James and Sexuality*. New York: Cambridge University Press, 1998. Study of the depiction of sexuality in James's work, including discussions of homosexuality and gender roles. Chapter 4 examines the eroticism of prohibition, masochism, and the law in *Roderick Hudson*.

The Romance of Leonardo da Vinci

Author: Dmitry Merezhkovsky (1865-1941)
First published: Voskresshiye bogi: Leonardo da Vinci,
    1901 (English translation, 1902)
Type of work: Novel
Type of plot: Historical
Time of plot: 1494-1519
Locale: Italy and France

Principal characters:
LEONARDO DA VINCI, a Renaissance artist
GIOVANNI BELTRAFFIO, his pupil
CESARE BORGIA, Leonardo's patron
MONNA CASSANDRA, a sorceress
FRANCESCO MELZI, another pupil of Leonardo
MONNA LISA GIOCONDA, a model for a portrait by
    Leonardo

The Story:

In 1494 the fear of the coming of the Antichrist prophesied in the New Testament begins to make itself felt in Italy. Greek and Roman statues, which were recently excavated and accepted as supreme works of art by such men as Leonardo da Vinci, are considered by the common people to be pagan deities returning to prepare the world for the reign of the Antichrist.

Leonardo is a member of the court of Duke Moro in Milan. Besides acting as chief architect for the duke, he interests himself in teaching his pupils, Giovanni Beltraffio and Andrea Salaino, and in working on whatever catches his fancy. Most of the money he receives from the duke's treasury goes to buy pieces of amber with insects embedded in them, old shells, live birds that he studies and then frees, and other curious objects that distract his attention and keep him from completing his painting, *The Last Supper.*

The student Giovanni is attracted to Monna Cassandra, a beautiful girl who lives in the neighborhood. Unknown to him, she practices the black arts and is a favorite of suspected witches. The duke of Milan calls upon the king of France to help protect and support his dukedom. Louis XII of France, however, soon proves false to his friendship with the duke and overruns the duchy. The French forces use a clay statue of a mounted warrior, which Leonardo did not yet cast in bronze, as a target for a shooting contest, and a flood causes the walls on which *The Last Supper* is painted to bulge and crack. Realizing that these two works of art can never be finished, Leonardo decides to leave Milan and go to the court of Cesare Borgia, the son of Pope Alexander VI.

As Borgia's adviser, Leonardo designs many pieces of war equipment and machinery, which Borgia uses in his attempt to seize all of Italy for the pope. None of Leonardo's pupils approves of his working for Borgia, whose cruelties and vices make him hated throughout Italy.

One day one of Leonardo's students, a blacksmith named Zoroastro da Peretola, goes against his orders and tries to fly in Leonardo's only partly completed airplane. Falling from a considerable height, he receives such a jolt that his mind is never again sound. Leonardo leaves Borgia's services and, with the help of his friend, Niccolò Machiavelli, receives a commission from the city of Florence to plan a system of waterways that would divert the course of the Arno River. Machiavelli underestimates the expense of the work, and Leonardo is soon in trouble with the authorities. The canal project is abandoned, and Leonardo is asked instead to paint a large picture depicting the battle of Anghiari. At that time Michelangelo is also working in Florence, and a great jealousy grows up between admirers of the two artists. Leonardo tries to make friends with Michelangelo, but the passionate artist will have nothing to do with the mild Leonardo. Raphael, at that time only a young man, is friendly with both artists. His works are more popular with artistically minded Pope Leo X than those of either of the older men.

During his stay in Florence, Leonardo begins the portrait of a young married woman of the town named Monna Lisa Gioconda. As she sits for him, day after day, he amuses her by telling her stories as he works or converses with her on any subject in order to keep her interested in the dull task of posing. As the months pass, Monna Lisa and Leonardo are more and more drawn to each other. Both are essentially secretive persons who seem to understand each other intuitively. Months pass into years, and still Monna Lisa comes to the studio to pose. No one suspects anything improper of the meetings, but it becomes a source of amusement in Florence that the gentle artist, who never before took an interest in women, seems to be in love. Monna Lisa's sudden death shocks Leonardo to the bottom of his soul. He hoped to finish her portrait, to finish this one work at least, but with Monna Lisa's death his hopes fall. He tried to show in her face the mystery of the universe, for he found that the mystery of Monna Lisa and the mystery of the universe are one.

As a result of the trouble over the canal and the unfinished picture of the battle of Anghiari, Leonardo is dismissed from the service of the city of Florence. He returns to Milan to serve under the new ruler of that city, Louis XII of France. There Giovanni Beltraffio again meets Monna Cassandra. One day, she promises to show him the answers to his deepest questions. He is to meet her late that same night. As Giovanni leaves her, he is shocked to see in her face the expression of the White She-Demon, a specter that haunted him since childhood.

Before the time for their meeting, however, Monna Cassandra is taken prisoner by the Most Holy Inquisition. Thinking her completely innocent, Giovanni visits all of his old friends in an effort to secure her release. The more he tries to help her, however, the more convinced he becomes that there are indeed evil spirits who inhabit the forms of human beings and that the White She-Demon is one of them. Unable to prevent Monna's death, Giovanni walks about the streets disconsolately. Suddenly he realizes that the strange odor he was smelling is the scent of burning flesh. Monna and 129 others accused as witches are being burned at the stake. Terror-stricken, he almost loses his mind. Later, still haunted by the White She-Demon, Giovanni commits suicide.

The loss of his favorite pupil would be a more terrible blow to Leonardo if Francesco Melzi did not recently join his group of students. Melzi, who is to be the true and faithful friend of the old artist, helps him through the final years of his life, especially in that trying period when the death of Louis XII leaves Leonardo without a patron, but the new French king, Francis I, soon afterward calls Leonardo to Paris. In 1516 Leonardo and his small group leave Italy for France, and the artist is never to see his home country again.

In France he is well treated despite his inability to finish anything he begins. He takes up the Monna Lisa portrait again and almost finishes it to his satisfaction from memory. One day King Francis visits him in his studio. Seeing the portrait, the king purchases it but agrees that Leonardo can keep his beloved portrait until he dies.

King Francis does not have long to wait. A few years later Leonardo, old and weak, grows sick and dies. His faithful pupil, Melzi, sees to it that Leonardo receives the rites of the Church before his death. He also arranges to have the artist buried in a style which, he hopes, will forever still the whispering tongues that called Leonardo a disciple of the Antichrist to come.

Critical Evaluation:

Dmitry Merezhkovsky is frequently associated with the Symbolist movement of the late nineteenth century. He be- lieved art should be recognized as humanity's highest metaphysical activity. Symbolism elevated idealism above materialism, aesthetics above science, imagination above reason, and subjectivity above objectivity. Drawing examples from ancient Greece, medieval Europe, Renaissance Italy, and Russia, Merezhkovsky argued that all great art is motivated by religious strivings. Greek tragedy was an attempt to place humanity in the cosmos. Gothic cathedrals indicate the desire for ascension. Michelangelo and Leonardo da Vinci were motivated by religious questions to develop a new theology. Likewise, Merezhkovsky considered Symbolist art theurgy, a means to higher truth, and the basis for spiritual revival in Russia. With the artist as spiritual guide, religion becomes a source of unity between artists and people.

The incompatibility of artists and the people became apparent as Symbolism grew as a cultural movement. Within the framework of Friedrich Nietzsche's theory of the superman, Merezhkovsky developed a new theology over the course of several decades. For Merezhkovsky, historical Christianity scorned the world and exalted selflessness, asceticism, and humility. Instead, he admired Christ as a superman who overcame death. He considered the next step in religious consciousness as the development of godmanhood, a process of spiritual evolution occurring in three distinct historical phases. The first humanity is the pre-Christian world of the flesh, depicted in the Old Testament. The second revelation, in the New Testament, revealed that spiritual love is truth. In the third revelation, the Holy Mother, who symbolizes the union of divine spirit and earthly flesh, ends human religious duality. The outcome is apocalyptic; a new humanity is created on earth, the world is transformed, and a new church is born.

Christ and Antichrist, the trilogy of novels in which *The Romance of Leonardo da Vinci* is the second, was Merezhkovsky's attempt to recapitulate the stages of world history and to delineate the features of the godman who appears at the end. Each work in the trilogy focuses on a titanic figure who epitomizes humanity in his own time. Taken together, the three volumes demonstrate Merezhkovsky's conviction that history is a dialectic between the two principles of paganism and Christianity, a dialectic that must ultimately be resolved. The work was written at different stages in Merezhkovsky's spiritual development, so the volumes are not unified and, ultimately, reflect the failure of his religious creation.

The first volume, *Smert bogov: Yulian Otstupnik* (1896; *The Death of the Gods: Or, Julian the Apostate*, 1929), is essentially a Nietzschean tract. Based on the Roman emperor who attempted to restore paganism, it exalted courage, beauty, and defiance of death. The novel was successful throughout Europe due to its scandalous portrayal of sexuality and violent revelry. Julian embodies the Nietzschean ideal of sensuality. Paganism is the principle of happiness on earth, and it values personal freedom, beauty, sensuality, and prosperity.

The second volume, *The Romance of Leonardo da Vinci*, depicts the resurgence of paganism and an attempted reconciliation with Christianity by a godman. Leonardo harmonizes the principles of pagan beauty and sensuality and Christian spiritual tranquillity. As opposed to his contemporary, Michelangelo, who was ruled entirely by the flesh, Leonardo expresses a desire for ascension. Leonardo's plan for a flying machine indicates both the Christian desire for heaven and the pagan desire for superhuman powers. His paintings illustrate the harmonious combination of divergent elements. Their detailed accuracy stems from the careful observation of the world, but the details serve to recapture the living spirit of the subject. Leonardo combines masculine and feminine elements in himself and finds his feminine counterpart in Monna Lisa. Prefiguring the godman, Leonardo unites perfect love and perfect knowledge, strength and compassion, daring and humility, sensuality and intellect, idealism and practicality, art and science, love of beauty and spiritual yearning. His new religious consciousness was inconsistent; he wavered between Christian humility and pagan ideals of sensuality and personal freedom. Furthermore, his artistic efforts had to submit to political machinations. Leonardo ultimately emerges as a prophet of a new religion, not its fulfillment. The novel combines stylistic elements typical of the Symbolist period with the copious detail of historical romance. The demonic motifs of the Symbolists, represented by Monna Cassandra and the White She-Devil, express a religious desire to explore evil's place in the divine scheme. The sun and its golden hue, prominent in *The Romance of Leonardo da Vinci*, signified paganism for the Symbolist poets. Images of scientific complexity and technology, such as mathematical calculations, architectural plans, and the camera obscura, reflect the futuristic bent of the art of Merezhkovsky's time. The novel makes no attempt at historical accuracy but does re-create the wealth of art, literature, and politics in Renaissance Italy. The uneasy relationship between art and politics also presents a powerful critique of the literature of late nineteenth century Russia.

Although the novel's historical interest and relevant political commentary made it an international success, its characters are not fully developed. The novel is told primarily from Leonardo's point of view, but the narrator frequently interprets the action. *The Romance of Leonardo da Vinci* reads as a vehicle for Merezhkovsky's religious ideas rather than convincing fiction. He did, however, bring Italian Renaissance to the consciousness of Russians.

In later years, Merezhkovsky considered Leonardo a transition figure between the pagan past of art and beauty and the pagan future of science and reason. From this perspective, the pagan elements he represented were destined to grow until they overshadowed the Christian elements. The last novel of the trilogy, *Antikhrist: Pyotri Aleksey* (1905; *Peter and Alexis*, 1905), describes the dissolution of the synthesis prefigured by Leonardo. Christian and pagan beliefs are represented by noble and idealistic figures, rendering their final incompatibility even more tragic. The novel reflects Merezhkovsky's growing disillusion with the Religious Philosophic Society he founded with his wife, poet Zinaida Hippius, and with the growing social turbulence in Russia. Merezhkovsky initiated a religious search, but he did not see its fulfillment.

"Critical Evaluation" by Pamela Pavliscak

Further Reading

Bedford, Charles. *The Seeker: D. S. Merezhkovsky.* Lawrence: University Press of Kansas, 1975. Explores Merezhkovsky's religion and ethics. Examines the synthesis of Christianity and paganism attempted in Merezhkovsky's trilogy of historical novels and finds that *The Romance of Leonardo Da Vinci* most successfully combines the two.

Fedotov, Georgy. *The Russian Religious Mind.* 2 vols. Belmont, Mass.: Norland, 1975. Surveys Russian religious thought and practice. Provides valuable background to Merezhkovsky's literary efforts by summarizing contemporary religious beliefs.

Frajlich, Anna. "The Contradictions of the Northern Pilgrim: Dmitry Merezhkovsky." In *The Legacy of Ancient Rome in the Russian Silver Age.* New York: Rodopi, 2007. Frajlich describes how the renewal of classical scholarship in nineteenth century Russia led Merezhkovsky and other Russian Symbolists to find inspiration in ancient Rome. Includes discussion of some of Merezhkovsky's novels and poems.

Hellman, Ben. *Poets of Hope and Despair: The Russian Symbolists in War and Revolution, 1914-1918.* Helsinki: Institute for Russian and East European Studies, 1995. This study of Russian Symbolism includes a chapter on Merezhkovsky. The book describes how he and other symbolists interpreted the deeper meaning of the events of World War I and the Russian Revolution.

Hippius, Zinaida. *Between Paris and St. Petersburg: Selected Diaries of Zinaida Hippius.* Translated by Temira

Pachmuss. Champaign: University of Illinois Press, 1975. Merezhkovsky's wife outlines literary events in the lives of both authors and gives valuable insight into their religious and social ideas.

Pachmuss, Temira. *D. S. Merezhkovsky in Exile: The Master of the Genre of Biographie Romancée.* New York: Peter Lang, 1990. One of the few works on Merezhkovsky in English to devote attention primarily to his prose. Defines the genre of biographical romance and considers Merezhkovsky's historical novels as an example of the genre. Includes analysis of narrative structure, point of view, and characterization.

Rosenthal, Bernice G. *Dmitri Sergeevich Merezhkovsky and the Silver Age: The Development of a Revolutionary Mentality.* The Hague, the Netherlands: Martinus Nijhoff, 1975. Offers an overview of the historical novels within the context of Merezhkovsky's philosophical thinking. Elaborates upon Friedrich Nietzsche's direct and indirect influence on Merezhkovsky. Provides an analysis of narrative structure, important themes, and characters.

The Romance of the Forest

Author: Ann Radcliffe (1764-1823)
First published: 1791
Type of work: Novel
Type of plot: Gothic
Time of plot: Seventeenth century
Locale: France and Savoy

Principal characters:
ADELINE, a victim of intrigue
PIERRE DE LA MOTTE, her benefactor and a fugitive from justice
MADAME DE LA MOTTE, his wife
LOUIS, their son
THEODORE PEYROU, a young soldier
THE MARQUIS DE MONTALT, a villainous nobleman
ARNAUD LA LUC, a cleric and scholar
CLARA, his daughter
PETER, a loyal servant

The Story:

On a tempestuous night, Pierre de la Motte leaves Paris to escape his creditors and prosecution by the law. Descended from an ancient house, he is a man whose passions often prove stronger than his conscience. Having dissipated his own fortune and that of his wife, he has engaged in various questionable schemes that have brought him at last to disgrace and made this flight necessary. Leaving Paris with his wife and two faithful servants, he hopes to find a refuge in some village of the southern provinces. The departure is so sudden that the couple have had no time to say farewell to their son Louis, who is on duty with his regiment in Germany.

Several leagues from the city, the coachman, Peter, loses his way while driving them across a wild heath. La Motte sees in the distance the lighted window of a small, ancient house. He dismounts and walks there in the hope of securing directions from the residents. A grim-visaged man opens the door at his knock, ushers him into a desolate apartment, and abruptly leaves, locking the door behind him. Over the howling of the wind, la Motte can hear rough voices close at hand and the muffled sobbing of a woman.

The door is at last unlocked, and the forbidding ruffian reappears, dragging by the hand a beautiful girl of about eighteen. The man puts a pistol to la Motte's chest and offers him his choice between death or taking the girl with him. When the girl begs him to take pity on her, la Motte is moved by her tears as much as by his own danger, and he readily assents. Other men appear, and the now blindfolded prisoners are taken on horseback to the edge of the heath, where la Motte's carriage waits. La Motte and the girl are put into the carriage, and Peter quickly drives them away from the threats and curses of the wild crew. The agitated girl, thrust so strangely into the company of la Motte and his wife, gives her name only as Adeline. Not wishing to add to her distress and filled with pity for her, they do not pursue any further questioning.

Several days later, the travelers reach the vast forest of Fontanville. As the sun is setting, they are awed to see against the ruddy sky the towers of an ancient abbey. Soon after, when one of the carriage wheels breaks and the vehicle is overturned, they decide to return to the abbey. During their explorations of the empty building, they discover a suite of apartments still habitable and of more modern date than the rest of the structure. Despite his wife's misgivings, la Motte decides to make the secluded abbey his place of refuge.

Peter is dispatched to a nearby village for provisions and furniture, and he returns with the report that the ruins are the property of a nobleman living on a distant estate. The country people also claim that a mysterious prisoner was once confined there, and although no one knows his fate, his ghost is said to haunt the scene of his imprisonment. For seventeen years, the natives of the region have not dared to approach the old abbey.

La Motte is well pleased with all that he hears; before long, he and his household have made their quarters comfortable. La Motte spends most of his mornings out of doors, either hunting or fishing, and his afternoons and evenings with his family. Sometimes he reads, but more often he simply sits in gloomy silence. Only Adeline has the power to enliven his spirits when he grows moody and depressed. She has fully recovered from her terrifying experience and has a sweet, lively disposition and diligent habits. After a time, she confides the story of her life to Madame de la Motte, whom she has begun to look upon as a mother.

She is the only child of the poor but reputable Chevalier de St. Pierre. With her mother dead, she was reared in a convent, after which her father had intended that she should marry. When she refused, he rebuked her for her obstinacy, and one day he took her not to his magnificent house in Paris but to that lonely house on the heath. There she had been turned over to the care of brutal keepers. Only the arrival of la Motte, she believes, saved her from an unknown but terrible fate.

After a month in the forest refuge, la Motte regains a measure of his tranquillity and even cheerfulness, much to the delight of his wife and their ward. Then his mood suddenly changes again. As if he were being preyed upon by some guilty secret or deep remorse, he avoids his family and spends many hours alone in the forest. Peter, the faithful servant, tries to follow his master on more than one occasion, but la Motte always eludes his follower and, at one particular place, disappears as if the trees and rocks have swallowed him. About that time, Peter brings a report from the village that a stranger in the neighborhood has been inquiring for his master. Greatly disturbed, la Motte remembers a trapdoor he

had observed in one of the decaying chambers of the abbey. With the hope that it might lead to a good hiding place, he explores the passageway to which the trapdoor gives access and finally comes to a room containing a large chest of ancient design. Throwing open the lid, he is horrified to find a human skeleton. He insists that his family join him in the hidden apartments he has discovered, but he tells the others nothing about the gruesome remains in the chest.

When he ventures out of hiding the next day, la Motte sees a stranger in the abbey and returns quickly to his place of concealment. The group's provisions are running low, however, and at last it is decided that Adeline should reconnoiter the ruins to learn whether the stranger, assumed to be an officer of the law, has gone away. In the cloisters, she encounters a young man in military uniform. Although she tries to flee, he overtakes her and demands to know the whereabouts of Pierre de la Motte. Adeline's relief is as great as her joy when the stranger turns out to be Louis de la Motte, whose filial affection has drawn him to his father's side.

Unfortunately, Louis's growing fondness for Adeline completely destroys Madame de la Motte's liking for her. To avoid the older woman's coldness, Adeline begins to spend much of her time in the forest, where she composes poems inspired by the beauty of the landscape and her own gentle melancholy. One day, while she is singing some stanzas of her own composition, a strange voice echoes hers. Startled to find a young man in hunter's dress close at hand, she is about to flee in fright when she realizes that the stranger has paused respectfully on seeing her agitation. As she leaves the forest, Adeline decides to refrain for a time from walking so far from the abbey. On her return to the abbey, Madame de la Motte adds to her confusion by greeting her suspiciously.

About a month later, a party of horsemen arrive at the abbey during a violent midnight storm. When no one responds to their knocking, they push the decayed door from its hinges and stalk into the hall. Overcome by fear for her benefactor, Adeline faints. When she revives, she finds the young man of the forest in the room and learns from the conversation that his name is Theodore Peyrou and that his older companion, a chevalier of haughty demeanor, is the Marquis de Montalt, the owner of the abbey, who is staying at his hunting lodge on the edge of the forest. La Motte, who had fled when the knocking began, returns to the room. Immediately, he and the marquis regard each other in great confusion, and the nobleman puts his hand threateningly on his sword. He agrees, however, when la Motte requests a private discussion in another room. Madame de la Motte overhears enough of their conversation to realize that there is some secret between the two men.

The marquis and his retinue depart early in the morning. Returning the next day, the nobleman, after inquiring for la Motte, pays courteous attention to Adeline. When he and la Motte have disappeared into the forest on an errand of their own, Theodore remains with the ladies. Adeline suddenly realizes that she is falling in love with the young man. Louis de la Motte prepares to return to his regiment. The marquis continues to visit the abbey almost every day. Adeline meets Theodore in the forest, and he promises to meet her again the next evening, but he is unable to do so when the marquis suddenly orders him to return to duty.

That night, Adeline dreams that she is in a strange chamber of the abbey, where a cloaked guide conducts her to a coffin covered with a pall. When her guide lifts the covering, she sees a dead man lying within, blood gushing from his side. The next day, the marquis comes for dinner and consents with reluctance to sleep at the abbey. A rearrangement of the private apartments is necessary to accommodate the guests, and Adeline retires to a small chamber usually occupied by Madame de la Motte's maid. Behind a tapestry, she discovers a door that leads into the chamber she saw in her dream. A rusted dagger lies on the floor, and in a moldering bed, she finds a small roll of manuscript.

On her return to her room, Adeline hears voices coming from the room below. To her horror, she hears the marquis declare his passionate intention to make her his. She retires in great distress of mind, to be aroused again when the nobleman, in evident alarm, leaves the abbey unceremoniously before daybreak. Later that same morning, the marquis returns and, over Adeline's protests, declares his suit. When she turns to la Motte for aid, he assures her that he is unable to help her, because his safety depends on the nobleman. So great is Adeline's despair that she almost forgets about the manuscript she found in the abandoned room. She has read enough of the despairing document, however, to realize that it was written by the mysterious prisoner of the abbey, who had been a victim of the marquis. She also learns from Peter that the marquis has a wife still living.

To save the helpless young woman, Peter promises to take her to his native village in Savoy. She is to meet him at an old tomb in the forest, but when she arrives there, a strange horseman appears and, despite her struggles, captures her and carries her to the marquis's hunting lodge. She manages to escape from the lodge through a window, and Theodore, who returned from his regiment when he learned of the marquis's evil plans, joins her in her flight. In a carriage that he had waiting, they drive all night in the direction of the frontier. When they stop at an inn for some refreshment, they are overtaken by officers who try to arrest Theodore in the king's

name. Resisting, he receives a saber cut in the head. He has almost recovered from his wound when the Marquis de Montalt appears and orders his men to seize Theodore on a charge of treason. Theodore, snatching up a sergeant's cutlass, wounds the marquis. During the confusion, Adeline is hustled into a chaise and driven back to the abbey, where la Motte locks her in her room. Anxious for word of Theodore, she is told a short time later that the young officer has been returned under arrest to his regiment.

By the time the marquis is able to travel, his passion for Adeline has turned to hate, and he orders la Motte to kill the girl. The unscrupulous nobleman's hold over la Motte is strong, for during his early days at the abbey, driven to desperation by his lack of funds, la Motte had robbed the marquis, whom he mistook for a chance traveler. Although he is completely in the marquis's power, la Motte refuses to stain his hands with blood. Instead, he orders the faithful Peter to take Adeline to Leloncourt, in Savoy, where she will be safe from the marquis's agents. When her flight is revealed, the nobleman has la Motte arrested for highway robbery and imprisoned.

Shortly after her arrival in Leloncourt, Adeline becomes ill, and Arnaud la Luc, a scholarly clergyman, takes her into his home. During her convalescence, she forms a close friendship with his daughter, Clara. Her grief over Theodore is so deep that she never mentions him to her new friends. Then la Luc's health begins to fail, and Adeline and Clara accompany him to the Mediterranean seacoast. There Adeline encounters Louis de la Motte and learns that he is on his way to Leloncourt on an errand for Theodore. To her great surprise, it is revealed that the man she knows as Theodore Peyrou is in reality the son of Arnaud la Luc. The travelers immediately hasten to Vaceau, where the young officer is being held under sentence of death.

Meanwhile, la Motte has been taken to Paris for trial on the charges brought against him by the marquis. The prisoner is in despair when an unexpected witness appears in his behalf. The man is Du Bosse, one of the ruffians hired to dispose of Adeline while she was held prisoner in the lonely house on the heath. His story starts an investigation that reveals that Adeline may be the natural daughter of the Marquis de Montalt, who had never seen the girl before he met her at the ruined abbey. In the past, one of his agents had always played the part of her father. The marquis is arrested, and Adeline is summoned to Paris for his trial. With the marquis's arrest, other activities he has engaged in come to light. He ordered the murder of his older brother, whose skeleton la Motte found in the abbey. The confederate also testifies that Adeline is not the nobleman's natural daughter but his older brother's legitimate child, an heir whom the marquis had tried to conceal from the world. The manuscript Adeline found in the abbey provides further evidence of her uncle's villainy. He is sentenced to death for his crimes.

When the extent of the marquis's evil schemes becomes known, Theodore receives a royal pardon and is restored to his military rank. Pierre de la Motte is sentenced to exile in England, and with her newfound inheritance, Adeline is able to provide for his comfort and that of his wife in their old age. She arranges for the burial of her father's skeleton, with all respect, in the vault of his ancestors. A short time later, she and Theodore marry and go to live at Leloncourt. Clara marries Monsieur Verneuil, Adeline's distant kinsman, who has been helpful to her and the la Lucs during the time of their distress over Theodore and la Motte. Before many years have passed, Louis de la Motte and his bride settle in a house nearby, and there in Leloncourt the three deserving couples live out their lives in happiness and prosperity.

Critical Evaluation:

The Romance of the Forest, a popular eighteenth century romance, marks Ann Radcliffe's contribution to the development of the novel genre. In each of her gothic tales, a damsel in distress must usually endure various trials involving danger, terror, and mystery. Underlying the plot is the opposition of good and evil. Radcliffe may employ such traditional elements of gothic fiction as dungeons, decaying castles, ghosts, and villains, but the conflict she portrays is between virtue and vice, and the novel sets up a fixed system of punishments and rewards. Powers of evil, whether natural or supernatural, are ultimately overruled.

Radcliffe's characters represent varying degrees of good and evil. Adeline, the heroine, is the most virtuous. She does not rebel against the evil forces that seek to destroy her but trusts her safety to divine providence. Her moral strength enables her to triumph despite her feminine vulnerability. Adeline, who faces both physical and emotional isolation, has mysterious origins; she spent her childhood in a convent, apart from family. Later, her supposed father rejected her and placed her in the hands of strangers. Radcliffe does not reveal Adeline's heritage and the facts regarding her father's identity and murder until the close of the novel.

Adeline is also isolated physically. Each time she tries to escape disaster, she is somehow imprisoned. After leaving the convent, she is first locked in a dark chamber with barred windows, then sent away with strangers to live in exile in the abbey ruins of the forest. There she is abducted from a black tomb by the marquis's servant and eventually returned to confinement in the abbey towers.

She escapes these physical barricades only when she flees France to seek asylum in the mountains of Savoy. Her new location is not only at a higher altitude but also on higher moral ground. The darkness of the forest and the plots to abduct her are here replaced by sunlight, open scenery, and the kindness of the la Luc family. Even here, however, her emotional isolation continues. The la Lucs care for her, but she remains separated from the knowledge of her true identity and from the man she loves.

Theodore, Adeline's lover and rescuer, is a virtuous young man who left home to study for the ministry but finds himself ill suited for the role of clergyman. He seeks a more active vocation (and perhaps a less devout life) by joining the military and finds himself in service to the villainous Marquis de Montalt. Theodore attempts to save Adeline, but because he leaves his military post and later physically attacks the Marquis de Montalt he is arrested for desertion and assault. He cannot rely on his innocence and virtue to save him because he has broken the law. Theodore faces a death sentence more imminent than the threats Adeline has endured, but since Theodore's motives were honorable, he is eventually released from prison and rewarded with the love of the heroine.

Unlike Theodore, who breaks rules to save Adeline, Pierre de la Motte and his wife often commit wrongs for selfish ends. La Motte, who lost the family fortune through self-indulgence, finds that he is capable of ever greater evil—cheating, stealing, and finally attacking and robbing innocent victims—to preserve his own welfare. Thus he conspires to deliver Adeline into the hands of the marquis to save himself. La Motte is not totally depraved, however; Radcliffe asserts that his heart was betrayed by "weakness rather than natural depravity." He had fallen victim to the temptations of the "dissipations of Paris." Madame de la Motte too is weak. She at first befriends Adeline but then rejects her when she succumbs to jealousy and suspicion. Later, when she learns of the Marquis's plot to abduct Adeline, she acquiesces in the scheme even though she knows that Adeline is innocent of any offense.

The la Mottes have a capacity for both good and evil. Their natural inclination toward politeness and pity is their redeeming quality, which surfaces when they are called on to save Adeline's life. Radcliffe rejuvenates the couple's moral reputations by using them to resolve the plot, for it is their information that leads to Theodore's acquittal and the marquis's demise. Ultimately, the la Mottes cannot be pardoned as Theodore is because their transgressions are more serious. The couple escape prison sentences and the death penalty, but they must face exile.

The greatest evil is embodied in the character of the Marquis de Montalt, who has no redeeming qualities. Unlike the la Mottes, the marquis is not capable of good impulses. He is the antithesis of Adeline, who possesses no title, birthright, or position but is virtuous. The marquis has the appearance of virtue but is evil. His "elegance of manners" merely "veiled the depravity of his heart." He identifies Adeline as his niece and restores her inheritance, but these actions reflect defeat rather than repentance.

Radcliffe's tale presents a picture of a fallen world. Original sin has fostered moral decay, temptation, and death. The wild, overgrown forest resembles the corruption of Eden. The lost manuscript and rusty dagger that Adeline finds in the abbey are symbols of the excesses that eventually destroy the marquis. Even Adeline is affected by her fallen world. She is deceived about her own identity and becomes a victim of those who are less upright. Virtue ultimately triumphs, however, and each character receives a proper reward. Radcliffe thus assures her readers that justice, however long delayed, will overtake the guilty.

"Critical Evaluation" by Paula M. Miller

Further Reading

Bruce, Donald Williams. "Ann Radcliffe and the Extended Imagination." *Contemporary Review* 258 (June, 1991): 300-308. Discusses Radcliffe's use of imagination in shaping her descriptions of landscape to correlate with the development of her heroines. Includes historical information regarding her study of Italian travelogues.

Cottom, Daniel. *The Civilized Imagination: A Study of Ann Radcliffe, Jane Austen, and Sir Walter Scott.* 1985. Reprint. New York: Cambridge University Press, 2009. Scholarly work examines the link between Radcliffe's novels and eighteenth century English society. Focuses on the relationships of the female protagonists and social values.

Durant, David. "Ann Radcliffe and the Conservative Gothic." *Studies in English Literature* 22, no. 3 (Summer, 1982): 519-530. Proposes that Radcliffe's gothic fiction is a reaction against romanticism and the irrational. Discusses Radcliffe's heroines and their rejection of the "fallen world."

Haggerty, George E. "The Pleasures of Victimization in *The Romance of the Forest.*" In *Unnatural Affections: Women and Fiction in the Later Eighteenth Century.* Bloomington: Indiana University Press, 1998. Argues that Radcliffe creates an alternative fiction "of male vulnerability and emasculation," rewriting "masculinity in a female mold" that "attempts to eroticize the very fact of victimization."

Miles, Robert. *Ann Radcliffe: The Great Enchantress.* New York: Manchester University Press, 1995. Explores the historical and aesthetic context of Radcliffe's fiction, with separate chapters on her early works and her mature novels; *The Romance of the Forest* is discussed in chapter 6. Considers Radcliffe's role as a woman writer and her place in society.

Tracy, Ann B. *The Gothic Novel, 1790-1830: Plot Summaries and Index to Motifs.* Lexington: University Press of Kentucky, 1981. Opens with a very strong introductory chapter that discusses the common themes and important elements of gothic fiction. Contains synopses of Radcliffe's major novels, including *The Romance of the Forest.*

Romance of the Three Kingdoms

Author: Luo Guanzhong (c. 1320-c. 1380)
First published: Sanguo zhi yanyi, fourteenth century
    (English translation, 1925)
Type of work: Novel
Type of plot: Historical
Time of plot: c. 180-c. 280
Locale: China

Principal characters:
LIU PEI, a distant descendant of the royal family of the
    Han Dynasty and the founder of the Shu Kingdom
KUAN YÜ, Liu Pei's sworn brother, later apotheosized as
    the god of war
CHANG FEI, the sworn brother of Liu and Kuan and a blunt
    soldier of great prowess
CHU-KO LIANG, chief strategist and eventually the prime
    minister to Liu Pei and to his weakling successor
TS'AO TS'AO, the founder of the Wei Kingdom, noted for
    his unscrupulous resourcefulness
SUN CH'ÜAN, the founder of the Wu Kingdom
CHOU YÜ, Sun Ch'üan's brilliant military commander,
    perpetually piqued by Chu-ko Liang's superior
    intelligence
CHAO YÜN, a brave general of the Shu Han Kingdom
LÜ PU, an unprincipled and matchless warrior famous for
    his romantic involvement with the beauty Tiao Ch'an
SSU-MA I, the founder of the all-powerful Ssu-ma family in
    the Wei Kingdom
CHIANG WEI, Chu-ko Liang's successor

The Story:

When the Yellow Turban rebellion is finally quashed, the many soldiers of fortune who take part in its suppression seize power for themselves, thus precipitating the downfall of the Eastern Han Dynasty. Among these the most shrewd and successful politician is Ts'ao Ts'ao, who already attracted a large following of able strategists and warriors. After the systematic elimination of his many rivals, such as Tung Cho, Lü Pu, Yuan Shao, and Yuan Shu, he rules over North China as the king of Wei, subjecting the Han Emperor and his court to great indignity.

Liu Pei, who also rose to fame during the Yellow Turban rebellion, is for a long time doing very poorly, despite the legendary prowess of his sworn brothers, Kuan Yü and Chang Fei. It is not until he seeks out Chu-ko Liang and makes him his chief strategist that his fortunes begin to improve. In time he rules over Szechwan as the king of Shu.

While Liu Pei is beginning to mend his fortunes, the only man who blocks Ts'ao Ts'ao's territorial ambitions is Sun Ch'üan, who inherited from his father and older brother the rich kingdom of Wu, south of the Yangtze. When Ts'ao Ts'ao finally decides to cross the Yangtze and subdue Wu, Sun Ch'üan and Liu Pei form an alliance, and the combined strategy of their respective military commanders, Chou Yü

and Chu-ko Liang, subject Ts'ao Ts'ao's forces to a crushing defeat in the Battle of Red Cliff. After this victory Liu Pei goes to Szechwan, and the precarious balance of power of the Three Kingdoms is established. The friendly relationship between Shu and Wu does not last long. Kuan Yü, entrusted with the vital task of governing the province of Hupeh, adjacent to the Wu territory, antagonizes Sun Ch'üan, and in the subsequent military struggle he is killed. Liu Pei now vows to conquer Wu; against the sage advice of Chu-ko Liang, who wants to conciliate Wu so as to counter their more dangerous common enemy, Wei, he leads a personal expedition against Wu and suffers a disastrous defeat. Liu Pei dies soon afterward.

Liu Pei's son and successor is a moronic weakling. Out of loyalty to his late master, however, Chu-ko Liang is determined to serve him and to improve the fortunes of Shu. He makes peace with Wu and leads several expeditions against Wei. These campaigns end in a stalemate. Overburdened with work and handicapped by the lack of able generals (of the "Five Tiger Warriors" of Liu Pei's day, only Chao Yün remains, an old fighter as intrepid as ever), Chu-ko Liang can no longer direct his campaigns with his usual brilliance. Moreover, the Wei commander, Ssu-ma I, whose family becomes increasingly powerful in the Wei court following the death of Ts'ao Ts'ao, is in many ways his match. Finally Chu-ko Liang dies of physical exhaustion.

By that time the Ssu-mas usurp the power of Wei and subject Ts'ao Ts'ao's descendants to as much cruelty and torture as Ts'ao Ts'ao and his immediate successor subjected the Han emperors. Wu and Shu weaken. Although Chiang Wei, the Shu general, try bravely to stem the tide, he is overwhelmed by the numerical strength of the invading Wei forces, under the command of T'eng Ai and Chung Hui. Soon after the death of Chiang Wei, the kings of Shu and Wu surrender. Ssu-ma Yen, Ssu-ma I's grandson, now rules as the first Emperor of China.

Critical Evaluation:

Instead of maintaining a single imperial family line from millennium to millennium, as in Japan, China traditionally had a succession of ruling houses, or dynasties, which rose and fell in a cyclical pattern. Whenever a dynasty reached the point of collapse, the field was thrown open for the era's most talented and ambitious soldiers of fortune to form alliances and fight with rival camps in struggles that led to the establishment of a new dynasty. Periods of dynastic change occasionally stretched into decades if no single camp could prevail over all its competitors, as was the case in the time in which this story is set. Ironically, the highly talented first generation of contenders witnessed a protracted stalemate in the struggle. Its members eventually died off, while the much weaker second generation blundered its way into the reunification of the empire.

The bulk of *Romance of the Three Kingdoms* deals with the extraordinary accomplishments and tragic shortcomings of the first generation of strategists and warriors. Epic grandeur suffuses Luo Guanzhong's novelistic synthesis of historical accounts and folk story cycles. For reasons about which scholars can only speculate, China lacked the sort of grand verse epic found in most of the great ancient civilizations. *Romance of the Three Kingdoms*, however, emerged to an ascendant position as the nation's enduring epic in prose. The epic warrior hero, Kuan Yü, even achieved the status of a deity in the popular mind. By the late imperial age, China housed more temples devoted to the worship of Lord Kuan Yü, god of war, than to any other deity aside from the local earth god.

Long before his ascent to the throne as the ruler of Shu Han in the southwest, Liu Pei emerged as the most sympathetic contender in the grand struggle. As a humble provincial member of the Liu clan that produced all of the Han Dynasty emperors, Liu Pei entered the fray not out of personal ambition but rather as a result of an altruistic yearning to thwart the Machiavellian usurper, Chancellor Ts'ao Ts'ao, and thereby restore the house of Han. Unlike Ts'ao Ts'ao of Wei and Sun Ch'üan of Wu, Liu Pei repeatedly placed the imperative of virtue and benevolence above the dictates of expediency, even when this prevented him from securing various important military objectives. Although the loss of these military objectives resulted in temporary setbacks for Liu Pei from time to time, his principled conduct strengthened the ties of loyalty and dedication that bonded him with his sworn brothers, scholarly military advisers, rank-and-file soldiers, and civilian subjects.

At the levels of elite and popular culture in China, Liu Pei has long been revered as a model of kingly virtue and benevolence. Liu Pei's sworn brothers Kuan Yü and Chang Fei have similarly been celebrated as beacons of martial courage and loyalty, while the military strategist and ministerial adviser Chu-ko Liang has long fired the imagination of Chinese readers and theatergoers as an embodiment of wisdom and of shrewd statecraft. These men, however, were not the stick figures of a morality play, but characters whose failings loomed almost as large as their strengths. Kuan Yü's fame for bravery often went to his head, and his arrogant dismissal of Sun Ch'üan's proposal to strengthen the ties between the Shu and Wu with intermarriage led to the deterioration of relations between the two states and to his eventual capture and decapitation at the hands of Sun Ch'üan. Liu Pei placed his personal oath of sworn loyalty to Kuan Yü above the long-term collective interests of restoring the Han Dynasty, and, over Chu-ko Liang's strong objections, he led an abortive attack on Wu simply to avenge Kuan Yü's execution. After the ensuing military debacle and chaotic retreat back to Shu, Liu Pei's health failed. When he expressed his deathbed wish that Chu-ko Liang ascend the throne of Shu rather than let it pass to Liu Pei's moronic son, Chu-ko Liang doggedly insisted on serving as the foolish son's adviser, even though he knew that the son's succession would lead to the rapid and irreversible decline of Shu as a serious contender in the struggle to reunite China. Chu-ko Liang thus epitomizes the unwavering dedication to a noble but unrealizable enterprise of the sort that Confucius had long ago linked to the life of virtue.

"Critical Evaluation" by Philip F. Williams

Further Reading

Besio, Kimberly, and Constantine Tung, eds. *"Three Kingdoms" and Chinese Culture.* Albany: State University of New York Press, 2007. Collection of essays interpreting the cultural, historical, and literary significance of *Ro-*

mance of the Three Kingdoms. Includes an introduction providing an overview of the novel; an article on values in the Ming novel by Moss Roberts, who has translated the novel into English; and discussions of the novel's "structure of tragic consciousness," its notion of appropriateness, and its historical sources and contexts.

Hsia, C. T. *The Classic Chinese Novel: A Critical Introduction.* New York: Columbia University Press, 1968. Contains an introductory analysis of *Romance of the Three Kingdoms* that is one of the best starting points for appreciation of this novel. Insightful regarding the conflict between the claims of statecraft and of personal loyalties.

Lu Xun. *A Brief History of Chinese Fiction.* Translated by Yang Hsien-yi and Gladys Yang. Peking: Foreign Languages Press, 1976. The section on *Romance of the Three Kingdoms* includes an interesting comparison of the early version of the novel with the finished version.

McGreal, Ian P., ed. "*Romance of the Three Kingdoms.*" In *Great Literature of the Eastern World: The Major Works of Prose, Poetry, and Drama from China, India, Japan, Korea, and the Middle East.* New York: HarperCollins, 1996. Discusses Luo Guanzhong's life and the major themes of his novel. Provides a critical evaluation of the novel and bibliographies of his works in English translation and of secondary sources about him.

Plaks, Andrew H. *The Four Masterworks of the Ming Novel.* Princeton, N.J.: Princeton University Press, 1987. Insightful and in-depth interpretations of *Romance of the Three Kingdoms* and the other three novels of the Ming Dynasty.

_____, ed. *Chinese Narrative: Critical and Theoretical Essays.* Princeton, N.J.: Princeton University Press, 1977. Two essays compare *Romance of the Three Kingdoms* with other Chinese literary masterpieces.

Rolston, David L., ed. *How to Read the Chinese Novel.* Princeton, N.J.: Princeton University Press, 1990. A pioneering collection of translated essays by major premodern Chinese critics. The essay on *Romance of the Three Kingdoms* provides a vivid sense of how the Chinese interpreted this novel centuries ago.

The Romantic Comedians

Author: Ellen Glasgow (1873-1945)
First published: 1926
Type of work: Novel
Type of plot: Fiction of manners
Time of plot: 1920's
Locale: Queenborough, Virginia

Principal characters:
JUDGE GAMALIEL BLAND HONEYWELL, a widower of sixty-five
ANNABEL, his twenty-three-year-old second wife
MRS. UPCHURCH, Annabel's mother
EDMONIA BREDALBANE, the Judge's sister
AMANDA LIGHTFOOT, the Judge's childhood sweetheart

The Story:

As Judge Honeywell walks home from church on the first Easter morning after his wife's death, he is surprised by his own reactions to the Virginia springtime. He feels quite young for sixty-five, and his life with his wife, now dead, seems so remote as never to have happened. In fact, he feels relieved, for his wife had seldom let him lead an existence of his own.

The Judge has for some time hospitably looked after Mrs. Upchurch and her daughter, Annabel, because they are kinswomen of his late wife, but shortly after this memorable Easter morning, he begins to think of twenty-three-year-old Annabel in quite another way. His change in attitude had begun because he is secretly sorry for her. She had been engaged to a young man who left her almost at the altar, and this had hurt her bitterly, as the Judge and her mother know.

As time passes, Judge Honeywell finds himself thinking more and more of Annabel Upchurch and also of Amanda Lightfoot, his childhood sweetheart. Unfortunately, the Judge's sister, Mrs. Bredalbane, tries to convince him that falling in love with Amanda would be the sensible thing to do. The Judge promptly closes his mind to Amanda and begins thinking more of Annabel, who has asked the Judge to help her open a flower shop.

Soon the Judge has purchased a house with a large garden for Mrs. Upchurch and her daughter so that Annabel might practice landscape gardening. When he tells the girl about the house, he adds that the only reward he expects is that of seeing her happy; however, when she takes her leave, he kisses her.

By the time Mrs. Upchurch and Annabel are settled in their new home, the Judge knows that he is in love with Annabel, who is more than forty years younger than he. He buys new clothes and has his hair and beard trimmed to lessen the amount of gray that shows in them. He feels that he could give Annabel everything she needs—love, tenderness, security, and wealth.

The number and quality of the Judge's gifts soon make apparent to Annabel and her mother what is on the old man's mind. Annabel thinks at first that it would be more suitable for him to marry her mother; however, as she informs her mother, marrying an older man is certainly better than living in an atmosphere of shabby gentility. Annabel decides to visit Amanda Lightfoot. Knowing that Amanda has never married because she had been in love with the Judge, Annabel wishes to find out if the older woman still loves him. If she does not, Annabel decides, she herself will marry him. Amanda, however, almost refuses to say anything at all. Annabel is disappointed but secretly relieved. When she arrives home, Judge Honeywell is waiting with a present for her, a sapphire bracelet. Before he leaves the house, he tells Annabel that he loves her, and she accepts him.

After they are married, the Judge and Annabel travel in England and in continental Europe. The Judge feels that he is as fine a man as he was at thirty-five, although his nerves are jarred a little on occasion when someone assumes that Annabel is his daughter. That she often dances with young men does not bother him. He feels no envy of their youth; after all, she is his wife.

Following their honeymoon, the Judge is glad to be back in his home in Virginia. The dyspepsia he suffered in Europe soon disappears after he begins to eat familiar cooking once more, and he feels at peace to be living in the familiar old house, which has not been refurnished in more than thirty years.

The couple dine out frequently and attend many dances. The Judge, after noting how silly his contemporaries appear on the dance floor, abstains from dancing, but he encourages Annabel to enjoy herself. He always goes to the dances with her, not from jealousy but because he feels that he has to keep up with her life. This costs him a great deal of effort—on some of their evenings out he thinks that he never before knew what fatigue is really like.

At home, Annabel brings changes into the house. While he does not approve, Judge Honeywell says nothing—that is, until she tries to change the furniture in his own room. She learns then that he will not let her meddle with his own privacy.

When the Judge comes down with bronchitis, Annabel proves an able and attentive nurse. During his convalescence,

however, she finds it difficult to remain at home reading night after night. The Judge notices her restlessness and tells her that she should begin going out again, even though he cannot go with her. Annabel does resume going out, and on those evenings she is away her mother or the Judge's sister joins the Judge for dinner and stays with him until Annabel returns.

The passing weeks bring a change in Annabel that many people notice. Previously noted for her boisterous spirit and lack of reticence, she becomes increasingly vague about her comings and goings. At the same time, their acquaintances compliment the Judge on how happy she seems. The compliments make the old gentleman content, for, as he says, Annabel's happiness is what he wants most.

Slowly, Judge Honeywell begins to feel that all is not right in his home. Annabel is distant in her manner, but when he talks with his sister and Annabel's mother, both reassure him of his wife's devotion. Still, he knows that something is not right, and he receives proof that his suspicions are warranted one day when he finds Annabel kissing a young man, Dabney Birdsong. Dabney belongs to an old family in the community, and Annabel has resolved to have him at whatever the cost. The Judge's greatest concern is that Annabel's relationship with Dabney might be only an infatuation that will not make her happy. Annabel, on the other hand, thinks that if she does not have Dabney, she will die.

Annabel and her lover run away to New York City, and the Judge follows them. Unable to understand his young wife, he feels sorry for her because she has defied convention and thinks that he himself is to blame for what has happened. After a talk with Annabel, he leaves New York, defeated, to return to Virginia.

After traveling home from New York on a drafty train, the Judge comes down with a cold that turns into influenza, and he is seriously ill and confined to bed for several weeks. During his convalescence, he discovers that spring has once more arrived. With the stirring in nature, he feels a resurgence of life in his weary body. Once again, the season of freshness and greenery gives him the feeling of youthfulness that he had on the previous Easter Sunday morning. He finds himself beginning to look with new, eager interest at the young nurse who is attending him during his illness.

Critical Evaluation:

Ellen Glasgow has been largely overlooked by students of American literature. Her output was prodigious, and her penetrating analysis of the social history of Virginia from 1850 to 1930, her insight into the position of women, and her brilliant use of ironic characterization are qualities that set her apart from the mass of popular novelists of the first third of the twentieth century and necessitate a reevaluation of her work.

It was Glasgow's colleague James Branch Cabell who first called her a social historian; reviewing her novel *Barren Ground* (1925), he said that her books, taken collectively, are a "portrayal of all social and economic Virginia since the War Between the States." Other critics and Glasgow herself accepted the label, but despite its accuracy, the phrase "social historian" is too narrow to describe the wide range of Glasgow's talents. Her work has also suffered from commentary by antagonistic male critics. Never one to accept a "woman's role," Glasgow often attacked those whose writing or person she did not admire. This penchant, as well as her creation of less-than-admirable male characters, has led to some highly questionable commentary about both her life and her work.

Properly, Glasgow should be seen as an early writer in the literary movement known as the Southern Renaissance. In 1931, she helped to organize a conference of southern writers at the University of Virginia that was attended by William Faulkner, Sherwood Anderson, and Allen Tate, among others. She was always interested in her native Virginia and wrote perceptively about the South's various epochs and social classes. If her view is often an ironic one, it nevertheless helps the reader to see the love-hate relationship that she had with the South. She judges, but with a sympathetic voice.

The Romantic Comedians was published soon after the more famous *Barren Ground* and is, like Glasgow's succeeding work *They Stooped to Folly* (1929), a novel of manners. Like all such works, *The Romantic Comedians* depends for much of its impact on tone and point of view, for neither its plot nor its characters are unique. The novel relies on the reader's knowledge of similar situations and characters in making its ironic commentary. From the outset, the narrator directs the reader's attitudes. Character names satirically reveal inner traits: Bland Honeywell, Upchurch, Bredalbane, Lightfoot. Judge Honeywell is seen as a slightly ridiculous figure, interested in the outward demonstration of his grief and unable to understand his own emotions: "'I am a bird with a broken wing,' he sighed to himself." This romantic outward show of grief over his dead wife lacks sincerity, for simultaneously, he "felt an odd palpitation . . . where his broken wing was helplessly trying to flutter." Glasgow shows herself to be a writer in the great tradition of Jane Austen and George Eliot, two other ironic critics of society.

Judge Honeywell is portrayed as a man of a bygone era, unable to understand or adjust to new ideas, yet somewhat naïvely excited by the prospect of Annabel's youth and beauty. He has firm values that nevertheless do not alter his self-interested actions. His most endearing characteristic is his willingness to forgive Annabel, but this too he carries to excess, needlessly accepting the guilt for her unhappiness.

Like Judge Honeywell, all the other characters are both romantic and a bit ridiculous. Annabel is deluded in imagining that ultimate personal happiness is attainable and of primary importance. Her amoral attitude does, however, cut through the hypocrisy and moral sham of people like her mother and Amanda Lightfoot. Annabel asserts that perfect ladies "lie as perfectly as they behave." Edmonia Bredalbane carries her "scandalous" behavior to an extreme that, even in its refreshing lack of convention, is shown to be silly. Glasgow reverses the generally accepted roles in the relationship of the Judge and his twin sister; here the woman is emancipated and the man tied by convention.

The theme of the novel is voiced by Mrs. Upchurch, who muses on "the popular superstition that love and happiness are interchangeable terms." She notes that both old and young, old-fashioned and modern, are "enslaved" by this illusion. The Judge, Amanda, Annabel, Dabney—"all this company of happiness-hunters appeared to be little better than a troupe of romantic comedians." This attitude seems to be the view of the narrator as well, but Mrs. Upchurch is not always the narrator's mouthpiece. In fact, Mrs. Upchurch's pragmatic morality, which shifts radically depending on the situation, is as often laughed at as is the Judge's unyielding system. Mrs. Upchurch, however, has a more realistic view of life than any other character in the novel.

Glasgow displays skill not only in the consistency of her tone but also in her use of images to suggest character. The Judge often thinks of Annabel in terms of nature ("fields and streams," "tall wind-blown grasses," the "April mist" in her eyes), yet these very qualities in Annabel—her "natural" freedom and amorality—doom their marriage; wild nature cannot become domestic and maternal. As their relationship deteriorates, the Judge begins to think of Annabel in terms of images of light without heat: She lacks the warmth he craves. She is like "the fire at the heart of an opal"; her head is like "November leaves in the sunlight." After she runs off with Dabney, she looks alive "not as a flower, but as a jewel."

Although the novel's point of view is most often centered in Judge Honeywell's consciousness, the narrator sometimes inserts commentary to make her attitude more obvious. Usually this is unobtrusive, but occasionally it becomes an affectation of style or a violation of the convention already established. An example is the use of the phrase "like most lawyers and all vestrymen" in the beginning of a comment on the Judge. In general, however, Glasgow's ironic tone is consistent, pungent, and entertaining. Each of the female characters—including the Judge's late first wife, Cordelia—

represents a distinctive way of dealing with the role assigned to women in the American South of the 1920's. Glasgow's accomplishment in this novel shows her to be more than a social historian and suggests that she deserves a higher place in the hierarchy of American letters than she is sometimes given.

"Critical Evaluation" by Margaret McFadden-Gerber

Further Reading

Beilke, Debra. "'The Courage of Her Appetites': The Ambivalent Grotesque in Ellen Glasgow's *Romantic Comedians*." In *Scenes of the Apple: Food and the Female Body in Nineteenth- and Twentieth-Century Women's Writing*, edited by Tamar Heller and Patricia Moran. Albany: State University of New York Press, 2003. Focuses on the relationship between food and the body images of the female characters in Glasgow's novel.

Godbold, E. Stanly, Jr. *Ellen Glasgow and the Woman Within*. Baton Rouge: Louisiana State University Press, 1972. Reliable biography offers informative commentary on Glasgow's major novels.

Hall, Caroline King Barnard. "'Telling the Truth About Themselves': Women, Form, and Idea in *The Romantic Comedians*." In *Ellen Glasgow: New Perspectives*, edited by Dorothy M. Scura. Knoxville: University of Tennessee Press, 1995. Provides a feminist interpretation of the novel.

Holman, C. Hugh. "The Comedies of Manners." In *Ellen Glasgow: Centennial Essays*, edited by M. Thomas Inge. Charlottesville: University Press of Virginia, 1976. Contrasts the comedy of Glasgow's Queenborough trilogy—*The Romantic Comedians, They Stooped to Folly*, and *The Sheltered Life* (1932)—with the didacticism of her earlier realistic novels. Focuses on Glasgow's narrative techniques and points out similarities and differences among the novels of the trilogy.

Patterson, Martha H. "Mary Johnston, Ellen Glasgow, and the Evolutionary Logic of Progressive Reform." In *Beyond the Gibson Girl: Reimagining the American New Woman, 1895-1915*. Urbana: University of Illinois Press, 2005. Chapter discussing Glasgow's work is part of a larger examination of how writers at the end of the nineteenth century and the beginning of the twentieth challenged the image of the "New Woman"—who was well educated, progressive, and white—by creating women characters who were African American, southern, and in other ways different from that image.

Raper, Julius Rowan. *From the Sunken Garden: The Fiction of Ellen Glasgow, 1916-1945*. Baton Rouge: Louisiana State University Press, 1980. Offers thoughtful commentary on all of Glasgow's major novels. Argues that *The Romantic Comedians* displays a classic comic pattern of subversion of gerontocracy by youth.

Rouse, Blair. *Ellen Glasgow*. New York: Twayne, 1962. Provides a good introduction to Glasgow's fiction. Views Glasgow's fictional Queenborough as the essence of several Virginia towns and suggests tragic overtones within the comedy of *The Romantic Comedians*.

Taylor, Welford Dunaway, and George C. Longest, eds. *Regarding Ellen Glasgow: Essays for Contemporary Readers*. Richmond: Library of Virginia, 2001. Collection of essays includes examinations of such topics as Glasgow and southern history, Glasgow and Calvinism, Glasgow's depictions of southern women, and the feminist elements in her work.

Romeo and Juliet

Author: William Shakespeare (1564-1616)
First produced: c. 1595-1596; first published, 1597
Type of work: Drama
Type of plot: Tragedy
Time of plot: Fifteenth century
Locale: Verona, Italy

The Story:

In Verona, Italy, there live two famous families, the Montagues and the Capulets. These two houses are deadly enemies, and their enmity does not stop at harsh words, but

Principal characters:
ROMEO, son of the house of Montague
JULIET, daughter of the house of Capulet
FRIAR LAWRENCE, a Franciscan
MERCUTIO, Romeo's friend
TYBALT, Lady Capulet's nephew

extend to bloody duels. Romeo, son of old Montague, thinks himself in love with haughty Rosaline, a beautiful girl who does not return his affection. Hearing that Rosaline is to attend a great feast at the house of Capulet, Romeo and his trusted friend, Mercutio, don masks and enter the great hall of their enemy as guests. Romeo is no sooner in the ballroom than he notices the exquisite Juliet, Capulet's daughter, and instantly forgets his disdainful Rosaline. Romeo never saw Juliet before, and in asking her name he arouses the suspicion of Tybalt, a fiery member of the Capulet clan. Tybalt draws his sword and faces Romeo. Old Capulet, coming upon the two men, parts them, and with the gentility that comes with age requests that they have no bloodshed at the feast. Tybalt, however, is angered that a Montague should take part in Capulet festivities and afterward nurses a grudge against Romeo.

Romeo goes to Juliet, speaks in urgent courtliness to her, and asks if he might kiss her hand. She gives her permission, much impressed by this unknown gentleman whose affection for her is so evident. Romeo then begs to kiss her lips, and when she has no breath to object, he presses her to him. They are interrupted by Juliet's nurse, who sends the young girl off to her mother. When she goes, Romeo learns from the nurse that Juliet is a Capulet. He is stunned, for he is certain that this fact will mean his death. He can never give her up. Juliet, who fell instantly in love with Romeo, discovers that he is a Montague, the son of a hated house.

That night Romeo, too much in love to go home to sleep, steals to Juliet's house and stands in the orchard beneath a balcony that leads to her room. To his surprise, he sees Juliet leaning over the railing above him. Thinking herself alone, she begins to talk of Romeo and wishes aloud that he were not a Montague. Hearing her words, Romeo can contain himself no longer, but speaks to her. She is frightened at first, and when she sees who it is she is confused and ashamed that he overheard her confession. It is too late to pretend reluctance. Juliet freely admits her passion, and the two exchange vows of love. Juliet tells Romeo that she will marry him and will send him word by nine o'clock the next morning to arrange for their wedding.

Romeo then goes off to the monastery cell of Friar Lawrence to enlist his help in the ceremony. The good friar is much impressed with Romeo's devotion. Thinking that the union of a Montague and a Capulet will dissolve the enmity between the two houses, he promises to marry Romeo and Juliet.

Early the next morning, while he is in company with his two friends, Benvolio and Mercutio, Romeo receives Juliet's message, brought by her nurse. He tells the old woman of his arrangement with Friar Lawrence and bids her carry the word back to Juliet. The nurse gives her mistress the message. When Juliet appears at the friar's cell at the appointed time, she and Romeo are married. Time is short, however, and Juliet has to hurry home. Before she leaves, Romeo promises that he will meet her in the orchard underneath the balcony after dark that night.

That same day, Romeo's friends, Mercutio and Benvolio, are loitering in the streets when Tybalt comes by with some other members of the Capulet house. Tybalt, still holding his grudge against Romeo, accuses Mercutio of keeping company with the hateful and villainous young Montague. Mercutio, proud of his friendship with Romeo, cannot take insult lightly, for he is as hot-tempered when provoked as Tybalt. The two are beginning their heated quarrel when Romeo, who just returned from his wedding, appears. He is appalled at the situation because he knows that Juliet is fond of Tybalt, and he wishes no injury to his wife's people. He tries in vain to settle the argument peaceably. Mercutio is infuriated by Romeo's soft words, and when Tybalt calls Romeo a villain, Mercutio draws his sword and rushes to his friend's defense. Tybalt, the better swordsman, gives Mercutio a mortal wound. Romeo can try to settle the fight no longer. Enraged at the death of his friend, he rushes at Tybalt with drawn sword and kills him quickly. The fight soon brings crowds of people to the spot. For his part in the fray, Romeo is banished from Verona.

Hiding out from the police, he goes, grief-stricken, to Friar Lawrence's cell. The friar advises him to go to his wife that night, and then at dawn to flee to Mantua until the friar sees fit to publish the news of the wedding. Romeo consents to follow this advice. As darkness falls, he goes to meet Juliet. When dawn appears, heartsick Romeo leaves for Mantua.

Meanwhile, Juliet's father decides that it is time for his daughter to marry. Having not the slightest idea of her love for Romeo, the old man demands that she accept her handsome and wealthy suitor, Paris. Juliet is horrified at her father's proposal but dares not tell him of her marriage because of Romeo's part in Tybalt's death. She fears that her husband will be instantly sought out and killed if her family learned of the marriage.

At first she tries to put off her father with excuses. Failing to persuade him, she goes in dread to Friar Lawrence to ask the good monk what she could do. Telling her to be brave, the friar gives her a small flask of liquid which he tells her to swallow the night before her wedding to Paris. This liquid will make her appear to be dead for a certain length of time; her seemingly lifeless body will then be placed in an open tomb for a day or two, and during that time the friar would send for Romeo, who would rescue his bride when she awakens from the powerful effects of the draught. Then, together, the two will be able to flee Verona. Juliet almost loses courage over this desperate venture, but she promises to obey the friar. On the way home she meets Paris and modestly promises to be his bride.

The great house of the Capulets no sooner prepares for a lavish wedding than it becomes the scene of a mournful funeral. Juliet swallows the strong liquid and seems lifeless. Her anguished family sadly places her body in the tomb.

Meanwhile Friar Lawrence writes to Romeo in Mantua, telling him of the plan by which the lovers can make their escape together. These letters, however, fail to reach Romeo before word of Juliet's death arrives. He determines to go to Verona and take his last farewell of her as she lies in her tomb, and there, with the help of poison procured from an apothecary, to die by her side.

Reaching the tomb at night, Romeo is surprised to find a young man there. It is Paris, who comes to weep over his lost bride. Thinking Romeo a grave robber, he draws his sword. Romeo, mistaking Paris for a hated Capulet, warns him that he is desperate and armed. Paris, in loyalty to Juliet, falls upon Romeo, but Romeo kills him. By the light of a lantern, Romeo recognizes Paris and, taking pity on one who also loved Juliet, draws him into the tomb so that Paris, too, can be near her. Then Romeo goes to the bier of his beautiful bride. Taking leave of her with a kiss, he drinks the poison he brought with him and soon dies by her side.

It is near the time for Juliet to awaken from her deathlike sleep. The friar, hearing that Romeo never received his letters, goes himself to deliver Juliet from the tomb. When he arrives, he finds Romeo dead. Juliet, waking, asks for her husband. Then, seeing him lying near her with an empty cup in his hands, she guesses what he did. She tries to kiss some of the poison from his lips that she, too, might die, but failing in this, she unsheathes his dagger and without hesitation plunges it into her breast.

By this time a guard comes up. Seeing the dead lovers and the body of Paris, he rushes off in horror to spread the news. When the Capulets and Montagues arrives at the tomb, the friar tells them of the unhappy fate that befell Romeo and Juliet, whose only sin was to love. His account of their tender and beautiful romance shames the two families, and over the bodies of their dead children they swear to end the feud of many years.

Critical Evaluation:

This story of star-crossed lovers is one of William Shakespeare's tenderest dramas. Shakespeare is sympathetic toward Romeo and Juliet, and in attributing their tragedy to fate, rather than to a flaw in their characters, he raises them to heights near perfection, as well as running the risk of creating pathos, not tragedy. They are both sincere, kind, brave, loyal, virtuous, and desperately in love, and their tragedy is greater because of their innocence. The feud between the lovers' families represents the fate that Romeo and Juliet are powerless to overcome. The lines capture in poetry the youthful and simple passion that characterizes the play. One of the most popular plays of all time, *Romeo and Juliet* was Shakespeare's second tragedy (after *Titus Andronicus* of 1594, a failure). Consequently, the play shows the sometimes artificial lyricism of early comedies such as *Love's Labour's Lost* (pr. c. 1594-1595, pb. 1598) and *A Midsummer Night's Dream* (pr. c. 1595-1596, pb. 1600), while its character development predicts the direction of the playwright's artistic maturity. In Shakespeare's usual fashion, he based his story on sources that were well known in his day: Masuccio Salernitano's *Novellino* (1475), William Painter's *The Palace of Pleasure* (1566-1567), and, especially, Arthur Brooke's poetic *The Tragical History of Romeus and Juliet* (1562). Shakespeare reduces the time of the action from the months it takes in Brooke's work to a few compact days.

In addition to following the conventional five-part structure of a tragedy, Shakespeare employs his characteristic alternation, from scene to scene, between taking the action forward and retarding it, often with comic relief, to heighten the dramatic impact. Although in many respects the play's structure recalls that of the genre of the fall of powerful men, its true prototype is tragedy as employed by Geoffrey Chaucer in *Troilus and Criseyde* (c. 1382)—a fall into unhappiness, on the part of more or less ordinary people, after a fleeting period of happiness. The fall is caused traditionally and in Shakespeare's play by the workings of fortune. Insofar as *Romeo and Juliet* is a tragedy, it is a tragedy of fate rather than of a tragic flaw. Although the two lovers have weaknesses, it is not their faults, but their unlucky stars, that destroy them. As the friar comments at the end, "A greater power than we can contradict/ Hath thwarted our intents."

Shakespeare succeeds in having the thematic structure closely parallel the dramatic form of the play. The principal theme is that of the tension between the two houses, and all the other oppositions of the play derive from that central one. Thus, romance is set against revenge, love against hate, day against night, sex against war, youth against age, and "tears to fire." Juliet's soliloquy in act 3, scene 2 makes it clear that it is the strife between her family and Romeo's that has turned Romeo's love to death. If, at times, Shakespeare seems to forget the family theme in his lyrical fascination with the lovers, that fact only sets off their suffering all the more poignantly against the background of the senseless and arbitrary strife between the Capulets and Montagues. For the families, after all, the story has a classically comic ending; their feud is buried with the lovers—which seems to be the intention of the fate that compels the action.

The lovers never forget their families; their consciousness of the conflict leads to another central theme in the play, that of identity. Romeo questions his identity to Benvolio early in the play, and Juliet asks him, "Wherefore art thou Romeo?" At her request he offers to change his name and to be defined only as one star-crossed with her. Juliet, too, questions her identity, when she speaks to the nurse after Romeo's slaying of Tybalt. Romeo later asks the friar to help him locate the lodging of his name so that he may cast it from his "hateful mansion," bringing a plague upon his own house in an ironic fulfillment of Mercutio's dying curse. Only when they are in their graves, together, do the two lovers find peace from the persecution of being Capulet and Montague; they are remembered by their first names only, an ironic proof that their story has the beneficial political influence the Prince, who wants the feud to end, wishes.

Likewise, the style of the play alternates between poetic gymnastics and pure and simple lines of deep emotion. The unrhymed iambic pentameter is filled with conceits, puns, and wordplay, presenting both lovers as very well-spoken youngsters. Their verbal wit, in fact, is not Shakespeare's rhetorical excess but part of their characters. It fortifies the impression the audience has of their spiritual natures, showing their love as an intellectual appreciation of beauty combined with physical passion. Their first dialogue, for example, is a sonnet divided between them. In no other early play is the imagery as lush and complex, making unforgettable the balcony speech in which Romeo describes Juliet as the sun, Juliet's nightingale-lark speech, her comparison of Romeo to the "day in night," which Romeo then develops as he observes, at dawn, "more light and light, more dark and dark our woes."

At the beginning of the play Benvolio describes Romeo as a "love-struck swain" in the typical pastoral fashion. He is, as the cliché has it, in love with love (Rosaline's name is not even mentioned until much later). He is youthful energy seeking an outlet, sensitive appreciation seeking a beautiful object. Mercutio and the friar comment on his fickleness. The sight of Juliet immediately transforms Romeo's immature and erotic infatuation to true and constant love. He matures more quickly than anyone around him realizes; only the audience understands the process, since Shakespeare makes Romeo introspective and articulate in his monologues. Even in love, however, Romeo does not reject his former romantic ideals. When Juliet comments, "You kiss by th' book," she is

being astutely perceptive; Romeo's death is the death of an idealist, not of a foolhardy youth. He knows what he is doing, his awareness growing from his comment after slaying Tybalt, "O, I am Fortune's fool."

Juliet is equally quick-witted and also has early premonitions of their sudden love's end. She is made uniquely charming by her combination of girlish innocence with a winsome foresight that is "wise" when compared to the superficial feelings expressed by her father, mother, and Count Paris. Juliet, moreover, is realistic as well as romantic. She knows how to exploit her womanly softness, making the audience feel both poignancy and irony when the friar remarks, at her arrival in the wedding chapel, "O, so light a foot/ Will ne'er wear out the everlasting flint!" It takes a strong person to carry out the friar's stratagem, after all; Juliet succeeds in the ruse partly because everyone else considers her weak in body and in will. She is a subtle actor, telling the audience after dismissing her mother and the nurse, "My dismal scene I needs must act alone." Her quiet intelligence makes the audience's tragic pity all the stronger when her "scene" becomes reality.

Shakespeare provides his lovers with effective dramatic foils in the characters of Mercutio, the nurse, and the friar. The play, nevertheless, remains forever that of "Juliet and her Romeo."

"Critical Evaluation" by Kenneth John Atchity

Further Reading

Battenhouse, Roy W. *Shakespearean Tragedy: Its Art and Its Christian Premises.* Bloomington: Indiana University Press, 1969. Argues that in *Romeo and Juliet*, Shakespeare shows a mistrust of carnal love, which leads the protagonists to suicide and damnation; the suicides in the tomb at the end of the play are an inversion of the Easter story.

Bloom, Harold, ed. *William Shakespeare's "Romeo and Juliet."* Philadelphia: Chelsea House, 2005. Includes a biographical sketch of Shakespeare, a plot summary and analysis, a list of characters, and several essays interpreting the play. Some of the essays examine the motivations of Friar Laurence, the Capulets' role in their daughter's death, the play's integration of speech and action, and Shakespeare and adolescence.

Cartwright, Kent. *Shakespearean Tragedy and Its Double: The Rhythms of Audience Response.* University Park: Pennsylvania State University Press, 1991. Examines how audiences respond to Shakespeare's tragedies. Shows how an audience of *Romeo and Juliet* usually identifies strongly with the lovers, although the play compels detachment.

Evans, Robert. *The Osier Cage: Rhetorical Devices in "Romeo and Juliet."* Lexington: University of Kentucky Press, 1966. Explores the style of *Romeo and Juliet*, particularly Shakespeare's use of opposites, such as love and violence, darkness and light, and appearance and reality.

Gibson, Rex. *Shakespeare: "Romeo and Juliet."* New York: Cambridge University Press, 2002. Guidebook designed for advanced-level students of English literature. Provides a commentary on the text; discusses the play's historical, cultural, and social contexts and use of language; offers a survey of critical interpretation.

Jackson, Russell. *"Romeo and Juliet."* London: Arden Shakespeare in association with the Shakespeare Birthplace Trust, 2003. Analyzes how different directors, scenic designers, and actors have interpreted and adapted the play for productions mounted by the Royal Shakespeare Company since 1945. Includes photographs of company productions.

Leggatt, Alexander. *"Romeo and Juliet*: What's in a Name?"* In *Shakespeare's Tragedies: Violation and Identity.* New York: Cambridge University Press, 2005. Examines how acts of violence in *Romeo and Juliet* and six other tragedies generate questions about the identities of the victims, the perpetrators, and the acts themselves.

Watts, Cedric. *Romeo and Juliet.* Boston: Twayne, 1991. One of the best starting places. Contains information on the history of the play and discusses its themes, sources, and characters.

Wells, Stanley, ed. *The Cambridge Companion to Shakespeare Studies.* New York: Cambridge University Press, 1986. All studies of Shakespeare should begin with this book. Includes excellent chapters on the poet's life, the beliefs of Elizabethan England, and reviews of scholarship in the field.

White, R. S., ed. *"Romeo and Juliet."* New York: Palgrave, 2001. Collection of essays providing various interpretations of the play, including "The Servants" by playwright Bertolt Brecht. Among the other essays are White's introduction, "What Is This Thing Called Love?" and discussions of the ideology of romantic love, love and hatred in Romeo and Juliet's relationship, and director Baz Luhrmann's film adaptation of the play.

Romola

Author: George Eliot (1819-1880)
First published: 1862-1863
Type of work: Novel
Type of plot: Historical realism
Time of plot: 1492-1498
Locale: Italy

Principal characters:
BARDO, a Florentine scholar
ROMOLA, his daughter
TITO MELEMA, an adventurer
TESSA, a peasant
BALDASSARE CALVO, Tito's benefactor
GIROLAMO SAVONAROLA, a Dominican friar

The Story:

Tito Melema arrives in the Florence of the Medicis penniless and unknown, but the sale of some rare jewels in his possession soon brings him into the circle of the wealthy, learned men of the city, among them Bardo, a blind antiquarian. Bardo is a great scholar who continues his annotations of Greek and Roman books through the eyes of his beautiful daughter, Romola. Bardo's only interests in life are his library and his museum, and he has reared his daughter in innocence of the outside world. Bardo accepts Tito eagerly, for he is always glad to meet a scholar who has traveled widely. He tells Tito of a son whom he had lost.

Tito's fortune has at last come to him with the sale of all his jewels except a single ring. He recalls that the money properly belongs to Baldassare Calvo, the man who has been almost a father to him and who might now be a slave in the hands of the Turks. If Baldassare is alive, Tito tells himself, he will spend the money for the old man's ransom, but he is not sure his foster father still lives.

Tito quickly entrenches himself in the learned society of Florence. While sitting at a window with a friend during the yearly festival of San Giovanni, patron saint of Florence, Tito fancies that a monk in the crowd below is looking at him with malice. Also glancing up at Tito from below is the beautiful Tessa, daughter of a milk vendor, whom Tito had met on the day of his arrival in Florence.

Later, as he walks through the crowded streets, Tito rescues Tessa from some jostling revelers. When he leaves her, he meets the strange monk he had seen gazing at him from the crowd earlier in the afternoon. The monk, Fra Luca, gives him a note that has been brought from a pilgrim in the Near East; Tito wonders why he finds the monk's face so familiar. The note is from Baldassare, who pleads with Tito to rescue him from slavery. Unwilling to give up his happy life in Florence, Tito ignores his foster father's plea.

Attracted to the lovely, grave Romola, Tito spends many hours reading and writing manuscripts with her blind father. One day, when Tito has the opportunity to be alone with Romola for a moment, he declares his love to her, and Romola shyly confesses her love for him. That same day, Monna Brigida pays a call on her cousin Bardo. When she accidentally mentions the name of a Dominican monk, Dino, Tito discovers that the lost son of Bardo is not dead; rather, he has been banished from his father's house. Tito realizes that Fra Luca is Dino, and he fears exposure of his benefactor's slavery. He feels the time is right for him to ask the old man for permission to marry Romola; he does so, and Bardo readily consents to the marriage.

Tito learns that Fra Luca is dangerously ill at Fiesole. One evening, Romola tells him that her dying brother has sent for her. Tito fears that Fra Luca will tell her about Baldassare's plea for help—a story that Tito hopes will die with him. In despair, he wanders through the city and accidentally meets Tessa. The two take part in a ribald mock marriage ceremony that amuses a gaping crowd, and Tito allows Tessa to believe that he has really married her. Unwilling to undeceive her, he makes her promise to keep the marriage a secret. Meanwhile, Dino dies without revealing to Romola the story of Baldassare and the ungrateful Tito. Tito and Romola are married.

Bardo dies, leaving Romola to carry on his scholarly work. Meanwhile, as the Medicis struggle to maintain control of their city, the political situation deteriorates. The Medicis' troubles are made worse by the charismatic preaching of Savonarola, who proclaims that the impending arrival of the French is God's will. This situation helps to advance Tito's fortunes; he becomes an interpreter in negotiations with the French. On the day the French king arrives in the city, the soldiers lead through the streets a group of prisoners who beg their ransoms from the Florentines. The mocking mob cuts an old man loose from his fetters and allows him to escape into the crowd. The prisoner runs blindly into Tito, who is standing with a group of dignitaries. Tito turns and finds himself looking into the face of Baldassare Calvo, who then disappears into the crowd.

Fearing Baldassare's revenge, Tito buys a coat of mail to wear under his clothes. He begs Romola to sell her father's library and leave Florence with him, and when Romola refuses, he secretly sells the library. Betrayed by her husband, Romola flees Florence, only to be met outside the city by Savonarola, who persuades her to honor her marriage vows and return to Tito.

In his search for a place to stay, Baldassare comes by chance to the house where Tessa and her children by Tito live with a deaf old peasant woman. The deaf woman gives the old man permission to sleep in the hayloft. Tessa eagerly confides in Baldassare, telling him that Tito sent her to live with the old peasant woman, whom he pays well for the care she gives Tessa and his children, and that he has sworn the two women to secrecy. While Baldassare lies in the loft, Tito arrives to see Tessa. Suspecting from her description the identity of the old man, Tito goes to his foster father to ask his forgiveness—he has decided that Baldassare should come to live with him and share his comfort. The old man cannot forgive, however; he lunges at Tito with a knife, which breaks against the chain mail Tito is wearing. He then threatens to expose Tito and ruin him.

At a dinner in Florence, Baldassare appears to denounce Tito before his politically important friends. The trembling old man is pronounced mad, however, and is sent to prison. During a plague, the prison is emptied to make room for the sick, and Baldassare is released. He spies on Tito until he learns about Romola; he then approaches Romola and tells her of Tito's relationship with Tessa. When Romola learns of Tito's betrayal, she is able to piece together all the suspicions she has had about her husband—his long absences from home, his strange moods, and his secret fears. One day, she finds little Lillo, Tessa's son, wandering lost in the streets. She takes the child to his home, and there she realizes that she has discovered Tessa.

The final blow comes to Romola when her godfather, Bernardo Del Nero, the only person in the world she still loves, is arrested for helping the Medicis in their plotting to return to Florence. Romola knows that Tito has been a spy for both political factions; he has gained his own safety by betraying others. Romola reveals to Tito her knowledge of Baldassare's story and the truth of the old man's accusations against him. Romola tries to prevent Bernardo's execution by pleading with Savonarola to intervene and gain his release, but the preacher refuses. Disillusioned and sorrowful over her godfather's death, Tito's betrayals, and Savonarola's falseness, Romola leaves Florence to seek a new life.

Tito also plans to flee Florence, for his double-dealing has been discovered. As a mob pursues him out of the city, he throws away his money belt, and while those in the crowd scramble for it, he jumps into the river. Weakly, he pulls himself ashore on the opposite side. There Baldassare, now a starving beggar, finds him. In a final effort, the old man flings himself onto his exhausted enemy and strangles him.

After spending many months in another city, Romola returns to Florence, where she learns of her husband's murder at the hands of an old man who had long been his enemy. Romola understands the justice of Tito's violent end. She finds Tessa and the children and brings them to live with her, as she is determined to repair the damage that Tito's deceptions have wrought.

Critical Evaluation:

Of her novels, George Eliot once said, *Romola* stood out as "having been written with my best blood." This is a revealing statement coming from the author of *Middlemarch* (1871-1872) and *The Mill on the Floss* (1860), novels considered by most critics to be superior works. Why did Eliot shower *Romola* with such high praise? *Romola* is Eliot's most ambitious historical novel. Readers find themselves transported back to fifteenth century Florence, where politics and religion intermingle; this is illustrated by the expulsion of the Medicis from power, an act in part inspired by the fervent preaching of Fra Girolamo Savonarola. Eliot spent many months studying Florentine history, both at home and during a trip to Italy in 1861. Her research resulted in a solid and reliable account of the period the novel portrays. Unfortunately, her meticulous attention to detail sometimes makes for cumbersome and difficult prose.

In addition to the painstaking re-creation of Italian history, Eliot presents her readers with a cast of both fictional and historical characters. One of her most intriguing creations is Tito Melema, the young man who quickly curries favor with the Florentine elite. No other Eliot character manifests the selfishness and deceit of Tito, a man with great personal charm. His unmatched skills in manipulating people, language, and politics drive the plot forward and provide the reader with a fascinating study of the devastating effects of rationalization and egotism.

In apparent contrast to the fictional Tito, Eliot portrays the historical Fra Girolamo Savonarola, a Dominican friar whose calls for reform captivated Florence from 1491 to 1498. Savonarola is also a man of great charisma and influence, whose moral convictions are revealed by his religious zeal. Savonarola believes that God is working through him, carrying out heavenly justice through a human channel. Unlike Tito, Savonarola acts with the best of intentions, but he too is unwilling to contemplate the effects of his deeds. Consequently, Tito and Savonarola are revealed to be cut from the same moral cloth. Both men misuse their power and breed mistrust in those who rely on their judgment. Together, these characters offer a rich resource for reflection on questions of intentionality, morality, human will, and the appropriate use of political power.

In distinction to Tito and Savonarola stand the two main female characters in the book, Tessa and Romola. Tessa, in particular, seems to represent traits commonly associated with femininity in the nineteenth century. She is beautiful, naïve, and uneducated, and she easily falls prey to the charming and unscrupulous Tito. Unlike Tito, for whom every situation is an opportunity to deceive, Tessa takes everything literally. She is unable to see beyond appearances.

In contrast, Romola is educated and poised but lacks life experience. Like Tessa, Romola is seduced by Tito's magnetism. Unlike Tessa, however, Romola is attracted to Tito's worldliness and scholarly capabilities. He is a man who can understand her dedication to intellectual pursuits. Both Romola and Tessa experience the same disrespectful treatment from Tito and from their culture at large. Only Romola, however, is aware of the strictures placed on her because of her sex. Tessa is happy to perform the duties of wife and mother; Romola chafes under the prohibitions that forbid her to follow her father's path. Romola is continually ignored or punished by a society that refuses to listen to her or take her seriously. She shares with Eliot's other heroines (for example Dorothea Brooke in *Middlemarch* and Maggie Tulliver in *The Mill on the Floss*) a sense of estrangement from her culture.

This particular aspect of the novel—its presentation of an autonomous and capable woman repressed and alienated by her culture—led many of the novel's critics to reprimand its author for using a fifteenth century setting to discuss nineteenth century problems. The historical setting provided Eliot with a contrast that allowed the reader to see with clarity that fifteenth century restrictions were quite relevant to the situation of women in the nineteenth century. Medieval Florence provided Eliot with the perfect opportunity not only to explore and instruct with regard to women's capabilities but also to illustrate the educational value of history.

The use of history as an instructional guide in *Romola* has led many critics to argue that this work contains Eliot's expression of a nineteenth century philosophy known as positivism. Developed by the French thinker Auguste Comte, positivism espouses the idea that in its growth and development over time, human society has participated in a moral evolution. According to Comte, in the manner that a child grows and learns to develop a sophisticated moral sense, so do cultures. From this perspective, fifteenth century Florence represents the painful transition from societal childhood to maturity. Romola represents this broader change, beginning the novel with a childish naïveté that grows into a moral sense that surpasses even that of the most devoted Christians. Taught the necessity of blind obedience to external authority, Romola struggles throughout the novel to discover her own inner strength and moral vision. Romola's efforts to use her intellect in service of others and to develop a sense of moral duty without God form a major theme in the novel.

Although *Romola*—with its blend of history and fiction along with thematic explorations of egoism and piety, religious mysticism and political intrigue, and duty and rebellion—is a grand artistic achievement, the novel's critical reception has been less than enthusiastic. Outside the English milieu that is more typical of her work, Eliot seems to lose, among the years that separate her from her subject, some of the acerbic wit and shrewd insight that characterize her other novels. However, one may say that it is precisely because Eliot attempted to create a work that would embody the philosophical, literary, and historical ideals she valued that she regarded *Romola* as one of her best works.

"Critical Evaluation" by Susan E. Hill

Further Reading

Armstrong, Heather V. *Character and Ethical Development in Three Novels of George Eliot: "Middlemarch," "Romola," "Daniel Deronda."* Lewiston, N.Y.: Edwin Mellen Press, 2001. Focuses on the encounters between characters in the three novels, applying philosophical concepts to an analysis of these works. Examines Eliot's ideas about morality, duty, sympathy, and imagination.

Barrett, Dorothea. *Vocation and Desire: George Eliot's Heroines.* London: Routledge & Kegan Paul, 1989. Includes a chapter on *Romola* that discusses the influence of Auguste Comte's positivist philosophy on the novel. Offers superb feminist readings of Eliot's novels.

Bonaparte, Felicia. *The Triptych and the Cross: The Central Myths of George Eliot's Poetic Imagination.* New York: New York University Press, 1979. This first book-length study of *Romola* presents a thorough analysis of the historical, mythic, and classical influences in the novel. Includes discussion of *Romola* in the context of Eliot's other novels.

Eliot, George. *The George Eliot Letters.* 9 vols. Edited by Gordon Haight. New Haven, Conn.: Yale University Press, 1954-1956, 1978. Offers commentary on the dynamics of Eliot's writing process. A number of letters from readers reveal how the novel was received by the public when it first appeared. Most of the letters concerning *Romola* can be found in volumes 4 and 8.

Hardy, Barbara. *George Eliot: A Critic's Biography.* London: Continuum, 2006. Presents an examination of Eliot's life combined with an analysis of her works that is particularly informative for readers with some prior knowledge of her writings. Includes an outline of Eliot's works and the events in her life.

_____, ed. *Critical Essays on George Eliot.* New York: Barnes & Noble, 1970. Collection edited by a pioneer in Eliot studies played a part in interesting feminist critics in examining her work. One of the essays is devoted to an analysis of *Romola*.

Levine, Caroline, and Mark W. Turner, eds. *From Author to Text: Re-reading George Eliot's "Romola."* Brookfield, Vt.: Ashgate, 1998. Collection of essays seeks to reappraise the novel from the point of view of the late twentieth century. Includes articles on topics such as the character of Romola, Eliot's depiction of gender issues, and *Romola* and the paintings of Florence.

Levine, George, ed. *The Cambridge Companion to George Eliot.* New York: Cambridge University Press, 2001. Collection of essays presents analyses of Eliot's work from various perspectives, including discussions of her early and late novels. Topics addressed include realism, philosophy, science, politics, religion, and gender.

Thompson, Andrew. *George Eliot and Italy: Literary, Cultural, and Political Influences from Dante to the Risorgimento.* New York: St. Martin's Press, 1998. Examines the influence of Dante and the Risorgimento (the nineteenth century Italian nationalist movement) on Eliot's work. Chapters 4 and 5 focus on Italian mythmaking and Dante in *Romola*.

Room at the Top

Author: John Braine (1922-1986)
First published: 1957
Type of work: Novel
Type of plot: Social realism
Time of plot: 1947
Locale: Warley, Yorkshire, England

Principal characters:
JOE LAMPTON, an ambitious young accountant eager to shed his working-class background by rising to the top in Warley's establishment
ALICE AISGILL, an older woman with whom Joe has an affair
SUSAN BROWN, the attractive but vacuous daughter of Warley's most powerful businessman
JACK WALES, the handsome young son of a rich industrialist, Joe's rival for Susan's affections
MR. BROWN, Susan's father, a self-made man

The Story:

The story of Joe Lampton's rise to prosperity begins in a railway compartment. Joe, slightly hung over and wearing cheap clothes, is leaving his home in Dufton for a job in the municipal government of Warley. Ambitious to escape his working-class background, Joe used his stint in a German prisoner-of-war camp during World War II to study accounting. The move to Warley gives him the chance to rise into the middle class and even to aspire to wealth.

Joe joined the Warley Thespians, a little theater group, as a way of becoming refined and of mixing with important people. There he meets the thirty-four-year-old Alice Aisgill, frustrated that she gave up an acting career for an unhappy marriage to a local industrialist. Joe and Alice fall in love and have an affair. At the same time, however, Joe is attracted to Susan Brown, the nineteen-year-old daughter of Warley's most important businessman. Joe understands that his future success lies in winning and marrying Susan, yet he cannot give up Alice. He tries to have both by continuing his affair with Alice while developing a calculated strategy to woo Susan.

The great obstacle to Joe's future is the presence of Jack Wales. Jack is almost everything that Joe is not: rich, self-assured, a student at a prestigious university, a war hero, and destined for a place in the family firm. Jack is at home in the Leddersford Conservative Club (the haunt of Warley's elite), drives a nice car, and dresses well. However, despite his shortcomings, Joe wins Susan. Joe knows how to use his sexual attractiveness to get his way. Jack is solid but unexciting and, to Susan's dismay, comes with her mother's approval.

At this juncture, Susan's parents decide to act. Mr. Brown has a word with the Warley Treasurer, Joe's superior, and the Treasurer in turn speaks to Joe. Speaking purely hypotheti-

cally, the Treasurer tells Joe that a good future is in store for him in Warley, that he might expect promotion in local government, but that all this might be lost if he persists in seeing Susan. The Treasurer advises him to find a suitable girl—that is, a girl of a lower class than Susan—and to get married. Joe is furious as he realizes that Warley's establishment conspires against him, that he might lose his expectations of a good future, and that he has no hope of marrying Susan. He continues to date her, however, even as his affair with Alice grows more intense. Its intensity enables Joe to accept Susan's breaking off of their relationship when she finds out about his relationship with Alice.

Joe then thinks he wants to marry Alice. The couple go away together on a long weekend and feel like husband and wife. However, knowing that marriage with Alice will prevent his rise in society, Joe reconciles with Susan. Alice develops a serious medical condition that requires surgery; while she is in the hospital, Joe and Susan consummate their love. Two months later, the day Alice is discharged from the hospital, Mr. Brown calls Joe and orders him to have lunch with him at the Leddersford Conservative Club. Over lunch, Brown offers to set Joe up in business if he agrees never to see Susan again. Joe indignantly refuses to be bought. That is what Mr. Brown wants to hear. He says that Joe and Susan can get married and that the first thing is to fix the date. Joe, puzzled, asks Mr. Brown why he is in such a hurry for them to get married when he was against their marrying from the start. The reason, Joe quickly learns, is that Susan is pregnant. The lunch ends with Mr. Brown's ordering Joe to break off relations with Alice, who, he says, is "an old whore" who slept with other young men, including Jack.

Joe tells Alice that he no longer loves her and announces

his engagement to Susan. In despair, Alice goes on a drinking binge and drives her car so fast that it leaves the road at a curve. The following morning, Joe learns of Alice's death. No one blames Joe for her death, but he knows that she committed suicide and that he is responsible. Guilty with his knowledge, he leaves work and goes to a nearby town to drink away his guilt. He stops in a pub frequented by gays and allows a man to buy him drinks. Then he slips away, has dinner, and drinks at another pub. He picks up Mavis, a working-class girl, takes her to a secluded place, and has sex with her. On his way home, friends of hers attack him, but he fights back and escapes. The book ends with Joe's return to Warley, mourning Alice but accepting his future life as Susan's husband.

Critical Evaluation:

Room at the Top is one of several novels and plays of the 1950's by authors who had been born during the 1920's. Other works from this group include the plays *Look Back in Anger* (1956) by John Osborne and *A Taste of Honey* (1958) by Shelagh Delaney and the novels *Saturday Night and Sunday Morning* (1958) by Alan Sillitoe, *Hurry on Down* (1953) by John Wain, and *Lucky Jim* (1953) by Kingsley Amis. This generation of writers came to be called Angry Young Men largely because of Osborne's play, although women were also writing. Their themes included the realistic depiction of working-class life and complaints about how little of the social structure government welfare programs had changed. Angry writers rejected both the literary formulas and what they considered to be the deadness of feeling of postwar literature, yet they did not use their writing to espouse causes, as had the authors of the 1930's. John Braine neither espoused left-wing causes nor challenged the status quo. Osborne made Jimmy Porter, the protagonist of *Look Back in Anger*, scream and whine about the mediocrity of the era. Braine, in contrast, gave Joe Lampton self-awareness and made him want to find a place in the existing establishment.

Braine certainly did not write *Room at the Top* with a view to social criticism. He denied that it was the writer's job to pass judgment on either individuals or on society. The writer is to say what is, not what should be. Thus, Braine believed that novels should be marked by "a vigorous realism"; in this case, he was careful to describe clearly and to fill his descriptions with brand names. Braine himself thought that what drew attention to *Room at the Top* was its realism, its "true feeling of living in the present, or at least in the just-past Forties." Braine also believed that writers should write from their own experience. Certainly, one of the novel's

strengths is its clear presentation of life in the north of England.

The novel's theme is that of the young man who rises in the world by his own exertions. Joe wants to become what he calls a Zombie, a person who sells himself to the powerful in society in order to find a niche in that society. Unlike others, however, Joe wants to sell himself for the highest price possible. He wants to be a "Grade Two Zombie" with power and wealth, not a Grade Eight or Ten one who sells himself for a modest, lower-middle-class standard of living. "In business, I ruminated, I'd have to soft-soap people whom I despised, I'd have to steer the conversation towards their favourite subjects, I'd have to stand them meals and drinks. But the game was worth the candle; if I sold my independence, at least I'd get a decent price for it." To achieve his goal, Joe plots out careful, calculated strategies for both his personal relationships and his work life. However, Braine includes hints, as Joe reflects on the position he gains, that perhaps the cost of selling himself is too high.

Room at the Top is written in first-person narrative; Joe narrates the events of his own story, in chronological order, from the vantage point of ten years later. Occasionally, however, Braine has Joe step back and take an objective look at himself. In these passages, Braine uses the third person—not the third person of the outside narrator, however, but rather the voice of Joe taking a clinical, objective look at himself.

Joe and Alice are the two best-drawn characters. Alice is admirable in her honesty and realism about their relationship. Joe is a somewhat more complex and ambiguous character. He, too, is mostly honest about his own actions, yet he does terrible things. Readers are meant to recognize his amorality, yet they are meant to sympathize with him as well. The other main characters are less well realized. One does not understand why Joe is attracted to Susan Brown, other than for her father's influence, for she is drawn as superficial and vacuous. Jack Wales is a cardboard cutout of the handsome son of privilege. Mr. Brown, although a more real character, partakes somewhat of the stereotype of a self-made man. Joe is drawn to Mr. Brown largely because the two are alike in having shed their working-class backgrounds. When they have lunch, Joe remarks that his father, a staunch member of the British Labour Party, would turn in his grave if he could see Joe at the Conservative Club. Mr. Brown says, "So would mine, lad. But we're not bound by our fathers."

The novel reflects attitudes of its day in its treatment of gays and in its double standard of sexual morality. In the scene in which Joe is in the pub, gays are discussed in disparaging terms and depicted stereotypically. Throughout the novel, also, women who are sexually active are depicted in less-approving ways than men who are sexually active. Despite, and in part because of, these outdated attitudes, *Room at the Top* offers one of the finest depictions of the life of a young man in Great Britain immediately after World War II.

D. G. Paz

Further Reading

Allsop, Kenneth. *The Angry Decade: A Survey of the Cultural Revolt of the Nineteen-Fifties.* London: Peter Owen, 1958. Although this book was written at the end of the very decade it discusses, it remains the single best study of that period in British literary history. Its chapter on Braine uses interviews with the author.

Braine, John. *Writing a Novel.* New York: Coward, McCann & Geoghegan, 1974. Braine's own explanation of how he crafts fiction, the result of reflections on his teaching of creative writing, provides insights into the development of *Room at the Top.* Essential reading, in which Braine includes examples of how he planned and revised this novel.

Carpenter, Humphrey. *The Angry Young Men: A Literary Comedy of the 1950's.* London: Allen Lane, 2002. Entertaining book about Braine, Kingsley Amis, John Osborne, and the other writers dubbed Angry Young Men. Carpenter maintains there was no such thing as a movement of angry young men and that it was a creation of the media.

Fjagesund, Peter. "John Braine's *Room at the Top*: The Stendhal Connection." *English Studies* 80, no. 3 (June, 1999): 247. Points out similarities between Braine's novel and Stendhal's *The Red and the Black* (1830). Compares the protagonists of both novels and argues that these men are responding to similar dilemmas within their respective historical periods.

Frazer, G. S. *The Modern Writer and His World.* Baltimore: Penguin Books, 1964. Includes a highly negative evaluation of *Room at the Top* and, hence, is useful as a counterweight to more laudatory views. Frazer finds in Braine's work a cheap style, inadequate understanding of the characters of Joe Lampton and Susan Brown, and silliness in thinking that a thirty-four-year-old woman is decrepit.

Lee, James W. *John Braine.* New York: Twayne, 1968. A balanced survey of Braine's background and upbringing in the north of England and a consideration of the four novels that he had published by 1968. The chapter on *Room at the Top* is a good analysis of the novel's themes and literary style.

Schoene-Harwood, Berthold. "The Successful Zombie: John Braine's *Room at the Top.*" In *Writing Men: Literary Masculinities from Frankenstein to the New Man.* Edinburgh: Edinburgh University Press, 2000. Traces how masculinity has been depicted in literature in the nineteenth and twentieth centuries. Part 2 contains a detailed analysis of *Room at the Top* and other works written in the 1950's and early 1960's.

Sinfield, Alan. *Literature, Politics, and Culture in Postwar Britain.* Berkeley: University of California Press, 1989. A survey, written from a left-wing perspective, of the relationships between political change and literary production in Britain since 1945. It includes a chapter on left-wing writing.

A Room of One's Own

Author: Virginia Woolf (1882-1941)
First published: 1929
Type of work: Literary criticism

Set at Oxbridge (a veiled Oxford University) and at sites in London, *A Room of One's Own* critically examines the intersection of women, writing, fiction, and gender. The work is nontraditional in terms of its format (the chapters can be read as one continuous essay or independently), content (historical facts mix with stories and memoir), point of view (an intimate first-person female voice), and audience (by a woman for women; male readers must read through women's eyes in a reversal of the male gaze). *A Room of One's Own* is a groundbreaking, genre-expanding inquiry into the effects of gender on literary production.

Based on lectures Virginia Woolf delivered at Newnham

and Girton colleges in 1928, the six interrelated essays seek to answer why, historically, fewer women than men have written. The title of the book refers to Woolf's belief that a woman writer needs privacy, space, and sufficient financial means to practice her craft. Additionally, Woolf calls for an expansion of the literary canon to include "room" for works by women. Initially, Woolf announces that she will speak in the persona of another—"call me Mary Beton, Mary Seton, Mary Carmichael or by any name you please"—but the author's musings supersede these personas, each of whom will make an appearance in a chapter—while Woolf's presence is felt throughout.

Several incidents that Woolf recounts in *A Room of One's Own*, including being driven from male-exclusive university turf, are drawn from her own experiences as a woman barred from men's venues. In the essays, Woolf approaches the literary canon as a male realm from which women have been excluded.

Woolf begins her first chapter with an apologia. She informs readers that she will not be able to provide them with either the truth about women or about literature. Instead, she offers her opinion that "a woman must have money and a room of her own if she is to write fiction." The arguments presented in this and subsequent chapters support her assertion of these two requirements. Woolf continues her discussion by contrasting the education of men and women; her visits to representative colleges reveal the wealth of the first and the poverty of the second. The men's abodes have private rooms; the women share tight quarters. Men's colleges boast well-stocked libraries; women's colleges provide sparse classrooms. Male students feast; female students sup. Woolf observes, "One cannot think well, love well, sleep well, if one has not dined well."

Woolf explains this disparity as one based on tradition, whereby, for centuries, women have been legally barred from possessing wealth, and their education has been held in low regard by society. While it appears that Woolf scolds the founders of women's colleges for not providing more amenities, in actuality she honors them for making the effort despite social custom and female penury.

In chapter 2, Woolf relocates her investigation of women and fiction to the British Museum in London. Searching the card catalog, she is amazed by the multitude of works about women composed by men, but notes that few women have written books about men. Men, it seems, cannot agree on what they think of women. Depending on the reference one consults, women have either little character or characters that surpass those of men. These texts agree, however, on the general superiority of men over women.

Woolf next refers to and consults a fictitious reference book called *The Mental, Moral, and Physical Inferiority of the Female Sex* and concludes that the professor who composed it had been angry. (She wonders why all the professors who have written about women were angry.) Drawing upon the practice of psychology, she reasons that men have demeaned women to inflate their own sense of importance. Woolf concludes that labeling one gender inferior grants superior status to the other gender by default. In short, male superiority is not proven or earned; it is simply stated.

Chapter 3 finds the narrator consulting works of history and literature in search of answers to the question of gender and the economy, including how women's poverty affects their creativity. She finds abundant references to women in fiction written by men, but only two references to women as historical persons. From the work of historians, she reads that women had few freedoms, little education, and were the legal property of their fathers and husbands. In contrast, from the works of playwrights and poets, she finds images of powerful, yet beautiful or evil, women in the extreme. Almost absent from history, women are abundant in fiction.

To explain the disparity, Woolf presents the story of Judith Shakespeare, William Shakespeare's fictional sister. Woolf imagines Judith to be sixteen years old with creative gifts equal to those of her brother. Unlike William, though, she is denied an education and her days are occupied by menial chores. Judith writes in secret, hiding her poems in an apple loft. When her father insists that she marry a local boy of his choosing, she escapes to London, where she is mocked by men during her search for employment in the theater. Crazed by the passion of her suppressed art, pregnant with a stage manager's child, and alive in a time and place that is not ready for female genius, Judith commits suicide. The story reveals what might have happened to a woman with Shakespeare's talent in Shakespeare's day.

In chapter 4, Woolf considers the matriarchy of women writers that began with seventeenth century playwright Aphra Behn. Restoration society had considered women like Behn immoral for earning their livelihoods as writers. Woolf discusses how chastity, a virtue bestowed distinctly upon women, relates to their silencing. A chaste woman does not express her ideas in public; she certainly does not publish them in a book or parade them on the stage. However, to beget succeeding generations of poets, playwrights, and novelists, there must be a lineage of great voices; Woolf believes men have the advantage over women in this regard. She credits fourteenth century playwright Geoffrey Chaucer for preparing the way for William Shakespeare and credits Shakespeare for inspiring other male writers of note. She decries women's brief lineage but praises modern literary foremothers such as Jane Austen, sisters Charlotte Brontë and Emily Brontë, and George Elliot. With the exception of Austen, these women published under male pseudonyms, for even in the nineteenth century chastity was a factor inhibiting female expression. Woolf credits Austen and Emily Brontë with possessing minds as incandescent as that of Shakespeare, for they did not let gender inequalities impede their craft. Additionally, Woolf praises Austen for crafting sentences uniquely suited to a woman's voice and for adapting the novel to a female form. Charlotte Brontë and Elliot had been constricted, Woolf believes, by their anger at the limitations society placed upon women.

Chapter 5 finds Woolf exploring works by women of her time. In addition to composing novels, her contemporaries produced works that include biography, travel, philosophy, and aesthetics. This chapter, however, concentrates on one novel—a fictional work called *Life's Adventure* by the fictional Mary Carmichael—and Woolf assumes the role of literary critic, assessing the work's merits. Initially, her response to the novel is negative, citing terse sentences and jarring sequences, until she notes something new: the words "Chloe liked Olivia," a statement suggestive of female friendship and perhaps even lesbian attraction. Woolf believes that relationships between women have been glossed over or omitted in works about women written by men. She finds that not until the time of Austen are such relationships authentically presented in literature. Men, Woolf concludes, have the tendency to see women through their own eyes and not through the eyes of women, a precursor to her discussion of androgyny in the final chapter.

In chapter 6, Woolf employs the image of a man and a woman entering a taxicab to symbolize a mind that is androgynous. According to Woolf, only men who write without male biases and women who write unimpeded by female constraints are able to create authentic male and female characters. In such writers, both genders reside and govern their creative faculties. Woolf credits Shakespeare with possessing such a mind.

Casting off pseudonyms and claiming her own voice, Woolf challenges her readers. Her parting words exhort readers, ostensibly the same college women who made up her audiences at Newnham and Girton colleges, but by extension all women who have had the benefit of a formal or informal education, to prepare the way for the arrival of a female Shakespeare.

Dorothy Dodge Robbins

Further Reading

Brackett, Virginia. *Restless Genius: The Story of Virginia Woolf.* Greensboro, N.C.: Morgan Reynolds, 2004. A biographical account written especially for younger readers. Discusses Woolf's life and work clearly and succinctly. Includes a chapter on *A Room of One's Own.*

Briggs, Julia. "Between the Texts: Virginia Woolf's Acts of Revision." In *Reading Virginia Woolf.* Edinburgh: Edinburgh University Press, 2006. In this larger study of Woolf's writings, Briggs examines changes that Woolf made to the manuscript of *A Room of One's Own.*

_____. *Virginia Woolf: An Inner Life.* Orlando, Fla: Harcourt, 2005. A biography focusing on Woolf's work and her fascination with the workings of the mind. Briggs traces the creation of each of Woolf's books, combining literary analysis with details of Woolf's life.

Caughie, Pamela. "The Artist Figure in Woolf's Writings." In *Virginia Woolf and Postmodernism.* Chicago: Illinois University Press, 1991. Caughie considers Woolf's depiction of the woman writer in terms of postmodern theory.

Gan, Wendy. "Solitude and Community: Virginia Woolf, Spatial Privacy, and *A Room of One's Own.*" *Literature and History* 18, no. 1 (Spring, 2009): 68-80. Posits Woolf's preference for gender-neutral, private writing spaces through an examination of *A Room of One's Own.*

Roe, Sue, and Susan Sellers, eds. *The Cambridge Companion to Virginia Woolf.* New York: Cambridge University Press, 2009. A collection of essays by leading scholars that addresses Woolf's life and work from a range of intellectual perspectives. Includes discussions of Woolf and modernism, feminism, and psychoanalysis.

Rosenbaum, S. P. "The Philosophical Realism of Virginia Woolf." In *Aspects of Bloomsbury: Studies in Modern English Literature and Intellectual History.* New York: St. Martin's Press, 1998. Examines Woolf's philosophy of life in the context of her ideas presented in *A Room of One's Own.*

A Room with a View

Author: E. M. Forster (1879-1970)
First published: 1908
Type of work: Novel
Type of plot: Social realism
Time of plot: Early twentieth century
Locale: Florence, Italy; Surrey, England

Principal characters:
MISS LUCY HONEYCHURCH, a young Englishwoman
MISS CHARLOTTE BARTLETT, her cousin and chaperone
MR. EMERSON, an Englishman
GEORGE EMERSON, his son
THE REVEREND ARTHUR BEEBE, an acquaintance of Lucy
MRS. HONEYCHURCH, Lucy's mother
FREDDY HONEYCHURCH, Lucy's brother
CECIL VYSE, Lucy's fiancé
MISS CATHERINE ALAN, a guest at the Pension Bertolini
MISS TERESA ALAN, her sister
MISS ELEANOR LAVISH, a novelist

The Story:

Lucy Honeychurch and Charlotte Bartlett are disappointed by the Pension Bertolini, where they are staying in Florence, and by the fact that their rooms have no view. They are embarrassed at dinner at the pension when Mr. Emerson offers for himself and his son to exchange rooms with the two women, as their rooms have a view. Lucy and Charlotte's unhappiness decreases when the Reverend Arthur Beebe, whom they had known previously, and who has been appointed rector of Lucy's home parish, joins them at dinner. After dinner, he manages to convince Charlotte that the exchange of rooms will not put the women under any obligation to the Emersons. The change, although effected, merely confirms Charlotte's opinion that the Emersons are ill-bred.

At Santa Croce Church, Lucy meets the Emersons, who guide her to the Giotto frescoes that she has come to see. She finds that she is more at ease with Mr. Emerson than she had expected to be, although she is confused by his rejection of artistic and religious cant and his concern about his son.

Late one afternoon, Lucy declares that she is going for a walk alone. She buys some photographs of paintings that she has seen and then walks through the Piazza Signoria. As she does so, she passes two men who are arguing over a debt. One stabs the other, and the stricken man, bleeding from the mouth, dies at her feet. At that moment, she sees George Emerson watching from across the square. As he reaches her side, she faints. After she has recovered, she sends him to get her photographs, which she had dropped. Disturbed because they are covered with blood, he tosses them into the Arno on the way home. When Lucy asks why he has thrown the pictures away, he is forced to tell her. He feels that something very significant has happened to him in the piazza. Lucy and George stop near the pension, and Lucy leans beside him

over a parapet and asks him to tell no one that he had been there. Perturbed by their enforced intimacy, she is puzzled and amazed when George says that the murder has made him want to live.

In a large party, the visitors at the pension, together with a resident English chaplain, drive toward Fiesole. Lucy, excluded from Miss Lavish's conversation with Charlotte, asks one of the drivers to direct her to the clergyman. Instead, he leads her to George. Lucy finds at the end of a path a terrace covered with violets. While she stands there, radiant with joy at the beauty of the place, George steps forward and kisses her. Charlotte, whom neither Lucy nor George had seen at first, calls to her cousin to return to the group.

Charlotte tells Lucy that George is a cad and that obviously he is accustomed to stealing kisses. She takes advantage of Lucy's need for sympathy to indicate that George's way of life, as she sees it, is merely brutal. In the morning, Lucy and Charlotte leave the pension, taking the train for Rome.

Back at her home in Surrey, England, Lucy becomes engaged to Cecil Vyse, whom she had visited in Rome. When Mr. Beebe comes to the house for tea, he is perturbed by the news of the engagement. Returning from a party with Lucy and Mrs. Honeychurch, Cecil notices a pair of ugly villas that have been put up by a local builder. When the village residents become alarmed as they consider what type of person might rent the villas, they are assured that Sir Harry Otway has bought them and intends to lease them only to suitable tenants. Lucy suggests that the sisters Miss Catherine Alan and Miss Teresa Alan, whom she met in Florence, would be such tenants. After seeing the villas, Cecil and Lucy walk on through the woods. By a pond where Lucy had bathed as a child, Cecil, for the first time, asks if he might kiss her. Their embrace is not successful and only reminds Lucy of the Emersons, whom she then mentions to Cecil.

Shortly before the Misses Alans's occupancy has been arranged, Cecil meets the Emersons in London and suggests that they take one of the villas. Not connecting the father and son with Lucy, he hopes thereby to disrupt the local social order. After the Emersons have moved into their house, Mr. Beebe takes Lucy's brother, Freddy Honeychurch, to meet them. The boy immediately asks George to go swimming with him. Together with Mr. Beebe, they strip off their clothes and swim and race happily at the pond in the woods. There Lucy, out walking with her mother and Cecil, comes upon George again. Although he greets her joyously, she bows stiffly and moves on.

While George is visiting the Honeychurch house one Sunday, Cecil, who is also visiting, loftily refuses to play tennis. Lucy, George, Freddy, and a friend of Freddy play while Cecil reads. After the game, Cecil reads aloud to the group from the novel he has been reading. Written by Miss Lavish, it contains a scene describing George and Lucy's kiss. Cecil is ignorant of the fact that the scene depicts them, but George and Lucy are profoundly moved. On the way into the house, George again kisses Lucy. Charlotte is staying in the house at the time, and Lucy is furious that Charlotte has betrayed what she saw in Italy to Miss Lavish. She speaks to Charlotte, and then together they go to George, and Lucy asks him to leave. Before he obeys, he tells Lucy that he loves her and that it would be disastrous for her to marry Cecil, who is incapable of intimacy with anyone.

Although she denies to herself that she is attracted to George, Lucy breaks her engagement to Cecil that evening. In the meantime, Mr. Beebe receives a letter from the Misses Alan, who are planning to visit Athens. To escape her confusion, Lucy decides that she must go with them, and Charlotte joins Mr. Beebe in persuading Mrs. Honeychurch to let Lucy go. Lucy, afraid that George will hear of her rejection of Cecil and return to see her, hopes in this manner to avoid another meeting with him.

As Lucy and her mother are returning from a day in London, Charlotte meets them as she is coming out of Mr. Beebe's house and asks them to go with her to church. Lucy declines and goes into Mr. Beebe's house to await their return. There she finds Mr. Emerson in the library. George, feeling utterly lost, has gone to London. Lucy finally admits that she is not going to marry Cecil, but when Mr. Emerson reveals his intuitive knowledge that she loves George, she becomes angry and weeps. Although she gradually perceives that all he has said is true, she is upset at the prospect of dis-

tressing everyone afresh if she acts on her new knowledge. Strengthened by Mr. Emerson's passion, sincerity, and confidence, however, she promises to attempt to live the truth she has learned.

With her family opposing the marriage, but not insistently, Lucy marries George. They spend their honeymoon at the Pension Bertolini, where they wonderingly realize that, subconsciously, Charlotte had been on their side. She had known that Mr. Emerson was in Mr. Beebe's house, and she also must have realized how he would speak to Lucy when they met there.

Critical Evaluation:

E. M. Forster and Virginia Woolf were the literary leaders of the Bloomsbury Group, a circle of intellectuals who gathered regularly in London in the first two decades of the twentieth century to discuss art and aesthetics. The circle also included the economist John Maynard Keynes, the painters Vanessa and Clive Bell, and the philosopher and critic Lytton Strachey. From the group's wide-ranging discussions, Forster often received ideas about art that he later incorporated into his fiction. Forster became noted for his deft style, complex characters, and important themes.

Although he is best remembered for his acknowledged masterpieces *Howards End* (1910) and *A Passage to India* (1924), Forster's earlier novels and short stories often point in the direction to which his later fiction turned. These earlier works are usually concerned with how people living in a modern world lack the passion necessary for a complete life. To make his point, Forster often contrasts the passionate intensity of people in southern European countries with the flaccid people of his native England. Typically, a character in one of these stories travels from England to Greece or Rome and there undergoes a revelation. In Forster's famous short story "The Road from Colonus" (1903), for example, Mr. Lucas discovers passion at an idyllic spring in Greece. His daughter forces him to return to England, however, and he subsequently dies a miserable and lonely old man. In *A Room with a View*, on which Forster was working as he finished "The Road from Colonus," Lucy Honeychurch discovers the passion of Italy. Lucy is more fortunate in her fate than is Mr. Lucas. Although she initially rejects the passion that Italy represents (indeed, she is shocked by it), she later comes to accept it as a fundamental part of life. The novel consequently ends happily with her in George Emerson's arms as they honeymoon in Florence.

Forster struggled to write *A Room with a View*. Although he initially conceived it and started taking notes during a trip to Italy in 1902, he did not complete the novel until 1908, after he had already published two other novels, *Where Angels Fear to Tread* (1905) and *The Longest Journey* (1907). His struggles with *A Room with a View* stemmed partially from the book's odd structure—the first half is set in Florence, while the majority of the second half is set in the English countryside of Surrey, with a brief return to Florence in the final chapter. Furthermore, Forster was undecided as to whether he wanted the novel to end happily or tragically. He opted for the happy ending to ensure that his theme of personal growth would be clear to his readers.

It is perhaps most useful to read *A Room with a View* symbolically in order to understand Forster's primary theme. In such a reading, Lucy Honeychurch is a person intended to serve as an example for the reader and one with whom the reader may identify. Charlotte Bartlett and Cecil Vyse represent the forces of oppression that try to stifle Lucy's growing sense of passion. The Emersons represent the forces of good, encouraging her to follow her inner conviction that passion is essential to life. Lucy initially obeys the dictates of Charlotte and Cecil, which is no great surprise because they are the voices of English convention. When she chooses later to listen to Mr. Emerson (who knows instinctively that she and his son are in love), Lucy ignores the voices of convention and decides to follow her heart and marry George. Consequently, Lucy grows into a whole person, one who recognizes the necessity of passion in her life. At the beginning of the novel, Lucy complains that her room in Florence lacks a view, that she cannot "see." By novel's end, she "sees" very well indeed, having gained insight into human nature and herself.

Throughout his novel, Forster continually juxtaposes staid Christianity—represented by the Reverends Cuthbert Eager and Arthur Beebe—with the richness of pagan myth. To Forster, Pan, the Greek god of fertility and vigor, represents the passion missing from the daily lives of most people. Consequently, his early short stories and novels are replete with symbols that point to Pan's importance. A scene central to *A Room with a View* serves as an example. Near the Honeychurch residence is a small pond, nicknamed the Sacred Lake, and after George and his father move into the neighborhood, Lucy's brother impetuously invites George and the Reverend Beebe for a swim, to which they agree. During the course of their riotous skinny-dipping, which seems governed by Pan himself, the three men engage in a celebration of life that does not end until Lucy, her mother, and Cecil happen by the pond. Forster intends for the reader to contrast the pure, free passion evident in this scene with the artificial existence found in the next chapter, in which Lucy feels stifled by her mother and her fiancé Cecil, and to

conclude—as Lucy does later in the novel—that such displays of passion are essential for a full life.

Although reviews were generally flattering when *A Room with a View* was released, sales of the novel disappointed Forster. Enough copies sold, however, for his publisher, Edward Arnold, to agree to publish his next novel, *Howards End*. This work proved to be a qualified critical and financial success and assured Forster's reputation as a writer of importance.

"Critical Evaluation" by Jim McWilliams

Further Reading

Bradshaw, David, ed. *The Cambridge Companion to E. M. Forster*. New York: Cambridge University Press, 2007. Collection of essays presents analyses of various aspects of Forster's life and work, including discussions of Forster's depictions of women, Forsterian sexuality, and postcolonial Forster.

Dowling, David. *Bloomsbury Aesthetics and the Novels of Forster and Woolf*. New York: St. Martin's Press, 1985. Includes discussion of *A Room with a View* that demonstrates the iconographic significance of the paintings mentioned in the novel and analyzes the change that Lucy Honeychurch undergoes through her meetings with the Emersons.

Edwards, Mike. *E. M. Forster: The Novels*. New York: Palgrave, 2002. Shows how analysis of four of Forster's novels—*A Room with a View*, *Howards End*, A *Passage to India*, and *The Longest Journey*—can help readers to understand his treatment of characters, locations, relationships, and other aspects of these works. Also examines Forster's life and provides examples of how four literary critics have approached Forster's writing.

Furbank, P. N. *E. M. Forster: A Life*. 1978. Reprint. San Diego, Calif.: Harcourt Brace, 1994. Definitive biography is detailed, well written, and copiously illustrated. Demonstrates how a trip Forster made to Florence in late 1901 inspired him to attempt a novel about English tourists in Italy. Recounts his subsequent struggles in writing *A Room with a View* and summarizes the novel's critical reception.

Land, Stephen K. *Challenge and Conventionality in the Fiction of E. M. Forster*. New York: AMS Press, 1990. Explains how *A Room with a View* fits into a pattern established by Forster's other novels by positioning Lucy as the heroine, Charlotte and Cecil as villains, George as a challenger, and Miss Lavish as a "rebel woman." Argues that the novel's conclusion is unsatisfying.

Medalie, David. *E. M. Forster's Modernism*. New York: Palgrave, 2002. Examines the relationship of Forster's writings to modernism, analyzing his works to demonstrate their modernist elements. Places Forster's work within the context of early twentieth century social, political, and aesthetic developments.

Rosecrance, Barbara. *Forster's Narrative Vision*. Ithaca, N.Y.: Cornell University Press, 1982. Analyzes the quirky narrative voice in *A Room with a View* and concludes that its effects on a reader are primarily comic; points out that the voice functions as a type of stage manager.

Roots
The Saga of an American Family

Author: Alex Haley (1921-1992)
First published: 1976
Type of work: Novel
Type of plot: Historical realism
Time of plot: 1750-twentieth century
Locale: Gambia and the American South

Principal characters:
KUNTA KINTE, an African who is enslaved
BELL, Kunta's wife
KIZZY, Bell and Kunta's daughter
CHICKEN GEORGE, Kizzy's son
TOM, Chicken George's son
ALEX HALEY, Kunta Kinte's descendant

The Story:

In the spring of 1750, Kunta Kinte is born in Juffure in The Gambia, Africa. His father is Omoro; his mother is Binta. Kunta learns the Mandinka village's customs and its religion—Islam. At five years of age, he graduates to the second *kafo*, donning clothes, attending school, and herding goats. He learns that some people in Juffure are slaves and that *toubob*—white people—sometimes capture Africans and sell them into slavery.

At ten years of age, he enters the third *kafo*, when boys receive manhood training, learning how to hunt, to use their wits, and to make war. They study sacred writings—the Qurʾān, the Pentateuch, and the Psalms. The boys then are circumcised and sent back to the village as men. Kunta moves from his mother's hut into his own. He, his younger brother, Lamin, and some friends go to hunt for gold. He listens to the Council of Elders discussing village business.

One day after sentry duty, Kunta looks for wood for a drum. Some *toubob* and their black assistants ambush and capture him. He and people from other tribes are shackled in a ship's hold, where many die. The stench of vomit, urine, feces, and death is overwhelming. Kunta becomes very ill but survives the four-month journey.

Sold to a white man, Kunta cannot understand why other black men do not free him. He runs away but is recaptured by men and dogs. Kunta works in the fields and watches the ways of both *toubob* and black people in this new land, where

tobacco and butchered hogs offend his Muslim nose. Kunta's master calls him Toby. He secretly learns some *toubob* words and pretends to obey, but when his leg irons are removed, he again runs away. Again he is captured; again he runs. This time he is shot. He recovers and runs again; his captors cut off half of his foot.

A *toubob* man of medicine and a black woman, Bell, help Kunta's foot heal. A man called Fiddler befriends him and begins teaching him English. When Kunta is well enough, he helps the gardener, taking over his duties after the old man becomes ill. The Fiddler tells Kunta he is in Virginia; the old gardener talks about slavery and about the rebellion against the king. The slaves discuss white people's fear that the English will encourage slaves to fight their masters. The gardener also talks about their owner, whose wife and baby died. Massa Waller bought Kunta from Waller's brother.

Kunta becomes Waller's driver, taking the doctor to call on patients, friends, and relatives. At Waller's parents' plantation, Kunta meets another African. Kunta realizes that, although keeping his dignity, he is losing his African identity. Partly because the old African encourages him to have children, Kunta considers marrying. He and Bell spend time together and finally "jumped the broom." Marriage agrees with him; Bell tells him what she read in the master's newspaper (although slaves are forbidden to read), and Kunta tells her about Africa. Kunta and Bell have a daughter, Kizzy. Massa

Waller's niece, Anne, adores her, infuriating Kunta. Kunta begins teaching Kizzy Mandinka, although Bell fears it will endanger the child.

News of slave uprisings interest Kunta and his friends, partly because revolts so terrify white people. Kizzy loves a slave named Noah, who runs away. When caught, he confesses that Kizzy forged his pass. Waller sells Kizzy; Kunta and Bell never see her again.

Tom Lea, a North Carolinian, buys Kizzy and rapes her repeatedly. She has a son, George. Kizzy and Lea's other slaves—Malizy, Pompey, and Sarah—care for George. Kizzy teaches George about his grandfather. George begins spending time with Mingo, a slave who trains fighting cocks. Finally, Lea has Mingo build George a shack and train him as an assistant. Upset, Kizzy bursts out with the truth about George's father's identity.

George becomes such an excellent rooster trainer that he is called Chicken George. Chicken George marries Matilda, a girl from a neighboring plantation, and Massa Lea buys her. The couple have eight children. Chicken George begins saving to buy the family's freedom, but Massa Lea loses him in a chicken fight. By the time Chicken George returns from England, Massa Lea has sold Matilda and their children to the Murrays.

Chicken George and Matilda's son Tom, a blacksmith, begins saving to buy his grandmother and the other Lea slaves, except Uncle Pompey, who has died. When Chicken George returns to Lea's farm, he finds Kizzy and Sarah dead also. He gets his father drunk and finds his hidden manumission paper, then tracks down his family, including new in-laws and grandchildren. He stays briefly on the Murray farm, telling his grandson about their African ancestor, but leaves because of the law that a freed slave can stay in North Carolina only sixty days.

When the Civil War begins, a white boy, George Johnson, comes begging for food; Murray makes him an overseer. The family, who like his honesty and hard work, teach him his job. George leaves and returns with his pregnant wife, Martha, who is so weak their baby is born dead.

Despite the Emancipation Proclamation, freedom comes only with the war's end in 1865. Chicken George returns and takes the family, with other freed people and the Johnsons, to Tennessee. Matilda dies; a few years later Chicken George falls into a fire and is killed. Tom and his wife Irene's daughter Cynthia marries Will Palmer, who manages a lumber mill. They tell their daughter, Bertha, the story of the African. At college, Bertha meets Simon Alexander Haley. They marry and have a son, Alex Haley.

As a boy, Haley listens to relatives talk about their ances-tor, Kunta Kinte. He uses his journalistic skills, developed in the U.S. Coast Guard, to track down his ancestors. *The Reader's Digest* finances his search, which takes him to the Gambian village of Juffure, where a *griot*—an oral historian—tells the Kinte family's story. When the *griot* tells about young Kunta Kinte who went out to cut wood and was never seen again, Haley knows he has finished his ancestor's tale. Haley and the Mandingos are ecstatic. Haley finds records of the ship on which Kunta was transported and of Kunta's sale from John to William Waller. Haley spends ten nights on a plank in a freighter's hold to get a hint of his ancestor's experience.

Critical Evaluation:

Alex Haley's *Roots: The Saga of an American Family* has been both lauded for giving African American people a sense of identity and condemned for amateurish style and sloppy scholarship. It deserves both the praise and the criticism. Haley called it a "novelized amalgam" of factual history and of fiction.

Spawning perhaps the most important television mini-series of the late twentieth century, *Roots* reminded black Americans of the value of their African heritage and the strength of their ancestors, who endured the grueling journey from Africa and the agony of slavery. The book prompted many African Americans to search for their own heritage. In short, it promoted black pride. The book and miniseries also made white Americans more aware of their ancestors' culpability for the plight of their black compatriots. In the light of history, especially when based on fact and presented so vividly, black anger made more sense.

Critics have pointed out that almost all of the black characters are strong and noble, and almost all of the white characters are weak, evil, foolish, or all three. For example, Kunta Kinte's father, Omoro, is brave, handsome, respectable, and perfect as a role model for his four healthy sons, while the slave traders and owners (who include most white characters in the book) beat, shackle, rape, and mutilate people.

Roots is also criticized for its adolescent style. Haley includes some references to sex, including masturbation, to aim for mature audiences, but the work is generally most appropriate for high school readers. The style is often amateurish, and the book lacks the subtlety and complexity of character to make it great literature. For example, in chapter 67, after a fight with Bell, Kunta Kinte has the following reverie:

It pained him to think how grievously he had underestimated her and the other blacks. Though they never showed it except to those they loved, and sometimes not even then, he realized at last that they felt—and hated—no less than he the oppressiveness under which they all lived. He wished he could find a way to tell her how sorry he was, how he felt her pain, how grateful he was to feel her love, how strong he felt the bond between them growing deep within himself.

Historical references are often clumsy, and Haley has been roundly criticized for sloppy scholarship, such as having Kunta Kinte working in huge cotton fields in Virginia, where almost no cotton was grown; having Mandinka people kiss children, a use of the mouth they would have considered dirty; and having Chicken George not know he was free after going to England and being in New York.

The book also becomes much less interesting near the end, when Haley briefly chronicles his last few ancestors. His final chapter, which describes his research, would be more appropriate as an introduction or an epilogue. *Roots* is not a particularly well-written book. It has not received much scholarly or critical attention. It is, however, an extremely important work in American culture for its attention to slavery and African heritage.

M. Katherine Grimes

Further Reading

Baldwin, James. "How One Black Man Came to Be an American." *The New York Times Book Review*, September 26, 1976. This important African American writer compliments Haley's re-creation of Kinte's Africa. Emphasizes the impact of generations on succeeding ones and history's effects on individuals.

Blayney, Michael Steward. "*Roots* and the Noble Savage." *North Dakota Quarterly* 54 (Winter, 1986): 1-17. Provides a correlation between the popularity of the novel and the American fascination with the Romantic ideal of the noble savage. Sees Kunta Kinte as a character in that tradition. Shows how Haley inverts the notion of the American Eden: Africa, not America, represents the Edenic paradise in the novel.

Cooke, Michael G. "Roots as Placebo." *The Yale Review* 67 (Autumn, 1977): 144-146. Criticizes Haley's writing as adolescent, neither subtle nor complex. Asserts that its magic comes from sentimentality, from promising more than it delivers, and from a placebo effect: It pretends to deal with American disease and to offer a strong cure, but it is too mild to heal.

Courlander, Harold. "Kunta Kinte's Struggle to Be African." *Phylon* 47 (December, 1986): 294-302. Questions Haley's scholarship. Asserts that Kinte, although unbelievable, is "an unreconstructed African."

Gerber, David. "Haley's *Roots* and Our Own: An Inquiry into the Nature of Popular Phenomenon." *Journal of Ethnic Studies* 5 (Fall, 1977): 87-111. A review essay that analyzes the popular cultural phenomenon generated by the novel and the subsequent airing of the television miniseries. Analyzes Haley's treatment of historical material in general and his treatment of slavery in particular.

Huntzicker, William E. "Alex Haley's *Roots*: The Fiction of Fact." In *Memory and Myth: The Civil War in Fiction and Film from "Uncle Tom's Cabin" to "Cold Mountain,"* edited by David B. Sachsman, S. Kittrell Rushing, and Roy Morris, Jr. West Lafayette, Ind.: Purdue University Press, 2007. *Roots* is one of the works included in this examination of how American writers and filmmakers have sought to make sense of the Civil War.

Miller, R. Baxter. "Kneeling at the Fireplace: Black Vulcan—*Roots* and the Double Artificer." *MELUS* 9 (Spring, 1982): 73-84. Analyzes Haley's attempt to celebrate the artisan within the novel. The use of the figures of painters, blacksmiths, and fireworkers subtly alludes to the Hephaestus/Vulcan story of ancient mythology.

Othow, Helen Chavis. "*Roots* and the Heroic Search for Identity." *College Language Association Journal* 26 (March, 1983): 311-324. Offers a discussion of the organic unity of the novel. Cites as problematic the shifting of protagonists, abrupt endings of generational episodes, and authorial intrusion. The work is viewed as an epic in a tradition found in Greek classical literature.

Pinsker, Sanford. "Magic Realism, Historical Truth, and the Quest for a Liberating Identity: Reflections on Alex Haley's *Roots* and Toni Morrison's *Song of Solomon*." In *Black American Prose Theory*, edited by Joe Weixlmann and Chester J. Fontenot. Vol. 1 in *Studies in Black American Literature*. Greenwood, Fla.: Penkevill, 1984. Examines the role of the storyteller in conjunction with African American identity in *Roots* and in Toni Morrison's *Song of Solomon* (1977).

Taylor, Helen. "'The Griot from Tennessee': The Saga of Alex Haley's *Roots*." *Critical Quarterly* 37, no. 3 (Summer, 1995): 46. Considers the critical reception of the novel in relation to its commercial success and its legendary status within American popular culture. Views the novel as an African American autobiography and compares it with other best-selling novels set in the antebellum South.

The Rope

Author: Plautus (c. 254-184 B.C.E.)
First produced: Rudens, third or second century B.C.E.
   (English translation, 1694)
Type of work: Drama
Type of plot: Comedy
Time of plot: Late third century B.C.E.
Locale: Cyrene, Libya

Principal characters:
DAEMONES, an aged Athenian
PALAESTRA, his daughter
AMPELISCA, a slave woman
PLESIDIPPUS, a young man in love with Palaestra
LABRAX, a procurer
CHARMIDES, an aged Sicilian, his guest
GRIPUS, a servant of Daemones
TRACHALIO, a servant of Plesidippus

The Story:

Daemones, an old Athenian exiled from Athens, has come to Cyrene to spend his waning years. He is a kindly man, and his exile has come about as a result of his excessive generosity to others and consequent indebtedness rather than from any sort of dishonorable activity on his part. Further, his impoverishment and exile are not his only misfortunes. Some years before, his daughter Palaestra, then a girl, was stolen from him and sold by the thief to the procurer Labrax, who brought her, unknown to her father, to Cyrene, where she has been reared and educated by Labrax. As Palaestra is approaching maturity, the young Plesidippus sees her and falls in love with her. Wanting to secure her freedom, he arranges to buy her from Labrax for thirty minae. He gives the procurer a retainer and binds him by oath to turn Palaestra over to him when he has paid the full sum agreed upon.

Labrax is as unscrupulous as his profession would suggest. When Charmides, a Sicilian, suggests that the procurer could get a much better price out of his women by taking them to Sicily, Labrax decides to ignore his contract with Plesidippus. He contrives to get the young man out of the way by arranging to meet him before the temple of Venus for a sacrificial breakfast. The night before, however, he moves Palaestra and her fellow slave, Ampelisca, together with all his belongings aboard ship. Then, accompanied by Charmides, he sets sail. A storm arises during the night, wrecking the ship and casting Labrax and his guest on the rocks; Palaestra and Ampelisca manage to escape in a small boat. The two young women land near the temple of Venus, not far from the house of Daemones. After asking sanctuary of the priest, they go inside.

A short time later, Ampelisca is sent to Daemones' house for water. On her way, she encounters Plesidippus's servant, Trachalio, who has come to the temple looking for his master. She sends him inside to see Palaestra. While Ampelisca is waiting for the servant of Daemones to bring her the water, however, she spies Labrax and Charmides, whom she had be-

lieved dead, laboriously making their way to the temple from the place where the sea washed them up on the rocks. Terrified, she hastens back to the temple to warn her friend.

When Labrax and Charmides arrive, wet and tattered, they devote most of their remaining energy to mutual recriminations for their plight until the procurer learns from a servant that his two slaves did not drown but are inside the temple. He rushes in, intent on saving at least that much of his property, and attempts to drag the two young women away from the statue of Venus at whose feet they have sought sanctuary. Trachalio witnesses this violence and calls out for someone to aid the outraged suppliants. Daemones hears him and brings his servants to the slaves' assistance. Labrax is soundly beaten, but he remains determined to get his two slaves back. Then, while Daemones' men hold the struggling procurer, Trachalio goes to find Plesidippus and bring him to the temple. On his arrival the young Athenian, angry at the outrageous trick Labrax has nearly succeeded in playing on him, drags the scoundrel to justice.

Daemones takes the two young women home with him; on the previous night he had dreamed that he prevented a she-ape from stealing the fledglings from a swallow's nest. He believes that the episode with Labrax has been in some way a fulfillment of that dream and that the slaves, therefore, are somehow important to him. He has no sooner escorted the two young women inside the door than his wife, jealous of their youth and beauty, creates an intolerable furor on the grounds that he has brought harlots into the house.

Meanwhile, Daemones' servant, Gripus, is making his way home from a morning's fishing, elated at having pulled up in his nets a large container that, unknown to him, had been lost by Labrax the night before and that contains, in addition to the procurer's own wealth, certain tokens that will help Palaestra to identify her parents if she should ever encounter them. Gripus intends to keep the contents of the container for himself, but on his way home Trachalio overtakes him, recognizes the container, and raises such a clamor that Daemones is finally brought out to arbitrate between them. Trachalio tells the old man that the container belongs to Labrax and that it holds, among other things, the identifying trinkets of Palaestra. To test Trachalio's story, Daemones asks Palaestra to describe the trinkets. Her description both fits the contents of the container and reveals that the slave is Daemones' long-lost daughter. Father and daughter, united in great joy, ignore Gripus's claims to ownership of the remainder of the container's contents and go together into Daemones' house.

The case of Labrax is tried by the court, and it is decided that the procurer has no legal title to Palaestra, for she was born free. Ampelisca, however, is adjudged rightfully his, and he returns to the temple to look for her. Overhearing Gripus grumbling about the container, Labrax questions him and, to his joy, learns that it was recovered. Promising Gripus a talent of silver for identifying the container's present possessor, he is directed to Daemones, who, scrupulously honest, returns the container willingly. The procurer is about to go off when Gripus protests that the talent of silver has not yet been paid. Although Labrax swore on the altar of Venus that he would give the money to the servant, who wants to buy his freedom, the procurer is about to leave Gripus nothing for his pains when Daemones intervenes. The old man suggests that Labrax give Gripus only half a talent and give Ampelisca her freedom for the remainder. To this suggestion Labrax agrees. Even Gripus is content with it when he learns that Daemones is willing to give him his freedom for the half talent.

One of the first things that Daemones does in his newly recovered status as father is to betroth his daughter to Plesidippus. In addition, he agrees to encourage the young man to give Trachalio his freedom and permit him to marry Ampelisca if she is willing. Then everyone, including Labrax, has a hearty dinner with Daemones.

Critical Evaluation:

The Rope is one of Plautus's longer plays. Some scholars think that it is also his finest play. In some respects, it is not a typical play. For one thing, the setting, on the African seacoast, is distinctly exotic compared with the typical urban settings of much Roman comedy. In general tone, the play is more poetic than the Plautine comedies, which tend to be raucous. The emotions are serious in this play, with an ending that reintegrates all the characters, even the villainous pimp. The storm and the shipwreck and the final universal forgiveness evoke the atmosphere of romance found in plays such as William Shakespeare's *The Tempest* (pr. 1611, pb. 1623).

In other ways, *The Rope* has some elements typical of Plautus's work. As the prologue reminds the audience, the play is based on a Greek play by Diphilus, who named the town Cyrene. This is a reminder to any audience of the standard practice of Plautus's times: The Roman playwrights translated the Greek originals, creating a category called *comoediae palliatae*, or comedies in Greek dress. The translation is from Greek to Latin and includes changes in the details of locales and customs. This must have enabled the Roman dramatists to enjoy at least two advantages: They could amuse their audiences with the essential comic tool of incongruity achieved with anachronisms, and, if their satire and jokes gave offense, they could always claim they were poking fun at the Greeks, not at their Roman audiences.

Greek New Comedy, the most influential comedic formula in Western literature, has survived for thousands of years and continues to appeal to audiences primarily through its transmission in the works of Latin playwrights, including Plautus. Certain aspects of *The Rope* are typical of this traditional comedy: the kidnapped child, the tokens of high birth, the villain, the thwarting of young love, the recognition scene, and the reuniting of families.

Plautus is known for creating memorably clever servants who engineer much of the comic action. In this respect, the servants in *The Rope* are typical, for Trachalio and Gripus provide most of the comedy. It is not unusual for memorable characterizations and speeches, such as Gripus's daydream of power and wealth or the dialogue of the fishermen, to have little to do with the action; however, they can distinguish a play.

A distinctive aspect of *The Rope*, in keeping with its air of romance and fantasy, is the mystical element, much stronger here than in most of Plautus's other surviving works. The mystical element begins with the setting, which has two human habitations: Daemones' humble farmhouse and the temple of Venus. The prologue is spoken by Arcuturus, a bright star in the constellation, who, before telling the tale, provides a strong clue to its moral nature. The gods, he informs the audience, watch closely over human affairs, and they keep track of the good and the evil. He and other stars report back to Jove so that Jove may "confer prosperity" on the deserving.

In the story that follows, the gods do not directly arrange matters; still, a spiritual element pervades. The two women, miraculously saved from the storm and shipwreck, arrive at the temple of Venus. A minor character in the play, the priest of Venus, provides them with shelter and refuge. The temple becomes a focal point in the action as the pimp tries to reclaim his "property" and the women fight him off.

In that respect, the women may be said to be "reborn" because of the storm, from their pathetic state as slaves to free women. Their rebirth, as one scholar has observed, takes on a mythic note: The goddess Venus was born from the tempestuous sea. Different versions of her birth have her coming either from the foam or from a seashell. This play may well contain the first literary allusion in classical literature to the Venus-rising-from-a-shell version. Another mystical element is Daemones' dream of the ape and the fledglings in the swallow's nest. The dream inspires him to protect the two slaves.

An indirect allusion to rebirth continues in the matter of the container that is recovered from the sea. The tug-of-war between the servants—which includes the rope referred to in the title—while a fine bit of comic business, also brings in the box containing the proof that Palaestra is Daemones' daughter. Curiously for a young female character, compared with those in similar comedies, Palaestra is more concerned with her identity and with finding her family than she is interested in her hardworking, faithful lover, Plesidippus. When the box also survives the storm and reappears, her fond wish is granted, for Daemones recognizes his long-lost daughter, and the family, so long separated and broken, is reunited and whole again.

Plautus's plays were very popular in his lifetime and have continued to be enjoyed by audiences. The plays are so popular, in fact, that Plautus's name has been attached to about one hundred plays. Whether or not he wrote that many, over the years about twenty complete plays that have survived have come to be accepted as his. To describe a typical Plautine comedy or even a typical New Comedy is, therefore, to describe the comedy on the basis of incomplete knowledge. Many plays have not survived or have not yet been discovered.

The surviving plays of Plautus have not always pleased and delighted audiences. In the Middle Ages in Europe, for example, his works were considered too boisterous. Although Latin scholars have appreciated his enormous talent for colloquial Latin and his wordplay, not all have respected his work. Much of it has seemed too lighthearted and superficial; the works are amusing, but they lack significant social commentary.

The Rope is an interesting example of Plautus's work because it has the trademark humor, comic characters, plot elements, and more. The myth of Venus's rebirth, a story that balances the destructive power of the sea with its benign, productive power, weaves throughout the play. This allusion flavors the conventional comedic story of family loss and reunion with a spirituality unusual in Plautus's extant comedies.

"Critical Evaluation" by Shakuntala Jayaswal

Further Reading

Arnott, W. Geoffrey. *Menander, Plautus, Terence.* New York: Oxford University Press, 1975. Introductory survey of New Comedy presents brief comparisons to show the similarities and differences between the Greek playwright Menander and his Latin successors.

Duckworth, George. *The Nature of Roman Comedy: A Study in Popular Entertainment.* 2d ed. Norman: University of Oklahoma Press, 1994. Classic study of Roman comedy provides a comprehensive introduction to Latin playwrights, including Plautus.

Fraenkel, Eduard. *Plautine Elements in Plautus.* Translated by Tomas Drevikovsky and Frances Muecke. New York: Oxford University Press, 2007. In the first English translation of a German study initially published in 1922, Fraenkel, an influential twentieth century classicist, provides an analytic overview of Plautus's plays, including their motifs of transformation and identification, mythological material, and dialogue.

Konstan, David. "*Rudens*: City-State and Utopia." In *Roman Comedy.* Ithaca, N.Y.: Cornell University Press, 1983. Examines the plays of Plautus and Terence in the light of the cultural system in the ancient city-state society. Sees the theme of *The Rope* as an attempt to extend the boundaries beyond the city-state to include heaven and nature.

Leach, Eleanor Winsor. "Plautus' *Rudens*: Venus Born from a Shell." *Texas Studies in Literature and Language* 15, no. 5 (1974): 915-931. Analyzes the use of myth in Plautus's play, discussing the work as a reenactment of the birth of Venus, with her restorative powers, from the chaotic sea.

Leigh, Matthew. *Comedy and the Rise of Rome.* New York: Oxford University Press, 2004. Analyzes the comedies of Plautus and Terence, placing them within the context of political and economic conditions in Rome during the third and second centuries B.C.E. Discusses how audiences of that time responded to these comedies.

Segal, Erich. *Roman Laughter: The Comedy of Plautus.* Cambridge, Mass.: Harvard University Press, 1968. Valuable study of Plautus's work addresses the social and cultural contexts in which the plays were written and originally performed and comments on their appeal to Roman audiences. Argues that all of Plautus's comedies were meant to make the Romans laugh by reversing Roman values.

_____, ed. *Oxford Readings in Menander, Plautus, and Terence.* New York: Oxford University Press, 2001. Includes essays on Plautus and the public stage, the response of Plautus's audience, and traditions, theatrical improvisation, and mastery of comic language in his plays.

A Rose for Emily

Author: William Faulkner (1897-1962)
First published: 1930
Type of work: Short fiction
Type of plot: Gothic
Time of plot: c. 1865-1924
Locale: Jefferson, Yoknapatawpha County, Mississippi

Principal characters:
MISS EMILY GRIERSON, an eccentric aristocrat
HOMER BARRON, her lover, and a construction supervisor
COLONEL SARTORIS, Jefferson's mayor, a war hero
THE TOWNSPEOPLE OF JEFFERSON
TOBE, Miss Emily's servant

The Story:

As a child, Miss Emily Grierson had been cut off from most social contact and all courtship by her father. When he dies, she refuses to acknowledge his death for three days. After the townspeople intervene and bury her father, Emily is further isolated by a mysterious illness, possibly a mental breakdown.

Homer Barron's crew comes to town to build sidewalks, and Emily is seen with him. He tells his drinking buddies that he is not the marrying kind. The townspeople consider their relationship improper because of differences in values, social class, and regional background. Emily buys arsenic and refuses to say why. The ladies in town convince the Baptist minister to confront Emily and attempt to persuade her to break off the relationship. When he refuses to discuss their conversation or to try again to persuade Miss Emily, his wife writes to Emily's Alabama cousins. They come to Jefferson, but the townspeople find them even more haughty and disagreeable than Miss Emily. The cousins leave town.

Emily buys a men's silver toiletry set, and the townspeople assume marriage is imminent. Homer is seen entering the house at dusk one day, but is never seen again. Shortly afterward, complaints about the odor emanating from her house lead Jefferson's aldermen to surreptitiously spread lime around her yard, rather than confront Emily, but they discover her openly watching them from a window of her home.

Miss Emily's servant, Tobe, seems the only one to enter and exit the house. No one sees Emily for approximately six months. By this time she is fat and her hair is short and graying. She refuses to set up a mailbox and is denied postal delivery. Few people see inside her house, though for six or seven years she gives china-painting lessons to young women whose parents send them to her out of a sense of duty.

The town mayor, Colonel Sartoris, tells Emily an implausible story when she receives her first tax notice: The city of Jefferson is indebted to her father, so Emily's taxes are waived forever. However, a younger generation of aldermen later confronts Miss Emily about her taxes, and she tells them to see Colonel Sartoris (now long dead, though she refuses to acknowledge his death). Intimidated by Emily and her ticking watch, the aldermen leave, but they continue to send tax notices every year, all of which are returned without comment.

In her later years, it appears that Emily lives only on the bottom floor of her house. She is found dead there at the age of seventy-four. Her Alabama cousins return to Jefferson for the funeral, which is attended by the entire town out of duty and curiosity. Emily's servant, Tobe, opens the front door for them, then disappears out the back. After the funeral, the townspeople break down a door in Emily's house that, it turns out, had been locked for forty years. They find a skeleton on a bed, along with the remains of men's clothes, a tarnished silver toiletry set, and a pillow with an indentation and one long iron-gray hair.

Critical Evaluation:

In "A Rose For Emily," William Faulkner imitates associative Southern storytelling style as an unnamed first-person narrator speaks for the entire town of Jefferson, relating what all the townspeople know or believe. Unlike typical Faulkner stories that employ multiple individual narrators, "A Rose for Emily" achieves the effect of multiple narrators by combining them into a single narrative voice, an unnamed (and not always consistent) narrator. First-person plural pronouns emphasize that this narrator represents the consciousness of the town. This style is similar to that used in Greek tragedy, wherein chorus and chorus leader provide the reader/audience with information, interpret the characters' actions, and express public opinion; thus, the narrator in "A Rose for Emily," whose age and gender are never identified, can be designated a choric character.

The narrative sequence in this story is not chronological; the reader learns Miss Emily's history in much the same way a newcomer to Jefferson might hear about her history. As the story opens, Miss Emily apparently has just died, and the townspeople are discussing her strange and sad life. Faulkner relates various incidents in her life, but these incidents are related thematically, not chronologically. Faulkner builds suspense by imitating the southern storyteller's style of describing people and events through situation-triggered memories; hence, the plot is associative rather than chronological.

The story's primary theme—the destructive effects of time, most notably change and decay—is familiar to readers of Faulkner. Change is Miss Emily's enemy, so she refuses to acknowledge it, whether that change is the death of her father, the arrival of tax bills, the decay of her house, or even the beginning of residential mail delivery. Furthermore, her attitude toward the death of her father (and later the death of Colonel Sartoris) foreshadows her attitude toward the death of Homer Barron. Because Miss Emily is associated with the passage of time (her ticking watch is concealed in her bosom—heard but never seen), one might consider her to be living outside the normal limitations of time or, perhaps, simply not existing. Thus, she appears to combine life and death in her own person.

A minor theme in the story is the social structure of the early twentieth century American South, as it is being eroded by the industrialized New South. To avoid embarrassing Miss Emily, Colonel Sartoris devises a convoluted explanation of Jefferson's pre-Civil War debt to the Griersons, but this same man, also, had authored an edict that any African American woman appearing on Jefferson's streets without an apron could be beaten. Likewise, to avoid appearing to give Miss Emily charity, the families of Jefferson send their young daughters to Miss Emily's house for china-painting lessons. Most significant, though, is the change in Jefferson's attitude toward the relationship between Miss Emily (a descendant of Southern gentility) and Homer (a working man, and a Northerner). Initially, the townspeople are horrified by their coupling, but gradually they come to accept Homer as a good choice for Miss Emily, perhaps as a matter of necessity.

Like most Faulkner stories, "A Rose for Emily" is highly symbolic. Miss Emily is described as a fallen monument to the chivalric American South. Reenforcing the themes of change and decay, her house, once an elegant mansion, has become a decaying eyesore in the middle of a neighborhood that has changed from residential to industrial. Another prominent symbol is the crayon portrait of Miss Emily's father, associated with the oppressive hold of the past on the present. Although less elegant than an oil portrait, the crayon portrait is important to Miss Emily, and it is seen by the rare visitor who enters her house.

The pseudo-chivalry of the townspeople comes out in several symbolic actions, such as when parents send their daughters to Miss Emily for china-painting lessons, when civic leaders spread lime around her yard to deal with the foul odor emanating from her house, and when Colonel Sartoris

decrees that she will never have to pay local taxes. In contrast, Homer's carriage—considered gaudy by the townspeople—symbolizes the difference between the town's old-fashioned attitudes (reflective of the Old South) and Homer's more modern one (reflective of the emerging New South).

In this gothic story, though, perhaps the most vivid symbols are the locked room in Miss Emily's house and the long iron-gray hair found on a pillow inside. The room symbolizes the secrecy and mystery associated with Miss Emily's house and her relationship with Homer. The location of the hair as well as its color and length suggest a continuing interaction between Miss Emily and the corpse of Homer, again indicating her refusal to acknowledge the finality of death.

In Faulkner's youth, a popular literary genre was the reconciliation story, in which a Southern lady and a Northern man fall in love, thus helping to resolve the sectional conflict remaining after the Civil War. Faulkner's story can be read as a reaction against this sentimentality. Faulkner never describes the actual relationship between Miss Emily and Homer; thus, readers must decide whether "A Rose for Emily" is a gothic psychological tale or a tragic story of unrequited love.

In various stories and novels, Faulkner focuses on both individuals and their cultural milieu, and he repeatedly uses Jefferson as a microcosm for the early twentieth century South. In "A Rose for Emily," Jefferson also is a microcosm for the United States after World War I and its transition from an agrarian society to the beginnings of an urban-industrial society. The cotton gin near Miss Emily's house bridges this transition, as it combines the cotton culture of the antebellum South with the emerging industrialism of the increasingly urban New South. The tension arising from the collision of these cultures has given rise to a creative outburst of which Faulkner and "A Rose for Emily" are significant parts.

Charmaine Allmon Mosby

Further Reading

Brooks, Cleanth. *William Faulkner: The Yoknapatawpha County*. New Haven, Conn.: Yale University Press, 1963. This venerable classic of Faulkner criticism is one of the best introductions, treating Faulkner's characteristic themes and historical and social background and offering detailed readings of the major novels and stories. Includes carefully prepared notes, appendixes, and a character index.

Kirk, Robert W., and Marvin Klotz. "A Rose for Emily." In *Faulkner's People: A Complete Guide and Index to the Characters in the Fiction of William Faulkner*. Berkeley:

University of California Press, 1963. Identifies all the named characters in "A Rose for Emily" and describes the role of each character in terms of the plot.

Porter, Carolyn. *William Faulkner.* New York: Oxford University Press, 2007. A concise and informative biographical work that spans Faulkner's entire life but focuses primarily on his most prolific period, from 1929 to 1940. Offers insightful analysis of his major works.

Skei, Hans H. "A Rose for Emily." In *Reading Faulkner's Best Short Stories.* Columbia: University of South Carolina Press, 1999. Skei addresses critical questions about apparent inconsistencies in the narrator's voice and the appropriate genre designation for this story.

Towner, Theresa M. *The Cambridge Introduction to William Faulkner.* New York: Cambridge University Press, 2008.

An accessible resource, aimed at students and general readers. Provides detailed analyses of Faulkner's works and information about the critical reception for his fiction.

Towner, Theresa M., and James Carothers. "A Rose for Emily." In *Reading Faulkner's Collected Stories.* Jackson: University Press of Mississippi, 1999. Towner and Carothers survey criticism about the story, including criticism of Miss Emily's personality. Also explains key phrases used in the story.

Wagner-Martin, Linda, ed. *William Faulkner: Six Decades of Criticism.* East Lansing: Michigan State University Press, 2002. A collection of critical essays interpreting Faulkner's work from perspectives such as language theory, feminism, deconstruction, and psychoanalysis.

Rosencrantz and Guildenstern Are Dead

Author: Tom Stoppard (1937-)
First produced: 1966; first published, 1967
Type of work: Drama
Type of plot: Existential
Time of plot: 1600
Locale: Denmark

Principal characters:
ROSENCRANTZ, a courtier to the Danish throne
GUILDENSTERN, a courtier to the Danish throne
THE PLAYER, an actor and manager of a troupe of traveling players
ALFRED, one of the players
TRAGEDIANS, actors in the troupe of traveling players
HAMLET, prince of Denmark
CLAUDIUS, king of Denmark and Hamlet's uncle
GERTRUDE, queen of Denmark and Hamlet's mother
POLONIUS, adviser to the king
OPHELIA, his daughter

The Story:

In nondescript surroundings, Rosencrantz and Guildenstern gamble at tossing coins. Rosencrantz keeps winning but remains calm about his unusual lucky streak. Guildenstern reflects uneasily about this apparent suspension of the laws of probability, which causes him to begin questioning the nature of the reality into which he and Rosencrantz are plunged. They have no memory of past events, except for a vague recollection of having been sent for. Dismayed at being unable to account for themselves or their situation, they feels stranded and without direction.

Their speculations are interrupted by the arrival of a band of motley players on their way to the Danish court. The principal player greets Rosencrantz and Guildenstern enthusias-

tically, for he hopes they will pay for a performance. The Player informs them that his company does on stage what other people do off stage. Guildenstern is offended by this suggestion of a lewd performance. He requests that the players perform something more traditional.

Hamlet and Ophelia pass by; Hamlet is disheveled and Ophelia distraught. They are followed by Claudius and Gertrude, who seem to know who the courtiers are but are unable to distinguish between them. Claudius tells them that Hamlet is transformed and that they are to "glean" what afflicts him. Gertrude promises them a royal reward. The king's adviser, Polonius, tells Claudius and Gertrude that he knows the cause of Hamlet's lunacy.

Rosencrantz and Guildenstern are disquieted by all this activity. Guildenstern remarks that they are caught up in events beyond their comprehension. Guildenstern pretends to be Hamlet while Rosencrantz practices the art of "gleaning." Then they overhear Hamlet telling Polonius that he can be the same age as Hamlet if he can walk backward like a crab. Polonius leaves in a state of confusion. Hamlet greets them as two old friends, but he, too, confuses their identities. They attempt to "delve" into the cause of Hamlet's lunacy but discover nothing except that Hamlet can tell a hawk from a handsaw when the wind is southerly. Hamlet leaves the courtiers and then returns with the tragedians and Polonius. Hamlet plans to have the players enact "The Murder of Gonzago" for the Danish court. The Player leaves to study the extra lines written by Hamlet.

After Claudius and Gertrude question Rosencrantz and Guildenstern and discover that they were unsuccessful as spies, they determine that Polonius is to spy on Hamlet and Ophelia. Claudius decides that he must send Hamlet to England. Rosencrantz and Guildenstern are completely confused by the events they witness. The tragedians rehearse the play to be performed before the court, and Rosencrantz and Guildenstern, though without realizing it, witness an enactment of their own fate, death at the hands of the king of England.

Claudius is displeased by the play. On the way to hide the body of the murdered Polonius, Hamlet drags the corpse past Rosencrantz and Guildenstern. Then Claudius gives Rosencrantz and Guildenstern the task of escorting Hamlet to England. Rosencrantz and Guildenstern find themselves on board a ship headed for England. Guildenstern summarizes their situation: They are Rosencrantz and Guildenstern bearing a letter from one king to another and they are taking Hamlet to England. They rehearse their audience with the king of England and in the process discover that the letter given to them by Claudius condemns Hamlet to death. Once again, they are terribly disconcerted.

They hear music coming from barrels on the ship's deck and discover that the tragedians are on board as well. The Player tells them the play offended the king. Guildenstern struggles to discover a pattern in these events. Pirates attack the ship. After the skirmish, Rosencrantz and Guildenstern discover that Hamlet is missing. Having a letter to the English king but no Hamlet makes them very uneasy. Once again, they rehearse their audience with the king of England. When they come to the part about the letter, they discover that the letter condemns not Hamlet, but them, to death. Guildenstern is enraged by the senselessness of their situation and by the Player's calm reaction to their impending

deaths. He snatches up the Player's dagger and stabs him in the throat. The Player dies in a theatrical manner. The tragedians, who are watching with interest, applaud with enthusiasm. The befuddled Guildenstern examines the Player's dagger and discovers that it has a retractable blade. The Player modestly evaluates his performance as merely competent, informing the courtiers that enactments of death, not death itself, are all that people really believe in. Resigned to his fate, a weary Guildenstern reflects that death is essentially absence. Rosencrantz declares that he is relieved to be done with it. With these words, he disappears. Still puzzled by the circumstances of his existence, Guildenstern ceases to exist. The ambassador from England returns to the Danish court and announces that "Rosencrantz and Guildenstern are dead."

Critical Evaluation:

Tom Stoppard's plays revolutionized twentieth century theater with their combination of comic wit and serious themes. His first major dramatic work, *Rosencrantz and Guildenstern Are Dead*, was first performed on April 11, 1966, at the Old Vic Theatre in London, by the National Theatre Company. That same year, the work received the Play and Players Award for best new play in England, and in 1968 it received the Antoinette Perry (Tony) Award for best play and the New York Drama Critics Circle Award for best play. In the years that followed, Stoppard's work ranged from a collaboration with Terry Gilliam (of Monty Python fame) on the screenplay of *Brazil* (1985, Los Angeles Critics Circle Award for best original screenplay) to screen adaptations of works by Vladimir Nabokov, Graham Greene, and E. L. Doctorow. A prolific and brilliant writer, Stoppard also continued to write plays, including *Travesties* (1974) and *The Real Thing* (1982).

In William Shakespeare's *Hamlet, Prince of Denmark* (pr. c. 1600-1601, pb. 1603), Rosencrantz and Guildenstern, the two courtiers summoned by Claudius to spy on Hamlet, bear to the English king the order for their own execution. As characters, they remain undefined, functioning in tandem as ciphers for a sort of banal treachery, their services purchased by the promise of reward. As spies they prove clumsy and inept. As foils for Hamlet, they are beheaded by the English king. In *Rosencrantz and Guildenstern Are Dead*, Stoppard turns *Hamlet* inside out by retelling the story from the courtiers' point of view, a very different one indeed. The Player reminds the confused courtiers that there is a design in all art, a finality toward which all events point. This is appropriate for the characters in *Hamlet*, who sweep across the stage with a sense of sureness and identity, but it totally bewilders

Rosencrantz and Guildenstern, who have no memory of the past nor comprehension of the future. Although they struggle to make sense of their situation, for them existence is episodic and without pattern. The vaguely menacing Player informs them that all events lead to death, "the bad end unhappily, the good unluckily." In response to Guildenstern's inquiry, "Who decides?" the Player responds, "It is written." Rosencrantz and Guildenstern are unaware of their fictive existence. They must fill in the time between their brief appearances in *Hamlet* until they meet death at the hands of the English king. Thus they are seen tossing coins on the road to Elsinore. When they encounter the tragedians on their way to court, it is as part of the *Hamlet* script, which defines and controls them.

Stoppard imparts individual quirks of character to the virtually indistinguishable Rosencrantz and Guildenstern of Shakespeare's play. The simple and uninquiring Rosencrantz and the perpetually perplexed Guildenstern charm the audience. Their efforts to extricate themselves from a situation beyond their comprehension engenders uncomfortable laughter, for the audience is aware of their fate and the futility of their situation. Rosencrantz and Guildenstern engage the audience's sympathy because they have ceased to be nonentities; moreover, their plight mirrors the confused alienation present in much of modern life. It is this realization that contributes to the poignancy of the announcement of their deaths by the English ambassador at the end of Stoppard's play, which is in sharp contrast to the feelings engendered by their deaths in *Hamlet*. Stoppard gives the existential dilemma a new twist. For Rosencrantz and Guildenstern, essence precedes existence. The course of their lives is predetermined; consequently, choosing between alternatives is meaningless. For them, alternatives do not really exist. Guildenstern is vaguely aware that the reality they inhabit is of a different order when the tossed coin invariably comes up heads in defiance of the laws of probability. The Player, who provides the bridge between *Hamlet* and *Rosencrantz and Guildenstern Are Dead*, understands the situation perfectly. He was through all this before, his memory of events unimpeded by a scripted death. He knows not only the fictional nature of his existence but also the fate of the doomed courtiers. The unfortunate Rosencrantz and Guildenstern mistake themselves for real people, which is why their search for meaning elicits sympathy from an audience that shares the Player's knowledge of the senseless deaths awaiting them.

Unlike Rosencrantz and Guildenstern, the audience exists in a reality where choice appears to affect outcome. Knowing that Rosencrantz and Guildenstern are unaware that they share a predetermined end suggests the notion that human-

kind might be in the same boat, a metaphor that Stoppard employs in the third act. Because they are free to move about and improvise on board the boat that bears them to England, Rosencrantz and Guildenstern share the illusion of freedom as they move toward their rendezvous with death.

Rosencrantz and Guildenstern Are Dead contradicts Arthur Miller's contention that attention must be paid to the tragedy of the common man. Stoppard's play suggests that the ennobling qualities of tragedy may be limited to principal characters. Hamlet goes to his death secure in the knowledge that he acted within the scope of a provident deity. However, Rosencrantz and Guildenstern cease to exist without having acquired the wisdom of experience or the dignity of meaning. For Stoppard their comic search for meaning within an incomprehensible context more closely parallels the human condition than does the dramatic death of a tragic hero. When Rosencrantz and Guildenstern simply cease to exist, the audience is moved by their absence, for Stoppard endows them with a humanity that transcends the pointlessness of their existence. In this sense their fictive lives parallel Stoppard's work, wherein comedy is to be taken seriously, and tragedy is leavened with comic wit.

David Sundstrand

Further Reading

Brassell, Tim. *Tom Stoppard: An Assessment*. New York: St. Martin's Press, 1985. An excellent discussion of Stoppard's themes that includes a chapter on *Rosencrantz and Guildenstern Are Dead*.

Corballis, Richard. *Stoppard: The Mystery and the Clockwork*. Oxford, England: Amber Lane Press, 1984. Suggests that, with the death of tragedy in the twentieth century, Hamlet had to be redefined and that Guildenstern is the existential hero.

Fleming, John. *Stoppard's Theatre: Finding Order Amid Chaos*. Austin: University of Texas Press, 2001. Analyzes all of Stoppard's plays from their first productions through their revivals. Charts Stoppard's evolution as a playwright by considering both his work and his personal opinions as expressed in correspondence and interviews. Chapter 2 is devoted to *Rosencrantz and Guildenstern Are Dead*.

Hunter, Jim. *Tom Stoppard's Plays*. New York: Grove Press, 1982. Discusses Stoppard's work from the perspective of staging, playing, talking, and thinking. Provides a study guide with page references to listed discussions.

_____. *Tom Stoppard: "Rosencrantz and Guildenstern Are Dead," "Jumpers," "Travesties," "Arcadia."* London: Faber & Faber, 2000. A critical guide providing close readings of four plays. Examines the interplay between comedy and "the most basic and serious challenges to human understanding" in Stoppard's work.

Jenkins, Anthony. *The Theatre of Tom Stoppard*. New York: Cambridge University Press, 1987. Offers thematic interpretations of Stoppard's work, with an interesting discussion of *Rosencrantz and Guildenstern Are Dead* that explores the characters' plight as a game where the rules are not understood by all the players.

Kelly, Katherine E., ed. *The Cambridge Companion to Tom Stoppard*. New York: Cambridge University Press, 2001. Collection of essays examining Stoppard's life and plays written for the stage, screen, radio, and television. The references to *Rosencrantz and Guildenstern Are Dead* are listed in the index.

Nadel, Ira Bruce. *Tom Stoppard: A Life*. New York: Palgrave Macmillan, 2002. Comprehensive critical biography. The numerous references to *Rosencrantz and Guildenstern Are Dead* are listed in the index.

Schlueter, Jane. *Metafictional Characters in Modern Drama*. Columbia: Columbia University Press, 1979. Includes the chapter "Stoppard's Moon and Birdboot, Rosencrantz and Guildenstern," an excellent discussion of the way in which Stoppard handles characters who move between different fictive realities.

Rosmersholm

Author: Henrik Ibsen (1828-1906)
First produced: 1887; first published, 1886 (English translation, 1889)
Type of work: Drama
Type of plot: Social realism
Time of plot: Mid-nineteenth century
Locale: A small coastal town in western Norway

Principal characters:
JOHANNES ROSMER, a former clergyman
REBECCA WEST, his friend
RECTOR KROLL, the schoolmaster
ULRIC BRENDEL, a disillusioned liberal
PETER MORTENSGARD, a publisher
MADAM HELSETH, housekeeper at Rosmersholm

The Story:

Since the death of his wife, Beata, Johannes Rosmer turns more and more to his friend, Rebecca West. Rosmer had an unhappy marriage with an unsympathetic, neurotic wife who took her own life in a millpond. Rebecca was her friend as well as the husband's. Beata's brother, Rector Kroll, the schoolmaster, also is Rosmer's close friend.

Kroll calls on Rosmer to get him to join a political drive against the new liberal party that is gaining power in the village. The party is controlled by Peter Mortensgard, publisher of the *Beacon*, a paper Kroll considers radical and dangerous because it criticizes the conservative party, which he represents. Kroll is disappointed to learn that Rosmer no longer holds his former static views on politics and social structures but, instead, supports the liberals. Rosmer's real concern is not with politics at all, but only with encouraging people to ennoble their souls; he feels the new party is a step toward this goal. Rebecca supports him in his belief.

While they talk, Madam Helseth, the housekeeper, announces Ulric Brendel, a self-styled genius who is going to the village to offer his services to the liberal party. Brendel is in rags and obviously without a livelihood, and to Kroll he epitomizes the liberals. To Rosmer and Rebecca, however, Brendel is a man living and working as his conscience directs, and they help him with clothing and money.

This act turns Kroll against them. He now turns on Rosmer savagely and accuses him of betraying his class. Rosmer was a clergyman, and Kroll attempts to plead with him from a religious point of view, but Rosmer claims that he renounced the church and became a freethinker. He feels that people are growing so bitter in political struggles that they must be brought back to tolerance and good will. It is his hope that he can aid in this task by renouncing his way of life and working with the new leaders.

Kroll then accuses Rosmer of living in sin with Rebecca, even though he defended Rosmer and Rebecca when town gossips whispered about them. He accuses Rebecca of influencing Rosmer in his new attitude and suggests that she was responsible for the suicide of Rosmer's wife. He says his sister believed that Rosmer wished to wed Rebecca, and for that reason she drowned herself. Kroll maintains he did not speak up before because he did not know that Rebecca is an emancipated woman, and he did not believe her capable of such actions. His worst thoughts about Rosmer and Rebecca are confirmed when Mortensgard appears at Rosmer's home in answer to a note Rebecca writes him in Brendel's behalf. When Kroll leaves, he promises to inform the town of Rosmer's treachery.

Mortensgard comes to solicit Rosmer's aid in the liberal cause, but when he learns that Rosmer left the church, he does not want the former clergyman's help. He needs Christians, not freethinkers, as he himself is, and so Rosmer is left with no one to support. Mortensgard, too, slyly accuses Rosmer and Rebecca of indiscretions and of causing the death of Rosmer's wife.

From that time on Rosmer begins to feel guilty about his part in her death and fears that he did not conceal his true feelings for Rebecca from his wife. Determined not to let the past rule his life, he asks Rebecca to marry him. She flees from him sobbing, swearing that she can never marry him, that if he ever asks her again she will die the way his wife died.

Kroll does his work well. The paper supporting his party accuses Rosmer of betraying his class to gain favor with the liberals. The article links Rebecca and Rosmer in a debasing way. Rosmer wants to fight back, if only to free people's minds from pettiness and mass thinking, but he believes that he cannot accomplish this task because he no longer feels innocent of his wife's death; only the innocent can lead others.

Rebecca decides to give him back his purity of conscience. In Kroll's presence she tells Rosmer that she alone is responsible for his wife's suicide. She says that she came to Rosmersholm for the sole purpose of converting Rosmer to the liberal party. She knows that Brendel once had great influence over Rosmer, and she hoped to renew that influence and win him to the emancipators. With victory in sight, his wife was a stumbling block. To overcome that obstacle, she made that sick woman believe that she was going to have a child by Rosmer. In desperation the wife threw herself into the millpond. Rebecca's love for Rosmer makes her confess so that he can clear his own conscience of all guilt. Kroll and Rosmer leave her alone after her confession, and she prepares to leave Rosmersholm forever.

While she packs, Rosmer returns and tells her his old friends persuaded him that the task of ennobling people's minds is not for him or for anyone. He tells her that he knew she used him only to attain her own goals. Then she makes her greatest confession to him. She says that she was at first moved by physical passion. She plotted to get rid of his wife.

Then, after the suicide, Rebecca came to feel such deep and quiet love for Rosmer that it took her spirit from her. He ennobled her soul.

Rosmer cannot quite believe her story; he fears that she is again using him for her own purposes. As they talk, Brendel appears and tells them that he is leaving town, that his genius is gone, and he is bankrupt. He tells them, too, that Mortensgard is the only one who can win their cause, for he is without ideals. Only those without ideals can gain a victory. He says also that Rosmer can gain victory if the woman who loves him will convince him of her loyalty. After Brendel leaves them, Rosmer asks Rebecca to prove that he ennobled her soul. The price is high. He asks her to throw herself into the millpond as she caused his wife to do. Only her self-inflicted death can give him back his faith in himself, so she agrees to his plan. Since they no longer believe in a judgment after death, they must punish themselves for their love. At the last minute, Rosmer decides to join Rebecca in death. They stand with their arms entwined, then throw themselves into the pond.

Critical Evaluation:

The last of Henrik Ibsen's social dramas, *Rosmersholm* gives readers a glimpse of the psychological studies he was to write later. In this play, Ibsen continues the attempt to arouse his readers to raise themselves above the mass, not to be pulled down to the level of the popular majority. This work is written with the dramatist's usual skill and ranks with his other great plays.

Rosmersholm is literally the home of Rosmer, but in keeping with the temper of the play, the title actually signifies a spiritual homecoming for Johannes Rosmer. His life, both personal and political, is stormy. Almost without realizing it, he finds himself associated with unpopular political causes and movements by his friendship with Ulric Brendel and Peter Mortensgard. In a similar vein, his relationship with Rebecca West, after his wife Beata's suicide, further alienates him from the mainstream. Former friends and colleagues—notably Rector Kroll—desert him, forsake him, and betray him. His admission of religious lapse only exacerbates the situation. When all of his life seems to tumble about him like a house of cards, Rosmer seeks reassurance by asking Rebecca to make the ultimate sacrifice of her life. At the decisive moment, Rosmer elects to join her in suicide. In so doing, Rosmer finds his home—his spiritual home, Rosmersholm—that formerly eluded him.

In reality, Rosmer only toys with politics. He does not have the committed revolutionary's dedicated zeal; he is not capable of the self-sacrifice involved in giving himself over to a cause. His loyalties are divided between public issues and personal gratification. In the end, he chooses the latter, an important decision signifying a shift in Ibsen's focus and emphasis. Ibsen's earlier work deals with social issues of consequence to masses of people. *Rosmersholm* is a transitional piece that marks a change from social issues, which are a feature of his earlier dramas, to personal and individual concerns, which characterize Ibsen's later dramas.

Still, *Rosmersholm* is a politically charged play, for Rosmer's social ostracizing is more a consequence of his political philosophy than of his presumed unconventional lifestyle. In fact, the latter is attributed to the former, and much of the action in the play revolves around political philosophy and meetings with political figures, creating an onus from which even Rebecca is not exempt. The liberal-versus-conservative argument is the fulcrum of the conflict, with the issue of the so-called emancipated woman—Rebecca—serving as a microcosm of the entire macrocosm of the dispute. Rosmer's loyalties are thus ground between the Scylla of public principle and the Charybdis of personal passion. Ibsen offers the only logical possible solution to the dilemma: in effect, a mutual suicide pact. The inevitability of this conclusion is not clear from the start; it only emerges in the unfolding of the play. As a consequence of such subtlety, the dramatic dimensions of *Rosmersholm* are enhanced to tragic proportions, making the play, despite its ambivalent stance, a genuine classic of its kind.

Further Reading

Durbach, Errol. *"Ibsen the Romantic": Analogues of Paradise in the Later Plays.* Athens: University of Georgia Press, 1982. A tracing of romantic elements in Ibsen's later plays. The section on *Rosmersholm*, a play that Durbach considers bleak and depressing, discusses how joy nevertheless can be found in the midst of despair.

Holtan, Orley I. *Mythic Patterns in Ibsen's Last Plays.* Minneapolis: University of Minnesota Press, 1970. An overview of the mythic content in Ibsen's last seven plays. Contains a good discussion of the echoes from ancient Scandinavian mythology that can be heard in *Rosmersholm*.

Johnston, Brian. *The Ibsen Cycle: The Design of the Plays from "Pillars of Society" to "When We Dead Awaken."*

Boston: Twayne, 1975. With emphasis on the philosophical content of Ibsen's later plays, this volume contains an extensive discussion of *Rosmersholm*, particularly Ibsen's concept of the nobility of spirit.

McFarlane, James, ed. *The Cambridge Companion to Ibsen.* New York: Cambridge University Press, 1994. Collection of essays, including discussions of Ibsen's dramatic apprenticeship, historical drama, comedy, realistic problem drama, and working methods. The references to *Rosmersholm* are listed in the index.

Meyer, Michael. *Ibsen: A Biography.* Garden City, N.Y.: Doubleday, 1971. A standard biography of Ibsen. Contains a good discussion of *Rosmersholm* and its place in Ibsen's canon, in which, according to Meyer, it marks the transition from a concern with matters of society to a focus on the internal life of individuals.

Moi, Toril. "Losing Faith in Language: Fantasies of Perfect Communication in *Rosmersholm*." In *Henrik Ibsen and the Birth of Modernism: Art, Theater, Philosophy.* New York: Oxford University Press, 2006. A reevaluation of Ibsen, in which Moi refutes the traditional definition of Ibsen as a realistic and naturalistic playwright and describes him as an early modernist.

Robinson, Michael, ed. *Turning the Century: Centennial Essays on Ibsen.* Norwich, England: Norvik Press, 2006. Collection of the essays published in the journal *Scandinavica* during the past four decades, including discussions of Ibsen's style, his language, and the reception of his plays in England. One of the essays analyzes *Rosmersholm*.

Templeton, Joan. *Ibsen's Women.* New York: Cambridge University Press, 1997. Templeton examines the women characters in Ibsen's plays and their relationship to the women in the playwright's life and career. Chapter 8 includes an analysis of *Rosmersholm*.

Weigand, Hermann J. *The Modern Ibsen: A Reconsideration.* New York: Henry Holt, 1925. Reprint. Salem, N.H.: Ayer, 1984. Long a standard of Ibsen criticism, this volume covers each of the last twelve plays. The section on *Rosmersholm* offers a detailed and incisive explication, with emphasis on the psychological motivations of each of the characters, and serves as an excellent introduction for the general reader.

Roughing It

Author: Mark Twain (1835-1910)
First published: 1872
Type of work: Autobiography

Roughing It is a partly fictional account of Mark Twain's travel to the Nevada Territory and to California, his varied life there, colorful personalities he encountered, and his visit to the Hawaiian Islands (then called the Sandwich Islands). Interspersed throughout are factual and semifactual journalistic reports as well as tall tales. The book covers Twain's stagecoach trip with his brother Orion Clemens, the newly appointed secretary of the Nevada Territory, from St. Joseph, Missouri, to Carson City, Nevada (July to August, 1861); Twain's unsuccessful efforts to stake a timber claim and to prospect for silver (until August, 1862); his reporting and freelance writing for the *Territorial Enterprise* of Virginia City, Nevada (until May, 1864); his reporting for the *San Francisco Morning Call* (1864 to 1865); his trip to Hawaii (March to August, 1866); his work in San Francisco (until December, 1866); and—much more briefly—his return to the East Coast through the isthmus of Panama (December, 1866, to January, 1867).

Between the time of his return to the United States and the publication of *Roughing It*, Twain enjoyed a varied life. Details of his trip in 1867 to Europe and the Holy Land were converted into his best seller *The Innocents Abroad*, published in 1869. Soon after Twain married Olivia Langdon of Elmira, New York, his publisher persuaded him to follow up on the success of *The Innocents Abroad* with an account of his earlier travels in the Far West. Promising to deliver a manuscript in January, 1871, Twain wrote furiously for a time, but his work was interrupted by his father-in-law's death and his wife's illness. He then grew so dissatisfied with his writing that he extensively revised and padded the work with additional source material, partly by including some of his own Western journalistic pieces, to make a substantial book—for he always felt that it was necessary for a subscription book to be both a critical and a financial success. The final version, delivered to the publisher in November, 1871, was flawed and uneven, but when it appeared in the United States and London in February, 1872, *Roughing It* was a success. Critical opinion regards *Roughing It* as one of Twain's best travel books, along with *The Innocents Abroad*. Furthermore, because *Roughing It* reveals a great deal about the United States at a crucial period in its history, it is a more significant cultural document than *The Innocents Abroad*, which mainly relates the responses of a set of unrepresentative American tourists in the Old World.

The seventy-nine chapters of *Roughing It* fall into six separate and uneven parts. Getting to Carson City occupies chapters 1 through 20. Twain's wandering, timber work, and efforts at mining are covered in chapters 21 through 41. Chapters 42 through 61 describe Twain's work as a reporter in Virginia City, Nevada, and his renewed attempts to strike it rich, this time in the California mine fields. The parts concerning the Hawaiian Islands (chapters 62 through 77) betray both haste and padding, and represent little in the way of "roughing it." Ever desirous to swell his production, Twain added three appendices: "Brief Sketch of Mormon History"; "The Mountain Meadows Massacre," about the Mormon slaughter of travelers in a California-bound wagon train in September, 1857; and "Concerning a Frightful Assassination That Was Never Consummated," about the alleged near murder in 1870 of Conrad Wiegand, a naïvely idealistic, whistle-blowing journalist from Gold Hill, Nevada.

An excellent way of enjoying *Roughing It* is to notice how skillfully the narrator traces his evolution from a tenderfoot to an old-timer. After naïvely dreaming of "Indians, deserts, and silver bars," he gladly agrees to accompany his brother to Nevada and plans to have fun in the Far West for three months. Twain, a lover of numbers and arithmetic, regularly records distances covered and successive stops during their glorious twenty-day stagecoach trek. For example, he reports that on the tenth day they arrive at Green River, then proceed to Fort Bridger, 1,025 miles away; next, a two-day stop at Salt Lake City, with 600 final miles to go. Early in the going, they discard unneeded items of fancy dress, ineptly strap on weapons, and stand in awe of Homeric stagecoach drivers, picturesque way stations, and colorful workers.

Four episodes combine to demonstrate the foolishness of Mark Twain's eastern training. A coyote, "not a pretty creature, or respectable," is observed; he stays just out of pistol range, teases a town-bred dog with his "fraudful smile" only to outrun him, and thus becomes a symbolic King of the West—scrubby-looking, perhaps, but certainly in charge of the situation (chapter 5). Later, the narrator is persuaded by an auctioneer to buy a horse, the "Genuine Mexican Plug," which immediately bucks him off, darts away, throws other riders, and is finally given away to a passing emigrant more ignorant than its unhappy owner (chapter 24). (Here, Twain parades his genius in describing animals, as he does again in chapter 61, which features the biography of Tom Quartz, a pocket-miner's cat.) Caught overnight in a Nevada snowstorm later, the narrator and two friends find their booklearning of no use: They cannot start a fire by discharging their pistols, and their horses do not stand loyally by (chapters 32 to 33). In "The Great Landslide Case," which is often anthologized separately, conniving Westerners relish fooling a pompous attorney from the East into thinking that his client must lose his ranch when a neighbor's ranch has slid downhill intact and buried it (chapter 34).

Twain gradually recasts his narrator—first as a prospector and then as a journalist. In both endeavors the fellow sheds his greenhorn personality and grows pro-Western and knowledgeable—though often remaining humorously unsuccessful in his new pursuits. So mature and acclimated does he eventually become that he can simultaneously appreciate Western storytellers and report their vernacular style a bit superciliously. When, for example, the miner Scotty Briggs goes to a Virginia City parson at his "gospel-mill" to arrange for the funeral of his lamented partner Buck Fanshaw, the conversation is a mixture of colorful Western slang and sacerdotal locutions. The episode spoofs both men's speech patterns and inability to understand each other, even while remaining aware of Scotty's total and utter sincerity (chapter 47).

Western topics covered in the chapters preceding the narrator's Hawaiian junket are quite varied and include criticism of the Western jury system, respect for education and professionalism, grudging admiration for a burly sea captain's hanging of his black mate's killer, proof of flush-time vices (gambling, crime, brothels, jails, and "the birth of the 'literary' paper"), and praise of Chinese laborers for their many admirable traits and their contempt for the politicians and police officers who abuse them. Twain surely reveals his writer's fatigue when he invites the reader to skip chapter 52, which he announces will discuss silver mines in detail. The chapter that follows is graced with one of his most lovable literary triumphs—the story of Jim Blaine's grandfather's ram. Admirers get Jim "comfortably and sociably drunk" and then invite him to talk about the ram. Jim drones on and on, with each topic reminding him of another: a woman who loans her glass eye to a friend, a coffin peddler's bewigged wife, a deacon whose first wife's daughter married a missionary and "died in grace—et up by the savages," a dog that upsets Calvinistic theories of predestination by nimbly avoiding an accident that cripples a fated human victim, a man "nipped" by

a carpet-weaving machine that speedily turned him into a fourteen-yard rug, and so on. Old Jim discusses no fewer than twenty-seven named characters but nods off without ever getting to that ram.

Twain enjoys the Hawaiian Islands because he can respond to their pristine scenery, criticize soul-deadening missionary work there, visit sites of historic importance, describe native tattoos and poi and hula dances, and report how he generously guarded lady bathers on whose clothes he sat to prevent their being stolen. He probably expends too many words on Hawaiian politics, in a section of the book that seems dated and somewhat stale now, but his thrilling description of volcanic eruptions—a stylish set piece reminiscent of several in *The Innocents Abroad*—is positively Miltonic. With fatigue clearly evident, Twain closes *Roughing It* with quick accounts of lecturing about Hawaii back in Nevada and California, and then returning aboard a cholera-infected steamer to New York, where he lugubriously notes many changes. Children he once knew now sport "whiskers or waterfalls," and many grown friends have been jailed or hanged.

Roughing It defies easy categorization. Above all, it is a touched-up autobiography, the main purpose of which is to be a vehicle for Mark Twain's boastful account of his troubled maturation under Western skies. It is also a travel narrative that satirizes sentimental examples of the moribund genre even while it is a pioneering example of what became known as New Journalism, or the nonfiction novel. Above all it is a mini-anthology of delightful Western tall tales and anecdotes. Twain wrote three more travel books: *A Tramp Abroad* (1880), *Life on the Mississippi* (1883), and *Following the Equator* (1897). The first part of *Life on the Mississippi* contains some of his best reminiscences, but the second part, as well as the other two travel books, betray a strained falling-off in quality. *Roughing It*, flawed though it is, remains universally regarded as one of the most durable books in its genre.

Robert L. Gale

Further Reading

Camfield, Gregg. *The Oxford Companion to Mark Twain.* New York: Oxford University Press, 2003. Comprehensive collection of original essays presents discussion of Twain's individual works, covering topics such as themes, characters, language, and subjects that interested Twain. Includes an appendix on researching Twain that lists useful secondary sources and an extensive annotated bibliography of Twain's novels, plays, poems, and other writings.

Coulombe, Joseph L. "Mark Twain as Western Outlaw: Masculine Language, Violence, and Success in *Roughing It*." In *Mark Twain and the American West*. Columbia: University of Missouri Press, 2003. Analyzes *Roughing It* and some of Twain's other works to describe how he deliberately altered nineteenth century concepts of the American West. Describes the central role of the West in Twain's creation of his public persona.

Emerson, Everett. *Mark Twain: A Literary Life*. Philadelphia: University of Pennsylvania Press, 2000. Masterful work—a complete revision of Emerson's *The Authentic Mark Twain* (1984)—traces the development of Twain's writing against the events in his life and provides illuminating discussions of many individual works.

Gerber, John. *Mark Twain*. Boston: Twayne, 1988. Includes a concise introduction to *Roughing It*, with discussion of the work's composition, its autobiographical elements, the narrator's inconsistency, the comic styles and devices Twain uses, and the book's resemblances to *The Innocents Abroad*.

Hellwig, Harold H. *Mark Twain's Travel Literature: The Odyssey of a Mind*. Jefferson, N.C.: McFarland, 2008. Analyzes *Roughing It* and Twain's other travel literature, describing his depictions of time, place, and identity. Demonstrates how the travel literature reflects Twain's nostalgia for a disappearing America, his concern about Native American assimilation, and his own quest for personal and national identity. Argues that the theme of travel is also central to Twain's fictional works.

Messent, Peter B. "Travel and Travel Writing: *Innocents Abroad*, *A Tramp Abroad*, *Roughing It*, *Life on the Mississippi*." In *The Cambridge Introduction to Mark Twain*. New York: Cambridge University Press, 2007. Provides a solid overview of Twain's travel writing, placing it within the context of his other works.

Rasmussen, R. Kent. *Bloom's How to Write About Mark Twain*. New York: Bloom's Literary Criticism, 2008. Designed for students, this volume contains a chapter offering clear guidelines on how to write essays on literature, a chapter on writing about Twain, and chapters providing specific advice on individual works, including *Roughing It*.

Smith, Henry Nash. "Mark Twain as an Interpreter of the Far West: The Structure of *Roughing It*." In *The Frontier in Perspective*, edited by Walker D. Wyman and Clifton B. Kroeber. Madison: University of Wisconsin Press, 1957. Discusses the inconsistent voices of Twain's narrator, the naïve tenderfoot changing into an old-timer, satirist and parodist, observant reporter, custodian of official values, pompous moralist, and short-story teller.

Rouse Up O Young Men of the New Age!

Author: Kenzaburō Ōe (1935-   )
First published: Atarashii hito yo mezameyo, 1983
    (English translation, 2002)
Type of work: Novel
Type of plot: Psychological
Time of plot: Early 1980's
Locale: Setagaya, Tokyo, Japan

Principal characters:
K, a novelist
EEYORE, his mentally disabled son
MR. SHUMATA, a swimming instructor
MARTHA CROWLEY, an American graduate student
UNAMI and INADA, student radicals who kidnap Eeyore

The Story:

While traveling in Europe with a television crew, K picks up a copy of the *Complete Works of William Blake* because he was inspired by a line from Blake's poetry that he had read in a novel by Malcolm Lowry. Blake was a nineteenth century British Romantic poet who wrote prophetic poems and lyrics that redefined the major themes of Christianity, and he illustrated his poetry with engravings of mystical creatures. K remembers that he had previously translated a Blake poem, a significant creative act for K. This act reminds K of his demanding relationship with his son Eeyore, whose real name is Hikari.

Eeyore is mentally disabled, and K uses the imaginative world of Blake to mediate between himself and Eeyore's bizarre antics and behaviors. One day, when K was away from Japan on a trip, Eeyore had become physically violent, attacking his mother with a judo kick that made her fall to the ground. Later, Eeyore grabbed a butcher knife from the kitchen and made suspicious comments. Eeyore is almost twenty years old and is a powerful physical presence of equal height and weight when compared with his father. He is a child in the body of a fully developed adult. He makes irrational statements, believing that his father is dead when he is only attending a conference or on another trip. K is afraid Eeyore is becoming increasingly unpredictable and that he might need to be institutionalized.

K successfully convinces Eeyore that he is still alive by allowing him to stroke his bare foot, thus giving Eeyore a new definition for "foot." K had promised to write a book of definitions for everything in the world that would help disabled children like his son, and this promise underlines his desire to pass on his accumulated wisdom to Eeyore.

K was born and raised in a small village on Shikoku, the smallest and most rural of Japan's four main islands. When he entered Tokyo University, he felt marginalized by the giant city and its sophistication, until one day, when he accidentally discovered some lines from Blake's prophetic poem *The Four Zoas* in a book lying open in a library. The poem made K recall the dark valley of his childhood and how imagination is crucial to the process of learning and renewal. K remembers childhood experiences such as swimming underwater inside Carp Cave and nearly drowning before being rescued by his mother. His "rebirth" from near-death reminds K of the epileptic seizures suffered by his son and of Eeyore's second birth following brain surgery to remove a large growth inside his skull. K continues to look for ways in which he can use Blake's poetry to re-create the world for his son. K worries that his son lacks imagination and the ability to dream and will not be able to understand the modern world.

Eeyore, in middle school, is taking swimming lessons at a private health club. K thought the physical experience of moving in the water would increase the emotional bond with his son because they would need to verbalize instructions and emotions. However, a military group is training in the same pool under the direction of Mr. Shumata, a former Olympic athlete. The military men resemble Yukio Mishima's private army and are planning a celebration of the tenth anniversary of Mishima's aborted attempt to overthrow the Japanese government and his subsequent suicide in 1970. K is troubled by Mishima's use of violence as political expression and by the young men's apparent admiration for militarism. Suddenly, Eeyore begins to have trouble swimming, and Mr. Shumata dives in to rescue K's son, just as K had been rescued by his mother as a child. K is humiliated that he could not act quickly enough to rescue his own son.

A young American graduate student named Martha Crowley has been researching theories of sex and violence, and she is in Japan to interview K about Mishima and his desire to resurrect the Japanese imperial empire. Crowley worries that the memory of Mishima's suicide will damage Eeyore's fragile identity because Eeyore remembers the photograph of Mishima's severed head appearing in the newspaper. K recalls several troubling episodes of Eeyore's youth, including his own wish to kill Eeyore as an infant when he discovered the extent of his son's abnormalities. He also remembers a trip to the family cabin on the Izu peninsula. A typhoon forced father and son to shelter each other as the storm knocked down trees and battered the cabin. As Eeyore grew up, he learned to recognize bird calls and became a gifted musician and composer.

K and Eeyore are now collaborating on a drama called "Gulliver's Foot and the Country of the Little People," about the role of the weak in preventing the horrors of war. The drama is performed at Eeyore's special school. The script, written by K, depicts Gulliver as a weapon in a war between two nations. The king of one country asks Gulliver to destroy the ships and people of the neighboring country, but Gulliver refuses, and the two nations disarm.

K has celebrity status, in part because of his antinuclear politics. One day, two students, Unami and Inada, kidnap Eeyore in hopes of forcing K to reexamine his views. Eeyore is returned unharmed. K writes a story about a transcendental experience with a rain tree in Bali, and he realizes that his spirit will eventually merge with Eeyore's after his death, much as Blake had foretold.

As Eeyore answers to his real name, Hikari, while being called to dinner by his brother, K realizes that Eeyore has indeed become Hikari, which means "light" in Japanese. Though still mentally challenged, Hikari has matured into a young man of the new age.

Critical Evaluation:

Kenzaburō Ōe, who gained a reputation as one of Japan's greatest modern authors, is the second Japanese writer to win the Nobel Prize in Literature. His writings explore the political, psychological, and spiritual aspects of the modern world in a way that is distinctly Japanese but not without universal appeal. Ōe often bases his novels on intimate experiences from his life, such as sexual escapades, memories of family humiliation during wartime, and the challenges of parenting a mentally disabled child.

When Ōe began his education in the 1940's, he was taught to believe that Emperor Hirohito was a god and that every child should be willing to sacrifice his or her life for the benefit of the emperor and Japan. After he began studying French literature at Tokyo University, Ōe began writing stories on the themes of hope and rebirth in the face of death. His writing is a search for hope and redemption in a modern world devoid of stability and peace, and he advocates for the expansion of human rights, for political freedom, and against the proliferation of nuclear weapons. Ōe discovers hope through his intimate soul-searching and engagement with the world. Perhaps it is Ōe's optimism, emerging from the horrors of Japan's destruction in World War II, including the nuclear incineration of Hiroshima and Nagasaki, that gives *Rouse Up O Young Men of the New Age!* its moral authority and creative energy.

Each of the seven chapters takes its title from a line in a William Blake poem, including the lines "A Cold Babe Stands in the Furious Air" or "The Soul Descends as a Falling Star, to the Bone at my Heel" from *Vala: Or, The Four Zoas* (wr. 1795-1804, pb. 1963; best known as *The Four Zoas*) or the lyric poems *Songs of Innocence and of Experience* (1794) or the painting titled "The Ghost of a Flea." Clearly the driving force behind the novel, Blake's prophetic and imaginative engagement of the world provides a model for K, a thinly veiled autobiographic persona for the novelist Kenzaburō Ōe.

The protagonist with the single-letter name alludes to the novel *Kokoro* (1914; English translation, 1941) by Sōseki Natsume. In *Kokoro*, which is perhaps the finest Japanese novel in the bildungsroman tradition, the character K commits suicide after being defeated in a competition with another young man for the hand of an attractive young woman. As K in *Rouse Up O Young Men of the New Age!* attempts to understand Eeyore's world, he uses Blake's imaginative mythology to explain life's ironies and the difficulty of parenting a mentally disabled son. Eeyore provides many moments of uncertainty and a constant stream of humorous and offbeat pronouncements.

To re-create the modern world for his son, K must reconsider the most basic tenets of life, including the definition of "river" or the concepts of birth, maturation, and death. K's re-creation of the universe through the lens of Blake is the reason for his desire to write a new book of definitions for Eeyore (and, ultimately, for himself). To gain a new appreciation for the definition of one word is to understand the nature of the universe. In other words, the division between the personal and the universal is obliterated in Ōe's *Rouse Up O Young Men of the New Age!* K's self-understanding comes

under the microscope because the self is the most accessible object of consideration, which leads to a broader understanding of the world. K wants to help Eeyore by providing him with new definitions, but as the story progresses, he realizes that he cannot do this without a fundamental reexamination of himself. It is here that imagination as well as the poetry of Blake become essential to the re-creation of the self.

In a dazzling final chapter, K strives to understand a mystical experience of transcendence. He stares at a rain tree in a botanical garden for three hours, visits his friend who is dying of leukemia, and remembers sexual experiences as a college student. Ultimately, he realizes that the spirit will transcend the body and that his knowledge will transfer to Eeyore. This realization leads K to acknowledge Eeyore's real name: Hikari.

Jonathan Thorndike

Further Reading

Bradbury, Steven, Donald Pease, Rob Wilson, and Kenzaburō Ōe. "A Conversation with Ōe Kenzaburō." *Boundary 2* 20, no. 2 (Summer, 1993): 1-23. An interview conducted by Pease and Wilson with the author in Tokyo in 1991. Ōe explains his fascination with William Blake and his views on nonviolence in the aftermath of the demise of the Soviet Union and the beginning of the first Gulf War.

Claremont, Yasuko. *The Novels of Kenzaburō Ōe.* New York: Routledge, 2009. A full-length critical study that covers Ōe's career from 1957 to 2006, including analysis of his later novels. Claremont documents the philosophical journey of Ōe through postwar nihilism, atonement for Japan's errors, and redemption in the modern world through myth and imagination.

Napier, Susan J. "Death and the Emperor: Mishima, Ōe, and the Politics of Betrayal." *Journal of Asian Studies* 48, no. 1 (February, 1989): 71-89. A fascinating article about the resurrection of the emperor system in modern Japan under the leadership of Yukio Mishima, which is critiqued extensively in the work of Ōe.

Wilson, Michiko N. *The Marginal World of Ōe Kenzaburō: A Study in Themes and Techniques.* Armonk, N.Y.: M. E. Sharpe, 1986. A critical study of the themes of the outsider, cultural boundaries, and marginalization in Ōe's fiction through the lenses of semiotics and poststructuralism.

Roxana

Author: Daniel Defoe (1660-1731)
First published: 1724
Type of work: Novel
Type of plot: Picaresque
Time of plot: Eighteenth century
Locale: England and continental Europe

Principal characters:
ROXANA, a courtesan
AMY, her maid
MR. ——, her landlord
THE PRINCE DE ——
A MERCHANT

The Story:

Born in France, from which her parents fled because of religious persecution, Roxana grew to adolescence in England. At the age of fifteen, she married a handsome but conceited man. After eight years of marriage, during which time her husband went through all of their money, Roxana is left penniless with five children. She appeals for aid to her husband's relatives, all of whom refuse her except one old aunt, who is in no position to help her materially. Amy, Roxana's maid, refuses to leave her mistress although she receives no wages for her work. Another poor old woman whom Roxana had aided during her former prosperity adds her efforts to those of the old aunt and Amy. These good people manage to extract money from the relatives of the children's father, and all five of the little ones are given over to the care of the poor old woman.

Roxana is penniless and at the point of despair when Mr. ——, her landlord, after expressing his admiration for her, praises her fortitude under all of her difficulties and offers to set her up in housekeeping. He returns all the furniture he had confiscated, gives her food and money, and generally conducts himself with such kindness and candor that Amy urges Roxana to become the gentleman's mistress should he ask it. Roxana, however, clings to her virtuous independence. Fearing that the gentleman's kindness will go unrewarded, Amy, because she loves her mistress, offers to lie with the landlord in Roxana's place. This offer, however, Roxana refuses to consider. The two women talk much about the merits of the landlord, his motive in befriending Roxana, and the moral implications of his attentions.

When the landlord comes to take residence as a boarder in Roxana's house, he proposes, since his wife has deserted him, that he and Roxana live as husband and wife. To show his good faith, he offers to share his wealth with her, bequeathing her five hundred pounds in his will and promising seven thousand pounds if he leaves her. There is a festive celebration that evening and a little joking about Amy's offer to lie with the gentleman. Finally Roxana, her conscience still bothering her, yields to his protestations of love and has sex with him.

After a year and a half has passed and Roxana has not conceived a child, Amy chides her mistress for her barrenness. Feeling that Mr. —— is not her true husband, Roxana sends Amy to him to beget a child. Amy does bear a child, which Roxana takes as her own to save the maid embarrassment. Two years later, Roxana has a daughter, who dies within six months. A year later, she pleases her lover with a son.

Mr. —— takes Roxana with him to Paris on business. There they live in great style until he is robbed and murdered for the jewels he carries on his person. Roxana manages to retain the gentleman's wealth and secure it against the possible claims of his wife, who is still living.

In France, the Prince de —— hopes to make amends to Roxana for the murder of her protector by lavishing gifts upon her and flattering her beauty until she consents to be his mistress, this time allowing her virtue to be sullied not because of poverty but because of vanity. In order to suppress gossip, Roxana pretends that she has gone back to England on business, confines herself to her quarters, and instructs Amy to admit only Prince de ——.

Roxana's new lover showers her bountifully with gifts. When she gives birth to a son, he promises to acknowledge the child as his own and to provide adequately for him. After the birth of the child, Roxana sees a man, a member of the gendarmes, whom she thinks she recognizes as her husband. Amy visits the man and finds him to be the same worthless scoundrel who, years before, had abandoned his wife and five children. When the prince has to go to Italy on an official assignment, he takes Roxana with him. They remain there for two years. She has another son, who lives only two months. Then the prince's wife dies, and he, repenting his sins, parts from Roxana, who has been his faithful mistress for eight years.

Roxana and her maid sail for England after engaging a merchant to handle Roxana's wealth. Roxana has to go to Holland to receive her money from the merchant, who arrives in Holland from Paris and takes lodgings in the same house as Roxana. He and Roxana become well acquainted. The merchant wants to marry her, but she, too avaricious and calculating to risk her wealth for a mere caprice of love, suspects his motives. She does allow him to seduce her, however, for she feels she owes him some token of gratitude for his assistance. She is already pregnant with his child when they part.

Returning to London, Roxana settles her financial affairs and gives birth to a boy. She establishes herself in a handsome apartment and is courted by numerous fortune hunters, but her philosophy, as she chooses to call it, will not permit her to marry anyone. As a wife, she would have to share her wealth; as a mistress, she receives riches, and she is determined to amass a fortune.

Roxana gives lavish parties that are attended by many of the fashionable people of London. Soon her name becomes famous, and her purpose is fulfilled when a rich lord offers her a substantial income if she will become his mistress. She retires from society, takes a new apartment, and sees only the lord. She passes several years in this fashion, by which time she is fifty years old. Tiring at last of her lover, she begins to see her friends again.

With Amy's help, she begins to live a different kind of life so that eventually she can assist her children. She takes a room in another part of the city with a Quaker lady, and Amy lets people believe that her mistress has gone to Europe. By chance, Roxana meets the merchant whom she had known in Holland and whose son she had borne, and the merchant renews his suit. Although Amy sends word from Europe that Prince de —— is trying to find Roxana and wishes to marry her, Roxana, having learned that her husband is dead, accepts the merchant's proposal. The pair plans to return to Holland and take residence there. They will declare themselves eleven years married in order to legitimate their son.

One of Roxana's legitimate daughters is also her maid while Roxana lives in London. At first, Roxana tries to help her daughter by giving her, through Amy, money and advantages above her station. When the girl begins to suspect that her employer is her mother, Roxana is distressed, for she will be undone if her past is revealed. When Amy, infuriated with the prying girl, threatens to murder her, Roxana, after many years' friendship, dismisses her faithful maid. At last, however, the persistent daughter's inquiries are silenced, and Roxana is able to go to Holland with her new husband.

Critical Evaluation:

The Fortunate Mistress: Or, A History of the Life and Vast Variety of Fortunes of Mademoiselle de Beleau, Afterwards *Call'd the Countess de Wintselsheim, in Germany, Being the Person Known by the Name of the Lady Roxana, in the Time of King Charles II*, commonly known as *Roxana*, is the last novel in Daniel Defoe's series of great fictional works written between 1719 and 1724, which included *Robinson Crusoe* (1719), *Moll Flanders* (1722), and *A Journal of the Plague Year* (1722). Like its predecessors, it reflects the author's preoccupation with economic individualism and middle-class values as well as his dissenting Protestant orientation. Like other Defoe novels, *Roxana* is written in Defoe's characteristically robust style. At the same time, this prose work is unique, as it departs from the earlier novels to some degree in its point of view, its thematic variations, and its plot structure.

In *Roxana*, as in all of his works of fiction, Defoe is preoccupied with his characters' struggles for economic independence; Roxana, like Robinson Crusoe and Moll Flanders, is faced with poverty and starvation, but through her ambition, practicality, and shrewd business sense she overcomes tremendous obstacles, eventually amassing a fortune. Roxana and her predecessors are fiercely individual entrepreneurs. In order to stress their independence, Defoe typically isolates his heroes and heroines in some drastic way—Crusoe is shipwrecked; Moll and Roxana are social outcasts as a result of their criminal careers. Given these dire circumstances, Defoe shows how sheer necessity operates to make his characters act as they do.

Roxana is driven to a variety of criminal activities when she and her five children are abandoned by a worthless husband. Defoe had more than ample factual evidence on which to base such a portrait. It was during his age that modern urban civilization first devised large police forces, detective networks complete with organized informant systems, and a complex court system for handling the huge new criminal population. Not only in his fiction but also in countless journalistic pieces and pamphlets, Defoe argued passionately for the repeal of inhumane debtor laws, which he recognized as the cause of much crime and injustice. As he asserted in one eloquent plea, "Necessity will make us all Thieves." At least partly connected with this intense social concern was Defoe's Protestant background. He did not believe in the religious tenets of Puritanism, but he inherited its conception of human existence as a continual struggle, its habit of viewing everyday events as charged with moral significance, and its tendency toward introspection.

In *Roxana*, Defoe's social conscience and ethical underpinnings combine to produce a unique and, in many ways, brilliant novel that is difficult to classify. On the surface, the work resembles a picaresque tale, and it shares many features with other works of that category. In other ways, however, *Roxana* is radically different from a traditional picaresque narrative, most significantly in the depth of its characterizations and in the implications of its plot. A picaro is typically the tool through which an author presents a series of comic episodes for the purpose of satirizing society and human folly. Defoe's heroine, however, is a multidimensional individual. Roxana is a woman shaped by her environment and constantly striving to get the better of it. In contrast to the picaro, whose misadventures never pose a serious threat to his or her life, Roxana is placed in situations in which the danger is real. She need only be apprehended to run the risk of hanging.

Roxana's fears, pains, pleasures, and ambitions make her a human and sympathetic heroine. This quality of realism is further heightened by Defoe's distinctive style, which shows all the influences of his journalist's profession. He has a reporter's eye for detail, and he crowds his scenes with particulars, all described in plain, straightforward prose. His objective, unadorned language creates a powerful effect of verisimilitude. Defoe always insisted that his fictions are not romances (what modern-day readers might also call adventure stories). Defoe's social and moral orientation, coupled with his wonderful capacity for "lying like the truth," places *Roxana* far beyond the realm of typical eighteenth century romances.

There is a strongly autobiographical flavor to all of Defoe's novels, which results largely from the author's close identification with his main characters. In its beginning sections, *Roxana* is no exception. Later in the narrative, a curious thing begins to happen. As Defoe develops Roxana's character—which he modeled closely on the actual careers of several real-life criminals—she begins to act in ways of which he cannot approve, and he loses his sympathy for and close imaginative identification with her. This shifting sympathy occurs repeatedly throughout the novel and results in a curious vacillation on the author's part between admiring and approving of his heroine and being deeply shocked at her behavior. The basic reason for Defoe's ambivalence toward Roxana lies in the fact that in this novel, the same basic theme used in *Moll Flanders*—that of the innocent woman being corrupted by the pressures of poverty—is carried to much greater lengths. Moll is to be forgiven because she abandons her life of crime once she has gained sufficient wealth to be independent. Roxana continues her illicit activities long after the demands of economic necessity are met.

Roxana also differs from its author's other works in the relative tightness of the plot, which is particularly unified by the threat of possible exposure and consequent ruin for the heroine. This threat is reinforced so often, and the daughter is so persistent a presence in the later narrative, that exposure seems, indeed, the only natural conclusion to which the plot can proceed—but it does not. Defoe is not willing to have his heroine hanged any more than he can in right conscience allow her to live happily ever after. This conflict between sympathy and justice generates much of the dramatic tension in the novel. The solution to which Defoe resorts at the end of the novel solves not only the problem of plot but also that of the author's shifting attitude toward Roxana. In an insightful psychological twist, he imposes Roxana's punishment in the form of haunting guilt over her daughter's murder and consuming fear that her evil past will be revealed. Therefore, at the end of the novel, Roxana suffers the fate of Tantalus. Surrounded by wealth and friends, she can never enjoy them. Her peace is poisoned as she realizes that the simple pleasures of her friend the Quaker woman are forever unattainable for herself.

"Critical Evaluation" by Nancy G. Ballard

Further Reading

Backscheider, Paula R. *Daniel Defoe: Ambition and Innovation.* Louisville: University of Kentucky Press, 1986. Provides biographical information as well as critical interpretations of Defoe's novels.

Bell, Ian A. *Defoe's Fiction.* New York: Barnes & Noble, 1985. Examines the elements of Defoe's writing style and discusses his characters, including Roxana.

Boardman, Michael M. *Defoe and the Use of Narrative.* New Brunswick, N.J.: Rutgers University Press, 1985. Provides a discussion of Defoe's technique of storytelling, with a focus on how the author structures his stories.

Lund, Roger D., ed. *Critical Essays on Daniel Defoe.* New York: G. K. Hall, 1997. Collection of essays addresses the full range of Defoe's writings, including his domestic conduct manuals, his travel books, and his novels, with two essays devoted to *Roxana*. Among the topics discussed are Defoe's treatment of slavery and his treatment of the city.

Novak, Maximillian E. *Daniel Defoe: Master of Fictions—His Life and Ideas.* New York: Oxford University Press, 2001. Comprehensive biographical study by a leading Defoe scholar places Defoe's work within the context of the events of his life. Includes analysis of *Robinson Crusoe, Moll Flanders,* and other novels as well as discussion of Defoe's works in other genres.

Richetti, John J. *Daniel Defoe.* Boston: Twayne, 1987. Looks at Defoe's process of writing and his development of plot and characters, using *Roxana* and *Moll Flanders* as examples.

_____. *Life of Daniel Defoe: A Critical Biography.* Malden, Mass.: Blackwell, 2005. Presents a thorough examination of Defoe's writing within the context of his life and opinions, including analysis of his fiction and his political and religious journalism. Focuses on Defoe's distinctive literary style.

_____, ed. *The Cambridge Companion to Daniel Defoe.* New York: Cambridge University Press, 2008. Collection of essays includes analyses of Defoe's political and religious journalism as well as examinations of the topics of money and character in his fiction, Defoe as a narrative innovator, and gender issues in *Moll Flanders* and *Roxana.*

Rubáiyát of Omar Khayyám

Author: Edward FitzGerald (1809-1883)
First published: 1859; revised, 1868, 1872, 1879
Type of work: Poetry

Although Edward FitzGerald was a friend of such writers as Alfred, Lord Tennyson, and Thomas Carlyle, FitzGerald himself published few works. His principal one was a translation of the rubáiyát (quatrains) of a twelfth century Persian mathematician-astronomer, Omar Khayyám. Barely noticed when it first appeared in 1859, the work became popular on both sides of the Atlantic soon after Dante Gabriel Rossetti found a copy of the book and urged his friends to read it. A second edition appeared nine years after the first, expanded from 75 quatrains to 110. FitzGerald continued to make changes in a third and fourth edition, finally reducing the work to 101 quatrains.

It is widely acknowledged that the poem is much more than a translation. FitzGerald freely adapted the original quatrains, adding many of his own images and giving disconnected stanzas a unity of theme, tone, and style. He stayed with the four-line stanza of the original *Rubáiyát*, rhyming on all but the third line, though in a few instances all four lines rhyme. The result, known as the Rubáiyát stanza, employs an iambic pentameter line (ten syllables, five of them accented) and is crafted so that the third line, FitzGerald explained, "seems to lift and suspend the Wave that falls over the last." The final line usually gives the quatrain an epigrammatic force. FitzGerald also combined parts of some quatrains and arranged the whole collection into what he called "something of an Eclogue," a poem with a rustic setting that uses dialogue or soliloquy. He also gave the poem a framework appropriate to its astronomer author, opening at dawn and ending at nightfall on the same day, when the moon rises

and the narrator, who identifies himself along the way as "old Khayyám," is no more.

The poem begins not only at the break of a new day but also on New Year's Day, which occurred in Khayyám's time at the vernal equinox, the beginning of spring. This season provides the poet with useful symbols—the grape, the rose, the nightingale, and the verdant garden—and the spring setting inspires the poet to ponder the mystery of creation, life's brevity, the futility of trying to understand life's purpose, and the wisdom of enjoying life while it lasts.

As the sun drives out the night, the poet bids his companion to rise and accompany him. This companion is addressed later as "Love" and is the famous "thou" whom the poet finds "enow" (enough) in the wilderness along with a book of verses and a loaf of bread. She acts as a foil to the poet's meditations on their journey through the day, and this artful device gives the impression that the poet is addressing the reader as a familiar person. The narrator's voice becomes the principal unifying element in the poem. By the eleventh stanza (in the first edition), the personal element is established, and one cannot resist the poet's invitation to "come with old Khayyám."

Eager to begin the day, the poet says he might hear a voice within the tavern chiding the drowsy ones for tarrying outside. He sees others waiting impatiently to enter the tavern, impatient because time is wasting and, when they are dead, they shall not return. The tavern, which symbolizes for the poet the world at large, is a place where one's cup is filled with the "Wine of Life," and one had better hurry to drink it, for the wine keeps draining away slowly. If the rose dies, others will take its place, the companion answers, implying that spring renews life, but the poet makes it clear that the rose symbolizes people who will be gone forever.

Put such thoughts away, old Khayyám urges, and go with him to the garden, where the names of kings and slaves are forgotten, where one can see, in the natural setting, images that teach how to enjoy the brief stay on earth. There, all the poet sees reminds him that life is short; everyone becomes dust and never returns. One is therefore well advised to live today and not worry about yesterday or tomorrow. In this verdant setting, the poet is reminded of the cyclic nature of life. Spring renews the earth, but the rose and the hyacinth are nurtured by the buried bodies of those who have come and gone. No one is exempt, not the hero, the sultan, or Caesar himself.

The poet's skepticism regarding the usefulness of learning is brought to light as he recalls how little he learned from "Doctor and Saint." All he learned from them is that the individual has no control over his or her existence. One is but a pawn in the hands of a seemingly whimsical Creator. In this way, the individual is no different from nature's abundant manifestations: the rose, water, and wind. Although humans can reason, compute, ask questions, and seek causes, reason cannot penetrate the veil that separates the living from the dead. Futile is the search for life's purpose and futile is the hope for existence in the afterlife—if, indeed, there is an afterlife. All the poet learns is that wine is the best antidote for reason's inability to see into the darkness.

Wine offers the hedonist a quick escape from a meaningless life, but the grape also, for old Khayyám, symbolizes nature's abundant resources and, as such, offers a way of escaping *into* life, abandoning the arid, futile speculations of saint and Sufi (mystic). The tavern is a haven in which the weary traveler may find respite from the knowledge that life is brief and one is doomed to join those countless numbers who sink beneath the earth, never to return. Grimly, the poet sees that humans are like bubbles in the wine that the Eternal Saki pours, desert travelers in a Phantom Caravan.

Reminded of his own intellectual abilities and accomplishments, the poet dismisses their significance. Though he can calculate and use logic, he abandons reason and puts his faith in wine, which is all in which he was ever rich. This potent liquid confutes warring sectarians and transmutes life's base metal into gold. The only certainty, the poet discovers, is that life is brief and once one is dead, one is dead forever. Heaven and hell are within the individual, who is in the hands of an unknowable master. Using his reason to refute reason's

power to understand the meaning of existence, old Khayyám explains that it is absurd to think that the individual is punished in heaven for being made imperfect or expected to repay God in "pure gold" for an existence that was "drossalloyed." It is equally absurd to think that God will sue to collect a debt from one who has no part in making the contract.

These thoughts remind the poet of an earlier experience, a dream or a fantasy, in which he finds himself in the house of a potter surrounded by pots of all shapes and sizes, a loquacious lot that has the same concerns many humans have, the purpose of their existence, why some are misshapen and others are not, and who the Potter is. These vessels, it seems, were made to hold wine, the spirit of life, and they eagerly await the winebearer. They, too, come to the same realization as old Khayyám: Wine enables one to endure a life of unanswered questions. The poet acknowledges that his devotion to the potion tarnishes his reputation. He even repents, but when spring returns, his penitent spirit vanishes, and he returns to the grape.

The plaintive voices of the vessels bring to mind once again the vanishing rose, youth, and spring itself, and though spring will return, one day the poet will not. This melancholy thought makes him wish he could spring forth from the ground like the harvest, rewrite what Fate has written for him, or obliterate Fate altogether. Addressing his companion, he says that if they could re-create the world, they would surely mold it closer to their hearts' desire. The passage of time, however, is inexorable. Often, he says, the moon will wax and wane, returning again and again. On one of those rounds, in the darkness of night while other guests are "starscattered on the grass," it will be discovered that he is gone.

The day's journey from morning to evening, from the bedchamber to a pleasant garden, is also a journey through the mind of a philosophical poet pondering the mystery of human existence. In the lush garden that reminds him of nature's poignant beauty, of creation, and of the remorseless finality of death, the poet cannot find a satisfying, rational answer to his questions. Answers, if they exist, lie beyond the power of human reason. Impatient with the explanations of others, the poet concludes that it is best simply to live for today and drink oneself into oblivion.

Wine, the tavern, and intoxication, however, have symbolic value for the poet. In one sense, the tavern represents the world at large and includes the garden to which the poet and his companion journey. Wine, representing life itself or the spirit, impels one, not *from* life but *into* it. Commitment to the grape represents commitment to living intensely in the moment, becoming intoxicated by the spirit of life. In that state, one becomes oblivious to those questions that baffle saint and doctor alike. One escapes from the world of futile rationality into a world of sensory awareness.

FitzGerald considered Omar Khayyám a "material Epicurean," yet FitzGerald's translation suggests that Khayyám offered something beyond a refinement of life's pleasures, beyond a refined enjoyment of wine, women, and song. Without pushing the symbols too far, one could find the rose to be more than a dying flower that reminds one of life's brevity and the wine to be more than a temporary escape into oblivion. Clearly, old Khayyám of the quatrains sees in the rose a beauty that sustains life and reminds one of that nature that restores and enriches. Clearly, too, he sees the tavern as a metaphor of the larger world of nature, and he believes, finally, that the power of wine to intoxicate is the individual's only and best reward.

Bernard E. Morris

Further Reading

Aminrazavi, Mehdi. *The Wine of Wisdom*. Oxford, England: Oneworld, 2005. A biography of Omar Khayyám, covering his life, his poetry and philosophical writings, and his impact in the West. Includes original translations and the full text of FitzGerald's *Rubáiyát*.

Avery, Peter, and John Heath-Stubbs. Introduction to *The Rubáiyát of Omar Khayyám*, translated by Avery and Heath-Stubbs. New York: Penguin Books, 1981. Avery and Heath-Stubbs stay close to the original in their translation of 235 quatrains. Their introduction broadens readers' understanding of Omar Khayyám, and the translations, attractively illustrated, enhance appreciation of Khayyám's *Rubáiyát* without diminishing FitzGerald's achievement.

Bloom, Harold, ed. *Edward FitzGerald's "The Rubáiyát of Omar Khayyám."* Philadelphia: Chelsea House, 2004. Collection of essays analyzing the work, including "The Fin de Siècle Cult of FitzGerald's 'Rubáiyát' of Omar Khayyam" by John D. Yohannan, comparisons of FitzGerald with Spanish playwright Pedro Calderón de la Barca and English poet Alfred, Lord Tennyson, and "The Discovery of the Rubáiyát" by Robert Bernard Martin.

Bowen, John Charles Edward. *A New Selection from the Rubáiyát of Omar Khayyám*. Warminster, England: Aris & Phillips, 1976. The chief value of this work is that it includes a literal translation of the quatrains Bowen renders into verse and, along with Bowen's, many of FitzGerald's translations from the first and fourth editions. One is therefore able to compare four different versions of some of the quatrains.

Dashti, Ali. *In Search of Omar Khayyám*. Translated by L. P. Elwell-Sutton. New York: Columbia University Press, 1971. Dashti describes the character of Omar Khayyám by examining the writings of Khayyám's contemporaries. On the basis of this portrait, Dashti authenticates thirty-six quatrains with some confidence, translates them along with other quatrains, and examines their literary style.

Garrard, Garry. *A Book of Verse: The Biography of the "Rubáiyát of Omar Khayyám."* Stroud, England: Sutton, 2007. Chronicles the book's history, its reception over the years, and how it served as a source of inspiration for artists, writers, and musicians.

Untermeyer, Louis, ed. *Rubáiyát of Omar Khayyám: Translated into English Quatrains by Edward FitzGerald*. New York: Random House, 1947. Although FitzGerald's inimitable translation is often printed, this edition of all but the second edition has a fine introduction by Louis Untermeyer and contains FitzGerald's prefaces and notes together with attractive illustrations.

Yogananda, Paramhansa. *The Rubáiyát of Omar Khayyám Explained*. Nevada City, Calif.: Crystal Clarity, 1994. This contemporary mystic interprets the *Rubáiyát* as an allegory of the human spirit, not as the work of a hedonist. Though his reading contrasts sharply with FitzGerald's, Yogananda nevertheless uses the first edition of FitzGerald's translation as his text.

Rubyfruit Jungle

Author: Rita Mae Brown (1944-   )
First published: 1973
Type of work: Novel
Type of plot: Social realism
Time of plot: Early 1950's through late 1960's
Locale: Pennsylvania, Florida, and New York City

Principal characters:
MOLLY BOLT, the narrator
CARRIE, Molly's mother by adoption
CARL, Molly's father by adoption
LEROY DENMAN, Molly's cousin and friend
LEOTA B. BISLAND, Molly's first love

The Story:

Molly Bolt at the age of seven is already tough and lively. She had taught herself to read at the age of three and is brighter and more assertive than most children in Coffee Hollow, Pennsylvania. When a classmate, "Broccoli" Detwiler, urinates in front of her, she notices that his penis looks different from others she had seen (he was not circumcised), and she soon decides they could make money by showing it off to classmates after school for a nickel a look. The project is a big hit, and Molly realizes that money conveys power and popularity. Little Earl Stambach tells the teacher and the teacher contacts Molly's parents. Molly's mother, Carrie, angrily berates Molly for thinking she is clever, belittling her further by yelling that Molly is not even her daughter, that she is a bastard. Molly's response is immediate: "I don't care. It makes no difference where I came from. I'm here, ain't I?"

Molly continues to live by this principle of self-assertion throughout her life. She learns to accomplish her goals in whatever way necessary, whether or not that means following the restrictive views of others. She retaliates against Earl's tattling by tricking him into eating rabbit droppings he thinks are raisins and then blackmailing him into ceasing to tattle against her.

Leroy Denman is Molly's cousin and close friend. When his mother dies of cancer, Molly realizes that Leroy's family, and her own family, had built its views on a rigid standard that does not actually fit the actions of family members. Except for her father, Carl, most of the extended family tries to ignore realities that do not match their pretended standards of human behavior. After the funeral, Carl hugs the grieving husband in sympathy, yet this sympathy contradicts the American social custom that men should not hug other men. Molly knows that there are times when rules need to be broken.

School and home life provide Molly with many opportunities to learn about hypocrisy and how to circumvent rules. During a Christmas play in which Molly had been assigned the role of the Virgin Mary, a snobbish classmate improvises through the presentation to give herself a larger role. Molly ends up kicking her off the stage, much to the shocked delight of the audience. At home, when Carrie decides that Molly is too much of a tomboy and insists she stay indoors and do household chores, Molly retaliates by locking Carrie in the cellar. Molly considers such actions necessary to preserve her independence and her right to be herself.

When Molly is in the sixth grade, she develops a crush on her friend, Leota B. Bisland. They spend time together after school kissing each other, and one night at Leota's house they learn that touching bodies in other ways is even more fun. Rather than feel ashamed that her first love experimentation had been with another girl, Molly recognizes that love does not always follow society's norms. Years later, when Molly visits Leota as an adult, she finds that Leota is married to a man and denies having any homoerotic thoughts. Molly has had sex with both women and men but is not willing to label herself or condemn herself for her actions.

Molly, Carrie, Carl, and cousin Leroy and his family move to Florida in search of greater economic opportunity. Molly makes friends at school because of her sense of humor and her quick brain. Leroy has a sexual friendship with an older boy but cannot face that this might mean he is gay. Molly tells him not to worry about labels. She and Leroy have sex together, and Molly has affairs with other boys at school, but she also has an affair with her classmate, Carolyn Simpson. Carolyn, like Leroy, cannot accept feelings that contradict social customs, and she bows to the social norms.

At college in Gainesville, Florida, Molly encounters the same patterns. She falls in love with her roommate, Faye, but when others learn of their affair, Molly is chastised by the dean of women students (herself a closeted lesbian), sent to a psychologist to be "cured," and would have been kicked out of school had she not been within a few weeks of graduation. Faye, fearing that her rich parents would cut off their financial support, deserts Molly and acquiesces to social pressure. When Molly returns home, she is kicked out of the house by Carrie, who says Molly is "a dirty queer."

Molly hitchhikes her way from Florida to Greenwich Village in New York City, having heard that the Village is more accepting of varied lifestyles. Lacking money, she stays the first night in a deserted car on the street. Calvin, a young gay man who had been using the car as a sleeping space, too, leads Molly to a restaurant, where a friend gives them free food, and then takes her to a man who pays her one hundred dollars for throwing grapefruit at him while he is naked. Molly continues to learn that there are many different kinds of people in the world, and many ways to survive. She rents a small apartment, works at a movie theater and later a restaurant and other places, and enrolls in a local university to study filmmaking.

During her years as a part-time student and full-time worker, Molly comes to understand that there are many types of lesbians. One of her lovers was Holly, a tall black woman who was being supported financially by an older wealthy lesbian. Molly rejected such a situation for herself, preferring self-sufficiency. She then had an affair with the forty-one-year-old Polina Bellantoni and briefly during this time also with Polina's sixteen-year-old daughter, Alice. Polina also was having an affair with Paul, an extremely unattractive man, and Molly learned that when Polina and Paul had sex, they verbalized scenarios of themselves as the opposite gender. At the same time, Polina claimed that she was heterosexual and that Molly was perverted.

Near the end of her college years, Molly revisits her rural town in Pennsylvania, where Leota, now married, denies that there had been any childhood romance. Later, Molly goes to Florida to see Carrie and make a film of her for her senior filmmaking project. Leroy is there with his wife and children. He envies Molly's courage in living her life. Carrie claims that she had never disowned Molly, and Molly accepts Carrie for who she is.

Molly shows her documentary film alongside the films of rape and violence made by her classmates, but no one acknowledges her work. Molly vows to become a filmmaker who gives women visibility—"then watch out world."

Critical Evaluation:

Rita Mae Brown created a fictional character to teach diversity, and she made the story entertaining and compelling with the use of youthful slang and Molly's bravado wit. *Rubyfruit Jungle* was first published in 1973 by a small feminist publishing house, Daughters, Inc., and the book went through seven printings before 1977. When Bantam Books bought the rights and published the novel in 1977 (with repeated subsequent printings), it became a mainstream best seller.

Rubyfruit Jungle was the first lesbian novel published with a positive view of lesbian sexuality by a major press. The novel became a classic in contemporary lesbian literature and brought Brown national recognition. As a bildungsroman, *Rubyfruit Jungle* is often compared to Mark Twain's *Adventures of Huckleberry Finn* (1884) and the picaresque tradition of a character on a journey of self-discovery. In this coming-of-age novel, Brown emphasizes the individual spirit; she also shows how society shapes the self and challenges personal freedom. In many ways, Molly is an outsider who moves from innocence to experience as she learns to exist in a hostile world. The novel also is considered both a contribution to and a product of the women's movement. Molly's odyssey shows the need for mutual respect among all classes, races, and genders. Her story is lesbian, but her determination applies to many other struggles.

Critics have often noted that Brown is a Southern writer with a keen sense of place. Carol M. Ward wrote that the four sections of the novel, which show changes in time, location, and sexual partners, all reveal transformations in Molly. Brown contrasts rural and natural with city and artificial environments, and she structures Molly's journeys in such a way as to contrast North and South. Molly herself often expresses criticism of the artificial boundaries that separate.

Molly's family was always poor, and Molly constantly struggles to have enough money to pursue her dreams, sometimes simply for enough to survive. Her father, Carl, encouraged her to make of her life something different from the trap he felt his life to be. Carrie, bitter about the economic restrictions that she had endured, was jealous of Molly's ambition and her ability to act on her needs. When Molly returns from self-exile to see her, however, Carrie is clearly pleased at Molly's successes, which allows Molly to be reconciled and to accept the mother-daughter relationship. The film Molly makes is a tribute to that love and to the resilience of the human spirit, just as the film's negative reception in New York is symbolic of society's inability to see the value of that spirit.

Brown fought for women's rights from a young age, writing essays and lesbian poetry while active in feminist politics. Her other novels, including several volumes of detective fiction, present a variety of characters and situations. *Rubyfruit Jungle* remains her most influential work, her most widely read and widely acclaimed literary success. Molly is a daring, uninhibited heroine, and her wit and determination make her a character who reflects the eternal longing for a better world.

Lois A. Marchino

Further Reading

Abel, Elizabeth, Marianne Hirsch, and Elizabeth Langland, eds. *The Voyage In: Fictions of Female Development.* Hanover, N.H.: University Press of New England, 1983. This valuable collection of essays examines developmental novels by women. Brown and *Rubyfruit Jungle* are discussed at length in Bonnie Zimmerman's "Exiting from the Patriarchy: The Lesbian Novel of Development." Zimmerman's 1990 book *The Safe Sea of Women* expands many ideas from this essay.

Alexander, Delores. "Rita Mae Brown: 'The Issue for the Future Is Power.'" *Ms.*, September, 1974, 110-113. In this magazine article, published shortly after the publication of *Rubyfruit Jungle*, Alexander discusses Brown's writing and her perspectives on the contemporary women's movement.

Boyle, Sharon D. "Rita Mae Brown." In *Contemporary Lesbian Writers of the United States: A Bio-Bibliographical Critical Sourcebook*, edited by Sandra Pollack and Denise D. Knight. Westport, Conn.: Greenwood Press, 1993. Boyle's article profiles Brown's life and work, including an extended discussion of *Rubyfruit Jungle* and a useful bibliography.

Chew, Martha. "Rita Mae Brown: Feminist Theorist and Southern Novelist." In *Women Writers of the Contemporary South*, edited by Peggy Whitman Prenshaw. Jackson: University Press of Mississippi, 1984. Chew examines the connections between Brown's political essays and her fiction. She places Brown in the context of Southern writers who are also active in the realm of politics.

Day, Frances Ann. "Molly Bolts and Lifelines: Rita Mae Brown's *Rubyfruit Jungle*." In *Women in Literature: Reading Through the Lens of Gender*, edited by Jerilyn Fisher and Ellen S. Silber. Westport, Conn.: Greenwood Press, 2003. This brief feminist analysis of *Rubyfruit Jungle* is included in a collection of feminist interpretations of ninety-six works of fiction. This book is designed for middle-school students and older.

Elliott, Jane. "Promiscuous Times: *Rubyfruit Jungle*, *Fear of Flying*, and the Desire for the Event." In *Popular Feminist Fiction as American Allegory: Representing National Time*. New York: Palgrave Macmillan, 2008. Elliott explores how *Rubyfruit Jungle* and other feminist novels depict women as trapped in time and unable to access positive futures—an allegory for the perceived decline of American progress after the 1960's.

Palmer, Paulina. "Contemporary Lesbian Feminist Fiction: Texts for Everywoman." In *Plotting Change: Contemporary Women's Fiction*, edited by Linda Anderson. London: Edward Arnold, 1990. Palmer argues that *Rubyfruit Jungle* is representative of early lesbian feminist fiction, which "generally utilized the form of the bildungsroman and concentrated, somewhat narrowly, on the theme of Coming Out."

Perry, Carolyn, and Mary Louise Weaks, eds. *The History of Southern Women's Literature*. Baton Rouge: Louisiana State University Press, 2002. An analysis of Brown's work is included in this study that examines the distinctive nature of literature written by southern women from the years before the American Civil War through the twentieth century.

Stimpson, Catharine R. "Zero Degree Deviancy: The Lesbian Novel in English." In *Writing and Sexual Difference*, edited by Elizabeth Abel. Chicago: University of Chicago Press, 1982. This groundbreaking essay describes and distinguishes between the "dying fall" and "enabling escape" patterns of lesbian narrative, using *Rubyfruit Jungle* as a prime example of the second category.

Ward, Carol M., ed. *Rita Mae Brown*. New York: Twayne, 1993. An excellent full-length discussion of Brown and her works arranged according to individual books. Includes a discussion of *Rubyfruit Jungle* in the chapter "The Grand Canyon Between First Person Narrative and Third Person Narrative." Includes an extensive bibliography of reviews and criticism about the novels.

Zimmerman, Bonnie. *The Safe Sea of Women: Lesbian Fiction, 1969-1989*. Boston: Beacon Press, 1990. This insightful, classic study of contemporary lesbian prose literature explores the interaction between fiction and community—specifically, how lesbian novels and short stories have both reflected and shaped lesbian communities. Zimmerman describes *Rubyfruit Jungle* as the quintessential coming-out novel, a bildungsroman.

Rumble Fish

Author: S. E. Hinton (1948-   )
First published: 1975
Type of work: Young adult fiction
Type of plot: Social realism
Time of plot: 1960's
Locale: Tulsa, Oklahoma

Principal characters:
RUSTY-JAMES, a teenage boy
MOTORCYCLE BOY, his older brother
PATTY, Rusty's girlfriend
STEVE HAYS, Rusty's best friend
SMOKEY BENNET, and
B. J. JACKSON, Rusty's other friends
BIFF WILCOX, Rusty's rival
CASSANDRA, Motorcycle Boy's girlfriend

The Story:

Rusty-James, or Rusty, runs into his old friend, Steve Hays, at the beach. Five or six years have passed since they last saw each other. Steve is in college and Rusty is not long out of the reformatory. Rusty's memory is not very good these days. When Steve looks at the scar on Rusty's side, Rusty tells him that he got it in a knife fight. Steve remembers. He tells Rusty he was there when it happened several years before. When Steve mentions that Rusty looks just like someone from their past, Rusty thinks he could have been happy to see Steve again if he had not made him remember everything.

Rusty tells his story. At the age of fourteen, Rusty is hanging around Benny's, playing pool with his friends when he learns that Biff Wilcox wants to kill him. Rusty is not afraid of Biff and seems to be annoyed that Biff wants to kill him for the comments he made about a girl named Anita. He tells his friends what he said, and when the gang agrees that Rusty is telling the truth, the notion of fighting about it seems silly. Some of the boys, though, are holding on to the past, the days when gang fights were common. Steve tries to impart a warning to Rusty about gang fights, a warning handed down by Rusty's older brother, Motorcycle Boy, a former gang leader.

Rusty gets angry with Steve for bringing up Motorcycle Boy and makes plans to fight Biff. Rusty kills a few hours before the fight by spending some time with his girlfriend, Patty. He falls asleep while there, nearly missing the fight. Later, Rusty arrives to fight Biff, and is accompanied by his friends Steve, Smokey Bennet, and B. J. Jackson. Biff, too, brings some friends for backup. Biff's erratic behavior leads Rusty to believe that he is on drugs, which causes him to worry that the fight will not be a fair one. Rusty's fears are confirmed when Biff pulls a knife. Rusty is able to knock the knife away from Biff and beats him until it appears the fight is over. Motorcycle Boy arrives and announces his return. Rusty is momentarily distracted and vulnerable to being at-

tacked. Biff seizes the opportunity to grab the knife and stabs Rusty in the side. Motorcycle Boy steps in and ends the fight by breaking Biff's wrist.

Motorcycle Boy and Steve manage to get Rusty home to the apartment the boys share with their mostly absent alcoholic father. They bandage Rusty's wounds. Motorcycle Boy talks about his recent trip to California. Rusty falls asleep and dreams about his older brother. Rusty is uncomfortable being himself and is preoccupied with becoming just like his brother.

Despite the knife wound, Rusty shows up for school the next day. After school, he steals a set of hubcaps from a car near Benny's, while Steve talks about his mother's recent hospitalization. The owner of the car notices the theft in progress and begins chasing the boys, accompanied by a couple of his friends. Rusty and Steve barely escape. The ordeal scares Steve, and he cries as they walk home. His crying scares Rusty because he has never seen a guy cry before. Rusty assumes that Steve is crying about his mother, but Rusty never knew his own mother, so he cannot relate.

Later that evening, Rusty and Motorcycle Boy chat with their father about the older son's trip to California; his girlfriend, Cassandra; and one of the local cops, who has issues with the brothers. Rusty goes to a late-night party at the beach. He ditches school the next morning and gets expelled. When Patty finds out that Rusty had been with another girl at the party, she breaks up with him. Rusty feels there is nothing he can do to change what has happened, so he copes by "forgetting" these events. He also recruits Steve and Motorcycle Boy to go out drinking, also to help him forget this terrible day.

Motorcycle Boy tells Rusty that while he was in California, he saw their mother. Rusty has only vague memories of her because she abandoned the family when he was two years old. Rusty's father had begun drinking when his mother left, even going on a three-day drinking binge and leaving Rusty home alone. Motorcycle Boy surmises that this is why Rusty fears being alone now.

After watching Motorcycle Boy play pool, Rusty and Steve get separated from him and end up in an unfamiliar part of town. The boys are mugged and Rusty is beaten. Once again, Motorcycle Boy saves them. The following day, Rusty notices that his vision is not quite right, most likely because of the head injury he suffered in the mugging. Rusty goes to Steve's house and discovers that Steve's father had beaten his friend severely for staying out past curfew the night before. Rusty tells Steve that he is worried about his brother, but is not sure why. He asks Steve to help keep an eye on him. Steve refuses because he cannot afford to do anything that would cause him to get into more trouble at home. Rusty leaves, and he will not see Steve until they meet at the beach in five years.

Rusty goes to Benny's and finds out that Patty is now dating his friend Smokey. Smokey had set Rusty up by inviting the other girls to get Patty to break up with him. Instead of being angry, Rusty envies Smokey for being smart enough to think up that kind of a plan. B. J. tells Rusty that Motorcycle Boy is in the pet store looking at the fish. Rusty goes to the pet store, and the two watch the fish. Motorcycle Boy calls them rumble fish because they would kill each other if they could. He wonders if the fish would still act that way if they were in the river.

Later that night, Motorcycle Boy breaks into the pet store and starts setting the animals free. Rusty tries to stop him, but it is no use. Motorcycle Boy grabs the rumble fish and heads for the river as police arrive. An officer fires a warning shot that hits him. He dies near the river with the rumble fish flopping on the ground, dying beside him. Rusty knows the shooting was intentional. He screams and smashes his fists through the window of the police car.

Rusty is back on the beach with Steve, five years later. Steve asks him if he ever went back home after his brother's death. Rusty says no. Steve invites him out for dinner and tells him where to meet later. Rusty decides that he never wants to see Steve again, so that he can start forgetting about Motorcycle Boy, but it is taking Rusty longer than expected to forget his older brother.

Critical Evaluation:

S. E. Hinton had cut out a photograph of a boy and a motorcycle in a magazine, and kept the picture. The image stuck with her, and it inspired her to write a story. *Rumble Fish* was originally published in October, 1968, as a short story in *Nimrod*, a literary supplement to the *University of Tulsa*

Magazine. This early work is an encapsulated version of the novel; the main difference between the two versions is the viewpoint narrator.

In the short story, Hinton switches viewpoints several times. When Hinton first attempted to convert the short story into a novel, she struggled with the decision of which character to use as her narrator. She wrote a draft using Steve Hays as her narrator, but did not like the completed manuscript. Steve was too smart, too well spoken, and too observant. He reminded her too much of Ponyboy Curtis and Bryon Douglas, the narrators from her first two novels, respectively. She decided to tell the story from Rusty-James's point of view because he was a wholly different character than the ones she had devised in the past. Hinton considers *Rumble Fish* to be her most literary work.

In terms of themes and imagery, *Rumble Fish* is ambitious. Fate and destiny are the forces guiding Rusty-James's life. Hinton explores this theme, too, in the characters of Dallas "Dally" Winston in *The Outsiders* (1967) and Mark Jennings in *That Was Then, This Is Now* (1971). In both cases, Hinton sets the reader up to accept that these characters were doomed from the start. However, because the reader sees Dally and Mark through Ponyboy's and Bryon's eyes, there is still some shred of hope for them. Hinton's choice to make Rusty-James a predestined failure and show the reader the world through his eyes creates a tone for the story of hopelessness.

Rusty-James has given up on living even before the story begins. If there is nothing he can do to change his fate, why would anyone care about what happens to him? Hinton disproves the notion of fate by showing readers what has become of Steve in the five years that have passed since Motorcycle Boy's death. Steve could have easily become like Rusty-James, but instead chose to leave their hometown and go to college. The difference between Steve and Rusty-James is a difference in attitude. Steve believes one can make his or her own luck, Rusty-James does not.

Hinton uses animal imagery to further identify her characters. Steve is often referred to as a rabbit; Motorcycle Boy as a panther. Rusty-James often refers to himself as a dog. Rusty-James's choice illustrates that he sees himself as someone who is loyal. However, Motorcycle Boy calls Rusty-James a chameleon. This would imply that he sees Rusty-James as the kind of person who is always trying to fit in, compromising himself to be accepted.

In the pet store, the rumble fish are separated, one fish to a bowl. If two fish are put in the same bowl, they will fight to the death. They must be detached from others to survive, much like Motorcycle Boy. However, as Rusty-James and

Motorcycle Boy's father points out, Motorcycle Boy is not crazy; he had been born too late. He has an acute awareness of the state of the world. He might have fared better in life had he been born in a different era. Fate has played a cruel joke on Motorcycle Boy, and on the rumble fish.

Critical reaction to *Rumble Fish* has been mixed. Some critics fault Hinton for not writing another Ponyboy, and others do not like that Rusty-James is unable to fully express or understand what is happening around him. One review compares Hinton's career to one of her characters, claiming her future in writing is as bleak as Rusty-James's life. However, not all critics agree. Some consider her a brilliant novelist, and some praise Hinton for not sugarcoating her characters' problems. Others like Rusty-James for the same reasons other reviewers do not. Despite the criticism, *Rumble Fish* has won many awards, including the American Library Association's Best Books for Young Adults citation in 1975.

Martel Sardina

Further Reading

Abrams, Dennis. *S. E. Hinton*. New York: Chelsea House, 2009. An introductory book on Hinton's life and fiction written especially for younger readers. Part of the Who Wrote That? series. Includes a chronology, a bibliography, photographs, and an index.

Daly, Jay. *Presenting S. E. Hinton*. Boston: Twayne, 1989. A comprehensive analysis of Hinton's works. Contains an author biography, individual chapters focused on each of her young adult novels, literary criticism, and supplemental information about the film adaptations.

Hinton, S. E. *Some of Tim's Stories*. New York: Penguin Books, 2007. Although the first half of this book consists of short stories, the second half contains interviews of the author not published elsewhere, offering retrospective insights into the author's early writing years. Discusses her young adult novels and their film adaptations, and her latest works.

Kjelle, Marylou Morano. *S. E. Hinton: Author of "The Outsiders."* Berkeley Heights, N.J.: Enslow, 2008. This biography intersperses analysis of Hinton's work with facts about her life. Includes transcripts of speeches, interviews, and some photographs.

Wilson, Antoine. *S. E. Hinton*. New York: Rosen Central, 2003. Provides an overview of Hinton's works, including *Rumble Fish*. Contains an author interview, selected book reviews, and a list of awards each of her books has received. Part of the Library of Author Biographies series.

R.U.R.
Rossum's Universal Robots

Author: Karel Čapek (1890-1938)
First produced: 1921; first published, 1920 (English translation, 1923)
Type of work: Drama
Type of plot: Social satire
Time of plot: The future
Locale: An unnamed island

Principal characters:
HARRY DOMIN, the general manager of Rossum's Universal Robots
HELENA GLORY, his wife
DR. GALL, a scientist
MR. ALQUIST, the head of the works department of R.U.R.
PRIMUS, a robot
HELENA, a robot

The Story:

The Rossum Universal Robot Factory perfects the production of mechanical men and women. The formula was developed originally by old Rossum, but it was left to his son, an engineer, to manufacture the robots. Robots know no joy, no desire to take a solitary walk, no personal wish of any kind. They are highly developed, with mechanisms devised for only one purpose: work.

The robots manufactured by Rossum's Universal Robot Factory are so lifelike, however, that when the president's daughter, Helena Glory, calls at the factory and is shown around by Harry Domin, general manager, she can hardly believe that the robots are not human. Helena was sent by the Humanity League on a mission to gain better living conditions for the robots. Helena knows that when the robots begin to act strangely, as they sometimes do, they are destroyed and their parts are used to make new robots. She is dismayed to find that the robots she meets and talks with in the factory do not care whether they are killed or are starved. They think of nothing but their work. They talk rationally, answering her questions, but they seem to have no desires or feelings beyond their given jobs. Domin and the other executives are willing to have her preach to the robots all she wishes.

In the warehouses are hundreds of thousands of robots waiting to be shipped all over the world. Domin tries to convince Helena of the rightness of the new era. Now, humanity is no longer effective. People are too imperfect, too expensive, too immature. Although Domin cannot agree that robots should be freed and allowed human rights, he admits that sometimes they act oddly. Often one would gnash its teeth, throw things about, and then stand still. The attack is similar to epilepsy, and the robot has to go to the stamping-mill to be destroyed. Helena believes these are signs of developing a soul. The managers are working on a pain-nerve. They think that if the robots were to feel pain, these attacks could be foreseen and treated.

The executives try also to convince Helena of the virtue of robots by pointing out to her that the prices of all manufactured and farm goods drop almost to nothing. Where Helena can see only the millions of humans out of work, the managers can see a world in which no human being has to work. People can then sit back and enjoy the labors of mechanical workers. Only Mr. Alquist, head of the works department, disagrees with that notion. Alquist can see the joy that people find only in working and creating. The others quickly vote him down.

Without prior warning, Domin tells Helena that he loves her and cannot bear to lose her. Puzzling even herself, she accepts him. Ten years pass. The managers try to keep from Helena the news that the robots are causing trouble. All over the world small groups of robots revolt against their masters. Some governments turn the robots into soldiers and terrible wars are fought. Learning of these revolts, she begs Domin and the others to close the factory while there is still time. The men laugh at her fears. They have a gunboat standing by that will protect them from any rebels in the warehouses. Only Alquist agrees with Helena. He even prays that God will destroy the robots and let humanity return to work. He knows, as Helena does, that people stopped reproducing; there were no births recorded in the past week.

Dr. Gall, the physiologist, begins to fear the results when he learns that some of the more intelligent robots, according to their different grades, begin to feel pain and to have heart flutters. They also begin to show definite signs of hating and

of loving. The R.U.R. shareholders, however, are making too much money, and world governments are growing too powerful with robot soldiers to permit their discontinuation, even if Domin and the others accepted Helena and Alquist's views. Feeling that the end is near, Dr. Gall warns Helena to look out for herself. The scientist believes they are all doomed.

The only weapon the managers can use against the robots, should they rebel, is the secret of their manufacture, the secret that promises to end a world organization of robots. As soon as the current trouble is over, each country will begin to manufacture its own robots. The differences in language and customs will prevent a world union in the future.

The trouble soon grows into a real danger. A mail boat arrives with leaflets announcing that the world organization orders all robots to kill every man, woman, and child in the world. The robots claim that humanity is now a parasite, that robots are now smarter than humanity and must rule the world. The orders are to be carried out immediately.

After a gallant fight the humans in the factory are overpowered. Even when he knows death is near, Domin has no regrets. He wanted to free humanity from the restrictions of an unfair social system, from poverty, from the slavery of working for another; something went wrong. Somehow the robots began to care about the things that people cared about. The mystery is solved when Helena confesses that she persuaded Dr. Gall to give the robots souls. She hoped that if the robots were more like human beings both groups could understand each other better. Now the robots are so human that they act like humans. This similarity includes killing.

The only hope is to persuade the robots that they dare not kill the men who know the secret of their manufacture. Domin prefers death rather than to give up his dream, but the others, hoping to use the formula in their bargaining, outvote him. Then they learn that Helena, hoping to put an end to the factory and to help children be born again, burned the formula.

All the humans are killed except Alquist, spared by the robots because he also works with his hands. Alquist, unable to duplicate the formula, cannot save the robots, who are dying by the millions. Before long they will be extinct. The irony is that Alquist needs human beings to study and experiment with in order to rediscover the formula, but there are no humans left.

One day Alquist decides that there is hope. Primus, a robot, and Helena, a robot made in Helena's image, exhibit all the symptoms of love. At first Alquist plans to dissect them, to see what makes them feel human love. When he learns that they are willing to die for each other, but that they will not be parted, he knows that he needs search no longer for the secret of robot life. Their love will bring forth new life, and the world will know humanity once more.

Critical Evaluation:

Early translations of *R.U.R.* gave the word "robot"—derived from the Czech word for forced labor—to the English language. Subsequent users have, however, shifted its meaning. Rossum's robots are slaves manufactured from artificial flesh and blood, but the word is currently applied in industry to refer to machines that mimic the actions of a human limb. The shift in meaning was begun when Fritz Lang's film *Metropolis* (1926) extended the term to embrace a humanoid creature made of metal. It was taken a stage further when some science fiction writers who wished to discriminate between humanoid machines and humanoids made of artificial organic materials—and who were more familiar with *Metropolis* than *R.U.R.*—chose to restrict the term "robot" to metallic humanoids while calling fleshy humanoids "androids."

The fact that people associate the term "robot" with machinery led some commentators to interpret *R.U.R.* as an allegory about mechanization. It can, indeed, be decoded in this way, but that was certainly not what Karel Čapek intended. He used a very similar plot in the novel *Válka s mloky* (1936; *The War with the Newts*, 1937), in which the role played by Rossum's robots is played by a newly discovered race of intelligent animals. A novel that does feature marvelous machinery, *Továrna na absolutno* (1922; *The Absolute at Large*, 1927), proceeds in a rather different manner. It is true that Čapek was suspicious of the march of technology, but he was far more suspicious of the follies and mistaken ambitions of human beings, as can easily be seen in *Ze ivota hmyzu* (1920; *And So Infinitam: The Life of the Insects*, 1923), a satire he wrote with his brother Josef shortly after writing *R.U.R.*

R.U.R.'s primary target is the attitude of mind that Harry Domin represents: that human beings are—or ought to be—eager to be released from the burden of labor, for which they are in any case ill-adapted by virtue of their appetite for play and other diversions. Labor, according to Domin, ought instead to be done by beings specifically adapted to that task: beings without ambition or distraction and hence without rights to enable them to pursue ambitions or distractions. This description can far more readily be applied to the attitude of the leisured classes toward the servant classes, whose labor supports the leisured classes' lifestyle than it can to the relationship between humanity as a whole and machinery. The common view in Čapek's day—as exemplified by the imagery of *Metropolis*—was not that machines were slaves but rather that the majority of people were in the process of becoming slaves of machinery.

If *R.U.R.* is seen as a political allegory, Čapek's drama is a call for the recognition that those who are condemned to eternal labor actually have the same needs and desires as those who remain free, and a warning that willful blindness to those needs and desires will eventually provoke violent rebellion. Through the character of Alquist, the author adds to this proposal the further judgment that the leisured classes are mistaken in their assessment of their own needs, because people who do not labor at all are forsaking their own creativity; creativity is not expressed without work. Creativity, not idleness, is humanity's most precious possession.

The "souls" that Dr. Gall imports into the robots at Helena's request are metaphorical. What the robots are given is a means of feeling, not in the sense that emotions that were not there before are grafted on, but in the sense that a potential that was always there is now activated. While the robots remain robots (that is, laborers), however, this release of feeling can only be turned to destructive ends. Ironically, the rebellion of the robots is hardly necessary, given that their masters—having forsaken their creativity—ceased even to practice the most fundamental creative act of reproducing themselves. The world within the play gets twisted so far out of shape that a new beginning is required before a new order may be secured. That new beginning is—as, in Čapek's view, it must be—the rediscovery of the power of love by those whose feelings were previously channeled into hatred. It is the robots rather than their masters, according to Čapek, who retain this potential; Harry Domin's love for Helena and hers for him have been wasted in secret conflict.

Čapek was active in politics for a little while after the creation of Czechoslovakia in the wake of World War I, but he preferred to make use of his talents and energies as a writer. He did not survive to experience the country's annexation by Adolf Hitler, although his brother Josef died in a concentration camp. Answering critics, Čapek denied that his view of the world was entirely cynical and pessimistic, but such works as *R.U.R.* and *War with the Newts*—both of which feature the extinction of the human race—seem to some observers to undermine his denial. It is important to notice, however, that the "humans" who are swept away in these allegories are humans who lose sight of their own humanity, and that they are succeeded by other beings who discover the real meaning of "humanity" and therefore become human beings.

Seen in this light, Čapek's works–*R.U.R.* in particular—are certainly awful warnings, but they are not despairing.

After its fashion, *R.U.R.* seeks to help its audiences recover their authentic humanity which, as members of the leisured theatergoing classes, they may perhaps be in danger of losing.

"Critical Evaluation" by Brian Stableford

Further Reading

Bradbrook, Bohuslava R. *Karel Čapek: In Pursuit of Truth, Tolerance, and Trust.* Brighton, England: Sussex Academic Press, 1998. Comprehensive English-language account of Čapek's life and work. A lengthy treatment of *R.U.R.* is included in chapter 3, "The Dramatist."

Čapek, Karel. *Toward the Radical Center: A Karel Capek Reader.* Edited and introduced by Peter Kussi. Translated by Norma Comrada et al. Highland Park, N.J.: Catbird Press, 1990. Includes a brief but informative biography. Evaluates existing translations of Čapek's works and provides many new translations, including one of *R.U.R.* Discusses Čapek's philosophy, politics, and use of language.

Harkins, William Edward. *Karel Capek.* New York: Columbia University Press, 1962. Good introduction to *R.U.R.*, discussing the play's philosophy, artistic structure, theme, character, literary influences, and innovations in form.

King, Sharon D. "A Better Eve: Women and Robots in Capek's *R.U.R.* and Pavlovsky's *El Robot.*" In *Women in Theatre*, edited by James Redmond. New York: Cambridge University Press, 1989. Interesting, detailed analysis of the character of Helena, including discussion of the play's male-female roles and attitudes about childbirth and sterility.

Klíma, Ivan. *Karel Čapek: Life and Work. Translated by Norma Comrada.* North Haven, Conn.: Catbird Press, 2002. Klíma, a Czech novelist and scholar, provides a detailed account of Čapek's life and work. *R.U.R.* is discussed in the chapter entitled "The First Report on the End of Civilization: *R.U.R.*"

Matuska, Alexander. *Karel Capek: An Essay.* Translated by Cathryn Alan. London: Allen & Unwin, 1964. A clear introduction to Čapek's life and philosophy. Discusses *R.U.R.* as an analysis of human nature and of labor.

Schubert, Peter Z. *The Narratives of Čapek and Cexov: A Typological Comparison of the Authors' World Views.* Bethesda, Md.: International Scholars, 1997. Although this is a somewhat difficult work for beginning students, it proves valuable with its discussion of the themes of freedom, lack of communication, justice, and truth. There is also a separate section discussing critical views of Čapek and of his worldview. The comprehensive bibliography alone makes this a volume well worth consulting.

Wellek, Rene. *Essays on Czech Literature.* The Hague, the Netherlands: Mouton, 1963. Divides Čapek's writing into three periods, discussing changes in style and subject matter. Evaluates *R.U.R.*'s theatrical qualities, traces its popularity, and analyzes the play's emphasis on the dangers of mechanization.

Ruslan and Lyudmila

Author: Alexander Pushkin (1799-1837)
First published: Ruslan i Lyudmila, 1820 (English translation, 1936)
Type of work: Poetry
Type of plot: Mock epic
Time of plot: Late tenth century
Locale: Russia

Principal characters:
RUSLAN, a knight
LYUDMILA, Kievan princess, Ruslan's bride
CHERNOMOR, an evil sorcerer
THE FINN, a benevolent sorcerer
NAINA, a witch
ROGDAY,
FARLAF, and
RATMIR, Ruslan's rivals
VLADIMIR, prince of Kiev

The Poem:

As Vladimir and his warrior retinue feast in celebration of Lyudmila's marriage, the amorous bridegroom Ruslan plucks at his mustache and waits impatiently for the ceremonies to end. Just as uneasy are his rivals Rogday, Farlaf, and Ratmir, who sit brooding over their love for Lyudmila and their hatred of Ruslan. Finally the newlyweds retire to the bridal chamber, and soon only the rustle of discarded clothing and lovers' murmurs are to be heard—until suddenly, in a flash of lightning, a roll of thunder, and a puff of smoke, Lyudmila vanishes. A frustrated and puzzled Ruslan is left to explain the mysterious disappearance of his bride. Vladimir, prince of Kiev, blames Ruslan for failing to protect her and offers Lyudmila's still-virginal hand to whichever knight succeeds in bringing her back. Ruslan, Rogday, Farlaf, and Ratmir at once mount their horses and gallop off; they soon part ways.

A dejected Ruslan finds himself at the cave of the Finn, a serene old hermit who greets him by name. The Finn explains that it is the sorcerer Chernomor who has spirited Lyudmila away for his own lustful ends, but Ruslan need not fear—his bride will remain unharmed and he will get her back in the end. The Finn also tells Ruslan his own story of love and misplaced enchantment and warns that his old love Naina, now a witch, will turn her malice on him too. Ruslan, emboldened by hope, continues his quest.

Meanwhile, Rogday has decided to first do away with Ruslan and then pursue Lyudmila. After chasing down the cowardly Farlaf by mistake, then leaving in amused disgust, Rogday encounters an old woman who directs him further; this same old woman, promising that the girl will not escape, advises Farlaf to go home and bide his time.

Lyudmila awakens to find herself in Chernomor's castle, in a splendid chamber hung with precious brocades and redolent of incense. Wandering through the enchanted gardens outside the castle, utterly alone, she contemplates throwing herself from a bridge but thinks better of it; she also considers starving herself rather than eating the sumptuous dinner that is miraculously set before her, but in the end she eats. At nightfall, as she waits in terror to see what will befall her, the door to her bedchamber opens to reveal a procession of slaves carrying a long gray beard on pillows; at the end of the beard pompously strides Chernomor, the hunchbacked dwarf. Lyudmila leaps from the bed, snatches the dwarf's cap from his head, shakes her fist, and screams so deafeningly that the entire parade falls into confusion and Chernomor tangles himself in his own beard. The slaves then scoop him up and carry him off to untangle him.

Far away, after a bloody battle by moonlight, Ruslan manages to unhorse Rogday and hurl him into the river, where he is immediately pulled to the bottom by a mermaid. Lyudmila, meanwhile, discovers that wearing Chernomor's cap makes her invisible.

Ruslan, who has been disarmed in the struggle with Rogday, wanders gloomily among the ruins of an old battleground; although he finds himself a new mail shield and a new lance, he cannot find a proper sword. That same night he encounters an enormous helmeted head that he takes at first for a hill. After exchanging insults with the head, Ruslan strikes it, and it rolls away to reveal a magical sword. The enchanted head is that of Chernomor's giant brother, who has been betrayed by the dwarf. The head reveals Chernomor's secret—that all his magical power resides in his beard.

As Ruslan proceeds north, overcoming witches, giants, and various spirits, Ratmir is distracted from his pursuit of Lyudmila by a magical castle and twelve voluptuous maidens. Lyudmila teases her captors by leaving traces of her invisible presence, until Chernomor manages to trick her into showing herself by taking the form of Ruslan. As she falls into an enchanted swoon, Chernomor begins to paw her, but the sound of a horn interrupts him—Ruslan has arrived.

Chernomor flies to the attack, but Ruslan grabs the dwarf's beard and holds on as they soar over mountain, forest, and sea. Ruslan finally forces Chernomor back to the castle, where he cuts off the beard, packs the dwarf behind his saddle, and quickly finds Lyudmila. The voice of the Finn advises Ruslan to take the sleeping girl back to Kiev, where she will recover. On the way back, Ruslan meets his former rival Ratmir, now a fisherman leading an idyllic life with the young wife who wooed him away from the maidens. Naina, however, now leads treacherous Farlaf to the sleeping Ruslan's camp, where Farlaf runs the knight through with his sword and then carries Lyudmila off to Kiev to claim his prize. As Ruslan lies dying, the city waits for Lyudmila's enchantment to lift, but it does not. Meanwhile, a crisis is at hand—Kiev is under attack by the nomad raiders the Pechenegs.

The wise Finn then goes to a magical spring from which he fetches water of death to close Ruslan's wounds and water of life to restore him. Ruslan arrives in Kiev in time to rally the Kievans to defeat the Pechenegs, and he then revives Lyudmila. The city rejoices, Farlaf confesses and is pardoned, and the couple live happily ever.

Critical Evaluation:

When *Ruslan and Lyudmila* appeared in 1820, it caused a sensation in Russian literature. It also made young Alexander Pushkin's name and helped make Russian a literary language. Given the fact that Russia had had a written language—and writers—for centuries, that might seem an odd statement, but it was Pushkin whose work demonstrated the range and flexibility of contemporary Russian. Pushkin showed that the language could accommodate formal and informal diction alike, that it was an instrument that could be played in any number of styles.

With its victory over Napoleon Bonaparte, the Russian Empire was an indisputable military and political power on the European scene. Many Russian writers thought, however, that they did not yet have a culture, let alone a literary culture, of their own, and some of them consciously set about to create one. That meant that in Russia, Western literary movements such classicism, sentimentalism, and Romanticism—themselves, by the late eighteenth century, not so neatly divided—were all telescoped into a few decades. A question that faced Russian writers was whether western European literary models were the right models. The question of language was a question of cultural identity. The Slavophile camp looked nostalgically back to a mythic pre-Petrine Slavic past. The Westernizers favored adapting the western European literary legacy. In the arguments over the direction Russian literature was to take, Pushkin came down on the side of the Westernizers; *Ruslan and Lyudmila* was, in its own lighthearted way, a blow to the cause of the Slavophiles. Who, after this brilliant mock epic, could possibly write a serious Slavic epic?

For all its nearly three thousand lines, its six cantos plus an epilogue, the poem moves along at a sprightly, dancing pace. Pushkin's choice of iambic tetrameter, a relatively short line, is one reason for this. Another is Pushkin's particular genius at varying his rhyme scheme to advance or retard the movement. The basic verse form of the poem is an alternating quatrain (*abab*), but Pushkin also uses enveloping rhyme (*abba*), occasional couplets, and a five- or six-line unit. Add to that the fact that all Russian words, long or short, have only one accent (unlike English, which has primary and secondary accents on longer words), and the result is that even very formal poetry in Russian is less likely to have the monotonous, jingling quality of serious English poetry at its worst. Pushkin has a pattern at work, but it is a fluid and shifting one that corresponds to changes in action or narrative tone.

Pushkin seems to have borrowed from everyone, from high literature and low, in writing the poem. Russian folktales, songs, epics, and works of popular literature have their influence, as does, for example, Ludovico Ariosto's *Orlando furioso* (1516, 1521, 1532; English translation, 1591), yet *Ruslan and Lyudmila* is a work of dazzling originality, a piece that is at home in the Western tradition and at the same time is unmistakably Russian. On one hand, Pushkin draws on native Russian sources that tell of an exotic, heroic, even barbarous past. Vladimir did rule in Kiev and Novgorod in the late tenth century, and the grim battlefield where Ruslan rummages among the bones of long-dead warriors recalls a famous passage from Russian chronicles. A warrior named Rokhday is listed as a guest at one of Vladimir's famous feasts. The name Ruslan comes from historical sources.

Finns were famed as sorcerers in those times. The magic cap, the "living water" and the "dead water," and the enchanted head all appear in folktale and epic. Furthermore, in the 1828 edition, Pushkin added a prologue straight out of the folktale tradition:

> There is a green oak by the bay,
> And on that oak a golden chain,
> And day and night a learned cat
> On that chain length paces round.

Like a storyteller closing the circle in traditional fashion, he ends the poem with the same words that end his prologue.

Despite all this, there is no direct plot link connecting *Ruslan and Lyudmila* with the Russian folk epics. Such epics involve trials undertaken by pure-hearted knights seeking to rescue virtuous maidens. These epics, ironically, come straight out of Western chivalric romance, not out of Russian tradition.

Pushkin's audience was made up of the young women and men of the St. Petersburg salons, to whom the poem's playful combination of innocence, eroticism, and wit would certainly appeal. Lyudmila's charm and common sense have more to do with nineteenth century sensibility than with tenth century mores. The narrator might as well be talking about a young lady of his acquaintance. Ruslan and Ratmir's encounter provides another example; Ruslan greets his former rival as "dear prince" and continues to chat as if they had just seen each other at the theater the week before. The narrator undercuts Ruslan's sense of injured honor and manhood—which in the traditional epic was grounds for war—by comparing Ruslan's feelings to those of a rooster whose favorite hen has just been snatched away by a passing vulture. This and other digressions give the poem a casual, insouciant tone that prevents the reader from taking seriously any of what otherwise might be serious or even tragic themes—sorcery, betrayal, abduction, and murder. This tone has also prevented many scholars from assigning too much weight to Pushkin's most buoyant and fanciful work.

Jane Ann Miller

Further Reading

Bayley, John. *Pushkin: A Comparative Commentary*. New York: Cambridge University Press, 1971. Devotes a number of pages to *Ruslan and Lyudmila* and its impact. Discusses the poem in the context of Pushkin's later fairy tales in verse.

Bethea, David M. *Realizing Metaphors: Alexander Pushkin*

and the Life of the Poet. Madison: University of Wisconsin Press, 1998. Describes the relationship between Pushkin's life and his art and discusses why, more than two hundred years after the poet's birth, his work remains relevant. Includes index and illustrations.

Binyon, T. J. *Pushkin: A Biography*. New York: Knopf, 2004. Prizewinning biography chronicles Pushkin's literary success alongside his personal failures. Describes how the writer included small pieces of his life in his novel *Evgeny Onegin* (1825-1832, 1833; *Eugene Onegin*, 1881) and other works.

Briggs, A. D. P. *Alexander Pushkin: A Critical Study*. New York: Barnes & Noble, 1983. Provides an excellent introduction to Pushkin's work. Especially valuable for an explanation of the formal aspects of Pushkin's poetry aimed at readers who do not speak Russian.

Kahn, Andrew, ed. *The Cambridge Companion to Pushkin*. New York: Cambridge University Press, 2006. Collection of essays by Pushkin scholars offers discussion of the writer's life and his works in various genres. Topics addressed include politics and history in Pushkin's work and Pushkin's position as an author in Soviet and post-Soviet culture.

O'Bell, Leslie. "Young Pushkin: *Ruslan and Liudmila* in Its Lyric Context." *Russian Review* 44, no. 2 (April, 1985): 139-155. Discusses the poem in light of Pushkin's earlier lyrics and takes issue with the common critical evaluation of the poem as sparkling entertainment but less-than-profound poetry.

Pushkin, Alexander. "Ruslan and Lyudmila." In *Collected Narrative and Lyrical Poetry*. Translated by Walter Arndt. Ann Arbor, Mich.: Ardis, 1984. Examines Pushkin's sources for the poem, with special attention to the vogue for gothic tales and translated ballads. Discusses contemporary reaction to the poem.

Vickery, Walter. *Alexander Pushkin Revisited*. Rev. ed. New York: Maxwell Macmillan International, 1992. The chapter "Early Verse and *Ruslan and Lyudmila*" analyzes the poem and gives a good overview of the state of Russian literature when Pushkin entered the scene.

S

The Sacred Fount

Author: Henry James (1843-1916)
First published: 1901
Type of work: Novel
Type of plot: Psychological realism
Time of plot: 1890's
Locale: Newmarch, England

Principal characters:
THE NARRATOR
GILBERT LONG and GUY BRISSENDEN, former
  acquaintances of the narrator
GRACE BRISSENDEN or MRS. BRISS, Guy Brissenden's wife,
FORD OBERT, a painter,
MRS. MAY SERVER and LADY JOHN, houseguests at
  Newmarch

The Story:

The nameless narrator encounters two former acquaintances, Gilbert Long and Grace Brissenden, both of whom are also going to the party at Newmarch, and both of whom appear considerably changed to the narrator. Long, who previously struck the narrator as a handsome clod, seems suddenly to have become clever, and Mrs. Brissenden, who is supposedly at least forty, seems to have grown younger or at least not to have aged. In conversation with Mrs. Briss, as she is called, the narrator receives the idea for what is to become his theory, that Long's intellectual improvement is the result of his having entered into a relationship with a clever woman, identified by Mrs. Briss as Lady John, another guest at Newmarch. Lady John is coming on a later train with Guy Brissenden, her screen, as that gentleman's wife intimates, for her affair with Long.

Arriving at the party, the narrator fails, just as he initially failed to recognize Mrs. Briss, to recognize Guy, who, although only in his late twenties, looks older now than his wife. Guy appears, in fact, "quite sixty." This discovery completes the narrator's theory that as one party to a relationship gains, either physically or intellectually, the other loses, is drained by the "sacrificer" until quite depleted. The narrator communicates this theory to Ford Obert, who assumes Mrs. Briss to be considerably younger than her husband.

The narrator attempts to corroborate his theory. His discovery that Lady John is as witty and superficial as ever leads him to reject her, in a conversation with Mrs. Briss, as Long's "victim," for the partner to such a relationship will of necessity lack her former attributes. At this juncture, the two conspirators discovers in colloquy two figures who prove to be Guy and May Server, the latter presumably using Guy as a screen, just as Lady John was formerly said to have done. Mrs. Briss happily proves to be the very woman for whom they are looking to serve as the replacement for the now unacceptable Lady John. Mrs. Server is "all over the place," flitting from man to man in an attempt to mask the loss of her faculties, or so Mrs. Briss confides to the narrator in their next interview. Her description tallies remarkably with that given the narrator by Obert, who sees Mrs. Server greatly changed from the self-possessed woman she was when she sat for him to have her portrait painted. By this time, the narrator, on the grounds of both Mrs. Briss's and Obert's testimony and of an encounter with Mrs. Server herself, comes around to accepting Mrs. Briss's account, but his tender feeling for Mrs. Server, his sense that he and his collaborator are poking into a matter that is none of their business, and perhaps also his pique that Mrs. Briss is beating him at his own game, prevents him from acknowledging to her fully the degree of conviction to which she brings him.

The amount of data with which the narrator is confronted becomes prodigious, but the theory expands to accommodate all of it: Lady John makes up to Guy to conceal the fact that she is in love with Long; Mrs. Server's single appearance with Long (the point is actually made by Mrs. Briss) is the exception that proves the rule; Mrs. Server's avoidance of the narrator, out of all the men at the party, indicates her awareness that he is on to her predicament. (It never strikes him that she could find his inquisitiveness obnoxious.) Mrs. Server's frequent juxtaposition with Guy is less Mrs. Briss's postulated screen than the mutual tacit commiseration of the two victims, each conscious of the other's depletion. (The narrator's hypothesis is that victims know of their condition while victimizers do not.) A conversation with Guy, who tells the narrator that Mrs. Server has nothing to say and who confesses a certain terror of and yet fascination with her, confirms the narrator's view of their condition and mutual relation—although Guy's confusion might as easily have been sincere, and Mrs. Server's evidently morbid state could not be attributable to the loss of her three children. Guy, however, can be covering an actual affair that he is having with Mrs. Server. Next, the narrator himself engages in talk with Mrs. Server, hinting in a veiled manner at her relation with Guy and gleaning that she took comfort in his awareness of her plight and his tolerant sympathy. Mrs. Server's participation in the dialogue was, however, so vague and so slight that in "truth" she gave evidence of everything or nothing. Lady John then confronts the narrator with the fact that his super-subtlety and his passion for reading meanings into everything put the rest of the company in great upset, and she chastises him for sending Guy off to Mrs. Server when it is perfectly obvious to everyone the loathing that she inspires in him. The narrator, in an elaborate subterfuge, attempts to convince Lady John that as long as Long is in love with her and he himself with Mrs. Server, she ought to relinquish Guy so that the narrator might at least have the pleasure of seeing the woman he loves, Mrs. Server, get the man she loves, Guy. Their conversation is halted when they see Mrs. Briss and Long deep in talk, a fact that leads the narrator to speculate that Lady John benightedly and jealously conceives a liaison between the two, whereas he, by dint of his "superior wisdom," knows them now to come to a knowledge, and by the very agency of his inquiries, of their "bloated" or victimizing conditions, and to be joining together for mutual protection. As their talk ends, Mrs. Briss approaches him and briefly informs him that she wishes to speak to him later in the evening, after the other guests retire.

The narrator's theory begins to crumble. First, Obert appears to inform him that Mrs. Server is no longer in her drained condition and that the man, whoever he is, is out of the question, since she gave him up. To top this blow, Mrs. Briss arrives to demolish what is left of the narrator's theory. There is nothing in what he says, she informs him, and she speculates along his lines only while under his spell. Mrs. Server is not the woman because there is no woman. Long, as her conversation with him amply testifies, is as stupid as he ever has been. As a matter of fact, he and Lady John are lovers, a fact that squares perfectly with his theory because she is

not drained (there being very little to drain) or he improved. Moreover, she has it from Guy that Lady John and Long are intimate. What the narrator thinks he sees is simply his insanity. Finally, to clinch her argument, to explain, in fact, her wriggling and self-contradiction throughout the course of the interview, Mrs. Server is not using Guy as a screen; she is—and this from Guy's own lips—making love to him. In addition, Mrs. Server is sharply perceptive. At the narrator's amazed gasp, Mrs. Briss asks if that is not the very thing he maintains. She then tells him he is crazy and bids him good night. The narrator can only wanly observe that she has the last word.

Clearly disinvited, he will have to leave. The facts toward which the narrator works, then, are finally unknowable. Whether Mrs. Briss is telling the truth at the end, lying in collusion with Long to protect their status, or attempting to shield the fact that she is actually carrying on an affair with Long, cannot be resolved. The theory, it seems, rests on the unstable base of the narrator's ego.

Critical Evaluation:

Critical interest in *The Sacred Fount* centers on the credibility of the inquisitive and sometimes intrusive unnamed narrator who tells the story of a weekend gathering at an English country manor. From his perspective, the guests who gather at Newmarch all have hidden lives, and he is determined to discover the truth about them. He is particularly obsessed with determining how Grace Brissenden grew younger as a result of her marriage, while her husband seems to have withered. Equally intriguing to him is the fact that the same pattern seems to have affected two other characters who are not supposed to be attached in any way: Gilbert Long, who suddenly becomes interesting and exciting after being considered a dullard for years, and May Server, once a vibrant creature but now exhausted and near the point of a breakdown. The qualities of such relationships intrigue the narrator, and he spends all of his time concocting theories about romantic relationships (including a number of illicit affairs among the various characters) that can account for the changes he observes. The narrator commits himself to discover "the sacred fount," that source of inspiration from which people such as Mrs. Brissenden and Long draw their power.

Viewed in this fashion, the novel is a kind of detective story in which the narrator serves as the sleuth. The problem, however, is not so simple as who did it. Far from being the insightful Sherlockian figure of typical detective fictions, Henry James's narrator often finds himself making assumptions that are not shared by others. In fact, as he learns at the end of the story, his conclusions about a number of characters are off the mark, assuming that Mrs. Brissenden's final indictment is to be believed. Whether she is simply setting the narrator straight so that he will quit his meddling, or creating an elaborate fiction to preserve the reputations of the party at Newmarch, is also not clear. The narrator in *The Sacred Fount* is either a perceptive observer of society, capable of detecting meaning and motive in the slightest gesture, or a hopelessly deluded intruder whose incessant pursuit of evil wrecks the lives of those he believes he is protecting. *The Sacred Fount* does not reward the reader with the certainties of detective fiction, in which the truth is discovered. Rather, *The Sacred Fount* is a lesson on the inability of one mind to know the truth. Critical opinion about the narrator has been divided. Some have seen James's narrator as a sensible, sensitive figure who reveals the sordid details of the lives of people who are supposedly respectable. If this is who the narrator is, then he is a speaker through whom James is satirizing the British upper classes. Other critics, however, have suggested that the narrator is completely untrustworthy, even to the point of being insane. His intrusions and wild speculations lead to nothing but trouble, and his expulsion from Newmarch at the end of the novel is fit punishment for someone who is no better than the snake in Paradise.

The novelist does not make it easy for readers to determine which view to take. Like many of James's later novels, *The Sacred Fount* is obscure and difficult to read. The writer's decision to maintain the point of view inside the consciousness of a narrator who is himself not clear about the implications of what he sees going on around him, and who is prone to find sinister meaning in even the most innocent or the most innocuous word or gesture, leads some readers almost to despair. James relies on this obscurity to create the effect he wishes to produce on his readers. It suggests the opacity of humanity, attempting to glimpse what lies beneath the surface statements, movements, gestures, and actions that characterize the observed lives of others. No one, James asserts, can really know for sure what another human being is really like, because the outward signs of behavior are often masks deliberately constructed to hide the true feelings and motivations of men and women who do not wish to reveal themselves as they really are.

The issue is not only social but also epistemological: If James is right in his view of human nature, then human existence is solipsistic, and no person can ever really know another. Far from being a distraction, then, the obscurity created by the novelist—the work's "inaccessibility," to use critic R. P. Blackmur's term—is the work's greatest strength. In this case, technique reinforces theme.

The lesson of the novel is not simply epistemological, however; the work is also a cautionary tale about the limits of fiction. As he illustrates in other works as well as this one, James believes that the function of the novelist is much like that of the narrator in *The Sacred Fount*: to penetrate the layers of opacity that obscure a person's true self to lay bare human personality in all its complexities. Such examinations are fraught with danger, since the act of revelation can invade not only the privacy of individuals on a social level but also the psychological integrity of individuals subjected to such scrutiny. How successful a novelist can be in revealing human character without violating the integrity of those portrayed or misrepresenting them is one of the key questions addressed in this haunting and perplexing tale.

Laurence W. Mazzeno

Further Reading

Blackall, Jean Frantz. *Jamesian Ambiguity and "The Sacred Fount."* Ithaca, N.Y.: Cornell University Press, 1965. Uses the novel as the principal example to illustrate James's handling of ambiguity in his fiction. Blackall calls the novel an "intellectual detective story" in which the reader, not the narrator, is cast in the role of the detective, tasked to determine where truth lies in this complex tale of social relationships.

Coulson, Victoria. *Henry James, Women, and Realism.* New York: Cambridge University Press, 2007. Examines James's important friendships with three women: his sister Alice James, and the novelists Constance Fenimore Woolson and Edith Wharton. These three women writers and James shared what Coulson describes as an "ambivalent realism," or a cultural ambivalence about gender identity, and she examines how this idea is manifest in James's works, including *The Sacred Fount*.

Freedman, Jonathan, ed. *The Cambridge Companion to Henry James.* New York: Cambridge University Press, 1998. A collection of essays that provides extensive information on James's life and literary influences and describes his works and the characters in them.

Gargano, James W., ed. *Critical Essays on Henry James: The Late Novels.* Boston: G. K. Hall, 1987. Includes excerpts from three reviews by James's contemporaries as well as a twentieth century essay justifying the novelist's narrative method and defending the sanity of the narrator.

Hutchinson, Hazel. "The Unapproachable Face: Difference in *The Sacred Fount*." In *Seeing and Believing: Henry James and the Spiritual World.* New York: Palgrave Macmillan, 2006. Describes how *The Sacred Fount* and some of James's other works reflect the Victorian-era theological debate over Darwinism.

Jones, Granville H. *Henry James's Psychology of Experience: Innocence, Responsibility, and Renunciation in the Fiction of Henry James*. Hawthorne, N.Y.: Mouton, 1975. Psychological analysis of James's major fiction. Includes an extensive discussion of the narrator's role in *The Sacred Fount* and provides useful commentary from earlier critics of the novelist's complex method of presenting his story.

Kappeler, Susanne. *Writing and Reading in Henry James*. New York: Columbia University Press, 1980. A major section of this study is devoted to an examination of *The Sacred Fount*. Kappeler explores the function of the narrator, who serves not only to record but also to interpret experience; she claims that James breaks down traditional barriers between writer, critic, and reader.

Sicker, Philip. *Love and the Quest for Identity in the Fiction of Henry James*. Princeton, N.J.: Princeton University Press, 1980. Concentrates on the psychological dimensions of the novel. Believes the source of the ambiguity lies in James's "presentation of two differing views of identity." Discusses the role of the narrator. Claims the novel reveals James's vision of love in human relationships.

The Sacred Hoop
Recovering the Feminine in American Indian Traditions

Author: Paula Gunn Allen (1939-2008)
First published: 1986; revised, 1992
Type of work: Literary theory and social criticism

Paula Gunn Allen's *The Sacred Hoop* is a landmark work both in American Indian studies and in literary theory. Allen posits, with ample documentation from the written and oral histories of white Americans as well as of American Indians, that many indigenous beliefs and traditions had been either suppressed or altered by the conquering phallocentric culture of Euro-Americans. She argues that Euro-Americans have not respected or even recognized the "gynocratic" nature of many indigenous American cultures, in which women held positions of tribal leadership.

Allen's authority as a literary critic began with her participation in the landmark 1977 curriculum-development seminar on American Indian studies at Northern Arizona University (sponsored by the Modern Language Association of America, or MLA). In the years that followed this seminar, there was an overwhelming demand for notes and handouts from the gathering. Allen compiled materials from the seminar and edited the collection *Studies in American Indian Literature: Critical Essays and Course Designs* (1983), which laid the foundation for the study of American Indian literature. While pursuing parallel careers as a poet and novelist, Allen completed her next work of literary criticism, *The Sacred Hoop*. The book merits the attention and acclaim it has received.

In *The Sacred Hoop*'s introductory chapter, Allen outlines seven essential themes or issues that are critical to her work: Indians and spirits are always found together; Indians endure; traditional tribal lifestyles are usually gynocratic; the physical and cultural genocide of American Indian tribes was due mostly to a patriarchal fear of gynocracy; the definition of American Indian literature necessarily includes both traditional literature and the genre literature of the present; Western studies of American Indian tribal systems are culturally biased and essentially erroneous because of a predilection to "discount, degrade or conceal gynocratic features or recontextualize those features so that they will appear patriarchal"; and the sacred, ritual ways of American Indian peoples are similar to sacred cultures elsewhere on the planet. Although most of these assumptions have been accepted by many contemporary artists and critics working within American Indian studies, Allen's gender-specific premises, on the other hand, have at times been met with polemics rather than collaboration and learning.

In "The Ways of Our Grandmothers," the first section of the text, Allen establishes the context and poetics of her gynocratic Indian perspective. In two essays she sequentially describes the mythic and cosmogonic female traditions of Indian America in general and the Keresan people of Laguna

Pueblo in particular, the historical influence of European culture—after contact—on matriarchal Indian societies. A third essay is a personal chronicle that provides a human illustration of a representative life. Furthermore, Allen essentially teaches Keresan cosmogony and cosmology as she introduces Ts'its'tsi'nako (Thought Woman) as the prime mover and informing spirit of the universe.

> She [Thought Woman] is the Old Woman who tends the fires of life. She is the Old Woman Spider who weaves us together in a fabric of interconnection. . . . [W]e endure into the present, alive, certain of our significance, certain of her centrality, her identity as the Sacred Hoop of Be-ing.

The primary potency is, therefore, female. Allen assumes an interpretive perspective that considers gender to be essential to the tradition, not marginal. She laments the demise of pre-contact Indian cultures that had healthy, collaborative, peace-centered, and ritual-oriented systems that also were female-centered. The status of women had declined, Allen argues, because the dominant and encroaching Euro-American culture considered matriarchy to be a system that societies grew out of as they matured and became more complex.

"The Word Warriors" section includes eight essays examining myth and vision in Indian literature. "The Sacred Hoop: A Contemporary Perspective" helped solidify Allen's reputation as an exemplary teacher and facilitator of a then-new ethnic American literature that demanded interpretive apparatus different from that used in other areas of the white American curriculum. Allen writes, for example, that Indian literature springs from a knowledge that all people can experience sincere and deep emotion, so, therefore, art can celebrate sincerity and deep emotion without reference to a sole individual. Contemporary American Indian literature, she argues, should have its value and significance "determined by its relation to creative empowerment, its reflection of tribal understandings, and its relation to the unitary nature of reality."

Aware of her status as an academic Kochinnenako (Yellow Woman), a role model of sorts, Allen introduces five American Indian poets, all women, in her essay "The Wilderness In My Blood: Spiritual Foundations of the Poetry of Five American Indian Women." Secured as part of the multicultural canon was Joy Harjo, Linda Hogan, Mary TallMountain, Wendy Rose, and Carol Lee Sanchez. During a period in which Leslie Marmon Silko's remarkable novel *Ceremony* (1977) became one of the most widely taught texts on American college and university campuses, Allen's essay on Silko's novel provided teachers at all educational levels with a close reading of one of the controlling features of *Ceremony*. The essay affected the novel's reputation, and related discussions, for decades to follow.

The section "Pushing Up the Sky" includes the essay "Angry Women Are Building: Issues and Struggles Facing American Indian Women Today," in which she helps to set the agenda for and the future direction of American Indian literature and women's studies. "Gynosophy" is the term Allen uses to describe her American Indian feminist perspective. In "Red Roots of White Feminism" she documents instances of tribal tolerance, if not celebration, of gay and lesbian individuals that persisted until the time of contact and colonization. Women's leadership roles were reduced or eliminated, and new expectations for social community had been imposed.

In the essay "Stealing the Thunder: Future Visions for American Indian Women, Tribes, and Literary Studies," Allen asserts that she is committed to "putting women at the center of the tribal universe." She also hopes the contemporary idea of the American Indian "will shift from warrior/brave/hunter/chief to grandmother/mother/Peacemaker/farmer."

With *The Sacred Hoop*, Allen has secured her place as a pioneer in ethnic literature, literary theory, women's studies, and American Indian studies. Even after her death in 2008, her reputation as a critic and her achievements as a poet and novelist have not waned. Her opinions continue to matter to readers, teachers and scholars, and students.

Richard Sax

Further Reading

Allen, Paula Gunn. *Grandmothers of the Light: A Medicine Woman's Sourcebook*. Boston: Beacon Press, 1991. A collection of Allen's essays and traditional tales. A good source for understanding Allen's overall philosophy and worldview.

_____. *Studies in American Indian Literature: Critical Essays and Course Designs*. New York: Modern Language Association of America, 1983. This text, in addition to setting the foundation for studies of American Indian literature in academe, served as a template for professors, most of whom were new to the field. Includes multiple course designs, essays, and study and teaching resources.

Lincoln, Kenneth. *Native American Renaissance*. 1985. Reprint. Berkeley: University of California Press, 1992. Insights into the texts and contexts of American Indian poets and prose writers of the 1980's who constituted a flourishing new generation of Indian literary artists writing in English. Much of chapter 8, "The New Day Indi'ns," includes discussion of Allen's early work, namely her poetry.

Mihesuah, Devon, ed. *Natives and Academics: Researching and Writing About American Indians.* Lincoln: University of Nebraska Press, 1998. Essays by twelve American Indian scholars and artists, including "Special Problems in Teaching Leslie Marmon Silko's *Ceremony*" by Allen, that examines topics and concerns that overlap with those in *The Sacred Hoop.*

Pulitano, Elvira. *Toward a Native American Critical Theory.* Lincoln: University of Nebraska Press, 2003. The first book-length study of the foundations of a distinctive American Indian critical theory. Pulitano examines "the theoretical underpinnings" of this critical theory, including the writings of Allen. Features the chapter "Back to a Woman-Centered Universe: The Gynosophical Perspective of Paula Gunn Allen's Critical Narrative." For advanced readers.

Warrior, Robert Allen. *Tribal Secrets: Recovering American Indian Intellectual Traditions.* Minneapolis: University of Minnesota Press, 1995. In this study of American Indian intellectuals, including Vine Deloria, Jr., and John Joseph Mathews, Warrior creates a framework for a contemporary and interdisciplinary Indian studies. Includes references to Allen's literary criticism and reviews.

The Saga of Grettir the Strong

Author: Unknown
First transcribed: Grettis Saga, c. 1300 (English translation, 1869)
Type of work: Folklore
Type of plot: Adventure
Time of plot: Eleventh century
Locale: Iceland, Norway, and Constantinople

Principal characters:
GRETTIR THE STRONG, an outlaw
ASMUND LONGHAIR, his father
ILLUGI, his youngest brother
THORBJORN OXMAIN, Grettir's enemy
THORBJORN SLOWCOACH, Oxmain's kinsman, killed by Grettir
THORIR OF GARD, an Icelandic chief
THORBJORN ANGLE, Grettir's slayer
THORSTEINN DROMUND, Grettir's half brother and avenger

The Story:

Grettir the strong is descended from Onund, a Viking famed for enemies killed in war and the taking of booty from towns plundered on far sea raids. In a battle at Hafrsfjord, Onund loses a leg and is thereafter known as Onund Treefoot. His wife is Aesa, the daughter of Ofeig. Thrand, a great hero, is his companion in arms. During a time of great trouble in Norway, the two heroes sail to Iceland to be free of injustice in their homeland, where the unscrupulous can rob without fear of redress. Onund lives in quiet and plenty in the new land, and his name becomes renowned, for he is valiant. At last he dies. His sons fight after his death, and his lands are divided.

Grettir of the line of Onund is born at Biarg. As a child he shows strange intelligence. He quarrels constantly with Asmund Longhair, his father, and he is very lazy, never doing anything cheerfully or without urging. When he is fourteen years old, grown big in body, he kills Skeggi in a quarrel over a provision bag that falls from his horse, and for that deed his father pays blood money to the kinsmen of Skeggi. Then the Lawman declares that he must leave Iceland for three years. In that way the long outlawry of Grettir begins.

Grettir sets sail for Norway. The ship is wrecked on rocks off the Norwegian coast, but all get safely ashore on land that belongs to Thorfinn, a wealthy landsman of the district. Grettir makes his home with him for a time. At Yuletide, Thorfinn, with most of his household, goes to a merrymaking and leaves Grettir to look after the farm. In Thorfinn's absence, a party of berserks, or raiders, led by Thorir and Ogmund, come to rob and lay waste to the district. Grettir tricks them by locking them in a storehouse. When they break through the wooden walls, Grettir, armed with sword and spear, kills Thorir and Ogmund and puts the rest to flight.

Sometime before this adventure, he entered the tomb of Karr-the-Old, father of Thorfinn, a long-dead chieftain who guarded a hidden treasure. For his brave deed in killing the berserks, Thorfinn gives him an ancient sword from the treasure hoard of Karr-the-Old.

Next Grettir kills a great bear that was carrying off the sheep. In doing so he incurs the wrath of Bjorn, who is jealous of Grettir's strength and bravery. Then Grettir kills Bjorn and is summoned before Jarl Sveinn. Friends of Bjorn plot to take Grettir's life. After he kills two of his enemies, his friends save him from the wrath of the jarl, who wishes to banish him. His term of outlawry ends, Grettir sails back to Iceland in the spring.

At this time in Iceland, young Thorgils Maksson, Asmund's kinsman, is slain in a quarrel over a whale, and Asmund takes up the feud against those who killed him. The murderers are banished.

When Grettir returns, Asmund gives him the welcome that is his due because of his fame as a brave hero. Shortly after his return, Grettir battles with some men after a horse fight. The struggle is halted by a man named Thorbjorn Oxmain. The feud would be forgotten if Thorbjorn Oxmain's kinsman, Thorbjorn Slowcoach, did not sneer at the hero.

Word comes that a fiend took possession of the corpse of Glam, a shepherd. At night Glam ravages the countryside. He can find no man with whom he can prove his strength, so Grettir goes to meet Glam. They struggle in the house of Thorhall and rip down beams and rafters in their angry might. At last Glam falls exhausted. Defeated, he predicts that Grettir will have no greater strength and less honor in arms from that day on and that he will grow afraid of the dark. Grettir cuts off Glam's head and burns the body to destroy the evil spirit that possesses the dead shepherd.

Grettir decides to return to Norway. Among the passengers on the boat is Thorbjorn Slowcoach; they fight, and Grettir kills his foe. The travelers land on a barren shore where they are without fire to warm themselves, and Grettir swims across the cove to get burning brands at an inn where the sons of Thorir of Gard, an Icelandic chieftain, are holding a drunken feast. He has to fight to get the fire he wants; in the struggle, hot coals set fire to the straw on the inn floor and the house burns. Charged with deliberately setting fire to the inn and burning those within, Grettir goes to lay the matter before the king. To prove his innocence of the charge of willful burning, he is sentenced to undergo trial by fire in the church, but the ordeal ends when Grettir becomes angry and throws a bystander into the air. The king then banishes him from Norway, but because no ships can sail to Iceland before the spring, Grettir is allowed to remain in the country that winter.

He lives some time with a man named Einar, on a lonely farm to which comes the berserk Snaekoll, a wild man who pretends great frenzy during his lawless raids. Grettir seizes him in his mad fit and kills the robber with his own sword. Grettir falls in love with Einar's beautiful daughter, but he knows that Einar will never give his child to a man of Grettir's reputation. Giving up his suit, he goes to stay with his half brother, Thorsteinn Dromund. They are men of the same blood, and Thorsteinn swears to avenge Grettir if he is ever killed.

Grettir's father Asmund dies. On his deathbed he says that little good will come of his son. Grettir's time of bad luck in Iceland begins. Thorbjorn Oxmain kills Atli, Grettir's brother, in revenge for the slaying of Thorbjorn Slowcoach, and Thorir of Gard, hearing that his sons were killed in the burning of the inn, charges Grettir with their murder before the court of the Althing. By the time Grettir returns, he is proclaimed an outlaw throughout Iceland. He has little worry over his outlawry from the inn burning. Determined to avenge his brother, he goes alone to Thorbjorn Oxmain's farm and kills both the man and his son. Grettir's mother is delighted with his deed, but she predicts that Grettir will not live freely to enjoy his victory. Thorir of Gard and Thorodd, Thorbjorn Oxmain's kinsman, each put a price of three silver marks upon his head. Soon afterward Grettir is captured by some farmers, but he is released by a wise woman named Thorbjorg.

Avoided by most of his former friends, who will no longer help him, Grettir goes far north to find a place to live. In the forest, he meets another outlaw named Grim, but a short time later, he is forced to kill his companion because Grim intends to kill Grettir for the reward. About that time there is a fear of the dark growing upon Grettir, as Glam prophesied. Thorir of Gard hires Redbeard, another outlaw, to kill Grettir, but Grettir discovers the outlaw's plans and kills him instead. At last Grettir realizes that he cannot take any forest men into his trust, and yet he is afraid to live alone because of his fear of the dark.

Thorir of Gard attacks Grettir with eighty men, but the outlaw is able to hold them off for a time. Unknown to him, a friend named Hallmund attacks Thorir's men from the rear, and the attempt to capture Grettir fails. Nevertheless, Grettir can not stay long in any place, for all men turn against him. Hallmund is treacherously slain for the aid he gave Grettir; as he dies, he hopes that the outlaw will avenge his death.

One night a troll woman attacks a traveler named Gest in the room where he lies sleeping. They struggle all night, but at last Gest is able to cut off the monster's right arm. Then Gest reveals himself as Grettir. Steinvor of Sandhauger gives birth to a boy whom many call Grettir's son, but he dies when he is seventeen years old and leaves no personal saga.

Thorodd then tries to gain favor by killing Grettir, but the outlaw soon overcomes him and refuses to kill his enemy. Grettir goes north once more, but his fear of the dark increases so that he can no longer live alone, even to save his life. At last, with his youngest brother, Illugi, and a servant, he settles on Drangey, an island that has no inlet so that men have to climb to its grassy summit by rope ladders. There Grettir, who was an outlaw for some sixteen years, is safe for a time, because no one can climb the steep cliffs to attack him. For several years he and his companions live on the sheep that were put there to graze and on eggs and birds. His enemies try in vain to lure him from the island. At last an old woman puts magic runes upon a piece of driftwood that floats to the island. When Grettir attempts to chop the log, his ax slips, gashing his leg. He feels that his end is near, for the wound becomes swollen and painful.

Thorbjorn Angle, who paid the old woman to cast a spell upon the firewood, leads an attack upon the island while Grettir lies near death. Grettir is already dying when he strikes his last blows at his enemies. Illugi and the servant die with him. After Thorbjorn cuts off Grettir's head as proof of the outlaw's death, Steinn the Lawman decrees that the murderer cut off the head of a man already dead and that he cannot collect the reward because he used witchcraft to overcome Grettir. Outlawed for his deed, Thorbjorn goes to Constantinople, where he enlists in the emperor's guard. There Thorsteinn Dromund follows him and cuts off the murderer's head with a sword Grettir took years before from the treasure hoard of Karr-the-Old.

Critical Evaluation:

There are several types of sagas: family sagas, legendary sagas, and sagas of notable individuals. *The Saga of Grettir the Strong* is one of the longest, and possibly the best known of the third category. It is also one of the last of the great sagas, by an author thoroughly familiar with the saga tradition. He makes reference to earlier sagas throughout the work. Grettir's story is semihistorical; locations are nearly all identifiable, and many characters also appear in other sagas. The overall feel is realistic, in spite of a number of supernatural beings and events. These may seem highly improbable to the modern reader, but the direction of the story is determined by Grettir's character, not by the specific incidents, and these are all revealing of his nature, whether natural or supernatural.

The Saga of Grettir the Strong begins with Grettir's ancestors. This section takes up thirteen of the ninety-three chapters and centers on Grettir's great-grandfather Onund Tree-Foot. Onund is a Viking of the heathen era, who loses a leg during a turbulent and violent career. In old age he exchanges a good farm in Norway for the harsh climate of Iceland to escape the repressive rule of Harald Hairfair, the first king of Norway. Grettir is much like his ancestor, and even more violent and unruly, but he has no Iceland to which to escape. The Viking era is dying, and Christianity conquered the North. Grettir is an anachronism in a world becoming ever more settled and civilized.

The author is a master of characterization. One sees Grettir's cruelty and his impatience with authority and routine in his childhood rebellion against his father, especially when he mutilates the favorite horse he is assigned to tend. It is not only rebellion against his father but also impatience with the horse's leisurely grazing while Grettir waits in the cold. He is not always the instigator, but he seldom makes a situation better, and he insists upon satisfying his honor even when he has every reason to accept an offer of peace. Grettir's behavior often seems thuggish, and yet he is honorable, intelligent, resourceful, and witty. He is physically big, but he has a big spirit as well. Though an outlaw himself, he is unlike the several outlaws he befriends and who try to murder him for the reward.

An important concept of the Viking age is "luck," and one of the monsters Grettir kills predicts that his luck will henceforth grow worse. Many events in Grettir's later career seem unlucky, but again fate is character. Grettir seldom ameliorates bad fortune or takes advantage of good. For example, he swims across an icy estuary to get fire for the merchants with whom he is traveling. A scuffle takes place at the house he goes to for fire, and the people inside are burned. The merchants then accuse Grettir of murder. He is attacked first, but he might have retreated and tried to explain that, in spite of his appearance, he is not a troll and not there for an evil motive. The next day, when the merchants find the burned house, Grettir could stress his innocence. After all that, he is given a chance by King Olaf to clear himself by ordeal, but he loses his temper in the church and commits an act of violence so that the trial cannot take place, and he cannot clear himself. At the end, when terms are offered to Grettir and he refuses them, a witch calls him luckless because, "there are few things which lead to more certain disaster than not to want what is good." She later contributes to his downfall by magic, but the ultimate cause is not magic, but Grettir's unwillingness to seize an opportunity.

As the story progresses, Grettir's sphere of action narrows. He is outlawed in Norway, returns to Iceland, and is immediately outlawed there. As fewer and fewer dare or are willing to take him in, he is reduced to robbing travelers, something he would not do earlier. At last he takes refuge with his brother and a slave on a small island with cliffs all around. Here he shows his growth in maturity by his patience in adversity, by his love for his brother, and by his surprising tolerance for his lazy and irresponsible slave. When he kills a lamb to eat, he is deeply touched by the mother ewe's grief, a considerable advance in his humanity from his boyhood cruelty to animals. He remains on the island for more than two years, but the witch's charm causes him to wound himself in the leg. As he lies near death, his enemies finally manage to scale the cliff and to kill him.

The last eleven chapters form a sort of prologue in which Grettir's one surviving brother follows the killer to Constantinople and avenges Grettir. He then marries a lady of that city and returns to Norway wealthy. At last, to expiate their sins, they go to Rome, set up separate huts, and finish their lives as hermits. They end, like Grettir, in isolation, but theirs is an isolation of peace with their world and with themselves.

In spite of its understated tone and seemingly episodic structure, *The Saga of Grettir the Strong* is a masterpiece of construction, with its many, seemingly random episodes contributing to an understanding of Grettir's motivations and character. It is also a sophisticated exploration of such themes as the collective and the individual, Christianity and heathenism, luck and character, freedom and responsibility, honor and social obligation. Compared to the conventional novel—with its descriptions, atmosphere, analyses of character and action, and elaborately developed scenes—the saga formula may seem bare, objective, and austere. Nevertheless, in terms of literary excellence and sophistication, the best sagas can stand with the best of the world's novels, and *The Saga of Grettir the Strong* makes a strong showing.

"Critical Evaluation" by Jack Hart

Further Reading

Andersson, Theodore M. *The Icelandic Family Saga: An Analytic Reading*. Cambridge, Mass.: Harvard University Press, 1967. Unlike the many saga studies that focus on history and origin, this book examines sagas as narrative. Chapters on structure, rhetoric, and heroic legacy are followed by insightful commentary.

Arent, A. Margaret. "The Heroic Pattern: Old Germanic Helmets, *Beowulf*, and *Grettis Saga*." In *Old Norse Literature and Mythology*, edited by Edgar C. Polomé. Austin: University of Texas Press, 1969. Discussion of the pictorial ornamentations found on Germanic helmets, and how the cultural and religious themes depicted on typical helmets shed light on the literature. Includes twenty-seven illustrations.

Fjalldal, Magnús. *The Long Arm of Coincidence: The Frustrated Connection Between "Beowulf" and "Grettis Saga."* Toronto, Ont.: University of Toronto Press, 1998. Fjalldal examines other scholars' arguments that the Old Norse and Old English sagas are linked. While he explains how these theories may have originated, his close analysis refutes the idea that the two works are connected.

Hastrup, Kirsten. "Tracing Tradition: An Anthropological Perspective on *Grettis Saga Ásmundarsonar*." In *Structure and Meaning in Old Norse Literature*, edited by John Lindow et al. Odense, Denmark: Odense University Press, 1986. Traces how Icelanders have perceived Grettir the Strong over the past seven hundred years, showing how the meaning of the outcast-hero has changed.

Hume, Kathryn. "The Thematic Design of *Grettis Saga*." *Journal of English and Germanic Philology* 73, no. 4 (October, 1974): 469-486. Explains the puzzling contrasts in Grettir's character and the narrative tone between different episodes. Hunt demonstrates how the theme of the unacceptability of the heroic in a modern society accounts for the differences.

The Saga of Grettir the Strong. Translated by Bernard Scudder. Edited with an introduction and notes by Örnólfur Thorsson. New York: Penguin, 2005. In addition to a new translation of the saga, this edition features a plot summary, family trees, a glossary, maps, and an index of characters, as well as discussions of the saga's narrative, social, political, and legal structures. Thorsson's introduction examines the influence of Christianity on the work.

Schach, Paul. *Icelandic Sagas*. Boston: Twayne, 1984. Contains a brief but excellent introduction to this saga, including a discussion of its authorship, structure, and themes of intergenerational conflict and tragic isolation. Other sections provide historical and literary contexts, a chronology, and a bibliography.

The Sailor Who Fell from Grace with the Sea

Author: Yukio Mishima (1925-1970)
First published: Gogo no eikō, 1963 (English translation, 1965)
Type of work: Novel
Type of plot: Psychological realism
Time of plot: After World War II
Locale: Yokohama, Japan

Principal characters:
NOBORU KURODA, an adolescent male
FUSAKO KURODA, his widowed mother
RYUJI TSUKAZAKI, second mate of a tramp vessel
CHIEF, anonymous leader of a band of boys to which Noboru belongs

The Story:

Part 1. Noboru, a precocious boy of thirteen, convinced of his own genius, spends much of his time in his bedroom, looking out over Yokohama Bay and listening to the sound of ships' horns. His personal philosophy, like that of the German philosopher Arthur Schopenhauer, comprises distrust of authority and women, concentration on death and nihilism, and faith in universal order. One night he discovers a peephole in his bedroom wall through which he is able to observe his mother's boudoir. Several days later, his mother, Fusako, who is only thirty-three years old and retains much of her beauty, invites a sailor named Ryuji to dinner, and they pass the night in lovemaking. Noboru, through his peephole, observes their most intimate moments. At first, he finds nothing objectionable, merely a verification of his philosophy of universal order. In his mind, he is encroaching on the mother, the mother on the man, the man on the sea, and the sea on the boy in a purposeful design.

Superficially, Fusako, as the wealthy proprietress of an exclusive male boutique, has nothing in common with Ryuji, the rough sailor. About her own age, he always lived as a loner, hating both the land and the sea as types of a prison. From his youth, he cherished the illusion of a special destiny leading him to glory. Becoming a sailor to escape a boring life such as his father led, Ryuji did not, like the conventional seafarer, engage in easy and frequent sex. His image of perfect love consists of idyllic courtship ending in death.

On the morning after Noboru's spying on his mother, he tells her that he is going swimming, but instead he spends the day denouncing the insignificance of ordinary life with a band of six schoolfellows, all top students. They are ranked according to leadership; their chief is number one, and Noboru is number three. In boasting of his spying exploits, Noboru portrays the sailor as a hero, a man dominating a woman, but the chief disagrees on the grounds that such a relationship is unimportant. He inculcates as a principle that the band should remain absolutely apathetic concerning all things sexual. By means of a therapy of showing pictures that portray every physical aspect of intercourse, he makes the band completely dispassionate. Part of their ritual at this meeting consists of killing a kitten as a symbol of the emptiness of existence. Selected as executioner, Noboru bashes the kitten against a log. The boys strip off the animal's skin and dissect its organs in order to experience the sensation of absolute nakedness. Noboru compares the nakedness of the kitten with the nakedness of his mother.

A chance meeting with Ryuji on his way home turns Noboru's rapture into embarrassment. Since he told his mother that his destination was elsewhere in the city, he is forced to admit his deception to the sailor, who good-naturedly promises not to expose his lie. Instead of feeling gratitude, Noboru looks down upon Ryuji as a fawning adult, seeking to ingratiate himself. As they talk about sailing and the sea on their way to Noboru's home, however, he has another change of heart, impressed by the sailor's masculinity and experience. Fusako is similarly attracted by Ryuji's manliness, but she struggles against being trapped in the conventional role of a grieving woman deserted by a sailor lover.

During their final encounter before his next voyage, Ryuji has the fantasy that one of their kisses is the kiss of death and that Fusako should, therefore, feel that their parting is like dying happily. Previously, in his dreams, he associated the notion of final glory with abandoning a woman. Their actual farewell on the docks, however, is formal, without emotion on either side.

Part 2. When Ryuji returns to Yokohama in time for the New Year festivities, Fusako takes him straight to her home. During his absence, she was chaste, dissipating her energies through work and exercise. By this time, Ryuji, having reached the age of thirty-three, realizes that his dream of a grand future will never come to pass and considers giving up the sea. Although the sea represents freedom, it also involves a monotonous existence with no tangible glory. In the midst of indecision, he asks Fusako to marry him, at the same time offering to give her all of his money, whether or not she accepts his proposal. Fusako, touched by this artless generosity, agrees immediately.

After the holidays, when Noboru rejoins his band in an enormous abandoned crate on the harbor front, he expresses his disgust at Ryuji's decision to settle down as a landsman. The chief first asks whether he would like to participate in turning the sailor back into a hero, but then without saying more on the subject, he launches into a generalized diatribe against fathers and father figures, boasting that he is capable of making his own world die, an achievement equivalent to glory.

Ryuji takes up permanent residence with Fusako, and, soon after, she informs Noboru of their imminent marriage. Conditions in the household grow tense. Fusako discovers the existence of the peephole and angrily confronts Noboru. Expecting Ryuji to administer bodily punishment, she is shocked when he merely delivers a verbal rebuke. Noboru is even more upset by this placid reaction, which completely shatters his image of the sailor as hero and glory-figure. Angrily, he asks the chief to call an emergency meeting of the band to discuss the situation. They decide that Ryuji's example represents an affront to order and that he has to be eliminated. They decide that he should be drugged and then disemboweled in line with their previous ritual with the kitten. They have no fear of consequences, since none is yet the age of fourteen, and the penal code clearly states that acts of juveniles under that age are not punishable by law.

On the day of execution, Noboru succeeds in delivering Ryuji to the appointed meeting place under the pretext that his companions want to hear tales of the sea. Ryuji willingly begins a narrative combining nautical and personal reminiscences. Although sensing that something is not quite right, he unhesitatingly drinks a cup of poisoned tea that is offered to him. It has an odd taste, a sensation he associates with the bitterness of glory. His romantic association of love, death, and glory vanishes with him into nothingness.

Critical Evaluation:

Widely regarded as one of the most philosophical and thought-provoking novelists of the post-World War II period, Yukio Mishima produced twenty-five major works of fiction, concentrating on contemporary Japan but embracing universal literary and philosophical themes. These themes he presents in such dichotomies as art and nature, literature and life, asceticism and hedonism, mind and body, and Eastern and Western culture. His portrayals of art and beauty, love and death, nearly always involved some shocking exposure of deviant sexuality, such as Noboru's voyeurism. Unlike conventional authors, Mishima sought to remain in the pub-

lic eye, advertising both his aestheticism and his political conservatism. As a final act of staged publicity, he committed suicide in full military regalia watched by thousands on television.

The original Japanese title *Gogo no eikō*, literally meaning "towing in the afternoon," conceals a pun on *eikō*, which stands for "glory" as well as "towing." Since this pun cannot be translated into English, Mishima selected the English title that the novel now bears from a list devised by his translator. It presumably means that Ryuji, by abandoning the sea, deviated from his destined role in the universal order and therefore fell from an approved position. Throughout the novel, the sea is a metaphor for woman, sex, glory, and death, elements that are continually interwoven.

Events are narrated from the perspective of only two characters, Ryuji and Noboru. They are foils for each other, Ryuji representing bodily development and romantic optimism, and Noboru standing for intellect, youth, and carnal nihilism. Ryuji may be seen as an idealistic figure, hopelessly obsessed by the trinity of the sea, feminine beauty, and death. These elements are united in his recurrent dream of a man lured by a perfect woman into a passionate embrace in which a kiss of death is accompanied by the sound of the sea. Ryuji's quest for glory, with which this dream is associated, is by itself highly romantic, but his actions fall sadly short of his mission. The high degree of erotic satisfaction provided by Fusako compensates for his lack of fulfillment, but it leads to his abandoning the sea, a further retreat from his vision of glory. His death, moreover, does not represent a tragic resistance to destiny or, as he fantasizes it should be, a glorious and triumphant finale to a storm-tossed career. It comes instead as the result of the commonplace act of drinking a cup of tea. Since each member of the band is instructed to bring a knife to the meeting place, it is clear that Ryuki's body, like that of the kitten, will be dissected after his death. At this moment, the figure of Ryuki symbolizes the pessimistic philosophy of Schopenhauer instead of the romantic optimism that had until then been associated with him.

Noboru, who is Ryuki's antithesis, observes and criticizes him and, eventually, starts in motion the machinery leading to Ryuki's destruction. At first, Noboru highly approves of the sailor when he finds him in bed with his mother. For him, the sight is "like being part of a miracle." He admires the sailor's muscular body and sexual prowess, but when the latter exchanges the sea for a subordinate position in Fusako's boutique, Ryuki is converted from his mother's conqueror into her ally. Although seeing himself as the instrument of Ryuji's destruction, Noboru is forced to turn to the chief for energy to carry out the actual deed. Noboru's antagonism toward Ryuji is linked with his personal development and his coming-of-age. In part 1, his bedroom door is locked by his mother at night, a sign of childhood dependence; in part 2, on the advice of Ryuji, it is left unlocked. This symbolizes both Noboru's emancipation and the role he will play in Ryuji's ultimate demise. It also represents a choice in life between retreating to a safe haven and taking arms against turbulent reality. Noboru clearly indicates these alternatives when he wonders whether there is any way that he could remain in the room and at the same time be out in the hall locking the door.

Although the characters of the novel lend themselves to a psychological interpretation, the key elements in the plot are implausible from a realistic perspective, particularly the thirteen-year-old boy's commitment to nihilistic philosophy, the contemplated marriage between the rough sailor and the wealthy owner of a luxury boutique, and the effortless massacre of the sailor as the joint act of a group of schoolboys. On this level, the novel is best understood as an exquisitely wrought allegory, expounding the doctrines of nihilism.

A. Owen Aldridge

Further Reading

Keene, Donald. *Five Modern Japanese Novelists*. New York: Columbia University Press, 2003. Keene devotes a chapter to Mishima in his examination of five Japanese novelists with whom he was acquainted. He provides his personal recollections of the writers as well as literary and cultural analyses of their works.

Napier, Susan J. *Escape from the Wasteland: Romanticism and Realism in the Fiction of Mishima Yukio and Ōe Kenzaburō*. Cambridge, Mass.: Harvard University Press, 1991. Does not treat *The Sailor Who Fell from Grace with the Sea* separately but offers many insights and suggestions.

Nathan, John. *Mishima: A Biography*. Boston: Little, Brown, 1974. Reprint. Cambridge, Mass.: Da Capo Press, 2000. Nathan provides a new preface for the 2000 reprint of his classic biography. Nathan knew Mishima personally and professionally, and he provides a detailed and balanced portrait of the writer.

Petersen, Gwenn Boardman. *The Moon in the Water: Understanding Tanizaki, Kawabata, and Mishima*. Honolulu: University of Hawaii Press, 1979. Provides a lucid interpretation of the sexual and aesthetic elements in *The Sailor Who Fell from Grace with the Sea*.

Piven, Jerry S. *The Madness and Perversion of Yukio Mishima*. Westport, Conn.: Praeger, 2004. A psychological study of Mishima. Piven traces the events of Mishima's life—most notably his early childhood, spent largely in his grandmother's sick room—in order to provide a better understanding of the author and his works. Chapter 7 is devoted to a discussion of *The Sailor Who Fell from Grace with the Sea*.

Starrs, Roy. *Deadly Dialectics: Sex, Violence, and Nihilism in the World of Yukio Mishima*. Honolulu: University of Hawaii Press, 1994. Starrs provides a critical and interpretive look at Mishima's work, focusing on its elements of sex, violence, and nihilism. He examines Mishima's intellectual background, including the influences of Thomas Mann and Friedrich Nietzsche, and describes the quality of Mishima's thought. Includes bibliography and index

Ueda, Makoto. *Modern Japanese Writers and the Nature of Literature*. Stanford, Calif.: Stanford University Press, 1976. Discerning analysis of Mishima's fiction by a Japanese scholar.

Viglielmo, Valdo H. "The Sea as Metaphor: An Aspect of the Modern Japanese Novel." In *Poetics of the Elements in the Human Condition*, edited by Anna-Teresa Tyrnieniecke. Dordrecht, the Netherlands: Reidel, 1985. Offers an ingenious and credible interpretation of the multiple meanings of the sea.

Wolfe, Peter. *Yukio Mishima*. New York: Continuum, 1989. Excellent criticism of the novel and one of the best critiques in English. The novel is portrayed as "a work of warped genius" that "opens exciting realms of response, but only to slam them shut."

Saint Joan

Author: George Bernard Shaw (1856-1950)
First produced: 1923; first published, 1924
Type of work: Drama
Type of plot: Historical
Time of plot: Fifteenth century
Locale: France

Principal characters:
JOAN, the Maid, a teenage French country girl
CHARLES, THE DAUPHIN, heir to the French throne
ARCHBISHOP OF RHEIMS, a political prelate
JACK DUNOIS, a French general
PETER CAUCHON, the bishop of Beauvais
EARL OF WARWICK, an English nobleman
STOGUMBER, an English chaplain

The Story:

At Vaucouleurs castle, Robert de Baudricourt berates his steward for claiming that the hens stopped laying. The steward insists they will not lay until Robert talks to Joan, the Maid, who demands to see him. Robert finally admits Joan. She promptly requests a horse, armor, and some soldiers to take her to the dauphin. She already persuaded several soldiers to accompany her and convinced them that God sent her to save France from the English occupying force. Robert yields, and the hens immediately begin laying again.

At Chinon, the archbishop and the Lord Chamberlain complain about the dauphin's irresponsibility. Bluebeard, a nobleman, tells about a cursing soldier who died after being cautioned by an angel dressed as a soldier. Charles appears, looking browbeaten but excited about Robert's surprise. Almost everyone advises Charles not to see Joan, but he insists. They then decide that Bluebeard will pretend to be Charles, to see if Joan can pick out the real dauphin; the archbishop cynically remarks that such seeming miracles could be as useful as real ones. When Joan enters, she immediately spots Charles and tells him that she is sent by God to help him drive the English from France and to crown him king. Charles, full of doubts, tries to escape her but finally yields and gives Joan command of the army. Cheering, the knights prepare to head for Orléans.

Two months later at Orléans, Dunois's French forces still did not attack the English because the east wind prevents their ships from going up the river. When Joan arrives, Dunois explains the military situation. Joan grasps the problem immediately and agrees to pray for a west wind to make the French attack possible. As she speaks, a page sneezes and everyone suddenly notices that the wind changed. Joan, overwhelmed by this sign, rushes with Dunois into battle.

In the English camp, Chaplain Stogumber and the Earl of Warwick consider France's recent military victories. Stogumber resents seeing Englishmen beaten by French "foreigners." Warwick complains that people are beginning

to define themselves by their country rather than by local allegiances—a danger to both feudal lords and the Church. Warwick therefore hopes to collaborate with Bishop Cauchon, who represents the rival Burgundian faction in France. When Cauchon arrives, he and Warwick agree that neither feels happy about the imminent crowning of Charles, that they prefer to limit his future progress, and that capturing Joan offers the best chance of success. The three men then debate the precise nature of Joan's threat and the possible remedies. Cauchon considers her a heretic for her belief that God communicates with her directly; if people insist on their own interpretation of God's will rather than that of the Church, there will be religious and social chaos. His ideal solution is to compel Joan to abandon her heretical belief. In Warwick's opinion, Joan spreads a secular belief that he defines as Protestantism and that he considers dangerous to the feudal social structure—the idea of "nations" under autocratic kings who hold their power directly from God. Warwick and Cauchon, who define Joan's belief as nationalism, agree that Joan must at least recant her heresy; if she can be thoroughly neutralized they are willing to spare her life, but Stogumber is prepared to burn her as a witch.

At Rheims Cathedral, Charles is crowned king of France. Joan wonders to Dunois why everyone suddenly seems to hate her. She says that once she conquers Paris, she will return to the country. Dunois expresses doubts about more fighting, but Joan insists that her "voices"—the saints' voices she hears and obeys—tell her she must continue. When Charles and others arrive, Joan suggests that she return to her father's farm. Everyone seems much relieved, but it is obvious that she wants to continue fighting for France. When the archbishop comes, he counsels that her stubborn confidence in her own beliefs will lead to her destruction. Dunois reveals that the English offer a reward for whoever captures Joan. Joan finally realizes that, if she is captured, none of her old supporters will try to save her.

In May, 1431, Joan is about to be tried for heresy in Rouen. Stogumber and a French priest complain that many charges were dropped, but the Inquisitor and Cauchon insist that the crucial ones remain. Warwick reveals that English soldiers are guarding the site, ready for trouble. Soldiers bring Joan into court. When questioned, Joan does not understand the charges, insisting that she loves the Church and therefore cannot be a heretic. Some suggest that she be tortured to make her confess, but the Inquisitor refuses. Joan continues to assert that everything she did was at God's command and that she trusts her own judgment of what God wants of her. Her insistence on her own judgment condemns her as a heretic. Several people beg her to recant, and, when she realizes the punishment is death, she does so. When she learns, however, that her alternative punishment will be life in prison, she denies her recantation and chooses death at the stake. English soldiers lead her away and execute her. Those who see her die, including Stogumber, are transformed.

In 1456, Charles is reading in bed when Ladvenu, who helped Joan at the trial, brings word that Joan's verdict was overturned: The judges were ruled corrupt and Joan declared innocent. Several people from twenty-five years earlier, including some who died in the meantime, appear, including Joan, Cauchon, Dunois, an English soldier who gave Joan a makeshift cross, Stogumber, and Warwick. They reveal their subsequent fates. A twentieth century man appears, announcing Joan's canonization in 1920. Strangely, no one wants a living Joan, and, one by one, the ghostly spirits disappear. Alone, Joan wonders when this world will be ready to receive God's living saints.

Critical Evaluation:

Like most of George Bernard Shaw's dramatic works, *Saint Joan* has a didactic purpose. By the 1920's, Shaw was disillusioned about many political programs, including aspects of his own Fabian Socialism, and he developed the concept of the "evolutionary appetite" or Creative Evolution. According to this belief, the Life Force itself needs to keep evolving and developing, thereby producing individuals who, by embodying new ideas, force humanity to the next evolutionary stage; such individuals include Jesus, Muhammad, Oliver Cromwell, and Saint Joan. New concepts necessarily threaten the existing social order, and people in power often try to suppress the ideas by killing those who embody them. Nevertheless, such powerful evolutionary ideas eventually triumph, as they must if humanity is to fulfill its destiny. Shaw believed that Joan forced the people of her time to confront two central tenets of modern consciousness: Protestantism and nationalism, both of which give greater scope to individual conscience. He discusses this theme at length in the preface (nearly half as long as the play itself) and presents it most explicitly in the confrontation between Warwick and Cauchon in scene 4. This scene was criticized for being too wordy and for its implausibility. After all, intelligent medieval people, for whom the social structure of feudalism and the power of the Catholic Church were completely self-evident, might well struggle with the exact nature of Joan's threat, but there would have been no need for them to explain their fundamental worldviews to each other in such detail. Anticipating this criticism, Shaw insisted that twentieth century audiences, who were profoundly ignorant of history, had to have the medieval perspective spelled out for them if the play were to make any sense.

Joan's trial (scene 6) also drew criticism for compressing historical events, for blending comedy (Stogumber's extraneous charges) and tragedy (Joan's excommunication and death), as well as, occasionally, for the uninspired poetry of Joan's last speeches. However, these two scenes display one of Shaw's greatest strengths—his ability convincingly to express points of view completely different from his own. In the preface, he insists that Joan received a fair trial from Cauchon and the Inquisitor; he therefore gives these men wonderfully persuasive speeches, even though the characters embody what Shaw considered doomed ideas. Shaw's Joan dies because she is, in truth, a heretic from the prevailing system of thought. With typical Shavian perversity, her heresy is the necessary precondition for her sanctity.

Chronologically, *Saint Joan* follows the despairing play about war (*Heartbreak House*, 1919) and his massive five-play cycle about Creative Evolution (*Back to Methuselah*, 1921), which reflects Shaw's disgust with the postwar world and traces human life from the Garden of Eden to the year 31,920. Compared with these two works, *Saint Joan* is simple and direct, and it reflects real affection for its heroine. Like the earlier plays, however, it also reflects contemporary issues that concern Shaw. Shaw chooses, for example, to contemplate Joan's era from the perspective of one who observed the horrors of trench warfare; the implicit comparison of old cruelties with new ones allows him to present Warwick and Cauchon more sympathetically. Shaw also implies that society still persecutes anyone who resists the prevailing orthodoxy. Thus, in the preface, he equates the twentieth century belief in science and medicine with the unthinking medieval faith in the Church, noting the modern condemnation of those who refused inoculations. In the epilogue, he has Cauchon wonder if Christ (and, by extension, any truly original but disruptive individual) "must perish in torment in every age to save those that have no imaginations." He questions traditional gender roles by focusing on a heroine who sensibly rejects them, and he uses Stogumber's mindless English chauvinism to criticize British imperialism, especially in his own native Ireland.

Structurally, this historical play presents a mixture of romance, tragedy, and farce; the combination of styles underscores Shaw's ironic approach to his subject. The first three scenes, in which Joan moves from triumph to triumph, have a fairy-tale quality that vanishes as the forces of conventionality converge to destroy her. Both the inevitability and the cruelty of her approaching death make the last three scenes dark indeed. The epilogue, by contrast, turns her suffering into a cosmic joke. First, her just conviction is overturned in a politically motivated show trial. Then, her former friends and enemies, living and dead, gather in Charles's dream to consider their past actions with detached amusement. Finally, a ridiculous man in twentieth century clothing appears, rather like a space alien, to inform the people of 1456 that Joan the heretic has become a saint. When Joan suggests a miracle to make her live again, however, everyone flees in panic. For ordinary humans, Shaw sardonically implies, the only good saint is a dead one.

Susan Wladaver-Morgan

Further Reading

Dukore, Bernard F. *Shaw's Theater*. Gainesville: University Press of Florida, 2000. Focuses on the performance of Shaw's plays and how *Saint Joan* and other plays call attention to elements of the theater, such as the audience, characters directing other characters, and plays within plays. Includes a section on "Bernard Shaw, Director," and another section in which Shaw describes how a director should interpret *Pygmalion* for theatrical production.

Hill, Holly. *Playing Joan: Actresses on the Challenge of Shaw's "Saint Joan."* New York: Theatre Communications Group, 1987. Compilation of twenty-six interviews with women who have played the role of Joan, sometimes in languages other than English. Partly anecdotal, the collection provides insight into the varied interpretations of the play.

Holroyd, Michael. *The Lure of Fantasy, 1918-1950*. Vol. 3 in *Bernard Shaw*. New York: Random House, 1991. Part of Holroyd's magisterial four-volume biography of Shaw. Provides a brief analysis of *Saint Joan* as well as a great deal of information about the circumstances surrounding its creation and production. Includes an excellent examination of the development of Shaw's ideas.

Innes, Christopher, ed. *The Cambridge Companion to George Bernard Shaw*. New York: Cambridge University Press, 1998. Collection of scholarly essays examining Shaw's work, including discussions of Shaw's feminism, Shavian comedy and the shadow of Oscar Wilde, his "discussion plays," and his influence on modern theater. *Saint Joan* is analyzed in Matthew H. Wikander's essay "Reinventing the History Play: *Caesar and Cleopatra*, *Saint Joan*, 'In Good King Charles's Golden Days.'"

Nightingale, Benedict. *A Reader's Guide to Fifty Modern British Plays*. Totowa, N.J.: Barnes & Noble, 1982. Considers Shaw and thirty-three other British playwrights and thus provides a historical, comparative context for Shaw's work. Includes a concise analysis of *Saint Joan* and four other Shaw plays.

Pagliaro, Harold E. *Relations Between the Sexes in the Plays of George Bernard Shaw*. Lewiston, N.Y.: Edwin Mellen Press, 2004. Demonstrates how the relationship between men and women is a key element in Shaw's plays. Notes a pattern in how Shaw depicts these relationships, including lovers destined by the "life force" to procreate; relations between fathers and daughters, and mothers and sons; and the sexuality of politically, intellectually, and emotionally strong men.

Silver, Arnold. *"Saint Joan": Playing with Fire*. New York: Twayne, 1993. Thorough analysis of the play, discussing its themes of the individual versus society, change versus stability, the limits of tolerance, and patriotism. Demonstrates how Shaw's experiences during World War I and his support for the Russian Revolution are reflected in the play.

Tyson, Brian. *The Story of Shaw's "Saint Joan."* Kingston, Ont.: McGill-Queen's University Press, 1982. Detailed scene-by-scene analysis of the play based on examination of Shaw's original manuscript in the British Museum. Covers Joan's miracles in one chapter, then focuses on the Warwick-Cauchon confrontation, the trial, and the epilogue.

Weintraub, Stanley, ed. *Saint Joan: Fifty Years After, 1923/24-1973/74*. Baton Rouge: Louisiana State University Press, 1973. A collection of twenty-five essays that analyze Joan from Marxist, feminist, Irish nationalist, and many other perspectives, including a consideration of Joan as a 1920's flapper. The authors include T. S. Eliot and Luigi Pirandello.

St. Peter's Umbrella

Author: Kálmán Mikszáth (1847-1910)
First published: Szent Péter esernyöje, 1895 (English translation, 1900)
Type of work: Novel
Type of plot: Comic realism
Time of plot: Second half of nineteenth century
Locale: Hungary

Principal characters:
PÁL GREGORICS, a wealthy bachelor
ANNA WIBRA, his housekeeper and cook
GYURY or GYÖRGY WIBRA, the illegitimate son of Anna Wibra
JÁNOS BÉLYI, a priest in Glogova
VERONICA BÉLYI, his sister
WIDOW ADAMECZ, the priest's housekeeper
JÁNOS SZTOLARIK, a lawyer
JÓNÁS MÜNCZ, a Jewish merchant

The Story:

When the new priest, young János Bélyi, arrives in Glogova, prospects for an enjoyable life are extremely dim. The little Hungarian town is a forlorn place where impoverished peasants live out their lives trying to get as much as possible out of the poor soil. No provisions are made for the priest's subsistence, and church property is almost nonexistent. While the priest contemplates the fact that he will have to eat less and pray more, the situation becomes more critical with the arrival of his baby sister. His parents died and somebody decided to send little Veronica to her nearest relative, the priest; thus, a baby in a basket is suddenly put at the doorstep of his modest home. In order to find a solution to his problems, he takes a prayerful walk.

A heavy rain begins to fall. Suddenly he remembers the baby, still lying in front of his house, and he is certain the child will be soaking wet before he can arrive. To his surprise he finds her completely dry, protected by an old red umbrella. The priest cannot imagine who was so kind to his little sister; however, the townspeople soon find all sorts of explanations. Since the only stranger seen lately is an old Jew, the peasants come to the conclusion that St. Peter came to show his mercy for the poor child.

At the next funeral on a rainy day the priest uses the red umbrella. The men carrying the coffin stumble, and the supposedly dead man, who was merely in a trance, becomes very much alive. To the villagers this incident is another sign of the supernatural character of the umbrella. As a result of the umbrella, the priest's conditions improve rapidly, and all kinds of gifts arrive at his house for the baby who caused St. Peter to come to Glogova. Even Widow Adamecz offers her services as housekeeper free of charge, additional proof of the miraculous power of the umbrella to all who know the money-conscious widow.

In the beginning the priest tries to resist continuous requests for the presence of the umbrella during church ceremonies, but his parishioners feel so offended when he refuses that he finally gives in and uses the umbrella on all occasions. Pilgrims come from far away to look at the umbrella, and brides insist on being married under it. Soon the town feels the need for building an inn that carries the name Miraculous Umbrella. The priest wonders how the umbrella came to Glogova; he waits many years for an answer.

In the town of Besztercebanya lives a wealthy bachelor, Pál Gregorics. A spy during the war, he was seen many times with a red umbrella. Pál is in love with his housekeeper, Anna Wibra, who gives birth to an illegitimate son, Gyury Wibra. The townspeople observe how Pál devotes all of his time to the child. Pál's two brothers and his sister do not like the possibility that they might someday have to share Pál's estate with an illegitimate child. For this reason Pál, afraid that his relatives might try to harm young Gyury, decides to trick them by pretending he does not care for the boy, and he sends Gyury to a distant school. To deceive his brothers and sister, he acts as if he invested all of his money in several estates that require inspection from time to time, but in reality he visits his son.

Despite great love for his father, Gyury reproaches Pál for making himself a laughingstock by always carrying the old red umbrella. Pál disregards the complaints and promises his son he will one day inherit the umbrella. When Pál feels he is going to die, he asks his lawyer János Sztolarik to prepare his will. Mysteriously, he asks two masons, under strict order of secrecy, to break a wall in order to place a caldron into the wall and finish the masonry as it was before. Although he tells his housekeeper to notify Gyury of his illness, she fails to do so, and Pál dies, without seeing his son, with the red umbrella in his hands.

When Sztolarik reads the will, Pál's brothers and sister are horrified to hear nothing about the rich estates that their brother supposedly owned. They spend much time and money to find out what Pál did with the money. They suspect a secret bequest to Gyury, but investigators report that the boy is studying and living on a meager income. Finally they discover the two masons, who reveal for a large sum of money the secret of the caldron in the wall. Certain they found the answer to their riddle, they buy the house, which was willed to Gyury, for an extremely high price. When they break the wall open, they find the caldron filled with rusty nails.

Soon afterward Gyury completes his education and becomes a lawyer in Besztercebanya. He hears about the frantic search for his father's estate, and he begins to wonder where it could be. The first clue is given by the dying mayor, who tells how Pál carried secret documents in the hollow handle of his umbrella during the war. Gyury's suspicion is confirmed when his mother tells him how Pál, even in death, still clutched the umbrella. The search for the umbrella then begins. Gyury's investigations points to an old Jew, Jónás Müncz, who bought for a few coins those odds and ends belonging to his father that the relatives did not want. Further inquiries establish that the Jew died but that his wife owned a small store in Babaszek. Gyury and his coachman hurry to that town. An interview with Frau Müncz reveals that her husband was fond of the umbrella and carried it around at all times. Gyury hears from Frau Müncz's son that the old Jew was seen putting the umbrella over a little baby in Glogova.

As he is about to leave for Glogova, Gyury finds a lost earring for which, according to the town crier, the mayor is searching. Returning the earring to the mayor, he is introduced to its owner, a young and extremely beautiful woman. Furthermore, he learns she is Veronica Bélyi, sister of the village priest in Glogova. She was on her way home when an accident damaged her vehicle.

Gyury gladly offers to conduct Veronica and her traveling companion in his carriage, but the two women decide that it is now too late for departure, and Gyury agrees to postpone his trip until morning. During a party in the mayor's house, Gyury hears about the miraculous umbrella in Glogova and realizes that the umbrella he seeks is identical to the priest's umbrella. Throughout the night he can hardly sleep from thinking how near and yet how far away the umbrella is. During the night he dreams that St. Peter advises him to marry the priest's sister; thus he will have a beautiful wife and a legal claim on the umbrella.

On the trip to Glogova, Gyury considers the advantages of the suggestion offered to him in his dream, but he is afraid Veronica might not love him. The carriage breaks down not far away from the town. Searching for some wood needed for repair, he hears faint cries for help; a man fell into a deep hole. After several attempts he succeeds in lifting out the unfortunate man, who turns out to be the priest of Glogova; he fell into the hole while waiting for Veronica on the previous night. Deeply grateful, the priest wants to know whether there is anything he can do for his rescuer. Gyury tells him he has something in his carriage belonging to the priest. The priest is surprised to find his sister in the vehicle; he informs Veronica of his promise, and she becomes engaged to Gyury.

In Glogova the young man has a conversation with the lawyer Sztolarik, who heard from Gyury about his successful search. The lawyer is concerned because he feels that Gyury cannot be sure whether love for Veronica or for the umbrella is the primary motive for his marriage. Veronica, overhearing the conversation, runs away heartbroken.

Gyury is eager to see the umbrella, which the priest gladly shows him; but the old handle was replaced by a new one of silver. Gyury's last hope for recovering the old handle is crushed when the priest's housekeeper informs him that she burned it. Meanwhile, the priest begins to worry about the absence of his sister. Hearing of her disappearance, Gyury is also greatly upset. Suddenly he realizes that he can overcome the loss of the umbrella but not the loss of Veronica. Church bells give the fire alarm signal, and everybody in Glogova appears for the search. When Gyury finds Veronica and tells her about the burned handle, she recognizes his greater love for her, and she and Gyury are married in the grandest wedding Glogova ever saw. Although Gyury never knows whether the handle contained the key to his inheritance, the umbrella remains a treasured relic in his family.

Critical Evaluation:

Kálmán Mikszáth was a country squire, lawyer, magistrate, journalist, member of parliament, and novelist; his forte, however, was undoubtedly the ability for superb storytelling. He draws his characters with the certainty of a man who knows and understands the people about whom he writes, mainly the Hungarian peasantry. The ease with which he transforms everyday life into unusual stories reminds one strongly of Guy de Maupassant; his sense of humor, as demonstrated in this novel, makes reading a pleasure. The author became a member of the Hungarian Academy and of the Hungarian Parliament, but his parliamentary speeches will be long forgotten while the hilarious episodes of *St. Peter's Umbrella* will be still remembered.

Sometimes called the Hungarian Mark Twain, Mikszáth established his fame as a short-story writer before he turned to writing novels, the first of which was *St. Peter's Umbrella*.

Like much of Twain's work, the novel reveals a bittersweet, jauntily pessimistic tone in Mikszáth's attitude toward the human condition. Although Mikszáth wanted to believe in essential human goodness, he was empirically convinced that human flaws and failings were innate and ineradicable. Thus, the well-meaning priest becomes party to a heretical superstition about the umbrella. So, too, the otherwise inoffensive brothers and sister of Pál Gregorics become greedy vultures who begrudge Gyury a share of his father's estate.

Yet, for all this, *St. Peter's Umbrella* is not a Dickensian tale of unrelieved gloom but a lighthearted fable with the makings of a modern legend—literary rather than folk in its origins, for it does not stem from the ethnic lore of Hungary. The unifying factor in the story is the umbrella, a symbol of protection from inclement weather. As the plot unfolds, the umbrella gains additional symbolic significance: It mysteriously appears in Glogova, bringing good fortune. It becomes even more intriguing as the object of Gyury's search. Hence, the umbrella is the stuff from which fable and legend are made. In fact, throughout the novel, Mikszáth follows the conventions of Hungarian fables and consequently invests the story with an air of authenticity.

The aura of authenticity in *St. Peter's Umbrella* is so strong that the improbable coincidences are often overlooked. How likely is it that a passerby would place an umbrella over an untended baby in a rainstorm? How likely is it that a putative corpse being buried on a rainy day by a priest with an umbrella should prove to be very much alive? How likely is it that Gyury would find the widow of Jónás Müncz? How likely is it that Gyury would find a lost earring, which coincidentally belongs to Veronica Bélyi, sister of the priest who possesses the umbrella for which Gyury is searching? How likely is Gyury's falling in love with Veronica? It is a tribute to Mikszáth's storytelling powers that the reader never asks such questions, enjoying the fable on its own terms.

Further Reading

Czigány, Lóránt. "The Decline of the Gentry and the Novel." In *The Oxford History of Hungarian Literature from the Earliest Times to the Present*. New York: Oxford University Press, 1984. Provides an overview of Mikszáth's work.

Reményi, Joseph. "Kálmän Mikszáth: Novelist and Satirist." In *Hungarian Writers and Literature*. New Brunswick, N.J.: Rutgers University Press, 1964. Pages 154 to 164 introduce and establish a context for Mikszáth's works.

Scheer, Steven C. *Kálmän Mikszáth*. Boston: Twayne, 1977. A good starting place in the study of Mikszáth's life and work. Includes a bibliography.

Śakuntalā
Or, The Lost Ring

Author: Kālidāsa (c. 340-c. 400)
First produced: Abhijñānaśākuntala, c. 395 C.E.; first transcribed, c. 395 C.E. (English translation, 1789)
Type of work: Drama
Type of plot: Love
Time of plot: Golden Age of India
Locale: India

Principal characters:
ŚAKUNTALĀ, the beautiful daughter of a Brahman and a nymph
KANWA, Śakuntalā's foster father and a wise hermit
DUSHYANTA, the king of India, in love with Śakuntalā
MATHAVYA, the court jester

The Story:

Dushyanta, the king of India, is hunting one day when his chariot takes him into the sacred grounds of a religious establishment. A hermit stops the king and reminds him that he has sworn to protect the religious people who live there. The king leaves his chariot and wanders through the hallowed groves. As he walks, he hears voices and then sees three young women passing through the grove to water the plants growing there. When a bee, angered by their presence, flies at one of the young women, she playfully calls out for Dushyanta to rescue her, not knowing that the king is anywhere near.

Dushyanta, stepping from his hiding place, announces himself, but not as the king; rather, he says that he is the king's representative appointed to oversee the safety of the grove and its inhabitants. While they talk, Dushyanta learns that Śakuntalā, the young woman who had cried out, is no ordinary maid but the child of a Brahman and a water nymph. Dushyanta falls in love with her. Śakuntalā also feels the first pangs of love for the king and believes that the Hindu god of love has struck her with his five flower-tipped arrows.

Mathavya, the king's jester, complains to his master that the king and his retinue spend too much time in hunting and that this life is too hard on him. Ostensibly to humor the jester, but actually to have more time to seek out Śakuntalā, the king calls off any further hunting and orders his retinue to camp near the sacred grove in which Śakuntalā lives with her foster father, a hermit wise man named Kanwa. A short time later, word comes to the camp that the king's mother wishes him to return to the capital to take part in certain ceremonies, but Dushyanta is so smitten with love for Śakuntalā that he sends his retinue back while he remains at the sacred grove in the hope of seeing Śakuntalā again.

Since their first meeting, both the king and Śakuntalā have languished with love. At last Dushyanta finds an excuse and opportunity to revisit the grove, and there he meets Śakuntalā again. Both are clearly in love, but neither knows how to tell the other. One of Śakuntalā's attendants finally conceives the idea of having her send a love note to the king. As Śakuntalā writes the note, Dushyanta hears her speaking the words aloud. He steps from his place of concealment and tells her of his determination to make her his consort and the head of his household, above all his other wives. Śakuntalā leaves, telling him that she will have to talk over the subject of marriage with her attendants, for her foster father, Kanwa, is absent and so cannot give his consent.

Sometime later, a scurrilous and eccentric sage comes to the sacred grove. He feels himself slighted by Śakuntalā, who had not heard of his arrival and so has not accomplished the rites of hospitality to suit him. In his anger, he calls down a curse on the young woman, although she does not know of it. The curse is that her lover will not remember her until he sees once again the ring of recognition that he will give her. The attendants who hear the curse are afraid to tell Śakuntalā for fear she will become ill with worry.

Before Dushyanta leaves the sacred grove to return to his palace, Śakuntalā agrees to a secret marriage and becomes his wife, but she decides to remain at the grove until the return of her foster father. Before he leaves, the king gives her a ring as a sign of her new status. Not long after Dushyanta's departure, Kanwa returns. Having the gift of omniscience, he knows all that has taken place, and as he reenters the sacred grove, a supernatural voice tells him that Śakuntalā shall give

birth to a son destined to rule the world. Kanwa, thus assured of the future, gives his blessing to the union of Śakuntalā and Dushyanta. He has his people make the necessary preparations for sending the bride to her husband, to appear as the royal consort.

When the time comes for her departure, Śakuntalā is filled with regret, for she loves the sacred grove where she was reared. In addition, she has premonitions that her future will not be a happy one. Kanwa insists, however, that she make ready to leave, so that her son can be born in his father's palace.

When the hermits of the sacred wood appear in Dushyanta's presence with Śakuntalā, the curse proved true, for the king fails to remember Śakuntalā and his marriage to her. The hermits, feeling that they have done their duty in escorting Śakuntalā to her husband, leave her in the king's household. Śakuntalā, heartbroken at her husband's failure to remember her, looks for the ring of recognition he had given her, but the ring has been lost during the journey from the sacred wood to the palace.

Not long after Dushyanta has sent Śakuntalā from his presence, his courtiers come to tell him that a strange, winged being was seen flying into the palace gardens, where it picked up Śakuntalā and carried her away into the heavens. The king is much disturbed by this, but he resolves to put the event from his mind. Later, the ring of recognition, bearing the king's crest, is discovered in the hands of a poor fisherman, who had found it in the belly of a carp. The ring is carried to Dushyanta; no sooner has he set eyes on it than he remembers Śakuntalā and their secret marriage, for the sight of the ring removes the curse.

Remembering Śakuntalā does him no good; when she was snatched from the palace garden, she was lost to mortal eyes. Dushyanta grows sad and refuses to be comforted. Meanwhile, the nymph who stole Śakuntalā from the palace garden keeps watch and takes note of the king's unhappiness. Finally she takes pity on him and has the chariot of the god Indra sent down to earth to convey Dushyanta to heaven for a reunion with Śakuntalā.

In heaven the king finds a young boy playing with a lion. He is amazed to see what the child is doing and feels a strong attraction toward him. While Dushyanta watches, an amulet falls from the child's neck. The king picks it up and replaces it on the boy's shoulders, much to the surprise of the boy's heavenly attendants, for the amulet is deadly to all but the child's parents. Dushyanta, recognized as the boy's true father, is taken to Śakuntalā, who readily forgives her husband, for she has heard the story of the curse. The gods, happy to see the pair reunited, send them back to earth, along with their little son Bharata, to live many years in happiness together.

Critical Evaluation:

The greatness of the drama *Śakuntalā* lies in its tremendous lyric power. The play was originally written in a combination of verse and prose, a form that most modern translators from the original Sanskrit have tried to emulate, although not always successfully. While almost nothing is known of the playwright, Kālidāsa, legend has it that he was the son of a good family of high caste, but that he was abandoned as a baby and reared as a common laborer. In spite of that handicap, says the legend, he became a great poet and dramatist as well as the favorite of an Indian princess.

The story of Śakuntalā stems from an ancient Hindu legend recounted in book 1 of the *Mahabharata* (200 B.C.E.-200 C.E.). When Kālidāsa dramatized this well-known legend, he was not presenting an unfamiliar tale but artfully retelling an old one. Greek writers had Homer's *Iliad* (c. 750 B.C.E.; English translation, 1611) and *Odyssey* (c. 725 B.C.E.; English translation, 1614) for their sources; Indian writers went to the two great Hindu epics, the *Mahabharata* (c. 400 B.C.E.-200 C.E.) and the *Ramayana* (c. 500 B.C.E.) for theirs. In the West and in the East, writers usually adhered to the main story lines of the originals but varied the plot structures slightly and added subplots and details of psychological insight. The advantages of working within an accepted cultural framework are immediately evident. The audience instantly recognizes the story, correctly identifies allusions in it, and knows the story's place in the larger mythological context, freeing the writer from the need to provide lengthy description and explanation. The writer thus may concentrate on intricacies of plot and on the characters' spiritual and psychological development.

In addition to this common use of tradition, there are crucial differences. The first is material: The contents of the two mythologies of East and West are vastly different. More important is a subtle and complex difference in dramaturgy. Aristotelian Western drama places top priority on plot (imitation of action); characterization, setting, and other embellishments are subordinate to the action. Sanskrit drama, however, emphasizes *rasa* (a dominant emotion or flavor, a "sympathy"). It imitates emotion; the action is thus subordinated to the progressive evocation of an emotional state. Hence priorities are shifted from action to feeling, from an accumulation of episodes to a series of moods, a movement from plot to dominant emotion.

In *Śakuntalā*, the dominant emotion is love, in all its varieties and flavors. The playwright has Śakuntalā fare badly at the hands of the gods and of human beings in order to intensify the depiction of her emotional state, to bring out in stark relief the multifaceted depths of her love. Śakuntalā's love—its intensity, its depth, its breadth—is what the play is all about. The work's examination of this emotional state is so compelling that it overwhelms all other considerations.

Herein lies the core of Sanskrit drama at its best in Kālidāsa's masterpiece: Feeling takes precedence over rationality. The Western reader must therefore adjust to the Hindu scale of dramatic values instead of imposing Western standards on this non-Western play. The rewards of reading *Śakuntalā* in the appropriate cultural context are well worth the effort.

Further Reading

Bose, Mandakranta. *Supernatural Intervention in "The Tempest" and "Śakuntalā."* Salzburg, Austria: Institut für Anglistik und Amerikanistik, Universitat Salzburg, 1980. Explains the basis for comparing Kālidāsa's play with William Shakespeare's *The Tempest* (pr. 1611, pb. 1623), focusing on the important structural function of supernatural forces in the two works. Notes how the structures of the societies in which playwrights live affect the use of mythic devices in their dramas.

Harris, Mary B. *Kalidasa: Poet of Nature.* Boston: Meador Press, 1936. Thematic study of Kālidāsa's use of nature in his plays remains a valuable resource. Presents analysis of *Śakuntalā* as well as the writer's other major dramatic works and several of his nondramatic writings.

Knapp, Bettina L. "Kalidasa's Sanskrit Drama, *Sakuntala*: From Passivity to Adamantine Essence." In *Women, Myth, and the Feminine Principle.* Albany: State University of New York Press, 1998. Describes the development of Śakuntalā's character, tracing how she evolves from a passive, unconscious, and archetypal maiden to a conscious, decisive, and spiritual mother.

Krishnamoorthy, K. *Kālidāsa.* New York: Twayne, 1972. Offers an introduction to the writer and his works. Describes *Śakuntalā* as a play about the raptures and torments of love, highlighting the important Indian values of "duty, property, love, and spiritual good."

Miller, Barbara Stoler, ed. *Theater of Memory: The Plays of Kālidāsa.* New York: Columbia University Press, 1984. Provides an excellent introduction to Kālidāsa's major dramatic works. Includes the full text of *Śakuntalā*, translated into English by Miller, and offers commentary that emphasizes the work's major themes and the playwright's mastery of dramatic techniques.

Sinha, Biswajit. *Kalidasa.* Vol. 3 in *Encyclopaedia of Indian*

Theatre. Delhi: Raj, 2002. Presents information about Kālidāsa's life as well as discussion of his plays and their various productions, including cinematic adaptations.

Thapar, Romila. *Śakuntalā: Texts, Readings, Histories*. New Delhi: Kali for Women, 1999. Examines various versions of the legend of Śakuntalā, tracing the transformation of the autonomous, assertive figure of Śakuntalā in the *Mahabharata* to the more submissive woman in Kālidāsa's play.

Wells, Henry W. "Theatrical Techniques on the Sanskrit Stage." In *The Classical Drama of India: Studies in Its Values for the Literature and Theatre of the World*. 1963. Reprint. Westport, Conn.: Greenwood Press, 1975. Examines the theatrical qualities of *Śakuntalā*, focusing on the construction of scenes, dialogue, and development of dramatic tensions that reach a climax in the final act.

Salammbô

Author: Gustave Flaubert (1821-1880)
First published: 1862 (English translation, 1886)
Type of work: Novel
Type of plot: Historical
Time of plot: Third century B.C.E.
Locale: Carthage

Principal characters:
HAMILCAR, Suffete of Carthage
SALAMMBÔ, his daughter
MATHÔ, a Libyan chief
SPENDIUS, a Greek slave
NARR' HAVAS, a Numidian chief

The Story:

Inside the walls of Carthage a vast army of mercenaries gathers in the gardens of Hamilcar. There are Ligurians, Lusitanians, nomadic barbarians from North Africa, Romans, Greeks, Gauls, and Egyptians. A feast for these thousands of hired warriors is in preparation. Odors of cooking food come from Hamilcar's kitchens, and the Council of Elders provides many oxen to roast over the open fires in the gardens. The men, tired from their defeat at the hands of the Romans and weary from the sea journey over the Mediterranean, wait with ill-concealed impatience for the feasting to begin.

More than that, they are in an ugly mood because they were not paid. Hamilcar, their beloved leader even in defeat, promises them their pay many times. The city elders, however, parsimonious and afraid of this huge assembly of fierce foreigners, withholds the pay. Offers of token payment are angrily refused.

While the revelry is at its height, many men are emboldened by drink and began to pillage the palace of Hamilcar. In a private lake, surrounded by a heavy hedge, they find fish with jewels in their gill flaps. With joy they ruthlessly tear off the gems and boil the sacred fish for their feast. The slaves bring new foods and fresh casks of wine for the drunken revelers. Then above them on a high balcony appears Salammbô, the priestess of the moon goddess and daughter of Hamilcar. Her great beauty stills the wild barbarians. She calls down a malediction on their heads and in a wailing refrain laments the sad state of Carthage.

Among those who watch the young girl, none is more attracted than Narr' Havas, a Numidian chief sent by his father to Carthage to serve with Hamilcar. Although he was in Carthage for six months, this is his first sight of Salammbô. Watching her keenly, too, is Mathô, a gigantic Libyan. He heard of Salammbô and already loves her. With Mathô is Spendius, a former Greek slave who, tricky and shrewd, plays the jackal to brave Mathô. Spendius is long in service to Carthage, and he whispers the delights of Salammbô to his master.

The elders give each soldier a piece of gold if he promises to go to Sicca and wait for the rest of his money to be sent to him. The gold and the solemn promises entice many, and finally all the mercenaries and barbarians join the march to Sicca. Many of their leaders distrust the words of the elders, but they are sure of better treatment when Hamilcar returns to Carthage.

Mathô lies in his tent all day long at Sicca. He is in love, and since he has no prospect of ever seeing Salammbô again, he despairs. Finally the wily Spendius profits greatly by Mathô's inaction, ingratiating himself with Mathô.

At Sicca the enormous Hanno appears in his costly litter. Hanno, one of the Council of Elders, is tremendously fat; the fat on his legs even covers his toenails, and his body is covered with weeping sores. He pompously addresses the crowd, telling them of Carthage's intent to pay later and urging them all to return to their homes. The Gauls and the Campanians and the rest, however, understand not a word of Hanno's address, which is in Punic. Spendius leaps up beside Hanno and offers to translate. Falsely he tells the soldiers that Hanno is exalting his own gods and reviling theirs. The mob becomes unruly, and Hanno barely escapes with his life.

Soon the inflamed barbarians are on the march again, this time to besiege Carthage. At their head rides Mathô, Narr' Havas, and Spendius, now a leader. The mob camps at the gates of Carthage. The city sends Gisco, a famous warrior, to deal with them. In fear the Carthaginians raise a little money and begin to pay the soldiers. They feel powerless without Hamilcar. The payment is slow. Gisco has insufficient funds, and many barbarians claim more pay than they merit.

As the unrest grows, Spendius goes to Mathô with a project of his own. He is sure he finds a way into the city, and if Mathô will follow his lead and help him in his own private errand, he will take Mathô to Salammbô. Outside the walls Spendius finds a loose stone in the pavement over the aqueduct that supplies the city with water. With his giant's strength, Mathô lifts the stone, and the two swim with the current in the darkness until they come to a reservoir inside the city itself. Then Spendius reveals his project. He and Mathô are to steal the zaïmph, the mysterious veil of Tanit, goddess of the moon. The Carthaginians put their trust in Tanit and Tanit's strength lies in the veil, so Spendius hopes to demoralize the city. Mathô is fearful of committing sacrilege, but he is obliged to take the veil in order to see Salammbô.

While the female guards sleep, the two steal into Tanit's sanctuary and Mathô seizes the veil. Then quietly Spendius leads the trembling Mathô, who wears the sacred robe, into Salammbô's sleeping chamber.

As Mathô advances with words of love to Salammbô's bed, the terrified girl awakens and shouts an alarm. Instantly servants come running. Mathô flees, but while he wears the sacred veil no one dares to lay a hand on him. Mathô leaves the city and returns to the barbarians with his prize.

Hamilcar returns to Carthage in time to organize the defense of the city, and the siege melts away. The barbarians are short of food, so they march to Utica to demand supplies. Only loosely bound to Carthage, Utica is glad to harass Carthage by aiding its enemies. Newly supplied with arms and food, the barbarians are a more formidable host. Hamilcar, however, brings his army out of Carthage and joins the battle on the plain. Although the Carthaginians are few in number, they are disciplined and well led. They engage the

barbarians several times, always indecisively. Finally, by a stroke of luck, the army of Hamilcar is trapped, and the barbarians surround the city's defenders.

Meanwhile Salammbô is goaded by the high priest into retrieving the sacred veil. Disguised and with a guide, she makes her way into the barbarian camp, under priestly injunction to do whatever might be necessary to reclaim the robe. Finding Mathô's tent, she goes in and asks for the veil, which hangs among his trophies of war. Mathô is thunderstruck and stammers eager protestations of love. Remembering the commands of the priest, Salammbô submits to Mathô. While the Libyan sleeps, she takes the veil and goes unmolested into her father's camp.

Hamilcar notices immediately that the thin golden chain linking her ankles is broken, and in his shame he promises her to Narr' Havas, who long since deserted the barbarians and returned to help Hamilcar. The marriage, however, is delayed until after the final defeat of Hamilcar's enemies. Hamilcar, wary of the stalemate in the battle, leads his followers back to Carthage, and the barbarians again lay siege to the city. Spendius seeks to end the siege by breaking the aqueduct. Thirst and famine threaten the city from within. When pestilence breaks out, the children of Carthage are burned in sacrifice to Moloch. Moloch is appeased, and torrential rains save the city.

With help from his allies, Hamilcar begins to reduce the forces of the enemy. A large part of the army is trapped in a defile in the mountains and left to starve. Mathô is taken prisoner.

On the wedding day of Narr' Havas and Salammbô, Mathô is led through the city and tortured by the mob. Still alive but with most of his flesh torn away, he staggers up to the nuptial dais of Salammbô. There he falls dead. Salammbô recalls how he knelt before her, speaking gentle words. When the drunken Narr' Havas embraces her in token of possession and drinks to the greatness of Carthage, she lifts a cup and drinks also. A moment later she falls back on the wedding dais, dead. So dies the warrior and the priestess who by their touch profaned the sacred robe of Tanit.

Critical Evaluation:

Salammbô is one of the great historical romances of French literature. Following Théophile Gautier's "Une Nuit de Cléopatre" (1838; "One of Cleopatra's Nights," 1888) and *Le Roman de la momie* (1856; *Romance of the Mummy*, 1863), which were set in different eras of Egypt's remote history, Gustave Flaubert's novel brought a new level of sophistication to the French historical novel. Many French writers were fascinated by the ancient history of the lands surrounding the Mediterranean. French historical novelists were particularly entranced with decadence, which makes for entertaining reading and into which the great empires of the ancient world fell before being sacked by barbarians. Although in Flaubert's novel the barbarians lose, the book strongly implies that Carthage will soon fall as a result of its moral decline.

Decadence was not only a topic; it became a writing style. Gautier defined a decadent style in writing in his introduction to the posthumous third edition of Charles Baudelaire's *Les Fleurs du mal* (1857, 1861, 1868; *Flowers of Evil*, 1931), which had first been published in 1857—the year in which Flaubert visited Tunisia to collect material for *Salammbô*. Flaubert, however, was not at all interested in decadent style. He had recently completed the profoundly antiromantic *Madame Bovary* (1857), and he approached his new task in the same careful, literal-minded, scrupulous manner. He stated that his intention was "to perpetuate a mirage by applying to antiquity the methods of the modern novel." The Carthage that he desired to reproduce in the pages of his novel might have been trembling on the brink of decline, but Flaubert had no wish to submit his powers of description to the glamour of its decay. The novel, nevertheless, may be considered to betray its author's intentions, in that its lush, sensuous, and exuberant description lend glamour to an extremely unglamorous dirty little war.

No one else ever managed to combine the lush exoticism of the ancient world with such brilliantly detailed and realistic descriptions as are found in *Salammbô*. The fact that Carthage, unlike Rome or Alexandria, had been so obliterated by its conquerors that nothing substantial survived for modern contemplation makes Flaubert's feat of re-creation all the more remarkable. Continued scholarly reports have added much information to those Flaubert studied relentlessly, but it is improbable in the extreme that anyone will ever manage to draw them together into an image as sharp, as rich, and as clear as the one that Flaubert constructed. The tale told in *Salammbô* is a very violent one that includes several episodes of hideous cruelty. These are brought to a climax in the extraordinary concluding passage, in which Mathô is virtually torn apart by the citizens of Carthage as he makes his way to the place where Salammbô and her husband are celebrating their wedding day, there to have his heart torn out. This end is symbolic as well as literal: Salammbô has already torn his heart out. It is her dazzling erotic allure rather than the cunning encouragements of Spendius that overwhelm Mathô's fear of committing sacrilege and give him the nerve to steal the veil of Tanit. Flaubert was always fascinated by the femme fatale. He produced his

own account of the story of Salomé, who asked for John the Baptist's head on a platter, in "Hérodias" (1877), and his *The Temptation of Saint Anthony* (1874) includes an archetypal femme fatale figure in Ennoïa. As he does in *Salammbô*, however, he implies in these works that there is no real triumph to be gained in seducing men to their doom, and that both parties to any such transaction are ruined by it.

The mirage that Flaubert perpetuates in his plot is not so much an image of lost Carthage, seeming to hover above the desert sands, but rather an illusion of the power of human emotion. *Salammbô* relentlessly smashes the idols of romantic fiction: true love, honor, cunning, bravery in battle, and other such staples of public and individual mythology all are shown to be nonsense. Few of the later writers who imitated *Salammbô*, however, retained Flaubert's clear-sighted awareness of where the mirage ends and the desert begins.

The distinction between civilization and barbarism, which seemed so clear to the Greeks and Romans—and to many later writers who looked back with regret on the collapse that brought about the Dark Ages—is deliberately blurred in *Salammbô*. The barbarians fight Carthage's—civilization's—battles, but they do not get paid for it. When they demand reparation their forces are riven by internal dissent and eventually split by the offer of selective bribes. In courage and honesty of emotion, if not in table manners, they often outshine the Carthaginians. Their strike is broken with an amoral cynicism that the captains of industry of contemporary times can only emulate. Narr' Havas never gets to enjoy his promised bride; readers are not told whether he ever gets to collect all his back pay, but one is inclined to suspect that he does not. *Salammbô* agrees with many other fictitious accounts of the classical world in presuming that civilization won its temporary victory by offering promises of leisure and luxury that it could not keep. Flaubert, however—unlike most of the novelists who contemplated the decadence of the ancient world—was cynical, or realistic, enough to suppose that the bankruptcy that eventually brought about the fall of civilization was actual as well as merely moral. Flaubert was one of Western civilization's great demythologizers; *Salammbô* explores the mythologies of the romantic war story.

"Critical Evaluation" by Brian Stableford

Further Reading

Brombert, Victor. *The Novels of Flaubert: A Study of Themes and Techniques*. Princeton, N.J.: Princeton University Press, 1966. Chapter 3 discusses "*Salammbô*: The Epic of Immobility."

Culler, Jonathan. *Flaubert: The Uses of Uncertainty*. Rev. ed.

Ithaca, N.Y.: Cornell University Press, 1985. *Salammbô* is discussed in chapter 3.

Curry, Corrada Biazzo. *Description and Meaning in Three Novels by Gustave Flaubert*. New York: Peter Lang, 1997. Focuses on Flaubert's use of imagery in *Madame Bovary, Salammbô*, and *A Sentimental Education*. Demonstrates how his descriptive passages are subject to various possibilities of meaning and nonmeaning.

Green, Anne. *Flaubert and the Historical Novel: Salammbô Reassessed*. New York: Cambridge University Press, 1982. A detailed study of the text and its literary context.

Sherrington, R. J. *Three Novels by Flaubert: A Study of Techniques*. Oxford, England: Clarendon Press, 1970. Chapter 4 is a lengthy analysis of *Salammbô*.

Hohl, Anne Mullen. *Exoticism in "Salammbô": The Languages of Myth, Religion, and War*. Birmingham, Ala.: Summa, 1995. Analyzes the elements of the exotic in the novel, including Flaubert's use of language and of figures of speech and the novel's structure.

Porter, Laurence M., ed. *A Gustave Flaubert Encyclopedia*. Westport, Conn.: Greenwood Press, 2001. An alphabetically arranged collection of articles that focus on Flaubert's literary works and their sources, as well as information about the places and the characters in his fiction, nineteenth century history, and the writers who influenced and were influenced by Flaubert. Each article includes a bibliography.

Troyat, Henri. *Flaubert*. Translated by Joan Pinkham. New York: Viking Press, 1992. Troyat, an accomplished biographer, provides a thorough, engrossing book that reconstructs Flaubert's life based on the novelist's prodigious correspondence with his family and friends.

Unwin, Timothy, ed. *The Cambridge Companion to Flaubert*. New York: Cambridge University Press, 2004. Collection of essays analyzing all of Flaubert's works and discussing his life, place in literary history, writing process, and other aspects of his fiction. In the final essay, "Flaubert, Our Contemporary," noted novelist Mario Vargas Llosa assesses Flaubert's continued relevance.

Wall, Geoffrey. *Flaubert: A Life*. New York: Farrar, Straus and Giroux, 2002. A critically acclaimed narrative biography. Offers many new details and is a great read.

'Salem's Lot

Author: Stephen King (1947-　　)
First published: 1975
Type of work: Novel
Type of plot: Horror
Time of plot: 1975-1976
Locale: Jerusalem's Lot, Maine; Los Zapatos, Mexico

Principal characters:
KURT BARLOW, a powerful vampire
BENJAMAN MEARS, a young novelist
JIMMY CODY, a young doctor
MARK PETRIE, a twelve-year-old boy
SUSAN NORTON, an attractive aspiring artist
MATTHEW BURKE, a sixty-three-year-old high school English teacher
FATHER DONALD CALLAHAN, an alcoholic Catholic priest
RICHARD THROCKETT STRAKER, Barlow's human assistant
RALPHIE and DANNY GLICK, young victims
BONNIE SAWYER, an adulterous young wife
COREY BRYANT, a telephone repairman and Bonnie's lover
FLOYD TIBBITS, a young man who has dated Susan
MICHAEL COREY RYERSON, a groundskeeper
SANDY McDOUGALL, a young mother

The Story:

In Mexico in 1976, a nameless man and boy pass as father and son, though they are unrelated. The man, once a novelist, maintains an interest in Maine, and he obtains regional newspapers to keep apprised of current events there. He pays particular attention to a lengthy story describing the town of Jerusalem's Lot, now abandoned. A priest, to whom the boy makes a confession, reveals that the boy wept terribly during confession. Though no details of the confession are revealed, a week later the pair decide to return to Maine.

In 1975, the novelist, Ben Mears, nears the town of Jerusalem's Lot, pausing at the decrepit Marsten house on its out-skirts. Hubie Marsten was a mobster; he killed his wife and hanged himself in the house. When Ben was a boy, he entered the Marsten house on a dare and saw Marsten's hanged ghost, which opened its eyes as he approached. The house has re-mained vacant, and the returning Ben, who believes it holds Marsten's psychic residue, has attempted to rent it, not know-ing that Richard Straker has purchased it.

In town, Ben meets aspiring artist Susan Norton, who rec-ognizes him from a dust-jacket photograph. They share ice cream, and Ben reveals he has returned to write about the town: He lost both parents before he was fourteen and was raised by his aunt, a resident of 'Salem's Lot. They left the town during a devastating fire. Ben's arrival is noted by the local police, who also note that Susan has been dating Floyd Tibbits; her relationship with Tibbits is also noted by her overprotective mother, who is relieved to learn that Ben is staying in a conservative rooming house.

The town experiences a seemingly typical day: An ado-lescent dislikes his morning farm chores; the milkman makes his rounds; the landlady at Ben's rooming house prepares breakfast; young Sandy McDougall hates her noisy baby, Randy; cemetery groundskeeper Mike Ryerson discovers a dead dog hanging on a fence; the child-hating schoolbus driver abuses his passengers; by keeping calm, young Mark Petrie confronts and defeats the school bully; Bonnie Sawyer continues her adulterous affair with young Corey Bryant; and Ralphie Glick vanishes while walking with Danny: At midnight, his corpse is made an offering to the Lord of the Flies.

Straker meets the realtor who sold him the Marsten house and gives instructions concerning the delivery of a sideboard to the house. He and his partner Barlow intend to open an an-tique shop in Jerusalem's Lot. One of the delivery men sees something in the basement that might be Ralphie Glick's clothes, but he is dissuaded from reporting this to the police. After seeming to recover from pernicious anemia, Danny Glick dies in the hospital. Ben, who assisted in the search for Ralphie, goes out on a date with Susan. Afterward, he has a drink in the local roadhouse, where he meets Matt Burke, who likes the loud music.

Danny Glick's grave is readied. Father Callahan officiates at the burial and, later, drinks; his faith is waning. Mark Petrie concludes that death is when monsters get you, and the police receive reports on Ben, Straker, and Barlow, concluding that there is no connection between them. Ben and Matt discuss current events and decide to visit the Marsten house with Su-san, ostensibly to welcome the new owners. Somewhat later, Matt is concerned about the listless Ryerson, who is now his

houseguest; he witnesses the man being killed by Danny Glick. He calls Ben, whose advice is to report the death but say nothing about vampires. Local doctor Jimmy Cody pro-nounces Ryerson dead.

As this is occurring, Susan fights with her mother, who wants her to marry Tibbits. Susan realizes she must leave home, after which she receives a telephone call in which she learns that Tibbits has attacked and hospitalized Ben. She visits Ben, who instructs her to visit Matt. Matt tells her about Ryerson and vampires. As they talk, he hears something, goes upstairs, and confronts the vampiric Ryerson; he repels Ryerson, but the stress causes a nonfatal heart attack.

The fire that drove Ben from 'Salem's Lot is revealed to have been set intentionally. The arsonist graduated as class valedictorian and amassed a fortune on Wall Street before dying young. Meanwhile, the vampires are increasing: Ryerson takes the mortuary attendant; Danny Glick takes Randy McDougall; the Glick children take their parents; Floyd Tibbits dies in his cell; Bonnie Sawyer and Corey Bryant are surprised by Bonnie's husband, who tells Bryant to leave town, after which Bryant is taken by Barlow. Mark repels Danny Glick with a cross. Jimmy Cody pronounces Ben healthy and is told about vampires. He wants evidence and agrees to conduct an autopsy of Danny Glick under the pretense of looking for infectious encephalitis. They visit the mortuary: Mrs. Glick awakens as a vampire, attacking and biting Jimmy before vanishing.

Without consulting Matt or Ben, Susan decides to visit the Marsten house, and Mark encounters her outside. They enter together, and Straker catches them. He ties Mark in the attic where Marsten hanged himself, and he leaves Susan in the basement, near Barlow's coffin. Mark escapes just as Barlow awakens. Matt broaches the subject of vampires to Father Callahan.

The vampires overwhelm Jerusalem's Lot. Mark intro-duces himself to Ben and informs him of Susan's fate. They meet Matt and Jimmy and learn what must be done. Father Callahan blesses and confesses them, and he accompanies Ben, Jimmy, and Mark to the Marsten house. They find Straker bled dry by Barlow, along with a note from Barlow welcoming, mocking, and threatening them each by name. Ben drives a stake through Susan's body. As Ben and Jimmy confer with the hospitalized Matt, Father Callahan takes Mark home and talks to his disbelieving parents. Barlow ar-rives, kills the Petries, and confronts Father Callahan, whose faith falters: Barlow defeats and subjugates him, and he leaves town. Mark flees to the hospital and tells Ben, Jimmy, and Matt what has occurred, but Barlow does not attack them.

The next day, as Mark, Jimmy, and Ben wearily look for Barlow and make stakes, Matt has a fatal heart attack. Jimmy realizes that Barlow is in the basement of the rooming house and goes there with Mark, only to be killed by a trap. As night is falling, Ben drives a stake through Barlow. The next day, he returns to town, buries Jimmy and the Petries, and flees with Mark. A year later, they return to burn the town and battle the vampires.

Critical Evaluation:

Although displaying flaws in plotting and some unfortunately sloppy writing, *'Salem's Lot* is a major novel. Stephen King's panoramic narrative approach and colloquial narrative style permitted him to create dozens of recognizable characters and to address issues and develop subtexts that previous vampire novels, because of their composition time or limited narrative focus, could not. *'Salem's Lot* was a best seller and did much to make King a household name, and it was one of the seminal works in the horror publishing boom of the late 1970's and the 1980's. Numerous writers copied King's narrative techniques and attempted to replicate his style, but few succeeded, and none of their works has *'Salem's Lot* narrative drive or reaches its level of suspense.

King stated in "On Becoming a Brand Name," his foreword to *Fear Itself* (1982), that *'Salem's Lot* was inspired by a conversation about "what might happen if Dracula returned today," by memories of the town in which he grew up, and by Thornton Wilder's *Our Town* (pr., pb. 1938), which he was then teaching in high school. King set about creating a Maine town in which "people could drop out of sight, disappear, perhaps even come back as the living dead"; he was later, in his 2002 book *On Writing*, to describe *'Salem's Lot* as "a peculiar combination of *Peyton Place* and *Dracula*."

Perhaps because King did not want to stray far from his literary models, *'Salem's Lot* is a deeply conservative work on all levels. King's vampires are entirely traditional: evil, undead, nocturnal, bloodsucking beings bound by arbitrary rules that cannot withstand scrutiny. The major subtext of *'Salem's Lot* concerns the death of small-town America. The cause of this death, however, remains intriguingly unresolved and multivalent, for King deliberately establishes several equally valid (and conservative) subtexts. In the first, it is significant that Barlow and Straker, like Dracula in England, are not natives but foreigners. Indeed, their seemingly innocent antique store sells foreign materials, and through this store they infiltrate and fatally corrupt Jerusalem's Lot by exploiting the greed and venality of its residents. Thus, external mercantile forces are what destroy small-town America.

In a second subtext, *'Salem's Lot* depicts a war in the epic and unending religious battle between white (good) and black (evil). Although Father Callahan several times witnesses the extraordinary power of the white, particularly when it blasts the lock from the door as they enter the Marsten house, his doubts and dwindling faith become moral and spiritual failures that permit the black (Barlow) to emerge triumphant. It is the decline in traditional faith and its accompanying spiritual values that leads to the destruction of the town.

A third subtext involves sex and sexuality, and to establish this theme King deliberately emphasizes the erotic aspects of vampirism that *Dracula* (1897) author Bram Stoker and other writers were unable or unwilling to develop. The many scenes of vampiric attack and seduction are sexually charged, and victims go to their deaths sexually aroused. In addition, the relationship between Barlow and Straker is that of a cultured homosexual couple: They are "partners," Barlow is repeatedly described as "effeminate" while Straker is "not effeminate in the least," and they intend to live together in the town after having traveled the world together. The conservative subtext in this case is that emergent sexuality and exposure to and acceptance of deviant behavior (in 1976 terms) will lead not only to personal corruption but also to the destruction of traditional small-town values.

Whatever the subtext, King's narrative is informed, culturally literate, and carefully structured. He not only draws upon the classic text (*Dracula*) but also makes explicit reference to Wallace Steven's classic poem about death, "The Emperor of Ice-Cream" (1922), and he draws heavily upon the presence of vampires in American popular culture: *'Salem's Lot* depicts vampires by cereal boxes, plastic models, television shows, and motion pictures. Barlow does not appear for the first third of *'Salem's Lot*, but he is expertly and ominously foreshadowed, his corruption depicted as a natural part of American culture as a whole.

In early interviews, King stated that he intended to write a sequel to *'Salem's Lot*, perhaps beginning in New York City with Father Callahan receiving a summons to return. To date he has not done this, although the short story "One for the Road," published in *Maine* in 1977 and in *Night Shift* (1978), is a quasi-sequel and offers a memorable and moving description of a child vampire. "Night Flier" (1987) is a traditional vampire story, largely unexceptional but for the concept and description of a vampire's bloody urine. Moreover, Father Callahan does reappear in the later books of the *Dark Tower* series (1982-2004). *'Salem's Lot* remains one of King's strongest works.

Richard Bleiler

Further Reading

Bleiler, Richard. "Stephen King." In *Supernatural Fiction Writers: Contemporary Fantasy and Horror*, edited by Bleiler. New York: Charles Scribner's Sons/Thomson Gale, 2003. Analysis of the writer's life and work.

Joshi, S. T. *The Modern Weird Tale*. Jefferson, N.C.: McFarland, 2001. Contemporary discussion of horror and fantasy, analyzing the evolution of traditional and established tropes over time.

King, Stephen. "On Becoming a Brand Name." Foreword to *Fear Itself: The Horror Fiction of Stephen King*. Edited by Tim Underwood and Chuck Miller. San Francisco: Underwood-Miller, 1982. King talks about the peculiar phenomenon in which a person is transformed into a brand in order to sell books.

_____. *On Writing*. New York: Scribners, 2002. King discusses the craft of writing, both his own creative process and literary practice more generally.

Magistrale, Tony. *Landscape of Fear: Stephen King's American Gothic*. Bowling Green, Ohio: Bowling Green State University Popular Press, 1988. Analyzes King's novels from the perspective of popular culture studies, and places them in the context of distinctively American literature.

Reino, Joseph. *Stephen King: The First Decade, "Carrie" to "Pet Sematary."* Boston: Twayne, 1988. Details the beginning of the novelists' career and analyzes his early works, including *'Salem's Lot*.

Russell, Sharon A. *Stephen King: A Critical Companion*. Westport, Conn.: Greenwood Press, 1996. Provides an overview of King's work and his prevalent themes and concerns.

The Salt Eaters

Author: Toni Cade Bambara (1939-1995)
First published: 1980
Type of work: Novel
Type of plot: Magical Realism
Time of plot: Late 1970's
Locale: Claybourne, a town in the American South

Principal characters:
VELMA HENRY, a community organizer
MINNIE RANSOM, a healer
OLD WIFE, her spirit guide
JAMES LEE "OBIE" HENRY, Velma's husband
PALMA, Velma's sister
FRED HOLT, a bus driver
DR. MEADOWS, a physician

The Story:

Two women are seated on stools in the middle of a circle of onlookers in the Southwest Community Infirmary in Claybourne, a town in the American South. One of the women is Velma Henry, a woman with a husband, a son, a full-time job as a computer programmer and an avocation for community organizing. She has been a strong political and artistic force in her community, but strains in her marriage as well as exhaustion caused by continuing a struggle that seems to promise no results have led her to attempt suicide. Now she sits, dirty and unkempt, wearing only a hospital gown, facing but withdrawn from Minnie Ransom, a healer who sits on the other stool.

Minnie is dressed in a bright red dress, a hot-pink head scarf, two waist bands of kenti cloth, a fringed shawl, and several wrist bangles. She warns Velma that spiritual healing can come only to those who truly want it; as she coaxes Velma, a prayer group, a medical doctor, and visiting interns and nurses look on.

As Velma fades in and out of awareness, she thinks about her activities at the Academy of Seven Arts, a community center she and her husband, James Lee "Obie" Henry had founded to preserve African American arts and culture and to teach job skills and home economics. Typically, at the center, the men have been the loudest voices in meetings devoted to politics, while the women have quietly done most of the organizing, clerical work, cooking, and cleaning. It is the late 1970's in the United States, and the community is concerned about job equality, apartheid in South Africa, and pollution caused by the local chemical company. Feminism remains a powerful but largely unspoken idea among the activists. As the 1970's draws to a close, the community is coming apart, pulled in too many directions at once—just as Velma is herself. It will soon be time for the annual Claybourne Mardi Gras Festival, and many hope that the event will draw the community back together.

As Minnie focuses on Velma, she also engages in a conversation with Old Wife, her guide in the spirit world. Both women realize that Velma's problem is in part sexual; she and Henry have not been as intimate as they once were, and Henry has cheated on Velma. For Minnie, sexuality is an important part of a woman's power; she dresses provocatively and flirts with the physician at the clinic. Minnie remembers her younger days, before she had discovered her gift for healing, when everyone around her thought she was losing her mind. Wandering the woods, she met Old Wife and began an apprenticeship with her. At first she resisted the gift. Now she tells Velma that she believes she also has the ability to connect with the spiritual world, but that she is resisting the gift as Minnie once did.

Meanwhile, the women of the Seven Sisters performance troupe, including Velma's sister, Palma, are on a bus headed to Claybourne. Palma has had a dream about Velma being in trouble, so to check on her sister she arranged for the women of the troupe to perform at the festival. The women are politically aware, and as they ride they discuss plans for a program that could include references to U.S. president Jimmy Carter, to nuclear weapons, and to the Ku Klux Klan. Their driver is Fred Holt, whose good friend, Porter, has just died and who is tempted to end his own life rather than face a lonely retirement. He decides to drive the bus into a swamp, but two of the women sense his plan and will him and the bus to stay on the road. Nearly on schedule, they all reach Claybourne in time for the festival, amid rumors that the Academy of Seven Arts is also a center for militant activity and the repository of a large supply of weapons; there are rumors as well that something dramatic is going to happen.

Everyone continues preparations for the festival in the middle of a dramatic thunderstorm. Soon, there is an explosion at the Transchemical Company plant that sends radioactive material over the area. Few people realize what has happened. Hoo Doo Man leads the parade as the festival begins. Minnie finally does break through to Velma, urging her to claim her power and to claim the responsibility that comes with choosing life. She will reconnect with her husband and will resume leadership of the community, but this time, she will do so with the strength of her healing gifts and her spiritual connection.

Critical Evaluation:

Toni Cade Bambara lived a multilayered life, as a short-story writer, a novelist, a filmmaker, a dancer, a community organizer, and a critic. She is perhaps best known for her short stories, including the collection *Gorilla, My Love* (1972); one of its stories, "The Lesson," is widely anthologized in high school and college textbooks. Her first novel, *The Salt Eaters*, also is multilayered, telling several stories simultaneously, presenting characters' conversations, and relating their dreams, memories, and stream-of-consciousness musings. This "layeredness" is not merely structural: one of the themes of the novel is the necessity of integrating or reintegrating the layers of individuals and their communities.

As the novel opens, Velma has attempted suicide because she is overwhelmed by her many responsibilities, her husband's infidelity, and her sense that further struggle for social justice is futile. At the same time, her community, represented by the Academy of Seven Arts, is coming apart as well—divided by sexism, power struggles, and too many causes being adopted by too many individuals. Bambara's lesson through the story is that Velma must literally "pull herself together" by embracing her spiritual gifts and claiming the power that resides in an integrated whole. By her example and through her leadership, the community will survive as well.

In Bambara's work, as it had been in her life, African American culture and black community activism are essential. The author believed that radical grassroots political organizations could bring change, and she was herself active in the Civil Rights movement and various Black Nationalist groups. Many of her characters in *The Salt Eaters* are activists, too, and are members of groups and organizations including the Academy of Seven Arts, the Seven Sisters improvisational group, the YWCA, the Ida B. Wells Club, the Coalition of Black Trade Unionists, and local churches. They work to address social issues that are prominent in the late 1970's, including the 1978 Humphrey-Hawkins Bill, which addressed unemployment; nuclear proliferation; the junta in Chile; and the illegal activities of U.S. counterintelligence programs. Activism is critical to the black community, and it strengthens individuals. However, community organizations are only as strong as its often frail members can make them; the women of Claybourne are among Bambara's characters who have suffered from and been limited by, for example, the sexism of the Civil Rights movement.

Another theme of the novel is healing. Salt, used to treat wounds, is a symbol of healing, but too much of it can be poisonous. The wide variety of healing gifts is made clear from the opening chapter, which shows Minnie Ransom and her spirit guide conducting a healing ceremony in an otherwise conventional infirmary, as a prayer group and a skeptical medical doctor look on. Minnie's spirit guide, Old Wife, is

Christian; other characters in the novel find wisdom and healing in tarot cards, acupressure, obeah, astrology, cowrie shells, and tent revivals. Dr. Meadows, director of the Southwest Community Infirmary, is amused by Minnie's rituals and impatient with those of Velma. Successful and self-important, he has lost all touch with his community until an accidental encounter with poor African Americans shows him that there are things in the world he does not understand. He remains committed to Western medicine, but becomes more tolerant of other approaches to healing. Treating Velma's wounds, and the wounds of her community, is at the heart of the novel, but Bambara makes clear that there are many paths to healing.

The Salt Eaters is, by every measure, a difficult novel that is much admired but seldom read or taught. Readers looking for linearity and plot are easily confused by the novel's free movement between past, present, and future; between real and imagined; and between spoken and unspoken. Allusions to specific events from the 1970's have become increasingly obscure with the passing of time, as have references to music and literature. Even critics are divided about what actually happens in the novel—whether the explosion at the Transchemical plant, for example, is a real event in the story or only imagined by the novel's characters. Many critics state that the town of Claybourne is in Georgia, while others think the author leaves the state unclear. The world, Bambara seems to be saying, is not linear or logical, it is not sequential, it is not broken into discrete people and events. The world is a web, a network—everything is connected. The only way to live in it is to stand in the center and be open to everything at once.

Cynthia A. Bily

Further Reading

Bambara, Toni Cade. *Deep Sightings and Rescue Missions: Fiction, Essays, and Conversations.* Edited by Toni Morrison. New York: Pantheon, 1996. A posthumous collection, mostly of previously uncollected pieces. Includes the illuminating essay "Language and the Writer," about the colonization of the creative imagination, and "The Education of a Storyteller," about the author's lessons from her grandmother.

Butler-Evans, Elliott. *Race, Gender, and Desire: Narrative Strategies in the Fiction of Toni Cade Bambara, Toni Morrison, and Alice Walker.* Philadelphia: Temple University Press, 1989. The first two chapters examine the aesthetic context of these African American women novelists, setting up feminist readings such as that in chapter 6, "Rewriting and Revising in the 1980's: *Tar Baby, The Color Purple*, and *The Salt Eaters*."

Holmes, Linda Janet, and Cheryl A. Wall, eds. *Savoring the Salt: The Legacy of Toni Cade Bambara.* Philadelphia: Temple University Press, 2008. Thirty essays on Bambara's life and work, including her activism and her film career. Several of the authors refer to *The Salt Eaters*, examining its themes of despair and healing.

Kelley, Margot Anne. "'Damballah Is the First Law of Thermodynamics': Modes of Access to Toni Cade Bambara's *The Salt Eaters*." *African American Review* 27, no. 3 (Fall, 1993): 479-493. Kelley explains how she uses the science of chaos theory as a model for helping students understand Bambara's approach to metaphysical wholeness.

Vertreace, Martha M. *Toni Cade Bambara.* New York: Macmillan Library Reference, 1998. The first full-length resource devoted to the entirety of Bambara's career. Provides information useful for students of the author's works.

Wilentz, Gay. *Healing Narratives: Women Writers Curing Cultural Dis-ease.* New Brunswick, N.J.: Rutgers University Press, 2000. Includes Bambara among a diverse group of writers who intend to heal themselves and their communities through their writing. In *The Salt Eaters*, Wilentz demonstrates, the connection between individual and community healing is particularly foregrounded.

Samson Agonistes

Author: John Milton (1608-1674)
First published: 1671
Type of work: Poetry
Type of plot: Tragedy
Time of plot: c. 1100 B.C.E.
Locale: Palestine

Principal characters:
SAMSON, a Hebrew champion, one of the Judges
MANOA, his father
DALILA, a Philistine woman, Samson's wife
HARAPHA, a Philistine giant
CHORUS OF HEBREW ELDERS

The Poem:

Samson, eyeless in Gaza, is given a holiday from his labors during the season of a Philistine religious festival. He sits alone before the prison, lamenting his fallen state. His hair grows long again and his physical strength returns, but to him life seems hopeless. He wonders why God chose him, who seems destined to live out his days as a miserable, blinded wretch, but he nevertheless blames his misfortunes on himself. He should not have trusted in his strength without also seeing to it that he gained the wisdom to protect him from the wiles of Philistine women. He mourns also the blindness that makes him live a life only half alive.

A chorus of Hebrew elders joins him. It recalls his past great deeds and speak of the present state of Israel, subject to Philistine rule. Samson accuses his people of loving bondage more than liberty because they refused to take advantage of the victories he won for them in the days of his strength. Manoa, Samson's aged father, also comes to see his son, whose fate gives him great distress. He brings news that plunges Samson still deeper into his depression: The Philistine feast is being given to thank the idol Dagon for delivering the mighty Hebrew into the hands of his enemies. Samson realizes then the dishonor he brought to God, yet he is able to find hope in the thought that the contest now is between Jehovah and Dagon. He foresees no good for himself, cast off by God, and he prays only for speedy death.

As the chorus muses over God's treatment of his chosen ones, Dalila approaches. When she offers Samson help as recompense for her betrayal of him, he scorns her. She tries to excuse herself, pleading weakness and patriotism, but Samson refuses to compound his sins by yielding to her again; he is regaining spiritual as well as physical might. He again accepts his position as God's champion when Harapha, a Philistine giant, comes to gloat over his misfortune. It is too bad that Samson is now so weak, says Harapha; had he met him sooner he would have won great honor by defeating him. Harapha cannot defile himself by combat with a slave. Samson, enraged, invites Harapha to come within his reach. The giant refuses to accept the challenge, however, saying that such a contest would be beneath his dignity, and leaves.

When a public officer comes to summon Samson to the feast, the blind man refuses to go. His presence there would violate Hebrew law, and he has no desire to have the Philistine mob make sport of his blindness. As Samson tells the chorus why he will not go, however, he feels a sudden inner compulsion to follow the messenger. He senses that the day will mark some remarkable deed in his life. When the officer brings a second, more imperative summons, Samson accompanies him.

Manoa, returning with the news that he was able to persuade the Philistine lords to ransom his son, gladly plans to sacrifice his patrimony and spend his old age caring for Samson. As he is speaking of his hopes that Samson will recover his sight, horrible shouting breaks out in the temple. A Hebrew messenger, fleeing the awful spectacle, tells Manoa and the chorus that he just saw Samson pull the temple down upon himself and thousands of Philistines. Manoa decides that Samson conducted himself like Samson and heroically ended a heroic life.

Critical Evaluation:

Samson Agonistes is John Milton's profound treatment of a biblical story in the form of the classical Greek tragedy. The poetic play, published with *Paradise Regained* in 1671, was not designed for the stage (such a play is known as a closet play); the author modeled his work on Greek tragedy because he found it "the gravest, moralest, and most profitable of all other poems." The story of Samson is one of the most dramatic episodes in the Old Testament; the parallels between the life of the blind Hebrew hero and Milton's own must have encouraged him to base his last work on the story of the man singled out before his birth as a servant of God. Milton opens his play during Samson's imprisonment. He refers frequently to the biblical accounts of the events of Samson's youth, but the episodes that make up most of the play are his own creation. Each affects Samson's character, renewing his faith in God and influencing his decision to go to the Philistine temple to die.

Samson Agonistes is a powerful and moving drama. The

poetry is majestic and simple, different from the rich verse of *Paradise Lost* (1667, 1674) and *Paradise Regained* but perfectly suited to the subject. The play is the masterpiece of an old man, one who suffered like Samson and who has, in his own way, triumphed over suffering. *Samson Agonistes* was published in the same volume as *Paradise Regained*, three years before Milton's death, so tradition ascribes its composition to the late years of his life and marks the drama as the last of his three great poems. More recently, however, various theories place the date of the work as far back as the 1640's. Generally, support for the earlier date of composition is related to the critical opinion that the artistry of *Samson Agonistes* is of a lower order than that of *Paradise Lost* and *Paradise Regained*. In other words, by placing *Samson Agonistes* at a greater chronological distance from the other poems, it is easier to support a theory that it is an inferior work of art. It is certain from manuscript evidence that as early as the 1640's Milton planned a series of five Samson plays; so it is by no means impossible that at least a first draft of *Samson Agonistes* was written at that time. The traditional view that *Samson Agonistes* belongs to the end of Milton's canon is still widely held, and whether the drama was written shortly before publication or nearly thirty years earlier, scholars know that it was initially conceived long before it appeared.

Perhaps the origin of the view that *Samson Agonistes* is inferior to Milton's other major poems lies in Samuel Johnson's criticism of its tragic form. Ever since he said that the play has a beginning and an end but no middle, critics have been addressing themselves to the problem of viewing the poem as a classical Greek tragedy. Milton set the stage for later arguments by prefacing the poem with an essay discussing Aristotle's concept of tragedy and extolling classical tragedy. By harking back to the ancients as his models rather than his own Elizabethan predecessors, he hoped to reestablish the "classical" pattern of tragedy, purging the abuses into which the genre fell through the English habit of mixing comedy and lowborn persons into the plot of a tragic play. The difference between Milton and the ancients is also established in the prefatory essay, however, when he says that *Samson Agonistes* was never meant for the stage. Those who sided with Johnson find that, in spite of Milton's attempt to follow the classical pattern, the play is flawed by the static and lifeless quality they see in the central episodes.

What the drama lacks, however, is not life but action. All the famous acts of the protagonist occur either in the past or "offstage." Samson's actions as the hero of the Israelites and his subsequent fall are over before the poem begins, and his final triumph over the Philistines is narrated, not shown.

There is no physical action during the episodes with Manoa, Dalila, and Harapha, but there is much psychological action. These episodes provide readers with the background of Samson's present dilemma and reveal the progressive revitalization of Samson's willingness to fulfill his role as the hero and the deliverer of his people. The three episodes in the middle of the play may be seen as temptations to betray his faith, fortitude, and patience. The action of the drama may be seen as the psychological process by which Samson meets and overcomes these temptations. Through these episodes, which some have found dramatically empty, Samson moves from despair to courage and to the final heroic act of self-sacrifice. Johnson's critical mistake was in not accepting inner conflicts and resolutions as action.

Beyond the structural problems that complicate *Samson Agonistes'* claim to being a tragedy, there is an additional difficulty arising from the basic difference in theological perspective between Milton and his Greek counterparts. The question is whether it is possible to write such a thing as Christian tragedy. Is it possible, within the Christian view of the human experience as a comedy, to have an ultimately tragic event? One of the paradoxes in the drama then is that while the play ends with death, it is a death-in-victory, like that of Jesus Christ. Therefore, it may be argued that the play is not a tragedy.

In a sense, the tragedy already took place before readers meet Samson "eyeless in Gaza." Samson already fell, and the fall was precipitated by hubris, his tragic flaw of excessive pride. Samson's death results from a conscious willful act, not from a personal flaw or from an act of the indifferent Fates. Through his death Samson triumphs over his enemies and fulfills his destiny. This victorious tragedy, too, has parallels among the classics. Certainly the Oedipus cycle presents the similar pattern of a protagonist who falls first through a flaw and then later, in a tragedy resulting from the first fall, transcends the disaster of death with a spiritual victory.

Granting the classical parallels in Milton's poem, readers are left with the issue of fitting tragedy into Milton's Christian view of history. Critics are right to say that tragedy is not ultimately possible for a Christian hero in a Christian universe. That is not to deny, however, that tragedy may exist in human terms. Thus, on one level the deaths of Samson and Christ are tragic, but the paradox of the Christian faith is that one who loses his life shall find it. Although individual tragedies can exist, they are ultimately subsumed in the larger cosmic framework of the divine design. That is, they become a part of a larger pattern in which death is followed by resurrection. Hence, readers can see Milton's tragic poem as the union of a biblical theme and a classical literary form, just as *Paradise Lost* is the union of the classical epic form and the Christian vision of creation.

"Critical Evaluation" by Timothy E. Bollinger

Further Reading

Campbell, Gordon, and Thomas N. Corns. *John Milton: Life, Work, and Thought*. New York: Oxford University Press, 2008. Insightful and comprehensive biography written by the editors of the *Oxford Milton* that is based in part on new information about seventeenth century English history. Sheds light on Milton's ideas and the turbulent times in which he lived.

Crump, Galbraith M., ed. *Twentieth Century Interpretations of "Samson Agonistes."* Englewood Cliffs, N.J.: Prentice-Hall, 1968. Assembles seven seminal articles and eight shorter selections of critical commentary. Following an introductory critical survey, the selections offer a wide range of literary criticism dealing with the tragedy's biographical significance, structure, style, themes, and genre.

Duran, Angelica, ed. *A Concise Companion to Milton*. Malden, Mass.: Blackwell, 2007. Collection of essays analyzing Milton's works, including discussions of his legacy, a survey of more than three hundred years of Milton criticism, and "The Nightmare of History: *Samson Agonistes*" by Louis Schwartz.

Hanford, James Holly, and James G. Taaffe. *A Milton Handbook*. 5th ed. East Norwalk, Conn.: Appleton-Century-Crofts, 1970. Presents an overview of the tragedy and a survey of previous criticism. An excellent starting point. Includes bibliography.

Hunter, William B., ed. *Milton's English Poetry*. Cranbury, N.J.: Bucknell University Press, 1986. Reprints articles on Milton's poetry from *A Milton Encyclopedia*, written by distinguished scholars. The long entry on *Samson Agonistes* provides a detailed survey of the numerous important critical issues and controversies associated with the tragedy.

Kelley, Mark R., and Joseph Wittreich, eds. *Altering Eyes: New Perspectives on "Samson Agonistes."* Newark: University of Delaware Press, 2002. Collection of eleven essays offering new interpretations of the poem, including discussions of redemption in the work, the character of Dalila, and Samson and the homeless women of Israel.

Low, Anthony. *The Blaze of Noon: A Reading of "Samson Agonistes."* Ithaca, N.Y.: Columbia University Press, 1974. Offers a scholarly analysis of the origins, style, and characters of this tragedy. The extended scholarly discussion is developed with the general reader in mind; the book is accessible and erudite.

Mayer, Joseph G. *Between Two Pillars: The Hero's Plight in "Samson Agonistes" and "Paradise Regained."* Lanham, Md.: University Press of America, 2004. Describes the dilemmas facing the protagonists in both works. Samson Agonistes is caught between two opposing forces: his election by God to perform great deeds and his inability to perform these feats after he becomes blind.

Wittreich, Joseph. *Interpreting "Samson Agonistes."* Princeton, N.J.: Princeton University Press, 1986. A challenging but highly informative book that surveys the biblical and the Renaissance traditions related to Milton's tragedy. Furnishes a comprehensive assessment of modern criticism.

Sanctuary

Author: William Faulkner (1897-1962)
First published: 1931
Type of work: Novel
Type of plot: Melodrama
Time of plot: 1929
Locale: Mississippi; Memphis, Tennessee

Principal characters:
POPEYE, a racketeer
HORACE BENBOW, a lawyer
TEMPLE DRAKE, a woman raped and kidnapped by Popeye
TOMMY, a moonshiner killed by Popeye
LEE GOODWIN, a moonshiner accused of Tommy's murder
RUBY LAMAR, Goodwin's woman
REBA RIVERS, the madam of a Memphis bawdy house
GOWAN STEVENS, a college student

The Story:

Horace Benbow, on his way to Jefferson one afternoon, stops to drink from a spring on the Old Frenchman place. When he rises, he sees an undersized man in a black suit watching him; the man's hand is in a pocket that holds his gun. Satisfied at last that the lawyer is not a revenue officer, Popeye leads Benbow to the gutted ruins of a plantation house. That night the lawyer drinks moonshine and eats with Popeye, several moonshiners, and a blind and deaf old man, the father of Lee Goodwin, one of the moonshiners. They are fed by Ruby, Goodwin's woman. Later, Benbow is given a lift into Jefferson on a truck loaded with whiskey on its way to Memphis.

The next afternoon, at his widowed sister's home, Benbow watches her walking in the garden with young Gowan Stevens. Stevens leaves that evening after supper because he has a date with a woman at the state university the following night. The woman is Temple Drake.

After a dance, Stevens gets drunk. He awakens the next morning in front of the railroad station. A special train taking university students to a baseball game already left. Driving rapidly, Stevens catches up with the train in the next town. Temple jumps from the train and climbs into his car. Disgusted with his disheveled appearance, she orders him to drive her back to the university. Stevens insists that he promised to drive her to the game. On the way, he decides to stop at Goodwin's place to buy more whiskey.

Stevens wrecks his car when he strikes a tree across the lane leading to the house. Popeye takes Temple and Stevens to the house. Temple goes into the kitchen, where Ruby sits smoking and watching the door. When Temple sees Stevens again, he is drunk. Then Popeye refuses to drive them back to town. Temple is frightened. Ruby tells Temple to go into the dining room to eat with the men.

One of the men tries to seize her, and Temple runs from the room and hides in a back room. Tommy, one of the moonshiners, follows her with a plate of food. The men begin to quarrel, and Stevens is knocked unconscious and carried into the house. Goodwin and a moonshiner named Van tussle until Popeye stops them. When Van finds Temple in one of the bedrooms, Goodwin knocks him down.

Then begins a series of comings and goings in the bedroom. Ruby comes to stand quietly in the darkness. Later, Popeye appears and stands silently over the girl. After he goes, Goodwin enters to claim a raincoat in which Temple wrapped herself. Popeye returns once more, followed noiselessly by Tommy, who squats in the dark beside Ruby. When the men finally leave the house to load the truck for its run to Memphis, Ruby takes Temple out to the barn and stays with her until daylight.

Stevens awakens early and starts out for the nearest house to hire a car. Feeling that he cannot face Temple again after his drunken night, he pays a farmer to drive to the house for Temple, while he thumbs a ride into town. Learning that Stevens already left, Temple goes into the kitchen with Ruby. When she leaves the house again, she sees the shadowy outline of a man who is squatting in the bushes and watching her. She returns to the house. Seeing Goodwin coming toward the house, she runs to the barn and hides in the corncrib. Watching, Popeye sees Goodwin looking from the house toward the barn. In the barn, Popeye finds Tommy at the door of the corncrib. While Tommy stands watching Goodwin, Popeye shoots him. Popeye rapes Temple with a corncob and kidnaps her. A short time later, Goodwin tells Ruby that Tommy is shot. He sends her to the nearest house to phone for the sheriff.

Benbow stays with his sister for two days. When Goodwin is brought in, charged with Tommy's murder, Benbow agrees to defend the prisoner. Goodwin, afraid of Popeye, claims only that he did not shoot Tommy. It is Ruby who tells Benbow that Popeye took Temple away in his car.

Benbow attempts to trace the woman's whereabouts. State Senator Snopes tells him that Judge Drake's daughter is supposed to be visiting an aunt in Michigan after an attempted runaway marriage.

A week before the opening of the court session, Benbow meets Senator Snopes again. For a price the politician is willing to reveal that Temple is in Reba Rivers's bawdy house in Memphis. Benbow goes at once to see the girl. Temple, although reluctant to talk, confirms many details of Ruby's story. The lawyer realizes that without Temple's testimony he cannot prove that Goodwin is innocent of Popeye's crime.

One morning, Temple bribes Reba's black servant to let her out of the house to make a phone call. That evening she manages to sneak out again, just as a car with Popeye in it pulls up at the curb. When she refuses to go back to her room, he takes her to the Grotto, where Temple arranged to meet a young man called Red, whom Popeye took to her room. At the Grotto, she dances with Red while Popeye plays at the crap table. She begs Red to take her away with him. Later in the evening, two of Popeye's henchmen force Temple into a car waiting outside. As they drive away, Temple sees Popeye sitting in a parked car.

Red's funeral is held in the Grotto. For the occasion, the tables are draped in black, and a downtown orchestra is hired to play hymns. Drinks are on the house. The night before the trial, Benbow learns from Reba that Popeye and Temple left her house. Ruby takes the witness stand the next day, and she tells the story of Tommy's murder. She and Benbow spend that night in the jail cell with Goodwin, who is afraid that Popeye might shoot him from one of the buildings across the street.

Temple, located through the efforts of Senator Snopes, is called to testify the next morning. She indicates that Goodwin is the man who attacked her on the day of Tommy's murder. Goodwin is convicted. That night a mob drags the prisoner from the jail and burns him. Popeye, on his way to Pensacola, is arrested for the murder of a police officer in Birmingham. The murder occurred the same night that Red was shot outside the Grotto. Popeye makes no defense, and his only claim is that he knows nothing about the Birmingham shooting. Convicted, he is executed for a crime he did not commit. Judge Drake takes his daughter to Europe. In Paris's Luxembourg Gardens with her father, listening in boredom to the band, Temple sits in quiet, sullen discontent.

Critical Evaluation:

William Faulkner, who was awarded the Nobel Prize, the Pulitzer Prize, and two National Book Awards, was one of the best fiction writers in America. Unsuccessful in his early attempts at poetry, Faulkner began selling his short stories to national magazines. This enabled him to support his family, in a manner of speaking, as he pursued fame. His first published short story, "A Rose for Emily," was his favorite and it is perhaps his most often anthologized. *Sartoris* (1929), whose plot retells events in Faulkner's grandfather's life, was rather successful and so the soft-spoken southerner began to discover his "own postage stamp of soil," Yoknapatawpha County (based on his hometown of Oxford, Mississippi, and its environs).

Faulkner is known for the complexities of his novels, which are usually not told chronologically. Rather, the story of events is filtered through one or more observers who interpret these actions in the context of their own biases, needs, and confusions. In Faulkner's world, the reader is often a witness at second hand. *Sanctuary* is an example of this element of his work. Although Faulkner claimed that he wrote *Sanctuary* as a cheap, lurid tale to make money, critics have come to recognize that it is as significant to his canon as *Light in August* (1932) or *The Sound and the Fury* (1929), which focus on the nature of evil and the influence of past actions on the present. As in other Faulkner works, the story of *Sanctuary* is told by a seemingly innocent bystander (Horace Benbow) who becomes enmeshed in the drama.

In one draft, Faulkner's tale focused almost totally on Benbow, whose incestuous love of his sister becomes transferred first to a married woman he eventually marries (Belle),

and then to her daughter (whose sexual adventures lead Benbow to see her as a twin of Temple Drake). Faulkner revised the book to focus more clearly on Temple and her encounter with her evil. Benbow's judgment of her and her actions affects the reader's reactions as he struggles to find justice in the courts and as he strives to find Temple's basic decency, her goodness. Readers see everything through Benbow's scornful, twisted, and disillusioned psyche. He is a witness corrupted by knowledge, and Temple is witness and victim. She becomes a victimizer as well when she testifies against Lee Goodwin. Together she and Benbow are guilty of complicity in evil. To see evil, Faulkner implies, is to be corrupted by it.

The characters seem trapped in a past action that hovers over their present circumstances. For the idealistic Benbow, as for Temple, that singular past action will continue to define him as he struggles against the unyielding, senseless evil and meaninglessness of modern life. For Temple, this past is her rape and her witnessing of Tommy's murder at the hands of Popeye. To Benbow, it is his idealistic yet self-centered and pathetic love for his sister, wife, and stepdaughter, all of whom flaunt their sexual escapades. Benbow's disillusioned despair will haunt him as long as he lives.

Readers see the story through Benbow's eyes, and so are influenced to believe that women are the source of all evil. At first idealistic and irrational, Benbow imbues women and the law with every virtue. Later, disillusioned, he declares, almost gleefully, that the "inherent evil" of women corrupts even the courts of justice. He can thereby believe that Popeye's rape of Temple is her fault.

If Faulkner's characters are destined to suffer the violent fates they meet, it is not through external forces, but rather through their own inner demons, that they become so destined. In every case, the characters' internal evil emerges to vanquish others and then themselves. So, Temple's rape releases her carnal corruption, which in turn leads to the deaths of four men—Tommy, Red, Lee, and Popeye—and to the disillusionment of Benbow and of her boyfriend Gowan Stevens. Though she senses that something is wrong, Temple does not comprehend her fate. She is aware only that "something is happening to [her.]" Temple never seems to suspect that she is the cause of the evil that befalls her. This lack of insight characterizes most evil people. Like Popeye, Temple seems to have no conscience, no sense of right and wrong.

Popeye is not just a bad man. He has been called the epitome of pure evil, while other readers say he is simply amoral. Like other evil men in Faulkner's works, Popeye is described as if he were a robot. He has rubber knobs for eyes; his frame is angular, like a lamp; he has a permanent sneer on a face that looks like melted wax; and he is inhuman—he has such a delicate stomach he cannot drink the whiskey he sells, and he is unable to have sex. However, his evil seems less severe than Temple's.

Sanctuary may be more than just a horrific tale of murder and rape. Faulkner's characters and their vile actions may symbolize Faulkner's vision of the rape and corruption of the South by the mechanized industries, politicians, and fortune-hunters who descended upon it after the Civil War. Faulkner indicates that evil has a power stronger than that of goodness, that this evil is made possible by the weakness of good men and women who hide in their private illusions of justice and goodness.

"Critical Evaluation" by Linda L. Labin

Further Reading

Bassett, John, ed. *William Faulkner: The Critical Heritage.* London: Routledge & Kegan Paul, 1975. Contains eight essays on *Sanctuary*, all written within two years of the novel's publication.

Brooks, Cleanth. *William Faulkner: The Yoknapatawpha Country.* New Haven, Conn.: Yale University Press, 1963. Contains chapters on most of the Faulkner novels and a section comparing *Sanctuary* and *Requiem for a Nun*, calling them Faulkner's discovery of evil. One of the most helpful and accessible books for information on Faulkner.

Clarke, Deborah. *Robbing the Mother: Women in Faulkner.* Jackson: University Press of Mississippi, 1994. Argues that female sexuality threatens a male-dominated cultural order in *Sanctuary*. Delineates women in Faulkner's novels and finds women treated poorly. Makes some reference to the women in Faulkner's life.

Dore, Florence. "Counting as Decent: Obscenity and Masculinity in William Faulkner's *Sanctuary*." In *The Novel and the Obscene: Sexual Subjects in American Modernism.* Stanford, Calif.: Stanford University Press, 2005. Dore contradicts the common view that modernist fiction was sexually progressive and openly represented sexuality. She examines how Faulkner's novel and other modernist works were restricted by censorship laws and other limitations on sexual openness.

Dowling, David. *William Faulkner.* New York: St. Martin's Press, 1989. Includes a chronology and sections describing the major works completed during different periods in Faulkner's life. Finds *Sanctuary* to be the darkest of all of Faulkner's novels and compares it to his other novels of the 1930's. Provides a history of Yoknapatawpha County, extended bibliography, and index.

Marius, Richard. *Reading Faulkner: Introduction to the First Thirteen Novels.* Compiled and edited by Nancy Grisham Anderson. Knoxville: University of Tennessee Press, 2006. A collection of the lectures that Marius, a novelist, biographer, and Faulkner scholar, presented during an undergraduate course. Provides a friendly and approachable introduction to Faulkner. Includes a chapter on *Sanctuary*.

Page, Sally R. *Faulkner's Women: Characterization and Meaning.* Deland, Fla.: Everett/Edwards, 1972. A survey of the women characters in Faulkner's novels, with attention to their individuality and to the stereotypes they represent. Finds that Faulkner depicts women favorably.

Porter, Carolyn. *William Faulkner.* New York: Oxford University Press, 2007. Concise and informative, this resource spans Faulkner's entire life, but focuses on his most prolific period, from 1929 to 1940. It examines his childhood and personal struggles and offers insightful analyses of his major works. *Sanctuary* is discussed in chapter 2.

Towner, Theresa M. *The Cambridge Introduction to William Faulkner.* New York: Cambridge University Press, 2008. An accessible book aimed at students and general readers. Focusing on Faulkner's work, the book provides detailed analyses of his nineteen novels, discussion of his other works, and information about the critical reception for his fiction.

Sanine

Author: Mikhail Artsybashev (1878-1927)
First published: Sanin, 1907 (English translation, 1914)
Type of work: Novel
Type of plot: Philosophical
Time of plot: 1906
Locale: Russia

Principal characters:
VLADIMIR PETROVITCH SANINE, an individualistic young Russian
LIDA PETROVNA, his sister
MARIA IVANOVNA, his mother
CAPTAIN ZARUDIN, in love with Lida
DR. NOVIKOV, also in love with Lida
SINA KARSAVINA, briefly the mistress of Sanine
YURI SVAROZHICH, in love with Sina Karsavina

The Story:

During the formative years of his life, Vladimir Petrovitch Sanine is away from the influence of his family and their home. When he returns as a young man to his mother's house in a provincial garrison town, he comes as a person believing only in himself, his strength, and the desirability of following his inclinations, wherever they might lead him. His mother, Maria Ivanovna, cannot understand her son. His sister Lida, however, finds him strangely attractive, even though she distrusts and fears his thinking and its influence.

Lida, having many admirers among young civilians and the junior army officers, is the belle of the little garrison town. Her two most serious admirers are Dr. Novikov, who wishes sincerely to marry her but is awkward as a suitor, and Captain Zarudin, a brutal and lascivious army officer who wishes only to make a sexual conquest and is well on his way to success with the young woman. Sanine, giving the same freedoms to others as he believes in for himself, makes no serious attempt to interfere in his sister's affairs.

Before long Sanine is caught up in the social life among the young intelligentsia of the town. Among those in the group are Sina Karsavina and Yuri Svarozhich. The former is a pretty young schoolteacher of strong emotions who finds herself drawn strangely to Sanine, although she is very much in love with Yuri, a young student who was exiled to the provinces for his part in revolutionary activities. Although attracted to Sina, Yuri feels that his political duties and ambitions would be hampered if he were married. As a result of his beliefs in political duty, and as a result of bashfulness as well, he avoids becoming emotionally involved with the young schoolteacher.

As the weeks pass, Lida draws closer to Captain Zarudin. So strong is his physical attraction that she refuses a proposal of marriage from Dr. Novikov, whose jealousy almost becomes hate. Soon afterward, Lida becomes Captain Zaru-

din's mistress. Discovering that she is pregnant, she turns for help to her lover, only to learn that he is now finished with her, having made his conquest. Lida is distraught and thinks of drowning herself, but she is found by her brother in time. He convinces her that she needs to live and that she should become Dr. Novikov's wife. Having his sister's agreement, Sanine goes to Dr. Novikov, who is about to leave the town. Little persuasion is needed, even with a knowledge of the facts, to get the doctor's agreement to marry Lida.

About this time Captain Zarudin has a visitor from St. Petersburg. When Captain Zarudin and his friend pay a visit to the Sanine home so that the officer might show off the beautiful woman he seduced, Sanine orders the captain to leave the house and suggests further that he leave town. Captain Zarudin, true to the code of his corps, challenges Sanine to a duel. Sanine believes that dueling proves nothing and so refuses the challenge. He learns that his sister, on the other hand, expects him to fight the duel. Realizing that his sister, like his mother, is a conformist to opinion and tradition, Sanine feels alienated from them because of their attitudes and their failure to understand his ideas.

Even more angered by the refusal of his challenge, Captain Zarudin fears that his failure to avenge his honor might put him in a disgraceful position with his brother officers. That he disgraced himself in some people's eyes by his treatment of Lida does not enter his mind. One evening, as Sanine and some friends are strolling along the boulevard, they unexpectedly meet Captain Zarudin and several of his fellow officers. Captain Zarudin speaks harshly to Sanine and threatens him with a riding crop. In self-defense, Sanine knocks down the officer with his fist. Not much hurt physically but humiliated by the indignity of the blow, Captain Zarudin almost goes out of his mind. Taken back to his quarters, he refuses to see even his friends or his orderly.

After the brief but violent encounter, Sanine walks home with a Jewish friend, Soloveitchik. The two sit for a long time discussing human life and its meaning. Sanine refuses to accept any blame for his behavior, although it might ruin Captain Zarudin's career and life. The Jew asks Sanine if a man who worries and thinks too much might not be better off dead. Sanine replies that a man or woman who cannot enjoy life is already dead. Shortly afterward, he leaves. On his way home he meets Captain Zarudin's orderly, who informs him that the officer committed suicide by shooting himself. The next morning word comes, too, that Soloveitchik hanged himself. The two sudden deaths cause a great furor in the little town, but Sanine steadfastly refuses to admit that he is in any way responsible.

One morning Yuri receives a letter from Sina asking him to meet her at a monastery near the town. He meets her as requested, and a tender but awkward love scene ensues. Yuri hates to admit he needs the woman, and his conscience bothers him in strange ways. When Sina is suddenly called back to town that evening, Sanine, who is also visiting at the monastery, offers to escort her. On the way both Sanine and Sina are overcome by their emotions, and she surrenders to him. Though she is upset afterward, she decides that the best thing for her to do is to forget what happened. In the meantime Yuri's sister tries to persuade her brother to marry. The problems that marriage raise for him are so great that the young man cannot face them, and he shoots himself. At the funeral Sanine is asked to say a few words, and he declares that there is one fool less in the world. His response horrifies everyone. Soon afterward, Sanine leaves the town again by train. Early one morning, as the train is crossing the plains, he jumps off to glory in the beauty of an autumn sunrise.

Critical Evaluation:

Sanine centers on the title character and the profound effect he produces on his family and acquaintances. At the end of the novel, Sanine vanishes into the limbo from which he originated. The hero exists in a vacuum; little information is given about his past activities or his future plans. His physical presence is powerful, however, as is made clear by repeated mention of his prominent muscles and mocking eyes. By limiting Sanine's existence to the novel's present, Mikhail Artsybashev demonstrates Sanine's appreciation of life's immediacy. Sanine is a mouthpiece for the author's views and a didactic figure who considers it his duty to become involved in the lives of others and to demonstrate his convictions. Anarchical individuality guides his philosophy. For Sanine, Christianity has left humans ill-equipped for everyday living because Christianity directs attention inward.

Its emphasis on humility deprives the underprivileged of the will to protest against the established order. Abstractions of law, morality, and government, in turn, which are also founded on hierarchical authority, suppress self-will. The development of egoism and the denial of any higher power will, and should, in Sanine's view, lead to the rejection of domination.

Sanine consistently critiques intellectual achievement. Life is sensations, emotions, and sensual pleasure, but thought is empty conceptions and vain speech, powerless against the mystery of life and death. Sanine excepts literature, with its potential to ameliorate the human condition, from his contempt for intellectual activity. Nature, on the other hand, is a constant presence in the novel. Artsybashev shows the cyclical quality of life in the change of seasons. Although his style is cumbersome, the pictorial quality of Artsybashev's natural scenes reveals a sensitivity to color and detail. Sanine's intense physical response to nature demonstrates his pagan enjoyment of the earth.

The technology student, Svarozhich, acts as a foil to Sanine and demonstrates unnatural living. The two represent opposite camps among the Russian intelligentsia, which is emphasized by Sanine and Svarozhich both having their own followers. Sanine's behavior testifies to physical joy, and Svarozhich's thoughts reveal profound pessimism. Like Sanine, he was formerly active in revolutionary circles. Svarozhich, however, spent six months in prison and remains under police surveillance. Obsessed with the futility of human endeavor and engaging in the morbid introspection typical of Fyodor Dostoevski's characters, he toys with the idea of suicide throughout the novel and eventually kills himself.

Sanine considers Svarozhich a representative of the second phase of human development, characterized by the re-evaluation of human desires. Svarozhich's agonizing self-scrutiny abstracts him from natural impulses. According to Sanine, humans should give themselves freely to pleasure and enjoy love without fear or constraint. Sanine addresses his judgment to Karsavina, with whom Svarozhich fails sexually and whom Sanine is seducing. When asked to say a few words at Svarozhich's grave, Sanine declares that Svarozhich lived foolishly and died an idiotic death. Soloveichik's pacifism, which Artsybashev associates with Judaism, and subsequent suicide put him in the same psychological category as Svarozhich. The ingratiating Soloveichik was probably intended to critique the doctrine of nonresistance to evil.

Although Artsybashev focuses primarily on young representatives of the middle class, he also portrays the military.

The military's status as a select and autonomous caste in Russian society was a central public concern. Unlike his literary predecessors, he shows soldiers stationed in remote provinces during peacetime. The soldiers are arrogant and vain, holding others in contempt and pursuing false honor. In the novel, soldiers, as do intellectuals, lead incomplete existences. Compared to Sanine, who is sexually desirous but also appreciative of women, Zarudin is consistently lascivious and callous to women. After he is humiliated by Sanine's blow, he is abandoned by his fellow officers and confronted with the spiritual bankruptcy of his existence. Recalling his rejection of Lida, he regrets the suffering he caused her and vows to renounce his former ways. Renunciation proves impossible, however, and his life ends in suicide.

The rash of suicides at the end of the novel suggests social instability. Each suicide represents a significant element of Russian society at the turn of the century. The army enables the government to maintain the status quo, the student body questions autocratic rule, and the Jews take the blame for public discontent. Zarudin realizes his military life is empty, Svarozhich fails to justify his own existence, and Soloveichik finds his continual suffering intolerable. Those who remain alive by the end of the novel are generally the mediocre ones. Sanine is the only character who is not paralyzed with inadequacy by the end of the novel.

The structure of the novel is chronological, punctuated with long diatribes, primarily initiated by Sanine. Psychological motivation is scant. Characters are sketched primarily as vehicles for Artsybashev's debate. Given Sanine's advocacy of primal response to the world, he and the other characters exhibit little emotional reaction to events. Artsybashev relies heavily on coincidence to bring Sanine into situations in which his behavior can be demonstrated or his views expressed at length. Given the complex character groupings and Sanine's involvement with them all, narrative momentum often flags.

Artsybashev gained wide notoriety with *Sanine*, mainly because of its polemical content. Publishers in several countries were quick to respond to the public demand for titillating reading. Translations appeared throughout Western Europe within a year of its publication in Russia. Artsybashev's alleged affront to public morality resulted in a number of court cases, myriad literary imitations, and an avalanche of reviews. The novel's graphic violence and sexuality, not its literary or philosophical merits, attracted most of the attention.

The novel reflects the Russian intelligentsia's disenchantment with public ideals, particularly after the failure of the 1905 Revolution, and the extreme sexual freedom of the times. Other controversial issues, such as abortion, incest, and women's rights, are debated in the text.

Artsybashev's work also represents the spiritual questions of the time. *Sanine* is frequently viewed as a vulgarization of Dostoevski's *Zapiski iz podpolya* (1864; *Notes from the Underground*, 1913) since it features an amoral, cynical, antihero who rationalizes his behavior in long-winded discussions. For the most part, Sanine's behavior fails to provide the model Artsybashev intended. His critique of intellectual discussion takes the form of intellectual discussion, and his arguments lapse into sensationalism. Despite these problems, *Sanine* embodies contemporary debate and suggests the bankruptcy of empty convictions and false priorities.

"Critical Evaluation" by Pamela Pavliscak

Further Reading

Artsybashev, Mikhail. *Sanin: A Novel.* Translated by Michael R. Katz. Ithaca, N.Y.: Cornell University Press, 2001. Includes an excellent introduction by Otto Boele recounting the scandal set off by the novel's publication, placing the book within the context of fin de siècle Russia, and providing analysis of the novel and information about Artsybashev's literary career.

Boele, Otto. "The Pornographic *Roman à Thèse*: Mikhail Artsybashev's *Sanin*." In *Eros and Pornography in Russian Culture*, edited by Marcus Levitt and Andreí Toporkov. Moscow: Ladomir, 1999. Boele focuses on the novel's depiction of sexuality, which caused many Russians to denounce the book as pornographic.

Engelstein, Laura. *The Keys to Happiness: Sex and the Search for Modernity in Fin-de-Siècle Russia.* Ithaca, N.Y.: Cornell University Press, 1992. Surveys popular culture in early twentieth century Russia. Elaborates Artsybashev's role as literary innovator.

Luker, Nicholas. *In Defense of a Reputation: Essays on the Early Prose of Mikhail Artsybashev.* Nottingham, England: Astra Press, 1990. A balanced consideration of Artsybashev's major novels and a thorough summary of earlier criticism of Artsybashev's works, most of which are available only in Russian. Emphasizing the careful structure of *Sanine*, Luker makes a convincing case for considering Artsybashev a serious author.

Phelps, William. *Essays on Russian Novelists.* New York: Macmillan, 1911. A contemporary account of the sensation *Sanine* made abroad as an affront to morality and as a pagan appreciation of nature.

Rosenthal, Bernice G., ed. *Nietzsche in Russia.* Princeton,

N.J.: Princeton University Press, 1986. Collection of essays about the influence of Friedrich Nietzsche on Russian authors of the late nineteenth and early twentieth centuries. Several essays discuss Artsybashev, including one that considers Sanine as a Nietzschean superman.

Todd, William Mills, ed. *Literature and Society in Imperial Russia, 1800-1914.* Stanford, Calif.: Stanford University Press, 1978. Examines the relations between Russian literature and mass readership. *Sanine*'s success is considered in the broader context of works read by the middle classes.

Sappho

Author: Alphonse Daudet (1840-1897)
First published: Sapho, 1884 (English translation, 1886)
Type of work: Novel
Type of plot: Naturalism
Time of plot: Nineteenth century
Locale: Paris

Principal characters:
JEAN GAUSSIN, a student
FANNY LEGRAND, his mistress
IRÈNE, his fiancé
BOUCHEREAU, a famous physiologist
DÉCHELETTE, a wealthy engineer
LA GOURNERIE, a poet
DE POTTER, a composer
ROSA, de Potter's mistress
FLAMANT, a convicted counterfeiter
CÉSAIRE, Jean's uncle

The Story:

Déchelette, a vigorous but aging engineer, spends all but two months of the year on construction projects far from Paris. Each summer, however, he returns to the carefree city to compress into two months enough pleasure to make up for his enforced absences. Jean Gaussin, a young student from the south of France, attends one of Déchelette's masquerade parties and finds himself bewildered at the extravagant affair. Unhappy and lost, he wanders into a gallery, where he encounters a woman dressed as an Egyptian. When he is ready to leave, the woman stops him and asks her to take her to his room. In this way, he becomes her lover. Her name, she tells him, is Fanny Legrand.

Fanny continues to visit Jean in his room frequently. When he finally goes to see her at her apartment, he is astonished at the luxury of the place. In the morning, before he and Fanny arise from bed, the servant announces a visitor. Fanny goes into another room to see the early caller, and Jean is horrified to overhear a violent quarrel. Fanny is shouting insults and curses at the man in the language of the gutter. Finally, the man begins to sob and presses money on Fanny. He begs her not to dismiss him, whatever else she does. Following this incident, Jean goes back to his classes much disturbed.

Unable to end the affair, he rents an apartment and sets up

housekeeping with Fanny. She proves to be a capable homemaker as well as a demanding mistress. Jean feels settled and at ease, and he makes good progress in his consular studies. The following summer, he meets Déchelette and Caoudal, a sculptor, at a café and learns the past history of his mistress. Twenty years before, she had lived with Caoudal and had been the model for his well-known sculpture of Sappho. She had also lived with Déchelette at various times, and La Gournerie, the poet, had kept her for some years. Jean feels nauseated when he comes to understand that Fanny owes her imaginative diction to La Gournerie, her graceful gestures to Caoudal, and her ample spending money to Déchelette. One of her latest lovers had been Flamant. The poor man, an engraver, had counterfeited some banknotes and had been sentenced to prison. Jean learns that Fanny is nearly forty years of age, almost twenty years older than he.

When he confronts Fanny with his knowledge, she readily admits her past. When she protests that she loves him alone, Jean asks to see her box of keepsakes. From the letters she has saved, he traces her history of loose love for nearly thirty years. The farewell letter from Flamant asks Fanny to look after his young son. Jean suspects that the child is also Fanny's. Despite this knowledge, Jean cannot leave his mistress after Fanny meekly submits to his reproaches. They continue to live together.

Césaire, Jean's uncle, arrives in Paris with news that Jean's family has been ruined by failure of the grape crop; he has been sent to Paris to collect an old debt of eight thousand francs. With Fanny's help, Césaire collects the money but soon loses it gambling. Fanny volunteers to get more money from Déchelette. As Jean and Césaire await her return from her meeting with Déchelette, Jean tortures himself by imagining how she will get the money from him. After some hours, Fanny returns with the money and Césaire leaves for home, loudly asserting Fanny's goodness and promising to keep silent to Jean's family about his loose life.

With the decline in the Gaussin family fortunes, Jean and Fanny decide to separate. Fanny goes to work managing an apartment for Rosa, the mistress of de Potter, a wealthy composer. She and Jean see each other every Sunday on her day off. After evaluating his economic situation, Jean finds that his decreased allowance will allow them to take a small hut in the country. He is sure that they can exist there for a year while he finishes his course of study. Jean, however, hates their life in the country. The grumbling old servant that Fanny had hired previously, now gone, is revealed to have been her stepmother. Her father, a dissolute cab driver, comes to visit them. Flamant's child, a savage boy six years of age, lives with them. Jean counts on receiving an appointment to a consular office so that he can break away from Fanny.

On his trips into town, Jean becomes acquainted with Bouchereau, an eminent physiologist. He then meets and falls in love with Bouchereau's niece, Irène. Jean hopes that he will receive an appointment to a post in South America and that Irène will go with him as his wife. As he is gradually permitted to see Irène more often, Jean becomes troubled. Her innocent enjoyment of simple things is disturbing, for he has become so satiated with his experienced courtesan that other women have little attraction for him. When he tells Fanny of his approaching marriage, a furious quarrel breaks out.

Shortly afterward, Jean meets de Potter, who congratulates him on his approaching marriage. De Potter's story is a horrible warning to Jean: The composer has never been able to get away from his mistress, Rosa, and the attraction of her flesh has held him fast for many years; de Potter's wife rarely sees him, and his children are almost strangers. De Potter is bitter about his wasted life, but he cannot leave the aging Rosa, whom he supports in luxury.

Despite de Potter's example, and despite his engagement to Irène, Jean resolves to keep Fanny as his mistress. On the eve of his departure for his post in South America, he breaks

his engagement to Irène and writes to Fanny to join him in Marseilles. Waiting with tense expectancy in a hotel room in the Mediterranean port, Jean receives a letter from Fanny. She has gone back to Flamant, who has been released from prison. She says that she is too old to go traveling about—she cannot leave her beloved Paris.

Critical Evaluation:

Already a noted novelist and an acknowledged leader in the naturalist movement before he wrote *Sappho*, Alphonse Daudet chose for this novel a subject of great personal interest. Having been engaged himself in a lengthy affair with a Parisian courtesan, the novelist dramatizes in *Sappho* the bohemian lifestyle characteristic of the denizens of certain sections of the city. This subject was of great interest to contemporary readers, whose curiosity was aroused by tales of young men caught up in the web of sex and degradation. French readers were insatiable in their appetite for stories of *collages*, relationships between unmarried lovers, especially when the woman was one of ill repute. Despite its reputation as a salacious work, Daudet's novel contains little to satisfy the baser interests of readers; instead, the relationship between the young Jean Gaussin and the older Fanny Legrand is handled with a sensitivity and decorum not normally associated with naturalistic fiction.

As one might expect, the central interest in the novel is the relationship between Jean and the worldly-wise courtesan who seduces him and leads him into the relationship that will govern his life for years to come. Daudet has often been commended for his ability to create strong female and weak male characters, and for his penetrating insights into love relationships. Drawing on his personal experiences for this novel, he is particularly successful in delineating his protagonists. Nevertheless, Jean is not simply a fictionalized portrait of the artist as a young lover. Instead, Daudet gives him little of the artistic sensitivity that his creator possessed, instead providing him the kind of career aspirations more common among young men in France in the late nineteenth century. Bound for a career in the diplomatic service, Jean is initially fascinated with the lifestyle represented by Fanny; he pursues her initially merely to fulfill some juvenile romantic fantasy. He does not realize the power of such a woman until it is much too late for him to avoid her clutches.

Fanny Legrand is one of those "vampire" characters who fascinated nineteenth century readers throughout Europe. Like the figure in gothic legend that gives the name to the term, Fanny metaphorically draws her life from her lovers: Her manners, her imaginative language, even her money come from the men with whom she has consorted. Jean finds that he, too, is being sucked dry by his relationship with the courtesan, but he is powerless to flee from her. Like a vampire, she has mesmerized him with her fatal attractiveness; although he is aware on an intellectual level that he should break off his relationship with her, he finds he does not have the emotional strength to do so. Even when he becomes engaged to another, he remains drawn to Fanny; his desperate plea at the end of the novel that she join him on his journey to South America shows the hold she has over him.

Fanny, too, depends on such relationships for her own strength, just as she depends on the milieu in which she lives to keep up her lifestyle; like a vampire who cannot stray too far from her coffin, Fanny cannot leave the confines of Paris lest she lose her powers. Unable to go with Jean, she sends him an ironic letter in which she sets him free with "a kiss, the last one, on your neck." Within her sphere, Fanny is a powerful creature whose animal magnetism draws men to her and causes them to lose their sensibility as they satisfy their sensual desires. Daudet's portrait of his heroine is psychologically convincing, displaying his exceptional ability to render human emotion and motivation.

Although Daudet espoused the tenets of naturalism, in *Sappho* he does not always adhere strictly to the notion that the writer must become a transparent chronicler of events. Instead, the novel contains numerous authorial comments intended to tell readers how to react to situations and characters. For example, when Jean finds he cannot escape the hold that Fanny has over him, he declares that he loves her. At this point, Daudet observes: "There is in certain words that we ordinarily use a hidden spring which suddenly opens them down to the base. . . . Love is one of these words. Only those for whom its clearness has once been felt, translated in its entirety, will understand the delightful anguish in which Jean lived." Such authorial intrusion is reminiscent more of Anthony Trollope and Charles Dickens than of Émile Zola and other proponents of objectivity in fiction.

Daudet introduced such passages deliberately, because he wished *Sappho* to be more than a mere portrait of French life as he had experienced it. His dedication for the novel makes his authorial intentions clear: "For my sons when they are twenty." The novel is Daudet's lesson about the pitfalls that await young men whose very nature makes them susceptible to the charms of women like Fanny. The novel reveals the secret of man: that he is vulnerable in his sensuality rather than in his capacity for love. Critics have commented on the di-

dactic nature of the work since it appeared in 1884. Unquestionably, the novelist meant the work to be instructive; while it offers no strong moralistic statement, *Sappho* provides a lesson for those who have not yet had the experiences Daudet chronicles.

"Critical Evaluation" by Laurence W. Mazzeno

Further Reading

Daudet, Léon. *Alphonse Daudet*. Translated by Charles De Kay. 1901. Reprint. Rockville, Md.: Wildside Press, 2007. Biography by Daudet's son, a journalist, provides information on how the events of the author's life influenced his writing.

Dobie, G. V. *Alphonse Daudet*. 1949. Reprint. Norwood, Pa.: Norwood Editions, 1977. Biographical study presents critical commentary interwoven with the story of Daudet's career. Discusses the novelist's attempt to create a believable story of an ordinary man in love with a Parisian courtesan and asserts that *Sappho* is Daudet's greatest contribution to the naturalist movement.

Gosse, Edmund. *French Profiles*. 1913. Reprint. Freeport, N.Y.: Books for Libraries Press, 1970. Includes an overview of Daudet's career that notes the particular strengths of *Sappho*, described as the novelist's contribution to a French tradition that highlights the "obsession of the feminine."

Roche, Alphonse. *Alphonse Daudet*. Boston: Twayne, 1976. Offers an introduction to the writer's major works for general readers. Discusses Daudet's handling of the relationship between his principal characters in *Sappho* and comments on the publication history of the novel, including the stir created by its appearance in nineteenth century France.

Sachs, Murray. *The Career of Alphonse Daudet*. Cambridge, Mass.: Harvard University Press, 1965. Discusses Daudet's place as a major figure in French literature. Analyzes the novelist's handling of the love relationship in *Sappho*, calling it exceptionally well done and psychologically realistic.

Vitaglione, Daniel. *The Literature of Provence: An Introduction*. Jefferson, N.C.: McFarland, 2000. Focuses on the works of authors whose lives and careers have been devoted to depicting the region of Provence. Chapter 3 discusses Daudet's work.

Sappho

Author: Franz Grillparzer (1791-1872)
First produced: 1818; first published, 1819 (English translation, 1928)
Type of work: Drama
Type of plot: Tragedy
Time of plot: Sixth century B.C.E.
Locale: Lesbos, Greece

Principal characters:
SAPPHO, a renowned Greek poet
PHAON, a young man loved by Sappho
MELITTA, Sappho's young and beautiful slave
RHAMNES, an elderly male slave owned by Sappho

The Story:

Sappho, beloved by all and treated as if she were the queen of her native island of Lesbos, goes to Olympia to compete for the prize to be awarded for poetry and song. As the result of her genius, she wins the laurel wreath accorded the victor and returns in triumph to her island home. To the surprise of those on Lesbos, she brings back with her a handsome, pleasant, but very young man named Phaon, with whom she fell deeply in love. Phaon, having heard the poems of Sappho read in his father's home, had great admiration for the poet before he journeyed to Olympia to compete in the games as a charioteer. There he and Sappho met and fell in love.

Phaon, a young man of simple tastes, is almost overwhelmed by Sappho's home, her way of life, and her place of importance on the island. Sappho, deeply in love with Phaon, tries to make him comfortable and at ease in his new environment by constantly expressing her love for him and telling him how much he means to her happiness.

In Sappho's household is a beautiful young female slave named Melitta, who was taken into Sappho's home as a small child. For some years, the girl is very close to her mistress. When Sappho returns from Olympia, she suddenly realizes that the child is a woman. This realization causes Sappho some pangs, for it brings home the fact that Sappho herself is no longer young. For the first time, the poet wishes she were younger again, for the sake of Phaon.

One day, Phaon, who still is ill at ease in the luxurious household of his mistress, finds refuge in a grotto from the noisy merrymaking of Sappho's guests. While he is enjoying the silence of the place, Melitta wanders nearby, having been sent to the gardens to pick some flowers. As she walks along, she voices her grief at being a slave in a foreign land, lonely for a home and family. Phaon, hearing Melitta's lamentations, is greatly moved, for he, too, is lonesome in a strange land. He goes to the slave and tries to cheer her. This leads to a kiss, which is observed by Sappho as she comes looking for Phaon. Upset, she does not reveal her presence and leaves Phaon to himself for a time. Later, she finds him asleep in the grotto and awakens him with a kiss. As he awakens, Phaon murmurs Melitta's name. Fully awake, he tells Sappho of a dream in which he saw himself in love with Melitta, who usurped the place of Sappho. Sappho tells him not to believe in lying dreams.

Although she conceals the fact from him, Sappho's pride is badly hurt by his account of the dream and by the kiss she saw him bestow upon Melitta. Coming upon Melitta, Sappho accuses the slave of maliciously trying to steal Phaon's love. After heated words pass between the mistress and Melitta, Sappho draws a dagger and threatens Melitta's life. Phaon's appearance saves the woman from injury at Sappho's hands. Phaon then announces his love for the slave and accuses Sappho of trying to weave magic spells with her poetry to make him believe he loves her.

Later that day, Sappho calls her most trusted slave, Rhamnes, to her and commanded him to take Melitta away from Lesbos to Chios, across the sea, to be placed in the household of one of Sappho's friends. That night, Rhamnes tries to lure the woman from her quarters to a boat on the beach. Melitta, suspecting a trap, protests. Phaon, fearful for Melitta's safety, remains awake and hears Rhamnes enter Melitta's quarters. When he discovers Rhamnes' trickery, he makes him relinquish Melitta.

Alarmed by what happens, Phaon decides to flee Lesbos and Sappho's household. Taking Melitta with him, he embarks in the boat Rhamnes planned to use in spiriting the young beauty away.

As soon as he is free of the threat of Phaon's dagger, Rhamnes sounds the alarm and tells of Phaon's flight with Melitta. Planning revenge, Sappho calls the people of the island to her and promises a handsome reward of gold for the return of the fugitives. Spurred by the reward and their love for Sappho, the islanders hurry after Phaon and Melitta. When they come up with the fugitives upon the sea, Melitta is struck on the head by an oar during the struggle. Phaon then yields to their captors.

Back in Sappho's house, Phaon demands to know why she should be given the privilege of judging him, as if she were a queen. The islanders tell him that they regard her as their queen. When Sappho demands the return of Melitta, Phaon said that, in threatening the slave's life, Sappho relinquished all her rights to the girl. Sappho then accuses Phaon of being a deceiver in love. Phaon defends himself by saying that he was mistaken in his love, that the love he feels for Sappho is the love of her genius. He adds that he really loves her as a goddess, not as a woman, not knowing the difference until after he met and fell in love with Melitta.

Sappho is disturbed by what happened and by what Phaon said. At first, thinking that she is being asked too great a price for having poetic gifts, she wishes to disown her genius in order to live and to love as an ordinary woman. She leaves the company to think in solitude. As she looks out across the sea, her lyre suddenly clangs loudly, as if warning her, and she decides not to try to escape the genius given her by the gods. She asks the gods only to keep her from being an object of men's derision. Returning, she forgives the young lovers with a kiss and then walks to an altar of Aphrodite that stands on a cliff overlooking the sea. Calling upon the gods to take her to them, Sappho hurls herself over the brink into the water below. Phaon and Sappho's people run to rescue her, but they are too late. The ocean currents dash her to her death against the rocks.

Critical Evaluation:

Like so many of his contemporaries in the Romantic movement, Franz Grillparzer found early inspiration for a number of his creative works in classical mythology. For centuries, the tale of the Greek poet Sappho's unrequited love for the young Phaon served as the subject for works that emphasized the comic qualities inherent in the story of an older woman attempting to secure the love of a younger man. Grillparzer found something else entirely in the tale. For him, the story of Sappho and Phaon was appealing because it permitted him to explore a topic of personal interest: the fate of artists in a world that does not understand or appreciate them.

Structurally, *Sappho* follows closely the form of Greek tragedy. Grillparzer is careful to observe the classical unities (a practice he abandons in later works), concentrating the dramatic action on the climactic scenes in which Sappho confronts her lover, Phaon, and his new beloved, Melitta. Through this series of altercations, and through the skillful presentation of much-needed background material in a series of lengthy speeches by a number of characters, the playwright vivifies the central conflict in his drama. Neither the

conflict nor its resolution is classical, however; instead, in *Sappho* Grillparzer dramatizes the conflict the Romantic artist faces in dealing with those who are unable to understand or to appreciate the psychological demands placed on those who have the power to create art. The heroine desperately wants to synthesize her desires for a normal life as a wife and a lover with her vocation as a poet. Unfortunately, her beloved Phaon sees her only in the latter role, revering her as an artist but transferring his love to the younger Melitta. The heroine's decision to end her life when she finds she cannot keep Phaon as her lover is carried out as a means of demonstrating that she has the will to determine her own fate.

The central critical issue in Grillparzer's play revolves around an important issue that has both technical and moral overtones: whether the dramatic action justifies the ending. More than one critic observed that the choice Grillparzer gives his heroine seems forced, and her fate too extreme. She seems to love Phaon deeply, and his failure to return that love leaves her desolate. Nevertheless, her status as a poet is in no way diminished by this rejection; she should be able to go on without him, still revered for her artistry, which everyone recognizes. The play suggests, however, that Sappho does not wish to settle for one or the other option: She wishes to have both her fame as an artist and her life as a wife to the man she loves. As a result, some critics have dismissed her as unbalanced, which may be normal for a poet but is unsatisfactory in terms of dramatic characterization.

While such a reading can be plausibly constructed from the text, it does not do justice to Grillparzer's understanding of his character or the tradition in which he is working. As a Romantic tragedy, *Sappho* shares affinities with other great works in the tradition. Comparisons with Johann Wolfgang von Goethe's *Faust: Eine Tragödie* (1808; *The Tragedy of Faust*, 1823) and Percy Bysshe Shelley's *The Cenci* (1819) are not inappropriate. More noteworthy are what the play shares with the greatest of all Romantic love stories, *Tristan and Isolde* (Richard Wagner's opera, 1857-1859). The love triangle in Grillparzer's play is an ironic reversal of the legend, in that Grillparzer gives to his aging heroine the qualities that the young lovers in the medieval tale possess: a fine sensitivity for life that allows them to rise above the mundane, and an artistic temperament that makes their love greater than the simple sensual affairs of mere mortals. The story in *Sappho* also parallels an even more famous love triangle, that of Arthur, Guinevere, and Lancelot in the Arthurian legends. In all of these cases, the lovers find no optimal means of compromising their feelings.

The common thread that unites these tragedies, and which runs through all of Romantic literature, is the struggle of the hero to transcend the limitations of time. Certainly this is the case with Grillparzer's Sappho. The poet realizes that she is growing older; she can understand Phaon's desire to take a younger bride in Melitta, but she is unable to accept it. On more than one occasion, she makes it clear that her efforts to keep her lover are motivated by her desire to stop time. In her art, she is able to do that; the poems she produces are monuments that will transcend time, providing pleasure and insight not only to her contemporaries but also to generations who will follow her. They are not Sappho herself, of course; although she lives through her art, she cannot be fully actualized as a person except through human love. When Sappho realizes that she cannot arrest time, she chooses what, for her, seems the only possible option: She determines for herself when the moment of death will come, demonstrating—in a Romantic statement—that she is in control of her life just as she is in control of her art. Whether or not this choice seems believable to readers of subsequent generations, it represents accurately the Romantic attitude that places the greatest value on the integrity of the self and the right of choice.

"Critical Evaluation" by Laurence W. Mazzeno

Further Reading

Coenen, Frederic. *Franz Grillparzer's Portraiture of Men.* Chapel Hill: University of North Carolina Press, 1951. Focuses on the depiction of Phaon and Rhamnes in *Sappho*. Calls the former a "delightfully youthful figure" who grows in self-knowledge during the drama; asserts the latter figure is better drawn than most servants in similar dramas.

Henn, Marianne, Clemens Ruthner, and Raleigh Whitinger, eds. *Aneignungen, Entfremdungen: The Austrian Playwright Franz Grillparzer, 1791-1872.* New York: Peter Lang, 2007. Collection of essays, the majority of them in English, about Grillparzer's plays. Examines his representation of women; his attitude toward the state, nation, and nationalism; and productions of his plays in both the Habsburg era and in Austria since 1930.

Menhennet, Alan. "The Emergence of Austria: Franz Grillparzer." In *The Historical Experience in German Drama: From Gryphius to Brecht.* Rochester, N.Y.: Camden House, 2003. A study of the drama of Grillparzer and other German playwrights that convey a historical experience. Places these plays within the broader context of German history and literature.

Roe, Ian F. *Franz Grillparzer: A Century of Criticism.* Columbia, S.C.: Camden House, 1995. Examines the critical reception for Grillparzer's plays from their initial appearance to their political appropriation by the Nazis and their postwar sociological and psychoanalytical interpretations.

Thompson, Bruce. *Franz Grillparzer.* Boston: Twayne, 1981. Surveys Grillparzer's poetry, prose, and drama. Reviews the critical reception of *Sappho* and examines Grillparzer's handling of the psychological dimensions of his heroine. Concludes the work exemplifies Grillparzer's treatment of the theme of the artist's tragedy.

Wagner, Eva. *An Analysis of Franz Grillparzer's Dramas: Fate, Guilt, and Tragedy.* Lewiston, N.Y.: E. Mellen Press, 1992. Focuses on Grillparzer the tragedian, discussing theories of tragic drama and how they relate to his plays. Examines the tragic nature, fate, and concepts of guilt expressed in ten plays, including *Sappho*.

Wells, George A. *The Plays of Grillparzer.* London: Pergamon Press, 1969. Excellent scholarly analysis of *Sappho*, summarizing earlier critical opinion and providing detailed examination of character, plot, and structure. Notes the technical advancements over Grillparzer's earlier work.

Yates, W. E. *Grillparzer: A Critical Introduction.* New York: Cambridge University Press, 1972. Provides a brief sketch of Grillparzer's life. Analyzes his works, focusing on themes such as love, duty, and the role of the artist. Describes the genesis of *Sappho* and provides extensive discussion of character development, showing how the heroine achieves self-knowledge through her tragedy.

Sartor Resartus

Author: Thomas Carlyle (1795-1881)
First published: 1833-1834, serial; 1836, book
Type of work: Philosophy

Many scholars of Thomas Carlyle refer to *Sartor Resartus* as fiction, but readers who think of the nineteenth century novel when they think of fiction would hardly agree. Although *Sartor Resartus* does have a putative hero, Diogenes Teufelsdröckh, whose life and opinions become the substance of the book, he is only the mouthpiece through whom Carlyle unleashes a torrent of criticism about the materialism and philosophical rationalism of his age. Writing about the German humorist Jean Paul Richter, Carlyle observes that "every work, be it fiction or serious treatise, is embaled in some fantastic wrappage," and he refers to Richter's "perfect Indian jungle" of a style. This precisely describes Carlyle's prose as well.

Sartor Resartus is divided into three books of eleven, ten, and twelve chapters, respectively. The title means, literally, "the Tailor Retailored," and the whole work elaborates a long metaphor suggested by Jonathan Swift's question in the second book of *A Tale of a Tub* (1704): "What is Man himself but a *Micro-Coat*, or rather a compleat Suit of Cloaths with all its Trimmings?" In Carlyle's view, civilization—that is, religion, government, and all the other institutional garments that human beings weave to clothe themselves—is frayed and shabby and needs retailoring. For the transcendentalist Carlyle, clothes also become the shroud of matter by which all spirit makes its appearance in this world of sensible experience.

Carlyle adopts the conventional apprenticeship novel to his own purposes in *Sartor Resartus*. His chosen hero, the young man who goes out into the world and meets its challenges, has the fantastic name of Diogenes Teufelsdröckh, or Born-of-God Devil's-Dung. This improbably named character becomes professor of Allerley-Wissenschaft at the University of Weissnichtwo, or Professor of Things in General at the University of Know-Not-Where.

Carlyle's complicated narrative begins with praise for "deep-thinking Germany" and its Idealist tradition in philosophy, its expounding of a transcendental supersensible realm closed off from the five senses. This admiration for German thought permeates *Sartor Resartus*, appearing not only in Teufelsdröckh's nationality but also in the repeated German phrases and in the penchant for beginning nouns with capital letters. Given this predilection, the narrator responds eagerly to the arrival of Professor Teufelsdröckh's new book on the origin and influence of clothes.

After months of perusing Teufelsdröckh's opus, the narrator unexpectedly receives a letter from Teufelsdröckh's associate, Herr Hofrath Heuschrecke (Mr. Councilor Grasshopper), announcing that he is sending materials for a "Life and Opinions of Herr Teufelsdröckh." Before these materials arrive, however, the narrator muses on the character of Teufelsdröckh and on passages from the volume on clothes. In book 1, chapter 5, for instance, Carlyle attacks one of his favorite targets, Enlightenment rationalism, when his narrator quotes Teufelsdröckh's sneer at the Cause-and-Effect Philosopher.

The chapter "The World out of Clothes" stresses the inadequacy of rational systems, praising Teufelsdröckh's broad, intuitive approach to understanding the spiritual basis of nature, an infinitely complex system, but one that faith convinces readers reveals a plan. Humans live as in a dream, perceiving only in "rare half-waking moments" the spiritual reality behind the mask of matter in the creation.

This same theme is pursued in a chapter that renounces "vulgar Logic" in favor of "Pure Reason"; that is, logic views the human being simply as an "omnivorous Biped that wears Breeches," whereas Pure Reason, or direct, unmediated intuition, apprehends in humans "A Soul, a Spirit, and divine Apparition." Matter, however, should not be denigrated, for it is everywhere the manifestation of Spirit. Science threatens the reverence for Spirit, however, because its curiosity about matter dampens the sense of wonder at the mystery of existence.

Book 1 ends with the narrator's receipt of six large paper bags stuffed with Teufelsdröckh's manuscripts. The narrator's subsequent absorption in the story of the philosopher's life and opinions will form the substance of book 2, told mostly in long passages quoted from Teufelsdröckh's papers.

The hero's origins in the village of Entepfuhl (Duck Pond) are mysterious; an enigmatic stranger brings the infant in a basket to a childless, aging couple, Andreas and Gretchen Futteral. The young Diogenes' childhood is idyllic, his intellectual development prodigious. In his adolescence, he loses both Andreas and Gretchen, but in learning the puzzle of his birth, he miraculously discovers his individuality: "*I was like no other*," he exults. His university experience disillusions him, and the narrator digresses to blister one of Carlyle's favorite targets, the barrenness of rationalism. However, Teufelsdröckh's youthful skepticism is a natural rite of passage, for

> first must the dead Letter of Religion own itself dead, and drop piecemeal into dust, if the living Spirit of Religion, freed from this its charnelhouse, is to arise on us, newborn of Heaven, and with new healing under its wings.

This passage well illustrates Carlyle's unrelieved practice of narrating by metaphor.

After the young Teufelsdröckh leaves the university, he follows a ragged course. He flounders in a legal career before suffering through his first great love interest, the collapse of which turns him into a Byronic pilgrim wandering in the mountains. At this point in book 2, Carlyle subjects his hero to an ordeal of religious despair through which the hero fights his way. Chapter 7, "The Everlasting No," finds Teufelsdröckh mired in spiritual sloth but still clinging to his belief in a transcendent Truth and the demands of duty. Finally, he rouses himself and looks outward at the world, the "*Not-me*," finding great relief in this escape from the burden of solipsism, or absorption in self.

In chapter 8, "Centre of Indifference," the revitalized Teufelsdröckh plunges into the give-and-take of great events and great scenes, and Carlyle expands on one of his favorite themes, the importance of the great person in shaping history. This was a topic on which Carlyle was to write at length in *On Heroes and Hero-Worship* (1841). By chapter's end, Teufelsdröckh has banished spiritual pride and can ask himself, "Pshaw! what is this paltry little Dog-cage of an Earth; what art thou that sittest whining there?"

Chapter 10, "The Everlasting Yea," relates Teufelsdröckh's emergence whole on the far side of the slough of despond. He reports that "Annihilation of Self . . . had been happily accomplished; and my mind's eyes were now unsealed, and its hands ungyved." He suddenly enjoys knowledge of a living universe full of the immanent God, a nature he calls the Living Garment of God. This mystical breakthrough inspires in him infinite love and pity for his fellow human beings, and it frees him from Calvinist fretting about Original Sin. The insight he achieves owes a debt to Johann Wolfgang von Goethe's *Faust* (part 1, 1808): People's unhappiness derives from the source of their greatness, their finite soul's

striving for the infinite. Once they overcome their preoccupation with happiness and turn their attention to God, they shall achieve peace. Carlyle's famous command is "Close thy *Byron*; open thy *Goethe*." In an apostrophe to Voltaire, Teufelsdröckh tells Voltaire that his work is over; Christian superstition is dead. These three chapters are the centerpiece of *Sartor Resartus*, and they conclude resoundingly: "Work while it is called To-day, for the Night cometh wherein no man can work."

The remaining chapters return to the same ideas, fashioning them in different metaphors. "Incident in Modern History" celebrates the life of George Fox (1624-1691), founder of the Society of Friends (Quakers). "Church Clothes" elaborates on a conceit in which government appears as the outer skin of society, and religion becomes "the inmost Pericardial and Nervous Tissue, which ministers Life and warm Circulation to the whole." Utilitarians, or "Motive-Millwrights," take a couple of punches in "Symbols," a chapter that also lauds as the highest of all symbols the artist or poet who emerges as a prophet in whom "all men can recognise a present God." Jesus is cited as "our divinest Symbol." Clearly, Carlyle aspired to be the artist-prophet of his age.

Liberal, rationalist contempt for the Church and its hierarchical authority is condemned in "The Phoenix," which predicts that a saving remnant will revitalize the institution. This revitalization is enabled by the "organic filaments" that connect the dying elements of the old generation to the elements being born in the new generation. Humankind is a unity that gives sequence and continuity to life. The new age will need new titles, but kings will remain kings. The true basis for organizing society will always be hero worship, which elevates great individuals to their proper positions. Even with the old religion in retreat, there remain "Fragments of a genuine Church-*Homiletic*" scattered amid "this immeasurable froth ocean we name *Literature*." Paramount among the prophets of literature is Goethe.

One of Carlyle's longest chapters is "Natural Supernaturalism," in which he sneers at science as petty in the face of the miracles witnessed daily: "the true inexplicable God-revealing Miracle lies in this," he insists, "that I can stretch forth my hand at all." God's presence shines through the universe, and each person lives as a ghost, "a shadow-system gathered round our Me." Humans come into this world and take a bodily shape before disappearing again, "through Mystery to Mystery, from God and to God."

A chapter entitled "Circumspective" expounds a semiotics of spirit, and "The Dandiacal Body" contrasts, rather meanly, the sect of self-absorbed dandies whose "*Fashionable Novels*" constitute their sacred books, with the "Poor-Slaves," that is "Rhizophagous," or potato-eating, Irish-Catholic peasantry. Two final chapters, repeating the same metaphors, conclude the hyperbolic musings of Carlyle's modern Diogenes.

Two years after Carlyle published *Sartor Resartus*, the American transcendentalist Ralph Waldo Emerson published his famous meditation *Nature* (1836), in which he announces his own version of the Idealism that Carlyle celebrated; in "Self-Reliance" (1841), Emerson gives his most eloquent testimony in support of Carlyle's hero-worship. In their fierce defense of a supersensible realm of Spirit, their condemnation of the positivism of their times, and their proclamation of the individual's freedom to achieve greatness through efforts of the will, these two sages contributed greatly to nineteenth century intellectual history.

Frank Day

Further Reading

Carlyle, Thomas. *Sartor Resartus: The Life and Opinions of Herr Teufelsdröckh in Three Books*. Introduction and notes by Rodger L. Tarr. Berkeley: University of California Press, 2000. This edition uses all extant versions to create an authentic text. It also includes a helpful introduction that discusses the work and places it in its historical context. Also includes extensive textual annotations.

Kaplan, Fred. *Thomas Carlyle: A Biography*. Ithaca, N.Y.: Cornell University Press, 1983. Comprehensive biography. Presents Carlyle's circumstances while writing *Sartor Resartus* and his dealings with publishers. Vividly depicts Carlyle's relations with notable figures, such as Harriet Martineau and John Stuart Mill, and shows clear affinities with American readers. Includes many illustrations.

LaValley, Albert J. *Carlyle and the Idea of the Modern*. New Haven, Conn.: Yale University Press, 1968. Studies Carlyle's prophetic writings in relation to William Blake and other prophets of his day, including Friedrich Nietzsche and Karl Marx. Argues that *Sartor Resartus* presents Christianity as exhausted and asserts that the self will be the new basis of religion.

Levine, George. *The Boundaries of Fiction: Carlyle, Macaulay, Newman*. Princeton, N.J.: Princeton University Press, 1968. Pointing to the use in *Sartor Resartus* of symbols and images, and to its satire and didacticism, Levine treats it not as a novel but as a "confession-anatomy-romance" in Northrop Frye's system of classification.

Morrow, John. *Thomas Carlyle*. New York: Hambledon Continuum, 2006. This updated biography chronicles Carlyle's personal life and intellectual career and discusses his works.

Seigel, Jules Paul, ed. *Thomas Carlyle: The Critical Heritage*. London: Routledge & Kegan Paul, 1971. A collection of contemporary reviews. John Sterling praises the "genius and moral energy" of *Sartor Resartus*, Alexander Hill Everett calls the book a "philosophical romance," and Nathaniel Frothingham admires its "humane cast of thought."

Tennyson, G. B. *Sartor Called Resartus*. Princeton, N.J.: Princeton University Press, 1965. Invaluable study of *Sartor Resartus*. Includes chapters on the book's German background and on its composition, structure, texture, and style. The final chapter illustrates the book's philosophy in the context of the period. Appendix includes a chronology of the composition of Carlyle's works.

Trela, D. J., and Rodger L. Tarr, eds. *The Critical Response to Thomas Carlyle's Major Works*. Westport, Conn.: Greenwood Press, 1997. Collection of reviews and essays about *Sartor Resartus* and Carlyle's other major works that date from their initial publication through the twentieth century. The introduction discusses how Carlyle responded to his critics.

Sartoris

Author: William Faulkner (1897-1962)
First published: 1929
Type of work: Novel
Type of plot: Psychological realism
Time of plot: Immediately following World War I
Locale: Mississippi

Principal characters:
YOUNG BAYARD SARTORIS, a self-destructive veteran
AUNT JENNY DEPRE, his caustic aunt
OLD BAYARD SARTORIS, his irascible grandfather
NARCISSA BENBOW, a friend of Jenny who reluctantly falls in love with young Bayard
HORACE BENBOW, her effete and absent-minded brother, also a veteran
SIMON STROTHER, a black retainer of the Sartoris family
BYRON SNOPES, a Peeping Tom and Narcissa's secret admirer

The Story:

Shortly after the conclusion of World War I, Will Falls, an ancient veteran of the Civil War, comes to visit old Bayard Sartoris in his Jefferson, Mississippi, bank, bringing a pipe that belonged to John Sartoris, Bayard's father and a colonel in the Confederacy. John's heroic ghost seems to fill the room as they reminisce.

The bank day over, Simon Strother, a Sartoris family servant, comes to drive old Bayard home in the family carriage and reports that Bayard's grandson, also named Bayard, was seen arriving on a train that afternoon. Young Bayard is a Royal Air Force pilot along with his twin brother John. John died foolishly in the skies over France. Juxtaposed with young Bayard's reported sighting is another story of the past, this one about a third Bayard Sartoris, who fought in the Civil War. Colonel John Sartoris's brother died vaingloriously in the service of Jeb Stuart. His Civil War exploits, as did his brother John's, became part of the Sartoris family legend. The repository of the Sartoris legends is eighty-year-old Aunt Jenny Depre, who keeps house for the Sartorises. The sister of John and Bayard Sartoris of the Civil War, she alternated between paying homage to and scoffing at the deeds of her brothers. A no-nonsense person with an acidic tongue, she attributed the violence and foolishness of the World War I generation of brothers to the same streak of Sartoris bullheadedness that ran through the Sartoris men of the Civil War.

Safely returned home to the care of Aunt Jenny and his grandfather, young Bayard still cannot find peace. He is filled with guilt over his brother's death and is driven to self-destructive behavior. He foolishly tries to ride an untrained stallion and is thrown. Rather than return home, he becomes drunk with some country folks and then serenades all the eligible ladies in town, including Narcissa Benbow. He also races recklessly through the county in an automobile, running wagons off the road. Although warned to avoid the automobile because of a bad heart, the elder Bayard rides along, ostensibly to restrain his grandson's recklessness but really, according to Miss Jenny, because, as another Sartoris male, he desires the same thrill of danger as his grandson. Narcissa is Jenny's friend and formerly was in love with Bayard's brother John. Visiting one day, she confides to Jenny that she was receiving anonymous and obscene love letters. For all of her ladylike decorum, however, she is secretly flattered by the letters. The sender, Byron Snopes, is a stealthy, animalistic bookkeeper at the Sartorises' bank, who dictates his missives to a schoolboy, as if they were business correspondence. The boy blackmails Snopes into giving him an air rifle.

Narcissa welcomes home another returning veteran, her brother Horace Benbow. A noncombatant during the war, he served in the YMCA and learned glassblowing in Italy. Impractical and absent-minded, Horace finds that his love of beauty is a thin disguise for his cowardice. He adores his sister, even naming one of his glass vases after her, but he falls out of favor with her when he resumes an affair with Belle Mitchell, a discontented married woman.

A third returning veteran is Caspey Strother, son of Simon, who comes to believe that, given their equal status in France, blacks need no longer accept a servile position in southern society. Caspey's war tales are exaggerated, and the only real wounds he suffered were in a crap game. Old Bayard regards Caspey's notions of his rights as insolent. In the meantime, old Bayard develops a wen on his face, which, much to Aunt Jenny's exasperation, he allows Will Falls to treat with an ancient Indian remedy. Fearful that Bayard will get blood poisoning, she takes him to a pretentious but ineffectual specialist. Falls's salve ultimately works perfectly, much to the dismay of Jenny and the doctors. Eventually, young Bayard has an automobile accident in which he breaks his ribs. Narcissa, with conflicting feelings of attraction and revulsion, reads to him as he recovers, although he has no interest whatsoever in books. The relationship develops further until they agree to marry. On the eve of the wedding, Byron Snopes breaks into Narcissa's bedroom, steals the anonymous letters he wrote her, robs the Sartorises' bank, and leaves town.

Simon gets into trouble with his church congregation, which entrusts him with money being collected to build a new church building. Simon gave the money away to a mistress, claiming, in imitation of his employer, that he lent the money out. He assures the congregation that the elder Bayard will restore the money, much to his employer's outrage. Young Bayard finds a momentary contentment in marriage, Narcissa's pregnancy, and the rhythms of seasonal plantation life. He and Narcissa watch the sharecroppers make sorghum molasses, go possum hunting with Caspey, and share Thanksgiving dinner with family and friends. Memories of his twin brother, however, drive him to despair again. Driving recklessly off the road one December day, he causes his grandfather to die of a heart attack. Ashamed of his conduct, he does not return home but escapes into the country to stay with the MacCallums, with whom he and his brother often hunted. This return to a wholesome life close to the earth reminds him of better times, but it cannot restore his spirits. On Christmas Eve he leaves the MacCallums', spends the night and Christmas morning with a black sharecropping family, and then takes a train away from his home forever.

At the conclusion of the novel, Narcissa receives a letter from Horace, who went off to live with Belle. Jenny and she also receive, from various parts of the country, Bayard's requests for money. Bayard eventually agrees to test-fly a dangerously designed airplane and is killed on the day his son is born to Narcissa. Jenny announces that the child's name must be John, but in an effort to evade the Sartoris heritage of violence and self-destructiveness, Narcissa insists on naming the child Benbow Sartoris. Simon Strother is eventually murdered as the result of his adulterous affair. Jenny tends to Simon's and the Sartoris men's graves. Picking up the pieces left behind by the destructive Sartoris men seems to be her lot in life, a role that she stoically accepts.

Critical Evaluation:

The juxtaposition of modern themes and the mythology of a southern family's past resulted in William Faulkner's first important novel. He wrote two prior books, *Soldiers'*

Pay (1926) and *Mosquitoes* (1927), whose modernism was fairly typical of their time, but they lacked the rich texture of *Sartoris*. In this novel, Faulkner imparts to his alienated modern heroes a long tradition of Sartoris glory and vainglory. His dramatization is deepened by positioning it in the context of southern history and by creating a strong sense of place.

Some critics see family history as a burden that young Bayard must bear, an impossibly high standard to which he must aspire. Others argue that, in the modern, mechanized world, Bayard is prevented from shouldering that burden and following in the heroic footsteps of his ancestors. In either case, his life epitomizes the despair so often associated with modern protagonists. Lacking meaning in their lives, the protagonists of many modern novels find themselves alienated from their society and from life itself.

Sartoris is about the South's entering the modern world, taking one last backward glance into the past as it does so. The novel displays a double consciousness about the Southern past. From the beginning, when Will Falls visits old Bayard, the influence of the Civil War and the heroic Sartoris legend pervades the book. Various devices, such as narrative commentary, the reminiscences of Falls and Aunt Jenny, and the opening of the chest in the attic containing Sartoris relics, combine to underscore the past's influence on the present. The novel's attitude toward the past is a mixture of romantic nostalgia and modern skepticism. Miss Jenny, for example, speaks tartly of the antics of the male line of her family even as she keeps their legends alive. She is simultaneously contemptuous and tender.

The novel is not only concerned with romanticized views of the Southern past but with romantic notions generally. Faulkner depicts the romantic attitudes of a variety of characters, and he employs satire to undercut those notions. For instance, the idealized brother-and-sister relationship of Horace and Narcissa is undermined by both her willingness to keep Snopes's obscene letters and his sordid affair with a married woman. In *Sartoris*, Faulkner seems eager to explore the many possibilities of his fictional world. In fact, one of the problems noted by critics of this work is that, in it, he tries to do too much. There are too many stories, and they are only superficially related to each other. The novel has been called episodic and lacking a center. The first draft of the book, called "Flags in the Dust," was even longer and had to be edited before a publisher would agree to print it. The material is so rich that Faulkner revisits many of the same characters, or similar ones, in later novels. He later devoted a trilogy of novels (*The Hamlet*, 1940; *The Town*, 1957; and *The Mansion*, 1959) to the wily Snopes family. He writes of Horace and Narcissa in *Sanctuary* (1931). He returns to common people such as V. K. Suratt (who later becomes V. K. Ratliff) and the MacCallums in various novels. He also returns to black characters in books such as *The Sound and the Fury* (1929) and *Go Down, Moses* (1942). For all its artistic flaws, *Sartoris* is exciting because of the richness of its material and the tangible enthusiasm of its author as he discovers the characters and the setting that will occupy him for the rest of his career.

William L. Howard

Further Reading

Hoffman, Frederick J. *William Faulkner.* 2d rev. ed. Boston: Twayne, 1966. A basic study of Faulkner's work and life. Notes that *Sartoris* is the beginning of his great novels about his own "postage stamp of native soil," Yoknapatawpha County and shows a deeper insight into the cultural context in which his characters operate than his previous novels.

Howe, Irving. *William Faulkner: A Critical Study.* 3d ed. Chicago: University of Chicago Press, 1975. Divided into two parts, one addressing Faulkner's "world and his work" and the other evaluating his achievement in the major novels. *Sartoris* is treated as an apprentice work.

Millgate, Michael. *The Achievement of William Faulkner.* New York: Random House, 1966. Includes a chapter on Faulkner's career, separate chapters on each of his novels, and a chapter assessing his achievement. Sees *Sartoris* as a bridge between his apprenticeship and his mature novels. Millgate notes that in this novel, Faulkner successfully captured the spirit of a place for the first time.

Towner, Theresa M. *The Cambridge Introduction to William Faulkner.* New York: Cambridge University Press, 2008. An accessible book aimed at students and general readers. Focusing on Faulkner's work, the book provides detailed analyses of his nineteen novels, discussion of his other works, and information about the critical reception for his fiction.

Tuck, Dorothy. *Crowell's Handbook of Faulkner.* New York: Thomas Y. Crowell, 1964. An excellent source for basic information about each of Faulkner's novels. Provides a synopsis of *Sartoris* as well as essays on the history of Yoknapatawpha County and Faulkner's style of writing.

Vickery, Olga W. *The Novels of William Faulkner.* Rev. ed. Baton Rouge: Louisiana State University Press, 1964. Treats Faulkner's novels separately, then discusses themes that pervade a number of them. Sees *Sartoris* as about mythmaking and the deflation of myths.

The Satanic Verses

Author: Salman Rushdie (1947-   )
First published: 1988
Type of work: Novel
Type of plot: Fantasy
Time of plot: Late twentieth and early seventh centuries
Locale: London, India, and Jahilia

Principal characters:

GIBREEL FARISHTA, an Indian film star
SALADIN CHAMCHA, an English actor, the man of a thousand and one voices
PAMELA LOVELACE, his wife
ALLELUIA CONE, a mountain climber, Gibreel's lover
MAHOUND, a pejorative Christian name for the Prophet Muḥammad
HIND, queen of Jahilia
THE IMAM, an exiled religious figure
AYESHA, a young woman who leads her followers on a fatal pilgrimage to Mecca
ZEENY VIKAL, a medical doctor, art critic, and political activist
SALMAN, Mahound's scribe
BAAL, a satirist

The Story:

Odd-numbered chapters. Around New Year's Day, just before dawn, Sikh terrorists destroy an Air India jumbo jet in flight. Two passengers miraculously, or fantastically, fall safely into the English Channel, one flapping his arms and singing, the other desperately, doubtfully, clinging to his companion. Forty-year-old Gibreel Farishta, née Ismail Najruddin, is a poor orphan who has grown up to become India's biggest film star. "Fortyish" Saladin Chamcha, née Salahuddin Chamchawala, the estranged Anglophile son of a prominent Bombay businessman, is also an actor; a master mimic, he is the costar of the popular English television series *The Aliens*. The two men interpret their salvation differently, and, once ashore, they experience very different receptions. Unable to prove his identity and having begun to assume a goatlike appearance and smell, Chamcha is arrested and verbally and physically abused by racist police officers. Gibreel, dressed in the clothes of his host's (Rosa Diamond's) late husband, is allowed to go free.

Chamcha's situation worsens. Escaping from a migrants-only ward of the mental hospital, where he was committed once the police discovered that he was what he claimed to be, a British citizen, he returns home to find his very proper-sounding and proper-looking English wife, Pamela Lovelace, in bed with another man, Jamsheed Joshi. He also finds he is without a job, the role of Maxim Alien having been cut by the show's Thatcherite producer, Hal Valence. With "Jumpy" Joshi's help, he secures temporary lodgings in the kind of immigrant neighborhood that he has spent much of his life trying to avoid. As his anger and helplessness grow, so does Chamcha. Local activists transform the satanic-looking eight-foot-tall satyr into an immigrant hero. Not until he vents his rage in a local nightspot where Asians, West Indians, and others dance alongside wax effigies of developing world heroes and their English oppressors (including Margaret Thatcher) is he able to resume his earlier form.

Gibreel, meanwhile, fares much better. Transformed into his namesake, the Angel of the Recitation, he seeks refuge in the bed of his English lover, the fair-skinned climber of Mount Everest Alleluia Cone (originally Cohen), whom he had met immediately after his near-fatal illness several months earlier and before his mysterious disappearance from Bombay. Spurned by England and his English wife alike, Chamcha, transmogrified into Shaitan as well as the angel Azraeel, avenges his fall from grace by destroying Gibreel's happiness, undermining his faith in Alleluia Cone, and thus pushing Gibreel one step closer to madness.

Leaving Alleluia does not mean Gibreel can leave behind the dreams that have been troubling him since his recovery

from the Phantom Bug. From her home, he walks straight into a nightmarish London beset by racial strife and police cover-ups that leave several people dead, including Pamela Lovelace and her lover. Chamcha nearly dies trying to save the Bangladeshi couple with whom he stayed earlier, but he is saved by Gibreel, despite the fact that Gibreel realizes that it is Chamcha who scripted his breakup with Alleluia.

Chamcha's life improves. He survives a heart attack, returns to Bombay, and becomes reconciled not only with his dying father but also with India, to the point of taking an interest in local politics, or at least in one political activist, Zeeny Vikal. Gibreel's fortunes, meanwhile, take a downward turn. His films are unsuccessful; his cynicism grows. A chance encounter ends with Gibreel shooting Whisky Sisodia, the stuttering film producer and erstwhile Good Samaritan, and then throwing Alleluia Cone off a high-rise roof in a virtual replay of the suicide of his former mistress Rekha Merchant two years earlier. After telling his tale, Gibreel kills himself as Chamcha looks helplessly on.

Even-numbered chapters. The angel Gibreel has troubling dreams. In the first, Abu Simbel, leader of Jahilia (pre-Islamic Arabia), offers to make a deal with Mahound: He will accept the new monotheistic religion if Mahound will grant subordinate but still divine status to three local goddesses. After consulting the angel Gibreel, Mahound accepts the offer. Later, however, after the number of his followers has grown, Mahound claims that the concession was the work of Shaitan and that the verses in the revelation conceding semidivine status to the three goddesses are satanic in origin and effect and therefore must be corrected. In Gibreel's second dream, an exiled Imam returns to Desh (Iran) and commands Gibreel to defeat Ayesha (a version of the whore of Babylon, or, alternately, the Great Satan, the United States). In the third dream, Mahound completes his conquest of Jahilia, ordering the closing of its most famous brothel and the executions of its prostitutes, who have adopted the names of Mahound's twelve wives. In the fourth, Gibreel orders a young woman, Ayesha, to lead a group of pilgrims to the sea and on to Mecca. When the sea fails to part as the angel told her it would, all but a few of the pilgrims drown.

Critical Evaluation:

Upon its publication, *The Satanic Verses* elicited the harshest of reviews, a death sentence, from Iran's Ayatollah Ruhollah Khomeini, whose familiarity with the novel was apparently limited to secondhand reports of Gibreel's "blasphemous" dreams. The fatwa, or decree, of death, which was issued on February 14, 1989, had less to do with Salman

Rushdie and his novel than it did with the power struggle then going on in Iran between hard-liners such as Khomeini and moderates. The author and his book suffered greatly as a result. Rushdie was effectively made a hostage to a new form of international terrorism backed by the promise of financial and heavenly rewards for the assassin. He had to go into hiding. His novel, when not either burned or banned, was initially discussed almost exclusively with reference to the fatwa.

In its intricate and provocative exploration of postmodern and postcolonial sensibilities, *The Satanic Verses* celebrates and extends what one character calls "the eclectic, hybridized nature of the Indian artistic tradition." Its multiplicity of styles and stories, its blurring of the boundaries separating reality from dream, fact from fiction, its "pitting levity against gravity," and its allowing characters' names to migrate, as it were, from one narrative to another, do more than confuse some readers and entertain others. Metaphorically, such techniques work much the same way as the novel's intertextuality does in drawing on a wide variety of ceaselessly metamorphosing texts—the Qurʾān, the Bible, the *Mahabharata* (200 B.C.E.-200 C.E.), and Homer's *Odyssey* (c. 725 B.C.E.; English translation, 1614) on one hand and Hindi films and British television shows on the other. "Democracy can only thrive in a turbulent environment," Rushdie has noted, and *The Satanic Verses* is a narratively turbulent novel in which pyrotechnic style is put to political purpose as Rushdie considers both the chances for and challenges to democracy in an increasingly intolerant and multicultural world. Not even a writer as ambitious as Rushdie can hope to be completely democratic.

Rushdie has written that the telling of one story in effect censors the telling of others. In *The Satanic Verses* Rushdie does, however, imply the existence of these other tales and, more important, make clear what happens in a world ruled by a "terrifying singularity" where "and, or, maybe" has no place, no voice.

The stasis and "purity" of Mahound's "Rule" and "the Untime of the Imam" (Khomeini's "revolt against history"), Rushdie believes, pervert one of Muḥammad's greatest achievements, his having situated himself in the actual historical circumstances of his time and place. *The Satanic Verses* may be critical of religion, but it is not antireligious and certainly not blasphemous. "Fact is," the stuttering but good-hearted Whisky Sisodia tells Chamcha, "religious fafaith, which encodes the highest ass ass aspirations of human race, is now, in our cocountry, the servant of lowest instincts, and gogo God is the creature of evil." The novel views these aspirations in secular terms and religious move-

ments—whether Islam in the early seventh century or Muslim and Hindu fundamentalism in the late twentieth—as responses to specific economic and political problems. Rushdie is, however, equally critical of the West, whose freedoms he embraces but whose racism he deplores in all its forms. These range all the way from physical assaults to more subtle variations on the old Asian theme. Chamcha learns from another transmogrified immigrant, "They have the power of description, and we conform to the pictures they construct." The most insidious form of racism is the creation of the monoculture of multinational capitalism, what Rushdie only half-jokingly calls "the Coca-Colonization of the planet."

Metamorphosis at all levels is at the heart of *The Satanic Verses*. The questions it asks—"Who am I?" and "How does newness come into the world?"—may be old, but Rushdie gives them a new urgency as he ponders "the migrant condition." Rushdie has argued that mass migration has created radically new types of human beings: people who root themselves in ideas rather than in places, in memories as much as in material things. Such people have been obliged to define themselves, because they are so defined by others, by their otherness. In a melting pot, strange mixes are made. *The Satanic Verses* succeeds on many fronts—managing to be at once narratively compelling, stylistically flamboyant, psychologically insightful, and sociopolitically relevant—and it succeeds most in that it creates a space where postcolonial and postmodern sensibilities intersect, where the migrant condition becomes a metaphor for all humanity.

Robert A. Morace

Further Reading

Brennan, Timothy. *Salman Rushdie and the Third World: Myths of the Nation*. New York: St. Martin's Press, 1989. Discusses both the strengths and weaknesses of Rushdie's cosmopolitanism and the ways in which his fiction draws on materials from the developing world but does not adequately represent the concerns of developing nations.

Gurnah, Abdulrazak, ed. *The Cambridge Companion to Salman Rushdie*. New York: Cambridge University Press, 2007. Collection of essays presents assessment of Rushdie's importance for postcolonial literature and analysis of specific works. Two of the essays focus on *The Satanic Verses*: "The Fatwa and Its Aftermath," by Ruvani Ranasinha, and "*The Satanic Verses*: 'To Be Born Again, First You Have to Die,'" by Joel Kuortti.

Harrison, James. *Salman Rushdie*. New York: Twayne, 1992.

Provides a good general introduction to the author's work. Includes biographical material, background on India, and chapters devoted to individual novels.

Hassumani, Sabrina. *Salman Rushdie: A Postmodern Reading of His Major Works*. Madison, N.J.: Fairleigh Dickinson University Press, 2002. Presents a close reading of *The Satanic Verses* as well as analyses of four other of Rushdie's major novels.

Kimmich, Matt. *Offspring Fictions: Salman Rushdie's Family Novels*. New York: Rodopi, 2008. Examines the depiction of families and the parent-child relationship in *The Satanic Verses* and three other novels. Argues that Rushdie's concepts of the family are variations on the ideas of Sigmund Freud; describes how his portrayals of children and parents reflect his concern with nationalism, religion, history, and authorship.

MacDonogh, Steve, ed. *The Rushdie Letters: Freedom to Speak, Freedom to Write*. Lincoln: University of Nebraska Press, 1993. Collection features the letters written to Rushdie by twenty-seven prominent writers concerning the fatwa as well as essays by Rushdie and Tom Stoppard and Carmel Bedford's compilation, "Fiction, Fact, and the Fatwa."

Rushdie, Salman. *Imaginary Homelands: Essays and Criticism, 1981-1991*. New York: Penguin Books, 1991. Offers several essays that deal specifically with *The Satanic Verses* and the fatwa.

Teverson, Andrew. *Salman Rushdie*. New York: Manchester University Press, 2007. Examines the intellectual, biographical, literary, and cultural contexts of Rushdie's novels. One chapter is devoted to satire in *The Satanic Verses*.

Satires

Author: Nicolas Boileau-Despréaux (1636-1711)
First published: Les Satires, 1666-1711 (English translation, 1711-1713)
Type of work: Poetry

The name of Nicolas Boileau-Despréaux, is often linked only to *L'Art poétique* (1674; *The Art of Poetry*, 1683), his critical treatise setting down the rules and unities of French classicism. He received the mantle of prophet and lawgiver for that movement, which is something of a false emphasis. *The Art of Poetry* was a summary and compendium of standard poetic practices, of the rules French literature had been operating under for the entire century.

The modern student of literature may not realize the importance of Boileau-Despréaux in the development of literary taste. The subjects of Boileau-Despréaux's satires resemble those of his classical predecessors and of his contemporaries in seventeenth century France. Modeling his work on the giants of the past, most noticeably Juvenal, Boileau-Despréaux attacks contemporary fashion and its excesses with a vitriol exceeding that of many less perceptive and less daring satirists. While only a dozen of his writings are formally designated satires, the satiric point of view colors all his writings, including *The Art of Poetry*.

The influence of Boileau-Despréaux on the development of literature should not be underestimated. For more than a hundred years Boileau-Despréaux was upheld as something like a literary dictator of Europe. His influence extended over England during the late seventeenth and throughout the eighteenth centuries. His work established on the Continent and in England a feeling of reverence for the authors of Greece and Rome. His support of the ancients over the moderns in his discussion of literary merit may seem strange, since on numerous occasions he expressed great admiration for his contemporaries Jean Racine and Molière. He was nevertheless a vigorous defender of the classical methods of balance and restraint, contrasting their reserve with what he found to be the silly exuberances of most contemporary writing (especially the multivolume romances that were exceptionally popular in France). His pronouncements on the necessity to "follow nature"—which, in turn, meant to follow the practices of the great classical writers whose works mirrored nature—became dogma for authors both in France and abroad for the next century.

Despite his great influence on European ideas of what literature should be, Boileau-Despréaux may be best remembered as a practitioner, not a theoretician, of French verse.

His *Satires* are a notable example of the skill with which he returned French poetry to a character of imitation of nature. Seventeenth century poetry had turned chiefly to the burlesque and the heroic styles, which were highly conceited and artificial. With *Satires*, written with common sense as a norm and the expression of truth as a goal, Boileau-Despréaux did much to purify his medium.

He had a genius for satire and ample opportunity to find subjects for his verse in the brilliant and sophisticated court of Louis XIV, the Sun King. The monarchy had become absolute in France, and the ideal of the courtier—the aristocratic, gracious, elegant, witty, refined, accomplished man—afforded ideal occasion for a satirist to comment upon the vanity, ambition, intrigue, and posturings that invariably accompany competition for royal favor.

Boileau-Despréaux was presented to the king in 1669. Despite his trenchant criticisms of the vices and foibles of society, he remained in favor at the court for thirty years. His frank and courageous outspokenness was notable as well as his benevolence, generosity, and kindliness. Accordingly, his satirical writings are not stinging lashes of vice, as with Juvenal, but a gentler ridiculing of humanity's failings. His twelve satires touch on many facets of the fashionable life of his times and give a lively indication of what it was like to live in seventeenth century Parisian society.

The second, seventh and ninth satires are concerned with the art and craft of the satirist and with Boileau-Despréaux's own fortunes in that calling. Boileau-Despréaux liberally criticizes his fellow poets and makes no pretense of acceding to public opinion about the merit of any writer. However high a poet's fashionable reputation may be, if he cannot rhyme Boileau-Despréaux says so. He attacks many of his contemporaries, but seldom drops into ad hominem criticism. Moreover, time has proven his opinions to be remarkably just: The names that receive most of Boileau-Despréaux's scorn have become as obscure to the present day as their poetry is mediocre. Likewise, those whom he praised remain as the outstanding seventeenth century French authors.

Satire 2, addressed to Molière, laments the difficulties of finding rhymes without having them tyrannize over the sense in a poem. In mock despair, and in perfectly rhymed Alexandrines, Boileau-Despréaux rehearses the poet's plight, the necessity of either glib and vapid epithets to match a rhyme or else wrenched syntax and broken phrases. In the seventh satire, Boileau-Despréaux discusses a tentative plan to banish satire from his writing, saying it is a malicious style that makes the author many enemies. He would much prefer to write poems of praise. Alas, however, all his poetic powers desert him at such an attempt; his talent, he concludes, lies in

the exposure of folly, and a satirical poet he will have to remain. The ninth satire has a similar tone: The author affects to scold himself for his feeble efforts to reform the city by his verse. He points out the vanity of any hope for esteem of his work and says that the fools he castigates are not even worth spilling ink over. As the poem develops, it shifts subtly into an ironic ridicule of all the people who are the just subjects of the satirist's pen and becomes a triumph, not a reproach, to Boileau-Despréaux.

Another group of satires is directed toward the life of the city, with its would-be aristocrats and pseudosophisticates. Satire 1 demonstrates how the poet is abused and neglected in the city, while the lackey, the toady, the pedant are all exalted, and all vices flourish. Satire 6 continues this theme with an account of the noise, dirt, confusion, and crime that surround the city dweller. These two were originally composed as one poem, in imitation of Juvenal's Satire 3. Boileau-Despréaux's third satire tells the uproarious tale of a feast given by a gourmand who pretends to be a gourmet and of the ridiculous pretensions to elegance and erudition of the host and his country-bumpkin guests. The execrable repast is reduced to shambles by a hair-pulling scuffle between the guests: one an absurdly aspiring poet, the other an absurdly aspiring literary critic.

Satires 5 and 6 catalog the excesses of the town by an inquiry into what constitutes true nobility and true honor. In Satire 5, hereditary nobility is ridiculed, along with its trappings of heraldry and elaborate equipage. Boileau-Despréaux shows how the bearer of a name famous of old for courage and daring may be an arrogant coward, retaining nothing of the virtue of his ancestors. On the other hand, a truly valorous man who is of humble descent ought to be able to adopt Achilles, Alexander, or Caesar for his ancestors, the author says, since he behaves like them. Ancient days, when nobility was a valid indication of virtue, are contrasted to the present, whose wretched aristocrats are so deep in debt that they must barter their titles for enough gold to maintain the ostentation considered essential for a peer. Satire 11 exposes similar abuses of the ideal of honor. This was written considerably later than the preceding poems, in 1698, at a time when Boileau-Despréaux's family was engaged in a lawsuit over the validity of their own hereditary title to the nobility (which was finally proven to be false). Various erroneous ideas about honor are shown: ambition, avarice, vanity. For Boileau-Despréaux, honor resides ultimately only in justice, and he castigates the inability of the self-interested and contentious to understand or to practice justice.

To this point, the satires have all been directed against the specific personal failings and vices of people. In Satires 4 and 8, Boileau-Despréaux takes a broader view and attacks the condition of being human. Satire 4 argues that all people are mad, but all believe that they are sane. The theme developed is a perennial: one's ability to see the mote in another's eye but not the beam in one's own. All are mad in their attachment to something: learning, refined manners, religion, atheism, wisdom, money, gambling, poetry. He concludes that it is probably better for people to be mad and happy than coldly reasonable with nothing to give them joy. Satire 8 takes a sharper tone on the same subject, the universal folly of humanity. Boileau-Despréaux adopts a mordant disdain for all human accomplishments, comparing people to beasts and finding the latter more humane in their activities. Depravity and corruption are everywhere, and even one's capacity for reason is so abused and ignored as to set one beneath the irrational animals. These two broader-ranging satires approach a kind of misanthropy not seen in the witty ridicule of foppery and the vanities of the others. All the poems, however, are in the traditional voice of the satirist, who is the gadfly of society, attempting to correct humanity's faults by turning on them the bright clear light of reason and common sense.

Another time-honored subject for the satirist is woman, and she has her place in the Boileau-Despréaux canon. His Satire 10 on women is the longest of the twelve. Not published until 1693, it is prefaced by an apology to the fair sex for the unkind portraits drawn therein, suggesting that since they are such near-perfect creatures, they cannot surely resent a well-meaning attempt to refine them a trifle more. The poem is a dialogue between Boileau-Despréaux and a friend, Alcippes, who has decided to take a wife. Boileau-Despréaux depicts the consequences of marrying various kinds of women: the adulterer, the coquette, the card-player, the penny-pincher, the shrew, the hypochondriac, the pedant, the falsely pious. All these character vignettes are artfully and vividly portrayed and have a devastating effect upon the poor lover, Alcippes. When he vows his lady is none of these, the poet declares that he has not told a quarter of the vices women can have. The confused would-be bridegroom protests that in any case he can always divorce her if she should be so bad. Boileau-Despréaux then triumphantly adduces woman's final villainy: Once her claws are in a man, she will never let him go.

The twelfth and last of Boileau-Despréaux's satires is quite different from the others. The satire is a serious attack on the problem of ambiguity in language deliberately used for evil ends. The meaning of *equivoque* (ambiguity, duplicity) expands through the poem, to indicate not only verbal ambiguity but also confusion of intentions, thoughts, expres-

sions—all sorts of misconceptions of the human mind and, most seriously, the way these have altered and corrupted Christianity from its original purity and holiness. As a theological argument, the poem attacks everything that Boileau-Despréaux considered heresies, particularly Jansenism and Jesuitism. The sincerity of this piece is beyond doubt, for Boileau-Despréaux was all his life a good Catholic; but its poetic power is perhaps less than in some of the earlier pieces. For several years after its composition, the poem was not permitted publication.

Taken as a whole, the satires of Boileau-Despréaux are characterized more by a genial gaiety than any deep bitterness or spite toward their victims. There is malicious wit but no indignant rage, and the butt of the joke is ridiculed rather than condemned. In all, *Satires* is a delightful account of one person's view of a fascinating and glamorous era of French civilization.

"Critical Evaluation" revised by Laurence W. Mazzeno

Further Reading

Colton, Robert E. *Studies of Classical Influence on Boileau and La Fontaine.* Hildesheim, Germany: G. Olms, 1996. Assesses the influence of Horace on Boileau-Despréaux's sixth, seventh, and eighth satires and some of his other work.

Corum, Robert T. *Reading Boileau: An Integrative Study of the Early "Satires."* West Lafayette, Ind.: Purdue University Press, 1998. An analysis of the first nine satires, discussing their sources, genesis, relation to each other, coherence, and continuity. Corum argues that Boileau-Despréaux was a gifted poet and not a mere "versifier."

Haight, Jeanne. *The Concept of Reason in French Classical Literature: 1635-1690.* Toronto, Ont.: University of Toronto Press, 1982. Examines Boileau-Despréaux's efforts to associate reason with socially accepted behavior in seventeenth century France. Describes the connection between aesthetics and sociology in Boileau-Despréaux's writing.

Moriarty, Michael. *Taste and Ideology in Seventeenth-Century France.* New York: Cambridge University Press, 1988. Explores the connection between Boileau-Despréaux's literary taste and his political ideology. Explains why Boileau-Despréaux's association of taste with an admiration for high culture caused him to reject representations of popular culture.

Pocock, Gordon. *Boileau and the Nature of Neo-Classicism.* New York: Cambridge University Press, 1980. Examines the general themes and structures in the satires. Stresses

Boileau-Despréaux's creative imitation of Horace and other classical Roman satirists.

White, Julian E. *Nicolas Boileau*. New York: Twayne, 1969. Introduction to Boileau-Despréaux's literary career and a fine annotated bibliography of important critical studies on his work. Examines his satires within the classical tradition of comedy of manners and describes Boileau-Despréaux's originality as a satiric poet.

Yarrow, P. J. *The Seventeenth Century: 1600-1715*. Vol. 2 in *A Literary History of France*. New York: Barnes & Noble, 1967. Traces the general evolution of French neoclassical literature during the seventeenth century. The chapter on Boileau-Despréaux describes the unity of his aesthetic and moral vision as expressed in his satires and in his theoretical writings.

Satires

Author: Juvenal (c. 60-c. 130)
First published: Saturae, 100-127 C.E. (English translation, 1693)
Type of work: Poetry

Juvenal is one of the greatest satirists in the literary tradition. An examination of the poet's influence on writers of generations succeeding his own bears out such an assessment. Often imitated, and even more frequently quoted, Juvenal has been venerated as one of the founding practitioners of satire and one of the most penetrating commentators on the human condition. His stance is that of the "angry" satirist who is driven to expression by a sense of indignation at the corruption he sees around him.

Juvenal's poems are rich in lurid description and vituperative rhetoric. The angry persona he adopts in his poems has spawned a tradition of satire that has run for nearly two thousand years through European literature. Perhaps more than any other figure, he is the source of inspiration for perhaps the greatest of English satirists, Jonathan Swift.

Writing at the height of the Roman Empire, Juvenal's principal target is the city of Rome and its inhabitants. Born during the reign of Nero, he lived under nine other emperors, including the tyrannical Domitian, of whom he was especially critical. In addition to the court of the emperors, he turns his critical gaze on the Roman nobility, a host of professions, as well as ordinary citizens, whose lives he sees being wasted in the vain pursuit of pleasure and wealth. As succeeding generations have noted, the failings he exposes are not unique to the Roman Empire: avarice, sycophancy, lewdness, treachery, and self-centeredness exist in every society, and Juvenal's satires speak to readers of any age who can see the analogies between the satirist's times and their own.

Juvenal was born in Aquinum, southeast of Rome, and may have worked in minor governmental positions, perhaps abroad in Egypt for a time. Few facts about him have survived outside those provided by his own writings, although a biography written in the fourth century indicates that he was the son of a freedman and had practiced rhetoric until middle age for his own amusement—perhaps until he took up poetry. He was clearly well-versed in both Greek and Latin literature and mythology, to which he constantly alludes. His favorite genre appears to have been epic, as he writes in hexameters and uses many words and phrases from Vergil's *Aeneid*. As far as satire is concerned, he tells readers in his opening lines that he models himself on Lucilius, who was renowned for his outspokenness and fearless attacks on powerful men.

Juvenal's pictures of life in Rome are colorful and brilliantly observed. He is the master of the telling detail and the piquant metaphor, all deployed in the service of skewering those whom he targets. He resents the growing power of the moneyed classes, the traders, and the freedmen and the displacement of traditional Roman centers of power. He disapproves of the softening influences of Greek and Eastern cultures and the vices they introduce into the hardy and self-reliant Roman character that had made the empire great. He despises the Roman aristocracy for its weakness and degeneracy and for its abandonment of the patron-client relationship in favor of naked self-interest. Last but by no means least, he presents himself as revolted by men who do not behave as men should, but have adopted womanly ways and, conversely, women who have abandoned Roman ideals of modesty and chastity and who take on masculine roles, such as that of gladiator in the arena.

Juvenal explains his choice of medium in his first satire. Having no desire to rewrite old plays or endless epics, and having seen a barber become wealthier than a patrician and a social-climbing Egyptian advance himself at the expense of the Romans, he declares that "it is difficult not to write satires." His writing was little appreciated during his lifetime. Indeed, his satires disappeared for several centuries. Rediscovered, Juvenal was esteemed as an epigrammatist and social historian because of his vivid pictures of Roman life. Sixteen satires, totaling 3,775 lines, make up the total preserved work of Juvenal. The poems vary in length from the little more than sixty lines of the unfinished satire 16, which deals with the prerogatives of a soldier, to the 661 lines of satire 6, directed against women, a poem that is long enough to fill a papyrus roll.

Juvenal's first book, containing 690 lines, includes his first five satires, of which satire 1, appropriately, explains why he has turned to this form of literary activity. He declares that he is writing to pay back the many poets who have bored him, from crude Cordus, with his interminable epics, to the writers of bad comedies and elegies. Since depravities on every side "rate the midnight oil of Horace," the writer of satires charges onto the plain like a new Lucilius. Pondering, however, the advice of those who have warned him against the wrath and punishment he may incur from the powerful if he attacks them, he declares his intention to dedicate his attention to the dead, those whose ashes lie along the roads outside Rome.

The third satire, a lengthy tirade against life in Rome, is justly famous for its vivid account of the sordid aspects of urban life; delivered through the mouthpiece of Juvenal's friend Umbricius, who is leaving for the quiet seaside town of Cumae, it presents Rome as a place in which no "decent Roman" now belongs. Satire 4 is the story of Domitian and a giant fish caught in the Adriatic Sea and sent to the imperial palace for consumption; in this satire, Juvenal captures the fear, hypocrisy, and brutality of tyrannical regimes.

Underlying Juvenal's satirical ire in these opening poems is a profound anxiety about the violation of traditional boundaries and the permeability of borders. His hostility to Greeks and Egyptians, as well as to foreigners generally, reflects a sense that Rome is losing its "Romanness" and, along with it, the old values upon which society depends. Thus, in satire 2, Juvenal attacks Roman aristocratic males who have adopted the manly guise of Stoic philosophers and walk around grim-faced, while, in the secrecy of their homes, they engage in the most effeminate activities imaginable. Similarly, in satire 5, he describes a dinner-party hosted by a rich patron for his friends and clients that is a nightmare of abuse and humiliation. The poor client without means is served cheap and disgusting dishes and rancid wine, while the wealthy host dines on exotic fare and drinks fine vintage. This encapsulates the perversion of networks of friendship and patronage that has occurred with the influx of new wealth and the rise of nouveaux riches.

The approaching marriage of Postumus gives the poet a motive for a coarse diatribe against the women of Rome in satire 6. This is the longest poem in the collection, taking up the entire second book. In primitive times, Juvenal asserts, the goddess Chastity existed on Earth, but not among the Roman matrons of his time. He then launches into a catalog of examples of women behaving badly, from Eppia who ran off to Egypt with a gladiator; to Maura, who gets drunk and cavorts lewdly around the statue of Chastity at night; to the empress Messalina having sex with multiple men in a brothel. No aspect of Roman womanhood is spared in this extended outburst: clothing, make-up, exercise, chit-chat, shopping, theatre-going, all come under Juvenal's jaundiced scrutiny. While this poem is a counterpart to the attack of satire 2 on inappropriately behaving men, it is a much more substantial depiction of the atrophying of traditional gender roles. It ends with examples of women who poison step-children and murder husbands, and it has a final message to convey to Postumus and any other Roman man: do not get married, as there is no woman who is chaste.

With the third book, Juvenal's tone becomes slightly less angry and more resigned and cynical. Some have detected a more philosophical turn in these satires. Juvenal offers in the remaining poems of the collection various versions of the same rather bleak message, namely that one looks in vain for the traditional Roman values as anchors of moral stability. Family lineage is no guarantee of noble character and, hence, no reason for expecting respect, he argues in satire 8. Retraced a few generations, even the noblest blood is mixed with the common. Deeds are more important.

The famous satire 10, adapted in 1749 by Samuel Johnson as *The Vanity of Human Wishes: The Tenth Satire of Juvenal Imitated*, shows that few human beings know what is good or bad for them. Most people wish for health or honor. Students of rhetoric crave eloquence, the ruin of Demosthenes and Cicero. The ambitions of Alexander and Xerxes were their undoing. People desire long life, which brings ills, or beauty, which causes unhappiness. If people were wise, they would let the gods make the decisions. As Johnson writes, "So raise for good the supplicating voice,/ But leave to Heaven the measure and the choice." If people must pray, they should ask for a healthy mind in a healthy body and a spirit reconciled to trouble or death.

Extravagance is the theme of satire 11, sent to Persicus along with an invitation to dinner. Many in Rome beggar themselves for pleasure, says Juvenal, but at Juvenal's table, his friend will eat what he can afford, simply served, and without lavish entertainment. Satire 15 is a disturbing parable about the rivalry of two neighboring Egyptian towns and an incidence of cannibalism born of religious fanaticism; but others should guard against feeling superior because, he shows, things every bit as violent and appalling happen in Rome as well.

The final, unfinished, satire 16 appears to be shaping into an attack on the Roman army and the special privileges enjoyed by soldiers; it then breaks off. No more of the collection exists. It is likely that it continued in a similar vein. There is debate as to whether or not Juvenal offers any real corrective to the behavior he observes and condemns; some think he attacks vices to make his readers change their ways, but that is probably too simplistic: Although Juvenal does give glimpses into an alternative way of living—a simple, rustic life without acquisitiveness and ambition—he has a tendency to deflate even that which he apparently admires.

In the end, Juvenal's satires are most remarkable for their descriptive power, their flashes of bitter humor, and their unsparing portrayal of corruption. Even with the intolerance and prejudice that underpins many of his criticisms, Juvenal holds up a mirror to his own society and to humankind in general.

Revised by David H. J. Larmour

Further Reading

Coffey, Michael. *Roman Satire.* London: Methuen, 1976. Groups the major Roman satirists according to various traditions. Examines Juvenal's *Satires* with discussion of prevalent themes and such stylistic considerations as imagery and rhetoric. Includes extensive notes.

Freudenburg, Kirk. *Satires of Rome: Threatening Poses from Lucilius to Juvenal.* New York: Cambridge University Press, 2001. Analyzes Juvenal's satire and its relationship to other satirical writings by Lucilius, Horace, and Persius. Describes the audience for the work of these ancient Roman satirists.

_____, ed. *The Cambridge Companion to Roman Satire.* New York: Cambridge University Press, 2005. "The Poor Man's Feast: Juvenal" by Victoria Remell provides a lengthy analysis of the *Satires*, and the other essays in the collection contain references to Juvenal that are listed in the index.

Green, Peter. *The Shadow of the Parthenon.* Berkeley: University of California Press, 1972. Includes the essay, "Juvenal and His Age," which discusses the elusiveness of the writer and his obsession with avarice and luxury. Explores the difficulty of finding an overall structure or order for the sixteen *Satires*.

Highet, Gilbert. *Juvenal the Satirist.* Oxford, England: Clarendon Press, 1954. Provides a definitive volume on Juvenal's life and work. The bulk of this scholarly tome analyzes the sixteen *Satires* and looks at their influence and appraisal through various later ages. Provides useful indexes to persons, places, things, and passages in the works.

Jones, Frederick. *Juvenal and the Satiric Genre.* London: Duckworth, 2007. Examines how Juvenal manipulated the genre of ancient Roman satire, as well as the epic and other literary forms of his time, to create his works.

Knoche, Ulrich. *Roman Satire.* Translated by Edwin S. Ramage. Bloomington: Indiana University Press, 1975. In the chapter on Juvenal, Knoche calls him the most serious of the satirists, focusing on social conditions rather than individuals. Included are summaries of the *Satires* and evaluations of modern editions.

Satires

Author: Lucian (c. 120-c. 180)

First transcribed: second century C.E.; includes
   Nekrikoi dialogoi (*Dialogues of the Dead*, 1684);
   Enalioi dialogoi (*Dialogues of the Sea Gods*, 1684);
   Theōn dialogoi (*Dialogues of the Gods*, 1684);
   Hetairikoi dialogoi (*Dialogues of the Courtesans*, 1684)

Type of work: Essays

Although Lucian was but one of many satirists who attacked the excesses of the Roman empire in the second century, he has the distinction of being one of the most influential of all practitioners of the genre. His works often seem motivated by personal animosity and inspired by self-serving principles, but he rises above invective to achieve a vision of humanity that inspired countless writers who have followed him. Best known for his development of the satiric dialogue, in which characters reveal their own deficiencies as they defend themselves, Lucian managed to make from the many foibles and hypocrisies of his own day material for timeless analysis of humankind's greatest follies.

Condemned by Christian writers (and ultimately by the Catholic Church) as an atheist for his scathing portrait of the deities in *Dialogues of the Gods*, he fell into disrepute in the West for more than a millennium; however, with the rediscovery of classical writings in the Renaissance, Lucian's reputation grew rapidly, and by the sixteenth century he was one of the most widely read and influential satirists of all time.

The list of literary figures indebted to Lucian is long and contains the names of some of the most distinguished writers in the European tradition. Desiderius Erasmus and Thomas More fell under his spell. The rhetoricians and the dramatists of Renaissance England found his works compelling subjects for study. His satires, especially his work about Timon the misanthrope, inspired a number of works during this period, including plays by Ben Jonson, Francis Beaumont, and John Fletcher. William Shakespeare borrowed from Lucian not only for *Timon of Athens* (pr. c. 1607-1608, pb. 1623) but also for the famous graveyard scene in *Hamlet, Prince of Denmark* (pr. c. 1600-1601, pb. 1603). John Dryden found him a useful mentor and wrote a brief biography for an edition of Lucian produced at the end of the seventeenth century. Lucian's *True History* is the model for Jonathan Swift's *Gulliver's Travels* (1726), the greatest of all English satires. In France, both François Rabelais in the sixteenth century and Voltaire two centuries later found inspiration in his writings.

Prolific and caustic, Lucian fulfills admirably the role of the satirist, using humor and invective to promote social change.

The satires of Lucian are directed not so much against social customs and manners as against the ideological attitudes of men in the Roman empire. Of a conservative spirit, Lucian wanted to recall people to old ethical standards and values by exposing the shams and affectations of religion, philosophy, pedantry, and superstition. So vehement does he become in his attacks, it often seems that he is condemning not only the abuse of the thing but also the thing itself, particularly in the satires on philosophy.

The *Dialogues of the Gods* is composed of twenty-six conversations among the Olympian deities. Their own words condemn them, for in their bickering, gossip, complaints, and flatteries they show themselves to be as prideful and ignorant as human beings, and as much enslaved by their ignoble passions, so that they are not at all worthy of the awe and reverence that the mortals on earth accord them. Hera nags at Zeus because of his myriad love affairs; Asclepius and Herakles argue over precedence in seating at the dinner table; Hermes whines over all his work as messenger to the gods; Zeus scolds Helius for giving the sun-chariot to Phaeton; Apollo and Hermes chat about the similarity of the twins Castor and Pollux; Ares whispers sedition behind Zeus's back; the Judgment of Paris is enacted. Each vignette develops its own little drama, and through them Olympus is lowered to the level of the common marketplace.

The *Dialogues of the Sea Gods* follows the same pattern. Poseidon comforts his son Cyclops after Odysseus dupes and blinds him; the river Alpheus rehearses his protestations of love for the river Arethusa; the metamorphoses of Proteus are marveled at by his friends as if he were a circus magician; nymphs and Nereids talk about their lovers and gossip about one another.

The satire in the *Dialogues of the Dead* is more penetrating and mordant. The residents of the Underworld, newly dead and long-dead, live together in uneasy fellowship. They still dispute over the petty things that concerned them when they were alive. Men who on earth were highly honored, fabulously wealthy, physically beautiful, are leveled to dry and uniform bones, but still they squabble over reputation, appearances, precedence. Cynics argue with epicureans, the once-poor taunt the once-rich, and Charon prays for war or plague on earth so he may collect more fares on his ferry. Achilles learns there is no glory on the far side of the Styx, but Alexander the Great tries unsuccessfully to impress his magnificence on his fellow shades. Menippus, the Cynic philosopher, thrives in Hades because all his earthly activities are directed against the vanities that people lose at death. Socrates and Diogenes appear, also Agamemnon, Ajax, Tiresias, Menelaus, Paris—soldiers, courtiers, kings, and philosophers reduced to wandering shades who can do nothing but talk of the past.

Menippus the Cynic is one of Lucian's favorite characters, and he is frequently used as a touchstone for satirizing pretentiousness in philosophy and in religion. In the dialogue that bears his name, Menippus tells his friend of a necromantic experiment he makes in order to visit Hades. Troubled by the great discrepancy between the licentious freedom of the gods—as the poets describe them committing murders, rapes, incest, usurpations—and the strict laws forbidding mortals to engage in the same activities, Menippus goes to the philosophers to have the situation explained to him. He discovers them to be as helpless and vicious as ordinary people, and sometimes even more ignorant. Finally he decides to seek out the seer Tiresias in Hades and ask him how one should live. With the help of a Chaldean soothsayer, Menippus gains entrance to Hades; he sees the judgment of the dead and their punishments. In the Acherusian Plain of Hell he sees the common dead and the demigods, all indistinguishable, all reduced to dusty bones. Men who were kings on earth occupy, in Hades, the same allowance of space as beggars, and they are forced to tutor or to sell fish or to cobble shoes. The philosophers indefatigably carry on their learned disquisitions. While Menippus is in Hades, an assembly is called, which he attends. A decree is sent out against rich men on earth, that their souls after death be sent to inhabit asses for a quarter-million years, to learn humility. Finally finding Tiresias, Menippus explains his dilemma. The sage tells him the life of the ordinary person is best; one should shun clever logic and metaphysical speculation, live cheerfully, and work productively. Convinced, Menippus returns to earth.

In a companion piece to this satire, Menippus tells a friend of an aerial expedition he made to visit Heaven. After observing the vices and follies of mortals, and their ignoble goals and contemptible behavior, he vows to find a worthier occupation: to discover the divine order of the universe. When he observes the workings of the stars and the nature of earth, however, he can make no sense out of them. Again he goes to the philosophers, only to find them as confused as himself but too proud to admit it. Menippus then fashions a pair of wings for himself, one from an eagle, the other from a vulture, and from the top of Mount Olympus he launches himself heavenward, hoping to get some firsthand information about the universe. A rest stop at the moon and a chat with Empedocles, whom he finds there, enables him to look down on the entire earth and its inhabitants going antlike and self-importantly about their affairs. All their crimes are revealed to him. Continuing on, he arrives in Heaven, is admitted to the presence of mighty Zeus, and explains his mission. The god, forgoing his mighty mien, quizzes Menippus about weather conditions, the price of wheat, social news, and Zeus's own popularity among the people. Menippus is invited to a banquet, at which Zeus denounces to the company those philosophers about whom Menippus complains. The gods decide to annihilate them all in four months' time. Menippus is returned to earth and deprived of his wings, for the gods cannot have mortals disturbing them whenever the mortals' fancy moves them. Finishing the narrative to his friend, Menippus goes off to tell the philosophers of the doom pronounced on them.

Another story of a journey is the dialogue of Charon and Hermes. Tired of his ferryman work, Charon takes a holiday to visit the earth and to see what life is like, because he has long been impressed at how the dead so lament the loss of it when he conducts them to the underworld. Charon persuades Hermes to assist him, and the two pile up four mountains to give Charon a view of the world from a good vantage point. The greatest cities seem to him nothing but little animal dens. A charm of Hermes sharpens Charon's eyesight enough to see all human activities. He observes people striving for fame, glory, power, and wealth, never thinking of the death that broods over them, even as Charon broods. Solon, a wise man, is the only one aware of mortality, and Charon watches him vainly trying to warn King Croesus to take less interest in his gold. Charon, who hears the dooms of many mortals pronounced by the Fates, watches the mortals and comments on the vanity of their strivings. He looks at the ostentatious tombs that the great provide for themselves and derides this worldly display. He asks to be shown the cities of Babylon, Ninevah, and Tyre, but Hermes tells him they are long destroyed. Wonderingly, Charon concludes that people are utter fools: Nothing they do either comes with them after death or endures after them on earth.

Philosophy receives another drubbing in another dialogue. Zeus auctions off philosophers: Pythagoras, Diogenes, Heraclitus, Socrates, Democritus, Epicureans, and Stoics. Various dealers question them and bid on them. Philosophy is sold as if it were any other commodity. In another dialogue, the philosophers, granted a day's respite from Hades, come up to earth to murder Lucian for his cavalier treatment of them. Lucian protests that he is a faithful admirer of philosophy and proposes that his case be formally tried, with Philosophy herself as the judge and the several philosophers as the jury. Philosophy agrees and brings her waiting-ladies, Virtue, Temperance, Justice, Culture, and Truth. The trial opens with Diogenes speaking for the prosecution. He accuses Lucian of ridiculing, parodying, and scorning philosophy and of teaching his audiences to flout and to jeer at philosophy also. Lucian replies that he never abused the true philosophers, but only those who corrupt the doctrines, the hypocrites who want to be honored as philosophers but behave like rogues. He describes the corruptions of philosophy he sees around him in the world, and he appeals at last to Truth to confirm his words. Truth and Philosophy agree, and even the philosophers are convinced; they acquit Lucian. Together they decide to separate the true practitioners and punish the false ones. They call all who claim to be philosophers to the Acropolis, to make their defense before Virtue, Philosophy, and Justice. Very few appear. Then Lucian calls out that gifts are to be distributed to philosophers, and a horde rushes in to receive the gifts. The latter group looks more like philosophers than the honest ones. When Lucian takes a fishing rod baited with gold and figs and dangles it over the city, he catches a variety of specimens, all described according to the branch of philosophy they claim to represent, all like monstrous fish. There are so many of them that Philosophy decides to send Lucian out with Exposure to crown or to brand them all as needed.

Lucian's other satires are numerous and equally pointed. In another, a cobbler's rooster turns out to be a reincarnation of Pythagoras. The cobbler complains about the injustice of his poverty, and the bird answers, showing the misery that often accompanies riches and the vices of wealthy men. The cobbler, Mycyllus, learns to be content with his station in life. The gods are again satirized and their dignities punctured in more dialogues. Further dialogues inspect superstitions and prejudices. Still not through, Lucian again attacks, in additional dialogues, philosophy, oratory, the gods, ego-

tists, and parasites. Lucian's satire occasionally becomes so personal and venomous that it seems more a venting of spleen than a social corrective. It is always vivid and entertaining, however, and often uncomfortably just.

"Critical Evaluation" revised by Laurence W. Mazzeno

Further Reading

Allinson, Francis G. *Lucian: Satirist and Artist*. New York: Longmans, Green, 1927. Excellent on the topic of the supernatural in Lucian, discussing his work in terms of its treatment of the ancient gods, superstition, and Christianity. Spells out the major influences on Lucian.

Baldwin, Barry. *Studies in Lucian*. Toronto, Ont.: Hakkert, 1973. Traces the scant evidence concerning Lucian's life and speculates on who may have been Lucian's important friends and enemies. Strong emphasis is placed on Lucian's satire in comparison with that of other notable contemporaries. Stresses Lucian's intense involvement with "fashions and living issues" of his time.

Craig, Hardin. *The Written Word, and Other Essays*. Chapel Hill: University of North Carolina Press, 1953. The essay on "The Vitality of an Old Classic: Lucian and Lucianism" is a graceful appreciation of the best features of Lucian. The discussion of Lucian's skill with the dialogue is excellent.

Gilhuly, Kate. "Bronze for Gold: Subjectivity in Lucian's *Dialogues of the Courtesans*." *American Journal of Philology* 128, no. 1 (Spring, 2007): 59-94. Focuses on dialogue 6, describing how Lucian manipulates his audience's expectations by combining comedic characters with a philosophical form.

Jones, C. P. *Culture and Society in Lucian*. Cambridge, Mass.: Harvard University Press, 1986. Separate chapters discuss, among other topics, Lucian's inconsistent treatment of philosophy, the "concealed victims" of the satires, and the gods and the oracles.

Marsh, David. *Lucian and the Latins: Humor and Humanism in the Early Renaissance*. Ann Arbor: University of Michigan Press, 1998. Describes how European authors in the fifteenth and sixteenth centuries rediscovered Lucian's comic writings, tracing how the themes and structures of his works were adapted by Renaissance writers. Chapters 2, 3, and 4 focus on *The Dialogue of the Dead* and *The Dialogue of the Gods*.

Satires

Author: Persius (34-62 C.E.)
First published: Saturae, first century C.E. (English
   translation, 1616)
Type of work: Poetry

The *Satires* of Persius belong to a rich tradition in Roman literature. According to an ancient biography attached to the manuscripts of the *Satires*, Persius was born into an affluent family associated with Rome. His short life spanned the reigns of Tiberius, Caligula, Claudius, and Nero, a time characterized by increasing constraints on literary and personal freedom. Although Persius preferred a quiet domestic life to the busyness of urban literary and intellectual circles, he nevertheless shared friendships with many influential writers of his day, including the epic poet Lucan, the lyric poet Caesius Bassus, and, to some degree, the philosopher and politician Seneca.

It is impossible to understand Persius's intent in composing the *Satires* without a proper understanding of the philosophy of Stoicism, which so influenced his opinions. When sixteen years of age, Persius became the student of Lucius Annaeus Cornutus, an important Stoic philosopher and a freedman of Seneca's family. Stoicism was the preeminent philosophy among Roman writers and intellectuals, and its proponents were often at odds with the mechanisms of the imperial political regime. The basic tenet of Stoicism is that one should live a virtuous life with the soul in accord with the principle of divine reason; denial of passions that disrupt the soul and living free from extremes are of fundamental importance. Thus Persius, combining a philosophical conviction with poetic skills in satire, sought to expose and criticize those vices rampant in his own society.

In the first satire, Persius diagnoses the decay of Roman literary tastes concurrent with a decline in morality. He presents this satire as a dialogue between himself and a friend. The argument ensues after Persius recites a line of "superior" poetry, probably from Gaius Lucilius (a founder of Roman satire), and his friend remarks that too few people in Rome would spend time reading such fine literature. Persius responds that he is not concerned with the tastes of most Romans and initiates his critique along Stoic lines.

To his friend's argument that one should be recognized for one's learning, Persius promptly suggests that the real benefit of knowledge is private, by which he implies that improvement of the soul is the goal. Persius notes that praise is most often mere remembrance in gossip. The friend accuses Persius of being prudish, but Persius responds that he is desirous of honest praise only, not that secured by favor or bribery.

Persius then sharpens his criticism of the writing produced in his own time. He complains that it is artificial and obsessed with rhetoric as a justified end, and that grandiose heroic acts are composed by writers who could not muster the attention to describe a mere grove in fine detail. The criticism of rhetoric—which succeeds only when passions are inflamed and people are dragged along—is especially important, because rhetorical precision was of fundamental importance for public life under the emperors. Although Persius does not—and could not—criticize the increasing constraints on freedom of speech, he does manage to criticize their outcome.

Persius argues against other literary habits in vogue at that time, which he believed threatened direct and honest writing. Eventually he agrees to keep quiet, but only after he recalls Gaius Lucilius's observation that humanity has a great propensity for foolishness. This satire concludes with a petition from Persius for his readers to join him in celebration of superior writers and abandon the poor tastes of their society. The first satire is thus marked by the nostalgia common when a person attempts to distinguish good literature from inane competition, but it further carries the serious conviction of Stoic philosophy.

The second satire is critical of the hidden intentions behind most prayers. Persius wrote it to commemorate the birthday of a friend, Plotius Macrinus, and immediately names Macrinus as one who offers genuine prayers. Most men, Persius argues, offer the most selfless prayers in public and in private wish for the opposite: A man may publicly petition for his uncle's good health while he privately waits for the uncle's death and the inheritance. Persius insists that Jupiter (the king of the gods in the Roman pantheon) finds no pleasure in these petitions or in the scant offerings traditionally made to secure the god's favor.

Persius turns his criticism from this depravity of saying one thing and intending another to human inconsistencies.

He strikes quickly at superstitious beliefs and, in a superbly constructed point, takes aim at the person who eats lavishly but prays for health and at the man who makes expensive sacrifices but prays for wealth. Finally, he attacks the belief that the gods are subject to the same desires as humanity and may thus be bribed accordingly. The second satire closes with a recommendation that the individual cultivate a soul of noble generosity and integrity and not offer vain sacrifices with petitions for shallow gain.

The third satire condemns living without the benefits of a philosophical attitude and restraint, and reveals the appalling consequences of such a life. The poet seems to include himself among those who live poorly when they know better, but such self-criticism is typical of Stoic ethics. The poem begins with a call to awaken from sleep, a metaphor that must not be overlooked. Persius notes all the common excuses given for procrastination, but his interlocutor reprimands such inactivity as mere childishness, which is not suitable as one matures. He warns that to continue on a path of indolence is to spoil one's opportunity to achieve a virtuous life. It is especially wicked for the person who encounters philosophy and learns to distinguish proper living from poor to neglect such duties. Thus one must construct a plan for one's life and not live subject to the whims of each day.

From line 63 to the end, the third satire turns to those people who have not yet enjoyed the benefits of a philosophical life, and Persius makes a conservative and dire observation regarding their imminent eternal slavery to ignorance. He insists that one must learn the general issues at stake in philosophy as soon as possible and dedicate one's life to them. The list of issues Persius provides reveals his own conviction regarding Stoicism's necessity, and he reflects on the ill treatment a philosopher receives from the common people. Persius does not offer a solution to this ridicule or criticize the foolishness of the crowd, but he implies that the lives of such people are deprived of true virtue and joy.

Persius concludes the third satire with a story of a man who falls ill after returning to his poor habits, once cured by his doctor, and dies indulging in his lavish behavior. The third satire closes by arguing that those base impulses that stir one to indulge in desires are a clear sign that although perhaps one is not yet gravely ill, symptoms do exist that only the sober life may rectify.

The fourth satire is the shortest, fifty-two lines. In it, Persius turns his attention to self-examination and opens with a criticism of those who put more stock in public affairs than in the virtuous improvement of their own lives. He initially addresses the poem to Alcibiades, the Athenian statesman, playboy, and maverick student of the philosopher Soc-rates. Alcibiades, the ward of the Athenian statesman Pericles, was blessed with an excellent upbringing and skill in speaking, but he never knew his own psychological pitfalls. Persius's criticism is directed at both this type of person and the multitude who ignorantly follow such a person, passionately stirred up by his charms.

The poem then turns to a more general lament over the human habit of criticizing and gossiping about others while knowing so little of oneself, along with the fault that Persius terms "covering a secret wound behind a golden belt," the confusion of the public opinion of a person with the real person. The fourth satire closes with advice to shun the opinions of the crowd and hold oneself accountable to high personal standards. The final image is succinct and compelling: One should tend to one's own house, having realized how empty it is.

The fifth satire is the longest, at 191 lines. As does the second satire, it closely imitates Horace with respect to style and theme. The poem is dedicated to Persius's friend and mentor Lucius Annaeus Cornutus, whose influence the poet joyfully recognizes in all aspects of his life. Persius first recalls his study under Cornutus at sixteen years of age, when he performed his coming-of-age ceremony and found himself at the mercy of adolescent temperament. He credits Cornutus's teaching with saving his soul and setting straight his ethical standards. Persius respectfully suggests that the two were fated to meet each other.

The remainder of the fifth satire turns with a critical eye to the vices of other people. Persius argues that each person is distinguished by his or her particular desires and laments that so few follow the proper path of the Stoic's life, as Cornutus did. He offers that all people seek liberty, but few understand the genuine object of freedom; therefore, most people are slaves to their passions. The Stoic knows the best remedy: One must dedicate oneself to proper living, distinguish truth, and employ reason to live a moderate and self-controlled life, freed from inane desires that weaken the soul, especially the vices of avarice and lust. Persius satirizes those people whom he is accustomed to criticize: candidates for office who seduce the mob, the superstitious, and, finally, ignorant soldiers. The poem closes abruptly, following a list of senseless activities that bind the soul into some form of slavery.

The sixth satire is addressed to the lyric poet Caesius Bassus. In it, Persius assesses the virtues of moderate living and the difficulty such a life may cause for those not so inclined. Persius remarks that he has a good life, keeps at his estate away from the crowd, and meets his daily needs without great concern for hoarding wealth or, conversely, indulgence in trivial expenditures. He then turns his criticism toward common arguments against his way of life, most notably those offered by the fault-finding troublemaker (he uses the name Bestius, taken from Horace) or the heir who threatens to neglect proper funeral rites—which the Romans perceived as a dishonor and threat to the deceased's final rest—unless his avarice is fed. To this heir, Persius offers a discussion that meanders in presentation but essentially argues that he would not starve himself in the present so that someone in the future may grow fat. In this way, Persius presents the Stoic emphasis on moderation. The poem closes with a satiric encouragement of vice, by which he emphasizes the imminent danger of such a life.

Persius's style is difficult and, as mentioned before, often imitates Horace. His moderate lifestyle, distant from the rigors of urban demands, helped to establish a secure, if not grand, reputation for him. Persius's contributions are important to the legacy of Roman satire and reveal much about his society and the nature of philosophical and literary protest in imperial Rome. They further present a fine study of Stoicism's potential influence on the young, and their insistence on moderation attracted many subsequent writers, most notably the seventeenth century English poet John Dryden, who made one of the earliest translations.

Stephen C. Olbrys

Further Reading

Coffey, Michael. *Roman Satire*. New York: Barnes & Noble, 1976. Introduces the basic issues of classical scholarship at stake in Persius's work and places Persius within his literary and historical context. Chapter 6 offers a particularly thorough summary of the *Satires*.

Dessen, Cynthia S. *The Satires of Persius: Iunctura callidus acri*. 2d ed. London: Bristol Classical Press, 1996. Demonstrates how Persius's satires are unified and understandable through his use of controlling metaphors, imagery, and word repetition.

Freudenburg, Kirk. *Satires of Rome: Threatening Poses from Lucilius to Juvenal*. New York: Cambridge University Press, 2001. Analyzes Persius's *Satires* and the work's relationship to other satirical writings by Horace, Juvenal, and Lucilius. Describes the audience for the work of these ancient Roman satirists.

_____, ed. *The Cambridge Companion to Roman Satire*. New York: Cambridge University Press, 2005. Collection of essays provides wide-ranging discussion of the satire of ancient Rome. "Speaking from Silence: The Stoic Paradoxes of Persius," by Andrea Cucchiarelli, provides an analysis of the *Satires*.

Morford, Mark. *Persius*. Boston: Twayne, 1984. Presents a superbly detailed explanation of the *Satires* and discussion of Persius's style and influence. Includes a copious bibliography of primary and secondary sources, interesting notes, a chronology, and an index. One of the best books for a beginner's study of Persius.

Nisket, R. G. M. "Persius." In *Satire: Critical Essays on Roman Literature*, edited by J. P. Sullivan. Bloomington: Indiana University Press, 1968. Places Persius and the *Satires* within their literary context. Thought-provoking source for a thorough introduction to Persius.

Rudd, Niall, trans. *The Satires of Horace and Persius*. New York: Penguin Books, 1973. Superior translation of the *Satires* in blank verse is preceded by an introduction that provides useful information about Persius's life and craft.

Satiromastix
Or, The Untrussing of the Humourous Poet

Author: Thomas Dekker (c. 1572-1632)
First produced: 1601; first published, 1602
Type of work: Drama
Type of plot: Satire
Time of plot: c. 1100
Locale: England

Principal characters:
WILLIAM RUFUS, king of England
SIR WALTER TERRILL, his noble follower
CAELESTINE, Sir Walter's bride
SIR QUINTILIAN SHORTHOSE, the bride's father
MISTRESS MINIVER, a wealthy widow
SIR VAUGHAN AP REES, a Welshman, suitor of the widow
SIR ADAM PRICKSHAFT, another suitor of the widow
CRISPINUS, a poet
DEMETRIUS, another poet
HORACE, the humorous poet
ASINIUS BUBO, Horace's admiring follower
CAPTAIN TUCCA, a roaring roisterer

The Story:

While Sir Quintilian Shorthose supervises the preparations for the marriage of his daughter Caelestine to Sir Walter Terrill, three guests arrive to share in the festivities: Sir Adam Prickshaft, Sir Vaughan ap Rees, and Mistress Miniver, a wealthy widow. All three of the older knights are enamored of the widow. When the bridal party enters, the groom-to-be announces that King William Rufus will grace the wedding with his presence. He also announces that he has sent to the poet Horace for a wedding song.

Horace is laboring by candlelight, surrounded by books, when his admiring friend Asinius Bubo visits him. Bubo warns that Crispinus and Demetrius plan to put Horace in a play as a bricklayer. To the great embarrassment of Horace, Crispinus and Demetrius enter and accuse him of unfair attacks on them.

Soon Blunt, accompanied by Captain Tucca, arrives to get the wedding verses, but Horace confesses that he was not able to finish them in the three days allotted him. Captain Tucca blasts Horace with a stream of Rabelaisian abuse for writing satires about him, and Horace, quivering with fear, apologizes and promises future good behavior. The captain tips him generously, and the visitors leave.

At the wedding dance, the three knights urge Mistress Miniver to choose one of them for her second husband, but their talk is interrupted by the arrival of King William Rufus and his train. The king greets the bride with a kiss, obviously taken with her beauty and charm. During the dance he manages to single her out frequently and engages her in risqué banter. When the ladies withdraw, the king dares Sir Walter to postpone the wedding night and to trust his bride at court alone with the king. Goaded by accusations

that he lacks faith in her, Sir Walter unwisely promises to send her.

The widow refuses Sir Vaughan, in spite of the love letters he has given her, which he purchased from Horace; she favors Sir Adam. Enraged, Sir Vaughan asks Horace to write a satire on baldness, as Sir Adam is bald. Sir Quintilian, needing a messenger to speak to the widow for him, turns to the raucous, foul-mouthed Captain Tucca. The captain also agrees to carry rich gifts to the widow from Sir Adam. However, Captain Tucca woos for himself. Later, he is shown a new series of satirical epigrams by Horace of which the captain is the subject.

Sir Vaughan entertains the widow at a banquet at which Horace reads his satire on baldness, and Mistress Miniver announces that she could never be "enameled" of a baldheaded man again. Captain Tucca bursts in and threatens Horace; Sir Vaughan drives him out, but Mistress Miniver calls after the captain, demanding that he return the money she has lent him. Sir Vaughan rushes after the captain to punish him, and Bubo shows Horace a challenge left by the captain.

Captain Tucca promises Sir Adam that he will have Crispinus and Demetrius praise baldness in verse. Bubo and Horace come to the captain for a parley, and the three make peace again. Captain Tucca convinces Sir Vaughan that his borrowing the money was part of his plan to help the knight win the widow. At the next gathering of the widow's friends, Crispinus reads his praise of baldness; then Captain Tucca arouses the whole group to take Horace to court and punish him for his sharp satires.

Sir Walter, Sir Quintilian, and Caelestine lament the danger she is in, and Sir Quintilian proposes that she drink poison. Grief-stricken, Sir Walter consents to the loss of his wife in order to save her honor. When revelers come to escort the couple to court, Sir Walter announces his wife's death and requests that they go with him in procession to the king.

King William Rufus, laughing at the gullibility of Sir Walter, waits eagerly for the coming of the bride. Sir Walter, dressed in black, escorts the body into the king's presence. Seeing Caelestine lifeless, the king cries out in horror. Sir Walter accuses the king of tyranny and explains that Caelestine chose to die rather than lose her honor; Sir Walter's oath is kept by his bringing her body to the king. Shame overcomes the repentant monarch. Caelestine then revives, and Sir Quintilian tells how he provided her a potion that gave her the appearance of death, though both Sir Walter and she had believed it poison. The king restores the wife unharmed to her husband.

Crispinus offers an interlude of comic relief after this serious situation is resolved. Captain Tucca leads Horace and Bubo, both wearing horns, into the royal presence. Bubo is made to swear that he will abandon Horace and his poetry; upon swearing this, he is released. Horace, crowned with nettles instead of laurels, promises at great length to reform as a writer and to give up sour criticisms and complaints. Captain Tucca announces that he and Mistress Miniver are to be married. The disgruntled knights accept defeat, and Captain Tucca promises to repay them what they have given him for their wooing of the widow. A dance follows, and all ends happily. Captain Tucca delivers an epilogue that promises future theatrical battles between Horace and the poetasters.

Critical Evaluation:

Satiromastix owes its fame to its attack on Ben Jonson. Apparently the play was patched up in some haste in order to reply to Jonson's *Poetaster: Or, His Arraignment* (pr. 1601), which caricatures Thomas Dekker and John Marston. The literary community of Renaissance London was a relatively small but highly active arena in which personal and professional egos frequently collided. Clashes such as the "Harvey-Nashe controversy" and dueling pamphlets and verses were numerous. Conflicts were even more frequent among playwrights and actors.

During the 1599-1600 theatrical season, London experienced what came to be called the War of the Theatres, in which rival stage companies sniped at one another through increasingly sharp and satirical attacks written into their new productions. The playwright who became the acknowledged leader in these attacks was Ben Jonson. Already known as a satirist, Jonson created highly unflattering portraits of his fellow dramatists in works that reached a climax in *Poetaster*, in which he singled out Marston (as Crispinus) and Dekker

(as Demetrius Fannius) for special attack. Jonson scored points against the two as being incompetent as writers, unlearned as scholars, and unsuccessful as businessmen. The two writers, with Dekker apparently doing most of the composition, responded with *Satiromastix*, which contains their own powerful assault on Jonson. This particular aspect of the play—its intensely topical, transitory, and highly specific satire—has caused problems for critics and scholars since the initial production in 1601; they frequently cite Dekker's "unbalanced" dramatic structure, which restricts the main plot to relatively few scenes while allowing a subplot and the satirical lampoon on Jonson to overwhelm the action.

Satiromastix has three plot lines. The first centers on the marriage of Sir Walter Terrill and his bride, Caelestine. At their wedding feast, the young couple is accosted by William Rufus, king of England, who demands that Caelestine spend her wedding night at his palace. He clearly intends to seduce the young bride, but, because of his royal rank, his request cannot be denied. Caelestine's father gives her a drug that causes her to fall into a swoon that mimics death, and when her supposedly lifeless body is delivered to William Rufus and he is told she took poison to preserve her honor, the king is overcome by guilt. He confesses his ignoble intentions and begs forgiveness, at which point Caelestine revives. This plot line, which supposedly contains the major action of the play, is stretched through five acts, with the story being told in small bits and pieces often interrupted by other activity.

The secondary plot concerns the wealthy widow Mistress Miniver, who is being wooed by an assortment of suitors. Through an increasingly bawdy and suggestive string of puns and other wordplay, this comedic subplot becomes the major force of the play.

Finally, there is the attack on Jonson, known as the poet "Horace." Horace is introduced into the action when Sir Walter hires him to compose wedding verses for his marriage to Caelestine. Later, Mistress Miniver's suitors also employ Horace to write letters and epigrams for them. Horace is a hack, and not a very good one at that.

Dekker vigorously assaults Horace (that is, Jonson) for a variety of faults and failings, including poetic incompetence, moral and artistic bankruptcy, personal cowardice, and physical ugliness. Specifics of Jonson's past—his early career as a bricklayer, his notorious ill temper, even the fact that he once killed a fellow actor in a duel and was tried for manslaughter—are made attributes of Horace, who is portrayed as a bumbling, bragging artistic fraud. In an especially telling stroke, Dekker lifts the character of Captain Tucca, created by Jonson in *Poetaster*, and uses this figure, already closely associated with Jonson and his work, to attack Jonson. The bombastic captain, who carries much of the assault on Dekker and Marston in *Poetaster*, has his character completely reversed, his strokes now aimed at Jonson, his creator.

The attacks on Jonson are meant to answer to charges made in *Poetaster*. *Satiromastix* may actually have preceded Jonson's play in production, thus serving as a first strike in the War of the Theatres. Dekker's play is uninhibited and unreserved in its unflattering portrait of Jonson and, while *Satiromastix* is considerably inferior to *Poetaster* in artistic achievement, it seems to have been an effective response to Jonson, for Jonson attempted no answer to Dekker.

The successful satirical attacks on Jonson weaken *Satiromastix* as a drama. Critics generally agree that Dekker, or Dekker and Marston as collaborators, took an almost-completed work by Dekker and adapted it into a response to *Poetaster*. The result was a series of individually well-written satirical scenes that, hastily inserted, disrupt the dramatic progress and development of the original play. By the final act, the attacks on Horace almost completely dominate the stage, reducing the resolution of the story of Sir Walter and Caelestine to a rapid summary quickly and not quite convincingly presented.

In *Satiromastix* Dekker creates one of his typical dramas, a tragicomedy that combines an intriguing plot with a fairly light examination of moral and ethical issues. This play is loosely connected to two extensive subplots that are overlaid with an extensive, highly personal assault on Ben Jonson as a person and as a writer. The result is an interweaving of some excellent, telling satire with a conventional drama.

"Critical Evaluation" by Michael Witkoski

Further Reading

Champion, Larry S. *Thomas Dekker and the Traditions of English Drama*. New York: Peter Lang, 1985. Provides a good general overview of Dekker's writings and a helpful guide to his place in the dramatic literature of the time.

Hoy, Cyrus Henry. Introduction to *The Dramatic Works of Thomas Dekker*. Edited by Fredson Bowers. New York: Cambridge University Press, 1980. Presents a well-rounded survey of Dekker's stage works, with emphasis on their composition and production.

McLuskie, Kathleen. *Dekker and Heywood: Professional Dramatists*. New York: St. Martin's Press, 1994. Focuses on the performances of the two playwrights' works, examining the relationship between their plays and the cultural moment when the plays were produced

Price, George. *Thomas Dekker*. New York: Twayne, 1969. Covers Dekker's life and writing and is especially good at placing him within the context of his times. Valuable resource for beginning students of Dekker's work.

Wells, Stanley W. "Thomas Dekker and London." In *Shakespeare and Co.: Christopher Marlowe, Thomas Dekker, Ben Jonson, Thomas Middleton, John Fletcher, and the Other Players in His Story*. New York: Penguin Books, 2007. Examines the plays of William Shakespeare by placing them within the broader context of Elizabethan theater, discussing other playwrights of the period, including Dekker, the work of acting companies, and the staging of theatrical productions. Chapter on Dekker recounts his life and career, discusses his collaborations, and analyzes some of his plays; another chapter on Ben Jonson includes information on *Satiromastix*.

The Satyricon

Author: Petronius (c. 20-c. 66 C.E.)
First transcribed: c. 60 C.E. (English translation, 1694)
Type of work: Short fiction
Type of plot: Satire
Time of plot: First century
Locale: Italy

Principal characters:
ENCOLPIUS, the narrator
ASCYLTUS, his friend
GITO, their attendant
EUMOLPUS, a poet
TRIMALCHIO, a wealthy vulgarian

The Story:

Encolpius rails at the growth of artificiality in modern rhetoric and the ill-prepared students who come to the school. Agamemnon, the professor, agrees with him but places the blame entirely on parents who refuse to make their children study. Weary of the dispute and far gone in drink, Encolpius flees the school. An old woman, who makes indecent proposals to him, shows him the way back to his inn.

Gito, Encolpius's sixteen-year-old slave, has prepared

supper, but the comely boy is crying: Ascyltus has made violent love to him. Encolpius is soothing the boy with caresses and tender words when Ascyltus breaks in on them. A quarrel ensues between the two friends as to who should enjoy Gito's favors. The dispute is settled only when all three agree to pay a visit to Lycurgus, a rich friend of Ascyltus. Lycurgus receives them most cordially and introduces them to Lichas, his friend. Lichas, completely taken with Encolpius, insists that Encolpius and Gito come home with him. On the way, Tryphaena, a beautiful woman attached to Lichas's entourage, makes surreptitious love to Encolpius, who resolves to have little to do with Lichas. When the party arrives at Lichas's villa, Tryphaena deserts Encolpius for the bewitching Gito. Smarting under her desertion, Encolpius makes love to Doris, Lichas's attractive wife. All goes fairly well until Gito tires of Tryphaena—she then accuses both Gito and Encolpius of making improper advances, and the two return in haste to Lycurgus's house.

Lycurgus at first supports the two adventurers, but as the jealous Lichas increases his complaints, Lycurgus turns against the pair. At the suggestion of Ascyltus, the three set out again to seek whatever love affairs and plunder they can find. They are well supplied with gold, for Encolpius plundered one of Lichas's ships before leaving.

A fair is in progress at a nearby small town, where they come upon a groom who is saddling a rich man's horse. When the groom leaves for a moment, Encolpius steals the rich man's riding cloak. Soon afterward, Ascyltus finds a bag of coins on the ground. The two friends hide the gold by sewing it under the lining of Encolpius's threadbare tunic. Just as they finish, the rich man's retainers give chase to recover the riding cloak. Dashing through a wood, Encolpius is separated from his friend and loses the tunic. When they meet again later at a market, they see the tunic up for sale there, with the gold pieces still hidden in the lining. They offer to trade the riding cloak for the tunic, but the bystanders become suspicious and try to make the two friends appear before a judge. Dropping the riding cloak and seizing the tunic, they flee.

After telling Gito to follow later on, they set out for the next town. Seeing the dim forms of two comely women hurrying through the dusk, Encolpius and Ascyltus follow them, unobserved, into an underground temple. There the two men see a company of women in Bacchanalian garb, each with a phallic emblem in her hand, preparing to worship Priapus. They are discovered by the horrified women and chased back to their inn.

As they are dining with Gito in their rooms, the maid of one of the women they had followed to the sacred rites comes

in and begs them to listen to her mistress, who is a respectable matron. Even though Encolpius swears never to tell of the forbidden rites, the matron has the three seized and taken to her villa. The men are bound and given powerful love potions, and then all the women of the household have sex with them. After escaping from the love-maddened ladies, Encolpius has to rest for three days; Gito seems little affected.

Next the three attend a huge banquet given by Trimalchio, a rich and vulgar freedman. After hours of eating and drinking, they are glad even for the respite of storytelling. Trimalchio starts off with a boring elucidation of the signs of the zodiac, and many of the guests tell pointless anecdotes. From Niceros, however, they hear an absorbing tale. While still a slave, Niceros was staying at an inn where he was in love with the landlord's complaisant wife, Melissa. One day he induced a soldier to go for a walk with him. When they came to a graveyard, the soldier took off his clothes and threw them beside the path. Making a magic circle around the clothes, he straightaway turned into a wolf and went howling away. When Niceros saw to his horror that the clothes had turned to stone, he hurried home to Melissa. She told him that a wolf had just come into the yard and killed some sheep. A servant drove a spear through the wolf's neck but the animal escaped. Niceros ran back to the cemetery, where he found that the stone clothes had dissolved in blood. When he went to the soldier's room in the morning, he found a physician there stanching the blood from a wound in the soldier's neck.

Encolpius, Ascyltus, and Gito are finally so stuffed and bored they can stand no more. To their relief, the company moves outdoors to exercise. They learn from the conversation that another banquet is to follow, this one given by Trimalchio's wife, and they leave hurriedly. Following another quarrel over Gito, Encolpius and Ascyltus part company. To the distress of Encolpius, Gito elects to go with Ascyltus.

After sorrowing uselessly for days, Encolpius falls in with an old man, the poet Eumolpus. When the two go to the baths to cement their friendship, Encolpius is overjoyed to find Gito acting as attendant for Ascyltus, who is in another room. Gito confesses that he really likes Encolpius better; in a happy mood, Encolpius takes the boy back to his apartment.

Later, Encolpius makes the mistake of trying to make love to Circe. As a result of his past tribulations and hardships, he has no strength for her ardors, and she suspects him of trifling with her. She raises such an outcry that Encolpius judges it wise to leave town. On Eumolpus's advice, the comrades embark secretly at night on a ship lying in the harbor. In the morning, Encolpius discovers to his chagrin that they are aboard Lichas's ship, and the owner and Tryphaena are also on board. Eumolpus tries to disguise Encolpius and Gito by darkening their skin with burned cork, but their subterfuge is discovered, and for a while it looks as though they will be flogged. Lichas, however, remembers his old attraction to Encolpius, and Tryphaena is smitten anew with Gito, so they are spared.

When Lichas's ship is wrecked in a storm, the three comrades land ashore at Croton. There Eumolpus poses as a rich landowner, and Encolpius and Gito pass as his slaves. By cleverly deluding the inhabitants, the three live luxuriously as guests of the town. After a year, however, suspicion grows as to Eumolpus's supposed wealth. Seeing an end to their pleasant stay, Encolpius and Gito escape just in time. The aroused townspeople use Eumolpus as a scapegoat, first decking him with boughs and sacred vestments and leading him through the city before hurling him from a cliff.

Critical Evaluation:

The Satyricon is a mere fragment of an extremely complex medley of stories that, in the complete version, perhaps were part of a mock-epic prose romance. Attached to the manuscript of *The Satyricon*, which was discovered in 1663 at Trau in Dalmatia, was a scribe's note describing the contents as taken from the "fifteenth and sixteenth books." If this information is correct, the original work must have been enormously long.

For centuries, scholars have disputed the purpose, scope, and meaning of the whole work. Not even the name of the author is accepted for certain. By tradition, *The Satyricon* is attributed to Gaius Petronius—better known as Petronius Arbiter, the arbiter of the court of Nero. Tacitus's famous description of the death of Gaius Petronius seems to correspond well with the reader's perception of the writer of such a book: a refined voluptuary, clever but cynical, practical, sophisticated in his knowledge of the pleasures and vices of ancient Rome. Apart from Tacitus's brief account concerning Petronius, nothing is known for certain about the origin or reception of his book, and the fragment that remains has often been misinterpreted.

One major problem in reading *The Satyricon* in English is that many translations, particularly those of the nineteenth and early twentieth centuries, are corrupt. Some translators, because of prudery, have cut from the text whole portions that they consider offensive. Others have interpolated sections that are clearly not Petronius's; these additions, for the most part, err in the opposite direction: They are passages of deliberately and crudely obscene material that surpass in indelicacy the author's refined erotic language. In general, one of the best translations of *The Satyricon* is that by William Arrowsmith, whose vigorous, honest, and sensitive version closely approximates the qualities of the Latin original. Readers of Latin may examine with confidence the modern scholarly editions by Alfred Ernout and E. T. Sage, or the older but still useful edition by W. D. Lowe. The reader, however, must be cautioned about poor English translations that markedly alter the content or misconstrue the tone of the Petronius model. These inadequate translations, for the most part, cut out all or most of the poetical selections. A simple test to determine whether or not a given translation is faithful to the source is to check Eumolpus's long verse passage titled "The Civil War"; accurate translations include the whole passage, although the poem, allusive and rhetorically pompous, may seem tedious to some readers.

In its context, Eumolpus's poem imitates or parodies heroic style. Petronius delights to parody conventions of language or literary form. The title of his work has been variously translated as "medley" (from *satura*, a mixed dish, from which the word "satire" is derived) and as "satyr-book" (from *saturika*, that is, concerned with satyrs and hence lecherous). From the fragment that exists, *The Satyricon* may be taken in both senses, as a Roman "satire"—a farrago of mixed stories using a multitude of styles—and as a book of comic-erotic adventures pleasing to satyrs. Within the main plot concerning the adventures of Encolpius are interwoven many stories or parts of stories, in the manner of popular Greek tales and of their imitated Roman counterparts, of which Lucius Apuleius's early second century *Metamorphoses* (*The Golden Ass*, 1566) is a famous example. The most remarkable of the stories is Eumolpus's "The Widow of Ephesus," a cynical narrative that has served many later writers and dramatists, including—to choose only English authors—George Chapman and Christopher Frye. Although Eumolpus's story may be extracted from the plot as a perfect short piece, in the context of the action (Encolpius, Gito, and Eumolpus are aboard the ship of their enemies, Lichas and Tryphaena), the anecdote takes on additional ironic meanings. Similarly, the stories that abound within stories of *The Satyricon* acquire richer tones of irony, satire, or comedy, depending upon the context at the moment. Petronius's chief device is parody, either to amuse or to ridicule, and the stories furnish ample subjects for literary and social burlesques.

Although *The Satyricon* belongs to the genre of Menippean satire—a mixture of verse with prose, philosophy with low comedy, romance with realism—the word "satire," as it is commonly understood, should not be applied to the book.

Troubled by Petronius's outspoken and often coarsely erotic subject matter, some prudish commentators have attempted to apologize for the work on the grounds of its supposed moral satire. To be sure, the picture of Roman manners and morals that the author provides is one of vulgarity and excess. Petronius, however, is neither a Christian moralist nor, for that matter, a moralist in the stamp of Juvenal. Far from ridiculing the corruption of contemporary morals, he approaches his subject with amused tolerance. Even the great scene of Trimalchio's banquet, widely regarded as a keen satire on Roman debauchery, may be seen in a different light as a comic burlesque on vulgar ostentation. The tone of Petronius's irony is sprightly rather than censorious. If the author has a moral argument to demonstrate, he skillfully conceals it.

Similarly, any notion that *The Satyricon* is intended as a social satire—one concerned with the degradation of Roman culture—must be examined cautiously in terms of Petronius's moral ambivalence. Although his major characters are clearly homosexual (some are less clearly bisexual) and parasitical, they are not treated as objects of ridicule; instead, they are shown as amusing rogues, foolish or crafty, successful or unfortunate. The main character, Encolpius (whose name is roughly translated as "the crotch"), is easily misled, especially by the guile of his homosexual partner, the sixteen-year-old, narcissistic Gito; Encolpius is cheated and abused by his rival for Gito's affections, the devious Ascyltus; another rival is the old pederast Eumolpus, the poet. In the world of *The Satyricon*, homosexual intrigues are taken as a norm and are treated casually. As a youth, Trimalchio began to earn his fortune through his sexual compliance with his master. To be evenhanded, Petronius treats heterosexual relations with the same casual tolerance. The women in the work are as sexually assertive as the men. Quartilla, Tryphaena, Circe, Chrysis, Corax—all are aggressive, earthy, lusty types quite the equal of their lovers.

The reader should not conclude from the evidence of the story that Petronius judges Roman society harshly. Rather, he takes men and women as he finds them, observes their habits with cool, realistic detachment, and—in the section dealing with obscenity, following the Circe episode—refutes the charges that his book is obscene. The matter rests ultimately with the reader, who may regard Petronius's fragment as a work either of social criticism or of mock-epic romance.

Judged from the second point of view, *The Satyricon* describes the fortunes of Encolpius, who has apparently aroused the wrath of the sex god Priapus. Throughout the book, the god's vengeance pursues his hapless victim. Against his will, Encolpius must take part in the orgy of Quartilla, priest of the cult of Priapus; with Circe he is humiliated by his impotence. He always tries to free himself from blame but only manages to offend Priapus more seriously (as when he kills a pet goose sacred to the god). Encolpius's adventures may be understood as a parody of Odysseus's in the Homeric epic. Just as Odysseus outraged the god Poseidon and suffered from mistreatment as a consequence, so Encolpius apparently is tormented by Priapus. If the comparison drawn from the fragment is apt, the complete *Satyricon* must have been a prose mock epic of great scope and richness, recalling the later James Joyce's *Ulysses* (1922), which, modeled on *Odyssey* (c. 725 B.C.E.; English translation, 1614), parodies heroic and literary conventions. Both *Ulysses* and *The Satyricon* are replete with puns, verbal games, and innovative stylistic techniques, and, through myth and symbolic action, each creates its own moral universe.

"Critical Evaluation" by Leslie B. Mittleman

Further Reading

Connors, Catherine. *Petronius the Poet: Verse and Literary Tradition in "The Satyricon."* New York: Cambridge University Press, 1998. Examines the thirty-two short and two long poems that are part of *The Satyricon* in their fictional and literary historical contexts.

Courtney, Edward. *A Companion to Petronius*. New York: Oxford University Press, 2001. Provides an introductory overview of *The Satyricon*, including discussion of the author's use of first-person narrative, parody, and symbolism.

Rimell, Victoria. *Petronius and the Anatomy of Fiction*. New York: Cambridge University Press, 2002. Focuses on the metaphors of corporeality in *The Satyricon*, arguing that Petronius uses this imagery to mirror apparent paradoxes.

Slater, Niall W. *Reading Petronius*. Baltimore: Johns Hopkins University Press, 1990. Explores the humor of *The Satyricon* through an initial linear reading, a reading that focuses on various language systems, and a reading that examines Petronius's comedic purpose, or lack thereof.

Sullivan, J. P. *"The Satyricon" of Petronius: A Literary Study.* Bloomington: Indiana University Press, 1968. Discusses authorship and date of *The Satyricon*; Petronius's choice of form; satire, criticism, and parody in the work; the author's humor; and the work's sexual themes.

Todd, Frederick Augustus. *"The Satiricon of Petronius."* In *Some Ancient Novels: "Leucippe and Clitophon," "Daphnis and Chloe," "The Satiricon," "The Golden Ass."* Freeport, N.Y.: Books for Libraries Press, 1968.

Contrasts *The Satyricon* with earlier classical romances and declares Petronius's work to be unique in its use of common, highly individualistic characters, realistic scenes, and lack of rhetorical flourish. Notes that Petronius's work is one of the chief sources of information about spoken Latin.

Whitmarsh, Tim, ed. *The Cambridge Companion to the Greek and Roman Novel.* New York: Cambridge University Press, 2008. Collection of essays about the works of long fiction produced in ancient Greece and Rome helps to place *The Satyricon* in historical context.

Saul

Author: Vittorio Alfieri (1749-1803)
First produced: 1794; first published, 1788 (English translation, 1815)
Type of work: Drama
Type of plot: Tragedy
Time of plot: Eleventh century B.C.E.
Locale: Gilboa, Israel

Principal characters:
SAUL, the aging king of Israel
DAVID, the exiled commander of Saul's forces
JONATHAN, Saul's son and friend of David
MICHAL, Saul's daughter and David's wife
ABNER, Saul's cousin and present commander of his forces
AHIMELECH, the priest of Nob

The Story:

After his famous victories over the Philistines, which began with his triumph over the giant Goliath, David rose to great power in Saul's kingdom. He became the best friend of Saul's son and heir, Jonathan, entertained Saul with his music, and married Saul's daughter, Michal. David's success and popularity, however, made Saul so jealous and envious that he has driven David from Israel and threatened to kill him if he returns from exile. Saul has fallen from favor with God (Jehovah) because he failed to execute the captured Amalekite king, Agag, but he does not blame himself. Instead, in his madness he has come to fear that David is scheming to assassinate him.

Knowing of the upcoming battle with the Philistines, David slips into the Israelite camp in the night and meets with Jonathan and with Michal, whom he has not seen for a long time. Jonathan informs him that Abner, the king's cousin and a conniving courtier, is deceiving the insane king and encouraging him to kill David. David's plan is to abase himself before Saul and beg his pardon, although he knows he has done no wrong.

When Saul appears, he complains about his age and the loss of his champion, but Abner insists that David is the cause of Saul's misfortunes, along with the now-dead priest Samuel, who had anointed David. The confused Saul has come to hate David, but he still admires his qualities of character. In a dream, Saul has seen Samuel take the crown from Saul's head and offer it to David, but David refused it

and placed it back on Saul's head. Michal and Jonathan appear before Saul to announce David's return, and David convinces Saul of his innocence by presenting a piece he cut from Saul's robe when he was in a cave at En Gedi, his point being that he could easily have killed the king then if he had wanted to.

David shows both modesty and good sense by appealing to Abner to continue in his role as commander, and he offers to act as Abner's subordinate. When Saul becomes suspicious of David's sword, which was given to David by priests at the temple, David sings to him as in the old days, and the king is at ease for a while. Saul then once again flies into a rage against David and the priests, and Jonathan cannot convince his father of his friend's innocence, so David has to hide.

The priest Ahimelech then appears to warn Saul, but the furious king orders Abner to kill him and to massacre the other priests and their families at Nob as well. After that, David cannot fight against the Philistines because the kingdom has become contaminated by Saul's sinfulness and violence. In the battle the Israelites are soundly defeated and Jonathan is killed. Michal comes to her father as the enemy approaches, but he is hallucinating and sees in her his old enemy Samuel, appealing for the return of David even if it means his own death. At last, Saul orders Abner to take care of Michal and, left alone as the Philistines appear, kills himself by falling on his sword.

Critical Evaluation:

Regarded as one of Italy's major poets, Vittorio Alfieri helped define the Italian drama of his age, particularly the tragedy, of which he wrote nineteen between 1776 and 1786. *Saul* was written in 1782. Alfieri also wrote an engaging autobiography, one that accounts for various love affairs in which he engaged while traveling throughout Europe, and his published writings include a treatise on tyranny, several comedies, lyric poetry, and satires. His best work, however, is in the genre of tragedy, and *Saul* is generally considered his best play.

In the late eighteenth century and throughout the nineteenth century, Alfieri was admired as one of Italy's foremost Romantic writers, an opponent of tyranny, a spokesman for Italian political unity and identity, and a libertarian. Although he was not inclined toward religious subjects for his work, his reading of the Bible in 1782 led him to write *Saul* with great rapidity. His personal inclination toward depression (melancholy) and his sense of his own aloneness may be detected in Saul, for whom he creates genuine stature as a tragic hero. In 1793, Alfieri himself appeared onstage in the play's title role.

Although Alfieri's acquaintance with William Shakespeare's tragedies was not extensive (he knew them mostly in French translation), *Saul* is somewhat reminiscent of *King Lear* (pr. c. 1605-1606, pb. 1608). In both plays one encounters the motif of an aging monarch who turns against his own best interests, including the good of his people and even his own children, and in the process goes mad and brings destruction on himself and his kingdom. Lear is manipulated by two of his daughters, Saul by his cousin, the "perfidious" Abner, who is ambitious and deeply envious of David.

Although David is a victim of Saul's insanity, he is not especially appealing, in spite of his obvious virtue and strength of character. David, who opens the play with a soliloquy in which he states his determination to fight the Philistines even if Saul will have him executed, is courageous to the point of audacity. He seems perhaps too aware of his heroism. In act 2 he directly confronts the unstable king and boldly demonstrates his innocence. In the third act he also shows his compassion by singing to soothe Saul's troubled mind.

The four substantial lyrical poems sung by David, which Alfieri inserts into act 3, scene 4, are noteworthy in their own right. The remainder of the tragedy is composed in unrhymed hexameter, a conventional meter in Italian and French plays, and it is typically translated into English as blank verse (unrhymed iambic pentameter). Alfieri's style in his plays has been characterized as "severely simple," which is somewhat surprising for a lyric poet. Extensive descriptive passages

and metaphoric language are not common in his dramatic writing, so the lyrics in the third act of *Saul* are exceptional. A note Alfieri includes with the play indicates that if the actor portraying David is not also a capable singer, then an instrumental passage before each stanza would be appropriate, followed by David reciting "with majesty and gravity."

Perhaps in an effort to build sympathy for David, Alfieri elaborates on his love for Michal, but the result is that while one may feel compassion for her, one is not quite convinced that their separation has been or will be as painful for him. At the end of the first act, David confidently informs Michal, "I am impell'd/ By a sure instinct; I at random act not." When he suddenly appears before Saul in act 2, the king himself says, "In thee speaks a God." Even his proper, devout humility ("Saul gave my life; Saul takes that life away") seems somehow too pat. "O virtue of a David!" Jonathan exclaims in act 1, "God's elect/ Thou art assuredly." Near the end of the play, when he and Michal share a "last embrace," David is moved, but his grief is slight and fleeting compared to hers.

Against the confidence and boldness of the mighty, youthful, and perhaps overly virtuous David, Alfieri constructs the deeply flawed Saul, a type of Romantic hero who recalls Christopher Marlowe's overreachers, such as Faustus and Tamerlane. Johann Wolfgang von Goethe was to refashion the type in *Faust: Eine Tragödie* (pb. 1808; *The Tragedy of Faust*, 1823); Percy Bysshe Shelley's Prometheus and several of Lord Byron's protagonists were to epitomize it in the next century. Saul's heroism resides in the fact that he has defied God in sparing the Amalekite king, Agag. In the process he has incurred the wrath of Samuel and other priests. The proper response would have been to act as Abraham did with his son Isaac, as David implies in the third scene of act 2. Even his pursuit of David, the Lord's anointed, has heroic implications, as it, too, suggests Saul's defiance.

What makes Saul a captivating character for a playgoer, however, is his psychological complexity. Unlike the conventionally heroic David, whose weaknesses are not hinted at in the play, Saul is human and vulnerable. When he appears at the start of act 2, his mind seems lucid as he admires the beauty of the dawn but laments his age and loss of strength. "How many years," he asks Abner, "have pass'd now, since a smile/ Was seen to play on my lips?" Saul clearly perceives his own mental disorder: "I am a burden to myself and others;/ In peace I wish for war, in war for peace." He sees that God has rejected him, and he even detects that Abner can be "hostile, invidious, crafty, and a traitor."

Saul's inability to resist the ministrations of David may suggest that he is as open to the potential for good as he is to the potential for evil in the form of Abner, and it is fairly easy to understand his jealousy over David's heroism. When Jonathan reasons with him about David, Saul confesses, "A strange inexplicable mystery/ This David is to me. . . ./ . . . he pleased/ My eyes; but never, never won my heart." Even his son's assurances as to David's virtue and trustworthiness cannot untangle Saul's feelings of mixed love and hatred.

Ultimately, perhaps, it is Saul's inability to deal with the spiritual and moral arrogance of the self-righteous that undoes him. When the priest Ahimelech scorns him—"thou art but a crown'd heap of dust"—and repeats his threat, "tremble, Saul," Saul gives vent to his mad craving for vengeance and orders the priest's execution along with the deaths of the other priests and their families at Nob. Ahimelech's courage is admirable but conventional, the typical attitude of the willing martyr: "No king can hinder me/ From dying like a just man; whence my death/ Will be as welcome as it is illustrious."

When he reaches out to Jonathan in act 4 ("Jonathan,/ Lov'st thou thy father?") and to Michal at the end of the play, Saul shows another facet of his character, that of the caring but hurt father. Even as his son prepares to fight by his side (to the death, although the play makes no mention of that), Saul says, "I have no children." His last concern is for Michal's safety, which he regards as assured so long as she is presented not as Saul's daughter but as David's wife.

Not a religious man himself, Alfieri portrays sinful Saul as the sympathetic "tragic hero" and virtuous David as a traditional but unappealing "epic hero." Not surprisingly, his depiction of God, as seen by David, Ahimelech, and Saul, is of the foreboding Lord of wrath, judgment, and vengeance. David points out to Jonathan in the first act that "in the fierce career/ Of His retributory punishments,/ He hath involved the guiltless with the guilty." God, says Ahimelech, "writes His vengeance in adamant." Left alone at the end, Saul asks, "Inexorable God,/ Is Thy retributory wrath appeased?"

Ron McFarland

Further Reading

Betti, Franco. *Vittorio Alfieri*. Boston: Twayne, 1984. Presents discussion of *Saul* that reflects on the title character's nobility gained through struggle, on the "touching figure of Michal," and on the play's theme of the past (Saul's age versus David's youth). Notes that in his suicide, Saul demonstrates the power of his will as a hero—neither the Philistines nor God can take credit for striking him down.

Bondanella, Peter, and Julia Conaway, eds. *Dictionary of Italian Literature*. Westport, Conn.: Greenwood Press, 1979. Collection of essays includes an informative brief entry on Alfieri by Giancarlo Maiorino. Concludes with comments on *Saul*, described as "the only character capable of expressing the superhuman passions of Alfieri himself."

Fido, Franco. "Alfieri and Pre-Romanticism." In *The Cambridge History of Italian Literature*, edited by Peter Brand and Lino Pertile. Rev. ed. New York: Cambridge University Press, 1999. Essay on Alfieri is part of a collection that provides an overview of Italian literature. Describes Alfieri's work as a link between eighteenth century neoclassicism and nineteenth century Romanticism.

Hallock, Ann H. "The Religious Aspects of Alfieri's *Saul*." *Forum Italicum* 18 (Spring, 1984): 43-64. One of the most thorough commentaries on the play available in English. Summarizes previous criticism of *Saul* from autobiographical, politico-philosophical, and psychological perspectives and argues that the fundamental issue of the play is "the nature of man without God."

Hillary, Richard B. "Biblical Exegesis in Alfieri's *Saul*." *South Atlantic Bulletin* 38 (March, 1973): 3-7. Focuses on the Old Testament concept of sin as it relates to Saul's insanity.

Mazzaro, Jerome. "Alfieri's *Saul* as Enlightenment Tragedy." In *Tragedy's Insights: Identity, Polity, Theodicy*, edited by Luis R. Gámez. West Cornwall, Conn.: Locust Hill Press, 1999. Analyzes the play, discussing its representation of King Saul, its depiction of the conflict between hero and tyrant, and the relation of pity and fear to the essence of tyranny.

Wilkins, Ernest Hatch. *A History of Italian Literature*. Rev. ed. Cambridge, Mass.: Harvard University Press, 1974. Presents a chapter on Alfieri that sets him and his work within the context of Italian literature and includes comments on *Saul*.